TEXAS PHARMACY LAWS AND REGULATIONS

2020 EDITION

QUESTIONS ABOUT THIS PUBLICATION?

For CUSTOMER SERVICE ASSISTANCE concerning replacement pages,
shipments, billing, reprint permission, or other matters,
    please contact Customer Support at our self-service portal
    available 24/7 at *support.lexisnexis.com/print*
    or call us at 800-833-9844.

For EDITORIAL **content questions** concerning this publication,
    email: *LLP.CLP@lexisnexis.com*

For **information on other LEXISNEXIS MATTHEW BENDER publications**,
    please call us at 800-223-1940
    or visit our online bookstore at *www.lexisnexis.com/bookstore*

ISBN: 978-1-5221-8780-6

 **LexisNexis®**

Matthew Bender & Company, Inc.
Editorial Offices
701 E. Water Street
Charlottesville, VA 22902
800-446-3410
www.lexisnexis.com

(Pub. 33510)

TEXAS PHARMACY LAWS AND REGULATIONS*

TABLE OF CONTENTS

*   includes all amendments and revisions effective prior to 12/1/2019

**   T.A.C. is Texas Administrative Code (a compilation of all regulations adopted by agencies in the state of Texas)

Texas Pharmacy Laws and Regulations is published by:

LexisNexis®
701 E. Water Street, Charlottesville, VA 22902
800/833-9844
www.lexisnexis.com

In consultation with:

Texas State Board of Pharmacy
William P. Hobby Building
333 Guadalupe Street, Suite 3-500
Austin, TX 78701
(512) 305-8000
www.pharmacy.texas.gov

LexisNexis® is pleased to provide you with the 2020 Edition of *Texas Pharmacy Laws and Regulations*. This publication is produced in December of each year. In this Edition you will find the latest legislative changes through the 2019 Regular Session, 86th Legislature, and the regulations are current through October 31, 2019.

Table of Contents

OCCUPATIONS CODE

TITLE 3. HEALTH PROFESSIONS

SUBTITLE J. PHARMACY AND PHARMACISTS
[EXPIRES SEPTEMBER 1, 2029]

Phr. Act

Phr. Act

Phr. Act

OCCUPATIONS CODE

TITLE 3. HEALTH PROFESSIONS

SUBTITLE J. PHARMACY AND PHARMACISTS
[EXPIRES SEPTEMBER 1, 2029]

CHAPTER 551. GENERAL PROVISIONS
[EXPIRES SEPTEMBER 1, 2029]

Sec. 551.001. [Expires September 1, 2029] Short Title.

This subtitle may be cited as the Texas Pharmacy Act.

Leg.H. Stats. 1999 76th Leg. Sess. Ch. 388, effective September 1, 1999; Stats. 2013, 83rd Leg., ch. 583 (S.B. 869), § 2, effective June 14, 2013.

Editor's note.- See Tex. Occ. Code Ann. § 551.005 for sunset provision.

Sec. 551.002. [Expires September 1, 2029] Legislative Declaration; Purpose.

(a) This subtitle shall be liberally construed to regulate in the public interest the practice of pharmacy in this state as a professional practice that affects the public health, safety, and welfare.

(b) It is a matter of public interest and concern that the practice of pharmacy merits and receives the confidence of the public and that only qualified persons be permitted to engage in the practice of pharmacy in this state.

(c) The purpose of this subtitle is to promote, preserve, and protect the public health, safety, and welfare through:
    (1) effectively controlling and regulating the practice of pharmacy; and
    (2) licensing pharmacies engaged in the sale, delivery, or distribution of prescription drugs and devices used in diagnosing and treating injury, illness, and disease.

Leg.H. Stats. 1999 76th Leg. Sess. Ch. 388, effective September 1, 1999.

Sec. 551.003. [Expires September 1, 2029] Definitions.

In Chapters 551-566:

(1) "Administer" means to directly apply a prescription drug to the body of a patient by any means, including injection, inhalation, or ingestion, by:
    (A) a person authorized by law to administer the drug, including a practitioner or an authorized agent under a practitioner's supervision; or
    (B) the patient at the direction of a practitioner.

(2) "Board" means the Texas State Board of Pharmacy.

(3) "Class A pharmacy license" or "community pharmacy license" means a license described by Section 560.051.

(4) "Class B pharmacy license" or "nuclear pharmacy license" means a license described by Section 560.051.

(5) "Class C pharmacy license" or "institutional pharmacy license" means a license described by Section 560.051.

(6) "Class D pharmacy license" or "clinic pharmacy license" means a license described by Section 560.051.

(7) "Class E pharmacy license" or "nonresident pharmacy license" means a license described by Section 560.051.

(8) "College of pharmacy" means a school, university, or college of pharmacy that:
    (A) satisfies the accreditation standards of the American Council on Pharmaceutical Education as adopted by the board; or
    (B) has degree requirements that meet the standards of accreditation set by the board.

(9) "Compounding" means the preparation, mixing, assembling, packaging, or labeling of a drug or device:
    (A) as the result of a practitioner's prescription drug order based on the practitioner-patient-pharmacist relationship in the course of professional practice;
    (B) for administration to a patient by a practitioner as the result of a practitioner's initiative based on the practitioner-patient-pharmacist relationship in the course of professional practice;
    (C) in anticipation of a prescription drug order based on a routine, regularly observed prescribing pattern; or
    (D) for or as an incident to research, teaching, or chemical analysis and not for selling or dispensing, except as allowed under Section 562.154 or Chapter 563.

(10) "Confidential record" means a health-related record, including a patient medication record, prescription drug order, or medication order, that:
    (A) contains information that identifies an individual; and
    (B) is maintained by a pharmacy or pharmacist.

(11) "Controlled substance" means a substance, including a drug:
    (A) listed in Schedule I, II, III, IV, or V, as established by the commissioner of public health under Chapter 481, Health and Safety Code, or in Penalty Group 1, 1-A, 2, 3, or 4, Chapter 481; or
    (B) included in Schedule I, II, III, IV, or V of the Comprehensive Drug Abuse Prevention and Control Act of 1970 (21 U.S.C. Section 801 et seq.).

(12) "Dangerous drug" means a drug or device that:
    (A) is not included in Penalty Group 1, 2, 3, or 4, Chapter 481, Health and Safety Code, and is unsafe for self-medication; or
    (B) bears or is required to bear the legend:

    (i) "Caution: federal law prohibits dispensing without prescription" or "Rx only" or another legend that complies with federal law; or

    (ii) "Caution: federal law restricts this drug to use by or on the order of a licensed veterinarian."

 (13) "Deliver" or "delivery" means the actual, constructive, or attempted transfer of a prescription drug or device or controlled substance from one person to another, with or without consideration.

 (14) "Designated agent" means:

  (A) an individual, including a licensed nurse, physician assistant, or pharmacist:

   (i) who is designated by a practitioner and authorized to communicate a prescription drug order to a pharmacist; and

   (ii) for whom the practitioner assumes legal responsibility;

  (B) a licensed nurse, physician assistant, or pharmacist employed in a health care facility to whom a practitioner communicates a prescription drug order; or

  (C) a registered nurse or physician assistant authorized by a practitioner to administer a prescription drug order for a dangerous drug under Subchapter B, Chapter 157.

 (15) "Device" means an instrument, apparatus, implement, machine, contrivance, implant, in vitro reagent, or other similar or related article, including a component part or accessory, that is required under federal or state law to be ordered or prescribed by a practitioner.

 (15-a) "Direct supervision" means supervision by a pharmacist who directs the activities of a pharmacist-intern, pharmacy technician, or pharmacy technician trainee to a sufficient degree to ensure the activities are performed accurately, safely, and without risk of harm to patients, as specified by board rule.

 (16) "Dispense" means to prepare, package, compound, or label, in the course of professional practice, a prescription drug or device for delivery to an ultimate user or the user's agent under a practitioner's lawful order.

 (17) "Distribute" means to deliver a prescription drug or device other than by administering or dispensing.

 (18) "Drug" means:

  (A) a substance recognized as a drug in a drug compendium, including the current official United States Pharmacopoeia, official National Formulary, or official Homeopathic Pharmacopoeia, or in a supplement to a drug compendium;

  (B) a substance intended for use in the diagnosis, cure, mitigation, treatment, or prevention of disease in a human or another animal;

  (C) a substance, other than food, intended to affect the structure or a function of the body of a human or another animal;

  (D) a substance intended for use as a component of a substance specified in Paragraph (A), (B), or (C);

  (E) a dangerous drug; or

  (F) a controlled substance.

 (19) "Drug regimen review" includes evaluation of prescription drug or medication orders and a patient medication record for:

  (A) a known allergy;

  (B) a rational therapy-contraindication;

  (C) a reasonable dose and route of administration;

  (D) reasonable directions for use;

  (E) duplication of therapy;

  (F) a drug-drug interaction;

  (G) drug-food interaction;

  (H) drug-disease interaction;

  (I) adverse drug reaction; and

  (J) proper use, including overuse or underuse.

 (20) "Internship" means a practical experience program that is approved by the board.

 (21) "Label" means written, printed, or graphic matter on the immediate container of a drug or device.

 (22) "Labeling" means the process of affixing a label, including all information required by federal and state statute or regulation, to a drug or device container. The term does not include:

  (A) the labeling by a manufacturer, packer, or distributor of a nonprescription drug or commercially packaged prescription drug or device; or

  (B) unit dose packaging.

 (23) "Manufacturing" means the production, preparation, propagation, conversion, or processing of a drug or device, either directly or indirectly, by extraction from a substance of natural origin or independently by a chemical or biological synthesis. The term includes packaging or repackaging a substance or labeling or relabeling a container and promoting and marketing the drug or device and preparing and promoting a commercially available product from a bulk compound for resale by a person, including a pharmacy or practitioner. The term does not include compounding.

 (24) "Medication order" means an order from a practitioner or a practitioner's designated agent for administration of a drug or device.

 (25) "Nonprescription drug" means a nonnarcotic drug or device that may be sold without a prescription and that is labeled and packaged in compliance with state or federal law.

 (26) "Patient counseling" means communication by a pharmacist of information, as specified by board rule, to a patient or caregiver to improve therapy by ensuring proper use of a drug or device.

 (27) "Pharmaceutical care" means providing drug therapy and other pharmaceutical services defined by board rule and intended to assist in curing or preventing a disease, eliminating or reducing a patient's symptom, or arresting or slowing a disease process.

 (28) "Pharmacist" means a person licensed by the board to practice pharmacy.

 (29) "Pharmacist-in-charge" means the pharmacist designated on a pharmacy license as the pharmacist who has the authority or responsibility for the pharmacy's compliance with statutes and rules relating to the practice of pharmacy.

 (30) "Pharmacist-intern" means:

  (A) an undergraduate student who is enrolled in the professional sequence of a college of pharmacy approved by the board and who is participating in a board-approved internship program; or

  (B) a graduate of a college of pharmacy who is participating in a board-approved internship.

(31) "Pharmacy" means a facility at which a prescription drug or medication order is received, processed, or dispensed under this subtitle, Chapter 481 or 483, Health and Safety Code, or the Comprehensive Drug Abuse Prevention and Control Act of 1970 (21 U.S.C. Section 801 et seq.). The term does not include a narcotic drug treatment program that is regulated under Chapter 466, Health and Safety Code.

(32) "Pharmacy technician" means an individual employed by a pharmacy whose responsibility is to provide technical services that do not require professional judgment regarding preparing and distributing drugs and who works under the direct supervision of and is responsible to a pharmacist. The term does not include a pharmacy technician trainee.

(32-a) "Pharmacy technician trainee" means an individual who is registered with the board as a pharmacy technician trainee and is authorized to participate in a pharmacy technician training program.

(33) "Practice of pharmacy" means:

  (A) providing an act or service necessary to provide pharmaceutical care;

  (B) interpreting or evaluating a prescription drug order or medication order;

  (C) participating in drug or device selection as authorized by law, and participating in drug administration, drug regimen review, or drug or drug-related research;

  (D) providing patient counseling;

  (E) being responsible for:

    (i) dispensing a prescription drug order or distributing a medication order;

    (ii) compounding or labeling a drug or device, other than labeling by a manufacturer, repackager, or distributor of a nonprescription drug or commercially packaged prescription drug or device;

    (iii) properly and safely storing a drug or device; or

    (iv) maintaining proper records for a drug or device;

  (F) performing for a patient a specific act of drug therapy management delegated to a pharmacist by a written protocol from a physician licensed in this state in compliance with Subtitle B; or

  (G) administering an immunization or vaccination under a physician's written protocol.

(34) "Practitioner" means:

  (A) a person licensed or registered to prescribe, distribute, administer, or dispense a prescription drug or device in the course of professional practice in this state, including a physician, dentist, podiatrist, or veterinarian but excluding a person licensed under this subtitle;

  (B) a person licensed by another state, Canada, or the United Mexican States in a health field in which, under the law of this state, a license holder in this state may legally prescribe a dangerous drug;

  (C) a person practicing in another state and licensed by another state as a physician, dentist, veterinarian, or podiatrist, who has a current federal Drug Enforcement Administration registration number and who may legally prescribe a Schedule II, III, IV, or V controlled substance, as specified under Chapter 481, Health and Safety Code, in that other state; or

  (D) an advanced practice registered nurse or physician assistant to whom a physician has delegated the authority to prescribe or order a drug or device under Section 157.0511, 157.0512, or 157.054.

(35) "Preceptor" has the meaning assigned by Section 558.057.

(36) "Prescription drug" means:

  (A) a substance for which federal or state law requires a prescription before the substance may be legally dispensed to the public;

  (B) a drug or device that under federal law is required, before being dispensed or delivered, to be labeled with the statement:

    (i) "Caution: federal law prohibits dispensing without prescription" or "Rx only" or another legend that complies with federal law; or

    (ii) "Caution: federal law restricts this drug to use by or on the order of a licensed veterinarian"; or

  (C) a drug or device that is required by federal or state statute or regulation to be dispensed on prescription or that is restricted to use by a practitioner only.

(37) "Prescription drug order" means:

  (A) an order from a practitioner or a practitioner's designated agent to a pharmacist for a drug or device to be dispensed; or

  (B) an order under Subchapter B, Chapter 157.

(38) "Prospective drug use review" means the review of a patient's drug therapy and prescription drug order or medication order, as defined by board rule, before dispensing or distributing a drug to the patient.

(39) "Provide" means to supply one or more unit doses of a nonprescription drug or dangerous drug to a patient.

(40) "Radioactive drug" means a drug that exhibits spontaneous disintegration of unstable nuclei with the emission of nuclear particles or photons, including a nonradioactive reagent kit or nuclide generator that is intended to be used in the preparation of the substance.

(41) "Substitution" means the dispensing of a drug or a brand of drug other than the drug or brand of drug ordered or prescribed.

(42) "Texas trade association" means a cooperative and voluntarily joined statewide association of business or professional competitors in this state designed to assist its members and its industry or profession in dealing with mutual business or professional problems and in promoting their common interest.

(42-a) "Therapeutic contact lens" means a contact lens that contains one or more drugs and that delivers the drugs into the wearer's eye.

(43) "Ultimate user" means a person who obtains or possesses a prescription drug or device for the person's own use or for the use of a member of the person's household or for administering to an animal owned by the person or by a member of the person's household.

(44) "Unit dose packaging" means the ordered amount of drug in a dosage form ready for administration to a particular patient, by the prescribed route at the prescribed time, and properly labeled with the name, strength, and expiration date of the drug.

(45) "Written protocol" means a physician's order, standing medical order, standing delegation order, or other order or protocol as defined by rule of the Texas Medical Board under Subtitle B.

Leg.H. Stats. 1999, 76th Leg., ch. 388 (H.B. 3155), § 1, effective September 1, 1999; am. Acts 2001, 77th Leg., ch. 112 (S.B. 1166), § 5, effective May 11, 2001; am. Acts 2001, 77th Leg., ch. 1254 (S.B. 768), § 1, effective September 1, 2001; am. Acts 2003, 78th Leg., ch. 88 (H.B. 1095), § 8, effective May 20, 2003; am. Acts 2005, 79th Leg., ch. 28 (S.B. 492), § 1, effective September 1, 2005; am. Acts 2005, 79th Leg., ch. 1345 (S.B. 410), § 2, effective September 1, 2005; am. Acts 2009, 81st Leg., ch. 396 (H.B. 1740), § 1, effective June 19, 2009; am. Acts 2013, 83rd Leg., ch. 418 (S.B. 406), § 19, effective November 1, 2013; am. Acts 2013, 83rd Leg., ch. 583 (S.B. 869), § 3, effective June 14, 2013; am. Acts 2017, 85th Leg., ch. 929 (S.B. 1633), § 1, effective September 1, 2017.

Sec. 551.004. [Expires September 1, 2029] Applicability of Subtitle.

(a) This subtitle does not apply to:
   (1) a practitioner licensed by the appropriate state board who supplies a patient of the practitioner with a drug in a manner authorized by state or federal law and who does not operate a pharmacy for the retailing of prescription drugs;
   (2) a member of the faculty of a college of pharmacy recognized by the board who is a pharmacist and who performs the pharmacist's services only for the benefit of the college;
   (3) a person who procures prescription drugs for lawful research, teaching, or testing and not for resale;
   (4) a home and community support services agency that possesses a dangerous drug as authorized by Section 142.0061, 142.0062, or 142.0063, Health and Safety Code; or
   (5) a dispensing organization, as defined by Section 487.001, Health and Safety Code, that cultivates, processes, and dispenses low-THC cannabis, as authorized by Chapter 487, Health and Safety Code, to a patient listed in the compassionate-use registry established under that chapter.
(b) This subtitle does not prevent a practitioner from administering a drug to a patient of the practitioner.
(c) This subtitle does not prevent the sale by a person, other than a pharmacist, firm, joint stock company, partnership, or corporation, of:
   (1) a nonprescription drug that is harmless if used according to instructions on a printed label on the drug's container and that does not contain a narcotic;
   (2) an insecticide, a fungicide, or a chemical used in the arts if the insecticide, fungicide, or chemical is properly labeled; or
   (3) an insecticide or fungicide that is mixed or compounded only for an agricultural purpose.
(d) A wholesaler or manufacturer may distribute a prescription drug as provided by state or federal law.
(e) This subtitle does not prevent a physician or therapeutic optometrist from dispensing and charging for therapeutic contact lenses. This subsection does not authorize a therapeutic optometrist to prescribe, administer, or dispense a drug that is otherwise outside the therapeutic optometrist's scope of practice.

Leg.H. Stats. 1999 76th Leg. Sess. Ch. 388, effective September 1, 1999; Stats. 2009 81st Leg. Sess. Ch. 396, effective June 19, 2009; am. Acts 2015, 84th Leg., ch. 301 (S.B. 339), § 5, effective June 1, 2015.

Sec. 551.005. [Expires September 1, 2029] Application of Sunset Act.

The Texas State Board of Pharmacy is subject to Chapter 325, Government Code (Texas Sunset Act). Unless continued in existence as provided by that chapter, the board is abolished and this subtitle expires September 1, 2029.

Leg.H. Stats. 1999 76th Leg. Sess. Ch. 388, effective September 1, 1999; Stats. 2005 79th Leg. Sess. Ch. 1345, effective September 1, 2005; am. Acts 2017, 85th Leg., ch. 485 (H.B. 2561), § 8, effective September 1, 2017.

Sec. 551.006. [Expires September 1, 2029] Exclusive Authority.

Notwithstanding any other law, a pharmacist has the exclusive authority to determine whether or not to dispense a drug.

Leg.H. Stats. 2017, 85th Leg., ch. 485 (H.B. 2561), § 9, effective September 1, 2017.

Sec. 551.008. [Expires September 1, 2029] Prohibition on Rule Violating Sincerely Held Religious Belief.

(a) All rules, regulations, or policies adopted by the board may not violate Chapter 110, Civil Practice and Remedies Code.
(b) A person may assert a violation of Subsection (a) as an affirmative defense in an administrative hearing or as a claim or defense in a judicial proceeding under Chapter 37, Civil Practice and Remedies Code.

Leg.H. Stats. 2017, 85th Leg., ch. 485 (H.B. 2561), § 9, effective September 1, 2017.

CHAPTER 552. TEXAS STATE BOARD OF PHARMACY
[EXPIRES SEPTEMBER 1, 2029]

Sec. 552.001. [Expires September 1, 2029] Membership.

(a) The Texas State Board of Pharmacy consists of 11 members appointed by the governor with the advice and consent of the senate as follows:
   (1) seven members who are pharmacists;
   (2) one member who is a pharmacy technician; and
   (3) three members who represent the public.
(b) Appointments to the board shall be made without regard to the race, color, disability, sex, religion, age, or national origin of the appointee.

Leg.H. Stats. 1999 76th Leg. Sess. Ch. 388, effective September 1, 1999; Stats. 2013, 83rd Leg., ch. 26 (S.B. 500), § 1, effective September 1, 2013.

Sec. 552.002. [Expires September 1, 2029] Qualifications.

(a)   The board must include representation for pharmacists who are primarily employed in Class A pharmacies and Class C pharmacies.

(b)   A pharmacist board member must, at the time of appointment:
   (1)   be a resident of this state;
   (2)   have been licensed for the five years preceding appointment;
   (3)   be in good standing to practice pharmacy in this state; and
   (4)   be practicing pharmacy in this state.

(b-1) A pharmacy technician board member must, at the time of appointment:
   (1)   be a resident of this state;
   (2)   have been registered as a pharmacy technician for the five years preceding appointment;
   (3)   be in good standing to act as a pharmacy technician in this state; and
   (4)   be acting as a pharmacy technician in this state.

(c)   Each person appointed to the board shall, not later than the 15th day after the date of appointment, qualify by taking the constitutional oath of office.

Leg.H. Stats. 1999 76th Leg. Sess. Ch. 388, effective September 1, 1999; Stats. 2013, 83rd Leg., ch. 26 (S.B. 500), § 2, effective September 1, 2013.

Sec. 552.003. [Expires September 1, 2029] Public Membership Eligibility.

A person is not eligible for appointment as a public member of the board if the person or the person's spouse:
   (1)   is registered, certified, or licensed by an occupational regulatory agency in the field of health care;
   (2)   is employed by or participates in the management of a business entity or other organization regulated by or receiving funds from the board;
   (3)   owns or controls, directly or indirectly, more than a 10 percent interest in a business entity or other organization regulated by or receiving funds from the board; or
   (4)   uses or receives a substantial amount of tangible goods, services, or funds from the board, other than compensation or reimbursement authorized by law for board membership, attendance, or expenses.

Leg.H. Stats. 1999 76th Leg. Sess. Ch. 388, effective September 1, 1999.

Sec. 552.004. [Expires September 1, 2029] Membership Restrictions.

(a)   A person may not be a member of the board if the person is required to register as a lobbyist under Chapter 305, Government Code, because of the person's activities for compensation on behalf of a profession related to the operation of the board.

(b)   A person may not be a member of the board if:
   (1)   the person is an officer, employee, or paid consultant of a Texas trade association in the field of health care; or
   (2)   the person's spouse is an officer, manager, or paid consultant of a Texas trade association in the field of health care.

Leg.H. Stats. 1999 76th Leg. Sess. Ch. 388, effective September 1, 1999; Stats. 2005 79th Leg. Sess. Ch. 1345, effective September 1, 2005.

Sec. 552.005. [Expires September 1, 2029] Terms; Vacancy.

(a)   Members of the board are appointed for staggered six-year terms, with either three or four members' terms, as applicable, expiring every other year at midnight on the last day of the state fiscal year in the last year of the member's term.

(b)   If a vacancy occurs during a member's term, the governor shall appoint a replacement to fill the unexpired term.

(c)   A board member may not serve more than two consecutive full terms. The completion of the unexpired portion of a full term is not service for a full term for purposes of this subsection.

(d)   A person appointed by the governor to a full term before the expiration of the term of the member being succeeded becomes a member of the board on the first day of the next state fiscal year following the appointment.

(e)   A person appointed to an unexpired portion of a full term becomes a member of the board on the day after the date of appointment.

Leg.H. Stats. 1999 76th Leg. Sess. Ch. 388, effective September 1, 1999; Stats. 2013, 83rd Leg., ch. 26 (S.B. 500), § 3, effective September 1, 2013.

Sec. 552.006. [Expires September 1, 2029] Board Member Training.

(a)   A person who is appointed to and qualifies for office as a member of the board may not vote, deliberate, or be counted as a member in attendance at a meeting of the board until the person completes a training program that complies with this section.

(b)   The training program must provide the person with information regarding:
   (1)   the law governing the board's operations;
   (2)   the programs, functions, rules, and budget of the board;
   (3)   the scope of and limitations on the rulemaking authority of the board;
   (4)   the types of board rules, interpretations, and enforcement actions that may implicate federal antitrust law by limiting competition or impacting prices charged by persons engaged in a profession or business the board regulates, including rules, interpretations, and enforcement actions that:
      (A)   regulate the scope of practice of persons in a profession or business the board regulates;
      (B)   restrict advertising by persons in a profession or business the board regulates;

      (C) affect the price of goods or services provided by persons in a profession or business the board regulates; and

      (D) restrict participation in a profession or business the board regulates;

    (5) the results of the most recent formal audit of the board;

    (6) the requirements of:

      (A) laws relating to open meetings, public information, administrative procedure, and disclosing conflicts of interest; and

      (B) other laws applicable to members of the board in performing their duties; and

    (7) any applicable ethics policies adopted by the board or the Texas Ethics Commission.

(c) A person appointed to the board is entitled to reimbursement, as provided by the General Appropriations Act, for the travel expenses incurred in attending the training program regardless of whether the attendance at the program occurs before or after the person qualifies for office.

(d) The executive director shall create a training manual that includes the information required by Subsection (b). The executive director shall distribute a copy of the training manual annually to each board member. On receipt of the training manual, each board member shall sign and submit to the executive director a statement acknowledging receipt of the training manual. The board shall publish a copy of each signed statement on the board's Internet website.

Leg.H. Stats. 1999, 76th Leg., ch. 388 (H.B. 3155), § 1, effective September 1, 1999; am. Acts 2005, 79th Leg., ch. 1345 (S.B. 410), § 4, effective September 1, 2005; am. Acts 2017, 85th Leg., ch. 485 (H.B. 2561), § 10, effective September 1, 2017.

Sec. 552.007. [Expires September 1, 2029] Officers.

(a) The governor shall designate a member of the board as the president of the board to serve in that capacity at the pleasure of the governor. The board shall elect from its members for one-year terms a vice president, treasurer, and other officers the board considers appropriate and necessary to conduct board business.

(b) The board's president shall preside at each board meeting and is responsible for the performance of the board's duties and functions under this subtitle.

(c) An officer, other than the president, shall perform the duties normally associated with the officer's position and other duties assigned to the officer by the board.

(d) The term of an officer begins on the first day of the state fiscal year following the officer's election and ends on election of a successor.

(e) A member elected as an officer may not serve more than two consecutive full terms in each office to which the member is elected.

Leg.H. Stats. 1999 76th Leg. Sess. Ch. 388, effective September 1, 1999; Stats. 2005 79th Leg. Sess. Ch. 1345, effective September 1, 2005.

Sec. 552.008. [Expires September 1, 2029] Grounds for Removal.

(a) It is a ground for removal from the board that a member:

    (1) does not have at the time of appointment the qualifications required for appointment to the board;

    (2) does not maintain during service on the board the qualifications required for appointment to the board;

    (3) violates a prohibition established by Section 552.004;

    (4) cannot, because of illness or disability, discharge the member's duties for a substantial part of the member's term; or

    (5) is absent from more than half of the regularly scheduled board meetings the member is eligible to attend during a calendar year, unless the absence is excused by majority vote of the board.

(b) If the executive director has knowledge that a potential ground for removal exists, the executive director shall notify the president of the board of the ground. The president shall then notify the governor that a potential ground for removal exists.

(c) The validity of an action of the board is not affected by the fact that the action is taken when a ground for removal of a board member exists.

Leg.H. Stats. 1999 76th Leg. Sess. Ch. 388, effective September 1, 1999.

Sec. 552.009. [Expires September 1, 2029] Per Diem; Reimbursement.

(a) Each member of the board is entitled to a per diem set by legislative appropriation for each day the member engages in board business.

(b) A member is entitled to reimbursement for travel expenses as prescribed by the General Appropriations Act.

Leg.H. Stats. 1999 76th Leg. Sess. Ch. 388, effective September 1, 1999; Stats. 2005 79th Leg. Sess. Ch. 1345, effective September 1, 2005.

Sec. 552.010. [Expires September 1, 2029] Meetings.

(a) The board shall meet at least once every four months to transact board business.

(b) The board may meet at other times at the call of the board's president or two-thirds of the board's members.

Leg.H. Stats. 1999 76th Leg. Sess. Ch. 388, effective September 1, 1999; Stats. 2013, 83rd Leg., ch. 26 (S.B. 500), § 4, effective September 1, 2013.

Sec. 552.011. [Expires September 1, 2029] Executive Session.

(a) The board may, in accordance with Chapter 551, Government Code, conduct a portion of a board meeting in executive session.

(b) The board may conduct in executive session a deliberation relating to discipline of a license holder. At the conclusion of the deliberation, in open session the board shall vote and announce the board's decision relating to the license holder.

(c) The board may conduct in executive session a disciplinary hearing relating to a pharmacist or pharmacy student who is impaired because of chemical abuse or mental or physical illness.

Leg.H. Stats. 1999 76th Leg. Sess. Ch. 388, effective September 1, 1999.

Sec. 552.012. [Expires September 1, 2029] Quorum; Validity of Board Action.

Except when a greater number is required by this subtitle or by board rule, an action of the board must be by a majority of a quorum.

Leg.H. Stats. 1999 76th Leg. Sess. Ch. 388, effective September 1, 1999.

CHAPTER 553. EXECUTIVE DIRECTOR AND OTHER BOARD PERSONNEL
[EXPIRES SEPTEMBER 1, 2029]

Sec. 553.001. [Expires September 1, 2029] Executive Director.

The board shall employ an executive director.

Leg.H. Stats. 1999 76th Leg. Sess. Ch. 388, effective September 1, 1999.

Sec. 553.002. [Expires September 1, 2029] Qualifications of Executive Director.

The executive director must be a pharmacist.

Leg.H. Stats. 1999 76th Leg. Sess. Ch. 388, effective September 1, 1999.

Sec. 553.003. [Expires September 1, 2029] General Duties of Executive Director.

(a) The executive director is an ex officio member of the board without vote.
(b) The executive director is a full-time employee of the board and shall:
    (1) serve as secretary to the board;
    (2) perform the regular administrative functions of the board and any other duty as the board directs; and
    (3) under the direction of the board, perform the duties required by this subtitle or designated by the board.
(c) The executive director may not perform a discretionary or decision-making function for which the board is solely responsible.
(d) The executive director shall keep the seal of the board. The executive director may affix the seal only in the manner prescribed by the board.

Leg.H. Stats. 1999, 76th Leg., ch. 388 (H.B. 3155), § 1, effective September 1, 1999; am. Acts 2017, 85th Leg., ch. 485 (H.B. 2561), § 11, effective September 1, 2017.

Sec. 553.004. [Expires September 1, 2029] Personnel.

The board may employ persons in positions or capacities the board considers necessary to properly conduct the board's business and fulfill the board's responsibilities under this subtitle.

Leg.H. Stats. 1999 76th Leg. Sess. Ch. 388, effective September 1, 1999.

Sec. 553.005. [Expires September 1, 2029] Employee Restrictions.

(a) A person may not be an employee of the board employed in a "bona fide executive, administrative, or professional capacity," as that phrase is used for purposes of establishing an exemption to the overtime provisions of the federal Fair Labor Standards Act of 1938 (29 U.S.C. Section 201 et seq.), if:
    (1) the person is an officer, employee, or paid consultant of a Texas trade association in the field of health care; or
    (2) the person's spouse is an officer, manager, or paid consultant of a Texas trade association in the field of health care.
(b) A person may not act as general counsel to the board if the person is required to register as a lobbyist under Chapter 305, Government Code, because of the person's activities for compensation on behalf of a profession related to the operation of the board.

Leg.H. Stats. 1999 76th Leg. Sess. Ch. 388, effective September 1, 1999; Stats. 2005 79th Leg. Sess. Ch. 1345, effective September 1, 2005.

Sec. 553.006. [Expires September 1, 2029] Possession by Employee of Regulated Substance.

A board employee may possess a dangerous drug or controlled substance when acting in the employee's official capacity.

Leg.H. Stats. 1999 76th Leg. Sess. Ch. 388, effective September 1, 1999.

Sec. 553.007. [Expires September 1, 2029] Division of Responsibilities.

The board shall develop and implement policies that clearly define the responsibilities of the board and the staff of the board.

Leg.H. Stats. 1999 76th Leg. Sess. Ch. 388, effective September 1, 1999.

Sec. 553.008. [Expires September 1, 2029] Qualifications and Standards of Conduct Information.

The board shall provide, as often as necessary, to its members and employees information regarding their:

(1) qualifications for office or employment under this subtitle; and
(2) responsibilities under applicable laws relating to standards of conduct for state officers or employees.

Leg.H. Stats. 1999 76th Leg. Sess. Ch. 388, effective September 1, 1999.

Sec. 553.009. [Expires September 1, 2029] Career Ladder Program; Performance Evaluations.
(a) The executive director or the executive director's designee shall develop an intra-agency career ladder program. The program must require intra-agency postings of all nonentry level positions concurrently with any public posting.
(b) The executive director or the executive director's designee shall develop a system of annual performance evaluations. All merit pay for board employees must be based on the system established under this subsection.

Leg.H. Stats. 1999 76th Leg. Sess. Ch. 388, effective September 1, 1999.

Sec. 553.010. [Expires September 1, 2029] Equal Employment Opportunity Policy; Report.
(a) The executive director or the executive director's designee shall prepare and maintain a written policy statement to ensure implementation of an equal employment opportunity program under which all personnel transactions are made without regard to race, color, disability, sex, religion, age, or national origin. The policy statement must include:
(1) personnel policies, including policies related to recruitment, evaluation, selection, appointment, training, and promotion of personnel that are in compliance with Chapter 21, Labor Code;
(2) a comprehensive analysis of the board workforce that meets federal and state guidelines;
(3) procedures by which a determination can be made of significant underuse in the board workforce of all persons for whom federal or state guidelines encourage a more equitable balance; and
(4) reasonable methods to appropriately address those areas of significant underuse.
(b) A policy statement prepared under Subsection (a) must:
(1) cover an annual period;
(2) be updated annually;
(3) be reviewed by the Commission on Human Rights for compliance with Subsection (a)(1); and
(4) be filed with the governor.
(c) The governor shall deliver a biennial report to the legislature based on the information received under Subsection (b). The report may be made separately or as a part of other biennial reports made to the legislature.

Leg.H. Stats. 1999 76th Leg. Sess. Ch. 388, effective September 1, 1999.

CHAPTER 554. BOARD POWERS AND DUTIES; RULEMAKING AUTHORITY
[EXPIRES SEPTEMBER 1, 2029]

SUBCHAPTER A. POWERS AND DUTIES
[EXPIRES SEPTEMBER 1, 2029]

Sec. 554.001. [Expires September 1, 2029] General Powers and Duties of Board.
(a) The board shall:
(1) administer and enforce this subtitle and rules adopted under this subtitle and enforce other laws relating to the practice of pharmacy and other powers and duties granted under other law;
(2) cooperate with other state and federal agencies in the enforcement of any law relating to the practice of pharmacy or any drug or drug-related law;
(3) maintain an office in which permanent records are kept; and
(4) preserve a record of the board's proceedings.
(b) The board may:
(1) join a professional organization or association organized to promote the improvement of the standards of the practice of pharmacy for protecting the health and welfare of the public; and
(2) appoint committees from the board's membership, an advisory committee from the pharmacy profession, and any other group to assist in administering this subtitle.
(c) The board may:
(1) issue a duplicate copy of a license to practice pharmacy or a license renewal certificate on a request from the holder and on payment of a fee determined by the board; and
(2) inspect a facility licensed under this subtitle for compliance with this subtitle.
(d) The board may be represented by counsel, including the attorney general, district attorney, or county attorney, if necessary in a legal action taken under this subtitle.
(e) The board shall develop formal policies outlining the structure, role, and responsibilities of each committee established under Subsection (b)(2) that contains board members. The board may adopt rules to implement this subsection.

Leg.H. Stats. 1999 76th Leg. Sess. Ch. 388, effective September 1, 1999; Stats. 2005 79th Leg. Sess. Ch. 1345, effective September 1, 2005.

Sec. 554.0011. [Expires September 1, 2029] Use of Alternative Rulemaking and Dispute Resolution.
(a) The board shall develop a policy to encourage the use of:

(1) negotiated rulemaking procedures under Chapter 2008, Government Code, for the adoption of board rules; and
(2) appropriate alternative dispute resolution procedures under Chapter 2009, Government Code, to assist in the resolution of internal and external disputes under the board's jurisdiction.
(b) The board's procedures relating to alternative dispute resolution must conform, to the extent possible, to any model guidelines issued by the State Office of Administrative Hearings for the use of alternative dispute resolution by state agencies.
(c) The board shall:
(1) coordinate the implementation of the policy adopted under Subsection (a);
(2) provide training as needed to implement the procedures for negotiated rulemaking or alternative dispute resolution; and
(3) collect data concerning the effectiveness of those procedures.

Leg.H. Stats 2017, 85th Leg., ch. 485 (H.B. 2561), § 12, effective September 1, 2017.

Sec. 554.002. [Expires September 1, 2029] Regulation of Practice of Pharmacy.

The board shall regulate the practice of pharmacy in this state by:
(1) issuing a license after examination or by reciprocity to an applicant qualified to practice pharmacy and issuing a license to a pharmacy under this subtitle;
(2) renewing a license to practice pharmacy and a license to operate a pharmacy;
(3) determining and issuing standards for recognizing and approving degree requirements of colleges of pharmacy whose graduates are eligible for a license in this state;
(4) specifying and enforcing requirements for practical training, including an internship;
(5) enforcing the provisions of this subtitle relating to:
   (A) the conduct or competence of a pharmacist practicing in this state and the conduct of a pharmacy operating in this state; and
   (B) the suspension, revocation, retirement, or restriction of a license to practice pharmacy or to operate a pharmacy or the imposition of an administrative penalty or reprimand on a license holder;
(6) regulating the training, qualifications, and employment of a pharmacist-intern, pharmacy technician, and pharmacy technician trainee; and
(7) determining and issuing standards for recognizing and approving a pharmacy residency program for purposes of Subchapter W, Chapter 61, Education Code.

Leg.H. Stats. 1999 76th Leg. Sess. Ch. 388, effective September 1, 1999; Stats. 2001 77th Leg. Sess. Ch. 1420, effective September 1, 2001; Stats. 2013, 83rd Leg., ch. 583 (S.B. 869), § 4, effective June 14, 2013.

Sec. 554.0021. [Expires September 1, 2029] Recognition and Approval of Pharmacist Certification Programs.

(a) The board shall determine and issue standards for recognizing and approving pharmacist certification programs.
(b) In adopting standards under Subsection (a), the board shall include a requirement that a pharmacist may not use the designation "board certified" unless the pharmacist has successfully completed a certification program that meets the board's standards.

Leg.H. Stats. 2001 77th Leg. Sess. Ch. 1420, effective September 1, 2001.

Sec. 554.003. [Expires September 1, 2029] Procedures.

The board by rule shall specify:
(1) the licensing procedures to be followed, including specification of forms to be used, in applying for a pharmacy license; and
(2) fees for filing an application for a pharmacy license.

Leg.H. Stats. 1999 76th Leg. Sess. Ch. 388, effective September 1, 1999.

Sec. 554.004. [Expires September 1, 2029] Administration of Medication.

(a) The board shall specify conditions under which a pharmacist may administer medication, including an immunization and vaccination. The conditions must ensure that:
(1) a licensed health care provider authorized to administer the medication is not reasonably available to administer the medication;
(2) failure to administer the medication, other than an immunization or vaccination, might result in a significant delay or interruption of a critical phase of drug therapy;
(3) the pharmacist possesses the necessary skill, education, and certification as specified by the board to administer the medication;
(4) within a reasonable time after administering medication, the pharmacist notifies the licensed health care provider responsible for the patient's care that the medication was administered;
(5) the pharmacist may not administer medication to a patient at the patient's residence, except at a licensed nursing home or hospital;
(6) the pharmacist administers an immunization or vaccination under a physician's written protocol and meets the standards established by the board; and
(7) the authority of a pharmacist to administer medication may not be delegated.
(b) This section does not prohibit a pharmacist from preparing or manipulating a biotechnological agent or device.

(c)   This section does not prohibit a pharmacist from performing an act delegated by a physician in accordance with Chapter 157. The pharmacist performing a delegated medical act under that chapter is considered to be performing a medical act and not to be engaging in the practice of pharmacy.

Leg.H. Stats. 1999 76th Leg. Sess. Ch. 388, effective September 1, 1999.

Sec. 554.005. [Expires September 1, 2029] Prescription Drugs and Devices.

(a)   In regulating the practice of pharmacy and the use in this state of prescription drugs and devices in the diagnosis, mitigation, or treatment or prevention of injury, illness, or disease, the board shall:
     (1)   regulate the delivery or distribution of a prescription drug or device;
     (2)   specify minimum standards for the professional environment, technical equipment, and security in a prescription dispensing area;
     (3)   specify minimum standards for:
         (A)   drug storage;
         (B)   maintenance of prescription drug records; and
         (C)   procedures for the:
             (i)   delivering and dispensing in a suitable, appropriately labeled container;
             (ii)   providing of prescription drugs or devices;
             (iii)   monitoring of drug therapy; and
             (iv)   counseling of patients on proper use of a prescription drug or device in the practice of pharmacy;
     (4)   adopt rules regulating a prescription drug order or medication order transmitted by electronic means; and
     (5)   register a balance used for compounding drugs in a pharmacy licensed in this state and periodically inspect the balance to verify accuracy.
(b)   In implementing Subsection (a)(1), the board may, after notice and hearing, seize any prescription drug or device that poses a hazard to the public health and welfare.
(c)   In implementing Subsection (a)(1), the board may not regulate:
     (1)   any manufacturer's representative or employee acting in the normal course of business;
     (2)   a person engaged in the wholesale drug business and licensed by the commissioner of public health as provided by Chapter 431, Health and Safety Code; or
     (3)   an employee of a person described by Subdivision (2) if the employee is acting in the normal course of business.

Leg.H. Stats. 1999 76th Leg. Sess. Ch. 388, effective September 1, 1999; Stats. 2001 77th Leg. Sess. Ch. 1420, effective September 1, 2001.

Sec. 554.006. [Expires September 1, 2029] Fees.

(a)   The board by rule shall establish reasonable and necessary fees so that the fees, in the aggregate, produce sufficient revenue to cover the cost of administering this subtitle.
(b)   The board by rule shall establish reasonable and necessary fees so that the fees, in the aggregate, produce sufficient revenue to cover the cost of establishing and maintaining the program described by Sections 481.075, 481.076, and 481.0761, Health and Safety Code.
(c)   The board may assess the fee described by Subsection (b) on individuals or entities authorized to prescribe or dispense controlled substances under Chapter 481, Health and Safety Code, and to access the program described by Sections 481.075, 481.076, and 481.0761, Health and Safety Code.
(d)   Each agency that licenses individuals or entities authorized to prescribe or dispense controlled substances under Chapter 481, Health and Safety Code, and to access the program described by Sections 481.075, 481.076, and 481.0761, Health and Safety Code, shall increase the occupational license, permit, or registration fee of the license holders or use available excess revenue in an amount sufficient to operate that program as specified by the board.
(e)   A fee collected by an agency under Subsection (d) shall be transferred to the board for the purpose of establishing and maintaining the program described by Sections 481.075, 481.076, and 481.0761, Health and Safety Code.
(f)   Grants received by the board to implement or operate the program described by Sections 481.075, 481.076, and 481.0761, Health and Safety Code, may be used by the board to offset or reduce the amount of fees paid by each agency that licenses individuals or entities who are or may be authorized to prescribe or dispense controlled substances under Chapter 481, Health and Safety Code.

Leg.H. Stats. 1999 76th Leg. Sess. Ch. 388, effective September 1, 1999; am. Acts 2015, 84th Leg., ch. 1268 (S.B. 195), § 23, effective September 1, 2016.

Sec. 554.007. [Expires September 1, 2029] Funds.

(a)   The board shall deposit revenue collected under this subtitle to the credit of the general revenue fund.
(b)   The board may receive and spend money, or use gifts, grants, and other funds and assets, in addition to money collected under Subsection (a), in accordance with state law.

Leg.H. Stats. 1999 76th Leg. Sess. Ch. 388, effective September 1, 1999; Stats. 2005 79th Leg. Sess. Ch. 1345, effective September 1, 2005; Stats. 2013, 83rd Leg., ch. 583 (S.B. 869), § 5, effective June 14, 2013.

Sec. 554.008. Repealed.

Repealed Stats. 2003 78th Leg. Sess. Ch. 285, effective September 1, 2003.

Sec. 554.009. [Expires September 1, 2029] Lease or Purchase of Vehicles.

(a) The board may lease or purchase vehicles for use in official board business.

(b) A vehicle acquired under Subsection (a) is exempt from a requirement to bear state government identification.

(c) The board may register a vehicle with the Texas Department of Motor Vehicles in an alias name only for investigative personnel.

Leg.H. Stats. 1999 76th Leg. Sess. Ch. 388, effective September 1, 1999; Stats. 2009 81st Leg. Sess. Ch. 933, effective September 1, 2009.

Sec. 554.010. [Expires September 1, 2029] Peace Officers.

(a) The board may commission as a peace officer to enforce this subtitle an employee who has been certified as qualified to be a peace officer by the Texas Commission on Law Enforcement.

(b) An employee commissioned as a peace officer under this subtitle has the powers, privileges, and immunities of a peace officer while carrying out duties as a peace officer under this subtitle.

Leg.H. Stats. 1999 76th Leg. Sess. Ch. 388, effective September 1, 1999; Stats. 2009 81st Leg. Sess. Ch. 1361, effective June 19, 2009; Stats. 2013, 83rd Leg., ch. 93 (S.B. 686), § 2.57, effective May 18, 2013.

Sec. 554.011. [Expires September 1, 2029] Pilot and Demonstration Research Projects.

(a) The board may approve pilot and demonstration research projects for innovative applications in the practice of pharmacy.

(b) The board shall specify the procedures to be followed in applying for approval of a project.

(c) The approval may include a provision granting an exception to any rule adopted under this subtitle. The board may extend the time an exception to a rule is granted as necessary for the board to adopt an amendment or modification of the rule. The board may condition approval of a project on compliance with this section and rules adopted under this section.

(d) A project may not include therapeutic substitution or substitution of a medical device used in patient care.

(e) This section does not expand the definition of pharmacy under this subtitle.

Leg.H. Stats. 1999 76th Leg. Sess. Ch. 388, effective September 1, 1999; Stats. 2001 77th Leg. Sess. Ch. 1420, effective September 1, 2001.

Sec. 554.012. [Expires September 1, 2029] Notification Relating to Therapeutic Optometrists.

The board shall inform each holder of a license to practice pharmacy and each holder of a license to operate a pharmacy of the authority of a therapeutic optometrist to prescribe a drug under Section 351.357 by annually mailing to each license holder a notice that:

(1) describes the authority of a therapeutic optometrist to prescribe a drug; and

(2) lists each drug that a therapeutic optometrist may lawfully prescribe.

Leg.H. Stats. 1999 76th Leg. Sess. Ch. 388, effective September 1, 1999.

Sec. 554.013. Repealed.

Repealed Stats. 2011 82nd Leg. Ch. 1083, effective June 17, 2011.

Sec. 554.014. [Expires September 1, 2029] Information Provided to License Holders.

At least once each biennium, the board shall provide to license holders information on:

(1) prescribing and dispensing pain medications, with particular emphasis on Schedule II and Schedule III controlled substances;

(2) abusive and addictive behavior of certain persons who use prescription pain medications;

(3) common diversion strategies employed by certain persons who use prescription pain medications, including fraudulent prescription patterns; and

(4) the appropriate use of pain medications and the differences between addiction, pseudo-addiction, tolerance, and physical dependence.

Leg.H. Stats. 2003 78th Leg. Sess. Ch. 1163, effective September 1, 2003.

Sec. 554.015. [Expires September 1, 2029] Poison Control Center Information.

The board shall provide to license holders information regarding the services provided by poison control centers.

Leg.H. Stats. 2003 78th Leg. Sess. Ch. 1163, effective September 1, 2003.

Sec. 554.016. [Expires September 1, 2029] Canadian Pharmacy Inspection; Designation; Fees; Information.

(a) The board shall designate at least one and not more than 10 Canadian pharmacies whose primary business is to dispense prescription drugs under prescription drug orders to Canadian residents, as having passed inspection by the board for shipping, mailing, or delivering to this state a prescription dispensed under a prescription drug order to a resident in this state.

(b) The board by rule shall set fees in amounts reasonable and necessary to cover the costs incurred by the board in inspecting Canadian pharmacies as provided by Subsection (a).

(c) The board shall establish and maintain an Internet website to provide information necessary to enable residents of this state to conveniently order prescription drugs from Canadian pharmacies designated by the board as having passed inspection to dispense prescription drugs to residents in this state in accordance with this subtitle and board rules. The board shall include on the website a statement that the board is not liable for any act or omission of a Canadian pharmacy designated as having passed inspection to dispense prescription drugs to residents in this state.

Leg.H. Stats. 2005 79th Leg. Sess. Ch. 1345, effective September 1, 2005.

Sec. 554.017. [Expires September 1, 2029] List of Pharmacists Authorized to Sign Prescription Drug Orders.

The board shall provide on its Internet website a list of pharmacists who are authorized to sign a prescription drug order under Section 157.101(b-1), including the name of the pharmacist's delegating physician under the protocol required under that subsection.

Leg.H. Stats. 2009 81st Leg. Sess. Ch. 271, effective September 1, 2009.

SUBCHAPTER B. RULEMAKING
[EXPIRES SEPTEMBER 1, 2029]

Sec. 554.051. [Expires September 1, 2029] Rulemaking: General Powers and Duties.

(a) The board shall adopt rules consistent with this subtitle for the administration and enforcement of this subtitle.

(a-1) The board may adopt rules to administer Sections 481.073, 481.074, 481.075, 481.076, 481.0761, 481.0762, 481.0763, 481.0764, 481.0765, and 481.0766, Health and Safety Code.

(b) If the board determines it necessary to protect the health and welfare of the citizens of this state, the board may make a rule concerning the operation of a licensed pharmacy located in this state applicable to a pharmacy licensed by the board that is located in another state.

(c) The board shall adopt rules regarding records to be maintained by a pharmacist performing a specific act under a written protocol.

(d) The board by rule shall specify minimum standards for professional responsibility in the conduct of a pharmacy.

Leg.H. Stats. 1999, 76th Leg., ch. 388 (H.B. 3155), § 1, effective September 1, 1999; am. Acts 2015, 84th Leg., ch. 1268 (S.B. 195), § 24, effective September 1, 2016; am. Acts 2017, 85th Leg., ch. 485 (H.B. 2561), § 13, effective September 1, 2017.

Sec. 554.052. [Expires September 1, 2029] Immunizations and Vaccinations; Physician Supervision.

(a) The board by rule shall require a pharmacist to notify a physician who prescribes an immunization or vaccination within 24 hours after the pharmacist administers the immunization or vaccination.

(b) The board shall establish minimum education and continuing education standards for a pharmacist who administers an immunization or vaccination. The standards must include Centers for Disease Control and Prevention training, basic life support training, and hands-on training in techniques for administering immunizations and vaccinations.

(c) Supervision by a physician is adequate if the delegating physician:

(1) is responsible for formulating or approving an order or protocol, including the physician's order, standing medical order, or standing delegation order, and periodically reviews the order or protocol and the services provided to a patient under the order or protocol;

(2) except as provided by Subsection (c-1), has established a physician-patient relationship with each patient under 14 years of age and referred the patient to the pharmacist;

(3) is geographically located to be easily accessible to the pharmacy where an immunization or vaccination is administered;

(4) receives, as appropriate, a periodic status report on the patient, including any problem or complication encountered; and

(5) is available through direct telecommunication for consultation, assistance, and direction.

(c-1) A pharmacist may administer an influenza vaccination to a patient over seven years of age without an established physician-patient relationship.

(d) The Texas Medical Board by rule shall establish the minimum content of a written order or protocol. The order or protocol may not permit delegation of medical diagnosis.

Leg.H. Stats. 1999 76th Leg. Sess. Ch. 388, effective September 1, 1999; Stats. 2009 81st Leg. Sess. Ch. 375, effective September 1, 2009.

Sec. 554.053. [Expires September 1, 2029] Rulemaking: Pharmacy Technician and Pharmacy Technician Trainee.

(a) The board shall establish rules for the use and the duties of a pharmacy technician and pharmacy technician trainee employed by a pharmacy licensed by the board. A pharmacy technician and pharmacy technician trainee shall be responsible to and must be directly supervised by a pharmacist.

(b) The board may not adopt a rule establishing a ratio of pharmacists to pharmacy technicians and pharmacy technician trainees in a Class C pharmacy or limiting the number of pharmacy technicians or pharmacy technician trainees that may be used in a Class C pharmacy.

(c) The board shall determine and issue standards for recognition and approval of a training program for pharmacy technicians and maintain a list of board-approved training programs that meet those standards.

Leg.H. Stats. 1999, 76th Leg., ch. 388 (H.B. 3155), § 1, effective September 1, 1999; am. Acts 2001, 77th Leg., ch. 1420 (H.B. 2812), § 14.303(a), effective September 1, 2001; am. Acts 2013, 83rd Leg., ch. 583 (S.B. 869), §§ 6, 7, effective June 14, 2013; am. Acts 2017, 85th Leg., ch. 929 (S.B. 1633), § 2, effective September 1, 2017.

Sec. 554.054. [Expires September 1, 2029] Rules Restricting Advertising or Competitive Bidding.

(a) The board may not adopt rules restricting advertising or competitive bidding by a person regulated by the board except to prohibit false, misleading, or deceptive practices by that person.

(b) The board may not include in rules to prohibit false, misleading, or deceptive practices by a person regulated by the board a rule that:

    (1) restricts the use of any advertising medium;

    (2) restricts the person's personal appearance or use of the person's voice in an advertisement;

    (3) relates to the size or duration of an advertisement used by the person; or

    (4) restricts the use of a trade name in advertising by the person.

Leg.H. Stats. 1999 76th Leg. Sess. Ch. 388, effective September 1, 1999.

Sec. 554.055. [Expires September 1, 2029] Rulemaking; Electronic Media.

The board shall adopt rules regarding the sale and delivery of drugs by use of electronic media, including the Internet.

Leg.H. Stats. 2001 77th Leg. Sess. Ch. 972, effective September 1, 2001.

Sec. 554.056. [Expires September 1, 2029] Rulemaking; Addition of Flavoring to Commercial Product.

The board may adopt rules governing the procedures for a pharmacist, as part of compounding, to add flavoring to a commercial product at the request of a patient or a patient's agent.

Leg.H. Stats. 2007, 80th Leg. Sess. Ch. 550, effective September 1, 2007.

Sec. 554.057. [Expires September 1, 2029] Rulemaking; Implementation of Drug Therapy Under Protocol.

The board, with the advice of the Texas Medical Board, shall adopt rules that allow a pharmacist to implement or modify a patient's drug therapy pursuant to a physician's delegation under Section 157.101(b-1).

Leg.H. Stats. 2009 81st Leg. Sess. Ch. 271, effective September 1, 2009.

CHAPTER 555. PUBLIC INTEREST INFORMATION AND COMPLAINT PROCEDURES
[EXPIRES SEPTEMBER 1, 2029]

Sec. 555.001. [Expires September 1, 2029] Public Interest Information.

(a) The board shall prepare information of public interest describing the functions of the board and procedures by which complaints are filed with and resolved by the board.

(b) The board shall make the information available to the public and appropriate state agencies.

(c) The board shall provide on its website a list of all Internet pharmacies licensed by the board and shall provide information about each pharmacy, including the pharmacy's name, license number, and state of physical location. In this subsection, an Internet pharmacy is a pharmacy physically located in this state or another state that:

    (1) dispenses a prescription drug or device under a prescription drug order in response to a request received by way of the Internet to dispense the drug or device; and

    (2) delivers the drug or device to a patient in this state by United States mail, common carrier, or delivery service.

(d) Information regarding the home address or home telephone number of a person licensed or registered under this subtitle, including a pharmacy owner, is confidential and not subject to disclosure under Chapter 552, Government Code, but each person licensed or registered must provide the board with a business address or address of record that is subject to disclosure under Chapter 552, Government Code, and that may be posted on the board's Internet site or in the board's licensure verification database.

Leg.H. Stats. 1999 76th Leg. Sess. Ch. 388, effective September 1, 1999; Stats. 2005 79th Leg. Sess. Ch. 1345, effective September 1, 2005.

Sec. 555.002. [Expires September 1, 2029] Complaints.

(a) The board by rule shall establish methods by which consumers and service recipients are notified of the name, mailing address, and telephone number of the board for the purpose of directing complaints to the board. The board may provide for that notice:

    (1) on each registration form, application, or written contract for services of a person regulated by the board;

    (2) on a sign prominently displayed in the place of business of each person regulated by the board;

    (3) on an electronic messaging system in a font specified by board rule prominently displayed in the place of business of each person regulated by the board; or

    (4) in a bill for service provided by a person regulated by the board.

(b) The board shall list with its regular telephone number any toll-free telephone number established under other state law that may be called to present a complaint about a health professional.

(c) Any person who has knowledge relating to an action or omission of a pharmacist or pharmacy licensed by the board that constitutes a ground for disciplinary action under Section 565.001 or 565.002, or a rule adopted under one of those sections, may provide relevant records, report relevant information, or provide assistance to the board.

(d) A complaint directed to the board under this section may be made through the Internet.

Leg.H. Stats. 1999 76th Leg. Sess. Ch. 388, effective September 1, 1999; Stats. 2001 77th Leg. Sess. Ch. 972, effective September 1, 2001; am. Acts 2015, 84th Leg., ch. 599 (S.B. 460), § 2, effective September 1, 2015.

Sec. 555.003. [Expires September 1, 2029] Complaint Form.

The board by rule shall adopt a form on which a person may file a complaint with the board.

Leg.H. Stats. 1999 76th Leg. Sess. Ch. 388, effective September 1, 1999.

Sec. 555.004. [Expires September 1, 2029] Assistance with Complaint.

The board shall provide reasonable assistance to a person who wants to file a complaint with the board.

Leg.H. Stats. 1999 76th Leg. Sess. Ch. 388, effective September 1, 1999.

Sec. 555.005. [Expires September 1, 2029] Records of Complaints.

For each complaint received by the board, the board shall maintain information about parties to the complaint, including the complainant's identity, the subject matter of the complaint, a summary of the results of the review or investigation of the complaint, and the disposition of the complaint.

Leg.H. Stats. 1999 76th Leg. Sess. Ch. 388, effective September 1, 1999; Stats. 2005 79th Leg. Sess. Ch. 1345, effective September 1, 2005; Stats. 2013, 83rd Leg., ch. 522 (S.B. 404), § 1, effective September 1, 2013.

Sec. 555.006. [Expires September 1, 2029] Notification Concerning Complaint.

(a) The board shall notify the complainant not later than the 30th day after the date the board receives the complaint and shall provide an estimated time for resolution of the complaint.

(b) If a written complaint is filed with the board that the board has authority to resolve, the board, at least every four months and until final disposition of the complaint, shall notify the parties to the complaint of the status of the complaint unless the notice would jeopardize an undercover investigation.

Leg.H. Stats. 1999 76th Leg. Sess. Ch. 388, effective September 1, 1999.

Sec. 555.007. [Expires September 1, 2029] General Rules Regarding Complaint Investigation and Disposition.

(a) The board shall adopt policies and procedures concerning the investigation of a complaint filed with the board. The policies and procedures must:
   (1) determine the seriousness of the complaint;
   (2) ensure that a complaint is not closed without appropriate consideration;
   (3) ensure that a letter is sent to the person who filed the complaint explaining the action taken on the complaint;
   (4) ensure that the person who filed the complaint has an opportunity to explain the allegations made in the complaint;
   (5) prescribe guidelines concerning the types of complaints that require the use of a private investigator and the procedures for the board to obtain the services of a private investigator; and
   (6) allow appropriate employees of the board to dismiss a complaint if an investigation shows that:
      (A) no violation occurred; or
      (B) the subject of the complaint is outside the board's jurisdiction.

(b) The board shall:
   (1) dispose of a complaint in a timely manner; and
   (2) establish a schedule for conducting each phase of the investigation or disposition that is under the control of the board.

(c) At each public meeting of the board, the executive director shall report to the board each complaint dismissed under Subsection (a)(6) since the board's last public meeting.

(d) The board may not consider or act on a complaint involving a violation alleged to have occurred more than seven years before the date the complaint is received by the board.

Leg.H. Stats. 1999 76th Leg. Sess. Ch. 388, effective September 1, 1999; Stats. 2005 79th Leg. Sess. Ch. 1345, effective September 1, 2005; Stats. 2013, 83rd Leg., ch. 522 (S.B. 404), § 2, effective September 1, 2013.

Sec. 555.008. [Expires September 1, 2029] Notice to Board Concerning Complaints.

(a) The executive director shall notify the board of the number of complaints that are unresolved after two years after the date of the filing of the complaint. The executive director shall provide the board with an explanation of the reason that a complaint has not been resolved.

(b) The executive director shall provide the notice and explanation required under Subsection (a) periodically at regularly scheduled board meetings.

Leg.H. Stats. 1999 76th Leg. Sess. Ch. 388, effective September 1, 1999.

Sec. 555.009. [Expires September 1, 2029] Public Participation.

(a) The board shall develop and implement policies that provide the public with a reasonable opportunity to appear before the board and to speak on an issue under the board's jurisdiction.

(b) The board shall prepare and maintain a written plan that describes how a person who does not speak English may be provided reasonable access to the board's programs.

Leg.H. Stats. 1999 76th Leg. Sess. Ch. 388, effective September 1, 1999.

Sec. 555.010. [Expires September 1, 2029] Confidentiality.

The identity of a person who reports to or assists the board under Section 555.002(c) and a document that could disclose the identity of that person are confidential and are not considered public information for the purposes of Chapter 552, Government Code.

Leg.H. Stats. 1999 76th Leg. Sess. Ch. 388, effective September 1, 1999.

Sec. 555.011. [Expires September 1, 2029] Immunity.

(a) A person who provides information or assistance under Section 555.002(c) is immune from civil liability arising from providing the information or assistance.

(b) Subsection (a) shall be liberally construed to accomplish the purposes of this chapter, and the immunity provided under that subsection is in addition to any other immunity provided by law.

(c) A person who provides information or assistance to the board under this chapter is presumed to have acted in good faith. A person who alleges a lack of good faith has the burden of proof on that issue.

Leg.H. Stats. 1999 76th Leg. Sess. Ch. 388, effective September 1, 1999.

Sec. 555.012. [Expires September 1, 2029] Counterclaim or Suit.

(a) A person who provides information or assistance under Section 555.002(c) and who is named as a defendant in a civil action filed as a result of the information or assistance may file a counterclaim in a pending action or may prove a cause of action in a subsequent suit to recover defense costs, including court costs, attorney's fees, and damages incurred as a result of the civil action, if the plaintiff's original suit is determined to be frivolous, unreasonable, without foundation, or brought in bad faith.

(b) A board employee or member or an agent of the board who is named as a defendant in a civil action filed as a result of an action taken in the person's official capacity or in the course and scope of employment may file a counterclaim in a pending action or may prove a cause of action in a subsequent suit to recover defense costs, including court costs, attorney's fees, and damages incurred as a result of the civil action, if the plaintiff's original suit is determined to be frivolous, unreasonable, without foundation, or brought in bad faith.

Leg.H. Stats. 1999 76th Leg. Sess. Ch. 388, effective September 1, 1999.

CHAPTER 556. ADMINISTRATIVE INSPECTIONS AND WARRANTS
[EXPIRES SEPTEMBER 1, 2029]

SUBCHAPTER A. GENERAL PROVISIONS
[EXPIRES SEPTEMBER 1, 2029]

Sec. 556.001. [Expires September 1, 2029] Definition.

In this chapter, "facility" means a place:

(1) for which an application has been made for a pharmacy license under this subtitle;

(2) at which a pharmacy licensed under this subtitle is located;

(3) at which a pharmacy is being operated in violation of this subtitle; or

(4) where the practice of pharmacy occurs.

Leg.H. Stats. 1999 76th Leg. Sess. Ch. 388, effective September 1, 1999.

SUBCHAPTER B. INSPECTIONS
[EXPIRES SEPTEMBER 1, 2029]

Sec. 556.051. [Expires September 1, 2029] Authorization to Enter and Inspect.

(a) The board or a representative of the board may enter and inspect a facility relative to the following:

(1) drug storage and security;

(2) equipment;

(3) components used in compounding, finished and unfinished products, containers, and labeling of any item;

(4) sanitary conditions;

(5) records, reports, or other documents required to be kept or made under this subtitle, Chapter 481 or 483, Health and Safety Code, or the Comprehensive Drug Abuse Prevention and Control Act of 1970 (21 U.S.C. Section 801 et seq.) or rules adopted under one of those laws; or

(6) subject to Subsection (b), financial records relating to the operation of the facility.

(b) The board or a representative of the board may inspect financial records under Subsection (a) only in the course of the investigation of a specific complaint. The board or representative may inspect only records related to the specific complaint. The inspection is subject to Section 565.055.

Leg.H. Stats. 1999 76th Leg. Sess. Ch. 388, effective September 1, 1999; Stats. 2005 79th Leg. Sess. Ch. 28, effective September 1, 2005; am. Acts 2015, 84th Leg., ch. 599 (S.B. 460), § 3, effective September 1, 2015.

Phr. Act

Sec. 556.052. [Expires September 1, 2029] Requirements Before Entry and Inspection.

(a) Before an entry and inspection of the facility, the person authorized to represent the board must:

    (1) state the purpose for the inspection; and

    (2) present to the owner, pharmacist, or agent in charge of the facility:

        (A) appropriate credentials; and

        (B) written notice of the authority for the inspection.

(b) If an inspection is required by or is supported by an administrative inspection warrant, the warrant is the notice for purposes of Subsection (a)(2)(B).

Leg.H. Stats. 1999 76th Leg. Sess. Ch. 388, effective September 1, 1999.

Sec. 556.053. [Expires September 1, 2029] Extent of Inspection; Confidentiality.

(a) Except as otherwise provided in an inspection warrant, the person authorized to represent the board may:

    (1) inspect and copy documents, including records or reports, required to be kept or made under this subtitle, Chapter 481 or 483, Health and Safety Code, or the Comprehensive Drug Abuse Prevention and Control Act of 1970 (21 U.S.C. Section 801 et seq.) or rules adopted under one of those laws;

    (2) inspect, within reasonable limits and in a reasonable manner, a facility's storage, equipment, security, prescription drugs or devices, components used in compounding, finished and unfinished products, or records; or

    (3) perform an inventory of any stock of prescription drugs or devices, components used in compounding, or finished and unfinished products in a facility and obtain samples of those substances.

(b) Reports, records, formulas, and test results of samples of products compounded by pharmacies obtained by the board may be provided to the pharmacy that compounded the product but otherwise are confidential and do not constitute public information for purposes of Chapter 552, Government Code. The board may create, use, or disclose statistical information from the test results of samples of compounded products.

(c) The board may disclose information confidential under Subsection (b):

    (1) in a disciplinary hearing before the board or in a subsequent trial or appeal of a board action or order;

    (2) to a pharmacist licensing or disciplinary authority of another jurisdiction; or

    (3) under a court order.

(d) The board shall require a pharmacy to recall a compounded product and may release the results of the tests of the samples of the compounded product if the board determines that:

    (1) the test results indicate a patient safety problem that may involve potential harm to a patient; and

    (2) the release of the test results is necessary to protect the public.

(e) The board shall release the test results described by Subsection (d) if a pharmacy is unable to or does not recall the compounded product within 48 hours after the board's request under that subsection.

Leg.H. Stats. 1999 76th Leg. Sess. Ch. 388, effective September 1, 1999; Stats. 2005 79th Leg. Sess. Ch. 28, effective September 1, 2005; Stats. 2009 81st Leg. Sess. Ch. 785, effective June 19, 2009.

Sec. 556.054. [Expires September 1, 2029] Confidentiality of Certain Information.

The following information obtained by the board during an inspection of a facility is confidential and not subject to disclosure under Chapter 552, Government Code:

    (1) financial data;

    (2) sales data, other than shipment data; and

    (3) pricing data.

Leg.H. Stats. 1999 76th Leg. Sess. Ch. 388, effective September 1, 1999; am. Acts 2015, 84th Leg., ch. 599 (S.B. 460), § 4, effective September 1, 2015.

Sec. 556.055. [Expires September 1, 2029] Inspections with Warning Notice.

Before a complaint may be filed with the board as the result of a written warning notice that is issued during an inspection authorized by this chapter and that lists a specific violation of this subtitle or a rule adopted under this subtitle, the license holder must be given a reasonable time, as determined by the board, to comply with this subtitle or rules adopted under this subtitle.

Leg.H. Stats. 1999 76th Leg. Sess. Ch. 388, effective September 1, 1999.

Sec. 556.0551. [Expires September 1, 2029] Inspection of Licensed Nonresident Pharmacy.

(a) The board may inspect a nonresident pharmacy licensed by the board that compounds sterile preparations as necessary to ensure compliance with the safety standards and other requirements of this subtitle and board rules.

(b) A nonresident pharmacy shall reimburse the board for all expenses, including travel, incurred by the board in inspecting the pharmacy as provided by Subsection (a).

Leg.H. Stats. 2013, 83rd Leg., ch. 608 (S.B. 1100), § 1, effective September 1, 2013.

Sec. 556.0555. [Expires September 1, 2029] Inspections.

(a) At least annually, the board shall conduct random inspections of Canadian pharmacies designated under Section 554.016 as necessary to ensure compliance with the safety standards and other requirements of this subtitle and board rules.

(b)   Notwithstanding the requirements of this chapter, the board by rule may establish the standards and procedures for inspections under this section.

(c)   The board may enter into a written agreement with another state for an agency or employee of the state to perform services for the board related to inspecting a Canadian pharmacy designated by the board under Section 554.016 to dispense prescription drugs to residents in this state. This subsection does not apply to the initial inspection of the pharmacy.

Leg.H. Stats. 2005 79th Leg. Sess. Ch. 1345, effective September 1, 2005.

Sec. 556.056. [Expires September 1, 2029] Code of Professional Responsibility.

(a)   The board shall adopt a code of professional responsibility to regulate the conduct of a representative of the board authorized to inspect and survey a pharmacy.

(b)   The code must contain:

    (1)   a procedure to be followed by a person authorized to represent the board:

        (A)   on entering a pharmacy;

        (B)   during inspection of the pharmacy; and

        (C)   during an exit conference; and

    (2)   standards of conduct that the person must follow in dealing with the staff and management of the pharmacy and the public.

(c)   The board shall establish a procedure for receiving and investigating a complaint of a code violation. The board shall investigate each complaint of a code violation. The board shall forward results of an investigation to the complainant.

(d)   The board may adopt rules establishing sanctions for code violations.

Leg.H. Stats. 1999 76th Leg. Sess. Ch. 388, effective September 1, 1999.

Sec. 556.057. [Expires September 1, 2029] Inspection of Pharmacist Records.

A pharmacist shall provide to the board, on request, records of the pharmacist's practice that occurs outside of a pharmacy. The pharmacist shall provide the records at a time specified by board rule.

Leg.H. Stats. 2015, 84th Leg., ch. 599 (S.B. 460), § 5, effective September 1, 2015.

SUBCHAPTER C. WARRANTS
[EXPIRES SEPTEMBER 1, 2029]

Sec. 556.101. [Expires September 1, 2029] Warrant Not Required.

A warrant is not required under this chapter to:

    (1)   inspect books or records under an administrative subpoena issued under this subtitle; or

    (2)   enter a facility or conduct an administrative inspection of a facility if:

        (A)   the owner, pharmacist, or agent in charge of the facility consents to the inspection;

        (B)   the situation presents imminent danger to the public health and safety;

        (C)   the situation involves inspection of a conveyance, if there is reasonable cause to believe that the mobility of the conveyance makes it impracticable to obtain a warrant; or

        (D)   any other exceptional situation or emergency exists involving an act of God or natural disaster in which time or opportunity to apply for a warrant is lacking.

Leg.H. Stats. 1999 76th Leg. Sess. Ch. 388, effective September 1, 1999.

Sec. 556.102. [Expires September 1, 2029] Compliance with Chapter.

An administrative inspection warrant may be issued and executed only in accordance with this chapter.

Leg.H. Stats. 1999 76th Leg. Sess. Ch. 388, effective September 1, 1999.

Sec. 556.103. [Expires September 1, 2029] Issuance of Warrant.

(a)   In this section, "probable cause" means a valid public interest exists in the effective enforcement of this subtitle or a rule adopted under this subtitle that is sufficient to justify an administrative inspection of the facility, area, building, or conveyance, or its contents in the circumstances specified in the application for the warrant.

(b)   A district judge may, on proper oath or affirmation that shows probable cause, issue a warrant to:

    (1)   conduct an administrative inspection authorized by this chapter or rules adopted under this subtitle; and

    (2)   seize property appropriate to the inspection.

(c)   A warrant may be issued only on an affidavit that:

    (1)   is given by a board representative who has knowledge of the facts alleged;

    (2)   is sworn to before the judge; and

    (3)   establishes the grounds for issuance of the warrant.

(d)   The judge shall issue a warrant if the judge is satisfied that grounds for the application exist or that there is probable cause to believe they exist.

Leg.H. Stats. 1999 76th Leg. Sess. Ch. 388, effective September 1, 1999.

Sec. 556.104. [Expires September 1, 2029] Contents of Warrant.

The warrant must:
  (1) identify:
    (A) the facility, area, building, or conveyance to be inspected;
    (B) the purpose of the inspection;
    (C) the type of property to be inspected, if appropriate; and
    (D) each item or type of property to be seized, if any;
  (2) state the grounds for issuance of the warrant and the name of each person whose affidavit has been taken in support of the warrant;
  (3) be directed to a person authorized under this chapter to execute the warrant;
  (4) command the person to whom the warrant is directed to inspect the facility, area, building, or conveyance identified for the purpose specified;
  (5) direct the seizure of the property specified, if appropriate;
  (6) direct that the warrant be served during normal business hours; and
  (7) designate the judge to whom the warrant is to be returned.

Leg.H. Stats. 1999 76th Leg. Sess. Ch. 388, effective September 1, 1999.

Sec. 556.105. [Expires September 1, 2029] Execution and Return of Warrant.

  (a) A warrant issued under this chapter must be executed and returned not later than the 10th day after the date of the warrant's issuance unless the judge allows additional time in the warrant after a showing by the board of a need for additional time.
  (b) A person who seizes property under a warrant shall provide a copy of the warrant and a receipt for the property taken by:
    (1) giving the copy and receipt to the person from whom or from whose facility the property was taken; or
    (2) leaving the copy and receipt at the facility from which the property was taken.
  (c) The return of the warrant shall be made promptly and be accompanied by a written inventory of any property taken. The inventory shall be:
    (1) prepared in the presence of the person executing the warrant and of:
      (A) the person from whose possession or facility the property was taken, if present; or
      (B) at least one credible person other than the person preparing the inventory; and
    (2) verified by the person executing the warrant.
  (d) The judge, on request, shall deliver a copy of the inventory to:
    (1) the person from whose possession or facility the property was taken; and
    (2) the applicant for the warrant.

Leg.H. Stats. 1999 76th Leg. Sess. Ch. 388, effective September 1, 1999.

Sec. 556.106. [Expires September 1, 2029] Filing with District Court.

  (a) A judge who issues a warrant under this chapter shall attach to the warrant:
    (1) a copy of the return; and
    (2) the papers filed in connection with the warrant.
  (b) The judge shall file the copy of the return and the papers with the clerk of the district court with jurisdiction of the area in which the inspection was conducted.

Leg.H. Stats. 1999 76th Leg. Sess. Ch. 388, effective September 1, 1999.

Sec. 556.107. [Expires September 1, 2029] Disposal of Seized Property.

Property seized under this chapter must be disposed of in a manner considered appropriate by the board if the board has jurisdiction over the property or the district court if the court has jurisdiction over the property.

Leg.H. Stats. 1999 76th Leg. Sess. Ch. 388, effective September 1, 1999.

CHAPTER 557. PHARMACIST-INTERNS
[EXPIRES SEPTEMBER 1, 2029]

Sec. 557.001. [Expires September 1, 2029] Pharmacist-Intern Registration.

A person must register with the board before beginning a board-approved internship in this state.

Leg.H. Stats. 1999 76th Leg. Sess. Ch. 388, effective September 1, 1999.

Sec. 557.002. [Expires September 1, 2029] Application for Registration.

An application for registration as a pharmacist-intern must be on a form prescribed by the board.

Leg.H. Stats. 1999 76th Leg. Sess. Ch. 388, effective September 1, 1999.

Phr. Act

Sec. 557.003. [Expires September 1, 2029] Duration of Registration.

A person's registration as a pharmacist-intern remains in effect as long as the person meets the qualifications for an internship specified by board rule.

Leg.H. Stats. 1999 76th Leg. Sess. Ch. 388, effective September 1, 1999.

Sec. 557.004. [Expires September 1, 2029] Limitations on Registration.

(a) The board may:
    (1) refuse to issue a registration to an applicant; or
    (2) restrict, suspend, or revoke a pharmacist-intern registration for a violation of this subtitle.
(b) The board may take disciplinary action against an applicant for a pharmacist-intern registration or the holder of a current or expired pharmacist-intern registration in the same manner as against an applicant for a license or a license holder by imposing a sanction authorized under Section 565.051 if the board finds that the applicant or registration holder has engaged in conduct described by Section 565.001.

Leg.H. Stats. 1999 76th Leg. Sess. Ch. 388, effective September 1, 1999; Stats. 2013, 83rd Leg., ch. 583 (S.B. 869), § 8, effective June 14, 2013.

CHAPTER 558. LICENSE TO PRACTICE PHARMACY
[EXPIRES SEPTEMBER 1, 2029]

SUBCHAPTER A. LICENSE
[EXPIRES SEPTEMBER 1, 2029]

Sec. 558.001. [Expires September 1, 2029] License Required.

(a) A person may not practice pharmacy unless the person holds a license to practice pharmacy under this subtitle.
(b) A person may not:
    (1) impersonate a pharmacist; or
    (2) use the title "Registered Pharmacist" or "R.Ph.," or words of similar intent, unless the person is licensed to practice pharmacy in this state.
(c) A person may not dispense or distribute prescription drugs unless the person:
    (1) is a pharmacist; or
    (2) is otherwise authorized by this subtitle to dispense or distribute prescription drugs.

Leg.H. Stats. 1999 76th Leg. Sess. Ch. 388, effective September 1, 1999.

Sec. 558.002. [Expires September 1, 2029] Unauthorized Acquisition of License.

A person may not:
    (1) impersonate before the board an applicant applying for a license under this subtitle; or
    (2) acquire, with the intent to fraudulently acquire the license, a license in a manner other than the manner provided by this subtitle.

Leg.H. Stats. 1999 76th Leg. Sess. Ch. 388, effective September 1, 1999.

SUBCHAPTER B. LICENSING BY EXAMINATION
[EXPIRES SEPTEMBER 1, 2029]

Sec. 558.051. [Expires September 1, 2029] Qualifications for License by Examination.

(a) To qualify for a license to practice pharmacy, an applicant for licensing by examination must submit to the board:
    (1) a license fee set by the board; and
    (2) a completed application on a form prescribed by the board with satisfactory sworn evidence that the applicant:
        (A) is at least 18 years of age;
        (B) has completed a minimum of a 1,000-hour internship or other program that has been approved by the board or has demonstrated, to the board's satisfaction, experience in the practice of pharmacy that meets or exceeds the board's minimum internship requirements;
        (C) has graduated and received a professional practice degree, as defined by board rule, from an accredited pharmacy degree program approved by the board;
        (D) has passed the examination required by the board; and
        (E) has not had a pharmacist license granted by another state restricted, suspended, revoked, or surrendered, for any reason.
(b) Each applicant must obtain practical experience in the practice of pharmacy concurrent with college attendance or after college graduation, or both, under conditions the board determines.

Leg.H. Stats. 1999, 76th Leg., ch. 388 (H.B. 3155), § 1, effective September 1, 1999; am. Acts 2017, 85th Leg., ch. 485 (H.B. 2561), § 14, effective September 1, 2017.

Sec. 558.052. [Expires September 1, 2029] Content, Preparation, and Validation of Examination.

(a) The board shall determine the content and subject matter of a licensing examination.

(b) The examination shall be prepared to measure the competence of the applicant to practice pharmacy.

(c) The board may employ and cooperate with an organization or consultant in preparing an appropriate examination.

(d) A written examination prepared or offered by the board, including a standardized national examination, must be validated by an independent testing professional.

Leg.H. Stats. 1999 76th Leg. Sess. Ch. 388, effective September 1, 1999.

Sec. 558.053. [Expires September 1, 2029] Grading of Examination.

(a) The board may employ and cooperate with an organization or consultant in grading the examination.

(b) The board shall determine whether an applicant has passed the examination. The board has sole discretion and responsibility for that determination.

Leg.H. Stats. 1999 76th Leg. Sess. Ch. 388, effective September 1, 1999.

Sec. 558.054. [Expires September 1, 2029] Frequency of Offering Examination.

The board shall give the examination at least two times during each state fiscal year.

Leg.H. Stats. 1999 76th Leg. Sess. Ch. 388, effective September 1, 1999.

Sec. 558.055. [Expires September 1, 2029] Failure to Pass; Reexamination.

(a) An applicant who on the applicant's first attempt fails the examination may take the examination four additional times.

(b) Before an applicant who has failed the examination five times is allowed to retake the examination, the applicant must provide documentation from a college of pharmacy that the applicant has successfully completed additional college course work in each examination subject area the applicant failed.

(c) If requested in writing by a person who fails the examination, the board shall furnish the person with an analysis of the person's performance on the examination.

Leg.H. Stats. 1999 76th Leg. Sess. Ch. 388, effective September 1, 1999; am. Acts 2015, 84th Leg., ch. 599 (S.B. 460), § 6, effective September 1, 2015.

Sec. 558.056. [Expires September 1, 2029] Notification.

The board shall notify each person taking an examination of the results of the examination not later than the 30th day after the date the board receives the results from a national testing service if the board uses a national testing service.

Leg.H. Stats. 1999 76th Leg. Sess. Ch. 388, effective September 1, 1999.

Sec. 558.057. [Expires September 1, 2029] Internship or Other Program to Qualify for Examination.

(a) In this section, "preceptor" means a pharmacist licensed in this state to practice pharmacy or another health care professional who meets the preceptor requirements specified by rule and who is recognized by the board to supervise and be responsible for the activities and functions of a pharmacist-intern in an internship program.

(b) The board shall:
(1) establish standards for an internship or other program necessary to qualify an applicant for the licensing examination; and
(2) determine the qualifications necessary for a preceptor used in the program.

Leg. H. Stats. 1999 76th Leg. Sess. Ch. 388, effective September 1, 1999; Stats. 2005 79th Leg. Sess. Ch. 1345, effective September 1, 2005.

Sec. 558.058. [Expires September 1, 2029] Accessibility of Examination.

The board by rule shall ensure that an examination under this subchapter is administered to applicants with disabilities in compliance with the Americans with Disabilities Act of 1990 (42 U.S.C. Section 12101 et seq.).

Leg. H. Stats. 2005 79th Leg. Sess. Ch. 1345, effective September 1, 2005.

Sec. 558.059. [Expires September 1, 2029] Examination Fee Refund.

(a) The board may retain all or part of an examination fee paid by an applicant who is unable to take the examination.

(b) The board shall adopt policies allowing the board to refund the examination fee paid by an applicant who:
(1) provides advance notice of the applicant's inability to take the examination; or
(2) is unable to take the examination because of an emergency.

(c) The board's policy must establish the required notification period and the emergencies that warrant a refund.

(d) The board shall make efforts to ensure that the policy does not conflict with the policy of a national testing body involved in administering the examination.

Leg. H. Stats. 2005 79th Leg. Sess. Ch. 1345, effective September 1, 2005.

SUBCHAPTER C. LICENSING BY RECIPROCITY
[EXPIRES SEPTEMBER 1, 2029]

Sec. 558.101. [Expires September 1, 2029] Qualifications for License by Reciprocity.

(a) To qualify for a license to practice pharmacy, an applicant for licensing by reciprocity must:
  (1) submit to the board:
    (A) a reciprocity fee set by the board; and
    (B) a completed application in the form prescribed by the board, given under oath;
  (2) have graduated and received a professional practice degree, as defined by board rule, from an accredited pharmacy degree program approved by the board;
  (3) have presented to the board:
    (A) proof of current or initial licensing by examination; and
    (B) proof that the current license and any other license granted to the applicant by another state has not been restricted, suspended, revoked, or surrendered for any reason; and
  (4) pass the Texas Pharmacy Jurisprudence examination.
(b) An applicant is not eligible for licensing by reciprocity unless the state in which the applicant is currently or was initially licensed as a pharmacist grants reciprocal licensing to pharmacists licensed by examination in this state, under like circumstances and conditions.

Leg.H. Stats. 1999, 76th Leg., ch. 388 (H.B. 3155), § 1, effective September 1, 1999; am. Acts 2005, 79th Leg., ch. 1345 (S.B. 410), § 16, effective September 1, 2005; am. Acts 2017, 85th Leg., ch. 485 (H.B. 2561), § 15, effective September 1, 2017.

SUBCHAPTER D. PROVISIONAL AND TEMPORARY LICENSING
[EXPIRES SEPTEMBER 1, 2029]

Sec. 558.151. [Expires September 1, 2029] Qualifications for Provisional License.

(a) The board may grant a provisional license to practice pharmacy to an applicant licensed in another state who seeks a license in this state. An applicant for a provisional license under this section must:
  (1) pay a fee set by the board;
  (2) be licensed in good standing as a pharmacist in another state that has professional standards and licensing requirements that the board considers to be substantially equivalent to the requirements of this subtitle;
  (3) have passed a national or other examination recognized by the board relating to pharmacy; and
  (4) be sponsored by a person licensed under this subtitle with whom the provisional license holder may practice under this subchapter.
(b) The board may waive the requirement of Subsection (a)(4) for an applicant if the board determines that compliance with that subsection constitutes a hardship to the applicant.

Leg.H. Stats. 1999 76th Leg. Sess. Ch. 388, effective September 1, 1999.

Sec. 558.152. [Expires September 1, 2029] Duration of Provisional License.

A provisional license is valid until the date the board approves or denies the license application under this subtitle.

Leg.H. Stats. 1999 76th Leg. Sess. Ch. 388, effective September 1, 1999.

Sec. 558.153. [Expires September 1, 2029] Processing of License Application.

The board must complete the processing of a provisional license holder's application for a license not later than the 180th day after the date the provisional license is issued or at the time licenses are issued following the successful completion of the examination, whichever date is later.

Leg.H. Stats. 1999 76th Leg. Sess. Ch. 388, effective September 1, 1999.

Sec. 558.154. [Expires September 1, 2029] Issuance of License to Provisional License Holder.

The board shall issue a license to practice pharmacy under this subtitle to the holder of a provisional license if:
  (1) the provisional license holder passes the jurisprudence examination required under this subtitle;
  (2) the board verifies that the provisional license holder has the academic and experience requirements for a license to practice pharmacy under this subtitle; and
  (3) the provisional license holder satisfies all other requirements for a license to practice pharmacy under this subtitle.

Leg.H. Stats. 1999 76th Leg. Sess. Ch. 388, effective September 1, 1999.

Sec. 558.155. [Expires September 1, 2029] Temporary License.

The board by rule may provide for the issuance of a temporary license.

Leg.H. Stats. 1999 76th Leg. Sess. Ch. 388, effective September 1, 1999.

SUBCHAPTER E. CERTAIN PROHIBITED PRACTICES
[EXPIRES SEPTEMBER 1, 2029]

Sec. 558.201. [Expires September 1, 2029] Duplicating License or Certificate.

Except as expressly provided under this subtitle, a person may not in any manner duplicate a license to practice pharmacy or a license renewal certificate.

Leg.H. Stats. 1999 76th Leg. Sess. Ch. 388, effective September 1, 1999.

Sec. 558.202. [Expires September 1, 2029] False Affidavit.

A person who falsely makes the affidavit prescribed by Section 558.051 or 558.101 is guilty of fraudulent and dishonorable conduct and malpractice.

Leg.H. Stats. 1999 76th Leg. Sess. Ch. 388, effective September 1, 1999.

CHAPTER 559. RENEWAL OF LICENSE TO PRACTICE PHARMACY
[EXPIRES SEPTEMBER 1, 2029]

SUBCHAPTER A. GENERAL PROVISIONS
[EXPIRES SEPTEMBER 1, 2029]

Sec. 559.001. [Expires September 1, 2029] Expiration of License.

(a) Except as provided by Subsection (b), a license to practice pharmacy expires December 31 of each year or of every other year, as determined by the board.

(b) The board may adopt a system under which licenses to practice pharmacy expire on various dates during the year.

(c) If the board changes the expiration date of a license, the board shall prorate the license renewal fee to cover the months for which the license is valid for the year in which the date is changed. The total license renewal fee is due on the new expiration date.

Leg.H. Stats. 1999 76th Leg. Sess. Ch. 388, effective September 1, 1999.

Sec. 559.002. [Expires September 1, 2029] Renewal Period.

A license to practice pharmacy may be renewed for one or two years, as determined by the board.

Leg.H. Stats. 1999 76th Leg. Sess. Ch. 388, effective September 1, 1999.

Sec. 559.003. [Expires September 1, 2029] Requirements for Renewal.

(a) To renew a license to practice pharmacy, the license holder must before the expiration date of the license:
    (1) pay a renewal fee as determined by the board;
    (2) comply with the continuing education requirements prescribed by the board; and
    (3) file with the board a completed application for a license renewal certificate that:
        (A) is given under oath; and
        (B) is accompanied by a certified statement executed by the license holder that attests that the license holder has satisfied the continuing education requirements during the preceding license period.

(b) A person whose license has been expired for 90 days or less may renew the expired license by paying to the board a renewal fee that is equal to one and one-half times the normally required renewal fee for the license.

(c) A person whose license has been expired for more than 90 days but less than one year may renew the expired license by paying to the board a renewal fee that is equal to two times the normally required renewal fee for the license.

(d) A person whose license has been expired for one year or more may not renew the license. The person may obtain a new license by complying with the requirements and procedures for obtaining an original license, including the examination requirement.

(e) A person may not renew a license to practice pharmacy if the person holds a license to practice pharmacy in another state that has been suspended, revoked, canceled, or subject to an action that prohibits the person from practicing pharmacy in that state.

(f) The board may refuse to renew a license to practice pharmacy for a license holder who is in violation of a board order.

Leg.H. Stats. 1999, 76th Leg., ch. 388 (H.B. 3155), § 1, effective September 1, 1999; am. Acts 2001, 77th Leg., ch. 1254 (S.B. 768), § 2, effective September 1, 2001; am. Acts 2005, 79th Leg., ch. 1345 (S.B. 410), § 17, effective September 1, 2005; am. Acts 2013, 83rd Leg., ch. 583 (S.B. 869), § 9, effective June 14, 2013; am. Acts 2017, 85th Leg., ch. 485 (H.B. 2561), § 16, effective September 1, 2017.

Sec. 559.004. [Expires September 1, 2029] Issuance of License Renewal Certificate.

(a) The board shall issue a license renewal certificate to an applicant after the board has received, in a time prescribed by Section 559.003:
    (1) the completed application;
    (2) the renewal fee; and
    (3) proof of completion of the continuing education requirements prescribed by Subchapter B.

(b) The renewal certificate must contain:
    (1) the pharmacist's license number;

(2) the period for which the license is renewed; and

(3) other information the board determines necessary.

Leg.H. Stats. 1999 76th Leg. Sess. Ch. 388, effective September 1, 1999.

Sec. 559.005. [Expires September 1, 2029] Issuance of New License.

(a) The board may issue a new license to practice pharmacy to a person who is prohibited under Section 559.003(d) from renewing a license if the person has not had a license granted by any other state restricted, suspended, revoked, canceled, or surrendered for any reason and qualifies under this section.

(b) A person qualifies for a license under this section if the person:

(1) was licensed as a pharmacist in this state, moved to another state, and is licensed and has been practicing pharmacy in the other state for the two years preceding the date the application for a new license is submitted;

(2) pays to the board an amount equal to the examination fee for the license; and

(3) passes the Texas Pharmacy Jurisprudence examination.

(c) A person qualifies for a license under this section if the person:

(1) was licensed as a pharmacist in this state;

(2) pays to the board an amount equal to the examination fee for the license; and

(3) passes the Texas Pharmacy Jurisprudence examination and any other examination required by the board and in addition to or instead of passing the examination as required by the board, participates in continuing pharmacy education and practices under conditions set by the board.

(d) A person qualifies for a license under this section if the person:

(1) submits to reexamination; and

(2) complies with the requirements and procedures for obtaining an original license.

Leg.H. Stats. 1999 76th Leg. Sess. Ch. 388, effective September 1, 1999.

Sec. 559.006. [Expires September 1, 2029] License Expiration Notice.

At least 30 days before the expiration of a person's license, the board shall send written notice of the impending license expiration to the person at the license holder's last known address according to the board's records.

Leg.H. Stats. 1999 76th Leg. Sess. Ch. 388, effective September 1, 1999.

Sec. 559.007. [Expires September 1, 2029] Practicing Pharmacy without Renewal Certificate.

A person who practices pharmacy without a current license renewal certificate as required by this chapter is practicing pharmacy without a license and is subject to all penalties for practicing pharmacy without a license.

Leg.H. Stats. 1999 76th Leg. Sess. Ch. 388, effective September 1, 1999.

SUBCHAPTER B. MANDATORY CONTINUING EDUCATION
[EXPIRES SEPTEMBER 1, 2029]

Sec. 559.051. [Expires September 1, 2029] Satisfaction of Continuing Education Requirement.

(a) A holder of a license to practice pharmacy may meet the continuing education requirement by:

(1) completing continuing education programs approved by the board; or

(2) passing a standardized pharmacy examination approved by the board.

(b) A license holder who takes the examination under Subsection (a)(2) must pay the examination fee assessed by the board under Section 554.006.

Leg.H. Stats. 1999 76th Leg. Sess. Ch. 388, effective September 1, 1999.

Sec. 559.052. [Expires September 1, 2029] Rules Relating to Continuing Education.

(a) The board shall adopt rules relating to:

(1) the adoption or approval of mandatory continuing education programs;

(2) the approval of providers and the operation of continuing education programs; and

(3) the evaluation of the effectiveness of continuing education programs and a license holder's participation and performance in those programs.

(b) In establishing the requirement for continuing education, the board shall consider:

(1) factors that lead to the competent performance of professional duties; and

(2) the continuing education needs of license holders.

(c) In adopting rules relating to the approval of continuing education programs or providers, the board may consider:

(1) programs approved by the Texas Pharmacy Foundation; and

(2) providers approved by the American Council on Pharmaceutical Education.

(d) The board shall approve home study courses, correspondence courses, or other similar programs.

(e) The board by rule may grant an extension for the completion of a continuing education requirement for good cause.

(f) The board by rule may exempt a person from all or part of the continuing education requirements.

Leg.H. Stats. 1999 76th Leg. Sess. Ch. 388, effective September 1, 1999.

Sec. 559.0525. [Expires September 1, 2029] Continuing Education Relating to Opioid Drugs.

(a) The board shall develop a continuing education program regarding opioid drug abuse and the delivery, dispensing, and provision of tamper-resistant opioid drugs after considering input from interested persons.

(b) The board by rule may require a license holder to satisfy a number of the continuing education hours required by Section 559.053 through attendance of a program developed under this section.

Leg.H. Stats. 2013, 83rd Leg., ch. 518 (S.B. 316), § 1, effective June 14, 2013.

Sec. 559.053. [Expires September 1, 2029] Program Hours Required.

A license holder satisfies the continuing education requirement by presenting evidence satisfactory to the board of completion of at least 30 hours of continuing education during the preceding 24 months of the person's license period.

Leg.H. Stats. 1999 76th Leg. Sess. Ch. 388, effective September 1, 1999; Stats. 2001 77th Leg. Sess. Chs. 1254, 1420, effective September 1, 2001.

Sec. 559.054. [Expires September 1, 2029] Certificate of Completion.

Each continuing education program approved by the board shall issue a certificate of completion to a license holder who satisfactorily completes the program.

Leg.H. Stats. 1999 76th Leg. Sess. Ch. 388, effective September 1, 1999.

Sec. 559.055. [Expires September 1, 2029] Records.

Each license holder shall maintain records for three years showing the continuing education programs completed by the license holder.

Leg.H. Stats. 1999 76th Leg. Sess. Ch. 388, effective September 1, 1999.

Sec. 559.056. [Expires September 1, 2029] Demonstration of Compliance.

On an audit by the board, a license holder is in compliance with the continuing education requirements if the license holder submits to the board:

(1) an affidavit stating that the license holder has complied with those requirements; and

(2) records showing completion of the continuing education programs.

Leg.H. Stats. 1999 76th Leg. Sess. Ch. 388, effective September 1, 1999.

SUBCHAPTER C. INACTIVE STATUS
[EXPIRES SEPTEMBER 1, 2029]

Sec. 559.101. [Expires September 1, 2029] Eligibility for Inactive Status.

The board by rule shall adopt a system for placing on inactive status a license held by a person who:

(1) is licensed by the board to practice pharmacy;

(2) is not eligible to renew the license because of failure to comply with the continuing education requirements under Subchapter B; and

(3) is not practicing pharmacy in this state.

Leg.H. Stats. 1999 76th Leg. Sess. Ch. 388, effective September 1, 1999.

Sec. 559.102. [Expires September 1, 2029] Restriction on Length of Inactive Status.

The board may restrict the length of time a license may remain on inactive status.

Leg.H. Stats. 1999 76th Leg. Sess. Ch. 388, effective September 1, 1999.

Sec. 559.103. [Expires September 1, 2029] Application for Inactive Status.

A license holder may place the holder's license on inactive status by:

(1) applying for inactive status on a form prescribed by the board before the expiration date of the license; and

(2) complying with all other requirements for renewal of a license other than the continuing education requirements under Subchapter B.

Leg.H. Stats. 1999 76th Leg. Sess. Ch. 388, effective September 1, 1999.

Sec. 559.104. [Expires September 1, 2029] Return to Active Status.

A holder of a license that is on inactive status may return the license to active status by:

(1) applying for active status on a form prescribed by the board; and

(2)   providing evidence satisfactory to the board that the license holder has completed the number of hours of continuing education, up to 36 hours, that would otherwise have been required for renewal of the license.

Leg.H. Stats. 1999 76th Leg. Sess. Ch. 388, effective September 1, 1999.

Sec. 559.105. [Expires September 1, 2029] Practicing Pharmacy During Inactive Status.

(a)   A holder of a license that is on inactive status may not practice pharmacy in this state.

(b)   A license holder who practices pharmacy while the holder's license is on inactive status is practicing pharmacy without a license.

Leg.H. Stats. 1999 76th Leg. Sess. Ch. 388, effective September 1, 1999.

CHAPTER 560. LICENSING OF PHARMACIES
[EXPIRES SEPTEMBER 1, 2029]

SUBCHAPTER A. LICENSE REQUIRED
[EXPIRES SEPTEMBER 1, 2029]

Sec. 560.001. [Expires September 1, 2029] License Required.

(a)   A person may not operate a pharmacy in this state unless the pharmacy is licensed by the board.

(b)   A pharmacy located in another state may not ship, mail, or deliver to this state a prescription drug or device dispensed under a prescription drug order, or dispensed or delivered as authorized by Subchapter D, Chapter 562, unless the pharmacy is licensed by the board or is exempt under Section 560.004.

(c)   A pharmacy located in Canada may not ship, mail, or deliver to this state a prescription drug dispensed under a prescription drug order to a resident of this state unless the pharmacy is designated by the board under Section 554.016.

Leg.H. Stats. 1999 76th Leg. Sess. Ch. 388, effective September 1, 1999; Stats. 2005 79th Leg. Sess. Ch. 1345, effective September 1, 2005; Stats. 2013, 83rd Leg., ch. 608 (S.B. 1100), § 2, effective September 1, 2013.

Sec. 560.002. [Expires September 1, 2029] Use of "Pharmacy"; Providing Pharmacy Services without License.

(a)   A person may not display in or on a place of business the word "pharmacy" or "apothecary" in any language, any word or combination of words of the same or similar meaning, or a graphic representation that would lead or tend to lead the public to believe that the business is a pharmacy unless the facility is a pharmacy licensed under this chapter.

(b)   A person may not advertise a place of business as a pharmacy or provide pharmacy services unless the facility is a pharmacy licensed under this chapter.

Leg.H. Stats. 1999 76th Leg. Sess. Ch. 388, effective September 1, 1999; Stats. 2001 77th Leg. Sess. Ch. 1254, effective September 1, 2001.

Sec. 560.003. [Expires September 1, 2029] Prohibited Advertising of Pharmacy.

(a)   A pharmacy that is not licensed under this chapter may not advertise the pharmacy's services in this state.

(b)   A person who is a resident of this state may not advertise the pharmacy services of a pharmacy that is not licensed by the board if the pharmacy or person makes the advertisement with the knowledge that the advertisement will or is likely to induce a resident of this state to use the pharmacy to dispense a prescription drug order.

Leg.H. Stats. 1999 76th Leg. Sess. Ch. 388, effective September 1, 1999.

Sec. 560.004. [Expires September 1, 2029] Exemption.

The board may grant an exemption from the licensing requirements of this chapter on the application of a pharmacy located in another state that restricts to isolated transactions the pharmacy's dispensing of a prescription drug or device to a resident of this state.

Leg.H. Stats. 1999 76th Leg. Sess. Ch. 388, effective September 1, 1999.

SUBCHAPTER B. PHARMACY CLASSIFICATION
[EXPIRES SEPTEMBER 1, 2029]

Sec. 560.051. [Expires September 1, 2029] License Classifications.

(a)   Each applicant for a pharmacy license shall apply for a license in one or more of the following classifications:

     (1)   Class A;

     (2)   Class B;

     (3)   Class C;

     (4)   Class D;

     (5)   Class E; or

     (6)   another classification established by the board under Section 560.053.

(b)   A Class A pharmacy license or community pharmacy license authorizes a pharmacy to dispense a drug or device to the public under a prescription drug order.

(c) A Class B pharmacy license or nuclear pharmacy license authorizes a pharmacy to dispense a radioactive drug or device for administration to an ultimate user.

(d) A Class C pharmacy license or institutional pharmacy license may be issued to a pharmacy located in:

(1) an inpatient facility, including a hospital, licensed under Chapter 241 or 577, Health and Safety Code;

(2) a hospital maintained or operated by the state;

(3) a hospice inpatient facility licensed under Chapter 142, Health and Safety Code; or

(4) an ambulatory surgical center licensed under Chapter 243, Health and Safety Code.

(e) A Class D pharmacy license or clinic pharmacy license authorizes a pharmacy to dispense a limited type of drug or device under a prescription drug order.

(f) A Class E pharmacy license or nonresident pharmacy license may be issued to a pharmacy located in another state whose primary business is to:

(A) dispense a prescription drug or device under a prescription drug order; and

(B) deliver the drug or device to a patient, including a patient in this state, by United States mail, common carrier, or delivery service.

(g) The board may determine the classification under which a pharmacy may be licensed.

Leg.H. Stats. 1999 76th Leg. Sess. Ch. 388, effective September 1, 1999; Stats. 2001 77th Leg. Sess. Ch. 1420, effective September 1, 2001; Stats. 2003 78th Leg. Sess. Ch. 941, effective September 1, 2003.

Sec. 560.052. [Expires September 1, 2029] Qualifications.

(a) The board by rule shall establish the standards that each pharmacy and the pharmacy's employees involved in the practice of pharmacy must meet to qualify for licensing as a pharmacy in each classification.

(b) To qualify for a pharmacy license, an applicant must submit to the board:

(1) a license fee set by the board, except as provided by Subsection (d); and

(2) a completed application that:

(A) is on a form prescribed by the board;

(B) is given under oath;

(C) includes proof that:

(i) a pharmacy license held by the applicant in this state or another state, if applicable, has not been restricted, suspended, revoked, or surrendered for any reason; and

(ii) no owner of the pharmacy for which the application is made has held a pharmacist license in this state or another state, if applicable, that has been restricted, suspended, revoked, or surrendered for any reason; and

(D) includes a statement of:

(i) the ownership;

(ii) the location of the pharmacy;

(iii) the license number of each pharmacist who is employed by the pharmacy, if the pharmacy is located in this state, or who is licensed to practice pharmacy in this state, if the pharmacy is located in another state;

(iv) the pharmacist license number of the pharmacist-in-charge; and

(v) any other information the board determines necessary.

(c) A pharmacy located in another state that applies for a license, in addition to satisfying the other requirements of this chapter, must provide to the board:

(1) evidence that the applicant holds a pharmacy license, registration, or permit in good standing issued by the state in which the pharmacy is located;

(2) the name of the owner and pharmacist-in-charge of the pharmacy for service of process;

(3) evidence of the applicant's ability to provide to the board a record of a prescription drug order dispensed or delivered as authorized by Subchapter D, Chapter 562, by the applicant to a resident of or practitioner in this state not later than 72 hours after the time the board requests the record;

(4) an affidavit by the pharmacist-in-charge that states that the pharmacist has read and understands the laws and rules relating to the applicable license;

(5) proof of creditworthiness;

(6) an inspection report issued:

(A) not more than two years before the date the license application is received; and

(B) by the pharmacy licensing board in the state of the pharmacy's physical location, except as provided by Subsection (f); and

(7) any other information the board determines necessary.

(d) A pharmacy operated by the state or a local government that qualifies for a Class D pharmacy license is not required to pay a fee to obtain a license.

(e) With respect to a Class C pharmacy license, the board may issue a license to a pharmacy on certification by the appropriate agency that the facility in which the pharmacy is located has substantially completed the requirements for licensing.

(f) A Class E pharmacy may submit an inspection report issued by an entity other than the pharmacy licensing board of the state in which the pharmacy is physically located if:

(1) the state's licensing board does not conduct inspections;

(2) the inspection is substantively equivalent to an inspection conducted by the board, as determined by board rule; and

(3) the inspecting entity meets specifications adopted by the board for inspecting entities.

(g) A license may not be issued to a pharmacy that compounds sterile preparations unless the pharmacy has been inspected by the board to ensure the pharmacy meets the safety standards and other requirements of this subtitle and board rules.

(h) The board may accept, as satisfying the inspection requirement in Subsection (g) for a pharmacy located in another state, an inspection report issued by the pharmacy licensing board in the state in which the pharmacy is located if:
   (1) the board determines that the other state has comparable standards and regulations applicable to pharmacies, including standards and regulations related to health and safety; and
   (2) the pharmacy provides to the board any requested documentation related to the inspection.

Leg.H. Stats. 1999 76th Leg. Sess. Ch. 388, effective September 1, 1999; Stats. 2001 77th Leg. Sess. Ch. 1420, effective September 1, 2001; Stats. 2005 79th Leg. Sess. Ch. 1345, effective September 1, 2005; Stats. 2013, 83rd Leg., ch. 583 (S.B. 869), § 10, effective June 14, 2013; Stats. 2013, 83rd Leg., ch. 608 (S.B. 1100), § 3, effective September 1, 2013; am. Acts 2015, 84th Leg., ch. 599 (S.B. 460), § 7, effective September 1, 2015.

Sec. 560.0525. [Expires September 1, 2029] Additional Qualification Requirements for Canadian Pharmacies.

(a) To pass an inspection by the board, a Canadian pharmacy must meet Texas licensing standards.
(b) In addition to satisfying the other requirements of this chapter, to qualify for designation by the board under Section 554.016, a Canadian pharmacy applicant must submit to the board:
   (1) evidence satisfactory to the board that the applicant holds a pharmacy license, registration, or permit in good standing issued by Canada or the Canadian province in which the pharmacy is located and is not subject to any pending disciplinary action or legal action by any regulatory authority;
   (2) the name and address of the pharmacy's owner and pharmacist-in-charge for service of process;
   (3) evidence of the applicant's ability to provide to the board, not later than 72 hours after the time the board requests the record, a record of a prescription drug order authorizing the pharmacy to dispense a prescription drug to a resident of this state;
   (4) an affidavit by the pharmacist-in-charge that states the pharmacist has read and understands this subtitle and the rules adopted under this subtitle that relate to a Canadian pharmacy designated by the board as having passed inspection to dispense prescription drugs to residents in this state;
   (5) evidence satisfactory to the board that the applicant meets the standards established by board rule to ensure customer safety for each order filled and in the dispensing, storing, packaging, shipping, and delivering of prescription drugs; and
   (6) evidence satisfactory to the board that the applicant's employees hold the appropriate Canadian licenses required to dispense prescription drugs in Canada.
(c) Before a Canadian pharmacy is designated as having passed inspection to dispense prescription drugs to residents in this state, a representative of the board shall visit the pharmacy's facilities and review the pharmacy's compliance with the requirements and safety standards established under this subtitle.

Leg.H. Stats. 2005 79th Leg. Sess. Ch. 1345, effective September 1, 2005.

Sec. 560.053. [Expires September 1, 2029] Establishment of Additional Pharmacy Classifications.

The board by rule may establish classifications of pharmacy licenses in addition to the classifications under Section 560.051 if the board determines that:
   (1) the practice setting will provide pharmaceutical care services to the public;
   (2) the existing classifications of pharmacy licenses are not appropriate for that practice setting; and
   (3) establishment of a new classification of pharmacy license is necessary to protect the public health, safety, and welfare.

Leg.H. Stats. 2003 78th Leg. Sess. Ch. 941, effective September 1, 2003.

SUBCHAPTER C. RESTRICTIONS ON LICENSE
[EXPIRES SEPTEMBER 1, 2029]

Sec. 560.101. [Expires September 1, 2029] License Not Transferable.

A pharmacy license issued under this chapter is not transferable or assignable.

Leg.H. Stats. 1999 76th Leg. Sess. Ch. 388, effective September 1, 1999.

Sec. 560.102. [Expires September 1, 2029] Separate License for Each Location.

(a) A separate pharmacy license is required for each principal place of business of a pharmacy.
(b) Only one pharmacy license may be issued for a specific location.

Leg.H. Stats. 1999 76th Leg. Sess. Ch. 388, effective September 1, 1999.

SUBCHAPTER D. CERTAIN PROHIBITED PRACTICES
[EXPIRES SEPTEMBER 1, 2029]

Sec. 560.103. [Expires September 1, 2029] False Affidavit.

A person who falsely makes the affidavit prescribed by Section 560.052 is guilty of fraudulent and dishonorable conduct and malpractice.

Leg.H. Stats. 1999 76th Leg. Sess. Ch. 388, effective September 1, 1999.

CHAPTER 561. RENEWAL OF PHARMACY LICENSE
[EXPIRES SEPTEMBER 1, 2029]

Sec. 561.001. [Expires September 1, 2029] Expiration of License.

(a)   A pharmacy license expires May 31 of each year.

(b)   The board may adopt a system under which pharmacy licenses expire on various dates during the year or every other year, as appropriate.

(c)   If the board changes the expiration date of a license, the board shall prorate the license renewal fee to cover the number of months for which the license is valid for the year in which the date is changed. The total license renewal fee is due on the new expiration date.

Leg.H. Stats. 1999 76th Leg. Sess. Ch. 388, effective September 1, 1999; Stats. 2001 77th Leg. Sess. Ch. 1420, effective September 1, 2001.

Sec. 561.002. [Expires September 1, 2029] Pharmacy License Renewal.

A pharmacy license must be renewed annually or biennially as determined by the board.

Leg.H. Stats. 1999 76th Leg. Sess. Ch. 388, effective September 1, 1999; Stats. 2001 77th Leg. Sess. Ch. 1420, effective September 1, 2001.

Sec. 561.003. [Expires September 1, 2029] Requirements for Renewal.

(a)   The board by rule shall establish:

    (1)   procedures to be followed for renewal of a pharmacy license;

    (2)   the fees to be paid for renewal of a pharmacy license; and

    (3)   the standards in each classification that each pharmacy and the pharmacy's employees involved in the practice of pharmacy must meet to qualify for relicensing as a pharmacy.

(b)   A pharmacy license may be renewed by:

    (1)   payment of a renewal fee set by the board; and

    (2)   filing with the board a completed application for a license renewal certificate given under oath before the expiration date of the license or license renewal certificate.

(c)   A pharmacy whose license has been expired for 90 days or less may renew the expired license by paying to the board a renewal fee that is equal to one and one-half times the normally required renewal fee for the license.

(d)   [Repealed by Acts 2015, 84th Leg., ch. 599 (S.B. 460), § 14(1), effective September 1, 2015.]

(e)   If a pharmacy's license has been expired for 91 days or more, the pharmacy may not renew the license. The pharmacy may obtain a new license by complying with the requirements and procedures for obtaining an original license.

(f)   A pharmacy may not renew a license under this section if the pharmacy's license to operate in another state has been suspended, revoked, canceled, or subject to an action that prohibits the pharmacy from operating in that state.

Leg.H. Stats. 1999 76th Leg. Sess. Ch. 388, effective September 1, 1999; Stats. 2005 79th Leg. Sess. Ch. 1345, effective September 1, 2005; Stats. 2013, 83rd Leg., ch. 583 (S.B. 869), § 11, effective June 14, 2013; am. Acts 2015, 84th Leg., ch. 599 (S.B. 460), § 8, 14(1), effective September 1, 2015.

Sec. 561.0031. [Expires September 1, 2029] Additional Renewal Requirement for Class E Pharmacy.

(a)   In addition to the renewal requirements under Section 561.003, the board shall require that a Class E pharmacy have on file with the board an inspection report issued:

    (1)   not more than three years before the date the renewal application is received; and

    (2)   by the pharmacy licensing board in the state of the pharmacy's physical location, except as provided by Subsection (b).

(b)   A Class E pharmacy may have on file with the board an inspection report issued by an entity other than the pharmacy licensing board of the state in which the pharmacy is physically located if the requirements of Section 560.052(f) are met.

Leg.H. Stats. 2005 79th Leg. Sess. Ch. 1345, effective September 1, 2005.

Sec. 561.0032. [Expires September 1, 2029] Additional Renewal Requirement for Compounding Pharmacy.

(a)   In addition to the renewal requirements under Section 561.003, a pharmacy that compounds sterile preparations may not renew a pharmacy license unless the pharmacy:

    (1)   has been inspected as provided by board rule; and

    (2)   if the pharmacy is located in another state, has reimbursed the board for all expenses, including travel, incurred by the board in inspecting the pharmacy during the term of the expiring license.

(b)   The board may accept, as satisfying the inspection requirement in Subsection (a) for a pharmacy located in another state, an inspection report issued by the pharmacy licensing board in the state in which the pharmacy is located if:

    (1)   the board determines that the other state has comparable standards and regulations applicable to pharmacies, including standards and regulations related to health and safety; and

    (2)   the pharmacy provides to the board any requested documentation related to the inspection.

Leg.H. Stats. 2013, 83rd Leg., ch. 608 (S.B. 1100), § 4, effective September 1, 2013.

Sec. 561.004. [Expires September 1, 2029] Issuance of License Renewal Certificate.

On timely receipt of a completed application and renewal fee, the board shall issue a license renewal certificate that contains:

    (1)   the pharmacy license number;

(2) the period for which the license is renewed; and

(3) other information the board determines necessary.

Leg.H. Stats. 1999 76th Leg. Sess. Ch. 388, effective September 1, 1999.

Sec. 561.005. [Expires September 1, 2029] Suspension of Pharmacy License for Nonrenewal.

(a) The board shall suspend the license and remove from the register of licensed pharmacies the name of a pharmacy that does not file a completed application and pay the renewal fee on or before the date the license expires.

(b) After review by the board, the board may determine that Subsection (a) does not apply if the license is the subject of a pending investigation or disciplinary action.

Leg.H. Stats. 1999 76th Leg. Sess. Ch. 388, effective September 1, 1999; Stats. 2001 77th Leg. Sess. Chs. 1254, 1420, effective September 1, 2001.

CHAPTER 562. PRACTICE BY LICENSE HOLDER
[EXPIRES SEPTEMBER 1, 2029]

SUBCHAPTER A. PRESCRIPTION AND SUBSTITUTION REQUIREMENTS
[EXPIRES SEPTEMBER 1, 2029]

Sec. 562.001. [Expires September 1, 2029] Definitions.

In this subchapter:

(1) "Biological product" has the meaning assigned by Section 351, Public Health Service Act (42 U.S.C. Section 262).

(1-a) "Generically equivalent" means a drug that is pharmaceutically equivalent and therapeutically equivalent to the drug prescribed.

(1-b) "Interchangeable," in reference to a biological product, has the meaning assigned by Section 351, Public Health Service Act (42 U.S.C. Section 262), or means a biological product that is designated as therapeutically equivalent to another product by the United States Food and Drug Administration in the most recent edition or supplement of the United States Food and Drug Administration's Approved Drug Products with Therapeutic Equivalence Evaluations, also known as the Orange Book.

(2) "Pharmaceutically equivalent" means drug products that have identical amounts of the same active chemical ingredients in the same dosage form and that meet the identical compendial or other applicable standards of strength, quality, and purity according to the United States Pharmacopoeia or another nationally recognized compendium.

(3) "Therapeutically equivalent" means pharmaceutically equivalent drug products that, if administered in the same amounts, will provide the same therapeutic effect, identical in duration and intensity.

Leg.H. Stats. 1999 76th Leg. Sess. Ch. 388, effective September 1, 1999; am. Acts 2015, 84th Leg., ch. 1007 (H.B. 751), § 1, effective September 1, 2015.

Sec. 562.002. [Expires September 1, 2029] Legislative Intent.

It is the intent of the legislature to save consumers money by allowing the substitution of lower-priced generically equivalent drug products for certain brand name drug products and the substitution of interchangeable biological products for certain biological products and for pharmacies and pharmacists to pass on the net benefit of the lower costs of the generically equivalent drug product or interchangeable biological product to the purchaser.

Leg.H. Stats. 1999 76th Leg. Sess. Ch. 388, effective September 1, 1999; am. Acts 2015, 84th Leg., ch. 1007 (H.B. 751), § 2, effective September 1, 2015.

Sec. 562.003. [Expires September 1, 2029] Disclosure of Price; Patient's Option.

If the price of a drug or biological product to a patient is lower than the amount of the patient's copayment under the patient's prescription drug insurance plan, the pharmacist shall offer the patient the option of paying for the drug or biological product at the lower price instead of paying the amount of the copayment.

Leg.H. Stats. 2005 79th Leg. Sess. Ch. 943, effective September 1, 2005; am. Acts 2015, 84th Leg., ch. 1007 (H.B. 751), § 3, effective September 1, 2015.

Sec. 562.004. [Expires September 1, 2029] Prescription Transmitted Orally by Practitioner.

A pharmacist to whom a prescription is transmitted orally shall:

(1) note on the file copy of the prescription the dispensing instructions of the practitioner or the practitioner's agent; and

(2) retain the prescription for the period specified by law.

Leg.H. Stats. 1999 76th Leg. Sess. Ch. 388, effective September 1, 1999.

Sec. 562.005. [Expires September 1, 2029] Record of Dispensed Drug or Biological Product.

A pharmacist shall record on the prescription form the name, strength, and manufacturer or distributor of a drug or biological product dispensed as authorized by this subchapter.

Leg.H. Stats. 1999 76th Leg. Sess. Ch. 388, effective September 1, 1999; am. Acts 2015, 84th Leg., ch. 1007 (H.B. 751), § 4, effective September 1, 2015.

Sec. 562.0051. [Expires September 1, 2029] Communication Regarding Certain Dispensed Biological Products.

(a)   Not later than the third business day after the date of dispensing a biological product, the dispensing pharmacist or the pharmacist's designee shall communicate to the prescribing practitioner the specific product provided to the patient, including the name of the product and the manufacturer or national drug code number.

(b)   The communication must be conveyed by making an entry into an interoperable electronic medical records system or through electronic prescribing technology or a pharmacy benefit management system or a pharmacy record, which may include information submitted for the payment of claims, that a pharmacist reasonably concludes is electronically accessible by the prescribing practitioner. Otherwise, the pharmacist or the pharmacist's designee shall communicate the biological product dispensed to the prescribing practitioner, using facsimile, telephone, electronic transmission, or other prevailing means, provided that communication is not required if:

     (1)   there is no interchangeable biological product approved by the United States Food and Drug Administration for the product prescribed; or

     (2)   a refill prescription is not changed from the product dispensed on the prior filling of the prescription.

(c)   This section expires September 1, 2019.

Leg.H. Stats 2015, 84th Leg., ch. 1007 (H.B. 751), § 5, effective September 1, 2015.

Sec. 562.006. [Expires September 1, 2029] Label.

(a)   Unless otherwise directed by the practitioner, the label on the dispensing container must indicate the actual drug or biological product dispensed, indicated by either:

     (1)   the brand name; or

     (2)   if there is not a brand name, the drug's generic name or the name of the biological product, the strength of the drug or biological product, and the name of the manufacturer or distributor of the drug or biological product.

(b)   In addition to the information required by Subsection (a), the label on the dispensing container of a drug or biological product dispensed by a Class A or Class E pharmacy must indicate:

     (1)   the name, address, and telephone number of the pharmacy;

     (2)   the date the prescription is dispensed;

     (3)   the name of the prescribing practitioner;

     (4)   the name of the patient or, if the drug or biological product was prescribed for an animal, the species of the animal and the name of the owner;

     (5)   instructions for use;

     (6)   the quantity dispensed;

     (7)   if the drug or biological product is dispensed in a container other than the manufacturer's original container, the date after which the prescription should not be used, determined according to criteria established by board rule based on standards in the United States Pharmacopeia-National Formulary; and

     (8)   any other information required by board rule.

(c)   The information required by Subsection (b)(7) may be recorded on any label affixed to the dispensing container.

(d)   Subsection (b) does not apply to a prescription dispensed to a person at the time of release from prison or jail if the prescription is for not more than a 10-day supply of medication.

(e)   If a drug or biological product has been selected other than the one prescribed, the pharmacist shall place on the container the words "Substituted for brand prescribed" or "Substituted for 'brand name'" where "brand name" is the name of the brand name drug or biological product prescribed.

(f)   The board shall adopt rules requiring the label on a dispensing container to be in plain language and printed in an easily readable font size for the consumer.

Leg.H. Stats. 1999 76th Leg. Sess. Ch. 388, effective September 1, 1999; Stats. 2007, 80th Leg. Sess. Ch. 457, effective September 1, 2007; Stats. 2009 81st Leg. Sess. Ch. 289, effective September 1, 2009; am. Acts 2015, 84th Leg., ch. 1007 (H.B. 751), § 6, effective September 1, 2015.

Sec. 562.0061. [Expires September 1, 2029] Other Prescription Information.

The board shall adopt rules specifying the information a pharmacist must provide to a consumer when dispensing a prescription to the consumer for self-administration. The information must be:

     (1)   written in plain language;

     (2)   relevant to the prescription; and

     (3)   printed in an easily readable font size.

Leg.H. Stats. 2007, 80th Leg. Sess. Ch. 457, effective September 1, 2007.

Sec. 562.0062. [Expires September 1, 2029] Required Statement Regarding Medication Disposal.

The board by rule shall require pharmacists, when dispensing certain drugs, to include on the dispensing container label or in the information required by Section 562.0061 the statement "Do not flush unused medications or pour down a sink or drain."

Leg.H. Stats. 2009 81st Leg. Sess. Ch. 289, effective September 1, 2009.

Sec. 562.007. [Expires September 1, 2029] Refills.

Except as provided by Section 562.0545, a properly authorized prescription refill shall follow the original dispensing instruction unless otherwise indicated by the practitioner or the practitioner's agent.

Leg.H. Stats. 1999 76th Leg. Sess. Ch. 388, effective September 1, 1999; Stats. 2011 82nd Leg. Ch. 303, effective September 1, 2011.

Sec. 562.008. [Expires September 1, 2029] Generic Equivalent or Interchangeable Biological Product Authorized.

(a) If a practitioner certifies on the prescription form that a specific prescribed brand is medically necessary, the pharmacist shall dispense the drug or biological product as written by the practitioner. The certification must be made as required by the dispensing directive adopted under Section 562.015. This subchapter does not permit a pharmacist to substitute a generically equivalent drug or interchangeable biological product unless the substitution is made as provided by this subchapter.

(b) Except as otherwise provided by this subchapter, a pharmacist who receives a prescription for a drug or biological product for which there is one or more generic equivalents or one or more interchangeable biological products may dispense any of the generic equivalents or interchangeable biological products.

Leg.H. Stats. 1999 76th Leg. Sess. Ch. 388, effective September 1, 1999; Stats. 2001 77th Leg. Sess. Ch. 1254, effective September 1, 2001; am. Acts 2015, 84th Leg., ch. 1007 (H.B. 751), § 7, effective September 1, 2015.

Sec. 562.009. [Expires September 1, 2029] Requirements Concerning Selection of Generically Equivalent Drug or Interchangeable Biological Product.

(a) Before delivery of a prescription for a generically equivalent drug or interchangeable biological product, a pharmacist must personally, or through the pharmacist's agent or employee:
  (1) inform the patient or the patient's agent that a less expensive generically equivalent drug or interchangeable biological product is available for the brand prescribed; and
  (2) ask the patient or the patient's agent to choose between the generically equivalent drug or interchangeable biological product and the brand prescribed.

(a-1) Repealed by Acts 2015, 84th Leg., ch. 599 (S.B. 460), § 14(2), effective September 1, 2015.

(b) A pharmacy is not required to comply with the provisions of Subsection (a):
  (1) in the case of the refill of a prescription for which the pharmacy previously complied with Subsection (a) with respect to the same patient or patient's agent; or
  (2) if the patient's physician or physician's agent advises the pharmacy that:
    (A) the physician has informed the patient or the patient's agent that a less expensive generically equivalent drug or interchangeable biological product is available for the brand prescribed; and
    (B) the patient or the patient's agent has chosen either the brand prescribed or the less expensive generically equivalent drug or interchangeable biological product.

(c) A pharmacy that supplies a prescription by mail is considered to have complied with the provisions of Subsection (a) if the pharmacy includes on the prescription order form completed by the patient or the patient's agent language that clearly and conspicuously:
  (1) states that if a less expensive generically equivalent drug or interchangeable biological product is available for the brand prescribed, the patient or the patient's agent may choose between the generically equivalent drug or interchangeable biological product and the brand prescribed; and
  (2) allows the patient or the patient's agent to indicate the choice between the generically equivalent drug or interchangeable biological product and the brand prescribed.

(d) If the patient or the patient's agent fails to indicate otherwise to a pharmacy on the prescription order form under Subsection (c), the pharmacy may dispense a generically equivalent drug or interchangeable biological product.

(e) If the prescription is for an immunosuppressant drug, as defined by Section 562.0141(a)(1), the pharmacist must comply with the provisions of Section 562.0141. This subsection expires if Section 562.0141 expires under the requirements of Section 562.0142.

Leg.H. Stats. 1999 76th Leg. Sess. Ch. 388, effective September 1, 1999; Stats 2005 79th Leg. Sess. Ch. 943, effective September 1, 2005; Stats 2007, 80th Leg. Sess. Ch. 385, effective June 15, 2007; am. Acts 2015, 84th Leg., ch. 599 (S.B. 460), § 14(2), effective September 1, 2015; am. Acts 2015, 84th Leg., ch. 1007 (H.B. 751), § 8, 9, effective September 1, 2015.

Sec. 562.010. [Expires September 1, 2029] Responsibility Concerning Generically Equivalent Drug or Interchangeable Biological Product; Liability.

(a) A pharmacist who selects a generically equivalent drug or interchangeable biological product to be dispensed under this subchapter assumes the same responsibility for selecting the generically equivalent drug or interchangeable biological product as the pharmacist does in filling a prescription for a drug prescribed by generic or biological product name.

(b) The prescribing practitioner is not liable for a pharmacist's act or omission in selecting, preparing, or dispensing a drug or biological product under this subchapter.

Leg.H. Stats. 1999 76th Leg. Sess. Ch. 388, effective September 1, 1999; am. Acts 2015, 84th Leg., ch. 1007 (H.B. 751), § 10, effective September 1, 2015.

Sec. 562.011. [Expires September 1, 2029] Restriction on Selection of and Charging for Generically Equivalent Drug or Interchangeable Biological Product.

(a) A pharmacist may not select a generically equivalent drug or interchangeable biological product unless the generically equivalent drug or interchangeable biological product selected costs the patient less than the prescribed drug or biological product.

(b) A pharmacist may not charge for dispensing a generically equivalent drug or interchangeable biological product a professional fee higher than the fee the pharmacist customarily charges for dispensing the brand name drug or biological product prescribed.

Leg.H. Stats. 1999 76th Leg. Sess. Ch. 388, effective September 1, 1999; am. Acts 2015, 84th Leg., ch. 1007 (H.B. 751), § 11, effective September 1, 2015.

Sec. 562.012. [Expires September 1, 2029] Substitution of Dosage Form Permitted.

With the patient's consent, a pharmacist may dispense a dosage form of a drug different from that prescribed, such as a tablet instead of a capsule or a liquid instead of a tablet, if the dosage form dispensed:

(1) contains the identical amount of the active ingredients as the dosage prescribed for the patient;

(2) is not an enteric-coated or timed release product; and

(3) does not alter desired clinical outcomes.

Leg.H. Stats. 1999 76th Leg. Sess. Ch. 388, effective September 1, 1999; Stats. 2013, 83rd Leg., ch. 583 (S.B. 869), § 12, effective June 14, 2013.

Sec. 562.013. [Expires September 1, 2029] Applicability of Subchapter.

Unless a drug is determined to be generically equivalent to, or a biological product is determined to be interchangeable with, the brand prescribed, drug or biological product selection as authorized by this subchapter does not apply to:

(1) an enteric-coated tablet;

(2) a controlled release product;

(3) an injectable suspension, other than an antibiotic;

(4) a suppository containing active ingredients for which systemic absorption is necessary for therapeutic activity; or

(5) a different delivery system for aerosol or nebulizer drugs.

Leg.H. Stats. 1999 76th Leg. Sess. Ch. 388, effective September 1, 1999; am. Acts 2015, 84th Leg., ch. 1007 (H.B. 751), § 12, effective September 1, 2015.

Sec. 562.014. [Expires September 1, 2029] Narrow Therapeutic Index Drugs.

(a) Except as provided by this section, drug selection as authorized by this subchapter does not apply to the refill of a prescription for a narrow therapeutic index drug. The board, in consultation with the Texas Medical Board, shall by rule establish a list of narrow therapeutic index drugs to which this subsection applies. A prescription for a narrow therapeutic index drug may be refilled only by using the same drug product by the same manufacturer that the pharmacist last dispensed under the prescription, unless otherwise agreed to by the prescribing practitioner. If a pharmacist does not have the same drug product by the same manufacturer in stock to refill the prescription, the pharmacist may dispense a drug product that is generically equivalent if the pharmacist, before dispensing the generically equivalent drug product, notifies:

(1) the patient, at the time the prescription is dispensed, that a substitution of the prescribed drug product has been made; and

(2) the prescribing practitioner of the drug product substitution by telephone, facsimile, or mail, at the earliest reasonable time, but not later than 72 hours after dispensing the prescription.

(b) The board and the Texas Medical Board shall establish a joint committee to recommend to the board a list of narrow therapeutic index drugs and the rules, if any, by which this section applies to those drugs. The committee must consist of an equal number of members from each board. The committee members shall select a member of the committee to serve as presiding officer for a one year term. The presiding officer may not represent the same board as the presiding officer's predecessor.

(c), (d) [Expired pursuant to Acts 2007, 80th Leg., ch. 385 (S.B. 625), § 1, effective December 1, 2008.]

Leg.H. Stats. 1999 76th Leg. Sess. Ch. 388, effective September 1, 1999; Stats 2007, 80th Leg. Sess. Ch. 385, effective June 15, 2007.

Sec. 562.0141. [Expires September 1, 2029] Transplant Immunosuppressant Drug Product Selection Prohibited.

(a) In this section:

(1) "Immunosuppressant drug" means any drug prescribed for immunosuppressant therapy following a transplant.

(2) "Interchange" means the substitution of one version of the same immunosuppressant drug, including a generic version for the prescribed brand, a brand version for the prescribed generic version, a generic version by one manufacturer for a generic version by a different manufacturer, a different formulation of the prescribed immunosuppressant drug, or a different immunosuppressant drug for the immunosuppressant drug originally prescribed.

(b) A pharmacist may not interchange an immunosuppressant drug or formulation of an immunosuppressant drug, brand or generic, for the treatment of a patient following a transplant without prior consent to the interchange from the prescribing practitioner.

(c) To comply with Subsection (b), a pharmacist shall notify a prescribing practitioner orally or electronically to secure permission to interchange an immunosuppressant drug or formulation of an immunosuppressant drug, brand or generic. The practitioner's authorization or denial of authorization must be documented by the pharmacist and by the practitioner.

(d) If a pharmacist does not have the same drug product by the same manufacturer in stock to refill the prescription, or if the practitioner is unavailable to give authorization, the pharmacist may dispense a drug product that is generically equivalent if the pharmacist, before dispensing the generally equivalent drug product:

(1) notifies and receives consent from the patient, at the time the prescription is dispensed, to substitute the prescribed drug product; and

(2) notifies the prescribing practitioner of the drug product substitution orally or electronically at the earliest reasonable time, but not later than 24 hours after dispensing the prescription.

(e) This section is only effective subject to the conditions established by Section 562.0142.

Leg.H. Stats. 2007, 80th Leg. Sess. Ch. 385, effective June 15, 2007.

Sec. 562.0142. [Expires September 1, 2029] Adoption of Rules.

(a) If, not later than October 1, 2007, a drug manufacturer requests that the joint committee under Section 562.014 conduct a hearing and make a recommendation to include a drug listed in Section 562.014(c) on the list of narrow therapeutic index drugs, the joint committee shall make a recommendation to the board to enable the board to adopt a rule and issue findings not later than July 1, 2008.

(b) If, not later than October 1, 2007, no drug manufacturer requests that the joint committee conduct a hearing and make recommendations to the board to include a drug listed in Section 562.014(c) on the list of narrow therapeutic index drugs, Section 562.0141 expires October 1, 2007.

(c) If all drug manufacturers that request, before October 1, 2007, the joint committee to conduct a hearing and make a recommendation to the board to include a drug listed in Section 562.014(c) on the list of narrow therapeutic index drugs subsequently withdraw those requests before the date the joint committee makes a recommendation to include the drug on that list, Section 562.0141 expires effective on the date of the manufacturers' withdrawal of those requests.

(d) If the joint committee receives a request under Subsection (a), the recommendation of the joint committee under that subsection may include the drugs listed in Section 562.014(c) or the joint committee may recommend that no drug should be added to the list of narrow therapeutic index drugs following the review by the joint committee.

(e) If the joint committee receives a request under Subsection (a) and, not later than July 1, 2008, the board adopts a rule to include any drug listed in Section 562.014(c) on the list of narrow therapeutic index drugs or determines by rule that no drug should be added to the list of narrow therapeutic index drugs, Section 562.0141 expires on July 1, 2008.

(f) If the joint committee receives a request under Subsection (a) and the board does not before July 1, 2008, adopt a rule to include any drug listed in Section 562.014(c) on the list of narrow therapeutic index drugs or determine by rule that no drug should be added to the list of narrow therapeutic index drugs, Section 562.0141 takes effect July 1, 2008.

(g) If the joint committee receives a request under Subsection (a) and litigation or a request for an attorney general's opinion regarding this section, Section 562.014, or Section 562.0141 is filed by a drug manufacturer between the effective date of this section and July 1, 2008, the time limits established by Subsections (e) and (f) are tolled until the litigation is resolved or the attorney general renders an opinion.

(h) For purposes of this section, notice of the following must be published in the Texas Register not later than the third business day after the date of occurrence:

(1) a request by a drug manufacturer for inclusion of a drug on the list of narrow therapeutic index drugs;

(2) withdrawal of a request described by Subdivision (1);

(3) litigation described by Subsection (g);

(4) resolution of litigation described by Subsection (g); and

(5) a request for an attorney general's opinion described by Subsection (g).

Leg.H. Stats. 2007, 80th Leg. Sess. Ch. 385, effective June 15, 2007.

Sec. 562.015. [Expires September 1, 2029] Dispensing Directive; Compliance with Federal Law.

(a) The board shall adopt rules to provide a dispensing directive to instruct pharmacists on the manner in which to dispense a drug or biological product according to the contents of a prescription. The rules adopted under this section must:

(1) require the use of the phrase "brand necessary" or "brand medically necessary" on a prescription form to prohibit the substitution of a generically equivalent drug or interchangeable biological product for a brand name drug or biological product;

(2) be in a format that protects confidentiality as required by the Health Insurance Portability and Accountability Act of 1996 (Pub. L. No. 104-191) and its subsequent amendments;

(3) comply with federal and state law, including rules, with regard to formatting and security requirements;

(4) be developed to coordinate with 42 C.F.R. Section 447.512; and

(5) include an exemption for electronic prescriptions as provided by Subsection (b).

(b) The board shall provide an exemption from the directive adopted under this section for prescriptions transmitted electronically. The board may regulate the use of electronic prescriptions in the manner provided by federal law, including rules.

Leg.H. Stats. 2001 77th Leg. Sess. Ch. 1254, effective September 1, 2001; am. Acts 2015, 84th Leg., ch. 1007 (H.B. 751), § 13, effective September 1, 2015.

Sec. 562.016. [Expires September 1, 2029] List of Approved Interchangeable Biological Products.

The board shall maintain on the board's Internet website a link to the United States Food and Drug Administration's list of approved interchangeable biological products.

Leg.H. Stats. 2015, 84th Leg., ch. 1007 (H.B. 751), § 14, effective September 1, 2015.

SUBCHAPTER B. OTHER PRACTICE BY PHARMACIST
[EXPIRES SEPTEMBER 1, 2029]

Sec. 562.051. Repealed.

Repealed by Acts 2015, 84th Leg., ch. 599 (S.B. 460), § 14(3), effective September 1, 2015.

Sec. 562.052. [Expires September 1, 2029] Release of Confidential Records.

A confidential record is privileged and a pharmacist may release a confidential record only to:

(1)　the patient or the patient's agent;

(2)　a practitioner or another pharmacist if, in the pharmacist's professional judgment, the release is necessary to protect the patient's health and well-being;

(3)　the board or to a person or another state or federal agency authorized by law to receive the confidential record;

(4)　a law enforcement agency engaged in investigation of a suspected violation of Chapter 481 or 483, Health and Safety Code, or the Comprehensive Drug Abuse Prevention and Control Act of 1970 (21 U.S.C. Section 801 et seq.);

(5)　a person employed by a state agency that licenses a practitioner, if the person is performing the person's official duties; or

(6)　an insurance carrier or other third party payor authorized by the patient to receive the information.

Leg.H. Stats. 1999 76th Leg. Sess. Ch. 388, effective September 1, 1999.

Sec. 562.053. [Expires September 1, 2029] Reports to Board.

A pharmacist shall report in writing to the board not later than the 10th day after the date of a change of address or place of employment.

Leg.H. Stats. 1999 76th Leg. Sess. Ch. 388, effective September 1, 1999.

Sec. 562.054. [Expires September 1, 2029] Emergency Refills.

(a)　A pharmacist may exercise the pharmacist's professional judgment in refilling a prescription for a prescription drug, other than a controlled substance listed in Schedule II as established by the commissioner of state health services under Chapter 481, Health and Safety Code, without the authorization of the prescribing practitioner if:

(1)　failure to refill the prescription might result in an interruption of a therapeutic regimen or create patient suffering;

(2)　either:

(A)　a natural or manmade disaster has occurred that prohibits the pharmacist from being able to contact the practitioner; or

(B)　the pharmacist is unable to contact the practitioner after reasonable effort;

(3)　the quantity of prescription drug dispensed does not exceed a 72-hour supply;

(4)　the pharmacist informs the patient or the patient's agent at the time of dispensing that the refill is being provided without the practitioner's authorization and that authorization of the practitioner is required for a future refill; and

(5)　the pharmacist informs the practitioner of the emergency refill at the earliest reasonable time.

(b)　Notwithstanding Subsection (a), in the event of a natural or manmade disaster, a pharmacist may dispense not more than a 30-day supply of a prescription drug, other than a controlled substance listed in Schedule II as established by the commissioner of state health services under Chapter 481, Health and Safety Code, without the authorization of the prescribing practitioner if:

(1)　failure to refill the prescription might result in an interruption of a therapeutic regimen or create patient suffering;

(2)　the natural or manmade disaster prohibits the pharmacist from being able to contact the practitioner;

(3)　the governor has declared a state of disaster under Chapter 418, Government Code; and

(4)　the board, through the executive director, has notified pharmacies in this state that pharmacists may dispense up to a 30-day supply of a prescription drug.

(c)　The prescribing practitioner is not liable for an act or omission by a pharmacist in dispensing a prescription drug under Subsection (b).

Leg.H. Stats. 1999 76th Leg. Sess. Ch. 388, effective September 1, 1999; Stats 2007, 80th Leg. Sess. Ch. 567, effective September 1, 2007.

Sec. 562.0545. [Expires September 1, 2029] 90-day Supply and Accelerated Refills.

A pharmacist may dispense up to a 90-day supply of a dangerous drug pursuant to a valid prescription that specifies the dispensing of a lesser amount followed by periodic refills of that amount if:

(1) the total quantity of dosage units dispensed does not exceed the total quantity of dosage units authorized by the prescriber on the original prescription, including refills;

(2) the patient consents to the dispensing of up to a 90-day supply and the physician has been notified electronically or by telephone;

(3) the physician has not specified on the prescription that dispensing the prescription in an initial amount followed by periodic refills is medically necessary;

(4) the dangerous drug is not a psychotropic drug; and

(5) the patient is at least 18 years of age.

Leg.H. Stats. 2011 82nd Leg. Ch. 303, effective September 1, 2011.

Sec. 562.055. [Expires September 1, 2029] Report to Texas Department of Health.

A pharmacist shall report to the Texas Department of Health any unusual or increased prescription rates, unusual types of prescriptions, or unusual trends in pharmacy visits that may be caused by bioterrorism, epidemic or pandemic disease, or novel and highly fatal infectious

agents or biological toxins that might pose a substantial risk of a significant number of human fatalities or incidents of permanent or long-term disability. Prescription-related events that require a report include:
  (1) an unusual increase in the number of:
     (A) prescriptions to treat respiratory or gastrointestinal complaints or fever;
     (B) prescriptions for antibiotics; and
     (C) requests for information on over-the-counter pharmaceuticals to treat respiratory or gastrointestinal complaints or fever; and
  (2) any prescription that treats a disease that is relatively uncommon and has bioterrorism potential.

Leg.H. Stats. 2003 78th Leg. Sess. Ch. 1312, effective June 22, 2003.

Sec. 562.056. [Expires September 1, 2029] Practitioner-Patient Relationship Required.

  (a) Before dispensing a prescription, a pharmacist shall determine, in the exercise of sound professional judgment, that the prescription is a valid prescription. A pharmacist may not dispense a prescription drug if the pharmacist knows or should know that the prescription was issued without a valid practitioner-patient relationship.
  (a-1) To be a valid prescription, a prescription must be issued for a legitimate medical purpose by a practitioner acting in the usual course of the practitioner's professional practice. The responsibility for the proper prescribing and dispensing of prescription drugs is on the prescribing practitioner, but a corresponding responsibility rests with the pharmacist who fills the prescription.
  (b) This section does not prohibit a pharmacist from dispensing a prescription when a valid practitioner-patient relationship is not present in an emergency.
  (c) For purposes of this section, a valid practitioner-patient relationship is present between a practitioner providing telemedicine medical services and the patient receiving the telemedicine medical services if the practitioner has complied with the requirements for establishing such a relationship in accordance with Section 111.005.

Leg.H. Stats. 2005, 79th Leg., ch. 1345 (S.B. 410), § 21, effective September 1, 2005; am. Acts 2013, 83rd Leg., ch. 583 (S.B. 869), § 13, effective June 14, 2013; am. Acts 2015, 84th Leg., ch. 599 (S.B. 460), § 9, effective September 1, 2015; am. Acts 2017, 85th Leg., ch. 205 (S.B. 1107), § 4, effective May 27, 2017.

Sec. 562.057. [Expires September 1, 2029] Administration of Epinephrine.

  (a) A pharmacist may administer epinephrine through an auto-injector device in accordance with this section.
  (b) The board shall adopt rules designed to protect the public health and safety to implement this section. The rules must provide that a pharmacist may administer epinephrine through an auto-injector device to a patient in an emergency situation.
  (c) A pharmacist may maintain, administer, and dispose of epinephrine auto-injector devices only in accordance with rules adopted by the board under this section.
  (d) A pharmacist who administers epinephrine through an auto-injector device to a patient shall report the use to the patient's primary care physician, as identified by the patient, if the patient has a primary care physician.
  (e) A pharmacist who in good faith administers epinephrine through an auto-injector device in accordance with the requirements of this section is not liable for civil damages for an act performed in the administration unless the act is wilfully or wantonly negligent. A pharmacist may not receive remuneration for the administration of epinephrine through an auto-injector device but may seek reimbursement for the cost of the epinephrine auto-injector device.
  (f) The administration of epinephrine through an auto-injector device to a patient in accordance with the requirements of this section does not constitute the unlawful practice of any health care profession.

LegH. Stats. 2015, 84th Leg., ch. 1253 (H.B. 1550), § 1, effective January 1, 2016.

SUBCHAPTER C. PRACTICE BY PHARMACY
[EXPIRES SEPTEMBER 1, 2029]

Sec. 562.101. [Expires September 1, 2029] Supervision of Pharmacy.

  (a) A pharmacy is required to be under the supervision of a pharmacist as provided by this section.
  (b) A Class A or Class B pharmacy is required to be under the continuous on-site supervision of a pharmacist during the time the pharmacy is open for pharmacy services.
  (c) A Class C pharmacy that is in an institution with more than 100 beds is required to be under the continuous on-site supervision of a pharmacist during the time the pharmacy is open for pharmacy services.
  (d) A Class C pharmacy that is in an institution with 100 beds or fewer is required to have the services of a pharmacist on a part-time or consulting basis according to the needs of the institution.
  (e) A Class D pharmacy is required to be under the continuous supervision of a pharmacist whose services are required according to the needs of the pharmacy.
  (f) A Class E pharmacy is required to be under the continuous on-site supervision of a pharmacist and shall designate one pharmacist licensed to practice pharmacy by the regulatory or licensing agency of the state in which the Class E pharmacy is located to serve as the pharmacist-in-charge of the Class E pharmacy.
  (f-1) A Canadian pharmacy designated by the board as having passed inspection to dispense prescription drugs to residents in this state is required to be under the continuous on-site supervision of a pharmacist and shall designate one pharmacist licensed to practice pharmacy by the regulatory or licensing agency of Canada or of the Canadian province in which the Canadian pharmacy is located to serve as the pharmacist-in-charge of the Canadian pharmacy.

(g) For a pharmacy license classification established under Section 560.053, the board shall adopt rules that provide for the supervision of the pharmacy by a pharmacist. Supervision under the board rules must require at least continuous supervision by a pharmacist according to the needs of the pharmacy.

Leg.H. Stats. 1999 76th Leg. Sess. Ch. 388, effective September 1, 1999; Stats. 2003 78th Leg. Sess. Ch. 941, effective September 1, 2003; Stats. 2005 79th Leg. Sess. Ch. 1345, effective September 1, 2005.

Sec. 562.1011. [Expires September 1, 2029] Operation of Class C Pharmacy in Certain Rural Hospitals.

(a) In this section:
    (1) "Nurse" has the meaning assigned by Section 301.002. The term includes a nurse who is also registered as a pharmacy technician.
    (2) "Rural hospital" means a licensed hospital with 75 beds or fewer that:
        (A) is located in a county with a population of 50,000 or less; or
        (B) has been designated by the Centers for Medicare and Medicaid Services as a critical access hospital, rural referral center, or sole community hospital.

(b) If a practitioner orders a prescription drug or device for a patient in a rural hospital when the hospital pharmacist is not on duty or when the institutional pharmacy is closed, a nurse or practitioner may withdraw the drug or device from the pharmacy in sufficient quantity to fill the order.

(c) The hospital pharmacist shall verify the withdrawal of a drug or device under Subsection (b) and perform a drug regimen review not later than the seventh day after the date of the withdrawal.

(d) In a rural hospital that uses a floor stock method of drug distribution, a nurse or practitioner may withdraw a prescription drug or device from the institutional pharmacy in the original manufacturer's container or a prepackaged container.

(e) The hospital pharmacist shall verify the withdrawal of a drug or device under Subsection (d) and perform a drug regimen review not later than the seventh day after the date of the withdrawal.

(f) A rural hospital may allow a pharmacy technician to perform the duties specified in Subsection (g) if:
    (1) the pharmacy technician is registered and meets the training requirements specified by the board;
    (2) a pharmacist is accessible at all times to respond to any questions and needs of the pharmacy technician or other hospital employees, by telephone, answering or paging service, e-mail, or any other system that makes a pharmacist accessible; and
    (3) a nurse or practitioner or a pharmacist by remote access verifies the accuracy of the actions of the pharmacy technician.

(g) If the requirements of Subsection (f) are met, the pharmacy technician may, during the hours that the institutional pharmacy in the hospital is open, perform the following duties in the pharmacy without the direct supervision of a pharmacist:
    (1) enter medication order and drug distribution information into a data processing system;
    (2) prepare, package, or label a prescription drug according to a medication order if a licensed nurse or practitioner verifies the accuracy of the order before administration of the drug to the patient;
    (3) fill a medication cart used in the rural hospital;
    (4) distribute routine orders for stock supplies to patient care areas;
    (5) access and restock automated medication supply cabinets; and
    (6) perform any other duty specified by the board by rule.

(h) The pharmacist-in-charge of an institutional pharmacy in a rural hospital shall develop and implement policies and procedures for the operation of the pharmacy when a pharmacist is not on-site.

(i) On or after September 1, 2011, the board may establish, by rule, a requirement for prospective and retrospective drug use review by a pharmacist for each new drug order. A drug use review is not required when a delay in administration of the drug would harm the patient in an urgent or emergency situation, including sudden changes in a patient's clinical status.

(j) Rural hospitals may establish standing orders and protocols, to be developed jointly by the pharmacist and medical staff, that may include additional exceptions to instances in which prospective drug use review is required.

(k) This section does not restrict or prohibit the board from adopting a rule related to authorizing the withdrawal of a drug or device by a nurse or practitioner from, or the supervision of a pharmacy technician in, an institutional pharmacy not located in a rural hospital. As part of the rulemaking process, the board shall consider the effect that a proposed rule, if adopted, would have on access to pharmacy services in hospitals that are not rural hospitals.

(l) The board shall adopt rules to implement this section, including rules specifying:
    (1) the records that must be maintained under this section;
    (2) the requirements for policies and procedures for operation of a pharmacy when a pharmacist is not on-site; and
    (3) the training requirements for pharmacy technicians.

Leg.H. Stats. 2009 81st Leg. Sess. Ch. 1128, effective June 19, 2009.

Sec. 562.102. [Expires September 1, 2029] Confidential Record.

A pharmacy shall comply with Section 562.052 concerning the release of a confidential record.

Leg.H. Stats. 1999 76th Leg. Sess. Ch. 388, effective September 1, 1999.

Sec. 562.103. [Expires September 1, 2029] Display of Licenses by Pharmacy.

(a) A pharmacy shall display in the pharmacy in full public view the license under which the pharmacy operates.
(b) A Class A or Class C pharmacy that serves the public shall:
    (1) display the word "pharmacy" or a similar word or symbol as determined by the board in a prominent place on the front of the pharmacy; and
    (2) display in public view the license of the pharmacist-in-charge of the pharmacy.

(c) A pharmacy shall maintain and make available to the public on request proof that each pharmacist, pharmacist-intern, pharmacy technician, and pharmacist technician trainee working in the pharmacy holds the appropriate license or registration.

Leg.H. Stats. 1999 76th Leg. Sess. Ch. 388, effective September 1, 1999; Stats. 2013, 83rd Leg., ch. 583 (S.B. 869), § 14, effective June 14, 2013.

Sec. 562.104. [Expires September 1, 2029] Toll-Free Telephone Number Required.

A pharmacy whose primary business is to dispense a prescription drug or device under a prescription drug order to a patient located outside the area covered by the pharmacy's telephone area code shall provide a toll-free telephone line that is answered during normal business hours to enable communication between a patient or the patient's physician and a pharmacist at the pharmacy who has access to the patient's records.

Leg.H. Stats. 1999 76th Leg. Sess. Ch. 388, effective September 1, 1999.

Sec. 562.1045. [Expires September 1, 2029] Linking Internet Sites.

(a) This section applies only to a pharmacy that:
    (1) maintains a generally accessible Internet site; and
    (2) sells or distributes drugs through the Internet.
(b) A pharmacy subject to this section shall link its site to the Internet site maintained by the board. The link must be:
    (1) on the pharmacy's initial home page; and
    (2) if the pharmacy sells drugs through its site, on the page where the sale occurs.
(c) A pharmacy subject to this section shall post:
    (1) on its initial home page general information on how to file a complaint about the pharmacy with the board; and
    (2) specific information on how to file a complaint with the board not more than two links away from its initial home page.
(d) Information under Subsection (c) must include the board's telephone number, mailing address, and Internet website address.

Leg.H. Stats. 2001 77th Leg. Sess. Ch. 972, effective November 1, 2001; Stats. 2005 79th Leg. Sess. Ch. 1345, effective September 1, 2005.

Sec. 562.105. [Expires September 1, 2029] Maintenance of Records.

A pharmacy shall maintain a permanent record of:
    (1) any civil litigation initiated against the pharmacy by a resident of this state; or
    (2) a complaint that arises out of a prescription for a resident of this state that was lost during delivery.

Leg.H. Stats. 1999 76th Leg. Sess. Ch. 388, effective September 1, 1999.

Sec. 562.106. [Expires September 1, 2029] Notification.

(a) A pharmacy shall report in writing to the board not later than the 10th day after the date of:
    (1) a permanent closing of the pharmacy;
    (2) a change of ownership of the pharmacy;
    (3) a change of the person designated as the pharmacist-in-charge of the pharmacy;
    (4) a sale or transfer of any controlled substance or dangerous drug as a result of the permanent closing or change of ownership of the pharmacy;
    (5) any matter or occurrence that the board requires by rule to be reported;
    (6) as determined by the board, an out-of-state purchase of any controlled substance;
    (7) a final order against the pharmacy license holder by the regulatory or licensing agency of the state in which the pharmacy is located if the pharmacy is located in another state; or
    (8) a final order against a pharmacist who is designated as the pharmacist-in-charge of the pharmacy by the regulatory or licensing agency of the state in which the pharmacy is located if the pharmacy is located in another state.
(a-1) A pharmacy shall report in writing to the board not later than the 30th day before the date of a change of location of the pharmacy.
(b) A pharmacy shall report in writing to the board a theft or significant loss of any controlled substance immediately on discovery of the theft or loss. The pharmacy shall include with the report a list of all controlled substances stolen or lost.
(c) A pharmacy shall report in writing to the board a disaster, accident, or emergency that may affect the strength, purity, or labeling of a drug, medication, device, or other material used in the diagnosis or treatment of injury, illness, or disease, immediately on the occurrence of the disaster, accident, or emergency.
(d) The reporting pharmacy shall maintain a copy of any notification required by this section or Section 562.053 for two years and make the copy available for inspection.

Leg.H. Stats. 1999 76th Leg. Sess. Ch. 388, effective September 1, 1999; Stats. 2013, 83rd Leg., ch. 608 (S.B. 1100), § 5, effective September 1, 2013; am. Acts 2015, 84th Leg., ch. 599 (S.B. 460), § 10, effective September 1, 2015.

Sec. 562.107. [Expires September 1, 2029] Written Consumer Information Required.

(a) Each pharmacy shall make available to a consumer written information designed for the consumer that provides at a minimum:
    (1) the therapeutic use of a drug; and
    (2) the names of generically equivalent drugs.
(b) The information must be in a conspicuous location that is easily accessible to pharmacy customers. The information shall be periodically updated, as necessary, to reflect a change in the information.

(c)   On request by a consumer, the pharmacy shall make available to the consumer the cost index ratio of the prescribed drug and any generic equivalents of the prescribed drug.

Leg.H. Stats. 1999 76th Leg. Sess. Ch. 388, effective September 1, 1999.

Sec. 562.108. [Expires September 1, 2029] Emergency Medication Kits.

(a)   A Class A or Class C pharmacy, or a Class E pharmacy located not more than 20 miles from any institution in this state that is licensed under Chapter 242 or 252, Health and Safety Code, may maintain controlled substances and dangerous drugs in an emergency medication kit used at an institution licensed under those chapters. A United States Department of Veterans Affairs pharmacy or another federally operated pharmacy may maintain controlled substances and dangerous drugs in an emergency medication kit used at an institution licensed under Chapter 242, Health and Safety Code, that is a veterans home, as defined by Section 164.002, Natural Resources Code. The controlled substances and dangerous drugs may be used only for the emergency medication needs of a resident at the institution. A Class F pharmacy may not maintain drugs in an emergency medication kit for an institution that is located more than 20 miles from a pharmacy.

(b)   The board shall adopt rules relating to emergency medication kits, including:

     (1)   the amount and type of dangerous drugs and controlled substances that may be maintained in an emergency medication kit;

     (2)   procedures regarding the use of drugs from an emergency medication kit;

     (3)   recordkeeping requirements; and

     (4)   security requirements.

Leg.H. Stats. 2001 77th Leg. Sess. Ch. 1254, effective September 1, 2001; Stats. 2003 78th Leg. Sess. Chs. 582, 914, effective June 20, 2003; Stats. 2005 79th Leg. Sess. Ch. 728, effective September 1, 2005.

Sec. 562.1085. [Expires September 1, 2029] Unused Drugs Returned by Certain Pharmacists.

(a)   A pharmacist who practices in or serves as a consultant for a health care facility or a licensed health care professional responsible for administration of drugs in a penal institution, as defined by Section 1.07, Penal Code, in this state may return to a pharmacy certain unused drugs, other than a controlled substance as defined by Chapter 481, Health and Safety Code, purchased from the pharmacy as provided by board rule. The unused drugs must:

     (1)   be approved by the federal Food and Drug Administration and be:

         (A)   sealed in unopened tamper-evident packaging and either individually packaged or packaged in unit-dose packaging;

         (B)   oral or parenteral medication in sealed single-dose containers approved by the federal Food and Drug Administration;

         (C)   topical or inhalant drugs in sealed units-of-use containers approved by the federal Food and Drug Administration; or

         (D)   parenteral medications in sealed multiple-dose containers approved by the federal Food and Drug Administration from which doses have not been withdrawn; and

     (2)   not be the subject of a mandatory recall by a state or federal agency or a voluntary recall by a drug seller or manufacturer.

(b)   A pharmacist for the pharmacy shall examine a drug returned under this section to ensure the integrity of the drug product. A health care facility or penal institution may not return a drug that:

     (1)   has been compounded;

     (2)   appears on inspection to be adulterated;

     (3)   requires refrigeration; or

     (4)   has less than 120 days until the expiration date or end of the shelf life.

(c)   The pharmacy may restock and redistribute unused drugs returned under this section.

(d)   The pharmacy shall reimburse or credit the state Medicaid program for an unused drug returned under this section.

(e)   The board shall adopt the rules, policies, and procedures necessary to administer this section, including rules that require a health care facility to inform the Health and Human Services Commission of medicines returned to a pharmacy under this section.

(f)   The tamper-evident packaging required under Subsection (a)(1) for the return of unused drugs is not required to be the manufacturer's original packaging unless that packaging is required by federal law.

Leg.H. Stats. 2003 78th Leg. Sess. Ch. 198, effective September 1, 2003; Stats. 2003 78th Leg. Sess. Ch. 321, effective June 18, 2003; Stats. 2005 79th Leg. Sess. Ch. 349, effective September 1, 2005; Stats. 2007, 80th Leg. Sess. Ch. 820, effective June 15, 2007.

Sec. 562.1086. [Expires September 1, 2029] Limitation on Liability.

(a)   A pharmacy that returns unused drugs and a manufacturer that accepts the unused drugs under Section 562.1085 and the employees of the pharmacy or manufacturer are not liable for harm caused by the accepting, dispensing, or administering of drugs returned in strict compliance with Section 562.1085 unless the harm is caused by:

     (1)   wilful or wanton acts of negligence;

     (2)   conscious indifference or reckless disregard for the safety of others; or

     (3)   intentional conduct.

(b)   This section does not limit, or in any way affect or diminish, the liability of a drug seller or manufacturer under Chapter 82, Civil Practice and Remedies Code.

(c)   This section does not apply if harm results from the failure to fully and completely comply with the requirements of Section 562.1085.

(d)   This section does not apply to a pharmacy or manufacturer that fails to comply with the insurance provisions of Chapter 84, Civil Practice and Remedies Code.

Leg.H. Stats. 2003 78th Leg. Sess. Ch. 198, effective September 1, 2003; Stats. 2003 78th Leg. Sess. Ch. 321, effective June 18, 2003.

Sec. 562.109. [Expires September 1, 2029] Automated Pharmacy Systems.

(a) In this section, "automated pharmacy system" means a mechanical system that:
    (1) dispenses prescription drugs; and
    (2) maintains related transaction information.

(b) A Class A or Class C pharmacy may provide pharmacy services through an automated pharmacy system in a facility that is not at the same location as the Class A or Class C pharmacy. The pharmacist in charge of the Class A or Class C pharmacy is responsible for filling and loading the storage containers for medication stored in bulk at the facility.

(c) An automated pharmacy system is required to be under the continuous supervision of a pharmacist as determined by board rule. To qualify as continuous supervision for an automated pharmacy system, the pharmacist is not required to be physically present at the site of the automated pharmacy system and may supervise the system electronically.

(d) An automated pharmacy system may be located only at a health care facility regulated by the state.

(e) The board shall adopt rules regarding the use of an automated pharmacy system under this section, including:
    (1) the types of health care facilities at which an automated pharmacy system may be located, which shall include a facility regulated under Chapter 142, 242, or 252, Health and Safety Code;
    (2) recordkeeping requirements; and
    (3) security requirements.

Leg.H. Stats. 2001 77th Leg. Sess. Ch. 92, effective May 11, 2001.

Sec. 562.110. [Expires September 1, 2029] Telepharmacy Systems.

(a) In this section:
    (1) "Provider pharmacy" means a Class A pharmacy that provides pharmacy services through a telepharmacy system at a remote dispensing site.
    (2) "Remote dispensing site" means a location licensed as a telepharmacy that is authorized by a provider pharmacy through a telepharmacy system to store and dispense prescription drugs and devices, including dangerous drugs and controlled substances.
    (3) "Telepharmacy system" means a system that monitors the dispensing of prescription drugs and provides for related drug use review and patient counseling services by an electronic method, including the use of the following types of technology:
        (A) audio and video;
        (B) still image capture; and
        (C) store and forward.

(b) A Class A or Class C pharmacy located in this state may provide pharmacy services, including the dispensing of drugs, through a telepharmacy system at locations separate from the Class A or Class C pharmacy.

(c) A telepharmacy system is required to be under the continuous supervision of a pharmacist as determined by board rule. To qualify as continuous supervision for a telepharmacy system, the pharmacist is not required to be physically present at the site of the telepharmacy system. The pharmacist shall supervise the system electronically by audio and video communication.

(d) A telepharmacy system may be located only at:
    (1) a health care facility in this state that is regulated by this state or the United States; or
    (2) a remote dispensing site.

(e) The board shall adopt rules regarding the use of a telepharmacy system under this section, including:
    (1) the types of health care facilities at which a telepharmacy system may be located under Subsection (d)(1), which must include the following facilities:
        (A) a clinic designated as a rural health clinic regulated under 42 U.S.C. Section 1395x(aa); and
        (B) a health center as defined by 42 U.S.C. Section 254b;
    (2) the locations eligible to be licensed as remote dispensing sites, which must include locations in medically underserved areas, areas with a medically underserved population, and health professional shortage areas determined by the United States Department of Health and Human Services;
    (3) licensing and operating requirements for remote dispensing sites, including:
        (A) a requirement that a remote dispensing site license identify the provider pharmacy that will provide pharmacy services at the remote dispensing site;
        (B) a requirement that a provider pharmacy be allowed to provide pharmacy services at not more than two remote dispensing sites;
        (C) a requirement that a pharmacist employed by a provider pharmacy make at least monthly on-site visits to a remote dispensing site or more frequent visits if specified by board rule;
        (D) a requirement that each month the perpetual inventory of controlled substances at the remote dispensing site be reconciled to the on-hand count of those controlled substances at the site by a pharmacist employed by the provider pharmacy;
        (E) a requirement that a pharmacist employed by a provider pharmacy be physically present at a remote dispensing site when the pharmacist is providing services requiring the physical presence of the pharmacist, including immunizations;
        (F) a requirement that a remote dispensing site be staffed by an on-site pharmacy technician who is under the continuous supervision of a pharmacist employed by the provider pharmacy;
        (G) a requirement that all pharmacy technicians at a remote dispensing site be counted for the purpose of establishing the pharmacist-pharmacy technician ratio of the provider pharmacy, which, notwithstanding Section 568.006, may not exceed three pharmacy technicians for each pharmacist providing supervision;
        (H) a requirement that, before working at a remote dispensing site, a pharmacy technician must:
            (i) have worked at least one year at a retail pharmacy during the three years preceding the date the pharmacy technician begins working at the remote dispensing site; and

        (ii)　have completed a board-approved training program on the proper use of a telepharmacy system;

    (I)　a requirement that pharmacy technicians at a remote dispensing site may not perform extemporaneous sterile or nonsterile compounding but may prepare commercially available medications for dispensing, including the reconstitution of orally administered powder antibiotics; and

    (J)　any additional training or practice experience requirements for pharmacy technicians at a remote dispensing site;

    (4)　the areas that qualify under Subsection (f);

    (5)　recordkeeping requirements; and

    (6)　security requirements.

(f)　A telepharmacy system located at a health care facility under Subsection (d)(1) may not be located in a community in which a Class A or Class C pharmacy is located as determined by board rule. If a Class A or Class C pharmacy is established in a community in which a telepharmacy system has been located under this section, the telepharmacy system may continue to operate in that community.

(g)　[2 Versions: As added by Acts 2017, 85th Leg., ch. 929] A telepharmacy system located at a remote dispensing site under Subsection (d)(2) may not dispense a controlled substance listed in Schedule II as established by the commissioner of state health services under Chapter 481, Health and Safety Code.

(g)　[2 Versions: As added by Acts 2017, 85th Leg., ch. 485] A telepharmacy system located at a remote dispensing site under Subsection (d)(2) may not dispense a controlled substance listed in Schedule II as established by the commissioner of state health services under Chapter 481, Health and Safety Code, and may not be located within 22 miles by road of a Class A pharmacy.

(h)　[2 Versions: As added by Acts 2017, 85th Leg., ch. 929] Except as provided by Subsection (j), a telepharmacy system located at a remote dispensing site under Subsection (d)(2) may not be located within 25 miles by road of a Class A pharmacy.

(h)　[2 Versions: As added by Acts 2017, 85th Leg., ch. 485] If a Class A pharmacy is established within 22 miles by road of a remote dispensing site that is currently operating, the remote dispensing site may continue to operate at that location.

(i)　[2 Versions: As added by Acts 2017, 85th Leg., ch. 929] Except as provided by Subsection (j), if a Class A pharmacy is established within 25 miles by road of a remote dispensing site that is currently operating, the remote dispensing site may continue to operate at that location.

(i)　[2 Versions: As added by Acts 2017, 85th Leg., ch. 485] The board by rule shall require and develop a process for a remote dispensing site to apply for classification as a Class A pharmacy if the average number of prescriptions dispensed each day the remote dispensing site is open for business is more than 125, as calculated each calendar year.

(j)　A telepharmacy system located at a remote dispensing site under Subsection (d)(2) in a county with a population of at least 13,000 but not more than 14,000 may not be located within 22 miles by road of a Class A pharmacy. If a Class A pharmacy is established within 22 miles by road of a remote dispensing site described by this subsection that is currently operating, the remote dispensing site may continue to operate at that location.

(k)　The board by rule shall require and develop a process for a remote dispensing site to apply for classification as a Class A pharmacy if the average number of prescriptions dispensed each day the remote dispensing site is open for business is more than 125, as calculated each calendar year.

Leg.H. Stats. 2001, 77th Leg., ch. 1220 (S.B. 65), § 1, effective September 1, 2001; am. Acts 2017, 85th Leg., ch. 485 (H.B. 2561), § 17, effective September 1, 2017; am. Acts 2017, 85th Leg., ch. 929 (S.B. 1633), § 3, effective September 1, 2017.

Sec. 562.111. [Expires September 1, 2029] Prescription Drug Order for Consumer.

(a)　A pharmacy in this state may order for a consumer a prescription drug from a Canadian pharmacy designated by the board under Section 554.016 to dispense prescription drugs to residents in this state.

(b)　A pharmacy may order a prescription drug under this section only with the knowledge and clear consent of the consumer.

Leg.H. Stats. 2005 79th Leg. Sess. Ch. 1345, effective September 1, 2005.

Sec. 562.112. [Expires September 1, 2029] Practitioner-Patient Relationship Required.

(a)　A pharmacy shall ensure that its agents and employees, before dispensing a prescription, determine in the exercise of sound professional judgment that the prescription is a valid prescription. A pharmacy may not dispense a prescription drug if an agent or employee of the pharmacy knows or should know that the prescription was issued on the basis of an Internet-based or telephonic consultation without a valid practitioner-patient relationship.

(b)　Subsection (a) does not prohibit a pharmacy from dispensing a prescription when a valid practitioner-patient relationship is not present in an emergency.

Leg.H. Stats. 2005 79th Leg. Sess. Ch. 1345, effective September 1, 2005; Stats 2007, 80th Leg. Sess. Ch. 921, effective September 1, 2007 (renumbered from Sec. 562.111).

SUBCHAPTER D. COMPOUNDED AND PREPACKAGED DRUGS
[EXPIRES SEPTEMBER 1, 2029]

Sec. 562.151. [Expires September 1, 2029] Definitions.

In this subchapter:

    (1)　"Office use" means the provision and administration of a compounded drug to a patient by a practitioner in the practitioner's office or by the practitioner in a health care facility or treatment setting, including a hospital, ambulatory surgical center, or pharmacy in accordance with Chapter 563.

(2) "Prepackaging" means the act of repackaging and relabeling quantities of drug products from a manufacturer's original container into unit dose packaging or a multiple dose container for distribution within a facility licensed as a Class C pharmacy or to other pharmacies under common ownership for distribution within those facilities. The term as defined does not prohibit the prepackaging of drug products for use within other pharmacy classes.

(3) "Reasonable quantity" with reference to drug compounding means an amount of a drug that:
    (A) does not exceed the amount a practitioner anticipates may be used in the practitioner's office before the expiration date of the drug;
    (B) is reasonable considering the intended use of the compounded drug and the nature of the practitioner's practice; and
    (C) for any practitioner and all practitioners as a whole, is not greater than an amount the pharmacy is capable of compounding in compliance with pharmaceutical standards for identity, strength, quality, and purity of the compounded drug that are consistent with United States Pharmacopoeia guidelines and accreditation practices.

Leg.H. Stats. 2005 79th Leg. Sess. Ch. 28, effective September 1, 2005.

Sec. 562.152. [Expires September 1, 2029] Compounding for Office Use.

A pharmacy may dispense and deliver a reasonable quantity of a compounded drug to a practitioner for office use by the practitioner in accordance with this chapter.

Leg.H. Stats. 2005 79th Leg. Sess. Ch. 28, effective September 1, 2005.

Sec. 562.153. [Expires September 1, 2029] Requirements for Office Use Compounding.

To dispense and deliver a compounded drug under Section 562.152, a pharmacy must:
    (1) verify the source of the raw materials to be used in a compounded drug;
    (2) comply with applicable United States Pharmacopoeia guidelines, including the testing requirements, and the Health Insurance Portability and Accountability Act of 1996 (Pub. L. No. 104-191);
    (3) comply with all applicable competency and accrediting standards as determined by the board; and
    (4) comply with board rules, including rules regarding the reporting of adverse events by practitioners and recall procedures for compounded products.

Leg.H. Stats. 2005 79th Leg. Sess. Ch. 28, effective September 1, 2005.

Sec. 562.154. [Expires September 1, 2029] Distribution of Compounded and Prepackaged Products to Certain Pharmacies.

    (a) A Class A pharmacy licensed under Chapter 560 is not required to register or be licensed under Chapter 431, Health and Safety Code, to distribute compounded pharmaceutical products to a Class C pharmacy licensed under Chapter 560.
    (b) A Class C pharmacy licensed under Chapter 560 is not required to register or be licensed under Chapter 431, Health and Safety Code, to distribute compounded and prepackaged pharmaceutical products that the Class C pharmacy has compounded or prepackaged to other Class C pharmacies licensed under Chapter 560 and under common ownership.

Leg.H. Stats. 2005 79th Leg. Sess. Ch. 28, effective September 1, 2005.

Sec. 562.155. [Expires September 1, 2029] Compounding Service and Compounded Drug Products.

A compounding pharmacist or pharmacy may advertise or promote:
    (1) nonsterile prescription compounding services provided by the pharmacist or pharmacy; and
    (2) specific compounded drug products that the pharmacy or pharmacist dispenses or delivers.

Leg.H. Stats. 2005 79th Leg. Sess. Ch. 28, effective September 1, 2005.

Sec. 562.156. [Expires September 1, 2029] Compounded Sterile Preparation; Notice to Board.

    (a) A pharmacy may not compound and dispense a sterile preparation unless the pharmacy holds a license as required by board rule.
    (b) A pharmacy that compounds a sterile preparation shall notify the board:
        (1) immediately of any adverse effects reported to the pharmacy or that are known by the pharmacy to be potentially attributable to a sterile preparation compounded by the pharmacy; and
        (2) not later than 24 hours after the pharmacy issues a recall for a sterile preparation compounded by the pharmacy.

Leg.H. Enacted Stats. 2013, 83rd Leg., ch. 608 (S.B. 1100), § 6, effective September 1, 2013.

SUBCHAPTER E. PRACTICE BY CANADIAN PHARMACY
[EXPIRES SEPTEMBER 1, 2029]

Sec. 562.201. [Expires September 1, 2029] Additional Practice Requirements.

In addition to complying with the other requirements of this chapter, a Canadian pharmacy designated by the board under Section 554.016 shall:
    (1) dispense a prescription drug to a resident of this state only under the lawful order of a practitioner licensed in the United States;

(2) dispense to a resident of this state only a prescription drug that is approved by Canada's Therapeutic Products Directorate for sale to residents of Canada;

(3) dispense to a resident of this state a prescription drug in the original, unopened manufacturer's packaging whenever possible; and

(4) dispense to a resident of this state only drugs prescribed for long-term use.

Leg.H. Stats. 2005 79th Leg. Sess. Ch. 1345, effective September 1, 2005.

Sec. 562.202. [Expires September 1, 2029] Limitations on Practice.

A Canadian pharmacy designated by the board under Section 554.016 to dispense prescription drugs to residents in this state may not:

(1) dispense to a resident of this state a prescription drug for which there is not an equivalent drug approved by the United States Food and Drug Administration for sale in the United States;

(2) dispense to a resident of this state a prescription drug that cannot be safely shipped by mail, common carrier, or delivery service;

(3) dispense in one order to a resident of this state a quantity of a prescription drug that exceeds:

    (A) a three-month supply; or

    (B) the amount ordered by the practitioner;

(4) fill a prescription drug order for a consumer who is a resident of this state that the consumer indicates is the consumer's first prescription for that drug; or

(5) dispense to a resident of this state any of the following:

    (A) a substance designated as a controlled substance under Chapter 481, Health and Safety Code (Texas Controlled Substances Act);

    (B) a biological product, as described by Section 351, Public Health Service Act (42 U.S.C. Section 262);

    (C) an infused drug, including a peritoneal dialysis solution;

    (D) an intravenously injected drug; or

    (E) a drug that is inhaled during surgery.

Leg.H. Stats. 2005 79th Leg. Sess. Ch. 1345, effective September 1, 2005.

Sec. 562.203. [Expires September 1, 2029] Complaint Report.

A Canadian pharmacy designated by the board under Section 554.016 to dispense prescription drugs to residents in this state shall provide to the board periodic reports in accordance with board rules on each complaint received by the pharmacy from a consumer in this state who purchases a prescription drug from the pharmacy.

Leg.H. Stats. 2005 79th Leg. Sess. Ch. 1345, effective September 1, 2005.

Sec. 562.204. [Expires September 1, 2029] Price List.

A Canadian pharmacy designated by the board under Section 554.016 shall:

(1) compile and maintain a current price list for prescription drugs provided to residents in this state; and

(2) guarantee those prices for not less than 30 days from the date the list is effective.

Leg.H. Stats. 2005 79th Leg. Sess. Ch. 1345, effective September 1, 2005.

CHAPTER 563. PRESCRIPTION REQUIREMENTS; DELEGATION OF ADMINISTRATION AND PROVISION OF DANGEROUS DRUGS
[EXPIRES SEPTEMBER 1, 2029]

SUBCHAPTER A. PRESCRIPTION REQUIREMENTS FOR PRACTITIONERS
[REPEALED]

Sec. 563.001. Repealed.

Repealed Stats. 2001 77th Leg. Sess. Ch. 1254, effective June 1, 2002.

Sec. 563.002. Repealed.

Repealed Stats. 2001 77th Leg. Sess. Ch. 1254, effective June 1, 2002.

SUBCHAPTER B. DELEGATION OF ADMINISTRATION AND PROVISION OF DANGEROUS DRUGS
[EXPIRES SEPTEMBER 1, 2029]

Sec. 563.051. [Expires September 1, 2029] General Delegation of Administration and Provision of Dangerous Drugs.

(a) A physician may delegate to any qualified and properly trained person acting under the physician's supervision the act of administering or providing dangerous drugs in the physician's office, as ordered by the physician, that are used or required to meet the immediate needs of the physician's patients. The administration or provision of the dangerous drugs must be performed in compliance with laws relating to the practice of medicine and state and federal laws relating to those dangerous drugs.

(b) A physician may also delegate to any qualified and properly trained person acting under the physician's supervision the act of administering or providing dangerous drugs through a facility licensed by the board, as ordered by the physician, that are used or required to meet the needs of the physician's patients. The administration of those dangerous drugs must be in compliance with laws relating to the practice of medicine, professional nursing, and pharmacy and state and federal drug laws. The provision of those dangerous drugs must be in compliance with:

    (1) laws relating to the practice of medicine, professional nursing, and pharmacy;

    (2) state and federal drug laws; and

    (3) rules adopted by the board.

(c) The administration or provision of the drugs may be delegated through a physician's order, a standing medical order, a standing delegation order, or another order defined by the Texas State Board of Medical Examiners.

(d) This section does not authorize a physician or a person acting under the supervision of a physician to keep a pharmacy, advertised or otherwise, for the retail sale of dangerous drugs, other than as authorized under Section 158.003, without complying with the applicable laws relating to the dangerous drugs.

(e) A practitioner may designate a licensed vocational nurse or a person having education equivalent to or greater than that required for a licensed vocational nurse to communicate the prescriptions of an advanced practice nurse or physician assistant authorized by the practitioner to sign prescription drug orders under Subchapter B, Chapter 157.

Leg.H. Stats. 1999 76th Leg. Sess. Ch. 388, effective September 1, 1999; Stats. 2001 77th Leg. Sess. Ch. 1420, effective September 1, 2001.

Sec. 563.052. [Expires September 1, 2029] Suitable Container Required.

A drug or medicine provided under this subchapter must be supplied in a suitable container labeled in compliance with applicable drug laws. A qualified and trained person, acting under the supervision of a physician, may specify at the time of the provision of the drug the inclusion on the container of the date of the provision and the patient's name and address.

Leg.H. Stats. 1999 76th Leg. Sess. Ch. 388, effective September 1, 1999.

Sec. 563.053. [Expires September 1, 2029] Dispensing of Dangerous Drugs in Certain Rural Areas.

(a) In this section, "reimbursement for cost" means an additional charge, separate from that imposed for the physician's professional services, that includes the cost of the drug product and all other actual costs to the physician incidental to providing the dispensing service. The term does not include a separate fee imposed for the act of dispensing the drug itself.

(b) This section applies to an area located in a county with a population of 5,000 or less, or in a municipality or an unincorporated town with a population of less than 2,500, that is within a 15-mile radius of the physician's office and in which a pharmacy is not located. This section does not apply to a municipality or an unincorporated town that is adjacent to a municipality with a population of 2,500 or more.

(c) A physician who practices medicine in an area described by Subsection (b) may:

    (1) maintain a supply of dangerous drugs in the physician's office to be dispensed in the course of treating the physician's patients; and

    (2) be reimbursed for the cost of supplying those drugs without obtaining a license under Chapter 558.

(d) A physician who dispenses dangerous drugs under Subsection (c) shall:

    (1) comply with each labeling provision under this subtitle applicable to that class of drugs; and

    (2) oversee compliance with packaging and recordkeeping provisions applicable to that class of drugs.

(e) A physician who desires to dispense dangerous drugs under this section shall notify both the board and the Texas State Board of Medical Examiners that the physician practices in an area described by Subsection (b). The physician may continue to dispense dangerous drugs in the area until the board determines, after notice and hearing, that the physician no longer practices in an area described by Subsection (b).

Leg.H. Stats. 1999 76th Leg. Sess. Ch. 388, effective September 1, 1999.

Sec. 563.054. [Expires September 1, 2029] Administration of Dangerous Drugs.

(a) A veterinarian may:

    (1) administer or provide dangerous drugs to a patient in the veterinarian's office, or on the patient's premises, if the drugs are used or required to meet the needs of the veterinarian's patients;

    (2) delegate the administration or provision of dangerous drugs to a person who:

        (A) is qualified and properly trained; and

        (B) acts under the veterinarian's supervision; and

    (3) itemize and receive compensation for the administration or provision of the dangerous drugs under Subdivision (1).

(b) This section does not permit a veterinarian to maintain a pharmacy for the retailing of drugs without complying with applicable laws.

(c) The administration or provision of dangerous drugs must comply with:

    (1) laws relating to the practice of veterinary medicine; and

    (2) state and federal laws relating to dangerous drugs.

Leg.H. Stats. 1999 76th Leg. Sess. Ch. 388, effective September 1, 1999.

CHAPTER 564. PROGRAM TO AID IMPAIRED PHARMACISTS AND PHARMACY STUDENTS; PHARMACY PEER REVIEW
[EXPIRES SEPTEMBER 1, 2029]

SUBCHAPTER A. REPORTING AND CONFIDENTIALITY
[EXPIRES SEPTEMBER 1, 2029]

Sec. 564.001. [Expires September 1, 2029] Reports.

(a) An individual or entity, including a pharmaceutical peer review committee, who has knowledge relating to an action or omission of a pharmacist in this state or a pharmacy student who is enrolled in the professional sequence of an accredited pharmacy degree program approved by the board that might provide grounds for disciplinary action under Section 565.001(a)(4) or (7) may report relevant facts to the board.

(b) A committee of a professional society composed primarily of pharmacists, the staff of the committee, or a district or local intervenor participating in a program established to aid pharmacists or pharmacy students impaired by chemical abuse or mental or physical illness may report in writing to the board the name of an impaired pharmacist or pharmacy student and the relevant information relating to the impairment.

(c) The board may report to a committee of the professional society or the society's designated staff information that the board receives relating to a pharmacist or pharmacy student who may be impaired by chemical abuse or mental or physical illness.

Leg.H. Stats. 1999 76th Leg. Sess. Ch. 388, effective September 1, 1999; Stats. 2011 82nd Leg.Sess. Ch. 923, effective June 17, 2011.

Sec. 564.002. [Expires September 1, 2029] Confidentiality.

(a) All records and proceedings of the board, an authorized agent of the board, or a pharmaceutical organization committee relating to the administration of this chapter are confidential and are not considered public information for purposes of Chapter 552, Government Code. Records considered confidential under this section include:

    (1) information relating to a report made under Section 564.001, including the identity of the individual or entity making the report;

    (2) the identity of an impaired pharmacist or pharmacy student participating in a program administered under this chapter, except as provided by Section 564.003;

    (3) a report, interview, statement, memorandum, evaluation, communication, or other information possessed by the board, an authorized agent of the board, or a pharmaceutical organization committee, related to a potentially impaired pharmacist or pharmacy student;

    (4) a policy or procedure of an entity that contracts with the board relating to personnel selection; and

    (5) a record relating to the operation of the board, an authorized agent of the board, or a pharmaceutical organization committee, as the record relates to a potentially impaired pharmacist or pharmacy student.

(b) A record or proceeding described by this section is not subject to disclosure, subpoena, or discovery, except to a member of the board or an authorized agent of the board involved in the discipline of an applicant or license holder.

Leg.H. Stats. 1999 76th Leg. Sess. Ch. 388, effective September 1, 1999; Stats. 2011 82nd Leg. Sess. Ch. 923, effective June 17, 2011.

Sec. 564.003. [Expires September 1, 2029] Disclosure of Certain Information.

(a) The board may disclose information confidential under Section 564.002 only:

    (1) during a proceeding conducted by the State Office of Administrative Hearings, the board, or a panel of the board, or in a subsequent trial or appeal of a board action or order;

    (2) to a pharmacist licensing or disciplinary authority of another jurisdiction;

    (3) under a court order;

    (4) to a person providing a service to the board, including an expert witness, investigator, or employee of an entity that contracts with the board, related to a disciplinary proceeding against an applicant or license holder, if the information is necessary for preparation for, or a presentation in, the proceeding; or

    (5) as provided by Subsection (b).

(a-1) Information that is disclosed under Subsection (a) remains confidential and is not subject to discovery or subpoena in a civil suit and may not be introduced as evidence in any action other than an appeal of a board action.

(a-2) Information that is confidential under Section 564.002 and that is admitted under seal in a proceeding conducted by the State Office of Administrative Hearings is confidential information for the purpose of a subsequent trial or appeal.

(b) The board may disclose that the license of a pharmacist who is the subject of an order of the board that is confidential under Section 564.002 is suspended, revoked, canceled, restricted, or retired or that the pharmacist is in any other manner limited in the practice of pharmacy. The board may not disclose the nature of the impairment or other information that resulted in the board's action.

Leg.H. Stats. 1999 76th Leg. Sess. Ch. 388, effective September 1, 1999; Stats. 2001 77th Leg. Sess. Ch. 1420, effective September 1, 2001; Stats. 2011 82nd Leg. Ch. 923, effective June 17, 2011.

Sec. 564.004. [Expires September 1, 2029] Immunity.

(a) Any person, including a board employee or member, peer review committee member, pharmaceutical organization committee member, or pharmaceutical organization district or local intervenor, who provides information, reports, or records under Section

564.001 to aid an impaired pharmacist or pharmacy student is immune from civil liability if the person provides the information in good faith.

(b)   Subsection (a) shall be liberally construed to accomplish the purposes of this subchapter, and the immunity provided under that subsection is in addition to any other immunity provided by law.

(c)   A person who provides information or assistance to the board under this subchapter is presumed to have acted in good faith. A person who alleges a lack of good faith has the burden of proof on that issue.

Leg.H. Stats. 1999 76th Leg. Sess. Ch. 388, effective September 1, 1999; Stats. 2011 82nd Leg. Sess. Ch. 923, effective June 17, 2011.

Sec. 564.005. [Expires September 1, 2029] Record of Report.

On a determination by the board that a report submitted by a peer review committee or pharmaceutical organization committee under Section 564.001 (a) or (b) is without merit, the board shall expunge the report from the pharmacist's or pharmacy student's individual record in the board's office.

Leg.H. Stats. 1999 76th Leg. Sess. Ch. 388, effective September 1, 1999.

Sec. 564.006. [Expires September 1, 2029] Examination of Report.

A pharmacist, a pharmacy student, or an authorized representative of the pharmacist or student is entitled on request to examine the peer review or the pharmaceutical organization committee report submitted to the board and to place into the record a statement of reasonable length of the pharmacist's or pharmacy student's view concerning information in the report.

Leg.H. Stats. 1999 76th Leg. Sess. Ch. 388, effective September 1, 1999.

SUBCHAPTER B. PROGRAM ADMINISTRATION
[EXPIRES SEPTEMBER 1, 2029]

Sec. 564.051. [Expires September 1, 2029] Program Authorization; Funding.

(a)   The board may add a surcharge of not more than $10 for each 12 months in a license period to a license or license renewal fee authorized under this subtitle to fund a program to aid impaired pharmacists and pharmacy students.

(b)   The board may accept, transfer, and spend funds from the federal or state government, from another public source, or from a private source to be used in the program authorized by this section.

(c)   Funds and surcharges collected under this section shall be deposited in the general revenue fund and may only be used by the board to administer the program authorized by this section, including providing for initial evaluation and referral of an impaired pharmacist or pharmacy student by a qualified health professional and paying the administrative costs incurred by the board in connection with that funding. The money may not be used for costs incurred for treatment or rehabilitation after initial evaluation and referral.

Leg.H. Stats. 1999 76th Leg. Sess. Ch. 388, effective September 1, 1999; Stats. 2001 77th Leg. Sess. Ch. 1420, effective September 1, 2001; Stats. 2005 79th Leg. Sess. Ch. 1345, effective September 1, 2005.

Sec. 564.052. [Expires September 1, 2029] Rules or Criteria.

In administering and enforcing this subchapter, the board shall adopt rules or minimum criteria that are at least as strict as the rules or minimum criteria for the administration or enforcement of a peer assistance program adopted by the Texas Commission on Alcohol and Drug Abuse under Chapter 467, Health and Safety Code.

Leg.H. Stats. 1999 76th Leg. Sess. Ch. 388, effective September 1, 1999.

SUBCHAPTER C. PHARMACY PEER REVIEW
[EXPIRES SEPTEMBER 1, 2029]

Sec. 564.101. [Expires September 1, 2029] Definitions.

In this subchapter:

(1)   "Pharmacy peer review committee" means:

     (A)   a pharmacy peer review, judicial, or grievance committee of a pharmacy society or association that is authorized to evaluate the quality of pharmacy services or the competence of pharmacists and suggest improvements in pharmacy systems to enhance patient care; or

     (B)   a pharmacy peer review committee established by a person who owns a pharmacy or employs pharmacists that is authorized to evaluate the quality of pharmacy services or the competence of pharmacists and suggest improvements in pharmacy systems to enhance patient care.

(2)   "Pharmacy society or association" means a membership organization of pharmacists that is incorporated under the Texas Non-Profit Corporation Act (Article 1396-1.01 et seq., Vernon's Texas Civil Statutes) or that is exempt from the payment of federal income taxes under Section 501(c) of the Internal Revenue Code of 1986.

Leg.H. Stats. 2001 77th Leg. Sess. Ch. 1420, effective September 1, 2001.

Sec. 564.102. [Expires September 1, 2029] Pharmacy Peer Review Committee.

(a) A pharmacy peer review committee may be established to evaluate the quality of pharmacy services or the competence of pharmacists and suggest improvements in pharmacy systems to enhance patient care.

(b) The committee may review documentation of quality-related activities in a pharmacy, assess system failures and personnel deficiencies, determine facts, and make recommendations or issue decisions in a written report that can be used for continuous quality improvement purposes.

(c) A pharmacy peer review committee includes the members, employees, and agents of the committee, including assistants, investigators, attorneys, and any other agent that serves the committee in any capacity.

Leg.H. Stats. 2001 77th Leg. Sess. Ch. 1420, effective September 1, 2001.

Sec. 564.103. [Expires September 1, 2029] Confidentiality.

(a) Except as otherwise provided by this subchapter, all proceedings and records of a pharmacy peer review committee are confidential and all communications made to a pharmacy peer review committee are privileged.

(b) If a court makes a preliminary finding that a proceeding, record, or communication described by Subsection (a) is relevant to an anticompetitive action or an action brought under federal civil rights provisions under 42 U.S.C. Section 1983, then the proceeding, record, or communication is not confidential to the extent it is considered to be relevant.

(c) The final report of, and any written or oral communication made to, a pharmacy peer review committee and the records and proceedings of the committee may be disclosed to another pharmacy peer review committee, appropriate state or federal agencies, national accreditation bodies, or the state board of registration or licensure of this or any other state.

(d) Disclosure to the affected pharmacist of confidential pharmacy peer review committee information pertinent to the matter under review does not constitute waiver of the confidentiality provisions provided by this section.

(e) If a pharmacy peer review committee takes action that could result in censure, license suspension, restriction, limitation, or revocation by the board or denial of membership or privileges in a health care entity, the affected pharmacist must be provided a written copy of the recommendation of the pharmacy peer review committee and a copy of the pharmacy peer review committee's final decision, including a statement of the basis for the decision.

(f) Unless disclosure is required or authorized by law, records or determinations of, or communications to, a pharmacy peer review committee are not subject to subpoena or discovery and are not admissible as evidence in any civil, judicial, or administrative proceeding without waiver of the privilege of confidentiality executed in writing by the committee. The evidentiary privilege created by this section may be invoked by any person or organization in any civil, judicial, or administrative proceeding unless the person or organization has secured a waiver of the privilege executed in writing by the presiding officer, assistant presiding officer, or secretary of the affected pharmacy peer review committee.

(g) Reports, information, or records received and maintained by the board under this subchapter are considered investigative files and are confidential and may only be released as specified in Section 565.055.

Leg.H. Stats. 2001 77th Leg. Sess. Ch. 1420, effective September 1, 2001.

Sec. 564.104. [Expires September 1, 2029] Use of Information in Civil and Criminal Actions.

(a) If a pharmacy peer review committee, a person participating in peer review, or any organization named as a defendant in any civil action filed as a result of participation in peer review may use otherwise confidential information in the committee's, person's, or organization's own defense or in a claim or suit under Section 564.106(b), a plaintiff in the proceeding may disclose records or determinations of, or communications to, a peer review committee in rebuttal to information supplied by the defendant.

(b) Any person seeking access to privileged information must plead and prove waiver of the privilege.

(c) A member, employee, or agent of a pharmacy peer review committee who provides access to otherwise privileged communications or records in cooperation with a law enforcement authority in a criminal investigation is not considered to have waived any privilege established under this subchapter.

Leg.H. Stats. 2001 77th Leg. Sess. Ch. 1420, effective September 1, 2001.

Sec. 564.105. [Expires September 1, 2029] Compliance with Subpoena.

All persons, including governing bodies and medical staffs of health care entities, shall comply fully with a subpoena issued by the board for documents or information as otherwise authorized by law. The disclosure of documents or information under the subpoena does not constitute a waiver of the privilege associated with a pharmacy peer review committee proceeding. Failure to comply with the subpoena is grounds for disciplinary action against the facility or individual by the appropriate licensing board.

Leg.H. Stats. 2001 77th Leg. Sess. Ch. 1420, effective September 1, 2001.

Sec. 564.106. [Expires September 1, 2029] Immunity.

(a) A cause of action does not accrue against the members, agents, or employees of a pharmacy peer review committee from any act, statement, determination, or recommendation made or act reported, without malice, in the course of peer review according to this subchapter.

(b) A pharmacy peer review committee, a person participating in peer review, or a health care entity named as a defendant in any civil action filed as a result of participation in peer review may use otherwise confidential information obtained for legitimate internal business and professional purposes, including use in the committee's, person's, or entity's own defense. The use of the information does not waive the confidential and privileged nature of pharmacy peer review committee proceedings.

Leg.H. Stats. 2001 77th Leg. Sess. Ch. 1420, effective September 1, 2001.

CHAPTER 565. DISCIPLINARY ACTIONS AND PROCEDURES; REINSTATEMENT OF LICENSE
[EXPIRES SEPTEMBER 1, 2029]

SUBCHAPTER A. GROUNDS FOR DISCIPLINE OF APPLICANT OR LICENSE HOLDER
[EXPIRES SEPTEMBER 1, 2029]

Sec. 565.001. [Expires September 1, 2029] Applicant for or Holder of License to Practice Pharmacy.

(a) The board may discipline an applicant for or the holder of a current or expired license to practice pharmacy if the board finds that the applicant or license holder has:

(1) violated this subtitle or a board rule adopted under this subtitle;

(2) engaged in unprofessional conduct as defined by board rule;

(3) engaged in gross immorality as defined by board rule;

(4) developed an incapacity that prevents or could prevent the applicant or license holder from practicing pharmacy with reasonable skill, competence, and safety to the public;

(5) engaged in fraud, deceit, or misrepresentation, as defined by board rule, in practicing pharmacy or in seeking a license to practice pharmacy;

(6) been convicted of or placed on deferred adjudication community supervision or deferred disposition or the applicable federal equivalent for:

    (A) a misdemeanor:

        (i) involving moral turpitude; or

        (ii) under Chapter 481 or 483, Health and Safety Code, or the Comprehensive Drug Abuse Prevention and Control Act of 1970 (21 U.S.C. Section 801 et seq.); or

    (B) a felony;

(7) used alcohol or drugs in an intemperate manner that, in the board's opinion, could endanger a patient's life;

(8) failed to maintain records required by this subtitle or failed to maintain complete and accurate records of purchases or disposals of drugs listed in Chapter 481 or 483, Health and Safety Code, or the Comprehensive Drug Abuse Prevention and Control Act of 1970 (21 U.S.C. Section 801 et seq.);

(9) violated any provision of:

    (A) Chapter 481 or 483, Health and Safety Code, or the Comprehensive Drug Abuse Prevention and Control Act of 1970 (21 U.S.C. Section 801 et seq.), or rules relating to one of those laws; or

    (B) Section 485.031, 485.032, 485.033, or 485.034, Health and Safety Code;

(10) aided or abetted an unlicensed person in the practice of pharmacy if the pharmacist knew or reasonably should have known that the person was unlicensed at the time;

(11) refused entry into a pharmacy for an inspection authorized by this subtitle if the pharmacist received notification from which the pharmacist knew or reasonably should have known that the attempted inspection was authorized;

(12) violated any pharmacy or drug statute or rule of this state, another state, or the United States;

(13) been negligent in the practice of pharmacy;

(14) failed to submit to an examination after hearing and being ordered to do so by the board under Section 565.052;

(15) dispensed a prescription drug while acting outside the usual course and scope of professional practice;

(16) been disciplined by a pharmacy board or by another health regulatory board of this state or another state for conduct substantially equivalent to conduct described under this subsection;

(17) violated a disciplinary order, including a confidential order or contract under the program to aid impaired pharmacists and pharmacy students under Chapter 564;

(18) failed to adequately supervise a task delegated to a pharmacy technician or pharmacy technician trainee;

(19) inappropriately delegated a task delegated to a pharmacy technician or pharmacy technician trainee;

(20) been responsible for a drug audit shortage; or

(21) been convicted or adjudicated of a criminal offense that requires registration as a sex offender under Chapter 62, Code of Criminal Procedure.

(b) A certified copy of the record of the state taking action described by Subsection (a)(16) is conclusive evidence of the action taken by that state.

Leg.H. Stats. 1999 76th Leg. Sess. Ch. 388, effective September 1, 1999; Stats. 2001 77th Leg. Sess. Chs. 1254, 1463, effective September 1, 2001; Stats. 2005 79th Leg. Sess. Ch. 1345, effective September 1, 2005; Stats. 2013, 83rd Leg., ch. 583 (S.B. 869), § 15, effective June 14, 2013.

Sec. 565.002. [Expires September 1, 2029] Applicant for or Holder of Pharmacy License.

(a) The board may discipline an applicant for or the holder of a pharmacy license, including a Class E pharmacy license subject to Section 565.003, if the board finds that the applicant or license holder has:

(1) been convicted of or placed on deferred adjudication community supervision or deferred disposition or the applicable federal equivalent for:

    (A) a misdemeanor:

        (i) involving moral turpitude; or

        (ii) under Chapter 481 or 483, Health and Safety Code, or the Comprehensive Drug Abuse Prevention and Control Act of 1970 (21 U.S.C. Section 801 et seq.); or

    (B) a felony;

(2) advertised a prescription drug or device in a deceitful, misleading, or fraudulent manner;

(3) violated any provision of this subtitle or any rule adopted under this subtitle or that an owner or employee of a pharmacy has violated any provision of this subtitle or any rule adopted under this subtitle;

(4) sold without legal authorization a prescription drug or device to a person other than:
- (A) a pharmacy licensed by the board;
- (B) a practitioner;
- (C) a person who procures a prescription drug or device for lawful research, teaching, or testing, and not for resale;
- (D) a manufacturer or wholesaler licensed by the commissioner of public health as required by Chapter 431, Health and Safety Code; or
- (E) a carrier or warehouseman;

(5) allowed an employee who is not a pharmacist to practice pharmacy;

(6) sold an adulterated or misbranded prescription or nonprescription drug;

(7) failed to engage in or ceased to engage in the business described in the application for a license;

(8) failed to maintain records as required by this subtitle, Chapter 481 or 483, Health and Safety Code, the Comprehensive Drug Abuse Prevention and Control Act of 1970 (21 U.S.C. Section 801 et seq.), or any rule adopted under this subtitle or Chapter 483, Health and Safety Code;

(9) failed to establish and maintain effective controls against diversion of prescription drugs into other than a legitimate medical, scientific, or industrial channel as provided by this subtitle, another state statute or rule, or a federal statute or rule;

(10) engaged in fraud, deceit, or misrepresentation as defined by board rule in operating a pharmacy or in applying for a license to operate a pharmacy;

(11) violated a disciplinary order;

(12) been responsible for a drug audit shortage;

(13) been disciplined by the regulatory board of another state for conduct substantially equivalent to conduct described under this subsection; or

(14) waived, discounted, or reduced, or offered to waive, discount, or reduce, a patient copayment or deductible for a compounded drug in the absence of:
- (A) a legitimate, documented financial hardship of the patient; or
- (B) evidence of a good faith effort to collect the copayment or deductible from the patient.

(b) This subsection applies only to an applicant or license holder that is a legal business entity. The board may discipline an applicant for or the holder of a pharmacy license, including a Class E pharmacy license, if the board finds that a managing officer of the applicant or license holder has been convicted of or placed on deferred adjudication community supervision or deferred disposition or the applicable federal equivalent for:
- (1) a misdemeanor:
  - (A) involving moral turpitude; or
  - (B) under Chapter 481 or 483, Health and Safety Code, or the Comprehensive Drug Abuse Prevention and Control Act of 1970 (21 U.S.C. Section 801 et seq.); or
- (2) a felony.

(c) A certified copy of the record of the state taking action described by Subsection (a)(13) is conclusive evidence of the action taken by that state.

Leg.H. Stats. 1999 76th Leg. Sess. Ch. 388, effective September 1, 1999; Stats. 2005 79th Leg. Sess. Ch. 1345, effective September 1, 2005; am. Acts 2015, 84th Leg., ch. 599 (S.B. 460), § 11, effective September 1, 2015.

Sec. 565.003. [Expires September 1, 2029] Additional Grounds for Discipline Regarding Applicant for or Holder of Nonresident Pharmacy License.

Unless compliance would violate the pharmacy or drug statutes or rules in the state in which the pharmacy is located the board may discipline an applicant for or the holder of a nonresident pharmacy license if the board finds that the applicant or license holder has failed to comply with:
- (1) Section 481.074 or 481.075, Health and Safety Code;
- (2) Texas substitution requirements regarding:
  - (A) the practitioner's directions concerning generic substitution;
  - (B) the patient's right to refuse generic substitution; or
  - (C) notification to the patient of the patient's right to refuse substitution;
- (3) any board rule relating to providing drug information to the patient or the patient's agent in written form or by telephone; or
- (4) any board rule adopted under Section 554.051(a) and determined by the board to be applicable under Section 554.051(b).

Leg.H. Stats. 1999 76th Leg. Sess. Ch. 388, effective September 1, 1999; Stats. 2005 79th Leg. Sess. Ch. 1345 (S.B. 410), § 45, effective September 1, 2005; Stats. 2013, 83rd Leg., ch. 608 (S.B. 1100), § 7, effective September 1, 2013.

SUBCHAPTER B. DISCIPLINARY ACTIONS AND PROCEDURES
[EXPIRES SEPTEMBER 1, 2029]

Sec. 565.051. [Expires September 1, 2029] Discipline Authorized.

On a determination that a ground for discipline exists under Subchapter A, or that a violation of this subtitle or a rule adopted under this subtitle has been committed by a license holder or applicant for a license or renewal of a license, the board may:
- (1) suspend the person's license;
- (2) revoke the person's license;

(3) restrict the person's license to prohibit the person from performing certain acts or from practicing pharmacy or operating a pharmacy in a particular manner for a term and under conditions determined by the board;

(4) impose an administrative penalty under Chapter 566;

(5) refuse to issue or renew the person's license;

(6) place the offender's license on probation and supervision by the board for a period determined by the board and impose a requirement that the license holder:

  (A) report regularly to the board on matters that are the basis of the probation;

  (B) limit practice to the areas prescribed by the board;

  (C) continue or review professional education until the license holder attains a degree of skill satisfactory to the board in each area that is the basis of the probation; or

  (D) pay the board a probation fee to defray the costs of monitoring the license holder during the period of probation;

(7) reprimand the person;

(8) retire the person's license as provided by board rule; or

(9) impose more than one of the sanctions listed in this subsection.

Leg.H. Stats. 1999 76th Leg. Sess. Ch. 388, effective September 1, 1999; Stats. 2005 79th Leg. Sess. Ch. 1345, effective September 1, 2005.

Sec. 565.052. [Expires September 1, 2029] Submission to Mental or Physical Examination.

(a) In enforcing Section 565.001(a)(4) or (7), the board or an authorized agent of the board on probable cause, as determined by the board or agent, shall request a pharmacist, pharmacist applicant, pharmacist-intern, or pharmacist-intern applicant to submit to a mental or physical examination by a physician or other health care professional designated by the board.

(b) If the pharmacist, pharmacist applicant, pharmacist-intern, or pharmacist-intern applicant refuses to submit to the examination, the board or the executive director of the board shall issue an order requiring the pharmacist, pharmacist applicant, pharmacist-intern, or pharmacist-intern applicant to show cause why the pharmacist, pharmacist applicant, pharmacist-intern, or pharmacist-intern applicant will not submit to the examination and shall schedule a hearing before a panel of three members of the board appointed by the president of the board on the order not later than the 30th day after the date notice is served on the pharmacist, pharmacist applicant, pharmacist-intern, or pharmacist-intern applicant. The pharmacist, pharmacist applicant, pharmacist-intern, or pharmacist-intern applicant shall be notified by either personal service or certified mail with return receipt requested.

(c) At the hearing, the pharmacist, pharmacist applicant, pharmacist-intern, or pharmacist-intern applicant and an attorney are entitled to present testimony or other evidence to show why the pharmacist, pharmacist applicant, pharmacist-intern, or pharmacist-intern applicant should not be required to submit to the examination. The pharmacist, pharmacist applicant, pharmacist-intern, or pharmacist-intern applicant has the burden of proof to show why the pharmacist, pharmacist applicant, pharmacist-intern, or pharmacist-intern applicant should not be required to submit to the examination.

(d) After the hearing, the panel shall by order require the pharmacist, pharmacist applicant, pharmacist-intern, or pharmacist-intern applicant to submit to the examination not later than the 60th day after the date of the order or withdraw the request for examination, as applicable.

Leg.H. Stats. 1999 76th Leg. Sess. Ch. 388, effective September 1, 1999; Stats. 2011 82nd Leg. Sess. Ch. 923, effective June 17, 2011.

Sec. 565.053. [Expires September 1, 2029] Discipline of Nonresident Pharmacy; Notice to Resident State.

The board shall give notice of a disciplinary action by the board against a license holder located in another state to the regulatory or licensing agency of the state in which the pharmacy is located.

Leg.H. Stats. 1999 76th Leg. Sess. Ch. 388, effective September 1, 1999; Stats. 2005 79th Leg. Sess. Ch. 1345, effective September 1, 2005; Stats. 2013, 83rd Leg., ch. 608 (S.B. 1100), § 8, effective September 1, 2013.

Sec. 565.054. [Expires September 1, 2029] Service of Process on Nonresident Pharmacy.

(a) Service of process on a nonresident pharmacy under Section 565.058 or 566.051 or for disciplinary action taken by the board under Section 565.061 shall be on the owner and pharmacist-in-charge of the pharmacy, as designated on the pharmacy's license application.

(b) The complaining party shall mail by certified mail, return receipt requested and postage prepaid, a copy of the process served to the license holder at the address of the license holder designated on the license application.

Leg.H. Stats. 1999 76th Leg. Sess. Ch. 388, effective September 1, 1999; Stats. 2013, 83rd Leg., ch. 608 (S.B. 1100), §§ 9, 10, effective September 1, 2013.

Sec. 565.055. [Expires September 1, 2029] Investigation; Confidentiality of Information.

(a) The board or the board's authorized representative may investigate and gather evidence concerning any alleged violation of this subtitle or a board rule.

(b) Information or material compiled by the board in connection with an investigation, including an investigative file of the board, is confidential and not subject to:

  (1) disclosure under Chapter 552, Government Code; or

  (2) any means of legal compulsion for release, including disclosure, discovery, or subpoena, to anyone other than the board or a board employee or board agent involved in discipline of a license holder.

(c) Notwithstanding Subsection (b), information or material compiled by the board in connection with an investigation may be disclosed:

(1) during any proceeding conducted by the State Office of Administrative Hearings, to the board, or a panel of the board, or in a subsequent trial or appeal of a board action or order;

(2) to a person providing a service to the board, including an expert witness, investigator, or employee of an entity that contracts with the board, related to a disciplinary proceeding against an applicant or license holder, or a subsequent trial or appeal, if the information is necessary for preparation for, or a presentation in, the proceeding;

(3) to an entity in another jurisdiction that:
  (A) licenses or disciplines pharmacists or pharmacies; or
  (B) registers or disciplines pharmacy technicians or pharmacy technician trainees;

(4) to a pharmaceutical or pharmacy peer review committee as described under Chapter 564;

(5) to a law enforcement agency;

(6) to a person engaged in bona fide research, if all information identifying a specific individual has been deleted; or

(7) to an entity that administers a board-approved pharmacy technician certification examination.

Leg.H. Stats. 1999 76th Leg. Sess. Ch. 388, effective September 1, 1999; Stats. 2001 77th Leg. Sess. Ch. 1420, effective September 1, 2001; Stats. 2011 82nd Leg. Sess. Ch. 923, effective June 17, 2011; Stats. 2013, 83rd Leg., ch. 583 (S.B. 869), § 16, effective June 14, 2013.

Sec. 565.056. [Expires September 1, 2029] Informal Proceedings.

(a) The board by rule shall adopt a procedure governing:
  (1) informal disposition of a contested case under Chapter 2001, Government Code; and
  (2) an informal proceeding held in compliance with Chapter 2001, Government Code.

(b) A rule adopted under this section must:
  (1) provide the complainant, if applicable and permitted by law, and the license holder an opportunity to be heard;
  (2) require the presence of an attorney to advise the board or a board employee; and
  (3) if an informal meeting will be held, require notice of the time and place of the informal meeting to be given to the license holder not later than the 45th day before the date the informal meeting is held.

(c) The attorney must be a member of the board's legal staff, if the board has a legal staff. If the board does not have a legal staff, the attorney must be an employee of the office of the attorney general.

(d) The notice required by Subsection (b)(3) must be accompanied by a written statement of the nature of the allegations against the license holder and the information the board intends to use at the informal meeting. If the board does not provide the statement or information when the notice is provided, the license holder may use that failure as grounds for rescheduling the informal meeting. The license holder must provide to the board the license holder's rebuttal not later than the 15th day before the date of the meeting in order for that information to be considered at the meeting.

(e) On request by a license holder under review, the board shall make a recording of the informal meeting. The recording is a part of the investigative file and may not be released to a third party unless authorized under this subtitle. The board may charge the license holder a fee to cover the cost of recording the meeting. The board shall provide a copy of the recording to the license holder on the license holder's request.

Leg.H. Stats. 1999 76th Leg. Sess. Ch. 388, effective September 1, 1999; Stats. 2013, 83rd Leg., ch. 522 (S.B. 404), § 3, effective September 1, 2013.

Sec. 565.057. [Expires September 1, 2029] Monitoring of License Holder.

(a) The board shall develop a policy and procedure for monitoring a license holder's compliance with this subtitle.

(b) A policy or procedure adopted under this section must include a procedure to:
  (1) monitor for compliance a license holder who is ordered by the board to perform a certain act; and
  (2) identify and monitor a license holder who represents a risk to the public.

Leg.H. Stats. 1999 76th Leg. Sess. Ch. 388, effective September 1, 1999.

Sec. 565.058. [Expires September 1, 2029] Subpoena Authority.

(a) The board or an officer of the board may:
  (1) issue subpoenas ad testificandum or subpoenas duces tecum to compel the attendance of witnesses or the production of items, including books, records, or documents;
  (2) administer oaths; and
  (3) take testimony concerning matters in the board's or officer's jurisdiction.

(b) A person designated in the subpoena may serve the subpoena.

Leg.H. Stats. 1999 76th Leg. Sess. Ch. 388, effective September 1, 1999.

Sec. 565.059. [Expires September 1, 2029] Temporary Suspension or Restriction of License.

(a) The president of the board shall appoint a three-member disciplinary panel consisting of board members to determine whether a license under this subtitle should be temporarily suspended or restricted. If a majority of the disciplinary panel determines from evidence or information presented to the panel that the holder of a license by continuation in the practice of pharmacy or in the operation of a pharmacy would constitute a continuing threat to the public welfare, the panel shall temporarily suspend or restrict the license as provided by Subsection (b).

(b) The disciplinary panel may temporarily suspend or restrict the license:
  (1) after a hearing conducted by the panel after the 10th day after the date notice of the hearing is provided to the license holder; or

(2) without notice or hearing if, at the time the suspension or restriction is ordered, a hearing before the panel is scheduled to be held not later than the 14th day after the date of the temporary suspension or restriction to determine whether the suspension or restriction should be continued.

(c) Not later than the 90th day after the date of the temporary suspension or restriction, the board shall initiate a disciplinary action against the license holder, and a contested case hearing shall be held by the State Office of Administrative Hearings. If the State Office of Administrative Hearings does not hold the hearing in the time required by this subsection, the suspended or restricted license is automatically reinstated.

(d) Notwithstanding Chapter 551, Government Code, the disciplinary panel may hold a meeting by telephone conference call if immediate action is required and convening of the panel at one location is inconvenient for any member of the disciplinary panel.

Leg.H. Stats. 1999 76th Leg. Sess. Ch. 388, effective September 1, 1999; Stats. 2005 79th Leg. Sess. Ch. 1345, effective September 1, 2005; Stats. 2011 82nd Leg. Sess. Ch. 923, effective June 17, 2011.

Sec. 565.060. [Expires September 1, 2029] Remedial Plan.

(a) The board may issue and establish the terms of a remedial plan to resolve the investigation of a complaint relating to this subtitle.

(b) A remedial plan may not be imposed to resolve a complaint:
  (1) concerning:
    (A) a death;
    (B) a hospitalization;
    (C) the commission of a felony; or
    (D) any other matter designated by board rule; or
  (2) in which the appropriate resolution may involve a restriction on the manner in which a license holder practices pharmacy.

(c) The board may not issue a remedial plan to resolve a complaint against a license holder if the license holder has entered into a remedial plan with the board in the preceding 24 months for the resolution of a different complaint relating to this subtitle.

(d) If a license holder complies with and successfully completes the terms of a remedial plan, the board shall remove all records of the remedial plan from the board's records at the end of the state fiscal year in which the fifth anniversary of the date the board issued the terms of the remedial plan occurs.

(e) The board may assess a fee against a license holder participating in a remedial plan in an amount necessary to recover the costs of administering the plan.

(f) The board shall adopt rules necessary to implement this section.

Leg.H. Stats. 2013, 83rd Leg., ch. 522 (S.B. 404), § 4, effective September 1, 2013; am. Acts 2015, 84th Leg., ch. 599 (S.B. 460), § 12, effective September 1, 2015.

Sec. 565.061. [Expires September 1, 2029] Administrative Procedure.

(a) Except as provided by Chapter 564, a disciplinary action taken by the board on the basis of a ground for discipline under Subchapter A is governed by Chapter 2001, Government Code, and the rules of practice and procedure before the board.

(b) A final decision of the board under this chapter is subject to judicial review under Chapter 2001, Government Code.

Leg.H. Stats. 1999 76th Leg. Sess. Ch. 388, effective September 1, 1999; am. Acts 2015, 84th Leg., ch. 599 (S.B. 460), § 13, effective September 1, 2015.

Sec. 565.062. [Expires September 1, 2029] Burden of Proof.

(a) In a proceeding under this subtitle, including a trial or hearing, the state is not required to negate an exemption or exception set forth by this subtitle in a pleading, including in a complaint, information, or indictment.

(b) The burden of going forward with the evidence with respect to an exemption or exception is on the person claiming the benefit of the exemption or exception.

(c) In the absence of proof that a person is the authorized holder of an appropriate license issued under this subtitle, the person is presumed not to be the holder of the license. The presumption is subject to rebuttal by a person charged with an offense under this subtitle.

Leg.H. Stats. 1999 76th Leg. Sess. Ch. 388, effective September 1, 1999.

Sec. 565.063. [Expires September 1, 2029] Liability.

This subtitle does not impose liability on an authorized board employee or person acting under the supervision of a board employee, or on a state, county, or municipal officer, engaged in the lawful enforcement of this subtitle.

Leg.H. Stats. 1999 76th Leg. Sess. Ch. 388, effective September 1, 1999.

Sec. 565.064. [Expires September 1, 2029] Construction.

This subtitle does not bar a criminal prosecution for a violation of this subtitle if the violation is a criminal offense under another law of this state or a law of the United States.

Leg.H. Stats. 1999 76th Leg. Sess. Ch. 388, effective September 1, 1999.

SUBCHAPTER C. PETITION FOR REINSTATEMENT OR REMOVAL OF RESTRICTION
[EXPIRES SEPTEMBER 1, 2029]

Sec. 565.101. [Expires September 1, 2029] Petition for Reinstatement or Removal of Restriction.

(a) A person whose pharmacy license, license to practice pharmacy, pharmacy technician registration, or pharmacy technician trainee registration in this state has been revoked or restricted under this subtitle, whether voluntarily or by board action, may, after the first anniversary of the effective date of the revocation or restriction, petition the board for reinstatement or removal of the restriction of the license or registration.

(b) The petition must be in writing and in the form prescribed by the board.

(c) A person petitioning for reinstatement or removal of a restriction has the burden of proof.

Leg.H. Stats. 1999 76th Leg. Sess. Ch. 388, effective September 1, 1999; Stats. 2001 77th Leg. Sess. Ch. 1420, effective September 1, 2001; Stats. 2013, 83rd Leg., ch. 583 (S.B. 869), § 17, effective June 14, 2013.

Sec. 565.102. [Expires September 1, 2029] Action by Board.

(a) On investigation and review of a petition under this subchapter, the board may grant or deny the petition or may modify the board's original finding to reflect a circumstance that has changed sufficiently to warrant the modification.

(b) If the board denies the petition, the board may not consider a subsequent petition from the petitioner until the first anniversary of the date of denial of the previous petition.

Leg.H. Stats. 1999 76th Leg. Sess. Ch. 388, effective September 1, 1999; Stats. 2001 77th Leg. Sess. Ch. 1420, effective September 1, 2001.

Sec. 565.103. [Expires September 1, 2029] Condition for Reinstatement or Removal of Restriction.

The board may require a person to pass one or more examinations to reenter the practice of pharmacy.

Leg.H. Stats. 1999 76th Leg. Sess. Ch. 388, effective September 1, 1999; Stats. 2001 77th Leg. Sess. Ch. 1420, effective September 1, 2001.

CHAPTER 566. PENALTIES AND ENFORCEMENT PROVISIONS
[EXPIRES SEPTEMBER 1, 2029]

SUBCHAPTER A. ADMINISTRATIVE PENALTY
[EXPIRES SEPTEMBER 1, 2029]

Sec. 566.001. [Expires September 1, 2029] Imposition of Penalty.

The board may impose an administrative penalty on a person licensed or regulated under this subtitle who violates this subtitle or a rule or order adopted under this subtitle.

Leg.H. Stats. 1999 76th Leg. Sess. Ch. 388, effective September 1, 1999.

Sec. 566.002. [Expires September 1, 2029] Amount of Penalty.

(a) The amount of the administrative penalty may not exceed $5,000 for each violation, including a violation involving the diversion of a controlled substance.

(b) Each day a violation continues or occurs is a separate violation for purposes of imposing the penalty.

(c) The amount, to the extent possible, shall be based on:

   (1) the seriousness of the violation, including the nature, circumstances, extent, and gravity of any prohibited act, and the hazard or potential hazard created to the health, safety, or economic welfare of the public;

   (2) the economic harm to property or the environment caused by the violation;

   (3) the history of previous violations;

   (4) the amount necessary to deter a future violation;

   (5) efforts to correct the violation; and

   (6) any other matter that justice may require.

(d) The board by rule shall adopt an administrative penalty schedule for violations of this subtitle or board rules to ensure that the amounts of penalties imposed are appropriate to the violation.

Leg.H. Stats. 1999 76th Leg. Sess. Ch. 388, effective September 1, 1999; Stats. 2005 79th Leg. Sess. Ch. 1345, effective September 1, 2005.

Sec. 566.003. [Expires September 1, 2029] Notice of Violation.

(a) If the board by order determines that a violation occurred and imposes an administrative penalty, the board shall give notice of the board's order to the person found to have committed the violation.

(b) The notice must include a statement of the person's right to judicial review of the order.

Leg.H. Stats. 1999 76th Leg. Sess. Ch. 388, effective September 1, 1999.

Sec. 566.004. [Expires September 1, 2029] Options Following Decision: Pay or Appeal.

(a) Not later than the 30th day after the date the board's order becomes final, the person shall:
    (1) pay the administrative penalty;
    (2) pay the penalty and file a petition for judicial review contesting the fact of the violation, the amount of the penalty, or both; or
    (3) without paying the penalty, file a petition for judicial review contesting the fact of the violation, the amount of the penalty, or both.

(b) Within the 30-day period, a person who acts under Subsection (a)(3) may:
    (1) stay enforcement of the penalty by:
        (A) paying the penalty to the court for placement in an escrow account; or
        (B) giving to the court a supersedeas bond that is approved by the court and that:
            (i) is for the amount of the penalty; and
            (ii) is effective until judicial review of the board's order is final; or
    (2) request the court to stay enforcement of the penalty by:
        (A) filing with the court a sworn affidavit of the person stating that the person is financially unable to pay the penalty and is financially unable to give the supersedeas bond; and
        (B) giving a copy of the affidavit to the executive director by certified mail.

(c) If the executive director receives a copy of an affidavit under Subsection (b)(2), the executive director may file with the court a contest to the affidavit not later than the fifth day after the date the copy is received.

(d) The court shall hold a hearing on the facts alleged in the affidavit as soon as practicable and shall stay the enforcement of the penalty on finding that the alleged facts are true. The person who files an affidavit has the burden of proving that the person is financially unable to pay the penalty and to give a supersedeas bond.

Leg.H. Stats. 1999 76th Leg. Sess. Ch. 388, effective September 1, 1999.

Sec. 566.005. [Expires September 1, 2029] Collection of Penalty.

If the person does not pay the administrative penalty and the enforcement of the penalty is not stayed, the executive director may refer the matter to the attorney general for collection of the penalty.

Leg.H. Stats. 1999 76th Leg. Sess. Ch. 388, effective September 1, 1999.

Sec. 566.006. [Expires September 1, 2029] Determination by Court.

(a) If the court sustains the determination that a violation occurred on appeal, the court may uphold or reduce the amount of the administrative penalty and order the person to pay the full or reduced penalty.

(b) If the court does not sustain the determination that a violation occurred, the court shall order that a penalty is not owed.

Leg.H. Stats. 1999 76th Leg. Sess. Ch. 388, effective September 1, 1999.

Sec. 566.007. [Expires September 1, 2029] Remittance of Penalty and Interest.

(a) If after judicial review, the administrative penalty is reduced or is not upheld by the court, the court shall, after the judgment becomes final:
    (1) order that the appropriate amount, plus accrued interest, be remitted to the person if the person paid the penalty; or
    (2) order the release of the bond in full if the penalty is not upheld or order the release of the bond after the person pays the penalty imposed if the person gave a supersedeas bond.

(b) The interest paid under Subsection (a)(1) is the rate charged on loans to depository institutions by the New York Federal Reserve Bank. The interest shall be paid for the period beginning on the date the penalty is paid and ending on the date the penalty is remitted.

Leg.H. Stats. 1999 76th Leg. Sess. Ch. 388, effective September 1, 1999.

Sec. 566.008. [Expires September 1, 2029] Effect of Subchapter.

This subchapter does not limit the board's ability to impose an administrative penalty under a consent order entered in accordance with board rules and requirements adopted under Section 565.056.

Leg.H. Stats. 1999 76th Leg. Sess. Ch. 388, effective September 1, 1999.

Sec. 566.009. [Expires September 1, 2029] Administrative Procedure.

(a) The board by rule shall prescribe procedures, consistent with provisions of Chapter 2001, Government Code, relating to contested cases, by which the board may impose an administrative penalty.

(b) Chapter 2001, Government Code, applies to a proceeding under this subchapter.

Leg.H. Stats. 1999 76th Leg. Sess. Ch. 388, effective September 1, 1999.

SUBCHAPTER B. INJUNCTIVE RELIEF
[EXPIRES SEPTEMBER 1, 2029]

Sec. 566.051. [Expires September 1, 2029] Injunctive Relief.

(a) The attorney general at the request of the board may petition a district court for an injunction to prohibit a person who is violating this subtitle from continuing the violation.

(b) Venue in a suit for injunctive relief is in Travis County.

(c) After application and a finding that a person is violating this subtitle, the district court shall grant the injunctive relief the facts warrant.

Leg.H. Stats. 1999 76th Leg. Sess. Ch. 388, effective September 1, 1999; Stats. 2005 79th Leg. Sess. Ch. 1345, effective September 1, 2005.

Sec. 566.052. [Expires September 1, 2029] Cease and Desist Order.

(a) If it appears to the board that a person is engaging in an act or practice that constitutes the practice of pharmacy without a license or registration under this subtitle, the board, after notice and opportunity for a hearing, may issue a cease and desist order prohibiting the person from engaging in the activity.

(b) A violation of an order issued under this section constitutes grounds for imposing an administrative penalty under Subchapter A.

Leg.H. Stats. 2005 79th Leg. Sess. Ch. 1345, effective September 1, 2005.

SUBCHAPTER C. CIVIL PENALTY
[EXPIRES SEPTEMBER 1, 2029]

Sec. 566.101. [Expires September 1, 2029] Civil Penalty.

(a) A person who violates the license requirements of this subtitle is liable to the state for a civil penalty not to exceed $1,000 for each day the violation continues.

(b) A person found by the board to have unlawfully engaged in the practice of pharmacy or unlawfully operated a pharmacy is subject to a civil penalty under this section.

Leg.H. Stats. 1999 76th Leg. Sess. Ch. 388, effective September 1, 1999.

Sec. 566.102. [Expires September 1, 2029] Collection by Attorney General.

At the request of the board, the attorney general shall institute an action to collect a civil penalty from a person who has violated this subtitle or any rule adopted under this subtitle.

Leg.H. Stats. 1999 76th Leg. Sess. Ch. 388, effective September 1, 1999.

Sec. 566.103. [Expires September 1, 2029] Collection by District, County, or City Attorney.

(a) If the attorney general fails to take action before the 31st day after the date of referral from the board under Section 566.102, the board shall refer the case to the local district attorney, county attorney, or city attorney.

(b) The district attorney, county attorney, or city attorney shall file suit in a district court to collect and retain the penalty.

Leg.H. Stats. 1999 76th Leg. Sess. Ch. 388, effective September 1, 1999.

Sec. 566.104. [Expires September 1, 2029] Venue.

Venue for a suit under this subchapter is in Travis County.

Leg.H. Stats. 1999 76th Leg. Sess. Ch. 388, effective September 1, 1999.

SUBCHAPTER D. CRIMINAL OFFENSES
[EXPIRES SEPTEMBER 1, 2029]

Sec. 566.151. [Expires September 1, 2029] Offenses; Criminal Penalty.

(a) A person commits an offense if the person violates this subtitle or any rule adopted under this subtitle relating to unlawfully engaging in the practice of pharmacy or unlawfully operating a pharmacy.

(b) A person commits an offense if the person knowingly violates the licensing requirements of this subtitle or Section 558.001, 558.002, or 560.002.

(c) A person commits an offense if the person violates Section 560.001 or 560.003.

(d) Each day of violation under Subsection (b) or (c) is a separate offense.

(e) An offense under this section is a Class A misdemeanor.

Leg.H. Stats. 1999 76th Leg. Sess. Ch. 388, effective September 1, 1999.

CHAPTER 567. LABELING REQUIREMENTS FOR CERTAIN PRESCRIPTION DRUGS OR DRUG PRODUCTS
[REPEALED]

Sec. 567.001. Repealed.
Repealed Stats. 2013, 83rd Leg., ch. 583 (S.B. 869), § 33(1), effective June 14, 2013.

Sec. 567.002. Repealed.
Repealed Stats. 2013, 83rd Leg., ch. 583 (S.B. 869), § 33(1), effective June 14, 2013.

Sec. 567.003. Repealed.
Repealed Stats. 2013, 83rd Leg., ch. 583 (S.B. 869), § 33(1), effective June 14, 2013.

CHAPTER 568. PHARMACY TECHNICIANS AND PHARMACY TECHNICIAN TRAINEES
[EXPIRES SEPTEMBER 1, 2029]

Sec. 568.001. [Expires September 1, 2029] Rules; Qualifications.
(a) In establishing rules under Section 554.053(c), the board shall require that:
    (1) a pharmacy technician:
        (A) have a high school diploma or a high school equivalency certificate or be working to achieve an equivalent diploma or certificate; and
        (B) have passed a board-approved pharmacy technician certification examination; and
    (2) a pharmacy technician trainee have a high school diploma or a high school equivalency certificate or be working to achieve an equivalent diploma or certificate.
(b) The board shall adopt rules that permit a pharmacy technician and pharmacy technician trainee to perform only nonjudgmental technical duties under the direct supervision of a pharmacist.

Leg.H. Stats. 2001 77th Leg. Sess. Ch. 1420, effective September 1, 2001; Stats. 2013, 83rd Leg., ch. 583 (S.B. 869), § 19, effective June 14, 2013.

Sec. 568.002. [Expires September 1, 2029] Registration Required.
(a) A person must register with the board before beginning work in a pharmacy in this state as a pharmacy technician or a pharmacy technician trainee.
(b) The board may allow a pharmacy technician to petition the board for a special exemption from the pharmacy technician certification requirement if the pharmacy technician is in a county with a population of less than 50,000.
(c) An applicant for registration as a pharmacy technician or a pharmacy technician trainee must submit an application on a form prescribed by the board.
(d) A person's registration as a pharmacy technician or pharmacy technician trainee remains in effect as long as the person meets the qualifications established by board rule.

Leg.H. Stats. 2001, 77th Leg., ch. 1420 (H.B. 2812), § 14.313(a), effective September 1, 2001; am. Acts 2013, 83rd Leg., ch. 583 (S.B. 869), § 20, effective June 14, 2013; am. Acts 2017, 85th Leg., ch. 485 (H.B. 2561), § 18, effective September 1, 2017.

Sec. 568.003. [Expires September 1, 2029] Grounds for Disciplinary Action.
(a) The board may take disciplinary action under Section 568.0035 against an applicant for or the holder of a current or expired pharmacy technician or pharmacy technician trainee registration if the board determines that the applicant or registrant has:
    (1) violated this subtitle or a rule adopted under this subtitle;
    (2) engaged in gross immorality, as that term is defined by the rules of the board;
    (3) engaged in any fraud, deceit, or misrepresentation, as those terms are defined by the rules of the board, in seeking a registration to act as a pharmacy technician or pharmacy technician trainee;
    (4) been convicted of or placed on deferred adjudication community supervision or deferred disposition or the applicable federal equivalent for:
        (A) a misdemeanor:
            (i) involving moral turpitude; or
            (ii) under Chapter 481 or 483, Health and Safety Code, or the Comprehensive Drug Abuse Prevention and Control Act of 1970 (21 U.S.C Section 801 et seq.); or
        (B) a felony;
    (5) developed an incapacity that prevents the applicant or registrant from practicing as a pharmacy technician or pharmacy technician trainee with reasonable skill, competence, and safety to the public;
    (6) violated:
        (A) Chapter 481 or 483, Health and Safety Code, or rules relating to those chapters;
        (B) Sections 485.031-485.035, Health and Safety Code; or
        (C) a rule adopted under Section 485.011, Health and Safety Code;
    (7) violated the pharmacy or drug laws or rules of this state, another state, or the United States;

    (8) performed duties in a pharmacy that only a pharmacist may perform, as defined by the rules of the board;

    (9) used alcohol or drugs in an intemperate manner that, in the board's opinion, could endanger a patient's life;

    (10) engaged in negligent, unreasonable, or inappropriate conduct when working in a pharmacy;

    (11) violated a disciplinary order;

    (12) been convicted or adjudicated of a criminal offense that requires registration as a sex offender under Chapter 62, Code of Criminal Procedure; or

    (13) been disciplined by a pharmacy or other health regulatory board of this state or another state for conduct substantially equivalent to conduct described by this subsection.

(b) A certified copy of the record of a state taking action described by Subsection (a)(13) is conclusive evidence of the action taken by the state.

Leg.H. Stats. 2001 77th Leg. Sess. Ch. 1420, effective September 1, 2001; Stats. 2005 79th Leg. Sess. Ch. 1345, effective September 1, 2005; Stats. 2009 81st Leg. Sess. Ch. 837, effective June 19, 2009; Stats. 2013, 83rd Leg., ch. 583 (S.B. 869), § 21, effective June 14, 2013.

Sec. 568.0035. [Expires September 1, 2029] Discipline Authorized; Effect on Trainee.

(a) On a determination that a ground for discipline exists under Section 568.003, the board may:

    (1) suspend the person's registration;

    (2) revoke the person's registration;

    (3) restrict the person's registration to prohibit the person from performing certain acts or from practicing as a pharmacy technician or pharmacy technician trainee in a particular manner for a term and under conditions determined by the board;

    (4) impose an administrative penalty under Chapter 566;

    (5) refuse to issue or renew the person's registration;

    (6) place the offender's registration on probation and supervision by the board for a period determined by the board and impose a requirement that the registrant:

        (A) report regularly to the board on matters that are the basis of the probation;

        (B) limit practice to the areas prescribed by the board;

        (C) continue or review professional education until the registrant attains a degree of skill satisfactory to the board in each area that is the basis of the probation; or

        (D) pay the board a probation fee to defray the costs of monitoring the registrant during the period of probation;

    (7) reprimand the person;

    (8) retire the person's registration as provided by board rule; or

    (9) impose more than one of the sanctions listed in this section.

(b) A disciplinary action affecting the registration of a pharmacy technician trainee remains in effect if the trainee obtains registration as a pharmacy technician.

Leg.H. Stats. 2005 79th Leg. Sess. Ch. 1345, effective September 1, 2005; Stats. 2009 81st Leg. Sess. Ch. 837, effective June 19, 2009; Stats. 2013, 83rd Leg., ch. 583 (S.B. 869), § 22, effective June 14, 2013.

Sec. 568.0036. [Expires September 1, 2029] Submission to Mental or Physical Examination.

(a) This section applies to a pharmacy technician, pharmacy technician applicant, pharmacy technician trainee, or pharmacy technician trainee applicant.

(b) In enforcing Section 568.003(a)(5) or (7), the board or an authorized agent of the board on probable cause, as determined by the board or agent, may request a person subject to this section to submit to a mental or physical examination by a physician or other health care professional designated by the board.

(c) If the person refuses to submit to the examination, the board or the executive director of the board shall:

    (1) issue an order requiring the person to show cause why the person will not submit to the examination; and

    (2) schedule a hearing before a panel of three members of the board appointed by the president of the board on the order not later than the 30th day after the date notice of the order is served on the person under Subsection (d).

(d) The person shall be notified by either personal service or certified mail, return receipt requested.

(e) At the hearing, the person and the person's counsel may present testimony or other evidence to show why the person should not be required to submit to the examination. The person has the burden of proof to show why the person should not be required to submit to the examination.

(f) After the hearing, as applicable, the panel shall, by order:

    (1) require the person to submit to the examination not later than the 60th day after the date of the order; or

    (2) withdraw the request for examination.

Leg.H. Stats. 2009 81st Leg. Sess. Ch. 837, effective June 19, 2009; Stats. 2011 82nd Leg. Sess. Ch. 923, effective June 17, 2011.

Sec. 568.0037. [Expires September 1, 2029] Temporary Suspension or Restriction of Registration.

(a) The president of the board shall appoint a disciplinary panel consisting of three board members to determine whether a registration under this chapter should be temporarily suspended or restricted. If a majority of the panel determines from evidence or information presented to the panel that the registrant by continuation in practice as a pharmacy technician or pharmacy technician trainee would constitute a continuing threat to the public welfare, the panel shall temporarily suspend or restrict the registration as provided by Subsection (b).

(b) A disciplinary panel may temporarily suspend or restrict the registration:

    (1) after a hearing conducted by the panel after the 10th day after the date notice of the hearing is provided to the registrant; or

(2) without notice or hearing if, at the time the suspension or restriction is ordered, a hearing before the panel is scheduled to be held not later than the 14th day after the date of the temporary suspension or restriction to determine whether the suspension or restriction should be continued.

(c) Not later than the 90th day after the date of the temporary suspension or restriction, the board shall initiate a disciplinary action under this chapter, and a contested case hearing shall be held by the State Office of Administrative Hearings. If the State Office of Administrative Hearings does not hold the hearing in the time required by this subsection, the suspended or restricted registration is automatically reinstated.

(d) Notwithstanding Chapter 551, Government Code, the disciplinary panel may hold a meeting by telephone conference call if immediate action is required and convening the panel at one location is inconvenient for any member of the disciplinary panel.

Leg.H. Stats. 2011 82nd Leg. Sess. Ch. 923, effective June 17, 2011; Stats. 2013, 83rd Leg., ch. 583 (S.B. 869), § 23, effective June 14, 2013.

Sec. 568.004. [Expires September 1, 2029] Renewal of Registration.

(a) The board may adopt a system in which the registrations of pharmacy technicians and pharmacy technician trainees expire on various dates during the year.

(b) To renew a pharmacy technician registration, the registrant must, before the expiration date of the registration:
(1) pay a renewal fee as determined by the board under Section 568.005; and
(2) comply with the continuing education requirements prescribed by the board in accordance with Section 568.0045.

(c) A person whose pharmacy technician registration has been expired for 90 days or less may renew the expired registration by paying to the board a renewal fee that is equal to one and one-half times the normally required renewal fee for the registration.

(d) A person whose pharmacy technician registration has been expired for more than 90 days but less than one year may renew the expired registration by paying to the board a renewal fee that is equal to two times the normally required renewal fee for the registration.

(e) A person whose pharmacy technician registration has been expired for one year or more may not renew the registration. The person may register by complying with the requirements and procedures for initially registering, including the examination requirement.

(f) The board may refuse to renew a pharmacy technician registration for a registrant who is in violation of a board order.

Leg.H. Stats. 2001, 77th Leg., ch. 1420 (H.B. 2812), § 14.313(a), effective September 1, 2001; am. Acts 2013, 83rd Leg., ch. 583 (S.B. 869), § 24, effective June 14, 2013; am. Acts 2017, 85th Leg., ch. 485 (H.B. 2561), § 19, effective September 1, 2017.

Sec. 568.0045. [Expires September 1, 2029] Rules Relating to Continuing Education.

The board shall adopt rules relating to the continuing education required for pharmacy technicians. The rules must include requirements for:
(1) the number of hours of continuing education;
(2) the methods for meeting the continuing education requirements;
(3) the approval of continuing education programs;
(4) reporting completion of continuing education;
(5) records of completion of continuing education; and
(6) board audits to ensure compliance with the continuing education requirements.

Leg.H. Stats. 2017, 85th Leg., ch. 485 (H.B. 2561), § 20, effective September 1, 2017.

Sec. 568.005. [Expires September 1, 2029] Fees.

The board may adopt fees as necessary for the registration of pharmacy technicians and pharmacy technician trainees.

Leg.H. Stats. 2001 77th Leg. Sess. Ch. 1420, effective September 1, 2001; Stats. 2013, 83rd Leg., ch. 583 (S.B. 869), § 25, effective June 14, 2013.

Sec. 568.006. [Expires September 1, 2029] Ratio of Pharmacists to Pharmacy Technicians and Pharmacy Technician Trainees.

The ratio of pharmacists to pharmacy technicians and pharmacy technician trainees in a Class A pharmacy must be at least one pharmacist for every five pharmacy technicians or pharmacy technician trainees if the Class A pharmacy dispenses not more than 20 different prescription drugs and does not produce intravenous or intramuscular drugs on-site.

Leg.H. Stats. 2003 78th Leg. Sess. Ch. 1198, effective September 1, 2003; Stats. 2013, 83rd Leg., ch. 583 (S.B. 869), § 26, effective June 14, 2013.

Sec. 568.007. Repealed.

Repealed Stats. 2013, 83rd Leg., ch. 583 (S.B. 869), § 33(2), effective June 14, 2013.

Sec. 568.008. [Expires September 1, 2029] Pharmacy Technicians in Hospitals with Clinical Pharmacy Program.

(a) In this section, "clinical pharmacy program" means a program that provides pharmaceutical care services as specified by board rule.

(b) A Class C pharmacy that has an ongoing clinical pharmacy program may allow a pharmacy technician to verify the accuracy of work performed by another pharmacy technician relating to the filling of floor stock and unit dose distribution systems for a patient admitted to the hospital if the patient's orders have previously been reviewed and approved by a pharmacist.

(c) The pharmacist-in-charge of the clinical pharmacy program shall adopt policies and procedures for the verification process authorized by this section.

(d) A hospital must notify the board before implementing the verification process authorized by this section.

(e) The board shall adopt rules to implement this section, including rules specifying:

    (1) the duties that may be verified by another pharmacy technician;

    (2) the records that must be maintained for the verification process; and

    (3) the training requirements for pharmacy technicians who verify the accuracy of the work of other pharmacy technicians.

Leg.H. Stats. 2009 81st Leg. Sess. Ch. 1128, effective June 19, 2009; Stats. 2013, 83rd Leg., ch. 583 (S.B. 869), § 27, effective June 14, 2013.

Sec. 568.009. [Expires September 1, 2029] Change of Address or Employment.

Not later than the 10th day after the date of a change of address or employment, a pharmacy technician or a pharmacy technician trainee shall notify the board in writing of the change.

Leg.H. Stats. 2013, 83rd Leg., ch. 583 (S.B. 869), § 28, effective June 14, 2013.

CHAPTER 569. REPORTING REQUIREMENTS FOR PROFESSIONAL LIABILITY INSURERS [EXPIRES SEPTEMBER 1, 2029]

Sec. 569.001. [Expires September 1, 2029] Duty to Report.

(a) Every insurer or other entity providing pharmacist's professional liability insurance, pharmacy technician professional and supplemental liability insurance, or druggist's professional liability insurance covering a pharmacist, pharmacy technician, pharmacy technician trainee, or pharmacy license holder in this state shall submit to the board the information described in Section 569.002 at the time prescribed.

(b) The information shall be provided with respect to a notice of claim letter or complaint filed against an insured in a court, if the notice or complaint seeks damages relating to the insured's conduct in providing or failing to provide appropriate service within the scope of pharmaceutical care or services, and with respect to settlement of a claim or lawsuit made on behalf of the insured.

(c) If a pharmacist, pharmacy technician, pharmacy technician trainee, or pharmacy licensed in this state does not carry or is not covered by pharmacist's professional liability insurance, pharmacy technician professional and supplemental liability insurance, or druggist's professional liability insurance and is insured by a nonadmitted carrier or other entity providing pharmacy professional liability insurance that does not report under this subtitle, the duty to report information under Section 569.002 is the responsibility of the pharmacist, pharmacy technician, pharmacy technician trainee, or pharmacy license holder.

Leg.H. Stats. 2001 77th Leg. Sess. Ch. 1420, effective September 1, 2001; Stats. 2013, 83rd Leg., ch. 583 (S.B. 869), § 29, effective June 14, 2013.

Sec. 569.002. [Expires September 1, 2029] Information to Be Reported.

(a) The following information must be furnished to the board not later than the 30th day after receipt by the insurer of the notice of claim letter or complaint from the insured:

    (1) the name of the insured and the insured's state pharmacy technician registration number, pharmacy technician trainee registration number, or pharmacist or pharmacy license number;

    (2) the policy number; and

    (3) a copy of the notice of claim letter or complaint.

(b) The board shall, in consultation with the Texas Department of Insurance, adopt rules for reporting additional information as the board may require. Other claim reports required under state and federal law shall be considered in determining the information to be reported, the form of the report, and frequency of reporting under the rules. Additional information that the board may require may include:

    (1) the date of any judgment, dismissal, or settlement; and

    (2) whether an appeal has been taken and by which party.

Leg.H. Stats. 2001 77th Leg. Sess. Ch. 1420, effective September 1, 2001; Stats. 2013, 83rd Leg., ch. 583 (S.B. 869), § 30, effective June 14, 2013.

Sec. 569.003. [Expires September 1, 2029] Immunity from Liability.

An insurer reporting under this subchapter, its agents or employees, or the board or its employees or representatives are not liable for damages in a suit brought by any person or entity for reporting as required by this subchapter or for any other action taken under this subchapter.

Leg.H. Stats. 2001 77th Leg. Sess. Ch. 1420, effective September 1, 2001.

Sec. 569.004. [Expires September 1, 2029] Restriction on Use of Information Reported.

(a) Information submitted to the board under this subchapter and the fact that the information has been submitted to the board may not be:

    (1) offered in evidence or used in any manner in the trial of a suit described in this subchapter; or

    (2) used in any manner to determine the eligibility or credentialing of a pharmacy to participate in a health insurance plan defined by the Insurance Code.

(b) Information submitted under this subchapter is confidential and is not subject to disclosure under Chapter 552, Government Code.

(c)   The board shall adopt rules to ensure the confidentiality of information submitted under this subchapter.

Leg.H. Stats. 2001 77th Leg. Sess. Ch. 1420, effective September 1, 2001.

Sec. 569.005. [Expires September 1, 2029] Investigation of Report.

(a)   Except as otherwise provided in this section, a report received by the board under this subchapter is not a complaint for which a board investigation is required.

(b)   The board shall review the information relating to a pharmacist, pharmacy technician, pharmacy technician trainee, or pharmacy license holder against whom at least three professional liability claims have been reported within a five-year period in the same manner as if a complaint against the pharmacist, pharmacy technician, pharmacy technician trainee, or pharmacy license holder had been made under Chapter 555.

Leg.H. Stats. 2001 77th Leg. Sess. Ch. 1420, effective September 1, 2001; Stats. 2013, 83rd Leg., ch. 583 (S.B. 869), § 31, effective June 14, 2013.

Sec. 569.006. [Expires September 1, 2029] Sanctions Imposed on Insurer.

The Texas Department of Insurance may impose on any insurer subject to this subtitle sanctions authorized by Chapter 82, Insurance Code, if the insurer fails to report information as required by this subchapter.

Leg.H. Stats. 2001 77th Leg. Sess. Ch. 1420, effective September 1, 2001.

Phr. Act

CHAPTER 281. ADMINISTRATIVE PRACTICE AND PROCEDURES

SUBCHAPTER A. GENERAL PROVISIONS

SUBCHAPTER B. GENERAL PROCEDURES IN A CONTESTED CASE

SUBCHAPTER C. DISCIPLINARY GUIDELINES

CHAPTER 283. LICENSING REQUIREMENTS FOR PHARMACISTS

Phr. Rules

CHAPTER 291. PHARMACIES

SUBCHAPTER A. ALL CLASSES OF PHARMACIES

SUBCHAPTER B. COMMUNITY PHARMACY (CLASS A)

SUBCHAPTER C. NUCLEAR PHARMACY (CLASS B)

SUBCHAPTER D. INSTITUTIONAL PHARMACY (CLASS C)

SUBCHAPTER E. CLINIC PHARMACY (CLASS D)

SUBCHAPTER F. NON-RESIDENT PHARMACY (CLASS E)

SUBCHAPTER G. SERVICES PROVIDED BY PHARMACIES

SUBCHAPTER H. OTHER CLASSES OF PHARMACY

CHAPTER 295. PHARMACISTS

CHAPTER 297. PHARMACY TECHNICIANS AND PHARMACY TECHNICIAN TRAINEES

CHAPTER 303. DESTRUCTION OF DRUGS

CHAPTER 305. EDUCATIONAL REQUIREMENTS

CHAPTER 309. SUBSTITUTION OF DRUG PRODUCTS

Phr. Rules

CHAPTER 311. CODE OF CONDUCT

CHAPTER 315. CONTROLLED SUBSTANCES

CHAPTER 281. ADMINISTRATIVE PRACTICE AND PROCEDURES

SUBCHAPTER A. GENERAL PROVISIONS

§281.1 Objective and Scope

The objective of this chapter is to obtain a just, fair, and equitable determination of any matter within the jurisdiction of the board. To the end that this objective may be attained with as great expedition and at the least expense as possible to the parties and the state, the provisions of this chapter shall be given a liberal construction. The provisions of this chapter govern the procedure for the institution, conduct, and determination of all proceedings before the board. All actions taken by the board shall be in accordance with the Act, the Government Code, the Occupations Code, the board's rules and any other applicable laws or rules.

Source: The provisions of this §281.1 adopted to be effective December 30, 1998, 23 TexReg 13073; amended to be effective March 25, 2007, 32 TexReg 1507

§281.2 Definitions

The following words and terms, when used in this chapter, have the following meanings, unless the context clearly indicates otherwise:

(1) Act—The Texas Pharmacy Act, Chapters 551 – 566, Texas Occupations Code, as amended.

(2) Administrative law judge—A judge employed by the State Office of Administrative Hearings.

(3) Agency—The Texas State Board of Pharmacy, and its divisions, departments, and employees.

(4) Administrative Procedure Act (APA)—Government Code, Chapter 2001, as amended.

(5) Board—The Texas State Board of Pharmacy.

(6) Confidential address of record—The home address required to be provided by each individual, who is a licensee, registrant, or pharmacy owner and where service of legal notice will be sent. The address is confidential, as set forth in §555.001(d) of the Act, and not subject to disclosure under the Public Information Act.

(7) Contested case—A proceeding, including but not restricted to licensing, in which the legal rights, duties, or privileges of a party are to be determined by the board after an opportunity for adjudicative hearing.

(8) Diversion of controlled substances—An act or acts which result in the distribution of controlled substances from legitimate pharmaceutical or medical channels in violation of the Controlled Substances Act or rules promulgated pursuant to the Controlled Substances Act or rules relating to controlled substances promulgated pursuant to this Act.

(9) Diversion of dangerous drugs—An act or acts which result in the distribution of dangerous drugs from legitimate pharmaceutical or medical channels in violation of the Dangerous Drug Act or rules promulgated pursuant to the Dangerous Drug Act or rules relating to dangerous drugs promulgated pursuant to this Act.

(10) Executive director/secretary—The secretary of the board and executive director of the agency.

(11) License—The whole or part of any agency permit, certificate, approval, registration, or similar form of permission required by law.

(12) Licensee—Any individual or person to whom the agency has issued any permit, certificate, approved registration, or similar form of permission authorized by law.

(13) Licensing—The agency process relating to the granting, denial, renewal, revocation, suspension, annulment, withdrawal, or amendment of a license.

(14) Official act—Any act performed by the board pursuant to a duty, right, or responsibility imposed or granted by law, rule, or regulation.

(15) Person—An individual, corporation, government or governmental subdivision or agency, business trust, estate, trust, partnership, association, or any other legal entity.

(16) President—The president of the Texas State Board of Pharmacy.

(17) Presiding Officer—The president of the Texas State Board of Pharmacy or, in the president's absence, the highest ranking officer present at a board meeting.

(18) Publicly available address of record—The alternate address required to be provided by each licensee, registrant, or pharmacy owner, which will be released to the public, as set forth in §555.001(d) of the Act, and is subject to disclosure under the Public Information Act.

    (A) The alternate address must be a business address or other alternate address, such as the home address of the individual's relative, where mail can be received on a regular basis.

    (B) A pharmacy must provide the physical address of the pharmacy to be used for this purpose.

(19) Quorum—A majority of the members of the board appointed and serving on the board.

(20) State Office of Administrative Hearings (SOAH)—The agency to which contested cases are referred by the Texas State Board of Pharmacy.

(21) Sample—A prescription drug which is not intended to be sold and is intended to promote the sale of the drug.

(22) Texas Public Information Act—Government Code, Chapter 552.

Source: The provisions of this §281.2 adopted to be effective December 30, 1998, 23 TexReg 13073; amended to be effective December 27, 2000, 25 TexReg 12688; amended to be effective September 8, 2002, 27 TexReg 8212; amended to be effective March 25, 2007, 32 TexReg 1507; amended to be effective September 12, 2011, 36 TexReg 5845

§281.3 Construction of This Chapter

(a) In the construction of this chapter, a provision of a section referring to the board, or a provision referring to the presiding officer, is construed to apply to the board or the president if the matter is within the jurisdiction of the board.

Phr. Rules

(b) Unless otherwise provided by law, any duty imposed on the board or the president may be delegated to a duly authorized representative. In such case, the provisions of any section referring to the board or the president shall be construed to also apply to the duly authorized representative(s) of the board or the president.

Source: The provisions of this §281.3 adopted to be effective December 30, 1998, 23 TexReg 13073

§281.4 Official Acts in Writing and Open to the Public

(a) All official acts of the board shall be evidenced by a written record. Such writings shall be open to the public in accordance with the Act and the Texas Public Information Act, Government Code Chapter 552. Any hearing and any Board meeting shall be open to the public in accordance with the Texas Open Meetings Act, Government Code, Chapter 551, provided, however, that pursuant to §552.011, Texas Pharmacy Act, the board may, in its discretion, conduct deliberations relative to licensee disciplinary actions in a closed meeting. The board in a closed meeting may conduct disciplinary hearings relating to a pharmacist or pharmacy student who is impaired because of chemical abuse or mental or physical illness. At the conclusion of its deliberations relative to licensee disciplinary action, the board shall vote and announce its decision relative to the licensee in open session. All disciplinary hearings before the State Office of Administrative Hearings shall be open to the public, including those relating to a pharmacist or pharmacy student who is impaired because of chemical abuse or mental or physical illness. Official action of the board shall not be bound or prejudiced by any informal statement or opinion made by any member of the board or the employees of the agency.

(b) The president shall be the chairman and preside over all meetings of the board at which the president is present unless otherwise provided for under this chapter. In the absence of the president, the vice president shall preside. In the vice president's absence, one of the other Board members shall preside as acting chairman. The acting chairman shall be selected by mutual agreement of the board members present or, lacking mutual agreement, shall be the member senior in length of service on the board.

Source: The provisions of this §281.4 adopted to be effective December 30, 1998, 23 TexReg 13073; amended to be effective December 27, 2000, 25 TexReg 12688; amended to be effective September 8, 2002, 27 TexReg 8212; amended to be effective March 25, 2007, 32 TexReg 1507

§281.5 Initiating Proceedings Before the Board

(a) Rules. Any interested person may petition the board requesting the adoption of a rule. Petitions shall be sent to the executive director/secretary. Within 60 days after the submission of a petition, the board shall either deny the petition in writing, stating the reasons for the denial, or shall initiate rulemaking proceedings. Petitions shall be deemed sufficient if they contain:
   (1) the exact wording of the new, changed, or amended proposed rule;
   (2) specific reference to the existing rule which is proposed to be changed or amended in the case of a changed or amended rule; and
   (3) a justification for the proposed action set out in narrative form with sufficient particularity to inform the board and any other interested party of the reasons and arguments on which the petitioner is relying.

(b) Other. In any other matter, any person desiring that the board perform some official act permitted or required by law shall request such performance in writing. Such requests shall be directed to the executive director/secretary of the board. Any written request shall be deemed sufficient to initiate the proceedings and present the subject matter to the board for its official determination if the request reasonably gives notice to the board of the act desired. The board may also initiate proceedings on its own motion.

Source: The provisions of this §281.5 adopted to be effective December 30, 1998, 23 TexReg 13073; amended to be effective March 25, 2007, 32 TexReg 1507

§281.6 Mental or Physical Examination

For the purposes of the Act, §§ 565.001(a)(4), 565.052, 568.003(a)(5), and 568.0036, shall be applied as follows.
   (1) The board may discipline an applicant, licensee, or registrant if the board finds that the applicant, licensee, or registrant has developed an incapacity that in the estimation of the board would prevent a pharmacist from engaging in the practice of pharmacy or a pharmacy technician or pharmacy technician trainee from practicing with a level of skill and competence that ensures the public health, safety, and welfare.
   (2) Upon a finding of probable cause, as determined by the board or an authorized agent of the board, that the applicant, licensee, or registrant has developed an incapacity that in the estimation of the board would prevent a pharmacist from engaging in the practice of pharmacy or a pharmacy technician or pharmacy technician trainee from practicing with a level of skill and competence that ensures the public health, safety, and welfare, the following is applicable.
      (A) The executive director/secretary, legal counsel of the agency, or other representative of the agency as designated by the executive director/secretary, shall request the applicant, licensee, or registrant to submit to a mental or physical examination by a physician or other healthcare professional designated by the board. The individual providing the examination shall be approved by the board. Such examination shall be coordinated through the entity that contracts with the board to aid impaired pharmacists and pharmacy students. The applicant, licensee, or registrant shall:
         (i) provide the entity with written notice of the appointment at least three days prior to the appointment;
         (ii) execute and return to the entity an authorization for release of relevant information on the form required by the entity, within ten days of receipt of request for the release from the entity; and
         (iii) follow all other procedures of the entity for each examination.
      (B) The applicant, licensee, or registrant shall be notified in writing, by either personal service or certified mail with return receipt requested, of the request to submit to the examination.
      (C) The applicant, licensee, or registrant shall submit to the examination within 30 days of the date of the receipt of the request.
      (D) The applicant, licensee, or registrant shall authorize the release of the results of the examination and the results shall be submitted to the board within 15 days of the date of the examination.
   (3) If the applicant, licensee, or registrant does not comply with the provisions of paragraph (2) of this section, the following is applicable.
      (A) The executive director/secretary shall cause to be issued an order requiring the applicant, licensee, or registrant to show cause why he/she will not submit to the examination.

(B) The executive director/secretary shall schedule a hearing on the order before a panel of three members of the board appointed by the president of the board, within 30 days after notice is served on the applicant, licensee, or registrant.

(C) The applicant, licensee, or registrant shall be notified of the hearing by either personal service or certified mail with return receipt requested.

(D) At the hearing, the applicant, licensee, or registrant has the burden of proof once probable cause has been established by the board, as required by § 565.062 of the Act to rebut the probable cause. The applicant, licensee, or registrant, and if applicable, the applicant's, licensee's, or registrants' attorney, are entitled to present testimony and other evidence to show why probable cause has not been established requiring the applicant, licensee, or registrant to submit to the examination. An evaluation that has not been approved by the board and coordinated by the entity that contracts with the board to aid impaired pharmacist and pharmacy students according to its procedure cannot be admitted at the hearing in lieu of one that has been properly approved and coordinated.

(E) After the hearing, the panel shall issue an order either requiring the applicant, licensee, or registrant to submit to the examination not later than the 60th day after the date of the order or withdraw the request for examination, as applicable.

Source: The provisions of this §281.6 adopted to be effective December 30, 1998, 23 TexReg 13073; amended to be effective December 27, 2000, 25 TexReg 12688; amended to be effective March 25, 2007, 32 TexReg 1507; amended to be effective December 7, 2010, 35 TexReg 10689; amended to be effective June 7, 2012, 37 TexReg 4045; amended to be effective September 8, 2013, 38 TexReg 5720

§281.7   Grounds for Discipline for a Pharmacist License

(a) For the purposes of the Act, § 565.001(a)(2), "unprofessional conduct" is defined as engaging in behavior or committing an act that fails to conform with the standards of the pharmacy profession, including, but not limited to, criminal activity or activity involving moral turpitude, dishonesty, or corruption. This conduct shall include, but not be limited to:

(1) dispensing a prescription drug pursuant to a forged, altered, or fraudulent prescription;

(2) dispensing a prescription drug order pursuant to a prescription from a practitioner as follows:

(A) the dispensing of a prescription drug order not issued for a legitimate medical purpose or in the usual course of professional practice shall include the following:

(i) dispensing controlled substances or dangerous drugs to an individual or individuals in quantities, dosages, or for periods of time which grossly exceed standards of practice, approved labeling of the federal Food and Drug Administration, or the guidelines published in professional literature; or

(ii) dispensing controlled substances or dangerous drugs when the pharmacist knows or reasonably should have known that the controlled substances or dangerous drugs are not necessary or required for the patient's valid medical needs or for a valid therapeutic purpose;

(B) the provisions of subparagraph (A)(i) and (ii) of this paragraph are not applicable for prescriptions dispensed to persons with intractable pain in accordance with the requirements of the Intractable Pain Treatment Act, or to a narcotic drug dependent person in accordance with the requirements of Title 21, Code of Federal Regulations, § 1306.07, and the Regulation of Narcotic Drug Treatment Programs Act;

(3) delivering or offering to deliver a prescription drug or device in violation of this Act, the Controlled Substances Act, the Dangerous Drug Act, or rules promulgated pursuant to these Acts;

(4) acquiring or possessing or attempting to acquire or possess prescription drugs in violation of this Act, the Controlled Substances Act, the Dangerous Drug Act, or rules adopted pursuant to these Acts;

(5) distributing prescription drugs or devices to a practitioner or a pharmacy not in the course of professional practice or in violation of this Act, the Controlled Substances Act, Dangerous Drug Act, or rules adopted pursuant to these Acts;

(6) refusing or failing to keep, maintain or furnish any record, notification or information required by this Act, the Controlled Substances Act, the Dangerous Drug Act, or rules adopted pursuant to these Acts;

(7) refusing an entry into any pharmacy for any inspection authorized by the Act;

(8) making false or fraudulent claims to third parties for reimbursement for pharmacy services;

(9) operating a pharmacy in an unsanitary manner;

(10) making false or fraudulent claims concerning any drug;

(11) persistently and flagrantly overcharging for the dispensing of controlled substances;

(12) dispensing controlled substances or dangerous drugs in a manner not consistent with the public health or welfare;

(13) failing to practice pharmacy in an acceptable manner consistent with the public health and welfare;

(14) refilling a prescription upon which there is authorized "prn" refills or words of similar meaning, for a period of time in excess of one year from the date of issuance of such prescription;

(15) engaging in any act, acting in concert with another, or engaging in any conspiracy resulting in a restraint of trade, coercion, or a monopoly in the practice of pharmacy;

(16) sharing or offering to share with a practitioner compensation received from an individual provided pharmacy services by a pharmacist;

(17) obstructing a board employee in the lawful performance of his or her duties of enforcing the Act;

(18) engaging in conduct that subverts or attempts to subvert any examination or examination process required for a license to practice pharmacy. Conduct that subverts or attempts to subvert the pharmacist licensing examination process includes, but is not limited to:

(A) copying, retaining, repeating, or transmitting in any manner the questions contained in any examination administered by the board or questions contained in a question pool of any examination administered by the board;

(B) copying or attempting to copy another candidate's answers to any questions on any examination required for a license to practice pharmacy;

(C) obtaining or attempting to obtain confidential examination materials compiled by testing services or the board;

(D) impersonating or acting as a proxy for another in any examination required for a license to practice pharmacy;

(E) requesting or allowing another to impersonate or act as a proxy in any examination required for a license to practice pharmacy; or

(F) violating or attempting to violate the security of examination materials or the examination process in any manner;

(19) violating the provisions of an agreed board order or board order;

(20) dispensing a prescription drug while not acting in the usual course of professional pharmacy practice;

(21) failing to provide or providing false or fraudulent information on any application, notification, or other document required under this Act, the Dangerous Drug Act, the Controlled Substances Act, or rules adopted pursuant to those Acts;

(22) using abusive, intimidating, or threatening behavior toward a board member or employee during the performance of such member's or employee's lawful duties;

(23) failing to establish or maintain effective controls against the diversion or loss of controlled substances or dangerous drugs, loss of controlled substance or dangerous drug records, or failing to ensure that controlled substances or dangerous drugs are dispensed in compliance with state and federal laws or rules, by a pharmacist who is:

(A) a pharmacist-in-charge of a pharmacy;

(B) a sole proprietor or individual owner of a pharmacy;

(C) a partner in the ownership of a pharmacy; or

(D) a managing officer of a corporation, association, or joint-stock company owning a pharmacy. A pharmacist, as set out in subparagraphs (B) - (D) of this paragraph, is equally responsible with an individual designated as pharmacist-in-charge of such pharmacy to ensure that employee pharmacists and the pharmacy are in compliance with all state and federal laws or rules relating to controlled substances or dangerous drugs;

(24) failing to correct the issues identified in a warning notice by the specified time;

(25) being the subject of civil fines imposed by a federal or state court as a result of violating the Controlled Substances Act or the Dangerous Drug Act;

(26) selling, purchasing, or trading or offering to sell, purchase, or trade prescription drug samples; provided, however, this paragraph does not apply to:

(A) prescription drugs provided by a manufacturer as starter prescriptions or as replacement for such manufacturer's out-dated drugs;

(B) prescription drugs provided by a manufacturer in replacement for such manufacturer's drugs that were dispensed pursuant to written starter prescriptions; or

(C) prescription drug samples possessed by a pharmacy of a health care entity which provides health care primarily to indigent or low income patients at no or reduced cost and if:

(i)   the samples are possessed in compliance with the Prescription Drug Marketing Act of 1987;

(ii) the pharmacy is owned by a charitable organization described in the Internal Revenue Code of 1986, § 501(c)(3), or by a city, state or county government; and

(iii) the samples are for dispensing or provision at no charge to patients of such health care entity.

(27) selling, purchasing, or trading or offering to sell, purchase, or trade prescription drugs:

(A) sold for export use only;

(B) purchased by a public or private hospital or other health care entity; or

(C) donated or supplied at a reduced price to a charitable organization described in the Internal Revenue Code of 1986, § 501(c)(3);

(D) provided that subparagraphs (A) - (C) of this paragraph do not apply to:

(i)   the purchase or other acquisition by a hospital or other health care entity which is a member of a group purchasing organization or from other hospitals or health care entities which are members of such organization;

(ii) the sale, purchase, or trade of a drug or an offer to sell, purchase, or trade a drug by an organization described in subparagraph (C) of this paragraph to a nonprofit affiliate of the organization to the extent otherwise permitted by law;

(iii) the sale, purchase or trade of a drug or an offer to sell, purchase, or trade a drug among hospitals or other health care entities which are under common control;

(iv) the sale, purchase, or trade of a drug or an offer to sell, purchase, or trade a drug for emergency medical reasons including the transfer of a drug between pharmacies to alleviate temporary shortages of the drug arising from delays in or interruptions of regular distribution schedules; or

(v)   the dispensing of a prescription drug pursuant to a valid prescription drug order to the extent otherwise permitted by law;

(28) selling, purchasing, or trading, or offering to sell, purchase, or trade:

(A) misbranded prescription drugs; or

(B) prescription drugs beyond the manufacturer's expiration date;

(29) failing to repay a guaranteed student loan, as provided in Texas Education Code, § 57.491;

(30) failing to respond and to provide all requested records within the time specified in an audit of continuing education records under § 295.8 of this title (relating to Continuing Education Requirements); or

(31) allowing an individual whose license to practice pharmacy, either as a pharmacist or a pharmacist-intern, or a pharmacy technician/trainee whose registration has been disciplined by the board, resulting in the license or registration being revoked, canceled, retired, surrendered, denied or suspended, to have access to prescription drugs in a pharmacy.

(b) For the purposes of the Act, § 565.001(a)(3), the term "gross immorality" shall include, but not be limited to:

(1) conduct which is willful, flagrant, and shameless, and which shows a moral indifference to standards of the community;

(2) engaging in an act which is a felony;

(3) engaging in an act that constitutes sexually deviant behavior; or

(4) being required to register with the Department of Public Safety as a sex offender under Chapter 62, Code of Criminal Procedure.

(c) For the purposes of the Act, § 565.001(a)(5), the terms "fraud," "deceit," or "misrepresentation" in the practice of pharmacy or in seeking a license to act as a pharmacist shall be defined as follows.

(1) "Fraud" means an intentional perversion of truth for the purpose of inducing another in reliance upon it to part with some valuable thing belonging to him, or to surrender a legal right, or to issue a license; a false representation of a matter of fact, whether by words or by conduct, by false or misleading allegations, or by concealment of that which should have been disclosed, which deceives or is intended to deceive another.

(2) "Deceit" means the assertion, as a fact, of that which is not true by any means whatsoever to deceive or defraud another.

(3) "Misrepresentation" means a manifestation by words or other conduct which is a false representation of a matter of fact.

Source: The provisions of this § 281.7 adopted to be effective December 30, 1998, 23 TexReg 13073; amended to be effective December 27, 2000, 25 TexReg 12688; amended to be effective March 25, 2007, 32 TexReg 1507; amended to be effective September 9, 2012, 37 TexReg 6915; amended to be effective December 6, 2015, 40 TexReg 8763; amended to be effective June 20, 2019, 44 TexReg 2945

§281.8 Grounds for Discipline for a Pharmacy License

(a) For the purposes of § 565.002(a)(9) of the Act, a pharmacy fails to establish and maintain effective controls against diversion of prescription drugs when:
 (1) there is inadequate security or procedures to prevent unauthorized access to prescription drugs; or
 (2) there is inadequate security or procedures to prevent the diversion of prescription drugs.

(b) For the purposes of § 565.002(a)(3) of the Act, it is grounds for discipline for a pharmacy license when:
 (1) during the time an individual's license to practice pharmacy, either as a pharmacist or a pharmacist-intern, or a pharmacy technician's registration has been disciplined by the Board, resulting in the license or registration being revoked, canceled, retired, surrendered, denied or suspended, the pharmacy employs or allows such individual access to prescription drugs;
 (2) the pharmacy possesses or engages in the sale, purchase, or trade or the offer to sell, purchase, or trade prescription drug samples; provided however, this paragraph does not apply to:
  (A) prescription drugs provided by a manufacturer as starter prescriptions or as replacement for such manufacturer's outdated drugs;
  (B) prescription drugs provided by a manufacturer in replacement for such manufacturer's drugs that were dispensed pursuant to written starter prescriptions; or
  (C) prescription drug samples possessed by a pharmacy of a health care entity which provides health care primarily to indigent or low income patients at no or reduced cost and if:
   (i) the samples are possessed in compliance with the Prescription Drug Marketing Act of 1987;
   (ii) the pharmacy is owned by a charitable organization described in the Internal Revenue Code of 1986, § 501(c)(3), or by a city, state or county government; and
   (iii) the samples are for dispensing or provision at no charge to patients of such health care entity;
 (3) the pharmacy possesses or engages in the sale, purchase, or trade or the offer to sell, purchase, or trade of prescription drugs:
  (A) sold for export use only;
  (B) purchased by a public or private hospital or other health care entity; or
  (C) donated or supplied at a reduced price to a charitable organization described in the Internal Revenue Code of 1986, § 501(c)(3), and possessed by a pharmacy other than one owned by the charitable organization;
  (D) provided that subparagraphs (A) – (C) of this paragraph do not apply to:
   (i) the purchase or other acquisition by a hospital or other health care entity which is a member of a group purchasing organization or from other hospitals or health care entities which are members of such organization;
   (ii) the sale, purchase, or trade of a drug or an offer to sell, purchase, or trade a drug by an organization described in paragraph (2)(C)(ii) of this subsection to a nonprofit affiliate of the organization to the extent otherwise permitted by law;
   (iii) the sale, purchase or trade of a drug or an offer to sell, purchase, or trade a drug among hospitals or other health care entities which are under common control;
   (iv) the sale, purchase, or trade of a drug or an offer to sell, purchase, or trade a drug for emergency medical reasons including the transfer of a drug between pharmacies to alleviate temporary shortages of the drug arising from delays in or interruptions of regular distribution schedules;
   (v) the dispensing of a prescription drug pursuant to a valid prescription drug order to the extent otherwise permitted by law;
 (4) the pharmacy engages in the sale, purchase, or trade or the offer to sell, purchase, or trade of:
  (A) misbranded prescription drugs; or
  (B) prescription drugs beyond the manufacturer's expiration date.
 (5) the owner or managing officer has previously been disciplined by the board; or
 (6) a non-resident pharmacy fails to reimburse the board or its designee for all expenses, including travel, incurred by the board in inspecting the non-resident pharmacy as specified in § 556.0551 of the Act;
 (7) the owner, managing officer(s), or other pharmacy employee(s) displays abusive, intimidating, or threatening behavior toward a board member or employee during the performance of such member's or employee's lawful duties; or
 (8) the pharmacy waived, discounted, or reduced, or offered to waive, discount, or reduce, a patient copayment or deductible for a compounded drug in the absence of:
  (A) a legitimate, documented financial hardship of the patient; or
  (B) evidence of a good faith effort to collect the copayment or deductible from the patient.

(c) For the purposes of § 565.002(a)(10) of the Act, the terms "fraud," "deceit," or "misrepresentation" in operating a pharmacy or in seeking a license to operate shall be defined as follows:
 (1) "Fraud" means an intentional perversion of truth for the purpose of inducing another in reliance upon it to part with some valuable thing belonging to him, or to surrender a legal right, or to issue a license; a false representation of a matter of fact, whether by words or by conduct, by false or misleading allegations, or by concealment of that which should have been disclosed, which deceives or is intended to deceive another;

(2) "Deceit" means the assertion, as a fact, of that which is not true by any means whatsoever to deceive or defraud another; and

(3) "Misrepresentation" means a manifestation by words or other conduct which is a false representation of a matter of fact.

Source: The provisions of this § 281.8 adopted to be effective December 30, 1998, 23 TexReg 13073; amended to be effective July 14, 1999, 24 TexReg 5193; amended to be effective December 27, 2000, 25 TexReg 12688; amended to be effective March 12, 2003, 28 TexReg 2082; amended to be effective June 6, 2004, 29 TexReg 5347; amended to be effective March 25, 2007, 32 TexReg 1507; amended to be effective September 14, 2010, 35 TexReg 8355; amended to be effective March 15, 2015, 40 TexReg 1085; amended to be effective March 10, 2016, 41 TexReg 1689; amended to be effective September 11, 2016, 41 TexReg 6695

§281.9 Grounds for Discipline for a Pharmacy Technician or a Pharmacy Technician Trainee

(a) Pharmacy technicians and pharmacy technician trainees shall be subject to all disciplinary grounds set forth in § 568.003 of the Act.

(b) For the purposes of the Act, § 568.003(a)(10), "negligent, unreasonable, or inappropriate conduct" shall include, but not be limited to:

    (1) delivering or offering to deliver a prescription drug or device in violation of this Act, the Controlled Substances Act, the Dangerous Drug Act, or rules promulgated pursuant to these Acts;

    (2) acquiring or possessing or attempting to acquire or possess prescription drugs in violation of this Act, the Controlled Substances Act, or Dangerous Drug Act or rules adopted pursuant to these Acts;

    (3) failing to perform the duties of a pharmacy technician or pharmacy technician trainee in an acceptable manner consistent with the public health and welfare, which contributes to a prescription not being dispensed or delivered accurately;

    (4) obstructing a board employee in the lawful performance of his duties of enforcing the Act;

    (5) violating the provisions of an agreed board order or board order, including accessing prescription drugs with a revoked or suspended pharmacy technician or pharmacy technician trainee registration;

    (6) abusive, intimidating, or threatening behavior toward a board member or employee during the performance of such member's or employee's lawful duties;

    (7) failing to repay a guaranteed student loan, as provided in the Texas Education Code, § 57.491; or

    (8) failing to respond and to provide all requested records within the time specified in an audit of continuing education records under § 297.8 of this title (relating to Continuing Education Requirements).

(c) For the purposes of the Act, § 568.003(a)(2), the term "gross immorality" shall include, but not be limited to:

    (1) conduct which is willful, flagrant, and shameless, and which shows a moral indifference to standards of the community;

    (2) engaging in an act which is a felony;

    (3) engaging in an act that constitutes sexually deviant behavior; or

    (4) being required to register with the Department of Public Safety as a sex offender under Chapter 62, Code of Criminal Procedure.

(d) For the purposes of the Act, § 568.003(a)(3), the terms "fraud," "deceit," or "misrepresentation" shall apply to an individual seeking a registration as a pharmacy technician, as well as making an application to any entity that certifies or registers pharmacy technicians, and shall be defined as follows:

    (1) "Fraud" means an intentional perversion of truth for the purpose of inducing the board in reliance upon it to issue a registration; a false representation of a matter of fact, whether by words or by conduct, by false or misleading allegations, or by concealment of that which should have been disclosed, which deceives or is intended to deceive the board.

    (2) "Deceit" means the assertion, as a fact, of that which is not true by any means whatsoever to deceive or defraud the board.

    (3) "Misrepresentation" means a manifestation by words or other conduct which is a false representation of a matter of fact.

Source: The provisions of this § 281.9 adopted to be effective September 3, 2006, 31 TexReg 6721; amended to be effective March 25, 2007, 32 TexReg 1507; amended to be effective March 6 2008, 33 TexReg 1783; amended to be effective May 30, 2010, 35 TexReg 4163; amended to be effective September 12, 2011, 36 TexReg 5845; amended to be effective December 6, 2015, 40 TexReg 8763

§281.10 Denial of a License

If an applicant's original application or request for renewal of a license is denied, he shall have 30 days from the date of denial to make a written request for a hearing. If so requested, the hearing will be granted and the provisions of APA and this chapter with regard to a contested case shall apply.

Source: The provisions of this §281.10 adopted to be effective December 30, 1998, 23 TexReg 13073; amended to be effective March 25, 2007, 32 TexReg 1507

§281.11 Criminal History Evaluation Letter

(a) A person, who is enrolled or planning to enroll in an educational program that prepares the person for a license as a pharmacist or a registration as a pharmacy technician or trainee, or planning to take an examination required for such a license or registration, and who has reason to believe that he or she may be ineligible due to a conviction or deferred adjudication for a felony or misdemeanor offense, may request a criminal history evaluation letter regarding his or her eligibility for a license or registration.

(b) The person must submit an application for the criminal history evaluation letter on a form provided by the board which includes:

    (1) a statement indicating the reasons and basis for potential ineligibility, including each criminal offense for which the person was arrested, charged, convicted, or received deferred adjudication;

    (2) all legal documents related to the reasons and basis for potential ineligibility including, but not limited to, police reports, indictments, orders of deferred adjudication, judgments, probation records and evidence of completion of probation, if applicable;

    (3) all requirements necessary in order for the Board to access the criminal history record information, including submitting fingerprint information and paying the required fees; and

    (4) a non-refundable fee of $150 for processing the application.

(c) The application is considered complete when all documents and other information supporting the potential reasons and basis for potential ineligibility has been received by the board. If such documentation is not received within 120 days of the initial receipt of the application, the application is considered to be expired and must be refiled along with the appropriate fees.

(d) The board shall conduct an investigation of the application and the person's eligibility for a license or registration.

(e) The person or the Board may amend the application to include additional grounds for potential ineligibility at any time before a final determination is made.

(f)   A determination of eligibility will be made by the Board or its designees. Notification of the determination will be provided to the person in writing.

    (1)   If no grounds for ineligibility are identified, the notification shall address the determination regarding each ground of potential ineligibility.

    (2)   If grounds for ineligibility exist, the notification shall set out each basis for potential ineligibility and the corresponding determination.

(g)   The board shall mail the determination of eligibility no later than the 90th day after the complete application, as required by subsections (b) and (c) of this section, has been received by the board.

(h)   The determination of eligibility shall be made based on the law in effect on the date of receipt of a complete application.

(i)   Any information the person fails to disclose on the application or any information determined to be inaccurate or incomplete shall invalidate the determination of eligibility on the basis of the information, in the discretion of the board.

(j)   The administrative rules regarding disciplinary guidelines and regarding considerations and sanctions for criminal conduct apply in making the determination regarding eligibility.

(k)   If a person submits an application for license or registration at the same time or within 90 days after the receipt of a complete application for criminal history evaluation letter, board will process only the application for license or registration and will not issue a separate determination of eligibility.

Source: The provisions of this §281.11 adopted to be effective September 14, 2010, 35 TexReg 8355

§281.12 Rules Governing Cooperating Practitioners

For the purposes of the Act, §565.063, a person acting under the supervision of a Board employee engaged in the lawful enforcement of the Act shall include, but not be limited to, a practitioner who provides prescriptions for use in investigations of licensees when such prescriptions are issued by a practitioner at the request of and under the supervision of a Board investigator.

Source: The provisions of this §281.12 adopted to be effective September 14, 2010, 35 TexReg 8355

§281.13 Official Action by Majority

Any official act or decision of the board shall be concurred in by a majority of its members present at a meeting. Such act or decision shall be based upon information presented to members present at official meetings of the board. There shall be at least a quorum of the board members present at any official meeting of the board. Private solicitation of individual members in an effort to in any way influence their official actions through information or arguments not simultaneously presented to other members of the board is improper.

Source: The provisions of this §281.13 adopted to be effective December 30, 1998, 23 TexReg 13073.

§281.14 Vendor Protest Procedures

(a)   The purpose of this section is to establish procedures for resolving vendor protests relating to purchasing issues.

(b)   A vendor who submitted a written response to a solicitation may file a protest with the executive director for actions taken by the board on the following:

    (1)   the solicitation documents or actions associated with the publication of solicitation documents;

    (2)   the evaluation or method of evaluation for a solicitation; or

    (3)   the award of a contract.

(c)   Filing requirements.

    (1)   To be considered, a protest must be:

        (A)   in writing and contain:

            (i)   the specific rule, statute or regulation the protesting vendor alleges the solicitation, contract award, or tentative award violated;

            (ii)   a specific description of each action by the board that the protesting vendor alleges is a violation of the statutory or regulatory provision the protesting vendor identified in subparagraph (A)(i) of this paragraph;

            (iii)   a precise statement of the relevant facts including:

                (I)   sufficient documentation to establish that the protest has been timely filed;

                (II)   a description of the adverse impact to the board and the state; and

                (III)   a description of the resulting adverse impact to the protesting vendor;

            (iv)   a statement of the argument and authorities that the protesting vendor offers in support of the protest; and

            (v)   an explanation of the subsequent action the vendor is requesting;

        (B)   signed by an authorized representative and the signature notarized; and

        (C)   filed with the board in the time period specified in this section.

    (2)   To be considered timely, the protest must be filed:

        (A)   by the end of the posted solicitation period, if the protest concerns the solicitation documents or actions associated with the publication of solicitation documents;

        (B)   by the day of the award of a contract resulting from the solicitation, if the protest concerns the evaluation or method of evaluation for a solicitation; or

        (C)   no later than 10 days after the notice of award, if the protest concerns the award.

(d)   Timeliness of Protest.

    (1)   If a timely protest of a solicitation or contract award is filed under this section, the executive director may delay the solicitation or award of the contract if the executive director makes a determination that the contract must be awarded without delay to protect the best interests of the state.

    (2)   A protest that is filed untimely under this section shall not be considered unless the executive director determines that good cause for delay is shown or that a protest raises issues that are significant to the agency's procurement practices or procedures in general.

(e) Authority of the Executive Director to Settle the Protest.
   (1) Upon receipt of a protest, the executive director may dismiss the protest if it is not timely or does not meet the requirements of this section.
   (2) The executive director shall have the authority to settle and resolve the protest. The executive director may solicit written responses to the protest from other interested parties.
   (3) If the protest is not resolved through mutual agreement, the executive director shall issue a written determination responding to the protest.
(f) Appeal.
   (1) If a protest is based on a solicitation or contract award, the protesting party may appeal a determination of a protest by the executive director to the general counsel. An appeal of the executive director's determination must be in writing and received not later than 10 days after the date the executive director sent written notice of the executive director's determination. The scope of the appeal shall be limited to review of the executive director's determination. The protesting party must mail or deliver to all other interested parties a copy of the appeal, which must contain a certified statement that such copies have been provided.
   (2) The general counsel may refer the matter to the board for consideration or may issue a written decision that resolves the protest.
   (3) An appeal that is not filed timely shall not be considered unless good cause for delay is shown or the general counsel determines that an appeal raises issues that are significant to the agency's procurement practices or procedures in general.
   (4) A written decision issued by the general counsel or the board shall be the final administrative action of the board.
(g) The board shall maintain all documentation on the purchasing process that is the subject of a protest or appeal in accordance with the board's records retention schedule.
   Source: The provisions of this § 281.14 adopted to be effective September 10, 2019, 44 TexReg 4870

§281.15 Negotiated Rulemaking

(a) The board's policy is to encourage the use of negotiated rulemaking for the adoption of board rules in appropriate situations.
(b) The board's general counsel or the designee of the general counsel shall be the board's negotiated rulemaking coordinator (NRC). The NRC shall perform the following functions, as required:
   (1) coordinate the implementation of the policy set out in subsection (a) of this section and in accordance with the Negotiated Rulemaking Act, Chapter 2008, Government Code;
   (2) serve as a resource for any staff training or education needed to implement negotiated rulemaking procedures; and
   (3) collect data to evaluate the effectiveness of negotiated rulemaking procedures implemented by the board.
(c) The board or the executive director may direct the NRC to begin negotiated rulemaking procedures on a specified subject.
   Source: The provisions of this § 281.15 adopted to be effective September 10, 2019, 44 TexReg 4870

§281.16 Alternative Dispute Resolution

(a) The board's policy is to encourage the resolution and early settlement of internal and external disputes, including contested cases, through voluntary settlement processes, which may include any procedure or combination of procedures described by Chapter 154, Civil Practice and Remedies Code. Any ADR procedure used to resolve disputes before the board shall comply with the requirements of Chapter 2009, Government Code, and any model guidelines for the use of ADR issued by the State Office of Administrative Hearings.
(b) The board's general counsel or the designee of the general counsel shall be the board's dispute resolution coordinator (DRC). The DRC shall perform the following functions, as required:
   (1) coordinate the implementation of the policy set out in subsection (a) of this section;
   (2) serve as a resource for any staff training or education needed to implement the ADR procedures; and
   (3) collect data to evaluate the effectiveness of ADR procedures implemented by the board.
(c) The board, a committee of the board, a respondent in a disciplinary matter pending before the board, the executive director, or a board employee engaged in a dispute with the executive director or another employee, may request that the contested matter be submitted to ADR. The request must be in writing, be addressed to the DRC, and state the issues to be determined. The person requesting ADR and the DRC will determine which method of ADR is most appropriate. If the person requesting ADR is the respondent in a disciplinary proceeding, the executive director shall determine if the board will participate in ADR or proceed with the board's normal disciplinary processes.
(d) Any costs associated with retaining an impartial third party mediator, moderator, facilitator, or arbitrator, shall be borne by the party requesting ADR.
(e) Agreements of the parties to ADR must be in writing and are enforceable in the same manner as any other written contract. Confidentiality of records and communications related to the subject matter of an ADR proceeding shall be governed by § 154.073 of the Civil Practice and Remedies Code.
(f) If the ADR process does not result in an agreement, the matter shall be referred to the board for other appropriate disposition.
   Source: The provisions of this § 281.16 adopted to be effective September 10, 2019, 44 TexReg 4871

§281.17 Historically Underutilized Businesses

The Texas State Board of Pharmacy adopts by reference the rules promulgated by the Texas Building and Procurement Commission, which are set forth in Subchapter B of 1 TAC §111.11, et al. regarding Historically Underutilized Business Certification Program.
   Source: The provisions of this §281.17 adopted to be effective July 14, 1999, 24 TexReg 5193; amended to be effective September 8, 2002, 27 TexReg 8212; amended to be effective March 25, 2007, 32 TexReg 1507

§281.18 Reporting Professional Liability Claims

(a) Reporting responsibilities.

(1) Every insurer or other entity providing pharmacist's professional liability insurance, pharmacy technician professional and supplemental liability insurance, or druggist's professional liability insurance covering a pharmacist, pharmacy technician, or pharmacy license holder in this state shall submit to the board the information described in subsection (b) of this section at the time prescribed.

(2) The information shall be provided with respect to a notice of claim letter or complaint filed against an insured in a court, if the notice or complaint seeks damages relating to the insured's conduct in providing or failing to provide appropriate service within the scope of pharmaceutical care or services, and with respect to settlement of a claim or lawsuit made on behalf of the insured.

(3) If a pharmacist, pharmacy technician, or a pharmacy licensed in this state does not carry or is not covered by pharmacist's professional liability insurance, pharmacy technician professional and supplemental liability insurance, or druggist's professional liability insurance, or if a pharmacist, pharmacy technician, or a pharmacy licensed in this state is insured by a non-admitted carrier or other entity providing pharmacy professional liability insurance that does not report under this Act, the duty to report information under subsection (b) of this section is the responsibility of the particular pharmacist, pharmacy technician, or pharmacy license holder.

(4) For the purposes of this section a professional liability claim or complaint shall be defined as a cause of action against a pharmacist, pharmacy, or pharmacy technician for conduct in providing or failing to provide appropriate service within the scope of pharmaceutical care or services, which proximately results in injury to or death of the patient, whether the patient's claim or cause of action sounds in tort or contract, to include pharmacist's interns, pharmacy residents, supervising pharmacists, on-call pharmacists, consulting pharmacists.

(b) Information to be reported and due dates. The following reports are required for claims initiated or resolved on or after September 1, 1999.

(1) Initial report. Not later than the 30th day after receipt of the notice of claim letter or complaint by the insurer if the insurer has the duty to report, or by the pharmacist, pharmacy technician, or a pharmacy if the license holder has the duty to report, the following information must be furnished to the board on a form provided by the board:

(A) the name and address of the insurer;

(B) the name and address of the insured and type of license or registration held (pharmacist, pharmacy or pharmacy technician):

(C) the insured's Texas pharmacist or pharmacy license number or pharmacy technician registration number;

(D) certification, if applicable;

(E) the policy number;

(F) name(s) of plaintiff(s);

(G) date of injury;

(H) county of injury;

(I) cause of injury, e.g., dispensing error;

(J) nature of injury;

(K) type of action, e.g., claim only or lawsuit;

(L) name and phone number of the person filing the report; and

(M) a copy of the notice of claim letter or the lawsuit filed in court.

(2) Follow-up report. Within 105 days after disposition of the claim, the following information must be provided to the board on a form provided by the board:

(A) the name and address of the insured and type of license or registration held (pharmacist, pharmacy or pharmacy technician):

(B) the insured's Texas pharmacist or pharmacy license number or pharmacy technician registration number;

(C) name(s) of plaintiff(s);

(D) date of disposition;

(E) type of disposition, e.g., settlement, judgment;

(F) amount of disposition;

(G) whether an appeal has been taken and by which party; and

(H) name and phone number of the person filing the report.

(3) Definition. For the purpose of this section, disposition of a claim shall include circumstances where a court order has been entered, a settlement agreement has been reached, or the complaint has been dropped or dismissed.

(c) Report format

(1) Separate reports are required for each defendant licensee or registrant.

(2) The information shall be reported on a form provided by the board.

(3) A court order or settlement agreement may be submitted as an attachment to the follow-up report.

(d) Claims not required to be reported. Examples of claims that are not required to be reported under this section are the following:

(1) product liability claims (i.e., where a licensee invented a medical device which may have injured a patient but the licensee has no personal pharmacist-patient relationship with the specific patient claiming injury by the device);

(2) antitrust allegations;

(3) allegations involving improper peer review activities;

(4) civil rights violations; or

(5) allegations of liability for injuries occurring on a licensee's property, but not involving a breach of duty (i.e., slip and fall accidents).

(e) Liability. An insurer reporting under this section, its agents or employees, or the board or its employees or representatives are not liable for damages in a suit brought by any person or entity for reporting as required by this section or for any other action taken under this section.

(f) Limit on use of information reported.
  (1) Information submitted to the board under this section and the fact that the information has been submitted to the board may not be:
    (A) offered in evidence or used in any manner in the trial of a suit described in this section; or
    (B) used in any manner to determine the eligibility or credentialing of a pharmacy to participate in a health insurance plan defined by the Insurance Code.
  (2) A report received by the board under this section is not a complaint for which a board investigation is required except that the board shall review the information relating to a pharmacist, pharmacy technician, or pharmacy license holder against whom at least three professional liability claims have been reported within a five-year period in the same manner as if a complaint against the pharmacist, pharmacy technician, or pharmacy license holder had been made under Chapter 555 of the Act. The board may initiate an investigation of pharmacist, pharmacy technician, or pharmacy license holder based on the information received under this section.
  (3) The information received under this section may be used in any board proceedings as the board deems necessary.
(g) Confidentiality. Information submitted under this section is confidential, except as provided in subsection (f)(3) of this section, and is not subject to disclosure under Chapter 552, Government Code.
(h) Penalty. The Texas Department of Insurance may impose on any insurer subject to this Act sanctions authorized by §§82.051-82.055 (formerly §7, Article 1.10) of the Texas Insurance Code, if the insurer fails to report information as required by this section.
  Source: The provisions of this §281.18 adopted to be effective March 29, 2000, 25 TexReg 2572

§281.19 Vehicles

(a) Vehicle Inscription Information.
  (1) Exemption. As specified in § 554.009 of the Act and § 721.003 of the Transportation Code, vehicles assigned to or used by the compliance or investigation divisions for enforcement of pharmacy laws and rules are exempt from bearing the inscription required by § 721.002 of the Transportation Code. These vehicles are to be used primarily in the inspection of pharmacies and the investigation of violations of state and federal laws and rules relating to the practice of pharmacy. In addition, as specified in § 554.009 of the Act, the vehicles may be registered with the Texas Department of Motor Vehicles in an alias name for investigative personnel.
  (2) Purpose. The purpose of exempting these vehicles from the inscription requirements of § 721.002 of the Transportation Code is to increase the effectiveness of agency field employees in detecting and investigating violations of state and federal laws relating to the practice of pharmacy, thereby allowing compliance and investigative personnel to accomplish their tasks undetected, and to provide a greater degree of safety for these staff and the state property being used in the enforcement and a greater degree of case integrity.
(b) Restrictions on Assignments of Vehicles.
  (1) Each agency vehicle will be assigned to an individual field employee.
  (2) The agency may assign a vehicle to a board member or an individual administrative or executive employee:
    (A) on a temporary basis if field personnel are not available to assume responsibility for the car; or
    (B) on a regular basis only if the agency makes a written documented finding that the assignment is critical to the needs and mission of the agency.
  Source: The provisions of this § 281.19 adopted to be effective September 12, 2001, 26 TexReg 6890; amended to be effective September 10, 2019, 44 TexReg 4871

SUBCHAPTER B. GENERAL PROCEDURES IN A CONTESTED CASE

§281.20 Application of Other Laws

All disciplinary action shall be taken by the board in accordance with Chapters 2001 and 2003, Government Code, the State Office of Administrative Hearings Rules of Procedure, the board's rules, and any other applicable law or rule.
  Source: The provisions of this §281.20 adopted to be effective March 25, 2007, 32 TexReg 1508

§281.21 Complaints

Complaints may be filed with the agency in writing or by submitting a completed complaint form to the agency by mail or other method of delivery or through the Internet. A complaint form shall be maintained on the agency's Internet site and at the agency's office for use by a complainant. The complaint form shall request information necessary for the proper processing of the complaint by the agency, including, but not limited to:
  (1) complainant's name, address, and phone number;
  (2) name, address and phone number of subject of complaint, if known;
  (3) date of incident;
  (4) description of drug(s) involved, if any; and
  (5) description of incident giving rise to complaint.
  Source: The provisions of this §281.21 adopted to be effective December 30, 1998, 23 TexReg 13073; amended to be effective December 19, 2001, 26 TexReg 10299

§281.22 Informal Disposition of a Contested Case

(a) Unless precluded by law, informal disposition may be made of any contested case by stipulation, agreed settlement, consent order, default, or dismissal.
(b) Prior to the imposition of disciplinary sanction(s) against a respondent , the board shall provide the respondent with written notice of the matters asserted, including:

(1)   a statement of the legal authority, jurisdiction, and alleged conduct under which the enforcement action is based, with a reference to the particular section(s) of the statutes and rules involved;

(2)   information the board staff intends to use at an informal conference;

(3)   an offer for the respondent to attend an informal conference at a specified time and place and show compliance with all requirements of law, in accordance with §2001.054(c) of the Administrative Procedure Act;

(4)   a statement that the respondent has an opportunity for a hearing before the State Office of Administrative Hearings on the allegations; and

(5)   the following statement in capital letters in 12 point boldface type: FAILURE TO RESPOND TO THE ALLEGATIONS, BY EITHER PERSONAL APPEARANCE AT THE INFORMAL CONFERENCE OR IN WRITING, WILL RESULT IN THE ALLEGATIONS BEING ADMITTED AS TRUE AND THE RECOMMENDED SANCTION MADE AT THE INFORMAL CONFERENCE BEING GRANTED BY DEFAULT. The notice shall be served by delivering a copy to the respondent in person, by courier receipted delivery, by first class mail, or by certified or registered mail, return receipt requested to the respondent's last known address of record as shown by agency records.

(c)   The respondent will be provided the opportunity to appear at an informal conference prior to a hearing at the State Office of Administrative Hearings. The notice of the time and place of the informal conference, along with the written notice required in subsection (b) of this section, will be given to the respondent at least 45 days before the date of the informal conference. If such notice is not timely provided, the respondent may reschedule the informal conference.

(d)   The respondent shall respond either by personal appearance at the informal conference, or by providing a rebuttal in writing no later than 15 days before the date of the informal conference. If the respondent chooses to respond in writing, the response shall admit or deny each of the allegations. If the respondent intends to deny only a part of an allegation, the respondent shall specify so much of it is true and shall deny only the remainder. The response shall also include any other matter, whether of law or fact, upon which the respondent intends to rely upon as a defense. If the respondent fails to respond to the notice specified in subsection (b) of this section, the matter will be considered as a default case and the respondent will be deemed to have:

(1)   admitted all the factual allegations in the notice specified in subsection (b) of this section;

(2)   waived the opportunity to show compliance with the law;

(3)   waived notice of a hearing;

(4)   waived the opportunity for a hearing on the allegations; and

(5)   waived objection to the recommended sanctions made at the informal conference.

(e)   Default orders.

(1)   The informal conference panel may recommend that the board enter a default order, based upon the allegations set out in the notice specified in subsection (b) of this section, adopting the recommended sanctions made at the informal conference. Upon consideration of the case, the board may enter a default order under §2001.056 of the Administrative Procedure Act or direct that the case be set for a hearing at the State Office of Administrative Hearings.

(2)   For a contested case before the State Office of Administrative Hearings, the judge may announce a default upon receiving the required showing of proof to support a default, and then recess the hearing, issue an order dismissing the case from the docket of the State Office of Administrative Hearings, and return the file to the board for informal disposition on a default basis in accordance with §2001.056 of the Administrative Procedure Act. The board may then enter a default order or direct the case back to the State Office of Administrative Hearings.

(f)   Any default judgment granted under this section will be entered on the basis of the factual allegations in the notice specified in subsection (b) of this section, and upon proof of proper notice to the respondent's address of record. For purposes of this section, proper notice means notice sufficient to meet the provisions of §2001.054 of the Administrative Procedure Act and §281.30 of this title (relating to Pleadings and Notice in a Contested Case).

(g)   A motion for rehearing which requests that the board vacate its default order under this section shall be granted if the motion presents convincing evidence that the failure to respond to the notice specified in subsection (b) of this section was not intentional or the result of conscious indifference, but due to accident or mistake, provided that the respondent has a meritorious defense to the factual allegations contained in the notice specified in subsection (b) of this section and the granting thereof will not result in delay or injury to the public or the board.

(h)   Informal conferences shall be attended by the executive director/secretary or designated representative, legal counsel of the agency or an attorney employed by the office of the attorney general, and other representative(s) of the agency as the executive director/secretary and legal counsel may deem necessary for proper conduct of the conference. The respondent and/or the respondent's authorized representative(s) may attend the informal conference and shall be provided an opportunity to be heard. All communications from the respondent shall be directed to the legal counsel of the agency.

(i)   In any case where charges are based upon information provided by a person (complainant) who filed a complaint with the board, the complainant may attend the informal conference, unless the proceedings are confidential under §564.002 and §564.003 of the Texas Pharmacy Act or other applicable law. A complainant who chooses to attend an informal conference shall be provided an opportunity to be heard with regard to charges based upon the information provided by the complainant. Nothing herein requires a complainant to attend an informal conference.

(j)   Informal conferences shall not be deemed meetings of the board, and no formal record of the proceedings at such conferences shall be made or maintained unless the respondent requests such a recording in writing at least 15 days before the informal conference. Board staff will arrange for the presence of a court reporter to make the recording. The respondent shall be responsible for the cost of the recording. The recording will be part of the board's investigative file and will not be released to a third party unless authorized under §565.055 of the Act. The board will provide a copy of the recording to the respondent upon request.

(k)   Any proposed consent order shall be presented to the board in open meeting for its review. At the conclusion of its review, the board shall approve or disapprove the proposed consent order. Should the board approve the proposed consent order, the appropriate notation shall be made in minutes of the board and the proposed consent order shall be entered as an official action of the board. Should the board disapprove the proposed consent order, the matter shall be scheduled for public hearing.

Source: The provisions of this §281.22 adopted to be effective December 30, 1998, 23 TexReg 13073; amended to be effective December 27, 2000, 25 TexReg 12689; amended to be effective September 10, 2003, 28 TexReg 7708; amended to be effective December 4, 2005, 30 TexReg 7874; amended to be effective March 25, 2007, 32 TexReg 1508; amended to be effective September 14, 2010, 35 TexReg 8356; amended to be effective June 7, 2012, 37 TexReg 4045; amended to be effective September 9, 2012, 37 TexReg 6916; amended to be effective September 8, 2013, 38 TexReg 5721; amended to be effective December 10, 2013, 38 TexReg 8833

§281.23 Subpoenas

(a) A subpoena issued by the executive director/secretary under the authority of §565.058 of the Act is considered by the board to be a ministerial act. Such subpoena shall be used to obtain information and testimony at the request of board staff.

(b) If a subpoena is requested by an applicant, licensee, or registrant under §2001.089 of the APA, a showing of good cause shall be made to the executive director/secretary. Such a showing shall be by submission of a written request for the subpoena indicating the purpose of the subpoena and indicating that the subpoena is not requested in bad faith. In addition, the requesting party shall aver that the subpoena:

    (1) does not request information that is privileged;

    (2) requests information relevant to the contested case;

    (2) is not an undue burden; and

    (3) is sufficiently specific.

(c) Once the requesting party has complied with the requirements in subsection (b) of this section, the executive director/secretary may issue the subpoena.

(d) If the requesting party, the subpoenaed party, any other party to the contested case, or any person or entity affected by the subpoena objects, a challenge to the subpoena shall be filed with the Administrative Law Judge at the State Office of Administrative Hearings.

Source: The provisions of this §281.23 adopted to be effective December 7, 2010, 35 TexReg 10689

§281.30 Pleadings and Notice in a Contested Case

(a) The board initiates a contested case hearing at the State Office of Administrative Hearings by filing a complaint with notice of not less than 10 days as specified in subsection (b) of this section to the applicant, licensee, or registrant.

    (1) The complaint shall contain the matters asserted by the board, including the alleged conduct under which the enforcement action is based, and a statement of legal authority to the statutes or rules allegedly violated and those establishing jurisdiction.

    (2) The following statement in capital letters in 12 point boldface type shall be contained in the complaint: FAILURE TO RESPOND TO THE ALLEGATIONS IN WRITING WILL RESULT IN THE ALLEGATIONS BEING ADMITTED AS TRUE AND AN ORDER BEING ENTERED BY THE BOARD BY DEFAULT.

(b) The board may serve notice of the complaint initiating a contested case hearing at the State Office of Administrative Hearings by sending it to the party's current publicly available address of record and the party's current confidential address of record if the confidential address of record is different from the party's publicly available address of record as shown by the board's records. The notice shall be served by delivering a copy to the party either in person or by certified or registered mail, return receipt requested.

(c) The applicant, licensee, or registrant shall file a written answer with the State Office of Administrative Hearings in response to the complaint with service to the board within 23 days after the date of service of the complaint. The answer shall admit or deny each of the allegations. If the party intends to deny only a part of an allegation, the party shall specify so much of it is true and shall deny only the remainder. The response shall also include any other matter, whether of law or fact, upon which the licensee or registrant intends to rely for his or her defense. If the party fails to respond by filing a timely answer, the boards attorney files a motion to remand the case to the board for entry of a default order, and the matter will be considered as a default case and the party will be deemed to have:

    (1) admitted all the factual allegations in the notice specified in subsection (b) of this section;

    (2) waived notice of a hearing;

    (3) waived the opportunity for a hearing on the allegations; and

    (4) waived objection to the recommended sanctions made at the informal conference.

(d) If the contested case is remanded to the board by the State Office of Administrative Hearings as specified in subsection (c) of this section, the board may enter a default order under § 2001.056 of the Administrative Procedure Act.

(e) Any default judgment granted under this section will be entered on the basis of the factual allegations in the notice specified in subsection (b) of this section, and upon proof of proper notice to the party's address of record.

(f) The party may file a motion for rehearing to set aside the default order. The motion, which requests that the Board vacate its default order under this section, shall be granted if the motion presents convincing evidence that the failure to respond to the notice specified in subsection (b) of this section was not intentional or the result of conscious indifference, but due to accident or mistake, provided that the party has a meritorious defense to the factual allegations contained in the notice specified in subsection (b) of this section and the granting thereof will not result in delay or injury to the public or the Board.

Source: The provisions of this §281.30 adopted to be effective March 25, 2007, 32 TexReg 1508; amended to be effective September 12, 2011, 36 TexReg 5845; amended to be effective September 9, 2012, 37 TexReg 6916

§281.31 Burden of Proof

(a) In a contested case hearing at the State Office of Administrative Hearings involving grounds for disciplinary action, the board has the burden to prove that grounds to discipline respondent exist. However, the party that claims any exemption or exception, including mitigating factors as specified in § 281.62 of this chapter, has the burden to prove that the exemption or exception should be applied.

(b) In a contested case hearing at the State Office of Administrative Hearings involving a petition for reinstatement or removal of restriction, the petitioner has the burden to prove that the license should be reinstated or that a restriction on the license should be removed in accordance with § 281.66 of the chapter.

(c) In a show cause order hearing before a panel of the board involving an applicant, licensee, or registrant who has been previously ordered by the board to submit to a mental or physical examination under § 565.052 or § 568.0036 of the Act, the applicant, licensee, or registrant has the burden to prove that the applicant, licensee, or registrant should not be required to submit to the examination.

Source: The provisions of this § 281.31 adopted to be effective March 25, 2007, 32 TexReg 1508; amended to be effective December 7, 2010, 35 TexReg 10689; amended to be effective September 11, 2016, 41 TexReg 6696

§281.32 Failure to Attend Hearing and Default

(a) If a party who does not have the burden of proof fails to appear at a contested case hearing at the State Office of Administrative Hearings, the administrative law judge may announce a default upon receiving the required showing of proof to support a default, and then recess the hearing, issue an order dismissing the case from the docket of the State Office of Administrative Hearings, and return the file to the board for informal disposition on a default basis in accordance with § 2001.056 of the Administrative Procedure Act. In the alternative, the judge may issue a default proposal for decision, rather than continuing or dismissing the case and requiring the board to dispose of the case on a default basis as an informal disposition.

(b) If a party who does have the burden of proof fails to appear at a contested case hearing at the State Office of Administrative Hearings, the administrative law judge shall dismiss the case for want of prosecution, any relevant application will be withdrawn, and the board may not consider a subsequent petition from the party until the first anniversary of the date of dismissal of the case.

Source: The provisions of this §281.32 adopted to be effective March 25, 2007, 32 TexReg 1508; amended to be effective June 7, 2012, 37 TexReg 4045

§281.33 Proposal for Decision

(a) The administrative law judge shall submit a proposal for decision to the agency, and the board shall render the final decision in the contested case. The board may request that the proposal for decision be presented to the board by the administrative law judge at the next board meeting.

(b) If a party submitted proposed findings of fact, the proposal for decision shall include a ruling on each proposed finding by the administrative law judge.

(c) The parties may submit to the board for consideration, prior to the final decision, an alternative proposed board order with changes to the proposal for decision in compliance with the APA.

Source: The provisions of this §281.33 adopted to be effective March 25, 2007, 32 TexReg 1508

§281.34 Record of Hearing

(a) The board shall arrange for a stenographic recording of all contested case hearings before the State Office of Administrative Hearings on a regular basis. The administrative law judge may waive the requirement as authorized by the State Office of Administrative Hearings Rules of Procedure. Any party may request a written transcript of all or part of the hearing. The cost of a transcript shall be paid by the requesting party.

(b) A party who appeals a final decision in a hearing shall pay the cost of preparation of the original or a certified copy of the record of the board proceeding that is required to be sent to the reviewing court. A charge imposed under this section is a court cost and may be assessed by the court in accordance with the Texas Rules of Civil Procedure.

Source: The provisions of this §281.34 adopted to be effective March 25, 2007, 32 TexReg 1508

SUBCHAPTER C. DISCIPLINARY GUIDELINES

§281.60 General Guidance

(a) This subchapter is promulgated to:
   (1) promote consistency and guidance in the exercise of sound discretion by the agency in licensure and disciplinary matters;
   (2) provide notice as to the types of conduct that constitute violations of the Act and as to the disciplinary action that may be imposed; and
   (3) provide a framework of analysis for administrative law judges in making recommendations in licensure and disciplinary matters.

(b) Board's role. The board shall render the final decision in a contested case and has the responsibility to assess sanctions against licensees who are found to have violated the Act. The board welcomes recommendations of administrative law judges as to the sanctions to be imposed, but the board is not bound by such recommendations. A sanction should be consistent with sanctions imposed in other similar cases and should reflect the board's determination of the seriousness of the violation and the sanction required to deter future violations. A determination of the appropriate sanction is reserved to the board. The appropriate sanction is not a proper finding of fact or conclusion of law. This subchapter shall be construed and applied so as to preserve board member discretion in the imposition of sanctions and remedial measures pursuant to the APA and the Act's provisions related to types of discipline and administrative penalties. This subchapter shall be further construed and applied so as to be consistent with the Act, and shall be limited to the extent as otherwise proscribed by statute and board rule.

(c) Purpose of guidelines. These guidelines are designed to provide guidance in assessing sanctions for violations of the Act. The ultimate purpose of disciplinary sanctions is to protect and inform the public, deter future violations, offer opportunities for rehabilitation, if appropriate, punish violators, and deter others from violations. These guidelines are intended to promote consistent sanctions for similar violations, facilitate timely resolution of cases, and encourage settlements.
   (1) The standard sanctions outlined in the subchapter apply to cases involving a single violation of the Act, and in which there are no aggravating factors that apply. The board may impose more restrictive sanctions when there are multiple violations of the Act. In cases which do not have standard sanctions outlined in the subchapter, the board may consider any aggravating and/or mitigating factors listed in §281.62 of this title (relating to Aggravating and Mitigating Factors) that are found to apply in a particular case.
   (2) The standard and minimum sanctions outlined in the subchapter are applicable to first time violators. The board shall consider revoking the person's license if the person is a repeat offender.
   (3) The maximum sanction in all cases is revocation of the licensee's license, which may be accompanied by an administrative penalty of up to $5,000 per violation. Each day the violation continues is a separate violation.
   (4) Each statutory violation constitutes a separate offense, even if arising out of a single act.

Source: The provisions of this §281.60 adopted to be effective September 3, 2006, 31 TexReg 6722; amended to be effective December 7, 2010, 35 TexReg 10689

§281.61 Definitions of Discipline Authorized

For the purpose of the Act, § 565.051 and § 568.0035:

(1) "Probation" means a period of supervision by the board imposed against a license or registration for a term and under conditions as determined by the board, including a probation fee.

(2) "Reprimand" means a public and formal censure against a license or registration.

(3) "Restrict" means to limit, confine, abridge, narrow, or restrain a license or registration for a term and under conditions determined by the board.

(4) "Revoke" means a license or registration is void and may not be reissued; provided, however, upon the expiration of 12 months from and after the effective date of the order revoking a license or registration, the license or registration may be reinstated by the board upon the successful completion of any requirements determined by the board.

(5) "Suspend" means a license or registration is of no further force and effect for a period of time as determined by the board.

(6) "Retire" means a license or registration has been withdrawn and is of no further force and effect.

Source: The provisions of this § 281.61 adopted to be effective September 3, 2006, 31 TexReg 6722; amended to be effective June 12, 2013, 38 TexReg 3591; amended to be effective June 11, 2017, 42 TexReg 2928

§281.62 Aggravating and Mitigating Factors

The following factors may be considered in determining the disciplinary sanctions imposed by the board if the factors are applicable to the factual situation alleged. The factors are not applicable in situations involving criminal actions (in which case § 281.63 of this title (relating to Considerations for Criminal Offenses) applies).

(1) Aggravation. The following may be considered as aggravating factors so as to merit an increase in the severity of disciplinary sanction(s) to be imposed:

(A) extent and gravity of personal, economic, or public damage or harm;

(B) vulnerability of the patient(s);

(C) willful or reckless conduct, or as a result of a knowingly made professional omission, as opposed to negligent conduct;

(D) pattern of misconduct that serves as a basis of discipline;

(E) prior disciplinary action(s);

(F) attempted concealment of the conduct which serves as a basis for disciplinary action under the Act; and

(G) violation of a board order.

(2) Extenuation and Mitigation. The following may be considered as extenuating and mitigating factors so as to merit a reduction in the severity of disciplinary sanction(s) to be imposed:

(A) isolated incident that serves as a basis for disciplinary action;

(B) remorse for conduct;

(C) interim implementation of remedial measures to correct or mitigate harm from the conduct which serves as a basis for disciplinary action under the Act;

(D) remoteness of misconduct, when not based on delay attributable to actions by the respondent;

(E) extent to which respondent cooperated with board investigation;

(F) treatment and/or monitoring of an impairment;

(G) self-reported and voluntary admissions of the conduct which serves as a basis for disciplinary action under section 565.001(a)(4) and (7) of the Act; and

(H) if acting as pharmacist-in-charge, respondent did not personally engage, either directly or indirectly, in the conduct that serves as the basis for disciplinary action; did not permit or encourage, either by professional oversight or extreme negligence, the conduct that serves as the basis for disciplinary action; promptly reported the conduct to the board or other state or federal regulatory authorities or law enforcement upon identifying the conduct that serves as the basis for disciplinary action; and took all reasonable steps to mitigate or remediate the conduct that serves as the basis for disciplinary action.

Source: The provisions of this § 281.62 adopted to be effective September 3, 2006, 31 TexReg 6722; amended to be effective March 25, 2007, 32 TexReg 1508; amended to be effective September 7, 2008, 33 TexReg 7218; amended to be effective December 6, 2018, 43 TexReg 7770

§281.63 Considerations for Criminal Offenses

(a) The purpose of this section is to establish guidelines and criteria on the eligibility of persons with criminal backgrounds to obtain a license or registration from the board and on the disciplinary actions taken by the board. The section applies to all criminal convictions and to all deferred adjudication community supervisions or deferred dispositions, as authorized by the Act, for all types of licenses and registrations.

(b) The board may suspend, revoke, or impose other authorized disciplinary action on a current license or registration, disqualify a person from receiving a license or registration, or deny to a person the opportunity to be examined for a license or registration because of a person's conviction or deferred adjudication of a crime that serves as a ground for discipline under the Act, and that the board determines directly relates to the duties and responsibilities of a licensee, a registrant, or of an owner of a pharmacy. This subsection applies to persons who are not imprisoned at the time the board considers the conviction or deferred adjudication.

(c) The board shall revoke a license or registration upon the imprisonment of the licensee, the registrant, or the owner of a pharmacy following a felony conviction or deferred adjudication, or revocation of felony community supervision, parole, or mandatory supervision.

(d) A person in prison is not eligible for a license or registration.

(e) An applicant for a license or registration from the board shall disclose in writing to the board any conviction or deferred adjudication against him or her at the time of application. A current licensee or registrant shall disclose in writing to the board any conviction or deferred adjudication against him or her at the time of renewal.

(f) The board shall by rule determine and list in this section which criminal offenses directly relate to the occupation of a licensee or registrant, or the operation of a pharmacy. For all other offenses not listed in this section, in considering whether a criminal conviction or deferred adjudication directly relates to the occupation of a licensee or a registrant, or the operation of a pharmacy, the board shall consider:

(1) the nature and seriousness of the crime;

(2) the relationship of the crime to the purposes for requiring a license or registration to engage in the occupation of the licensee or registrant, or the operation of a pharmacy;

(3) the extent to which a license or registration might afford the licensee or registrant an opportunity to repeat the criminal activity in which the person had been involved; and

(4) the relationship of the crime to the ability, capacity, or fitness required to perform the duties and discharge the responsibilities of the licensee or registrant.

(g) The board has the authority to impose disciplinary action as authorized by the Act, for those criminal offenses that provide grounds for discipline under the Act. In reaching a decision regarding the severity of the disciplinary sanction to impose on a license or registration, the board shall, in its discretion and unless otherwise specified in § 281.64 of this title (relating to Sanctions for Criminal Offenses), also determine the person's fitness to perform the duties and discharge the responsibilities of a licensee or registrant by evaluating and balancing these factors in the following priority with the first being the highest priority:

(1) the extent and nature of the person's past criminal activity;

(2) the amount of time that has elapsed since the person's last criminal activity;

(3) the person's rehabilitation or rehabilitative effort while incarcerated or following release as corroborated by extrinsic evidence;

(4) the age of the person at the time of the commission of the crime, if younger than 21 years of age at the time of the crime;

(5) the conduct and work activity of the person prior to and following the criminal activity; and

(6) other evidence of the person's present fitness, including letters of recommendation from:

    (A) prosecution, law enforcement, and correctional officers who prosecuted, arrested, or had custodial responsibility for the person;

    (B) the sheriff and chief of police in the community where the person resides; and

    (C) any other persons in contact with the person.

(h) In order to establish the factors in subsection (g) of this section, a person with a conviction or deferred adjudication shall:

(1) to the extent possible, secure and provide to the board the recommendations of the prosecution, law enforcement, and correctional authorities specified in subsection (g)(6) of this section;

(2) cooperate with the board by providing the information required by this section, including proof that he or she has:

    (A) maintained a record of steady employment, as evidenced by salary stubs, income tax records or other employment records for the time since the conviction or deferred adjudication and/or release from imprisonment;

    (B) supported his or her dependents, as evidenced by salary stubs, income tax records or other employment records for the time since the conviction or deferred adjudication and/or release from imprisonment, and a recommendation from the spouse or either parent;

    (C) maintained a record of good conduct as evidenced by recommendations, absence of other criminal activity or documentation of community service since conviction or deferred adjudication;

    (D) paid all outstanding court costs, supervision fees, fines, and restitution as may have been ordered in all criminal cases in which he or she has been convicted, as evidenced by certified copies of a court release or other documentation from the court system that all monies have been paid; and

    (E) obtained appropriate treatment and/or counseling, if applicable.

(i) The board has determined that the following crimes directly relate to duties and responsibilities of board licensees or registrants. The commission of each indicates an inability or a tendency for the person to be unable to perform or to be unfit for licensure or registration, because commission of such crimes indicates a lack of integrity and respect for one's fellow human being and the community at large. Even if the commission of these crimes did not occur while the licensee or registrant was on-duty or employed at a pharmacy, the board has determined that the crimes directly relate to the practice of pharmacy based on a lack of integrity and good moral character exhibited by the commission of the crimes. In addition, the direct relationship to a license or registration is presumed when any crime occurs in connection with the practice of pharmacy or the operation of a pharmacy. The crimes are as follows:

(1) practicing or operating a pharmacy without a license or registration and other violations of the Pharmacy Act;

(2) deceptive business practices under the Texas Penal Code;

(3) Medicare or Medicaid fraud;

(4) a misdemeanor or felony offense under the Texas Penal Code involving:

    (A) murder;

    (B) assault;

    (C) burglary;

    (D) robbery;

    (E) theft;

    (F) sexual assault;

    (G) injury to a child;

    (H) injury to an elderly person;

    (I) child abuse or neglect;

    (J) tampering with a governmental record;

    (K) forgery;

    (L) perjury;

    (M) failure to report abuse;

    (N) bribery;

    (O) harassment;

    (P) insurance claim fraud;

    (Q) driving while intoxicated;

    (R) solicitation of professional employment under the *Penal Code § 38.12(d)* or Occupations Code, Chapter 102;

(S)   mail fraud; or

(T)   any criminal offense which requires the individual to register with the Department of Public Safety as a sex offender under Chapter 62, Code of Criminal Procedure.

(5)   any crime of moral turpitude;

(6)   a misdemeanor or felony offense under Chapters 431 and 481 through 486, Health and Safety Code and the Comprehensive Drug Abuse Prevention and Control Act of 1970; or

(7)   other misdemeanors or felonies which serve as grounds for discipline under the Act, including violations of the Penal Code, Titles 4, 5, 6, 7, 8, 9, and 10, which indicate an inability or tendency for the person to be unable to perform as a licensee or registrant, or to be unfit for licensure or registration, if action by the board will promote the intent of the Pharmacy Act, board rules including this chapter, and Occupations Code, Chapter 53.

Source: The provisions of this §281.63 adopted to be effective September 3, 2006, 31 TexReg 6722; amended to be effective March 25, 2007, 32 TexReg 1508; amended to be effective June 8, 2008, 33 TexReg 4304; amended to be effective September 7, 2009, 34 TexReg 7218; amended to be effective December 7, 2010, 35 TexReg 10689; amended to be effective September 8, 2013, 38 TexReg 5721

§281.64 Sanctions for Criminal Offenses

(a)   The guidelines for disciplinary sanctions apply to criminal convictions and to deferred adjudication community supervisions or deferred dispositions, as authorized by the Act, for all types of licensees and registrants including applicants for such licenses and registrations issued by the board. The board considers criminal behavior to be highly relevant to an individual's fitness to engage in pharmacy practice and has determined that the sanctions imposed by these guidelines promote the intent of § 551.002 of the Act. The "date of disposition," when referring to the number of years used to calculate the application of disciplinary sanctions, refers to the date a conviction, a deferred adjudication, or a deferred disposition is entered by the court. The use of the term "currently on probation" is construed to refer to individuals currently serving community supervision or any other type of probationary term imposed by an order of a court for a conviction, deferred adjudication, or deferred disposition.

(b)   The sanctions imposed by the guidelines can be used in conjunction with other types of disciplinary actions, including administrative penalties, as outlined in this section.

(c)   The board has determined that the nature and seriousness of certain crimes outweigh other factors to be considered in § 281.63(g) of this title (relating to Considerations for Criminal Offenses) and necessitate the disciplinary action listed in paragraphs (1) – (3) of this subsection. In regard to the crimes enumerated in this rule, the board has weighed the factors, which are required to be considered from § 281.63(g) of this title, in a light most favorable to the individual, and even if these factors were present, the board has concluded that the following sanctions apply to individuals with the criminal offenses as described in paragraphs (1) – (3) of this subsection:

(1)   Criminal offenses which require the individual to register with the Department of Public Safety as a sex offender under Chapter 62, Code of Criminal Procedure—denial or revocation;

(2)   Felony offenses:

(A)   Drug-related offenses, such as those listed in Chapter 481 or 483, Health and Safety Code:

(i)   Offenses involving manufacture, delivery, possession with intent to deliver, or illegal dispensing:

(I)   Currently on probation—denial or revocation;

(II)   0–5 years since date of disposition—denial or revocation;

(III) 6–10 years since date of disposition—denial or revocation;

(IV)   11–20 years since date of disposition—5 years probation;

(V)   Over 20 years since date of disposition—3 years probation;

(ii)   Offenses involving possession of drugs, fraudulent prescriptions, theft of drugs, or alcohol:

(I)   If the offense involved only the personal use of the drugs or alcohol and/or chemical impairment:

(-a-) Currently on probation—90-day to one-year suspension followed by 5 years probation;

(-b-) 0–5 years since date of disposition—5 years probation;

(-c-) 6–10 years since date of disposition—3 years probation;

(-d-) 11–20 years since date of disposition—1 year probation; or

(II)   Otherwise:

(-a-) Currently on probation—denial or revocation;

(-b-) 0–5 years since date of disposition—denial or one-year suspension followed by 5 years probation;

(-c-) 6–10 years since date of disposition—180-day suspension followed by 5 years probation;

(-d-) 11–20 years since date of disposition—3 years probation;

(-e-) Over 20 years since date of disposition—1 year probation;

(B)   Offenses involving sexual contact or violent acts, or offenses considered to be felonies of the first degree under the Texas Penal Code:

(i)   Currently on probation—denial or revocation;

(ii)   0–5 years since date of disposition—denial or revocation;

(iii) 6–10 years since date of disposition—denial or revocation;

(iv)   11–20 years since date of disposition—5 years probation;

(v)   Over 20 years since date of disposition—1 year probation;

(C)   Other felony offenses:

(i)   Currently on probation—denial, revocation, or 30- to 180-day suspension followed by 5 years probation;

(ii)   0–5 years since date of disposition—5 years probation;

(iii) 6–10 years since date of disposition—3 years probation;

(iv)   11–20 years since date of disposition—1 year probation;

(3)   Misdemeanor offenses:

(A)   Drug-related offenses, such as those listed in Chapter 481 or 483, Health and Safety Code:

(i)   Offenses involving manufacture, delivery, or possession with intent to deliver:

          (I)   Currently on probation—denial or revocation;

          (II) 0–10 years since date of disposition—30- to 180-day suspension followed by 5 years probation;

          (III) 11–20 years since date of disposition—1 year probation;

     (ii) Offenses involving possession of drugs, fraudulent prescriptions, or theft of drugs:

          (I)   Pharmacists:

             (-a-) 0–5 years since date of disposition—5 years probation;

             (-b-) 6–10 years since date of disposition—3 years probation;

          (II) Pharmacy Technicians and Pharmacy Technician Trainees:

             (-a-) 0–5 years since date of disposition and offense determined to be in violation of § 568.003(a)(5) or (9) of the Act—5 years probation;

             (-b-) 0 5 years since date of disposition and determined not to be in violation of § 568.003(a)(5) or (9) of the Act—1 year probation;

             (-c-) 6–10 years since date of disposition and offense determined to be in violation of § 568.003(a)(5) or (9) of the Act—3 years probation;

          (III) If 0-5 years since date of disposition, and the offense did not involve only personal use of the drugs and/or chemical impairment, an additional 30- to 90-day suspension will be imposed preceding the probation for the offenses in this clause;

    (B) Intoxication and alcoholic beverage offenses as defined in the Texas Penal Code, if two such offenses involving intoxication due to ingestion of alcohol occurred in the previous five years or if one such offense involving intoxication due to ingestion of controlled substances or dangerous drugs occurred in the previous five years:

     (i)   Pharmacists: 0-5 years since date of disposition and offense determined to be in violation of § 565.001(a)(4) or (7) of the Act—5 years probation;

     (ii) Pharmacy Technicians and Pharmacy Technician Trainees: 0-5 years since date of disposition and offense determined to be in violation of § 568.003(a)(5) or (9) of the Act—5 years probation;

    (C) Other misdemeanor offenses involving moral turpitude: 0-5 years since date of disposition—reprimand.

(d) When an individual has multiple criminal offenses or other violations, the board shall consider imposing additional more severe types of disciplinary sanctions, as deemed necessary.

(e) An individual who suffers from an impairment as described by § 565.001(a)(4) or (7) or § 568.003(a)(5) or (9), may provide mitigating information including treatment, counseling, and monitoring in order to mitigate the sanctions imposed.

Source: The provisions of this § 281.64 adopted to be effective September 3, 2006, 31 TexReg 6722; amended to be effective March 25, 2007, 32 TexReg 1508; amended to be effective March 6, 2008, 33 TexReg 1783; amended to be effective June 8, 2008, 33 TexReg 4304; amended to be effective September 7, 2008, 33 TexReg 7218; amended to be effective May 30, 2010, 35 TexReg 4164; amended to be effective September 14, 2010, 35 TexReg 8356; amended to be effective December 7, 2010, 35 TexReg 10689; amended to be effective June 7, 2012, 37 TexReg 4046; amended to be effective September 9, 2012, 37 TexReg 6916; amended to be effective June 19,2014, 39 TexReg 4655

§281.65 Schedule of Administrative Penalties

The board has determined that the assessment of an administrative penalty promotes the intent of § 551.002 of the Act. In disciplinary matters, the board may assess an administrative penalty in addition to any other disciplinary action in the circumstances and amounts as follows:

(1) The following violations by a pharmacist may be appropriate for disposition with an administrative penalty with or without additional sanctions or restrictions:

    (A) failing to provide patient counseling: $ 1,000;

    (B) failing to conduct a drug regimen review or inappropriate drug regimen reviews provided by § 291.33(c)(2)(A) of this title (relating to Operational Standards): $ 1,000;

    (C) failing to clarify a prescription with the prescriber: $ 1,000;

    (D) failing to properly supervise or improperly delegating a duty to a pharmacy technician: $ 1,000;

    (E) failing to identify the dispensing pharmacist on required pharmacy records: $ 500;

    (F) failing to maintain records of prescriptions: $ 500;

    (G) failing to respond or failing to provide all requested records within the time specified in a board audit of continuing education records: $ 100 per hour of continuing education credit not provided;

    (H) failing to provide or providing false or fraudulent information on any application, notification, or other document required under this Act, the Dangerous Drug Act, or Controlled Substances Act, or rules adopted pursuant to those Acts: $ 1,000;

    (I) dispensing a prescription drug pursuant to a forged, altered, or fraudulent prescription: up to $ 5,000;

    (J) dispensing unauthorized prescriptions: up to $ 5,000;

    (K) dispensing controlled substances or dangerous drugs to an individual or individuals in quantities, dosages, or for periods of time which grossly exceed standards of practice, approved labeling of the federal Food and Drug Administration, or the guidelines published in professional literature: up to $ 5,000;

    (L) violating a disciplinary order of the Board or a contract under the program to aid impaired pharmacists or pharmacy students under Chapter 564 of the Act: $ 500;

    (M) failing to report or to assure the report of a malpractice claim: $ 1,000;

    (N) practicing pharmacy with a delinquent license: $ 500;

    (O) operating a pharmacy with a delinquent license: $ 1,000;

    (P) allowing an individual to perform the duties of a pharmacy technician without a valid registration: $ 1,000;

    (Q) aiding and abetting the unlicensed practice of pharmacy, if the pharmacist knew or reasonably should have known that the person was unlicensed at the time: $ 2,500;

    (R) unauthorized substitutions: $ 1,000;

    (S) submitting false or fraudulent claims to third parties for reimbursement of pharmacy services: $ 1,000;

(T)   selling, purchasing, or trading, or offering to sell, purchase, or trade of misbranded prescription drugs or prescription drugs beyond the manufacturer's expiration date: $ 1,000;

(U)   selling, purchasing, or trading, or offering to sell, purchase, or trade of prescription drug samples as provided by § 281.7(a)(27) of this title (relating to Grounds for Discipline for a Pharmacist License): $ 1,000;

(V)   failing to keep, maintain or furnish an annual inventory as required by § 291.17 of this title (relating to Inventory Requirements): $ 1,000;

(W)   failing to obtain training on the preparation of sterile pharmaceutical compounding: $ 1,000;

(X)   failing to maintain the confidentiality of prescription records: $ 1,000;

(Y)   failing to inform the board of any notification or information required to be reported by the Act or rules: $ 500;

(Z)   failing to operate a pharmacy as provided by § 291.11 of this title (relating to Operation of a Pharmacy): $ 1,000; and

(AA) accessing information submitted to the Prescription Monitoring Program in violation of § 481.076 of the Controlled Substances Act: $ 1,000 - $ 2,500,

(2)   The following violations by a pharmacy may be appropriate for disposition with an administrative penalty with or without additional sanctions or restrictions:

(A)   failing to provide patient counseling: $ 1,500;

(B)   failing to conduct a drug regimen review or inappropriate drug regimen reviews provided by § 291.33(c)(2)(A) of this title: $ 1,500;

(C)   failing to clarify a prescription with the prescriber: $ 1,500;

(D)   failing to properly supervise or improperly delegating a duty to a pharmacy technician: $ 1,500;

(E)   failing to identify the dispensing pharmacist on required pharmacy records: $ 500;

(F)   failing to maintain records of prescriptions: $ 500;

(G)   failing to provide or providing false or fraudulent information on any application, notification, or other document required under this Act, the Dangerous Drug Act, or Controlled Substances Act, or rules adopted pursuant to those Acts: $ 1,000;

(H)   following an accountability audit, shortages of prescription drugs: dependent on the quantity involved with a minimum of $ 1,000;

(I)   dispensing a prescription drug pursuant to a forged, altered, or fraudulent prescription: up to $ 5,000;

(J)   dispensing unauthorized prescriptions: up to $ 5,000;

(K)   dispensing controlled substances or dangerous drugs to an individual or individuals in quantities, dosages, or for periods of time which grossly exceed standards of practice, approved labeling of the federal Food and Drug Administration, or the guidelines published in professional literature: up to $ 5,000;

(L)   violating a disciplinary order of the Board: $ 1,000;

(M)   failing to report or to assure the report of a malpractice claim: $ 1,500;

(N)   allowing a pharmacist to practice pharmacy with a delinquent license: $ 1,000;

(O)   operating a pharmacy with a delinquent license: $ 1,000;

(P)   allowing an individual to perform the duties of a pharmacy technician without a valid registration: $ 3,000;

(Q)   failing to comply with the reporting requirements to the Prescription Monitoring Program: $ 1,000;

(R)   aiding and abetting the unlicensed practice of pharmacy, if an employee of the pharmacy knew or reasonably should have known that the person engaging in the practice of pharmacy was unlicensed at the time: $ 5,000;

(S)   unauthorized substitutions: $ 1,000;

(T)   submitting false or fraudulent claims to third parties for reimbursement of pharmacy services: $ 1,000;

(U)   possessing or engaging in the sale, purchase, or trade or the offer to sell, purchase, or trade of misbranded prescription drugs or prescription drugs beyond the manufacturer's expiration date: $ 1,000;

(V)   possessing or engaging in the sale, purchase, or trade or the offer to sell, purchase, or trade of prescription drug samples as provided by § 281.8(b)(2) of this title (relating to Grounds for Discipline for a Pharmacy License): $ 1,000;

(W)   failing to keep, maintain or furnish an annual inventory as required by § 291.17 of this title: $ 2,500;

(X)   failing to obtain training on the preparation of sterile pharmaceutical compounding: $ 2,000;

(Y)   failing to maintain the confidentiality of prescription records: $ 1,000;

(Z)   failing to inform the board of any notification or information required to be reported by the Act or rules: $ 1,000;

(AA) failing to operate a pharmacy as specified in § 291.11 of this title: $ 3,000; and

(BB) operating a Class E or Class E-S pharmacy without a Texas licensed pharmacist-in-charge: $ 1,000.

(3)   The following violations by a pharmacy technician may be appropriate for disposition with an administrative penalty with or without additional sanctions or restrictions:

(A)   failing to respond or failing to provide all requested records within the time specified in a board audit of continuing education records: $ 30 per hour of continuing education credit not provided;

(B)   failing to provide or providing false or fraudulent information on any application, notification, or other document required under this Act, the Dangerous Drug Act, or Controlled Substances Act, or rules adopted pursuant to those Acts: $ 500;

(C)   violating a disciplinary Order of the Board: $ 250;

(D)   performing the duties of a pharmacy technician without a valid registration: $ 250;

(E)   failing to obtain training on the preparation of sterile pharmaceutical compounding: $ 500;

(F)   failing to maintain the confidentiality of prescription records: $ 500;

(G)   failing to inform the board of any notification or information required to be reported by the Act or rules: $ 250; and

(H)   accessing information submitted to the Prescription Monitoring Program in violation of § 481.076 of the Controlled Substances Act: $ 500 - $ 2,000.

(4)   Any of the violations listed in this section may be appropriate for disposition by the administrative penalties in this section in conjunction with any other penalties in § 281.61 of this title (relating to Definitions of Discipline Authorized).

(5)   Each day a violation continues or occurs is a separate violation for purposes of imposing a penalty or fine.

(6) The amount, to the extent possible, shall be based on:
  (A) the seriousness of the violation, including the nature, circumstances, extent, and gravity of any prohibited act, and the hazard or potential hazard created to the health, safety, or economic welfare of the public;
  (B) the aggravating and mitigating factors in § 281.62 of this title (relating to Aggravating and Mitigating Factors);
  (C) the amount necessary to deter a future violation; and
  (D) any other matter that justice may require.

Source: The provisions of this § 281.65 adopted to be effective September 3, 2006, 31 TexReg 6722; amended to be effective September 7, 2008, 33 TexReg 7218; amended to be effective June 7, 2009, 34 TexReg 3390; amended to be effective December 6, 2009, 34 TexReg 8690; amended to be effective December 19, 2016, 41 TexReg 9933; amended to be effective June 11, 2017, 42 TexReg 2928; amended to be effective December 6, 2018, 43 TexReg 7770

§281.66 Application for Reissuance or Removal of Restrictions of a License or Registration

(a) A person whose pharmacy license, pharmacy technician registration, or license or registration to practice pharmacy has been canceled, revoked, or restricted, whether voluntary or by action of the board, may, after 12 months from the effective date of such cancellation, revocation, or restriction, apply to the board for reinstatement or removal of the restriction of the license or registration.
  (1) The application shall be given under oath and on the form prescribed by the board.
  (2) A person applying for reinstatement or removal of restrictions may be required to meet all requirements necessary in order for the board to access the criminal history record information, including submitting fingerprint information and being responsible for all associated costs.
  (3) A person applying for reinstatement or removal of restrictions has the burden of proof.
  (4) On investigation and hearing, the board may in its discretion grant or deny the application or it may modify its original finding to reflect any circumstances that have changed sufficiently to warrant the modification.
  (5) If such application is denied by the board, a subsequent application may not be considered by the board until 12 months from the date of denial of the previous application.
  (6) The board in its discretion may require a person to pass an examination or examinations to reenter the practice of pharmacy.
  (7) The fee for reinstatement of a license or registration shall be $ 100 which is to be paid to the Texas State Board of Pharmacy and includes the processing of the reinstatement application.
(b) In reinstatement cases not involving criminal offenses, the board may consider the following items in determining the reinstatement of an applicant's previously revoked or canceled license or registration:
  (1) moral character in the community;
  (2) employment history;
  (3) financial support to his/her family;
  (4) participation in continuing education programs or other methods of maintaining currency with the practice of pharmacy;
  (5) criminal history record, including arrests, indictments, and convictions relating to felonies or misdemeanors involving moral turpitude;
  (6) offers of employment in pharmacy;
  (7) involvement in public service activities in the community;
  (8) failure to comply with the provisions of the board order revoking or canceling the applicant's license or registration;
  (9) action by other state or federal regulatory agencies;
  (10) any physical, chemical, emotional, or mental impairment;
  (11) the gravity of the offense for which the applicant's license or registration was canceled, revoked, or restricted and the impact the offense had upon the public health, safety and welfare;
  (12) the length of time since the applicant's license or registration was canceled, revoked or restricted, as a factor in determining whether the time period has been sufficient for the applicant to have rehabilitated himself/herself to be able to practice pharmacy in a manner consistent with the public health, safety and welfare;
  (13) competency to engage in the practice of pharmacy; or
  (14) other rehabilitation actions taken by the applicant.
(c) If a reinstatement case involves criminal offenses, the sanctions specified in § 281.64 of this chapter (relating to Sanctions for Criminal Offenses) apply.

Source: The provisions of this § 281.66 adopted to be effective March 25, 2007, 32 TexReg 1508; amended to be effective December 14, 2008, 33 TexReg 10026; amended to be effective December 6, 2009, 34 TexReg 8690; amended to be effective September 14, 2010, 35 TexReg 8356; amended to be effective September 8, 2013, 38 TexReg 5721; amended to be effective September 11, 2016, 41 TexReg 6696

§281.67 Sanctions for Out-of-State Disciplinary Actions

(a) When determining the appropriate sanction for a disciplinary action taken by a regulatory board of another state under § 565.001(a)(16), § 565.002(a)(13), or § 568.003(a)(13), the board has determined that the following shall be applicable for all types of licensees and registrants for such licenses and registrations issued by the board.
  (1) If the other state's disciplinary action resulted in the license or registration being restricted, suspended, revoked, or surrendered, the appropriate sanction shall be the same as the sanction imposed by the other state, such that the licensee or registrant has the same restriction against practice in Texas.
  (2) If the license or registration is subject to any other type of disciplinary sanctions, the appropriate sanction shall be equivalent to or less than that imposed by the other state unless contrary to board policy.
(b) The sanctions imposed by this chapter can be used in conjunction with other types of disciplinary actions, including administrative penalties, as outlined in this chapter.
(c) When a licensee or registrant has additional violations of the Texas Pharmacy Act, the board shall consider imposing additional more severe types of disciplinary sanctions, as deemed necessary.

Source: The provisions of this § 281.67 adopted to be effective June 7, 2012, 37 TexReg 4046; amended to be effective September 8, 2013, 38 TexReg 5721

§281.68 Remedial Plan

(a) The board may issue a remedial plan by agreement with the respondent to resolve the investigation of a complaint relating to the Act unless the complaint involves:

  (1) a death;

  (2) a hospitalization;

  (3) the commission of a felony;

  (4) the unlicensed practice of a licensee or registrant;

  (5) audit shortages;

  (6) diversion of controlled substances;

  (7) impairment by chemical abuse or mental or physical illness of a licensee or registrant;

  (8) unauthorized dispensing of a prescription drug;

  (9) gross immorality as defined by the board·

  (10) engaging in fraud, deceit, or misrepresentation as defined by board rule;

  (11) disciplinary action by another regulatory board of this state or another state; or

  (12) any other matter determined by the board.

(b) The board shall not impose a remedial plan if the appropriate resolution of the complaint involves a restriction on the manner in which a license holder practices pharmacy.

(c) The board may not issue a remedial plan to resolve a complaint against a license holder if the license holder has entered into a remedial plan with the board in the preceding 24 months for the resolution of a different complaint relating to this subtitle.

(d) If a license holder complies with and successfully completes the terms of a remedial plan, the board shall remove all records of the remedial plan from the board's records at the end of the fiscal year in which the fifth anniversary of the date the board issued the terms of the remedial plan occurs in accordance with § 565.060 of the Act.

(e) The board may assess a fee against a license holder participating in a remedial plan in the amount of $ 1,000 to recover the costs of administering the plan.

The provisions of this § 281.68 adopted to be effective December 10, 2013, 38 TexReg 8834; amended to be effective March 12, 2019, 44 TexReg 1316

CHAPTER 283. LICENSING REQUIREMENTS FOR PHARMACISTS

§283.1   Purpose

The purpose of this chapter is to provide a comprehensive, coherent regulatory scheme for the licensing of individuals wishing to engage in the practice of pharmacy in this state. The provisions of this chapter govern in conjunction with the Texas Pharmacy Act (Chapters 551 – 566, and 568 – 569, Occupations Code, as amended) the method for the issuance of a certificate to act as a pharmacist in Texas. This chapter also provides a framework for any board-approved internship program.

Source: The provisions of this §283.1 adopted to be effective February 17, 1988, 13 TexReg 610; amended to be effective June 13, 2002, 27 TexReg 4947; amended to be effective June 8, 2008, 33 TexReg 4304

§283.2   Definitions

The following words and terms, when used in this chapter, shall have the following meanings, unless the context clearly indicates otherwise.

  (1) ACPE—Accreditation Council for Pharmacy Education.

  (2) Applicant—An individual having applied for licensure to act as a pharmacist in Texas.

  (3) Approved continuing education—Continuing education which meets the requirements of § 295.8 of this title (relating to Continuing Education Requirements).

  (4) Board—The Texas State Board of Pharmacy; all members, divisions, departments, sections, and employees thereof.

  (5) College/School of pharmacy—A college/school of pharmacy whose professional degree program has been approved by the board and is either accredited by:

    (A) ACPE; or

    (B) the Canadian Council for Accreditation of Pharmacy Programs for 1993 – 2004 graduates.

  (6) Competency—A demonstrated state of preparedness for the realities of professional pharmacy practice.

  (7) Didactic—Systematic classroom instruction.

  (8) Direct supervision—A pharmacist preceptor or healthcare professional preceptor is physically present and on-site at the licensed location of the pharmacy where the pharmacist-intern is performing pharmacist-intern duties.

  (9) Extended-intern—An intern, registered with the board, who has:

    (A) applied to the board for licensure by examination and has successfully passed the NAPLEX and Texas Pharmacy Jurisprudence Examination but lacks the required number of hours of internship for licensure; or

    (B) applied to the board to take the NAPLEX and Texas Pharmacy Jurisprudence Examinations within six calendar months after graduation and has either:

      (i) graduated and received a professional degree from a college/school of pharmacy; or

      (ii) completed all of the requirements for graduation and for receipt of a professional degree from a college/school of pharmacy; or

    (C) applied to the board to take the NAPLEX and Texas Pharmacy Jurisprudence Examinations within six calendar months after obtaining full certification from the Foreign Pharmacy Graduate Equivalency Commission; or

    (D) applied to the Board for re-issuance of a pharmacist license which has been expired for more than two years but less than ten years and has successfully passed the Texas Pharmacy Jurisprudence Examination, but lacks the required number of hours of internship or continuing education required for licensure; or

    (E) been ordered by the Board to complete an internship.

(10) Foreign pharmacy graduate—An individual whose pharmacy degree was conferred by a pharmacy school whose professional degree program has not been accredited by ACPE and approved by the board. An individual whose pharmacy degree was conferred by a pharmacy school that was accredited by the Canadian Council for Accreditation of Pharmacy Programs between 1993 and 2004, inclusively, is not considered a foreign pharmacy graduate.

(11) FPGEC—The Foreign Pharmacy Graduate Equivalency Commission.

(12) Healthcare Professional—An individual licensed as:

   (A) a physician, dentist, podiatrist, veterinarian, advanced practice registered nurse, or physician assistant in Texas or another state; or

   (B) a pharmacist in a state other than Texas but not licensed in Texas.

(13) Healthcare Professional Preceptor—A healthcare professional serving as an instructor for a Texas college/school-based internship program who is recognized by a Texas college/school of pharmacy to supervise and be responsible for the activities and functions of a student-intern or intern-trainee in the internship program

(14) Intern-trainee—An individual registered with the board, who is enrolled in the first year of the professional sequence of a Texas college/school of pharmacy and who may only work during times and in sites assigned by a Texas college/school of pharmacy.

(15) Internship—A practical experience program that is approved by the board.

(16) MPJE—Multistate Pharmacy Jurisprudence Examination.

(17) NABP—The National Association of Boards of Pharmacy.

(18) NAPLEX—The North American Pharmacy Licensing Examination, or its predecessor, the National Association of Boards of Pharmacy Licensing Examination.

(19) Pharmaceutical care—The provision of drug therapy and other pharmaceutical services defined in the rules of the board and intended to assist in the cure or prevention of a disease, elimination or reduction of a patient's symptoms, or arresting or slowing of a disease process.

(20) Pharmacist-intern—An intern-trainee, a student-intern, a resident-intern, or an extended-intern who is participating in a board approved internship program.

(21) Pharmacist Preceptor—A pharmacist licensed in Texas to practice pharmacy who meets the requirements under board rules and is recognized by the board to supervise and be responsible for the activities and functions of a pharmacist-intern in an internship program.

(22) Resident-intern—An individual who is registered with the board and:

   (A) has graduated from a college/school of pharmacy; and

   (B) is completing a residency program in the state of Texas accredited by the American Society of Health-System Pharmacists.

(23) Preceptor—A pharmacist preceptor or a healthcare professional preceptor.

(24) Professional degree—A bachelor of science degree in pharmacy or a doctorate of pharmacy degree.

(25) State—One of the 50 United States of America, the District of Columbia, and Puerto Rico.

(26) Student-intern—An individual registered with the board who is enrolled in the professional sequence of a college/school of pharmacy, has completed the first professional year and obtained a minimum of 30 credit hours of work towards a professional degree in pharmacy, and is participating in a board-approved internship program.

(27) Texas Pharmacy Jurisprudence Examination—A licensing exam developed or approved by the Board which evaluates an applicant's knowledge of the drug and pharmacy requirements to practice pharmacy legally in the state of Texas.

Source: The provisions of this § 283.2 adopted to be effective February 17, 1988, 13 TEXREG 610; amended to be effective November 7, 1989, 14 TEXREG 5687; amended to be effective March 19, 1990, 15 TEXREG 1234; amended to be effective June 15, 1990, 15 TEXREG 3334; amended to be effective June 1, 1994, 19 TexReg 3920; amended to be effective February 1, 1996, 21 TexReg 110; amended to be effective December 31, 1996, 21 TexReg 12297; amended to be effective March 19, 1998, 23 TexReg 2814; amended to be effective December 27, 2000, 25 TexReg 12689; amended to be effective June 11, 2006, 31 TexReg 4628; amended to be effective June 8, 2008, 33 TexReg 4304; amended to be effective March 13, 2012, 37 TexReg 1705; amended to be effective December 6, 2015, 40 TexReg 8763; amended to be effective March 10, 2016, 41 TexReg 1689

§283.3 Educational and Age Requirements

An applicant for licensure as a pharmacist shall provide satisfactory evidence that the age of 18 years has been obtained and shall meet one of the following requirements:

   (1) have graduated and received a professional degree from a college of pharmacy; or

   (2) have graduated from a foreign college of pharmacy and obtained full certification from the FPGEC.

Source: The provisions of this § 283.3 adopted to be effective February 17, 1988, 13 TEXREG 610; amended to be effective December 31, 1996, 21 TexReg 12297; amended to be effective March 13, 2012, 37 TexReg 1705; amended to be effective March 7, 2018, 43 TexReg 1278

§283.4 Internship Requirements

(a) Goals and competency objectives of internship.

   (1) The goal of internship is for the pharmacist-intern to attain the knowledge, skills, and abilities to safely, efficiently, and effectively provide pharmacist-delivered patient care to a diverse patient population and practice pharmacy under the laws and regulations of the State of Texas.

   (2) The following competency objectives are necessary to accomplish the goal of internship in paragraph (1) of this subsection.

   (A) Provides drug products. The pharmacist-intern shall demonstrate competence in determining the appropriateness of prescription drug orders and medication orders; evaluating and selecting products; and assuring the accuracy of the product/prescription dispensing process.

   (B) Communicates with patients and/or patients' agents about prescription drugs. The pharmacist-intern shall demonstrate competence in interviewing and counseling patients, and/or the patients' agents, on drug usage, dosage, packaging, routes of administration, intended drug use, and storage; discussing drug cautions, adverse effects, and patient conditions; explaining policies on fees and services; relating to patients in a professional manner; and interacting to confirm patient understanding.

   (C) Communicates with patients and/or patients' agents about nonprescription products, devices, dietary supplements, diet, nutrition, traditional nondrug therapies, complementary and alternative therapies, and diagnostic aids. The pharmacist-intern shall demonstrate competence in interviewing and counseling patients and/or patients' agents on conditions, intended drug use, and adverse effects; assisting in and recommending drug selection; triaging and assessing the need for treatment or referral, including referral for a patient seeking pharmacist-guided self-care; providing information on medical/surgical devices and home diagnostic products; and providing poison control treatment information and referral.

(D) Communicates with healthcare professionals and patients and/or patients' agents. The pharmacist-intern shall demonstrate competence in obtaining and providing accurate and concise information in a professional manner and using appropriate oral, written, and nonverbal language.

(E) Practices as a member of the patient's interdisciplinary healthcare team. The pharmacist-intern shall demonstrate competence in collaborating with physicians, other healthcare professionals, patients, and/or patients' agents to formulate a therapeutic plan. The pharmacist-intern shall demonstrate competence in establishing and interpreting data-bases, identifying drug-related problems and recommending appropriate pharmacotherapy specific to patient needs, monitoring and evaluating patient outcomes, and devising follow-up plans.

(F) Maintains professional-ethical standards. The pharmacist-intern is required to comply with laws and regulations pertaining to pharmacy practice; to apply professional judgment; to exhibit reliability and credibility in dealing with others; to deal professionally and ethically with colleagues and patients; to demonstrate sensitivity and empathy for patients/care givers; and to maintain confidentiality.

(G) Compounds. The pharmacist-intern shall demonstrate competence in using acceptable professional procedures; selecting appropriate equipment and containers; appropriately preparing compounded non-sterile and sterile preparations; and documenting calculations and procedures. Pharmacist-interns engaged in compounding non-sterile preparations shall meet the training requirements for pharmacists specified in § 291.131 of this title (relating to Pharmacies Compounding Non-sterile Preparations). Pharmacist-interns engaged in compounding sterile preparations shall meet the training requirements for pharmacists specified in § 291.133 of this title (relating to Pharmacies Compounding Sterile Preparations).

(H) Retrieves and evaluates drug information. The pharmacist-intern shall demonstrate competence in retrieving, evaluating, managing, and using the best available clinical and scientific publications for answering a drug-related request in a timely fashion and assessing, evaluating, and applying evidence based information to promote optimal health care. The pharmacist-intern shall perform investigations on relevant topics in order to promote inquiry and problem-solving with dissemination of findings to the healthcare community and/or the public.

(I) Manages general pharmacy operations. The pharmacist-intern shall develop a general understanding of planning, personnel and fiscal management, leadership skills, and policy development. The pharmacist-intern shall have an understanding of drug security, storage and control procedures and the regulatory requirements associated with these procedures, and maintaining quality assurance and performance improvement. The pharmacist-intern shall observe and document discrepancies and irregularities, keep accurate records and document actions. The pharmacist-intern shall attend meetings requiring pharmacy representation.

(J) Participates in public health, community service or professional activities. The pharmacist-intern shall develop basic knowledge and skills needed to become an effective healthcare educator and a responsible participant in civic and professional organizations.

(K) Demonstrates scientific inquiry. The pharmacist-intern shall develop skills to expand and/or refine knowledge in the areas of pharmaceutical and medical sciences or pharmaceutical services. This may include data analysis of scientific, clinical, sociological, and/or economic impacts of pharmaceuticals (including investigational drugs), pharmaceutical care, and patient behaviors, with dissemination of findings to the scientific community and/or the public.

(b) Hours requirement.
(1) The board requires 1,500 hours of internship for licensure. These hours may be obtained through one or more of the following methods:
    (A) in a board approved student internship program, as specified in subsection (c) of this section;
    (B) in a board-approved extended-internship program as specified in subsection (d) of this section; and/or
    (C) graduation from a college/school of pharmacy after July 1, 2007. Persons graduating from such programs shall be credited 1,500 hours or the number of hours actually obtained and reported by the college; and/or
    (D) internship hours approved and certified to the board by another state board of pharmacy.
(2) Pharmacist-interns participating in an internship may be credited no more than 50 hours per week of internship experience.
(3) Internship hours may be used for the purpose of licensure for no longer than two years from the date the internship is completed.
(c) College-/School-Based Internship Programs.
(1) Internship experience acquired by student-interns.
    (A) An individual may be designated a student-intern provided he/she:
        (i) submits an application to the board that includes the following information:
            (I) name;
            (II) addresses, phone numbers, date of birth, and social security number;
            (III) college of pharmacy and expected graduation date; and
            (IV) any other information requested on the application;
        (ii) is enrolled in the professional sequence of a college/school of pharmacy;
        (iii) has successfully completed the first professional year and obtained a minimum of 30 credit hours of work towards a professional degree in pharmacy; and
        (iv) has met all requirements necessary for the board to access the criminal history records information, including submitting fingerprint information and being responsible for all associated costs.
    (B) The terms of the student internship shall be as follows.
        (i) The student internship shall be gained concurrent with college attendance, which may include:
            (I) partial semester breaks such as spring breaks;
            (II) between semester breaks; and

(III) whole semester breaks provided the student-intern attended the college/school in the immediate preceding semester and is scheduled with the college/school to attend in the immediate subsequent semester.

    (ii) The student internship shall be obtained in pharmacies licensed by the board, federal government pharmacies, or in a board-approved program.

    (iii) The student internship shall be in the presence of and under the supervision of a healthcare professional preceptor or a pharmacist preceptor.

(C) None of the internship hours acquired outside of a school-based program may be substituted for any of the hours required in a college/school of pharmacy internship program.

(2) Expiration date for student-intern designation.

  (A) The student-internship expires:

    (i) if the student-intern voluntarily or involuntarily ceases enrollment, including suspension, in a college/school of pharmacy;

    (ii) the student-intern fails either the NAPLEX or Texas Pharmacy Jurisprudence Examinations specified in this section; or

    (iii) the student-intern fails to take either the NAPLEX or Texas Pharmacy Jurisprudence Examinations or both within six calendar months after graduation.

  (B) The executive director of the board, in his/her discretion, may extend the term of the student internship if administration of the NAPLEX or Texas Pharmacy Jurisprudence Examinations is suspended or delayed.

(3) Texas colleges/schools of pharmacy internship programs.

  (A) Intern-trainees and student-interns completing a board-approved Texas college/school-based structured internship shall be credited the number of hours actually obtained and reported by the college. No credit shall be awarded for didactic experience.

  (B) No more than 600 hours of the required 1,500 hours may be obtained under a healthcare professional preceptor except when a pharmacist-intern is working in a federal government pharmacy.

  (C) Individuals enrolled in the professional sequence of a Texas college/school of pharmacy may be designated as an intern-trainee provided he/she:

    (i) submits an application to the board that includes the following information:

      (I) name;

      (II) addresses, phone numbers, date of birth, and social security number;

      (III) college of pharmacy and expected graduation date; and

      (IV) any other information requested on the application;

    (ii) is enrolled in the professional sequence of a college/school of pharmacy; and

    (iii) has met all requirements necessary for the board to access the criminal history records information, including submitting fingerprint information and being responsible for all associated costs. Such internship shall remain in effect during the time the intern-trainee is enrolled in the first year of the professional sequence and shall expire upon completion of the first year of the professional sequence or upon separation from the professional sequence.

(d) Extended-internship program.

(1) A person may be designated an extended-intern provided he/she has met one of the following requirements:

  (A) passed NAPLEX and the Texas Pharmacy Jurisprudence Examinations but lacks the required number of internship hours for licensure;

  (B) applied to the board to take the NAPLEX and Texas Jurisprudence Examinations within six calendar months after graduation and has:

    (i) graduated and received a professional degree from a college/school of pharmacy; or

    (ii) completed all of the requirements for graduation and receipt of a professional degree from a college/school of pharmacy;

  (C) applied to the board to take the NAPLEX and Texas Jurisprudence Examinations within six calendar months after obtaining full certification from the Foreign Pharmacy Graduate Equivalency Commission;

  (D) applied to the board for re-issuance of a pharmacist license which has expired for more than two years but less than ten years and has successfully passed the Texas Pharmacy Jurisprudence Examination, but lacks the required number of hours of internship or continuing education required for licensure;

  (E) is a resident in a residency program accredited by the American Society of Health-System Pharmacists in the state of Texas; or

  (F) been ordered by the Board to complete an internship.

(2) In addition to meeting one of the requirements in paragraph (1) of this subsection, an applicant for an extended-internship must:

  (A) submit an application to the board that includes the following information:

    (i) name;

    (ii) addresses, phone numbers, date of birth, and social security number;

    (iii) any other information requested on the application; and

  (B) meet all requirements necessary for the board to access the criminal history records information, including submitting fingerprint information and being responsible for all associated costs.

(3) The terms of the extended-internship shall be as follows.

  (A) The extended-internship shall be board-approved and gained in a pharmacy licensed by the board, or a federal government pharmacy participating in a board-approved internship program.

  (B) The extended-internship shall be in the presence of and under the direct supervision of a pharmacist preceptor.

(4) The extended internship remains in effect for two years. However, the internship expires immediately upon:

  (A) the failure of the extended-intern to take the NAPLEX and Texas Pharmacy Jurisprudence Examinations within six calendar months after graduation or FPGEC certification;

  (B) the failure of the extended-intern to pass the NAPLEX and Texas Pharmacy Jurisprudence Examinations specified in this section;

Phr. Rules

      (C) upon termination of the residency program; or

      (D) obtaining a Texas pharmacist license.

   (5) The executive director of the board, in his/her discretion, may extend the term of the extended internship if administration of the NAPLEX and/or Texas Pharmacy Jurisprudence Examinations is suspended or delayed.

   (6) An applicant for licensure who has completed less than 500 hours of internship at the time of application shall complete the remainder of the 1,500 hours of internship and have the preceptor certify that the applicant has met the objectives listed in subsection (a) of this section.

(e) Pharmacist-intern identification.

   (1) Pharmacist-interns shall keep documentation of designation as a pharmacist-intern with them at all times they are serving as a pharmacist-intern and make it available for inspection by board agents.

   (2) All pharmacist-interns shall wear an identification tag or badge which bears the person's name and identifies him or her as a pharmacist-intern.

(f) Change of address and/or name.

   (1) Change of address. A pharmacist-intern shall notify the board electronically or in writing within 10 days of a change of address, giving the old and new address.

   (2) Change of name. A pharmacist-intern shall notify the board in writing within 10 days of a change of name by:

      (A) sending a copy of the official document reflecting the name change (e.g., marriage certificate, divorce decree, etc.);

      (B) returning the current pharmacist-intern certificate which reflects the previous name; and

      (C) paying a fee of $ 20.

Source: The provisions of this § 283.4 adopted to be effective February 17, 1988, 13 TEXREG610; amended to be effective June 15, 1990, 15 TEXREG3334; amended to be effective June 1, 1994, 19 TexReg 3920; amended to be effective February 1, 1996, 21 TexReg 110; amended to be effective December 31, 1996, 21 TexReg 12297; amended to be effective June 30, 1997, 22 TexReg 5924; amended to be effective March 19, 1998, 23 TexReg 2814; amended to be effective December 27, 2000, 25 TexReg 12689; amended to be effective June 11, 2006, 31 TexReg 4628; amended to be effective September 3, 2006, 31 TexReg 6729; amended to be effective June 8, 2008, 33 TexReg 4304; amended to beeffective June 7, 2009, 34 TexReg 3390; amended to be effective September 12, 2011, 36 TexReg 5845; amended to be effective March 15, 2012, 37 TexReg 1705; amended to be effective June 12, 2016, 41 TexReg 4256; amended to be effective June 20, 2019, 44 TexReg 2945

§283.5 Pharmacist-Intern Duties

(a) A pharmacist-intern participating in a board-approved internship program may perform any duty of a pharmacist provided the duties are delegated by and under the supervision of:

   (1) a pharmacist licensed by the board and approved as a preceptor by the board; or

   (2) healthcare professional preceptor.

(b) A pharmacist preceptor serving as an instructor for a Texas college/school-based internship program, may delegate any duty of a pharmacist to an intern-trainee. An intern-trainee may only perform the duties of a pharmacist in a site assigned by a Texas college/school of pharmacy and the direct supervision of a pharmacist preceptor assigned by a Texas college/school of pharmacy.

(c) When not under the supervision of a pharmacist preceptor, a pharmacist-intern may function as a pharmacy technician and perform all of the duties of a pharmacy technician without registering as a pharmacy technician provided the pharmacist-intern:

   (1) is registered with the board as a pharmacist-intern;

   (2) is under the direct supervision of a pharmacist;

   (3) has completed the pharmacy's on-site technician training program;

   (4) has completed the training required for pharmacists in § 291.133 of this title (relating to Pharmacies Compounding Sterile Preparations) if the pharmacist-intern is involved in compounding sterile preparations; and

   (5) is not counted as a pharmacy technician in the ratio of pharmacists to pharmacy technicians. The ratio of pharmacists to pharmacist-interns shall be 1:1 when performing pharmacy technician duties.

(d) A pharmacist-intern may not:

   (1) present or identify himself/herself as a pharmacist;

   (2) sign or initial any document which is required to be signed or initialed by a pharmacist unless a preceptor cosigns the document; or

   (3) independently supervise pharmacy technicians or pharmacy technician trainees.

Source: The provisions of this § 283.5 adopted to be effective February 15, 1988, 13 TEXREG 610; amended to be effective February 1, 1996, 21 TexReg 110; amended to be effective June 30, 1997, 22 TexReg 5924; amended to be effective June 4, 2000, 25 TexReg 4777; amended to be effective June 20, 2001, 26 TexReg 4478; amended to be effective March 4, 2004, 29 TexReg 1949; amended to be effective June 8, 2008, 33 TexReg 4304; amended to be effective March 10, 2016, 41 TexReg 1689

§283.6 Preceptor Requirements and Ratio of Preceptors to Pharmacist-Interns

(a) Preceptor requirements.

   (1) Preceptors shall be:

      (A) a pharmacist whose license to practice pharmacy in Texas is current and not on inactive status with the board; or

      (B) a healthcare professional preceptor.

   (2) To be recognized as a pharmacist preceptor, a pharmacist must:

      (A) have at least:

         (i) one year of experience as a licensed pharmacist; or

         (ii) six months of residency training if the pharmacy resident is in a program accredited by the American Society of Health-System Pharmacists;

      (B) have completed:

         (i) for initial certification, three hours of pharmacist preceptor training provided by an ACPE approved provider within the previous two years. Such training shall be:

            (I) developed by a Texas college/school of pharmacy; or

            (II) approved by:

Phr. Rules

                       (-a-) a committee comprised of the Texas college/schools of pharmacy; or
                       (-b-) the board; or
               (ii)   to continue certification, three hours of pharmacist preceptor training provided by an ACPE approved provider within
                      the pharmacist's current license renewal period. Such training shall be:
                   (I)   developed by a Texas college/school of pharmacy; or
                   (II)   approved by:
                          (-a-) a committee comprised of the Texas college/schools of pharmacy; or
                          (-b-) the board; and
           (C) meet the requirements of subsection (c) of this section.
(b) Ratio of preceptors to pharmacist-interns.
     (1) A preceptor may supervise only one pharmacist-intern at any given time (1:1 ratio) except as provided in paragraph (2) of this
          subsection.
     (2) The following is applicable to Texas college/school of pharmacy internship programs only
          (A) Supervision. Supervision of a pharmacist-intern shall be:
               (i)   direct supervision when the student-intern or intern-trainee is engaged in functions associated with the preparation and
                      delivery of prescription or medication drug orders; and
               (ii)   general supervision when the student-intern or intern-trainee is engaged in functions not associated with the preparation
                      and delivery of prescription or medication drug orders.
          (B) Exceptions to the 1:1 ratio. There is no ratio requirement for preceptors supervising intern-trainees and student-interns as a
               part of a Texas college/school of pharmacy program.
(c) No pharmacist may serve as a pharmacist preceptor if his or her license to practice pharmacy has been the subject of an order of the
     board imposing any penalty set out in § 565.051 of the Act during the period he or she is serving as a pharmacist preceptor or within
     the three-year period immediately preceding application for approval as a pharmacist preceptor. Provided, however, a pharmacist who
     has been the subject of such an order of the board may petition the board, in writing, for approval to act as a pharmacist preceptor. The
     board may consider the following items in approving a pharmacist's petition to act as a pharmacist preceptor:
     (1) the type and gravity of the offense for which the pharmacist's license was disciplined;
     (2) the length of time since the action that caused the order;
     (3) the length of time the pharmacist has previously served as a preceptor;
     (4) the availability of other preceptors in the area;
     (5) the reason(s) the pharmacist believes he/she should serve as a preceptor;
     (6) a letter of recommendation from a Texas college/school of pharmacy if the pharmacist will be serving as a pharmacist preceptor
          for a Texas college/school of pharmacy; and
     (7) any other factor presented by the pharmacist demonstrating good cause why the pharmacist should be allowed to act as a
          pharmacist preceptor.
(d) The fee for issuance of a duplicate or amended preceptor certificate shall be $ 20.
     *Source: The provisions of this § 283.6 adopted to be effective February 17, 1988, 13 TEXREG610; amended to be effective February 1, 1996, 21 TexReg 110; amended to be
effective January 12, 1998, 23 TexReg 134; amended to be effective October 4, 1998, 23 TexReg 9745; amended to be effective June 20, 2001, 26 TexReg 4478; amended to be effective
June 13, 2002, 27 TexReg 4947; amended to be effective September 10, 2003, 28 TexReg 7709; amended to be effective March 4, 2004, 29 TexReg 1950; amended to be effective March
6, 2006, 31 TexReg 1439; amended to be effective June 11, 2006, 31 TexReg 4628; amended to be effective June8,2008, 33 TexReg 4304; amended to be effective June 7, 2009, 34
TexReg 3390; amended to be effective June 20, 2019, 44 TexReg 2945*

§283.7 Examination Requirements

Each applicant for licensure by examination shall pass the Texas Pharmacy Jurisprudence Examination and the NAPLEX. The examination
requirements shall be as follows:
     (1) Prior to taking the required examination, the applicant shall:
          (A) meet the educational and age requirements as set forth in § 283.3 of this title (relating to Educational and Age Requirements);
          (B) meet all requirements necessary in order for the Board to access the criminal history record information, including submitting
               fingerprint information and being responsible for all associated costs; and
          (C) submit an application to the board that includes the following information:
               (i)   name;
               (ii)   addresses, phone numbers, date of birth, and social security number; and
               (iii) any other information requested on the application.
     (2) All applicants shall pass NAPLEX, which includes, at a minimum, the following subject areas:
          (A) chemistry;
          (B) mathematics;
          (C) pharmacy;
          (D) pharmacology; and
          (E) practice of pharmacy.
     (3) Effective October 1, 1979, the following requirements apply.
          (A) To pass NAPLEX, an applicant shall make the following grades:
               (i)   a minimum grade of 60 on chemistry, mathematics, pharmacy, and pharmacology test;
               (ii)   a minimum grade of 75 on the practice of pharmacy test; and
               (iii) a minimum average grade of 75 on the NAPLEX.
          (B) Should the applicant fail to achieve a minimum grade of 60 in any of the tests set out in paragraph (2)(A) – (E) of this section
               or fail to achieve a minimum grade of 75 in the practice of pharmacy test or fail to achieve a minimum average grade of 75
               in the NAPLEX, such applicant, in order to be licensed, is required to retake all tests until such time as the minimum average
               grades are achieved.

(4) Effective June 1, 1986, the following requirements apply.
  (A) To pass the NAPLEX, an applicant shall make a minimum average grade of 75.
  (B) Should the applicant fail to achieve a minimum average grade of 75 in the NAPLEX, such applicant, in order to be licensed, shall retake the NAPLEX, as specified in § 283.11 of this title (relating to Examination Retake Requirements) until such time as a minimum average grade of 75 is achieved.

(5) To pass the Texas Pharmacy Jurisprudence Examination, an applicant shall make a minimum grade of 75. Should the applicant fail to achieve a minimum grade of 75 on the Texas Pharmacy Jurisprudence Examination, such applicant, in order to be licensed, shall retake the Texas Pharmacy Jurisprudence Examination as specified in § 283.11 of this title until such time as a minimum average grade of 75 is achieved.

(6) A passing grade on an examination may be used for the purpose of licensure for a period of two years from the date of passing the examination.

(7) Each applicant for licensure by examination utilizing NAPLEX scores transferred from another state shall meet the following requirements for licensure in addition to the requirements set out in paragraphs (1) – (6) of this section.
  (A) The applicant shall request NABP to transfer NAPLEX scores to the board. Such request shall be in accordance with NABP policy.
  (B) The applicant shall pay the fee set out in § 283.9 of this title.

(8) The NAPLEX and Texas Pharmacy Jurisprudence Examination shall be administered in compliance with the Americans with Disabilities Act of 1990 (42 U.S.C. Section 12101 et seq.) and in accordance with NABP policy.

(9) The board, in accordance with NABP policy, shall provide reasonable accommodations for an applicant diagnosed as having dyslexia, as defined in § 51.970, Texas Education Code. The applicant shall provide:
  (A) written documentation from a licensed physician which indicates that the applicant has been diagnosed as having dyslexia; and
  (B) a written request outlining the reasonable accommodations requested.

Source: The provisions of this § 283.7 adopted to be effective February 17, 1988, 13 TEXREG 610; amended to be effective March 23, 1994, 19 TexReg 1828; amended to be effective December 31, 1996, 21 TexReg 12297; amended to be effective June 30, 1997, 22 TexReg 5924; amended to be effective March 6, 2006, 31 TexReg 1440; amended to be effective September 3, 2006, 31 TexReg 6729; amended to be effective December 14, 2008, 33 TexReg 10026; amended to be effective September 12, 2011, 36 TexReg 5845; amended to be effective December 31, 1996, 21 TexReg 12297; amended to be effective November 24, 2011, 36 TexReg 7866; amended to be effective March 13, 2012, 37 TexReg 1705; amended to be effective June 12, 2016, 41 TexReg 4256

§283.8 Reciprocity Requirements

(a) All applicants for licensure by reciprocity shall:
  (1) meet the educational and age requirements specified in § 283.3 of this title (relating to Educational and Age Requirements);
  (2) meet all requirements necessary in order for the board to access the criminal history record information, including submitting fingerprint information and being responsible for all associated costs;
  (3) complete the Texas and NABP applications for reciprocity. Any fraudulent statement made in the application for reciprocity is grounds for denial of the application; if such application is granted, any fraudulent statement is grounds for suspension, revocation, and/or cancellation of any license so granted by the board. The Texas application includes the following information:
    (A) name;
    (B) addresses, phone numbers, dates of birth, and social security numbers; and
    (C) any other information requested on the application.
  (4) shall present to the board proof of initial licensing by examination and proof that their current license and any other license or licenses granted to the applicant by any other state have not been suspended, revoked, canceled, surrendered, or otherwise restricted for any reason; and
  (5) shall pass the Texas Pharmacy Jurisprudence Examination with a minimum grade of 75. (The passing grade may be used for the purpose of licensure by reciprocity for a period of two years from the date of passing the examination.) Should the applicant fail to achieve a minimum grade of 75 on the Texas Pharmacy Jurisprudence Examination, such applicant, in order to be licensed, shall retake the Texas Pharmacy Jurisprudence Examination as specified in § 283.11 of this title (relating to Examination Retake Requirements) until such time as a minimum grade of 75 is achieved.

(b) A reciprocity applicant originally licensed after January 1, 1978, and who has graduated and received a professional degree from a college of pharmacy, shall show proof such applicant has passed the NAPLEX or equivalent examination based on criteria no less stringent than the criteria in force in Texas.

(c) A reciprocity applicant who is a foreign pharmacy graduate shall provide written documentation that such applicant has:
  (1) obtained full certification from the FPGEC; and
  (2) passed NAPLEX or equivalent examination based on criteria no less stringent than the criteria in force in Texas.

(d) An applicant is not eligible for licensing by reciprocity unless the state in which the applicant is currently or was initially licensed as a pharmacist also grants reciprocal licensing to pharmacists duly licensed by examination in this state, under like circumstances and conditions.

Source: The provisions of this § 283.8 adopted to be effective February 17, 1988, 13 TEXREG 610; amended to be effective March 23, 1994, 19 TexReg 1828; amended to be effective December 31, 1996, 21 TexReg 12297; amended to be effective June 11, 2006, 31 TexReg 4628; amended to be effective December 3, 2006, 31 TexReg 9608; amended to be effective December 14, 2008, 33 TexReg 10026; amended to be effective September 12, 2011, 36 TexReg 5845; amended to be effective November 24, 2011, 36 TexReg 7866; amended to be effective March 13, 2012, 37 TexReg 1705; amended to be effective June 12, 2016, 41 TexReg 4256

§283.9 Fee Requirements for Licensure by Examination, Score Transfer and Reciprocity

(a) The fees for licensure by examination, score transfer, and reciprocity shall include one exam administration. The fees are as follows:
  (1) Examination Fee. The fee to submit an application for licensure by examination will include:
    (A) An examination processing fee of $ 103, which is to be paid to the Texas State Board of Pharmacy and includes the processing of the Texas application.

      (B) NAPLEX administrative and examination fees as determined by NABP, which are to be paid to NABP in accordance with NABP policy.

      (C) MPJE administrative and examination fees as determined by NABP, which are to be paid to NABP in accordance with NABP policy.

  (2) Reciprocity Fee. The fee to submit an application for licensure by reciprocity will include.

      (A) A reciprocity fee of $ 255, which is to be paid to the Texas State Board of Pharmacy.

      (B) MPJE administrative and examination fees as determined by NABP, which are to be paid to NABP in accordance with NABP policy.

      (C) A license verification fee as determined by NABP, which is to be paid to NABP in accordance with NABP policy.

  (3) Score Transfer Fee. The fees to transfer a score to Texas, using the NAPLEX Score Transfer system will include:

      (A) An examination processing fee of $ 103, which is to be paid to the Texas State Board of Pharmacy and includes the processing of the Texas application.

      (B) MPJE administrative and examination fees as determined by NABP, which are to be paid to NABP in accordance with NABP policy.

      (C) A score transfer fee as determined by NABP, which is to be paid to NABP in accordance with NABP policy.

(b) If an applicant fails an examination or is required to take an examination by the Board, the application fee is $ 103 for each examination the applicant is required to take.

(c) Rescheduling or canceling an examination appointment.

  (1) Refunds for fees charged by NABP for the administration of the NAPLEX and MPJE are in accordance with NABP policy. Rescheduling of an examination appointment shall be in accordance with NABP policy.

  (2) The Board may refund fifty percent of an examination fee paid to the Board by an applicant if the applicant:

      (A) provides advance notice of their inability to take the examination prior to the board providing authorization to take the examination; or

      (B) is unable to take the examination due to an emergency situation including but not limited to a manmade or natural disaster, documented serious medical illness, or other circumstance deemed an emergency by the Executive Director of the Board.

(d) A person who takes NAPLEX and/or the Texas Pharmacy Jurisprudence Examination will be notified of the results of the examination(s) within two weeks of receipt of the results of the examination(s) from the testing service. If both NAPLEX and the Texas Pharmacy Jurisprudence Examination are taken, the applicant will not be notified until the results of both examinations have been received. Such notification will be made within two weeks after receipt of the results of both examinations.

(e) Once an applicant has successfully completed all requirements of licensure, the applicant will be notified of licensure as a pharmacist and of his or her pharmacist license number and the following is applicable.

  (1) The notice letter shall serve as authorization for the person to practice pharmacy in Texas for a period of 30 days from the date of the notice letter.

  (2) The applicant shall complete a pharmacist license application and pay one pharmacist licensee fee as specified in § 295.5 of this title (relating to Pharmacist License or Renewal Fees).

  (3) The provisions of § 295.7 of this title (relating to Pharmacist License Renewal) apply to the timely receipt of an application and licensure fee.

  (4) If application and payment of the pharmacist license fee are not received by the board within 30 days from the date of the notice letter, the person's license to practice pharmacy shall expire. A person may not practice pharmacy with an expired license. The license may be renewed according to the following schedule.

      (A) If the notice letter has been expired for 90 days or less, the person may become licensed by making application and paying to the board one license fee and a fee that is one-half of the examination fee for the license.

      (B) If the notice letter has been expired for more than 90 days but less than one year, the person may become licensed by making application and paying to the board all unpaid renewal fees and a fee that is equal to the examination fee for the license.

      (C) If the notice letter has been expired for one year or more, the person shall apply for a new license.

Source: The provisions of this § 283.9 adopted to be effective December 27, 2000, 25 TexReg 12690; amended to be effective September 7, 2004, 29 TexReg 8516; amended to be effective June 11, 2006, 31 TexReg 4628; amended to be effective March 13, 2012, 37 TexReg 1705; amended to be effective September 14, 2015, 40 TexReg 6109

§283.10 Requirements for Application for a Pharmacist License Which Has Expired

(a) Expired less than 90 days. If a person's license has been expired for 90 days or less, the person may renew the license by:

  (1) paying to the board a renewal fee that is equal to one and one-half times the renewal fee for the license as specified in § 295.5 of this title (relating to Pharmacist License Renewal Fees); and

  (2) reporting completion of the required number of contact hours of approved continuing education.

(b) Expired more than 90 days. If a person's license has been expired for more than 90 days but less than one year, the person may renew the license by:

  (1) paying to the board all unpaid renewal fees and a renewal fee that is equal to two times the renewal fee for the license as specified in § 295.5 of this title; and

  (2) reporting completion of the required number of contact hours of approved continuing education.

(c) Expired for one year or more. If a person's license to practice pharmacy in Texas has been expired for one year or more, the person may not renew the license and shall apply for a new license.

(d) Reexamination. The board may issue a new license to a person if the person submits to reexamination and complies with the requirements and procedures for obtaining an original license as specified in § 283.7 of this title (relating to Examination Requirements).

(e) Alternatives to reexamination. In lieu of reexamination as specified in subsection (d) of this section, the board may issue a license to a person whose license has been expired for one year or more, if the person meets the requirements of subsection (f) or (g) of this section and has not had a license granted by any other state suspended, revoked, canceled, surrendered, or otherwise restricted for any reason.

(f) Persons practicing pharmacy in another state. Beginning January 1, 2002, the board may issue a license to a person who was licensed as a pharmacist in Texas, moved to another state, is licensed in the other state, and has been engaged in the practice of pharmacy in the other state for the two years preceding the application if the person meets the following requirements:

(1) makes application for licensure to the board on a form prescribed by the board;

(2) submits to the board certification that the applicant:

    (A) is licensed as a pharmacist in another state and that such license is in good standing;

    (B) has been continuously employed as a pharmacist in that state for the two years preceding the application; and

    (C) has completed a minimum of 30 contact hours of approved continuing education during the preceding two license years;

(3) passes the Texas Pharmacy Jurisprudence Examination with a grade of 75 (the passing grade may be used for the purpose of licensure for a period of two years from the date of passing the examination); and

(4) pays to the board the examination fee set out in § 283.9 of this title (relating to Fee Requirements for Licensure by Examination, Score Transfer and Reciprocity).

(g) Persons not practicing pharmacy. Beginning January 1, 2002, the board may issue a license to a person who was licensed as a pharmacist in this state, but has not practiced pharmacy for the two years preceding application for licensure under the following conditions.

(1) The person's Texas pharmacist license has been expired for less than 10 years, the person shall:

    (A) make application for licensure to the board on a form prescribed by the board;

    (B) pass the Texas Pharmacy Jurisprudence Examination with a grade of 75 (the passing grade may be used for the purpose of licensure for a period of two years from the date of passing the examination);

    (C) pay the examination fee set out in § 283.9 of this title; and

    (D) complete approved continuing education and/or board-approved internship requirements according to the following schedule:

        (i) if the Texas pharmacist license has been expired for more than one year but less than two years, the applicant shall complete 15 contact hours of approved continuing education;

        (ii) if the Texas pharmacist license has been expired for more than two years but less than three years, the applicant shall complete 30 contact hours of approved continuing education;

        (iii) if the Texas pharmacist license has been expired for more than three years but less than four years, the applicant shall complete 45 contact hours of approved continuing education;

        (iv) if the Texas pharmacist license has been expired for more than four years but less than five years, the applicant shall complete 45 contact hours of approved continuing education and 500 hours of internship in a board-approved internship program;

        (v) if the Texas pharmacist license has been expired for more than five years but less than six years, the applicant shall complete 45 contact hours of approved continuing education and 700 hours of internship in a board-approved internship program;

        (vi) if the Texas pharmacist license has been expired for more than six years but less than seven years, the applicant shall complete 45 contact hours of approved continuing education and 900 hours of internship in a board-approved internship program;

        (vii) if the Texas pharmacist license has been expired for more than seven years but less than eight years, the applicant shall complete 45 contact hours of approved continuing education and 1,100 hours of internship in a board-approved internship program;

        (viii) if the Texas pharmacist license has been expired for more than eight years but less than nine years, the applicant shall complete 45 contact hours of approved continuing education and 1,300 hours of internship in a board-approved internship program; and

        (ix) if the Texas pharmacist license has been expired for more than nine years but less than 10 years, the applicant shall complete 45 contact hours of approved continuing education and 1,500 hours of internship in a board-approved internship program.

(2) Any hours of approved continuing education earned within two years prior to the applicant successfully passing the Texas Pharmacy Jurisprudence Examination may be applied towards the continuing education requirement.

(3) Any hours worked as a licensed pharmacist in another state during the two years prior to the applicant successfully passing the Texas Pharmacy Jurisprudence examination may be applied towards the internship requirement.

(4) All requirements for licensure shall be completed within two years from the date the applicant successfully passes the Texas Pharmacy Jurisprudence Examination.

(5) If the person's Texas pharmacist license has been expired for 10 years or more, the applicant shall apply for licensure by examination as specified in § 283.7 of this title and § 283.4 of this title (relating to Internship Requirements).

Source: The provisions of this §283.10 adopted to be effective February 17, 1988, 13 TexReg 610; amended to be effective March 19, 1990, 15 TexReg 1234; amended to be effective January 4, 1994, 18 TexReg 9853; amended to be effective October 18, 1996, 21 TexReg 9832; amended to be effective December 31, 2001, 26 TexReg 10869; amended to be effective March 6, 2006, 31 TexReg 1440; amended to be effective March 13, 2012, 37 TexReg 1705

§283.11 Examination Retake Requirements

(a) Licensing by examination. Should an applicant fail to achieve the minimum grade on the NAPLEX or Texas Pharmacy Jurisprudence Examination or both, the following is applicable.

(1) If the applicant fails to achieve the minimum grade on NAPLEX as specified in § 283.7 of this title (relating to Examination Requirements), the applicant may retake NAPLEX four additional times for a total of five exam administrations. Prior to any subsequent retakes of NAPLEX, the applicant must:

    (A) complete course work in subject areas recommended by the board;

    (B) submit documentation to the board which specifies that the applicant has successfully completed the course work specified; and

    (C) comply with the requirements of § 283.7 of this title (relating to Examination Requirements).

(2) If the applicant fails to achieve the minimum grade on the Texas Pharmacy Jurisprudence Examination as specified in § 283.7 of this title (relating to Examination Requirements), the applicant may retake the examination four additional times for a total of five exam administrations. Prior to any subsequent retake of the Texas Pharmacy Jurisprudence Examination, the applicant must:
  (A) complete course work recommended by the board;
  (B) submit documentation to the board which specifies that the applicant has successfully completed the recommended course work; and
  (C) comply with the requirements of § 283.7 of this title (relating to Examination Requirements).
(3) If the applicant fails to achieve the minimum grade on both NAPLEX and the Texas Pharmacy Jurisprudence Examination, the applicant shall retake the examinations until a passing grade is achieved on one of the examinations. Such retakes shall be as specified in paragraphs (1) and (2) of this subsection.
(b) Licensing by reciprocity. If an applicant fails to achieve the minimum grade on the Texas Pharmacy Jurisprudence Examination as specified in § 283.8 of this title (relating to Reciprocity Requirements), the applicant may retake the examination four additional times for a total of five exam administrations. Prior to any subsequent retake of the Texas Pharmacy Jurisprudence Examination, the applicant must:
  (1) complete course work recommended by the board;
  (2) submit documentation to the board which specifies that the applicant has successfully completed the recommended course work; and
  (3) comply with the requirements of § 283.8 of this title (relating to Reciprocity Requirements).
(c) Course work. For the purpose of this subsection, course work shall be:
  (1) one or more standard courses or self-paced work offered in a college of pharmacy's academic program;
  (2) one or more courses presented by a board-approved provider of continuing pharmacy education as specified in § 295.8 of this title (relating to Continuing Education Requirements); or
  (3) any course specified by the board.

Source: The provisions of this § 283.11 adopted to be effective March 23, 1994, 19 TexReg 1828; amended to be effective December 31, 1996, 21 TexReg 12297; amended to be effective November 24, 2011, 36 TexReg 7866; amended to be effective March 13, 2012, 37 TexReg 1705; amended to be effective June 12, 2016, 41 TexReg 4256; amended to be effective September 10, 2019, 44 TexReg 4872

§283.12 Licenses for Military Service Members, Military Veterans, and Military Spouses

(a) Definitions. The following words and terms, when used in this section, shall have the following meanings, unless the context clearly indicates otherwise.
  (1) Active duty—Current full-time military service in the armed forces of the United States or active duty military service as a member of the Texas military forces, or similar military service of another state.
  (2) Armed forces of the United States—The army, navy, air force, coast guard, or marine corps of the United States or a reserve unit of one of those branches of the armed forces.
  (3) Military service member—A person who is on active duty.
  (4) Military spouse—A person who is married to a military service member.
  (5) Military veteran—A person who has served on active duty and who was discharged or released from active duty.
(b) Alternative licensing procedure. For the purpose of § 55.004, Occupations Code, an applicant for a pharmacist license who is a military service member, military veteran, or military spouse may complete the following alternative procedures for licensing as a pharmacist.
  (1) Requirements for licensing by reciprocity. An applicant for licensing by reciprocity who meets all of the following requirements may be granted a temporary license as specified in this subsection prior to completing the NABP application for pharmacist license by reciprocity, and taking and passing the Texas Pharmacy Jurisprudence Examination. The applicant shall:
    (A) complete the Texas application for pharmacist license by reciprocity that includes the following:
      (i) name;
      (ii) addresses, phone numbers, date of birth, and social security number; and
      (iii) any other information requested on the application;
    (B) meet the educational and age requirements as set forth in § 283.3 of this title (relating to Educational and Age Requirements);
    (C) present to the board proof of initial licensing by examination and proof that any current licenses and any other licenses granted to the applicant by any other state have not been suspended, revoked, canceled, surrendered, or otherwise restricted for any reason;
    (D) meet all requirements necessary for the board to access the criminal history records information, including submitting fingerprint information, and such criminal history check does not reveal any disposition for a crime specified in § 281.64 of this title (relating to Sanctions for Criminal Offenses) indicating a sanction of denial, revocation, or suspension; and
    (E) be exempt from the application and examination fees paid to the board set forth in § 283.9(a)(2)(A) and (b) of this title (relating to Fee Requirements for Licensure by Examination, Score Transfer and Reciprocity); and
    (F) provide documentation of eligibility, including:
      (i) military identification indicating that the applicant is a military service member, military veteran, or military dependent, if a military spouse; and
      (ii) marriage certificate, if a military spouse.
  (2) Requirements for an applicant whose Texas pharmacist license has expired. An applicant whose Texas pharmacist license has expired within five years preceding the application date:
    (A) shall complete the Texas application for licensing that includes the following:
      (i) name;
      (ii) addresses, phone numbers, date of birth, and social security number; and
      (iii) any other information requested on the application;
    (B) shall provide documentation of eligibility, including:

     (i) military identification indicating that the applicant is a military service member, military veteran, or military dependent, if a military spouse; and

     (ii) marriage certificate, if a military spouse;

  (C) shall pay the renewal fee specified in § 295.5 of this title (relating to Pharmacist License or Renewal Fees); however, the applicant shall be exempt from the fees specified in § 295.7(3) of this title (relating to Pharmacist License Renewal).

  (D) shall complete approved continuing education requirements according to the following schedule:

     (i) if the Texas pharmacist license has been expired for more than one year but less than two years, the applicant shall complete 15 contact hours of approved continuing education;

     (ii) if the Texas pharmacist license has been expired for more than two years but less than three years, the applicant shall complete 30 contact hours of approved continuing education; or

     (iii) if the Texas pharmacist license has been expired for more than three years but less than five years, the applicant shall complete 45 contact hours of approved continuing education; and

  (E) is not required to take the Texas Pharmacy Jurisprudence Examination.

  (3) A temporary license issued under this section is valid for no more than six months and may be extended, if disciplinary action is pending, or upon request, as otherwise determined reasonably necessary by the executive director of the board.

  (4) A temporary license issued under this section expires within six months of issuance if the individual fails to pass the Texas Pharmacy Jurisprudence Examination within six months or fails to take the Texas Pharmacy Jurisprudence Examination within six months.

  (5) An individual may not serve as pharmacist-in-charge of a pharmacy with a temporary license issued under this subsection.

(c) Expedited licensing procedure. For the purpose of § 55.005, Occupations Code, an applicant for a pharmacist license who is a military service member, military veteran, or military spouse and who holds a current license as a pharmacist issued by another state may complete the following expedited procedures for licensing as a pharmacist. The applicant shall:

  (1) meet the educational and age requirements specified in § 283.3 of this title (relating to Educational and Age Requirements);

  (2) meet all requirements necessary in order for the board to access the criminal history record information, including submitting fingerprint information and being responsible for all associated costs;

  (3) complete the Texas and NABP applications for reciprocity. Any fraudulent statement made in the application for reciprocity is grounds for denial of the application. If such application is granted, any fraudulent statement is grounds for suspension, revocation, and/or cancellation of any license so granted by the board. The Texas application includes the following information:

    (A) name;

    (B) addresses, phone numbers, date of birth, and social security number; and

    (C) any other information requested on the application.

  (4) present to the board proof of initial licensing by examination and proof that their current license and any other license or licenses granted to the applicant by any other state have not been suspended, revoked, canceled, surrendered, or otherwise restricted for any reason;

  (5) pass the Texas Pharmacy Jurisprudence Examination with a minimum grade of 75. (The passing grade may be used for the purpose of licensure by reciprocity for a period of two years from the date of passing the examination.) Should the applicant fail to achieve a minimum grade of 75 on the Texas Pharmacy Jurisprudence Examination, such applicant, in order to be licensed, shall retake the Texas Pharmacy Jurisprudence Examination as specified in § 283.11 of this title (relating to Examination Retake Requirements) until such time as a minimum grade of 75 is achieved; and

  (6) be exempt from the application and examination fees paid to the board set forth in § 283.9(a)(2)(A) and (b).

(d) License renewal. As specified in § 55.003, Occupations Code, a military service member who holds a pharmacist license is entitled to two years of additional time to complete any requirements related to the renewal of the military service member's license as follows:

  (1) A military service member who fails to renew their pharmacist license in a timely manner because the individual was serving as a military service member shall submit to the board:

    (A) name, address, and license number of the pharmacist;

    (B) military identification indicating that the individual is a military service member; and

    (C) a statement requesting up to two years of additional time to complete the renewal.

  (2) A military service member specified in paragraph (1) of this subsection shall be exempt from fees specified in § 295.7(3) of this title (relating to Pharmacist License Renewal).

  (3) A military service member specified in paragraph (1) of this subsection is entitled to two additional years of time to complete the continuing education requirements specified in § 295.8 of this title (relating to Continuing Education Requirements).

(e) Inactive status. The holder of a pharmacist license who is a military service member, a military veteran, or a military spouse who holds a pharmacist license and who is not engaged in the practice of pharmacy in this state may place the license on inactive status as specified in § 295.9 of this title (relating to Inactive License). The inactive license holder:

  (1) shall provide documentation to include:

    (A) military identification indicating that the pharmacist is a military service member, military veteran, or military dependent, if a military spouse; and

    (B) marriage certificate, if a military spouse;

  (2) shall be exempt from the fees specified in § 295.9(a)(1)(C) and § 295.9(a)(2)(C) of this title;

  (3) shall not practice pharmacy in this state; and

  (4) may reactivate the license as specified in § 295.9 of this title (relating to Inactive License).

Source: The provisions of this § 283.12 adopted to be effective March 13, 2012, 37 TexReg 1705; amended to be effective December 10, 2013, 38 TexReg 8834; amended to be effective December 6, 2015, 40 TexReg 8763; amended to be effective September 11, 2016, 41 TexReg 6696; amended to be effective March 12, 2019, 44 TexReg 1317

CHAPTER 291. PHARMACIES

SUBCHAPTER A. ALL CLASSES OF PHARMACIES

§291.1 Pharmacy License Application

(a) To qualify for a pharmacy license, the applicant must submit an application which includes any information requested on the application.

(b) The applicant may be required to meet all requirements necessary in order for the Board to access the criminal history record information, including submitting fingerprint information and being responsible for all associated costs. The criminal history information may be required for each individual owner, or if the pharmacy is owned by a partnership or a closely held corporation for each managing officer.

(c) A fee as specified in § 291.6 of this title (relating to Pharmacy License Fees) will be charged for the issuance of a pharmacy license.

(d) For purpose of this section, managing officers are defined as the top four executive officers, including the corporate officer in charge of pharmacy operations, who are designated by the partnership or corporation to be jointly responsible for the legal operation of the pharmacy.

(e) Prior to the issuance of a license for a pharmacy located in Texas, the board shall conduct an on-site inspection of the pharmacy in the presence of the pharmacist-in-charge and owner or representative of the owner, to ensure that the pharmacist-in-charge and owner can meet the requirements of the Texas Pharmacy Act and Board Rules.

(f) If the applicant holds an active pharmacy license in Texas on the date of application for a new pharmacy license or for other good cause shown as specified by the board, the board may waive the pre-inspection as set forth in subsection (e) of this section.

Source: The provisions of this § 291.1 adopted to be effective June 17, 1986, 11 TEXREG 2552; amended to be effective July 29, 1987, 12 TEXREG 2337; amended to be effective March 1, 2003, 27 TexReg 11535; amended to be effective December 23, 2003, 28 TexReg 11258; amended to be effective December 3, 2006, 31 TexReg 9609; amended to be effective June 7, 2009, 34 TexReg 3390; amended to be effective September 12, 2011, 36 TexReg 5846; amended to be effective March 15, 2015, 40 TexReg 1086; amended to be effective September 11, 2016, 41 TexReg 6697; amended to be effective September 16, 2018, 43 TexReg 5778

§291.2 Definitions

Any term not defined in this chapter shall have the definition set out in the Act, §551.003.

Source: The provisions of this §291.2 adopted to be effective September 18, 2007, 32 TexReg 6318

§291.3 Required Notifications

(a) Change of Location.

   (1) When a pharmacy changes location, the following is applicable:

      (A) A new completed pharmacy application containing the information outlined in § 291.1 of this title (relating to Pharmacy License Application), must be filed with the board not later than 30 days before the date of the change of location of the pharmacy.

      (B) The previously issued license must be returned to the board office.

      (C) An amended license reflecting the new location of the pharmacy will be issued by the board; and

      (D) A fee as specified in § 291.6 of this title (relating to Pharmacy License Fees) will be charged for issuance of the amended license.

   (2) At least 14 days prior to the change of location of a pharmacy that dispenses prescription drug orders, the pharmacist-in-charge shall post a sign in a conspicuous place indicating that the pharmacy is changing locations. Such sign shall be in the front of the prescription department and at all public entrance doors to the pharmacy and shall indicate the date the pharmacy is changing locations.

   (3) Disasters, accidents, and emergencies which require the pharmacy to change location shall be immediately reported to the board. If a pharmacy changes location suddenly due to disasters, accidents, or other emergency circumstances and the pharmacist-in-charge cannot provide notification 14 days prior to the change of location, the pharmacist-in-charge shall comply with the provisions of paragraph (2) of this subsection as far in advance of the change of location as allowed by the circumstances.

   (4) When a Class A-S, C-S, or E-S pharmacy changes location, the pharmacy's classification will revert to a Class A, Class C, or Class E unless or until the Board or its designee has inspected the new location to ensure the pharmacy meets the requirements as specified in § 291.133 of this title (relating to Pharmacies Compounding Sterile Preparations).

   (5) When a Class B pharmacy changes location, the Board shall inspect the pharmacy at the new location to ensure the pharmacy meets the requirements as specified in subchapter C of this title (relating to Nuclear Pharmacy (Class B)) prior to the pharmacy becoming operational.

(b) Change of Name. When a pharmacy changes its name, the following is applicable.

   (1) A new completed pharmacy application containing the information outlined in § 291.1 of this title (relating to Pharmacy License Application), must be filed with the board within 10 days of the change of name of the pharmacy.

   (2) The previously issued license must be returned to the board office.

   (3) An amended license reflecting the new name of the pharmacy will be issued by the board; and

   (4) A fee as specified in § 291.6 of this title (relating to Pharmacy License Fees) will be charged for issuance of the amended license.

(c) Change of Managing Officers.

   (1) The owner of a pharmacy shall notify the board in writing within 10 days of a change of any managing officer of a partnership or corporation which owns a pharmacy. The written notification shall include the effective date of such change and the following information for all managing officers:

      (A) name and title;

      (B) home address and telephone number;

      (C) date of birth;

(D) a copy of social security card or other official document showing the social security number as approved by the board; and

(E) a copy of current driver's license, state issued photo identification card, or passport.

(2) For purposes of this subsection, managing officers are defined as the top four executive officers, including the corporate officer in charge of pharmacy operations, who are designated by the partnership or corporation to be jointly responsible for the legal operation of the pharmacy.

(d) Change of Ownership.

(1) When a pharmacy changes ownership, a new pharmacy application must be filed with the board following the procedures as specified in § 291.1 of this title (relating to Pharmacy License Application). In addition, a copy of the purchase contract or mutual agreement between the buyer and seller must be submitted.

(2) The license issued to the previous owner must be returned to the board.

(3) A fee as specified in § 291.6 of this title will be charged for issuance of a new license.

(e) Change of Pharmacist Employment.

(1) Change of pharmacist employed in a pharmacy. When a change in pharmacist employment occurs, the pharmacist shall report such change in writing to the board within 10 days.

(2) Change of pharmacist-in-charge of a pharmacy. The incoming pharmacist-in-charge shall be responsible for notifying the board within 10 days in writing on a form provided by the board that a change of pharmacist-in-charge has occurred. The notification shall include the following:

(A) the name and license number of the departing pharmacist-in-charge;

(B) the name and license number of the incoming pharmacist-in-charge;

(C) the date the incoming pharmacist-in-charge became the pharmacist-in-charge; and

(D) a statement signed by the incoming pharmacist-in-charge attesting that:

(i) an inventory, as specified in § 291.17 of this title (relating to Inventory Requirements), has been conducted by the departing and incoming pharmacists-in-charge; if the inventory was not taken by both pharmacists, the statement shall provide an explanation; and

(ii) the incoming pharmacist-in-charge has read and understands the laws and rules relating to this class of pharmacy.

(f) Notification of Theft or Loss of a Controlled Substance or a Dangerous Drug.

(1) Controlled substances. For the purposes of the Act, § 562.106, the theft or significant loss of any controlled substance by a pharmacy shall be reported in writing to the board immediately on discovery of such theft or loss. A pharmacy shall be in compliance with this subsection by submitting to the board a copy of the Drug Enforcement Administration (DEA) report of theft or loss of controlled substances, DEA Form 106, or by submitting a list of all controlled substances stolen or lost.

(2) Dangerous drugs. A pharmacy shall report in writing to the board immediately on discovery the theft or significant loss of any dangerous drug by submitting a list of the name and quantity of all dangerous drugs stolen or lost.

(g) Fire or Other Disaster. If a pharmacy experiences a fire or other disaster, the following requirements are applicable.

(1) Responsibilities of the pharmacist-in-charge.

(A) The pharmacist-in-charge shall be responsible for reporting the date of the fire or other disaster which may affect the strength, purity, or labeling of drugs, medications, devices, or other materials used in the diagnosis or the treatment of the injury, illness, and disease; such notification shall be reported to the board, within 10 days from the date of the disaster.

(B) The pharmacist-in-charge or designated agent shall comply with the following procedures.

(i) If controlled substances, dangerous drugs, or Drug Enforcement Administration (DEA) order forms are lost or destroyed in the disaster, the pharmacy shall:

(I) notify the DEA and the board of the loss of the controlled substances or order forms immediately upon discovery; and

(II) notify the board in writing of the loss of the dangerous drugs by submitting a list of the dangerous drugs lost.

(ii) If the extent of the loss of controlled substances or dangerous drugs is not able to be determined, the pharmacy shall:

(I) take a new, complete inventory of all remaining drugs specified in § 291.17(c) of this title (relating to Inventory Requirements);

(II) submit to DEA a statement attesting that the loss of controlled substances is indeterminable and that a new, complete inventory of all remaining controlled substances was conducted and state the date of such inventory; and

(III) submit to the board a statement attesting that the loss of controlled substances and dangerous drugs is indeterminable and that a new, complete inventory of the drugs specified in § 291.17(c) of this title was conducted and state the date of such inventory.

(C) If the pharmacy changes to a new, permanent location, the pharmacist-in-charge shall comply with subsection (a) of this section.

(D) If the pharmacy moves to a temporary location, the pharmacist shall comply with subsection (a) of this section. If the pharmacy returns to the original location, the pharmacist-in-charge shall again comply with subsection (a) of this section.

(E) If the pharmacy closes due to fire or other disaster, the pharmacy may not be closed for longer than 90 days as specified in § 291.11 of this title (relating to Operation of a Pharmacy).

(F) If the pharmacy discontinues business (ceases to operate as a pharmacy), the pharmacist-in-charge shall comply with § 291.5 of this title (relating to Closing a Pharmacy).

(G) The pharmacist-in-charge shall maintain copies of all inventories, reports, or notifications required by this section for a period of two years.

(2) Drug stock.

(A) Any drug which has been exposed to excessive heat, smoke, or other conditions which may have caused deterioration shall not be dispensed.

(B) Any potentially adulterated or damaged drug shall only be sold, transferred, or otherwise distributed pursuant to the provisions of the Texas Food Drug and Cosmetics Act (Chapter 431, Health and Safety Code) administered by the Bureau of Food and Drug Safety of the Texas Department of State Health Services.

(h) Notification to Consumers.
  (1) Pharmacy.
    (A) Every licensed pharmacy shall provide notification to consumers of the name, mailing address, Internet site address, and telephone number of the board for the purpose of directing complaints concerning the practice of pharmacy to the board. Such notification shall be provided as follows.
      (i) If the pharmacy serves walk-in customers, the pharmacy shall either:
        (I) post in a prominent place that is in clear public view where prescription drugs are dispensed:
          (-a-) a sign which notifies the consumer that complaints concerning the practice of pharmacy may be filed with the board and list the board's name, mailing address, Internet site address, telephone number, and a toll-free telephone number for filing complaints; or
          (-b-) an electronic messaging system in a type size no smaller than ten-point Times Roman which notifies the consumer that complaints concerning the practice of pharmacy may be filed with the board and list the board's name, mailing address, Internet site address, telephone number, and a toll-free number for filing complaints; or
        (II) provide with each dispensed prescription a written notification in a type size no smaller than ten-point Times Roman which states the following: "Complaints concerning the practice of pharmacy may be filed with the Texas State Board of Pharmacy at: (list the mailing address, Internet site address, telephone number of the board, and a toll-free telephone number for filing complaints)."
      (ii) If the prescription drug order is delivered to patients at their residence or other designated location, the pharmacy shall provide with each dispensed prescription a written notification in type size no smaller than ten-point Times Roman which states the following: "Complaints concerning the practice of pharmacy may be filed with the Texas State Board of Pharmacy at: (list the mailing address, Internet site address, telephone number, and a toll-free telephone number for filing complaints)." If multiple prescriptions are delivered to the same location, only one such notice shall be required.
      (iii) The provisions of this subsection do not apply to prescriptions for patients in facilities where drugs are administered to patients by a person required to do so by the laws of the state (i.e., nursing homes).
    (B) A pharmacy that maintains a generally accessible site on the Internet that is located in Texas or sells or distributes drugs through this site to residents of this state shall post the following information on the pharmacy's initial home page and on the page where a sale of prescription drugs occurs.
      (i) Information on the ownership of the pharmacy, to include at a minimum, the:
        (I) owner's name or if the owner is a partnership or corporation, the partnership's or corporation's name and the name of the chief operating officer;
        (II) owner's address;
        (III) owner's telephone number; and
        (IV) year the owner began operating pharmacies in the United States.
      (ii) The Internet address and toll free telephone number that a consumer may use to:
        (I) report medication/device problems to the pharmacy; and
        (II) report business compliance problems.
      (iii) Information about each pharmacy that dispenses prescriptions for this site, to include at a minimum, the:
        (I) pharmacy's name, address, and telephone number;
        (II) name of the pharmacist responsible for operation of the pharmacy;
        (III) Texas pharmacy license number for the pharmacy and a link to the Internet site maintained by the Texas State Board of Pharmacy; and
        (IV) the names of all other states in which the pharmacy is licensed, the license number in that state, and a link to the Internet site of the entity that regulates pharmacies in that state, if available.
    (C) A pharmacy whose Internet site has been verified by the National Association of Boards of Pharmacy to be in compliance with the laws of this state, as well as in all other states in which the pharmacy is licensed shall be in compliance with subparagraph (B) of this paragraph.
  (2) Texas State Board of Pharmacy. On or before January 1, 2005, the board shall establish a pharmacy profile system as specified in § 2054.2606, Government Code.
    (A) The board shall make the pharmacy profiles available to the public on the agency's Internet site.
    (B) A pharmacy profile shall contain at least the following information:
      (i) name, address, and telephone number of the pharmacy;
      (ii) pharmacy license number, licensure status, and expiration date of the license;
      (iii) the class and type of the pharmacy;
      (iv) ownership information for the pharmacy;
      (v) names and license numbers of all pharmacists working at the pharmacy;
      (vi) whether the pharmacy has had prior disciplinary action by the board;
      (vii) whether the pharmacy's consumer service areas are accessible to disabled persons, as defined by law;
      (viii) the type of language translating services, including translating services for persons with impairment of hearing, that the pharmacy provides for consumers; and
      (ix) insurance information including whether the pharmacy participates in the state Medicaid program.
    (C) The board shall gather this information on initial licensing and update the information in conjunction with the license renewal for the pharmacy.
(i) Notification of Licensees or Registrants Obtaining Controlled Substances or Dangerous Drugs by Forged Prescriptions. If a licensee or registrant obtains controlled substances or dangerous drugs from a pharmacy by means of a forged prescription, the pharmacy shall report in writing to the board immediately on discovery of such forgery. A pharmacy shall be in compliance with this subsection by submitting to the board the following:

(1) name of licensee or registrant obtaining controlled substances or dangerous drugs by forged prescription;

(2) date(s) of forged prescription(s);

(3) name(s) and amount(s) of drug(s); and

(4) copies of forged prescriptions.

(j) Notification of Disciplinary Action. For the purpose of the Act, § 562.106, a pharmacy shall report in writing to the board not later than the 10th day after the date of:

(1) a final order against the pharmacy license holder by the regulatory or licensing agency of the state in which the pharmacy is located if the pharmacy is located in another state; or

(2) a final order against a pharmacist who is designated as the pharmacist-in-charge of the pharmacy by the regulatory or licensing agency of the state in which the pharmacy is located if the pharmacy is located in another state.

Source: The provisions of this § 291.3 adopted to be effective September 18, 2007, 32 TexReg 6318; amended to be effective June 7, 2009, 34 TexReg 3390; amended to be effective March 10, 2011, 36 TexReg 1511; amended to be effective June 7, 2012, 37 TexReg 4046; amended to be effective March 15, 2015, 40 TexReg 1086; amended to be effective December 6, 2015, 40 TexReg 8765; amended to be effective June 11, 2017, 42 TexReg 2931; amended to be effective January 4, 2018, 42 TexReg 7691; amended to be effective September 16, 2018, 43 TexReg 5779

§291.5   Closing a Pharmacy

(a) Prior to closing. At least 14 days prior to the closing of a pharmacy that dispenses prescription drug orders the pharmacist-in-charge shall:

(1) post a closing notice sign in a conspicuous place in the front of the prescription department and at all public entrance doors to the pharmacy. Such closing notice sign shall contain the following information:

(A) the date of closing; and

(B) the name, address, and telephone number of the pharmacy acquiring the prescription drug orders, including refill information and patient medication records of the pharmacy.

(2) notify DEA of any controlled substances being transferred to another registrant as specified in 21 CFR 1301.52(d).

(b) Closing day. On the date of closing, the pharmacist-in-charge shall comply with the following:

(1) take an inventory as specified in § 291.17 of this title (relating to Inventory Requirements);

(2) remove all prescription drugs from the pharmacy by one or a combination of the following methods:

(A) return prescription drugs to manufacturer or supplier (for credit/disposal);

(B) transfer (sell or give away) prescription drugs to a person who is legally entitled to possess drugs, such as a hospital, or another pharmacy; and

(C) destroy the prescription drugs following procedures specified in § 303.2 of this title (relating to Disposal of Stock Prescription Drugs);

(3) if the pharmacy dispenses prescription drug orders:

(A) transfer the prescription drug order files, including refill information, and patient medication records to a licensed pharmacy; and

(B) remove all signs or notify the landlord or owner of the property that it is unlawful to use the word "pharmacy" either in English or any other language, or any other word or combination of words of the same or similar meaning, or any graphic representation that would mislead or tend to mislead the public that a pharmacy is located at the address.

(c) After closing.

(1) Within ten days after the closing of the pharmacy, the pharmacist-in-charge shall forward to the board a written notice of the closing which includes the following information:

(A) the actual date of closing;

(B) the license issued to the pharmacy;

(C) a statement attesting:

(i) that an inventory as specified in § 291.17 of this title (relating to Inventory Requirements) has been conducted; and

(ii) the manner by which the dangerous drugs and controlled substances possessed by the pharmacy were transferred or disposed; and

(D) if the pharmacy dispenses prescription drug orders, the name and address of the pharmacy to which the prescription drug orders, including refill information, and patient medication records were transferred.

(2) If the pharmacy is registered to possess controlled substances, send notification to the appropriate DEA divisional office explaining that the pharmacy has closed and include the following items:

(A) DEA registration certificate; and

(B) all unused DEA order forms (222) with the word VOID written on the face of each order form.

(3) Once the pharmacy has notified the board that the pharmacy is closed, the license may not be renewed. The pharmacy may apply for a new license as specified in § 291.1 of this title (relating to Pharmacy License Application).

(d) Emergency closing. If pharmacy is closed suddenly due to fire, destruction, natural disaster, death, property seizure, eviction, bankruptcy, or other emergency circumstances and the pharmacist-in-charge cannot provide notification 14 days prior to the closing, the pharmacist-in-charge shall comply with the provisions of subsection (a) of this section as far in advance of the closing as allowed by the circumstances.

(e) Joint responsibility. If the pharmacist-in-charge is not available to comply with the requirements of this section, the owner shall be responsible for compliance with the provisions of this section.

Source: The provisions of this § 291.5 adopted to be effective June 17, 1986, 11 TEXREG 2553; amended to be effective July 29, 1987, 12 TEXREG 2337; amended to be effective September 30, 1993, 18 TexReg 6459; amended to be effective June 20, 1995, 20 TexReg 4121; amended to be effective March 25, 2007, 32 TexReg 1510; amended to be effective June 12, 2016, 41 TexReg 4257; amended to be effective January 4, 2018, 42 TexReg 7691

§291.6 Pharmacy License Fees

(a) Initial License Fee. The fee for an initial license shall be $ 507 for the initial registration period.
(b) Biennial License Renewal. The Texas State Board of Pharmacy shall require biennial renewal of all pharmacy licenses provided under the Act § 561.002.
(c) Renewal Fee. The fee for biennial renewal of a pharmacy license shall be $ 504 for the renewal period.
(d) Duplicate or Amended Certificates. The fee for issuance of a duplicate pharmacy license renewal certificate shall be $ 20. The fee for issuance of an amended pharmacy license renewal certificate shall be $ 100.

Source: The provisions of this § 291.6 adopted to be effective December 23, 2003, 28 TexReg 11260; amended to be effective September 1, 2004, 29 TexReg 5348; amended to be effective March 6, 2006, 31 TexReg 1440; amended to be effective November 1, 2006, 31 TexReg 6732; amended to be effective October 1, 2007, 32 TexReg 6318; amended to be effective October 1, 2009, 34 TexReg 6111 amended to be effective September 14, 2010, 35 TexReg 8357; amended to be effective December 1, 2011, 36 TexReg 5846; amended to be effective October 1, 2012, 37 TexReg 6917; amended to be effective January 1, 2014, 38 TexReg 8834; amended to be effective September 11, 2014, 39 TexReg 7093; amended to be effective October 1, 2015, 40 TexReg 6110; amended to be effective January 4, 2018, 42 TexReg 7691; amended to be effective October 1, 2019, 44 TexReg 4872

§291.7 Prescription Drug Recalls by the Manufacturer

(a) The pharmacist-in-charge shall develop and implement a written procedure for proper management of drug recalls by the manufacturer. Such procedures shall include, where appropriate, contacting patients to whom the recalled drug products have been dispensed.
(b) The written procedure shall include, but not be limited to, the following:
    (1) the pharmacist-in-charge shall reasonably ensure that a recalled drug has been removed from inventory no more than 24 hours after receipt of the recall notice, and quarantined until proper disposal or destruction of the drug; and
    (2) if the drug that is the subject to a recall is maintained by the pharmacy in a container without a lot number, the pharmacist-in-charge shall consider this drug included in the recall.

Source: The provisions of this §291.7 adopted to be effective May 30, 2010, 35 TexReg 4164

§291.8 Return of Prescription Drugs

(a) General prohibition on return of prescription drugs. As specified in §431.021(w), Health and Safety Code, a pharmacist may not accept an unused prescription or drug, in whole or in part, for the purpose of resale or re-dispensing to any person, after the prescription or drug has been originally dispensed, or sold except as provided in subsection (b) of this section.
(b) Return of prescription drugs from health care facilities.
    (1) Purpose. The purpose of this subsection is to outline procedures for the return of unused drugs from a health care facility or a penal institution to a dispensing pharmacy as specified in the §562.1085 of the Occupations Code. Nothing in this section shall require a consultant pharmacist, health care facility, penal institution, or pharmacy to participate in the return of unused drugs.
    (2) Definitions. The following words and terms, when used in this section, shall have the following meanings, unless the context clearly indicates otherwise.
        (A) Consultant pharmacist—A pharmacist who practices in or serves as a consultant for a health care facility in this state.
        (B) Health care facility—A facility regulated under Chapter 242, Health and Safety Code.
        (C) Licensed health care professional—A person licensed by the Texas Medical Board, Texas Board of Nurse Examiners, or the Texas State Board of Pharmacy.
        (D) Penal institution—A place designated by law for confinement of persons arrested for, charged with, or convicted of an offense. A penal institution includes a city, county or state jail or prison.
    (3) Responsibilities. A licensed health care professional in a penal institution or a consultant pharmacist may return to a pharmacy certain unused drugs, other than a controlled substance as defined by Chapter 481, Health and Safety Code, purchased from the pharmacy.
        (A) The unused drugs must:
            (i) be approved by the federal Food and Drug Administration and be:
                (I) sealed in unopened tamper-evident packaging and either individually packaged or packaged in unit-dose packaging;
                (II) oral or parenteral medication in sealed single-dose containers approved by the federal Food and Drug Administration;
                (III) topical or inhalant drugs in sealed unit-of-use containers approved by the federal Food and Drug Administration; or
                (IV) parenteral medications in sealed multiple-dose containers approved by the federal Food and Drug Administration from which doses have not been withdrawn.
            (ii) not be the subject of a mandatory recall by a state or federal agency or a voluntary recall by a drug seller or manufacturer; and
            (iii) have not been in the physical possession of the person for whom it was prescribed.
        (B) A healthcare facility or penal institution may not return any drug product that:
            (i) has been compounded;
            (ii) appears on inspection to be adulterated;
            (iii) requires refrigeration; or
            (iv) has less than 120 days until the expiration date or end of the shelf life.
        (C) The consultant pharmacist or licensed health care professional in a penal institution shall be responsible for assuring an inventory of the drugs to be returned to a pharmacy is completed. The following information shall be included on this inventory:
            (i) name and address of the facility or institution;
            (ii) name and pharmacist license number of the consultant pharmacist or name and license number of the licensed health care professional;
            (iii) date of return;
            (iv) date the prescription was dispensed;

Phr. Rules

     (v) unique identification number assigned to the prescription by the pharmacy;

     (vi) name of dispensing pharmacy;

     (vii) name, strength, and quantity of drug;

     (viii) signature of consultant pharmacist or licensed healthcare professional responsible for the administration of drugs in a penal institution.

  (D) The health care facility/penal institution shall send a copy of the inventory specified in subparagraph (C) of this paragraph to:

     (i) the pharmacy with the drugs returned; and

     (ii) the Health and Human Services Commission.

(4) Dispensing/Receiving pharmacy responsibilities. If a pharmacy accepts the return of unused drugs from a health care facility/penal institution, the following is applicable.

  (A) A pharmacist employed by the pharmacy shall examine the drugs to ensure the integrity of the drug product.

  (B) The pharmacy shall reimburse or credit the entity that paid for the drug including the state Medicaid program for an unused drug returned to the pharmacy. The pharmacy shall maintain a record of the credit or reimbursement containing the following information:

     (i) name and address of the facility or institution which returned the drugs;

     (ii) date and amount of the credit or reimbursement was issued;

     (iii) name of the person or entity to whom the credit or reimbursement was issued;

     (iv) date the prescription was dispensed;

     (v) unique identification number assigned to the prescription by the pharmacy;

     (vi) name, strength, and quantity of drug;

     (vii) signature of the pharmacist responsible for issuing the credit.

  (C) After the pharmacy has issued credit or reimbursement, the pharmacy may restock and redispense the unused drugs returned under this section.

(5) Limitation on Liability.

  (A) A pharmacy that returns unused drugs and a manufacturer that accepts the unused drugs under §562.1085, Occupations Code, and the employees of the pharmacy or manufacturer are not liable for harm caused by the accepting, dispensing, or administering of drugs returned in strict compliance with §562.1085, Occupations Code, unless the harm is caused by:

     (i) wilful or wanton acts of negligence;

     (ii) conscious indifference or reckless disregard for the safety of others; or

     (iii) intentional conduct.

  (B) This section does not limit, or in any way affect or diminish, the liability of a drug seller or manufacturer under Chapter 82, Civil Practice and Remedies Code.

  (C) This section does not apply if harm results from the failure to fully and completely comply with the requirements of §562.1085, Occupations Code.

  (D) This section does not apply to a pharmacy or manufacturer that fails to comply with the insurance provisions of Chapter 84, Civil Practice and Remedies Code.

Source: The provisions of this §291.8 adopted to be effective December 23, 2003, 28 TexReg 11261; amended to be effective September 18, 2007, 32 TexReg 6318; amended to be effective December 6, 2009, 34 TexReg 8690

§291.9 Prescription Pick Up Locations

(a) Except as provided in § 291.155 of this title (relating to Limited Prescription Delivery Pharmacy (Class H)), no person, firm, or business establishment may have, participate in, or permit an arrangement, branch, connection or affiliation whereby prescriptions are solicited, collected, picked up, or advertised to be picked up, from or at any location other than a pharmacy which is licensed and in good standing with the board.

(b) A pharmacist or pharmacy by means of its employee or by use of a common carrier or the U.S. Mail, at the request of the patient, may:

  (1) pick up prescription orders at the:

    (A) office or home of the prescriber;

    (B) residence or place of employment of the person for whom the prescription was issued; or

    (C) hospital or medical care facility in which the patient is receiving treatment; and

  (2) deliver prescription drugs to the:

    (A) office of the prescriber if the prescription is:

     (i) for a dangerous drug; or

     (ii) for a single dose of a controlled substance that is for administration to the patient in the prescriberas office;

    (B) residence of the person for whom the prescription was issued;

    (C) place of employment of the person for whom the prescription was issued, if the person is present to accept delivery; or

    (D) hospital or medical care facility in which the patient is receiving treatment.

Source: The provisions of this § 291.9 adopted to be effective November 5, 1982, 7 TEXREG 2916; amended to be effective September 14, 2010, 35 TexReg 8357; amended to be effective June 7, 2012, 37 TexReg 4046; amended to be effective June 7, 2018, 43 TexReg 3587

§291.10 Pharmacy Balance Registration/Inspection

(a) Definitions. The following words and terms, when used in this section, shall have the following meanings, unless the context clearly indicates otherwise. Pharmacy balance—An instrument for weighing including balances and scales.

(b) Registration.

  (1) A pharmacy shall annually or biennially register each pharmacy balance. The fee for the annual registration shall be $12.50 per pharmacy balance. The fee for the biennial registration shall be $25.00 per pharmacy balance.

  (2) The expiration date for pharmacy balance registrations shall coincide with the pharmacy license expiration date.

(c) Inspection.

(1)　The Board shall periodically inspect pharmacy balances to verify accuracy.
(2)　If a pharmacy balance fails the accuracy inspection, the following is applicable.
　　(A)　The pharmacy balance may not be used until it is repaired by an authorized repair person.
　　(B)　A tag indicating that the pharmacy balance failed the inspection and may not be used shall be placed on the pharmacy balance.

Source: The provisions of this §291.10 adopted to be effective January 23, 1996, 21 TexReg 261; amended to be effective July 16, 1999, 24 TexReg 5196; amended to be effective January 3, 2000, 24 TexReg 12066; amended to be effective September 18, 2007, 32 TexReg 6318

§291.11 Operation of a Pharmacy

(a)　For the purposes of §565.002(7) of the Texas Pharmacy Act, the following words and terms shall be defined as follows.
　　(1)　"Failure to engage in the business described in the application for a license" means the holder of a pharmacy license has not commenced operating the pharmacy within six months of the date of issuance of the license.
　　(2)　"Ceased to engage in the business described in the application for a license" means the holder of a pharmacy license, once it has been in operation, discontinues operating the pharmacy for a period of 30 days or longer unless the pharmacy experiences a fire or disaster, in which case the pharmacy must comply with §291.3(f) of this title (relating to Notifications).
(b)　For the purposes of this section, the term "operating the pharmacy" means the pharmacy shall demonstrate observable pharmacy business activity on a regular, routine basis, including a sufficient number of transactions of receiving, processing, or dispensing prescription drug orders or medication drug orders.
(c)　No person may operate a pharmacy in a personal residence.

Source: The provisions of this §291.11 adopted to be effective June 13, 2002, 27 TexReg 4947; amended to be effective March 10, 2011, 36 TexReg 1511

§291.14 Pharmacy License Renewal

(a)　Renewal requirements.
　　(1)　A license to operate a pharmacy expires on the last day of the assigned expiration month.
　　(2)　The provision of the Act, § 561.005, shall apply if the completed application and a renewal fee is not received in the board's office on or before the last day of the assigned expiration month.
　　(3)　An expired license may be renewed according to the following schedule:
　　　　(A)　If the license has been expired for 90 days or less, the license may be renewed by paying to the board a renewal fee that is equal to one and one-half times the required renewal fee as specified in § 291.6 of this title (relating to Pharmacy License Fees).
　　　　(B)　If the license has been expired for 91 days or more, the license may not be renewed. The pharmacy may apply for a new license as specified in § 291.1 of this title (relating to Pharmacy License Application).
(b)　If the board determines on inspection at the pharmacy's address on or after the expiration date of the license that no pharmacy is located or exists at the pharmacy's address (e.g., the building is vacated or for sale or lease, or another business is operating at the location), the board shall not renew the license.
(c)　Additional renewal requirements for Class E pharmacies. In addition to the renewal requirements in subsection (a) of this section, a Class E pharmacy shall have on file with the Board an inspection report issued:
　　(1)　not more than three years before the date the renewal application is received; and
　　(2)　by the pharmacy licensing board in the state of the pharmacy's physical location except as provided in § 291.104 of this title (relating to Operational Standards).

Source: The provisions of this § 291.14 adopted to be effective May 28, 1982, 7 TEXREG 1857; amended to be effective May 17, 1983, 8 TEXREG 1494; amended to be effective April 16, 1985, 10 TEXREG 1104; amended to be effective February 17, 1988, 13 TEXREG 613; amended to be effective May 31, 1995, 20 TexReg 1888; amended to be effective January 3, 2000, 24 TexReg 12066; amended to be effective March 12, 2003, 28 TexReg 2082; amended to be effective March 6, 2006, 31 TexReg 1440; amended to be effective June 12, 2016, 41 TexReg 4257

§291.15 Storage of Drugs

All drugs shall be stored at the proper temperature and conditions as defined by the following terms:
　　(1)　Freezer—A place in which the temperature is maintained thermostatically between minus 25 degrees Celsius and minus 10 degrees Celsius (minus 13 degrees Fahrenheit and 14 degrees Fahrenheit).
　　(2)　Cold—Any temperature not exceeding 8 degrees Celsius (46 degrees Fahrenheit). A refrigerator is a cold place in which the temperature is maintained thermostatically between 2 degrees Celsius and 8 degrees Celsius (36 degrees Fahrenheit and 46 degrees Fahrenheit).
　　(3)　Cool—Any temperature between 8 degrees Celsius and 15 degrees Celsius (46 degrees Fahrenheit and 59 degrees Fahrenheit). An article for which storage in a cool place is directed may, alternatively, be stored and distributed in a refrigerator, unless otherwise specified by the individual monograph.
　　(4)　Room temperature—The temperature prevailing in a working area.
　　(5)　Controlled room temperature—A temperature maintained thermostatically between 15 degrees Celsius and 30 degrees Celsius (59 degrees Fahrenheit and 86 degrees Fahrenheit).
　　(6)　Warm—Any temperature between 30 degrees Celsius and 40 degrees Celsius (86 degrees Fahrenheit and 104 degrees Fahrenheit).
　　(7)　Excessive heat—Any temperature above 40 degrees Celsius (104 degrees Fahrenheit).
　　(8)　Protection from freezing—Where, in addition to the risk of breakage of the container, freezing subjects a product to loss of strength or potency, or to destructive alteration of the dosage form, the container label bears an appropriate instruction to protect the product from freezing.
　　(9)　Dry place—A place that does not exceed 40% average relative humidity at controlled room temperature or the equivalent water vapor pressure at other temperatures.

Source: The provisions of this §291.15 adopted to be effective September 7, 2008, 33 TexReg 7218

§291.16 Samples

Unless otherwise specified, a pharmacy may not sell, purchase, trade or possess prescription drug samples, unless the pharmacy meets all of the following conditions:

    (1)   the pharmacy is owned by a charitable organization described in the Internal Revenue Code of 1986, or by a city, state or county government;

    (2)   the pharmacy is a part of a health care entity which provides health care primarily to indigent or low income patients at no or reduced cost;

    (3)   the samples are for dispensing or provision at no charge to patients of such health care entity; and

    (4)   the samples are possessed in compliance with the federal Prescription Drug Marketing Act of 1987.

Source: The provisions of this §291.16 adopted to be effective March 10, 2011, 36 TexReg 1511

§291.17 Inventory Requirements

(a)   General requirements.

    (1)   The pharmacist-in-charge shall be responsible for taking all required inventories, but may delegate the performance of the inventory to another person(s).

    (2)   The inventory shall be maintained in a written, typewritten, or printed form. An inventory taken by use of an oral recording device must be promptly transcribed.

    (3)   The inventory shall be kept in the pharmacy and shall be available for inspection for two years.

    (4)   The inventory shall be filed separately from all other records.

    (5)   The inventory shall be in a written, typewritten, or printed form and include all stocks of all controlled substances on hand on the date of the inventory (including any which are out-of-date).

    (6)   The inventory may be taken either as of the opening of business or as of the close of business on the inventory date.

    (7)   The inventory record shall indicate whether the inventory is taken as of the opening of business or as of the close of business on the inventory date. If the pharmacy is open 24 hours a day, the inventory record shall indicate the time that the inventory was taken.

    (8)   The person(s) taking the inventory shall make an exact count or measure of all controlled substances listed in Schedule II.

    (9)   The person(s) taking the inventory shall make an estimated count or measure of all controlled substances listed in Schedules III, IV, and V, unless the container holds more than 1,000 tablets or capsules in which case, an exact count of the contents must be made.

    (10)   The inventory of Schedule II controlled substances shall be listed separately from the inventory of Schedules III, IV, and V controlled substances.

    (11)   If the pharmacy maintains a perpetual inventory of any of the drugs required to be inventoried, the perpetual inventory shall be reconciled on the date of the inventory.

(b)   Initial inventory.

    (1)   A new Class A, Class A-S, Class C, Class C-S, or Class F pharmacy shall take an inventory on the opening day of business. Such inventory shall include all stocks of all controlled substances (including any out-of-date drugs).

    (2)   In the event the Class A, Class A-S, Class C, Class C-S, or Class F pharmacy commences business with no controlled substances on hand, the pharmacy shall record this fact as the initial inventory.

    (3)   The initial inventory shall serve as the pharmacy's inventory until the next May 1, or until the pharmacy's regular general physical inventory date, at which time the Class A, Class A-S, Class C, Class C-S, or Class F pharmacy shall take an annual inventory as specified in subsection (c) of this section.

(c)   Annual inventory.

    (1)   A Class A, Class A-S, Class C, Class C-S, or Class F pharmacy shall take an inventory on May 1 of each year, or on the pharmacy's regular general physical inventory date. Such inventory may be taken within four days of the specified inventory date and shall include all stocks of all controlled substances (including out-of-date drugs).

    (2)   A Class A, Class A-S, Class C, Class C-S, or Class F pharmacy applying for renewal of a pharmacy license shall include as a part of the pharmacy license renewal application a statement attesting that an annual inventory has been conducted, the date of the inventory, and the name of the person(s) taking the inventory.

    (3)   The person(s) taking the annual inventory and the pharmacist-in-charge shall indicate the time the inventory was taken (as specified in subsection (a)(7) of this section) and shall sign and date the inventory with the date the inventory was taken. The signature of the pharmacist-in-charge and the date of the inventory shall be notarized within three days after the day the inventory is completed, excluding Saturdays, Sundays, and federal holidays.

(d)   Change of ownership.

    (1)   A Class A, Class A-S, Class C, Class C-S, or Class F pharmacy that changes ownership shall take an inventory on the date of the change of ownership. Such inventory shall include all stocks of all controlled substances (including any out-of-date drugs).

    (2)   Such inventory shall constitute, for the purpose of this section, the closing inventory for the seller and the initial inventory for the buyer.

    (3)   Transfer of any controlled substances listed in Schedule II shall require the use of official DEA order forms (Form 222).

    (4)   The person(s) taking the inventory and the pharmacist-in-charge shall indicate the time the inventory was taken (as specified in subsection (a)(7) of this section) and shall sign and date the inventory with the date the inventory was taken. The signature of the pharmacist-in-charge and the date of the inventory shall be notarized within three days after the day the inventory is completed, excluding Saturdays, Sundays, and federal holidays.

(e)   Closed pharmacies.

    (1)   The pharmacist-in-charge of a Class A, Class A-S, Class C, Class C-S, or Class F pharmacy that ceases to operate as a pharmacy shall forward to the board, within 10 days of the cessation of operation, a statement attesting that an inventory of all controlled substances on hand has been conducted, the date of closing, and a statement attesting the manner by which the dangerous drugs and controlled substances possessed by such pharmacy were transferred or disposed.

Phr. Rules

(2)   The person(s) taking the inventory and the pharmacist-in-charge shall indicate the time the inventory was taken (as specified in subsection (a)(7) of this section) and shall sign and date the inventory with the date the inventory was taken. The signature of the pharmacist-in-charge and the date of the inventory shall be notarized within three days after the day the inventory is completed, excluding Saturdays, Sundays, and federal holidays.

(f)   Additional requirements for Class C and Class C-S pharmacies.
   (1)   Perpetual inventory.
      (A)   A Class C or Class C-S pharmacy shall maintain a perpetual inventory of all Schedule II controlled substances.
      (B)   The perpetual inventory shall be reconciled on the date of the annual inventory.
   (2)   Annual inventory. The inventory of the Class C or Class C-S pharmacy shall be maintained in the pharmacy. The inventory shall include all controlled substances located in the pharmacy and, if applicable, all controlled substances located in other departments within the institution. If an inventory is conducted in other departments within the institution, the inventory of the pharmacy shall be listed separately, as follows:
      (A)   the inventory of drugs on hand in the pharmacy shall be listed separately from the inventory of drugs on hand in the other areas of the institution; and
      (B)   the inventory of drugs on hand in all other departments shall be identified by department.

(g)   Change of pharmacist-in-charge of a pharmacy.
   (1)   On the date of the change of the pharmacist-in-charge of a Class A, Class A-S, Class C, Class C-S, or Class F pharmacy, an inventory shall be taken. Such inventory shall include all stocks of all controlled substances (including any out-of-date drugs).
   (2)   This inventory shall constitute, for the purpose of this section, the closing inventory of the departing pharmacist-in-charge and the beginning inventory of the incoming pharmacist-in-charge.
   (3)   If the departing and the incoming pharmacists-in-charge are unable to conduct the inventory together, a closing inventory shall be conducted by the departing pharmacist-in-charge and a new and separate beginning inventory shall be conducted by the incoming pharmacist-in-charge.
   (4)   The incoming pharmacist-in-charge shall be responsible for notifying the board within 10 days, as specified in § 291.3 of this title (relating to Required Notifications), that a change of pharmacist-in-charge has occurred.

   Source: The provisions of this § 291.17 adopted to be effective September 1, 1987, 12   TEXREG2568; amended to be effective September 30, 1993, 18 TexReg 6459; amended to be effective July 16, 1999, 24 TexReg 5196; amended to be effective June 4, 2000, 25 TexReg 4777; amended to be effective March 12, 2003, 28 TexReg 2082; amended to be effective March 10, 2011, 36 TexReg 1511; amended to be effective June 7, 2012, 37 TexReg 4046; amended to be effective December 5, 2012, 37 TexReg 9511; amended to be effective December 10, 2013, 38 TexReg 8835; amended to be effective December 6, 2015, 40 TexReg 8765; amended to be effective December 6, 2018, 43 TexReg 7772; amended to beeffective June 20, 2019, 44 TexReg 2946

§291.18 Time Limit for Filing a Complaint

For the purposes of the Act, §556.055, the board determines that a "reasonable time" to be no less than 10 days from the date of an inspection giving rise to a possible complaint; provided, however, in situations presenting imminent danger to the public health and safety, the board may obtain an injunction under the Act, §566.051, to restrain or enjoin a person from continuing to violate the Act or rules promulgated pursuant to the Act without waiting the 10-day period set out in this section.

   Source: The provisions of this §291.18 adopted to be effective June 11, 1982, 7 TexReg 2065; amended to be effective March 12, 2003, 28 TexReg 2082; amended to be effective September 18, 2007, 32 TexReg 6318

§291.19 Administrative Actions as a Result of a Compliance Inspection

As a result of a compliance inspection or compliance reinspection of a pharmacy wherein violations of the Texas Pharmacy Act, Controlled Substances Act, Dangerous Drug Act, Texas Food, Drug and Cosmetic Act, or rules adopted pursuant to such acts are observed:
   (1)   an agent of the board may issue a written report of areas of non-compliance that need improvement;
   (2)   an agent of the board may issue a written warning notice listing specific violations to which the licensee shall respond in writing to the board by the date stated on the warning notice, indicating that the violations listed in the warning notice will be corrected;
   (3)   an agent of the board may recommend the institution of disciplinary action against a licensee if such agent determines that:
      (A)   previously cited violations are continuing to occur; or
      (B)   violations observed are of a nature that written notice of non-compliance or a written warning notice would not be in the best interest of the public; or
   (4)   an agent of the board, upon determination that the violations observed are of a nature that pose an imminent peril to the public health, safety, or welfare, may recommend to the director of compliance, the institution of action by a district court in Travis County, Texas, to restrain or enjoin a licensee from continuing the violation, in addition to recommending the institution of disciplinary action against a licensee.

   Source: The provisions of this § 291.19 adopted to be effective December 18, 1985, 10 TEXREG 4692; amended to be effective September 18, 2007, 32 TexReg 6318; amended to be effective September 16, 2018, 43 TexReg 5779

§291.22 Petition to Establish an Additional Class of Pharmacy

(a)   Purpose. The purpose of this section is to specify the procedures to be followed in petitioning the board to establish an additional class of pharmacy as authorized by §560.053 of the Texas Pharmacy Act (Chapters 551 – 566 and 568 – 569, Texas Occupations Code). In reviewing petitions, the board will only consider petitions that provide pharmaceutical care services which contribute to positive patient outcomes. The board will not consider any petition intended only to provide a competitive advantage.

(b)   Procedures for petitioning the board to establish an additional class of pharmacy. A person who wishes the board to consider establishing an additional class of pharmacy shall submit to the board a petition that contains at least the following information:
   (1)   name, address, telephone number, and pharmacist's license number of the pharmacist responsible for submitting the petition;
   (2)   a detailed summary of the additional class of pharmacy which includes:
      (A)   a description of the type of pharmacy and the pharmaceutical care services provided to the public;
      (B)   if a pharmacy of this type currently exists, the name, address, and license number of the pharmacy;

       (C) a full explanation of the reasons:
          (i)   the existing classifications of pharmacy licenses are not appropriate for this practice setting; and
          (ii) that establishment of a new classification of pharmacy license is necessary to protect the public health, safety, and welfare.

(c) Review and approval or denial of the petition.
    (1) On receipt of a petition to establish an additional class of pharmacy, board staff shall initially review the petition for completeness and appropriateness. If the petition is incomplete or inappropriate for board consideration for any reason, board staff shall return the petition with a letter of explanation. Such review shall be completed within 30 working days of receipt of the petition.
    (2) Once board staff has determined that the petition is complete and appropriate, a task force composed of board staff, at least one board member and, if deemed necessary, resource personnel appointed by the board president, shall review the petition and make a written recommendation to the board regarding approval. Such recommendation shall be presented to the board at the next regularly scheduled meeting of the board that occurs at least three weeks after completion of the review and written recommendation.
    (3) A copy of the recommendation shall be provided to the petitioner and the board at least two weeks prior to the board meeting.
    (4) Both the petitioner and a representative of the task force shall be given equal time for presentations to the board.
    (5) Upon hearing the presentations, the board shall approve or deny the petition. If the board approves the petition, the board shall direct staff to develop rules for the new class of pharmacy or appoint a task force to work with the staff to assist in developing rules for the new class of pharmacy. The board shall approve or deny any petition to establish an additional class of pharmacy not later than the board meeting following the meeting at which the petition is heard.

Source: The provisions of this §291.22 adopted to be effective March 4, 2004, 29 TexReg 1950; amended to be effective September 18, 2007, 32 TexReg 6318

§291.23 Pilot or Demonstration Research Projects for Innovative Applications in the Practice of Pharmacy

(a) Purpose. The purpose of this section is to specify the procedures to be followed in applying for approval of a pilot or demonstration research project for innovative applications in the practice of pharmacy as authorized by §554.011 of the Texas Pharmacy Act (Chapters 551- 566 and 568 – 569, Texas Occupations Code). In reviewing projects, the board will only consider projects that expand pharmaceutical care services which contribute to positive patient outcomes. The board will not consider any project intended only to provide a competitive advantage.

(b) Scope of pilot or demonstration research projects and the board's approval of such projects.
    (1) Pilot or demonstration research projects may not:
       (A) expand the definition of the practice of pharmacy as provided in the Act; or
       (B) include therapeutic substitution or substitution of medical devices used in patient care.
    (2) The board's approval of pilot or demonstration research projects may include the granting of an exception to the rules adopted under the Texas Pharmacy Act, but may not include an exception from any law relating to the practice of pharmacy. Such exception to the rules shall be for a specified period of time and such period may not exceed 18 months.
    (3) The board may extend the time an exception to a rule is granted as necessary for the board to adopt an amendment or modification of the rule.

(c) Procedures for applying for approval of pilot or demonstration research projects. A person who wishes the board to consider approval of a pilot or demonstration research project shall submit to the board a petition for approval which contains at least the following information:
    (1) name, address, telephone number, and pharmacist's license number of the pharmacist responsible for overseeing the project;
    (2) specific location and, if a pharmacy, the pharmacy license number where the proposed pilot or demonstration project will be conducted;
    (3) a detailed summary of the proposed pilot or demonstration project which includes:
       (A) the goals, hypothesis, and/or objectives of the proposed project;
       (B) a full explanation of the project and how it will be conducted;
       (C) the time frame for the project including the proposed start date and length of study. Such time frame may not exceed 18 months;
       (D) background information and/or literature review to support the proposal;
       (E) the rule(s) that will have to be waived in order to complete the project and a request to waive the rule(s);
       (F) procedures to be used during the project to ensure that the public's health and safety are not compromised as a result of the rule waiver.

(d) Review and approval or denial of the proposed projects.
    (1) On receipt of a petition for approval of a pilot or demonstration research project, board staff shall initially review the petition for completeness and appropriateness. If the petition is incomplete or inappropriate for board consideration for any reason, staff shall return the petition with a letter of explanation. Such review shall be completed within 30 working days of receipt of the petition.
    (2) Once board staff has determined that the petition is complete and appropriate, a task force composed of board staff, at least one board member and, if deemed necessary, resource personnel appointed by the board president, shall review the petition and make a written recommendation to the board regarding approval. Such recommendation shall be presented to the board at the next regularly scheduled meeting of the board that occurs at least three weeks after completion of the review and written recommendation.
    (3) A copy of the recommendation shall be provided to the petitioner and the board at least two weeks prior to the board meeting.
    (4) Both the petitioner and a representative of the task force shall be given equal time for presentations to the board.
    (5) Upon hearing the presentations, the board shall either approve or deny the petition. If the board approves the petition, the approval:
       (A) shall be specific for that project and for a specific time period; and
       (B) may include conditions or qualifications, if deemed appropriate by the board.
    (6) The board or its representatives shall be allowed to inspect and review the project documentation and site at any time during the review process and after the project is approved.

(e) Presentation of results to the board.
  (1) The pharmacist responsible for overseeing the project shall forward to the board a summary of the results of the project and conclusions drawn from the results within three months after completion of the project.
  (2) A task force composed of board staff, at least one board member and, if deemed necessary, resource personnel appointed by the board president, shall review the results and make written recommendations to the board regarding the results of the project.
  (3) The board will receive the report of the task force at the next regularly scheduled meeting of the board that occurs at least three weeks after the task force has completed its review and issued written recommendations.
  (4) A copy of the task force recommendation shall be provided to the petitioner and the board at least two weeks prior to the board meeting.
  (5) Both the petitioner and a representative of the task force shall be given equal time for presentations to the board.
    Source: The provisions of this §291.23 adopted to be effective October 11, 1996, 21 TexReg 9441; amended to be effective December 27, 2000, 25 TexReg 12690; amended to be effective September 18, 2007, 32 TexReg 6318

§291.24 Pharmacy Residency Programs

For the purposes of Subchapter T, Chapter 61, Education Code, the standards for pharmacy residency programs shall be the standards required by the American Society of Health-System Pharmacists' Commission on Credentialing. The pharmacy residency programs approved by the Board shall be published periodically in the minutes of the Board.
    Source: The provisions of this §291.24 adopted to be effective September 18, 2007, 32 TexReg 6318

§291.27 Confidentiality

(a) A pharmacist shall provide adequate security of prescription drug orders, medication orders, and patient medication records to prevent indiscriminate or unauthorized access to confidential health information. If prescription drug orders, requests for refill authorization, or other confidential health information are not transmitted directly between a pharmacy and a physician but are transmitted through a data communication device, confidential health information may not be accessed or maintained by the operator of the data communication device unless specifically authorized to obtain the confidential information by this section.
(b) Confidential records are privileged and may be released only to:
  (1) the patient or the patient's agent;
  (2) a practitioner or another pharmacist if, in the pharmacist's professional judgement, the release is necessary to protect the patient's health and well being;
  (3) the board or to a person or another state or federal agency authorized by law to receive the confidential record;
  (4) a law enforcement agency engaged in investigation of a suspected violation of Chapter 481 or 483, Health and Safety Code, or the Comprehensive Drug Abuse Prevention and Control Act of 1970 (21 U.S.C. Section 801 et seq.);
  (5) a person employed by a state agency that licenses a practitioner, if the person is performing the person's official duties; or
  (6) an insurance carrier or other third party payor authorized by a patient to receive such information.
(c) A pharmacy shall provide written polices and procedures to prohibit the unauthorized disclosure of confidential records.
    Source: The provisions of this §291.27 adopted to be effective September 18, 2007, 32 TexReg 6318

§291.28 Access to Confidential Records

(a) Access to confidential records. A pharmacy shall comply with the request of a patient or a patient's agent to inspect or obtain a copy of the patient's confidential records maintained by the pharmacy, as defined in § 551.003(10) of the Act. A pharmacy shall comply with all relevant state and federal laws regarding release of confidential records to third party requestors.
(b) Form of request. The pharmacy may require a patient or a patient's agent or any authorized third party to make requests for confidential records in writing, provided such a requirement has been communicated to the requestor.
(c) Timely action by pharmacy. The pharmacy must respond to a request for confidential records in a timely manner.
  (1) The pharmacy must respond to a request for confidential records no later than fifteen days after receipt of the request by providing a copy of the records or, with the consent of the requestor, a summary or explanation of such information.
  (2) The pharmacy must provide confidential records as requested in a mutually agreed upon format.
  (3) Access to confidential records may be expedited at the request of a patient or a patient's agent if there is a medical emergency. The pharmacy must respond to a request for expedited access to confidential records within 24 hours if the records are maintained at the pharmacy or within 72 hours if the records are stored off-site. The pharmacy may charge a reasonable fee, in addition to the fees outlined in subsection (d) of this section, of no more than $ 25.00 for expediting a request for access to confidential records.
(d) Fees. The pharmacy may charge a reasonable, cost-based fee for providing a copy of confidential records or a summary or explanation of such information.
  (1) A reasonable fee shall be a charge of no more than $ 50.00 for the first twenty pages and $ 0.50 per page for every page thereafter. A reasonable fee shall include only the cost of:
    (A) copying, including the cost of supplies for and labor of copying;
    (B) postage, when the individual has requested the records be mailed; and
    (C) preparing an explanation or summary of the protected health information, if appropriate and consented to by the patient or patient's agent.
  (2) If an affidavit is requested certifying that the information is a true and correct copy of the records, a reasonable fee of no more than $ 15.00 may be charged for executing the affidavit.
  (3) If an affidavit or questionnaire accompanies the request, the pharmacy may charge a reasonable fee of no more than $ 50.00 to complete the written response.
    Source: The provisions of this § 291.28 adopted to be effective September 3, 2006, 31 TexReg 6732; amended to be effective December 6, 2009, 34 TexReg 8690; amended to be effective December 6, 2018, 43 TexReg 7774

§291.29 Professional Responsibility of Pharmacists

(a)   A pharmacist shall exercise sound professional judgment with respect to the accuracy and authenticity of any prescription drug order dispensed. If the pharmacist questions the accuracy or authenticity of a prescription drug order, the pharmacist shall verify the order with the practitioner prior to dispensing.

(b)   A pharmacist shall make every reasonable effort to ensure that any prescription drug order, regardless of the means of transmission, has been issued for a legitimate medical purpose by a practitioner in the course of medical practice. A pharmacist shall not dispense a prescription drug if the pharmacist knows or should have known that the order for such drug was issued without a valid pre-existing patient-practitioner relationship as defined by the Texas Medical Board in 22 Texas Administrative Code (TAC) § 190.8 (relating to Violation Guidelines) or without a valid prescription drug order.

    (1)   A prescription drug order may not be dispensed or delivered by means of the Internet unless pursuant to a valid prescription that was issued for a legitimate medical purpose in the course of medical practice by a practitioner, or practitioner covering for another practitioner.

    (2)   A prescription drug order may not be dispensed or delivered if the pharmacist has reason to suspect that the prescription drug order may have been authorized in the absence of a valid patient-practitioner relationship, or otherwise in violation of the practitioner's standard of practice to include that the practitioner:

        (A)   did not establish a diagnosis through the use of acceptable medical practices for the treatment of patient's condition;

        (B)   prescribed prescription drugs that were not necessary for the patient due to a lack of a valid medical need or the lack of a therapeutic purpose for the prescription drugs; or

        (C)   issued the prescriptions outside the usual course of medical practice.

    (3)   Notwithstanding the provisions of this subsection and as authorized by the Texas Medical Board in 22 TAC § 190.8, a pharmacist may dispense a prescription when a physician has not established a professional relationship with a patient if the prescription is for medications for:

        (A)   sexually transmitted diseases for partners of the physician's established patient; or

        (B)   a patient's family members if the patient has an illness determined by the Centers for Disease Control and Prevention, the World Health Organization, or the Governor's office to be pandemic.

(c)   If a pharmacist has reasons to suspect that a prescription was authorized solely based on the results of a questionnaire and/or in the absence of a documented patient evaluation including a physical examination, the pharmacist shall ascertain if that practitioner's standard of practice allows that practitioner to authorize a prescription under such circumstances. Reasons to suspect that a prescription may have been authorized in the absence of a valid patient-practitioner relationship or in violation of the practitioner's standard of practice include:

    (1)   the number of prescriptions authorized on a daily basis by the practitioner;

    (2)   a disproportionate number of patients of the practitioner receive controlled substances;

    (3)   the manner in which the prescriptions are authorized by the practitioner or received by the pharmacy;

    (4)   the geographical distance between the practitioner and the patient or between the pharmacy and the patient;

    (5)   knowledge by the pharmacist that the prescription was issued solely based on answers to a questionnaire;

    (6)   knowledge by the pharmacist that the pharmacy he/she works for directly or indirectly participates in or is otherwise associated with an Internet site that markets prescription drugs to the public without requiring the patient to provide a valid prescription order from the patients practitioner; or

    (7)   knowledge by the pharmacist that the patient has exhibited doctor-shopping or pharmacy-shopping tendencies.

(d)   A pharmacist shall ensure that prescription drug orders for the treatment of chronic pain have been issued in accordance with the guidelines set forth by the Texas Medical Board in 22 TAC § 170.3 (relating to Guidelines), prior to dispensing or delivering such prescriptions.

(e)   A prescription drug order may not be dispensed or delivered if issued by a practitioner practicing at a pain management clinic that is not in compliance with the rules of the Texas Medical Board in 22 TAC §§ 195.1 - 195.4 (relating to Pain Management Clinics). A prescription drug order from a practitioner practicing at a certified pain management clinic is not automatically valid and does not negate a pharmacist's responsibility to determine that the prescription is valid and has been issued for a legitimate or appropriate medical purpose.

(f)   A pharmacist shall not dispense a prescription drug if the pharmacist knows or should know the prescription drug order is fraudulent or forged. A pharmacist shall make every reasonable effort to prevent inappropriate dispensing due to fraudulent, forged, invalid, or medically inappropriate prescriptions in violation of a pharmacist's corresponding responsibility. The following patterns (i.e., red flag factors) are relevant to preventing the non-therapeutic dispensing of controlled substances and shall be considered by evaluating the totality of the circumstances rather than any single factor:

    (1)   the pharmacy dispenses a reasonably discernible pattern of substantially identical prescriptions for the same controlled substances, potentially paired with other drugs, for numerous persons, indicating a lack of individual drug therapy in prescriptions issued by the practitioner;

    (2)   the pharmacy operates with a reasonably discernible pattern of overall low prescription dispensing volume, maintaining relatively consistent 1:1 ratio of controlled substances to dangerous drugs and/or over-the-counter products dispensed as prescriptions;

    (3)   prescriptions by a prescriber presented to the pharmacy are routinely for controlled substances commonly known to be abused drugs, including opioids, benzodiazepines, muscle relaxants, psychostimulants, and/or cough syrups containing codeine, or any combination of these drugs;

    (4)   prescriptions for controlled substances by a prescriber presented to the pharmacy contain nonspecific or no diagnoses, or lack the intended use of the drug;

    (5)   prescriptions for controlled substances are commonly for the highest strength of the drug and/or for large quantities (e.g., monthly supply), indicating a lack of individual drug therapy in prescriptions issued by the practitioner;

    (6)   dangerous drugs or over-the-counter products (e.g., multi-vitamins or laxatives) are consistently added by the prescriber to prescriptions for controlled substances presented to the pharmacy, indicating a lack of individual drug therapy in prescriptions issued by the practitioner;

(7)   upon contacting the practitioner's office regarding a controlled substance prescription, the pharmacist is unable to engage in a discussion with the actual prescribing practitioner; the practitioner fails to appropriately address based on a reasonable pharmacist standard the pharmacist's concerns regarding the practitioner's prescribing practices with regard to the prescription; and/or the practitioner is unwilling to provide additional information, such as treatment goals and/or prognosis with prescribed drug therapy;

(8)   the practitioner's clinic is not registered as, and not exempted from registration as, a pain management clinic by the Texas Medical Board, despite prescriptions by the practitioner presented to the pharmacy indicating that the practitioner is mostly prescribing opioids, benzodiazepines, barbiturates, or carisoprodol, but not including suboxone, or any combination of these drugs;

(9)   the controlled substance(s) or the quantity of the controlled substance(s) prescribed are inconsistent with the practitioner's area of medical practice;

(10)   the Texas Prescription Monitoring Program indicates the person presenting the prescriptions is obtaining similar drugs from multiple practitioners, and/or that the persons is being dispensed similar drugs at multiple pharmacies;

(11)   multiple persons with the same address present substantially similar controlled substance prescriptions from the same practitioner;

(12)   persons consistently pay for controlled substance prescriptions with cash or cash equivalents more often than through insurance;

(13)   persons presenting controlled substance prescriptions are doing so in such a manner that varies from the manner in which persons routinely seek pharmacy services (e.g., persons arriving in the same vehicle with prescriptions from same practitioner; one person seeking to pick up prescriptions for multiple others; drugs referenced by street names;

(14)   the pharmacy charges and persons are willing to pay significantly more for controlled substances relative to nearby pharmacies;

(15)   the pharmacy routinely orders controlled substances from more than one drug supplier;

(16)   the pharmacy has been discontinued by a drug supplier related to controlled substance orders;

(17)   the pharmacy has a sporadic and inconsistent dispensing volume (including zero dispensing);

(18)   the pharmacy does not maintain normal operational hours each week from Monday through Friday; and

(19)   the pharmacy has been previously warned or disciplined by the Texas State Board of Pharmacy for inappropriate dispensing of controlled substances.

Source: The provisions of this § 291.29 adopted to be effective May 30, 2010, 35 TexReg 4164; amended to be effective September 12, 2011, 36 TexReg 5846; amended to be effective September 16, 2018, 43 TexReg 5779

SUBCHAPTER B. COMMUNITY PHARMACY (CLASS A)

§291.31 Definitions

The following words and terms, when used in this subchapter, shall have the following meanings, unless the context clearly indicates otherwise.

(1)   Accurately as prescribed—Dispensing, delivering, and/or distributing a prescription drug order:
     (A)   to the correct patient (or agent of the patient) for whom the drug or device was prescribed;
     (B)   with the correct drug in the correct strength, quantity, and dosage form ordered by the practitioner; and
     (C)   with correct labeling (including directions for use) as ordered by the practitioner. Provided, however, that nothing herein shall prohibit pharmacist substitution if substitution is conducted in strict accordance with applicable laws and rules, including Chapter 562 of the Texas Pharmacy Act.

(2)   Act—The Texas Pharmacy Act, Chapters 551 - 569, Occupations Code, as amended.

(3)   Advanced practice registered nurse—A registered nurse licensed by the Texas Board of Nursing to practice as an advanced practice registered nurse on the basis of completion of an advanced education program. The term includes nurse practitioner, nurse midwife, nurse anesthetist, and clinical nurse specialist. The term is synonymous with advanced nurse practitioner and advanced practice nurse.

(4)   Automated checking device—A device that confirms that the correct drug and strength has been labeled with the correct label for the correct patient prior to delivery of the drug to the patient.

(5)   Automated counting device—An automated device that is loaded with bulk drugs and counts and/or packages (i.e., fills a vial or other container) a specified quantity of dosage units of a designated drug product.

(6)   Automated pharmacy dispensing system—A system that automatically performs operations or activities, other than compounding or administration, relative to the storage, packaging, counting, and labeling for dispensing and delivery of medications, and that collects, controls, and maintains all transaction information. "Automated pharmacy dispensing system" does not mean "Automated compounding or counting device" or "Automated medication supply device."

(7)   Beyond use date—The date beyond which a product should not be used.

(8)   Board—The Texas State Board of Pharmacy.

(9)   Confidential record—Any health-related record that contains information that identifies an individual and that is maintained by a pharmacy or pharmacist, such as a patient medication record, prescription drug order, or medication order.

(10)   Controlled substance—A drug, immediate precursor, or other substance listed in Schedules I - V or Penalty Groups 1 - 4 of the Texas Controlled Substances Act, as amended (Chapter 481, Health and Safety Code), or a drug, immediate precursor, or other substance included in Schedules I, II, III, IV, or V of the Federal Comprehensive Drug Abuse Prevention and Control Act of 1970, as amended (Public Law 91-513).

(11)   Dangerous drug—A drug or device that:
     (A)   is not included in Penalty Groups 1 - 4 of the Texas Controlled Substances Act, as amended, (Chapter 481, Health and Safety Code), and is unsafe for self-medication; or
     (B)   bears or is required to bear the legend:
         (i)   "Caution: federal law prohibits dispensing without prescription" or "Rx only" or another legend that complies with federal law; or
         (ii)   "Caution: federal law restricts this drug to use by or on the order of a licensed veterinarian."

(12)   Data communication device—An electronic device that receives electronic information from one source and transmits or routes it to another (e.g., bridge, router, switch or gateway).

(13) Deliver or delivery—The actual, constructive, or attempted transfer of a prescription drug or device or controlled substance from one person to another, whether or not for a consideration.

(14) Designated agent—
   (A) a licensed nurse, physician assistant, pharmacist, or other individual designated by a practitioner to communicate prescription drug orders to a pharmacist;
   (B) a licensed nurse, physician assistant, or pharmacist employed in a health care facility to whom the practitioner communicates a prescription drug order;
   (C) an advanced practice registered nurse or physician assistant authorized by a practitioner to prescribe or order drugs or devices under Chapter 157 of the Medical Practice Act (Subtitle B, Occupations Code); or
   (D) a person who is a licensed vocational nurse or has an education equivalent to or greater than that required for a licensed vocational nurse designated by the practitioner to communicate prescriptions for an advanced practice registered nurse or physician assistant authorized by the practitioner to sign prescription drug orders under Chapter 157 of the Medical Practice Act (Subtitle B, Occupations Code).

(15) Dispense—Preparing, packaging, compounding, or labeling for delivery a prescription drug or device in the course of professional practice to an ultimate user or his agent by or pursuant to the lawful order of a practitioner.

(16) Dispensing error—An action committed by a pharmacist or other pharmacy personnel that causes the patient or patient's agent to take possession of a dispensed prescription drug and an individual subsequently discovers that the patient has received an incorrect drug product, which includes incorrect strength, incorrect dosage form, and/or incorrect directions for use.

(17) Dispensing pharmacist—The pharmacist responsible for the final check of the dispensed prescription before delivery to the patient.

(18) Distribute—The delivery of a prescription drug or device other than by administering or dispensing.

(19) Downtime—Period of time during which a data processing system is not operable.

(20) Drug regimen review—An evaluation of prescription drug orders and patient medication records for:
   (A) known allergies;
   (B) rational therapy-contraindications;
   (C) reasonable dose and route of administration;
   (D) reasonable directions for use;
   (E) duplication of therapy;
   (F) drug-drug interactions;
   (G) drug-food interactions;
   (H) drug-disease interactions;
   (I) adverse drug reactions; and
   (J) proper utilization, including overutilization or underutilization.

(21) Electronic prescription drug order—A prescription drug order that is generated on an electronic application and transmitted as an electronic data file.

(22) Electronic signature—A unique security code or other identifier which specifically identifies the person entering information into a data processing system. A facility which utilizes electronic signatures must:
   (A) maintain a permanent list of the unique security codes assigned to persons authorized to use the data processing system; and
   (B) have an ongoing security program which is capable of identifying misuse and/or unauthorized use of electronic signatures.

(23) Electronic verification process—an electronic verification, bar code verification, weight verification, radio frequency identification (RFID), or similar electronic process or system that accurately verifies that medication has been properly dispensed and labeled by, or loaded into, an automated pharmacy dispensing system.

(24) Full-time pharmacist—A pharmacist who works in a pharmacy from 30 to 40 hours per week or, if the pharmacy is open less than 60 hours per week, one-half of the time the pharmacy is open.

(25) Hard copy—A physical document that is readable without the use of a special device.

(26) Hot water—The temperature of water from the pharmacy's sink maintained at a minimum of 105 degrees F (41 degrees C).

(27) Medical Practice Act—The Texas Medical Practice Act, Subtitle B, Occupations Code, as amended.

(28) Medication order—A written order from a practitioner or a verbal order from a practitioner or his authorized agent for administration of a drug or device.

(29) New prescription drug order—A prescription drug order that has not been dispensed to the patient in the same strength and dosage form by this pharmacy within the last year.

(30) Original prescription—The:
   (A) original written prescription drug order; or
   (B) original verbal or electronic prescription drug order reduced to writing either manually or electronically by the pharmacist.

(31) Part-time pharmacist—A pharmacist who works less than full-time.

(32) Patient counseling—Communication by the pharmacist of information to the patient or patient's agent in order to improve therapy by ensuring proper use of drugs and devices.

(33) Patient med-pak—A package prepared by a pharmacist for a specific patient comprised of a series of containers and containing two or more prescribed solid oral dosage forms. The patient med-pak is so designed or each container is so labeled as to indicate the day and time, or period of time, that the contents within each container are to be taken.

(34) Pharmaceutical care—The provision of drug therapy and other pharmaceutical services intended to assist in the cure or prevention of a disease, elimination or reduction of a patient's symptoms, or arresting or slowing of a disease process.

(35) Pharmacist-in-charge—The pharmacist designated on a pharmacy license as the pharmacist who has the authority or responsibility for a pharmacy's compliance with laws and rules pertaining to the practice of pharmacy.

(36) Pharmacy technician—An individual who is registered with the board as a pharmacy technician and whose responsibility in a pharmacy is to provide technical services that do not require professional judgment regarding preparing and distributing drugs and who works under the direct supervision of and is responsible to a pharmacist.

(37) Pharmacy technician trainee—An individual who is registered with the board as a pharmacy technician trainee and is authorized to participate in a pharmacy's technician training program.

(38) Physician assistant—A physician assistant recognized by the Texas Medical Board as having the specialized education and training required under Subtitle B, Chapter 157, Occupations Code, and issued an identification number by the Texas Medical Board.

(39) Practitioner—

    (A) a person licensed or registered to prescribe, distribute, administer, or dispense a prescription drug or device in the course of professional practice in this state, including a physician, dentist, podiatrist, or veterinarian but excluding a person licensed under this Act;

    (B) a person licensed by another state, Canada, or the United Mexican States in a health field in which, under the law of this state, a license holder in this state may legally prescribe a dangerous drug;

    (C) a person practicing in another state and licensed by another state as a physician, dentist, veterinarian, or podiatrist, who has a current federal Drug Enforcement Administration registration number and who may legally prescribe a Schedule II, III, IV, or V controlled substance, as specified under Chapter 481, Health and Safety Code, in that other state; or

    (D) an advanced practice registered nurse or physician assistant to whom a physician has delegated the authority to prescribe or order drugs or devices under Chapter 157 of the Medical Practice Act (Subtitle B, Occupations Code) or, for the purpose of this subchapter, a pharmacist who practices in a hospital, hospital-based clinic, or an academic health care institution and to whom a physician has delegated the authority to sign a prescription for a dangerous drug under § 157.101, Occupations Code.

(40) Prepackaging—The act of repackaging and relabeling quantities of drug products from a manufacturer's original commercial container into a prescription container, unit-dose packaging, or multi-compartment container for dispensing by a pharmacist to the ultimate consumer, including dispensing through the use of an automated pharmacy dispensing system or automated checking device.

(41) Prescription department—The area of a pharmacy that contains prescription drugs.

(42) Prescription drug—

    (A) a substance for which federal or state law requires a prescription before the substance may be legally dispensed to the public;

    (B) a drug or device that under federal law is required, before being dispensed or delivered, to be labeled with the statement:

        (i) "Caution: federal law prohibits dispensing without prescription" or "Rx only" or another legend that complies with federal law; or

        (ii) "Caution: federal law restricts this drug to use by or on the order of a licensed veterinarian"; or

    (C) a drug or device that is required by federal or state statute or regulation to be dispensed on prescription or that is restricted to use by a practitioner only.

(43) Prescription drug order—

    (A) a written order from a practitioner or a verbal order from a practitioner or his authorized agent to a pharmacist for a drug or device to be dispensed; or

    (B) a written order or a verbal order pursuant to Subtitle B, Chapter 157, Occupations Code.

(44) Prospective drug use review—A review of the patient's drug therapy and prescription drug order or medication order prior to dispensing or distributing the drug.

(45) State—One of the 50 United States of America, a U.S. territory, or the District of Columbia.

(46) Texas Controlled Substances Act—The Texas Controlled Substances Act, Health and Safety Code, Chapter 481, as amended.

(47) Written protocol—A physician's order, standing medical order, standing delegation order, or other order or protocol as defined by rule of the Texas Medical Board under the Texas Medical Practice Act.

Source: The provisions of this § 291.31 adopted to be effective November 5, 1982, 7 TEXREG3830; amended to be effective March 31, 1986, 11 TEXREG1349; amended to be effective September 14, 1988, 13 TEXREG4305; amended to be effective September 5, 1990, 15 TEXREG4807; amended to be effective March 18, 1991, 16 TEXREG1365; amended to be effective January 1, 1993, 17 TexReg 9116; amended to be effective June 1, 1994, 19 TexReg 3921; amended to be effective December 1, 1994, 19 TexReg 9179; amended to be effective March 21, 1996, 21 TexReg 2227; amended to be effective April 7, 1997, 22 TexReg 3106; amended to be effective September 16, 1999, 24 TexReg 7227; amended to be effective March 29, 2000, 25 TexReg 2575; amended to be effective March 4, 2004, 29 TexReg 1951; amended to be effective June 6, 2004, 29 TexReg 5361; amended to be effective September 18, 2007, 32 TexReg 6319; amended to be effective September 7, 2008, 33 TexReg 7218; amended to be effective December 6, 2009, 34 TexReg 8691; amended to be effective March 17, 2013, 38 TexReg 1682; amended to be effective September 11, 2014, 39 TexReg 7094; amended to be effective December 7, 2014, 39 TexReg 9345; amended to be effective September 16, 2018, 43 TexReg 5783; amended to be effective March 12, 2019, 44 TexReg 1317

§291.32 Personnel

(a) Pharmacist-in-charge.

    (1) General.

        (A) Each Class A pharmacy shall have one pharmacist-in-charge who is employed on a full-time basis, who may be the pharmacist-in-charge for only one such pharmacy; provided, however, such pharmacist-in-charge may be the pharmacist-in-charge of:

            (i) more than one Class A pharmacy, if the additional Class A pharmacies are not open to provide pharmacy services simultaneously; or

            (ii) during an emergency, up to two Class A pharmacies open simultaneously if the pharmacist-in-charge works at least 10 hours per week in each pharmacy for no more than a period of 30 consecutive days.

        (B) The pharmacist-in-charge shall comply with the provisions of § 291.17 of this title (relating to Inventory Requirements).

        (C) The pharmacist-in-charge of a Class A pharmacy may not serve as the pharmacist-in-charge of a Class B pharmacy or a Class C pharmacy with 101 beds or more.

    (2) Responsibilities. The pharmacist-in-charge shall have responsibility for the practice of pharmacy at the pharmacy for which he or she is the pharmacist-in-charge. The pharmacist-in-charge may advise the owner on administrative or operational concerns. The pharmacist-in-charge shall have responsibility for, at a minimum, the following:

        (A) educating and training of pharmacy technicians and pharmacy technician trainees;

(B) supervising a system to assure appropriate procurement of prescription drugs and devices and other products dispensed from the Class A pharmacy;

(C) disposing of and distributing drugs from the Class A pharmacy;

(D) storing all materials, including drugs, chemicals, and biologicals;

(E) maintaining records of all transactions of the Class A pharmacy necessary to maintain accurate control over and accountability for all pharmaceutical materials required by applicable state and federal laws and sections;

(F) supervising a system to assure maintenance of effective controls against the theft or diversion of prescription drugs, and records for such drugs;

(G) adhering to policies and procedures regarding the maintenance of records in a data processing system such that the data processing system is in compliance with Class A (community) pharmacy requirements;

(H) legally operating the pharmacy, including meeting all inspection and other requirements of all state and federal laws or sections governing the practice of pharmacy; and

(I) if the pharmacy uses an automated pharmacy dispensing system, shall be responsible for the following:

    (i) consulting with the owner concerning and adherence to the policies and procedures for system operation, safety, security, accuracy and access, patient confidentiality, prevention of unauthorized access, and malfunction;

    (ii) inspecting medications in the automated pharmacy dispensing system, at least monthly, for expiration date, misbranding, physical integrity, security, and accountability;

    (iii) assigning, discontinuing, or changing personnel access to the automated pharmacy dispensing system;

    (iv) ensuring that pharmacy technicians, pharmacy technician trainees, and licensed healthcare professionals performing any services in connection with an automated pharmacy dispensing system have been properly trained on the use of the system and can demonstrate comprehensive knowledge of the written policies and procedures for operation of the system; and

    (v) ensuring that the automated pharmacy dispensing system is stocked accurately and an accountability record is maintained in accordance with the written policies and procedures of operation.

(b) Owner. The owner of a Class A pharmacy shall have responsibility for all administrative and operational functions of the pharmacy. The pharmacist-in-charge may advise the owner on administrative and operational concerns. The owner shall have responsibility for, at a minimum, the following, and if the owner is not a Texas licensed pharmacist, the owner shall consult with the pharmacist-in-charge or another Texas licensed pharmacist:

(1) establishing policies for procurement of prescription drugs and devices and other products dispensed from the Class A pharmacy;

(2) establishing policies and procedures for the security of the prescription department including the maintenance of effective controls against the theft or diversion of prescription drugs;

(3) if the pharmacy uses an automated pharmacy dispensing system, reviewing and approving all policies and procedures for system operation, safety, security, accuracy and access, patient confidentiality, prevention of unauthorized access, and malfunction;

(4) providing the pharmacy with the necessary equipment and resources commensurate with its level and type of practice; and

(5) establishing policies and procedures regarding maintenance, storage, and retrieval of records in a data processing system such that the system is in compliance with state and federal requirements.

(c) Pharmacists.

(1) General.

(A) The pharmacist-in-charge shall be assisted by sufficient number of additional licensed pharmacists as may be required to operate the Class A pharmacy competently, safely, and adequately to meet the needs of the patients of the pharmacy.

(B) All pharmacists shall assist the pharmacist-in-charge in meeting his or her responsibilities in ordering, dispensing, and accounting for prescription drugs.

(C) Pharmacists are solely responsible for the direct supervision of pharmacy technicians and pharmacy technician trainees and for designating and delegating duties, other than those listed in paragraph (2) of this subsection, to pharmacy technicians and pharmacy technician trainees. Each pharmacist shall be responsible for any delegated act performed by pharmacy technicians and pharmacy technician trainees under his or her supervision.

(D) Pharmacists shall directly supervise pharmacy technicians and pharmacy technician trainees who are entering prescription data into the pharmacy's data processing system by one of the following methods.

    (i) Physically present supervision. A pharmacist shall be physically present to directly supervise a pharmacy technician or pharmacy technician trainee who is entering prescription data into the data processing system. Each prescription entered into the data processing system shall be verified at the time of data entry. If the pharmacist is not physically present due to a temporary absence as specified in § 291.33(b)(3) of this title (relating to Operational Standards), on return the pharmacist must:

        (I) conduct a drug regimen review for the prescriptions data entered during this time period as specified in § 291.33(c)(2) of this title; and

        (II) verify that prescription data entered during this time period was entered accurately.

    (ii) Electronic supervision. A pharmacist may electronically supervise a pharmacy technician or pharmacy technician trainee who is entering prescription data into the data processing system provided the pharmacist:

        (I) has the ability to immediately communicate directly with the technician/trainee;

        (II) has immediate access to any original document containing prescription information or other information related to the dispensing of the prescription. Such access may be through imaging technology provided the pharmacist has the ability to review the original, hardcopy documents if needed for clarification; and

        (III) verifies the accuracy of the data entered information prior to the release of the information to the system for storage and/or generation of the prescription label.

    (iii) Electronic verification of data entry by pharmacy technicians or pharmacy technician trainees. A pharmacist may electronically verify the data entry of prescription information into a data processing system provided:

        (I) the pharmacist has the ability to immediately communicate directly with the technician/trainee;

        (II) the pharmacist electronically conducting the verification is either a:

          (-a-) Texas licensed pharmacist; or

          (-b-) pharmacist employed by a Class E pharmacy that:

              (-1-) has the same owner as the Class A pharmacy where the pharmacy technicians/trainees are located; or

              (-2-) has entered into a written contract or agreement with the Class A pharmacy, which outlines the services to be provided and the responsibilities and accountabilities of each pharmacy in compliance with federal and state laws and regulations;

        (III) the pharmacy establishes controls to protect the privacy and security of confidential records; and

        (IV) the pharmacy keeps permanent records of prescriptions electronically verified for a period of two years.

    (E) All pharmacists, while on duty, shall be responsible for the legal operation of the pharmacy and for complying with all state and federal laws or rules governing the practice of pharmacy.

    (F) A dispensing pharmacist shall be responsible for and ensure that the drug is dispensed and delivered safely and accurately as prescribed, unless the pharmacy's data processing system can record the identity of each pharmacist involved in a specific portion of the dispensing processing. If the system can track the identity of each pharmacist involved in the dispensing process, each pharmacist involved in the dispensing process shall be responsible for and ensure that the portion of the process the pharmacist is performing results in the safe and accurate dispensing and delivery of the drug as prescribed. The dispensing process shall include, but not be limited to, drug regimen review and verification of accurate prescription data entry, including prescriptions placed on hold, packaging, preparation, compounding, transferring, labeling, and performance of the final check of the dispensed prescription. An intern has the same responsibilities described in this subparagraph as a pharmacist but must perform his or her duties under the supervision of a pharmacist.

  (2) Duties. Duties which may only be performed by a pharmacist are as follows:

    (A) receiving oral prescription drug orders and reducing these orders to writing, either manually or electronically;

    (B) interpreting prescription drug orders;

    (C) selecting drug products;

    (D) performing the final check of the dispensed prescription before delivery to the patient to ensure that the prescription has been dispensed accurately as prescribed;

    (E) communicating to the patient or patient's agent information about the prescription drug or device which in the exercise of the pharmacist's professional judgment, the pharmacist deems significant, as specified in § 291.33(c) of this title;

    (F) communicating to the patient or the patient's agent on his or her request information concerning any prescription drugs dispensed to the patient by the pharmacy;

    (G) assuring that a reasonable effort is made to obtain, record, and maintain patient medication records;

    (H) interpreting patient medication records and performing drug regimen reviews;

    (I) performing a specific act of drug therapy management for a patient delegated to a pharmacist by a written protocol from a physician licensed in this state in compliance with the Medical Practice Act;

    (J) verifying that controlled substances listed on invoices are received by clearly recording his/her initials and date of receipt of the controlled substances; and

    (K) transferring or receiving a transfer of original prescription information on behalf of a patient.

  (3) Special requirements for compounding. All pharmacists engaged in compounding non-sterile preparations shall meet the training requirements specified in § 291.131 of this title (relating to Pharmacies Compounding Non-Sterile Preparations).

(d) Pharmacy Technicians and Pharmacy Technician Trainees.

  (1) General.

    (A) All pharmacy technicians and pharmacy technician trainees shall meet the training requirements specified in § 297.6 of this title (relating to Pharmacy Technician and Pharmacy Technician Trainee Training).

    (B) Special requirements for compounding. All pharmacy technicians and pharmacy technician trainees engaged in compounding non-sterile preparations shall meet the training requirements specified in § 291.131 of this title.

  (2) Duties.

    (A) Pharmacy technicians and pharmacy technician trainees may not perform any of the duties listed in subsection (c)(2) of this section.

    (B) A pharmacist may delegate to pharmacy technicians and pharmacy technician trainees any nonjudgmental technical duty associated with the preparation and distribution of prescription drugs provided:

      (i) unless otherwise provided under § 291.33 of this subchapter, a pharmacist verifies the accuracy of all acts, tasks, and functions performed by pharmacy technicians and pharmacy technician trainees;

      (ii) pharmacy technicians and pharmacy technician trainees are under the direct supervision of and responsible to a pharmacist; and

      (iii) only pharmacy technicians and pharmacy technician trainees who have been properly trained on the use of an automated pharmacy dispensing system and can demonstrate comprehensive knowledge of the written policies and procedures for the operation of the system may be allowed access to the system.

    (C) Pharmacy technicians and pharmacy technician trainees may perform only nonjudgmental technical duties associated with the preparation and distribution of prescription drugs, as follows:

      (i) initiating and receiving refill authorization requests;

      (ii) entering prescription data into a data processing system;

      (iii) taking a stock bottle from the shelf for a prescription;

      (iv) preparing and packaging prescription drug orders (i.e., counting tablets/capsules, measuring liquids and placing them in the prescription container);

      (v) affixing prescription labels and auxiliary labels to the prescription container;

      (vi) reconstituting medications;

      (vii) prepackaging and labeling prepackaged drugs;

      (viii) loading bulk unlabeled drugs into an automated dispensing system provided a pharmacist verifies that the system is properly loaded prior to use;

(ix) loading prepackaged containers previously verified by a pharmacist or manufacturer's unit of use packages into an automated dispensing system in accordance with § 291.33(i)(2)(D)(III) of this subchapter;

(x) compounding non-sterile prescription drug orders; and

(xi) compounding bulk non-sterile preparations.

(3) Ratio of on-site pharmacist to pharmacy technicians and pharmacy technician trainees.

(A) Except as provided in subparagraph (B) of this paragraph, the ratio of on-site pharmacists to pharmacy technicians and pharmacy technician trainees may be 1:4, provided the pharmacist is on-site and at least one of the four is a pharmacy technician. The ratio of pharmacists to pharmacy technician trainees may not exceed 1:3.

(B) As specified in § 568.006 of the Act, a Class A pharmacy may have a ratio of on-site pharmacists to pharmacy technicians/ pharmacy technician trainees of 1:5 provided:

(i) the Class A pharmacy:

(I) dispenses no more than 20 different prescription drugs; and

(II) does not produce sterile preparations including intravenous or intramuscular drugs on-site; and

(ii) the following conditions are met:

(I) at least four are pharmacy technicians and not pharmacy technician trainees; and

(II) The pharmacy has written policies and procedures regarding the supervision of pharmacy technicians and pharmacy technician trainees, including requirements that the pharmacy technicians and pharmacy technician trainees included in a 1:5 ratio may be involved only in one process at a time. For example, a technician/trainee who is compounding non-sterile preparations or who is involved in the preparation of prescription drug orders may not also call physicians for authorization of refills.

(e) Identification of pharmacy personnel. All pharmacy personnel shall be identified as follows.

(1) Pharmacy technicians. All pharmacy technicians shall wear an identification tag or badge that bears the person's name and identifies him or her as a pharmacy technician, or a certified pharmacy technician, if the technician maintains current certification with the Pharmacy Technician Certification Board or any other entity providing an examination approved by the board.

(2) Pharmacy technician trainees. All pharmacy technician trainees shall wear an identification tag or badge that bears the person's name and identifies him or her as a pharmacy technician trainee.

(3) Pharmacist interns. All pharmacist interns shall wear an identification tag or badge that bears the person's name and identifies him or her as a pharmacist intern.

(4) Pharmacists. All pharmacists shall wear an identification tag or badge that bears the person's name and identifies him or her as a pharmacist.

Source: The provisions of this § 291.32 adopted to be effective September 14, 1988, 13 TEXREG4306; amended to be effective October 27, 1989, 14 TEXREG5494; amended to be effective September 5, 1990, 15 TEXREG4807; amended to be effective January 29, 1992, 17 TexReg 323; amended to be effective January 1, 1993, 17 TexReg 9116; amended to be effective September 30, 1993, 18 TexReg 6460; amended to be effective June 1, 1994, 19 TexReg 3921; amended to be effective March 21, 1996, 21 TexReg 2227; amended to be effective April 7, 1997, 22 TexReg 3106; amended to be effective September 16, 1999, 24 TexReg 7227; amended to be effective March 29, 2000, 25 TexReg 2575; amended to beeffective June 4, 2000, 25 TexReg 4778; amended to be effective August 31, 2000, 25 TexReg 8405; amended to be effective December 27, 2000, 25 TexReg 12690; amended to be effective September 12, 2001, 26 TexReg 6891; amended to be effective September 8, 2002, 27 TexReg 8214; amended to be effective June 23, 2003, 28 TexReg 4637; amended to be effective March 4, 2004, 29 TexReg 1951; amended to be effective June 6, 2004, 29 TexReg 5361; amended to be effective September 18, 2007, 32 TexReg 6319; amended to be effective September 7, 2008, 33 TexReg 7218; amended to be effective September 13, 2009, 34 TexReg 6112; amended to be effective May 30, 2010, 35 TexReg 4165; amended to be effective December 8, 2010, 35 TexReg 10690; amended to be effective September 12, 2011, 36 TexReg 5847; amended to be effective June 7, 2012, 37 TexReg 4046; amended to be effective March 17, 2013, 38TexReg1682; amended to be effective March 26, 2014, 39 TexReg 2080; amended to be effective September 11, 2014, 39 TexReg 7094; amended to be effective December 6, 2015, 40 TexReg 8766; amended to be effective September 6, 2017, 42 TexReg 4466; amended to be effective September 16, 2018, 43 TexReg 5783; amended to be effective June 20, 2019, 44 TexReg 2946

§291.33 Operational Standards

(a) Licensing requirements.

(1) A Class A pharmacy shall register annually or biennially with the board on a pharmacy license application provided by the board, following the procedures as specified in § 291.1 of this title (relating to Pharmacy License Application).

(2) A Class A pharmacy which changes ownership shall notify the board within ten days of the change of ownership and apply for a new and separate license as specified in § 291.3 of this title (relating to Required Notifications).

(3) A Class A pharmacy which changes location and/or name shall notify the board as specified in § 291.3 of this title.

(4) A Class A pharmacy owned by a partnership or corporation which changes managing officers shall notify the board in writing of the names of the new managing officers within ten days of the change, following the procedures as specified in § 291.3 of this title.

(5) A Class A pharmacy shall notify the board in writing within ten days of closing, following the procedures as specified in § 291.5 of this title (relating to Closing a Pharmacy).

(6) A separate license is required for each principal place of business and only one pharmacy license may be issued to a specific location.

(7) A fee as specified in § 291.6 of this title (relating to Pharmacy License Fees) will be charged for the issuance and renewal of a license and the issuance of an amended license.

(8) A Class A pharmacy, licensed under the provisions of the Act, § 560.051(a)(1), which also operates another type of pharmacy which would otherwise be required to be licensed under the Act, § 560.051(a)(2) concerning Nuclear Pharmacy (Class B), is not required to secure a license for such other type of pharmacy; provided, however, such licensee is required to comply with the provisions of Subchapter C of this chapter (relating to Nuclear Pharmacy (Class B)), to the extent such sections are applicable to the operation of the pharmacy.

(9) A Class A pharmacy engaged in the compounding of non-sterile preparations shall comply with the provisions of § 291.131 of this title (relating to Pharmacies Compounding Non-Sterile Preparations).

(10) A Class A pharmacy shall not compound sterile preparations.

(11) A Class A pharmacy engaged in the provision of remote pharmacy services, including storage and dispensing of prescription drugs, shall comply with the provisions of § 291.121 of this title (relating to Remote Pharmacy Services).

(12) Class A pharmacy engaged in centralized prescription dispensing and/or prescription drug or medication order processing shall comply with the provisions of § 291.123 of this title (relating to Centralized Prescription Drug or Medication Order Processing) and/or § 291.125 of this title (relating to Centralized Prescription Dispensing)

(b) Environment.

  (1) General requirements.

    (A) The pharmacy shall be arranged in an orderly fashion and kept clean. All required equipment shall be clean and in good operating condition.

    (B) A Class A pharmacy shall have a sink with hot and cold running water within the pharmacy, exclusive of restroom facilities, available to all pharmacy personnel and maintained in a sanitary condition.

    (C) A Class A pharmacy which serves the general public shall contain an area which is suitable for confidential patient counseling.

      (i) Such counseling area shall be:

        (I) easily accessible to both patient and pharmacists and not allow patient access to prescription drugs; and

        (II) designed to maintain the confidentiality and privacy of the pharmacist/patient communication.

      (ii) In determining whether the area is suitable for confidential patient counseling and designed to maintain the confidentiality and privacy of the pharmacist/patient communication, the board may consider factors such as the following:

        (I) the proximity of the counseling area to the check-out or cash register area;

        (II) the volume of pedestrian traffic in and around the counseling area;

        (III) the presence of walls or other barriers between the counseling area and other areas of the pharmacy; and

        (IV) any evidence of confidential information being overheard by persons other than the patient or patient's agent or the pharmacist or agents of the pharmacist.

    (D) The pharmacy shall be properly lighted and ventilated.

    (E) The temperature of the pharmacy shall be maintained within a range compatible with the proper storage of drugs. The temperature of the refrigerator shall be maintained within a range compatible with the proper storage of drugs requiring refrigeration.

    (F) Animals, including birds and reptiles, shall not be kept within the pharmacy and in immediately adjacent areas under the control of the pharmacy. This provision does not apply to fish in aquariums, service animals accompanying disabled persons, or animals for sale to the general public in a separate area that is inspected by local health jurisdictions.

    (G) If the pharmacy has flammable materials, the pharmacy shall have a designated area for the storage of flammable materials. Such area shall meet the requirements set by local and state fire laws.

  (2) Security.

    (A) Each pharmacist while on duty shall be responsible for the security of the prescription department, including provisions for effective control against theft or diversion of prescription drugs, and records for such drugs.

    (B) The prescription department shall be locked by key, combination or other mechanical or electronic means to prohibit unauthorized access when a pharmacist is not on-site except as provided in subparagraphs (C) and (D) of this paragraph and paragraph (3) of this subsection. The following is applicable:

      (i) If the prescription department is closed at any time when the rest of the facility is open, the prescription department must be physically or electronically secured. The security may be accomplished by means such as floor to ceiling walls; walls, partitions, or barriers at least 9 feet 6 inches high; electronically monitored motion detectors; pull down sliders; or other systems or technologies that will secure the pharmacy from unauthorized entrance when the pharmacy is closed. Pharmacies licensed prior to June 1, 2009, shall be exempt from this provision unless the pharmacy changes location. Change of location shall include the relocation of the pharmacy within the licensed address. A pharmacy licensed prior to June 1, 2009 that files a change of ownership but does not change location shall be exempt from the provisions.

      (ii) The pharmacy's key, combination, or other mechanical or electronic means of locking the pharmacy may not be duplicated without the authorization of the pharmacist-in-charge or owner.

      (iii) At a minimum, the pharmacy must have a basic alarm system with off-site monitoring and perimeter and motion sensors. The pharmacy may have additional security by video surveillance camera systems.

    (C) Prior to authorizing individuals to enter the prescription department, the pharmacist-in-charge or owner may designate persons who may enter the prescription department to perform functions, other than dispensing functions or prescription processing, documented by the pharmacist-in-charge including access to the prescription department by other pharmacists, pharmacy personnel and other individuals. The pharmacy must maintain written documentation of authorized individuals other than individuals employed by the pharmacy who accessed the prescription department when a pharmacist is not on-site.

    (D) Only persons designated either by name or by title including such titles as "relief" or "floater" pharmacist, in writing by the pharmacist-in-charge may unlock the prescription department except in emergency situations. An additional key to or instructions on accessing the prescription department may be maintained in a secure location outside the prescription department for use during an emergency or as designated by the pharmacist-in-charge.

    (E) Written policies and procedures for the pharmacy's security shall be developed and implemented by the pharmacist-in-charge and/or the owner of the pharmacy. Such policies and procedures may include quarterly audits of controlled substances commonly abused or diverted; perpetual inventories for the comparison of the receipt, dispensing, and distribution of controlled substances; monthly reports from the pharmacy's wholesaler(s) of controlled substances purchased by the pharmacy; opening and closing procedures; product storage and placement; and central management oversight.

  (3) Temporary absence of pharmacist.

    (A) On-site supervision by pharmacist.

(i)   If a pharmacy is staffed by only one pharmacist, the pharmacist may leave the prescription department for short periods of time without closing the prescription department and removing pharmacy technicians, pharmacy technician trainees, and other pharmacy personnel from the prescription department provided the following conditions are met:

    (I)   at least one pharmacy technician remains in the prescription department;

    (II)   the pharmacist remains on-site at the licensed location of the pharmacy and is immediately available;

    (III)   the pharmacist reasonably believes that the security of the prescription department will be maintained in his or her absence. If in the professional judgment of the pharmacist, the pharmacist determines that the prescription department should close during his or her absence, then the pharmacist shall close the prescription department and remove the pharmacy technicians, pharmacy technician trainees, and other pharmacy personnel from the prescription department during his or her absence; and

    (IV)   a notice is posted which includes the following information:

      (-a-)   the pharmacist is on a break and the time the pharmacist will return; and

      (-b-)   pharmacy technicians may begin the processing of prescription drug orders or refills brought in during the pharmacist's absence, but the prescription or refill may not be delivered to the patient or the patient's agent until the pharmacist verifies the accuracy of the prescription.

(ii)   During the time a pharmacist is absent from the prescription department, only pharmacy technicians who have completed the pharmacy's training program may perform the following duties, provided a pharmacist verifies the accuracy of all acts, tasks, and functions performed by the pharmacy technicians prior to delivery of the prescription to the patient or the patient's agent:

    (I)   initiating and receiving refill authorization requests;

    (II)   entering prescription data into a data processing system;

    (III)   taking a stock bottle from the shelf for a prescription;

    (IV)   preparing and packaging prescription drug orders (e.g., counting tablets/capsules, measuring liquids, or placing them in the prescription container);

    (V)   affixing prescription labels and auxiliary labels to the prescription container; and

    (VI)   prepackaging and labeling prepackaged drugs.

(iii)   Upon return to the prescription department, the pharmacist shall:

    (I)   conduct a drug regimen review as specified in subsection (c)(2) of this section; and

    (II)   verify the accuracy of all acts, tasks, and functions performed by the pharmacy technicians prior to delivery of the prescription to the patient or the patient's agent.

(iv)   An agent of the pharmacist may deliver a previously verified prescription to the patient or his or her agent provided a record of the delivery is maintained containing the following information:

    (I)   date of the delivery;

    (II)   unique identification number of the prescription drug order;

    (III)   patient's name;

    (IV)   patient's phone number or the phone number of the person picking up the prescription; and

    (V)   signature of the person picking up the prescription.

(v)   Any prescription delivered to a patient when a pharmacist is not in the prescription department must meet the requirements for a prescription delivered to a patient as described in subsection (c)(1)(F) of this section.

(vi)   During the times a pharmacist is absent from the prescription department a pharmacist intern shall be considered a registered pharmacy technician and may perform only the duties of a registered pharmacy technician.

(vii)   In pharmacies with two or more pharmacists on duty, the pharmacists shall stagger their breaks and meal periods so that the prescription department is not left without a pharmacist on duty.

(B)   Pharmacist is off-site.

(i)   The prescription department must be secured with procedures for entry during the time that a pharmacy is not under the continuous on-site supervision of a pharmacist and the pharmacy is not open for pharmacy services.

(ii)   Pharmacy technicians and pharmacy technician trainees may not perform any duties of a pharmacy technician or pharmacy technician trainee during the time that the pharmacist is off-site.

(iii)   A pharmacy may use an automated storage and distribution device as specified in subsection (i)(4) of this section for pick-up of a previously verified prescription by a patient or patient's agent.

(iv)   An agent of the pharmacist may deliver a previously verified prescription to a patient or patient's agent during short periods of time when a pharmacist is off-site, provided the following conditions are met:

    (I)   short periods of time may not exceed two consecutive hours in a 24 hour period;

    (II)   a notice is posted which includes the following information:

      (-a-)   the pharmacist is off-site and not present in the pharmacy;

      (-b-)   no new prescriptions may be prepared at the pharmacy but previously verified prescriptions may be delivered to the patient or the patient's agent; and

      (-c-)   the date/time when the pharmacist will return;

    (III)   the pharmacy must maintain documentation of the absences of the pharmacist(s); and

    (IV)   the prescription department is locked and secured to prohibit unauthorized entry.

(v)   During the time a pharmacist is absent from the prescription department and is off-site, a record of prescriptions delivered must be maintained and contain the following information:

    (I)   date and time of the delivery;

    (II)   unique identification number of the prescription drug order;

    (III)   patient's name;

    (IV)   patient's phone number or the phone number of the person picking up the prescription; and

    (V)   signature of the person picking up the prescription.

(vi) Any prescription delivered to a patient when a pharmacist is not on-site at the pharmacy must meet the requirements for a prescription delivered to a patient as described in subsection (c)(1)(F) of this section.

(c) Prescription dispensing and delivery.
  (1) Patient counseling and provision of drug information.
    (A) To optimize drug therapy, a pharmacist shall communicate to the patient or the patient's agent information about the prescription drug or device which in the exercise of the pharmacist's professional judgment the pharmacist deems significant, such as the following:
        (i) name and description of the drug or device;
        (ii) dosage form, dosage, route of administration, and duration of drug therapy;
        (iii) special directions and precautions for preparation, administration, and use by the patient;
        (iv) common severe side or adverse effects or interactions and therapeutic contraindications that may be encountered, including their avoidance, and the action required if they occur;
        (v) techniques for self-monitoring of drug therapy;
        (vi) proper storage;
        (vii) refill information; and
        (viii) action to be taken in the event of a missed dose.
    (B) Such communication shall be:
        (i) provided to new and existing patients of a pharmacy with each new prescription drug order. A new prescription drug order is one that has not been dispensed by the pharmacy to the patient in the same dosage and strength within the last year;
        (ii) provided for any prescription drug order dispensed by the pharmacy on the request of the patient or patient's agent;
        (iii) communicated orally in person unless the patient or patient's agent is not at the pharmacy or a specific communication barrier prohibits such oral communication;
        (iv) documented by recording the initials or identification code of the pharmacist providing the counseling in the prescription dispensing record as follows:
            (I) on the original hard-copy prescription, provided the counseling pharmacist clearly records his or her initials on the prescription for the purpose of identifying who provided the counseling;
            (II) in the pharmacy's data processing system;
            (III) in an electronic logbook; or
            (IV) in a hard-copy log; and
        (v) reinforced with written information relevant to the prescription and provided to the patient or patient's agent. The following is applicable concerning this written information:
            (I) Written information must be in plain language designed for the patient and printed in an easily readable font size comparable to but no smaller than ten-point Times Roman. This information may be provided to the patient in an electronic format, such as by e-mail, if the patient or patient's agent requests the information in an electronic format and the pharmacy documents the request.
            (II) When a compounded preparation is dispensed, information shall be provided for the major active ingredient(s), if available.
            (III) For new drug entities, if no written information is initially available, the pharmacist is not required to provide information until such information is available, provided:
                (-a-) the pharmacist informs the patient or the patient's agent that the product is a new drug entity and written information is not available;
                (-b-) the pharmacist documents the fact that no written information was provided; and
                (-c-) if the prescription is refilled after written information is available, such information is provided to the patient or patient's agent.
            (IV) The written information accompanying the prescription or the prescription label shall contain the statement "Do not flush unused medications or pour down a sink or drain." A drug product on a list developed by the Federal Food and Drug Administration of medicines recommended for disposal by flushing is not required to bear this statement.
    (C) Only a pharmacist may verbally provide drug information to a patient or patient's agent and answer questions concerning prescription drugs. Non-pharmacist personnel and/or the pharmacy's computer system may not ask questions of a patient or patient's agent which are intended to screen and/or limit interaction with the pharmacist.
    (D) Nothing in this subparagraph shall be construed as requiring a pharmacist to provide consultation when a patient or patient's agent refuses such consultation. The pharmacist shall document such refusal for consultation.
    (E) In addition to the requirements of subparagraphs (A) - (D) of this paragraph, if a prescription drug order is delivered to the patient at the pharmacy, the following is applicable:
        (i) So that a patient will have access to information concerning his or her prescription, a prescription may not be delivered to a patient unless a pharmacist is in the pharmacy, except as provided in subsection (b)(3) of this section.
        (ii) Any prescription delivered to a patient when a pharmacist is not in the pharmacy must meet the requirements described in subparagraph (F) of this paragraph.
    (F) In addition to the requirements of subparagraphs (A) - (D) of this paragraph, if a prescription drug order is delivered to the patient or his or her agent at the patient's residence or other designated location, the following is applicable:
        (i) The information as specified in subparagraph (A) of this paragraph shall be delivered with the dispensed prescription in writing.
        (ii) If prescriptions are routinely delivered outside the area covered by the pharmacy's local telephone service, the pharmacy shall provide a toll-free telephone line which is answered during normal business hours to enable communication between the patient and a pharmacist.

(iii) The pharmacist shall place on the prescription container or on a separate sheet delivered with the prescription container in both English and Spanish the local and, if applicable, toll-free telephone number of the pharmacy and the statement: "Written information about this prescription has been provided for you. Please read this information before you take the medication. If you have questions concerning this prescription, a pharmacist is available during normal business hours to answer these questions at (insert the pharmacy's local and toll-free telephone numbers)."

(iv) The pharmacy shall maintain and use adequate storage or shipment containers and use shipping processes to ensure drug stability and potency. Such shipping processes shall include the use of appropriate packaging material and/or devices to ensure that the drug is maintained at an appropriate temperature range to maintain the integrity of the medication throughout the delivery process.

(v) The pharmacy shall use a delivery system which is designed to assure that the drugs are delivered to the appropriate patient.

(G) The provisions of this paragraph do not apply to patients in facilities where drugs are administered to patients by a person required to do so by the laws of the state (i.e., nursing homes).

(2) Pharmaceutical care services.

  (A) Drug regimen review.

    (i) For the purpose of promoting therapeutic appropriateness, a pharmacist shall, prior to or at the time of dispensing a prescription drug order, review the patient's medication record. Such review shall at a minimum identify clinically significant:

      (I) known allergies;

      (II) rational therapy-contraindications;

      (III) reasonable dose and route of administration;

      (IV) reasonable directions for use;

      (V) duplication of therapy;

      (VI) drug-drug interactions;

      (VII) drug-food interactions;

      (VIII) drug-disease interactions;

      (IX) adverse drug reactions; and

      (X) proper utilization, including overutilization or underutilization.

    (ii) Upon identifying any clinically significant conditions, situations, or items listed in clause (i) of this subparagraph, the pharmacist shall take appropriate steps to avoid or resolve the problem including consultation with the prescribing practitioner. The pharmacist shall document such occurrences as specified in subparagraph (C) of this paragraph.

    (iii) The drug regimen review may be conducted by remotely accessing the pharmacy's electronic database from outside the pharmacy by:

      (I) an individual Texas licensed pharmacist employee of the pharmacy provided the pharmacy establishes controls to protect the privacy of the patient and the security of confidential records; or

      (II) a pharmacist employed by a Class E pharmacy provided the pharmacies have entered into a written contract or agreement which outlines the services to be provided and the responsibilities and accountabilities of each pharmacy in compliance with federal and state laws and regulations.

    (iv) Prior to dispensing, any questions regarding a prescription drug order must be resolved with the prescriber and written documentation of these discussions made and maintained as specified in subparagraph (C) of this paragraph.

  (B) Other pharmaceutical care services which may be provided by pharmacists include, but are not limited to, the following:

    (i) managing drug therapy as delegated by a practitioner as allowed under the provisions of the Medical Practice Act;

    (ii) administering immunizations and vaccinations under written protocol of a physician;

    (iii) managing patient compliance programs;

    (iv) providing preventative health care services; and

    (v) providing case management of patients who are being treated with high-risk or high-cost drugs, or who are considered "high risk" due to their age, medical condition, family history, or related concern.

  (C) Documentation of consultation. When a pharmacist consults a prescriber as described in subparagraph (A) of this paragraph, the pharmacist shall document on the prescription or in the pharmacy's data processing system associated with the prescription such occurrences and shall include the following information:

    (i) date the prescriber was consulted;

    (ii) name of the person communicating the prescriber's instructions;

    (iii) any applicable information pertaining to the consultation; and

    (iv) initials or identification code of the pharmacist performing the consultation clearly recorded for the purpose of identifying the pharmacist who performed the consultation.

(3) Substitution of generically equivalent drugs or interchangeable biological products. A pharmacist may dispense a generically equivalent drug or interchangeable biological product and shall comply with the provisions of § 309.3 of this title (relating to Substitution Requirements).

(4) Substitution of dosage form.

  (A) As specified in § 562.012 of the Act, a pharmacist may dispense a dosage form of a drug product different from that prescribed, such as a tablet instead of a capsule or liquid instead of tablets, provided:

    (i) the patient consents to the dosage form substitution; and

    (ii) the dosage form so dispensed:

      (I) contains the identical amount of the active ingredients as the dosage prescribed for the patient;

      (II) is not an enteric-coated or time release product; and

      (III) does not alter desired clinical outcomes.

(B) Substitution of dosage form may not include the substitution of a product that has been compounded by the pharmacist unless the pharmacist contacts the practitioner prior to dispensing and obtains permission to dispense the compounded product.

(5) Therapeutic Drug Interchange. A switch to a drug providing a similar therapeutic response to the one prescribed shall not be made without prior approval of the prescribing practitioner. This paragraph does not apply to generic substitution. For generic substitution, see the requirements of paragraph (3) of this subsection.

(A) The patient shall be notified of the therapeutic drug interchange prior to, or upon delivery of, the dispensed prescription to the patient. Such notification shall include:

(i) a description of the change;

(ii) the reason for the change;

(iii) whom to notify with questions concerning the change; and

(iv) instructions for return of the drug if not wanted by the patient.

(B) The pharmacy shall maintain documentation of patient notification of therapeutic drug interchange which shall include:

(i) the date of the notification;

(ii) the method of notification;

(iii) a description of the change; and

(iv) the reason for the change.

(C) The provisions of this paragraph do not apply to prescriptions for patients in facilities where drugs are administered to patients by a person required to do so by the laws of this state if the practitioner issuing the prescription has agreed to use of a formulary that includes a listing of therapeutic interchanges that the practitioner has agreed to allow. The pharmacy must maintain a copy of the formulary including a list of the practitioners that have agreed to the formulary and the signature of these practitioners.

(6) Prescription containers.

(A) A drug dispensed pursuant to a prescription drug order shall be dispensed in a child-resistant container unless:

(i) the patient or the practitioner requests the prescription not be dispensed in a child-resistant container; or

(ii) the product is exempted from requirements of the Poison Prevention Packaging Act of 1970.

(B) A drug dispensed pursuant to a prescription drug order shall be dispensed in an appropriate container as specified on the manufacturer's container.

(C) Prescription containers or closures shall not be re-used. However, if a patient or patient's agent has difficulty reading or understanding a prescription label, a prescription container may be reused provided:

(i) the container is designed to provide audio-recorded information about the proper use of the prescription medication;

(ii) the container is reused for the same patient;

(iii) the container is cleaned; and

(iv) a new safety closure is used each time the prescription container is reused.

(7) Labeling.

(A) At the time of delivery of the drug, the dispensing container shall bear a label in plain language and printed in an easily readable font size, unless otherwise specified, with at least the following information:

(i) name, address and phone number of the pharmacy;

(ii) unique identification number of the prescription that is printed in an easily readable font size comparable to but no smaller than ten-point Times Roman;

(iii) date the prescription is dispensed;

(iv) initials or an identification code of the dispensing pharmacist;

(v) name of the prescribing practitioner;

(vi) if the prescription was signed by a pharmacist, the name of the pharmacist who signed the prescription for a dangerous drug under delegated authority of a physician as specified in Subtitle B, Chapter 157, Occupations Code;

(vii) name of the patient or if such drug was prescribed for an animal, the species of the animal and the name of the owner that is printed in an easily readable font size comparable to but no smaller than ten-point Times Roman. The name of the patient's partner or family member is not required to be on the label of a drug prescribed for a partner for a sexually transmitted disease or for a patient's family members if the patient has an illness determined by the Centers for Disease Control and Prevention, the World Health Organization, or the Governor's office to be pandemic;

(viii) instructions for use that are printed in an easily readable font size comparable to but no smaller than ten-point Times Roman;

(ix) quantity dispensed;

(x) appropriate ancillary instructions such as storage instructions or cautionary statements such as warnings of potential harmful effects of combining the drug product with any product containing alcohol;

(xi) if the prescription is for a Schedule II - IV controlled substance, the statement "Caution: Federal law prohibits the transfer of this drug to any person other than the patient for whom it was prescribed";

(xii) if the pharmacist has selected a generically equivalent drug or interchangeable biological product pursuant to the provisions of the Act, Chapter 562, the statement "Substituted for Brand Prescribed" or "Substituted for 'Brand Name'" where "Brand Name" is the actual name of the brand name product prescribed;

(xiii) the name and strength of the actual drug or biological product dispensed that is printed in an easily readable size comparable to but no smaller than ten-point Times Roman, unless otherwise directed by the prescribing practitioner;

(I) The name shall be either:

(-a-) the brand name; or

(-b-) if no brand name, then the generic drug or interchangeable biological product name and name of the manufacturer or distributor of such generic drug or interchangeable biological product. (The name of the manufacturer or distributor may be reduced to an abbreviation or initials, provided the abbreviation or initials are sufficient to identify the manufacturer or distributor. For combination drug products or non-sterile compounded drug preparations having no brand name, the principal active ingredients shall be indicated on the label.)

        (II)   Except as provided in clause (xii) of this subparagraph, the brand name of the prescribed drug or biological product shall not appear on the prescription container label unless it is the drug product actually dispensed.

    (xiv) if the drug is dispensed in a container other than the manufacturer's original container, the date after which the prescription should not be used or beyond-use-date. Unless otherwise specified by the manufacturer, the beyond-use-date shall be one year from the date the drug is dispensed or the manufacturer's expiration date, whichever is earlier. The beyond-use-date may be placed on the prescription label or on a flag label attached to the bottle. A beyond-use-date is not required on the label of a prescription dispensed to a person at the time of release from prison or jail if the prescription is for not more than a 10-day supply of medication; and

    (xv)   either on the prescription label or the written information accompanying the prescription, the statement "Do not flush unused medications or pour down a sink or drain." A drug product on a list developed by the Federal Food and Drug Administration of medicines recommended for disposal by flushing is not required to bear this statement.

  (B)   If the prescription label required in subparagraph (A) of this paragraph is printed in a type size smaller than ten-point Times Roman, the pharmacy shall provide the patient written information containing the information as specified in subparagraph (A) of this paragraph in an easily readable font size comparable to but no smaller than ten-point Times Roman.

  (C)   The label is not required to include the initials or identification code of the dispensing pharmacist as specified in subparagraph (A) of this paragraph if the identity of the dispensing pharmacist is recorded in the pharmacy's data processing system. The record of the identity of the dispensing pharmacist shall not be altered in the pharmacy's data processing system.

  (D)   The dispensing container is not required to bear the label as specified in subparagraph (A) of this paragraph if:

    (i)   the drug is prescribed for administration to an ultimate user who is institutionalized in a licensed health care institution (e.g., nursing home, hospice, hospital);

    (ii)   no more than a 90-day supply is dispensed at one time;

    (iii)   the drug is not in the possession of the ultimate user prior to administration;

    (iv)   the pharmacist-in-charge has determined that the institution:

        (I)   maintains medication administration records which include adequate directions for use for the drug(s) prescribed;

        (II)   maintains records of ordering, receipt, and administration of the drug(s); and

        (III)   provides for appropriate safeguards for the control and storage of the drug(s); and

    (v)   the dispensing container bears a label that adequately:

        (I)   identifies the:

            (-a-) pharmacy by name and address;

            (-b-) unique identification number of the prescription;

            (-c-) name and strength of the drug dispensed;

            (-d-) name of the patient; and

            (-e-) name of the prescribing practitioner or, if applicable, the name of the pharmacist who signed the prescription drug order;

        (II)   if the drug is dispensed in a container other than the manufacturer's original container, specifies the date after which the prescription should not be used or beyond-use-date. Unless otherwise specified by the manufacturer, the beyond-use-date shall be one year from the date the drug is dispensed or the manufacturer's expiration date, whichever is earlier. The beyond-use-date may be placed on the prescription label or on a flag label attached to the bottle. A beyond-use-date is not required on the label of a prescription dispensed to a person at the time of release from prison or jail if the prescription is for not more than a 10-day supply of medication; and

        (III)   sets forth the directions for use and cautionary statements, if any, contained on the prescription drug order or required by law.

 (8)   Returning Undelivered Medication to Stock.

  (A)   As specified in § 431.021(w), Health and Safety Code, a pharmacist may not accept an unused prescription or drug, in whole or in part, for the purpose of resale or re-dispensing to any person after the prescription or drug has been originally dispensed or sold, except as provided in § 291.8 of this title (relating to Return of Prescription Drugs). Prescriptions that have not been picked up by or delivered to the patient or patient's agent may be returned to the pharmacy's stock for dispensing.

  (B)   A pharmacist shall evaluate the quality and safety of the prescriptions to be returned to stock.

  (C)   Prescriptions returned to stock for dispensing shall not be mixed within the manufacturer's container.

  (D)   Prescriptions returned to stock for dispensing should be used as soon as possible and stored in the dispensing container. The expiration date of the medication shall be the lesser of one year from the dispensing date on the prescription label or the manufacturer's expiration date if dispensed in the manufacturer's original container.

  (E)   At the time of dispensing, the prescription medication shall be placed in a new prescription container and not dispensed in the previously labeled container unless the label can be completely removed. However, if the medication is in the manufacturer's original container, the pharmacy label must be removed so that no confidential patient information is released.

(d)   Equipment and supplies. Class A pharmacies dispensing prescription drug orders shall have the following equipment and supplies:

 (1)   data processing system including a printer or comparable equipment;

 (2)   refrigerator;

 (3)   adequate supply of child-resistant, light-resistant, tight, and if applicable, glass containers;

 (4)   adequate supply of prescription, poison, and other applicable labels;

 (5)   appropriate equipment necessary for the proper preparation of prescription drug orders; and

 (6)   metric-apothecary weight and measure conversion charts.

(e)   Library. A reference library shall be maintained which includes the following in hard-copy or electronic format:

 (1)   current copies of the following:

  (A)   Texas Pharmacy Act and rules;

(B) Texas Dangerous Drug Act and rules;

(C) Texas Controlled Substances Act and rules; and

(D) Federal Controlled Substances Act and rules (or official publication describing the requirements of the Federal Controlled Substances Act and rules);

(2) at least one current or updated reference from each of the following categories:

  (A) a patient prescription drug information reference text or leaflets which are designed for the patient and must be available to the patient;

  (B) at least one current or updated general drug information reference which is required to contain drug interaction information including information needed to determine severity or significance of the interaction and appropriate recommendations or actions to be taken; and

  (C) if the pharmacy dispenses veterinary prescriptions, a general reference text on veterinary drugs; and

(3) basic antidote information and the telephone number of the nearest Regional Poison Control Center.

(f) Drugs.

  (1) Procurement and storage.

    (A) The pharmacist-in-charge shall have the responsibility for the procurement and storage of drugs, but may receive input from other appropriate staff relative to such responsibility.

    (B) Prescription drugs and devices and nonprescription Schedule V controlled substances shall be stored within the prescription department or a locked storage area.

    (C) All drugs shall be stored at the proper temperature, as defined in the USP/NF and § 291.15 of this title (relating to Storage of Drugs).

  (2) Out-of-date drugs or devices.

    (A) Any drug or device bearing an expiration date shall not be dispensed beyond the expiration date of the drug or device.

    (B) Outdated drugs or devices shall be removed from dispensing stock and shall be quarantined together until such drugs or devices are disposed of properly.

  (3) Nonprescription Schedule V controlled substances.

    (A) Schedule V controlled substances containing codeine, dihydrocodeine, or any of the salts of codeine or dihydrocodeine may not be distributed without a prescription drug order from a practitioner.

    (B) A pharmacist may distribute nonprescription Schedule V controlled substances which contain no more than 15 milligrams of opium per 29.5729 ml or per 28.35 Gm provided:

      (i) such distribution is made only by a pharmacist; a nonpharmacist employee may not distribute a nonprescription Schedule V controlled substance even if under the supervision of a pharmacist; however, after the pharmacist has fulfilled professional and legal responsibilities, the actual cash, credit transaction, or delivery may be completed by a nonpharmacist:

      (ii) not more than 240 ml (eight fluid ounces), or not more than 48 solid dosage units of any substance containing opium, may be distributed to the same purchaser in any given 48-hour period without a prescription drug order;

      (iii) the purchaser is at least 18 years of age; and

      (iv) the pharmacist requires every purchaser not known to the pharmacist to furnish suitable identification (including proof of age where appropriate).

    (C) A record of such distribution shall be maintained by the pharmacy in a bound record book. The record shall contain the following information:

      (i) true name of the purchaser;

      (ii) current address of the purchaser;

      (iii) name and quantity of controlled substance purchased;

      (iv) date of each purchase; and

      (v) signature or written initials of the distributing pharmacist.

  (4) Class A Pharmacies may not sell, purchase, trade or possess prescription drug samples, unless the pharmacy meets the requirements as specified in § 291.16 of this title (relating to Samples).

(g) Prepackaging of drugs.

  (1) Drugs may be prepackaged in quantities suitable for internal distribution only by a pharmacist or by pharmacy technicians or pharmacy technician trainees under the direction and direct supervision of a pharmacist.

  (2) The label of a prepackaged unit shall indicate:

    (A) brand name and strength of the drug; or if no brand name, then the generic name, strength, and name of the manufacturer or distributor;

    (B) facility's lot number;

    (C) facility's beyond use date; and

    (D) quantity of the drug, if the quantity is greater than one.

  (3) Records of prepackaging shall be maintained to show:

    (A) name of the drug, strength, and dosage form;

    (B) facility's lot number;

    (C) manufacturer or distributor;

    (D) manufacturer's lot number;

    (E) manufacturer's expiration date;

    (F) quantity per prepackaged unit;

    (G) number of prepackaged units;

    (H) date packaged;

    (I) name, initials, or electronic signature of the prepacker; and

    (J) signature, or electronic signature of the responsible pharmacist.

  (4) Stock packages, repackaged units, and control records shall be quarantined together until checked/released by the pharmacist.

Phr. Rules

(h) Customized patient medication packages.

    (1) Purpose. In lieu of dispensing two or more prescribed drug products in separate containers, a pharmacist may, with the consent of the patient, the patient's caregiver, or the prescriber, provide a customized patient medication package (patient med-pak).

    (2) Label.

        (A) The patient med-pak shall bear a label stating:

            (i) the name of the patient;

            (ii) the unique identification number for the patient med-pak itself and a separate unique identification number for each of the prescription drug orders for each of the drug products contained therein;

            (iii) the name, strength, physical description or identification, and total quantity of each drug product contained therein;

            (iv) the directions for use and cautionary statements, if any, contained in the prescription drug order for each drug product contained therein;

            (v) if applicable, a warning of the potential harmful effect of combining any form of alcoholic beverage with any drug product contained therein;

            (vi) any storage instructions or cautionary statements required by the official compendia;

            (vii) the name of the prescriber of each drug product;

            (viii) the name, address, and telephone number of the pharmacy;

            (ix) the initials or an identification code of the dispensing pharmacist;

            (x) the date after which the prescription should not be used or beyond-use-date. Unless otherwise specified by the manufacturer, the beyond-use-date shall be one year from the date the med-pak is dispensed or the earliest manufacturer's expiration date for a product contained in the med-pak if it is less than one-year from the date dispensed. The beyond-use-date may be placed on the prescription label or on a flag label attached to the bottle. A beyond-use-date is not required on the label of a prescription dispensed to a person at the time of release from prison or jail if the prescription is for not more than a 10-day supply of medication;

            (xi) either on the prescription label or the written information accompanying the prescription, the statement "Do not flush unused medications or pour down a sink or drain." A drug product on a list developed by the Federal Food and Drug Administration of medicines recommended for disposal by flushing is not required to bear this statement; and

            (xii) any other information, statements, or warnings required for any of the drug products contained therein.

        (B) If the patient med-pak allows for the removal or separation of the intact containers therefrom, each individual container shall bear a label identifying each of the drug product contained therein.

        (C) The dispensing container is not required to bear the label as specified in subparagraph (A) of this paragraph if:

            (i) the drug is prescribed for administration to an ultimate user who is institutionalized in a licensed health care institution (e.g., nursing home, hospice, hospital);

            (ii) no more than a 90-day supply is dispensed at one time;

            (iii) the drug is not in the possession of the ultimate user prior to administration;

            (iv) the pharmacist-in-charge has determined that the institution:

                (I) maintains medication administration records which include adequate directions for use for the drug(s) prescribed;

                (II) maintains records of ordering, receipt, and administration of the drug(s); and

                (III) provides for appropriate safeguards for the control and storage of the drug(s); and

            (v) the dispensing container bears a label that adequately:

                (I) identifies the:

                    (-a-) pharmacy by name and address;

                    (-b-) name and strength of each drug product dispensed;

                    (-c-) name of the patient; and

                    (-d-) name of the prescribing practitioner of each drug product, or the pharmacist who signed the prescription drug order;

                (II) the date after which the prescription should not be used or beyond-use-date. Unless otherwise specified by the manufacturer, the beyond-use-date shall be one year from the date the med-pak is dispensed or the earliest manufacturer's expiration date for a product contained in the med-pak if it is less than one-year from the date dispensed. The beyond-use-date may be placed on the prescription label or on a flag label attached to the bottle. A beyond-use-date is not required on the label of a prescription dispensed to a person at the time of release from prison or jail if the prescription is for not more than a 10-day supply of medication; and

                (III) for each drug product sets forth the directions for use and cautionary statements, if any, contained on the prescription drug order or required by law.

    (3) Labeling. The patient med-pak shall be accompanied by a patient package insert, in the event that any drug contained therein is required to be dispensed with such insert as accompanying labeling. Alternatively, such required information may be incorporated into a single, overall educational insert provided by the pharmacist for the total patient med-pak.

    (4) Packaging. In the absence of more stringent packaging requirements for any of the drug products contained therein, each container of the patient med-pak shall comply with official packaging standards. Each container shall be either not reclosable or so designed as to show evidence of having been opened.

    (5) Guidelines. It is the responsibility of the dispensing pharmacist when preparing a patient med-pak, to take into account any applicable compendial requirements or guidelines and the physical and chemical compatibility of the dosage forms placed within each container, as well as any therapeutic incompatibilities that may attend the simultaneous administration of the drugs.

    (6) Recordkeeping. In addition to any individual prescription filing requirements, a record of each patient med-pak shall be made and filed. Each record shall contain, as a minimum:

        (A) the name and address of the patient;

        (B) the unique identification number for the patient med-pak itself and a separate unique identification number for each of the prescription drug orders for each of the drug products contained therein;

        (C) the name of the manufacturer or distributor and lot number for each drug product contained therein;

      (D) information identifying or describing the design, characteristics, or specifications of the patient med-pak sufficient to allow subsequent preparation of an identical patient med-pak for the patient;

      (E) the date of preparation of the patient med-pak and the beyond-use date that was assigned;

      (F) any special labeling instructions; and

      (G) the initials or an identification code of the dispensing pharmacist.

  (7) The patient med-pak label is not required to include the initials or identification code of the dispensing pharmacist as specified in paragraph (2)(A) of this subsection if the identity of the dispensing pharmacist is recorded in the pharmacy's data processing system. The record of the identity of the dispensing pharmacist shall not be altered in the pharmacy's data processing system.

(i) Automated devices and systems in a pharmacy.

  (1) Automated counting devices. If a pharmacy uses automated counting devices:

      (A) the pharmacy shall have a method to calibrate and verify the accuracy of the automated counting device and document the calibration and verification on a routine basis;

      (B) the devices may be loaded with bulk drugs only by a pharmacist or by pharmacy technicians or pharmacy technician trainees under the direction and direct supervision of a pharmacist;

      (C) the label of an automated counting device container containing a bulk drug shall indicate the brand name and strength of the drug; or if no brand name, then the generic name, strength, and name of the manufacturer or distributor;

      (D) records of loading bulk drugs into an automated counting device shall be maintained to show:

        (i) name of the drug, strength, and dosage form;

        (ii) manufacturer or distributor;

        (iii) manufacturer's lot number;

        (iv) expiration date;

        (v) date of loading;

        (vi) name, initials, or electronic signature of the person loading the automated counting device; and

        (vii) name, initials, or electronic signature of the responsible pharmacist; and

      (E) the automated counting device shall not be used until a pharmacist verifies that the system is properly loaded and affixes his or her name, initials, or electronic signature to the record as specified in subparagraph (D) of this paragraph.

  (2) Automated pharmacy dispensing systems.

      (A) Authority to use automated pharmacy dispensing systems. A pharmacy may use an automated pharmacy dispensing system to fill prescription drug orders provided that:

        (i) the pharmacist-in-charge is responsible for the supervision of the operation of the system;

        (ii) the automated pharmacy dispensing system has been tested by the pharmacy and found to dispense accurately. The pharmacy shall make the results of such testing available to the board upon request; and

        (iii) the pharmacy will make the automated pharmacy dispensing system available for inspection by the board for the purpose of validating the accuracy of the system.

      (B) Automated pharmacy dispensing systems may be stocked or loaded by a pharmacist or by a pharmacy technician or pharmacy technician trainee under the supervision of a pharmacist.

      (C) Quality assurance program. A pharmacy which uses an automated pharmacy dispensing system to fill prescription drug orders shall operate according to a quality assurance program of the automated pharmacy dispensing system which:

        (i) requires continuous monitoring of the automated pharmacy dispensing system; and

        (ii) establishes mechanisms and procedures to test the accuracy of the automated pharmacy dispensing system at least every twelve months and whenever any upgrade or change is made to the system and documents each such activity.

      (D) Policies and procedures of operation.

        (i) When an automated pharmacy dispensing system is used to fill prescription drug orders, it shall be operated according to written policies and procedures of operation. The policies and procedures of operation shall:

          (I) provide for a pharmacist's review, approval, and accountability for the transmission of each original or new prescription drug order to the automated pharmacy dispensing system before the transmission is made;

          (II) provide for access to the automated pharmacy dispensing system for stocking and retrieval of medications which is limited to licensed healthcare professionals or pharmacy technicians acting under the supervision of a pharmacist;

          (III) require that a pharmacist checks, verifies, and documents that the correct medication and strength of bulk drugs, prepackaged containers, or manufacturer's unit of use packages were properly stocked, filled, and loaded in the automated pharmacy dispensing system prior to initiating the fill process; alternatively, an electronic verification system may be used for verification of manufacturer's unit of use packages or prepacked medication previously verified by a pharmacist;

          (IV) provide for an accountability record to be maintained that documents all transactions relative to stocking and removing medications from the automated pharmacy dispensing system;

          (V) require a prospective drug regimen review is conducted as specified in subsection (c)(2) of this section; and

          (VI) establish and make provisions for documentation of a preventative maintenance program for the automated pharmacy dispensing system.

        (ii) A pharmacy that uses an automated pharmacy dispensing system to fill prescription drug orders shall, at least annually, review its written policies and procedures, revise them if necessary, and document the review.

      (E) Recovery Plan. A pharmacy that uses an automated pharmacy dispensing system to fill prescription drug orders shall maintain a written plan for recovery from a disaster or any other situation which interrupts the ability of the automated pharmacy dispensing system to provide services necessary for the operation of the pharmacy. The written plan for recovery shall include:

        (i) planning and preparation for maintaining pharmacy services when an automated pharmacy dispensing system is experiencing downtime;

        (ii) procedures for response when an automated pharmacy dispensing system is experiencing downtime; and

        (iii) procedures for the maintenance and testing of the written plan for recovery.

Phr. Rules

(F) Final check of prescriptions dispensed using an automated pharmacy dispensing system. For the purpose of § 291.32(c)(2) (D) of this title (relating to Personnel), a pharmacist must perform the final check of all prescriptions prior to delivery to the patient to ensure that the prescription is dispensed accurately as prescribed.

    (i) This final check shall be considered accomplished if:

        (I) a check of the final product is conducted by a pharmacist after the automated pharmacy dispensing system has completed the prescription and prior to delivery to the patient; or

        (II) the following checks are conducted:

            (-a-) if the automated pharmacy dispensing system contains bulk stock drugs, a pharmacist verifies that those drugs have been accurately stocked as specified in subparagraph (D)(i)(III) of this paragraph;

            (-b-) if the automated pharmacy dispensing system contains manufacturer's unit of use packages or prepackaged medication previously verified by a pharmacist, an electronic verification system has confirmed that the medications have been accurately stocked as specified in subparagraph (D)(i)(III) of this paragraph;

            (-c-) a pharmacist checks the accuracy of the data entry of each original or new prescription drug order entered into the automated pharmacy dispensing system; and

            (-d-) an electronic verification process is used to verify the proper prescription label has been affixed to the correct medication container, prepackaged medication or manufacturer unit of use package for the correct patient.

    (ii) If the final check is accomplished as specified in clause (i)(II) of this subparagraph, the following additional requirements must be met:

        (I) the dispensing process must be fully automated from the time the pharmacist releases the prescription to the automated pharmacy dispensing system until a completed, labeled prescription ready for delivery to the patient is produced;

        (II) the pharmacy has conducted initial testing and has a continuous quality assurance program which documents that the automated pharmacy dispensing system dispenses accurately as specified in subparagraph (C) of this paragraph;

        (III) the automated pharmacy dispensing system documents and maintains:

            (-a-) the name(s), initials, or identification code(s) of each pharmacist responsible for the checks outlined in clause (i)(II) of this subparagraph; and

            (-b-) the name(s), initials, or identification code(s) and specific activity(ies) of each pharmacist, pharmacy technician, or pharmacy technician trainee who performs any other portion of the dispensing process; and

        (IV) the pharmacy establishes mechanisms and procedures to test the accuracy of the automated pharmacy dispensing system at least every month rather than every twelve months as specified in subparagraph (C) of this paragraph.

(3) Automated checking device.

    (A) For the purpose of § 291.32(c)(2)(D) of this title, the final check of a dispensed prescription shall be considered accomplished using an automated checking device provided a check of the final product is conducted by a pharmacist prior to delivery to the patient or the following checks are performed:

        (i) the drug used to fill the order is checked through the use of an automated checking device which verifies that the drug is labeled and packaged accurately; and

        (ii) a pharmacist checks the accuracy of each original or new prescription drug order and is responsible for the final check of the order through the automated checking device.

    (B) If the final check is accomplished as specified in subparagraph (A) of this paragraph, the following additional requirements must be met:

        (i) the pharmacy has conducted initial testing of the automated checking device and has a continuous quality assurance program which documents that the automated checking device accurately confirms that the correct drug and strength has been labeled with the correct label for the correct patient;

        (ii) the pharmacy documents and maintains:

            (I) the name(s), initials, or identification code(s) of each pharmacist responsible for the checks outlined in subparagraph (A)(i) of this paragraph; and

            (II) the name(s) initials, or identification code(s) and specific activity(ies) of each pharmacist, or pharmacy technician, or pharmacy technician trainee who performs any other portion of the dispensing process;

        (iii) the pharmacy establishes mechanisms and procedures to test the accuracy of the automated checking device at least monthly; and

        (iv) the pharmacy establishes procedures to ensure that errors identified by the automated checking device may not be overridden by a pharmacy technician and must be reviewed and corrected by a pharmacist.

Source: The provisions of this § 291.33 adopted to be effective September 14, 1988, 13 TEXREG4306; amended to be effective February 1, 1989, 14 TEXREG453; amended to be effective September 5, 1990, 15 TEXREG4807; amended to be effective January 29, 1992, 17 TexReg 323; amended to be effective January 1, 1993, 17 TexReg 9116; amended to be effective January 4, 1994, 18 TexReg 9853; amended to be effective June 1, 1994, 19 TexReg 3921; amended to be effective December 1, 1994, 19 TexReg 9179; amended to be effective March 21, 1996, 21 TexReg 2227; amended to be effective April 7, 1997, 22 TexReg 3106; amended to be effective March 29, 2000, 25 TexReg 2575; amended to beeffective June 4, 2000, 25 TexReg 4778; amended to be effective August 31, 2000, 25 TexReg 8405; amended to be effective December 27, 2000, 25 TexReg 12690; amended to be effective June 20, 2001, 26 TexReg 4478; amended to be effective December 19, 2001, 26 TexReg 10311; amended to be effective June 1, 2002, 27 TexReg 1736; amended to be effective December 15, 2002, 27 TexReg 11537; amended to be effective June 23, 2003, 28 TexReg 4637; amended to be effective March 4, 2004, 29 TexReg 1951; amended to be effective June 6, 2004, 29 TexReg 5361; amended to be effective June 12, 2005, 30 TexReg 3208; amended to be effective June 11, 2006, 31 TexReg 4629; amended to be effective March 6, 2008, 33 TexReg 1784; amended to be effective September 7, 2008, 33 TexReg 7218; amended to be effective December 14, 2008, 33 TexReg 10027; amended to be effective March 12, 2009, 34 TexReg 1593; amendedto be effective June 7, 2009, 34 TexReg 3391; amended to be effective December 6, 2009, 34 TexReg 8691; amended to be effective May 30, 2010, 35 TexReg 4165; amended to be effective December 8, 2010, 35 TexReg 10690; amended to be effective March 10, 2011, 36 TexReg 1517; amended to be effective September 12, 2011, 36 TexReg 5847; amended to be effective June 7, 2012, 37 TexReg 4046; amended to be effective June 12, 2013, 38 TexReg 3592; amended to be effective December 10, 2013, 38 TexReg 8835; amended to be effective September 11, 2014, 39 TexReg 7094; amended to be effective December 7, 2014, 39 TexReg 9345; amended to be effective December 6, 2015, 40 TexReg 8766; amended to be effective September 11, 2016, 41 TexReg 6697; amended to be effective September 6, 2017, 42 TexReg 4466; amended to be effective June 7, 2018, 43 TexReg 3587; amended to be effective September 16,2018, 43TexReg 5783; amended to be effective March 12, 2019, 44 TexReg 1320

§291.34 Records

(a) Maintenance of records.

  (1) Every inventory or other record required to be kept under the provisions of Subchapter B of this chapter (relating to Community Pharmacy (Class A)) shall be:

    (A) kept by the pharmacy at the pharmacy's licensed location and be available, for at least two years from the date of such inventory or record, for inspecting and copying by the board or its representative and to other authorized local, state, or federal law enforcement agencies; and

    (B) supplied by the pharmacy within 72 hours, if requested by an authorized agent of the Texas State Board of Pharmacy. If the pharmacy maintains the records in an electronic format, the requested records must be provided in a mutually agreeable electronic format if specifically requested by the board or its representative. Failure to provide the records set out in this section, either on site or within 72 hours, constitutes prima facie evidence of failure to keep and maintain records in violation of the Act.

  (2) Records of controlled substances listed in Schedule II shall be maintained separately from all other records of the pharmacy.

  (3) Records of controlled substances, other than prescription drug orders, listed in Schedules III-V shall be maintained separately or readily retrievable from all other records of the pharmacy. For purposes of this subsection, readily retrievable means that the controlled substances shall be asterisked, red-lined, or in some other manner readily identifiable apart from all other items appearing on the record.

  (4) Records, except when specifically required to be maintained in original or hard copy form, may be maintained in an alternative data retention system, such as a data processing system or direct imaging system provided:

    (A) the records maintained in the alternative system contain all of the information required on the manual record; and

    (B) the data processing system is capable of producing a hard copy of the record upon the request of the board, its representative, or other authorized local, state, or federal law enforcement or regulatory agencies.

(b) Prescriptions.

  (1) Professional responsibility.

    (A) Pharmacists shall exercise sound professional judgment with respect to the accuracy and authenticity of any prescription drug order they dispense. If the pharmacist questions the accuracy or authenticity of a prescription drug order, he/she shall verify the order with the practitioner prior to dispensing.

    (B) Prior to dispensing a prescription, pharmacists shall determine, in the exercise of sound professional judgment, that the prescription is a valid prescription. A pharmacist may not dispense a prescription drug unless the pharmacist complies with the requirements of § 562.056 and § 562.112 of the Act, and § 291.29 of this title (relating to Professional Responsibility of Pharmacists).

    (C) Subparagraph (B) of this paragraph does not prohibit a pharmacist from dispensing a prescription when a valid patient-practitioner relationship is not present in an emergency situation (e.g., a practitioner taking calls for the patient's regular practitioner).

    (D) The owner of a Class A pharmacy shall have responsibility for ensuring its agents and employees engage in appropriate decisions regarding dispensing of valid prescriptions as set forth in § 562.112 of the Act.

  (2) Written prescription drug orders.

    (A) Practitioner's signature.

      (i) Dangerous drug prescription orders. Written prescription drug orders shall be:

        (I) manually signed by the practitioner; or

        (II) electronically signed by the practitioner using a system that electronically replicates the practitioner's manual signature on the written prescription, provided:

          (-a-) that security features of the system require the practitioner to authorize each use; and

          (-b-) the prescription is printed on paper that is designed to prevent unauthorized copying of a completed prescription and to prevent the erasure or modification of information written on the prescription by the prescribing practitioner. (For example, the paper contains security provisions against copying that results in some indication on the copy that it is a copy and therefore render the prescription null and void.)

      (ii) Controlled substance prescription orders. Prescription drug orders for Schedules II, III, IV, or V controlled substances shall be manually signed by the practitioner. Prescription drug orders for Schedule II controlled substances shall be issued on an official prescription form as required by the Texas Controlled Substances Act, § 481.075.

      (iii) Other provisions for a practitioner's signature.

        (I) A practitioner may sign a prescription drug order in the same manner as he would sign a check or legal document, e.g., J.H. Smith or John H. Smith.

        (II) Rubber stamped signatures may not be used.

        (III) The prescription drug order may not be signed by a practitioner's agent but may be prepared by an agent for the signature of a practitioner. However, the prescribing practitioner is responsible in case the prescription drug order does not conform in all essential respects to the law and regulations.

    (B) Prescription drug orders written by practitioners in another state.

      (i) Dangerous drug prescription orders. A pharmacist may dispense prescription drug orders for dangerous drugs issued by practitioners in a state other than Texas in the same manner as prescription drug orders for dangerous drugs issued by practitioners in Texas are dispensed.

      (ii) Controlled substance prescription drug orders.

        (I) A pharmacist may dispense prescription drug orders for Schedule II controlled substances issued by a practitioner in another state provided:

          (-a-) the prescription is dispensed as specified in § 315.9 of this title (relating to Pharmacy Responsibility - Out-of-State Practitioner - Effective September 1, 2016);

(-b-) the prescription drug order is an original written prescription issued by a person practicing in another state and licensed by another state as a physician, dentist, veterinarian, or podiatrist, who has a current federal Drug Enforcement Administration (DEA) registration number, and who may legally prescribe Schedule II controlled substances in such other state; and

(-c-) the prescription drug order is not dispensed after the end of the twenty-first day after the date on which the prescription is issued.

(II) A pharmacist may dispense prescription drug orders for controlled substances in Schedules III, IV, or V issued by a physician, dentist, veterinarian, or podiatrist in another state provided:

(-a-) the prescription drug order is issued by a person practicing in another state and licensed by another state as a physician, dentist, veterinarian, or podiatrist, who has a current federal DEA registration number, and who may legally prescribe Schedules III, IV, or V controlled substances in such other state;

(-b-) the prescription drug order is not dispensed or refilled more than six months from the initial date of issuance and may not be refilled more than five times; and

(-c-) if there are no refill instructions on the original prescription drug order (which shall be interpreted as no refills authorized) or if all refills authorized on the original prescription drug order have been dispensed, a new prescription drug order is obtained from the prescribing practitioner prior to dispensing any additional quantities of controlled substances.

(C) Prescription drug orders written by practitioners in the United Mexican States or the Dominion of Canada.

(i) Controlled substance prescription drug orders. A pharmacist may not dispense a prescription drug order for a Schedule II, III, IV, or V controlled substance issued by a practitioner in the Dominion of Canada or the United Mexican States.

(ii) Dangerous drug prescription drug orders. A pharmacist may dispense a dangerous drug prescription issued by a person licensed in the Dominion of Canada or the United Mexican States as a physician, dentist, veterinarian, or podiatrist provided:

(I) the prescription drug order is an original written prescription; and

(II) if there are no refill instructions on the original written prescription drug order (which shall be interpreted as no refills authorized) or if all refills authorized on the original written prescription drug order have been dispensed, a new written prescription drug order shall be obtained from the prescribing practitioner prior to dispensing any additional quantities of dangerous drugs.

(D) Prescription drug orders issued by an advanced practice registered nurse, physician assistant, or pharmacist.

(i) A pharmacist may dispense a prescription drug order that is:

(I) issued by an advanced practice registered nurse or physician assistant provided the advanced practice registered nurse or physician assistant is practicing in accordance with Subtitle B, Chapter 157, Occupations Code; and

(II) for a dangerous drug and signed by a pharmacist under delegated authority of a physician as specified in Subtitle B, Chapter 157, Occupations Code.

(ii) Each practitioner shall designate in writing the name of each advanced practice registered nurse or physician assistant authorized to issue a prescription drug order pursuant to Subtitle B, Chapter 157, Occupations Code. A list of the advanced practice registered nurses or physician assistants designated by the practitioner must be maintained in the practitioner's usual place of business. On request by a pharmacist, a practitioner shall furnish the pharmacist with a copy of the written authorization for a specific advanced practice registered nurse or physician assistant.

(E) Prescription drug orders for Schedule II controlled substances. No Schedule II controlled substance may be dispensed without a written prescription drug order of a practitioner on an official prescription form as required by the Texas Controlled Substances Act, § 481.075.

(3) Verbal prescription drug orders.

(A) A verbal prescription drug order from a practitioner or a practitioner's designated agent may only be received by a pharmacist or a pharmacist-intern under the direct supervision of a pharmacist.

(B) A practitioner shall designate in writing the name of each agent authorized by the practitioner to communicate prescriptions verbally for the practitioner. The practitioner shall maintain at the practitioner's usual place of business a list of the designated agents. The practitioner shall provide a pharmacist with a copy of the practitioner's written authorization for a specific agent on the pharmacist's request.

(C) A pharmacist may not dispense a verbal prescription drug order for a dangerous drug or a controlled substance issued by a practitioner licensed in the Dominion of Canada or the United Mexican States unless the practitioner is also licensed in Texas.

(4) Electronic prescription drug orders.

(A) Dangerous drug prescription orders.

(i) An electronic prescription drug order for a dangerous drug may be transmitted by a practitioner or a practitioner's designated agent:

(I) directly to a pharmacy; or

(II) through the use of a data communication device provided:

(-a-) the confidential prescription information is not altered during transmission; and

(-b-) confidential patient information is not accessed or maintained by the operator of the data communication device other than for legal purposes under federal and state law.

(ii) A practitioner shall designate in writing the name of each agent authorized by the practitioner to electronically transmit prescriptions for the practitioner. The practitioner shall maintain at the practitioner's usual place of business a list of the designated agents. The practitioner shall provide a pharmacist with a copy of the practitioner's written authorization for a specific agent on the pharmacist's request.

(B) Controlled substance prescription orders. A pharmacist may only dispense an electronic prescription drug order for a Schedule II, III, IV, or V controlled substance in compliance with the federal and state laws and the rules of the Drug

Enforcement Administration outlined in Part 1300 of the Code of Federal Regulations and Texas Department of Public Safety.

    (C) Prescriptions issued by a practitioner licensed in the Dominion of Canada or the United Mexican States. A pharmacist may not dispense an electronic prescription drug order for a dangerous drug or controlled substance issued by a practitioner licensed in the Dominion of Canada or the United Mexican States unless the practitioner is also licensed in Texas.

(5) Facsimile (faxed) prescription drug orders.
    (A) A pharmacist may dispense a prescription drug order for a dangerous drug transmitted to the pharmacy by facsimile.
    (B) A pharmacist may dispense a prescription drug order for a Schedule III-V controlled substance transmitted to the pharmacy by facsimile provided the prescription is manually signed by the practitioner and not electronically signed using a system that electronically replicates the practitioner's manual signature on the prescription drug order.
    (C) A pharmacist may not dispense a facsimile prescription drug order for a dangerous drug or controlled substance issued by a practitioner licensed in the Dominion of Canada or the United Mexican States unless the practitioner is also licensed in Texas.

(6) Original prescription drug order records.
    (A) Original prescriptions may be dispensed only in accordance with the prescriber's authorization as indicated on the original prescription drug order including clarifications to the order given to the pharmacist by the practitioner or the practitioner's agent and recorded on the prescription.
    (B) Notwithstanding subparagraph (A) of this paragraph, a pharmacist may dispense a quantity less than indicated on the original prescription drug order at the request of the patient or patient's agent.
    (C) Original prescriptions shall be maintained by the pharmacy in numerical order and remain legible for a period of two years from the date of filling or the date of the last refill dispensed.
    (D) If an original prescription drug order is changed, such prescription order shall be invalid and of no further force and effect; if additional drugs are to be dispensed, a new prescription drug order with a new and separate number is required. However, an original prescription drug order for a dangerous drug may be changed in accordance with paragraph (10) of this subsection relating to accelerated refills.
    (E) Original prescriptions shall be maintained in three separate files as follows:
        (i) prescriptions for controlled substances listed in Schedule II;
        (ii) prescriptions for controlled substances listed in Schedules III-V; and
        (iii) prescriptions for dangerous drugs and nonprescription drugs.
    (F) Original prescription records other than prescriptions for Schedule II controlled substances may be stored in a system that is capable of producing a direct image of the original prescription record, e.g., a digitalized imaging system. If original prescription records are stored in a direct imaging system, the following is applicable:
        (i) the record of refills recorded on the original prescription must also be stored in this system;
        (ii) the original prescription records must be maintained in numerical order and separated in three files as specified in subparagraph (D) of this paragraph; and
        (iii) the pharmacy must provide immediate access to equipment necessary to render the records easily readable.

(7) Prescription drug order information.
    (A) All original prescriptions shall bear:
        (i) the name of the patient, or if such drug is for an animal, the species of such animal and the name of the owner;
        (ii) the address of the patient, provided, however, a prescription for a dangerous drug is not required to bear the address of the patient if such address is readily retrievable on another appropriate, uniformly maintained pharmacy record, such as medication records;
        (iii) the name, address and telephone number of the practitioner at the practitioner's usual place of business, legibly printed or stamped, and if for a controlled substance, the DEA registration number of the practitioner;
        (iv) the name and strength of the drug prescribed;
        (v) the quantity prescribed numerically, and if for a controlled substance:
            (I) numerically, followed by the number written as a word, if the prescription is written;
            (II) numerically, if the prescription is electronic; or
            (III) if the prescription is communicated orally or telephonically, as transcribed by the receiving pharmacist;
        (vi) directions for use;
        (vii) the intended use for the drug unless the practitioner determines the furnishing of this information is not in the best interest of the patient;
        (viii) the date of issuance;
        (ix) if a faxed prescription:
            (I) a statement that indicates that the prescription has been faxed (e.g., Faxed to); and
            (II) if transmitted by a designated agent, the name of the designated agent;
        (x) if electronically transmitted:
            (I) the date the prescription drug order was electronically transmitted to the pharmacy, if different from the date of issuance of the prescription; and
            (II) if transmitted by a designated agent, the name of the designated agent; and
        (xi) if issued by an advanced practice nurse or physician assistant in accordance with Subtitle B, Chapter 157, Occupations Code:
            (I) the name, address, telephone number, and if the prescription is for a controlled substance, the DEA number of the supervising practitioner; and
            (II) the address and telephone number of the clinic where the prescription drug order was carried out or signed; and
        (xii) if communicated orally or telephonically:
            (I) the initials or identification code of the transcribing pharmacist; and
            (II) the name of the prescriber or prescriber's agent communicating the prescription information.

(B) At the time of dispensing, a pharmacist is responsible for documenting the following information on either the original hardcopy prescription or in the pharmacy's data processing system:
   (i)   the unique identification number of the prescription drug order;
   (ii)   the initials or identification code of the dispensing pharmacist;
   (iii) the initials or identification code of the pharmacy technician or pharmacy technician trainee performing data entry of the prescription, if applicable;
   (iv)   the quantity dispensed, if different from the quantity prescribed;
   (v)   the date of dispensing, if different from the date of issuance; and
   (vi)   the brand name or manufacturer of the drug or biological product actually dispensed, if the drug was prescribed by generic name or interchangeable biological name or if a drug or interchangeable biological product other than the one prescribed was dispensed pursuant to the provisions of the Act, Chapters 562 and 563,
(C) Prescription drug orders may be utilized as authorized in Title 40, Part 1, Chapter 19 of the Texas Administrative Code.
   (i)   A prescription drug order is not required to bear the information specified in subparagraph (A) of this paragraph if the drug is prescribed for administration to an ultimate user who is institutionalized in a licensed health care institution (e.g., nursing home, hospice, hospital). Such prescription drug orders must contain the following information:
      (I)   the full name of the patient;
      (II)   the date of issuance;
      (III) the name, strength, and dosage form of the drug prescribed;
      (IV)   directions for use; and
      (V)   the signature(s) required by 40 TAC § 19.1506.
   (ii)   Prescription drug orders for dangerous drugs shall not be dispensed following one year after the date of issuance unless the authorized prescriber renews the prescription drug order.
   (iii) Controlled substances shall not be dispensed pursuant to a prescription drug order under this subparagraph.
(8) Refills.
   (A) General information.
      (i)   Refills may be dispensed only in accordance with the prescriber's authorization as indicated on the original prescription drug order except as authorized in paragraph (10) of this subsection relating to accelerated refills.
      (ii)   If there are no refill instructions on the original prescription drug order (which shall be interpreted as no refills authorized) or if all refills authorized on the original prescription drug order have been dispensed, authorization from the prescribing practitioner shall be obtained prior to dispensing any refills and documented as specified in subsection (l) of this section.
   (B) Refills of prescription drug orders for dangerous drugs or nonprescription drugs.
      (i)   Prescription drug orders for dangerous drugs or nonprescription drugs may not be refilled after one year from the date of issuance of the original prescription drug order.
      (ii)   If one year has expired from the date of issuance of an original prescription drug order for a dangerous drug or nonprescription drug, authorization shall be obtained from the prescribing practitioner prior to dispensing any additional quantities of the drug.
   (C) Refills of prescription drug orders for Schedules III-V controlled substances.
      (i)   Prescription drug orders for Schedules III-V controlled substances may not be refilled more than five times or after six months from the date of issuance of the original prescription drug order, whichever occurs first.
      (ii)   If a prescription drug order for a Schedule III, IV, or V controlled substance has been refilled a total of five times or if six months have expired from the date of issuance of the original prescription drug order, whichever occurs first, a new and separate prescription drug order shall be obtained from the prescribing practitioner prior to dispensing any additional quantities of controlled substances.
   (D) Pharmacist unable to contact prescribing practitioner. If a pharmacist is unable to contact the prescribing practitioner after a reasonable effort, a pharmacist may exercise his professional judgment in refilling a prescription drug order for a drug, other than a Schedule II controlled substance, without the authorization of the prescribing practitioner, provided:
      (i)   failure to refill the prescription might result in an interruption of a therapeutic regimen or create patient suffering;
      (ii)   the quantity of prescription drug dispensed does not exceed a 72-hour supply;
      (iii) the pharmacist informs the patient or the patient's agent at the time of dispensing that the refill is being provided without such authorization and that authorization of the practitioner is required for future refills;
      (iv)   the pharmacist informs the practitioner of the emergency refill at the earliest reasonable time;
      (v)   the pharmacist maintains a record of the emergency refill containing the information required to be maintained on a prescription as specified in this subsection;
      (vi)   the pharmacist affixes a label to the dispensing container as specified in § 291.33(c)(7) of this title; and
      (vii) if the prescription was initially filled at another pharmacy, the pharmacist may exercise his professional judgment in refilling the prescription provided:
         (I)   the patient has the prescription container, label, receipt or other documentation from the other pharmacy that contains the essential information;
         (II)   after a reasonable effort, the pharmacist is unable to contact the other pharmacy to transfer the remaining prescription refills or there are no refills remaining on the prescription;
         (III) the pharmacist, in his professional judgment, determines that such a request for an emergency refill is appropriate and meets the requirements of clause (i) of this subparagraph; and
         (IV)   the pharmacist complies with the requirements of clauses (ii) - (vi) of this subparagraph.
   (E) Natural or manmade disasters. If a natural or manmade disaster has occurred that prohibits the pharmacist from being able to contact the practitioner, a pharmacist may exercise his professional judgment in refilling a prescription drug order for a drug, other than a Schedule II controlled substance, without the authorization of the prescribing practitioner, provided:

        (i)   failure to refill the prescription might result in an interruption of a therapeutic regimen or create patient suffering;

        (ii)   the quantity of prescription drug dispensed does not exceed a 30-day supply;

        (iii)   the governor has declared a state of disaster;

        (iv)   the board, through the executive director, has notified pharmacies that pharmacists may dispense up to a 30-day supply of prescription drugs;

        (v)   the pharmacist informs the patient or the patient's agent at the time of dispensing that the refill is being provided without such authorization and that authorization of the practitioner is required for future refills;

        (vi)   the pharmacist informs the practitioner of the emergency refill at the earliest reasonable time;

        (vii)   the pharmacist maintains a record of the emergency refill containing the information required to be maintained on a prescription as specified in this subsection;

        (viii)   the pharmacist affixes a label to the dispensing container as specified in § 291.33(c)(7) of this title; and

        (ix)   if the prescription was initially filled at another pharmacy, the pharmacist may exercise his professional judgment in refilling the prescription provided:

           (I)   the patient has the prescription container, label, receipt or other documentation from the other pharmacy that contains the essential information;

           (II)   after a reasonable effort, the pharmacist is unable to contact the other pharmacy to transfer the remaining prescription refills or there are no refills remaining on the prescription;

           (III)   the pharmacist, in his professional judgment, determines that such a request for an emergency refill is appropriate and meets the requirements of clause (i) of this subparagraph; and

           (IV)   the pharmacist complies with the requirements of clauses (ii) - (viii) of this subparagraph.

   (F)   Auto-Refill Programs. A pharmacy may use a program that automatically refills prescriptions that have existing refills available in order to improve patient compliance with and adherence to prescribed medication therapy. The following is applicable in order to enroll patients into an auto-refill program.

        (i)   Notice of the availability of an auto-refill program shall be given to the patient or patient's agent, and the patient or patient's agent must affirmatively indicate that they wish to enroll in such a program and the pharmacy shall document such indication.

        (ii)   The patient or patient's agent shall have the option to withdraw from such a program at any time.

        (iii)   Auto-refill programs may be used for refills of dangerous drugs, and Schedules IV and V controlled substances. Schedules II and III controlled substances may not be dispensed by an auto-refill program.

        (iv)   As is required for all prescriptions, a drug regimen review shall be completed on all prescriptions filled as a result of the auto-refill program. Special attention shall be noted for drug regimen review warnings of duplication of therapy and all such conflicts shall be resolved with the prescribing practitioner prior to refilling the prescription.

  (9)   Records Relating to Dispensing Errors. If a dispensing error occurs, the following is applicable.

   (A)   Original prescription drug orders:

        (i)   shall not be destroyed and must be maintained in accordance with subsection (a) of this section; and

        (ii)   shall not be altered. Altering includes placing a label or any other item over any of the information on the prescription drug order (e.g., a dispensing tag or label that is affixed to back of a prescription drug order must not be affixed on top of another dispensing tag or label in such a manner as to obliterate the information relating to the error).

   (B)   Prescription drug order records maintained in a data processing system:

        (i)   shall not be deleted and must be maintained in accordance with subsection (a) of this section;

        (ii)   may be changed only in compliance with subsection (e)(2)(B) of this section; and

        (iii)   if the error involved incorrect data entry into the pharmacy's data processing system, this record must be either voided or cancelled in the data processing system, so that the incorrectly entered prescription drug order may not be dispensed, or the data processing system must be capable of maintaining an audit trail showing any changes made to the data in the system.

  (10)   Accelerated refills. In accordance with § 562.0545 of the Act, a pharmacist may dispense up to a 90-day supply of a dangerous drug pursuant to a valid prescription that specifies the dispensing of a lesser amount followed by periodic refills of that amount if:

   (A)   the total quantity of dosage units dispensed does not exceed the total quantity of dosage units authorized by the prescriber on the original prescription, including refills;

   (B)   the patient consents to the dispensing of up to a 90-day supply and the physician has been notified electronically or by telephone;

   (C)   the physician has not specified on the prescription that dispensing the prescription in an initial amount followed by periodic refills is medically necessary;

   (D)   the dangerous drug is not a psychotropic drug used to treat mental or psychiatric conditions; and

   (E)   the patient is at least 18 years of age.

(c)   Patient medication records.

  (1)   A patient medication record system shall be maintained by the pharmacy for patients to whom prescription drug orders are dispensed.

  (2)   The patient medication record system shall provide for the immediate retrieval of information for the previous 12 months that is necessary for the dispensing pharmacist to conduct a prospective drug regimen review at the time a prescription drug order is presented for dispensing.

  (3)   The pharmacist-in-charge shall assure that a reasonable effort is made to obtain and record in the patient medication record at least the following information:

   (A)   full name of the patient for whom the drug is prescribed;

   (B)   address and telephone number of the patient;

   (C)   patient's age or date of birth;

   (D)   patient's gender;

   (E) any known allergies, drug reactions, idiosyncrasies, and chronic conditions or disease states of the patient and the identity of any other drugs currently being used by the patient which may relate to prospective drug regimen review;
   (F) pharmacist's comments relevant to the individual's drug therapy, including any other information unique to the specific patient or drug; and
   (G) a list of all prescription drug orders dispensed (new and refill) to the patient by the pharmacy during the last two years. Such lists hall contain the following information:
      (i) date dispensed;
      (ii) name, strength, and quantity of the drug dispensed;
      (iii) prescribing practitioner's name;
      (iv) unique identification number of the prescription; and
      (v) name or initials of the dispensing pharmacists.
   (4) A patient medication record shall be maintained in the pharmacy for two years. If patient medication records are maintained in a data processing system, all of the information specified in this subsection shall be maintained in a retrievable form for two years and information for the previous 12 months shall be maintained on-line. A patient medication record must contain documentation of any modification, change, or manipulation to a patient profile.
   (5) Nothing in this subsection shall be construed as requiring a pharmacist to obtain, record, and maintain patient information other than prescription drug order information when a patient or patient's agent refuses to provide the necessary information for such patient medication records.
(d) Prescription drug order records maintained in a manual system.
   (1) Original prescriptions shall be maintained in three files as specified in subsection (b)(6)(D) of this section.
   (2) Refills.
      (A) Each time a prescription drug order is refilled, a record of such refill shall be made:
         (i) on the back of the prescription by recording the date of dispensing, the written initials or identification code of the dispensing pharmacist, the initials or identification code of the pharmacy technician or pharmacy technician trainee preparing the prescription label, if applicable, and the amount dispensed. (If the pharmacist merely initials and dates the back of the prescription drug order, he or she shall be deemed to have dispensed a refill for the full face amount of the prescription drug order); or
         (ii) on another appropriate, uniformly maintained, readily retrievable record, such as medication records, that indicates by patient name the following information:
            (I) unique identification number of the prescription;
            (II) name and strength of the drug dispensed;
            (III) date of each dispensing;
            (IV) quantity dispensed at each dispensing;
            (V) initials or identification code of the dispensing pharmacist;
            (VI) initials or identification code of the pharmacy technician or pharmacy technician trainee preparing the prescription label, if applicable; and
            (VII) total number of refills for the prescription.
      (B) If refill records are maintained in accordance with subparagraph (A)(ii) of this paragraph, refill records for controlled substances in Schedules III-V shall be maintained separately from refill records of dangerous drugs and nonprescription drugs.
   (3) Authorization of refills. Practitioner authorization for additional refills of a prescription drug order shall be noted on the original prescription, in addition to the documentation of dispensing the refill as specified in subsection (l) of this section.
   (4) Each time a modification, change, or manipulation is made to a record of dispensing, documentation of such change shall be recorded on the back of the prescription or on another appropriate, uniformly maintained, readily retrievable record, such as medication records. The documentation of any modification, change, or manipulation to a record of dispensing shall include the identification of the individual responsible for the alteration.
(e) Prescription drug order records maintained in a data processing system.
   (1) General requirements for records maintained in a data processing system.
      (A) Compliance with data processing system requirements. If a Class A pharmacy's data processing system is not in compliance with this subsection, the pharmacy must maintain a manual record keeping system as specified in subsection (d) of this section.
      (B) Original prescriptions. Original prescriptions shall be maintained in three files as specified in subsection (b)(6)(D) of this section.
      (C) Requirements for backup systems.
         (i) The pharmacy shall maintain a backup copy of information stored in the data processing system using disk, tape, or other electronic backup system and update this backup copy on a regular basis, at least monthly, to assure that data is not lost due to system failure.
         (ii) Data processing systems shall have a workable (electronic) data retention system that can produce an audit trail of drug usage for the preceding two years as specified in paragraph (2)(H) of this subsection.
      (D) Change or discontinuance of a data processing system.
         (i) Records of dispensing. A pharmacy that changes or discontinues use of a data processing system must:
            (I) transfer the records of dispensing to the new data processing system; or
            (II) purge the records of dispensing to a printout that contains the same information required on the daily printout as specified in paragraph(2)(C) of this subsection. The information on this hard copy printout shall be sorted and printed by prescription number and list each dispensing for this prescription chronologically.
         (ii) Other records. A pharmacy that changes or discontinues use of a data processing system must:
            (I) transfer the records to the new data processing system; or
            (II) purge the records to a printout that contains all of the information required on the original document.

           (iii) Maintenance of purged records. Information purged from a data processing system must be maintained by the pharmacy for two years from the date of initial entry into the data processing system.

     (E) Loss of data. The pharmacist-in-charge shall report to the board in writing any significant loss of information from the data processing system within 10 days of discovery of the loss.

(2)   Records of dispensing.

     (A) Each time a prescription drug order is filled or refilled, a record of such dispensing shall be entered into the data processing system.

     (B) Each time a modification, change or manipulation is made to a record of dispensing, documentation of such change shall be recorded in the data processing system. The documentation of any modification, change, or manipulation to a record of dispensing shall include the identification of the individual responsible for the alteration. Should the data processing system not be able to record a modification, change, or manipulation to a record of dispensing, the information should be clearly documented on the hard copy prescription.

     (C) The data processing system shall have the capacity to produce a daily hard copy printout of all original prescriptions dispensed and refilled. This hard copy printout shall contain the following information:

           (i) unique identification number of the prescription;

           (ii) date of dispensing;

           (iii) patient name;

           (iv) prescribing practitioner's name; and the supervising physician's name if the prescription was issued by an advanced practice registered nurse, physician assistant or pharmacist;

           (v) name and strength of the drug product actually dispensed; if generic name, the brand name or manufacturer of drug dispensed;

           (vi) quantity dispensed;

           (vii) initials or an identification code of the dispensing pharmacist;

           (viii) initials or an identification code of the pharmacy technician or pharmacy technician trainee performing data entry of the prescription, if applicable;

           (ix) if not immediately retrievable via computer display, the following shall also be included on the hard copy printout:

               (I) patient's address;

               (II) prescribing practitioner's address;

               (III) practitioner's DEA registration number, if the prescription drug order is for a controlled substance;

               (IV) quantity prescribed, if different from the quantity dispensed;

               (V) date of issuance of the prescription drug order, if different from the date of dispensing; and

               (VI) total number of refills dispensed to date for that prescription drug order; and

           (x) any changes made to a record of dispensing.

     (D) The daily hard copy printout shall be produced within 72 hours of the date on which the prescription drug orders were dispensed and shall be maintained in a separate file at the pharmacy. Records of controlled substances shall be readily retrievable from records of non-controlled substances.

     (E) Each individual pharmacist who dispenses or refills a prescription drug order shall verify that the data indicated on the daily hard copy printout is correct, by dating and signing such document in the same manner as signing a check or legal document (e.g., J.H. Smith, or John H. Smith) within seven days from the date of dispensing.

     (F) In lieu of the printout described in subparagraph (C) of this paragraph, the pharmacy shall maintain a log book in which each individual pharmacist using the data processing system shall sign a statement each day, attesting to the fact that the information entered into the data processing system that day has been reviewed by him or her and is correct as entered. Such log book shall be maintained at the pharmacy employing such a system for a period of two years after the date of dispensing; provided, however, that the data processing system can produce the hard copy printout on demand by an authorized agent of the Texas State Board of Pharmacy. If no printer is available on site, the hard copy printout shall be available within 72 hours with a certification by the individual providing the printout, that states that the printout is true and correct as of the date of entry and such information has not been altered, amended, or modified.

     (G) The pharmacist-in-charge is responsible for the proper maintenance of such records and responsible that such data processing system can produce the records outlined in this section and that such system is in compliance with this subsection.

     (H) The data processing system shall be capable of producing a hard copy printout of an audit trail for all dispensings (original and refill) of any specified strength and dosage form of a drug (by either brand or generic name or both) during a specified time period.

           (i) Such audit trail shall contain all of the information required on the daily printout as set out in subparagraph (C) of this paragraph.

           (ii) The audit trail required in this subparagraph shall be supplied by the pharmacy within 72 hours, if requested by an authorized agent of the Texas State Board of Pharmacy.

     (I) Failure to provide the records set out in this subsection, either on site or within 72 hours constitutes prima facie evidence of failure to keep and maintain records in violation of the Act.

     (J) The data processing system shall provide on-line retrieval (via computer display or hard copy printout) of the information set out in subparagraph (C) of this paragraph of:

           (i) the original controlled substance prescription drug orders currently authorized for refilling; and

           (ii) the current refill history for Schedules III, IV, and V controlled substances for the immediately preceding six-month period.

     (K) In the event that a pharmacy that uses a data processing system experiences system downtime, the following is applicable:

           (i) an auxiliary procedure shall ensure that refills are authorized by the original prescription drug order and that the maximum number of refills has not been exceeded or authorization from the prescribing practitioner shall be obtained prior to dispensing a refill; and

           (ii) all of the appropriate data shall be retained for on-line data entry as soon as the system is available for use again.

(3) Authorization of refills. Practitioner authorization for additional refills of a prescription drug order shall be noted as follows:

    (A) on the hard copy prescription drug order;

    (B) on the daily hard copy printout; or

    (C) via the computer display.

(f) Limitation to one type of recordkeeping system. When filing prescription drug order information a pharmacy may use only one of the two systems described in subsection (d) or (e) of this section.

(g) Transfer of prescription drug order information. For the purpose of initial or refill dispensing, the transfer of original prescription drug order information is permissible between pharmacies, subject to the following requirements:

    (1) The transfer of original prescription drug order information for controlled substances listed in Schedule III, IV, or V for the purpose of refill dispensing is permissible between pharmacies on a one-time basis only. However, pharmacies electronically sharing a real-time, on-line database may transfer up to the maximum refills permitted by law and the prescriber's authorization

    (2) The transfer of original prescription drug order information for dangerous drugs is permissible between pharmacies without limitation up to the number of originally authorized refills.

    (3) The transfer is communicated orally by telephone or via facsimile directly by a pharmacist to another pharmacist; by a pharmacist to a pharmacist-intern; or by a pharmacist-intern to another pharmacist.

    (4) Both the original and the transferred prescription drug orders are maintained for a period of two years from the date of last refill.

    (5) The individual transferring the prescription drug order information shall ensure the following occurs:

        (A) write the word "void" on the face of the invalidated prescription or the prescription is voided in the data processing system;

        (B) record the name, address, if for a controlled substance, the DEA registration number of the pharmacy to which it was transferred, and the name of the receiving individual on the reverse of the invalidated prescription or stored with the invalidated prescription drug order in the data processing system;

        (C) record the date of the transfer and the name of the individual transferring the information; and

        (D) if the prescription is transferred electronically, provide the following information:

            (i) date of original dispensing and prescription number;

            (ii) number of refills remaining and if a controlled substance, the date(s) and location(s) of previous refills;

            (iii) name, address, and if a controlled substance, the DEA registration number of the transferring pharmacy;

            (iv) name of the individual transferring the prescription; and

            (v) if a controlled substance, name, address and DEA registration number, and prescription number from the pharmacy that originally dispensed the prescription, if different.

    (6) The individual receiving the transferred prescription drug order information shall:

        (A) write the word "transfer" on the face of the prescription or the prescription record indicates the prescription was a transfer; and

        (B) reduce to writing all of the information required to be on a prescription as specified in subsection (b)(7) of this section (relating to Prescriptions) and including the following information;

            (i) date of issuance and prescription number;

            (ii) original number of refills authorized on the original prescription drug order;

            (iii) date of original dispensing;

            (iv) number of valid refills remaining and if a controlled substance, date(s) and location(s) of previous refills;

            (v) name, address, and if for a controlled substance, the DEA registration number of the transferring pharmacy;

            (vi) name of the individual transferring the prescription; and

            (vii) name, address, and if for a controlled substance, the DEA registration number, of the pharmacy that originally dispensed the prescription, if different; or

        (C) if the prescription is transferred electronically, create an electronic record for the prescription that includes the receiving pharmacist's name and all of the information transferred with the prescription including all of the information required to be on a prescription as specified in subsection (b)(7) of this section (relating to Prescriptions) and the following:

            (i) date of original dispensing;

            (ii) number of refills remaining and if a controlled substance, the prescription number(s), date(s) and location(s) of previous refills;

            (iii) name, address, and if for a controlled substance, the DEA registration number;

            (iv) name of the individual transferring the prescription; and

            (v) name, address, and if for a controlled substance, the DEA registration number, of the pharmacy that originally filled the prescription.

    (7) Both the individual transferring the prescription and the individual receiving the prescription must engage in confirmation of the prescription information by such means as:

        (A) the transferring individual faxes the hard copy prescription to the receiving individual; or

        (B) the receiving individual repeats the verbal information from the transferring individual and the transferring individual verbally confirms that the repeated information is correct.

    (8) Pharmacies transferring prescriptions electronically shall comply with the following:

        (A) Prescription drug orders may not be transferred by non-electronic means during periods of downtime except on consultation with and authorization by a prescribing practitioner; provided however, during downtime, a hard copy of a prescription drug order may be made available for informational purposes only, to the patient or a pharmacist, and the prescription may be read to a pharmacist by telephone.

        (B) The original prescription drug order shall be invalidated in the data processing system for purposes of filling or refilling, but shall be maintained in the data processing system for refill history purposes.

        (C) If the data processing system does not have the capacity to store all the information as specified in paragraphs (5) and (6) of this subsection, the pharmacist is required to record this information on the original or transferred prescription drug order.

        (D) The data processing system shall have a mechanism to prohibit the transfer or refilling of controlled substance prescription drug orders that have been previously transferred.

(E) Pharmacies electronically accessing the same prescription drug order records may electronically transfer prescription information if the following requirements are met.
   (i)   The original prescription is voided and the pharmacies' data processing systems shall store all the information as specified in paragraphs (5) and (6) of this subsection.
   (ii) Pharmacies not owned by the same entity may electronically access the same prescription drug order records, provided the owner, chief executive officer, or designee of each pharmacy signs an agreement allowing access to such prescription drug order records.
   (iii) An electronic transfer between pharmacies may be initiated by a pharmacist intern, pharmacy technician, or pharmacy technician trainee acting under the direct supervision of a pharmacist.
(9) An individual may not refuse to transfer original prescription information to another individual who is acting on behalf of a patient and who is making a request for this information as specified in this subsection. The transfer of original prescription information must be completed within four business hours of the request.
(10) When transferring a compounded prescription, a pharmacy is required to provide all of the information regarding the compounded preparation including the formula unless the formula is patented or otherwise protected, in which case, the transferring pharmacy shall, at a minimum, provide the quantity or strength of all of the active ingredients of the compounded preparation.
(11) The electronic transfer of multiple or bulk prescription records between two pharmacies is permitted provided:
   (A) a record of the transfer as specified in paragraph (5) of this subsection is maintained by the transferring pharmacy;
   (B) the information specified in paragraph (6) of this subsection is maintained by the receiving pharmacy; and
   (C) in the event that the patient or patient's agent is unaware of the transfer of the prescription drug order record, the transferring pharmacy must notify the patient or patient's agent of the transfer and must provide the patient or patient's agent with the telephone number of the pharmacy receiving the multiple or bulk prescription drug order records.

(h) Distribution of controlled substances to another registrant. A pharmacy may distribute controlled substances to a practitioner, another pharmacy, or other registrant, without being registered to distribute, under the following conditions.
(1) The registrant to whom the controlled substance is to be distributed is registered under the Controlled Substances Act to dispense that controlled substance.
(2) The total number of dosage units of controlled substances distributed by a pharmacy may not exceed 5.0% of all controlled substances dispensed and distributed by the pharmacy during the 12-month period in which the pharmacy is registered; if at any time it does exceed 5.0%, the pharmacy is required to obtain an additional registration to distribute controlled substances.
(3) If the distribution is for a Schedule III, IV, or V controlled substance, a record shall be maintained that indicates:
   (A) the actual date of distribution;
   (B) the name, strength, and quantity of controlled substances distributed;
   (C) the name, address, and DEA registration number of the distributing pharmacy; and
   (D) the name, address, and DEA registration number of the pharmacy, practitioner, or other registrant to whom the controlled substances are distributed.
(4) If the distribution is for a Schedule II controlled substance, the following is applicable.
   (A) The pharmacy, practitioner, or other registrant who is receiving the controlled substances shall issue Copy 1 and Copy 2 of a DEA order form (DEA 222) to the distributing pharmacy.
   (B) The distributing pharmacy shall:
      (i)   complete the area on the DEA order form (DEA 222) titled "To Be Filled in by Supplier";
      (ii) maintain Copy 1 of the DEA order form (DEA 222) at the pharmacy for two years; and
      (iii) forward Copy 2 of the DEA order form (DEA 222) to the Divisional Office of the Drug Enforcement Administration.

(i) Other records. Other records to be maintained by a pharmacy:
(1) a log of the initials or identification codes that will identify each pharmacist, pharmacy technician, and pharmacy technician trainee who is involved in the dispensing process, in the pharmacy's data processing system (the initials or identification code shall be unique to ensure that each individual can be identified, i.e., identical initials or identification codes shall not be used). Such log shall be maintained at the pharmacy for at least seven years from the date of the transaction;
(2) copy 3 of DEA order forms (DEA 222) that have been properly dated, initialed, and filed, and all copies of each unaccepted or defective order form and any attached statements or other documents, and/or for each order filled using the DEA Controlled Substance Ordering System (CSOS), the original signed order and all linked records for that order;
(3) a copy of the power of attorney to sign DEA 222 order forms (if applicable);
(4) suppliers' invoices of dangerous drugs and controlled substances; a pharmacist shall verify that the controlled drugs listed on the invoices were actually received by clearly recording his/her initials and the actual date of receipt of the controlled substances;
(5) suppliers' credit memos for controlled substances and dangerous drugs;
(6) a copy of inventories required by § 291.17 of this title (relating to Inventory Requirements);
(7) reports of surrender or destruction of controlled substances and/or dangerous drugs to an appropriate state or federal agency;
(8) records of distribution of controlled substances and/or dangerous drugs to other pharmacies, practitioners, or registrants; and
(9) a copy of any notification required by the Texas Pharmacy Act or the sections in this chapter, including, but not limited to, the following:
   (A) reports of theft or significant loss of controlled substances to DEA and the board;
   (B) notifications of a change in pharmacist-in-charge of a pharmacy; and
   (C) reports of a fire or other disaster that may affect the strength, purity, or labeling of drugs, medications, devices, or other materials used in the diagnosis or treatment of injury, illness, and disease.

(j) Permission to maintain central records. Any pharmacy that uses a centralized recordkeeping system for invoices and financial data shall comply with the following procedures.
(1) Controlled substance records. Invoices and financial data for controlled substances may be maintained at a central location provided the following conditions are met.
   (A) Prior to the initiation of central recordkeeping, the pharmacy submits written notification by registered or certified mail to the divisional director of the Drug Enforcement Administration as required by Title 21, Code of Federal Regulations, §

1304.04(a), and submits a copy of this written notification to the Texas State Board of Pharmacy. Unless the registrant is informed by the divisional director of the Drug Enforcement Administration that permission to keep central records is denied, the pharmacy may maintain central records commencing 14 days after receipt of notification by the divisional director.

    (B) The pharmacy maintains a copy of the notification required in subparagraph (A) of this paragraph.

    (C) The records to be maintained at the central record location shall not include executed DEA order forms, prescription drug orders, or controlled substance inventories that shall be maintained at the pharmacy.

(2) Dangerous drug records. Invoices and financial data for dangerous drugs may be maintained at a central location.

(3) Access to records. If the records are kept on microfilm, computer media, or in any form requiring special equipment to render the records easily readable, the pharmacy shall provide access to such equipment with the records.

(4) Delivery of records. The pharmacy agrees to deliver all or any part of such records to the pharmacy location within two business days of written request of a board agent or any other authorized official.

(k) Ownership of pharmacy records. For the purposes of these sections, a pharmacy licensed under the Act is the only entity that may legally own and maintain prescription drug records.

(l) Documentation of consultation. When a pharmacist consults a prescriber as described in this section, the pharmacist shall document on the hard copy or in the pharmacy's data processing system associated with the prescription such occurrences and shall include the following information:

(1) date the prescriber was consulted;

(2) name of the person communicating the prescriber's instructions;

(3) any applicable information pertaining to the consultation; and

(4) initials or identification code of the pharmacist performing the consultation clearly recorded for the purpose of identifying the pharmacist who performed the consultation if the information is recorded on the hard copy prescription.

Source: The provisions of this § 291.34 adopted to be effective September 14, 1988, 13 TEXREG4306; amended to be effective September 5, 1990, 15 TEXREG4807; amended to be effective March 18, 1991, 16 TEXREG1365; amended to be effective January 29, 1992, 17 TexReg 323; amended to be effective January 1, 1993, 17 TexReg 9116; amended to be effective September 30, 1993, 18 TexReg 6460; amended to be effective June 1, 1994, 19 TexReg 3921; amended to be effective March 29, 1995, 20 TexReg 1888; amended to be effective June 20, 1995, 20 TexReg 4121; amended to be effective March 21, 1996, 21 TexReg 2227; amended to be effective April 7, 1997, 22 TexReg 3106; amended to be effectiveMarch29, 2000, 25 TexReg 2575; amended to be effective August 31, 2000, 25 TexReg 8405; amended to be effective March 7, 2001, 26 TexReg 1865; amended to be effective June 20, 2001, 26 TexReg 4478; amended to be effective June 1, 2002, 27 TexReg 1736; amended to be effective March 4, 2004, 29 TexReg 1951; amended to be effective June 6, 2004, 29 TexReg 5361; amended to be effective September 7, 2004, 29 TexReg 8516; amended to be effective March 10, 2005, 30 TexReg 1275; amended to be effective December 3, 2006, 31 TexReg 9610; amended to be effective March 25, 2007, 32 TexReg 1510; amended to be effective September 18, 2007, 32 TexReg 6319; amended to be effective March 6, 2008, 33 TexReg 1784; amended to be effective September 7, 2008, 33 TexReg 7218; amended to be effective June 7, 2009, 34 TexReg 3391; amended to be effective December 6,2009, 34 TexReg 8691; amended to be effective March 11, 2010, 35 TexReg 2005; amended to be effective July 11, 2011, 36 TexReg 4402; amended to be effective November 24, 2011, 36 TexReg 7867; amended to be effective March 13, 2012, 37 TexReg 1705; amended to be effective June 7, 2012, 37 TexReg 4046; amended to be effective September 8, 2013, 38 TexReg 5722; amended to be effective September 11, 2014, 39 TexReg 7094; amended to be effective December 7, 2014, 39 TexReg 9345; amended to be effective June 12, 2016, 41 TexReg 4257; amended to be effective December 19, 2016, 41 TexReg 9934; amended to be effective September 6, 2017, 42 TexReg 4466; amended to be effective September 16, 2018, 43 TexReg 5784; amended to be effective December 6, 2018, 43 TexReg 7774; amended to be effective June 20, 2019, 44 TexReg 2946

§291.35 Official Prescription Requirements

Class A pharmacies are subject to the rules set forth in chapter 315 of this title (relating to Controlled Substances).

Source: The provisions of this § 291.35 adopted to be effective January 3, 2000, 24 TexReg 12067; amended to be effective September 10, 2003, 28 TexReg 7710; amended to be effective March 12, 2019, 44 TexReg 1330

§291.36 Pharmacies Compounding Sterile Preparations (Class A-S).

Licensing Requirements. A community pharmacy engaged in the compounding of sterile preparations shall be designated as a Class A-S pharmacy.

(1) A Class A-S pharmacy shall register annually or biennially with the board on a pharmacy license application provided by the board, following the procedures as specified in §291.1 of this title (relating to Pharmacy License Application). A Class A-S license may not be issued unless the pharmacy has been inspected by the board to ensure the pharmacy meets the requirements as specified in §291.133 of this title (relating to Pharmacies Compounding Sterile Preparations).

(2) A Class A-S pharmacy may not renew a pharmacy license unless the pharmacy has been inspected by the board within the last renewal period.

(3) A Class A-S pharmacy which changes ownership shall notify the board within ten days of the change of ownership and apply for a new and separate license as specified in §291.3 of this title (relating to Required Notifications).

(4) A Class A-S pharmacy which changes location and/or name shall notify the board within ten days of the change and file for an amended license as specified in §291.3 of this title.

(5) A Class A-S pharmacy owned by a partnership or corporation which changes managing officers shall notify the board in writing of the names of the new managing officers within ten days of the change, following the procedures as specified in §291.3 of this title.

(6) A Class A-S pharmacy shall notify the board in writing within ten days of closing, following the procedures as specified in §291.5 of this title (relating to Closing a Pharmacy).

(7) A separate license is required for each principal place of business and only one pharmacy license may be issued to a specific location.

(8) A fee as specified in §291.6 of this title (relating to Pharmacy License Fees) will be charged for the issuance and renewal of a license and the issuance of an amended license.

(9) A Class A-S pharmacy which would otherwise be required to be licensed under the Act, §560.051(a)(1) concerning Community Pharmacy (Class A) is required to comply with the provisions of §291.31 of this title (relating to Definitions), §291.32 of this title (relating to Personnel), §291.33 of this title (relating to Operational Standards), §291.34 of this title (relating to Records), §291.35 of this title (relating to Official Prescription Requirements), and §291.133 of this title.

(10) A Class A-S pharmacy engaged in the compounding of non-sterile preparations shall comply with the provisions of §291.131 of this title (relating to Pharmacies Compounding Non-Sterile Preparations).

(11) A Class A-S pharmacy engaged in the provision of remote pharmacy services, including storage and dispensing of prescription drugs, shall comply with the provisions of §291.121 of this title (relating to Remote Pharmacy Services).

(12) A Class A-S pharmacy engaged in centralized prescription dispensing and/or prescription drug or medication order processing shall comply with the provisions of §291.123 of this title (relating to Centralized Prescription Drug or Medication Order Processing) and/or §291.125 of this title (relating to Centralized Prescription Dispensing).

Source: The provisions of this § 291.36 adopted to be effective December 10, 2013, 38 TexReg 8835

SUBCHAPTER C. NUCLEAR PHARMACY (CLASS B)

§291.51 Purpose

The purpose of this subchapter is to provide standards for the preparation, labeling, and distribution of radiopharmaceuticals by licensed nuclear pharmacies, pursuant to a radioactive prescription drug order. The intent of this subchapter is to establish a minimum acceptable level of pharmaceutical care to the patient so that the patient's health is protected while contributing to positive patient outcomes. The board has determined that this subchapter is necessary to protect the health and welfare of the citizens of this state.

Source: The provisions of this § 291.51 adopted to be effective March 19, 1998, 23 TexReg 2815; amended to be effective September 14, 2010, 35 TexReg 8357; amended to be effective September 14, 2015, 40 TexReg 6110

§291.52 Definitions

The following words and terms, when used in this subchapter, shall have the following meanings, unless the context clearly indicates otherwise. Any term not defined in this section shall have the definition set forth in the Act, § 551.003.

(1) Act—The Texas Pharmacy Act, Chapters 551 - 569, Occupations Code, as amended.

(2) Accurately as prescribed—Dispensing, delivering, and/or distributing a prescription drug order or radioactive prescription drug order:
  (A) to the correct patient (or agent of the patient) for whom the drug or device was prescribed;
  (B) with the correct drug in the correct strength, quantity, and dosage form ordered by the practitioner; and
  (C) with correct labeling (including directions for use) as ordered by the practitioner. Provided, however, that nothing herein shall prohibit pharmacist substitution if substitution is conducted in strict accordance with applicable laws and rules, including Subchapter A, Chapter 562 of the Act.

(3) ACPE—Accreditation Council for Pharmacy Education.

(4) Administer—The direct application of a prescription drug and/or radiopharmaceutical, by injection, inhalation, ingestion, or any other means to the body of a patient by:
  (A) a practitioner, an authorized agent under his supervision, or other person authorized by law; or
  (B) the patient at the direction of a practitioner.

(5) Authentication of product history—Identifying the purchasing source, the intermediate handling, and the ultimate disposition of any component of a radioactive drug.

(6) Authorized nuclear pharmacist—A pharmacist who:
  (A) has completed the specialized training requirements specified by this subchapter for the preparation and distribution of radiopharmaceuticals; and
  (B) is named on a Texas radioactive material license, issued by the Texas Department of State Health Services, Radiation Control Program.

(7) Authorized user—Any individual named on a Texas radioactive material license, issued by the Texas Department of State Health Services, Radiation Control Program.

(8) Board—The Texas State Board of Pharmacy.

(9) Component—Any ingredient intended for use in the compounding of a drug preparation, including those that may not appear in such preparation.

(10) Compounding—The preparation, mixing, assembling, packaging, or labeling of a drug or device:
  (A) as the result of a practitioner's prescription drug or medication order based on the practitioner-patient-pharmacist relationship in the course of professional practice;
  (B) for administration to a patient by a practitioner as the result of a practitioner's initiative based on the practitioner-patient-pharmacist relationship in the course of professional practice;
  (C) in anticipation of prescription drug or medication orders based on routine, regularly observed prescribing patterns; or
  (D) for or as an incident to research, teaching, or chemical analysis and not for sale or dispensing, except as allowed under § 562.154 or Chapter 563 of the Act.

(11) Controlled substance—A drug, immediate precursor, or other substance listed in Schedules I - V or Penalty Groups 1-4 of the Texas Controlled Substances Act, as amended, or a drug, immediate precursor, or other substance included in Schedule I, II, III, IV, or V of the Federal Comprehensive Drug Abuse Prevention and Control Act of 1970, as amended (Public Law 91-513).

(12) Dangerous drug—A drug or device that:
  (A) is not included in Penalty Group 1, 2, 3, or 4, Chapter 481, Health and Safety Code, and is unsafe for self-medication; or
  (B) bears or is required to bear the legend:
    (i) "Caution: federal law prohibits dispensing without prescription" or "Rx only" or another legend that complies with federal law; or
    (ii) "Caution: federal law restricts this drug to use by or on the order of a licensed veterinarian."

(13) Data communication device—An electronic device that receives electronic information from one source and transmits or routes it to another (e.g., bridge, router, switch, or gateway).

(14) Deliver or delivery—The actual, constructive, or attempted transfer of a prescription drug or device, radiopharmaceutical, or controlled substance from one person to another, whether or not for a consideration.

(15) Designated agent—
  (A) an individual, including a licensed nurse, physician assistant, nuclear medicine technologist, or pharmacist:
    (i) who is designated by a practitioner and authorized to communicate a prescription drug order to a pharmacist; and
    (ii) for whom the practitioner assumes legal responsibility;
  (B) a licensed nurse, physician assistant, or pharmacist employed in a health care facility to whom a practitioner communicates a prescription drug order; or
  (C) a registered nurse or physician assistant authorized by a practitioner to administer a prescription drug order for a dangerous drug under Subchapter B, Chapter 157 (Occupations Code).
(16) Device—An instrument, apparatus, implement, machine, contrivance, implant, in vitro reagent, or other similar or related articles, including any component parts or accessory that is required under federal or state law to be ordered or prescribed by a practitioner.
(17) Diagnostic prescription drug order—A radioactive prescription drug order issued for a diagnostic purpose.
(18) Dispense—Preparing, packaging, compounding, or labeling for delivery a prescription drug or device, or a radiopharmaceutical in the course of professional practice to an ultimate user or his agent by or pursuant to the lawful order of a practitioner.
(19) Dispensing pharmacist—The authorized nuclear pharmacist responsible for the final check of the dispensed prescription before delivery to the patient.
(20) Distribute—The delivering of a prescription drug or device, or a radiopharmaceutical other than by administering or dispensing.
(21) Electronic radioactive prescription drug order—A radioactive prescription drug order which is transmitted by an electronic device to the receiver (pharmacy).
(22) Full-time pharmacist—A pharmacist who works in a pharmacy at least 30 hours per week or, if the pharmacy is open less than 60 hours per week, one-half of the time the pharmacy is open.
(23) Hot water—The temperature of water from the pharmacy's sink maintained at a minimum of 105 degrees F (41 degrees C).
(24) Nuclear pharmacy technique—The mechanical ability required to perform the nonjudgmental, technical aspects of preparing and dispensing radiopharmaceuticals.
(25) Original prescription—The:
  (A) original written radioactive prescription drug orders; or
  (B) original verbal or electronic radioactive prescription drug orders maintained either manually or electronically by the pharmacist.
(26) Pharmacist-in-charge—The pharmacist designated on a pharmacy license as the pharmacist who has the authority or responsibility for a pharmacy's compliance with laws and rules pertaining to the practice of pharmacy.
(27) Pharmacy technician—An individual whose responsibility in a pharmacy is to provide technical services that do not require professional judgment regarding preparing and distributing drugs and who works under the direct supervision of and is responsible to a pharmacist.
(28) Pharmacy technician trainee—An individual who is registered with the board as a pharmacy technician trainee and is authorized to participate in a pharmacy's technician training program.
(29) Radiopharmaceutical—A prescription drug or device that exhibits spontaneous disintegration of unstable nuclei with the emission of a nuclear particle(s) or photon(s), including any nonradioactive reagent kit or nuclide generator that is intended to be used in preparation of any such substance.
(30) Radioactive drug service—The act of distributing radiopharmaceuticals; the participation in radiopharmaceutical selection and the performance of radiopharmaceutical drug reviews.
(31) Radioactive prescription drug order—An order from a practitioner or a practitioner's designated agent for a radiopharmaceutical to be dispensed.
(32) Sterile radiopharmaceutical—A dosage form of a radiopharmaceutical free from living micro-organisms.
(33) Therapeutic prescription drug order—A radioactive prescription drug order issued for a specific patient for a therapeutic purpose.
(34) Ultimate user—A person who has obtained and possesses a prescription drug or radiopharmaceutical for administration to a patient by a practitioner.

Source: The provisions of this § 291.52 adopted to be effective March 19, 1998, 23 TexReg 2815; amended to be effective September 16, 1999, 24 TexReg 7259; amended to be effective June 1, 2002, 27 TexReg 1781; amended to be effective March 4, 2004, 29 TexReg 1999; amended to be effective June 6, 2004, 29 TexReg 5362; amended to be effective September 14, 2010, 35 TexReg 8357; amended to be effective September 14, 2015, 40 TexReg 6110; amended to be effective June 11, 2017, 42 TexReg 2931

§291.53 Personnel

(a) Pharmacists-in-Charge.
  (1) General.
    (A) Every nuclear pharmacy shall have an authorized nuclear pharmacist designated on the nuclear pharmacy license as the pharmacist-in-charge who shall be responsible for a nuclear pharmacy's compliance with laws and regulations, both state and federal, pertaining to the practice of nuclear pharmacy.
    (B) The nuclear pharmacy pharmacist-in-charge shall see that directives from the board are communicated to the owner(s), management, other pharmacists, and interns of the nuclear pharmacy.
    (C Each Class B pharmacy shall have one pharmacist-in-charge who is employed on a full-time basis, who may be the pharmacist-in-charge for only one such pharmacy; provided, however, such pharmacist-in-charge may be the pharmacist-in-charge of:
      (i) more than one Class B pharmacy, if the additional Class B pharmacies are not open to provide pharmacy services simultaneously; or
      (ii) during an emergency, up to two Class B pharmacies open simultaneously if the pharmacist-in-charge works at least 10 hours per week in each pharmacy for no more than a period of 30 consecutive days.
    (D) The pharmacist-in-charge of a Class B pharmacy may not serve as the pharmacist-in-charge of a Class A pharmacy or a Class C pharmacy with 101 beds or more.
  (2) Responsibilities. The pharmacist-in-charge shall have the responsibility for, at a minimum, the following:

    (A) ensuring that radiopharmaceuticals are dispensed and delivered safely and accurately as prescribed;

    (B) developing a system to assure that all pharmacy personnel responsible for compounding and/or supervising the compounding of radiopharmaceuticals within the pharmacy receive appropriate education and training and competency evaluation;

    (C) determining that all pharmacists involved in compounding sterile radiopharmaceuticals obtain continuing education appropriate for the type of compounding done by the pharmacist;

    (D) supervising a system to assure appropriate procurement of drugs and devices and storage of all pharmaceutical materials including radiopharmaceuticals, components used in the compounding of radiopharmaceuticals, and drug delivery devices;

    (E) assuring that the equipment used in compounding is properly maintained;

    (F) developing a system for the disposal and distribution of drugs from the Class B pharmacy;

    (G) developing a system for bulk compounding or batch preparation of radiopharmaceuticals;

    (H) developing a system for the compounding, sterility assurance, and quality control of sterile radiopharmaceuticals;

    (I) maintaining records of all transactions of the Class B pharmacy necessary to maintain accurate control over and accountability for all pharmaceutical materials including radiopharmaceuticals, required by applicable state and federal laws and rules;

    (J) developing a system to assure the maintenance of effective controls against the theft or diversion of prescription drugs, and records for such drugs;

    (K) assuring that the pharmacy has a system to dispose of radioactive and cytotoxic waste in a manner so as not to endanger the public health; and

    (L) legally operating the pharmacy, including meeting all inspection and other requirements of all state and federal laws or rules governing the practice of pharmacy.

(b) Owner. The owner of a Class B pharmacy shall have responsibility for all administrative and operational functions of the pharmacy. The pharmacist-in-charge may advise the owner on administrative and operational concerns. The owner shall have responsibility for, at a minimum, the following, and if the owner is not a Texas licensed pharmacist, the owner shall consult with the pharmacist-in-charge or another Texas licensed pharmacist:

    (1) establishing policies for procurement of prescription drugs and devices and other products dispensed from the Class B pharmacy;

    (2) establishing policies and procedures for the security of the prescription department including the maintenance of effective controls against the theft or diversion of prescription drugs;

    (3) if the pharmacy uses an automated pharmacy dispensing system, reviewing and approving all policies and procedures for system operation, safety, security, accuracy and access, patient confidentiality, prevention of unauthorized access, and malfunction;

    (4) providing the pharmacy with the necessary equipment and resources commensurate with its level and type of practice; and

    (5) establishing policies and procedures regarding maintenance, storage, and retrieval of records in a data processing system such that the system is in compliance with state and federal requirements.

(c) Authorized nuclear pharmacists.

    (1) General.

        (A) The pharmacist-in-charge shall be assisted by a sufficient number of additional authorized nuclear pharmacists as may be required to operate the pharmacy competently, safely, and adequately to meet the needs of the patients of the pharmacy.

        (B) All personnel performing tasks in the preparation and distribution of radiopharmaceuticals shall be under the direct supervision of an authorized nuclear pharmacist. General qualifications for an authorized nuclear pharmacist are the following. A pharmacist shall:

            (i) meet minimal standards of training and experience in the handling of radioactive materials in accordance with the requirements of the Texas Regulations for Control of Radiation of the Radiation Control Program, Texas Department of State Health Services;

            (ii) be a pharmacist licensed by the board to practice pharmacy in Texas; and

            (iii) submit to the board either:

                (I) written certification that he or she has current board certification as a nuclear pharmacist by the Board of Pharmaceutical Specialties; or

                (II) written certification signed by a preceptor authorized nuclear pharmacist that he or she has achieved a level of competency sufficient to independently operate as an authorized nuclear pharmacist and has satisfactorily completed 700 hours in a structured educational program consisting of both:

                    (-a-) 200 hours of didactic training in a program accepted by the Radiation Control Program, Texas Department of State Health Services in the following areas:

                        (-1-) radiation physics and instrumentation;

                        (-2-) radiation protection;

                        (-3-) mathematics pertaining to the use and measurement of radioactivity;

                        (-4-) radiation biology; and

                        (-5-) chemistry of radioactive material for medical use; and

                    (-b-) 500 hours of supervised practical experience in a nuclear pharmacy involving the following:

                        (-1-) shipping, receiving, and performing related radiation surveys;

                        (-2-) using and performing checks for proper operation of instruments used to determine the activity of dosages, survey meters, and, if appropriate, instruments used to measure alpha- or beta-emitting radionuclides;

                        (-3-) calculating, assaying, and safely preparing dosages for patients or human research subjects;

                        (-4-) using administrative controls to avoid adverse medical events in the administration of radioactive material; and

                        (-5-) using procedures to prevent or minimize contamination and using proper decontamination procedures.

        (C) Authorized nuclear pharmacists are solely responsible for the direct supervision of pharmacy technicians and pharmacy technician trainees and for delegating nuclear pharmacy techniques and additional duties, other than those listed in paragraph (3) of this subsection, to pharmacy technicians and pharmacy technician trainees. Each authorized nuclear pharmacist shall:

Phr. Rules

          (i) verify the accuracy of all acts, tasks, or functions performed by pharmacy technicians and pharmacy technician trainees; and

          (ii) be responsible for any delegated act performed by pharmacy technicians and pharmacy technician trainees under his or her supervision.

      (D) All authorized nuclear pharmacists while on duty, shall be responsible for complying with all state and federal laws or rules governing the practice of pharmacy.

      (E) The dispensing pharmacist shall ensure that the drug is dispensed and delivered safely and accurately as prescribed.

    (2) Special requirements for compounding.

      (A) Non-sterile preparations. All pharmacists engaged in compounding non-sterile preparations, including radioactive preparations shall meet the training requirements specified in § 291.131 of this title (relating to Pharmacies Compounding Non-Sterile Preparations).

      (B) Sterile Preparations. All pharmacists engaged in compounding sterile preparations, including radioactive preparations shall meet the training requirements specified in § 291.133 of this title (relating to Pharmacies Compounding Sterile Preparations).

    (3) Duties. Duties which may only be performed by an authorized nuclear pharmacist are as follows:

      (A) receiving verbal therapeutic prescription drug orders and reducing these orders to writing, either manually or electronically;

      (B) receiving verbal, diagnostic prescription drug orders in instances where patient specificity is required for patient safety (e.g., radiolabeled blood products, radiolabeled antibodies) and reducing these orders to writing, either manually or electronically;

      (C) interpreting and evaluating radioactive prescription drug orders;

      (D) selecting drug products; and

      (E) performing the final check of the dispensed prescription before delivery to the patient to ensure that the radioactive prescription drug order has been dispensed accurately as prescribed.

(d) Pharmacy Technicians and Pharmacy Technician Trainees.

    (1) General. All pharmacy technicians and pharmacy technician trainees shall meet the training requirements specified in § 297.6 of this title (relating to Pharmacy Technician and Pharmacy Technician Trainee Training).

    (2) Special requirements for compounding.

      (A) Non-sterile preparations. All pharmacy technicians and pharmacy technician trainees engaged in compounding non-sterile preparations, including radioactive preparations shall meet the training requirements specified in § 291.131 of this title.

      (B) Sterile Preparations. All pharmacy technicians and pharmacy technician trainees engaged in compounding sterile preparations, including radioactive preparations shall meet the training requirements specified in § 291.133 of this title.

    (3) Duties.

      (A) Pharmacy technicians and pharmacy technician trainees may not perform any of the duties listed in subsection (c)(3) of this section.

      (B) An authorized nuclear pharmacist may delegate to pharmacy technicians and pharmacy technician trainees any nuclear pharmacy technique which is associated with the preparation and distribution of radiopharmaceuticals provided:

          (i) an authorized nuclear pharmacist verifies the accuracy of all acts, tasks, and functions performed by pharmacy technicians and pharmacy technician trainees; and

          (ii) pharmacy technicians and pharmacy technician trainees are under the direct supervision of and responsible to a pharmacist.

    (4) Ratio of authorized nuclear pharmacist to pharmacy technicians and pharmacy technician trainees.

      (A) The ratio of authorized nuclear pharmacists to pharmacy technicians and pharmacy technician trainees may be 1:4, provided at least one of the four is a pharmacy technician and is trained in the handling of radioactive materials.

      (B) The ratio of authorized nuclear pharmacists to pharmacy technician trainees may not exceed 1:3.

Source: The provisions of this § 291.53 adopted to be effective March 19, 1998, 23 TexReg 2815; amended to be effective September 16, 1999, 24 TexReg 7259; amended to be effective September 12, 2001, 26 TexReg 6920; amended to be effective March 4, 2004, 29 TexReg 1999; amended to be effective June 6, 2004, 29 TexReg 5362; amended to be effective September 14, 2010, 35 TexReg 8357; amended to be effective June 7, 2012, 37 TexReg 4047; amended to be effective March 26, 2014, 39 TexReg 2080; amended to be effective September 14, 2015, 40 TexReg 6110; amended to be effective December 6, 2015, 40 TexReg 8766

§291.54 Operational Standards

(a) Licensing requirements.

    (1) It is unlawful for a person to provide radioactive drug services unless such provision is performed by a person licensed to act as an authorized nuclear pharmacist, as defined by the board, or is a person acting under the direct supervision of an authorized nuclear pharmacist acting in accordance with the Act and its rules, and the regulations of the Texas Department of State Health Services, Radiation Control Program. Subsection (a) of this section does not apply to:

      (A) a licensed practitioner or his or her designated agent for administration to his or her patient, provided no person may receive, possess, use, transfer, own, acquire, or dispose of radiopharmaceuticals except as authorized in a specific or a general license as provided in accordance with the requirements of the Texas Department of State Health Services, Radiation Control Program, Texas Administrative Code, Title 25, Part 1, Subchapter F, § 289.252 relating to Licensing of Radioactive Material, or the Act;

      (B) institutions and/or facilities with nuclear medicine services operated by practitioners and who are licensed by the Texas Department of State Health Services, Radiation Control Program, to prescribe, administer, and dispense radioactive materials (drugs and/or devices).

    (2) An applicant for a Class B pharmacy shall provide evidence to the board of the possession of a Texas Department of State Health Services radioactive material license or proof of application for a radioactive material license.

    (3) A Class B pharmacy shall register with the board on a pharmacy license application provided by the board, following the procedures specified in § 291.1 of this title (relating to Pharmacy License Application).

    (4) A Class B pharmacy which changes ownership shall notify the board within ten days of the change of ownership and apply for a new and separate license as specified in § 291.3 of this title (relating to Required Notifications).

(5) A Class B pharmacy which changes location and/or name shall notify the board within ten days of the change and file for an amended license as specified in § 291.3 of this title.

(6) A Class B pharmacy owned by a partnership or corporation which changes managing officers shall notify the board in writing of the names of the new managing officers within ten days of the change, following the procedures in § 291.3 of this title.

(7) A Class B pharmacy shall notify the board in writing within ten days of closing, following the procedures in § 291.5 of this title (relating to Closing a Pharmacy).

(8) A separate license is required for each principal place of business and only one pharmacy license may be issued to a specific location.

(9) A fee as specified in § 291.6 of this title (relating to Pharmacy License Fees) will be charged for the issuance and renewal of a license and the issuance of an amended license.

(10) A Class B pharmacy, licensed under the provisions of the Act, § 560.051(a)(2), which also operates another type of pharmacy which would otherwise be required to be licensed under the Act, § 560.051(a)(1), concerning community pharmacy (Class A), is not required to secure a license for such other type of pharmacy; provided, however, such licensee is required to comply with the provisions of § 291.31 of this title (relating to Definitions); § 291.32 of this title (relating to Personnel); § 291.33 of this title (relating to Operational Standards); § 291.34 of this title (relating to Records); and § 291.35 of this title (relating to Official Prescription Requirements), to the extent such rules are applicable to the operation of the pharmacy.

(11) A Class B pharmacy engaged in the compounding of non-sterile preparations, including radioactive preparations, shall comply with the provisions of § 291.131 of this title (relating to Pharmacies Compounding Non-Sterile Preparations).

(12) A Class B pharmacy engaged in the compounding of sterile preparations, including radioactive preparations, shall comply with the provisions of § 291.133 of this title (relating to Pharmacies Compounding Sterile Preparations) using only radiopharmaceuticals from FDA-approved drug products.

(13) Effective June 1, 2016, a Class B pharmacy may not renew a pharmacy license unless the pharmacy has been inspected by the board within the last renewal period.

(b) Environment.
(1) General requirements.
(A) The pharmacy shall be arranged in an orderly fashion and kept clean. All required equipment shall be clean and in good operating condition.
(B) The pharmacy shall have a sink with hot and cold running water within the pharmacy, exclusive of restroom facilities, available to all pharmacy personnel and maintained in a sanitary condition.
(C) The pharmacy shall be properly lighted and ventilated.
(D) The temperature of the pharmacy shall be maintained within a range compatible with the proper storage of drugs. The temperature of the refrigerator shall be maintained within a range compatible with the proper storage of drugs requiring refrigeration.
(E) If the pharmacy has flammable materials, the pharmacy shall have a designated area for the storage of flammable materials. Such area shall meet the requirements set by local and state fire laws.

(2) Security requirements.
(A) All areas occupied by a pharmacy shall be capable of being locked by key, combination or other mechanical or electronic means to prohibit unauthorized access, when a pharmacist is not on-site except as provided in subparagraph (B) of this paragraph.
(B) The pharmacy may authorize personnel to gain access to that area of the pharmacy containing dispensed radiopharmaceuticals, in the absence of the pharmacist, for the purpose of retrieving the radiopharmaceuticals to be delivered patients. If the pharmacy allows such after-hours access, the area containing the dispensed radiopharmaceuticals shall be an enclosed and lockable area separate from the area containing undispensed prescription drugs. A list of the authorized personnel having such access shall be in the pharmacy's policy and procedure manual.
(C) Each pharmacist while on duty shall be responsible for the security of the prescription department, including provisions for effective control against theft or diversion of prescription drugs, and records for such drugs

(c) Prescription dispensing and delivery.
(1) Generic Substitution. A pharmacist may substitute on a prescription drug order issued for a brand name product provided the substitution is authorized and performed in compliance with Chapter 309 of this title (relating to Substitution of Drug Products).
(2) Prescription containers (immediate inner containers).
(A) A drug dispensed pursuant to a radioactive prescription drug order shall be dispensed in an appropriate immediate inner container as follows.
(i) If a drug is susceptible to light, the drug shall be dispensed in a light-resistant container.
(ii) If a drug is susceptible to moisture, the drug shall be dispensed in a tight container.
(iii) The container should not interact physically or chemically with the drug product placed in it so as to alter the strength, quality, or purity of the drug beyond the official requirements.
(B) Immediate inner prescription containers or closures shall not be re-used.
(3) Delivery containers (outer containers).
(A) Prescription containers may be placed in suitable containers for delivery which will transport the radiopharmaceutical safely in compliance with all applicable laws and regulations.
(B) Delivery containers may be re-used provided they are maintained in a manner to prevent cross contamination.
(4) Labeling.
(A) The immediate inner container of a radiopharmaceutical shall be labeled with:
(i) standard radiation symbol;
(ii) the words "caution-radioactive material" or "danger, radioactive material";
(iii) the name of the radiopharmaceutical or its abbreviation; and
(iv) the unique identification number of the prescription.
(B) The outer container of a radiopharmaceutical shall be labeled with:

(i) the name, address, and phone number of the pharmacy;

(ii) the date dispensed;

(iii) the directions for use, if applicable;

(iv) the unique identification number of the prescription;

(v) the name of the patient if known, or the statement, "for physician use" if the patient is unknown;

(vi) the standard radiation symbol;

(vii) the words "caution-radioactive material" or "danger, radioactive material";

(viii) the name of the radiopharmaceutical or its abbreviation;

(ix) the amount of radioactive material contained in millicuries (mCi), microcuries (uCi), or bequerels (Bq) and the corresponding time that applies to this activity, if different from the requested calibration date and time;

(x) the initials or identification codes of the person preparing the product and the authorized nuclear pharmacist who checked and released the final product unless recorded in the pharmacy's data processing system. The record of the identity of these individuals shall not be altered in the pharmacy's data processing system.

(xi) if a liquid, the volume in milliliters;

(xii) the requested calibration date and time; and

(xiii) the expiration date and/or time.

(C) The amount of radioactivity shall be determined by radiometric methods for each individual preparation immediately at the time of dispensing and calculations shall be made to determine the amount of activity that will be present at the requested calibration date and time, due to radioactive decay in the intervening period, and this activity and time shall be placed on the label per requirements set out in paragraph (4) of this subsection.

(d) Equipment. The following minimum equipment is required in a nuclear pharmacy:

(1) vertical laminar flow hood;

(2) dose calibrator;

(3) a calibrated system or device (i.e., thermometer) to monitor the temperature to ensure that proper storage requirements are met, if preparations are stored in the refrigerator;

(4) if applicable, a Class A prescription balance, or analytical balance and weights. Such balance shall be properly maintained and subject to periodic inspection by the board.

(5) scintillation analyzer;

(6) microscope and hemocytometer;

(7) equipment and utensils necessary for the proper compounding of prescription drug or medication orders. Such equipment and utensils used in the compounding process shall be:

(A) of appropriate design, appropriate capacity, and be operated within designed operational limits;

(B) of suitable composition so that surfaces that contact components, in-process material, or drug products shall not be reactive, additive, or absorptive so as to alter the safety, identity, strength, quality, or purity of the drug product beyond acceptable standards;

(C) cleaned and sanitized immediately prior to each use; and

(D) routinely inspected, calibrated (if necessary), or checked to ensure proper performance;

(8) appropriate disposal containers for used needles, syringes, etc., and if applicable, cytotoxic waste from the preparation of chemotherapeutic agents, and/or biohazardous waste;

(9) all necessary supplies, including:

(A) disposable needles, syringes, and other aseptic mixing;

(B) disinfectant cleaning solutions;

(C) hand washing agents with bactericidal action;

(D) disposable, lint free towels or wipes;

(E) appropriate filters and filtration equipment;

(F) radioactive spill kits, if applicable; and

(G) masks, caps, coveralls or gowns with tight cuffs, shoe covers, and gloves, as applicable.

(10) adequate glassware, utensils, gloves, syringe shields and remote handling devices, and adequate equipment for product quality control;

(11) adequate shielding material;

(12) data processing system including a printer or comparable equipment;

(13) radiation dosimeters for visitors and personnel and log entry book;

(14) exhaust/fume hood with monitor, for storage and handling of all volatile radioactive drugs if applicable, to be determined by the Texas Department of State Health Services, Radiation Control Program; and

(15) adequate radiation monitor(s).

(e) Library. A nuclear pharmacy shall maintain a reference library which shall include the following in hard copy or electronic format current or updated copies of the following:

(1) Texas Pharmacy Act and rules;

(2) Texas Dangerous Drug Act and rules;

(3) Texas Controlled Substances Act and rules; and

(4) Federal Controlled Substances Act and rules (or official publication describing the requirements of the Federal Controlled Substances Act and rules); and

(5) a minimum of one text dealing with nuclear medicine science.

(f) Radiopharmaceuticals and/or radioactive materials.

(1) General requirements.

(A) Radiopharmaceuticals may only be dispensed pursuant to a radioactive prescription drug order.

(B) An authorized nuclear pharmacist may distribute radiopharmaceuticals to authorized users for patient use. A nuclear pharmacy may furnish radiopharmaceuticals for departmental or physicians' use if such authorized users maintain a Texas radioactive materials license.

(C) An authorized nuclear pharmacist may transfer to authorized users radioactive materials not intended for drug use in accordance with the requirements of the Texas Department of State Health Services, Radiation Control Program, Texas Administrative Code, Title 25, Part 1, Subchapter F, § 289.252 relating to Licensing of Radioactive Material.

(D) The transportation of radioactive materials from the nuclear pharmacy must be in accordance with current state and federal transportation regulations.

(2) Procurement and storage.

(A) The pharmacist-in-charge shall have the responsibility for the procurement and storage of drugs, but may receive input from other appropriate staff relative to such responsibility.

(B) Prescription drugs and devices shall be stored within the prescription department or a locked storage area.

(C) All drugs shall be stored at the proper temperature, as defined in the USP/NF and § 291.15 of this title (relating to Storage of Drugs).

(D) The pharmacy's generator(s) shall be stored and eluted in an ISO Class 7 or ISO Class 8 environment as specified in § 291.133 of this title.

(3) Out-of-date and other unusable drugs or devices.

(A) Any drug or device bearing an expiration date shall not be dispensed beyond the expiration date of the drug or device.

(B) Outdated and other unusable drugs or devices shall be removed from dispensing stock and shall be quarantined together until such drugs or devices are disposed of properly.

Source: The provisions of this § 291.54 adopted to be effective March 19, 1998, 23 TexReg 2815; amended to be effective June 1, 2002, 27 TexReg 1781; amended to be effective June 23, 2003, 28 TexReg 4638; amended to be effective June 6, 2004, 29 TexReg 5362; amended to be effective September 14, 2010, 35 TexReg 8357; amended to be effective September 14, 2015, 40 TexReg 6110

§291.55 Records

(a) Maintenance of records.

(1) Every inventory or other record required to be kept under this section shall be:

(A) kept by the pharmacy and be available, for at least two years from the date of such inventory or record, for inspecting and copying by the board or its representative, and other authorized local, state, or federal law enforcement agencies; and

(B) supplied by the pharmacy within 72 hours, if requested by an authorized agent of the board. If the pharmacy maintains the records in an electronic format, the requested records must be provided in a mutually agreeable electronic format it specifically requested by the board or its representative. Failure to provide the records set out in this subsection, either on site or within 72 hours, constitutes prima facie evidence of failure to keep and maintain records in violation of the Act.

(2) Records of controlled substances listed in Schedules I and II shall be maintained separately from all other records of the pharmacy.

(3) Records of controlled substances, other than original prescription drug orders, listed in Schedules III - V shall be maintained separately or readily retrievable from all other records of the pharmacy. For purposes of this subsection, "readily retrievable" means that the controlled substances shall be asterisked, red-lined, or in some other manner readily identifiable apart from all other items appearing on the record.

(4) Records, except when specifically required to be maintained in original or hard copy form, may be maintained in an alternative data retention system, such as a data processing system or direct imaging system provided:

(A) the records maintained in the alternative system contain all of the information required on the manual record; and

(B) the data processing system is capable of producing a hard copy of the record upon request of the board, its representative, or other authorized local, state, or federal law enforcement or regulatory agencies.

(b) Prescriptions.

(1) Professional responsibility. Pharmacists shall exercise sound professional judgment with respect to the accuracy and authenticity of any radioactive prescription drug order they dispense. If the pharmacist questions the accuracy or authenticity of a radioactive prescription drug order, he/she shall verify the order with the practitioner prior to dispensing.

(2) Verbal radioactive prescription drug orders.

(A) Only an authorized nuclear pharmacist or a pharmacist-intern under the direct supervision of an authorized nuclear pharmacist may receive from a practitioner or a practitioner's designated agent:

(i) a verbal therapeutic prescription drug order; or

(ii) a verbal diagnostic prescription drug order in instances where patient specificity is required for patient safety (e.g., radiolabeled blood products, radiolabeled antibodies).

(B) A practitioner shall designate in writing the name of each agent authorized by the practitioner to communicate prescriptions verbally for the practitioner. The practitioner shall maintain at the practitioner's usual place of business a list of the designated agents. The practitioner shall provide a pharmacist with a copy of the practitioner's written authorization for a specific agent on the pharmacist's request.

(C) A pharmacist may not dispense a verbal radioactive prescription drug order for a dangerous drug or a controlled substance issued by a practitioner licensed in the Dominion of Canada or the United Mexican States unless the practitioner is also licensed in Texas.

(3) Radioactive prescription drug orders issued by practitioners in another state.

(A) Dangerous drug prescription orders. A pharmacist may dispense a radioactive prescription drug order for dangerous drugs issued by practitioners in a state other than Texas in the same manner as radioactive prescription drug orders for dangerous drugs issued by practitioners in Texas are dispensed.

(B) Controlled substance prescription drug orders. A pharmacist may dispense radioactive prescription drug orders for controlled substances in Schedule III, IV, or V issued by a practitioner in another state provided:

(i) the radioactive prescription drug order is written, oral, or telephonically or electronically communicated prescription as allowed by the DEA issued by a person practicing in another state and licensed by another state as a physician, dentist, veterinarian, or podiatrist, who has a current federal Drug Enforcement Administration registration number, and who may legally prescribe Schedule III, IV, or V controlled substances in such other state; and

(ii) the radioactive prescription drug order is not dispensed more than six months from the initial date of issuance.

(4) Radioactive prescription drug orders issued by practitioners in the United Mexican States or the Dominion of Canada.

(A) Controlled substance prescription drug orders. A pharmacist may not dispense a radioactive prescription drug order for a Schedule II, III, IV, or V controlled substance issued by a practitioner licensed in the Dominion of Canada or the United Mexican States.

(B) Dangerous drug prescription drug orders. A pharmacist may dispense a radioactive prescription drug order for a dangerous drug issued by a person licensed in the Dominion of Canada or the United Mexican States as a physician, dentist, veterinarian, or podiatrist provided the radioactive prescription drug order is an original written prescription.

(C) Prescription drug orders for Schedule II controlled substances. No Schedule II controlled substance may be dispensed without a written prescription drug order of a practitioner on an official prescription form as required by the Texas Controlled Substances Act, § 481.075.

(5) Electronic radioactive prescription drug orders. For the purpose of this paragraph, electronic radioactive prescription drug orders shall be considered the same as verbal radioactive prescription drug orders.

(A) An electronic radioactive prescription drug order may be transmitted by a practitioner or a practitioner's designated agent:

(i) directly to a pharmacy; or

(ii) through the use of a data communication device provided:

(I) the confidential prescription information is not altered during transmission; and

(II) confidential patient information is not accessed or maintained by the operator of the data communication device other than for legal purposes under federal and state law.

(B) A practitioner shall designate in writing the name of each agent authorized by the practitioner to electronically transmit prescriptions for the practitioner. The practitioner shall maintain at the practitioner's usual place of business a list of the designated agents. The practitioner shall provide a pharmacist with a copy of the practitioner's written authorization for a specific agent on the pharmacist's request.

(C) A pharmacist may not dispense an electronic radioactive prescription drug order for a:

(i) Schedule II controlled substance except as authorized for faxed prescriptions in § 481.074, Health and Safety Code; or

(ii) dangerous drug or controlled substance issued by a practitioner licensed in the Dominion of Canada or the United Mexican States unless the practitioner is also licensed in Texas.

(6) Original prescription drug order records.

(A) Original prescriptions shall be maintained and readily retrievable by the pharmacy and remain accessible for a period of two years from the date of filling.

(B) If an original prescription drug order is changed, such prescription order shall be invalid and of no further force and effect; if additional drugs are to be dispensed, a new prescription drug order with a new and separate number is required.

(C) Original prescriptions shall be maintained in one of the following formats:

(i) in three separate files as follows:

(I) prescriptions for controlled substances listed in Schedule II;

(II) prescriptions for controlled substances listed in Schedules III - V; and

(III) prescriptions for dangerous drugs and nonprescription drugs; or

(ii) within a patient medication record system provided that original prescriptions for controlled substances are maintained separate from original prescriptions for noncontrolled substances and prescriptions for Schedule II controlled substances are maintained separate from all other original prescriptions.

(D) Original prescription records other than prescriptions for Schedule II controlled substances may be stored on microfilm, microfiche, or other system which is capable of producing a direct image of the original prescription record, e.g., a digitalized imaging system. If original prescription records are stored in a direct imaging system, the following is applicable:

(i) The original prescription records must be maintained and readily retrievable as specified in subparagraph (C) of this paragraph.

(ii) The pharmacy must provide immediate access to equipment necessary to render the records easily readable.

(7) Prescription drug order information.

(A) All original radioactive prescription drug orders shall bear:

(i) the name of the patient, if applicable at the time of the order;

(ii) the name of the institution;

(iii) the name, and if for a controlled substance, the address and DEA registration number of the practitioner;

(iv) the name of the radiopharmaceutical;

(v) the amount of radioactive material contained in millicuries (mCi), microcuries (uCi), or bequerels (Bq) and the corresponding time that applies to this activity, if different than the requested calibration date and time;

(vi) the date and time of calibration; and

(vii) the date of issuance.

(B) At the time of dispensing, a pharmacist is responsible for the addition of the following information to the original prescription:

(i) the unique identification number of the prescription drug order;

(ii) the initials or identification code of the person who compounded the sterile radiopharmaceutical and the pharmacist who checked and released the product unless maintained in a readily retrievable format;

(iii) the name, quantity, lot number, and expiration date of each product used in compounding the sterile radiopharmaceutical; and

(iv) the date of dispensing, if different from the date of issuance.

    (8)   Refills. A radioactive prescription drug order must be filled from an original prescription which may not be refilled.

(c)   Policy and procedure manual.

    (1)   All nuclear pharmacies shall maintain a policy and procedure manual. The nuclear pharmacy policy and procedure manual is a compilation of written policy and procedure statements.

    (2)   A technical operations manual governing all nuclear pharmacy functions shall be prepared. It shall be continually revised to reflect changes in techniques, organizations, etc. All pharmacy personnel shall be familiar with the contents of the manual.

    (3)   The nuclear pharmacy policies and procedures manual shall be prepared by the pharmacist-in-charge with input from the affected personnel and from other involved staff and committees to govern procurement, preparation, distribution, storage, disposal, and control of all drugs used and the need for policies and procedures relative to procurement of multisource items, inventory, investigational drugs, and new drug applications.

(d)   Other records. Other records to be maintained by a pharmacy:

    (1)   a permanent log of the initials or identification codes which identifies each dispensing pharmacist by name (the initials or identification codes shall be unique to ensure that each pharmacist can be identified, i.e., identical initials or identification codes shall not be used);

    (2)   copy 3 of DEA order forms (DEA 222) which have been properly dated, initialed, and filed, and all copies of each unaccepted or defective order form and any attached statements or other documents;

    (3)   a hard copy of the power of attorney to sign DEA 222 order forms (if applicable);

    (4)   suppliers' invoices of controlled substances; a pharmacist shall verify that the controlled drugs listed on the invoices were actually received by clearly recording his/her initials and the actual date of receipt of the controlled substances;

    (5)   suppliers' credit memos for controlled substances and dangerous drugs;

    (6)   a hard copy of inventories required by § 291.17 of this title (relating to Inventory Requirements);

    (7)   hard copy reports of surrender or destruction of controlled substances and/or dangerous drugs to an appropriate state or federal agency;

    (8)   records of distribution of controlled substances and/or dangerous drugs to other pharmacies, practitioners, or registrants; and

    (9)   a hard copy of any notification required by the Texas Pharmacy Act or these sections, including, but not limited to, the following:

        (A)   reports of theft or significant loss of controlled substances to DEA and the board;

        (B)   notifications of a change in pharmacist-in-charge of a pharmacy; and

        (C)   reports of a fire or other disaster which may affect the strength, purity, or labeling of drugs, medications, devices, or other materials used in the diagnosis or treatment of injury, illness, and disease.

(e)   Permission to maintain central records. Any pharmacy that uses a centralized recordkeeping system for invoices and financial data shall comply with the following procedures.

    (1)   Controlled substance records. Invoices and financial data for controlled substances may be maintained at a central location provided the following conditions are met.

        (A)   Prior to the initiation of central recordkeeping, the pharmacy submits written notification by registered or certified mail to the divisional director of DEA as required by the Code of Federal Regulations, Title 21, § 1304.04(a), and submits a copy of this written notification to the board. Unless the registrant is informed by the divisional director of DEA that permission to keep central records is denied, the pharmacy may maintain central records commencing 14 days after receipt of notification by the divisional director.

        (B)   The pharmacy maintains a copy of the notification required in subparagraph (A) of this paragraph.

        (C)   The records to be maintained at the central record location shall not include executed DEA order forms, prescription drug orders, or controlled substance inventories, which shall be maintained at the pharmacy.

    (2)   Dangerous drug records. Invoices and financial data for dangerous drugs may be maintained at a central location.

    (3)   Access to records. If the records are kept on microfilm, computer media, or in any form requiring special equipment to render the records easily readable, the pharmacy shall provide access to such equipment with the records.

    (4)   Delivery of records. The pharmacy agrees to deliver all or any part of such records to the pharmacy location within two business days of written request of an authorized agent of the board or any other authorized official.

    (5)   Ownership of pharmacy records. For purposes of these sections, a pharmacy licensed under the Act is the only entity which may legally own and maintain prescription drug records.

Source: The provisions of this § 291.55 adopted to be effective March 19, 1998, 23 TexReg 2815; amended to be effective June 1, 2002, 27 TexReg 1781; amended to be effective June 6, 2004, 29 TexReg 5362; amended to be effective December 3, 2006, 31 TexReg 9610; amended to be effective September 14, 2010, 35 TexReg 8357; amended to be effective June 20, 2019, 44 TexReg 2947

SUBCHAPTER D. INSTITUTIONAL PHARMACY (CLASS C)

§291.71 Purpose

The purpose of these sections is to provide standards in the conduct, practice activities, and operation of a pharmacy located in a hospital or other inpatient facility that is licensed under the Texas Hospital Licensing Law, the Health and Safety Code, Chapter 241, or the Texas Mental Health Code, Chapter 6, Texas Civil Statutes, Article 5547-1 et seq., or a pharmacy located in a hospital maintained or operated by the state. The intent of these standards is to establish a minimum acceptable level of pharmaceutical care to the patient so that the patient's health is protected while contributing to positive patient outcomes.

Source: The provisions of this §291.71 adopted to be effective April 23, 1982, 7 TexReg 1469; amended to be effective September 14, 1988, 13 TexReg 4318; amended to be effective September 5, 1990, 15 TexReg 4810; amended to be effective March 16, 1995, 20 TexReg 1543.

§291.72 Definitions

The following words and terms, when used in this subchapter, shall have the following meanings, unless the context clearly indicates otherwise.

(1) Accurately as prescribed—Distributing and/or delivering a medication drug order:
   (A) to the correct patient (or agent of the patient) for whom the drug or device was prescribed;
   (B) with the correct drug in the correct strength, quantity, and dosage form ordered by the practitioner; and
   (C) with correct labeling as ordered by the practitioner and required by rule.
(2) Act—The Texas Pharmacy Act, Chapters 551 – 566 and 568 – 569, Occupations Code, as amended.
(3) Administer—The direct application of a prescription drug by injection, inhalation, ingestion, or any other means to the body of a patient by:
   (A) a practitioner, an authorized agent under his supervision, or other person authorized by law; or
   (B) the patient at the direction of a practitioner.
(4) Automated compounding or counting device—An automated device that compounds, measures, counts and/or packages a specified quantity of dosage units of a designated drug product.
(5) Automated medication supply system—A mechanical system that performs operations or activities relative to the storage and distribution of medications for administration and which collects, controls, and maintains all transaction information.
(6) Board—The State Board of Pharmacy.
(7) Clinical Pharmacy Program—An ongoing program in which pharmacists are on duty during the time the pharmacy is open for pharmacy services and pharmacists provide direct focused, medication-related care for the purpose of optimizing patients' medication therapy and achieving definite outcomes, which includes the following activities:
   (A) prospective medication therapy consultation, selection, and adjustment;
   (B) monitoring laboratory values and therapeutic drug monitoring;
   (C) identifying and resolving medication-related problems; and
   (D) disease state management.
(8) Confidential record—Any health-related record that contains information that identifies an individual and that is maintained by a pharmacy or pharmacist, such as a patient medication record, prescription drug order, or medication drug order.
(9) Consultant pharmacist—A pharmacist retained by a facility on a routine basis to consult with the facility in areas that pertain to the practice of pharmacy.
(10) Controlled substance—A drug, immediate precursor, or other substance listed in Schedules I – V or Penalty Groups 1 – 4 of the Texas Controlled Substances Act, as amended, or a drug, immediate precursor, or other substance included in Schedules I – V of the Federal Comprehensive Drug Abuse Prevention and Control Act of 1970, as amended (Public Law 91-513).
(11) Dangerous drug—A drug or device that:
   (A) is not included in Penalty Group 1, 2, 3, or 4, Chapter 481, Health and Safety Code, and is unsafe for self-medication; or
   (B) bears or is required to bear the legend:
      (i) "Caution: federal law prohibits dispensing without prescription" or "Rx only" or another legend that complies with federal law; or
      (ii) "Caution: federal law restricts this drug to use by or on the order of a licensed veterinarian."
(12) Device—An instrument, apparatus, implement, machine, contrivance, implant, in vitro reagent, or other similar or related article, including any component part or accessory, that is required under federal or state law to be ordered or prescribed by a practitioner.
(13) Direct copy—Electronic copy or carbonized copy of a medication order, including a facsimile (FAX) or digital image.
(14) Dispense—Preparing, packaging, compounding, or labeling for delivery a prescription drug or device in the course of professional practice to an ultimate user or his agent by or pursuant to the lawful order of a practitioner.
(15) Distribute—The delivery of a prescription drug or device other than by administering or dispensing.
(16) Distributing pharmacist—The pharmacist who checks the medication order prior to distribution.
(17) Downtime—Period of time during which a data processing system is not operable.
(18) Drug regimen review—
   (A) An evaluation of medication orders and patient medication records for:
      (i) known allergies;
      (ii) rational therapy—contraindications;
      (iii) reasonable dose and route of administration;
      (iv) reasonable directions for use;
      (v) duplication of therapy;
      (vi) drug-drug interactions;
      (vii) drug-food interactions;
      (viii) drug-disease interactions;
      (ix) adverse drug reactions; and
      (x) proper utilization, including overutilization or underutilization.
   (B) The drug regimen review may be conducted prior to administration of the first dose (prospective) or after administration of the first dose (retrospective).
(19) Electronic signature—A unique security code or other identifier which specifically identifies the person entering information into a data processing system. A facility which utilizes electronic signatures must:
   (A) maintain a permanent list of the unique security codes assigned to persons authorized to use the data processing system; and
   (B) have an ongoing security program which is capable of identifying misuse and/or unauthorized use of electronic signatures.
(20) Expiration date—The date (and time, when applicable) beyond which a product should not be used.
(21) Facility—
   (A) a hospital or other patient facility that is licensed under Chapter 241 or 577, Health and Safety Code;
   (B) a hospice patient facility that is licensed under Chapter 142, Health and Safety Code;
   (C) an ambulatory surgical center licensed under Chapter 243, Health and Safety Code; or
   (D) a hospital maintained or operated by the state.
(22) Floor stock—Prescription drugs or devices not labeled for a specific patient and maintained at a nursing station or other hospital department (excluding the pharmacy) for the purpose of administration to a patient of the facility.

(23) Formulary—List of drugs approved for use in the facility by the committee which performs the pharmacy and therapeutics function for the facility.

(24) Full-time pharmacist—A pharmacist who works in a pharmacy from 30 to 40 hours per week or if the pharmacy is open less than 60 hours per week, one-half of the time the pharmacy is open.

(25) Hard copy—A physical document that is readable without the use of a special device (i.e., data processing system, computer, etc).

(26) Hot water—The temperature of water from the pharmacy's sink maintained at a minimum of 105 degrees F (41 degrees C).

(27) Institutional pharmacy—Area or areas in a facility where drugs are stored, bulk compounded, delivered, compounded, dispensed, and distributed to other areas or departments of the facility, or dispensed to an ultimate user or his or her agent.

(28) Investigational new drug—New drug intended for investigational use by experts qualified to evaluate the safety and effectiveness of the drug as authorized by the Food and Drug Administration.

(29) Medical Practice Act—The Texas Medical Practice Act, Subtitle B, Occupations Code, as amended.

(30) Medication order—A written order from a practitioner or a verbal order from a practitioner or his authorized agent for administration of a drug or device.

(31) Number of beds—The total number of beds is determined by the:
- (A) number of beds for which the hospital is licensed by the Texas Department of State Health Services; or
- (B) average daily census as calculated by dividing the total number of inpatients admitted during the previous calendar year by 365 (or 366 if the previous calendar year is a leap year).

(32) Part-time pharmacist—A pharmacist either employed or under contract, who routinely works less than full-time.

(33) Patient—A person who is receiving services at the facility (including patients receiving ambulatory procedures and patients conditionally admitted as observation patients), or who is receiving long term care services or Medicare extended care services in a swing bed on the hospital premise or an adjacent, readily accessible facility that is under the authority of the hospital's governing body. For the purposes of this definition, the term "long term care services" means those services received in a skilled nursing facility which is a distinct part of the hospital and the distinct part is not licensed separately or formally approved as a nursing home by the state, even though it is designated or certified as a skilled nursing facility. A patient includes a person confined in any correctional institution operated by the state of Texas.

(34) Perpetual inventory—An inventory which documents all receipts and distributions of a drug product, such that an accurate, current balance of the amount of the drug product present in the pharmacy is indicated.

(35) Pharmaceutical care—The provision of drug therapy and other pharmaceutical services intended to assist in the cure or prevention of a disease, elimination or reduction of a patient's symptoms, or arresting or slowing of a disease process.

(36) Pharmacist-in-charge—Pharmacist designated on a pharmacy license as the pharmacist who has the authority or responsibility for a pharmacy's compliance with laws and rules pertaining to the practice of pharmacy.

(37) Pharmacy and therapeutics function—Committee of the medical staff in the facility which assists in the formulation of broad professional policies regarding the evaluation, selection, distribution, handling, use, and administration, and all other matters relating to the use of drugs and devices in the facility.

(38) Pharmacy technician—An individual who is registered with the board as a pharmacy technician and whose responsibility in a pharmacy is to provide technical services that do not require professional judgment regarding preparing and distributing drugs and who works under the direct supervision of and is responsible to a pharmacist.

(39) Pharmacy technician trainee—An individual who is registered with the board as a pharmacy technician trainee and is authorized to participate in a pharmacy's technician training program.

(40) Pre-packaging—The act of re-packaging and re-labeling quantities of drug products from a manufacturer's original container into unit-dose packaging or a multiple dose container for distribution within the facility except as specified in § 291.74(f)(3)(B) of this title (relating to Operational Standards).

(41) Prescription drug—
- (A) A substance for which federal or state law requires a prescription before it may be legally dispensed to the public;
- (B) A drug or device that under federal law is required, prior to being dispensed or delivered, to be labeled with either of the following statements:
  - (i) Caution: federal law prohibits dispensing without prescription or "Rx only" or another legend that complies with federal law; or
  - (ii) Caution: federal law restricts this drug to use by or on order of a licensed veterinarian; or
- (C) A drug or device that is required by any applicable federal or state law or regulation to be dispensed on prescription only or is restricted to use by a practitioner only.

(42) Prescription drug order—
- (A) a written order from a practitioner or a verbal order from a practitioner or his authorized agent to a pharmacist for a drug or device to be dispensed; or
- (B) a written order or a verbal order pursuant to Subtitle B, Chapter 157, Occupations Code.

(43) Rural hospital—A licensed hospital with 75 beds or fewer that:
- (A) is located in a county with a population of 50,000 or less as defined by the United States Census Bureau in the most recent U.S. census; or
- (B) has been designated by the Centers for Medicare and Medicaid Services as a critical access hospital, rural referral center, or sole community hospital.

(44) Sample—A prescription drug which is not intended to be sold and is intended to promote the sale of the drug.

(45) Supervision—
- (A) Physically present supervision—In a Class C pharmacy, a pharmacist shall be physically present to directly supervise pharmacy technicians or pharmacy technician trainees.
- (B) Electronic supervision—In a Class C pharmacy in a facility with 100 beds or less, a pharmacist licensed in Texas may electronically supervise pharmacy technicians or pharmacy technician trainees to perform the duties specified in § 291.73(e)(2) of this title (relating to Personnel) provided:

(i)   the pharmacy uses a system that monitors the data entry of medication orders and the filling of such orders by an electronic method that shall include the use of one or more the following types of technology:
  (I)   digital interactive video, audio, or data transmission;
  (II) data transmission using computer imaging by way of still-image capture and store and forward; and
  (III) other technology that facilitates access to pharmacy services;
(ii) the pharmacy establishes controls to protect the privacy and security of confidential records;
(iii) the pharmacist responsible for the duties performed by a pharmacy technician or pharmacy technician trainee verifies:
  (I)   the data entry; and
  (II) the accuracy of the filled orders prior to release of the order; and (iv)   the pharmacy keeps permanent digital records of duties electronically supervised and data transmissions associated with electronically supervised duties for a period of two years.
(C) If the conditions of subparagraph (B) of this paragraph are met, electronic supervision shall be considered the equivalent of direct supervision for the purposes of the Act.

(46) Tech-Check-Tech—Allowing a pharmacy technician to verify the accuracy of work performed by another pharmacy technician relating to the filling of floor stock and unit dose distribution systems for a patient admitted to the hospital if the patient's orders have previously been reviewed and approved by a pharmacist.

(47) Texas Controlled Substances Act—The Texas Controlled Substances Act, the Health and Safety Code, Chapter 481, as amended.

(48) Unit-dose packaging—The ordered amount of drug in a dosage form ready for administration to a particular patient, by the prescribed route at the prescribed time, and properly labeled with name, strength, and expiration date of the drug.

(49) Unusable drugs—Drugs or devices that are unusable for reasons, such as they are adulterated, misbranded, expired, defective, or recalled.

(50) Written protocol—A physician's order, standing medical order, standing delegation order, or other order or protocol as defined by rule of the Texas Medical Board under the Texas Medical Practice Act Subtitle B, Chapter 157, Occupations Code.

Source: The provisions of this § 291.72 adopted to be effective April 23, 1982, 7 TEXREG 1469; amended to be effective December 18, 1985, 10 TEXREG 4694; amended to be effective May 27, 1988, 13 TEXREG 2251; amended to be effective February 1, 1989, 14 TEXREG 453; amended to be effective October 27, 1989, 14 TEXREG 5494; amended to be effective September 5, 1990, 15 TEXREG 4810; amended to be effective September 30, 1993, 18 TexReg 6460; amended to be effective March 16, 1995, 20 TexReg 1543; amended to be effective March 21, 1996, 21 TexReg 2242; amended to be effective April 7, 1997, 22 TexReg 3106; amended to be effective September 16, 1999, 24 TexReg 7265; amended to be effective June 4, 2000, 25 TexReg 4816; amended to be effective August 31, 2000, 25 TexReg 8406; amended to be effective March 7, 2001, 26 TexReg 1865; amended to be effective March 4, 2004, 29 TexReg 2000; amended to be effective June 6, 2004, 29 TexReg 5376; amended to be effective September 18, 2007, 32 TexReg 6333; amended to be effective September 7, 2008, 33 TexReg 7241; amended to be effective September 20, 2009, 34 TexReg 6323; amended to be effective March 11, 2010, 35 TexReg 2005; amended to be effective May 30, 2010, 35 TexReg 4177; amended to be effective December 7, 2010, 35 TexReg 10693; amended to be effective December 7, 2014, 39 TexReg 9355

§291.73 Personnel

(a) Requirements for pharmacist services.
  (1) A Class C pharmacy in a facility with 101 beds or more shall be under the continuous on-site supervision of a pharmacist during the time it is open for pharmacy services; provided, however, that pharmacy technicians and pharmacy technician trainees may distribute prepackaged and prelabeled drugs from a drug storage area of the facility (e.g., a surgery suite), in the absence of physical supervision of a pharmacist, under the following conditions:
    (A) the distribution is under the control of a pharmacist; and
    (B) a pharmacist is on duty in the facility.
  (2) A Class C pharmacy in a facility with 100 beds or less shall have the services of a pharmacist at least on a part-time or consulting basis according to the needs of the facility except that a pharmacist shall be on-site at least once every seven days.
  (3) A pharmacist shall be accessible at all times to respond to other health professional's questions and needs. Such access may be through a telephone which is answered 24 hours a day, e.g., answering or paging service, a list of phone numbers where the pharmacist may be reached, or any other system which accomplishes this purpose.
(b) Pharmacist-in-charge.
  (1) General.
    (A) Each institutional pharmacy in a facility with 101 beds or more shall have one full-time pharmacist-in-charge, who may be pharmacist-in-charge for only one such pharmacy except as specified in subparagraph (C) of this paragraph.
    (B) Each institutional pharmacy in a facility with 100 beds or less shall have one pharmacist-in-charge who is employed or under contract, at least on a consulting or part-time basis, but may be employed on a full-time basis, if desired, and who may be pharmacist-in-charge for no more than three facilities or 150 beds.
    (C) A pharmacist-in-charge may be in charge of one facility with 101 beds or more and one facility with 100 beds or less, including a rural hospital, provided the total number of beds does not exceed 150 beds.
    (D) The pharmacist-in-charge shall be assisted by additional pharmacists, pharmacy technicians and pharmacy technician trainees commensurate with the scope of services provided.
    (E) If the pharmacist-in-charge is employed on a part-time or consulting basis, a written agreement shall exist between the facility and the pharmacist, and a copy of the written agreement shall be made available to the board upon request.
    (F) The pharmacist-in-charge of a Class C pharmacy with 101 beds or more, may not serve as the pharmacist-in-charge of a Class A pharmacy or a Class B pharmacy.
  (2) Responsibilities. The pharmacist-in-charge shall have the responsibility for, at a minimum, the following:
    (A) providing the appropriate level of pharmaceutical care services to patients of the facility;
    (B) ensuring that drugs and/or devices are prepared for distribution safely, and accurately as prescribed;
    (C) supervising a system to assure maintenance of effective controls against the theft or diversion of prescription drugs, and records for such drugs;
    (D) providing written guidelines and approval of the procedure to assure that all pharmaceutical requirements are met when any part of preparing, sterilizing, and labeling of sterile preparations is not performed under direct pharmacy supervision;

(E) participating in the development of a formulary for the facility, subject to approval of the appropriate committee of the facility;

(F) developing a system to assure that drugs to be administered to patients are distributed pursuant to an original or direct copy of the practitioner's medication order;

(G) developing a system for the filling and labeling of all containers from which drugs are to be distributed or dispensed;

(H) assuring that the pharmacy maintains and makes available a sufficient inventory of antidotes and other emergency drugs as well as current antidote information, telephone numbers of regional poison control center and other emergency assistance organizations, and such other materials and information as may be deemed necessary by the appropriate committee of the facility;

(I) maintaining records of all transactions of the institutional pharmacy as may be required by applicable law, state and federal, and as may be necessary to maintain accurate control over and accountability for all pharmaceutical materials including pharmaceuticals, components used in the compounding of preparations, and participate in policy decisions regarding prescription drug delivery devices;

(J) participating in those aspects of the facility's patient care evaluation program which relate to pharmaceutical utilization and effectiveness;

(K) participating in teaching and/or research programs in the facility;

(L) implementing the policies and decisions of the appropriate committee(s) relating to pharmaceutical services of the facility;

(M) providing effective and efficient messenger or delivery service to connect the institutional pharmacy with appropriate areas of the facility on a regular basis throughout the normal workday of the facility;

(N) developing a system for the labeling, storage, and distribution of investigational new drugs, including access to related drug information for healthcare personnel in the pharmacy and nursing station where such drugs are being administered, concerning the dosage form, route of administration, strength, actions, uses, side effects, adverse effects, interactions and symptoms of toxicity of investigational new drugs;

(O) assuring that records in a data processing system are maintained such that the data processing system is in compliance with Class C (Institutional) pharmacy requirements;

(P) assuring that a reasonable effort is made to obtain, record, and maintain patient medication records;

(Q) assuring the legal operation of the pharmacy, including meeting all inspection and other requirements of all state and federal laws or rules governing the practice of pharmacy; and

(R) if the pharmacy uses an automated medication supply system, shall be responsible for the following:

    (i) reviewing and approving all policies and procedures for system operation, safety, security, accuracy and access, patient confidentiality, prevention of unauthorized access, and malfunction;

    (ii) inspecting medications in the automated medication supply system, at least monthly, for expiration date, misbranding, physical integrity, security, and accountability; except that inspection of medications in the automated medication supply system may be performed quarterly if:

        (I) the facility uses automated medication supply systems that monitors expiration dates of prescription drugs; and

        (II) security of the system is checked at regularly defined intervals (e.g., daily or weekly);

    (iii) assigning, discontinuing, or changing personnel access to the automated medication supply system;

    (iv) ensuring that pharmacy technicians, pharmacy technician trainees, and licensed healthcare professionals performing any services in connection with an automated medication supply system have been properly trained on the use of the system and can demonstrate comprehensive knowledge of the written policies and procedures for operation of the system; and

    (v) ensuring that the automated medication supply system is stocked accurately and an accountability record is maintained in accordance with the written policies and procedures of operation.

(c) Consultant pharmacist.

  (1) The consultant pharmacist may be the pharmacist-in-charge.

  (2) A written agreement shall exist between the facility and any consultant pharmacist, and a copy of the written agreement shall be made available to the board upon request.

(d) Pharmacists.

  (1) General.

    (A) The pharmacist-in-charge shall be assisted by a sufficient number of additional licensed pharmacists as may be required to operate the institutional pharmacy competently, safely, and adequately to meet the needs of the patients of the facility.

    (B) All pharmacists shall assist the pharmacist-in-charge in meeting the responsibilities as outlined in subsection (b)(2) of this section and in ordering, administering, and accounting for pharmaceutical materials.

    (C) All pharmacists shall be responsible for any delegated act performed by pharmacy technicians or pharmacy technician trainees under his or her supervision.

    (D) All pharmacists while on duty, shall be responsible for complying with all state and federal laws or rules governing the practice of pharmacy.

    (E) A distributing pharmacist shall be responsible for and ensure that the drug is prepared for distribution safely, and accurately as prescribed unless the pharmacy's data processing system can record the identity of each pharmacist involved in a specific portion of the preparation of medication orders for distribution, in which case each pharmacist involved in the preparation of medication orders shall be responsible for and ensure that the portion of the process the pharmacist is performing results in the safe and accurate distribution and delivery of the drug as ordered. The preparation and distribution process for medication orders shall include, but not be limited to, drug regimen review, and verification of accurate medication order data entry, preparation, and distribution, and performance of the final check of the prepared medication.

  (2) Duties. Duties of the pharmacist-in-charge and all other pharmacists shall include, but need not be limited to the following:

    (A) providing those acts or services necessary to provide pharmaceutical care;

    (B) receiving, interpreting, and evaluating prescription drug orders, and reducing verbal medication orders to writing either manually or electronically;

(C) participating in drug and/or device selection as authorized by law, drug and/or device supplier selection, drug administration, drug regimen review, or drug or drug-related research;

(D) performing a specific act of drug therapy management for a patient delegated to a pharmacist by a written protocol from a physician licensed in this state in compliance with the Medical Practice Act Subtitle B, Chapter 157, Occupations Code;

(E) accepting the responsibility for:

   (i) distributing prescription drugs and devices with drug components pursuant to medication orders;

   (ii) compounding and labeling of prescription drugs and devices with drug components;

   (iii) proper and safe storage of prescription drugs and devices with drug components; and

   (iv) maintaining proper records for prescription drugs and devices with drug components.

(3) Special requirements for compounding. All pharmacists engaged in compounding non-sterile preparations shall meet the training requirements specified in § 291.131 of this title (relating to Pharmacies Compounding Non-sterile Preparations).

(c) Pharmacy technicians and pharmacy technician trainees.

(1) General.

(A) All pharmacy technicians and pharmacy technician trainees shall meet the training requirements specified in § 297.6 of this title (relating to Pharmacy Technician and Pharmacy Technician Trainee Training).

(B) A pharmacy technician performing the duties specified in paragraph (2)(C) of this subsection shall complete training regarding:

   (i) procedures for one pharmacy technician to verify the accuracy of actions performed by another pharmacy technician including required documentation; and

   (ii) the duties that may be performed by one pharmacy technician and checked by another pharmacy technician.

(C) In addition to the training requirements specified in subparagraph (A) of this paragraph, pharmacy technicians working in a rural hospital and performing the duties specified in paragraph (2)(D)(ii) of this subsection shall complete the following. Training on the:

   (i) procedures for verification of the accuracy of actions performed by pharmacy technicians including required documentation;

   (ii) duties which may and may not be performed by pharmacy technicians in the absence of a pharmacist; and

   (iii) the pharmacy technician's role in preventing dispensing and distribution errors.

(2) Duties. Duties may include, but need not be limited to, the following functions under the supervision of and responsible to a pharmacist:

(A) Facilities with 101 beds or more. The following functions must be performed under the physically present supervision of a pharmacist:

   (i) pre-packing and labeling unit and multiple dose packages, provided a pharmacist supervises and conducts a final check and affixes his or her name, initials or electronic signature to the appropriate quality control records prior to distribution;

   (ii) preparing, packaging, compounding, or labeling prescription drugs pursuant to medication orders, provided a pharmacist supervises and checks the preparation prior to distribution;

   (iii) bulk compounding or batch preparation provided a pharmacist supervises and conducts in-process and final checks and affixes his or her name, initials, or electronic signature to the appropriate quality control records prior to distribution;

   (iv) distributing routine orders for stock supplies to patient care areas;

   (v) entering medication order and drug distribution information into a data processing system, provided judgmental decisions are not required and a pharmacist checks the accuracy of the information entered into the system prior to releasing the order;

   (vi) loading unlabeled drugs into an automated compounding or counting device provided a pharmacist supervises, verifies that the system was properly loaded prior to use, and affixes his or her name, initials or electronic signature to the appropriate quality control records;

   (vii) accessing automated medication supply systems after proper training on the use of the automated medication supply system and demonstration of comprehensive knowledge of the written policies and procedures for its operation; and

   (viii) compounding non-sterile preparations pursuant to medication orders provided the pharmacy technicians or pharmacy technician trainees have completed the training specified in § 291.131 of this title.

(B) Facilities with 100 beds or less.

   (i) Physically present supervision. The following functions must be performed under the physically present supervision of a pharmacist unless the pharmacy meets the requirements for a rural hospital and has been approved by the board to allow pharmacy technicians to perform the duties specified in § 552.1011 of the Texas Pharmacy Act (Act) and subparagraph (D)(ii) of this paragraph:

     (I) pre-packing and labeling unit and multiple dose packages, provided a pharmacist supervises and conducts a final check and affixes his or her name, initials or electronic signature to the appropriate quality control records prior to distribution;

     (II) bulk compounding or batch preparation provided a pharmacist supervises and conducts in-process and final checks and affixes his or her name, initials, or electronic signature to the appropriate quality control records prior to distribution;

     (III) loading unlabeled drugs into an automated compounding or counting device provided a pharmacist supervises, verifies that the system was properly loaded prior to use, and affixes his or her name, initials, or electronic signature to the appropriate quality control records; and

     (IV) compounding medium-risk and high-risk sterile preparations pursuant to medication orders provided the pharmacy technicians or pharmacy technician trainees:

       (-a-) have completed the training specified in § 291.133 of this title; and

       (-b-) are supervised by a pharmacist who has completed the training specified in § 291.133 of this title and who conducts in-process and final checks, and affixes his or her name, initials, or electronic signature to the label or if batch prepared, to the appropriate quality control records. (The name, initials, initials or electronic signature are not required on the label if it is maintained in a permanent record of the pharmacy.)

    (ii)   Electronic supervision or physically present supervision. The following functions may be performed under the electronic supervision or physically present supervision of a pharmacist:

        (I)   preparing, packaging, or labeling prescription drugs pursuant to medication orders, provided a pharmacist checks the preparation prior to distribution;

        (II)   distributing routine orders for stock supplies to patient care areas;

        (III)   entering medication order and drug distribution information into a data processing system, provided judgmental decisions are not required and a pharmacist checks the accuracy of the information entered into the system prior to releasing the order;

        (IV)   accessing automated medication supply systems after proper training on the use of the automated medication supply system and demonstration of comprehensive knowledge of the written polices and procedures for its operation;

        (V)   compounding non-sterile preparations pursuant to medication orders provided the pharmacy technicians or pharmacy technician trainees have completed the training specified in § 291.131 of this title; and

        (VI)   compounding low-risk sterile preparations pursuant to medication orders provided the pharmacy technicians or pharmacy technician trainees:

            (-a-) have completed the training specified in § 291.133 of this title; and

            (-b-) are supervised by a pharmacist who has completed the training specified in § 291.133 of this title, and who conducts in-process and final checks, and affixes his or her name, initials, or electronic signature to the label or if batch prepared, to the appropriate quality control records. (The name, initials, or electronic signature are not required on the label if it is maintained in a permanent record of the pharmacy.)

  (C)   Facilities with an ongoing clinical pharmacy program. A Class C pharmacy with an ongoing clinical pharmacy program may allow a pharmacy technician to verify the accuracy of the duties specified in clause (ii) of this subparagraph when performed by another pharmacy technician, under the following conditions:

    (i)   The pharmacy technician:

        (I)   is a registered pharmacy technician and not a pharmacy technician trainee; and

        (II)   meets the training requirements specified in § 297.6 of this title and the training requirements specified in paragraph (1) of this subsection.

    (ii)   If the requirements of clause (i) of this subparagraph are met, a pharmacy technician may verify the accuracy of the following duties performed by another pharmacy technician:

        (I)   filling medication carts;

        (II)   distributing routine orders for stock supplies to patient care areas; and

        (III)   accessing and restocking automated medication supply systems after proper training on the use of the automated medication supply system and demonstration of comprehensive knowledge of the written policies and procedures for its operation; and

    (iii)   The patient's orders have previously been reviewed and approved by a pharmacist.

    (iv)   A pharmacist is on duty in the facility at all times that the pharmacy is open for pharmacy services.

  (D)   Rural Hospitals.

    (i)   A rural hospital may allow a pharmacy technician to perform the duties specified in clause (ii) of this subparagraph when a pharmacist is not on duty, if:

        (I)   the pharmacy technician:

            (-a-) is a registered pharmacy technician and not a pharmacy technician trainee; and

            (-b-) meets the training requirements specified in § 297.6 of this title and those specified in paragraph (1) of this subsection;

        (II)   a pharmacist is accessible at all times to respond to any questions and needs of the pharmacy technician or other hospital employees, by telephone, answering or paging service, e-mail, or any other system that makes a pharmacist immediately accessible;

        (III)   the pharmacy is appropriately staffed to meet the needs of the pharmacy; and

        (IV)   a nurse or practitioner at the rural hospital or a pharmacist through electronic supervision as specified in paragraph (2)(B)(ii) of this subsection, verifies the accuracy of the actions of the pharmacy technician.

    (ii)   If the requirements of clause (i) of this subparagraph are met, the pharmacy technician may, during the hours that the institutional pharmacy in the hospital is open, perform the following duties in the pharmacy without the direct supervision of a pharmacist:

        (I)   enter medication order and drug distribution information into a data processing system;

        (II)   prepare, package, or label a prescription drug according to a medication order if a licensed nurse or practitioner verifies the accuracy of the order before administration of the drug to the patient;

        (III)   fill a medication cart used in the rural hospital;

        (IV)   distribute routine orders for stock supplies to patient care areas; and

        (V)   access and restock automated medication supply cabinets.

  (3)   Procedures.

    (A)   Pharmacy technicians and pharmacy technician trainees shall handle medication orders in accordance with standard, written procedures and guidelines.

    (B)   Pharmacy technicians and pharmacy technician trainees shall handle prescription drug orders in the same manner as those working in a Class A pharmacy.

(f)   Owner. The owner of a Class C pharmacy shall have responsibility for all administrative and operational functions of the pharmacy. The pharmacist-in-charge may advise the owner on administrative and operational concerns. The owner shall have responsibility for, at a minimum, the following, and if the owner is not a Texas licensed pharmacist, the owner shall consult with the pharmacist-in-charge or another Texas licensed pharmacist:

    (1)   establishing policies for procurement of prescription drugs and devices and other products dispensed from the Class C pharmacy;

    (2)   establishing and maintaining effective controls against the theft or diversion of prescription drugs;

    (3)   if the pharmacy uses an automated pharmacy dispensing system, reviewing and approving all policies and procedures for system operation, safety, security, accuracy and access, patient confidentiality, prevention of unauthorized access, and malfunction;

    (4)   providing the pharmacy with the necessary equipment and resources commensurate with its level and type of practice; and

    (5)   establishing policies and procedures regarding maintenance, storage, and retrieval of records in a data processing system such that the system is in compliance with state and federal requirements.

(g)   Identification of pharmacy personnel. All pharmacy personnel shall be identified as follows.

    (1)   Pharmacy technicians. All pharmacy technicians shall wear an identification tag or badge that bears the person's name and identifies him or her as a pharmacy technician.

    (2)   Pharmacy technician trainees. All pharmacy technician trainees shall wear an identification tag or badge that bears the person's name and identifies him or her as a pharmacy technician trainee.

    (3)   Pharmacist interns. All pharmacist interns shall wear an identification tag or badge that bears the person's name and identifies him or her as a pharmacist intern.

    (4)   Pharmacists. All pharmacists shall wear an identification tag or badge that bears the person's name and identifies him or her as a pharmacist.

Source: The provisions of this § 291.73 adopted to be effective April 23, 1982, 7 TEXREG 1469; amended to be effective September 14, 1988, 13 TEXREG 4318; amended to be effective September 5, 1990, 15 TEXREG 4810; amended to be effective September 27, 1991, 16 TEXREG 5071; amended to be effective January 29, 1992, 17 TexReg 324; amended to be effective September 30, 1993, 18 TexReg 6460; amended to be effective March 16, 1995, 20 TexReg 1543; amended to be effective March 21, 1996, 21 TexReg 2242; amended to be effective October 11, 1996, 21 TexReg 9443; amended to be effective April 7, 1997, 22 TexReg 3106; amended to be effective September 16, 1999, 24 TexReg 7265; amendedtobe effective June 4, 2000, 25 TexReg 4816; amended to be effective August 31, 2000, 25 TexReg 8406; amended to be effective December 27, 2000, 25 TexReg 12728; amended to be effective September 12, 2001, 26 TexReg 6923; amended to be effective September 8, 2002, 27 TexReg 8242; amended to be effective March 4, 2004, 29 TexReg 2000; amended to be effective June 6, 2004, 29 TexReg 5376; amended to be effective September 11, 2005, 30 TexReg 5366; amended to be effective September 18, 2007, 32 TexReg 6333; amended to be effective September 7, 2008, 33 TexReg 7241; amended to be effective September 20, 2009, 34 TexReg 6323; amended to be effective March 11, 2010, 35 TexReg 2005; amended to be effective May 30, 2010, 35 TexReg 4177; amended to be effective December 7, 2010, 35 TexReg 10693; amended to be effective December 6, 2015, 40 TexReg 8766

§291.74 Operational Standards

(a)   Licensing requirements.

    (1)   A Class C pharmacy shall register annually or biennially with the board on a pharmacy license application provided by the board, following the procedures specified in § 291.1 of this title (relating to Pharmacy License Application).

    (2)   A Class C pharmacy which changes ownership shall notify the board within 10 days of the change of ownership and apply for a new and separate license as specified in § 291.3 of this title (relating to Required Notifications).

    (3)   A Class C pharmacy which changes location and/or name shall notify the board of the change as specified in § 291.3 of this title.

    (4)   A Class C pharmacy owned by a partnership or corporation which changes managing officers shall notify the board in writing of the names of the new managing officers within 10 days of the change following the procedures in § 291.3 of this title.

    (5)   A Class C pharmacy shall notify the board in writing within 10 days of closing, following the procedures in § 291.5 of this title (relating to Closing a Pharmacy).

    (6)   A fee as specified in § 291.6 of this title (relating to Pharmacy License Fees) will be charged for the issuance and renewal of a license and the issuance of an amended license.

    (7)   A separate license is required for each principal place of business and only one pharmacy license may be issued to a specific location.

    (8)   A Class C pharmacy, licensed under the Act, § 560.051(a)(3), which also operates another type of pharmacy which would otherwise be required to be licensed under the Act, § 560.051(a)(1) (Community Pharmacy (Class A)) or the Act, § 560.051(a)(2) (Nuclear Pharmacy (Class B)), is not required to secure a license for the such other type of pharmacy; provided, however, such licensee is required to comply with the provisions of § 291.31 of this title (relating to Definitions), § 291.32 of this title (relating to Personnel), § 291.33 of this title (relating to Operational Standards), § 291.34 of this title (relating to Records), and § 291.35 of this title (relating to Official Prescription Records), contained in Community Pharmacy (Class A), or § 291.51 of this title (relating to Purpose), § 291.52 of this title (relating to Definitions), § 291.53 of this title (relating to Personnel), § 291.54 of this title (relating to Operational Standards), and § 291.55 of this title (relating to Records), contained in Nuclear Pharmacy (Class B), to the extent such sections are applicable to the operation of the pharmacy.

    (9)   A Class C pharmacy engaged in the compounding of non-sterile preparations shall comply with the provisions of § 291.131 of this title (relating to Pharmacies Compounding Non-sterile Preparations).

    (10) Class C pharmacy personnel shall not compound sterile preparations unless the pharmacy has applied for and obtained a Class C-S pharmacy.

    (11) A Class C pharmacy engaged in the provision of remote pharmacy services, including storage and dispensing of prescription drugs, shall comply with the provisions of § 291.121 of this title (relating to Remote Pharmacy Services).

    (12) A Class C pharmacy engaged in centralized prescription dispensing and/or prescription drug or medication order processing shall comply with the provisions of § 291.123 of this title (relating to Central Prescription Drug or Medication Order Processing) and/ or § 291.125 of this title (relating to Centralized Prescription Dispensing).

    (13) A Class C pharmacy with an ongoing clinical pharmacy program that proposes to allow a pharmacy technician to verify the accuracy of work performed by another pharmacy technician relating to the filling of floor stock and unit dose distribution systems for a patient admitted to the hospital if the patient's orders have previously been reviewed and approved by a pharmacist shall make application to the board as follows.

        (A)   The pharmacist-in-charge must submit an application on a form provided by the board, containing the following information:

            (i)   name, address, and pharmacy license number;

            (ii)   name and license number of the pharmacist-in-charge;

    (iii) name and registration numbers of the pharmacy technicians;

    (iv) anticipated date the pharmacy plans to begin allowing a pharmacy technician to verify the accuracy of work performed by another pharmacy technician;

    (v) documentation that the pharmacy has an ongoing clinical pharmacy program; and

    (vi) any other information specified on the application.

  (B) The pharmacy may not allow a pharmacy technician to check the work of another pharmacy technician until the board has reviewed and approved the application and issued an amended license to the pharmacy.

  (C) Every two years, in connection with the application for renewal of the pharmacy license, the pharmacy shall provide updated documentation that the pharmacy continues to have an ongoing clinical pharmacy program as specified in subparagraph (A) (v) of this paragraph.

(14) A rural hospital that wishes to allow a pharmacy technician to perform the duties specified in § 291.73(e)(2)(D) of this title (relating to Personnel), shall make application to the board as follows.

  (A) Prior to allowing a pharmacy technician to perform the duties specified in § 291.73(e)(2)(D) of this title, the pharmacist-in-charge must submit an application on a form provided by the board, containing the following information:

    (i) name, address, and pharmacy license number;

    (ii) name and license number of the pharmacist-in-charge;

    (iii) name and registration number of the pharmacy technicians;

    (iv) proposed date the pharmacy wishes to start allowing pharmacy technicians to perform the duties specified in § 291.73(e)(2)(D) of this title;

    (v) documentation that the hospital is a rural hospital with 75 or fewer beds and that the rural hospital is either:

      (I) located in a county with a population of 50,000 or less as defined by the United States Census Bureau in the most recent U.S. census; or

      (II) designated by the Centers for Medicare and Medicaid Services as a critical access hospital, rural referral center, or sole community hospital; and

    (vi) any other information specified on the application.

  (B) A rural hospital may not allow a pharmacy technician to perform the duties specified in § 291.73(e)(2)(D) of this title until the board has reviewed and approved the application and issued an amended license to the pharmacy.

  (C) Every two years in conjunction with the application for renewal of the pharmacy license, the pharmacist-in-charge shall update the application for pharmacy technicians to perform the duties specified in § 291.73(e)(2)(D) of this title.

(b) Environment.

  (1) General requirements.

    (A) The institutional pharmacy shall have adequate space necessary for the storage, compounding, labeling, dispensing, and sterile preparation of drugs prepared in the pharmacy, and additional space, depending on the size and scope of pharmaceutical services.

    (B) The institutional pharmacy shall be arranged in an orderly fashion and shall be kept clean. All required equipment shall be clean and in good operating condition.

    (C) A sink with hot and cold running water exclusive of restroom facilities shall be available to all pharmacy personnel and shall be maintained in a sanitary condition at all times.

    (D) The institutional pharmacy shall be properly lighted and ventilated.

    (E) The temperature of the institutional pharmacy shall be maintained within a range compatible with the proper storage of drugs. The temperature of the refrigerator and/or freezer shall be maintained within a range compatible with the proper storage of drugs.

    (F) If the institutional pharmacy has flammable materials, the pharmacy shall have a designated area for the storage of flammable materials. Such area shall meet the requirements set by local and state fire laws.

    (G) The institutional pharmacy shall store antiseptics, other drugs for external use, and disinfectants separately from internal and injectable medications.

  (2) Security requirements.

    (A) The institutional pharmacy shall be enclosed and capable of being locked by key, combination or other mechanical or electronic means, so as to prohibit access by unauthorized individuals. Only individuals authorized by the pharmacist-in-charge shall enter the pharmacy.

    (B) Each pharmacist on duty shall be responsible for the security of the institutional pharmacy, including provisions for adequate safeguards against theft or diversion of dangerous drugs, controlled substances, and records for such drugs.

    (C) The institutional pharmacy shall have locked storage for Schedule II controlled substances and other drugs requiring additional security.

(c) Equipment and supplies. Institutional pharmacies distributing medication orders shall have the following equipment:

  (1) data processing system including a printer or comparable equipment; and

  (2) refrigerator and/or freezer and a system or device (e.g., thermometer) to monitor the temperature to ensure that proper storage requirements are met.

(d) Library. A reference library shall be maintained that includes the following in hard-copy or electronic format and that pharmacy personnel shall be capable of accessing at all times:

  (1) current copies of the following:

    (A) Texas Pharmacy Act and rules;

    (B) Texas Dangerous Drug Act and rules;

    (C) Texas Controlled Substances Act and regulations; and

    (D) Federal Controlled Substances Act and regulations (or official publication describing the requirements of the Federal Controlled Substances Act and regulations);

  (2) at least one current or updated reference from each of the following categories:

       (A) drug interactions. A reference text on drug interactions, such as Drug Interaction Facts. A separate reference is not required if other references maintained by the pharmacy contain drug interaction information including information needed to determine severity or significance of the interaction and appropriate recommendations or actions to be taken;

       (B) a general information reference text;

   (3) a current or updated reference on injectable drug products;

   (4) basic antidote information and the telephone number of the nearest regional poison control center;

   (5) metric-apothecary weight and measure conversion charts.

(e) Absence of a pharmacist.

   (1) Medication orders.

       (A) In facilities with a full-time pharmacist, if a practitioner orders a drug for administration to a bona fide patient of the facility when the pharmacy is closed, the following is applicable:

          (i) Prescription drugs and devices only in sufficient quantities for immediate therapeutic needs may be removed from the institutional pharmacy;

          (ii) Only a designated licensed nurse or practitioner may remove such drugs and devices;

          (iii) A record shall be made at the time of withdrawal by the authorized person removing the drugs and devices. The record shall contain the following information:

             (I) name of patient;

             (II) name of device or drug, strength, and dosage form;

             (III) dose prescribed;

             (IV) quantity taken;

             (V) time and date; and

             (VI) signature (first initial and last name or full signature) or electronic signature of person making withdrawal;

          (iv) The original or direct copy of the medication order may substitute for such record, providing the medication order meets all the requirements of clause (iii) of this subparagraph; and

          (v) The pharmacist shall verify the withdrawal of drugs from the pharmacy and perform a drug regimen review as specified in subsection (g)(1)(B) of this section as soon as practical, but in no event more than 72 hours from the time of such withdrawal.

       (B) In facilities with a part-time or consultant pharmacist, if a practitioner orders a drug for administration to a bona fide patient of the facility when the pharmacist is not on duty, or when the pharmacy is closed, the following is applicable:

          (i) Prescription drugs and devices only in sufficient quantities for therapeutic needs may be removed from the institutional pharmacy;

          (ii) Only a designated licensed nurse or practitioner may remove such drugs and devices;

          (iii) A record shall be made at the time of withdrawal by the authorized person removing the drugs and devices; the record shall meet the same requirements as specified in subparagraph (A)(iii) and (iv) of this paragraph;

          (iv) The pharmacist shall verify the withdrawal of drugs from the pharmacy after a reasonable interval, but in no event may such interval exceed seven days; and

          (v) The pharmacist shall perform a drug regimen review as specified in subsection (g)(1)(B) of this section as follows:

             (I) If the facility has an average daily inpatient census of ten or less, the pharmacist shall perform the drug review after a reasonable interval, but in no event may such interval exceed seven (7) days; or

             (II) If the facility has an average inpatient daily census above ten, the pharmacist shall perform the drug review after a reasonable interval, but in no event may such interval exceed 96 hours.

             (III) The average daily inpatient census shall be calculated by hospitals annually immediately following the submission of the hospital's Medicare Cost Report and the number used for purposes of subparagraph (B)(v)(I) and (II) of this paragraph shall be the average of the inpatient daily census in the report and the previous two reports for a three year period.

   (2) Floor stock. In facilities using a floor stock method of drug distribution, the following is applicable:

       (A) Prescription drugs and devices may be removed from the pharmacy only in the original manufacturer's container or prepackaged container.

       (B) Only a designated licensed nurse or practitioner may remove such drugs and devices.

       (C) A record shall be made at the time of withdrawal by the authorized person removing the drug or device; the record shall contain the following information:

          (i) name of the drug, strength, and dosage form;

          (ii) quantity removed;

          (iii) location of floor stock;

          (iv) date and time; and

          (v) signature (first initial and last name or full signature) or electronic signature of person making the withdrawal.

       (D) The pharmacist shall verify the withdrawal of drugs from the pharmacy after a reasonable interval, but in no event may such interval exceed seven days.

   (3) Rural hospitals. In rural hospitals when a pharmacy technician performs the duties listed in § 291.73(e)(2)(D) of this title, the following is applicable:

       (A) the pharmacy technician shall make a record of all drugs distributed from the pharmacy. The record shall be maintained in the pharmacy for two years and contain the following information:

          (i) name of patient or location where floor stock is distributed;

          (ii) name of device or drug, strength, and dosage form;

          (iii) dose prescribed or ordered;

          (iv) quantity distributed;

          (v) time and date of the distribution; and

      (vi) signature (first initial and last name or full signature) or electronic signature of nurse or practitioner that verified the actions of the pharmacy technician.
- (B) The original or direct copy of the medication order may substitute for the record specified in subparagraph (A) of this paragraph, provided the medication order meets all the requirements of subparagraph (A) of this paragraph.
- (C) The pharmacist shall:
  - (i) verify and document the verification of all distributions made from the pharmacy in the absence of a pharmacist as soon as practical, but in no event more than seven (7) days from the time of such distribution;
  - (ii) perform a drug regimen review for all medication orders as specified in subsection (g)(1)(B) of this section and document such verification including any discrepancies noted by the pharmacist as follows:
    - (I) If the facility has an average daily inpatient census of ten or less, the pharmacist shall perform the drug review as soon as practical, but in no event more than seven (7) days from the time of such distribution; or
    - (II) If the facility has an average daily inpatient census above ten, the pharmacist shall perform the drug review after a reasonable interval, but in no event may such interval exceed 96 hours;
    - (III) The average daily inpatient census shall be calculated by hospitals annually immediately following the submission of the hospital's Medicare Cost Report and the number used for purposes of subparagraph (C)(ii)(I) and (II) of this paragraph shall be the average of the inpatient daily census in the report and the previous two reports for a three year period;
  - (iii) review any discrepancy noted by the pharmacist with the pharmacy technician(s) and make any change in procedures or processes necessary to prevent future problems; and
  - (iv) report any adverse events that have a potential for harm to a patient to the appropriate committee of the hospital that reviews adverse events.
- (f) Drugs.
  - (1) Procurement, preparation and storage.
    - (A) The pharmacist-in-charge shall have the responsibility for the procurement and storage of drugs, but may receive input from other appropriate staff of the facility, relative to such responsibility.
    - (B) The pharmacist-in-charge shall have the responsibility for determining specifications of all drugs procured by the facility.
    - (C) Institutional pharmacies may not sell, purchase, trade or possess prescription drug samples, unless the pharmacy meets the requirements as specified in § 291.16 of this title (relating to Samples).
    - (D) All drugs shall be stored at the proper temperatures, as defined in the USP/NF and in § 291.15 of this title (relating to Storage of Drugs).
    - (E) Any drug bearing an expiration date may not be distributed beyond the expiration date of the drug.
    - (F) Outdated and other unusable drugs shall be removed from stock and shall be quarantined together until such drugs are disposed of properly.
  - (2) Formulary.
    - (A) A formulary shall be developed by the facility committee performing the pharmacy and therapeutics function for the facility. For the purpose of this section, a formulary is a compilation of pharmaceuticals that reflects the current clinical judgment of a facility's medical staff.
    - (B) The pharmacist-in-charge or pharmacist designated by the pharmacist-in-charge shall be a full voting member of the committee performing the pharmacy and therapeutics function for the facility, when such committee is performing the pharmacy and therapeutics function.
    - (C) A practitioner may grant approval for pharmacists at the facility to interchange, in accordance with the facility's formulary, for the prescribed drugs on the practitioner's medication orders provided:
      - (i) the pharmacy and therapeutics committee has developed a formulary;
      - (ii) the formulary has been approved by the medical staff committee of the facility;
      - (iii) there is a reasonable method for the practitioner to override any interchange; and
      - (iv) the practitioner authorizes pharmacists in the facility to interchange on his/her medication orders in accordance with the facility's formulary through his/her written agreement to abide by the policies and procedures of the medical staff and facility.
  - (3) Prepackaging of drugs.
    - (A) Distribution within a facility.
      - (i) Drugs may be prepackaged in quantities suitable for internal distribution by a pharmacist or by pharmacy technicians or pharmacy technician trainees under the direction and direct supervision of a pharmacist.
      - (ii) The label of a prepackaged unit shall indicate:
        - (I) brand name and strength of the drug; or if no brand name, then the generic name, strength, and name of the manufacturer or distributor;
        - (II) facility's unique lot number;
        - (III) expiration date based on currently available literature; and
        - (IV) quantity of the drug, if the quantity is greater than one.
      - (iii) Records of prepackaging shall be maintained to show:
        - (I) name of the drug, strength, and dosage form;
        - (II) facility's unique lot number;
        - (III) manufacturer or distributor;
        - (IV) manufacturer's lot number;
        - (V) expiration date;
        - (VI) quantity per prepackaged unit;
        - (VII) number of prepackaged units;
        - (VIII) date packaged;
        - (IX) name, initials, or electronic signature of the prepacker; and

(X) name, initials, or electronic signature of the responsible pharmacist.
- (iv) Stock packages, prepackaged units, and control records shall be quarantined together until checked/released by the pharmacist.
- (B) Distribution to other Class C (Institutional) pharmacies under common ownership.
  - (i) Drugs may be prepackaged in quantities suitable for distribution to other Class C (Institutional) pharmacies under common ownership by a pharmacist or by pharmacy technicians or pharmacy technician trainees under the direction and direct supervision of a pharmacist.
  - (ii) The label of a prepackaged unit shall indicate:
    - (I) brand name and strength of the drug; or if no brand name, then the generic name, strength, and name of the manufacturer or distributor;
    - (II) facility's unique lot number;
    - (III) expiration date based on currently available literature;
    - (IV) quantity of the drug, if the quantity is greater than one; and
    - (V) name of the facility responsible for prepackaging the drug.
  - (iii) Records of prepackaging shall be maintained to show:
    - (I) name of the drug, strength, and dosage form;
    - (II) facility's unique lot number;
    - (III) manufacturer or distributor;
    - (IV) manufacturer's lot number;
    - (V) expiration date;
    - (VI) quantity per prepackaged unit;
    - (VII) number of prepackaged units;
    - (VIII) date packaged;
    - (IX) name, initials, or electronic signature of the prepacker;
    - (X) name, initials, or electronic signature of the responsible pharmacist; and
    - (XI) name of the facility receiving the prepackaged drug.
  - (iv) Stock packages, prepackaged units, and control records shall be quarantined together until checked/released by the pharmacist.
  - (v) The pharmacy shall have written procedure for the recall of any drug prepackaged for another Class C Pharmacy under common ownership. The recall procedures shall require:
    - (I) notification to the pharmacy to which the prepackaged drug was distributed;
    - (II) quarantine of the product if there is a suspicion of harm to a patient;
    - (III) a mandatory recall if there is confirmed or probable harm to a patient; and
    - (IV) notification to the board if a mandatory recall is instituted.
- (4) Sterile preparations prepared in a location other than the pharmacy. A distinctive supplementary label shall be affixed to the container of any admixture. The label shall bear at a minimum:
  - (A) patient's name and location, if not immediately administered;
  - (B) name and amount of drug(s) added;
  - (C) name of the basic solution;
  - (D) name or identifying code of person who prepared admixture; and
  - (E) expiration date of solution.
- (5) Distribution.
  - (A) Medication orders.
    - (i) Drugs may be given to patients in facilities only on the order of a practitioner. No change in the order for drugs may be made without the approval of a practitioner except as authorized by the practitioner in compliance with paragraph (2)(C) of this subsection.
    - (ii) Drugs may be distributed only from the original or a direct copy of the practitioner's medication order.
    - (iii) Pharmacy technicians and pharmacy technician trainees may not receive verbal medication orders.
    - (iv) Institutional pharmacies shall be exempt from the labeling provisions and patient notification requirements of § 562.006 and § 562.009 of the Act, as respects drugs distributed pursuant to medication orders.
  - (B) Procedures.
    - (i) Written policies and procedures for a drug distribution system (best suited for the particular institutional pharmacy) shall be developed and implemented by the pharmacist-in-charge, with the advice of the committee performing the pharmacy and therapeutics function for the facility.
    - (ii) The written policies and procedures for the drug distribution system shall include, but not be limited to, procedures regarding the following:
      - (I) pharmaceutical care services;
      - (II) handling, storage and disposal of cytotoxic drugs and waste;
      - (III) disposal of unusable drugs and supplies;
      - (IV) security;
      - (V) equipment;
      - (VI) sanitation;
      - (VII) reference materials;
      - (VIII) drug selection and procurement;
      - (IX) drug storage;
      - (X) controlled substances;
      - (XI) investigational drugs, including the obtaining of protocols from the principal investigator;
      - (XII) prepackaging and manufacturing;

(XIII) stop orders;

(XIV) reporting of medication errors, adverse drug reactions/events, and drug product defects;

(XV) physician orders;

(XVI) floor stocks;

(XVII) drugs brought into the facility;

(XVIII) furlough medications;

(XIX) self-administration;

(XX) emergency drug supply;

(XXI) formulary;

(XXII) monthly inspections of nursing stations and other areas where drugs are stored, distributed, administered or dispensed;

(XXIII) control of drug samples;

(XXIV) outdated and other unusable drugs;

(XXV) routine distribution of patient medication;

(XXVI) preparation and distribution of sterile preparations;

(XXVII) handling of medication orders when a pharmacist is not on duty;

(XXVIII) use of automated compounding or counting devices;

(XXIX) use of data processing and direct imaging systems;

(XXX) drug administration to include infusion devices and drug delivery systems;

(XXXI) drug labeling;

(XXXII) recordkeeping;

(XXXIII) quality assurance/quality control;

(XXXIV) duties and education and training of professional and nonprofessional staff;

(XXXV) procedures for a pharmacy technician to verify the accuracy of work performed by another pharmacy technician, if applicable;

(XXXVI) operation of the pharmacy when a pharmacist in not on-site; and

(XXXVII) emergency preparedness plan, to include continuity of patient therapy and public safety.

(6) Discharge Prescriptions. Discharge prescriptions must be dispensed and labeled in accordance with § 291.33 of this title (relating to Operational Standards) except that certain medications packaged in unit-of-use containers, such as metered-dose inhalers, insulin pens, topical creams or ointments, or ophthalmic or otic preparation that are administered to the patient during the time the patient was a patient in the hospital, may be provided to the patient upon discharge provided the pharmacy receives a discharge order and the product bears a label containing the following information:

(A) name of the patient;

(B) name and strength of the medication;

(C) name of the prescribing or attending practitioner;

(D) directions for use;

(E) duration of therapy (if applicable); and

(F) name and telephone number of the pharmacy.

(g) Pharmaceutical care services.

(1) The pharmacist-in-charge shall assure that at least the following pharmaceutical care services are provided to patients of the facility.

(A) Drug utilization review. A systematic ongoing process of drug utilization review shall be developed in conjunction with the medical staff to increase the probability of desired patient outcomes and decrease the probability of undesired outcomes from drug therapy.

(B) Drug regimen review.

(i) For the purpose of promoting therapeutic appropriateness, a pharmacist shall evaluate medication orders and patient medication records for:

(I) known allergies;

(II) rational therapy--contraindications;

(III) reasonable dose and route of administration;

(IV) reasonable directions for use;

(V) duplication of therapy;

(VI) drug-drug interactions;

(VII) drug-food interactions;

(VIII) drug-disease interactions;

(IX) adverse drug reactions;

(X) proper utilization, including overutilization or underutilization; and

(XI) clinical laboratory or clinical monitoring methods to monitor and evaluate drug effectiveness, side effects, toxicity, or adverse effects, and appropriateness to continued use of the drug in its current regimen.

(ii) The drug regimen review shall be conducted on a prospective basis when a pharmacist is on duty, except for an emergency order, and on a retrospective basis as specified in subsection (e)(1) or (e)(3) of this section when a pharmacist is not on duty.

(iii) Any questions regarding the order must be resolved with the prescriber and a written notation of these discussions made and maintained.

(iv) The drug regimen review may be conducted by remotely accessing the pharmacy's electronic data base from outside the pharmacy by an individual Texas licensed pharmacist employee of the pharmacy, provided the pharmacy establishes controls to protect the privacy of the patient and the security of confidential records.

      (C) Education. The pharmacist-in-charge in cooperation with appropriate multi-disciplinary staff of the facility shall develop policies that assure that:

         (i)   the patient and/or patient's caregiver receives information regarding drugs and their safe and appropriate use; and

         (ii) health care providers are provided with patient specific drug information.

      (D) Patient monitoring. The pharmacist-in-charge in cooperation with appropriate multi-disciplinary staff of the facility shall develop policies to ensure that the patient's response to drug therapy is monitored and conveyed to the appropriate health care provider.

  (2) Other pharmaceutical care services which may be provided by pharmacists in the facility include, but are not limited to, the following:

      (A) managing drug therapy as delegated by a practitioner as allowed under the provisions of the Medical Practice Act;

      (B) administering immunizations and vaccinations under written protocol of a physician;

      (C) managing patient compliance programs;

      (D) providing preventative health care services; and

      (E) providing case management of patients who are being treated with high-risk or high-cost drugs, or who are considered "high risk" due to their age, medical condition, family history, or related concern.

(h) Emergency rooms.

  (1) During the times a pharmacist is on duty in the facility any prescription drugs supplied to an outpatient, including emergency department patients, may only be dispensed by a pharmacist.

  (2) When a pharmacist is not on duty in the facility, the following is applicable for supplying prescription drugs to be taken home by the patient for self-administration from the emergency room. If the patient has been admitted to the emergency room and assessed by a practitioner at the hospital, the following procedures shall be observed in supplying prescription drugs from the emergency room.

      (A) Dangerous drugs and/or controlled substances may only be supplied in accordance with the system of control and accountability for dangerous drugs and/or controlled substances administered or supplied from the emergency room; such system shall be developed and supervised by the pharmacist-in-charge or staff pharmacist designated by the pharmacist-in-charge.

      (B) Only dangerous drugs and/or controlled substances listed on the emergency room drug list may be supplied; such list shall be developed by the pharmacist-in-charge and the facility's emergency department committee (or like group or person responsible for policy in that department) and shall consist of dangerous drugs and/or controlled substances of the nature and type to meet the immediate needs of emergency room patients.

      (C) Dangerous drugs and/or controlled substances may only be supplied in prepackaged quantities not to exceed a 72-hour supply in suitable containers and appropriately prelabeled (including necessary auxiliary labels) by the institutional pharmacy.

      (D) At the time of delivery of the dangerous drugs and/or controlled substances, the practitioner or licensed nurse under the supervision of a practitioner shall appropriately complete the label with at least the following information:

         (i)   name, address, and phone number of the facility;

         (ii) date supplied;

         (iii) name of practitioner;

         (iv) name of patient;

         (v) directions for use;

         (vi) brand name and strength of the dangerous drug or controlled substance; or if no brand name, then the generic name, strength, and the name of the manufacturer or distributor of the dangerous drug or controlled substance;

         (vii) quantity supplied; and

         (viii) unique identification number.

      (E) The practitioner, or a licensed nurse under the supervision of the practitioner, shall give the appropriately labeled, prepackaged drug to the patient and explain the correct use of the drug.

      (F) A perpetual record of dangerous drugs and/or controlled substances supplied from the emergency room shall be maintained in the emergency room. Such record shall include the following:

         (i)   date supplied;

         (ii) practitioner's name;

         (iii) patient's name;

         (iv) brand name and strength of the dangerous drug or controlled substance; or if no brand name, then the generic name, strength, and the name of the manufacturer or distributor of the dangerous drug or controlled substance;

         (v) quantity supplied; and

         (vi) unique identification number.

      (G) The pharmacist-in-charge, or staff pharmacist designated by the pharmacist-in-charge, shall verify the correctness of this record at least once every seven days.

(i) Radiology departments.

  (1) During the times a pharmacist is on duty, any prescription drugs dispensed to an outpatient, including radiology department patients, may only be dispensed by a pharmacist.

  (2) When a pharmacist is not on duty, the following procedures shall be observed in supplying prescription drugs from the radiology department.

      (A) Prescription drugs may only be supplied to patients who have been scheduled for an x-ray examination at the facility.

      (B) Prescription drugs may only be supplied in accordance with the system of control and accountability for prescription drugs administered or supplied from the radiology department and supervised by the pharmacist-in-charge or staff pharmacist designated by the pharmacist-in-charge.

(C) Only prescription drugs listed on the radiology drug list may be supplied; such list shall be developed by the pharmacist-in-charge and the facility's radiology committee (or like group or persons responsible for policy in that department) and shall consist of drugs for the preparation of a patient for a radiological procedure.

(D) Prescription drugs may only be supplied in prepackaged quantities in suitable containers and prelabeled by the institutional pharmacy with the following information:

    (i) name and address of the facility;

    (ii) directions for use;

    (iii) name and strength of the prescription drug--if generic name, the name of the manufacturer or distributor of the prescription drug;

    (iv) quantity;

    (v) facility's lot number and expiration date; and

    (vi) appropriate ancillary label(s).

(E) At the time of delivery of the prescription drug, the practitioner or practitioner's agent shall complete the label with the following information:

    (i) date supplied;

    (ii) name of physician;

    (iii) name of patient; and

    (iv) unique identification number.

(F) The practitioner or practitioner's agent shall give the appropriately labeled, prepackaged prescription drug to the patient.

(G) A perpetual record of prescription drugs supplied from the radiology department shall be maintained in the radiology department. Such records shall include the following:

    (i) date supplied;

    (ii) practitioner's name;

    (iii) patient's name;

    (iv) brand name and strength of the prescription drug; or if no brand name, then the generic name, strength, dosage form, and the name of the manufacturer or distributor of the prescription drug;

    (v) quantity supplied; and

    (vi) unique identification number.

(H) The pharmacist-in-charge, or a pharmacist designated by the pharmacist-in-charge, shall verify the correctness of this record at least once every seven days.

(j) Automated devices and systems.

  (1) Automated compounding or counting devices. If a pharmacy uses automated compounding or counting devices:

    (A) the pharmacy shall have a method to calibrate and verify the accuracy of the automated compounding or counting device and document the calibration and verification on a routine basis;

    (B) the devices may be loaded with unlabeled drugs only by a pharmacist or by pharmacy technicians or pharmacy technician trainees under the direction and direct supervision of a pharmacist;

    (C) the label of an automated compounding or counting device container shall indicate the brand name and strength of the drug; or if no brand name, then the generic name, strength, and name of the manufacturer or distributor;

    (D) records of loading unlabeled drugs into an automated compounding or counting device shall be maintained to show:

      (i) name of the drug, strength, and dosage form;

      (ii) manufacturer or distributor;

      (iii) manufacturer's lot number;

      (iv) expiration date;

      (v) date of loading;

      (vi) name, initials, or electronic signature of the person loading the automated compounding or counting device; and

      (vii) signature or electronic signature of the responsible pharmacist; and

    (E) the automated compounding or counting device shall not be used until a pharmacist verifies that the system is properly loaded and affixes his or her signature to the record specified in subparagraph (D) of this paragraph.

  (2) Automated medication supply systems.

    (A) Authority to use automated medication supply systems. A pharmacy may use an automated medication supply system to fill medication orders provided that:

      (i) the pharmacist-in-charge is responsible for the supervision of the operation of the system;

      (ii) the automated medication supply system has been tested by the pharmacy and found to dispense accurately. The pharmacy shall make the results of such testing available to the Board upon request; and

      (iii) the pharmacy will make the automated medication supply system available for inspection by the board for the purpose of validating the accuracy of the system.

    (B) Quality assurance program. A pharmacy which uses an automated medication supply system to fill medication orders shall operate according to a written program for quality assurance of the automated medication supply system which:

      (i) requires continuous monitoring of the automated medication supply system; and

      (ii) establishes mechanisms and procedures to test the accuracy of the automated medication supply system at least every six months and whenever any upgrade or change is made to the system and documents each such activity.

    (C) Policies and procedures of operation.

      (i) When an automated medication supply system is used to store or distribute medications for administration pursuant to medication orders, it shall be operated according to written policies and procedures of operation. The policies and procedures of operation shall establish requirements for operation of the automated medication supply system and shall describe policies and procedures that:

        (I) include a description of the policies and procedures of operation;

(II) provide for a pharmacist's review and approval of each original or new medication order prior to withdrawal from the automated medication supply system:

(-a-) before the order is filled when a pharmacist is on duty except for an emergency order;

(-b-) retrospectively within 72 hours in a facility with a full-time pharmacist when a pharmacist is not on duty at the time the order is made; or

(-c-) retrospectively within 7 days in a facility with a part-time or consultant pharmacist when a pharmacist is not on duty at the time the order is made;

(III) provide for access to the automated medication supply system for stocking and retrieval of medications which is limited to licensed healthcare professionals, pharmacy technicians, or pharmacy technician trainees acting under the supervision of a pharmacist;

(IV) provide that a pharmacist is responsible for the accuracy of the restocking of the system. The actual restocking may be performed by a pharmacy technician or pharmacy technician trainee;

(V) provide for an accountability record to be maintained which documents all transactions relative to stocking and removing medications from the automated medication supply system;

(VI) require a prospective or retrospective drug regimen review is conducted as specified in subsection (g) of this section; and

(VII) establish and make provisions for documentation of a preventative maintenance program for the automated medication supply system.

(ii) A pharmacy which uses an automated medication supply system to fill medication orders shall, at least annually, review its written policies and procedures, revise them if necessary, and document the review.

(D) Automated medication supply systems used for storage and recordkeeping of medications located outside of the pharmacy department (e.g., Pyxis). A pharmacy technician or pharmacy technician trainee may restock an automated medication supply system located outside of the pharmacy department with prescription drugs provided:

(i) prior to distribution of the prescription drugs a pharmacist verifies that the prescription drugs pulled to stock the automated supply system match the list of prescription drugs generated by the automated medication supply system except as specified in § 291.73(e)(2)(C)(ii) of this title; or

(ii) all of the following occur:

(I) the prescription drugs to restock the system are labeled and verified with a machine readable product identifier, such as a barcode;

(II) either:

(-a-) the drugs are in tamper evident product packaging, packaged by an FDA registered repackager or manufacturer, that is shipped to the pharmacy; or

(-b-) if any manipulation of the product occurs in the pharmacy prior to restocking, such as repackaging or extemporaneous compounding, the product must be checked by a pharmacist; and

(III) quality assurance audits are conducted according to established policies and procedures to ensure accuracy of the process.

(E) Recovery Plan. A pharmacy which uses an automated medication supply system to store or distribute medications for administration pursuant to medication orders shall maintain a written plan for recovery from a disaster or any other situation which interrupts the ability of the automated medication supply system to provide services necessary for the operation of the pharmacy. The written plan for recovery shall include:

(i) planning and preparation for maintaining pharmacy services when an automated medication supply system is experiencing downtime;

(ii) procedures for response when an automated medication supply system is experiencing downtime;

(iii) procedures for the maintenance and testing of the written plan for recovery; and

(iv) procedures for notification of the Board and other appropriate agencies whenever an automated medication supply system experiences downtime for more than two days of operation or a period of time which significantly limits the pharmacy's ability to provide pharmacy services.

(3) Verification of medication orders prepared by the pharmacy department through the use of an automated medication supply system. A pharmacist must check drugs prepared pursuant to medication orders to ensure that the drug is prepared for distribution accurately as prescribed. This paragraph does not apply to automated medication supply systems used for storage and recordkeeping of medications located outside of the pharmacy department.

(A) This check shall be considered accomplished if:

(i) a check of the final product is conducted by a pharmacist after the automated system has completed preparation of the medication order and prior to delivery to the patient; or

(ii) the following checks are conducted by a pharmacist:

(I) if the automated medication supply system contains unlabeled stock drugs, a pharmacist verifies that those drugs have been accurately stocked; and

(II) a pharmacist checks the accuracy of the data entry of each original or new medication order entered into the automated medication supply system before the order is filled.

(B) If the final check is accomplished as specified in subparagraph (A)(ii) of this paragraph, the following additional requirements must be met.

(i) The medication order preparation process must be fully automated from the time the pharmacist releases the medication order to the automated system until a completed medication order, ready for delivery to the patient, is produced.

(ii) The pharmacy has conducted initial testing and has a continuous quality assurance program which documents that the automated medication supply system dispenses accurately as specified in paragraph (2)(A) and (B) of this subsection.

(iii) The automated medication supply system documents and maintains:

(I) the name(s), initials, or identification code(s) of each pharmacist responsible for the checks outlined in subparagraph (A)(ii) of this paragraph; and

(II) the name(s), initials, or identification code(s) and specific activity(ies) of each pharmacist or pharmacy technician or pharmacy technician trainee who performs any other portion of the medication order preparation process.

(iv) The pharmacy establishes mechanisms and procedures to test the accuracy of the automated medication supply system at least every month rather than every six months as specified in paragraph (2)(B) of this subsection.

(4) Automated checking device.

(A) For the purpose of this subsection, an automated checking device is a fully automated device which confirms, after a drug is prepared for distribution but prior to delivery to the patient, that the correct drug and strength has been labeled with the correct label for the correct patient.

(B) The final check of a drug prepared pursuant to a medication order shall be considered accomplished using an automated checking device provided:

(i) a check of the final product is conducted by a pharmacist prior to delivery to the patient or the following checks are performed by a pharmacist:

(I) the prepackaged drug used to fill the order is checked by a pharmacist who verifies that the drug is labeled and packaged accurately; and

(II) a pharmacist checks the accuracy of each original or new medication order.

(ii) the medication order is prepared, labeled, and made ready for delivery to the patient in compliance with Class C (Institutional) Pharmacy rules; and

(iii) prior to delivery to the patient:

(I) the automated checking device confirms that the correct drug and strength has been labeled with the correct label for the correct patient; and

(II) a pharmacist performs all other duties required to ensure that the medication order has been prepared safely and accurately as prescribed.

(C) If the final check is accomplished as specified in subparagraph (B) of this paragraph, the following additional requirements must be met.

(i) The pharmacy has conducted initial testing of the automated checking device and has a continuous quality assurance program which documents that the automated checking device accurately confirms that the correct drug and strength has been labeled with the correct label for the correct patient.

(ii) The pharmacy documents and maintains:

(I) the name(s), initials, or identification code(s) of each pharmacist responsible for the checks outlined in subparagraph (B)(i) of this paragraph; and

(II) the name(s), initials, or identification code(s) and specific activity(ies) of each pharmacist, pharmacy technician, or pharmacy technician trainee who performs any other portion of the medication order preparation process.

(iii) The pharmacy establishes mechanisms and procedures to test the accuracy of the automated checking device at least monthly.

Source: The provisions of this § 291.74 adopted to be effective April 23, 1982, 7 TEXREG1469; amended to be effective November 5, 1982, 7 TEXREG3839; amended to be effective August 30, 1984, 9 TEXREG4450; amended to be effective December 18, 1985, 10 TEXREG4694; amended to be effective July 29, 1987, 12 TEXREG2338; amended to be effective September 14, 1988, 13 TEXREG4318; amended to be effective October 27, 1989, 14 TEXREG5494; amended to be effective September 5, 1990, 15 TEXREG4810; amended to be effective September 27, 1991, 16 TEXREG5071; amended to be effective September 30, 1993, 18 TexReg 6460; amended to be effective March 16, 1995, 20 TexReg 1543; amended to be effective March 21, 1996, 21 TexReg 2242; amended to be effective June 4, 2000, 25 TexReg 4816; amended to be effective August 31, 2000, 25 TexReg 8406; amended to be effective December 27, 2000, 25 TexReg 12728; amended to be effective June 20, 2001, 26 TexReg 4512; amended to be effective December 19, 2001, 26 TexReg 10311; amended to be effective December 15, 2002, 27 TexReg 11541; amended to be effective June 23, 2003, 28 TexReg 4638; amended to be effective June 6, 2004, 29 TexReg 5376; amended to be effective September 11, 2005, 30 TexReg 5366; amended to be effective September 18, 2007, 32 TexReg 6333; amended to be effective March 6, 2008, 33 TexReg 1792; amended to be effective September 7, 2008, 33 TexReg 7241; amended to be effective September 20, 2009, 34 TexReg 6323; amended to be effective March 11, 2010, 35 TexReg 2005; amended to be effective May 30, 2010, 35 TexReg 4177; amended to be effective March 10, 2011, 36 TexReg 1528; amended to be effective July 11, 2011, 36 TexReg 4412; amended to be effective December 5, 2012, 37 TexReg 9513; amended to be effective December 10, 2013, 38 TexReg 8847; amended to be effective December 19, 2016, 41 TexReg 9934; amended to be effective January 4, 2018, 42 TexReg 7691; amended to be effective September 16, 2018, 43 TexReg 5784; amended to be effective December 6, 2018, 43 TexReg 7775

§291.75 Records

(a) Maintenance of records.

(1) Every inventory or other record required to be kept under the provisions of § 291.71 of this title (relating to Purpose), § 291.72 of this title (relating to Definitions), § 291.73 of this title (relating to Personnel), § 291.74 of this title (relating to Operational Standards), and this section contained in Institutional Pharmacy (Class C) shall be:

(A) kept by the institutional pharmacy and be available, for at least two years from the date of such inventory or record, for inspecting and copying by the board or its representative, and other authorized local, state, or federal law enforcement agencies; and

(B) supplied by the pharmacy within 72 hours, if requested by an authorized agent of the board. If the pharmacy maintains the records in an electronic format, the requested records must be provided in a mutually agreeable electronic format if specifically requested by the board or its representative. Failure to provide the records set out in this subsection, either on site or within 72 hours, constitutes prima facie evidence of failure to keep and maintain records in violation of the Act.

(2) Records of controlled substances listed in Schedules I and II shall be maintained separately from all other records of the pharmacy.

(3) Records of controlled substances listed in Schedules III - V shall be maintained separately or readily retrievable from all other records of the pharmacy. For purposes of this subsection, readily retrievable means that the controlled substances shall be asterisked, redlined, or in some other manner readily identifiable apart from all other items appearing on the record.

(4) Records, except when specifically required to be maintained in original or hard-copy form, may be maintained in an alternative data retention system, such as a data processing or direct imaging system, provided:

(A) the records in the alternative data retention system contain all of the information required on the manual record; and

    (B) the alternative data retention system is capable of producing a hard copy of the record upon the request of the board, its representative, or other authorized local, state, or federal law enforcement or regulatory agencies.

(b) Outpatient records.

    (1) Outpatient records shall be maintained as provided in § 291.34 (relating to Records), and § 291.35 (relating to Official Prescription Requirements), in chapter 291, subchapter B of this title.

    (2) Outpatient prescriptions, including, but not limited to, furlough and discharge prescriptions, that are written by a practitioner must be written on a form which meets the requirements of § 291.34(b)(7)(A) of this title. Medication order forms or copies thereof do not meet the requirements for outpatient forms.

    (3) Controlled substances listed in Schedule II must be written on an official prescription form in accordance with the Texas Controlled Substances Act, § 481.075, and rules promulgated pursuant to the Texas Controlled Substances Act, unless exempted by chapter 315 of this title (relating to Controlled Substances). Outpatient prescriptions for Schedule II controlled substances that are exempted from the official prescription requirement must be manually signed by the practitioner.

(c) Patient records.

    (1) Original medication orders.

        (A) Each original medication order shall bear the following information:

            (i)   patient name and room number or identification number;

            (ii) drug name, strength, and dosage form;

            (iii) directions for use;

            (iv) date; and

            (v)   signature or electronic signature of the practitioner or that of his or her authorized agent.

        (B) Original medication orders shall be maintained with the medication administration records of the patients.

    (2) Patient medication records (PMR). A patient medication record shall be maintained for each patient of the facility. The PMR shall contain at a minimum the following information:

        (A) Patient information:

            (i)   patient name and room number or identification number;

            (ii) gender, and date of birth or age;

            (iii) weight and height;

            (iv) known drug sensitivities and allergies to drugs and/or food;

            (v)   primary diagnoses and chronic conditions;

            (vi) primary physician; and

            (vii) other drugs the patient is receiving; and

        (B) Medication order information:

            (i)   date of distribution;

            (ii) drug name, strength, and dosage form; and

            (iii) directions for use.

    (3) Controlled substances records. Controlled substances records shall be maintained as follows:

        (A) All records for controlled substances shall be maintained in a readily retrievable manner; and

        (B) Controlled substances records shall be maintained in a manner to establish receipt and distribution of all controlled substances.

    (4) Schedule II controlled substances records. Records of controlled substances listed in Schedule II shall be maintained as follows:

        (A) Records of controlled substances listed in Schedule II shall be maintained separately from records of controlled substances in Schedules III, IV, and V, and all other records;

        (B) An institutional pharmacy shall maintain a perpetual inventory of any controlled substance listed in Schedule II; and

        (C) Distribution records for controlled substances listed in Schedule II shall bear the following information:

            (i)   patient's name;

            (ii) prescribing or attending practitioner;

            (iii) name of drug, dosage form, and strength;

            (iv) time and date of administration to patient and quantity administered;

            (v)   name, initials, or electronic signature of the individual administering the controlled substance;

            (vi) returns to the pharmacy; and

            (vii) waste (waste is required to be witnessed and cosigned, electronically or manually, by another individual).

    (5) Floor stock records.

        (A) Distribution records for Schedules II - V controlled substances floor stock shall include the following information:

            (i)   patient's name;

            (ii) prescribing or attending practitioner;

            (iii) name of controlled substance, dosage form, and strength;

            (iv) time and date of administration to patient;

            (v)   quantity administered;

            (vi) name, initials, or electronic signature of the individual administering drug;

            (vii) returns to the pharmacy; and

            (viii) waste (waste is required to be witnessed and cosigned, manually or electronically, by another individual).

        (B) The record required by subparagraph (A) of this paragraph shall be maintained separately from patient records.

        (C) A pharmacist shall review distribution records with medication orders on a periodic basis to verify proper usage of drugs, not to exceed 30 days between such reviews.

    (6) General requirements for records maintained in a data processing system.

        (A) Noncompliance with data processing requirements. If a hospital pharmacy's data processing system is not in compliance with the board's requirements, the pharmacy must maintain a manual recordkeeping system.

(B) Requirements for backup systems. The facility shall maintain a backup copy of information stored in the data processing system using disk, tape, or other electronic backup system and update this backup copy on a regular basis, at least monthly, to assure that data is not lost due to system failure.

(C) Change or discontinuance of a data processing system.

    (i) Records of distribution and return for all controlled substances. A pharmacy that changes or discontinues use of a data processing system must:

        (I) transfer the records to the new data processing system; or

        (II) purge the records to a printout which contains the same information as required on the audit trail printout as specified in paragraph (7)(B) of this subsection. The information on this printout shall be sorted and printed by drug name and list all distributions/returns chronologically.

    (ii) Other records. A pharmacy that changes or discontinues use of a data processing system must:

        (I) transfer the records to the new data processing system; or

        (II) purge the records to a printout which contains all of the information required on the original document.

    (iii) Maintenance of purged records. Information purged from a data processing system must be maintained by the pharmacy for two years from the date of initial entry into the data processing system.

(D) Loss of data. The pharmacist-in-charge shall report to the board in writing any significant loss of information from the data processing system within 10 days of discovery of the loss.

(7) Data processing system maintenance of records for the distribution and return of all controlled substances to the pharmacy.

(A) Each time a controlled substance is distributed from or returned to the pharmacy, a record of such distribution or return shall be entered into the data processing system.

(B) The data processing system shall have the capacity to produce a hard copy printout of an audit trail of drug distribution and return for any strength and dosage form of a drug (by either brand or generic name or both) during a specified time period. This printout shall contain the following information:

    (i) patient's name and room number or patient's facility identification number;

    (ii) prescribing or attending practitioner's name;

    (iii) name, strength, and dosage form of the drug product actually distributed;

    (iv) total quantity distributed from and returned to the pharmacy;

    (v) if not immediately retrievable via electronic image, the following shall also be included on the printout:

        (I) prescribing or attending practitioner's address; and

        (II) practitioner's DEA registration number, if the medication order is for a controlled substance.

(C) An audit trail printout for each strength and dosage form of the drugs distributed during the preceding month shall be produced at least monthly and shall be maintained in a separate file at the facility unless the pharmacy complies with subparagraph (D) of this paragraph. The information on this printout shall be sorted by drug name and list all distributions/returns for that drug chronologically.

(D) The pharmacy may elect not to produce the monthly audit trail printout if the data processing system has a workable (electronic) data retention system which can produce an audit trail of drug distribution and returns for the preceding two years. The audit trail required in this paragraph shall be supplied by the pharmacy within 72 hours, if requested by an authorized agent of the board, or other authorized local, state, or federal law enforcement or regulatory agencies.

(8) Failure to maintain records. Failure to provide records set out in this subsection, either on site or within 72 hours for whatever reason, constitutes prima facie evidence of failure to keep and maintain records.

(9) Data processing system downtime. In the event that a hospital pharmacy that uses a data processing system experiences system downtime, the pharmacy must have an auxiliary procedure which will ensure that all data is retained for on-line data entry as soon as the system is available for use again.

(10) Ongoing clinical pharmacy program records. If a pharmacy has an ongoing clinical pharmacy program and allows pharmacy technicians to verify the accuracy of work performed by other pharmacy technicians, the pharmacy must have a record of the pharmacy technicians and the duties performed.

(d) Distribution of controlled substances to another registrant. A pharmacy may distribute controlled substances to a practitioner, another pharmacy or other registrant, without being registered to distribute, under the following conditions:

(1) The registrant to whom the controlled substance is to be distributed is registered under the Controlled Substances Act to dispense that controlled substance; and

(2) The total number of dosage units of controlled substances distributed by a pharmacy may not exceed 5.0% of all controlled substances dispensed or distributed by the pharmacy during the 12-month period in which the pharmacy is registered; if at any time it does exceed 5.0%, the pharmacy is required to obtain an additional registration to distribute controlled substances.

(3) If the distribution is for a Schedule III, IV, or V controlled substance, a record shall be maintained which indicates:

(A) the actual date of distribution;

(B) the name, strength, and quantity of controlled substances distributed;

(C) the name, address, and DEA registration number of the distributing pharmacy; and

(D) the name, address, and DEA registration number of the pharmacy, practitioner, or other registrant to whom the controlled substances are distributed.

(4) If the distribution is for a Schedule I or II controlled substance, the following is applicable:

(A) The pharmacy, practitioner or other registrant who is receiving the controlled substances shall issue copy 1 and copy 2 of a DEA order form (DEA 222) to the distributing pharmacy; and

(B) The distributing pharmacy shall:

    (i) complete the area on the DEA order form (DEA 222) titled TO BE FILLED IN BY SUPPLIER;

    (ii) maintain copy 1 of the DEA order form (DEA 222) at the pharmacy for two years; and

    (iii) forward copy 2 of the DEA order form (DEA 222) to the divisional office of the Drug Enforcement Administration.

(e) Other records. Other records to be maintained by a pharmacy:

Phr. Rules

(1) a log of the initials or identification codes which identifies pharmacy personnel by name. The initials or identification code shall be unique to ensure that each person can be identified, i.e., identical initials or identification codes cannot be used. Such log shall be maintained at the pharmacy for at least seven years from the date of the transaction;

(2) copy 3 of DEA order forms (DEA 222) which have been properly dated, initialed, and filed, and all copies of each unaccepted or defective order form and any attached statements or other documents;

(3) a hard copy of the power of attorney to sign DEA 222 order forms (if applicable);

(4) suppliers' invoices of dangerous drugs and controlled substances; a pharmacist shall verify that the controlled drugs listed on the invoices were actually received by clearly recording his/her initials and the actual date of receipt of the controlled substances;

(5) suppliers' credit memos for controlled substances and dangerous drugs;

(6) a hard copy of inventories required by § 291.17 of this title (relating to Inventory Requirements) except that a perpetual inventory of controlled substances listed in Schedule II may be kept in a data processing system if the data processing system is capable of producing a hard copy of the perpetual inventory on-site;

(7) hard copy reports of surrender or destruction of controlled substances and/or dangerous drugs to an appropriate state or federal agency;

(8) a hard copy Schedule V nonprescription register book;

(9) records of distribution of controlled substances and/or dangerous drugs to other pharmacies, practitioners, or registrants; and

(10) a hard copy of any notification required by the Texas Pharmacy Act or these sections including, but not limited to, the following:

    (A) reports of theft or significant loss of controlled substances to DEA and the board;

    (B) notifications of a change in pharmacist-in-charge of a pharmacy; and

    (C) reports of a fire or other disaster which may affect the strength, purity, or labeling of drugs, medications, devices, or other materials used in diagnosis or treatment of injury, illness, and disease.

(f) Permission to maintain central records. Any pharmacy that uses a centralized recordkeeping system for invoices and financial data shall comply with the following procedures.

  (1) Controlled substance records. Invoices and financial data for controlled substances may be maintained at a central location provided the following conditions are met:

    (A) Prior to the initiation of central recordkeeping, the pharmacy submits written notification by registered or certified mail to the divisional director of DEA as required by Title 21, Code of Federal Regulations, § 1304.04(a), and submits a copy of this written notification to the board. Unless the registrant is informed by the divisional director of DEA that permission to keep central records is denied, the pharmacy may maintain central records commencing 14 days after receipt of notification by the divisional director;

    (B) The pharmacy maintains a copy of the notification required in subparagraph (A) of this paragraph; and

    (C) The records to be maintained at the central record location shall not include executed DEA order forms, prescription drug orders, or controlled substance inventories, which shall be maintained at the pharmacy.

  (2) Dangerous drug records. Invoices and financial data for dangerous drugs may be maintained at a central location.

  (3) Access to records. If the records are kept in any form requiring special equipment to render the records easily readable, the pharmacy shall provide access to such equipment with the records.

  (4) Delivery of records. The pharmacy agrees to deliver all or any part of such records to the pharmacy location within two business days of written request of a board agent or any other authorized official.

Source: The provisions of this § 291.75 adopted to be effective April 23, 1982, 7 TEXREG1469; amended to be effective August 30, 1984, 9 TEXREG4450; amended to be effective October 22, 1985, 10 TEXREG3896; amended to be effective December 18, 1985, 10 TEXREG4694; amended to be effective September 14, 1988, 13 TEXREG4318; amended to be effective September 5, 1990, 15 TEXREG4810; amended to be effective September 27, 1991, 16 TEXREG5071; amended to be effective September 30, 1993, 18 TexReg 6460; amended to be effective March 16, 1995, 20 TexReg 1543; amended to be effective June 4, 2000, 25 TexReg 4816; amended to be effective August 31, 2000, 25 TexReg 8406; amended to be effective June 6, 2004, 29 TexReg 5376; amended to be effective December 3, 2006, 31 TexReg 9610; amended to be effective September 18, 2007, 32 TexReg 6333; amended to be effective September 20, 2009, 34 TexReg 6323; amended to be effective March 11, 2010, 35 TexReg 2005; amended to be effective May 30, 2010, 35 TexReg 4177; amended to be effective June 7, 2018, 43 TexReg 3588; amended to be effective March 12, 2019, 44 TexReg 1331; amended to be effective June 20, 2019, 44 TexReg 2947

§291.76 Class C Pharmacies Located in a Freestanding Ambulatory Surgical Center

(a) Purpose. The purpose of this section is to provide standards in the conduct, practice activities, and operation of a pharmacy located in a freestanding ambulatory surgical center that is licensed by the Texas Department of State Health Services. Class C pharmacies located in a freestanding ambulatory surgical center shall comply with this section, in lieu of §§ 291.71 - 291.75 of this title (relating to Purpose; Definitions; Personnel; Operational Standards; and Records).

(b) Definitions. The following words and terms, when used in these sections, shall have the following meanings, unless the context clearly indicates otherwise.

  (1) Act—The Texas Pharmacy Act, Occupations Code, Subtitle J, as amended.

  (2) Administer—The direct application of a prescription drug by injection, inhalation, ingestion, or any other means to the body of a patient by:

    (A) a practitioner, an authorized agent under his supervision, or other person authorized by law; or

    (B) the patient at the direction of a practitioner.

  (3) Ambulatory surgical center (ASC) —A freestanding facility that is licensed by the Texas Department of State Health Services that primarily provides surgical services to patients who do not require overnight hospitalization or extensive recovery, convalescent time or observation. The planned total length of stay for an ASC patient shall not exceed 23 hours. Patient stays of greater than 23 hours shall be the result of an unanticipated medical condition and shall occur infrequently. The 23-hour period begins with the induction of anesthesia.

  (4) Automated medication supply system—A mechanical system that performs operations or activities relative to the storage and distribution of medications for administration and which collects, controls, and maintains all transaction information.

  (5) Board—The Texas State Board of Pharmacy.

  (6) Consultant pharmacist—A pharmacist retained by a facility on a routine basis to consult with the ASC in areas that pertain to the practice of pharmacy.

Phr. Rules

(7) Controlled substance—A drug, immediate precursor, or other substance listed in Schedules I - V or Penalty Groups 1 - 4 of the Texas Controlled Substances Act, as amended, or a drug immediate precursor, or other substance included in Schedules I - V of the Federal Comprehensive Drug Abuse Prevention and Control Act of 1970, as amended (Public Law 91-513).

(8) Dispense—Preparing, packaging, compounding, or labeling for delivery a prescription drug or device in the course of professional practice to an ultimate user or his agent by or pursuant to the lawful order of a practitioner.

(9) Distribute—The delivery of a prescription drug or device other than by administering or dispensing.

(10) Downtime—Period of time during which a data processing system is not operable.

(11) Electronic signature—A unique security code or other identifier which specifically identifies the person entering information into a data processing system. A facility which utilizes electronic signatures must:

    (A) maintain a permanent list of the unique security codes assigned to persons authorized to use the data processing system; and

    (B) have an ongoing security program which is capable of identifying misuse and/or unauthorized use of electronic signatures.

(12) Floor stock—Prescription drugs or devices not labeled for a specific patient and maintained at a nursing station or other ASC department (excluding the pharmacy) for the purpose of administration to a patient of the ASC.

(13) Formulary—List of drugs approved for use in the ASC by an appropriate committee of the ambulatory surgical center.

(14) Hard copy—A physical document that is readable without the use of a special device (i.e., data processing system, computer, etc.).

(15) Investigational new drug—New drug intended for investigational use by experts qualified to evaluate the safety and effectiveness of the drug as authorized by the federal Food and Drug Administration.

(16) Medication order—An order from a practitioner or his authorized agent for administration of a drug or device.

(17) Pharmacist-in-charge—Pharmacist designated on a pharmacy license as the pharmacist who has the authority or responsibility for a pharmacy's compliance with laws and rules pertaining to the practice of pharmacy.

(18) Pharmacy—Area or areas in a facility, separate from patient care areas, where drugs are stored, bulk compounded, delivered, compounded, dispensed, and/or distributed to other areas or departments of the ASC, or dispensed to an ultimate user or his or her agent.

(19) Prescription drug—

    (A) A substance for which federal or state law requires a prescription before it may be legally dispensed to the public;

    (B) A drug or device that under federal law is required, prior to being dispensed or delivered, to be labeled with either of the following statements:

        (i) Caution: federal law prohibits dispensing without prescription or "Rx only" or another legend that complies with federal law; or

        (ii) Caution: federal law restricts this drug to use by or on order of a licensed veterinarian; or

    (C) A drug or device that is required by any applicable federal or state law or regulation to be dispensed on prescription only or is restricted to use by a practitioner only.

(20) Prescription drug order—

    (A) An order from a practitioner or his authorized agent to a pharmacist for a drug or device to be dispensed; or

    (B) An order pursuant to Subtitle B, Chapter 157, Occupations Code.

(21) Full-time pharmacist—A pharmacist who works in a pharmacy from 30 to 40 hours per week or if the pharmacy is open less than 60 hours per week, one-half of the time the pharmacy is open.

(22) Part-time pharmacist—A pharmacist who works less than full-time.

(23) Pharmacy technician—An individual who is registered with the board as a pharmacy technician and whose responsibility in a pharmacy is to provide technical services that do not require professional judgment regarding preparing and distributing drugs and who works under the direct supervision of and is responsible to a pharmacist.

(24) Pharmacy technician trainee—An individual who is registered with the board as a pharmacy technician trainee and is authorized to participate in a pharmacy's technician training program.

(25) Texas Controlled Substances Act—The Texas Controlled Substances Act, Health and Safety Code, Chapter 481, as amended.

(c) Personnel.

  (1) Pharmacist-in-charge.

    (A) General. Each ambulatory surgical center shall have one pharmacist-in-charge who is employed or under contract, at least on a consulting or part-time basis, but may be employed on a full-time basis.

    (B) Responsibilities. The pharmacist-in-charge shall have the responsibility for, at a minimum, the following:

        (i) establishing specifications for procurement and storage of all materials, including drugs, chemicals, and biologicals;

        (ii) participating in the development of a formulary for the ASC, subject to approval of the appropriate committee of the ASC;

        (iii) distributing drugs to be administered to patients pursuant to the practitioner's medication order;

        (iv) filling and labeling all containers from which drugs are to be distributed or dispensed;

        (v) maintaining and making available a sufficient inventory of antidotes and other emergency drugs, both in the pharmacy and patient care areas, as well as current antidote information, telephone numbers of regional poison control center and other emergency assistance organizations, and such other materials and information as may be deemed necessary by the appropriate committee of the ASC;

        (vi) maintaining records of all transactions of the ASC pharmacy as may be required by applicable state and federal law, and as may be necessary to maintain accurate control over and accountability for all pharmaceutical materials;

        (vii) participating in those aspects of the ASC's patient care evaluation program which relate to pharmaceutical material utilization and effectiveness;

        (viii) participating in teaching and/or research programs in the ASC;

        (ix) implementing the policies and decisions of the appropriate committee(s) relating to pharmaceutical services of the ASC;

        (x) providing effective and efficient messenger and delivery service to connect the ASC pharmacy with appropriate areas of the ASC on a regular basis throughout the normal workday of the ASC;

Phr. Rules

        (xi) labeling, storing, and distributing investigational new drugs, including maintaining information in the pharmacy and nursing station where such drugs are being administered, concerning the dosage form, route of administration, strength, actions, uses, side effects, adverse effects, interactions, and symptoms of toxicity of investigational new drugs;

        (xii) meeting all inspection and other requirements of the Texas Pharmacy Act and this subsection;

        (xiii) maintaining records in a data processing system such that the data processing system is in compliance with the requirements for a Class C (institutional) pharmacy located in a freestanding ASC; and

        (xiv) ensuring that a pharmacist visits the ASC at least once each calendar week that the facility is open.

  (2) Consultant pharmacist.

    (A) The consultant pharmacist may be the pharmacist-in-charge.

    (B) A written contract shall exist between the ASC and any consultant pharmacist, and a copy of the written contract shall be made available to the board upon request.

  (3) Pharmacists

    (A) General.

      (i) The pharmacist-in-charge shall be assisted by a sufficient number of additional licensed pharmacists as may be required to operate the ASC pharmacy competently, safely, and adequately to meet the needs of the patients of the facility.

      (ii) All pharmacists shall assist the pharmacist-in-charge in meeting the responsibilities as outlined in paragraph (1)(B) of this subsection and in ordering, administering, and accounting for pharmaceutical materials.

      (iii) All pharmacists shall be responsible for any delegated act performed by pharmacy technicians or pharmacy technician trainees under his or her supervision.

      (iv) All pharmacists while on duty shall be responsible for complying with all state and federal laws or rules governing the practice of pharmacy.

    (B) Duties. Duties of the pharmacist-in-charge and all other pharmacists shall include, but need not be limited to, the following:

      (i) receiving and interpreting prescription drug orders and oral medication orders and reducing these orders to writing either manually or electronically;

      (ii) selecting prescription drugs and/or devices and/or suppliers; and

      (iii) interpreting patient profiles.

    (C) Special requirements for compounding non-sterile preparations. All pharmacists engaged in compounding non-sterile preparations shall meet the training requirements specified in § 291.131 of this title (relating to Pharmacies Compounding Non-Sterile Preparations).

  (4) Pharmacy technicians and pharmacy technician trainees.

    (A) General. All pharmacy technicians and pharmacy technician trainees shall meet the training requirements specified in § 297.6 of this title (relating to Pharmacy Technician and Pharmacy Technician Trainee Training).

    (B) Duties. Pharmacy technicians and pharmacy technician trainees may not perform any of the duties listed in paragraph (3)(B) of this subsection. Duties may include, but need not be limited to, the following functions, under the direct supervision of a pharmacist:

      (i) prepacking and labeling unit and multiple dose packages, provided a pharmacist supervises and conducts a final check and affixes his or her name, initials, or electronic signature to the appropriate quality control records prior to distribution;

      (ii) preparing, packaging, compounding, or labeling prescription drugs pursuant to medication orders, provided a pharmacist supervises and checks the preparation;

      (iii) compounding non-sterile preparations pursuant to medication orders provided the pharmacy technicians or pharmacy technician trainees have completed the training specified in § 291.131 of this title;

      (iv) bulk compounding, provided a pharmacist supervises and conducts in-process and final checks and affixes his or her name, initials, or electronic signature to the appropriate quality control records prior to distribution;

      (v) distributing routine orders for stock supplies to patient care areas;

      (vi) entering medication order and drug distribution information into a data processing system, provided judgmental decisions are not required and a pharmacist checks the accuracy of the information entered into the system prior to releasing the order or in compliance with the absence of pharmacist requirements contained in subsection (d)(6)(D) and (E) of this section;

      (vii) maintaining inventories of drug supplies;

      (viii) maintaining pharmacy records; and

      (ix) loading drugs into an automated medication supply system. For the purpose of this clause, direct supervision may be accomplished by physically present supervision or electronic monitoring by a pharmacist.

    (C) Procedures.

      (i) Pharmacy technicians and pharmacy technician trainees shall handle medication orders in accordance with standard written procedures and guidelines.

      (ii) Pharmacy technicians and pharmacy technician trainees shall handle prescription drug orders in the same manner as pharmacy technicians or pharmacy technician trainees working in a Class A pharmacy.

    (D) Special requirements for compounding non-sterile preparations. All pharmacy technicians and pharmacy technician trainees engaged in compounding non-sterile preparations shall meet the training requirements specified in § 291.131 of this title.

  (5) Owner. The owner of an ASC pharmacy shall have responsibility for all administrative and operational functions of the pharmacy. The pharmacist-in-charge may advise the owner on administrative and operational concerns. The owner shall have responsibility for, at a minimum, the following, and if the owner is not a Texas licensed pharmacist, the owner shall consult with the pharmacist-in-charge or another Texas licensed pharmacist:

    (A) establishing policies for procurement of prescription drugs and devices and other products dispensed from the ASC pharmacy;

    (B) establishing and maintaining effective controls against the theft or diversion of prescription drugs;

    (C) if the pharmacy uses an automated medication supply system, reviewing and approving all policies and procedures for system operation, safety, security, accuracy and access, patient confidentiality, prevention of unauthorized access, and malfunction;

    (D) providing the pharmacy with the necessary equipment and resources commensurate with its level and type of practice; and

    (E) establishing policies and procedures regarding maintenance, storage, and retrieval of records in a data processing system such that the system is in compliance with state and federal requirements.

  (6) Identification of pharmacy personnel. All pharmacy personnel shall be identified as follows:

    (A) Pharmacy technicians. All pharmacy technicians shall wear an identification tag or badge that bears the person's name and identifies him or her as a pharmacy technician.

    (B) Pharmacy technician trainees. All pharmacy technician trainees shall wear an identification tag or badge that bears the person's name and identifies him or her as a pharmacy technician trainee.

    (C) Pharmacist interns. All pharmacist interns shall wear an identification tag or badge that bears the person's name and identifies him or her as a pharmacist intern.

    (D) Pharmacists. All pharmacists shall wear an identification tag or badge that bears the person's name and identifies him or her as a pharmacist.

(d) Operational standards.

  (1) Licensing requirements.

    (A) An ASC pharmacy shall register annually or biennially with the board on a pharmacy license application provided by the board, following the procedures specified in § 291.1 of this title (relating to Pharmacy License Application).

    (B) An ASC pharmacy which changes ownership shall notify the board within 10 days of the change of ownership and apply for a new and separate license as specified in § 291.3 of this title (relating to Required Notifications).

    (C) An ASC pharmacy which changes location and/or name shall notify the board of the change within 10 days and file for an amended license as specified in § 291.3 of this title.

    (D) An ASC pharmacy owned by a partnership or corporation which changes managing officers shall notify the board in writing of the names of the new managing officers within 10 days of the change, following the procedures in § 291.3 of this title.

    (E) An ASC pharmacy shall notify the board in writing within 10 days of closing, following the procedures in § 291.5 of this title (relating to Closing a Pharmacy).

    (F) A fee as specified in § 291.6 of this title (relating to Pharmacy License Fees) will be charged for issuance and renewal of a license and the issuance of an amended license.

    (G) A separate license is required for each principal place of business and only one pharmacy license may be issued to a specific location.

    (H) An ASC pharmacy, licensed under the Act, § 560.051(a)(3), concerning institutional pharmacy (Class C), which also operates another type of pharmacy which would otherwise be required to be licensed under the Act, § 560.051(a)(1), concerning community pharmacy (Class A), or the Act, § 560.051(a)(2), concerning nuclear pharmacy (Class B), is not required to secure a license for the other type of pharmacy; provided, however, such license is required to comply with the provisions of § 291.31 of this title (relating to Definitions), § 291.32 of this title (relating to Personnel), § 291.33 of this title (relating to Operational Standards), § 291.34 of this title (relating to Records), and § 291.35 of this title (relating to Official Prescription Requirements), or § 291.51 of this title (relating to Purpose), § 291.52 of this title (relating to Definitions), § 291.53 of this title (relating to Personnel), § 291.54 of this title (relating to Operational Standards), and § 291.55 of this title (relating to Records), contained in Nuclear Pharmacy (Class B), to the extent such sections are applicable to the operation of the pharmacy.

    (I) An ASC pharmacy engaged in the compounding of non-sterile preparations shall comply with the provisions of § 291.131 of this title.

    (J) ASC pharmacy personnel shall not compound sterile preparations unless the pharmacy has applied for and obtained a Class C-S pharmacy license.

    (K) An ASC pharmacy engaged in the provision of remote pharmacy services, including storage and dispensing of prescription drugs, shall comply with the provisions of § 291.121 of this title (relating to Remote Pharmacy Services).

    (L) An ASC pharmacy engaged in centralized prescription dispensing and/or prescription drug or medication order processing shall comply with the provisions of § 291.123 of this title (relating to Central Prescription Drug or Medication Order Processing) and/or § 291.125 of this title (relating to Centralized Prescription Dispensing).

  (2) Environment.

    (A) General requirements.

      (i) Each ambulatory surgical center shall have a designated work area separate from patient areas, and which shall have space adequate for the size and scope of pharmaceutical services and shall have adequate space and security for the storage of drugs.

      (ii) The ASC pharmacy shall be arranged in an orderly fashion and shall be kept clean. All required equipment shall be clean and in good operating condition.

    (B) Special requirements.

      (i) The ASC pharmacy shall have locked storage for Schedule II controlled substances and other controlled drugs requiring additional security.

      (ii) The ASC pharmacy shall have a designated area for the storage of poisons and externals separate from drug storage areas.

    (C) Security.

      (i) The pharmacy and storage areas for prescription drugs and/or devices shall be enclosed and capable of being locked by key, combination, or other mechanical or electronic means, so as to prohibit access by unauthorized individuals. Only individuals authorized by the pharmacist-in-charge may enter the pharmacy or have access to storage areas for prescription drugs and/or devices.

Phr. Rules

(ii) The pharmacist-in-charge shall consult with ASC personnel with respect to security of the drug storage areas, including provisions for adequate safeguards against theft or diversion of dangerous drugs and controlled substances, and to security of records for such drugs.

(iii) The pharmacy shall have locked storage for Schedule II controlled substances and other drugs requiring additional security.

(3) Equipment and supplies. Ambulatory surgical centers supplying drugs for postoperative use shall have the following equipment and supplies:

(A) data processing system including a printer or comparable equipment;

(B) adequate supply of child-resistant, moisture-proof, and light-proof containers; and

(C) adequate supply of prescription labels and other applicable identification labels.

(4) Library. A reference library shall be maintained that includes the following in hard copy or electronic format and that pharmacy personnel shall be capable of accessing at all times:

(A) current copies of the following:

(i) Texas Pharmacy Act and rules;

(ii) Texas Dangerous Drug Act and rules;

(iii) Texas Controlled Substances Act and rules;

(iv) Federal Controlled Substances Act and rules or official publication describing the requirements of the Federal Controlled Substances Act and rules;

(B) at least one current or updated general drug information reference which is required to contain drug interaction information including information needed to determine severity or significance of the interaction and appropriate recommendations or actions to be taken; and

(C) basic antidote information and the telephone number of the nearest regional poison control center.

(5) Drugs.

(A) Procurement, preparation, and storage.

(i) The pharmacist-in-charge shall have the responsibility for the procurement and storage of drugs, but may receive input from other appropriate staff of the facility, relative to such responsibility.

(ii) The pharmacist-in-charge shall have the responsibility for determining specifications of all drugs procured by the facility.

(iii) ASC pharmacies may not sell, purchase, trade, or possess prescription drug samples, unless the pharmacy meets the requirements as specified in § 291.16 of this title (relating to Samples).

(iv) All drugs shall be stored at the proper temperatures, as defined in the USP/NF and in § 291.15 of this title (relating to Storage of Drugs).

(v) Any drug bearing an expiration date may not be dispensed or distributed beyond the expiration date of the drug.

(vi) Outdated drugs shall be removed from dispensing stock and shall be quarantined together until such drugs are disposed of.

(B) Formulary.

(i) A formulary may be developed by an appropriate committee of the ASC.

(ii) The pharmacist-in-charge or consultant pharmacist shall be a full voting member of any committee which involves pharmaceutical services.

(iii) A practitioner may grant approval for pharmacists at the ASC to interchange, in accordance with the facility's formulary, for the drugs on the practitioner's medication orders provided:

(I) a formulary has been developed;

(II) the formulary has been approved by the medical staff of the ASC;

(III) there is a reasonable method for the practitioner to override any interchange; and

(IV) the practitioner authorizes a pharmacist in the ASC to interchange on his/her medication orders in accordance with the facility's formulary through his/her written agreement to abide by the policies and procedures of the medical staff and facility.

(C) Prepackaging and loading drugs into automated medication supply system.

(i) Prepackaging of drugs.

(I) Drugs may be prepackaged in quantities suitable for distribution to other Class C pharmacies under common ownership or for internal distribution only by a pharmacist or by pharmacy technicians or pharmacy technician trainees under the direction and direct supervision of a pharmacist.

(II) The label of a prepackaged unit shall indicate:

(-a-) brand name and strength of the drug; or if no brand name, then the generic name, strength, and name of the manufacturer or distributor;

(-b-) facility's lot number;

(-c-) expiration date;

(-d-) quantity of the drug, if quantity is greater than one; and

(-e-) if the drug is distributed to another Class C pharmacy, name of the facility responsible for prepackaging the drug.

(III) Records of prepackaging shall be maintained to show:

(-a-) the name of the drug, strength, and dosage form;

(-b-) facility's lot number;

(-c-) manufacturer or distributor;

(-d-) manufacturer's lot number;

(-e-) expiration date;

(-f-) quantity per prepackaged unit;

(-g-) number of prepackaged units;

(-h-) date packaged;
(-i-) name, initials, or electronic signature of the prepacker;
(-j-) signature or electronic signature of the responsible pharmacist; and
(-k-) if the drug is distributed to another Class C pharmacy, name of the facility receiving the prepackaged drug.
  (IV) Stock packages, repackaged units, and control records shall be quarantined together until checked/released by the pharmacist.
  (ii) Loading bulk unit of use drugs into automated medication supply systems. Automated medication supply systems may be loaded with bulk unit of use drugs only by a pharmacist or by pharmacy technicians or pharmacy technician trainees under the direction and direct supervision of a pharmacist. For the purpose of this clause, direct supervision may be accomplished by physically present supervision or electronic monitoring by a pharmacist. In order for the pharmacist to electronically monitor, the medication supply system must allow for bar code scanning to verify the loading of drugs, and a record of the loading must be maintained by the system and accessible for electronic review by the pharmacist.
(6) Medication orders.
  (A) Drugs may be administered to patients in ASCs only on the order of a practitioner. No change in the order for drugs may be made without the approval of a practitioner except as authorized by the practitioner in compliance with paragraph (5)(B) of this subsection.
  (B) Drugs may be distributed only pursuant to the practitioner's medication order.
  (C) ASC pharmacies shall be exempt from the labeling provisions and patient notification requirements of § 562.006 and § 562.009 of the Act, as respects drugs distributed pursuant to medication orders.
  (D) In ASCs with a full-time pharmacist, if a practitioner orders a drug for administration to a bona fide patient of the facility when the pharmacy is closed, the following is applicable.
    (i) Prescription drugs and devices only in sufficient quantities for immediate therapeutic needs of a patient may be removed from the ASC pharmacy.
    (ii) Only a designated licensed nurse or practitioner may remove such drugs and devices.
    (iii) A record shall be made at the time of withdrawal by the authorized person removing the drugs and devices. The record shall contain the following information:
      (I) name of the patient;
      (II) name of device or drug, strength, and dosage form;
      (III) dose prescribed;
      (IV) quantity taken;
      (V) time and date; and
      (VI) signature or electronic signature of person making withdrawal.
    (iv) The medication order in the patient's chart may substitute for such record, provided the medication order meets all the requirements of clause (iii) of this subparagraph.
    (v) The pharmacist shall verify the withdrawal as soon as practical, but in no event more than 72 hours from the time of such withdrawal.
  (E) In ASCs with a part-time or consultant pharmacist, if a practitioner orders a drug for administration to a bona fide patient of the ASC when the pharmacist is not on duty, or when the pharmacy is closed, the following is applicable:
    (i) Prescription drugs and devices only in sufficient quantities for therapeutic needs may be removed from the ASC pharmacy;
    (ii) Only a designated licensed nurse or practitioner may remove such drugs and devices; and
    (iii) The pharmacist shall conduct an audit of the patient's medical record according to the schedule set out in the policy and procedures at a reasonable interval, but such interval must occur at least once in every calendar week that the pharmacy is open.
(7) Floor stock. In facilities using a floor stock method of drug distribution, the following is applicable for removing drugs or devices in the absence of a pharmacist.
  (A) Prescription drugs and devices may be removed from the pharmacy only in the original manufacturer's container or prepackaged container.
  (B) Only a designated licensed nurse or practitioner may remove such drugs and devices.
  (C) A record shall be made at the time of withdrawal by the authorized person removing the drug or device; the record shall contain the following information:
    (i) name of the drug, strength, and dosage form;
    (ii) quantity removed;
    (iii) location of floor stock;
    (iv) date and time; and
    (v) signature or electronic signature of person making the withdrawal.
  (D) A pharmacist shall verify the withdrawal according to the following schedule.
    (i) In facilities with a full-time pharmacist, the withdrawal shall be verified as soon as practical, but in no event more than 72 hours from the time of such withdrawal.
    (ii) In facilities with a part-time or consultant pharmacist, the withdrawal shall be verified after a reasonable interval, but such interval must occur at least once in every calendar week that the pharmacy is open.
    (iii) The medication order in the patient's chart may substitute for the record required in subparagraph (C) of this paragraph, provided the medication order meets all the requirements of subparagraph (C) of this paragraph.
(8) Policies and procedures. Written policies and procedures for a drug distribution system, appropriate for the ambulatory surgical center, shall be developed and implemented by the pharmacist-in-charge with the advice of the appropriate committee. The written policies and procedures for the drug distribution system shall include, but not be limited to, procedures regarding the following:
  (A) controlled substances;

     (B) investigational drugs;

     (C) prepackaging and manufacturing;

     (D) medication errors;

     (E) orders of physician or other practitioner;

     (F) floor stocks;

     (G) adverse drug reactions;

     (H) drugs brought into the facility by the patient;

     (I) self-administration;

     (J) emergency drug tray;

     (K) formulary, if applicable;

     (L) drug storage areas;

     (M) drug samples;

     (N) drug product defect reports;

     (O) drug recalls;

     (P) outdated drugs;

     (Q) preparation and distribution of IV admixtures;

     (R) procedures for supplying drugs for postoperative use, if applicable;

     (S) use of automated medication supply systems;

     (T) use of data processing systems; and

     (U) drug regimen review.

(9) Drugs supplied for postoperative use. Drugs supplied to patients for postoperative use shall be supplied according to the following procedures.

     (A) Drugs may only be supplied to patients who have been admitted to the ASC.

     (B) Drugs may only be supplied in accordance with the system of control and accountability established for drugs supplied from the ambulatory surgical center; such system shall be developed and supervised by the pharmacist-in-charge or staff pharmacist designated by the pharmacist-in-charge.

     (C) Only drugs listed on the approved postoperative drug list may be supplied; such list shall be developed by the pharmacist-in-charge and the medical staff and shall consist of drugs of the nature and type to meet the immediate postoperative needs of the ambulatory surgical center patient.

     (D) Drugs may only be supplied in prepackaged quantities not to exceed a 72-hour supply in suitable containers and appropriately prelabeled (including name, address, and phone number of the facility, and necessary auxiliary labels) by the pharmacy provided, however, that topicals and ophthalmics in original manufacturer's containers may be supplied in a quantity exceeding a 72-hour supply.

     (E) At the time of delivery of the drug, the practitioner shall complete the label, such that the prescription container bears a label with at least the following information:

         (i) date supplied;

         (ii) name of practitioner;

         (iii) name of patient;

         (iv) directions for use;

         (v) brand name and strength of the drug; or if no brand name, then the generic name of the drug dispensed, strength, and the name of the manufacturer or distributor of the drug; and

         (vi) unique identification number.

     (F) After the drug has been labeled, the practitioner or a licensed nurse under the supervision of the practitioner shall give the appropriately labeled, prepackaged medication to the patient.

     (G) A perpetual record of drugs which are supplied from the ASC shall be maintained which includes:

         (i) name, address, and phone number of the facility;

         (ii) date supplied;

         (iii) name of practitioner;

         (iv) name of patient;

         (v) directions for use;

         (vi) brand name and strength of the drug; or if no brand name, then the generic name of the drug dispensed, strength, and the name of the manufacturer or distributor of the drug; and

         (vii) unique identification number.

     (H) The pharmacist-in-charge, or a pharmacist designated by the pharmacist-in-charge, shall review the records at least once in every calendar week that the pharmacy is open.

(10) Drug regimen review.

     (A) A pharmacist shall evaluate medication orders and patient medication records for:

         (i) known allergies;

         (ii) rational therapy--contraindications;

         (iii) reasonable dose and route of administration;

         (iv) reasonable directions for use;

         (v) duplication of therapy;

         (vi) drug-drug interactions;

         (vii) drug-food interactions;

         (viii) drug-disease interactions;

         (ix) adverse drug reactions;

         (x) proper utilization, including overutilization or underutilization; and

(xi) clinical laboratory or clinical monitoring methods to monitor and evaluate drug effectiveness, side effects, toxicity, or adverse effects, and appropriateness to continued use of the drug in its current regimen.

    (B) A retrospective, random drug regimen review as specified in the pharmacy's policies and procedures shall be conducted on a periodic basis to verify proper usage of drugs not to exceed 31 days between such reviews.

    (C) Any questions regarding the order must be resolved with the prescriber and a written notation of these discussions made and maintained.

(e) Records.

  (1) Maintenance of records.

    (A) Every inventory or other record required to be kept under the provisions of this section (relating to Class C Pharmacies Located in a Freestanding Ambulatory Surgical Center) shall be:

      (i) kept by the pharmacy and be available, for at least two years from the date of such inventory or record, for inspecting and copying by the board or its representative, and other authorized local, state, or federal law enforcement agencies; and

      (ii) supplied by the pharmacy within 72 hours, if requested by an authorized agent of the board. If the pharmacy maintains the records in an electronic format, the requested records must be provided in a mutually agreeable electronic format if specifically requested by the board or its representative. Failure to provide the records set out in this subsection, either on site or within 72 hours, constitutes prima facie evidence of failure to keep and maintain records in violation of the Act.

    (B) Records of controlled substances listed in Schedule II shall be maintained separately and readily retrievable from all other records of the pharmacy.

    (C) Records of controlled substances listed in Schedules III - V shall be maintained separately or readily retrievable from all other records of the pharmacy. For purposes of this subparagraph, "readily retrievable" means that the controlled substances shall be asterisked, redlined, or in some other manner readily identifiable apart from all other items appearing on the record.

    (D) Records, except when specifically required to be maintained in original or hard copy form, may be maintained in an alternative data retention system, such as a data processing or direct imaging system provided:

      (i) the records in the alternative data retention system contain all of the information required on the manual record; and

      (ii) the alternative data retention system is capable of producing a hard copy of the record upon the request of the board, its representative, or other authorized local, state, or federal law enforcement or regulatory agencies.

    (E) Controlled substance records shall be maintained in a manner to establish receipt and distribution of all controlled substances.

    (F) An ASC pharmacy shall maintain a perpetual inventory of controlled substances listed in Schedules II - V which shall be verified for completeness and reconciled at least once in every calendar week that the pharmacy is open.

    (G) Distribution records for controlled substances, listed in Schedules II - V, shall include the following information:

      (i) patient's name;

      (ii) practitioner's name who ordered the drug;

      (iii) name of drug, dosage form, and strength;

      (iv) time and date of administration to patient and quantity administered;

      (v) signature or electronic signature of individual administering the controlled substance;

      (vi) returns to the pharmacy; and

      (vii) waste (waste is required to be witnessed and cosigned, manually or electronically, by another individual).

    (H) The record required by subparagraph (G) of this paragraph shall be maintained separately from patient records.

    (I) A pharmacist shall conduct an audit by randomly comparing the distribution records required by subparagraph (G) with the medication orders in the patient record on a periodic basis to verify proper administration of drugs not to exceed 30 days between such reviews.

  (2) Patient records.

    (A) Each medication order or set of orders issued together shall bear the following information:

      (i) patient name;

      (ii) drug name, strength, and dosage form;

      (iii) directions for use;

      (iv) date; and

      (v) signature or electronic signature of the practitioner or that of his or her authorized agent, defined as an employee or consultant/full or part-time pharmacist of the ASC.

    (B) Medication orders shall be maintained with the medication administration record in the medical records of the patient.

  (3) General requirements for records maintained in a data processing system.

    (A) If an ASC pharmacy's data processing system is not in compliance with the board's requirements, the pharmacy must maintain a manual recordkeeping system.

    (B) The facility shall maintain a backup copy of information stored in the data processing system using disk, tape, or other electronic backup system and update this backup copy on a regular basis to assure that data is not lost due to system failure.

    (C) A pharmacy that changes or discontinues use of a data processing system must:

      (i) transfer the records to the new data processing system; or

      (ii) purge the records to a printout which contains:

        (I) all of the information required on the original document; or

        (II) for records of distribution and return for all controlled substances, the same information as required on the audit trail printout as specified in subparagraph (F) of this paragraph. The information on the printout shall be sorted and printed by drug name and list all distributions and returns chronologically.

    (D) Information purged from a data processing system must be maintained by the pharmacy for two years from the date of initial entry into the data processing system.

(E) The pharmacist-in-charge shall report to the board in writing any significant loss of information from the data processing system within 10 days of discovery of the loss.

(F) The data processing system shall have the capacity to produce a hard copy printout of an audit trail of drug distribution and return for any strength and dosage form of a drug (by either brand or generic name or both) during a specified time period. This printout shall contain the following information:
  (i) patient's name and room number or patient's facility identification number;
  (ii) prescribing or attending practitioner's name;
  (iii) name, strength, and dosage form of the drug product actually distributed;
  (iv) total quantity distributed from and returned to the pharmacy;
  (v) if not immediately retrievable via electronic image, the following shall also be included on the printout:
    (I) prescribing or attending practitioner's address; and
    (II) practitioner's DEA registration number, if the medication order is for a controlled substance.

(G) An audit trail printout for each strength and dosage form of the drugs distributed during the preceding month shall be produced at least monthly and shall be maintained in a separate file at the facility. The information on this printout shall be sorted by drug name and list all distributions/returns for that drug chronologically.

(H) The pharmacy may elect not to produce the monthly audit trail printout if the data processing system has a workable (electronic) data retention system which can produce an audit trail of drug distribution and returns for the preceding two years. The audit trail required in this clause shall be supplied by the pharmacy within 72 hours, if requested by an authorized agent of the Texas State Board of Pharmacy, or other authorized local, state, or federal law enforcement or regulatory agencies.

(I) In the event that an ASC pharmacy which uses a data processing system experiences system downtime, the pharmacy must have an auxiliary procedure which will ensure that all data is retained for online data entry as soon as the system is available for use again.

(4) Distribution of controlled substances to another registrant. A pharmacy may distribute controlled substances to a practitioner, another pharmacy, or other registrant, without being registered to distribute, under the following conditions.

(A) The registrant to whom the controlled substance is to be distributed is registered under the Controlled Substances Act to possess that controlled substance.

(B) The total number of dosage units of controlled substances distributed by a pharmacy may not exceed 5.0% of all controlled substances dispensed by the pharmacy during the 12-month period in which the pharmacy is registered; if at any time it does exceed 5.0%, the pharmacy is required to obtain an additional registration to distribute controlled substances.

(C) If the distribution is for a Schedule III, IV, or V controlled substance, a record shall be maintained which indicates:
  (i) the actual date of distribution;
  (ii) the name, strength, and quantity of controlled substances distributed;
  (iii) the name, address, and DEA registration number of the distributing pharmacy; and
  (iv) the name, address, and DEA registration number of the pharmacy, practitioner, or other registrant to whom the controlled substances are distributed.

(D) If the distribution is for a Schedule II controlled substance, the following is applicable.
  (i) The pharmacy, practitioner, or other registrant who is receiving the controlled substances shall issue Copy 1 and Copy 2 of a DEA order form (DEA 222) to the distributing pharmacy.
  (ii) The distributing pharmacy shall:
    (I) complete the area on the DEA order form (DEA 222) titled "To Be Filled in by Supplier";
    (II) maintain Copy 1 of the DEA order form (DEA 222) at the pharmacy for two years; and
    (III) forward Copy 2 of the DEA order form (DEA 222) to the divisional office of DEA.

(5) Other records. Other records to be maintained by the pharmacy include:
(A) a log of the initials or identification codes which identifies each pharmacist by name. The initials or identification code shall be unique to ensure that each pharmacist can be identified, i.e., identical initials or identification codes cannot be used. Such log shall be maintained at the pharmacy for at least seven years from the date of the transaction;
(B) Copy 3 of DEA order forms (DEA 222), which have been properly dated, initialed, and filed, and all copies of each unaccepted or defective order form and any attached statements or other documents and/or for each order filled using the DEA Controlled Substance Ordering System (CSOS), the original signed order and all linked records for that order;
(C) a copy of the power of attorney to sign DEA 222 order forms (if applicable);
(D) suppliers' invoices of dangerous drugs and controlled substances dated and initialed or signed by the person receiving the drugs; a pharmacist shall verify that the controlled drugs listed on the invoices were added to the pharmacy's perpetual inventory by clearly recording his/her initials and the date of review of the perpetual inventory;
(E) supplier's credit memos for controlled substances and dangerous drugs;
(F) a copy of inventories required by § 291.17 of this title (relating to Inventory Requirements) except that a perpetual inventory of controlled substances listed in Schedule II may be kept in a data processing system if the data processing system is capable of producing a copy of the perpetual inventory on-site;
(G) reports of surrender or destruction of controlled substances and/or dangerous drugs to an appropriate state or federal agency;
(H) records of distribution of controlled substances and/or dangerous drugs to other pharmacies, practitioners, or registrants; and
(I) a copy of any notification required by the Texas Pharmacy Act or these rules, including, but not limited to, the following:
  (i) reports of theft or significant loss of controlled substances to DEA and the board;
  (ii) notification of a change in pharmacist-in-charge of a pharmacy; and
  (iii) reports of a fire or other disaster which may affect the strength, purity, or labeling of drugs, medications, devices, or other materials used in the diagnosis or treatment of injury, illness, and disease.

(6) Permission to maintain central records. Any pharmacy that uses a centralized recordkeeping system for invoices and financial data shall comply with the following procedures.

(A) Controlled substance records. Invoices and financial data for controlled substances may be maintained at a central location provided the following conditions are met:
  (i) Prior to the initiation of central recordkeeping, the pharmacy submits written notification by registered or certified mail to the divisional director of DEA as required by the Code of Federal Regulations, Title 21, § 1304(a), and submits a copy of this written notification to the board. Unless the registrant is informed by the divisional director of DEA that permission to keep central records is denied, the pharmacy may maintain central records commencing 14 days after receipt of notification by the divisional director;
  (ii) The pharmacy maintains a copy of the notification required in this subparagraph; and
  (iii) The records to be maintained at the central record location shall not include executed DEA order forms, prescription drug orders, or controlled substance inventories, which shall be maintained at the pharmacy.
(B) Dangerous drug records. Invoices and financial data for dangerous drugs may be maintained at a central location.
(C) Access to records. If the records are kept in any form requiring special equipment to render the records easily readable, the pharmacy shall provide access to such equipment with the records.
(D) Delivery of records. The pharmacy agrees to deliver all or any part of such records to the pharmacy location within two business days of written request of a board agent or any other authorized official.

Source: The provisions of this § 291.76 adopted to be effective October 7, 1986, 11 TEXREG4034; amended to be effective July 29, 1987, 12 TEXREG2337; amended to be effective September 14, 1988, 13 TEXREG4323; amended to be effective September 5, 1990, 15 TEXREG4810; amended to be effective September 27, 1991, 16 TEXREG5071; amended to be effective January 29, 1992, 17 TexReg 324; amended to be effective September 30, 1993, 18 TexReg 6460; amended to be effective August 31, 2000, 25 TexReg 8406; amended to be effective March 4, 2004, 29 TexReg 2000; amended to be effective June 6, 2004, 29 TexReg 5376; amended to be effective December 3, 2006, 31 TexReg 9611; amended to be effective September 18, 2007, 32 TexReg 6333; amended to be effective September 20, 2009, 34 TexReg 6323; amended to be effective March 10, 2011, 36 TexReg 1528; amended to be effective December 10, 2013, 38 TexReg 8847; amended to be effective September 11, 2014, 39 TexReg 7119; amended to be effective December 6, 2015, 40 TexReg 8766; amended to be effective September 11, 2016, 41 TexReg 6708; amended to be effective September 6, 2017, 42 TexReg 4467; amended to be effective June 7, 2018, 43 TexReg 3591; amended to be effective June 20, 2019, 44 TexReg 2950

§291.77 Pharmacies Compounding Sterile Preparations (Class C-S).

Licensing requirements. An institutional or ASC pharmacy engaged in the compounding of sterile preparations shall be designated as a Class C-S pharmacy.

(1) A Class C-S pharmacy shall register annually or biennially with the board on a pharmacy license application provided by the board, following the procedures specified in § 291.1 of this title (relating to Pharmacy License Application). A Class C-S license may not be issued unless the pharmacy has been inspected by the board to ensure the pharmacy meets the requirements as specified in § 291.133 of this title (relating to Pharmacies Compounding Sterile Preparations).

(2) A Class C-S pharmacy may not renew a pharmacy license unless the pharmacy has been inspected by the board within the last renewal period.

(3) A Class C-S pharmacy which changes ownership shall notify the board within 10 days of the change of ownership and apply for a new and separate license as specified in § 291.3 of this title (relating to Required Notifications).

(4) A Class C-S pharmacy which changes location and/or name shall notify the board within 10 days of the change and file for an amended license as specified in § 291.3 of this title.

(5) A Class C-S pharmacy owned by a partnership or corporation which changes managing officers shall notify the board in writing of the names of the new managing officers within 10 days of the change following the procedures in § 291.3 of this title.

(6) A Class C-S pharmacy shall notify the board in writing within 10 days of closing, following the procedures in § 291.5 of this title (relating to Closing a Pharmacy).

(7) A fee as specified in § 291.6 of this title (relating to Pharmacy License Fees) will be charged for the issuance and renewal of a license and the issuance of an amended license.

(8) A separate license is required for each principal place of business and only one pharmacy license may be issued to a specific location.

(9) A Class C-S pharmacy, licensed under the Act, § 560.051(a)(3), which also operates another type of pharmacy which would otherwise be required to be licensed under the Act, § 560.051(a)(1) (Community Pharmacy (Class A)) or the Act, § 560.051(a)(2) (Nuclear Pharmacy (Class B)), is not required to secure a license for the such other type of pharmacy; provided, however, such licensee is required to comply with the provisions of § 291.31 of this title (relating to Definitions), § 291.32 of this title (relating to Personnel), § 291.33 of this title (relating to Operational Standards), § 291.34 of this title (relating to Records), and § 291.35 of this title (relating to Official Prescription Requirements), contained in Community Pharmacy (Class A), or § 291.51 of this title (relating to Purpose), § 291.52 of this title (relating to Definitions), § 291.53 of this title (relating to Personnel), § 291.54 of this title (relating to Operational Standards), and § 291.55 of this title (relating to Records), contained in Nuclear Pharmacy (Class B), to the extent such sections are applicable to the operation of the pharmacy.

(10) A Class C-S pharmacy engaged in the compounding of non-sterile preparations shall comply with the provisions of § 291.131 of this title (relating to Pharmacies Compounding Non-Sterile Preparations).

(11) A Class C-S pharmacy engaged in the provision of remote pharmacy services, including storage and dispensing of prescription drugs, shall comply with the provisions of § 291.121 of this title (relating to Remote Pharmacy Services).

(12) A Class C-S pharmacy engaged in centralized prescription dispensing and/or prescription drug or medication order processing shall comply with the provisions of § 291.123 of this title (relating to Central Prescription Drug or Medication Order Processing) and/or § 291.125 of this title (relating to Centralized Prescription Dispensing).

(13) A Class C-S pharmacy with an ongoing clinical pharmacy program that proposes to allow a pharmacy technician to verify the accuracy of work performed by another pharmacy technician relating to the filling of floor stock and unit dose distribution systems for a patient admitted to the hospital if the patient's orders have previously been reviewed and approved by a pharmacist shall make application to the board as follows.
  (A) The pharmacist-in-charge must submit an application on a form provided by the board, containing the following information:
    (i) name, address, and pharmacy license number;
    (ii) name and license number of the pharmacist-in-charge;

      (iii) name and registration numbers of the pharmacy technicians;

      (iv) anticipated date the pharmacy plans to begin allowing a pharmacy technician to verify the accuracy of work performed by another pharmacy technician;

      (v) documentation that the pharmacy has an ongoing clinical pharmacy program; and

      (vi) any other information specified on the application.

   (B) The pharmacy may not allow a pharmacy technician to check the work of another pharmacy technician until the board has reviewed and approved the application and issued an amended license to the pharmacy.

   (C) Every two years, in connection with the application for renewal of the pharmacy license, the pharmacy shall provide updated documentation that the pharmacy continues to have an ongoing clinical pharmacy program as specified in subparagraph (A) (v) of this paragraph.

(14) A rural hospital that wishes to allow a pharmacy technician to perform the duties specified in § 291.73(e)(2)(D) of this title (relating to Personnel) shall make application to the board as follows.

   (A) Prior to allowing a pharmacy technician to perform the duties specified in § 291.73(e)(2)(D) of this title, the pharmacist-in-charge must submit an application on a form provided by the board, containing the following information:

      (i) name, address, and pharmacy license number;

      (ii) name and license number of the pharmacist-in-charge;

      (iii) name and registration number of the pharmacy technicians;

      (iv) proposed date the pharmacy wishes to start allowing pharmacy technicians to perform the duties specified in § 291.73(e)(2)(D) of this title;

      (v) documentation that the hospital is a rural hospital with 75 or fewer beds and that the rural hospital is either:

         (I) located in a county with a population of 50,000 or less as defined by the United States Census Bureau in the most recent U.S. census; or

         (II) designated by the Centers for Medicare and Medicaid Services as a critical access hospital, rural referral center, or sole community hospital; and (vi) any other information specified on the application.

   (B) A rural hospital may not allow a pharmacy technician to perform the duties specified in § 291.73(e)(2)(D) of this title until the board has reviewed and approved the application and issued an amended license to the pharmacy.

   (C) Every two years in conjunction with the application for renewal of the pharmacy license, the pharmacist-in-charge shall update the application for pharmacy technicians to perform the duties specified in § 291.73(e)(2)(D) of this title.

Source: The provisions of this § 291.77 adopted to be effective December 10, 2013, 38 TexReg 8847; amended to be effective September 6, 2017, 42 TexReg 4467

SUBCHAPTER E. CLINIC PHARMACY (CLASS D)

§291.91 Definitions

The following words and terms, when used in this chapter, shall have the following meanings, unless the context clearly indicates otherwise.

(1) Act—The Texas Pharmacy Act, Chapters 551 – 566, 568 – 569, Occupations Code as amended.

(2) Administer—The direct application of a prescription drug by injection, inhalation, ingestion, or any other means to the body of a patient by:

   (A) a practitioner or an authorized agent under his supervision; or

   (B) the patient at the direction of a practitioner.

(3) Board—The Texas State Board of Pharmacy.

(4) Clinic—A facility/location other than a physician's office, where limited types of dangerous drugs or devices restricted to those listed in and approved for the clinic's formulary are stored, administered, provided, or dispensed to outpatients.

(5) Consultant pharmacist—A pharmacist retained by a clinic on a routine basis to consult with the clinic in areas that pertain to the practice of pharmacy.

(6) Continuous supervision—Supervision provided by the pharmacist-in-charge, consultant pharmacist, and/or staff pharmacist, and consists of on-site and telephone supervision, routine inspection, and a policy and procedure manual.

(7) Controlled substance—A drug, immediate precursor, or other substance listed in Schedules I-V or Penalty Groups 1-4 of the Texas Controlled Substances Act, as amended, or a drug, immediate precursor, or other substance included in Schedule I, II, III, IV, or V of the Federal Comprehensive Drug Abuse Prevention and Control Act of 1970, as amended (Public Law 91-513).

(8) Dangerous drug—Any drug or device that is not included in Penalty Groups 1-4 of the Controlled Substances Act and that is unsafe for self-medication or any drug or device that bears or is required to bear the legend:

   (A) "Caution: federal law prohibits dispensing without prescription" or "Rx only";

   (B) "Caution: federal law restricts this drug to use by or on the order of a licensed veterinarian."

(9) Dispense—Preparing, packaging, compounding, or labeling for delivery a prescription drug or device in the course of professional practice to an ultimate user or his agent by or pursuant to the lawful order of a practitioner.

(10) Indigent—Person who meets or falls below 185% of federal poverty income guidelines as established from time to time by the United States Department of Health and Human Services.

(11) Limited type of device—An instrument, apparatus, implement, machine, contrivance, implant, in vitro reagent, or other similar or related article, including any component part or accessory, that is required under federal or state law to be ordered or prescribed by a practitioner, that is contained in the clinic formulary and is to be administered, dispensed, or provided according to the objectives of the clinic.

(12) Limited type of drug—A dangerous drug contained in the clinic formulary, and to be administered, dispensed, or provided according to the objectives of the clinic.

(13) Outpatient—An ambulatory patient who comes to a clinic to receive services related to the objectives of the clinic and departs the same day.

(14) Pharmacist—A person licensed by the board to practice pharmacy.

(15) Pharmacist-in-charge—The pharmacist designated on a pharmacy license as the pharmacist who is responsible for a pharmacy's compliance with laws and rules pertaining to the practice of pharmacy.

(16) Practitioner—

  (A) a person licensed or registered to prescribe, distribute, administer, or dispense a prescription drug or device in the course of professional practice in this state, including a physician, dentist, podiatrist, or veterinarian but excluding a person licensed under the Act;

  (B) a person licensed by another state, Canada, or the United Mexican States in a health field in which, under the law of this state, a license holder in this state may legally prescribe a dangerous drug;

  (C) a person practicing in another state and licensed by another state as a physician, dentist, veterinarian, or podiatrist, who has a current federal Drug Enforcement Administration registration number and who may legally prescribe a Schedule II, III, IV, or V controlled substance, as specified under Chapter 481, Health and Safety Code, in that other state; or

  (D) an advanced practice nurse or physician assistant to whom a physician has delegated the authority to carry out or sign prescription drug orders under §§157.0511, 157.052, 157.053, 157.054, 157.0541, or 157.0542, Occupations Code.

(17) Prepackaging—A method of packaging a drug product into a single container which contains more than one dosage unit and usually contains sufficient quantity of medication for one normal course of therapy.

(18) Provide—To supply one or more units of use of a nonprescription drug or dangerous drug to a patient.

(19) Standing delegation order—Written orders from a physician and designed for a patient population with specific diseases, disorders, health problems, or sets of symptoms, which provide authority for and a plan for use with patients presenting themselves prior to being examined or evaluated by a physician to assure that such acts are carried out correctly and are distinct from specific orders written for a particular patient.

(20) Standing medical order—Written orders from a physician or the medical staff of an institution for patients which have been examined or evaluated by a physician and which are used as a guide in preparation for and carrying out medical and/or surgical procedures.

(21) Supportive personnel—Individuals under the supervision of a pharmacist-in-charge, designated by the pharmacist-in-charge, and for whom the pharmacist-in-charge assumes legal responsibility, who function and perform under the instructions of the pharmacist-in-charge.

(22) Texas Controlled Substances Act—The Texas Controlled Substances Act, Health and Safety Code, Chapter 481, as amended.

(23) Unit of use—A sufficient quantity of a drug product for one normal course of therapy.

Source: The provisions of this §291.91 adopted to be effective January 7, 1987, 11 TexReg 5128; amended to be effective January 29, 1992, 17 TexReg 324; amended to be effective March 12, 2003, 28 TexReg 2082; amended to be effective September 7, 2008, 33 TexReg 7242; amended to be effective July 11, 2011, 36 TexReg 4412

§291.92 Personnel

(a) Pharmacist-in-charge.

  (1) General.

    (A) Each Class D pharmacy shall have one pharmacist-in-charge who is employed or under written agreement, at least on a part-time basis, but may be employed on a full-time basis if desired, and who may be pharmacist-in-charge of more than one clinic pharmacy.

    (B) A written agreement shall exist between the clinic and the pharmacist-in-charge, and a copy of the written agreement shall be made available to the board upon request.

  (2) Responsibilities. The pharmacist-in-charge shall have at a minimum, the responsibility for the following:

    (A) continuous supervision of registered nurses, licensed vocational nurses, physician assistants, pharmacy technicians, pharmacy technician trainees, and assistants carrying out the pharmacy related aspects of provision;

    (B) documented periodic on-site visits as specified in § 291.93(h) and § 291.94(b) of this title (relating to Operational Standards and Records), either personally or by the consultant pharmacist or staff pharmacist, to insure that the clinic is following set policies and procedures; documentation shall be as specified in § 291.94(b) of this title;

    (C) development of a formulary for the clinic, in conjunction with the clinic's pharmacy and therapeutics committee, consisting of drugs and/or devices needed to meet the objectives of the clinic;

    (D) procurement and storage of drugs and/or devices, but he or she may receive input from other appropriate staff of the clinic;

    (E) determining specifications of all drugs and/or devices procured by the clinic;

    (F) maintenance of records of all transactions of the pharmacy as may be required by applicable law and as may be necessary to maintain accurate control over and accountability for all drugs and/or devices;

    (G) development and at least annual review of a policy and procedure manual for the pharmacy in conjunction with the clinic's pharmacy and therapeutics committee;

    (H) meeting inspection and other requirements of the Texas Pharmacy Act and these sections;

    (I) dispensing of prescription orders; and

    (J) conducting inservice training at least annually for supportive personnel who provide drugs; such training shall be related to actions, contraindications, adverse reactions, and pharmacology of drugs contained in the formulary.

(b) Consultant pharmacist.

  (1) The consultant pharmacist may be the pharmacist-in-charge.

  (2) The consultant pharmacist may be retained by more than one clinic.

(c) Staff pharmacists.

  (1) The pharmacist-in-charge may be assisted by a sufficient number of additional pharmacists as may be required to operate the clinic pharmacy competently, safely, and adequately to meet the needs of the patients of the clinic.

  (2) Staff pharmacists and/or the consultant pharmacist shall assist the pharmacist-in-charge in meeting the responsibilities as outlined in subsection (a)(2) of this section and in ordering, supervising, and accounting for drugs and/or devices.

  (3) Staff pharmacists and/or the consultant pharmacist shall be responsible for any delegated act performed by supportive personnel under his or her supervision.

(d) Supportive personnel.
   (1) Qualifications.
     (A) Supportive personnel shall possess education and training necessary to carry out their responsibilities.
     (B) Supportive personnel shall be qualified to perform the pharmacy tasks assigned to them.
   (2) Duties. Duties may include:
     (A) prepackaging and labeling unit of use packages, under the direct supervision of a pharmacist with the pharmacist conducting in-process and final checks and affixing his or her signature to the appropriate quality control records;
     (B) maintaining inventories of drugs and/or devices; and
     (C) maintaining pharmacy records.
   (3) Absence of the pharmacist. The pharmacist-in-charge shall designate from among the supportive personnel a person to supervise the day-to-day pharmacy-related operations of the clinic.
(e) Owner. The owner of a Class D pharmacy shall have responsibility for all administrative and operational functions of the pharmacy. The pharmacist-in-charge may advise the owner on administrative and operational concerns. The owner shall have responsibility for, at a minimum, the following, and if the owner is not a Texas licensed pharmacist, the owner shall consult with the pharmacist-in-charge or another Texas licensed pharmacist:
   (1) establishment of policies for procurement of prescription drugs and devices and other products provided or dispensed from the Class D pharmacy;
   (2) establishment and maintenance of effective controls against the theft or diversion of prescription drugs;
   (3) providing the pharmacy with the necessary equipment and resources commensurate with its level and type of practice; and
   (4) establishment of policies and procedures regarding maintenance, storage, and retrieval of records in a data processing system such that the system is in compliance with state and federal requirements.

Source: The provisions of this §291.92 adopted to be effective January 7, 1987, 11 TexReg 5128; amended to be effective September 18, 2007, 32 TexReg 6348; amended to be effective September 7, 2008, 33 TexReg 7242

§291.93 Operational Standards
(a) Registration.
   (1) Licensing requirements.
     (A) All clinic pharmacies shall register with the board on a pharmacy license application provided by the board, following the procedures specified in § 291.1 of this title (relating to Pharmacy License Application).
     (B) All clinic pharmacies shall provide a copy of their policy and procedure manual, which includes the formulary, to the board with the initial license application.
     (C) The following fees will be charged.
       (i) A fee as specified in § 291.6 of this title (relating to Pharmacy License Fees) will be charged for the issuance of a new license and for each renewal.
       (ii) A pharmacy operated by the state or a local government that qualifies for a Class D license is not required to pay a fee to obtain a license.
     (D) A Class D pharmacy which changes ownership shall notify the board within ten days of the change of ownership and apply for a new and separate license as specified in § 291.3 of this title (relating to Required Notifications).
     (E) A clinic pharmacy shall notify the board in writing of any change in name or location as specified in § 291.3 of this title.
     (F) A separate license is required for each principal place of business and only one pharmacy license may be issued to a specific location.
     (G) A clinic pharmacy shall notify the board in writing within 10 days of a change of the pharmacist-in-charge or staff pharmacist or consultant pharmacist.
     (H) A Class D pharmacy shall notify the board in writing within ten days of closing, following the procedures as specified in § 291.5 of this title (relating to Closing a Pharmacy).
   (2) Registration requirements for facilities that operate at temporary clinic sites. A facility that operates a clinic at one or more temporary locations may be licensed as a Class D pharmacy and provide dangerous drugs from these temporary locations provided:
     (A) the Class D pharmacy complies with the registration requirements in paragraph (1) of this subsection;
     (B) the Class D pharmacy has a permanent location where all dangerous drugs and records are stored;
     (C) no dangerous drugs are stored or left for later pickup by the patient at the temporary location(s), and all drugs are returned to the permanent location each day and stored:
       (i) within the Class D pharmacy; or
       (ii) within the pharmacy's mobile unit provided the mobile clinic is parked at the location of the clinic pharmacy in a secure area with adequate measures to prevent unauthorized access, and the drugs are maintained at proper temperatures;
     (D) the permanent location is the address of record for the pharmacy;
     (E) the facility has no more than six temporary locations in operation simultaneously;
     (F) the Class D pharmacy notifies the board of the locations of the temporary locations where drugs will be provided and the schedule for operation of such clinics; and
     (G) the Class D pharmacy notifies the board within 10 days of a change in address or closing of a temporary location or a change in schedule of operation of a clinic.
(b) Environment.
   (1) General requirements.
     (A) The Class D pharmacy shall have a designated area(s) for the storage of dangerous drugs and/or devices.
     (B) No person may operate a pharmacy which is unclean, unsanitary, or under any condition which endangers the health, safety, or welfare of the public.
     (C) The Class D pharmacy shall comply with all federal, state, and local health laws and ordinances.

      (D) A sink with hot and cold running water shall be available to all pharmacy personnel and shall be maintained in a sanitary condition at all times.

    (2) Security.

      (A) Only authorized personnel may have access to storage areas for dangerous drugs and/or devices.

      (B) All storage areas for dangerous drugs and/or devices shall be locked by key, combination, or other mechanical or electronic means, so as to prohibit access by unauthorized individuals.

      (C) The pharmacist-in-charge shall be responsible for the security of all storage areas for dangerous drugs and/or devices including provisions for adequate safeguards against theft or diversion of dangerous drugs and devices, and records for such drugs and devices.

      (D) The pharmacist-in-charge shall consult with clinic personnel with respect to security of the pharmacy, including provisions for adequate safeguards against theft or diversion of dangerous drugs and/or devices, and records for such drugs and/or devices.

      (E) Housekeeping and maintenance duties shall be carried out in the pharmacy, while the pharmacist-in-charge, consultant pharmacist, staff pharmacist, or supportive personnel is on the premises.

(c) Equipment. Each Class D pharmacy shall maintain the following equipment and supplies:

    (1) if the Class D pharmacy prepackages drugs for provision:

      (A) a typewriter or comparable equipment; and

      (B) an adequate supply of child-resistant, moisture-proof, and light-proof containers and prescription, poison, and other applicable identification labels used in dispensing and providing of drugs;

    (2) if the Class D pharmacy maintains dangerous drugs requiring refrigeration and/or freezing, a refrigerator and/or freezer;

    (3) if the Class D pharmacy compounds prescription drug orders, a properly maintained Class A prescription balance (with weights) or equivalent analytical balance. It is the responsibility of the pharmacist-in-charge to have such balance inspected at least every three years by the appropriate authority as prescribed by local, state, or federal law or regulations.

(d) Library. A reference library shall be maintained which includes the following in hard copy or electronic format:

    (1) current copies of the following:

      (A) Texas Pharmacy Act and rules; and

      (B) Texas Dangerous Drug Act;

    (2) current copies of at least two of the following references:

      (A) Facts and Comparisons with current supplements;

      (B) AHFS Drug Information;

      (C) United States Pharmacopeia Dispensing Information (USPDI);

      (D) Physician's Desk Reference (PDR);

      (E) American Drug Index;

      (F) a reference text on drug interactions, such as Drug Interaction Facts. A separate reference is not required if other references maintained by the pharmacy contain drug interaction information including information needed to determine severity or significance of the interaction and appropriate recommendations or actions to be taken;

      (G) reference texts in any of the following subjects: toxicology, pharmacology, or drug interactions; or

      (H) reference texts pertinent to the major function(s) of the clinic.

(e) Drugs and devices.

    (1) Formulary.

      (A) Each Class D pharmacy shall have a formulary which lists all drugs and devices that are administered, dispensed, or provided by the Class D pharmacy.

      (B) The formulary shall be limited to the following types of drugs and devices, exclusive of injectable drugs for administration in the clinic and nonprescription drugs, except as provided in subparagraph (D) of this paragraph:

        (i) anti-infective drugs;

        (ii) musculoskeletal drugs;

        (iii) vitamins;

        (iv) obstetrical and gynecological drugs and devices;

        (v) topical drugs; and

        (vi) serums, toxoids, and vaccines.

      (C) The formulary shall not contain the following drugs or types of drugs:

        (i) Nalbuphine (Nubain);

        (ii) drugs used to treat erectile dysfunction; and

        (iii) Schedule I - V controlled substances.

      (D) Clinics with a patient population which consists of at least 80% indigent patients may petition the board to operate with a formulary which includes types of drugs and devices, other than those listed in subparagraph (B) of this paragraph based upon documented objectives of the clinic, under the following conditions.

        (i) Such petition shall contain an affidavit with the notarized signatures of the medical director, the pharmacist-in-charge, and the owner/chief executive officer of the clinic, and include the following documentation:

          (I) the objectives of the clinic;

          (II) the total number of patients served by the clinic during the previous fiscal year or calendar year;

          (III) the total number of indigent patients served by the clinic during the previous fiscal year or calendar year;

          (IV) the percentage of clinic patients who are indigent, based upon the patient population during the previous fiscal year or calendar year;

          (V) the proposed formulary and the need for additional types of drugs based upon objectives of the clinic; and

          (VI) if the provision of any drugs on the proposed formulary require special monitoring, the clinic pharmacy shall submit relevant sections of the clinic's policy and procedure manual regarding the provision of drugs that require special monitoring.

Phr. Rules

        (ii)   Such petition shall be resubmitted every two years in conjunction with the application for renewal of the pharmacy license.

           (I)   Such renewal petition shall contain the documentation required in clause (i) of this subparagraph.

           (II)   If at the time of renewal of the pharmacy license, the patient population for the previous fiscal year or calendar year is below 80% indigent patients, the clinic shall be required to submit an application for a Class A pharmacy license or shall limit the clinic formulary to those types of drugs and devices listed in subparagraph (B) of this paragraph.

        (iii) If a Class D pharmacy wishes to add additional drugs to the expanded formulary, the pharmacy shall petition the board in writing prior to adding such drugs to the formulary. The petition shall identify drugs to be added and the need for the additional drugs based upon objectives of the clinic as specified in clause (i) of this subparagraph

        (iv) The following additional requirements shall be satisfied for clinic pharmacies with expanded formularies.

           (I)   Supportive personnel who are providing drugs shall be licensed nurses or practitioners.

           (II)   The pharmacist-in-charge, consultant pharmacist, or staff pharmacist shall make on-site visits to the clinic at least monthly.

           (III) If the pharmacy provides drugs which require special monitoring (i.e., drugs which require follow-up laboratory work or drugs which should not be discontinued abruptly), the pharmacy shall have policies and procedures for the provision of the prescription drugs to patients and the monitoring of patients who receive such drugs.

           (IV) The pharmacist-in-charge, consultant pharmacists, or staff pharmacists shall conduct retrospective drug regimen reviews of a random sample of patients of the clinic on at least a quarterly basis. The pharmacist-in-charge shall be responsible for ensuring that a report regarding the drug regimen review, including the number of patients reviewed, is submitted to the clinic's medical director and the pharmacy and therapeutics committee of the clinic.

           (V) If a pharmacy provides antipsychotic drugs:

              (-a-) a practitioner of the clinic shall initiate the therapy;

              (-b-) a practitioner shall monitor and order ongoing therapy; and

              (-c-) the patient shall be physically examined by the practitioner at least on a yearly basis.

        (v)   The board may consider the following items in approving or disapproving a petition for an expanded formulary:

           (I)   the degree of compliance on past compliance inspections;

           (II)   the size of the patient population of the clinic;

           (III) the number and types of drugs contained in the formulary; and

           (IV) the objectives of the clinic.

  (2) Storage.

     (A) Drugs and/or devices which bear the words "Caution, Federal Law Prohibits Dispensing without prescription" or "Rx only" shall be stored in secured storage areas.

     (B) All drugs shall be stored at the proper temperatures, as defined in § 291.15 of this title (relating to Storage of Drugs).

     (C) Any drug or device bearing an expiration date may not be provided, dispensed, or administered beyond the expiration date of the drug or device.

     (D) Outdated drugs or devices shall be removed from stock and shall be quarantined together until such drugs or devices are disposed.

     (E) Controlled substances may not be stored at the Class D pharmacy.

  (3) Drug samples.

     (A) Drug samples of drugs listed on the Class D pharmacy's formulary and supplied by manufacturers shall be properly stored, labeled, provided, or dispensed by the Class D pharmacy in the same manner as prescribed by these sections for dangerous drugs.

     (B) Samples of controlled substances may not be stored, provided, or dispensed in the Class D pharmacy.

  (4) Prepackaging and labeling for provision.

     (A) Drugs may be prepackaged and labeled for provision in the Class D pharmacy. Such prepackaging shall be performed by a pharmacist or supportive personnel under the direct supervision of a pharmacist and shall be for the internal use of the clinic.

     (B) Drugs must be prepackaged in suitable containers.

     (C) The label of the prepackaged unit shall bear:

        (i)   the name, address, and telephone number of the clinic;

        (ii)   directions for use, which may include incomplete directions for use provided:

           (I)   labeling with incomplete directions for use has been authorized by the pharmacy and therapeutics committee;

           (II)   precise requirements for completion of the directions for use are developed by the pharmacy and therapeutics committee and maintained in the pharmacy policy and procedure manual; and

           (III) the directions for use are completed by practitioners, pharmacists, or licensed nurses in accordance with the precise requirements developed under subclause (II) of this clause;

        (iii) name and strength of the drug—if generic name, the name of the manufacturer or distributor of the drug;

        (iv) quantity;

        (v)   lot number and expiration date; and

        (vi) appropriate ancillary label(s).

     (D) Records of prepackaging shall be maintained according to § 291.94(c) of this title (relating to Records).

  (5) Labeling for provision of drugs and/or devices in an original manufacturer's container.

     (A) Drugs and/or devices in an original manufacturer's container shall be labeled prior to provision with the information set out in paragraph (4)(C) of this subsection.

     (B) Drugs and/or devices in an original manufacturer's container may be labeled by:

        (i)   a pharmacist in a pharmacy licensed by the board; or

        (ii)   supportive personnel in a Class D pharmacy, provided the drugs and/or devices and control records required by § 291.94(d) of this title are quarantined together until checked and released by a pharmacist.

      (C) Records of labeling for provision of drugs and/or devices in an original manufacturer's container shall be maintained according to § 291.94(d) of this title.

  (6) Provision.

      (A) Drugs and devices may only be provided to patients of the clinic.

      (B) At the time of the initial provision, a licensed nurse or practitioner shall provide verbal and written information to the patient or patient's agent on side effects, interactions, and precautions concerning the drug or device provided. If the provision of subsequent drugs is delivered to the patient at the patient's residence or other designated location, the following is applicable:

         (i) Written information as specified in subparagraph (B) of this paragraph shall be delivered with the medication.

         (ii) The pharmacy shall maintain and use adequate storage or shipment containers and use shipping processes to ensure drug stability and potency. Such shipping processes shall include the use of appropriate packaging material and/or devices to ensure that the drug is maintained at an appropriate temperature range to maintain the integrity of the medication throughout the delivery process.

         (iii) The pharmacy shall use a delivery system which is designed to ensure that the drugs are delivered to the appropriate patient.

      (C) The provision of drugs or devices shall be under the continuous supervision of a pharmacist according to standing delegation orders or standing medical orders and in accordance with written policies and procedures and completion of the label as specified in subparagraph (G) of this paragraph.

      (D) Drugs and/or devices may only be provided in accordance with the system of control and accountability for drugs and/or devices provided by the clinic; such system shall be developed and supervised by the pharmacist-in-charge.

      (E) Only drugs and/or devices listed in the clinic formulary may be provided.

      (F) Drugs and/or devices may only be provided in prepackaged quantities in suitable containers and/or original manufacturer's containers which are appropriately labeled as set out in paragraphs (4) and (5) of this subsection.

      (G) Such drugs and/or devices shall be labeled by a pharmacist licensed by the board; however, when drugs and/or devices are provided under the supervision of a physician according to standing delegation orders or standing medical orders, supportive personnel may at the time of provision print on the label the following information or affix an ancillary label containing the following information:

         (i) patient's name; however, the patient's partner or family member is not required to be on the label of a drug prescribed for a partner for a sexually transmitted disease or for a patient's family members if the patient has an illness determined by the Centers for Disease Control and Prevention, the World Health Organization, or the Governor's office to be pandemic;

         (ii) any information necessary to complete the directions for use in accordance with paragraph (4)(C)(ii) of this subsection;

         (iii) date of provision; and

         (iv) practitioner's name.

      (H) Records of provision shall be maintained according to § 291.94(e) of this title.

      (I) Controlled substances may not be provided or dispensed.

      (J) Non-sterile preparations may only be provided by the clinic pharmacy in accordance with § 291.131 of this title (relating to Pharmacies Compounding Non-sterile Preparations).

  (7) Dispensing. Dangerous drugs may only be dispensed by a pharmacist pursuant to a prescription order in accordance with §§ 291.31 - 291.35 of this title (relating to Community Pharmacy (Class A)) and § 291.131 of this title.

(f) Pharmacy and therapeutics committee.

  (1) The clinic pharmacy shall have a pharmacy and therapeutics committee, which shall be composed of at least three persons and shall include the pharmacist-in-charge, the medical director of the clinic, and a person who is responsible for provision of drugs and devices.

  (2) The pharmacy and therapeutics committee shall develop the policy and procedure manual.

  (3) The pharmacy and therapeutics committee shall meet at least annually to:

      (A) review and update the policy and procedure manual; and

      (B) review the retrospective drug utilization review reports submitted by the pharmacist-in-charge if the clinic pharmacy has an expanded formulary.

(g) Policies and procedures.

  (1) Written policies and procedures shall be developed by the pharmacy and therapeutics committee and implemented by the pharmacist-in-charge.

  (2) The policy and procedure manual shall include, but not be limited to, the following:

      (A) a current list of the names of the pharmacist-in-charge, consultant-pharmacist, staff pharmacist(s), supportive personnel designated to provide drugs or devices, and the supportive personnel designated to supervise the day-to-day pharmacy related operations of the clinic in the absence of the pharmacist;

      (B) functions of the pharmacist-in-charge, consultant pharmacist, staff pharmacist(s), and supportive personnel;

      (C) objectives of the clinic;

      (D) formulary;

      (E) a copy of written agreement between the pharmacist-in-charge and the clinic;

      (F) date of last review/revision of policy and procedure manual; and

      (G) policies and procedures for:

         (i) security;

         (ii) equipment;

         (iii) sanitation;

         (iv) licensing;

         (v) reference materials;

         (vi) storage;

         (vii) packaging-repackaging;

(viii) dispensing;
(ix) provision;
(x) retrospective drug regimen review;
(xi) supervision;
(xii) labeling-relabeling;
(xiii) samples;
(xiv) drug destruction and returns;
(xv) drug and device procuring;
(xvi) receiving of drugs and devices;
(xvii) delivery of drugs and devices;
(xviii) recordkeeping; and
(xix) inspection.

(h) Supervision. The pharmacist-in-charge, consultant pharmacist, or staff pharmacist shall personally visit the clinic on at least a monthly basis to ensure that the clinic is following established policies and procedures. However, clinics operated by state or local governments and clinics funded by government sources money may petition the board for an alternative visitation schedule under the following conditions.
(1) Such petition shall contain an affidavit with the notarized signatures of the medical director, the pharmacist-in-charge, and the owner/chief executive officer of the clinic, which states that the clinic has a current policy and procedure manual on file, has adequate security to prevent diversion of dangerous drugs, and is in compliance with all rules governing Class D pharmacies.
(2) The board may consider the following items in determining an alternative schedule:
(A) the degree of compliance on past compliance inspections;
(B) the size of the patient population of the clinic;
(C) the number and types of drugs contained in the formulary; and
(D) the objectives of the clinic.
(3) Such petition shall be resubmitted every two years in conjunction with the application for renewal of the pharmacy license.
Source: The provisions of this § 291.93 adopted to be effective January 7, 1987, 11 TEXREG 5128; amended to be effective July 29, 1987, 12 TEXREG 2339; amended to be effective February 17, 1988, 13 TEXREG 613; amended to be effective September 14, 1988, 13 TEXREG 4575; amended to be effective September 27, 1991, 16 TEXREG 5071; amended to be effective January 29, 1992, 17 TexReg 324; amended to be effective March 25, 1999, 24 TexReg 2022; amended to be effective June 20, 2001, 26 TexReg 4513; amended to be effective March 12, 2003, 28 TexReg 2082; amended to be effective September 7, 2008, 33 TexReg 7242; amended to be effective September 9, 2012, 37 TexReg 6917; amended to be effective December 5, 2012, 37 TexReg 9513; amended to be effective March 19, 2017, 42 TexReg 1127; amended to be effective September 6, 2017, TexReg 4467

§291.94 Records

(a) Maintenance of records.
(1) Every inventory or other record required to be kept under the provisions of § 291.91 of this title (relating to Definitions), § 291.92 of this title (relating to Personnel), § 291.93 of this title (relating to Operational Standards), and § 291.94 of this title (relating to Records), contained in Clinic Pharmacy (Class D) shall be:
(A) kept by the pharmacy and be available, for at least two years from the date of such inventory or record, for inspecting and copying by the board or its representative and to other authorized local, state, or federal law enforcement agencies; and
(B) supplied by the pharmacy within 72 hours, if requested by an authorized agent of the Texas State Board of Pharmacy. If the pharmacy maintains the records in an electronic format, the requested records must be provided in a mutually agreeable electronic format if specifically requested by the board or its representative. Failure to provide the records set out in this section, either on site or within 72 hours, constitutes prima facie evidence of failure to keep and maintain records in violation of the Act.
(2) Records, except when specifically required to be maintained in original or hard-copy form, may be maintained in an alternative data retention system, such as a data processing system or direct imaging system provided:
(A) the records maintained in the alternative system contain all of the information required on the manual record; and
(B) the data processing system is capable of producing a hard copy of the record upon the request of the board, its representative, or other authorized local, state, or federal law enforcement or regulatory agencies.
(3) Invoices and records of receipt may be kept at a location other than the pharmacy. Any such records not kept at the pharmacy shall be supplied by the pharmacy within 72 hours, if requested by an authorized agent of the Texas State Board of Pharmacy.
(b) On-site visits. A record of on-site visits by the pharmacist-in-charge, consultant pharmacist, or staff pharmacist shall be maintained and include the following information:
(1) date of the visit;
(2) pharmacist's evaluation of findings; and
(3) signature of the visiting pharmacist.
(c) Prepackaging. Records of prepackaging shall include the following:
(1) name, strength, and dosage form of drug;
(2) name of the manufacturer;
(3) manufacturer's lot number;
(4) expiration date;
(5) facility's lot number;
(6) quantity per package and number of packages;
(7) date packaged;
(8) name(s), signatures, or electronic signatures of the supportive personnel who prepackages the drug under direct supervision of a pharmacist; and
(9) name, signature, or electronic signature of the pharmacist who prepackages the drug or supervises the prepackaging and checks and releases the drug.

(d) Labeling. Records of labeling of drugs or devices in original manufacturer's containers shall include the following:
 (1) name and strength of the drug or device labeled;
 (2) name of the manufacturer;
 (3) manufacturer's lot number;
 (4) manufacturer's expiration date;
 (5) quantity per package and number of packages;
 (6) date labeled;
 (7) name of the supportive personnel affixing the label; and
 (8) the signature of the pharmacist who checks and releases the drug.

(e) Provision. Records of drugs and/or devices provided shall include logs, patient records, or other acceptable methods for documentation. Documentation shall include:
 (1) patient name;
 (2) name, signature, or electronic signature of the person who provides the drug or device;
 (3) date provided; and
 (4) the name of the drug or device and quantity provided.

(f) Dispensing. Record-keeping requirements for dangerous drugs dispensed by a pharmacist are the same as for a Class A pharmacy as set out in § 291.34 of this title (relating to Records).

Source: The provisions of this §291.94 adopted to be effective January 7, 1987, 11 TexReg 5128; amended to be effective September 7, 2008, 33 TexReg 7242

SUBCHAPTER F. NON-RESIDENT PHARMACY (CLASS E)

§291.101 Purpose

(a) The purpose of these rules is to provide standards for the operation of non-resident pharmacies (Class E) which dispense a prescription drug or device under a prescription drug order and deliver the drug or device to a patient in this state, by the United States mail, a common carrier, or a delivery service.

(b) These rules are in accordance with §554.051(a) and (b) of the Act which permit the board to make rules concerning the operation of licensed pharmacies in this state applicable to pharmacies licensed by the board that are located in another state. The board has determined that these rules are necessary to protect the health and welfare of the citizens of this state.

(c) Unless compliance would violate the pharmacy or drug laws or rules in the state in which the pharmacy is located, Class E Pharmacies are required to comply with the provisions of §§291.101-291.105 of this chapter (relating to Purpose, Definitions, Personnel, Operational Standards, and Records).

Source: The provisions of this §291.101 adopted to be effective September 1, 2000, 25 TexReg 2617

§291.102 Definitions

The following words and terms, when used in this subchapter, shall have the following meanings, unless the context clearly indicates otherwise.

 (1) Act—The Texas Pharmacy Act, Chapters 551-566, Occupations Code, as amended.
 (2) Accurately as prescribed—Dispensing, delivering, and/or distributing a prescription drug order:
  (A) to the correct patient (or agent of the patient) for whom the drug or device was prescribed;
  (B) with the correct drug in the correct strength, quantity, and dosage form ordered by the practitioner; and
  (C) with correct labeling (including directions for use) as ordered by the practitioner. Provided, however, that nothing herein shall prohibit pharmacist substitution if substitution is conducted in strict accordance with applicable laws and rules, including Subchapter A of Chapter 562 of the Texas Pharmacy Act relating to Prescription and Substitution Requirements.
 (3) Board—The Texas State Board of Pharmacy.
 (4) Class E pharmacy license or non-resident pharmacy license—a license issued to a pharmacy located in another state whose primary business is to:
  (A) dispense a prescription drug or device under a prescription drug order; and
  (B) to deliver the drug or device to a patient, including a patient in this state, by the United States mail, common carrier, or delivery service.
 (5) Confidential Record—Any health related record, including a patient medication record, prescription drug order, or medication order that:
  (A) contains information that identifies an individual; and
  (B) is maintained by a pharmacy or pharmacist.
 (6) Deliver or delivery—The actual, constructive, or attempted transfer of a prescription drug or device or controlled substance from one person to another, whether or not for a consideration.
 (7) Dispense—Preparing, packaging, compounding, or labeling, in the course of professional practice, a prescription drug or device for delivery to an ultimate user or the user's agent under a practitioner's lawful order.
 (8) Distribute—To deliver a prescription drug or device other than by administering or dispensing.
 (9) Generically equivalent—A drug that is "pharmaceutically equivalent" and "therapeutically equivalent" to the drug prescribed.
 (10) New prescription drug order—A prescription drug order that:
  (A) has not been dispensed to the patient in the same strength and dosage form by this pharmacy within the last year;
  (B) is transferred from another pharmacy; and/or
  (C) is a discharge prescription drug order. (Note: furlough prescription drug orders are not considered new prescription drug orders.)

(11) Pharmaceutically equivalent—Drug products which have identical amounts of the same active chemical ingredients in the same dosage form and which meet the identical compendial or other applicable standards of strength, quality, and purity according to the United States Pharmacopoeia or other nationally recognized compendium.

(12) Pharmacist—For the purpose of this subchapter, a person licensed to practice pharmacy in the state where the Class E pharmacy is located.

(13) Pharmacist-in-charge—The pharmacist designated on a pharmacy license as the pharmacist who has the authority or responsibility for a pharmacy's compliance with statutes and rules pertaining to the practice of pharmacy.

(14) Practitioner—

(A) a person licensed or registered to prescribe, distribute, administer, or dispense a prescription drug or device in the course of professional practice in this state, including a physician, dentist, podiatrist, or veterinarian but excluding a person licensed under the Act;

(B) a person licensed by another state, Canada, or the United Mexican States in a health field in which, under the law of this state, a license holder in this state may legally prescribe a dangerous drug; or

(C) a person practicing in another state and licensed by another state as a physician, dentist, veterinarian, or podiatrist, who has a current federal Drug Enforcement Administration registration number and who may legally prescribe a Schedule II, III, IV, or V controlled substance, as specified under Chapter 481, Health and Safety Code, in that other state.

(15) Prescription drug order—an order from a practitioner or a practitioner's designated agent to a pharmacist for a drug or device to be dispensed.

(16) Therapeutically equivalent—Pharmaceutically equivalent drug products which, when administered in the same amounts, will provide the same therapeutic effect, identical in duration and intensity.

Source: The provisions of this §291.102 adopted to be effective September 1, 2000, 25 TexReg 2617

§291.103 Personnel

As specified in § 562.101(f) of the Act (relating to Supervision of Pharmacy), a Class E pharmacy shall be under the continuous on-site supervision of a pharmacist and shall designate one pharmacist licensed to practice pharmacy by the regulatory or licensing agency of the state in which the Class E pharmacy is located and effective September 1, 2016, is licensed as a pharmacist in Texas to serve as the pharmacist-in-charge of the Class E pharmacy license.

Source: The provisions of this § 291.103 adopted to be effective September 1, 2000, 25 TexReg 2617; amended to be effective December 6, 2015, 40 TexReg 8779

§291.104 Operational Standards

(a) Licensing requirements.

(1) A Class E pharmacy shall register with the board on a pharmacy license application provided by the board, following the procedures specified in § 291.1 of this title (relating to Pharmacy License Application).

(2) On initial application, the pharmacy shall follow the procedures specified in § 291.1 of this title (relating to Pharmacy License Application) and then provide the following additional information specified in § 560.052(c) and (f) of the Act (relating to Qualifications):

(A) evidence that the applicant holds a pharmacy license, registration, or permit issued by the state in which the pharmacy is located;

(B) the name of the owner and pharmacist-in-charge of the pharmacy for service of process;

(C) evidence of the applicant's ability to provide to the board a record of a prescription drug order dispensed by the applicant to a resident of this state not later than 72 hours after the time the board requests the record;

(D) an affidavit by the pharmacist-in-charge which states that the pharmacist has read and understands the laws and rules relating to a Class E pharmacy;

(E) proof of creditworthiness; and

(F) an inspection report issued not more than two years before the date the license application is received and conducted by the pharmacy licensing board in the state of the pharmacy's physical location.

(i) A Class E pharmacy may submit an inspection report issued by an entity other than the pharmacy licensing board of the state in which the pharmacy is physically located if the state's licensing board does not conduct inspections as follows:

(I) an individual approved by the board who is not employed by the pharmacy but acting as a consultant to inspect the pharmacy;

(II) an agent of the National Association of Boards of Pharmacy;

(III) an agent of another State Board of Pharmacy; or

(IV) an agent of an accrediting body, such as the Joint Commission on Accreditation of Healthcare Organizations.

(ii) The inspection must be substantively equivalent to an inspection conducted by the board.

(3) On renewal of a license, the pharmacy shall complete the renewal application provided by the board and, as specified in § 561.0031 of the Act, provide an inspection report issued not more than three years before the date the renewal application is received and conducted by the pharmacy licensing board in the state of the pharmacy's physical location.

(A) A Class E pharmacy may submit an inspection report issued by an entity other than the pharmacy licensing board of the state in which the pharmacy is physically located if the state's licensing board does not conduct inspections as follows:

(i) an individual approved by the board who is not employed by the pharmacy but acting as a consultant to inspect the pharmacy;

(ii) an agent of the National Association of Boards of Pharmacy;

(iii) an agent of another State Board of Pharmacy; or

(iv) an agent of an accrediting body, such as the Joint Commission on Accreditation of Healthcare Organizations.

(B) The inspection must be substantively equivalent to an inspection conducted by the board.

(4) A Class E pharmacy which changes ownership shall notify the board within ten days of the change of ownership and apply for a new and separate license as specified in § 291.3 of this title (relating to Required Notifications).

(5) A Class E pharmacy which changes location and/or name shall notify the board of the change as specified in § 291.3 of this title.

(6) A Class E pharmacy owned by a partnership or corporation which changes managing officers shall notify the board in writing of the names of the new managing officers within ten days of the change, following the procedures in § 291.3 of this title.

(7) A Class E pharmacy shall notify the board in writing within ten days of closing.

(8) A separate license is required for each principal place of business and only one pharmacy license may be issued to a specific location.

(9) A fee as specified in § 291.6 of this title (relating to Pharmacy License Fees) will be charged for the issuance and renewal of a license and the issuance of an amended license.

(10) The board may grant an exemption from the licensing requirements of this Act on the application of a pharmacy located in a state of the United States other than this state that restricts its dispensing of prescription drugs or devices to residents of this state to isolated transactions.

(11) A Class E pharmacy engaged in the centralized dispensing of prescription drug or medication orders shall comply with the provisions of § 291.125 of this title (relating to Centralized Prescription Dispensing).

(12) A Class E pharmacy engaged in central processing of prescription drug or medication orders shall comply with the provisions of § 291.123 of this title (relating to Central Prescription or Medication Order Processing).

(13) A Class E pharmacy engaged in the compounding of non-sterile preparations shall comply with the provisions of § 291.131 of this title (relating to Pharmacies Compounding Non-Sterile Preparations).

(14) Class E pharmacy personnel shall not compound sterile preparations unless the pharmacy has applied for and obtained a Class E-S pharmacy.

(15) A Class E pharmacy, which operates as a community type of pharmacy which would otherwise be required to be licensed under the Act § 560.051(a)(1) (Community Pharmacy (Class A)), shall comply with the provisions of § 291.31 of this title (relating to Definitions), § 291.32 of this title (relating to Personnel), § 291.33 of this title (relating to Operational Standards), § 291.34 of this title (relating to Records), and § 291.35 of this title (relating to Official Prescription Requirements), contained in Community Pharmacy (Class A); or which operates as a nuclear type of pharmacy which would otherwise be required to be licensed under the Act § 560.051(a)(2) (Nuclear Pharmacy (Class B)), shall comply with the provisions of § 291.51 of this title (relating to Purpose), § 291.52 of this title (relating to Definitions), § 291.53 of this title (relating to Personnel), § 291.54 of this title (relating to Operational Standards), and § 291.55 of this title (relating to Records), contained in Nuclear Pharmacy (Class B), to the extent such sections are applicable to the operation of the pharmacy.

(b) Prescription dispensing and delivery.

(1) General.

(A) All prescription drugs and/or devices shall be dispensed and delivered safely and accurately as prescribed.

(B) The pharmacy shall maintain adequate storage or shipment containers and use shipping processes to ensure drug stability and potency. Such shipping processes shall include the use of packaging material and devices to ensure that the drug is maintained at an appropriate temperature range to maintain the integrity of the medication throughout the delivery process.

(C) The pharmacy shall utilize a delivery system which is designed to assure that the drugs are delivered to the appropriate patient.

(D) All pharmacists shall exercise sound professional judgment with respect to the accuracy and authenticity of any prescription drug order they dispense. If the pharmacist questions the accuracy or authenticity of a prescription drug order, he/she shall verify the order with the practitioner prior to dispensing.

(E) Prior to dispensing a prescription, pharmacists shall determine, in the exercise of sound professional judgment, that the prescription is a valid prescription. A pharmacist may not dispense a prescription drug if the pharmacist knows or should have known that the prescription was issued on the basis of an Internet-based or telephonic consultation without a valid patient-practitioner relationship.

(F) Subparagraph (E) of this paragraph does not prohibit a pharmacist from dispensing a prescription when a valid patient-practitioner relationship is not present in an emergency situation (e.g. a practitioner taking calls for the patient's regular practitioner).

(2) Drug regimen review.

(A) For the purpose of promoting therapeutic appropriateness, a pharmacist shall prior to or at the time of dispensing a prescription drug order, review the patient's medication record. Such review shall at a minimum identify clinically significant:

(i) inappropriate drug utilization;

(ii) therapeutic duplication;

(iii) drug-disease contraindications;

(iv) drug-drug interactions;

(v) incorrect drug dosage or duration of drug treatment;

(vi) drug-allergy interactions; and

(vii) clinical abuse/misuse.

(B) Upon identifying any clinically significant conditions, situations, or items listed in subparagraph (A) of this paragraph, the pharmacist shall take appropriate steps to avoid or resolve the problem including consultation with the prescribing practitioner. The pharmacist shall document such occurrences.

(3) Patient counseling and provision of drug information.

(A) To optimize drug therapy, a pharmacist shall communicate to the patient or the patient's agent, information about the prescription drug or device which in the exercise of the pharmacist's professional judgment the pharmacist deems significant, such as the following:

(i) the name and description of the drug or device;

(ii) dosage form, dosage, route of administration, and duration of drug therapy;

             (iii) special directions and precautions for preparation, administration, and use by the patient;

             (iv) common severe side or adverse effects or interactions and therapeutic contraindications that may be encountered, including their avoidance, and the action required if they occur;

             (v) techniques for self-monitoring of drug therapy;

             (vi) proper storage;

             (vii) refill information; and

             (viii) action to be taken in the event of a missed dose.

     (B) Such communication shall be:

             (i) provided to new and existing patients of a pharmacy with each new prescription drug order. A new prescription drug order is one that has not been dispensed by the pharmacy to the patient in the same dosage and strength within the last year;

             (ii) provided for any prescription drug order dispensed by the pharmacy on the request of the patient or patient's agent;

             (iii) communicated orally in person unless the patient or patient's agent is not at the pharmacy or a specific communication barrier prohibits such oral communication; and

             (iv) reinforced with written information. The following is applicable concerning this written information:

                  (I) Written information must be in plain language designed for the patient and printed in an easily readable font comparable to but no smaller than ten-point Times Roman. This information may be provided to the patient in an electronic format, such as by e-mail, if the patient or patient's agent requests the information in an electronic format and the pharmacy documents the request.

                  (II) When a compounded product is dispensed, information shall be provided for the major active ingredient(s), if available.

                  (III) For new drug entities, if no written information is initially available, the pharmacist is not required to provide information until such information is available, provided:

                     (-a-) the pharmacist informs the patient or the patient's agent that the product is a new drug entity and written information is not available;

                     (-b-) the pharmacist documents the fact that no written information was provided; and

                     (-c-) if the prescription is refilled after written information is available, such information is provided to the patient or patient's agent.

                  (IV) The written information accompanying the prescription or the prescription label shall contain the statement "Do not flush unused medications or pour down a sink or drain." A drug product on a list developed by the Federal Food and Drug Administration of medicines recommended for disposal by flushing is not required to bear this statement.

     (C) Only a pharmacist may orally provide drug information to a patient or patient's agent and answer questions concerning prescription drugs. Non-pharmacist personnel may not ask questions of a patient or patient's agent which are intended to screen and/or limit interaction with the pharmacist.

     (D) If prescriptions are routinely delivered outside the area covered by the pharmacy's local telephone service, the pharmacy shall provide a toll-free telephone line which is answered during normal business hours to enable communication between the patient and a pharmacist.

     (E) The pharmacist shall place on the prescription container or on a separate sheet delivered with the prescription container in both English and Spanish the local and toll-free telephone number of the pharmacy and the statement: "Written information about this prescription has been provided for you. Please read this information before you take the medication. If you have questions concerning this prescription, a pharmacist is available during normal business hours to answer these questions at (insert the pharmacy's local and toll-free telephone numbers)."

     (F) The provisions of this paragraph do not apply to patients in facilities where drugs are administered to patients by a person required to do so by the laws of the state (i.e., nursing homes).

     (G) Upon delivery of a refill prescription, a pharmacist shall ensure that the patient or patient's agent is offered information about the refilled prescription and that a pharmacist is available to discuss the patient's prescription and provide information.

     (H) Nothing in this subparagraph shall be construed as requiring a pharmacist to provide consultation when a patient or patient's agent refuses such consultation. The pharmacist shall document such refusal for consultation.

  (4) Labeling. At the time of delivery, the dispensing container shall bear a label that contains the following information:

     (A) the name, physical address, and phone number of the pharmacy;

     (B) if the drug is dispensed in a container other than the manufacturer's original container, the date after which the prescription should not be used or beyond-use-date. Unless otherwise specified by the manufacturer, the beyond-use-date shall be one year from the date the drug is dispensed or the manufacturer's expiration date, whichever is earlier. The beyond-use-date may be placed on the prescription label or on a flag label attached to the bottle. A beyond-use-date is not required on the label of a prescription dispensed to a person at the time of release from prison or jail if the prescription is for not more than a 10-day supply of medication;

     (C) either on the prescription label or the written information accompanying the prescription, the statement, "Do not flush unused medications or pour down a sink or drain." A drug product on a list developed by the Federal Food and Drug Administration of medicines recommended for disposal by flushing is not required to bear this statement; and

     (D) any other information that is required by the pharmacy or drug laws or rules in the state in which the pharmacy is located.

(c) Substitution requirements.

  (1) Unless compliance would violate the pharmacy or drug laws or rules in the state in which the pharmacy is located a pharmacist in a Class E pharmacy may dispense a generically equivalent drug or interchangeable biological product and shall comply with the provisions of § 309.3 of this title (relating to Substitution Requirements) and § 309.7 of this title (relating to Dispensing Responsibilities).

  (2) The pharmacy must include on the prescription order form completed by the patient or the patient's agent information that clearly and conspicuously:

(A) states that if a less expensive generically equivalent drug or interchangeable biological product is available for the brand prescribed, the patient or the patient's agent may choose between the generically equivalent drug or interchangeable biological product and the brand prescribed; and

(B) allows the patient or the patient's agent to indicate the choice of the generically equivalent drug or interchangeable biological product or the brand prescribed.

(d) Therapeutic Drug Interchange. A switch to a drug providing a similar therapeutic response to the one prescribed shall not be made without prior approval of the prescribing practitioner. This subsection does not apply to generic substitution. For generic substitution, see the requirements of subsection (c) of this section.

(1) The patient shall be notified of the therapeutic drug interchange prior to, or upon delivery, of the dispensed prescription to the patient. Such notification shall include:

(A) a description of the change;

(B) the reason for the change;

(C) whom to notify with questions concerning the change; and

(D) instructions for return of the drug if not wanted by the patient.

(2) The pharmacy shall maintain documentation of patient notification of therapeutic drug interchange which shall include:

(A) the date of the notification;

(B) the method of notification;

(C) a description of the change; and

(D) the reason for the change.

(e) Transfer of Prescription Drug Order Information. Unless compliance would violate the pharmacy or drug laws or rules in the state in which the pharmacy is located, a pharmacist in a Class E pharmacy may not refuse to transfer prescriptions to another pharmacy that is making the transfer request on behalf of the patient. The transfer of original prescription information must be done within four business hours of the request.

(f) Prescriptions for Schedules II - V controlled substances. Unless compliance would violate the pharmacy or drug laws or rules in the state in which the pharmacy is located, a pharmacist in a Class E pharmacy who dispenses a prescription for a Schedules II - V controlled substance for a resident of Texas shall electronically send the prescription information to the Texas State Board of Pharmacy as specified in § 315.6 of this title (relating to Pharmacy Responsibility - Electronic Reporting) not later than the next business day after the prescription is dispensed.

Source: The provisions of this § 291.104 adopted to be effective September 1, 2000, 25 TexReg 2617; amended to be effective December 15, 2002, 27 TexReg 11541; amended to be effective June 23, 2003, 28 TexReg 4638; amended to be effective June 6, 2004, 29 TexReg 5397; amended to be effective June 12, 2005, 30 TexReg 3209; amended to be effective March 6, 2006, 31 TexReg 1441; amended to be effective September 18, 2007, 32 TexReg 6348; amended to be effective June 8, 2008, 33 TexReg 4307; amended to be effective December 6, 2009, 34 TexReg 8703; amended to be effective May 30, 2010, 35 TexReg 4178; amended to be effective September 12, 2011, 36 TexReg 5847; amended tobe effective December 5, 2012, 37 TexReg 9514; amended to be effective December 10, 2013, 38 TexReg 8866; amended to be effective June 11, 2015, 40 TexReg 3646; amended to be effective December 6, 2015, 40 TexReg 8779; amended to be effective September 11, 2016, 41 TexReg 6717; amended to be effective December 6, 2018, 43 TexReg 7784

§291.105 Records

(a) Maintenance of records.

(1) Every record required to be kept under this section shall be:

(A) kept by the pharmacy and be available, for at least two years from the date of such record, for inspecting and copying by the board or its representative, and other authorized local, state, or federal law enforcement agencies; and

(B) supplied by the pharmacy within 72 hours, if requested by an authorized agent of the Texas State Board of Pharmacy. If the pharmacy maintains the records in an electronic format, the requested records must be provided in a mutually agreeable electronic format if specifically requested by the board or its representative. Failure to provide the records set out in this section, either on site or within 72 hours, constitutes prima facie evidence of failure to keep and maintain records in violation of the Act.

(2) Records, except when specifically required to be maintained in original or hard-copy form, may be maintained in an alternative data retention system, such as a data processing system or direct imaging system provided;

(A) the records maintained in the alternative system contain all of the information required on the manual record; and

(B) the data processing system is capable of producing a hard copy of the record upon the request of the board, its representative, or other authorized local, state, or federal law enforcement or regulatory agencies.

(b) Auto-Refill Programs. A pharmacy may use a program that automatically refills prescriptions that have existing refills available in order to improve patient compliance with and adherence to prescribed medication therapy. The following is applicable in order to enroll patients into an auto-refill program.

(1) Notice of the availability of an auto-refill program shall be given to the patient or patient's agent, and the patient or patient's agent must affirmatively indicate that they wish to enroll in such a program and the pharmacy shall document such indication.

(2) The patients or patient's agent shall have the option to withdraw from such a program at any time.

(3) Auto-refill programs may be used for refills of dangerous drugs, and schedule IV and V controlled substances. Schedule II and III controlled substances may not be dispensed by an auto-refill program.

(4) As is required for all prescriptions, a drug regimen review shall be completed on all prescriptions filled as a result of the auto-refill program. Special attention shall be noted for drug regimen review warnings of duplication of therapy and all such conflicts shall be resolved with the prescribing practitioner prior to refilling the prescription.

(c) Civil litigation and complaint records. A Class E pharmacy shall keep a permanent record of:

(1) any civil litigation commenced against the pharmacy by a Texas resident; and

(2) complaints that arise out of a prescription for a Texas resident lost during delivery.

Source: The provisions of this §291.105 adopted to be effective September 1, 2000, 25 TexReg 2617; amended to be effective June 6, 2004, 29 TexReg 5397; amended to be effective December 3, 2006, 31 TexReg 9611; amended to be effective September 18, 2007, 32 TexReg 6348; amended to be effective December 10, 2013, 38 TexReg 8866

§291.106 Pharmacies Compounding Sterile Preparations (Class E-S).

Licensing requirements. A non-resident pharmacy engaged in the compounding of sterile preparations shall be licensed as a Class E-S pharmacy.

(1) A Class E-S pharmacy shall register with the board on a pharmacy license application provided by the board, following the procedures specified in § 291.1 of this title (relating to Pharmacy License Application).

(2) A Class E-S license may not be issued unless the pharmacy has been inspected by the board or its designee to ensure the pharmacy meets the requirements as specified in § 291.133 of this title (relating to Pharmacies Compounding Sterile Preparations). A Class E-S pharmacy shall reimburse the board for all expenses, including travel, related to the inspection of the Class E-S pharmacy.

(3) On initial application, the pharmacy shall follow the procedures specified in § 291.1 of this title and then provide the following additional information specified in § 560.052(c) and (f) of the Act (relating to Qualifications):

   (A) evidence that the applicant holds a pharmacy license, registration, or permit issued by the state in which the pharmacy is located;

   (B) the name of the owner and pharmacist-in-charge of the pharmacy for service of process;

   (C) evidence of the applicant's ability to provide to the board a record of a prescription drug order dispensed by the applicant to a resident of this state not later than 72 hours after the time the board requests the record;

   (D) an affidavit by the pharmacist-in-charge which states that the pharmacist has read and understands the laws and rules relating to a Class E pharmacy; and

   (E) proof of creditworthiness.

(4) A Class E-S pharmacy may not renew a pharmacy license unless the pharmacy has been inspected by the board or its designee within the last renewal period.

(5) A Class E-S pharmacy which changes ownership shall notify the board within ten days of the change of ownership and apply for a new and separate license as specified in § 291.3 of this title (relating to Required Notifications).

(6) A Class E-S pharmacy which changes location and/or name shall notify the board as specified in § 291.3 of this title.

(7) A Class E-S pharmacy owned by a partnership or corporation which changes managing officers shall notify the board in writing of the names of the new managing officers within ten days of the change, as specified in § 291.3 of this title.

(8) A Class E-S pharmacy shall notify the board in writing within ten days of closing.

(9) A separate license is required for each principal place of business and only one pharmacy license may be issued to a specific location.

(10) A fee as specified in § 291.6 of this title (relating to Pharmacy License Fees) will be charged for the issuance and renewal of a license and the issuance of an amended license.

(11) The board may grant an exemption from the licensing requirements of this Act on the application of a pharmacy located in a state of the United States other than this state that restricts its dispensing of prescription drugs or devices to residents of this state to isolated transactions.

(12) A Class E-S pharmacy engaged in the centralized dispensing of prescription drug or medication orders shall comply with the provisions of § 291.125 of this title (relating to Centralized Prescription Dispensing).

(13) A Class E-S pharmacy engaged in central processing of prescription drug or medication orders shall comply with the provisions of § 291.123 of this title (relating to Central Prescription or Medication Order Processing).

(14) A Class E-S pharmacy engaged in the compounding of non-sterile preparations shall comply with the provisions of § 291.131 of this title (relating to Pharmacies Compounding Non-Sterile Preparations).

(15) A Class E-S pharmacy engaged in the compounding of sterile preparations shall comply with the provisions of § 291.133 of this title.

(16) A Class E-S pharmacy which would otherwise be required to be licensed under the Act, § 560.051(a)(5) concerning Non-Resident Pharmacy (Class E) is required to comply with the provisions of § 291.101 of this title (relating to Purpose), § 291.102 of this title (relating to Definitions), § 291.103 of this title (relating to Personnel), § 291.104 of this title (relating to Operational Standards) and § 291.105 of this title (relating to Records).

Source: The provisions of this § 291.106 adopted to be effective December 10, 2013, 38 TexReg 8866; amended to be effective June 11, 2015, 40 TexReg 3646; amended to be effective March 19, 2017, 42 TexReg 1127

SUBCHAPTER G. SERVICES PROVIDED BY PHARMACIES

§291.120 General

(a) Purpose. This subchapter applies to all classes of pharmacies except as otherwise noted.

(b) Definitions.

   (1) The Texas Pharmacy Act or Act—Subtitle J, other than Chapter 567, Occupations Code, as amended.

   (2) Board—The Texas State Board of Pharmacy.

Source: The provisions of this §291.120 adopted to be effective September 18, 2007, 32 TexReg 6352

§291.121 Remote Pharmacy Services

(a) Remote pharmacy services using automated pharmacy systems.

   (1) Purpose. The purpose of this section is to provide standards for the provision of pharmacy services by a Class A or Class C pharmacy in a facility that is not at the same location as the Class A or Class C pharmacy through an automated pharmacy system as outlined in § 562.109 of the Texas Pharmacy Act.

   (2) Definitions. The following words and terms, when used in this section, shall have the following meanings, unless the context clearly indicates otherwise. All other words and terms shall have the meanings defined in the Act.

      (A) Automated pharmacy system—A mechanical system that dispenses prescription drugs and maintains related transaction information.

(B) Prepackaging—The act of repackaging and relabeling quantities of drug products from a manufacturer's original commercial container, or quantities of unit dosed drugs, into another cartridge or container for dispensing by a pharmacist using an automated pharmacy system.

(C) Provider pharmacy—The community pharmacy (Class A) or the institutional pharmacy (Class C) providing remote pharmacy services.

(D) Remote pharmacy service—The provision of pharmacy services, including the storage and dispensing of prescription drugs, in remote sites.

(E) Remote site—A facility not located at the same location as a Class A or Class C pharmacy, at which remote pharmacy services are provided using an automated pharmacy dispensing system.

(F) Unit dose—An amount of a drug packaged in a dosage form ready for administration to a particular patient, by the prescribed route at the prescribed time, and properly labeled with name, strength, and expiration date of the drug.

(3) General requirements.

(A) A provider pharmacy may provide remote pharmacy services using an automated pharmacy system to a jail or prison operated by or for the State of Texas, a jail or prison operated by local government or a healthcare facility regulated under Chapter 142, 242, 247, or 252, Health and Safety Code, provided drugs are administered by a licensed healthcare professional working in the jail, prison, or healthcare facility.

(B) A provider pharmacy may only provide remote pharmacy services using an automated pharmacy system to inpatients of the remote site.

(C) A provider pharmacy may provide remote pharmacy services at more than one remote site.

(D) Before providing remote pharmacy services, the automated pharmacy system at the remote site must be tested by the provider pharmacy and found to dispense accurately. The provider pharmacy shall make the results of such testing available to the board upon request.

(E) A provider pharmacy which is licensed as an institutional (Class C) pharmacy is required to comply with the provisions of §§ 291.31 - 291.34 of this title (relating to Definitions, Personnel, Operational Standards, and Records for Class A (Community) Pharmacies) and this section.

(F) The pharmacist-in-charge of the provider pharmacy is responsible for all pharmacy operations involving the automated pharmacy system located at the remote site including supervision of the automated pharmacy system and compliance with this section.

(G) A pharmacist from the provider pharmacy shall be accessible at all times to respond to patient's or other health professionals' questions and needs pertaining to drugs dispensed through the use of the automated pharmacy system. Such access may be through a 24 hour pager service or telephone which is answered 24 hours a day.

(4) Operational standards.

(A) Application for permission to provide pharmacy services using an automated pharmacy system.

(i) A Class A or Class C Pharmacy shall file a completed application containing all information required by the board to provide remote pharmacy services using an automated pharmacy system.

(ii) Such application shall be resubmitted every two years in conjunction with the application for renewal of the provider pharmacy's license.

(iii) Upon approval of the application, the provider pharmacy will be sent a certificate which must be displayed at the remote site.

(B) Notification requirements.

(i) A provider pharmacy shall notify the board in writing within ten days of a discontinuance of service, or closure of:

(I) a remote site where an automated pharmacy system is operated by the pharmacy; or

(II) a remote pharmacy service at a remote site.

(ii) A provider pharmacy shall comply with appropriate federal and state controlled substance registrations for each remote site if controlled substances are maintained within an automated pharmacy system at the facility.

(iii) A provider pharmacy shall file a change of location and/or name of a remote site as specified in § 291.3 (relating to Notifications) of this title.

(C) Environment/Security.

(i) A provider pharmacy shall only store drugs at a remote site within an automated pharmacy system which is locked by key, combination or other mechanical or electronic means so as to prohibit access by unauthorized personnel.

(ii) An automated pharmacy system shall be under the continuous supervision of a provider pharmacy pharmacist. To qualify as continuous supervision, the pharmacist is not required to be physically present at the site of the automated pharmacy system if the system is supervised electronically by a pharmacist.

(iii) Automated pharmacy systems shall have adequate security and procedures to:

(I) comply with federal and state laws and regulations; and

(II) maintain patient confidentiality.

(iv) Access to the automated pharmacy system shall be limited to pharmacists or personnel who:

(I) are designated in writing by the pharmacist-in-charge; and

(II) have completed documented training concerning their duties associated with the automated pharmacy system.

(v) Drugs shall be stored in compliance with the provisions of § 291.15 of this title (relating to Storage of Drugs) and § 291.33(f)(2) of this title including the requirements for temperature and handling of outdated drugs.

(D) Prescription dispensing and delivery.

(i) Drugs shall only be dispensed at a remote site through an automated pharmacy system after receipt of an original prescription drug order by a pharmacist at the provider pharmacy in a manner authorized by § 291.34(b) of this title.

(ii) A pharmacist at the provider pharmacy shall control all operations of the automated pharmacy system and approve the release of the initial dose of a prescription drug order. Subsequent doses from an approved prescription drug order may be removed from the automated medication system after this initial approval. Any change made in the prescription drug order shall require a new approval by a pharmacist to release the drug.

        (iii) A pharmacist at the provider pharmacy shall conduct a drug regimen review as specified in § 291.33(c) of this title prior to releasing a prescription drug order to the automated pharmacy system.

        (iv) Drugs dispensed by the provider pharmacy through an automated pharmacy system shall comply with the labeling or labeling alternatives specified in § 291.33(c) of this title.

        (v) An automated pharmacy system used to meet the emergency medication needs for residents of a remote site must comply with the requirements for emergency medication kits in subsection (b) of this section.

  (E) Drugs.

        (i) Drugs for use in an automated pharmacy system shall be packaged in the original manufacturer's container or be prepackaged in the provider pharmacy and labeled in compliance with the board's prepackaging requirements for the class of pharmacy.

        (ii) Drugs dispensed from the automated pharmacy system may be returned to the pharmacy for reuse provided the drugs are in sealed, tamper evident packaging which has not been opened.

  (F) Stocking an automated pharmacy system.

        (i) Stocking of drugs in an automated pharmacy system shall be completed by a pharmacist, pharmacy technician, or pharmacy technician trainee under the direct supervision of a pharmacist, except as provided in clause (ii) of this subparagraph.

        (ii) If the automated pharmacy system uses removable cartridges or containers to hold drugs, the prepackaging of the cartridges or containers shall occur at the provider pharmacy unless provided by an FDA approved repackager. The prepackaged cartridges or containers may be sent to the remote site to be loaded into the machine by personnel designated by the pharmacist-in-charge provided:

           (I) a pharmacist verifies the cartridge or container has been properly filled and labeled;

           (II) the individual cartridges or containers are transported to the remote site in a secure, tamper-evident container; and

           (III) the automated pharmacy system uses bar-coding, microchip, or other technologies to ensure that the containers are accurately loaded in the automated pharmacy system.

        (iii) All drugs to be stocked in the automated pharmacy system shall be delivered to the remote site by the provider pharmacy.

  (G) Quality assurance program. A pharmacy that provides pharmacy services through an automated pharmacy system at a remote site shall operate according to a written program for quality assurance of the automated pharmacy system which:

        (i) requires continuous supervision of the automated pharmacy system; and

        (ii) establishes mechanisms and procedures to routinely test the accuracy of the automated pharmacy system at a minimum of every six months and whenever any upgrade or change is made to the system and documents each such activity.

  (H) Policies and procedures of operation.

        (i) A pharmacy that provides pharmacy services through an automated pharmacy system at a remote site shall operate according to written policies and procedures. The policy and procedure manual shall include, but not be limited to, the following:

           (I) a current list of the name and address of the pharmacist-in-charge and personnel designated by the pharmacist-in-charge to have access to the drugs stored in the automated pharmacy system;

           (II) duties which may only be performed by a pharmacist;

           (III) a copy of the portion of the written contract or agreement between the pharmacy and the facility which outlines the services to be provided and the responsibilities and accountabilities of each party relating to the operation of the automated pharmacy system in fulfilling the terms of the contract in compliance with federal and state laws and regulations;

           (IV) date of last review/revision of the policy and procedure manual; and

           (V) policies and procedures for:

               (-a-) security;

               (-b-) operation of the automated pharmacy system;

               (-c-) preventative maintenance of the automated pharmacy system;

               (-d-) sanitation;

               (-e-) storage of drugs;

               (-f-) dispensing;

               (-g-) supervision;

               (-h-) drug procurement;

               (-i-) receiving of drugs;

               (-j-) delivery of drugs; and

               (-k-) record keeping.

        (ii) A pharmacy that provides pharmacy services through an automated pharmacy system at a remote site shall, at least annually, review its written policies and procedures, revise them if necessary, and document the review.

        (iii) A pharmacy providing remote pharmacy services using an automated pharmacy system shall maintain a written plan for recovery from an event which interrupts the ability of the automated pharmacy system to dispense prescription drugs. The written plan for recovery shall include:

           (I) planning and preparation for maintaining pharmacy services when an automated pharmacy system is experiencing downtime;

           (II) procedures for response when an automated pharmacy system is experiencing downtime; and

           (III) procedures for the maintenance and testing of the written plan for recovery.

(5) Records.

  (A) Maintenance of records.

        (i) Every record required under this section must be:

     (I) kept by the provider pharmacy and be available, for at least two years for inspecting and copying by the board or its representative and to other authorized local, state, or federal law enforcement agencies; and

     (II) supplied by the provider pharmacy within 72 hours, if requested by an authorized agent of the Texas State Board of Pharmacy. If the pharmacy maintains the records in an electronic format, the requested records must be provided in an electronic format if specifically requested by the board or its representative. Failure to provide the records set out in this section, either on site or within 72 hours, constitutes prima facie evidence of failure to keep and maintain records in violation of the Act.

    (ii) The provider pharmacy shall maintain original prescription drug orders for drugs dispensed from an automated pharmacy system in compliance with § 291.34(b) of this title.

    (iii) if prescription drug records are maintained in a data processing system, the system shall have a workable (electronic) data retention system which can produce a separate audit trail of drug usage by the provider pharmacy and each remote site for the preceding two years as specified in § 291.34(e) of this title.

  (B) Prescriptions. Prescription drug orders shall meet the requirements of § 291.34(b) of this title.

  (C) Records of dispensing. Dispensing records for a prescription drug order shall be maintained by the provider pharmacy in the manner required by § 291.34(d) or (e) of this title.

  (D) Transaction information.

    (i) The automated pharmacy system shall electronically record all transactions involving drugs stored in, removed, or dispensed from the system.

    (ii) Records of dispensing from an automated pharmacy system for a patient shall be maintained by the providing pharmacy and include the:

     (I) identity of the system accessed;

     (II) identification of the individual accessing the system;

     (III) date of transaction;

     (IV) name, strength, dosage form, and quantity of drug accessed; and

     (V) name of the patient for whom the drug was accessed.

    (iii) Records of stocking or removal from an automated pharmacy system shall be maintained by the pharmacy and include the:

     (I) date;

     (II) name, strength, dosage form, and quantity of drug stocked or removed;

     (III) name, initials, or identification code of the person stocking or removing drugs from the system;

     (IV) name, initials, or identification code of the pharmacist who checks and verifies that the system has been accurately filled;

  (E) Patient medication records. Patient medication records shall be created and maintained by the provider pharmacy in the manner required by § 291.34(c) of this title.

  (F) Inventory.

    (i) A provider pharmacy shall:

     (I) keep a record of all drugs sent to and returned from a remote site separate from the records of the provider pharmacy and from any other remote site's records; and

     (II) keep a perpetual inventory of controlled substances and other drugs required to be inventoried under § 291.17 of this title (relating to Inventory Requirements for All Classes of Pharmacies) that are received and dispensed or distributed from each remote site.

    (ii) As specified in § 291.17 of this title, a provider pharmacy shall conduct an inventory at each remote site. The following is applicable to this inventory.

     (I) The inventory of each remote site and the provider pharmacy shall be taken on the same day.

     (II) The inventory of each remote site shall be included with, but listed separately from, the drugs of other remote sites and separately from the drugs of the provider pharmacy.

(b) Remote pharmacy services using emergency medication kits.

 (1) Purpose. The purpose of this section is to provide standards for the provision of pharmacy services by a Class A or Class C pharmacy in a facility that is not at the same location as the Class A or Class C pharmacy through an emergency medication kit as outlined in § 562.108 of the Texas Pharmacy Act.

 (2) Definitions. The following words and terms, when used in this subsection, shall have the following meanings, unless the context clearly indicates otherwise. All other words and terms shall have the meanings defined in the Act or § 291.31 of this title.

  (A) Automated pharmacy system—A mechanical system that dispenses prescription drugs and maintains related transaction information.

  (B) Emergency medication kits—Controlled substances and dangerous drugs maintained by a provider pharmacy to meet the emergency medication needs of a resident:

    (i) at an institution licensed under Chapter 242 or 252, Health and Safety Code; or

    (ii) at an institution licensed under Chapter 242, Health and Safety Code and that is a veterans home as defined by the § 164.002, Natural Resources Code, if the provider pharmacy is a United States Department of Veterans Affairs pharmacy or another federally operated pharmacy.

  (C) Prepackaging—The act of repackaging and relabeling quantities of drug products from a manufacturer's original commercial container, or quantities of unit dosed drugs, into another cartridge or container for dispensing by a pharmacist using an emergency medication kit.

  (D) Provider pharmacy—The community pharmacy (Class A), the institutional pharmacy (Class C), the non-resident (Class E) pharmacy located not more than 20 miles from an institution licensed under Chapter 242 or 252, Health and Safety Code, or the United States Department of Veterans Affairs pharmacy or another federally operated pharmacy providing remote pharmacy services.

    (E) Remote pharmacy service—The provision of pharmacy services, including the storage and dispensing of prescription drugs, in remote sites.

    (F) Remote site—A facility not located at the same location as a Class A, Class C, Class E pharmacy or a United States Department of Affairs pharmacy or another federally operated pharmacy, at which remote pharmacy services are provided using an emergency medication kit.

(3) General requirements.

    (A) A provider pharmacy may provide remote pharmacy services using an emergency medication kit to an institution regulated under Chapter 242, or 252, Health and Safety Code.

    (B) A provider pharmacy may provide remote pharmacy services at more than one remote site.

    (C) A provider pharmacy shall not place an emergency medication kit in a remote site which already has a kit from another provider pharmacy except as provided by paragraph (4)(B)(iii) of this subsection.

    (D) A provider pharmacy which is licensed as an institutional (Class C) or a non-resident (Class E) pharmacy is required to comply with the provisions of §§ 291.31 - 291.34 of this title and this section.

    (E) The pharmacist-in-charge of the provider pharmacy is responsible for all pharmacy operations involving the emergency medication kit located at the remote site including supervision of the emergency medication kit and compliance with this section.

(4) Operational standards.

    (A) Application for permission to provide pharmacy services using an emergency medication kit.

       (i) A Class A, Class C, or Class E Pharmacy shall file a completed application containing all information required by the board to provide remote pharmacy services using an emergency medication kit.

       (ii) Such application shall be resubmitted every two years in conjunction with the application for renewal of the provider pharmacy's license.

       (iii) Upon approval of the application, the provider pharmacy will be sent a certificate which must be displayed at the remote site.

    (B) Notification requirements.

       (i) A provider pharmacy shall notify the board in writing within ten days of a discontinuance of service, or closure of:

          (I) a remote site where an emergency medication kit is operated by the pharmacy; or

          (II) a remote pharmacy service at a remote site.

       (ii) A provider pharmacy shall comply with appropriate federal and state controlled substance registrations for each remote site if controlled substances are maintained within an emergency medication kit at the facility.

       (iii) If more than one provider pharmacy provides an emergency kit to a remote site, the provider pharmacies must enter into a written agreement as to the emergency medications supplied by each pharmacy. The provider pharmacies shall not duplicate drugs stored in the emergency medication kits. The written agreement shall include reasons why an additional pharmacy is required to meet the emergency medication needs of the residents of the institution.

       (iv) A provider pharmacy shall file a change of location and/or name of a remote site as specified in § 291.3 of this title.

    (C) Environment/Security.

       (i) Emergency medication kits shall have adequate security and procedures to:

          (I) prohibit unauthorized access;

          (II) comply with federal and state laws and regulations; and

          (III) maintain patient confidentiality.

       (ii) Access to the emergency medication kit shall be limited to pharmacists and licensed healthcare personnel employed by the facility.

       (iii) Drugs shall be stored in compliance with the provisions of § 291.15 and § 291.33(f)(2) of this title including the requirements for temperature and handling outdated drugs.

    (D) Prescription dispensing and delivery.

       (i) Drugs in the emergency medication kit shall be accessed for administration to meet the emergency medication needs of a resident of the remote site pursuant to an order from a practitioner. The prescription drug order for the drugs used from the emergency medication kit shall be forwarded to the provider pharmacy in a manner authorized by § 291.34(b) of this title.

       (ii) The remote site shall notify the provider pharmacy of each entry into an emergency medication kit. Such notification shall meet the requirements of paragraph (5)(D)(ii) of this subsection.

    (E) Drugs.

       (i) The contents of an emergency medication kit:

          (I) may consist of dangerous drugs and controlled substances; and

          (II) shall be determined by the consultant pharmacist, pharmacist-in-charge of the provider pharmacy, medical director, and the director of nurses and limited to those drugs necessary to meet the resident's emergency medication needs. For the purpose of this subsection, this shall mean a situation in which a drug cannot be supplied by a pharmacy within a reasonable time period.

       (ii) When deciding on the drugs to be placed in the emergency medication kit, the consultant pharmacist, pharmacist-in-charge of the provider pharmacy, medical director, and the director of nurses must determine, select, and record a prudent number of drugs for potential emergency incidents based on:

          (I) clinical criteria applicable to each facility's demographics;

          (II) the facility's census; and

          (III) the facility's healthcare environment.

       (iii) A current list of the drugs stored in each remote site's emergency medication kit shall be maintained by the provider pharmacy and a copy kept with the emergency medication kit.

       (iv) An automated pharmacy system may be used as an emergency medication kit provided the system limits emergency access to only those drugs approved for the emergency medication kit.

        (v) Drugs for use in an emergency medication kit shall be packaged in the original manufacturer's container or prepackaged in the provider pharmacy and labeled in compliance with the board's prepackaging requirements for the class of pharmacy.

    (F) Stocking emergency medication kits.

        (i) Stocking of drugs in an emergency medication kit shall be completed at the provider pharmacy or remote site by a pharmacist, pharmacy technician, or pharmacy technician trainee under the direct supervision of a pharmacist, except as provided in clause (ii) of this subparagraph.

        (ii) If the emergency medication kit is an automated pharmacy system which uses bar-coding, microchip, or other technologies to ensure that the containers or unit dose drugs are accurately loaded, the prepackaging of the containers or unit dose drugs shall occur at the provider pharmacy unless provided by a FDA approved repackager. The prepackaged containers or unit dose drugs may be sent to the remote site to be loaded into the machine by personnel designated by the pharmacist-in-charge provided:

            (I) a pharmacist verifies the container or unit dose drug has been properly filled and labeled;

            (II) the individual containers or unit dose drugs are transported to the remote site in a secure, tamper-evident container; and

            (III) the automated pharmacy system uses bar-coding, microchip, or other technologies to ensure that the containers or unit dose drugs are accurately loaded in the automated pharmacy system.

        (iii) All drugs to be stocked in the emergency medication kit shall be delivered to the remote site by the provider pharmacy.

    (G) Policies and procedures of operation.

        (i) A provider pharmacy that provides pharmacy services through an emergency medication kit at a remote site shall operate according to written policies and procedures. The policy and procedure manual shall include, but not be limited to, the following:

            (I) duties which may only be performed by a pharmacist;

            (II) a copy of the written contract or agreement between the pharmacy and the facility which outlines the services to be provided and the responsibilities and accountabilities of each party in fulfilling the terms of the contract in compliance with federal and state laws and regulations;

            (III) date of last review/revision of the policy and procedure manual; and

            (IV) policies and procedures for:

                (-a-) security;

                (-b-) operation of the emergency medication kit;

                (-c-) preventative maintenance of the automated pharmacy system if the emergency medication kit is an automated pharmacy system;

                (-d-) sanitation;

                (-e-) storage of drugs;

                (-f-) dispensing;

                (-g-) supervision;

                (-h-) drug procurement;

                (-i-) receiving of drugs;

                (-j-) delivery of drugs; and

                (-k-) record keeping.

        (ii) A pharmacy that provides pharmacy services through an emergency medication kit at a remote site shall, at least annually, review its written policies and procedures, revise them if necessary, and document the review.

        (iii) A pharmacy providing remote pharmacy services using an emergency medication kit which is an automated pharmacy system shall maintain a written plan for recovery from an event which interrupts the ability of the automated pharmacy system to provide emergency medications. The written plan for recovery shall include:

            (I) planning and preparation for maintaining pharmacy services when an automated pharmacy system is experiencing downtime;

            (II) procedures for response when an automated pharmacy system is experiencing downtime; and

            (III) procedures for the maintenance and testing of the written plan for recovery.

  (5) Records.

    (A) Maintenance of records.

        (i) Every record required under this section must be:

            (I) kept by the provider pharmacy and be available, for at least two years for inspecting and copying by the board or its representative and to other authorized local, state, or federal law enforcement agencies; and

            (II) supplied by the provider pharmacy within 72 hours, if requested by an authorized agent of the Texas State Board of Pharmacy. If the pharmacy maintains the records in an electronic format, the requested records must be provided in an electronic format if specifically requested by the board or its representative. Failure to provide the records set out in this section, either on site or within 72 hours, constitutes prima facie evidence of failure to keep and maintain records in violation of the Act.

        (ii) The provider pharmacy shall maintain original prescription drug orders for drugs dispensed from an emergency medication kit in compliance with § 291.34(b) of this title.

    (B) Prescriptions. Prescription drug orders shall meet the requirements of § 291.34(b) of this title.

    (C) Records of dispensing. Dispensing records for a prescription drug order shall be maintained by the provider pharmacy in the manner required by § 291.34(d) or (e) of this title.

    (D) Transaction information.

        (i) A prescription drug order shall be maintained by the provider pharmacy as the record of removal of a drug from an emergency medication kit for administration to a patient.

             (ii) The remote site shall notify the provider pharmacy electronically or in writing of each entry into an emergency medication kit. Such notification may be included on the prescription drug order or a separate document and shall include the name, strength, and quantity of the drug removed, the time of removal, and the name of the person removing the drug.

             (iii) A separate record of stocking, removal, or dispensing for administration from an emergency medication kit shall be maintained by the pharmacy and include the:

                (I) date;

                (II) name, strength, dosage form, and quantity of drug stocked, removed, or dispensed for administration;

                (III) name, initials, or identification code of the person stocking, removing, or dispensing for administration, drugs from the system;

                (IV) name, initials, or identification code of the pharmacist who checks and verifies that the system has been accurately filled; and

                (V) unique prescription number assigned to the prescription drug order when the drug is administered to the patient.

       (E) Inventory.

          (i) A provider pharmacy shall:

             (I) keep a record of all drugs sent to and returned from a remote site separate from the records of the provider pharmacy and from any other remote site's records; and

             (II) keep a perpetual inventory of controlled substances and other drugs required to be inventoried under § 291.17 of this title, that are received and dispensed or distributed from each remote site.

          (ii) As specified in § 291.17 of this title, a provider pharmacy shall conduct an inventory at each remote site. The following is applicable to this inventory.

             (I) The inventory of each remote site and the provider pharmacy shall be taken on the same day.

             (II) The inventory of each remote site shall be included with, but listed separately from, the drugs of other remote sites and separately from the drugs of the provider pharmacy.

(c) Remote pharmacy services using telepharmacy systems.

    (1) Purpose. The purpose of this section is to provide standards for the provision of pharmacy services by a Class A or Class C pharmacy in a healthcare facility that is not at the same location as a Class A or Class C pharmacy through a telepharmacy system as outlined in § 562.110 of the Texas Pharmacy Act.

    (2) Definitions. The following words and terms, when used in this section, shall have the following meanings, unless the context clearly indicates otherwise. All other words and terms shall have the meanings defined in the Act or § 291.31 of this title.

       (A) Provider pharmacy—

          (i) a Class A pharmacy that provides pharmacy services through a telepharmacy system at a remote dispensing site or at a healthcare facility that is regulated by this state or the United States; or

          (ii) a Class C pharmacy that provides pharmacy services though a telepharmacy system at a healthcare facility that is regulated by this state or the United States.

       (B) Remote dispensing site—a location licensed as a telepharmacy that is authorized by a provider pharmacy through a telepharmacy system to store and dispense prescription drugs and devices, including dangerous drugs and controlled substances.

       (C) Remote healthcare site—a healthcare facility regulated by this state or the United States that is a:

          (i) rural health clinic regulated under 42 U.S.C. Section 1395x(aa);

          (ii) health center as defined by 42 U.S.C. Section 254b;

          (iii) healthcare facility located in a medically underserved area as determined by the United States Department of Health and Human Services; or

          (iv) healthcare facility located in a health professional shortage area as determined by the United States Department of Health and Human Services.

       (D) Remote pharmacy service—The provision of pharmacy services, including the storage and dispensing of prescription drugs, drug regimen review, and patient counseling, at a remote site.

       (E) Remote site—a remote healthcare site or a remote dispensing site.

       (F) Still image capture—A specific image captured electronically from a video or other image capture device.

       (G) Store and forward—A video or still image record which is saved electronically for future review.

       (H) Telepharmacy system—A system that monitors the dispensing of prescription drugs and provides for related drug use review and patient counseling services by an electronic method which shall include the use of the following types of technology:

          (i) audio and video;

          (ii) still image capture; and

          (iii) store and forward.

    (3) General requirements.

       (A) A provider pharmacy may provide remote pharmacy services using a telepharmacy system at a:

          (i) remote healthcare site; or

          (ii) remote dispensing site.

       (B) A provider pharmacy may not provide remote pharmacy services at a remote healthcare site if a Class A or Class C pharmacy that dispenses prescription drug orders to out-patients is located in the same community. For the purposes of this subsection a community is defined as:

          (i) the census tract in which the remote site is located, if the remote site is located in a Metropolitan Statistical Area (MSA) as defined by the United States Census Bureau in the most recent U.S. Census; or

          (ii) within 10 miles of the remote site, if the remote site is not located in a MSA.

       (C) A provider pharmacy may not provide remote pharmacy services at a remote dispensing site if a Class A pharmacy is located within 22 miles by road of the remote dispensing site.

(D) If a Class A or Class pharmacy is established in a community in which a remote healthcare site has been located, the remote healthcare site may continue to operate.

(E) If a Class A pharmacy is established within 22 miles by road of a remote dispensing site that is currently operating, the remote dispensing site may continue to operate at that location.

(F) Before providing remote pharmacy services, the telepharmacy system at the remote site must be tested by the provider pharmacy and found to operate properly. The provider pharmacy shall make the results of such testing available to the board upon request.

(G) A provider pharmacy which is licensed as a Class C pharmacy is required to comply with the provisions of §§ 291.31 - 291.34 of this title and this section.

(H) A provider pharmacy can only provide pharmacy services at no more than two remote dispensing sites.

(4) Personnel.

(A) The pharmacist-in-charge of the provider pharmacy is responsible for all operations at the remote site including supervision of the telepharmacy system and compliance with this section.

(B) The provider pharmacy shall have sufficient pharmacists on duty such that each pharmacist may supervise no more two remote sites that are simultaneously open to provide services.

(C) The following duties shall be performed only by a pharmacist at the provider pharmacy:

(i) receiving an oral prescription drug order;

(ii) interpreting the prescription drug order;

(iii) verifying the accuracy of prescription data entry;

(iv) selecting the drug product to be stored and dispensed at the remote site;

(v) interpreting the patient's medication record and conducting a drug regimen review;

(vi) authorizing the telepharmacy system to print a prescription label at the remote site;

(vii) performing the final check of the dispensed prescription to ensure that the prescription drug order has been dispensed accurately as prescribed; and

(viii) counseling the patient.

(5) Operational standards.

(A) Application to provide remote pharmacy services using a telepharmacy system.

(i) A Class A or class C Pharmacy shall file a completed application containing all information required by the board to provide remote pharmacy services using a telepharmacy system.

(ii) Such application shall be resubmitted every two years in conjunction with the renewal of the provider pharmacy's license.

(iii) On approval of the application, the provider pharmacy will be sent a license for the remote site, which must be displayed at the remote site.

(iv) If the average number of prescriptions dispensed each day at a remote dispensing site is open for business is more than 125 prescriptions, as calculated each calendar year, the remote dispensing site shall apply for a Class A pharmacy license as specified in § 291.1 of this title (relating to Pharmacy License Application).

(B) Notification requirements.

(i) A provider pharmacy shall notify the board in writing within ten days of a discontinuance of service, or closure of a remote site where a telepharmacy system is operated by the pharmacy.

(ii) A provider pharmacy shall comply with appropriate federal and state controlled substance registrations for each remote site, if controlled substances are maintained.

(iii) A provider pharmacy shall file a change of location and/or name of a remote site as specified in § 291.3 of this title.

(C) Environment/Security.

(i) A remote site shall be under the continuous supervision of a provider pharmacy pharmacist at all times the site is open to provide pharmacy services. To qualify as continuous supervision, the pharmacist is not required to be physically present at the remote site and shall supervise electronically through the use of the following types of technology:

(I) audio and video;

(II) still image capture; and

(III) store and forward.

(ii) Drugs shall be stored in compliance with the provisions of § 291.15 and § 291.33(f)(2) of this title including the requirements for temperature and handling of outdated drugs.

(iii) Drugs for use in the telepharmacy system at a remote healthcare site shall be stored in an area that is:

(I) separate from any other drugs used by the healthcare facility; and

(II) locked by key, combination or other mechanical or electronic means, so as to prohibit access by unauthorized personnel.

(iv) Drugs for use in the telepharmacy system at a remote dispensing site shall be stored in an area that is locked by key, combination, or other mechanical or electronic means, so as to prohibit access by unauthorized personnel.

(v) Access to the area where drugs are stored at the remote site and operation of the telepharmacy system shall be limited to:

(I) pharmacists employed by the provider pharmacy;

(II) licensed healthcare providers, if the remote site is a remote healthcare site; and

(III) pharmacy technicians;

(vi) Individuals authorized to access the remote site and operate the telepharmacy system shall:

(I) be designated in writing by the pharmacist-in-charge; and

(II) have completed documented training concerning their duties associated with the telepharmacy pharmacy system.

(vii) Remote sites shall have adequate security and procedures to:

(I) comply with federal and state laws and regulations; and

(II) maintain patient confidentiality.

(D) Prescription dispensing and delivery.
  (i) A pharmacist at the provider pharmacy shall conduct a drug regimen review as specified in § 291.33(c) of this title prior to delivery of the dispensed prescription to the patient or patient's agent.
  (ii) The dispensed prescription shall be labeled at the remote site with the information specified in § 291.33(c) of this title.
  (iii) A pharmacist at the provider pharmacy shall perform the final check of the dispensed prescription before delivery to the patient to ensure that the prescription has been dispensed accurately as prescribed. This final check shall be accomplished through a visual check using electronic methods.
  (iv) A pharmacist at the provider pharmacy shall counsel the patient or patient's agent as specified in § 291.33(c) of this title. This counseling may be performed using electronic methods. Non-pharmacist personnel may not ask questions of a patient or patient's agent which are intended to screen and/or limit interaction with the pharmacist.
  (v) If the remote site has direct access to the provider pharmacy's data processing system, only a pharmacist or pharmacy technician may enter prescription information into the data processing system.
  (vi) Drugs which require reconstitution through the addition of a specified amount of water may be dispensed by the remote site only if a pharmacy technician, pharmacy technician trainee, or licensed healthcare provider reconstitutes the product.
  (vii) A telepharmacy system located at a remote dispensing site may not dispense a schedule II controlled substance.
  (viii) Drugs dispensed at the remote site through a telepharmacy system shall only be delivered to the patient or patient's agent at the remote site.
(E) Quality assurance program. A pharmacy that provides remote pharmacy services through a telepharmacy system at a remote site shall operate according to a written program for quality assurance of the telepharmacy system which:
  (i) requires continuous supervision of the telepharmacy system at all times the site is open to provide remote pharmacy services; and
  (ii) establishes mechanisms and procedures to routinely test the operation of the telepharmacy system at a minimum of every six months and whenever any upgrade or change is made to the system and documents each such activity.
(F) Policies and procedures.
  (i) A pharmacy that provides pharmacy services through a telepharmacy system at a remote site shall operate according to written policies and procedures. The policy and procedure manual shall include, but not be limited to, the following:
    (I) a current list of the name and address of the pharmacist-in-charge and personnel designated by the pharmacist-in-charge to have:
      (-a-) have access to the area where drugs are stored at the remote site; and
      (-b-) operate the telepharmacy system;
    (II) duties which may only be performed by a pharmacist;
    (III) if the remote site is located at a remote healthcare site, a copy of the written contact or agreement between the provider pharmacy and the healthcare facility which outlines the services to be provided and the responsibilities and accountabilities of each party in fulfilling the terms of the contract or agreement in compliance with federal and state laws and regulations;
    (IV) date of last review/revision of policy and procedure manual; and
    (V) policies and procedures for:
      (-a-) security;
      (-b-) operation of the telepharmacy system;
      (-c-) sanitation;
      (-d-) storage of drugs;
      (-e-) dispensing;
      (-f-) supervision;
      (-g-) drug and/or device procurement;
      (-h-) receiving of drugs and/or devices;
      (-i-) delivery of drugs and/or devices; and
      (-j-) recordkeeping
  (ii) A pharmacy that provides remote pharmacy services through a telepharmacy system at a remote site shall, at least annually, review its written policies and procedures, revise them if necessary, and document the review.
  (iii) A pharmacy providing remote pharmacy services through a telepharmacy system shall maintain a written plan for recovery from an event which interrupts the ability of a pharmacist to electronically supervise the telepharmacy system and the dispensing of prescription drugs at the remote site. The written plan for recovery shall include:
    (I) a statement that prescription drugs shall not be dispensed at the remote site, if a pharmacist is not able to electronically supervise the telepharmacy system and the dispensing of prescription drugs;
    (II) procedures for response when a telepharmacy system is experiencing downtime; and
    (III) procedures for the maintenance and testing of the written plan for recovery.
(6) Additional operational standards for remote dispensing sites.
  (A) A pharmacist employed by a provider pharmacy shall make at least monthly on-site visits to a remote site. The remote site shall maintain documentation of the visit.
  (B) A pharmacist employed by a provider pharmacy shall be physically present at a remote dispensing site when the pharmacist is providing services requiring the physical presence of the pharmacist, including immunizations.
  (C) A remote dispensing site shall be staffed by an on-site pharmacy technician who is under the continuous supervision of a pharmacist employed by the provider pharmacy.
  (D) All pharmacy technicians at a remote dispensing site shall be counted for the purpose of establishing the pharmacist-pharmacy technician ratio of the provider pharmacy which, notwithstanding Section 568.006 of the Act, may not exceed three pharmacy technicians for each pharmacist providing supervision.
  (E) A pharmacy technician working at a remote dispensing site must:

    (i) have worked at least one year at a retail pharmacy during the three years preceding the date the pharmacy technician begins working at the remote dispensing site; and

    (ii) have completed a training program on the proper use of a telepharmacy system.

  (F) A pharmacy technician at a remote dispensing site may not perform sterile or nonsterile compounding. However, a pharmacy technician may prepare commercially available medications for dispensing, including the reconstitution of orally administered powder antibiotics.

 (7) Records.

  (A) Maintenance of records.

   (i) Every record required under this section must be:

    (I) accessible by the provider pharmacy and be available, for at least two years for inspecting and copying by the board or its representative and to other authorized local, state, or federal law enforcement agencies; and

    (II) supplied by the provider pharmacy within 72 hours, if requested by an authorized agent of the Texas State Board of Pharmacy. If the pharmacy maintains the records in an electronic format, the requested records must be provided in an electronic format if specifically requested by the board or its representative. Failure to provide the records set out in this section, either on site or within 72 hours, constitutes prima facie evidence of failure to keep and maintain records in violation of the Act.

   (ii) The remote site shall maintain original prescription drug orders for medications dispensed from a remote site using a telepharmacy system in the manner required by § 291.34(b) of this title and the provider pharmacy shall have electronic access to all prescription records.

   (iii) If prescription drug records are maintained in a data processing system, the system shall have a workable (electronic) data retention system which can produce a separate audit trail of drug usage by the provider pharmacy and by each remote site for the preceding two years as specified in § 291.34(e) of this title.

  (B) Prescriptions. Prescription drug orders shall meet the requirements of § 291.34(b) of this title.

  (C) Patient medication records. Patient medication records shall be created and maintained at the remote site or provider pharmacy in the manner required by § 291.34(c) of this title. If such records are maintained at the remote site, the provider pharmacy shall have electronic access to those records.

  (D) Inventory.

   (i) A provider pharmacy shall:

    (I) keep a record of all drugs ordered and dispensed by a remote site separate from the records of the provider pharmacy and from any other remote site's records;

    (II) keep a perpetual inventory of all controlled substances that are received and dispensed or distributed from each remote site. The perpetual inventory shall be reconciled, by a pharmacist employed by the provider pharmacy, at least monthly.

   (ii) As specified in § 291.17 of this title. A provider pharmacy shall conduct an inventory at each remote site. The following is applicable to this inventory.

    (I) The inventory of each remote site and the provider pharmacy shall be taken on the same day.

    (II) The inventory of each remote site shall be included with, but listed separately from, the drugs of other remote sites and separately from the drugs at the provider pharmacy.

    (III) A copy of the inventory of the remote site shall be maintained at the remote site.

(d) Remote pharmacy services using automated storage and delivery systems.

 (1) Purpose. The purpose of this section is to provide standards for the provision of pharmacy services by a Class A or Class C pharmacy in a facility that is not at the same location as the Class A or Class C pharmacy through an automated storage and delivery system.

 (2) Definitions. The following words and terms, when used in this section, shall have the following meanings, unless the context clearly indicates otherwise. All other words and terms shall have the meanings defined in the Act.

  (A) Automated storage and delivery system—A mechanical system that delivers dispensed prescription drugs to patients at a remote delivery site and maintains related transaction information.

  (B) Deliver or delivery—The actual, constructive, or attempted transfer of a prescription drug or device or controlled substance from one person to another, whether or not for a consideration.

  (C) Dispense—Preparing, packaging, compounding, or labeling for delivery a prescription drug or device in the course of professional practice to an ultimate user or his agent by or pursuant to the lawful order of a practitioner.

  (D) Provider pharmacy—The community pharmacy (Class A) or the institutional pharmacy (Class C) providing remote pharmacy services.

  (E) Remote delivery site—A location at which remote pharmacy services are provided using an automated storage and delivery system.

  (F) Remote pharmacy service—The provision of pharmacy services, including the storage and delivery of prescription drugs, in remote delivery sites.

 (3) General requirements for a provider pharmacy to provide remote pharmacy services using an automated storage and delivery system to deliver a previously verified prescription that is dispensed by the provider pharmacy to a patient or patient's agent.

  (A) The pharmacist-in-charge of the provider pharmacy is responsible for all pharmacy operations involving the automated storage and delivery system located at the remote delivery site including supervision of the automated storage and delivery system and compliance with this section.

  (B) The patient or patient's agent shall receive counseling via a direct link to audio or video communication by a Texas licensed pharmacist who has access to the complete patient medication record (patient profile) maintained by the provider pharmacy prior to the release of any new prescription released from the system.

  (C) A pharmacist shall be accessible at all times to respond to patients' or other health professionals' questions and needs pertaining to drugs delivered through the use of the automated storage and delivery system. Such access may be through a 24 hour pager service or telephone which is answered 24 hours a day.

        12/1/2019

    (D) The patient or patient's agent shall be given the option whether to use the system.

    (E) An electronic notice shall be provided to the patient or patient's agent at the remote delivery site with the following information:

        (i)   the name and address of the pharmacy that verified the previously dispensed prescription; and

        (ii) a statement that a pharmacist is available 24 hours a day, 7 days a week through the use of telephonic communication.

    (F) Drugs stored in the automated storage and distribution system shall be stored at proper temperatures, as defined in the USP/NF and § 291.15 of this title (relating to Storage of Drugs).

    (G) A provider pharmacy may only provide remote pharmacy services using an automated storage and delivery system to patients at a board-approved remote delivery site.

    (H) A provider pharmacy may provide remote pharmacy services at more than one remote delivery site.

    (I) Before providing remote pharmacy services, the automated storage and delivery system at the remote delivery site must be tested by the provider pharmacy and found to deliver accurately. The provider pharmacy shall make the results of such testing available to the board upon request.

    (J) A provider pharmacy which is licensed as an institutional (Class C) pharmacy is required to comply with the provisions of §§ 291.31 - 291.34 of this title (relating to Definitions, Personnel, Operational Standards, and Records for Class A (Community) Pharmacies) and this section.

  (4) Operational standards.

    (A) Application to provide remote pharmacy services using an automated storage and delivery system.

        (i)   A community (Class A) or institutional (Class C) pharmacy shall file a completed application containing all information required by the board to provide remote pharmacy services using an automated storage and delivery system.

        (ii) Such application shall be resubmitted every two years in conjunction with the application for renewal of the provider pharmacy's license.

        (iii) Upon approval of the application, the provider pharmacy will be sent a certificate which must be displayed at the provider pharmacy.

    (B) Notification requirements.

        (i)   A provider pharmacy shall notify the board in writing within ten days of a discontinuance of service.

        (ii) A provider pharmacy shall comply with appropriate controlled substance registrations for each remote delivery site if dispensed controlled substances are maintained within an automated storage and delivery system at the facility.

        (iii) A provider pharmacy shall file an application for change of location and/or name of a remote delivery site as specified in § 291.3 of this title (relating to Notifications).

    (C) Environment/Security.

        (i)   A provider pharmacy shall only store dispensed drugs at a remote delivery site within an automated storage and delivery system which is locked by key, combination or other mechanical or electronic means so as to prohibit access by unauthorized personnel.

        (ii) Access to the automated storage and delivery system shall be limited to pharmacists, and pharmacy technicians or pharmacy technician trainees under the direct supervision of a pharmacist who:

            (I)   are designated in writing by the pharmacist-in-charge; and

            (II) have completed documented training concerning their duties associated with the automated storage and delivery system.

        (iii) Drugs shall be stored in compliance with the provisions of § 291.15 (relating to Storage of Drugs) and § 291.33(c)(8) (relating to Returning Undelivered Medication to Stock) of this title, including the requirements for temperature and the return of undelivered medication to stock.

        (iv) the automated storage and delivery system must have an adequate security system, including security camera(s), to prevent unauthorized access and to maintain patient confidentiality.

    (D) Stocking an automated storage and delivery system. Stocking of dispensed prescriptions in an automated storage and delivery system shall be completed under the supervision of a pharmacist.

    (E) Quality assurance program. A pharmacy that provides pharmacy services through an automated storage and delivery system at a remote delivery site shall operate according to a written program for quality assurance of the automated storage and delivery system which:

        (i)   requires continuous supervision of the automated storage and delivery system; and

        (ii) establishes mechanisms and procedures to routinely test the accuracy of the automated storage and delivery system at a minimum of every six months and whenever any upgrade or change is made to the system and documents each such activity.

    (F) Policies and procedures of operation.

        (i)   A pharmacy that provides pharmacy services through an automated storage and delivery system at a remote delivery site shall operate according to written policies and procedures. The policy and procedure manual shall include, but not be limited to, the following:

        (ii) A pharmacy that provides pharmacy services through an automated storage and delivery system at a remote delivery site shall, at least annually, review its written policies and procedures, revise them if necessary, and document the review.

        (iii) A pharmacy providing remote pharmacy services using an automated storage and delivery system shall maintain a written plan for recovery from an event which interrupts the ability of the automated storage and delivery system to deliver dispense prescription drugs. The written plan for recovery shall include:

            (I)   planning and preparation for maintaining pharmacy services when an automated storage and delivery system is experiencing downtime;

            (II) procedures for response when an automated storage and delivery system is experiencing downtime; and

            (III) procedures for the maintenance and testing of the written plan for recovery.

  (5) Records.

    (A) Maintenance of records.

(i) Every record required under this section must be:
  (I) kept by the provider pharmacy and be available, for at least two years for inspecting and copying by the board or its representative and to other authorized local, state, or federal law enforcement agencies; and
  (II) supplied by the provider pharmacy within 72 hours, if requested by an authorized agent of the Texas State Board of Pharmacy. If the pharmacy maintains the records in an electronic format, the requested records must be provided in an electronic format if specifically requested by the board or its representative. Failure to provide the records set out in this section, either on site or within 72 hours, constitutes prima facie evidence of failure to keep and maintain records in violation of the Act.
(ii) The provider pharmacy shall have a workable (electronic) data retention system which can produce a separate audit trail of drug delivery and retrieval transactions at each remote delivery site for the preceding two years.

(B) Transaction information.
  (i) The automated storage and delivery system shall electronically record all transactions involving drugs stored in, removed, or delivered from the system.
  (ii) Records of delivery from an automated storage and delivery system for a patient shall be maintained by the provider pharmacy and include the:
    (I) identity of the system accessed;
    (II) identification of the individual accessing the system;
    (III) date of transaction;
    (IV) prescription number, drug name, strength, dosage form;
    (V) number of prescriptions retrieved;
    (VI) name of the patient for whom the prescription was retrieved;
    (VII) name of prescribing practitioner; and
    (VIII) name of pharmacist responsible for consultation with the patient, if required, and documentation that the consultation was performed.
  (iii) Records of stocking or removal from an automated storage and delivery system shall be maintained by the pharmacy and include the:
    (I) date;
    (II) prescription number;
    (III) name of the patient;
    (IV) drug name;
    (V) number of dispensed prescription packages stocked or removed;
    (VI) name, initials, or identification code of the person stocking or removing dispensed prescription packages from the system; and
    (VII) name, initials, or identification code of the pharmacist who checks and verifies that the system has been accurately filled;

(C) the pharmacy shall make the automated storage and delivery system and any records of the system, including testing records, available for inspection by the board; and

(D) the automated storage and delivery system records a digital image of the individual accessing the system to pick-up a prescription and such record is maintained by the pharmacy for two years.

Source: The provisions of this § 291.121 adopted to be effective September 18, 2007, 32 TexReg 6352; amended to be effective September 14, 2010, 35 TexReg 8358; amended to be effective December 7, 2014, 39 TexReg 9358; amended to be effective January 4, 2018, 42 TexReg 7700; amended to be effective June 7, 2018, 43 TexReg 3591; amended to be effective March 12, 2019, 44 TexReg 1334

§291.123 Central Prescription Drug or Medication Order Processing

(a) Purpose.
  (1) The purpose of this section is to provide standards for centralized prescription drug or medication order processing by a Class A (Community), Class C (Institutional), or Class E (Non-Resident) pharmacy.
  (2) Any facility established for the purpose of processing prescription drug or medication drug orders shall be licensed as a Class A, Class C, or Class E pharmacy under the Act. However, nothing in this subsection shall prohibit an individual pharmacist employee, individual pharmacy technician employee, or individual pharmacy technician trainee employee who is licensed in Texas from remotely accessing the pharmacy's electronic data base from outside the pharmacy in order to process prescription or medication drug orders, provided the pharmacy establishes controls to protect the privacy and security of confidential records.

(b) Definitions. The following words and terms, when used in this section, shall have the following meanings, unless the context clearly indicates otherwise. Any term not defined in this section shall have the definition set out in the Act. Centralized prescription drug or medication order processing--the processing of a prescription drug or medication orders by a Class A, Class C, or Class E pharmacy on behalf of another pharmacy, a health care provider, or a payor. Centralized prescription drug or medication order processing does not include the dispensing of a prescription drug order but includes any of the following:
  (1) receiving, interpreting, or clarifying prescription drug or medication drug orders;
  (2) data entering and transferring of prescription drug or medication order information;
  (3) performing drug regimen review;
  (4) obtaining refill and substitution authorizations;
  (5) interpreting clinical data for prior authorization for dispensing;
  (6) performing therapeutic interventions; and
  (7) providing drug information concerning a patient's prescription.

(c) Operational Standards.
  (1) General requirements.

(A) A Class A, Class C, or Class E Pharmacy may outsource prescription drug or medication order processing to another Class A, Class C, or Class E pharmacy provided the pharmacies:
  (i) have:
    (I) the same owner; or
    (II) entered into a written contract or agreement which outlines the services to be provided and the responsibilities and accountabilities of each pharmacy in compliance with federal and state laws and regulations; and
  (ii) share a common electronic file or have appropriate technology to allow access to sufficient information necessary or required to process a non-dispensing function.
(B) A pharmacy that performs centralized prescription drug or medication order processing shall comply with the provisions applicable to the class of pharmacy contained in either §§ 291.31 - 291.35 of this title (relating to Definitions, Personnel, Operational Standards, Records, and Official Prescription Requirements in Class A (Community) Pharmacies), or §§ 291.72 - 291.75 of this title (relating to Definitions, Personnel, Operational Standards, and Records in a Class C (Institutional) Pharmacy), or §§ 291.102 - 291.105 of this title (relating to Definitions, Personnel, Operational Standards, and Records in a Class E (Non-Resident) Pharmacy) to the extent applicable for the specific processing activity and this section including:
  (i) duties which must be performed by a pharmacist; and
  (ii) supervision requirements for pharmacy technicians and pharmacy technician trainees.
(2) Notifications to patients.
  (A) A pharmacy that outsources prescription drug or medication order processing to another pharmacy shall prior to outsourcing their prescription:
    (i) notify patients that prescription processing may be outsourced to another pharmacy; and
    (ii) give the name of that pharmacy; or if the pharmacy is part of a network of pharmacies under common ownership and any of the network pharmacies may process the prescription, the patient shall be notified of this fact. Such notification may be provided through a one-time written notice to the patient or through use of a sign in the pharmacy.
  (B) The provisions of this paragraph do not apply to patients in facilities where drugs are administered to patients by a person required to do so by the laws of the state (i.e., hospitals or nursing homes).
(3) Policy and Procedures. A policy and procedure manual as it relates to central processing shall be maintained at all pharmacies involved in central processing and be available for inspection. Each pharmacy is required to maintain only those portions of the policy and procedure manual that relate to that pharmacy's operations. The manual shall:
  (A) outline the responsibilities of each of the pharmacies;
  (B) include a list of the name, address, telephone numbers, and all license/registration numbers of the pharmacies involved in centralized prescription drug or medication order processing; and
  (C) include policies and procedures for:
    (i) protecting the confidentiality and integrity of patient information;
    (ii) maintenance of appropriate records to identify the name(s), initials, or identification code(s) and specific activity(ies) of each pharmacist or pharmacy technician who performed any processing;
    (iii) complying with federal and state laws and regulations;
    (iv) operating a continuous quality improvement program for pharmacy services designed to objectively and systematically monitor and evaluate the quality and appropriateness of patient care, pursue opportunities to improve patient care, and resolve identified problems; and
    (v) annually reviewing the written policies and procedures and documenting such review.
(d) Records. All pharmacies shall maintain appropriate records which identify, by prescription drug or medication order, the name(s), initials, or identification code(s) of each pharmacist, pharmacy technician, or pharmacy technician trainee who performs a processing function for a prescription drug or medication order. Such records may be maintained:
  (1) separately by each pharmacy and pharmacist; or
  (2) in a common electronic file as long as the records are maintained in such a manner that the data processing system can produce a printout which lists the functions performed by each pharmacy and pharmacist.

Source: The provisions of this § 291.123 adopted to be effective September 18, 2007, 32 TexReg 6352; amended to be effective June 20, 2019, 44 TexReg 2951

§291.125 Centralized Prescription Dispensing

(a) Purpose. The purpose of this section is to provide standards for centralized prescription dispensing by a Class A (Community), Class C (Institutional) pharmacy, or Class E (Non-Resident) Pharmacy.
(b) Definitions. The following words and terms, when used in this section, shall have the following meanings, unless the context clearly indicates otherwise. Any term not defined in this section shall have the definition set out in the Act.
  (1) Central fill pharmacy—a Class A, Class A-S, Class C, Class C-S, Class E, or Class E-S pharmacy that prepares prescription drug orders for dispensing pursuant to a valid prescription transmitted to the central fill pharmacy by an outsourcing pharmacy.
  (2) Centralized prescription dispensing—the dispensing or refilling of a prescription drug order by a Class A, Class C, or Class E pharmacy at the request of another Class A or Class C pharmacy and the return of the dispensed prescriptions to the outsourcing pharmacy for delivery to the patient or patient's agent, or at the request of the outsourcing pharmacy for direct delivery to the patient.
  (3) Outsourcing pharmacy—a Class A or Class C pharmacy that transmits a prescription drug order via facsimile or communicates prescription information electronically to a central fill pharmacy to be dispensed by the central fill pharmacy.
(c) Operational standards.
  (1) General requirements.
    (A) A Class A or Class C pharmacy may outsource prescription drug order dispensing to a central fill pharmacy provided the pharmacies:
      (i) have:
        (I) the same owner; or

          (II) entered into a written contract or agreement which outlines the services to be provided and the responsibilities and accountabilities of each pharmacy in compliance with federal and state laws and regulations; and

      (ii) share a common electronic file or have appropriate technology to allow access to sufficient information necessary or required to dispense or process a prescription drug order.

    (B) The pharmacist-in-charge of the central fill pharmacy shall ensure that:

      (i) the pharmacy maintains and uses adequate storage or shipment containers and shipping processes to ensure drug stability and potency. Such shipping processes shall include the use of appropriate packaging material and/or devices to ensure that the drug is maintained at an appropriate temperature range to maintain the integrity of the medication throughout the delivery process; and

      (ii) the dispensed prescriptions are shipped in containers which are sealed in a manner as to show evidence of opening or tampering.

    (C) A Class A or Class C central fill pharmacy shall comply with the provisions of §§ 291.31 - 291.35 of this title (relating to Definitions, Personnel, Operational Standards, Records, and Official Prescription Requirements in Community Pharmacy (Class A) and this section.

    (D) A Class E central fill pharmacy shall comply with §§ 291.101 - 291.105 of this title (relating to Purpose, Definitions, Personnel, Operational Standards, and Records in Non-resident Pharmacy (Class E) and this section.

  (2) Notifications to patients.

    (A) A pharmacy that outsources prescription dispensing to a central fill pharmacy shall:

      (i) prior to outsourcing the prescription:

          (I) notify patients that their prescription may be outsourced to a central fill pharmacy; and

          (II) give the name of the central fill pharmacy or if the pharmacy is part of a network of pharmacies under common ownership and any of the network pharmacies may dispense the prescription, the patient shall be notified of this fact. Such notification may be provided through a one-time written notice to the patient or through use of a sign in the pharmacy; and

      (ii) if a prescription that is not for a controlled substance is delivered directly to the patient by the central fill pharmacy and not returned to the outsourcing pharmacy, place on the prescription container or on a separate sheet delivered with the prescription container, in both English and Spanish, the local, and if applicable, the toll-free telephone number of the pharmacy and the statement: "Written information about this prescription has been provided for you. Please read this information before you take the medication. If you have questions concerning this prescription, a pharmacist is available during normal business hours to answer these questions at (insert the pharmacy's local and toll-free telephone numbers)." A prescription for a controlled substance may not be delivered directly to the patient by the central fill pharmacy.

    (B) The provisions of this paragraph do not apply to patients in facilities where drugs are administered to patients by a person required to do so by the laws of the state (e.g., hospitals or nursing homes).

  (3) Prescription Labeling. The central fill pharmacy shall place on the prescription label, the name and address of the outsourcing pharmacy and a unique identifier (i.e., the central fill pharmacy's DEA registration number or, if the pharmacy does not have a DEA registration number, the central fill pharmacy's Texas license number) indicating that the prescription was dispensed by the central fill pharmacy; and comply with all other labeling requirements in § 291.33 of this title.

  (4) Policies and Procedures. A policy and procedure manual as it relates to centralized dispensing shall be maintained at both pharmacies and be available for inspection. Each pharmacy is required to maintain only those portions of the policy and procedure manual that relate to that pharmacy's operations. The manual shall:

    (A) outline the responsibilities of each of the pharmacies;

    (B) include a list of the name, address, telephone numbers, and all license/registration numbers of the pharmacies involved in centralized prescription dispensing; and

    (C) include policies and procedures for:

      (i) notifying patients that their prescription may be outsourced to a central fill pharmacy for dispensing and providing the name of that pharmacy;

      (ii) protecting the confidentiality and integrity of patient information;

      (iii) dispensing prescription drug orders when the dispensed order is not received or the patient comes in before the order is received;

      (iv) complying with federal and state laws and regulations;

      (v) operating a continuous quality improvement program for pharmacy services designed to objectively and systematically monitor and evaluate the quality and appropriateness of patient care, pursue opportunities to improve patient care, and resolve identified problems; and

      (vi) annually reviewing the written policies and procedures and documenting such review.

(d) Records.

  (1) Records may be maintained in an alternative data retention system, such as a data processing system or direct imaging system provided:

    (A) the records maintained in the alternative system contain all of the information required on the manual record; and

    (B) the data processing system is capable of producing a hard copy of the record upon the request of the board, its representative, or other authorized local, state, or federal law enforcement or regulatory agencies.

  (2) Each pharmacy shall comply with all the laws and rules relating to the maintenance of records and be able to produce an audit trail showing all prescriptions dispensed by the pharmacy.

  (3) The outsourcing pharmacy shall maintain records, in addition to the prescription drug order, which indicate the:

    (A) date:

      (i) the request for dispensing was transmitted to the central fill pharmacy; and

      (ii) the dispensed prescription was received by the outsourcing pharmacy, including the method of delivery (e.g., private, common, or contract carrier) and the name of the person accepting delivery; and

(B) name, address, license number, and the unique identifier of the central fill pharmacy.
(4) The central fill pharmacy shall maintain records, in addition to the prescription drug order, which indicate the:
    (A) date the prescription was shipped to the outsourcing pharmacy or the patient;
    (B) name and address where the prescription was shipped;
    (C) method of delivery (e.g., private, common, or contract carrier); and
    (D) name, address, and license number of the outsourcing pharmacy.

Source: The provisions of this § 291.125 adopted to be effective September 18, 2007, 32 TexReg 6352; amended to be effective March 26, 2014, 39 TexReg 2000, amended to be effective June 7, 2018, 43 TexReg 3592

§291.127 Emergency Remote Pharmacy License

(a) Definitions. The following words and terms, when used in this section, shall have the following meanings, unless the context clearly indicates otherwise. All other words and terms shall have the meanings defined in the Act.
    (1) Emergency remote pharmacy—A pharmacy not located at the same Texas location as a home pharmacy at which pharmacy services are provided during an emergency situation.
    (2) Emergency situation—An emergency caused by a natural or manmade disaster or any other exceptional situation that causes an extraordinary demand for pharmacy services.
    (3) Home pharmacy—A currently licensed Class A (Community), Class C (Institutional), or Class D (Clinic) pharmacy that is providing emergency pharmacy services through an emergency remote pharmacy.
(b) Emergency remote pharmacy license. In an emergency situation, the board may grant a holder of a Class A (Community), Class C (Institutional), or Class D (Clinic) pharmacy license, the authority to operate a pharmacy and provide pharmacy services at an alternate location. The following is applicable for the emergency remote pharmacy.
    (1) The emergency remote pharmacy will not be issued a separate pharmacy license, but shall operate under the license of the home pharmacy. To qualify for an emergency remote pharmacy license, the applicant must submit an application including the following information:
        (A) license number, name, address, and phone number of the home pharmacy;
        (B) name, address, and phone number of the emergency remote pharmacy;
        (C) name and Texas pharmacist license number of the pharmacist-in-charge of the home pharmacy and of the pharmacist-in-charge of the emergency remote pharmacy; and
        (D) any other information required by the board.
    (2) The board will notify the home pharmacy of the approval of an emergency remote pharmacy license.
    (3) The emergency remote pharmacy license shall be valid for a period as determined by the board not to exceed six months. The executive director of the board, in his/her discretion, may renew the remote license for an additional six months, if the emergency situation still exists and the holder of the license shows good cause for emergency remote pharmacy to continue operation.
    (4) The emergency remote pharmacy shall have a written contract or agreement with the home pharmacy which outlines the services to be provided and the responsibilities and accountabilities of the remote and home pharmacy in fulfilling the terms of the contract or agreement in compliance with federal and state laws and regulations.
    (5) The home pharmacy shall designate a pharmacist to serve as the pharmacist-in-charge of the emergency remote pharmacy.
    (6) The emergency remote pharmacy shall comply with the rules for the class of pharmacy under which the home pharmacy is licensed. A Class A pharmacy shall comply with the rules under Subchapter B of this chapter titled Community Pharmacy (Class A). A Class C pharmacy shall comply with the rules under Subchapter D of this chapter titled Institutional Pharmacy (Class C). A Class D pharmacy shall comply with the rules under Subchapter E of this chapter titled Clinic Pharmacy (Class D).
    (7) The records of services provided at the emergency remote pharmacy shall be:
        (A) kept by the home pharmacy and be available, for at least two years from the date of provision of the service, for inspecting and copying by the board or its representative and to other authorized local, state, or federal law enforcement agencies; and
        (B) supplied by the pharmacy within 72 hours, if requested by an authorized agent of the Texas State Board of Pharmacy. If the pharmacy maintains the records in an electronic format, the requested records must be provided in an electronic format if specifically requested by the board or its representative. Failure to provide the records set out in this section, either on site or within 72 hours, constitutes prima facie evidence of failure to keep and maintain records in violation of the Act.

Source: The provisions of this §291.127 adopted to be effective September 18, 2007, 32 TexReg 6352

§291.129 Satellite Pharmacy

(a) Purpose. The purpose of this section is to create a new class of pharmacy for the provision of pharmacy services by a Class A or Class C pharmacy in a location that is not at the same location as the Class A or Class C pharmacy through a satellite pharmacy and to provide standards for the operation of this class of pharmacy established under § 560.053 of the Texas Pharmacy Act.
(b) Definitions. The following words and terms, when used in this section, shall have the following meanings, unless the context clearly indicates otherwise. All other words and terms shall have the meanings as defined in the Act or in § 291.31 of this title.
    (1) Provider pharmacy—The Class A or Class C pharmacy providing satellite pharmacy services.
    (2) Satellite pharmacy—A facility not located at the same location as a Class A or Class C pharmacy at which satellite pharmacy services are provided.
    (3) Satellite pharmacy services—The provision of pharmacy services, including the storage and delivery of prescription drugs, in an alternate location.
(c) General requirements.
    (1) A Class A or Class C provider pharmacy may establish a satellite pharmacy in a location that is not at the same location as the Class A or Class C pharmacy.
    (2) The pharmacist-in-charge of the provider pharmacy is responsible for all pharmacy operations involving the satellite pharmacy including supervision of satellite pharmacy personnel and compliance with this section.

(3) A satellite pharmacy may not store bulk drugs and may only store prescription medications that have been previously verified and dispensed by the provider pharmacy.

(4) A Class C pharmacy that is a provider pharmacy dispensing outpatient prescriptions for a satellite pharmacy shall comply with the provisions of §§ 291.31 - 291.34 of this title (relating to Definitions, Personnel, Operational Standards, and Records for Class A (Community) pharmacies) and this section.

(5) The provider pharmacy and the satellite pharmacy must have:
  (A) the same owner; and
  (B) share a common electronic file or have appropriate technology to allow access to sufficient information necessary or required to process a non-dispensing function.

(d) Personnel.

(1) All individuals working at the satellite pharmacy shall be employees of the provider pharmacy and must report their employment to the board as such.

(2) A satellite pharmacy shall have sufficient pharmacists on duty to operate the satellite pharmacy competently, safely, and adequately to meet the needs of the patients of the pharmacy.

(3) Pharmacists are solely responsible for the direct supervision of pharmacy technicians and pharmacy technician trainees and for designating and delegating duties, other than those listed in paragraph (7) of this subsection, to pharmacy technicians and pharmacy technician trainees. Each pharmacist:
  (A) shall verify the accuracy of all acts, tasks, and functions performed by pharmacy technicians and pharmacy technician trainees; and
  (B) shall be responsible for any delegated act performed by pharmacy technicians and pharmacy technician trainees under his or her supervision.

(4) A pharmacist shall be physically present to directly supervise a pharmacy technician or pharmacy technician trainee who is entering prescription data into the data processing system. Each prescription entered into the data processing system shall be verified at the time of data entry.

(5) All pharmacists while on duty, shall be responsible for complying with all state and federal laws or rules governing the practice of pharmacy.

(6) A pharmacist shall ensure that the drug is dispensed and delivered safely and accurately as prescribed. A pharmacist shall ensure the safety and accuracy of the portion of the process the pharmacist is performing.

(7) Duties in a satellite pharmacy that may only be performed by a pharmacist are as follows:
  (A) receiving oral prescription drug orders and reducing these orders to writing, either manually or electronically;
  (B) interpreting or clarifying prescription drug orders;
  (C) communicating to the patient or patient's agent information about the prescription drug or device, which in the exercise of the pharmacist's professional judgment the pharmacist deems significant, as specified in § 291.33(c) of this title;
  (D) communicating to the patient or the patient's agent on his or her request for information concerning any prescription drugs dispensed to the patient by the pharmacy;
  (E) assuring that a reasonable effort is made to obtain, record, and maintain patient medication records;
  (F) interpreting patient medication records and performing drug regimen reviews; and
  (G) performing a specific act of drug therapy management for a patient when delegated to a pharmacist by a written protocol from a physician licensed in this state in compliance with the Medical Practice Act.

(8) Pharmacy technicians and pharmacy technician trainees may not perform any of the duties listed in paragraph (7) of this subsection. However, a pharmacist may delegate to pharmacy technicians and pharmacy technician trainees any nonjudgmental technical duty associated with the preparation and distribution of prescription drugs provided:
  (A) a pharmacist verifies the accuracy of all acts, tasks, and functions performed by pharmacy technicians and pharmacy technician trainees; and
  (B) pharmacy technicians and pharmacy technician trainees are under the direct supervision of, and responsible to, a pharmacist.

(9) Pharmacy technicians and pharmacy technician trainees in a satellite pharmacy may perform only nonjudgmental technical duties associated with the preparation and distribution of prescription drugs as follows:
  (A) initiating and receiving refill authorization requests;
  (B) entering prescription data into a data processing system; and
  (C) reconstituting medications.

(10) In a satellite pharmacy, the ratio of pharmacists to pharmacy technicians/pharmacy technician trainees may be 1:3, provided at least one of the three is a pharmacy technician and not a pharmacy technician trainee.

(11) All satellite pharmacy personnel shall wear identification tags or badges that bear the person's name and identifies him or her as a pharmacist, pharmacist intern, pharmacy technician, or pharmacy technician trainee.

(e) Operational requirements.

(1) Application for permission to provide satellite pharmacy services.
  (A) A Class A or Class C pharmacy shall make an application to the board to provide satellite pharmacy services. The application shall include the following:
    (i) the name, address, and license number of the provider pharmacy;
    (ii) the name and address of the facility where the satellite pharmacy will be located;
    (iii) the anticipated date of opening and hours of operation; and
    (iv) a copy of the lease agreement or if the location of the satellite pharmacy is owned by the applicant, a notarized statement certifying such location ownership.
  (B) A renewal application shall be resubmitted every two years in conjunction with the application for renewal of the provider pharmacy's license. The renewal application shall contain the documentation required in subparagraph (A) of this paragraph.
  (C) Upon approval of the application, the provider pharmacy will be sent a certificate which must be displayed at the satellite pharmacy.

(2) Notification requirements.

(A) A provider pharmacy shall notify the board in writing within ten days of a change of location, discontinuance of service, or closure of a satellite pharmacy that is operated by the pharmacy.

(B) A provider pharmacy shall comply with appropriate federal and state controlled substance registrations for each satellite pharmacy if controlled substances are maintained at the satellite pharmacy.

(3) Environment.

(A) The satellite pharmacy shall be arranged in an orderly fashion and kept clean. All required equipment shall be clean and in good operating condition.

(B) A satellite pharmacy shall contain an area which is suitable for confidential patient counseling.

(i)   Such counseling area shall:

(I)   be easily accessible to both the patient and pharmacists and not allow patient access to prescription drugs;

(II) be designed to maintain the confidentiality and privacy of the pharmacist/patient communication.

(ii) In determining whether the area is suitable for confidential patient counseling and designed to maintain the confidentiality and privacy of the pharmacist/patient communication, the board may consider factors such as the following:

(I)   the proximity of the counseling area to the check-out or cash register area;

(II) the volume of pedestrian traffic in and around the counseling area;

(III) the presence of walls or other barriers between the counseling area and other areas of the pharmacy; and

(IV) any evidence of confidential information being overheard by persons other than the patient or patient's agent or the pharmacist or agents of the pharmacist.

(C) The satellite pharmacy shall be properly lighted and ventilated.

(D) The temperature of the satellite pharmacy shall be maintained within a range compatible with the proper storage of drugs in compliance with the provisions of § 291.15 of this title (relating to storage of drugs). The temperature of the refrigerator shall be maintained within a range compatible with the proper storage of drugs requiring refrigeration.

(E) Animals, including birds and reptiles, shall not be kept within the pharmacy and in immediately adjacent areas under the control of the pharmacy. This provision does not apply to fish in aquariums, guide dogs accompanying disabled persons, or animals for sale to the general public in a separate area that is inspected by local health jurisdictions.

(4) Security.

(A) A satellite pharmacy shall be under the continuous, physically present supervision of a pharmacist at all times the satellite pharmacy is open to provide pharmacy services.

(B) The satellite pharmacy shall be enclosed by walls, partitions or other means of floor-to-ceiling enclosure. In addition to the security requirements outlined in § 291.33(b)(2) of this title, satellite pharmacies shall have adequate security and procedures to:

(i)   prohibit unauthorized access;

(ii) comply with federal and state regulations; and

(iii) maintain patient confidentiality.

(C) Access to the satellite pharmacy shall be limited to pharmacists, pharmacy technicians, and pharmacy technician trainees employed by the provider pharmacy and who are designated in writing by the pharmacist-in-charge.

(D) The provider pharmacy shall have procedures that specify that prescriptions may only be delivered to the satellite pharmacy by the provider pharmacy and shall:

(i)   be delivered in a sealed container with a list of the prescriptions delivered;

(ii) be signed for on receipt by the pharmacist at the satellite pharmacy;

(iii) be checked by personnel designated by the pharmacist-in-charge to verify that the prescriptions sent by the provider pharmacy were actually received. The designated person who checks the order shall document the verification by signing and dating the list of prescriptions delivered.

(5) Prescription dispensing and delivery. A satellite pharmacy shall comply with the requirements outlined in § 291.33(c) of this title with regard to prescription dispensing and delivery.

(6) Equipment and supplies. A satellite pharmacy shall have the following equipment and supplies:

(A) typewriter or comparable equipment;

(B) refrigerator, if storing drugs requiring refrigeration;

(C) metric-apothecary weight and measure conversion charts.

(7) Library. A reference library shall be maintained by the satellite pharmacy that includes the following in hard-copy or electronic format:

(A) current copies of the following:

(i)   Texas Pharmacy Act and rules;

(ii) Texas Dangerous Drug Act and rules;

(iii) Texas Controlled Substances Act and rules; and

(iv) Federal Controlled Substances Act and rules (or official publication describing the requirements of the Federal Controlled Substances Act and rules);

(B) at least one current or updated reference from each of the following categories:

(i)   patient information:

(I)   United States Pharmacopeia Dispensing Information, Volume II (Advice to the Patient); or

(II) a reference text or information leaflets which provide patient information;

(ii) drug interactions: a reference text on drug interactions, such as Drug Interaction Facts. A separate reference is not required if other references maintained by the satellite pharmacy contain drug interaction information including information needed to determine severity or significance of the interaction and appropriate recommendations or actions to be taken;

(iii) a general information reference text, such as:

(I)   Facts and Comparisons with current supplements;

(II) United States Pharmacopeia Dispensing Information Volume I (Drug Information for the Healthcare Provider);

(III) Clinical Pharmacology;

(IV) American Hospital Formulary Service with current supplements; or

(V) Remington's Pharmaceutical Sciences; and

(C) basic antidote information and the telephone number of the nearest Regional Poison Control Center.

(f) Records.

  (1) Maintenance of records.

    (A) Every record required to be kept under § 291.34 of this title and under this section shall be:

      (i) kept by the provider pharmacy and be available, for at least two years from the date of such inventory or record, for inspecting and copying by the board or its representative and to other authorized local, state, or federal law enforcement agencies; and

      (ii) supplied by the provider pharmacy within 72 hours, if requested by an authorized agent of the board. If the pharmacy maintains the records in an electronic format, the requested records must be provided in an electronic format if specifically requested by the board or its representative. Failure to provide the records set out in this section, either on site or within 72 hours, constitutes prima facie evidence of failure to keep and maintain records in violation of the Act.

    (B) Records, except when specifically required to be maintained in original or hard-copy form, may be maintained in an alternative data retention system, such as a data processing system or direct imaging system provided:

      (i) the records maintained in the alternative system contain all of the information required on the manual record; and

      (ii) the data processing system is capable of producing a hard copy of the record upon the request of the board, its representative, or other authorized local, state, or federal law enforcement or regulatory agencies.

    (C) Prescription drug orders shall be maintained by the provider pharmacy in the manner required by § 291.34(d) or (e) of this title.

  (2) Prescriptions.

    (A) Prescription drug orders shall meet the requirements of § 291.34(b) of this title.

    (B) The provider pharmacy must maintain appropriate records to identify the name(s), initials, or identification code(s) and specific activity(ies) of each pharmacist, pharmacy technician, or pharmacy technician trainee who performed any processing at the satellite pharmacy.

    (C) A provider pharmacy shall keep a record of all prescriptions sent and returned between the pharmacies separate from the records of the provider pharmacy and from any other satellite pharmacy's records.

    (D) A satellite pharmacy shall keep a record of all prescriptions received and returned between the pharmacies.

Source: The provisions of this § 291.129 adopted to be effective September 18, 2007, 32 TexReg 6352; amended to be effective June 7, 2009, 34 TexReg 3412; amended to be effective December 6, 2018, 43 TexReg 7787

§291.131 Pharmacies Compounding Non-Sterile Preparations

(a) Purpose. Pharmacies compounding non-sterile preparations, prepackaging pharmaceutical products and distributing those products shall comply with all requirements for their specific license classification and this section. The purpose of this section is to provide standards for the:

  (1) compounding of non-sterile preparations pursuant to a prescription or medication order for a patient from a practitioner in Class A (Community), Class C (Institutional), and Class E (Non-resident) pharmacies;

  (2) compounding, dispensing, and delivery of a reasonable quantity of a compounded non-sterile preparation in a Class A (Community), Class C (Institutional), and Class E (Non-resident) pharmacies to a practitioner's office for office use by the practitioner;

  (3) compounding and distribution of compounded non-sterile preparations by a Class A (Community) pharmacy for a Class C (Institutional) pharmacy; and

  (4) compounding of non-sterile preparations by a Class C (Institutional) pharmacy and the distribution of the compounded preparations to other Class C (Institutional) pharmacies under common ownership.

(b) Definitions. In addition to the definitions for specific license classifications, the following words and terms, when used in this section, shall have the following meanings, unless the context clearly indicates otherwise.

  (1) Beyond-use date—The date or time after which the compounded non-sterile preparation shall not be stored or transported or begin to be administered to a patient. The beyond-use date is determined from the date or time when the preparation was compounded.

  (2) Component—Any ingredient intended for use in the compounding of a drug preparation, including those that may not appear in such preparation.

  (3) Compounding—The preparation, mixing, assembling, packaging, or labeling of a drug or device:

    (A) as the result of a practitioner's prescription drug or medication order, based on the practitioner-patient-pharmacist relationship in the course of professional practice;

    (B) for administration to a patient by a practitioner as the result of a practitioner's initiative based on the practitioner-patient-pharmacist relationship in the course of professional practice;

    (C) in anticipation of prescription drug or medication orders based on routine, regularly observed prescribing patterns; or

    (D) for or as an incident to research, teaching, or chemical analysis and not for sale or dispensing, except as allowed under § 562.154 or Chapter 563 of the Occupations Code.

  (4) Hot water—The temperature of water from the pharmacy's sink maintained at a minimum of 105 degrees F (41 degrees C).

  (5) Reasonable quantity—An amount of a compounded drug that:

    (A) does not exceed the amount a practitioner anticipates may be used in the practitioner's office or facility before the beyond use date of the drug;

    (B) is reasonable considering the intended use of the compounded drug and the nature of the practitioner's practice; and

Phr. Rules

(C) for any practitioner and all practitioners as a whole, is not greater than an amount the pharmacy is capable of compounding in compliance with pharmaceutical standards for identity, strength, quality, and purity of the compounded drug that are consistent with United States Pharmacopoeia guidelines and accreditation practices.

(6) SOPs—Standard operating procedures.

(7) USP/NF—The current edition of the United States Pharmacopeia/National Formulary.

(c) Personnel.

  (1) Pharmacist-in-charge. In addition to the responsibilities for the specific class of pharmacy, the pharmacist-in-charge shall have the responsibility for, at a minimum, the following concerning non-sterile compounding:

    (A) determining that all personnel involved in non-sterile compounding possess the education, training, and proficiency necessary to properly and safely perform compounding duties undertaken or supervised;

    (B) determining that all personnel involved in non-sterile compounding obtain continuing education appropriate for the type of compounding done by the personnel;

    (C) assuring that the equipment used in compounding is properly maintained;

    (D) maintaining an appropriate environment in areas where non-sterile compounding occurs; and

    (E) assuring that effective quality control procedures are developed and followed.

  (2) Pharmacists. Special requirements for non-sterile compounding.

    (A) All pharmacists engaged in compounding shall:

      (i) possess the education, training, and proficiency necessary to properly and safely perform compounding duties undertaken or supervised; and

      (ii) obtain continuing education appropriate for the type of compounding done by the pharmacist.

    (B) A pharmacist shall inspect and approve all components, drug product containers, closures, labeling, and any other materials involved in the compounding process.

    (C) A pharmacist shall review all compounding records for accuracy and conduct in-process and final checks to ensure that errors have not occurred in the compounding process.

    (D) A pharmacist is responsible for the proper maintenance, cleanliness, and use of all equipment used in the compounding process.

  (3) Pharmacy technicians and pharmacy technician trainees. All pharmacy technicians and pharmacy technician trainees engaged in non-sterile compounding shall:

    (A) possess the education, training, and proficiency necessary to properly and safely perform compounding duties undertaken;

    (B) obtain continuing education appropriate for the type of compounding done by the pharmacy technician or pharmacy technician trainee; and

    (C) perform compounding duties under the direct supervision of and responsible to a pharmacist.

  (4) Training.

    (A) All training activities shall be documented and covered by appropriate SOPs as outlined in subsection (d)(8)(A) of this section.

    (B) All personnel involved in non-sterile compounding shall be well trained and must participate in continuing relevant training programs.

(d) Operational Standards.

  (1) General requirements.

    (A) Non-sterile drug preparations may be compounded in licensed pharmacies:

      (i) upon presentation of a practitioner's prescription drug or medication order based on a valid pharmacist/patient/prescriber relationship;

      (ii) in anticipation of future prescription drug or medication orders based on routine, regularly observed prescribing patterns; or

      (iii) in reasonable quantities for office use by a practitioner and for use by a veterinarian.

    (B) Non-sterile compounding in anticipation of future prescription drug or medication orders must be based upon a history of receiving valid prescriptions issued within an established pharmacist/patient/prescriber relationship, provided that in the pharmacist's professional judgment the quantity prepared is stable for the anticipated shelf time.

      (i) The pharmacist's professional judgment shall be based on the criteria used to determine a beyond-use date outlined in paragraph (5)(C) of this subsection.

      (ii) Documentation of the criteria used to determine the stability for the anticipated shelf time must be maintained and be available for inspection.

      (iii) Any preparation compounded in anticipation of future prescription drug or medication orders shall be labeled. Such label shall contain:

        (I) name and strength of the compounded preparation or list of the active ingredients and strengths;

        (II) facility's lot number;

        (III) beyond-use date as determined by the pharmacist using appropriate documented criteria as outlined in paragraph (5)(C) of this subsection; and

        (IV) quantity or amount in the container.

    (C) Commercially available products may be compounded for dispensing to individual patients provided the following conditions are met:

      (i) the commercial product is not reasonably available from normal distribution channels in a timely manner to meet patient's needs;

      (ii) the pharmacy maintains documentation that the product is not reasonably available due to a drug shortage or unavailability from the manufacturer; and

      (iii) the prescribing practitioner has requested that the drug be compounded as described in subparagraph (D) of this paragraph.

(D) A pharmacy may not compound preparations that are essentially copies of commercially available products (e.g., the preparation is dispensed in a strength that is only slightly different from a commercially available product) unless the prescribing practitioner specifically orders the strength or dosage form and specifies why the patient needs the particular strength or dosage form of the preparation. The prescribing practitioner shall provide documentation of a patient specific medical need and the preparation produces a clinically significant therapeutic response (e.g. the physician requests an alternate product due to hypersensitivity to excipients or preservative in the FDA-approved product, or the physician requests an effective alternate dosage form) or if the drug product is not commercially available. The unavailability of such drug product must be documented prior to compounding. The methodology for documenting unavailability includes maintaining a copy of the wholesaler's notification showing back-ordered, discontinued, or out-of-stock items. This documentation must be available in hard-copy or electronic format for inspection by the board.

(E) A pharmacy may enter into an agreement to compound and dispense prescription/medication orders for another pharmacy provided the pharmacy complies with the provisions of § 291.125 of this title (relating to Centralized Prescription Dispensing).

(F) Compounding pharmacies/pharmacists may advertise and promote the fact that they provide non-sterile prescription compounding services, which may include specific drug products and classes of drugs.

(G) A pharmacy may not compound veterinary preparations for use in food producing animals except in accordance with federal guidelines.

(H) A pharmacist may add flavoring to a prescription at the request of a patient, the patient's agent, or the prescriber. The pharmacist shall label the flavored prescription with a beyond-use-date that shall be no longer than fourteen days if stored in a refrigerator unless otherwise documented. Documentation of beyond-use-dates longer than fourteen days shall be maintained by the pharmacy electronically or manually and made available to agents of the board on request. A pharmacist may not add flavoring to an over-the-counter product at the request of a patient or patient's agent unless the pharmacist obtains a prescription for the over-the-counter product from the patient's practitioner.

(2) Library. In addition to the library requirements of the pharmacy's specific license classification, a pharmacy shall maintain a current copy, in hard-copy or electronic format, of Chapter 795 of the USP/NF concerning Pharmacy Compounding Non-Sterile Preparations.

(3) Environment.

(A) Pharmacies regularly engaging in compounding shall have a designated and adequate area for the safe and orderly compounding of non-sterile preparations, including the placement of equipment and materials. Pharmacies involved in occasional compounding shall prepare an area prior to each compounding activity which is adequate for safe and orderly compounding.

(B) Only personnel authorized by the responsible pharmacist shall be in the immediate vicinity of a drug compounding operation.

(C) A sink with hot and cold running water, exclusive of rest room facilities, shall be accessible to the compounding areas and be maintained in a sanitary condition. Supplies necessary for adequate washing shall be accessible in the immediate area of the sink and include:

(i) soap or detergent; and

(ii) air-driers or single-use towels.

(D) If drug products which require special precautions to prevent contamination, such as penicillin, are involved in a compounding operation, appropriate measures, including dedication of equipment for such operations or the meticulous cleaning of contaminated equipment prior to its use for the preparation of other drug products, must be used in order to prevent cross-contamination.

(4) Equipment and Supplies. The pharmacy shall:

(A) have a Class A prescription balance, or analytical balance and weights which shall be properly maintained and subject to periodic inspection by the Texas State Board of Pharmacy; and

(B) have equipment and utensils necessary for the proper compounding of prescription drug or medication orders. Such equipment and utensils used in the compounding process shall be:

(i) of appropriate design and capacity, and be operated within designed operational limits;

(ii) of suitable composition so that surfaces that contact components, in-process material, or drug products shall not be reactive, additive, or absorptive so as to alter the safety, identity, strength, quality, or purity of the drug product beyond the desired result;

(iii) cleaned and sanitized immediately prior and after to each use; and

(iv) routinely inspected, calibrated (if necessary), or checked to ensure proper performance.

(5) Labeling. In addition to the labeling requirements of the pharmacy's specific license classification, the label dispensed or distributed pursuant to a prescription drug or medication order shall contain the following.

(A) The generic name(s) or the official name(s) of the principal active ingredient(s) of the compounded preparation.

(B) A statement that the preparation has been compounded by the pharmacy. (An auxiliary label may be used on the container to meet this requirement).

(C) A beyond-use date after which the compounded preparation should not be used. The beyond-use date shall be determined as outlined in Chapter 795 of the USP/NF concerning Pharmacy Compounding Non-Sterile Preparations including the following:

(i) The pharmacist shall consider:

(I) physical and chemical properties of active ingredients;

(II) use of preservatives and/or stabilizing agents;

(III) dosage form;

(IV) storage containers and conditions; and

(V)   scientific, laboratory, or reference data from a peer reviewed source and retained in the pharmacy. The reference data should follow the same preparation instructions for combining raw materials and packaged in a container with similar properties.

(ii) In the absence of stability information applicable for a specific drug or preparation, the following maximum beyond-use dates are to be used when the compounded preparation is packaged in tight, light-resistant containers and stored at controlled room temperatures.

(I)   Nonaqueous liquids and solid formulations (Where the manufactured drug product is the source of active ingredient): 25% of the time remaining until the product's expiration date or 6 months, whichever is earlier.

(II) Water-containing formulations (Prepared from ingredients in solid form): Not later than 14 days when refrigerated between 2 - 8 degrees Celsius (36 - 46 degrees Fahrenheit).

(III) All other formulations: Intended duration of therapy or 30 days, whichever is earlier.

(iii) Beyond-use date limits may be exceeded when supported by valid scientific stability information for the specific compounded preparation.

(6)   Written drug information. Written information about the compounded preparation or its major active ingredient(s) shall be given to the patient at the time of dispensing. A statement which indicates that the preparation was compounded by the pharmacy must be included in this written information. If there is no written information available, the patient should be advised that the drug has been compounded and how to contact a pharmacist, and if appropriate the prescriber, concerning the drug.

(7)   Drugs, components, and materials used in non-sterile compounding.

(A)   Drugs used in non-sterile compounding shall be a USP/NF grade substances manufactured in an FDA-registered facility.

(B)   If USP/NF grade substances are not available, or when food, cosmetics, or other substances are, or must be used, the substance shall be of a chemical grade in one of the following categories:

(i)   Chemically Pure (CP);

(ii) Analytical Reagent (AR); or

(iii) American Chemical Society (ACS); or (iv) Food Chemical Codex; or

(C)   If a drug, component or material is not purchased from a FDA-registered facility, the pharmacist shall establish purity and stability by obtaining a Certificate of Analysis from the supplier and the pharmacist shall compare the monograph of drugs in a similar class to the Certificate of Analysis.

(D)   A manufactured drug product may be a source of active ingredient. Only manufactured drugs from containers labeled with a batch control number and a future expiration date are acceptable as a potential source of active ingredients. When compounding with manufactured drug products, the pharmacist must consider all ingredients present in the drug product relative to the intended use of the compounded preparation.

(E)   All components shall be stored in properly labeled containers in a clean, dry area, under proper temperatures.

(F)   Drug product containers and closures shall not be reactive, additive, or absorptive so as to alter the safety, identity, strength, quality, or purity of the compounded drug product beyond the desired result.

(G)   Components, drug product containers, and closures shall be rotated so that the oldest stock is used first.

(H)   Container closure systems shall provide adequate protection against foreseeable external factors in storage and use that can cause deterioration or contamination of the compounded drug product.

(I)   A pharmacy may not compound a preparation that contains ingredients appearing on a federal Food and Drug Administration list of drug products withdrawn or removed from the market for safety reasons.

(8) Compounding process.

(A)   All significant procedures performed in the compounding area shall be covered by written SOPs designed to ensure accountability, accuracy, quality, safety, and uniformity in the compounding process. At a minimum, SOPs shall be developed for:

(i)   the facility;

(ii) equipment;

(iii) personnel;

(iv) preparation evaluation;

(v)   quality assurance;

(vi) preparation recall;

(vii) packaging; and

(viii) storage of compounded preparations.

(B)   Any compounded preparation with an official monograph in the USP/NF shall be compounded, labeled, and packaged in conformity with the USP/NF monograph for the drug.

(C)   Any person with an apparent illness or open lesion that may adversely affect the safety or quality of a drug product being compounded shall be excluded from direct contact with components, drug product containers, closures, any materials involved in the compounding process, and drug products until the condition is corrected.

(D)   Personnel engaged in the compounding of drug preparations shall wear clean clothing appropriate to the operation being performed. Protective apparel, such as coats/jackets, aprons, hair nets, gowns, hand or arm coverings, or masks shall be worn as necessary to protect personnel from chemical exposure and drug preparations from contamination.

(E)   At each step of the compounding process, the pharmacist shall ensure that components used in compounding are accurately weighed, measured, or subdivided as appropriate to conform to the formula being prepared.

(9)   Quality Assurance.

(A)   Initial formula validation. Prior to routine compounding of a non-sterile preparation, a pharmacy shall conduct an evaluation that shows that the pharmacy is capable of compounding a product that contains the stated amount of active ingredient(s).

(B)   Finished preparation checks. The prescription drug and medication orders, written compounding procedure, preparation records, and expended materials used to make compounded non-sterile preparations shall be inspected for accuracy of correct identities and amounts of ingredients, packaging, labeling, and expected physical appearance before the non-sterile preparations are dispensed.

(10) Quality Control.

    (A) The pharmacy shall follow established quality control procedures to monitor the quality of compounded drug preparations for uniformity and consistency such as capsule weight variations, adequacy of mixing, clarity, or pH of solutions. When developing these procedures, pharmacy personnel shall consider the provisions of Chapter 795, concerning Pharmacy Compounding Non-Sterile Preparations, Chapter 1075, concerning Good Compounding Practices, and Chapter 1160, concerning Pharmaceutical Calculations in Prescription Compounding contained in the current USP/NF. Such procedures shall be documented and be available for inspection.

    (B) Compounding procedures that are routinely performed, including batch compounding, shall be completed and verified according to written procedures. The act of verification of a compounding procedure involves checking to ensure that calculations, weighing and measuring, order of mixing, and compounding techniques were appropriate and accurately performed.

    (C) Unless otherwise indicated or appropriate, compounded preparations are to be prepared to ensure that each preparation shall contain not less than 90.0 percent and not more than 110.0 percent of the theoretically calculated and labeled quantity of active ingredient per unit weight or volume and not less than 90.0 percent and not more than 110.0 percent of the theoretically calculated weight or volume per unit of the preparation.

(e) Records.

  (1) Maintenance of records. Every record required by this section shall be:

    (A) kept by the pharmacy and be available, for at least two years for inspecting and copying by the board or its representative and to other authorized local, state, or federal law enforcement agencies; and

    (B) supplied by the pharmacy within 72 hours, if requested by an authorized agent of the Texas State Board of Pharmacy. If the pharmacy maintains the records in an electronic format, the requested records must be provided in an electronic format. Failure to provide the records set out in this section, either on site or within 72 hours, constitutes prima facie evidence of failure to keep and maintain records in violation of the Act.

  (2) Compounding records.

    (A) Compounding pursuant to patient specific prescription drug or medication orders. Compounding records for all compounded preparations shall be maintained by the pharmacy electronically or manually as part of the prescription drug or medication order, formula record, formula book, or compounding log and shall include:

      (i) the date of preparation;

      (ii) a complete formula, including methodology and necessary equipment which includes the brand name(s) of the raw materials, or if no brand name, the generic name(s) and name(s) of the manufacturer(s) of the raw materials and the quantities of each;

      (iii) signature or initials of the pharmacist or pharmacy technician or pharmacy technician trainee performing the compounding;

      (iv) signature or initials of the pharmacist responsible for supervising pharmacy technicians or pharmacy technician trainees and conducting in-process and final checks of compounded preparations if pharmacy technicians or pharmacy technician trainees perform the compounding function;

      (v) the quantity in units of finished preparations or amount of raw materials;

      (vi) the container used and the number of units prepared;

      (vii) a reference to the location of the following documentation which may be maintained with other records, such as quality control records:

        (I) the criteria used to determine the beyond-use date; and

        (II) documentation of performance of quality control procedures. Documentation of the performance of quality control procedures is not required if the compounding process is done pursuant to a patient specific order and involves the mixing of two or more commercially available oral liquids or commercially available preparations when the final product is intended for external use.

    (B) Compounding records when batch compounding or compounding in anticipation of future prescription drug or medication orders.

      (i) Master work sheet. A master work sheet shall be developed and approved by a pharmacist for preparations prepared in batch. Once approved, a duplicate of the master work sheet shall be used as the preparation work sheet from which each batch is prepared and on which all documentation for that batch occurs. The master work sheet shall contain at a minimum:

        (I) the formula;

        (II) the components;

        (III) the compounding directions;

        (IV) a sample label;

        (V) evaluation and testing requirements;

        (VI) specific equipment used during preparation; and

        (VII) storage requirements.

      (ii) Preparation work sheet. The preparation work sheet for each batch of preparations shall document the following:

        (I) identity of all solutions and ingredients and their corresponding amounts, concentrations, or volumes;

        (II) lot number or each component;

        (III) component manufacturer/distributor or suitable identifying number;

        (IV) container specifications;

        (V) unique lot or control number assigned to batch;

        (VI) beyond use date of batch-prepared preparations;

        (VII) date of preparation;

        (VIII) name, initials, or electronic signature of the person(s) involved in the preparation;

        (IX) name, initials, or electronic signature of the responsible pharmacist;

Phr. Rules

(X) finished preparation evaluation and testing specifications, if applicable; and

(XI) comparison of actual yield to anticipated or theoretical yield, when appropriate.

(f) Office Use Compounding and Distribution of Compounded Preparations to Class C Pharmacies or Veterinarians in Accordance With § 563.054 of the Act.

   (1) General.

      (A) A pharmacy may dispense and deliver a reasonable quantity of a compounded preparation to a practitioner for office use by the practitioner in accordance with this subsection.

      (B) A Class A pharmacy is not required to register or be licensed under Chapter 431, Health and Safety Code, to distribute non-sterile compounded preparations to a Class C pharmacy.

      (C) A Class C pharmacy is not required to register or be licensed under Chapter 431, Health and Safety Code, to distribute non-sterile compounded preparations that the Class C pharmacy has compounded for other Class C pharmacies under common ownership.

      (D) To dispense and deliver a compounded preparation under this subsection, a pharmacy must:

         (i)   verify the source of the raw materials to be used in a compounded drug;

         (ii) comply with applicable United States Pharmacopoeia guidelines, including the testing requirements, and the Health Insurance Portability and Accountability Act of 1996 (Pub. L. No. 104-191);

         (iii) enter into a written agreement with a practitioner for the practitioner's office use of a compounded preparation;

         (iv) comply with all applicable competency and accrediting standards as determined by the board; and

         (v)   comply with the provisions of this subsection.

   (2) Written Agreement. A pharmacy that provides non-sterile compounded preparations to practitioners for office use or to another pharmacy shall enter into a written agreement with the practitioner or pharmacy. The written agreement shall:

      (A) address acceptable standards of practice for a compounding pharmacy and a practitioner and receiving pharmacy that enter into the agreement including a statement that the compounded preparations may only be administered to the patient and may not be dispensed to the patient or sold to any other person or entity except as authorized by § 563.054 of the Act;

      (B) state that the practitioner or receiving pharmacy should include on a separate log or in a patient's chart, medication order, or medication administration record, the lot number and beyond-use date of a compounded preparation administered to a patient; and

      (C) describe the scope of services to be performed by the pharmacy and practitioner or receiving pharmacy, including a statement of the process for:

         (i)   a patient to report an adverse reaction or submit a complaint; and

         (ii) the pharmacy to recall batches of compounded preparations.

   (3) Recordkeeping.

      (A) Maintenance of Records.

         (i)   Records of orders and distribution of non-sterile compounded preparations to a practitioner for office use or to a Class C pharmacy for administration to a patient shall:

            (I)   be kept by the pharmacy and be available, for at least two years from the date of the record, for inspecting and copying by the board or its representative and to other authorized local, state, or federal law enforcement agencies;

            (II) maintained separately from the records of products dispensed pursuant to a prescription or medication order; and

            (III) supplied by the pharmacy within 72 hours, if requested by an authorized agent of the Texas State Board of Pharmacy or its representative. If the pharmacy maintains the records in an electronic format, the requested records must be provided in an electronic format. Failure to provide the records set out in this subsection, either on site or within 72 hours for whatever reason, constitutes prima facie evidence of failure to keep and maintain records.

         (ii) Records may be maintained in an alternative data retention system, such as a data processing system or direct imaging system provided the data processing system is capable of producing a hard copy of the record upon the request of the board, its representative, or other authorized local, state, or federal law enforcement or regulatory agencies.

      (B) Orders. The pharmacy shall maintain a record of all non-sterile compounded preparations ordered by a practitioner for office use or by a Class C pharmacy for administration to a patient. The record shall include the following information:

         (i)   date of the order;

         (ii) name, address, and phone number of the practitioner who ordered the preparation and if applicable, the name, address and phone number of the Class C pharmacy ordering the preparation; and

         (iii) name, strength, and quantity of the preparation ordered.

      (C) Distributions. The pharmacy shall maintain a record of all non-sterile compounded preparations distributed pursuant to an order to a practitioner for office use or by a Class C pharmacy for administration to a patient. The record shall include the following information:

         (i)   date the preparation was compounded;

         (ii) date the preparation was distributed;

         (iii) name, strength and quantity in each container of the preparation;

         (iv) pharmacy's lot number;

         (v)   quantity of containers shipped; and

         (vi) name, address, and phone number of the practitioner or Class C pharmacy to whom the preparation is distributed.

      (D) Audit Trail.

         (i)   The pharmacy shall store the order and distribution records of preparations for all non-sterile compounded preparations ordered by and or distributed to a practitioner for office use or by a Class C pharmacy for administration to a patient in such a manner as to be able to provide a audit trail for all orders and distributions of any of the following during a specified time period.

            (I)   any strength and dosage form of a preparation (by either brand or generic name or both);

            (II) any ingredient;

            (III) any lot number;

Phr. Rules

(IV) any practitioner;
(V) any facility; and
(VI) any pharmacy, if applicable.
    (ii) The audit trail shall contain the following information:
      (I) date of order and date of the distribution;
      (II) practitioner's name, address, and name of the Class C pharmacy, if applicable;
      (III) name, strength and quantity of the preparation in each container of the preparation;
      (IV) name and quantity of each active ingredient;
      (V) quantity of containers distributed; and
      (VI) pharmacy's lot number;

(4) Labeling. The pharmacy shall affix a label to the preparation containing the following information:
  (A) name, address, and phone number of the compounding pharmacy;
  (B) the statement: "For Institutional or Office Use Only—Not for Resale"; or if the preparation is distributed to a veterinarian the statement: "Compounded Preparation";
  (C) name and strength of the preparation or list of the active ingredients and strengths;
  (D) pharmacy's lot number;
  (E) beyond-use date as determined by the pharmacist using appropriate documented criteria;
  (F) quantity or amount in the container;
  (G) appropriate ancillary instructions, such as storage instructions or cautionary statements, including hazardous drug warning labels where appropriate; and
  (H) device-specific instructions, where appropriate.

(g) Recall Procedures.
(1) The pharmacy shall have written procedures for the recall of any compounded non-sterile preparations provided to a patient, to a practitioner for office use, or a pharmacy for administration. Written procedures shall include, but not be limited to the requirements as specified in paragraph (3) of this subsection.
(2) The pharmacy shall immediately initiate a recall of any non-sterile preparation compounded by the pharmacy upon identification of a potential or confirmed harm to a patient.
(3) In the event of a recall, the pharmacist-in-charge shall ensure that:
  (A) each practitioner, facility, and/or pharmacy to which the preparation was distributed is notified, in writing, of the recall;
  (B) each patient to whom the preparation was dispensed is notified, in writing, of the recall;
  (C) if the preparation is prepared as a batch, the board is notified of the recall, in writing;
  (D) if the preparation is distributed for office use, the Texas Department of State Health Services, Drugs and Medical Devices Group, is notified of the recall, in writing;
  (E) the preparation is quarantined; and
  (F) the pharmacy keeps a written record of the recall including all actions taken to notify all parties and steps taken to ensure corrective measures.
(4) If a pharmacy fails to initiate a recall, the board may require a pharmacy to initiate a recall if there is potential for or confirmed harm to a patient.

Source: The provisions of this § 291.131 adopted to be effective September 18, 2007, 32 TexReg 6352; amended to be effective March 6, 2008, 33 TexReg 1801; amended to be effective September 9, 2012, 37 TexReg 6917; amended to be effective January 4, 2018, 42 TexReg 7700

§291.133 Pharmacies Compounding Sterile Preparations

(a) Purpose. Pharmacies compounding sterile preparations, prepackaging pharmaceutical products, and distributing those products shall comply with all requirements for their specific license classification and this section. The purpose of this section is to provide standards for the:
(1) compounding of sterile preparations pursuant to a prescription or medication order for a patient from a practitioner in Class A-S, Class B, Class C-S, and Class E-S pharmacies;
(2) compounding, dispensing, and delivery of a reasonable quantity of a compounded sterile preparation in Class A-S, Class B, Class C-S, and Class E-S pharmacies to a practitioner's office for office use by the practitioner;
(3) compounding and distribution of compounded sterile preparations by a Class A-S pharmacy for a Class C-S pharmacy; and
(4) compounding of sterile preparations by a Class C-S pharmacy and the distribution of the compounded preparations to other Class C or Class C-S pharmacies under common ownership.
(b) Definitions. In addition to the definitions for specific license classifications, the following words and terms, when used in this section, shall have the following meanings, unless the context clearly indicates otherwise.
(1) ACPE—Accreditation Council for Pharmacy Education.
(2) Airborne particulate cleanliness class—The level of cleanliness specified by the maximum allowable number of particles per cubic meter of air as specified in the International Organization of Standardization (ISO) Classification Air Cleanliness (ISO 14644-1). For example:
  (A) ISO Class 5 (formerly Class 100) is an atmospheric environment that contains less than 3,520 particles 0.5 microns in diameter per cubic meter of air (formerly stated as 100 particles 0.5 microns in diameter per cubic foot of air);
  (B) ISO Class 7 (formerly Class 10,000) is an atmospheric environment that contains less than 352,000 particles 0.5 microns in diameter per cubic meter of air (formerly stated as 10,000 particles 0.5 microns in diameter per cubic foot of air); and
  (C) ISO Class 8 (formerly Class 100,000) is an atmospheric environment that contains less than 3,520,000 particles 0.5 microns in diameter per cubic meter of air (formerly stated as 100,000 particles 0.5 microns in diameter per cubic foot of air).
(3) Ancillary supplies—Supplies necessary for the preparation and administration of compounded sterile preparations.
(4) Ante-area—An ISO Class 8 or better area where personnel may perform hand hygiene and garbing procedures, staging of components, order entry, labeling, and other high-particulate generating activities. It is also a transition area that:

(A) provides assurance that pressure relationships are constantly maintained so that air flows from clean to dirty areas; and

(B) reduces the need for the heating, ventilating and air conditioning (HVAC) control system to respond to large disturbances.

(5) Aseptic Processing—A mode of processing pharmaceutical and medical preparations that involves the separate sterilization of the preparation and of the package (containers-closures or packaging material for medical devices) and the transfer of the preparation into the container and its closure under at least ISO Class 5 conditions.

(6) Automated compounding device—An automated device that compounds, measures, and/or packages a specified quantity of individual components in a predetermined sequence for a designated sterile preparation.

(7) Batch—A specific quantity of a drug or other material that is intended to have uniform character and quality, within specified limits, and is produced during a single preparation cycle.

(8) Batch preparation compounding—Compounding of multiple sterile preparation units, in a single discrete process, by the same individual(s), carried out during one limited time period. Batch preparation/compounding does not include the preparation of multiple sterile preparation units pursuant to patient specific medication orders.

(9) Beyond-use date—The date or time after which the compounded sterile preparation shall not be stored or transported or begin to be administered to a patient. The beyond-use date is determined from the date or time the preparation is compounded.

(10) Biological Safety Cabinet, Class II—A ventilated cabinet for personnel, product or preparation, and environmental protection having an open front with inward airflow for personnel protection, downward HEPA filtered laminar airflow for product protection, and HEPA filtered exhausted air for environmental protection.

(11) Buffer Area—An ISO Class 7 or, if a Class B pharmacy, ISO Class 8 or better, area where the primary engineering control area is physically located. Activities that occur in this area include the preparation and staging of components and supplies used when compounding sterile preparations.

(12) Clean room—A room in which the concentration of airborne particles is controlled to meet a specified airborne particulate cleanliness class. Microorganisms in the environment are monitored so that a microbial level for air, surface, and personnel gear are not exceeded for a specified cleanliness class.

(13) Component—Any ingredient intended for use in the compounding of a drug preparation, including those that may not appear in such preparation.

(14) Compounding—The preparation, mixing, assembling, packaging, or labeling of a drug or device:

(A) as the result of a practitioner's prescription drug or medication order based on the practitioner-patient-pharmacist relationship in the course of professional practice;

(B) for administration to a patient by a practitioner as the result of a practitioner's initiative based on the practitioner-patient-pharmacist relationship in the course of professional practice;

(C) in anticipation of prescription drug or medication orders based on routine, regularly observed prescribing patterns; or

(D) for or as an incident to research, teaching, or chemical analysis and not for sale or dispensing, except as allowed under § 562.154 or Chapter 563 of the Occupations Code.

(15) Compounding Aseptic Isolator—A form of barrier isolator specifically designed for compounding pharmaceutical ingredients or preparations. It is designed to maintain an aseptic compounding environment within the isolator throughout the compounding and material transfer processes. Air exchange into the isolator from the surrounding environment shall not occur unless it has first passed through a microbial retentive filter (HEPA minimum).

(16) Compounding Aseptic Containment Isolator—A compounding aseptic isolator designed to provide worker protection from exposure to undesirable levels of airborne drug throughout the compounding and material transfer processes and to provide an aseptic environment for compounding sterile preparations. Air exchange with the surrounding environment should not occur unless the air is first passed through a microbial retentive filter (HEPA minimum) system capable of containing airborne concentrations of the physical size and state of the drug being compounded. Where volatile hazardous drugs are prepared, the exhaust air from the isolator should be appropriately removed by properly designed building ventilation.

(17) Compounding Personnel—A pharmacist, pharmacy technician, or pharmacy technician trainee who performs the actual compounding; a pharmacist who supervises pharmacy technicians or pharmacy technician trainees compounding sterile preparations, and a pharmacist who performs an intermediate or final verification of a compounded sterile preparation.

(18) Critical Area—An ISO Class 5 environment.

(19) Critical Sites—A location that includes any component or fluid pathway surfaces (e.g., vial septa, injection ports, beakers) or openings (e.g., opened ampules, needle hubs) exposed and at risk of direct contact with air (e.g., ambient room or HEPA filtered), moisture (e.g., oral and mucosal secretions), or touch contamination. Risk of microbial particulate contamination of the critical site increases with the size of the openings and exposure time.

(20) Device—An instrument, apparatus, implement, machine, contrivance, implant, in-vitro reagent, or other similar or related article, including any component part or accessory, that is required under federal or state law to be ordered or prescribed by a practitioner.

(21) Direct Compounding Area—A critical area within the ISO Class 5 primary engineering control where critical sites are exposed to unidirectional HEPA-filtered air, also known as first air.

(22) Disinfectant—An agent that frees from infection, usually a chemical agent but sometimes a physical one, and that destroys disease-causing pathogens or other harmful microorganisms but may not kill bacterial and fungal spores. It refers to substances applied to inanimate objects.

(23) First Air—The air exiting the HEPA filter in a unidirectional air stream that is essentially particle free.

(24) Hazardous Drugs—Drugs that, studies in animals or humans indicate exposure to the drugs, have a potential for causing cancer, development or reproductive toxicity, or harm to organs. For the purposes of this chapter, radiopharmaceuticals are not considered hazardous drugs.

(25) Hot water—The temperature of water from the pharmacy's sink maintained at a minimum of 105 degrees F (41 degrees C).

(26) HVAC—Heating, ventilation, and air conditioning.

(27) Immediate use—A sterile preparation that is not prepared according to USP 797 standards (i.e., outside the pharmacy and most likely not by pharmacy personnel) which shall be stored for no longer than one hour after completion of the preparation.

(28) IPA—Isopropyl alcohol (2-propanol).

Phr. Rules

(29) Labeling—All labels and other written, printed, or graphic matter on an immediate container of an article or preparation or on, or in, any package or wrapper in which it is enclosed, except any outer shipping container. The term "label" designates that part of the labeling on the immediate container.

(30) Media-Fill Test—A test used to qualify aseptic technique of compounding personnel or processes and to ensure that the processes used are able to produce sterile preparation without microbial contamination. During this test, a microbiological growth medium such as Soybean-Casein Digest Medium is substituted for the actual drug preparation to simulate admixture compounding. The issues to consider in the development of a media-fill test are the following: media-fill procedures, media selection, fill volume, incubation, time and temperature, inspection of filled units, documentation, interpretation of results, and possible corrective actions required.

(31) Multiple-Dose Container—A multiple-unit container for articles or preparations intended for potential administration only and usually contains antimicrobial preservatives. The beyond-use date for an opened or entered (e.g., needle-punctured) multiple-dose container with antimicrobial preservatives is 28 days, unless otherwise specified by the manufacturer.

(32) Negative Pressure Room—A room that is at a lower pressure compared to adjacent spaces and, therefore, the net flow of air is into the room.

(33) Office use—The administration of a compounded drug to a patient by a practitioner in the practitioner's office or by the practitioner in a health care facility or treatment setting, including a hospital, ambulatory surgical center, or pharmacy in accordance with Chapter 562 of the Act, or for administration or provision by a veterinarian in accordance with § 563.054 of the Act.

(34) Pharmacy Bulk Package—A container of a sterile preparation for potential use that contains many single doses. The contents are intended for use in a pharmacy admixture program and are restricted to the preparation of admixtures for infusion or, through a sterile transfer device, for the filling of empty sterile syringes. The closure shall be penetrated only one time after constitution with a suitable sterile transfer device or dispensing set, which allows measured dispensing of the contents. The pharmacy bulk package is to be used only in a suitable work area such as a laminar flow hood (or an equivalent clean air compounding area).

(35) Prepackaging—The act of repackaging and relabeling quantities of drug products from a manufacturer's original container into unit dose packaging or a multiple dose container for distribution within a facility licensed as a Class C pharmacy or to other pharmacies under common ownership for distribution within those facilities. The term as defined does not prohibit the prepackaging of drug products for use within other pharmacy classes.

(36) Preparation or Compounded Sterile Preparation—A sterile admixture compounded in a licensed pharmacy or other healthcare-related facility pursuant to the order of a licensed prescriber. The components of the preparation may or may not be sterile products.

(37) Primary Engineering Control—A device or room that provides an ISO Class 5 environment for the exposure of critical sites when compounding sterile preparations. Such devices include, but may not be limited to, laminar airflow workbenches, biological safety cabinets, compounding aseptic isolators, and compounding aseptic containment isolators.

(38) Product—A commercially manufactured sterile drug or nutrient that has been evaluated for safety and efficacy by the U.S. Food and Drug Administration (FDA). Products are accompanied by full prescribing information, which is commonly known as the FDA-approved manufacturer's labeling or product package insert.

(39) Positive Control—A quality assurance sample prepared to test positive for microbial growth.

(40) Quality assurance—The set of activities used to ensure that the process used in the preparation of sterile drug preparations lead to preparations that meet predetermined standards of quality.

(41) Quality control—The set of testing activities used to determine that the ingredients, components (e.g., containers), and final compounded sterile preparations prepared meet predetermined requirements with respect to identity, purity, non-pyrogenicity, and sterility.

(42) Reasonable quantity—An amount of a compounded drug that:
   (A) does not exceed the amount a practitioner anticipates may be used in the practitioner's office or facility before the beyond use date of the drug;
   (B) is reasonable considering the intended use of the compounded drug and the nature of the practitioner's practice; and
   (C) for any practitioner and all practitioners as a whole, is not greater than an amount the pharmacy is capable of compounding in compliance with pharmaceutical standards for identity, strength, quality, and purity of the compounded drug that are consistent with United States Pharmacopoeia guidelines and accreditation practices.

(43) Segregated Compounding Area—A designated space, either a demarcated area or room, that is restricted to preparing low-risk level compounded sterile preparations with 12-hour or less beyond-use date. Such area shall contain a device that provides unidirectional airflow of ISO Class 5 air quality for preparation of compounded sterile preparations and shall be void of activities and materials that are extraneous to sterile compounding.

(44) Single-dose container—A single-unit container for articles or preparations intended for parenteral administration only. It is intended for a single use. A single-dose container is labeled as such. Examples of single-dose containers include pre-filled syringes, cartridges, fusion-sealed containers, and closure-sealed containers when so labeled.

(45) SOPs—Standard operating procedures.

(46) Sterilizing Grade Membranes—Membranes that are documented to retain 100% of a culture of 107 microorganisms of a strain of Brevundimonas (Pseudomonas) diminuta per square centimeter of membrane surface under a pressure of not less than 30 psi (2.0 bar). Such filter membranes are nominally at 0.22-micrometer or 0.2-micrometer nominal pore size, depending on the manufacturer's practice.

(47) Sterilization by Filtration—Passage of a fluid or solution through a sterilizing grade membrane to produce a sterile effluent.

(48) Terminal Sterilization—The application of a lethal process, e.g., steam under pressure or autoclaving, to sealed final preparation containers for the purpose of achieving a predetermined sterility assurance level of usually less than 10-6 or a probability of less than one in one million of a non-sterile unit.

(49) Unidirectional Flow—An airflow moving in a single direction in a robust and uniform manner and at sufficient speed to reproducibly sweep particles away from the critical processing or testing area.

(50) USP/NF—The current edition of the United States Pharmacopeia/National Formulary.

(c) Personnel.
   (1) Pharmacist-in-charge.
      (A) General. The pharmacy shall have a pharmacist-in-charge in compliance with the specific license classification of the pharmacy.
      (B) Responsibilities. In addition to the responsibilities for the specific class of pharmacy, the pharmacist-in-charge shall have the responsibility for, at a minimum, the following concerning the compounding of sterile preparations:
         (i) developing a system to ensure that all pharmacy personnel responsible for compounding and/or supervising the compounding of sterile preparations within the pharmacy receive appropriate education and training and competency evaluation;
         (ii) determining that all personnel involved in compounding sterile preparations obtain continuing education appropriate for the type of compounding done by the personnel;
         (iii) supervising a system to ensure appropriate procurement of drugs and devices and storage of all pharmaceutical materials including pharmaceuticals, components used in the compounding of sterile preparations, and drug delivery devices;
         (iv) ensuring that the equipment used in compounding is properly maintained;
         (v) developing a system for the disposal and distribution of drugs from the pharmacy;
         (vi) developing a system for bulk compounding or batch preparation of drugs;
         (vii) developing a system for the compounding, sterility assurance, quality assurance, and quality control of sterile preparations; and
         (viii) if applicable, ensuring that the pharmacy has a system to dispose of hazardous waste in a manner so as not to endanger the public health.
   (2) Pharmacists.
      (A) General.
         (i) A pharmacist is responsible for ensuring that compounded sterile preparations are accurately identified, measured, diluted, and mixed and are correctly purified, sterilized, packaged, sealed, labeled, stored, dispensed, and distributed.
         (ii) A pharmacist shall inspect and approve all components, drug preparation containers, closures, labeling, and any other materials involved in the compounding process.
         (iii) A pharmacist shall review all compounding records for accuracy and conduct periodic in-process checks as defined in the pharmacy's policy and procedures.
         (iv) A pharmacist shall review all compounding records for accuracy and conduct a final check.
         (v) A pharmacist is responsible for ensuring the proper maintenance, cleanliness, and use of all equipment used in the compounding process.
         (vi) A pharmacist shall be accessible at all times, 24 hours a day, to respond to patients' and other health professionals' questions and needs.
      (B) Initial training and continuing education.
         (i) All pharmacists who compound sterile preparations or supervise pharmacy technicians and pharmacy technician trainees compounding sterile preparations shall comply with the following:
            (I) complete through a single course, a minimum of 20 hours of instruction and experience in the areas listed in paragraph (4)(D) of this subsection. Such training shall be obtained through completion of a recognized course in an accredited college of pharmacy or a course sponsored by an ACPE accredited provider;
            (II) complete a structured on-the-job didactic and experiential training program at this pharmacy which provides sufficient hours of instruction and experience in the facility's sterile compounding processes and procedures. Such training may not be transferred to another pharmacy unless the pharmacies are under common ownership and control and use a common training program; and
            (III) possess knowledge about:
               (-a-) aseptic processing;
               (-b-) quality control and quality assurance as related to environmental, component, and finished preparation release checks and tests;
               (-c-) chemical, pharmaceutical, and clinical properties of drugs;
               (-d-) container, equipment, and closure system selection; and
               (-e-) sterilization techniques.
         (ii) The required experiential portion of the training programs specified in this subparagraph must be supervised by an individual who is actively engaged in performing sterile compounding and is qualified and has completed training as specified in this paragraph or paragraph (3) of this subsection.
         (iii) In order to renew a license to practice pharmacy, during the previous licensure period, a pharmacist engaged in sterile compounding shall complete a minimum of:
            (I) two hours of ACPE-accredited continuing education relating to one or more of the areas listed in paragraph (4)(D) of this subsection if the pharmacist is engaged in compounding low and medium risk sterile preparations; or
            (II) four hours of ACPE-accredited continuing education relating to one or more of the areas listed in paragraph (4)(D) of this subsection if the pharmacist is engaged in compounding high risk sterile preparations.
   (3) Pharmacy technicians and pharmacy technician trainees.
      (A) General. All pharmacy technicians and pharmacy technician trainees shall meet the training requirements specified in § 297.6 of this title (relating to Pharmacy Technician and Pharmacy Technician Trainee Training).
      (B) Initial training and continuing education.
         (i) Pharmacy technicians and pharmacy technician trainees may compound sterile preparations provided the pharmacy technicians and/or pharmacy technician trainees are supervised by a pharmacist as specified in paragraph (2) of this subsection.
         (ii) All pharmacy technicians and pharmacy technician trainees who compound sterile preparations for administration to patients shall:

Phr. Rules

(I) have initial training obtained either through completion of:
(-a-) a single course, a minimum of 40 hours of instruction and experience in the areas listed in paragraph (4)(D) of this subsection. Such training shall be obtained through completion of a course sponsored by an ACPE accredited provider which provides 40 hours of instruction and experience; or
(-b-) a training program which is accredited by the American Society of Health-System Pharmacists.
(II) and
(-a-) complete a structured on-the-job didactic and experiential training program at this pharmacy which provides sufficient hours of instruction and experience in the facility's sterile compounding processes and procedures. Such training may not be transferred to another pharmacy unless the pharmacies are under common ownership and control and use a common training program; and
(-b-) possess knowledge about:
(-1-) aseptic processing;
(-2-) quality control and quality assurance as related to environmental, component, and finished preparation release checks and tests;
(-3-) chemical, pharmaceutical, and clinical properties of drugs;
(-4-) container, equipment, and closure system selection; and
(-5-) sterilization techniques.
(iii) Individuals enrolled in training programs accredited by the American Society of Health-System Pharmacists may compound sterile preparations in a licensed pharmacy provided the:
(I) compounding occurs only during times the individual is assigned to a pharmacy as a part of the experiential component of the American Society of Health-System Pharmacists training program;
(II) individual is under the direct supervision of and responsible to a pharmacist who has completed training as specified in paragraph (2) of this subsection;
(III) supervising pharmacist conducts periodic in-process checks as defined in the pharmacy's policy and procedures; and
(IV) supervising pharmacist conducts a final check.
(iv) The required experiential portion of the training programs specified in this subparagraph must be supervised by an individual who is actively engaged in performing sterile compounding, is qualified and has completed training as specified in paragraph (2) of this subsection or this paragraph.
(v) In order to renew a registration as a pharmacy technician, during the previous registration period, a pharmacy technician engaged in sterile compounding shall complete a minimum of:
(I) two hours of ACPE accredited continuing education relating to one or more of the areas listed in paragraph (4)(D) of this subsection if the pharmacy technician is engaged in compounding low and medium risk sterile preparations; or
(II) four hours of ACPE accredited continuing education relating to one or more of the areas listed in paragraph (4)(D) of this subsection if the pharmacy technician is engaged in compounding high risk sterile preparations.
(4) Evaluation and testing requirements.
(A) All pharmacy personnel preparing sterile preparations shall be trained conscientiously and skillfully by expert personnel through multimedia instructional sources and professional publications in the theoretical principles and practical skills of aseptic manipulations, garbing procedures, aseptic work practices, achieving and maintaining ISO Class 5 environmental conditions, and cleaning and disinfection procedures before beginning to prepare compounded sterile preparations.
(B) All pharmacy personnel preparing sterile preparations shall perform didactic review and pass written and media-fill testing of aseptic manipulative skills initially followed by:
(i) every 12 months for low- and medium-risk level compounding; and
(ii) every six months for high-risk level compounding.
(C) Pharmacy personnel who fail written tests or whose media-fill tests result in gross microbial colonization shall:
(i) be immediately re-instructed and re-evaluated by expert compounding personnel to ensure correction of all aseptic practice deficiencies; and
(ii) not be allowed to compound sterile preparations for patient use until passing results are achieved.
(D) The didactic and experiential training shall include instruction, experience, and demonstrated proficiency in the following areas:
(i) aseptic technique;
(ii) critical area contamination factors;
(iii) environmental monitoring;
(iv) structure and engineering controls related to facilities;
(v) equipment and supplies;
(vi) sterile preparation calculations and terminology;
(vii) sterile preparation compounding documentation;
(viii) quality assurance procedures;
(ix) aseptic preparation procedures including proper gowning and gloving technique;
(x) handling of hazardous drugs, if applicable;
(xi) cleaning procedures; and
(xii) general conduct in the clean room.
(E) The aseptic technique of each person compounding or responsible for the direct supervision of personnel compounding sterile preparations shall be observed and evaluated by expert personnel as satisfactory through written and practical tests, and challenge testing, and such evaluation documented. Compounding personnel shall not evaluate their own aseptic technique or results of their own media-fill challenge testing.

Phr. Rules

(F) Media-fill tests must be conducted at each pharmacy where an individual compounds low or medium risk sterile preparations. If pharmacies are under common ownership and control, the media-fill testing may be conducted at only one of the pharmacies provided each of the pharmacies are operated under equivalent policies and procedures and the testing is conducted under the most challenging or stressful conditions. In addition, each pharmacy must maintain documentation of the media-fill test. No preparation intended for patient use shall be compounded by an individual until the on-site media-fill tests indicate that the individual can competently perform aseptic procedures, except that a pharmacist may temporarily compound sterile preparations and supervise pharmacy technicians compounding sterile preparations without media-fill tests provided the pharmacist completes the on-site media-fill tests within seven days of commencing work at the pharmacy.

(G) Media-fill tests must be conducted at each pharmacy where an individual compounds high risk sterile preparations. No preparation intended for patient use shall be compounded by an individual until the on-site media-fill tests indicate that the individual can competently perform aseptic procedures, except that a pharmacist may temporarily compound sterile preparations and supervise pharmacy technicians compounding sterile preparations without media-fill tests provided the pharmacist completes the on-site media-fill tests within seven days of commencing work at the pharmacy.

(H) Media-fill testing procedures for assessing the preparation of specific types of sterile preparations shall be representative of the most challenging or stressful conditions encountered by the pharmacy personnel being evaluated and, if applicable, for sterilizing high-risk level compounded sterile preparations.

(I) Media-fill challenge tests simulating high-risk level compounding shall be used to verify the capability of the compounding environment and process to produce a sterile preparation.

(J) Commercially available sterile fluid culture media for low and medium risk level compounding or non-sterile fluid culture media for high risk level compounding shall be able to promote exponential colonization of bacteria that are most likely to be transmitted to compounding sterile preparations from the compounding personnel and environment. Media-filled vials are generally incubated at 20 to 25 degrees Celsius or at 30 to 35 degrees Celsius for a minimum of 14 days. If two temperatures are used for incubation of media-filled samples, then these filled containers should be incubated for at least 7 days at each temperature. Failure is indicated by visible turbidity in the medium on or before 14 days.

(K) The pharmacist-in-charge shall ensure continuing competency of pharmacy personnel through in-service education, training, and media-fill tests to supplement initial training. Personnel competency shall be evaluated:

   (i) during orientation and training prior to the regular performance of those tasks;

   (ii) whenever the quality assurance program yields an unacceptable result;

   (iii) whenever unacceptable techniques are observed; and

   (iv) at least on an annual basis for low- and medium-risk level compounding, and every six months for high-risk level compounding.

(L) The pharmacist-in-charge shall ensure that proper hand hygiene and garbing practices of compounding personnel are evaluated prior to compounding, supervising, or verifying sterile preparations intended for patient use and whenever an aseptic media fill is performed.

   (i) Sampling of compounding personnel glove fingertips shall be performed for all risk level compounding. If pharmacies are under common ownership and control, the gloved fingertip sampling may be conducted at only one of the pharmacies provided each of the pharmacies are operated under equivalent policies and procedures and the testing is conducted under the most challenging or stressful conditions. In addition, each pharmacy must maintain documentation of the gloved fingertip sampling of all compounding personnel.

   (ii) All compounding personnel shall demonstrate competency in proper hand hygiene and garbing procedures and in aseptic work practices (e.g., disinfection of component surfaces, routine disinfection of gloved hands).

   (iii) Sterile contact agar plates shall be used to sample the gloved fingertips of compounding personnel after garbing in order to assess garbing competency and after completing the media-fill preparation (without applying sterile 70% IPA).

   (iv) The visual observation shall be documented and maintained to provide a permanent record and long-term assessment of personnel competency.

   (v) All compounding personnel shall successfully complete an initial competency evaluation and gloved fingertip/thumb sampling procedure no less than three times before initially being allowed to compound sterile preparations for patient use. Immediately after the compounding personnel completes the hand hygiene and garbing procedure (i.e., after donning of sterile gloves and before any disinfecting with sterile 70% IPA), the evaluator will collect a gloved fingertip and thumb sample from both hands of the compounding personnel onto contact plates or swabs by having the individual lightly touching each fingertip onto the testing medium. The contact plates or swabs will be incubated for the appropriate incubation period and at the appropriate temperature. Results of the initial gloved fingertip evaluations shall indicate zero colony-forming units (0 CFU) growth on the contact plates or swabs, or the test shall be considered a failure. In the event of a failed gloved fingertip test, the evaluation shall be repeated until the individual can successfully don sterile gloves and pass the gloved fingertip evaluation, defined as zero CFUs growth. No preparation intended for patient use shall be compounded by an individual until the results of the initial gloved fingertip evaluation indicate that the individual can competently perform aseptic procedures except that a pharmacist may temporarily physically supervise pharmacy technicians compounding sterile preparations before the results of the evaluation have been received for no more than three days from the date of the test.

   (vi) Re-evaluation of all compounding personnel shall occur at least annually for compounding personnel who compound low and medium risk level preparations and every six months for compounding personnel who compound high risk level preparations. Results of gloved fingertip tests conducted immediately after compounding personnel complete a compounding procedure shall indicate no more than 3 CFUs growth, or the test shall be considered a failure, in which case, the evaluation shall be repeated until an acceptable test can be achieved (i.e., the results indicated no more than 3 CFUs growth).

(M) The pharmacist-in-charge shall ensure surface sampling shall be conducted in all ISO classified areas on a periodic basis. Sampling shall be accomplished using contact plates or swabs at the conclusion of compounding. The sample area shall be gently touched with the agar surface by rolling the plate across the surface to be sampled.

    (5) Documentation of Training. The pharmacy shall maintain a record of the training and continuing education on each person who compounds sterile preparations. The record shall contain, at a minimum, a written record of initial and in-service training, education, and the results of written and practical testing and media-fill testing of pharmacy personnel. The record shall be maintained and available for inspection by the board and contain the following information:

        (A) name of the person receiving the training or completing the testing or media-fill tests;

        (B) date(s) of the training, testing, or media-fill challenge testing;

        (C) general description of the topics covered in the training or testing or of the process validated;

        (D) name of the person supervising the training, testing, or media-fill challenge testing; and

        (E) signature or initials of the person receiving the training or completing the testing or media-fill challenge testing and the pharmacist-in-charge or other pharmacist employed by the pharmacy and designated by the pharmacist-in-charge as responsible for training, testing, or media-fill challenge testing of personnel.

(d) Operational Standards.

    (1) General Requirements.

        (A) Sterile preparations may be compounded:

           (i) upon presentation of a practitioner's prescription drug or medication order based on a valid pharmacist/patient/prescriber relationship;

           (ii) in anticipation of future prescription drug or medication orders based on routine, regularly observed prescribing patterns; or

           (iii) in reasonable quantities for office use by a practitioner and for use by a veterinarian.

        (B) Sterile compounding in anticipation of future prescription drug or medication orders must be based upon a history of receiving valid prescriptions issued within an established pharmacist/patient/prescriber relationship, provided that in the pharmacist's professional judgment the quantity prepared is stable for the anticipated shelf time.

           (i) The pharmacist's professional judgment shall be based on the criteria used to determine a beyond-use date outlined in paragraph (6)(G) of this subsection.

           (ii) Documentation of the criteria used to determine the stability for the anticipated shelf time must be maintained and be available for inspection.

           (iii) Any preparation compounded in anticipation of future prescription drug or medication orders shall be labeled. Such label shall contain:

              (I) name and strength of the compounded preparation or list of the active ingredients and strengths;

              (II) facility's lot number;

              (III) beyond-use date as determined by the pharmacist using appropriate documented criteria as outlined in paragraph (6)(G) of this subsection;

              (IV) quantity or amount in the container;

              (V) appropriate ancillary instructions, such as storage instructions or cautionary statements, including hazardous drug warning labels where appropriate; and

              (VI) device-specific instructions, where appropriate.

        (C) Commercially available products may be compounded for dispensing to individual patients or for office use provided the following conditions are met:

           (i) the commercial product is not reasonably available from normal distribution channels in a timely manner to meet individual patient's needs;

           (ii) the pharmacy maintains documentation that the product is not reasonably available due to a drug shortage or unavailability from the manufacturer; and

           (iii) the prescribing practitioner has requested that the drug be compounded as described in subparagraph (D) of this paragraph.

        (D) A pharmacy may not compound preparations that are essentially copies of commercially available products (e.g., the preparation is dispensed in a strength that is only slightly different from a commercially available product) unless the prescribing practitioner specifically orders the strength or dosage form and specifies why the individual patient needs the particular strength or dosage form of the preparation or why the preparation for office use is needed in the particular strength or dosage form of the preparation. The prescribing practitioner shall provide documentation of a patient specific medical need and the preparation produces a clinically significant therapeutic response (e.g., the physician requests an alternate preparation due to hypersensitivity to excipients or preservative in the FDA-approved product, or the physician requests an effective alternate dosage form) or if the drug product is not commercially available. The unavailability of such drug product must be documented prior to compounding. The methodology for documenting unavailability includes maintaining a copy of the wholesaler's notification showing back-ordered, discontinued, or out-of-stock items. This documentation must be available in hard-copy or electronic format for inspection by the board.

        (E) A pharmacy may enter into an agreement to compound and dispense prescription drug or medication orders for another pharmacy provided the pharmacy complies with the provisions of § 291.125 of this title (relating to Centralized Prescription Dispensing).

        (F) Compounding pharmacies/pharmacists may advertise and promote the fact that they provide sterile prescription compounding services, which may include specific drug preparations and classes of drugs.

        (G) A pharmacy may not compound veterinary preparations for use in food producing animals except in accordance with federal guidelines.

        (H) Compounded sterile preparations, including hazardous drugs and radiopharmaceuticals, shall be prepared only under conditions that protect the pharmacy personnel in the preparation and storage areas.

    (2) Microbial Contamination Risk Levels. Risk Levels for sterile compounded preparations shall be as outlined in Chapter 797, Pharmacy Compounding—Sterile Preparations of the USP/NF and as listed in this paragraph.

        (A) Low-risk level compounded sterile preparations.

(i)   Low-Risk conditions. Low-risk level compounded sterile preparations are those compounded under all of the following conditions:

    (I)   The compounded sterile preparations are compounded with aseptic manipulations entirely within ISO Class 5 or better air quality using only sterile ingredients, products, components, and devices;

    (II)   The compounding involves only transfer, measuring, and mixing manipulations using not more than three commercially manufactured packages of sterile products and not more than two entries into any one sterile container or package (e.g., bag, vial) of sterile product or administration container/device to prepare the compounded sterile preparation;

    (III)   Manipulations are limited to aseptically opening ampules, penetrating disinfected stoppers on vials with sterile needles and syringes, and transferring sterile liquids in sterile syringes to sterile administration devices, package containers of other sterile products, and containers for storage and dispensing;

    (IV)   For a low-risk level preparation, in the absence of passing a sterility test the storage periods cannot exceed the following time periods: before administration, the compounded sterile preparation is stored properly and are exposed for not more than 48 hours at controlled room temperature, for not more than 14 days if stored at a cold temperature, and for 45 days if stored in a frozen state between minus 25 degrees Celsius and minus 10 degrees Celsius. For delayed activation device systems, the storage period begins when the device is activated.

(ii)   Examples of Low-Risk Level Compounding. Examples of low-risk level compounding include the following:

    (I)   Single volume transfers of sterile dosage forms from ampules, bottles, bags, and vials using sterile syringes with sterile needles, other administration devices, and other sterile containers. The solution content of ampules shall be passed through a sterile filter to remove any particles;

    (II)   Simple aseptic measuring and transferring with not more than three packages of manufactured sterile products, including an infusion or diluent solution to compound drug admixtures and nutritional solutions.

(B)   Low-Risk Level compounded sterile preparations with 12-hour or less beyond-use date. Low-risk level compounded sterile preparations are those compounded pursuant to a physician's order for a specific patient under all of the following conditions:

   (i)   The compounded sterile preparations are compounded in compounding aseptic isolator or compounding aseptic containment isolator that does not meet the requirements described in paragraph (7)(C) or (D) of this subsection (relating to Primary Engineering Control Device) or the compounded sterile preparations are compounded in laminar airflow workbench or a biological safety cabinet that cannot be located within the buffer area;

   (ii)   The primary engineering control device shall be certified and maintain ISO Class 5 for exposure of critical sites and shall be located in a segregated compounding area restricted to sterile compounding activities that minimizes the risk of contamination of the compounded sterile preparation;

   (iii)   The segregated compounding area shall not be in a location that has unsealed windows or doors that connect to the outdoors or high traffic flow, or that is adjacent to construction sites, warehouses, or food preparation.

   (iv)   For a low-risk level preparation compounded as described in clauses (i) - (iii) of this subparagraph, administration of such compounded sterile preparations must commence within 12 hours of preparation or as recommended in the manufacturers' package insert, whichever is less. However, the administration of sterile radiopharmaceuticals, with documented testing of chemical stability, may be administered beyond 12 hours of preparation.

(C)   Medium-risk level compounded sterile preparations.

   (i)   Medium-Risk Conditions. Medium-risk level compounded sterile preparations, are those compounded aseptically under low-risk conditions and one or more of the following conditions exists:

    (I)   Multiple individual or small doses of sterile products are combined or pooled to prepare a compounded sterile preparation that will be administered either to multiple patients or to one patient on multiple occasions;

    (II)   The compounding process includes complex aseptic manipulations other than the single-volume transfer;

    (III)   The compounding process requires unusually long duration, such as that required to complete the dissolution or homogenous mixing (e.g., reconstitution of intravenous immunoglobulin or other intravenous protein products);

    (IV)   The compounded sterile preparations do not contain broad spectrum bacteriostatic substances and they are administered over several days (e.g., an externally worn infusion device); or

    (V)   For a medium-risk level preparation, in the absence of passing a sterility test the storage periods cannot exceed the following time periods: before administration, the compounded sterile preparations are properly stored and are exposed for not more than 30 hours at controlled room temperature, for not more than 9 days at a cold temperature, and for 45 days in solid frozen state between minus 25 degrees Celsius and minus 10 degrees Celsius.

   (ii)   Examples of medium-risk compounding. Examples of medium-risk compounding include the following:

    (I)   Compounding of total parenteral nutrition fluids using a manual or automated device during which there are multiple injections, detachments, and attachments of nutrient source products to the device or machine to deliver all nutritional components to a final sterile container;

    (II)   Filling of reservoirs of injection and infusion devices with more than three sterile drug products and evacuations of air from those reservoirs before the filled device is dispensed;

    (III)   Filling of reservoirs of injection and infusion devices with volumes of sterile drug solutions that will be administered over several days at ambient temperatures between 25 and 40 degrees Celsius (77 and 104 degrees Fahrenheit); and

    (IV)   Transfer of volumes from multiple ampules or vials into a single, final sterile container or product.

(D)   High-risk level compounded sterile preparations.

   (i) High-risk Conditions. High-risk level compounded sterile preparations are those compounded under any of the following conditions:

    (I)   Non-sterile ingredients, including manufactured products not intended for sterile routes of administration (e.g., oral) are incorporated or a non-sterile device is employed before terminal sterilization.

    (II)   Any of the following are exposed to air quality worse than ISO Class 5 for more than 1 hour:

           (-a-) sterile contents of commercially manufactured products;

           (-b-) CSPs that lack effective antimicrobial preservatives; and

           (-c-) sterile surfaces of devices and containers for the preparation, transfer, sterilization, and packaging of CSPs;

      (III) Compounding personnel are improperly garbed and gloved;

      (IV) Non-sterile water-containing preparations are exposed no more than 6 hours before being sterilized;

      (V) It is assumed, and not verified by examination of labeling and documentation from suppliers or by direct determination, that the chemical purity and content strength of ingredients meet their original or compendial specifications in unopened or in opened packages of bulk ingredients;

      (VI) For a sterilized high-risk level preparation, in the absence of passing a sterility test, the storage periods cannot exceed the following time periods: before administration, the compounded sterile preparations are properly stored and are exposed for not more than 24 hours at controlled room temperature, for not more than 3 days at a cold temperature, and for 45 days in solid frozen state between minus 25 degrees Celsius and minus 10 degrees Celsius; or

      (VII) All non-sterile measuring, mixing, and purifying devices are rinsed thoroughly with pyrogen-free or depyrogenated sterile water, and then thoroughly drained or dried immediately before use for high-risk compounding. All high-risk compounded sterile solutions subjected to terminal sterilization are prefiltered by passing through a filter with a nominal pore size not larger than 1.2 micron preceding or during filling into their final containers to remove particulate matter. Sterilization of high-risk level compounded sterile preparations by filtration shall be performed with a sterile 0.2 micrometer or 0.22 micrometer nominal pore size filter entirely within an ISO Class 5 or superior air quality environment.

    (ii) Examples of high-risk compounding. Examples of high-risk compounding include the following.

      (I) Dissolving non-sterile bulk drug powders to make solutions, which will be terminally sterilized;

      (II) Exposing the sterile ingredients and components used to prepare and package compounded sterile preparations to room air quality worse than ISO Class 5 for more than one hour;

      (III) Measuring and mixing sterile ingredients in non-sterile devices before sterilization is performed; and

      (IV) Assuming, without appropriate evidence or direct determination, that packages of bulk ingredients contain at least 95% by weight of their active chemical moiety and have not been contaminated or adulterated between uses.

(3) Immediate Use Compounded Sterile Preparations. For the purpose of emergency or immediate patient care, such situations may include cardiopulmonary resuscitation, emergency room treatment, preparation of diagnostic agents, or critical therapy where the preparation of the compounded sterile preparation under low-risk level conditions would subject the patient to additional risk due to delays in therapy. Compounded sterile preparations are exempted from the requirements described in this paragraph for low-risk level compounded sterile preparations when all of the following criteria are met:

    (A) Only simple aseptic measuring and transfer manipulations are performed with not more than three sterile non-hazardous commercial drug and diagnostic radiopharmaceutical drug products, including an infusion or diluent solution, from the manufacturers' original containers and not more than two entries into any one container or package of sterile infusion solution or administration container/device;

    (B) Unless required for the preparation, the compounding procedure occurs continuously without delays or interruptions and does not exceed 1 hour;

    (C) During preparation, aseptic technique is followed and, if not immediately administered, the finished compounded sterile preparation is under continuous supervision to minimize the potential for contact with nonsterile surfaces, introduction of particulate matter of biological fluids, mix-ups with other compounded sterile preparations, and direct contact with outside surfaces;

    (D) Administration begins not later than one hour following the completion of preparing the compounded sterile preparation;

    (E) When the compounded sterile preparations is not administered by the person who prepared it, or its administration is not witnessed by the person who prepared it, the compounded sterile preparation shall bear a label listing patient identification information such as name and identification number(s), the names and amounts of all ingredients, the name or initials of the person who prepared the compounded sterile preparation, and the exact 1-hour beyond-use time and date;

    (F) If administration has not begun within one hour following the completion of preparing the compounded sterile preparation, the compounded sterile preparation is promptly and safely discarded. Immediate use compounded sterile preparations shall not be stored for later use; and

    (G) Hazardous drugs shall not be prepared as immediate use compounded sterile preparations.

(4) Single-dose and multiple dose containers.

    (A) Opened or needle punctured single-dose containers, such as bags bottles, syringes, and vials of sterile products shall be used within one hour if opened in worse than ISO Class 5 air quality. Any remaining contents must be discarded.

    (B) Single-dose containers, including single-dose large volume parenteral solutions and single-dose vials, exposed to ISO Class 5 or cleaner air may be used up to six hours after initial needle puncture.

    (C) Opened single-dose fusion sealed containers shall not be stored for any time period.

    (D) Multiple-dose containers may be used up to 28 days after initial needle puncture unless otherwise specified by the manufacturer.

(5) Library. In addition to the library requirements of the pharmacy's specific license classification, a pharmacy shall maintain current or updated copies in hard-copy or electronic format of each of the following:

    (A) a reference text on injectable drug preparations, such as Handbook on Injectable Drug Products;

    (B) a specialty reference text appropriate for the scope of pharmacy services provided by the pharmacy, e.g., if the pharmacy prepares hazardous drugs, a reference text on the preparation of hazardous drugs;

    (C) the United States Pharmacopeia/National Formulary containing USP Chapter 71, Sterility Tests, USP Chapter 85, Bacterial Endotoxins Test, Pharmaceutical Compounding—Nonsterile Preparations, USP Chapter 795, USP Chapter 797, Pharmaceutical Compounding—Sterile Preparations, and USP Chapter 1163, Quality Assurance in Pharmaceutical Compounding; and

Phr. Rules

(D) any additional USP/NF chapters applicable to the practice of the pharmacy (e.g., USP Chapter 800, Hazardous Drugs—Handling in Healthcare Settings, USP Chapter 823, Positron Emission Tomography Drugs for Compounding, Investigational, and Research Uses).

(6) Environment. Compounding facilities shall be physically designed and environmentally controlled to minimize airborne contamination from contacting critical sites.

(A) Low and Medium Risk Preparations. A pharmacy that prepares low- and medium-risk preparations shall have a clean room for the compounding of sterile preparations that is constructed to minimize the opportunities for particulate and microbial contamination. The clean room shall:

(i) be clean, well lit, and of sufficient size to support sterile compounding activities;

(ii) be maintained at a temperature of 20 degrees Celsius or cooler and at a humidity below 60%;

(iii) be used only for the compounding of sterile preparations;

(iv) be designed such that hand sanitizing and gowning occurs outside the buffer area but allows hands-free access by compounding personnel to the buffer area;

(v) have non-porous and washable floors or floor covering to enable regular disinfection;

(vi) be ventilated in a manner to avoid disruption from the HVAC system and room cross-drafts;

(vii) have walls, ceilings, floors, fixtures, shelving, counters, and cabinets that are smooth, impervious, free from cracks and crevices (e.g., coved), non-shedding and resistant to damage by disinfectant agents;

(viii) have junctures of ceilings to walls coved or caulked to avoid cracks and crevices;

(ix) have drugs and supplies stored on shelving areas above the floor to permit adequate floor cleaning;

(x) contain only the appropriate compounding supplies and not be used for bulk storage for supplies and materials. Objects that shed particles shall not be brought into the clean room. A Class B pharmacy may use low-linting absorbent materials in the primary engineering control device;

(xi) contain an ante-area that contains a sink with hot and cold running water that enables hands-free use with a closed system of soap dispensing to minimize the risk of extrinsic contamination. A Class B pharmacy may have a sink with hot and cold running water that enables hands-free use with a closed system of soap dispensing immediately outside the ante-area if antiseptic hand cleansing is performed using a waterless alcohol-based surgical hand scrub with persistent activity following manufacturers' recommendations once inside the ante-area; and

(xii) contain a buffer area. The following is applicable for the buffer area:

(I) There shall be some demarcation designation that delineates the ante-area from the buffer area. The demarcation shall be such that it does not create conditions that could adversely affect the cleanliness of the area;

(II) The buffer area shall be segregated from surrounding, unclassified spaces to reduce the risk of contaminants being blown, dragged, or otherwise introduced into the filtered unidirectional airflow environment, and this segregation should be continuously monitored;

(III) A buffer area that is not physically separated from the ante-area shall employ the principle of displacement airflow as defined in Chapter 797, Pharmaceutical Compounding—Sterile Preparations, of the USP/NF, with limited access to personnel; and

(IV) The buffer area shall not contain sources of water (i.e., sinks) or floor drains other than distilled or sterile water introduced for facilitating the use of heat block wells for radiopharmaceuticals.

(B) High-risk Preparations.

(i) In addition to the requirements in subparagraph (A) of this paragraph, when high-risk preparations are compounded, the primary engineering control shall be located in a buffer area that provides a physical separation, through the use of walls, doors and pass-throughs and has a minimum differential positive pressure of 0.02 to 0.05 inches water column.

(ii) Presterilization procedures for high-risk level compounded sterile preparations, such as weighing and mixing, shall be completed in no worse than an ISO Class 8 environment.

(C) Automated compounding device.

(i) General. If automated compounding devices are used, the pharmacy shall have a method to calibrate and verify the accuracy of automated compounding devices used in aseptic processing and document the calibration and verification on a daily basis, based on the manufacturer's recommendations, and review the results at least weekly.

(ii) Loading bulk drugs into automated compounding devices.

(I) Automated compounding devices may be loaded with bulk drugs only by a pharmacist or by pharmacy technicians or pharmacy technician trainees under the direction and direct supervision of a pharmacist.

(II) The label of an automated compounding device container shall indicate the brand name and strength of the drug; or if no brand name, then the generic name, strength, and name of the manufacturer or distributor.

(III) Records of loading bulk drugs into an automated compounding device shall be maintained to show:

(-a-) name of the drug, strength, and dosage form;

(-b-) manufacturer or distributor;

(-c-) manufacturer's lot number;

(-d-) manufacturer's expiration date;

(-e-) quantity added to the automated compounding device;

(-f-) date of loading;

(-g-) name, initials, or electronic signature of the person loading the automated compounding device; and

(-h-) name, initials, or electronic signature of the responsible pharmacist.

(IV) The automated compounding device shall not be used until a pharmacist verifies that the system is properly loaded and affixes his or her signature or electronic signature to the record specified in subclause (III) of this clause.

(D) Hazardous drugs. If the preparation is hazardous, the following is also applicable:

(i) Hazardous drugs shall be prepared only under conditions that protect personnel during preparation and storage;

(ii) Hazardous drugs shall be stored separately from other inventory in a manner to prevent contamination and personnel exposure;

(iii) All personnel involved in the compounding of hazardous drugs shall wear appropriate protective apparel, such as gowns, face masks, eye protection, hair covers, shoe covers or dedicated shoes, and appropriate gloving at all times when handling hazardous drugs, including receiving, distribution, stocking, inventorying, preparation, for administration and disposal;

(iv) Appropriate safety and containment techniques for compounding hazardous drugs shall be used in conjunction with aseptic techniques required for preparing sterile preparations;

(v) Disposal of hazardous waste shall comply with all applicable local, state, and federal requirements;

(vi) Prepared doses of hazardous drugs must be dispensed, labeled with proper precautions inside and outside, and distributed in a manner to minimize patient contact with hazardous agents.

(E) Blood-labeling procedures. When compounding activities require the manipulation of a patient's blood-derived material (e.g., radiolabeling a patient's or donor's white blood cells), the manipulations shall be performed in a ISO Class 5 biological safety cabinet located in a buffer area and shall be clearly separated from routine material-handling procedures and equipment used in preparation activities to avoid any cross-contamination. The preparations shall not require sterilization.

(F) Cleaning and disinfecting the sterile compounding areas. The following cleaning and disinfecting practices and frequencies apply to direct and contiguous compounding areas, which include ISO Class 5 compounding areas for exposure of critical sites as well as buffer areas, ante-areas, and segregated compounding areas.

(i) The pharmacist-in-charge is responsible for developing written standard operating procedures (SOPs) for cleaning and disinfecting the direct and contiguous compounding areas and assuring the procedures are followed.

(ii) These procedures shall be conducted at the beginning of each work shift, before each batch preparation is started, when there are spills, and when surface contamination is known or suspected resulting from procedural breaches, and every 30 minutes during continuous compounding of individual compounded sterile preparations, unless a particular compounding procedure requires more than 30 minutes to complete, in which case, the direct compounding area is to be cleaned immediately after the compounding activity is completed.

(iii) Before compounding is performed, all items shall be removed from the direct and contiguous compounding areas and all surfaces are cleaned by removing loose material and residue from spills, followed by an application of a residue-free disinfecting agent (e.g., IPA), which is allowed to dry before compounding begins. In a Class B pharmacy, objects used in preparing sterile radiopharmaceuticals (e.g., dose calibrator) which cannot be reasonably removed from the compounding area shall be sterilized with an application of a residue-free disinfection agent.

(iv) Work surfaces in the buffer areas and ante-areas, as well as segregated compounding areas, shall be cleaned and disinfected at least daily. Dust and debris shall be removed when necessary from storage sites for compounding ingredients and supplies using a method that does not degrade the ISO Class 7 or 8 air quality.

(v) Floors in the buffer area, ante-area, and segregated compounding area shall be cleaned by mopping with a cleaning and disinfecting agent at least once daily when no aseptic operations are in progress. Mopping shall be performed by trained personnel using approved agents and procedures described in the written SOPs. It is incumbent on compounding personnel to ensure that such cleaning is performed properly.

(vi) In the buffer area, ante-area, and segregated compounding area, walls, ceilings, and shelving shall be cleaned and disinfected monthly. Cleaning and disinfecting agents shall be used with careful consideration of compatibilities, effectiveness, and inappropriate or toxic residues.

(vii) All cleaning materials, such as wipers, sponges, and mops, shall be non-shedding, and dedicated to use in the buffer area, ante-area, and segregated compounding areas and shall not be removed from these areas except for disposal. Floor mops may be used in both the buffer area and ante-area, but only in that order. If cleaning materials are reused, procedures shall be developed that ensure that the effectiveness of the cleaning device is maintained and that repeated use does not add to the bio-burden of the area being cleaned.

(viii) Supplies and equipment removed from shipping cartons must be wiped with a disinfecting agent, such as sterile IPA. After the disinfectant is sprayed or wiped on a surface to be disinfected, the disinfectant shall be allowed to dry, during which time the item shall not be used for compounding purposes. However, if sterile supplies are received in sealed pouches, the pouches may be removed as the supplies are introduced into the ISO Class 5 area without the need to disinfect the individual sterile supply items. No shipping or other external cartons may be taken into the buffer area or segregated compounding area.

(ix) Storage shelving emptied of all supplies, walls, and ceilings shall be cleaned and disinfected at planned intervals, monthly, if not more frequently.

(x) Cleaning must be done by personnel trained in appropriate cleaning techniques.

(xi) Proper documentation and frequency of cleaning must be maintained and shall contain the following:

    (I) date and time of cleaning;

    (II) type of cleaning performed; and

    (III) name of individual who performed the cleaning.

(G) Security requirements. The pharmacist-in-charge may authorize personnel to gain access to that area of the pharmacy containing dispensed sterile preparations, in the absence of the pharmacist, for the purpose of retrieving dispensed prescriptions to deliver to patients. If the pharmacy allows such after-hours access, the area containing the dispensed sterile preparations shall be an enclosed and lockable area separate from the area containing undispensed prescription drugs. A list of the authorized personnel having such access shall be in the pharmacy's policy and procedure manual.

(H) Storage requirements and beyond-use dating.

(i) Storage requirements. All drugs shall be stored at the proper temperature and conditions, as defined in the USP/NF and in § 291.15 of this title (relating to Storage of Drugs).

(ii) Beyond-use dating.

    (I) Beyond-use dates for compounded sterile preparations shall be assigned based on professional experience, which shall include careful interpretation of appropriate information sources for the same or similar formulations.

(II) Beyond-use dates for compounded sterile preparations that are prepared strictly in accordance with manufacturers' product labeling must be those specified in that labeling, or from appropriate literature sources or direct testing.

(III) When assigning a beyond-use date, compounding personnel shall consult and apply drug-specific and general stability documentation and literature where available, and they should consider the nature of the drug and its degradation mechanism, the container in which it is packaged, the expected storage conditions, and the intended duration of therapy.

(IV) The sterility and storage and stability beyond-use date for attached and activated container pairs of drug products for intravascular administration shall be applied as indicated by the manufacturer.

(7) Primary engineering control device. The pharmacy shall prepare sterile preparations in a primary engineering control device (PEC), such as a laminar air flow hood, biological safety cabinet, compounding aseptic isolator (CAI), or compounding aseptic containment isolator (CACI) which is capable of maintaining at least ISO Class 5 conditions for 0.5 micrometer particles while compounding sterile preparations.

(A) Laminar air flow hood. If the pharmacy is using a laminar air flow hood as its PEC, the laminar air flow hood shall:

(i) be located in the buffer area and placed in the buffer area in a manner as to avoid conditions that could adversely affect its operation such as strong air currents from opened doors, personnel traffic, or air streams from the heating, ventilating and air condition system;

(ii) be certified for operational efficiency using certification procedures, such as those outlined in the Certification Guide for Sterile Compounding Facilities (CAG-003-2006), which shall be performed by a qualified independent individual no less than every six months and whenever the device or room is relocated or altered or major service to the facility is performed;

(iii) have pre-filters inspected periodically and replaced as needed, in accordance with written policies and procedures and the manufacturer's specification, and the inspection and/or replacement date documented; and (iv) be located in a buffer area that has a minimum differential positive pressure of 0.02 to 0.05 inches water column. A buffer area that is not physically separated from the ante-area shall employ the principle of displacement airflow as defined in Chapter 797, Pharmaceutical Compounding—Sterile Preparations, of the USP/NF, with limited access to personnel.

(B) Biological safety cabinet.

(i) If the pharmacy is using a biological safety cabinet (BSC) as its PEC for the preparation of hazardous sterile compounded preparations, the biological safety cabinet shall be a Class II or III vertical flow biological safety cabinet located in an ISO Class 7 area that is physically separated from other preparation areas. The area for preparation of sterile chemotherapeutic preparations shall:

(I) have not less than 0.01 inches water column negative pressure to the adjacent positive pressure ISO Class 7 or better ante-area; and

(II) have a pressure indicator that can be readily monitored for correct room pressurization.

(ii) Pharmacies that prepare a low volume of hazardous drugs, are not required to comply with the provisions of clause (i) of this subparagraph if the pharmacy uses a device that provides two tiers of containment (e.g., closed-system vial transfer device within a BSC).

(iii) If the pharmacy is using a biological safety cabinet as its PEC for the preparation of non-hazardous sterile compounded preparations, the biological safety cabinet shall:

(I) be located in the buffer area and placed in the buffer area in a manner as to avoid conditions that could adversely affect its operation such as strong air currents from opened doors, personnel traffic, or air streams from the heating, ventilating and air condition system;

(II) be certified for operational efficiency using certification procedures, such as those outlined in the Certification Guide for Sterile Compounding Facilities (CAG-003-2006), which shall be performed by a qualified independent individual no less than every six months and whenever the device or room is relocated or altered or major service to the facility is performed;

(III) have pre-filters inspected periodically and replaced as needed, in accordance with written policies and procedures and the manufacturer's specification, and the inspection and/or replacement date documented; and

(IV) be located in a buffer area that has a minimum differential positive pressure of 0.02 to 0.05 inches water column.

(C) Compounding aseptic isolator.

(i) If the pharmacy is using a compounding aseptic isolator (CAI) as its PEC, the CAI shall provide unidirectional airflow within the main processing and antechambers, and be placed in an ISO Class 7 buffer area unless the isolator meets all of the following conditions:

(I) The isolator must provide isolation from the room and maintain ISO Class 5 during dynamic operating conditions including transferring ingredients, components, and devices into and out of the isolator and during preparation of compounded sterile preparations;

(II) Particle counts sampled approximately 6 to 12 inches upstream of the critical exposure site must maintain ISO Class 5 levels during compounding operations;

(III) The CAI must be certified for operational efficiency using certification procedures, such as those outlined in the Certification Guide for Sterile Compounding Facilities (CAG-003-2006), which shall be performed by a qualified independent individual no less than every six months and whenever the device or room is relocated or altered or major service to the facility is performed; and

(IV) The pharmacy shall maintain documentation from the manufacturer that the isolator meets this standard when located in worse than ISO Class 7 environments.

(ii) If the isolator meets the requirements in clause (i) of this subparagraph, the CAI may be placed in a non-ISO classified area of the pharmacy; however, the area shall be segregated from other areas of the pharmacy and shall:

(I) be clean, well lit, and of sufficient size;

(II) be used only for the compounding of low- and medium-risk, non-hazardous sterile preparations;

           (III) be located in an area of the pharmacy with non-porous and washable floors or floor covering to enable regular disinfection; and

           (IV) be an area in which the CAI is placed in a manner as to avoid conditions that could adversely affect its operation.

        (iii) In addition to the requirements specified in clauses (i) and (ii) of this subparagraph, if the CAI is used in the compounding of high-risk non-hazardous preparations, the CAI shall be placed in an area or room with at least ISO 8 quality air so that high-risk powders weighed in at least ISO-8 air quality conditions, compounding utensils for measuring and other compounding equipment are not exposed to lesser air quality prior to the completion of compounding and packaging of the high-risk preparation.

    (D) Compounding aseptic containment isolator.

        (i) If the pharmacy is using a compounding aseptic containment isolator (CACI) as its PEC for the preparation of low- and medium-risk hazardous drugs, the CACI shall be located in a separate room away from other areas of the pharmacy and shall:

           (I) provide at least 0.01 inches water column negative pressure compared to the other areas of the pharmacy;

           (II) provide unidirectional airflow within the main processing and antechambers, and be placed in an ISO Class 7 buffer area, unless the CACI meets all of the following conditions;

              (-a-) The isolator must provide isolation from the room and maintain ISO Class 5 during dynamic operating conditions including transferring ingredients, components, and devices into and out of the isolator and during preparation of compounded sterile preparations;

              (-b-) Particle counts sampled approximately 6 to 12 inches upstream of the critical exposure site must maintain ISO Class 5 levels during compounding operations;

              (-c-) The CACI must be certified for operational efficiency using certification procedures, such as those outlined in the Certification Guide for Sterile Compounding Facilities (CAG-003-2006), which shall be performed by a qualified independent individual no less than every six months and whenever the device or room is relocated or altered or major service to the facility is performed; and

              (-d-) The pharmacy shall maintain documentation from the manufacturer that the isolator meets this standard when located in worse than ISO Class 7 environments.

        (ii) If the CACI meets all conditions specified in clause (i) of this subparagraph, the CACI shall not be located in the same room as a CAI, but shall be located in a separate room in the pharmacy, that is not required to maintain ISO classified air. The room in which the CACI is located shall provide a minimum of 0.01 inches water column negative pressure compared with the other areas of the pharmacy and shall meet the following requirements:

           (I) be clean, well lit, and of sufficient size;

           (II) be maintained at a temperature of 20 degrees Celsius or cooler and a humidity below 60%;

           (III) be used only for the compounding of hazardous sterile preparations;

           (IV) be located in an area of the pharmacy with walls, ceilings, floors, fixtures, shelving, counters, and cabinets that are smooth, impervious, free from cracks and crevices, non-shedding and resistant to damage by disinfectant agents; and

           (V) have non-porous and washable floors or floor covering to enable regular disinfection.

        (iii) If the CACI is used in the compounding of high-risk hazardous preparations, the CACI shall be placed in an area or room with at least ISO 8 quality air so that high-risk powders, weighed in at least ISO-8 air quality conditions, are not exposed to lesser air quality prior to the completion of compounding and packaging of the high-risk preparation.

        (iv) Pharmacies that prepare a low volume of hazardous drugs, are not required to comply with the provisions of clauses (i) and (iii) of this subparagraph if the pharmacy uses a device that provides two tiers of containment (e.g., CACI that is located in a non-negative pressure room).

  (8) Additional Equipment and Supplies. Pharmacies compounding sterile preparations shall have the following equipment and supplies:

    (A) a calibrated system or device (i.e., thermometer) to monitor the temperature to ensure that proper storage requirements are met, if sterile preparations are stored in the refrigerator;

    (B) a calibrated system or device to monitor the temperature where bulk chemicals are stored;

    (C) a temperature-sensing mechanism suitably placed in the controlled temperature storage space to reflect accurately the true temperature;

    (D) if applicable, a Class A prescription balance, or analytical balance and weights. Such balance shall be properly maintained and subject to periodic inspection by the Texas State Board of Pharmacy;

    (E) equipment and utensils necessary for the proper compounding of sterile preparations. Such equipment and utensils used in the compounding process shall be:

        (i) of appropriate design, appropriate capacity, and be operated within designed operational limits;

        (ii) of suitable composition so that surfaces that contact components, in-process material, or drug products shall not be reactive, additive, or absorptive so as to alter the safety, identity, strength, quality, or purity of the drug preparation beyond the desired result;

        (iii) cleaned and sanitized immediately prior to and after each use; and

        (iv) routinely inspected, calibrated (if necessary), or checked to ensure proper performance;

    (F) appropriate disposal containers for used needles, syringes, etc., and if applicable, hazardous waste from the preparation of hazardous drugs and/or biohazardous waste;

    (G) appropriate packaging or delivery containers to maintain proper storage conditions for sterile preparations;

    (H) infusion devices, if applicable; and

    (I) all necessary supplies, including:

        (i) disposable needles, syringes, and other supplies for aseptic mixing;

        (ii) disinfectant cleaning solutions;

        (iii) sterile 70% isopropyl alcohol;

Phr. Rules

(iv)	sterile gloves, both for hazardous and non-hazardous drug compounding;

(v)	sterile alcohol-based or water-less alcohol based surgical scrub;

(vi)	hand washing agents with bactericidal action;

(vii)	disposable, lint free towels or wipes;

(viii)	appropriate filters and filtration equipment;

(ix)	hazardous spill kits, if applicable; and

(x)	masks, caps, coveralls or gowns with tight cuffs, shoe covers, and gloves, as applicable.

(9)	Labeling.

(A)	Prescription drug or medication orders. In addition to the labeling requirements for the pharmacy's specific license classification, the label dispensed or distributed pursuant to a prescription drug or medication order shall contain the following:

(i)	the generic name(s) or the official name(s) of the principal active ingredient(s) of the compounded sterile preparation;

(ii)	for outpatient prescription orders other than sterile radiopharmaceuticals, a statement that the compounded sterile preparation has been compounded by the pharmacy. (An auxiliary label may be used on the container to meet this requirement); and

(iii)	a beyond-use date. The beyond-use date shall be determined as outlined in Chapter 797, Pharmacy Compounding—Sterile Preparations of the USP/NF, and paragraph (7)(G) of this subsection;

(B)	Batch. If the sterile preparation is compounded in a batch, the following shall also be included on the batch label:

(i)	unique lot number assigned to the batch;

(ii)	quantity;

(iii)	appropriate ancillary instructions, such as storage instructions or cautionary statements, including hazardous drug warning labels where appropriate; and

(iv)	device-specific instructions, where appropriate.

(C)	Pharmacy bulk package. The label of a pharmacy bulk package shall:

(i)	state prominently "Pharmacy Bulk Package—Not for Direct Infusion;"

(ii)	contain or refer to information on proper techniques to help ensure safe use of the preparation; and

(iii)	bear a statement limiting the time frame in which the container may be used once it has been entered, provided it is held under the labeled storage conditions.

(10)	Written drug information for prescription drug orders only. Written information about the compounded preparation or its major active ingredient(s) shall be given to the patient at the time of dispensing a prescription drug order. A statement which indicates that the preparation was compounded by the pharmacy must be included in this written information. If there is no written information available, the patient shall be advised that the drug has been compounded and how to contact a pharmacist, and if appropriate, the prescriber, concerning the drug. This paragraph does not apply to the preparation of radiopharmaceuticals.

(11)	Pharmaceutical Care Services. In addition to the pharmaceutical care requirements for the pharmacy's specific license classification, the following requirements for sterile preparations compounded pursuant to prescription drug orders must be met. This paragraph does not apply to the preparation of radiopharmaceuticals.

(A)	Primary provider. There shall be a designated physician primarily responsible for the patient's medical care. There shall be a clear understanding between the physician, the patient, and the pharmacy of the responsibilities of each in the areas of the delivery of care, and the monitoring of the patient. This shall be documented in the patient medication record (PMR).

(B)	Patient training. The pharmacist-in-charge shall develop policies to ensure that the patient and/or patient's caregiver receives information regarding drugs and their safe and appropriate use, including instruction when applicable, regarding:

(i)	appropriate disposition of hazardous solutions and ancillary supplies;

(ii)	proper disposition of controlled substances in the home;

(iii)	self-administration of drugs, where appropriate;

(iv)	emergency procedures, including how to contact an appropriate individual in the event of problems or emergencies related to drug therapy; and

(v)	if the patient or patient's caregiver prepares sterile preparations in the home, the following additional information shall be provided:

(I)	safeguards against microbial contamination, including aseptic techniques for compounding intravenous admixtures and aseptic techniques for injecting additives to premixed intravenous solutions;

(II)	appropriate storage methods, including storage durations for sterile pharmaceuticals and expirations of self-mixed solutions;

(III)	handling and disposition of premixed and self-mixed intravenous admixtures; and

(IV)	proper disposition of intravenous admixture compounding supplies such as syringes, vials, ampules, and intravenous solution containers.

(C)	Pharmacist-patient relationship. It is imperative that a pharmacist-patient relationship be established and maintained throughout the patient's course of therapy. This shall be documented in the patient's medication record (PMR).

(D)	Patient monitoring. The pharmacist-in-charge shall develop policies to ensure that:

(i)	the patient's response to drug therapy is monitored and conveyed to the appropriate health care provider;

(ii)	the first dose of any new drug therapy is administered in the presence of an individual qualified to monitor for and respond to adverse drug reactions; and

(iii)	reports of adverse events with a compounded sterile preparation are reviewed promptly and thoroughly to correct and prevent future occurrences.

(12)	Drugs, components, and materials used in sterile compounding.

(A)	Drugs used in sterile compounding shall be a USP/NF grade substances manufactured in an FDA-registered facility.

(B)	If USP/NF grade substances are not available shall be of a chemical grade in one of the following categories:

(i)	Chemically Pure (CP);

(ii)	Analytical Reagent (AR);

           (iii) American Chemical Society (ACS); or

           (iv) Food Chemical Codex.

    (C) If a drug, component or material is not purchased from a FDA-registered facility, the pharmacist shall establish purity and stability by obtaining a Certificate of Analysis from the supplier and the pharmacist shall compare the monograph of drugs in a similar class to the Certificate of Analysis.

    (D) All components shall:

           (i) be manufactured in an FDA-registered facility; or

           (ii) in the professional judgment of the pharmacist, be of high quality and obtained from acceptable and reliable alternative sources; and

           (iii) be stored in properly labeled containers in a clean, dry area, under proper temperatures.

    (E) Drug preparation containers and closures shall not be reactive, additive, or absorptive so as to alter the safety, identity, strength, quality, or purity of the compounded drug preparation beyond the desired result.

    (F) Components, drug preparation containers, and closures shall be rotated so that the oldest stock is used first.

    (G) Container closure systems shall provide adequate protection against foreseeable external factors in storage and use that can cause deterioration or contamination of the compounded drug preparation.

    (H) A pharmacy may not compound a preparation that contains ingredients appearing on a federal Food and Drug Administration list of drug products withdrawn or removed from the market for safety reasons.

(13) Compounding process.

    (A) Standard operating procedures (SOPs). All significant procedures performed in the compounding area shall be covered by written SOPs designed to ensure accountability, accuracy, quality, safety, and uniformity in the compounding process. At a minimum, SOPs shall be developed and implemented for:

           (i) the facility;

           (ii) equipment;

           (iii) personnel;

           (iv) preparation evaluation;

           (v) quality assurance;

           (vi) preparation recall;

           (vii) packaging; and

           (viii) storage of compounded sterile preparations.

    (B) USP/NF. Any compounded formulation with an official monograph in the USP/NF shall be compounded, labeled, and packaged in conformity with the USP/NF monograph for the drug.

    (C) Personnel Cleansing and Garbing.

           (i) Any person with an apparent illness or open lesion, including rashes, sunburn, weeping sores, conjunctivitis, and active respiratory infection, that may adversely affect the safety or quality of a drug preparation being compounded shall be excluded from working in ISO Class 5, ISO Class 7, and ISO Class 8 compounding areas until the condition is remedied.

           (ii) Before entering the buffer area, compounding personnel must remove the following:

                (I) personal outer garments (e.g., bandanas, coats, hats, jackets, scarves, sweaters, vests);

                (II) all cosmetics, because they shed flakes and particles; and

                (III) all hand, wrist, and other body jewelry or piercings (e.g., earrings, lip or eyebrow piercings) that can interfere with the effectiveness of personal protective equipment (e.g., fit of gloves and cuffs of sleeves).

           (iii) The wearing of artificial nails or extenders is prohibited while working in the sterile compounding environment. Natural nails shall be kept neat and trimmed.

           (iv) Personnel shall don personal protective equipment and perform hand hygiene in an order that proceeds from the dirtiest to the cleanest activities as follows:

                (I) Activities considered the dirtiest include donning of dedicated shoes or shoe covers, head and facial hair covers (e.g., beard covers in addition to face masks), and face mask/eye shield. Eye shields are optional unless working with irritants like germicidal disinfecting agents or when preparing hazardous drugs.

                (II) After donning dedicated shoes or shoe covers, head and facial hair covers, and face masks, personnel shall perform a hand hygiene procedure by removing debris from underneath fingernails using a nail cleaner under running warm water followed by vigorous hand washing. Personnel shall begin washing arms at the hands and continue washing to elbows for at least 30 seconds with either a plain (non-antimicrobial) soap, or antimicrobial soap, and water while in the ante-area. Hands and forearms to the elbows shall be completely dried using lint-free disposable towels, an electronic hands-free hand dryer, or a HEPA filtered hand dryer.

                (III) After completion of hand washing, personnel shall don clean non-shedding gowns with sleeves that fit snugly around the wrists and enclosed at the neck.

                (IV) Once inside the buffer area or segregated compounding area, and prior to donning sterile powder-free gloves, antiseptic hand cleansing shall be performed using a waterless alcohol-based surgical hand scrub with persistent activity following manufacturers' recommendations. Hands shall be allowed to dry thoroughly before donning sterile gloves.

                (V) Sterile gloves that form a continuous barrier with the gown shall be the last item donned before compounding begins. Sterile gloves shall be donned using proper technique to ensure the sterility of the glove is not compromised while donning. The cuff of the sterile glove shall cover the cuff of the gown at the wrist. When preparing hazardous preparations, the compounder shall double glove or shall use single gloves ensuring that the gloves are sterile powder-free chemotherapy-rated gloves. Routine application of sterile 70% IPA shall occur throughout the compounding day and whenever non-sterile surfaces are touched.

           (v) When compounding personnel shall temporarily exit the buffer area during a work shift, the exterior gown, if not visibly soiled, may be removed and retained in the ante-area, to be re-donned during that same work shift only. However, shoe covers, hair and facial hair covers, face mask/eye shield, and gloves shall be replaced with new ones before re-entering the buffer area along with performing proper hand hygiene.

   (vi) During high-risk level compounding activities that precede terminal sterilization, such as weighing and mixing of non-sterile ingredients, compounding personnel shall be garbed and gloved the same as when performing compounding in an ISO Class 5 environment. Properly garbed and gloved compounding personnel who are exposed to air quality that is either known or suspected to be worse than ISO Class 7 shall re-garb personal protective equipment along with washing their hands properly, performing antiseptic hand cleansing with a sterile 70% IPA-based or another suitable sterile alcohol-based surgical hand scrub, and donning sterile gloves upon re-entering the ISO Class 7 buffer area.

   (vii) When compounding aseptic isolators or compounding aseptic containment isolators are the source of the ISO Class 5 environment, at the start of each new compounding procedure, a new pair of sterile gloves shall be donned within the CAI or CACI. In addition, the compounding personnel should follow the requirements as specified in this subparagraph, unless the isolator manufacturer can provide written documentation based on validated environmental testing that any components of personal protective equipment or cleansing are not required.

(14) Quality Assurance.

   (A) Initial Formula Validation. Prior to routine compounding of a sterile preparation, a pharmacy shall conduct an evaluation that shows that the pharmacy is capable of compounding a preparation that is sterile and that contains the stated amount of active ingredient(s).

      (i) Low risk level preparations.

         (I) Quality assurance practices include, but are not limited to the following:

            (-a-) Routine disinfection and air quality testing of the direct compounding environment to minimize microbial surface contamination and maintain ISO Class 5 air quality;

            (-b-) Visual confirmation that compounding personnel are properly donning and wearing appropriate items and types of protective garments and goggles;

            (-c-) Review of all orders and packages of ingredients to ensure that the correct identity and amounts of ingredients were compounded; and

            (-d-) Visual inspection of compounded sterile preparations, except for sterile radiopharmaceuticals, to ensure the absence of particulate matter in solutions, the absence of leakage from vials and bags, and the accuracy and thoroughness of labeling.

         (II) Example of a Media-Fill Test Procedure. This, or an equivalent test, is performed at least annually by each person authorized to compound in a low-risk level under conditions that closely simulate the most challenging or stressful conditions encountered during compounding of low-risk level sterile preparations. Once begun, this test is completed without interruption within an ISO Class 5 air quality environment. Three sets of four 5-milliliter aliquots of sterile fluid culture media are transferred with the same sterile 10-milliliter syringe and vented needle combination into separate sealed, empty, sterile 30-milliliter clear vials (i.e., four 5-milliliter aliquots into each of three 30-milliliter vials). Sterile adhesive seals are aseptically affixed to the rubber closures on the three filled vials. The vials are incubated within a range of 20 - 35 degrees Celsius for a minimum of 14 days. Failure is indicated by visible turbidity in the medium on or before 14 days. The media-fill test must include a positive-control sample.

      (ii) Medium risk level preparations.

         (I) Quality assurance procedures for medium-risk level compounded sterile preparations include all those for low-risk level compounded sterile preparations, as well as a more challenging media-fill test passed annually, or more frequently.

         (II) Example of a Media-Fill Test Procedure. This, or an equivalent test, is performed at least annually under conditions that closely simulate the most challenging or stressful conditions encountered during compounding. This test is completed without interruption within an ISO Class 5 air quality environment. Six 100-milliliter aliquots of sterile Soybean-Casein Digest Medium are aseptically transferred by gravity through separate tubing sets into separate evacuated sterile containers. The six containers are then arranged as three pairs, and a sterile 10-milliliter syringe and 18-gauge needle combination is used to exchange two 5-milliliter aliquots of medium from one container to the other container in the pair. For example, after a 5-milliliter aliquot from the first container is added to the second container in the pair, the second container is agitated for 10 seconds, then a 5-milliliter aliquot is removed and returned to the first container in the pair. The first container is then agitated for 10 seconds, and the next 5-milliliter aliquot is transferred from it back to the second container in the pair. Following the two 5-milliliter aliquot exchanges in each pair of containers, a 5-milliliter aliquot of medium from each container is aseptically injected into a sealed, empty, sterile 10-milliliter clear vial, using a sterile 10-milliliter syringe and vented needle. Sterile adhesive seals are aseptically affixed to the rubber closures on the three filled vials. The vials are incubated within a range of 20 - 35 degrees Celsius for a minimum of 14 days. Failure is indicated by visible turbidity in the medium on or before 14 days. The media-fill test must include a positive-control sample.

      (iii) High risk level preparations.

         (I) Procedures for high-risk level compounded sterile preparations include all those for low-risk level compounded sterile preparations. In addition, a media-fill test that represents high-risk level compounding is performed twice a year by each person authorized to compound high-risk level compounded sterile preparations.

         (II) Example of a Media-Fill Test Procedure for Compounded Sterile Preparations Sterilized by Filtration. This test, or an equivalent test, is performed under conditions that closely simulate the most challenging or stressful conditions encountered when compounding high-risk level compounded sterile preparations. Note: Sterility tests for autoclaved compounded sterile preparations are not required unless they are prepared in batches of more than 25 units. This test is completed without interruption in the following sequence:

            (-a-) Dissolve 3 grams of non-sterile commercially available fluid culture media in 100 milliliters of non-bacteriostatic water to make a 3% non-sterile solution.

(-b-) Draw 25 milliliters of the medium into each of three 30-milliliter sterile syringes. Transfer 5 milliliters from each syringe into separate sterile 10-milliliter vials. These vials are the positive controls to generate exponential microbial growth, which is indicated by visible turbidity upon incubation.

(-c-) Under aseptic conditions and using aseptic techniques, affix a sterile 0.2-micron porosity filter unit and a 20-gauge needle to each syringe. Inject the next 10 milliliters from each syringe into three separate 10-milliliter sterile vials. Repeat the process for three more vials. Label all vials, affix sterile adhesive seals to the closure of the nine vials, and incubate them at 20 to 35 degrees Celsius for a minimum of 14 days. Inspect for microbial growth over 14 days as described in Chapter 797 Pharmaceutical Compounding—Sterile Preparations, of the USP/NF.

(III) Filter Integrity Testing. Filters need to undergo testing to evaluate the integrity of filters used to sterilize high-risk preparations, such as Bubble Point Testing or comparable filter integrity testing. Such testing is not a replacement for sterility testing and shall not be interpreted as such. Such test shall be performed after a sterilization procedure on all filters used to sterilize each high-risk preparation or batch preparation and the results documented. The results should be compared with the filter manufacturer's specification for the specific filter used. If a filter fails the integrity test, the preparation or batch must be sterilized again using new unused filters.

(B) Finished preparation release checks and tests.

  (i) All high-risk level compounded sterile preparations that are prepared in groups of more than 25 identical individual single-dose packages (such as ampules, bags, syringes, and vials), or in multiple dose vials for administration to multiple patients, or are exposed longer than 12 hours at 2 - 8 degrees Celsius and longer than six hours at warmer than 8 degrees Celsius before they are sterilized shall be tested to ensure they are sterile and do not contain excessive bacterial endotoxins as specified in Chapter 71, Sterility Tests of the USP/NF before being dispensed or administered.

  (ii) All compounded sterile preparations, except for sterile radiopharmaceuticals, that are intended to be solutions must be visually examined for the presence of particulate matter and not administered or dispensed when such matter is observed.

  (iii) The prescription drug and medication orders, written compounding procedure, preparation records, and expended materials used to make compounded sterile preparations at all contamination risk levels shall be inspected for accuracy of correct identities and amounts of ingredients, aseptic mixing and sterilization, packaging, labeling, and expected physical appearance before they are dispensed or administered.

  (iv) Written procedures for checking compounding accuracy shall be followed for every compounded sterile preparation during preparation, in accordance with pharmacy's policies and procedures, and immediately prior to release, including label accuracy and the accuracy of the addition of all drug products or ingredients used to prepare the finished preparation and their volumes or quantities. A pharmacist shall ensure that components used in compounding are accurately weighed, measured, or subdivided as appropriate to conform to the formula being prepared.

(C) Environmental Testing.

  (i) Viable and nonviable environmental sampling testing. Environmental sampling shall occur, at a minimum, every six months as part of a comprehensive quality management program and under any of the following conditions:

    (I) as part of the commissioning and certification of new facilities and equipment;

    (II) following any servicing of facilities and equipment;

    (III) as part of the re-certification of facilities and equipment;

    (IV) in response to identified problems with end products or staff technique; or

    (V) in response to issues with compounded sterile preparations, observed compounding personnel work practices, or patient-related infections (where the compounded sterile preparation is being considered as a potential source of the infection).

  (ii) Total particle counts. Certification that each ISO classified area (e.g., ISO Class 5, 7, and 8), is within established guidelines shall be performed no less than every six months and whenever the equipment is relocated or the physical structure of the buffer area or ante-area has been altered. All certification records shall be maintained and reviewed to ensure that the controlled environments comply with the proper air cleanliness, room pressures, and air changes per hour. These certification records must include acceptance criteria and be made available upon inspection by the Board. Testing shall be performed by qualified operators using current, state-of-the-art equipment, with results of the following:

    (I) ISO Class 5 - not more than 3520 particles 0.5 micrometer and larger size per cubic meter of air;

    (II) ISO Class 7 - not more than 352,000 particles of 0.5 micrometer and larger size per cubic meter of air for any buffer area; and

    (III) ISO Class 8 - not more than 3,520,000 particles of 0.5 micrometer and larger size per cubic meter of air for any ante-area.

  (iii) Pressure differential monitoring. A pressure gauge or velocity meter shall be installed to monitor the pressure differential or airflow between the buffer area and the ante-area and between the ante-area and the general environment outside the compounding area. The results shall be reviewed and documented on a log at least every work shift (minimum frequency shall be at least daily) or by a continuous recording device. The pressure between the ISO Class 7 or ISO Class 8 and the general pharmacy area shall not be less than 0.02 inch water column.

  (iv) Sampling plan. An appropriate environmental sampling plan shall be developed for airborne viable particles based on a risk assessment of compounding activities performed. Selected sampling sites shall include locations within each ISO Class 5 environment and in the ISO Class 7 and 8 areas and in the segregated compounding areas at greatest risk of contamination. The plan shall include sample location, method of collection, frequency of sampling, volume of air sampled, and time of day as related to activity in the compounding area and action levels.

  (v) Viable air sampling. Evaluation of airborne microorganisms using volumetric collection methods in the controlled air environments shall be performed by properly trained individuals for all compounding risk levels. For low-, medium-, and high-risk level compounding, air sampling shall be performed at locations that are prone to contamination during compounding activities and during other activities such as staging, labeling, gowning, and cleaning. Locations shall include zones of air backwash turbulence within the laminar airflow workbench and other areas where air backwash turbulence may enter the compounding area. For low-risk level compounded sterile preparations within 12-hour or less beyond-use-date prepared in a primary engineering control that maintains an ISO Class 5, air sampling shall be performed at locations inside the ISO Class 5 environment and other areas that are in close proximity to the ISO Class 5 environment during the certification of the primary engineering control.

    (vi) Air sampling frequency and process. Air sampling shall be performed at least every 6 months as a part of the re-certification of facilities and equipment. A sufficient volume of air shall be sampled and the manufacturer's guidelines for use of the electronic air sampling equipment followed. At the end of the designated sampling or exposure period for air sampling activities, the microbial growth media plates are recovered and their covers secured and they are inverted and incubated at a temperature and for a time period conducive to multiplication of microorganisms. Sampling data shall be collected and reviewed on a periodic basis as a means of evaluating the overall control of the compounding environment. If an activity consistently shows elevated levels of microbial growth, competent microbiology or infection control personnel shall be consulted. A colony forming unit (cfu) count greater than 1 cfu per cubic meter of air for ISO Class 5, greater than 10 cfu per cubic meter of air for ISO Class 7, and greater than 100 cfu per cubic meter of air for ISO Class 8 or worse should prompt a re-evaluation of the adequacy of personnel work practices, cleaning procedures, operational procedures, and air filtration efficiency within the aseptic compounding location. An investigation into the source of the contamination shall be conducted. The source of the problem shall be eliminated, the affected area cleaned, and resampling performed. Counts of cfu are to be used as an approximate measure of the environmental microbial bioburden. Action levels are determined on the basis of cfu data gathered at each sampling location and trended over time. Regardless of the number of cfu identified in the pharmacy, further corrective actions will be dictated by the identification of microorganisms recovered by an appropriate credentialed laboratory of any microbial bioburden captured as a cfu using an impaction air sampler. Highly pathogenic microorganisms (e.g., gram-negative rods, coagulase positive staphylococcus, molds and yeasts) can be potentially fatal to patient receiving compounded sterile preparations and must be immediately remedied, regardless of colony forming unit count, with the assistance, if needed, of a competent microbiologist, infection control professional, or industrial hygienist.

    (vii) Compounding accuracy checks. Written procedures for checking compounding accuracy shall be followed for every compounded sterile preparation during preparation and immediately prior to release, including label accuracy and the accuracy of the addition of all drug products or ingredients used to prepare the finished preparation and their volumes or quantities. At each step of the compounding process, the pharmacist shall ensure that components used in compounding are accurately weighed, measured, or subdivided as appropriate to conform to the formula being prepared.

  (15) Quality control.

    (A) Quality control procedures. The pharmacy shall follow established quality control procedures to monitor the compounding environment and quality of compounded drug preparations for conformity with the quality indicators established for the preparation. When developing these procedures, pharmacy personnel shall consider the provisions of USP Chapter 71, Sterility Tests, USP Chapter 85, Bacterial Endotoxins Test, Pharmaceutical Compounding-Non-sterile Preparations, USP Chapter 795, USP Chapter 797, Pharmaceutical Compounding—Sterile Preparations, USP Chapter 800, Hazardous Drugs—Handling in Healthcare Settings, USP Chapter 823, Positron Emission Tomography Drugs for Compounding, Investigational, and Research Uses, USP Chapter 1160, Pharmaceutical Calculations in Prescription Compounding, and USP Chapter 1163, Quality Assurance in Pharmaceutical Compounding of the current USP/NF. Such procedures shall be documented and be available for inspection.

    (B) Verification of compounding accuracy and sterility.

      (i) The accuracy of identities, concentrations, amounts, and purities of ingredients in compounded sterile preparations shall be confirmed by reviewing labels on packages, observing and documenting correct measurements with approved and correctly standardized devices, and reviewing information in labeling and certificates of analysis provided by suppliers.

      (ii) If the correct identity, purity, strength, and sterility of ingredients and components of compounded sterile preparations cannot be confirmed such ingredients and components shall be discarded immediately. Any compounded sterile preparation that fails sterility testing following sterilization by one method (e.g., filtration) is to be discarded and not subjected to a second method of sterilization.

      (iii) If individual ingredients, such as bulk drug substances, are not labeled with expiration dates, when the drug substances are stable indefinitely in their commercial packages under labeled storage conditions, such ingredients may gain or lose moisture during storage and use and shall require testing to determine the correct amount to weigh for accurate content of active chemical moieties in compounded sterile preparations.

(e) Records. Any testing, cleaning, procedures, or other activities required in this subsection shall be documented and such documentation shall be maintained by the pharmacy.

  (1) Maintenance of records. Every record required under this section must be:

    (A) kept by the pharmacy and be available, for at least two years for inspecting and copying by the board or its representative and to other authorized local, state, or federal law enforcement agencies; and

    (B) supplied by the pharmacy within 72 hours, if requested by an authorized agent of the Texas State Board of Pharmacy. If the pharmacy maintains the records in an electronic format, the requested records must be provided in an electronic format. Failure to provide the records set out in this section, either on site or within 72 hours, constitutes prima facie evidence of failure to keep and maintain records in violation of the Act.

  (2) Compounding records.

    (A) Compounding pursuant to patient specific prescription drug orders or medication orders. Compounding records for all compounded preparations shall be maintained by the pharmacy and shall include:

      (i) the date and time of preparation;

      (ii) a complete formula, including methodology and necessary equipment which includes the brand name(s) of the raw materials, or if no brand name, the generic name(s) or official name and name(s) of the manufacturer(s) or distributor of the raw materials and the quantities of each; however, if the sterile preparation is compounded according to the manufacturer's labeling instructions, then documentation of the formula is not required;

        (iii) written or electronic signature or initials of the pharmacist or pharmacy technician or pharmacy technician trainee performing the compounding;

        (iv) written or electronic signature or initials of the pharmacist responsible for supervising pharmacy technicians or pharmacy technician trainees and conducting finals checks of compounded pharmaceuticals if pharmacy technicians or pharmacy technician trainees perform the compounding function;

        (v) the container used and the number of units of finished preparation prepared; and

        (vi) a reference to the location of the following documentation which may be maintained with other records, such as quality control records:

            (I) the criteria used to determine the beyond-use date; and

            (II) documentation of performance of quality control procedures.

    (B) Compounding records when batch compounding or compounding in anticipation of future prescription drug or medication orders.

        (i) Master work sheet. A master work sheet shall be developed and approved by a pharmacist for preparations prepared in batch. Once approved, a duplicate of the master work sheet shall be used as the preparation work sheet from which each batch is prepared and on which all documentation for that batch occurs. The master work sheet shall contain at a minimum:

            (I) the formula;

            (II) the components;

            (III) the compounding directions;

            (IV) a sample label;

            (V) evaluation and testing requirements;

            (VI) specific equipment used during preparation; and

            (VII) storage requirements.

        (ii) Preparation work sheet. The preparation work sheet for each batch of preparations shall document the following:

            (I) identity of all solutions and ingredients and their corresponding amounts, concentrations, or volumes;

            (II) lot number for each component;

            (III) component manufacturer/distributor or suitable identifying number;

            (IV) container specifications (e.g., syringe, pump cassette);

            (V) unique lot or control number assigned to batch;

            (VI) expiration date of batch-prepared preparations;

            (VII) date of preparation;

            (VIII) name, initials, or electronic signature of the person(s) involved in the preparation;

            (IX) name, initials, or electronic signature of the responsible pharmacist;

            (X) finished preparation evaluation and testing specifications, if applicable; and

            (XI) comparison of actual yield to anticipated or theoretical yield, when appropriate.

(f) Office Use Compounding and Distribution of Sterile Compounded Preparations

  (1) General.

    (A) A pharmacy may compound, dispense, deliver, and distribute a compounded sterile preparation as specified in Subchapter D, Texas Pharmacy Act Chapter 562.

    (B) A Class A-S pharmacy is not required to register or be licensed under Chapter 431, Health and Safety Code, to distribute sterile compounded preparations to a Class C or Class C-S pharmacy.

    (C) A Class C-S pharmacy is not required to register or be licensed under Chapter 431, Health and Safety Code, to distribute sterile compounded preparations that the Class C-S pharmacy has compounded for other Class C or Class C-S pharmacies under common ownership.

    (D) To compound and deliver a compounded preparation under this subsection, a pharmacy must:

        (i) verify the source of the raw materials to be used in a compounded drug;

        (ii) comply with applicable United States Pharmacopoeia guidelines, including the testing requirements, and the Health Insurance Portability and Accountability Act of 1996 (Pub. L. No. 104-191);

        (iii) enter into a written agreement with a practitioner for the practitioner's office use of a compounded preparation;

        (iv) comply with all applicable competency and accrediting standards as determined by the board; and

        (v) comply with the provisions of this subsection.

    (E) This subsection does not apply to Class B pharmacies compounding sterile radiopharmaceuticals that are furnished for departmental or physicians' use if such authorized users maintain a Texas radioactive materials license.

  (2) Written Agreement. A pharmacy that provides sterile compounded preparations to practitioners for office use or to another pharmacy shall enter into a written agreement with the practitioner or pharmacy. The written agreement shall:

    (A) address acceptable standards of practice for a compounding pharmacy and a practitioner and receiving pharmacy that enter into the agreement including a statement that the compounded drugs may only be administered to the patient and may not be dispensed to the patient or sold to any other person or entity except to a veterinarian as authorized by § 563.054 of the Act;

    (B) require the practitioner or receiving pharmacy to include on a patient's chart, medication order or medication administration record the lot number and beyond-use date of a compounded preparation administered to a patient; and

    (C) describe the scope of services to be performed by the pharmacy and practitioner or receiving pharmacy, including a statement of the process for:

        (i) a patient to report an adverse reaction or submit a complaint; and

        (ii) the pharmacy to recall batches of compounded preparations.

  (3) Recordkeeping.

    (A) Maintenance of Records.

      (i)   Records of orders and distribution of sterile compounded preparations to a practitioner for office use or to an institutional pharmacy for administration to a patient shall:

         (I)   be kept by the pharmacy and be available, for at least two years from the date of the record, for inspecting and copying by the board or its representative and to other authorized local, state, or federal law enforcement agencies;

         (II)   be maintained separately from the records of preparations dispensed pursuant to a prescription or medication order; and

         (III)   be supplied by the pharmacy within 72 hours, if requested by an authorized agent of the Texas State Board of Pharmacy or its representative. If the pharmacy maintains the records in an electronic format, the requested records must be provided in an electronic format. Failure to provide the records set out in this subsection, either on site or within 72 hours for whatever reason, constitutes prima facie evidence of failure to keep and maintain records.

      (ii)   Records may be maintained in an alternative data retention system, such as a data processing system or direct imaging system provided the data processing system is capable of producing a hard copy of the record upon the request of the board, its representative, or other authorized local, state, or federal law enforcement or regulatory agencies.

    (B)   Orders. The pharmacy shall maintain a record of all sterile compounded preparations ordered by a practitioner for office use or by an institutional pharmacy for administration to a patient. The record shall include the following information:

      (i)   date of the order;

      (ii)   name, address, and phone number of the practitioner who ordered the preparation and if applicable, the name, address and phone number of the institutional pharmacy ordering the preparation; and

      (iii)   name, strength, and quantity of the preparation ordered.

    (C)   Distributions. The pharmacy shall maintain a record of all sterile compounded preparations distributed pursuant to an order to a practitioner for office use or by an institutional pharmacy for administration to a patient. The record shall include the following information:

      (i)   date the preparation was compounded;

      (ii)   date the preparation was distributed;

      (iii)   name, strength and quantity in each container of the preparation;

      (iv)   pharmacy's lot number;

      (v)   quantity of containers shipped; and

      (vi)   name, address, and phone number of the practitioner or institutional pharmacy to whom the preparation is distributed.

    (D)   Audit Trail.

      (i)   The pharmacy shall store the order and distribution records of preparations for all sterile compounded preparations ordered by and or distributed to a practitioner for office use or by a pharmacy licensed to compound sterile preparations for administration to a patient in such a manner as to be able to provide an audit trail for all orders and distributions of any of the following during a specified time period:

         (I)   any strength and dosage form of a preparation (by either brand or generic name or both);

         (II)   any ingredient;

         (III)   any lot number;

         (IV)   any practitioner;

         (V)   any facility; and

         (VI)   any pharmacy, if applicable.

      (ii)   The audit trail shall contain the following information:

         (I)   date of order and date of the distribution;

         (II)   practitioner's name, address, and name of the institutional pharmacy, if applicable;

         (III)   name, strength and quantity of the preparation in each container of the preparation;

         (IV)   name and quantity of each active ingredient;

         (V)   quantity of containers distributed; and

         (VI)   pharmacy's lot number.

  (4)   Labeling. The pharmacy shall affix a label to the preparation containing the following information:

    (A)   name, address, and phone number of the compounding pharmacy;

    (B)   the statement: "For Institutional or Office Use Only—Not for Resale"; or if the preparation is distributed to a veterinarian the statement: "Compounded Preparation";

    (C)   name and strength of the preparation or list of the active ingredients and strengths;

    (D)   pharmacy's lot number;

    (E)   beyond-use date as determined by the pharmacist using appropriate documented criteria;

    (F)   quantity or amount in the container;

    (G)   appropriate ancillary instructions, such as storage instructions or cautionary statements, including hazardous drug warning labels where appropriate; and

    (H)   device-specific instructions, where appropriate.

(g)   Recall Procedures.

  (1)   The pharmacy shall have written procedures for the recall of any compounded sterile preparation provided to a patient, to a practitioner for office use, or a pharmacy for administration. Written procedures shall include, but not be limited to the requirements as specified in paragraph (3) of this subsection.

  (2)   The pharmacy shall immediately initiate a recall of any sterile preparation compounded by the pharmacy upon identification of a potential or confirmed harm to a patient.

  (3)   In the event of a recall, the pharmacist-in-charge shall ensure that:

    (A)   each practitioner, facility, and/or pharmacy to which the preparation was distributed is notified, in writing, of the recall;

    (B)   each patient to whom the preparation was dispensed is notified, in writing, of the recall;

    (C)   the board is notified of the recall, in writing, not later than 24 hours after the recall is issued;

   (D) if the preparation is distributed for office use, the Texas Department of State Health Services, Drugs and Medical Devices Group, is notified of the recall, in writing;

   (E) the preparation is quarantined; and

   (F) the pharmacy keeps a written record of the recall including all actions taken to notify all parties and steps taken to ensure corrective measures.

(4) If a pharmacy fails to initiate a recall, the board may require a pharmacy to initiate a recall if there is potential for or confirmed harm to a patient.

(5) A pharmacy that compounds sterile preparations shall notify the board immediately of any adverse effects reported to the pharmacy or that are known by the pharmacy to be potentially attributable to a sterile preparation compounded by the pharmacy.

Source: The provisions of this § 291.133 adopted to be effective December 10, 2013, 38 TexReg 8869; amended to be effective September 11, 2014, 39 TexReg 7128; amended to be effective June 11, 2015, 40 TexReg 3647; amended to be effective September 14, 2015, 40 TexReg 6111; amended to be effective June 12, 2016, 41 TexReg 4257; amended to be effective September 11, 2016, 41 TexReg 6718; amended to be effective January 4, 2018, 42 TexReg 7700; amended to be effective September 16, 2018, 43 TexReg 5784

SUBCHAPTER H. OTHER CLASSES OF PHARMACY

§291.151 Pharmacies Located in a Freestanding Emergency Medical Care Facility (Class F)

(a) Purpose. The purpose of this section is to provide standards in the conduct, practice activities, and operation of a pharmacy located in a freestanding emergency medical care facility that is licensed by the Texas Department of State Health Services or in a freestanding emergency medical care facility operated by a hospital that is exempt from registration as provided by § 254.052, Health and Safety Code. Class F pharmacies located in a freestanding emergency medical care facility shall comply with this section.

(b) Definitions. The following words and terms, when used in this section, shall have the following meanings, unless the context clearly indicates otherwise.

  (1) Act—The Texas Pharmacy Act, Occupations Code, Subtitle J, as amended.

  (2) Administer—The direct application of a prescription drug by injection, inhalation, ingestion, or any other means to the body of a patient by:

   (A) a practitioner, an authorized agent under his supervision, or other person authorized by law; or

   (B) the patient at the direction of a practitioner.

  (3) Automated medication supply system—A mechanical system that performs operations or activities relative to the storage and distribution of medications for administration and which collects, controls, and maintains all transaction information.

  (4) Board—The Texas State Board of Pharmacy.

  (5) Consultant pharmacist—A pharmacist retained by a facility on a routine basis to consult with the FEMCF in areas that pertain to the practice of pharmacy.

  (6) Controlled substance—A drug, immediate precursor, or other substance listed in Schedules I - V or Penalty Groups 1 - 4 of the Texas Controlled Substances Act, as amended, or a drug immediate precursor, or other substance included in Schedules I - V of the Federal Comprehensive Drug Abuse Prevention and Control Act of 1970, as amended (Public Law 91-513).

  (7) Dispense—Preparing, packaging, compounding, or labeling for delivery a prescription drug or device in the course of professional practice to an ultimate user or his agent by or pursuant to the lawful order of a practitioner.

  (8) Distribute—The delivery of a prescription drug or device other than by administering or dispensing.

  (9) Downtime—Period of time during which a data processing system is not operable.

  (10) Electronic signature—A unique security code or other identifier which specifically identifies the person entering information into a data processing system. A facility which utilizes electronic signatures must:

   (A) maintain a permanent list of the unique security codes assigned to persons authorized to use the data processing system; and

   (B) have an ongoing security program which is capable of identifying misuse and/or unauthorized use of electronic signatures.

  (11) Floor stock—Prescription drugs or devices not labeled for a specific patient and maintained at a nursing station or other FEMCF department (excluding the pharmacy) for the purpose of administration to a patient of the FEMCF.

  (12) Formulary—List of drugs approved for use in the FEMCF by an appropriate committee of the FEMCF.

  (13) Freestanding emergency medical care facility (FEMCF)—A freestanding facility that is licensed by the Texas Department of State Health Services pursuant to Chapter 254, Health and Safety Code, to provide emergency care to patients.

  (14) Hard copy—A physical document that is readable without the use of a special device (i.e., data processing system, computer, etc.).

  (15) Investigational new drug—New drug intended for investigational use by experts qualified to evaluate the safety and effectiveness of the drug as authorized by the federal Food and Drug Administration.

  (16) Medication order—An order from a practitioner or his authorized agent for administration of a drug or device.

  (17) Pharmacist-in-charge—Pharmacist designated on a pharmacy license as the pharmacist who has the authority or responsibility for a pharmacy's compliance with laws and rules pertaining to the practice of pharmacy.

  (18) Pharmacy—Area or areas in a facility, separate from patient care areas, where drugs are stored, bulk compounded, delivered, compounded, dispensed, and/or distributed to other areas or departments of the FEMCF, or dispensed to an ultimate user or his or her agent.

  (19) Prescription drug—

   (A) A substance for which federal or state law requires a prescription before it may be legally dispensed to the public;

   (B) A drug or device that under federal law is required, prior to being dispensed or delivered, to be labeled with either of the following statements:

    (i) Caution: federal law prohibits dispensing without prescription or "Rx only" or another legend that complies with federal law; or

    (ii) Caution: federal law restricts this drug to use by or on order of a licensed veterinarian; or

   (C) A drug or device that is required by any applicable federal or state law or regulation to be dispensed on prescription only or is restricted to use by a practitioner only.

(20) Prescription drug order—
    (A) An order from a practitioner or his authorized agent to a pharmacist for a drug or device to be dispensed; or
    (B) An order pursuant to Subtitle B, Chapter 157, Occupations Code.

(21) Full-time pharmacist—A pharmacist who works in a pharmacy from 30 to 40 hours per week or if the pharmacy is open less than 60 hours per week, one-half of the time the pharmacy is open.

(22) Part-time pharmacist—A pharmacist who works less than full-time.

(23) Pharmacy technician—An individual who is registered with the board as a pharmacy technician and whose responsibility in a pharmacy is to provide technical services that do not require professional judgment regarding preparing and distributing drugs and who works under the direct supervision of and is responsible to a pharmacist.

(24) Pharmacy technician trainee—An individual who is registered with the board as a pharmacy technician trainee and is authorized to participate in a pharmacy's technician training program.

(25) Texas Controlled Substances Act—The Texas Controlled Substances Act, Health and Safety Code, Chapter 481, as amended.

(c) Personnel.
  (1) Pharmacist-in-charge.
    (A) General. Each FEMCF shall have one pharmacist-in-charge who is employed or under contract, at least on a consulting or part-time basis, but may be employed on a full-time basis.
    (B) Responsibilities. The pharmacist-in-charge shall have the responsibility for, at a minimum, the following:
      (i) establishing specifications for procurement and storage of all materials, including drugs, chemicals, and biologicals;
      (ii) participating in the development of a formulary for the FEMCF, subject to approval of the appropriate committee of the FEMCF;
      (iii) distributing drugs to be administered to patients pursuant to the practitioner's medication order;
      (iv) filling and labeling all containers from which drugs are to be distributed or dispensed;
      (v) maintaining and making available a sufficient inventory of antidotes and other emergency drugs, both in the pharmacy and patient care areas, as well as current antidote information, telephone numbers of regional poison control center and other emergency assistance organizations, and such other materials and information as may be deemed necessary by the appropriate committee of the FEMCF;
      (vi) maintaining records of all transactions of the FEMCF pharmacy as may be required by applicable state and federal law, and as may be necessary to maintain accurate control over and accountability for all pharmaceutical materials;
      (vii) participating in those aspects of the FEMCF's patient care evaluation program which relate to pharmaceutical material utilization and effectiveness;
      (viii) participating in teaching and/or research programs in the FEMCF;
      (ix) implementing the policies and decisions of the appropriate committee(s) relating to pharmaceutical services of the FEMCF;
      (x) providing effective and efficient messenger and delivery service to connect the FEMCF pharmacy with appropriate areas of the FEMCF on a regular basis throughout the normal workday of the FEMCF;
      (xi) labeling, storing, and distributing investigational new drugs, including maintaining information in the pharmacy and nursing station where such drugs are being administered, concerning the dosage form, route of administration, strength, actions, uses, side effects, adverse effects, interactions, and symptoms of toxicity of investigational new drugs;
      (xii) meeting all inspection and other requirements of the Texas Pharmacy Act and this section; and
      (xiii) maintaining records in a data processing system such that the data processing system is in compliance with the requirements for an FEMCF; and
      (xiv) ensuring that a pharmacist visits the FEMCF at least once each calendar week that the facility is open.
  (2) Consultant pharmacist.
    (A) The consultant pharmacist may be the pharmacist-in-charge.
    (B) A written contract shall exist between the FEMCF and any consultant pharmacist, and a copy of the written contract shall be made available to the board upon request.
  (3) Pharmacists.
    (A) General.
      (i) The pharmacist-in-charge shall be assisted by a sufficient number of additional licensed pharmacists as may be required to operate the FEMCF pharmacy competently, safely, and adequately to meet the needs of the patients of the facility.
      (ii) All pharmacists shall assist the pharmacist-in-charge in meeting the responsibilities as outlined in paragraph (1)(B) of this subsection and in ordering, administering, and accounting for pharmaceutical materials.
      (iii) All pharmacists shall be responsible for any delegated act performed by pharmacy technicians or pharmacy technician trainees under his or her supervision.
      (iv) All pharmacists while on duty shall be responsible for complying with all state and federal laws or rules governing the practice of pharmacy.
    (B) Duties. Duties of the pharmacist-in-charge and all other pharmacists shall include, but need not be limited to, the following:
      (i) receiving and interpreting prescription drug orders and oral medication orders and reducing these orders to writing either manually or electronically;
      (ii) selecting prescription drugs and/or devices and/or suppliers; and
      (iii) interpreting patient profiles.
    (C) Special requirements for compounding non-sterile preparations. All pharmacists engaged in compounding non-sterile preparations shall meet the training requirements specified in § 291.131 of this title (relating to Pharmacies Compounding Non-Sterile Preparations).
  (4) Pharmacy technicians and pharmacy technician trainees.
    (A) General. All pharmacy technicians and pharmacy technician trainees shall meet the training requirements specified in § 297.6 of this title (relating to Pharmacy Technician and Pharmacy Technician Trainee Training).

    (B) Duties. Pharmacy technicians and pharmacy technician trainees may not perform any of the duties listed in paragraph (3)(B) of this subsection. Duties may include, but need not be limited to, the following functions, under the direct supervision of a pharmacist:
        (i) prepacking and labeling unit and multiple dose packages, provided a pharmacist supervises and conducts a final check and affixes his or her name, initials, or electronic signature to the appropriate quality control records prior to distribution;
        (ii) preparing, packaging, compounding, or labeling prescription drugs pursuant to medication orders, provided a pharmacist supervises and checks the preparation;
        (iii) compounding non-sterile preparations pursuant to medication orders provided the pharmacy technicians or pharmacy technician trainees have completed the training specified in § 291.131 of this title;
        (iv) bulk compounding, provided a pharmacist supervises and conducts in-process and final checks and affixes his or her name, initials, or electronic signature to the appropriate quality control records prior to distribution;
        (v) distributing routine orders for stock supplies to patient care areas;
        (vi) entering medication order and drug distribution information into a data processing system, provided judgmental decisions are not required and a pharmacist checks the accuracy of the information entered into the system prior to releasing the order or in compliance with the absence of pharmacist requirements contained in subsection (d)(6)(D) and (E) of this section;
        (vii) maintaining inventories of drug supplies;
        (viii) maintaining pharmacy records; and
        (ix) loading drugs into an automated medication supply system. For the purpose of this clause, direct supervision may be accomplished by physically present supervision or electronic monitoring by a pharmacist.
    (C) Procedures.
        (i) Pharmacy technicians and pharmacy technician trainees shall handle medication orders in accordance with standard written procedures and guidelines.
        (ii) Pharmacy technicians and pharmacy technician trainees shall handle prescription drug orders in the same manner as pharmacy technicians or pharmacy technician trainees working in a Class A pharmacy.
    (D) Special requirements for compounding non-sterile preparations. All pharmacy technicians and pharmacy technician trainees engaged in compounding non-sterile preparations shall meet the training requirements specified in § 291.131 of this title.
  (5) Owner. The owner of an FEMCF pharmacy shall have responsibility for all administrative and operational functions of the pharmacy. The pharmacist-in-charge may advise the owner on administrative and operational concerns. The owner shall have responsibility for, at a minimum, the following, and if the owner is not a Texas licensed pharmacist, the owner shall consult with the pharmacist-in-charge or another Texas licensed pharmacist:
    (A) establishing policies for procurement of prescription drugs and devices and other products dispensed from the FEMCF pharmacy;
    (B) establishing and maintaining effective controls against the theft or diversion of prescription drugs;
    (C) if the pharmacy uses an automated medication supply system, reviewing and approving all policies and procedures for system operation, safety, security, accuracy and access, patient confidentiality, prevention of unauthorized access, and malfunction;
    (D) providing the pharmacy with the necessary equipment and resources commensurate with its level and type of practice; and
    (E) establishing policies and procedures regarding maintenance, storage, and retrieval of records in a data processing system such that the system is in compliance with state and federal requirements.
  (6) Identification of pharmacy personnel. All pharmacy personnel shall be identified as follows:
    (A) Pharmacy technicians. All pharmacy technicians shall wear an identification tag or badge that bears the person's name and identifies him or her as a pharmacy technician.
    (B) Pharmacy technician trainees. All pharmacy technician trainees shall wear an identification tag or badge that bears the person's name and identifies him or her as a pharmacy technician trainee.
    (C) Pharmacist interns. All pharmacist interns shall wear an identification tag or badge that bears the person's name and identifies him or her as a pharmacist intern.
    (D) Pharmacists. All pharmacists shall wear an identification tag or badge that bears the person's name and identifies him or her as a pharmacist.
(d) Operational standards.
  (1) Licensing requirements.
    (A) An FEMCF pharmacy shall register annually or biennially with the board on a pharmacy license application provided by the board, following the procedures specified in § 291.1 of this title (relating to Pharmacy License Application).
    (B) An FEMCF pharmacy which changes ownership shall notify the board within 10 days of the change of ownership and apply for a new and separate license as specified in § 291.3 of this title (relating to Required Notifications).
    (C) An FEMCF pharmacy which changes location and/or name shall notify the board of the change within 10 days and file for an amended license as specified in § 291.3 of this title.
    (D) A pharmacy owned by a partnership or corporation which changes managing officers shall notify the board in writing of the names of the new managing officers within 10 days of the change, following the procedures in § 291.3 of this title.
    (E) An FEMCF pharmacy shall notify the board in writing within 10 days of closing, following the procedures in § 291.5 of this title (relating to Closing a Pharmacy).
    (F) A fee as specified in § 291.6 of this title (relating to Pharmacy License Fees) will be charged for issuance and renewal of a license and the issuance of an amended license.
    (G) A separate license is required for each principal place of business and only one pharmacy license may be issued to a specific location.
    (H) An FEMCF pharmacy, which also operates another type of pharmacy which would otherwise be required to be licensed under the Act, § 560.051(a)(1), concerning community pharmacy (Class A), is not required to secure a license for the other

type of pharmacy; provided, however, such license is required to comply with the provisions of § 291.31 of this title (relating to Definitions), § 291.32 of this title (relating to Personnel), § 291.33 of this title (relating to Operational Standards), § 291.34 of this title (relating to Records), and § 291.35 of this title (relating to Official Prescription Requirements), to the extent such sections are applicable to the operation of the pharmacy.

    (I)   An FEMCF pharmacy engaged in the compounding of non-sterile preparations shall comply with the provisions of § 291.131 of this title.

(2)   Environment.

    (A)   General requirements.

        (i)   Each FEMCF shall have a designated work area separate from patient areas, and which shall have space adequate for the size and scope of pharmaceutical services and shall have adequate space and security for the storage of drugs.

        (ii)   The FEMCF pharmacy shall be arranged in an orderly fashion and shall be kept clean. All required equipment shall be clean and in good operating condition.

    (B)   Special requirements.

        (i)   The FEMCF pharmacy shall have locked storage for Schedule II controlled substances and other controlled drugs requiring additional security.

        (ii)   The FEMCF pharmacy shall have a designated area for the storage of poisons and externals separate from drug storage areas.

    (C)   Security.

        (i)   The pharmacy and storage areas for prescription drugs and/or devices shall be enclosed and capable of being locked by key, combination, or other mechanical or electronic means, so as to prohibit access by unauthorized individuals. Only individuals authorized by the pharmacist-in-charge may enter the pharmacy or have access to storage areas for prescription drugs and/or devices.

        (ii)   The pharmacist-in-charge shall consult with FEMCF personnel with respect to security of the drug storage areas, including provisions for adequate safeguards against theft or diversion of dangerous drugs, controlled substances, and records for such drugs.

        (iii)   The pharmacy shall have locked storage for Schedule II controlled substances and other drugs requiring additional security.

(3)   Equipment and supplies. FEMCFs supplying drugs for outpatient use shall have the following equipment and supplies:

    (A)   data processing system including a printer or comparable equipment;

    (B)   adequate supply of child-resistant, moisture-proof, and light-proof containers; and

    (C)   adequate supply of prescription labels and other applicable identification labels.

(4)   Library. A reference library shall be maintained that includes the following in hard copy or electronic format and that pharmacy personnel shall be capable of accessing at all times:

    (A)   current copies of the following:

        (i)   Texas Pharmacy Act and rules;

        (ii)   Texas Dangerous Drug Act and rules;

        (iii)   Texas Controlled Substances Act and rules; and

        (iv)   Federal Controlled Substances Act and rules or official publication describing the requirements of the Federal Controlled Substances Act and rules;

    (B)   at least one current or updated general drug information reference which is required to contain drug interaction information including information needed to determine severity or significance of the interaction and appropriate recommendations or actions to be taken; and

    (C)   basic antidote information and the telephone number of the nearest regional poison control center.

(5)   Drugs.

    (A)   Procurement, preparation, and storage.

        (i)   The pharmacist-in-charge shall have the responsibility for the procurement and storage of drugs, but may receive input from other appropriate staff of the facility, relative to such responsibility.

        (ii)   The pharmacist-in-charge shall have the responsibility for determining specifications of all drugs procured by the facility.

        (iii)   FEMCF pharmacies may not sell, purchase, trade, or possess prescription drug samples, unless the pharmacy meets the requirements as specified in § 291.16 of this title (relating to Samples).

        (iv)   All drugs shall be stored at the proper temperatures, as defined in the USP/NF and in § 291.15 of this title (relating to Storage of Drugs).

        (v)   Any drug bearing an expiration date may not be dispensed or distributed beyond the expiration date of the drug.

        (vi)   Outdated drugs shall be removed from dispensing stock and shall be quarantined together until such drugs are disposed of.

    (B)   Formulary.

        (i)   A formulary may be developed by an appropriate committee of the FEMCF.

        (ii)   The pharmacist-in-charge, consultant pharmacist, or designee shall be a full voting member of any committee which involves pharmaceutical services.

        (iii)   A practitioner may grant approval for pharmacists at the FEMCF to interchange, in accordance with the facility's formulary, for the drugs on the practitioner's medication orders provided:

            (I)   a formulary has been developed;

            (II)   the formulary has been approved by the medical staff of the FEMCF;

            (III)   there is a reasonable method for the practitioner to override any interchange; and

            (IV)   the practitioner authorizes a pharmacist in the FEMCF to interchange on his/her medication orders in accordance with the facility's formulary through his/her written agreement to abide by the policies and procedures of the medical staff and facility.

    (C) Prepackaging and loading drugs into automated medication supply system.
       (i) Prepackaging of drugs.
         (I) Drugs may be prepackaged in quantities suitable for internal distribution only by a pharmacist or by pharmacy technicians or pharmacy technician trainees under the direction and direct supervision of a pharmacist.
         (II) The label of a prepackaged unit shall indicate:
           (-a-) brand name and strength of the drug; or if no brand name, then the generic name, strength, and name of the manufacturer or distributor;
           (-b-) facility's lot number;
           (-c-) expiration date; and
           (-d-) quantity of the drug, if quantity is greater than one.
         (III) Records of prepackaging shall be maintained to show:
           (-a-) the name of the drug, strength, and dosage form;
           (-b-) facility's lot number;
           (-c-) manufacturer or distributor;
           (-d-) manufacturer's lot number;
           (-e-) expiration date;
           (-f-) quantity per prepackaged unit;
           (-g-) number of prepackaged units;
           (-h-) date packaged;
           (-i-) name, initials, or electronic signature of the prepacker; and
           (-j-) signature or electronic signature of the responsible pharmacist.
         (IV) Stock packages, repackaged units, and control records shall be quarantined together until checked/released by the pharmacist.
       (ii) Loading bulk unit of use drugs into automated medication supply systems. Automated medication supply systems may be loaded with bulk unit of use drugs only by a pharmacist or by pharmacy technicians or pharmacy technician trainees under the direction and direct supervision of a pharmacist. For the purpose of this clause, direct supervision may be accomplished by physically present supervision or electronic monitoring by a pharmacist. In order for the pharmacist to electronically monitor, the medication supply system must allow for bar code scanning to verify the loading of drugs, and a record of the loading must be maintained by the system and accessible for electronic review by the pharmacist.
  (6) Medication orders.
    (A) Drugs may be administered to patients in FEMCFs only on the order of a practitioner. No change in the order for drugs may be made without the approval of a practitioner except as authorized by the practitioner in compliance with paragraph (5)(B) of this subsection.
    (B) Drugs may be distributed only pursuant to the copy of the practitioner's medication order.
    (C) FEMCF pharmacies shall be exempt from the labeling provisions and patient notification requirements of § 562.006 and § 562.009 of the Act, as respects drugs distributed pursuant to medication orders.
    (D) In FEMCFs with a full-time pharmacist, if a practitioner orders a drug for administration to a bona fide patient of the facility when the pharmacy is closed, the following is applicable.
       (i) Prescription drugs and devices only in sufficient quantities for immediate therapeutic needs of a patient may be removed from the FEMCF pharmacy.
       (ii) Only a designated licensed nurse or practitioner may remove such drugs and devices.
       (iii) A record shall be made at the time of withdrawal by the authorized person removing the drugs and devices. The record shall contain the following information:
         (I) name of the patient;
         (II) name of device or drug, strength, and dosage form;
         (III) dose prescribed;
         (IV) quantity taken;
         (V) time and date; and
         (VI) signature or electronic signature of person making withdrawal.
       (iv) The medication order in the patient's chart may substitute for such record, provided the medication order meets all the requirements of clause (iii) of this subparagraph.
       (v) The pharmacist shall verify the withdrawal as soon as practical, but in no event more than 72 hours from the time of such withdrawal.
    (E) In FEMCFs with a part-time or consultant pharmacist, if a practitioner orders a drug for administration to a bona fide patient of the FEMCF when the pharmacist is not on duty, or when the pharmacy is closed, the following is applicable.
       (i) Prescription drugs and devices only in sufficient quantities for therapeutic needs may be removed from the FEMCF pharmacy.
       (ii) Only a designated licensed nurse or practitioner may remove such drugs and devices.
       (iii) The pharmacist shall conduct an audit of the patient's medical record according to the schedule set out in the policy and procedures at a reasonable interval, but such interval must occur at least once in every calendar week that the pharmacy is open.
  (7) Floor stock. In facilities using a floor stock method of drug distribution, the following is applicable for removing drugs or devices in the absence of a pharmacist.
    (A) Prescription drugs and devices may be removed from the pharmacy only in the original manufacturer's container or prepackaged container.
    (B) Only a designated licensed nurse or practitioner may remove such drugs and devices.
    (C) A record shall be made at the time of withdrawal by the authorized person removing the drug or device; the record shall contain the following information:

(i)   name of the drug, strength, and dosage form;
(ii)   quantity removed;
(iii) location of floor stock;
(iv)   date and time; and
(v)   signature or electronic signature of person making the withdrawal.

(D) A pharmacist shall verify the withdrawal according to the following schedule.

(i)   In facilities with a full-time pharmacist, the withdrawal shall be verified as soon as practical, but in no event more than 72 hours from the time of such withdrawal.
(ii)   In facilities with a part-time or consultant pharmacist, the withdrawal shall be verified after a reasonable interval, but such interval must occur at least once in every calendar week that the pharmacy is open.
(iii) The medication order in the patient's chart may substitute for the record required in subparagraph (C) of this paragraph, provided the medication order meets all the requirements of subparagraph (C) of this paragraph.

(8) Policies and procedures. Written policies and procedures for a drug distribution system, appropriate for the freestanding emergency medical facility, shall be developed and implemented by the pharmacist-in-charge with the advice of the appropriate committee. The written policies and procedures for the drug distribution system shall include, but not be limited to, procedures regarding the following:

(A) controlled substances;
(B) investigational drugs;
(C) prepackaging and manufacturing;
(D) medication errors;
(E) orders of physician or other practitioner;
(F) floor stocks;
(G) adverse drug reactions;
(H) drugs brought into the facility by the patient;
(I) self-administration;
(J) emergency drug tray;
(K) formulary, if applicable;
(L) drug storage areas;
(M) drug samples;
(N) drug product defect reports;
(O) drug recalls;
(P) outdated drugs;
(Q) preparation and distribution of IV admixtures;
(R) procedures for supplying drugs for postoperative use, if applicable;
(S) use of automated medication supply systems;
(T) use of data processing systems; and
(U) drug regimen review.

(9) Drugs supplied for outpatient use. Drugs provided to patients for take home use shall be supplied according to the following procedures.

(A) Drugs may only be supplied to patients who have been admitted to the FEMCF.
(B) Drugs may only be supplied in accordance with the system of control and accountability established for drugs supplied from the FEMCF; such system shall be developed and supervised by the pharmacist-in-charge or staff pharmacist designated by the pharmacist-in-charge.
(C) Only drugs listed on the approved outpatient drug list may be supplied; such list shall be developed by the pharmacist-in-charge and the medical staff and shall consist of drugs of the nature and type to meet the immediate postoperative needs of the FEMCF patient.
(D) Drugs may only be supplied in prepackaged quantities not to exceed a 72-hour supply in suitable containers and appropriately prelabeled (including name, address, and phone number of the facility and necessary auxiliary labels) by the pharmacy, provided, however that topicals and ophthalmics in original manufacturer's containers may be supplied in a quantity exceeding a 72-hour supply.
(E) At the time of delivery of the drug, the practitioner shall complete the label, such that the prescription container bears a label with at least the following information:
(i)   date supplied;
(ii)   name of practitioner;
(iii) name of patient;
(iv)   directions for use;
(v)   brand name and strength of the drug; or if no brand name, then the generic name of the drug dispensed, strength, and the name of the manufacturer or distributor of the drug; and
(vi)   unique identification number.
(F) After the drug has been labeled, the practitioner or a licensed nurse under the supervision of the practitioner shall give the appropriately labeled, prepackaged medication to the patient.
(G) A perpetual record of drugs which are supplied from the FEMCF shall be maintained which includes:
(i)   name, address, and phone number of the facility;
(ii)   date supplied;
(iii) name of practitioner;
(iv)   name of patient;
(v)   directions for use;

(vi) brand name and strength of the drug; or if no brand name, then the generic name of the drug dispensed, strength, and the name of the manufacturer or distributor of the drug; and

(vii) unique identification number.

(H) The pharmacist-in-charge, or a pharmacist designated by the pharmacist-in-charge, shall review the records at least once in every calendar week that the pharmacy is open.

(10) Drug regimen review.

(A) A pharmacist shall evaluate medication orders and patient medication records for:

    (i) known allergies;

    (ii) rational therapy--contraindications;

    (iii) reasonable dose and route of administration;

    (iv) reasonable directions for use;

    (v) duplication of therapy;

    (vi) drug-drug interactions;

    (vii) drug-food interactions;

    (viii) drug-disease interactions;

    (ix) adverse drug reactions;

    (x) proper utilization, including overutilization or underutilization; and

    (xi) clinical laboratory or clinical monitoring methods to monitor and evaluate drug effectiveness, side effects, toxicity, or adverse effects, and appropriateness to continued use of the drug in its current regimen.

(B) A retrospective, random drug regimen review as specified in the pharmacy's policies and procedures shall be conducted on a periodic basis to verify proper usage of drugs not to exceed 31 days between such reviews.

(C) Any questions regarding the order must be resolved with the prescriber and a written notation of these discussions made and maintained.

(e) Records.

(1) Maintenance of records.

(A) Every inventory or other record required to be kept under the provisions of this section (relating to Pharmacies Located in a Freestanding Emergency Medical Care Facility (Class F) shall be:

    (i) kept by the pharmacy and be available, for at least two years from the date of such inventory or record, for inspecting and copying by the board or its representative, and other authorized local, state, or federal law enforcement agencies; and

    (ii) supplied by the pharmacy within 72 hours, if requested by an authorized agent of the board. If the pharmacy maintains the records in an electronic format, the requested records must be provided in a mutually agreeable electronic format if specifically requested by the board or its representative. Failure to provide the records set out in this subsection, either on site or within 72 hours, constitutes prima facie evidence of failure to keep and maintain records in violation of the Act.

(B) Records of controlled substances listed in Schedule II shall be maintained separately and readily retrievable from all other records of the pharmacy.

(C) Records of controlled substances listed in Schedules III - V shall be maintained separately or readily retrievable from all other records of the pharmacy. For purposes of this subparagraph, "readily retrievable" means that the controlled substances shall be asterisked, redlined, or in some other manner readily identifiable apart from all other items appearing on the record.

(D) Records, except when specifically required to be maintained in original or hard copy form, may be maintained in an alternative data retention system, such as a data processing or direct imaging system, provided:

    (i) the records in the alternative data retention system contain all of the information required on the manual record; and

    (ii) the alternative data retention system is capable of producing a hard copy of the record upon the request of the board, its representative, or other authorized local, state, or federal law enforcement or regulatory agencies.

(E) Controlled substance records shall be maintained in a manner to establish receipt and distribution of all controlled substances.

(F) An FEMCF pharmacy shall maintain a perpetual inventory of controlled substances listed in Schedules II - V which shall be verified for completeness and reconciled at least once in every calendar week that the pharmacy is open.

(G) Distribution records for controlled substances, listed in Schedules II - V shall include the following information:

    (i) patient's name;

    (ii) practitioner's name who ordered the drug;

    (iii) name of drug, dosage form, and strength;

    (iv) time and date of administration to patient and quantity administered;

    (v) signature or electronic signature of individual administering the controlled substance;

    (vi) returns to the pharmacy; and

    (vii) waste (waste is required to be witnessed and cosigned, manually or electronically, by another individual).

(H) The record required by subparagraph (G) of this paragraph shall be maintained separately from patient records.

(I) A pharmacist shall conduct an audit by randomly comparing the distribution records required by subparagraph (G) with the medication orders in the patient record on a periodic basis to verify proper administration of drugs not to exceed 30 days between such reviews.

(2) Patient records.

(A) Each medication order or set of orders issued together shall bear the following information:

    (i) patient name;

    (ii) drug name, strength, and dosage form;

    (iii) directions for use;

    (iv) date; and

        (v)   signature or electronic signature of the practitioner or that of his or her authorized agent, defined as a licensed nurse employee or consultant/full or part-time pharmacist of the FEMCF.

    (B)   Medication orders shall be maintained with the medication administration record in the medical records of the patient.

  (3)   General requirements for records maintained in a data processing system.

    (A)   If an FEMCF pharmacy's data processing system is not in compliance with the board's requirements, the pharmacy must maintain a manual recordkeeping system.

    (B)   The facility shall maintain a backup copy of information stored in the data processing system using disk, tape, or other electronic backup system and update this backup copy on a regular basis to assure that data is not lost due to system failure.

    (C)   A pharmacy that changes or discontinues use of a data processing system must:

        (i)   transfer the records to the new data processing system; or

        (ii)   purge the records to a printout which contains:

            (I)   all of the information required on the original document; or

            (II)   for records of distribution and return for all controlled substances, the same information as required on the audit trail printout as specified in subparagraph (F) of this paragraph. The information on the printout shall be sorted and printed by drug name and list all distributions and returns chronologically.

    (D)   Information purged from a data processing system must be maintained by the pharmacy for two years from the date of initial entry into the data processing system.

    (E)   The pharmacist-in-charge shall report to the board in writing any significant loss of information from the data processing system within 10 days of discovery of the loss.

    (F)   The data processing system shall have the capacity to produce a hard copy printout of an audit trail of drug distribution and return for any strength and dosage form of a drug (by either brand or generic name or both) during a specified time period. This printout shall contain the following information:

        (i)   patient's name or patient's facility identification number;

        (ii)   prescribing or attending practitioner's name;

        (iii)   name, strength, and dosage form of the drug product actually distributed;

        (iv)   total quantity distributed from and returned to the pharmacy;

        (v)   if not immediately retrievable via electronic image, the following shall also be included on the printout:

            (I)   prescribing or attending practitioner's address; and

            (II)   practitioner's DEA registration number, if the medication order is for a controlled substance.

    (G)   An audit trail printout for each strength and dosage form of the drugs distributed during the preceding month shall be produced at least monthly and shall be maintained in a separate file at the facility. The information on this printout shall be sorted by drug name and list all distributions/returns for that drug chronologically.

    (H)   The pharmacy may elect not to produce the monthly audit trail printout if the data processing system has a workable (electronic) data retention system which can produce an audit trail of drug distribution and returns for the preceding two years. The audit trail required in this clause shall be supplied by the pharmacy within 72 hours, if requested by an authorized agent of the board, or other authorized local, state, or federal law enforcement or regulatory agencies.

    (I)   In the event that an FEMCF pharmacy which uses a data processing system experiences system downtime, the pharmacy must have an auxiliary procedure which will ensure that all data is retained for online data entry as soon as the system is available for use again.

  (4)   Distribution of controlled substances to another registrant. A pharmacy may distribute controlled substances to a practitioner, another pharmacy, or other registrant, without being registered to distribute, under the following conditions.

    (A)   The registrant to whom the controlled substance is to be distributed is registered under the Controlled Substances Act to possess that controlled substance.

    (B)   The total number of dosage units of controlled substances distributed by a pharmacy may not exceed 5.0% of all controlled substances dispensed by the pharmacy during the 12-month period in which the pharmacy is registered; if at any time it does exceed 5.0%, the pharmacy is required to obtain an additional registration to distribute controlled substances.

    (C)   If the distribution is for a Schedule III, IV, or V controlled substance, a record shall be maintained which indicates:

        (i)   the actual date of distribution;

        (ii)   the name, strength, and quantity of controlled substances distributed;

        (iii)   the name, address, and DEA registration number of the distributing pharmacy; and

        (iv)   the name, address, and DEA registration number of the pharmacy, practitioner, or other registrant to whom the controlled substances are distributed.

    (D)   If the distribution is for a Schedule II controlled substance, the following is applicable.

        (i)   The pharmacy, practitioner, or other registrant who is receiving the controlled substances shall issue Copy 1 and Copy 2 of a DEA order form (DEA 222) to the distributing pharmacy.

        (ii)   The distributing pharmacy shall:

            (I)   complete the area on the DEA order form (DEA 222) titled "To Be Filled in by Supplier";

            (II)   maintain Copy 1 of the DEA order form (DEA 222) at the pharmacy for two years; and

            (III)   forward Copy 2 of the DEA order form (DEA 222) to the divisional office of DEA.

  (5)   Other records. Other records to be maintained by the pharmacy include:

    (A)   a permanent log of the initials or identification codes which identifies each pharmacist by name. The initials or identification code shall be unique to ensure that each pharmacist can be identified, i.e., identical initials or identification codes cannot be used;

    (B)   Copy 3 of DEA order form (DEA 222), which has been properly dated, initialed, and filed, and all copies of each unaccepted or defective order form and any attached statements or other documents and/or for each order filled using the DEA Controlled Substance Ordering System (CSOS), the original signed order and all linked records for that order;

    (C)   a copy of the power of attorney to sign DEA 222 order forms (if applicable);

(D) suppliers' invoices of dangerous drugs and controlled substances dated and initialed or signed by the person receiving the drugs; a pharmacist shall verify that the controlled drugs listed on the invoices were added to the pharmacy's perpetual inventory by clearly recording his/her initials and the date of review of the perpetual inventory;

(E) supplier's credit memos for controlled substances and dangerous drugs;

(F) a copy of inventories required by § 291.17 of this title (relating to Inventory Requirements) except that a perpetual inventory of controlled substances listed in Schedule II may be kept in a data processing system if the data processing system is capable of producing a hard copy of the perpetual inventory on site;

(G) reports of surrender or destruction of controlled substances and/or dangerous drugs to an appropriate state or federal agency;

(H) records of distribution of controlled substances and/or dangerous drugs to other pharmacies, practitioners, or registrants; and

(I) a copy of any notification required by the Texas Pharmacy Act or these rules, including, but not limited to, the following:

    (i) reports of theft or significant loss of controlled substances to DEA and the board;

    (ii) notification of a change in pharmacist-in-charge of a pharmacy; and

    (iii) reports of a fire or other disaster which may affect the strength, purity, or labeling of drugs, medications, devices, or other materials used in the diagnosis or treatment of injury, illness, and disease.

(6) Permission to maintain central records. Any pharmacy that uses a centralized recordkeeping system for invoices and financial data shall comply with the following procedures.

(A) Controlled substance records. Invoices and financial data for controlled substances may be maintained at a central location provided the following conditions are met:

    (i) Prior to the initiation of central recordkeeping, the pharmacy submits written notification by registered or certified mail to the divisional director of DEA as required by the Code of Federal Regulations, Title 21, § 1304(a), and submits a copy of this written notification to the board. Unless the registrant is informed by the divisional director of DEA that permission to keep central records is denied, the pharmacy may maintain central records commencing 14 days after receipt of notification by the divisional director;

    (ii) The pharmacy maintains a copy of the notification required in this subparagraph; and

    (iii) The records to be maintained at the central record location shall not include executed DEA order forms, prescription drug orders, or controlled substance inventories, which shall be maintained at the pharmacy.

(B) Dangerous drug records. Invoices and financial data for dangerous drugs may be maintained at a central location.

(C) Access to records. If the records are kept on microfilm, computer media, or in any form requiring special equipment to render the records easily readable, the pharmacy shall provide access to such equipment with the records.

(D) Delivery of records. The pharmacy agrees to deliver all or any part of such records to the pharmacy location within two business days of written request of a board agent or any other authorized official.

Source: The provisions of this § 291.151 adopted to be effective March 11, 2010, 35 TexReg 2005; amended to be effective September 14, 2010, 35 TexReg 8358; amended to be effective March 10, 2011, 36 TexReg 1547; amended to be effective September 11, 2014, 39 TexReg 7129; amended to be effective December 6, 2015, 40 TexReg 8780; amended to be effective September 11, 2016, 41 TexReg 6737; amended to be effective June 7, 2018, 43 TexReg 3592; amended to be effective June 20, 2019, 44 TexReg 2952

§291.153 Central Prescription Drug or Medication Order Processing Pharmacy (Class G)

(a) Purpose.

(1) The purpose of this section is to provide standards for a centralized prescription drug or medication order processing pharmacy.

(2) Any facility established for the primary purpose of processing prescription drug or medication drug orders shall be licensed as a Class G pharmacy under the Act. A Class G pharmacy shall not store bulk drugs, or dispense a prescription drug order. Nothing in this subsection shall prohibit an individual pharmacist employee, individual pharmacy technician employee, or individual pharmacy technician trainee employee who is licensed in Texas from remotely accessing the pharmacy's electronic data base from a location other than a licensed pharmacy in order to process prescription or medication drug orders, provided the pharmacy establishes controls to protect the privacy and security of confidential records, and the Texas-licensed pharmacist, pharmacy technician, or pharmacy technician trainee does not engage in the receiving of written prescription or medication orders or the maintenance of prescription or medication drug orders at the non-licensed remote location.

(b) Definitions. The following words and terms, when used in this section, shall have the following meanings, unless the context clearly indicates otherwise. Any term not defined in this section shall have the definition set out in the Act.

(1) Centralized prescription drug or medication order processing—The processing of a prescription drug or medication orders by a Class G pharmacy on behalf of another pharmacy, a health care provider, or a payor. Centralized prescription drug or medication order processing does not include the dispensing of a prescription drug but includes any of the following:

(A) receiving, interpreting, or clarifying prescription drug or medication drug orders;

(B) data entering and transferring of prescription drug or medication order information;

(C) performing drug regimen review;

(D) obtaining refill and substitution authorizations;

(E) verifying accurate prescription data entry;

(F) interpreting clinical data for prior authorization for dispensing;

(G) performing therapeutic interventions; and

(H) providing drug information concerning a patient's prescription.

(2) Full-time pharmacist—A pharmacist who works in a pharmacy from 30 to 40 hours per week or, if the pharmacy is open less than 60 hours per week, one-half of the time the pharmacy is open.

(c) Personnel.

(1) Pharmacist-in-charge.

(A) General. Each Class G pharmacy shall have one pharmacist-in-charge who is employed on a full-time basis, who may be the pharmacist-in-charge for only one such pharmacy.

    (B) Responsibilities. The pharmacist-in-charge shall have responsibility for the practice of pharmacy at the pharmacy for which he or she is the pharmacist-in-charge. The pharmacist-in-charge may advise the owner on administrative or operational concerns. The pharmacist-in-charge shall have responsibility for, at a minimum, the following:

        (i) educating and training pharmacy technicians and pharmacy technician trainees;

        (ii) maintaining records of all transactions of the Class G pharmacy required by applicable state and federal laws and sections;

        (iii) adhering to policies and procedures regarding the maintenance of records in a data processing system such that the data processing system is in compliance with Class G pharmacy requirements; and

        (iv) legally operating the pharmacy, including meeting all inspection and other requirements of all state and federal laws or sections governing the practice of pharmacy.

  (2) Owner. The owner of a Class G pharmacy shall have responsibility for all administrative and operational functions of the pharmacy. The pharmacist-in-charge may advise the owner on administrative and operational concerns. The owner shall have responsibility for, at a minimum, the following, and if the owner is not a Texas licensed pharmacist, the owner shall consult with the pharmacist-in-charge or another Texas licensed pharmacist:

    (A) providing the pharmacy with the necessary equipment and resources commensurate with its level and type of practice; and

    (B) establishing policies and procedures regarding maintenance, storage, and retrieval of records in a data processing system such that the system is in compliance with state and federal requirements.

  (3) Pharmacists.

    (A) General.

        (i) The pharmacist-in-charge shall be assisted by sufficient number of additional licensed pharmacists as may be required to operate the Class G pharmacy competently, safely, and adequately to meet the needs of the patients of the pharmacy.

        (ii) All pharmacists shall assist the pharmacist-in-charge in meeting his or her responsibilities.

        (iii) Pharmacists are solely responsible for the direct supervision of pharmacy technicians and pharmacy technician trainees and for designating and delegating duties, other than those listed in subparagraph (B) of this paragraph, to pharmacy technicians and pharmacy technician trainees. Each pharmacist shall be responsible for any delegated act performed by pharmacy technicians and pharmacy technician trainees under his or her supervision.

        (iv) Pharmacists shall directly supervise pharmacy technicians and pharmacy technician trainees who are entering prescription data into the pharmacy's data processing system by one of the following methods.

            (I) Physically present supervision. A pharmacist shall be physically present to directly supervise a pharmacy technician or pharmacy technician trainee who is entering prescription order or medication order data into the data processing system. Each prescription or medication order entered into the data processing system shall be verified at the time of data entry.

            (II) Electronic supervision. A pharmacist may electronically supervise a pharmacy technician or pharmacy technician trainee who is entering prescription order or medication order data into the data processing system provided the pharmacist:

                (-a-) the pharmacist has the ability to immediately communicate directly with the technician/trainee;

                (-b-) has immediate access to any original document containing prescription or medication order information or other information related to the dispensing of the prescription or medication order. Such access may be through imaging technology provided the pharmacist has the ability to review the original, hardcopy documents if needed for clarification; and

                (-c-) verifies the accuracy of the data entered information prior to the release of the information to the system for storage.

            (III) Electronic verification of data entry by pharmacy technicians or pharmacy technician trainees. A pharmacist may electronically verify the data entry of prescription information into a data processing system provided:

                (-a-) the pharmacist has the ability to immediately communicate directly with the technician/trainee;

                (-b-) the pharmacist electronically conducting the verification is either a:

                    (-1-) Texas licensed pharmacist; or

                    (-2-) pharmacist employed by a Class E pharmacy that has the same owner as the Class G pharmacy where the pharmacy technicians/trainees are located or that has entered into a written contract or agreement with the Class G pharmacy, which outlines the services to be provided and the responsibilities and accountabilities of each pharmacy in compliance with federal and state laws and regulations;

                (-c-) the pharmacy establishes controls to protect the privacy and security of confidential records; and

                (-d-) the pharmacy keeps permanent records of prescriptions electronically verified for a period of two years.

        (v) All pharmacists while on duty, shall be responsible for complying with all state and federal laws or rules governing the practice of pharmacy.

    (B) Duties. Duties which may only be performed by a pharmacist are as follows:

        (i) receiving oral prescription drug or medication orders and reducing these orders to writing, either manually or electronically;

        (ii) interpreting prescription drug or medication orders;

        (iii) selecting drug products;

        (iv) verifying the data entry of the prescription drug or medication order information at the time of data entry prior to the release of the information to a Class A, Class C, or Class E pharmacy for dispensing;

        (v) communicating to the patient or patient's agent information about the prescription drug or device which in the exercise of the pharmacist's professional judgment, the pharmacist deems significant, as specified in § 291.33(c) of this title (relating to Operational Standards);

        (vi) communicating to the patient or the patient's agent on his or her request information concerning any prescription drugs dispensed to the patient by the pharmacy;

        (vii) assuring that a reasonable effort is made to obtain, record, and maintain patient medication records; and

        (viii) interpreting patient medication records and performing drug regimen reviews.

    (4) Pharmacy Technicians and Pharmacy Technician Trainees.

        (A) General. All pharmacy technicians and pharmacy technician trainees shall meet the training requirements specified in § 297.6 of this title (relating to Pharmacy Technician and Pharmacy Technician Trainee Training).

        (B) Duties.

            (i) Pharmacy technicians and pharmacy technician trainees may not perform any of the duties listed in paragraph (3)(B) of this subsection.

            (ii) A pharmacist may delegate to pharmacy technicians and pharmacy technician trainees any nonjudgmental technical duty associated with the preparation and distribution of prescription drugs provided:

                (I) a pharmacist verifies the accuracy of all acts, tasks, and functions performed by pharmacy technicians and pharmacy technician trainees;

                (II) pharmacy technicians and pharmacy technician trainees are under the direct supervision of and responsible to a pharmacist; and

            (iii) Pharmacy technicians and pharmacy technician trainees may perform only nonjudgmental technical duties associated with the preparation of prescription drugs, as follows:

                (I) initiating and receiving refill authorization requests; and

                (II) entering prescription or medication order data into a data processing system.

        (C) Ratio of on-site pharmacists to pharmacy technicians and pharmacy technician trainees. A Class G pharmacy may have a ratio of on-site pharmacists to pharmacy technicians and pharmacy technician trainees of 1:8 provided:

            (i) at least seven are pharmacy technicians and not pharmacy technician trainees; and

            (ii) the pharmacy has written policies and procedures regarding the supervision of pharmacy technicians and pharmacy technician trainees.

    (5) Identification of pharmacy personnel. All pharmacy personnel shall be identified as follows.

        (A) Pharmacy technicians. All pharmacy technicians shall wear an identification tag or badge that bears the person's name and identifies him or her as a pharmacy technician, or a certified pharmacy technician, if the technician maintains current certification with the Pharmacy Technician Certification Board or any other entity providing an examination approved by the board.

        (B) Pharmacy technician trainees. All pharmacy technician trainees shall wear an identification tag or badge that bears the person's name and identifies him or her as a pharmacy technician trainee.

        (C) Pharmacist interns. All pharmacist interns shall wear an identification tag or badge that bears the person's name and identifies him or her as a pharmacist intern.

        (D) Pharmacists. All pharmacists shall wear an identification tag or badge that bears the person's name and identifies him or her as a pharmacist.

(d) Operational Standards.

    (1) General requirements.

        (A) A Class A, Class C, or Class E Pharmacy may outsource prescription drug or medication order processing to a Class G pharmacy provided the pharmacies:

            (i) have:

                (I) the same owner; or

                (II) entered into a written contract or agreement which outlines the services to be provided and the responsibilities and accountabilities of each pharmacy in compliance with federal and state laws and regulations; and

            (ii) share a common electronic file or have appropriate technology to allow access to sufficient information necessary or required to perform a non-dispensing function.

        (B) A Class G pharmacy shall comply with the provisions applicable to the class of pharmacy contained in either §§ 291.31 - 291.35 of this title (relating to Definitions, Personnel, Operational Standards, Records, and Official Prescription Requirements in Class A (Community) Pharmacies), or §§ 291.72 - 291.75 of this title (relating to Definitions, Personnel, Operational Standards, and Records in a Class C (Institutional) Pharmacy), or §§ 291.102 - 291.105 of this title (relating to Definitions, Personnel, Operational Standards, and Records in a Class E (Non-Resident) Pharmacy) to the extent applicable for the specific processing activity and this section including:

            (i) duties which must be performed by a pharmacist; and

            (ii) supervision requirements for pharmacy technicians and pharmacy technician trainees.

    (2) Licensing requirements.

        (A) A Class G pharmacy shall register with the board on a pharmacy license application provided by the board, following the procedures specified in § 291.1 of this title (relating to Pharmacy License Application).

        (B) A Class G pharmacy which changes ownership shall notify the board within 10 days of the change of ownership and apply for a new and separate license as specified in § 291.3 of this title (relating to Required Notifications).

        (C) A Class G pharmacy which changes location and/or name shall notify the board of the change within 10 days and file for an amended license as specified in § 291.3 of this title.

        (D) A Class G pharmacy owned by a partnership or corporation which changes managing officers shall notify the board in writing of the names of the new managing officers within 10 days of the change, following the procedures in § 291.3 of this title.

        (E) A Class G pharmacy shall notify the board in writing within 10 days of closing, following the procedures in § 291.5 of this title (relating to Closing a Pharmacy).

        (F) A fee as specified in § 291.6 of this title (relating to Pharmacy License Fees) will be charged for issuance and renewal of a license and the issuance of an amended license.

        (G) A separate license is required for each principal place of business and only one pharmacy license may be issued to a specific location.

Phr. Rules

(3) Environment.
   (A) General requirements.
      (i) The pharmacy shall be arranged in an orderly fashion and kept clean. All required equipment shall be in good operating condition.
      (ii) The pharmacy shall be properly lighted and ventilated.
   (B) Security.
      (i) Each pharmacist while on duty shall be responsible for the security of the prescription department, including provisions for effective control against theft or diversion of prescription drug records.
      (ii) Pharmacies shall employ appropriate measures to ensure that security of prescription drug records is maintained at all times to prohibit unauthorized access.
(4) Policy and Procedures. A policy and procedure manual shall be maintained by the Class G pharmacy and be available for inspection. The manual shall:
   (A) outline the responsibilities of each of the pharmacies;
   (B) include a list of the name, address, telephone numbers, and all license/registration numbers of the pharmacies involved in centralized prescription drug or medication order processing; and
   (C) include policies and procedures for:
      (i) protecting the confidentiality and integrity of patient information;
      (ii) maintaining appropriate records to identify the name(s), initials, or identification code(s) and specific activity(ies) of each pharmacist or pharmacy technician who performed any processing;
      (iii) complying with federal and state laws and regulations;
      (iv) operating a continuous quality improvement program for pharmacy services designed to objectively and systematically monitor and evaluate the quality and appropriateness of patient care, pursue opportunities to improve patient care, and resolve identified problems; and
      (v) annually reviewing the written policies and procedures and documenting such review.
(e) Records.
   (1) every record required to be kept under the provisions of this section shall be:
      (A) kept by the pharmacy and be available, for at least two years from the date of such inventory or record, for inspecting and copying by the board or its representative and to other authorized local, state, or federal law enforcement agencies; and
      (B) supplied by the pharmacy within 72 hours, if requested by an authorized agent of the Texas State Board of Pharmacy. If the pharmacy maintains the records in an electronic format, the requested records must be provided in a mutually agreeable electronic format if specifically requested by the board or its representative. Failure to provide the records set out in this section, either on site or within 72 hours, constitutes prima facie evidence of failure to keep and maintain records in violation of the Act.
   (2) The pharmacy shall maintain appropriate records which identify, by prescription drug or medication order, the name(s), initials, or identification code(s) of each pharmacist, pharmacy technician, or pharmacy technician trainee who performs a processing function for a prescription drug or medication order. Such records may be maintained:
      (A) separately by each pharmacy and pharmacist; or
      (B) in a common electronic file as long as the records are maintained in such a manner that the data processing system can produce a printout which lists the functions performed by each pharmacy and pharmacist.
   (3) In addition, the pharmacy shall comply with the record keeping requirements applicable to the class of pharmacy to the extent applicable for the specific processing activity and this section.

Source: The provisions of this § 291.153 adopted to be effective January 1, 2011, 35 TexReg 8358; amended to be effective July 11, 2011, 36 TexReg 4413; amended to be effective June 7, 2012, 37 TexReg 4047; amended to be effective March 26, 2014, 39 TexReg 2081; amended to be effective March 7, 2018, 43 TexReg 1278; amended to be effective June 20, 2019, 44 TexReg 2952

§291.155 Limited Prescription Delivery Pharmacy (Class H)
(a) Purpose.
   (1) The purpose of this section is to provide standards for a limited prescription delivery pharmacy.
   (2) Any facility established for the primary purpose of limited prescription delivery by a Class A pharmacy shall be licensed as a Class H pharmacy under the Act. A Class H pharmacy shall not store bulk drugs or dispense a prescription drug order.
   (3) A Class H pharmacy may deliver prescription drug orders for dangerous drugs. A Class H pharmacy may not deliver prescription drug orders for controlled substances.
(b) Definitions. Any term not defined in this chapter shall have the definition set out in the Act, §551.003.
(c) Personnel.
   (1) Pharmacist-in-charge.
      (A) General. Each Class H pharmacy shall have one pharmacist-in-charge who is employed or under written agreement, at least on a part-time basis, but may be employed on a full-time basis, and who may be the pharmacist-in-charge for more than one limited prescription delivery pharmacy.
      (B) Responsibilities. The pharmacist-in-charge shall have responsibility for the practice of pharmacy at the pharmacy for which he or she is the pharmacist-in-charge. The pharmacist-in-charge may advise the owner on administrative or operational concerns. The pharmacist-in-charge shall have responsibility for, at a minimum, the following:
         (i) educating and training pharmacy technicians and pharmacy technician trainees;
         (ii) maintaining records of all transactions of the Class H pharmacy required by applicable state and federal laws and sections;
         (iii) adhering to policies and procedures regarding the maintenance of records; and
         (iv) legally operating the pharmacy, including meeting all inspection and other requirements of all state and federal laws or sections governing the practice of pharmacy.

(2) Owner. The owner of a Class H pharmacy shall have responsibility for all administrative and operational functions of the pharmacy. The pharmacist-in-charge may advise the owner on administrative and operational concerns. The owner shall have responsibility for, at a minimum, the following, and if the owner is not a Texas licensed pharmacist, the owner shall consult with the pharmacist-in-charge or another Texas licensed pharmacist:

    (A) providing the pharmacy with the necessary equipment and resources commensurate with its level and type of practice; and

    (B) establishing policies and procedures regarding maintenance, storage, and retrieval of records in compliance with state and federal requirements.

(3) Pharmacists.

    (A) The pharmacist-in-charge shall be assisted by sufficient number of additional licensed pharmacists as may be required to operate the Class H pharmacy competently, safely, and adequately to meet the needs of the patients of the pharmacy.

    (B) All pharmacists shall assist the pharmacist-in-charge in meeting his or her responsibilities.

    (C) Pharmacists shall be responsible for any delegated act performed by the pharmacy technicians under his or her supervision.

(4) Pharmacy Technicians and Pharmacy Technician Trainees.

    (A) General. All pharmacy technicians and pharmacy technician trainees shall meet the training requirements specified in §297.6 of this title (relating to Pharmacy Technician and Pharmacy Technician Trainee Training).

    (B) Duties. Duties include:

        (i) delivering previously verified prescription drug orders to a patient or patient's agent provided a record of prescriptions delivered is maintained; and

        (ii) maintaining pharmacy records.

(5) Identification of pharmacy personnel. All pharmacy personnel shall be identified as follows:

    (A) Pharmacy technicians. All pharmacy technicians shall wear an identification tag or badge that bears the person's name and identifies him or her as a pharmacy technician, or a certified pharmacy technician, if the technician maintains current certification with the Pharmacy Technician Certification Board or any other entity providing an examination approved by the board.

    (B) Pharmacy technician trainees. All pharmacy technician trainees shall wear an identification tag or badge that bears the person's name and identifies him or her as a pharmacy technician trainee.

    (C) Pharmacist interns. All pharmacist interns shall wear an identification tag or badge that bears the person's name and identifies him or her as a pharmacist intern.

    (D) Pharmacists. All pharmacists shall wear an identification tag or badge that bears the person's name and identifies him or her as a pharmacist.

(d) Operational Standards.

(1) General requirements. A Class A or Class E Pharmacy may outsource limited prescription delivery to a Class H pharmacy provided the pharmacies have entered into a written contract or agreement which outlines the services to be provided and the responsibilities and accountabilities of each pharmacy in compliance with federal and state laws and regulations.

(2) Licensing requirements.

    (A) A Class H pharmacy shall register with the board on a pharmacy license application provided by the board, following the procedures specified in §291.1 of this title (relating to Pharmacy License Application).

    (B) A Class H pharmacy must be owned by a hospital district and located in a county without another pharmacy. If a Class A or Class C pharmacy is established in a county in which a Class H pharmacy has been located under this section, the Class H pharmacy may continue to operate in that county.

    (C) A Class H pharmacy that changes ownership shall notify the board within 10 days of the change of ownership and apply for a new and separate license as specified in §291.3 of this title (relating to Required Notifications).

    (D) A Class H pharmacy that changes location and/or name shall notify the board of the change and file for an amended license as specified in §291.3 of this title.

    (E) A Class H pharmacy shall notify the board in writing within 10 days of closing, following the procedures in §291.5 of this title (relating to Closing a Pharmacy).

    (F) A fee as specified in §291.6 of this title (relating to Pharmacy License Fees) will be charged for issuance and renewal of a license and the issuance of an amended license. However, a pharmacy operated by the state or a political subdivision of the state that qualifies for a Class H license is not required to pay a fee to obtain a license.

    (G) A separate license is required for each principal place of business and only one pharmacy license may be issued to a specific location.

(3) Environment.

    (A) General requirements.

        (i) The pharmacy shall have a designated area for the storage of previously verified prescription drug orders.

        (ii) The pharmacy shall be arranged in an orderly fashion and kept clean.

        (iii) A sink with hot and cold running water shall be available to all pharmacy personnel and shall be maintained in a sanitary condition at all times.

    (B) Security.

        (i) Only authorized personnel may have access to storage areas for dangerous drugs.

        (ii) When a pharmacist, pharmacy technician or pharmacy technician trainee is not present all storage areas for dangerous drugs devices shall be locked by key, combination, or other mechanical or electronic means, so as to prohibit access by unauthorized individuals.

        (iii) The pharmacist-in-charge shall be responsible for the security of all storage areas for dangerous drugs including provisions for adequate safeguards against theft or diversion of dangerous drugs, and records for such drugs.

        (iv) Housekeeping and maintenance duties shall be carried out in the pharmacy, while the pharmacist-in-charge, consultant pharmacist, staff pharmacist, or pharmacy technician/trainee is on the premises.

(4) Library. A reference library shall be maintained that includes current copies of the following in hard copy or electronic format:

    (A) Texas Pharmacy Act and rules;

    (B) Texas Dangerous Drug Act;
    (C) at least one current or updated patient information reference such as:
        (i) United States Pharmacopeia Dispensing Information, Volume II (Advice to the Patient); or
        (ii) a reference text or information leaflets which provide patient information; and
    (D) basic antidote information and the telephone number of the nearest Regional Poison Control Center.
  (5) Delivery of Drugs.
    (A) The pharmacist-in-charge, consultant pharmacist, staff pharmacist, pharmacy technician, or pharmacy technician trainee must be present at the pharmacy to deliver prescriptions.
    (B) Prescriptions for controlled substances may not be stored or delivered by the pharmacy.
    (C) Prescriptions may be stored at the pharmacy for no more than 15 days. If prescriptions are not picked up by the patient, the medications are to be destroyed utilizing a reverse distribution service.
    (D) The pharmacist-in-charge, consultant pharmacist, or staff pharmacist shall personally visit the pharmacy on at least a weekly basis and conduct monthly audits of prescriptions received and delivered by the pharmacy.
(e) Records.
  (1) Every record required to be kept under the provisions this section shall be:
    (A) kept by the pharmacy and be available, for at least two years from the date of such inventory or record, for inspecting and copying by the board or its representative and to other authorized local, state, or federal law enforcement agencies; and
    (B) supplied by the pharmacy within 72 hours, if requested by an authorized agent of the Texas State Board of Pharmacy. If the pharmacy maintains the records in an electronic format, the requested records must be provided in a mutually agreeable electronic format if specifically requested by the board or its representative. Failure to provide the records set out in this section, either on site or within 72 hours, constitutes prima facie evidence of failure to keep and maintain records in violation of the Act.
  (2) A record of on-site visits by the pharmacist-in-charge, consultant pharmacist, or staff pharmacist shall be maintained and include the following information:
    (A) date of the visit;
    (B) pharmacist's evaluation of findings; and
    (C) signature of the visiting pharmacist.
  (3) Records of prescription drug orders delivered to the Class H pharmacy shall include:
    (A) patient name;
    (B) name and quantity of drug delivered;
    (C) name of pharmacy and address delivering the prescription drug order; and
    (D) date received at the Class H pharmacy.
  (4) Records of drugs delivered to a patient or patient's agent shall include:
    (A) patient name;
    (B) name, signature, or electronic signature of the person who picks up the prescription drug;
    (C) date delivered; and
    (D) the name of the drug and quantity delivered.
  (5) Ownership of pharmacy records. For the purposes of these sections, a pharmacy licensed under the Act is the only entity that may legally own and maintain prescription drug records.
Source: The provisions of this § 291.155 adopted to be effective January 1, 2011, 35 TexReg 8362; amended to be effective December 19, 2016, 41 TexReg 9934

CHAPTER 295. PHARMACISTS

§295.1   Change of Address and/or Name
(a) Change of address. A pharmacist shall notify the board in writing within 10 days of a change of address, giving the old and new address and license number.
(b) Change of name.
  (1) A pharmacist shall notify the board in writing within 10 days of a change of name by:
    (A) sending a copy of the official document reflecting the name change (e.g., marriage certificate, divorce decree, etc.); and
    (B) paying a fee of $ 20.
  (2) Pharmacists who change their name may retain the original license to practice pharmacy (wall certificate). However, if the pharmacist wants an amended license (wall certificate) issued which reflects the pharmacist's name change, the pharmacist must:
    (A) return the original license (wall certificate); and
    (B) pay a fee of $ 35.
  (3) An amended electronic renewal certificate reflecting the new name of the pharmacist will be issued by the board without a fee.
Source: The provisions of this § 295.1 adopted to be effective January 1, 1976; amended to be effective February 20, 1991, 16 TEXREG773; amended to be effective January 3, 2000, 24 TexReg 12068; amended to be effective March 15, 2015, 40 TexReg 1089; amended to be effective June 20, 2019, 44 TexReg 2956

§295.2   Change of Employment
(a) A pharmacist shall report in writing to the board within 10 days of a change of employment and be responsible for seeing that his or her name is removed from the pharmacy license of last employment and added to the pharmacy license of new employment.
(b) For the purposes of this section, the term "employment" means the pharmacy at which the pharmacist engages in work on a regular and routine basis, whether remunerative or not, including the practice of pharmacy, administrative or managerial duties, supervisory tasks, or direct or indirect contractual services for pay. The term does not include an isolated case of practicing pharmacy on a temporary basis in order to relieve another pharmacist, unless such isolated cases become regular and routine.

Source: The provisions of this § 295.2 adopted to be effective January 1, 1976; amended to be effective April 3, 1987, 12 TEXREG 953; amended to be effective March 7, 2018, 43 TexReg 1278

§295.3 Responsibility of Pharmacist

(a) The pharmacist-in-charge shall insure that a pharmacy is in compliance with all state and federal laws and rules governing the practice of pharmacy.

(b) All pharmacists while on duty, shall be responsible for complying with all state and federal laws and rules governing the practice of pharmacy.

Source: The provisions of this §295.3 adopted to be effective April 3, 1987, 12 TexReg 953.

§295.4 Sharing Money Received for Prescription

No pharmacist may share or offer to share the money received from a customer for filling a prescription with the practitioner.

Source: The provisions of this §295.4 adopted to be effective January 1, 1976.

§295.5 Pharmacist License or Renewal Fees

(a) Biennial Registration. The Texas State Board of Pharmacy shall require biennial renewal of all pharmacist licenses provided under the Pharmacy Act, § 559.002.

(b) Initial License Fee.
    (1) The fee for the initial license shall be $ 332 for a two-year registration.
    (2) New pharmacist licenses shall be assigned an expiration date and initial fee shall be prorated based on the assigned expiration date.

(c) Renewal Fee. The fee for biennial renewal of a pharmacist license shall be $ 329 for a two-year registration.

(d) Exemption from fee. The license of a pharmacist who has been licensed by the Texas State Board of Pharmacy for at least 50 years or who is at least 72 years old shall be renewed without payment of a fee provided such pharmacist is not actively practicing pharmacy. The renewal certificate of such pharmacist issued by the board shall reflect an inactive status. A person whose license is renewed pursuant to this subsection may not engage in the active practice of pharmacy without first paying the renewal fee as set out in subsection (c) of this section.

Source: The provisions of this § 295.5 adopted to be effective December 23, 2003, 28 TexReg 11263; amended to be effective March 6, 2006, 31 TexReg 1444; amended to be effective November 1, 2006, 31 TexReg 6733; amended to be effective October 1, 2007, 32 TexReg 6374; amended to be effective October 1, 2009, 34 TexReg 6112; amended to be effective September 14, 2010, 35 TexReg 8364; amended to be effective December 1, 2011, 36 TexReg 5847; amended to be effective October 1, 2012, 37 TexReg 6938; amended to be effective January 1, 2014, 38 TexReg 8887; amended to be effective September 11, 2014, 39 TexReg 7138; amended to be effective October 1, 2015, 40 TexReg 6131; amended to be effective January 4, 2018, 42 TexReg 7709; amended to be effective June 20, 2019, 44 TexReg 2956; amended to be effective October 1, 2019, 44 TexReg 4872

§295.6 Emergency Temporary Pharmacist License

(a) Definitions. The following words and terms, when used in this chapter, shall have the following meanings, unless the context clearly indicates otherwise.
    (1) Emergency situation—an emergency caused by a natural or manmade disaster or any other exceptional situation that causes an extraordinary demand for pharmacist services.
    (2) State—One of the 50 United States of America, the District of Columbia, and Puerto Rico.

(b) Emergency Temporary Pharmacist license. In an emergency situation, the board may grant a pharmacist who holds a license to practice pharmacy in another state an emergency temporary pharmacist license to practice in Texas. The following is applicable for the emergency temporary pharmacist license.
    (1) An applicant for an emergency temporary pharmacist license under this section must hold a current pharmacist license in another state and that license and other licenses held by the applicant in any other state may not be suspended, revoked, canceled, surrendered, or otherwise restricted for any reason.
    (2) To qualify for an emergency temporary pharmacist license, the applicant must submit an application including the following information:
        (A) name, address, and phone number of the applicant; and
        (B) any other information the required by the board.
    (3) An emergency temporary pharmacist license shall be valid for a period as determined by the board not to exceed six months. The executive director of the board, in his/her discretion, may renew the license for an additional six months, if the emergency situation still exists.

(c) Exception. This section is not applicable to pharmacists enrolled in a volunteer health registry maintained by the Texas Department of State Health Services.

Source: The provisions of this § 295.6 adopted to be effective March 6, 2006, 31 TexReg 1445; amended to be effective June 11, 2015, 40 TexReg 3666

§295.7 Pharmacist License Renewal

For the purposes of the Act, Chapter 559, Subchapter A.
    (1) A license to practice pharmacy expires on the last day of the assigned expiration month.
    (2) Before the expiration date of the license means the receipt in the board's office of a completed application and renewal fee on or before the last day of the assigned expiration month.
    (3) As specified in §559.003, if the completed application and renewal fee is not received on or before the last day of the assigned expiration month, the person's license to practice pharmacy shall expire. A person shall not practice pharmacy with an expired license. An expired license may be renewed according to the following schedule.

Phr. Rules

    (A) If license has been expired for 90 days or less, the person may become licensed by making application and paying to the board a renewal fee that is equal to one and one-half times the renewal fee for the license as specified in §295.5 of this title (relating to Pharmacist License or Renewal Fees).

    (B) If license has been expired for more than 90 days but less than one year, the person may become licensed by making application and paying to the board a renewal fee that is equal to two times the renewal fee for the license as specified in §295.5 of this title.

    (C) If license has been expired for one year or more, the person shall apply for a new license as specified in §283.10 of this title (relating to Requirements for Application for a Pharmacist License Which Has Expired).

Source: The provisions of this §295.7 adopted to be effective May 28, 1982, 7 TexReg 1857; amended to be effective August 30 1984, 9 TexReg 4451; amended to be effective May 31, 1995, 20 TexReg 1888; amended to be effective January 3, 2000, 24 TexReg 12068; amended to be effective June 13, 2002, 27 TexReg 4947; amended to be effective March 6, 2006, 31 TexReg 1444

§295.8 Continuing Education Requirements

(a) Authority and purpose

    (1) Authority. In accordance with § 559.053 of the Texas Pharmacy Act, (Chapters 551 - 569, Occupations Code), all pharmacists must complete and report 30 contact hours (3.0 CEUs) of approved continuing education obtained during the previous license period in order to renew their license to practice pharmacy.

    (2) Purpose. The board recognizes that the fundamental purpose of continuing education is to maintain and enhance the professional competency of pharmacists licensed to practice in Texas, for the protection of the health and welfare of the citizens of Texas.

(b) Definitions. The following words and terms, when used in this section, shall have the following meanings, unless the context clearly indicates otherwise.

    (1) ACPE—Accreditation Council for Pharmacy Education.

    (2) Act—The Texas Pharmacy Act, Chapters 551 - 569, Occupations Code.

    (3) Approved programs—Live programs, home study, and other mediated instruction delivered by an approved provider or a program specified by the board and listed as an approved program in subsection (e) of this section.

    (4) Approved provider—An individual, institution, organization, association, corporation, or agency that is approved by the board.

    (5) Board—The Texas State Board of Pharmacy.

    (6) Certificate of completion—A certificate or other official document presented to a participant upon the successful completion of an approved continuing education program.

    (7) Contact hour—A unit of measure of educational credit which is equivalent to approximately 60 minutes of participation in an organized learning experience.

    (8) Continuing education unit (CEU)—A unit of measure of education credit which is equivalent to 10 contact hours (i.e., one CEU = 10 contact hours).

    (9) CPE Monitor—A collaborative service from the National Association of Boards of Pharmacy and ACPE that provides an electronic system for pharmacists to track their completed CPE credits.

    (10) Credit hour—A unit of measurement for continuing education equal to 15 contact hours.

    (11) Enduring Materials (Home Study)—Activities that are printed, recorded or computer assisted instructional materials that do not provide for direct interaction between faculty and participants.

    (12) Initial license period—The time period between the date of issuance of a pharmacist's license and the next expiration date following the initial 30 day expiration date. This time period ranges from eighteen to thirty months depending upon the birth month of the licensee.

    (13) License period—The time period between consecutive expiration dates of a license.

    (14) Live programs—Activities that provide for direct interaction between faculty and participants and may include lectures, symposia, live teleconferences, workshops, etc.

    (15) Standardized pharmacy examination—The North American Pharmacy Licensing Examination (NAPLEX).

(c) Methods for obtaining continuing education. A pharmacist may satisfy the continuing education requirements by either:

    (1) successfully completing the number of continuing education hours necessary to renew a license as specified in subsection (a)(1) of this section;

    (2) successfully completing during the preceding license period, one credit hour for each year of their license period, which is a part of the professional degree program in a college of pharmacy the professional degree program of which has been accredited by ACPE; or

    (3) taking and passing the standardized pharmacy examination (NAPLEX) during the preceding license period as a Texas licensed pharmacist, which shall be equivalent to the number of continuing education hours necessary to renew a license as specified in subsection (a)(1) of this section.

(d) Reporting Requirements.

    (1) Renewal of a pharmacist license. To renew a license to practice pharmacy, a pharmacist must report on the renewal application completion of at least thirty contact hours (3.0 CEUs) of continuing education. The following is applicable to the reporting of continuing education contact hours:

        (A) at least one contact hour (0.1 CEU) specified in paragraph (1) of this subsection shall be related to Texas pharmacy laws or rules;

        (B) at least one contact hour (0.1 CEU) specified in paragraph (1) of this subsection shall be related to opioid abuse; and

        (C) any continuing education requirements which are imposed upon a pharmacist as a part of a board order or agreed board order shall be in addition to the requirements of this section.

    (2) Failure to report completion of required continuing education. The following is applicable if a pharmacist fails to report completion of the required continuing education:

        (A) the license of a pharmacist who fails to report completion of the required number of continuing education contact hours shall not be renewed and the pharmacist shall not be issued a renewal certificate for the license period until such time as the pharmacist successfully completes the required continuing education and reports the completion to the board; and

(B) a pharmacist who practices pharmacy without a current renewal certificate is subject to all penalties of practicing pharmacy without a license including the delinquent fees specified in the Act, § 559.003.

(3) Extension of time for reporting. A pharmacist who has had a physical disability, illness, or other extenuating circumstances which prohibits the pharmacist from obtaining continuing education credit during the preceding license period may be granted an extension of time to complete the continued education requirement. The following is applicable for this extension:

(A) the pharmacist shall submit a petition to the board with his/her license renewal application which contains:
  (i) the name, address, and license number of the pharmacist;
  (ii) a statement of the reason for the request for extension;
  (iii) if the reason for the request for extension is health related, a statement from the attending physician(s) treating the pharmacist which includes the nature of the physical disability or illness and the dates the pharmacist was incapacitated; and
  (iv) if the reason for the request for the extension is for other extenuating circumstances, a detailed explanation of the extenuating circumstances and if because of military deployment, documentation of the dates of the deployment;

(B) after review and approval of the petition, a pharmacist may be granted an extension of time to comply with the continuing education requirement which shall not exceed one license renewal period;

(C) an extension of time to complete continuing education credit does not relieve a pharmacist from the continuing education requirement during the current license period; and

(D) if a petition for extension to the reporting period for continuing education is denied, the pharmacist shall:
  (i) have 60 days to complete and report completion of the required continuing education requirements; and
  (ii) be subject to the requirements of paragraph (2) of this subsection relating to failure to report completion of the required continuing education if the required continuing education is not completed and reported within the required 60-day time period.

(4) Exemptions from reporting requirements.

(A) All pharmacists licensed in Texas shall be exempt from the continuing education requirements during their initial license period.

(B) Pharmacists who are not actively practicing pharmacy shall be granted an exemption to the reporting requirements for continuing education provided the pharmacists submit a completed renewal application for each license period which states that they are not practicing pharmacy. Upon submission of the completed renewal application, the pharmacist shall be issued a renewal certificate which states that pharmacist is inactive. Pharmacists who wish to return to the practice of pharmacy after being exempted from the continuing education requirements as specified in this subparagraph must:
  (i) notify the board of their intent to actively practice pharmacy;
  (ii) pay the fee as specified in § 295.9 of this title (relating to Inactive License); and
  (iii) provide copies of completion certificates from approved continuing education programs as specified in subsection (e) of this section for 30 contact hours (3.0 CEUs). Approved continuing education earned within two years prior to the licensee applying for the return to active status may be applied toward the continuing education requirement for reactivation of the license but may not be counted toward subsequent renewal of the license.

(e) Approved Programs.

(1) Any program presented by an ACPE approved provider subject to the following conditions:

(A) pharmacists may receive credit for the completion of the same ACPE course only once during a license period;

(B) pharmacists who present approved ACPE continuing education programs may receive credit for the time expended during the actual presentation of the program. Pharmacists may receive credit for the same presentation only once during a license period; and

(C) proof of completion of an ACPE course shall contain the following information:
  (i) name of the participant;
  (ii) title and completion date of the program;
  (iii) name of the approved provider sponsoring or cosponsoring the program;
  (iv) number of contact hours and/or CEUs awarded;
  (v) the assigned ACPE universal program number and a "P" designation indicating that the CE is targeted to pharmacists; and
  (vi) either:
    (I) a dated certifying signature of the approved provider and the official ACPE logo; or
    (II) the CPE Monitor logo.

(2) Courses which are part of a professional degree program or an advanced pharmacy degree program offered by a college of pharmacy which has a professional degree program accredited by ACPE.

(A) Pharmacists may receive credit for the completion of the same course only once during a license period. A course is equivalent to one credit hour for each year of the renewal period.

(B) Pharmacists who teach these courses may receive credit towards their continuing education, but such credit may be received only once for teaching the same course during a license period.

(3) Basic cardiopulmonary resuscitation (CPR) courses which lead to CPR certification by the American Red Cross or the American Heart Association or its equivalent shall be recognized as approved programs. Pharmacists may receive credit for one contact hour (0.1 CEU) towards their continuing education requirement for completion of a CPR course only once during a license period. Proof of completion of a CPR course shall be the certificate issued by the American Red Cross or the American Heart Association or its equivalent.

(4) Advanced cardiovascular life support courses (ACLS) or pediatric advanced life support (PALS) courses which lead to initial ACLS or PALS certification by the American Heart Association or its equivalent shall be recognized as approved programs. Pharmacists may receive credit for twelve contact hours (1.2 CEUs) towards their continuing education requirement for completion of an ACLS or PALS course only once during a license period. Proof of completion of an ACLS or PALS course shall be the certificate issued by the American Heart Association or its equivalent.

(5) Advanced cardiovascular life support courses (ACLS) or pediatric advanced life support (PALS) courses which lead to ACLS or PALS recertification by the American Heart Association or its equivalent shall be recognized as approved programs. Pharmacists may receive credit for four contact hours (0.4 CEUs) towards their continuing education requirement for completion of an ACLS or PALS recertification course only once during a license period. Proof of completion of an ACLS or PALS recertification course shall be the certificate issued by the American Heart Association or its equivalent.

(6) Attendance at Texas State Board of Pharmacy Board Meetings shall be recognized for continuing education credit as follows:

    (A) pharmacists shall receive credit for three contact hours (0.3 CEUs) towards their continuing education requirement for attending a full, public board business meeting in its entirety;

    (B) a maximum of six contact hours (0.6 CEUs) are allowed for attendance at a board meeting during a license period; and

    (C) proof of attendance for a complete board meeting shall be a certificate issued by the Texas State Board of Pharmacy.

(7) Participation in a Texas State Board of Pharmacy appointed Task Force shall be recognized for continuing education credit as follows:

    (A) pharmacists shall receive credit for three contact hours (0.3 CEUs) towards their continuing education requirement for participating in a Texas State Board of Pharmacy appointed Task Force; and

    (B) proof of participation for a Task Force shall be a certificate issued by the Texas State Board of Pharmacy.

(8) Attendance at programs presented by the Texas State Board of Pharmacy or courses offered by the Texas State Board of Pharmacy as follows:

    (A) pharmacists shall receive credit for the number of hours for the program or course as stated by the Texas State Board of Pharmacy; and

    (B) proof of attendance at a program presented by the Texas State Board of Pharmacy or completion of a course offered by the Texas State Board of Pharmacy shall be a certificate issued by the Texas State Board of Pharmacy.

(9) Pharmacists shall receive credit toward their continuing education requirements for programs or courses approved by other state boards of pharmacy as follows:

    (A) pharmacists shall receive credit for the number of hours for the program or course as specified by the other state board of pharmacy; and

    (B) proof of attendance at a program or course approved by another state board of pharmacy shall be a certificate or other documentation that indicates:

        (i) name of the participant;

        (ii) title and completion date of the program;

        (iii) name of the approved provider sponsoring or cosponsoring the program;

        (iv) number of contact hours and/or CEUs awarded;

        (v) a dated certifying signature of the provider; and

        (vi) documentation that the program is approved by the other state board of pharmacy.

(10) Completion of an Institute for Safe Medication Practices' (ISMP) Medication Safety Self Assessment for hospital pharmacies or for community/ambulatory pharmacies shall be recognized for continuing education credit as follows:

    (A) pharmacists shall receive credit for three contact hours (0.3 CEUs) towards their continuing education requirement for completion of an ISMP Medication Safety Self Assessment; and

    (B) proof of completion of an ISMP Medication Safety Self Assessment shall be:

        (i) a continuing education certificate provided by an ACPE approved provider for completion of an assessment; or

        (ii) a document from ISMP showing completion of an assessment.

(11) Pharmacist shall receive credit for three contact hours (0.3 CEUs) toward their continuing education requirements for taking and successfully passing an initial Board of Pharmaceutical Specialties certification examination administered by the Board of Pharmaceutical Specialties. Proof of successfully passing the examination shall be a certificate issued by the Board of Pharmaceutical Specialties.

(12) Programs approved by the American Medical Association (AMA) as Category 1 Continuing Medical Education (CME) and accredited by the Accreditation Council for Continuing Medical Education subject to the following conditions:

    (A) pharmacists may receive credit for the completion of the same CME course only once during a license period;

    (B) pharmacists who present approved CME programs may receive credit for the time expended during the actual presentation of the program. Pharmacists may receive credit for the same presentation only once during a license period; and

    (C) proof of completion of a CME course shall contain the following information:

        (i) name of the participant;

        (ii) title and completion date of the program;

        (iii) name of the approved provider sponsoring or cosponsoring the program;

        (iv) number of contact hours and/or CEUs awarded; and

        (v) a dated certifying signature of the approved provider.

(f) Retention of continuing education records and audit of records by the board.

    (1) Retention of records. Pharmacists are required to maintain certificates of completion of approved continuing education for three years from the date of reporting the contact hours on a license renewal application. Such records may be maintained in hard copy or electronic format.

    (2) Audit of records by the board. The board shall audit the records of pharmacists for verification of reported continuing education credit. The following is applicable for such audits:

        (A) upon written request, a pharmacist shall provide to the board documentation of proof for all continuing education contact hours reported during a specified license period(s). Failure to provide all requested records during the specified time period constitutes prima facie evidence of failure to keep and maintain records and shall subject the pharmacist to disciplinary action by the board;

        (B) credit for continuing education contact hours shall only be allowed for approved programs for which the pharmacist submits documentation of proof reflecting that the hours were completed during the specified license period(s). Any other reported hours shall be disallowed. A pharmacist who has received credit for continuing education contact hours disallowed during an audit shall be subject to disciplinary action; and

(C) a pharmacist who submits false or fraudulent records to the board shall be subject to disciplinary action by the board.

Source: The provisions of this § 295.8 adopted to be effective March 19, 1990, 15 TexReg 1234; amended to be effective March 29, 1995, 20 TexReg 1889; amended to be effective March 25, 1999, 24 TexReg 2023; amended to be effective January 3, 2000, 24 TexReg 12068; amended to be effective June 20, 2001, 26 TexReg 4513; amended to be effective December 19, 2001, 26 TexReg 10311; amended to be effective June 23, 2003, 28 TexReg 4639; amended to be effective March 10, 2005, 30 TexReg 1284; amended to be effective November 21, 2007, 32 TexReg 8310; amended to be effective December 14, 2008, 33 TexReg 10027; amended to be effective September 13, 2009, 34 TexReg 6113; amended to be effectiveMarch 10, 2011, 36 TexReg 1556; amended to be effective September 9, 2012, 37 TexReg 6938; amended to be effective March 17, 2013, 38 TexReg 1682; amended to be effective March 7, 2018, 43 TexReg 1279; amended to be effective September 10, 2019, 44 TexReg 4873

§295.9   Inactive License

(a) Placing a license on inactive status. A person who is licensed by the board to practice pharmacy but who is not eligible to renew the license for failure to comply with the continuing education requirements of the Act, Chapter 559, Subchapter A, and who is not engaged in the practice of pharmacy in this state, may place the license on inactive status at the time of license renewal or during a license period as follows:

    (1) To place a license on inactive status at the time of renewal, the licensee shall:

        (A) complete and submit before the expiration date a pharmacist license renewal application provided by the board;

        (B) state on the renewal application that the license is to be placed on inactive status and that the licensee shall not practice pharmacy in Texas while the license is inactive; and

        (C) pay the fee for renewal of the license as specified in § 295.5 of this title (relating to Pharmacist License or Renewal Fees).

    (2) To place a license on inactive status at a time other than the time of license renewal, the licensee shall:

        (A) return the current renewal certificate to the board;

        (B) submit a signed statement stating that the licensee shall not practice pharmacy in Texas while the license is inactive, and the date the license is to be placed on inactive status; and

        (C) pay the fee for issuance of an amended license as specified in § 295.5(e) of this title (relating to Pharmacist License or Renewal Fees).

(b) Prohibition against practicing pharmacy in Texas with an inactive license. A holder of a license that is on inactive status shall not practice pharmacy in this state. The practice of pharmacy by a holder of a license that is on inactive status constitutes the practice of pharmacy without a license.

(c) Reactivation of an inactive license.

    (1) A holder of a license that is on inactive status may return the license to active status by:

        (A) applying for active status on a form prescribed by the board;

        (B) providing copies of completion certificates from approved continuing education programs as specified in § 295.8(e) of this title (relating to Continuing Education Requirements) for 30 hours including at least one contact hour (0.1 CEU) shall be related to Texas pharmacy laws or rules and at least one contact hour (0.1 CEU) shall be related to opioid abuse. Approved continuing education earned within two years prior to the licensee applying for the return to active status may be applied toward the continuing education requirement for reactivation of the license but may not be counted toward subsequent renewal of the license; and

        (C) paying the fee specified in paragraph (2) of this subsection.

    (2) If the application for reactivation of the license is made at the time of license renewal, the applicant shall pay the license renewal fee specified in § 295.5 of this title (relating to Pharmacist License or Renewal Fees). If the application for reactivation of the license is made at a time other than the time of license renewal, the applicant shall pay the fee for issuance of an amended license to practice pharmacy as specified in § 295.5(e) of this title (relating to Pharmacist License or Renewal Fees).

    (3) In an emergency caused by a natural or manmade disaster or any other exceptional situation that causes an extraordinary demand for pharmacist services, the executive director of the board, in his/her discretion, may allow a pharmacist whose license has been inactive for no more than two years to reactivate their license prior to obtaining the required continuing education specified in paragraph (1)(B) of this subsection, provided the pharmacist completes the continuing education requirement within six months of reactivation of the license. If the required continuing education is not provided within six months, the license shall return to an inactive status.

Source: The provisions of this § 295.9 adopted to be effective May 6, 1993, 18 TexReg 2625; amended to be effective January 3, 2000, 24 TexReg 12068; amended to be effective June 13, 2002, 27 TexReg 4947; amended to be effective March 6, 2006, 31 TexReg 1445; amended to be effective September 18, 2007, 32 TexReg 6375; amended to be effective June 11, 2015, 40 TexReg 3666; amended to be effective September 16, 2018, 43 TexReg 5804

§295.11 Notification to Consumers

(a) Pharmacist. Every pharmacist who practices pharmacy other than in a licensed pharmacy shall provide notification to consumers of the name, mailing address, internet site address and telephone number of the board for the purpose of directing complaints concerning the practice of pharmacy to the board. Such notification shall be provided as follows.

    (1) If the pharmacist maintains an office and provides pharmacy services to patients who come to the office, the pharmacist shall either:

        (A) post in a prominent place that is in clear public view where pharmacy services are provided:

            (i) a sign which notifies the consumer that complaints concerning the practice of pharmacy may be filed with the board and list the board's mailing address, internet site address, telephone number, and a toll-free telephone number for filing complaints; or

            (ii) an electronic messaging system in a type size no smaller than ten-point Times Roman which notifies the consumer that complaints concerning the practice of pharmacy may be filed with the board and list the board's name, mailing address, internet site address, and a toll-free number for filing complaints; or

      (B) provide to the patient each time pharmacy services are provided a written notification in type size no smaller than ten-point Times Roman which states the following: "Complaints concerning the practice of pharmacy may be filed with the Texas State Board of Pharmacy at: (list the mailing address, internet site address, telephone number of the board, and a toll-free telephone number for filing complaints)."

    (2) If the pharmacist provides pharmacy services to patients not at the pharmacist's office, the pharmacist shall provide to the patient each time pharmacy services are provided, a written notification in type size no smaller than ten-point Times Roman which states the following: "Complaints concerning the practice of pharmacy may be filed with the Texas State Board of Pharmacy at: (list the mailing address, telephone number of the board, internet site address, and a toll-free telephone number for filing complaints)." Such notification shall be included:

      (A) in each written contract for pharmacist services; or

      (B) on each bill for service provided by the pharmacist.

    (3) The provisions of this section do not apply to prescriptions for patients in facilities where drugs are administered to patients by a person required to do so by the laws of the state (i.e., nursing homes).

(b) Texas State Board of Pharmacy. On or before January 1, 2005, the board shall establish a pharmacist profile system as specified in § 2054.2606, Government Code.

    (1) The board shall make the pharmacist profiles available to the public on the agency's internet site

    (2) A pharmacist profile shall contain at least the following information:

      (A) pharmacist's name;

      (B) pharmacist's license number, licensure status, and expiration date of the license;

      (C) name, address, telephone number, and license number of all Texas pharmacies where the pharmacist works;

      (D) the number of years the person has practiced in Texas;

      (E) professional pharmacy degree held by the licensee, the year it was received, and the name of the institution that awarded the degree;

      (F) whether the pharmacist is preceptor;

      (G) any speciality certification held by the pharmacist; and

      (H) whether the pharmacist has had prior disciplinary action by the board.

    (3) The board shall gather this information on initial licensing and update the information in conjunction with the license renewal for the pharmacist.

Source: The provisions of this § 295.11 adopted to be effective April 1, 1994, 19 TexReg 1829; amended to be effective December 19, 2001, 26 TexReg 10312; amended to be effective September 16, 2018, 43 TexReg 5805

§295.12 Pharmacist Certification Programs

(a) Purpose. The purpose of this section is to provide standards for the recognition and approval of pharmacist certification programs as authorized by §554.0021, Occupations Code.

(b) Definitions. The following words and terms, when used in this section, shall have the following meanings, unless the context clearly indicates otherwise.

    (1) ACPE—The Accreditation Council for Pharmacy Education.

    (2) Approved Provider of Pharmacist Certificate Programs—An individual, institution, organization, association, corporation, or agency that is approved by the board and recognized by ACPE in accordance with its policy and procedures, as having:

      (A) met criteria indicative of the ability to provide quality continuing education programs; and

      (B) met the procedures outlines in the ACPE "Guidance Document for Practice Based Activities."

    (3) Board—The Texas State Board of Pharmacy.

(c) Board Certified Pharmacists.

    (1) The board shall recognize as certified, any pharmacist that successfully completes:

      (A) any program offered by an approved provider of pharmacist certificate programs;

      (B) any program that meets the requirements of §295.15 of this title (relating to Administration of Immunizations or Vaccinations by a Pharmacist under Written Protocol of a Physician);

      (C) any certification offered by the:

        (i) Board of Pharmaceutical Specialties;

        (ii) American Society of Consultant Pharmacists;

        (iii) American Board of Clinical Pharmacology;

        (iv) American Board of Applied Toxicology; and

        (v) American Academy of Pain Management; or

      (D) any additional certifications as published on the board's website.

    (2) Texas pharmacists may not identify themselves as certified unless they have completed one of the programs specified in paragraph (1) of this subsection.

Source: The provisions of this §295.12 adopted to be effective December 19, 2001, 26 TexReg 10312; amended to be effective December 10, 2013, 38 TexReg 8888

§295.13 Drug Therapy Management by a Pharmacist under Written Protocol of a Physician

(a) Purpose. The purpose of this section is to provide standards for the maintenance of records of a pharmacist engaged in the provision of drug therapy management as authorized in Chapter 157 of the Medical Practice Act and §554.005 of the Act.

(b) Definitions. The following words and terms, when used in this section, shall have the following meanings, unless the context clearly indicates otherwise.

    (1) Act—The Texas Pharmacy Act, Chapter 551 – 566 and 568 – 569, Occupations Code, as amended.

    (2) Board—The Texas State Board of Pharmacy.

    (3) Confidential record—Any health-related record maintained by a pharmacy or pharmacist, such as a patient medication record, prescription drug order, or medication order.

(4) Drug therapy management—The performance of specific acts by pharmacists as authorized by a physician through written protocol. Drug therapy management does not include the selection of drug products not prescribed by the physician, unless the drug product is named in the physician initiated protocol or the physician initiated record of deviation from a standing protocol. Drug therapy management may include the following:

    (A) collecting and reviewing patient drug use histories;

    (B) ordering or performing routine drug therapy related patient assessment procedures including temperature, pulse, and respiration;

    (C) ordering drug therapy related laboratory tests;

    (D) implementing or modifying drug therapy following diagnosis, initial patient assessment, and ordering of drug therapy by a physician as detailed in the protocol; or

    (E) any other drug therapy related act delegated by a physician.

(5) Medical Practice Act—The Texas Medical Practice Act, Subtitle B, Occupations Code, as amended.

(6) Written protocol—A physician's order, standing medical order, standing delegation order, or other order or protocol as defined by rule of the Texas State Board of Medical Examiners under the Medical Practice Act.

    (A) A written protocol must contain at a minimum the following:

        (i) a statement identifying the individual physician authorized to prescribe drugs and responsible for the delegation of drug therapy management;

        (ii) a statement identifying the individual pharmacist authorized to dispense drugs and to engage in drug therapy management as delegated by the physician;

        (iii) a statement identifying the types of drug therapy management decisions that the pharmacist is authorized to make which shall include:

            (I) a statement of the ailments or diseases involved, drugs, and types of drug therapy management authorized; and

            (II) a specific statement of the procedures, decision criteria, or plan the pharmacist shall follow when exercising drug therapy management authority;

        (iv) a statement of the activities the pharmacist shall follow in the course of exercising drug therapy management authority, including the method for documenting decisions made and a plan for communication or feedback to the authorizing physician concerning specific decisions made. Documentation shall be recorded within a reasonable time of each intervention and may be performed on the patient medication record, patient medical chart, or in a separate log book; and

        (v) a statement that describes appropriate mechanisms and time schedule for the pharmacist to report to the physician monitoring the pharmacist's exercise of delegated drug therapy management and the results of the drug therapy management.

    (B) A standard protocol may be used or the attending physician may develop a drug therapy management protocol for the individual patient. If a standard protocol is used, the physician shall record what deviations, if any, from the standard protocol are ordered for that patient.

(c) Physician delegation to a pharmacist.

    (1) As specified in Chapter 157 of the Texas Medical Practices Act, a physician may delegate to a properly qualified and trained pharmacist acting under adequate physician supervision the performance of specific acts of drug therapy management authorized by the physician through the physician's order, standing medical order, standing delegation order, or other order or protocol.

    (2) A delegation under paragraph (1) of this subsection may include the implementation or modification of a patient's drug therapy under a protocol, including the authority to sign a prescription drug order for dangerous drugs, if:

        (A) the delegation follows a diagnosis, initial patient assessment, and drug therapy order by the physician;

        (B) the pharmacist practices in a hospital, hospital-based clinic, or an academic health care institution; and

        (C) the hospital, hospital-based clinic, or academic health care institution in which the pharmacist practices has bylaws and a medical staff policy that permit a physician to delegate to a pharmacist the management of a patient's drug therapy.

    (3) A pharmacist who signs a prescription for a dangerous drug under authority granted under paragraph (2) of this subsection shall:

        (A) notify the board that a physician has delegated the authority to sign a prescription for dangerous drugs. Such notification shall:

            (i) be made on an application provided by the board;

            (ii) occur prior to signing any prescription for a dangerous drug;

            (iii) be updated annually; and

            (iv) include a copy of the written protocol.

        (B) include the pharmacist's name, address, and telephone number as well as the name, address, and telephone number of the delegating physician on each prescription for a dangerous drug signed by the pharmacist.

    (4) The board shall post the following information on its web-site:

        (A) the name and license number of each pharmacist who has notified the board that a physician has delegated authority to sign a prescription for a dangerous drug;

        (B) the name and address of the physician who delegated the authority to the pharmacist; and

        (C) the expiration date of the protocol granting the authority to sign a prescription.

(d) Pharmacist Training Requirements.

    (1) Initial requirements. A pharmacist shall maintain and provide to the Board within 24 hours of request a statement attesting to the fact that the pharmacist has within the last year:

        (A) completed at least six hours of continuing education related to drug therapy offered by a provider approved by the Accreditation Council for Pharmacy Education (ACPE); or

        (B) engaged in drug therapy management as allowed under previous laws or rules. A statement from the physician supervising the acts shall be sufficient documentation.

    (2)   Continuing requirements. A pharmacist engaged in drug therapy management shall annually complete six hours of continuing education related to drug therapy offered by a provider approved by the Accreditation Council for Pharmacy Education (ACPE). (These hours may be applied towards the hours required for renewal of a license to practice pharmacy.)

(e) Supervision. Physician supervision shall be as specified in the Medical Practice Act, Chapter 157 and shall be considered adequate if the delegating physician:

    (1)   is responsible for the formulation or approval of the written protocol and any patient-specific deviations from the protocol and review of the written protocol and any patient-specific deviations from the protocol at least annually and the services provided to a patient under the protocol on a schedule defined in the written protocol;

    (2)   has established and maintains a physician-patient relationship with each patient provided drug therapy management by a delegated pharmacist and informs the patient that drug therapy will be managed by a pharmacist under written protocol;

    (3)   is geographically located so as to be able to be physically present daily to provide medical care and supervision;

    (4)   receives, on a schedule defined in the written protocol, a periodic status report on the patient, including any problem or complication encountered;

    (5)   is available through direct telecommunication for consultation, assistance, and direction; and

    (6)   determines that the pharmacist to whom the physician is delegating drug therapy management establishes and maintains a pharmacist-patient relationship with the patient.

(f) Records.

    (1)   Maintenance of records.

        (A)   Every record required to be kept under this section shall be kept by the pharmacist and be available, for at least two years from the date of such record, for inspecting and copying by the board or its representative and to other authorized local, state, or federal law enforcement or regulatory agencies.

        (B)   Records may be maintained in an alternative data retention system, such as a data processing system or direct imaging system provided:

            (i)   the records maintained in the alternative system contain all of the information required on the manual record; and

            (ii)   the data processing system is capable of producing a hard copy of the record upon the request of the board, its representative, or other authorized local, state, or federal law enforcement or regulatory agencies.

    (2)   Written protocol.

        (A)   A copy of the written protocol and any patient-specific deviations from the protocol shall be maintained by the pharmacist.

        (B)   A pharmacist shall document all interventions undertaken under the written protocol within a reasonable time of each intervention. Documentation may be maintained in the patient medication record, patient medical chart, or in a separate log.

        (C)   A standard protocol may be used or the attending physician may develop a drug therapy management protocol for the individual patient. If a standard protocol is used, the physician shall record what deviations, if any, from the standard protocol are ordered for that patient. A pharmacist shall maintain a copy of any deviations from the standard protocol ordered by the physician.

        (D)   Written protocols, including standard protocols, any patient-specific deviations from a standard protocol, and any individual patient protocol, shall be reviewed by the physician and pharmacist at least annually and revised if necessary. Such review shall be documented in the pharmacist's records. Documentation of all services provided to the patient by the pharmacist shall be reviewed by the physician on the schedule established in the protocol.

(g) Confidentiality.

    (1)   In addition to the confidentiality requirements specified in §291.27 of this title (relating to Confidentiality) a pharmacist shall comply with:

        (A)   the privacy provisions of the federal Health Insurance Portability and Accountability Act of 1996 (Pub. L. No. 104-191) and any rules adopted pursuant to this act;

        (B)   the requirements of Medical Records Privacy contained in Chapter 181, Health and Safety Code;

        (C)   the Privacy of Health Information requirements contained in Chapter 28B of the Insurance Code; and

        (D)   any other confidentiality provisions of federal or state laws.

    (2)   This section shall not affect or alter the provisions relating to the confidentiality of the physician-patient communication as specified in the Medical Practice Act, Chapter 159.

(h) Construction and Interpretation.

    (1)   As specified in the Medical Practice Act, Chapter 157, this section does not restrict the use of a pre-established health care program or restrict a physician from authorizing the provision of patient care by use of a pre-established health care program if the patient is institutionalized and the care is to be delivered in a licensed hospital with an organized medical staff that has authorized standing delegation orders, standing medical orders, or protocols.

    (2)   As specified in the Medical Practice Act, Chapter 157, this section may not be construed to limit, expand, or change any provision of law concerning or relating to therapeutic drug substitution or administration of medication, including the Act, §554.004.

Source: The provisions of this §295.13 adopted to be effective April 7, 1997, 22 TexReg 3112; amended to be effective December 19, 2001, 26 TexReg 10313; amended to be effective June 12, 2005, 30 TexReg 3209; amended to be effective December 6, 2009, 34 TexReg 8721

§295.14 Dispensing of Opioid Antagonist by Pharmacist

(a) Purpose. The purpose of this section is to provide standards for pharmacists engaged in the dispensing of opioid antagonists as authorized in Chapter 483 of the Health and Safety Code.

(b) Definitions.

    (1)   Opioid antagonist—Any drug that binds to opioid receptors and blocks or otherwise inhibits the effects of opioids acting on those receptors.

    (2)   Opioid-related drug overdose—A condition, evidenced by symptoms such as extreme physical illness, decreased level of consciousness, constriction of the pupils, respiratory depression, or coma, that a layperson would reasonably believe to be the result of the consumption or use of an opioid.

(3) Prescriber—A person authorized by law to prescribe an opioid antagonist.
(c) Dispensing.
  (1) A pharmacist may dispense an opioid antagonist under a valid prescription, including a prescription issued by a standing order, to:
    (A) a person at risk of experiencing an opioid-related drug overdose; or
    (B) a family member, friend, or other person in a position to assist a person described by subparagraph (A) of this paragraph.
  (2) A prescription dispensed under this section is considered as dispensed for a legitimate medical purpose in the usual course of professional practice.
  (3) A pharmacist who, acting in good faith and with reasonable care, dispenses or does not dispense an opioid antagonist under a valid prescription is not subject to any criminal or civil liability or any professional disciplinary action for:
    (A) dispensing or failing to dispense the opioid antagonist; or
    (B) if the pharmacist chooses to dispense an opioid antagonist, any outcome resulting from the eventual administration of the opioid antagonist.

Source: The provisions of this § 295.14 adopted to be effective December 19, 2016, 41 TexReg 9935

§295.15 Administration of Immunizations or Vaccinations by a Pharmacist under Written Protocol of Physician

(a) Purpose. The purpose of this section is to provide standards for pharmacists engaged in the administration of immunizations or vaccinations as authorized in Chapter 554 of the Act.
(b) Definitions. The following words and terms, when used in this section, shall have the following meanings, unless the context clearly indicates otherwise.
  (1) ACPE—The Accreditation Council for Pharmacy Education.
  (2) Act—The Texas Pharmacy Act, Chapter 551 – 566 and 568 – 569, Occupations Code, as amended.
  (3) Administer—The direct application of a prescription drug by injection, inhalation, ingestion, or any other means to the body of a patient by:
    (A) a practitioner, an authorized agent under his supervision, or other person authorized by law; or
    (B) the patient at the direction of a practitioner.
  (4) Antibody—A protein in the blood that is produced in response to stimulation by a specific antigen. Antibodies help destroy the antigen that produced them. Antibodies against an antigen usually equate to immunity to that antigen.
  (5) Antigen—A substance "recognized" by the body as being foreign; it results in the production of specific antibodies directed against it.
  (6) Board—The Texas State Board of Pharmacy.
  (7) Confidential record—Any health-related record that contains information that identifies an individual and that is maintained by a pharmacy or pharmacist such as a patient medication record, prescription drug order, or medication order.
  (8) Data communication device—An electronic device that receives electronic information from one source and transmits or routes it to another (e.g., bridge, router, switch, or gateway).
  (9) Immunization—The act of inducing antibody formation, thus leading to immunity.
  (10) Medical Practice Act—The Texas Medical Practice Act, Subtitle B, Occupations Code, as amended.
  (11) Vaccination—Administration of any antigen in order to induce immunity; is not synonymous with immunization since vaccination does not imply success.
  (12) Vaccine—A specially prepared antigen, which upon administration to a person will result in immunity.
  (13) Written Protocol—A physician's order, standing medical order, standing delegation order, or other order or protocol as defined by rule of the Texas Medical Board under the Medical Practice Act.
    (A) A written protocol must contain, at a minimum, the following:
      (i) a statement identifying the individual physician authorized to prescribe drugs and responsible for the delegation of administration of immunizations or vaccinations;
      (ii) a statement identifying the individual pharmacist authorized to administer immunizations or vaccinations as delegated by the physician;
      (iii) a statement identifying the location(s) (i.e., address) at which the pharmacist may administer immunizations or vaccinations;
      (iv) a statement identifying the immunizations or vaccinations that may be administered by the pharmacist;
      (v) a statement identifying the activities the pharmacist shall follow in the course of administering immunizations or vaccinations, including procedures to follow in the case of reactions following administration; and
      (vi) a statement that describes the content of, and the appropriate mechanisms for the pharmacist to report the administration of immunizations or vaccinations to the physician issuing the written protocol within the time frames specified in this section.
    (B) A standard protocol may be used or the physician may develop an immunization or vaccination protocol for the individual patient. If a standard protocol is used, the physician shall record what deviations, if any, from the standard protocol are ordered for the patient.
(c) Pharmacist certification requirements. Pharmacist who enter into a written protocol with a physician to administer immunizations or vaccinations shall:
  (1) complete a course provided by an ACPE approved provider which:
    (A) requires documentation by the pharmacist of current certification in the American Heart Association's Basic Cardiac Life Support for Health-Care Providers or its equivalent;
    (B) is an evidence-based course which:
      (i) includes study material;
      (ii) includes hands-on training in techniques for administering immunizations or vaccines; and
      (iii) requires testing with a passing score; and

    (C) meets current Center for Disease Control training guidelines and provides a minimum of 20 hours of instruction and experiential training in the following content areas:
        (i) standards for pediatric, adolescent, and adult immunization practices;
        (ii) basic immunology and vaccine protection;
        (iii) vaccine-preventable diseases;
        (iv) recommended immunization schedules (pediatric/adolescent/adult);
        (v) vaccine storage and management;
        (vi) informed consent;
        (vii) physiology and techniques for vaccine administration;
        (viii) pre and post-vaccine assessment and counseling;
        (ix) immunization record management; and
        (x) adverse events:
            (I) identification and appropriate response; and
            (II) documentation and reporting; and
  (2) maintain documentation of:
    (A) completion of the initial course specified in paragraph (1) of this subsection;
    (B) 3 hours of continuing education every 2 years which are designed to maintain competency in the disease states, drugs, and administration of immunizations or vaccinations; and
    (C) current certification in the American Heart Association's Basic Cardiac Life Support for Health-Care Providers or its equivalent.

(d) Supervision. Pharmacists involved in the administration of immunizations or vaccinations shall be under the supervision of a physician. Physician supervision shall be considered adequate if the delegating physician:
  (1) is responsible for the formulation or approval of the physician's order, standing medical order, standing delegation order, or other order or protocol and periodically reviews the order or protocol and the services provided to a patient under the order or protocol;
  (2) has established a physician-patient relationship with each patient under 14 years of age and referred the patient to the pharmacist; except a pharmacist may administer an influenza vaccination to a patient over seven years of age without an established physician-patient relationship;
  (3) is geographically located so as to be easily accessible to the pharmacist administering the immunization or vaccination;
  (4) receives, as appropriate, a periodic status report on the patient, including any problem or complication encountered; and
  (5) is available through direct telecommunication for consultation, assistance, and direction.

(e) Special Provisions. Pharmacists involved in the administration of immunizations or vaccinations under their license to practice pharmacy shall meet the following restrictions and requirements.
  (1) Pharmacists may only administer immunizations or vaccinations pursuant to a written protocol from a physician authorizing the administration.
  (2) Pharmacists may administer immunizations or vaccinations to a patient under 14 years of age only upon a referral from a physician who has an established physician-patient relationship with each patient. However, a pharmacist may administer an influenza vaccination to a patient over seven years of age without an established physician-patient relationship.
  (3) Pharmacists may administer immunizations or vaccinations under written protocol of a physician within a pharmacy or at any other location specifically identified in the written protocol. Such other location may not include where the patient resides, except for a licensed nursing home or hospital.
  (4) The authority of a pharmacist to administer immunizations or vaccinations may not be delegated.
  (5) Pharmacists may administer immunizations and vaccinations only when a licensed health-care provider authorized to administer the medication is not reasonably available to administer the medication. For the purpose of this section, "reasonably available" means those times when the licensed health-care provider is immediately available to administer the immunization or vaccine and is specifically tasked to do so.
  (6) Under the provisions of the National Vaccine Injury Compensation Program (NVICP), the health-care provider under whose authority a covered vaccine is administered (i.e., the physician issuing the written protocol) must maintain certain information in the patient's permanent record. In order for the physician to comply with the provisions of the NVICP, the pharmacist shall provide the physician with the information specified in subsection (g) of this section.
  (7) Before preparing an immunization or vaccine and between each patient contact, the pharmacist shall cleanse his or her hands with an alcohol-based waterless antiseptic hand rub or shall wash his or her hands with soap and water. If gloves are worn, the pharmacist shall change gloves between patients.
  (8) The pharmacist shall comply with all other state and federal requirements regarding immunizations or vaccinations.

(f) Drugs.
  (1) Drugs administered by a pharmacist under the provisions of this section shall be in the legal possession of:
    (A) a pharmacy, which shall be the pharmacy responsible for drug accountability, including the maintenance of records of administration of the immunization or vaccination; or
    (B) a physician who shall be responsible for drug accountability, including the maintenance of records of administration of the immunization or vaccination.
  (2) Drugs shall be transported and stored at the proper temperatures indicated for each drug.
  (3) Pharmacists while actively engaged in the administration of immunizations or vaccinations under written protocol, may have in their custody and control the drugs for immunization or vaccination that are identified in the written protocol and any other dangerous drugs listed in the written protocol to treat adverse reactions.
  (4) After administering immunizations or vaccinations at a location other than a pharmacy, the pharmacist shall return all unused prescription medications to the pharmacy or physician responsible for the drugs.

(g) Notifications.
  (1) A pharmacist engaged in the administration of immunizations or vaccinations shall provide notification of the administration to:
    (A) the physician who issued the written protocol within 24 hours of administering the immunization or vaccination; and

  (B) the primary care physician of the patient, as provided by the patient or patient's agent, within 14 days of administering the immunization or vaccination.

 (2) The notifications required in paragraph (1) of this subsection shall include the:

  (A) name and address of the patient;

  (B) age of the patient if under 14 years of age;

  (C) name of the patient's primary care physician as provided by the patient or patient's agent;

  (D) name, manufacturer, and lot number of the vaccine administered;

  (E) amount administered;

  (F) date the vaccine was administered;

  (G) site of the immunization or vaccination (e.g., right arm, left leg, right upper arm);

  (H) route of administration of the immunization or vaccination (e.g., intramuscular, subcutaneous, by mouth); and

  (I) name, address, and title of the person administering the immunization or vaccination.

(h) Records.

 (1) Maintenance of records.

  (A) Every record, including notifications, required to be made under this section shall be kept by the pharmacist administering the immunization or vaccination and by the pharmacy when in legal possession of the drugs administered. Such records shall be available for at least two years from the date of such record, for inspecting and copying by the board or its representative and to other authorized local, state, or federal law enforcement or regulatory agencies.

  (B) Records, including notifications, may be maintained in an alternative data retention system, such as a data processing system or direct imaging system provided:

   (i) the records maintained in the alternative system contain all of the information required on the manual record; and

   (ii) the data processing system is capable of producing a hard copy of the record upon request of the board, its representative, or other authorized local, state, or federal law enforcement or regulatory agencies.

 (2) Records of administration under written protocol.

  (A) Records of administration shall be maintained by the pharmacist administering immunizations or vaccinations. Such records shall include:

   (i) all of the administration record requirements of subparagraph (B) of this paragraph; and

   (ii) include the name and address of the pharmacy or physician in legal possession of the immunization or vaccination administered.

  (B) A pharmacy, when responsible for drug accountability, shall maintain a record of administration of immunizations or vaccinations by a pharmacist. The records shall be kept and maintained by patient name. This record shall include:

   (i) a copy of the written protocol under which the immunization or vaccination was administered and any patient-specific deviations from the protocol;

   (ii) name and address of the patient;

   (iii) age of the patient if under 14 years of age;

   (iv) name of the patient's primary care physician as provided by the patient or patient's agent;

   (v) name, manufacturer, and lot number of the vaccine administered;

   (vi) amount administered;

   (vii) date the vaccine was administered;

   (viii) site of the immunization or vaccination (e.g., right arm, left leg, right upper arm);

   (ix) route of administration of the immunization or vaccination (e.g., intramuscular, subcutaneous, by mouth); and

   (x) name, address, and title of the person administering the immunization or vaccination.

 (3) Written protocol.

  (A) A copy of the written protocol and any patient-specific deviations from the protocol shall be maintained in accordance with paragraph (2) of this subsection.

  (B) A standard protocol may be used or the attending physician may develop an immunization/vaccination protocol for the individual patient. If a standard protocol is used, the physician shall record what deviations, if any, from the standard protocol are ordered for the patient. The pharmacy that is in possession of the vaccines administered shall maintain a copy of any deviations from the standard protocol ordered by the physician.

  (C) Written protocols, including standard protocols, any patient-specific deviations from a standard protocol, and any individual patient protocol, shall be reviewed by the physician and pharmacist at least annually and revised if necessary. Such review shall be documented in the records of the pharmacy that is in possession of the vaccines administered.

(i) Confidentiality.

 (1) In addition to the confidentiality requirements specified in § 291.27 of this title (relating to Confidentiality) a pharmacist shall comply with:

  (A) the privacy provisions of the federal Health Insurance Portability and Accountability Act of 1996 (Pub. L. No. 104-191) and any rules adopted pursuant to this act;

  (B) the requirements of Medical Records Privacy contained in Chapter 181, Health and Safety Code;

  (C) the Privacy of Health Information requirements contained in Chapter 28B of the Insurance Code; and

  (D) any other confidentiality provisions of federal or state laws.

 (2) This section shall not affect or alter the provisions relating to the confidentiality of the physician-patient communication as specified in the Medical Practice Act, Chapter 159.

Source: The provisions of this § 295.15 adopted to be effective October 4, 1998, 23 TexReg 9745; amended to be effective December 19, 2001, 26 TexReg 10313; amended to be effective December 6, 2009, 34 TexReg 8721; amended to be effective January 1, 2016, 40 TexReg 8788

Phr. Rules

§295.16 Administration of Epinephrine by a Pharmacist

(a) Purpose. The purpose of this section is to allow pharmacists to administer epinephrine through an auto-injector device to a patient in an emergency situation as authorized in Chapter 562 of the Act.

(b) Definitions. The following words and terms, when used in this section, shall have the following meanings, unless the context clearly indicates otherwise.

    (1) Act—The Texas Pharmacy Act, Chapter 551 – 569, Occupations Code, as amended.

    (2) Administer—The direct application of a prescription drug to the body of an individual by any means, including injection, by a pharmacist.

    (3) Anaphylaxis—A sudden, severe, and potentially life-threatening allergic reaction that occurs when a person is exposed to an allergen. Symptoms may include shortness of breath, wheezing, difficulty breathing, difficulty talking or swallowing, hives, itching, swelling, shock, or asthma. Causes may include, but are not limited to, an insect sting, food allergy, drug reaction, and exercise.

    (4) Epinephrine auto-injector—A disposable drug delivery system that contains a premeasured single dose of epinephrine that is used to treat anaphylaxis in an emergency situation.

(c) Administration requirements.

    (1) Pharmacists may administer epinephrine through an auto-injector to a patient in an emergency situation.

    (2) The authority of a pharmacist to administer epinephrine through an auto-injector may not be delegated.

    (3) Epinephrine administered by a pharmacist under the provisions of this section shall be in the legal possession of a pharmacist or the legal possession of a pharmacy which shall be the pharmacy responsible for drug accountability, including the maintenance of records of administration of the epinephrine.

(d) Limitation on liability.

    (1) A pharmacist who in good faith administers epinephrine through an auto-injector in accordance with this section and Chapter 562 of the Act is not liable for civil damages for an act performed in the administration unless the act is willfully or wantonly negligent.

    (2) A pharmacist may not receive remuneration for the administration of epinephrine through an auto-injector but may seek reimbursement for the cost of the epinephrine auto-injector.

    (3) The administration of epinephrine through an auto-injector to a patient in accordance with the requirements of this section and Chapter 562 of the Act does not constitute the unlawful practice of any health care profession.

(e) Notifications.

    (1) A pharmacist who administers epinephrine through an auto-injector to a patient shall report the use to the patient's primary care physician, as identified by the patient, as soon as practical, but in no event more than 72 hours from the time of administering the epinephrine.

    (2) Immediately, after administering the epinephrine auto-injector, the pharmacist shall ensure that 911 is called and the patient is evaluated by emergency personnel for possible transfer to the nearest emergency department for additional evaluation, monitoring, and treatment.

    (3) The notifications required in paragraph (1) of this subsection shall include the:

        (A) name of the patient;

        (B) age of the patient if under 8 years of age;

        (C) name and manufacturer of the epinephrine auto-injector;

        (D) date the epinephrine was administered;

        (E) name and title of the person administering the epinephrine; and

        (F) name, address, and telephone number of the pharmacy.

(f) Records.

    (1) The notification required to be made under this section shall be kept by the pharmacy and such records shall be available for at least two years from the date of such record, for inspecting and copying by the board or its representative and to other authorized local, state, or federal law enforcement or regulatory agencies.

    (2) The notification may be maintained in an alternative data retention system, such as a data processing system or direct imaging system provided:

        (A) the records maintained in the alternative system contain all of the information required on the manual record; and

        (B) the data processing system is capable of producing a hard copy of the record upon request of the board, its representative, or other authorized local, state, or federal law enforcement or regulatory agencies.

Source: The provisions of this § 295.16 adopted to be effective January 1, 2016, 40 TexReg 8788; amended to be effective December 19, 2016, 41 TexReg 9935

CHAPTER 297. PHARMACY TECHNICIANS AND PHARMACY TECHNICIAN TRAINEES

§297.1 Purpose

The purpose of this chapter is to provide a comprehensive, coherent regulatory scheme for the registration and training of pharmacy technicians and pharmacy technician trainees in this state. The provisions of this chapter, in conjunction with the Texas Pharmacy Act (Chapters 551 – 566 and 568 – 569, Texas Occupations Code, as amended), govern the method for the issuance of a registration to a pharmacy technician and a pharmacy technician trainee in Texas.

Source: The provisions of this §297.1 adopted to be effective December 23, 2003, 28 TexReg 11264; amended to be effective June 11, 2006, 31 TexReg 4640

§297.2 Definitions

The following words and terms, when used in this chapter, shall have the following meanings, unless the context clearly indicates otherwise.

    (1) Act—The Texas Pharmacy Act, Chapters 551 – 566 and 568 – 569, Texas Occupations Code, as amended.

    (2) Board—The Texas State Board of Pharmacy.

Phr. Rules

 (3) Pharmacy technician—An individual who is registered with the Board as a pharmacy technician and whose responsibility in a pharmacy is to provide technical services that do not require professional judgment regarding preparing and distributing drugs and who works under the direct supervision of and is responsible to a pharmacist.

 (4) Pharmacy technician trainee—An individual who is registered with the board as a pharmacy technician trainee and is authorized to participate in a pharmacy's technician training program.

Source: The provisions of this §297.2 adopted to be effective December 23, 2003, 28 TexReg 11264; amended to be effective December 5, 2004, 29 TexReg 11031; amended to be effective June 11, 2006, 31 TexReg 4640

§297.3 Registration Requirements

(a) General.

 (1) Individuals who are not registered with the Board may not be employed as or perform the duties of a pharmacy technician or pharmacy technician trainee.

 (2) Individuals who have previously applied and registered as a pharmacy technician, regardless of the pharmacy technician's current registration status, may not register as a pharmacy technician trainee.

 (3) Individuals who apply and are qualified for both a pharmacy technician trainee registration and a pharmacy technician registration concurrently will not be considered for a pharmacy technician trainee registration.

(b) Registration for pharmacy technician trainees. An individual may register as a pharmacy technician trainee only once and the registration may not be renewed.

 (1) Each applicant for pharmacy technician trainee registration shall:

  (A) have a high school or equivalent diploma (e.g., GED), or be working to achieve a high school or equivalent diploma. For the purposes of this subparagraph, an applicant for registration may be working to achieve a high school or equivalent diploma for no more than two years;

  (B) complete the Texas application for registration that includes the following information:

   (i) name;

   (ii) addresses, phone numbers, date of birth, and social security number; and

   (iii) any other information requested on the application.

  (C) meet all requirements necessary in order for the Board to access the criminal history record information, including submitting fingerprint information and paying the required fees.

 (2) Once an applicant has successfully completed all requirements of registration, and the board has determined there are no grounds to refuse registration, the applicant will be notified of registration as a pharmacy technician trainee and of his or her pharmacy technician trainee registration number.

 (3) Pharmacy technician trainee registrations expire two years from the date of registration or upon issuance of registration as a registered pharmacy technician, whichever is earlier.

(c) Initial registration for pharmacy technicians.

 (1) Each applicant for pharmacy technician registration shall:

  (A) have a high school or equivalent diploma (e.g., GED), or be working to achieve a high school or equivalent diploma. For the purpose of this clause, an applicant for registration may be working to achieve a high school or equivalent diploma for no more than two years; and

  (B) either have:

   (i) taken and passed a pharmacy technician certification examination approved by the board and have a current certification certificate; or

   (ii) been granted an exemption from certification by the board as specified in § 297.7 of this title (relating to Exemption from Pharmacy Technician Certification Requirements); and

  (C) complete the Texas application for registration that includes the following information:

   (i) name;

   (ii) addresses, phone numbers, date of birth, and social security number; and

   (iii) any other information requested on the application.

  (D) meet all requirements necessary in order for the Board to access the criminal history record information, including submitting fingerprint information and paying the required fees; and

  (E) pay the registration fee specified in § 297.4 of this title (relating to Fees).

 (2) Once an applicant has successfully completed all requirements of registration, and the board has determined there are no grounds to refuse registration, the applicant will be notified of registration as a registered pharmacy technician and of his or her pharmacy technician registration number. If the pharmacy technician applicant was registered as a pharmacy technician trainee at the time the pharmacy technician registration is issued, the pharmacy technician trainee registration expires.

(d) Renewal.

 (1) All applicants for renewal of a pharmacy technician registration shall:

  (A) complete the Texas application for registration that includes the following information:

   (i) name;

   (ii) addresses, phone numbers, date of birth, and social security number;

   (iii) meet all requirements necessary in order for the Board to access the criminal history record information, including submitting fingerprint information and being responsible for all associated costs; and

   (iv) any other information requested on the application.

  (B) pay the renewal fee specified in § 297.4 of this title; and

  (C) complete 20 contact hours of continuing education per renewal period as specified in § 297.8 of this title (relating to Continuing Education).

 (2) A pharmacy technician registration expires on the last day of the assigned expiration month.

(3) As specified in § 568.004 of the Act, if the completed application and renewal fee are not received in the board's office on or before the last day of the assigned expiration month, the person's pharmacy technician registration shall expire. An expired registration shall be renewed according to the following schedule.

    (A) If a pharmacy technician registration has expired for 90 days or less, the person may become registered by making application and paying to the board a renewal fee that is equal to one and one-half times the renewal fee for the registration as specified in § 297.4 of this title (relating to Fees).

    (B) If a pharmacy technician registration has been expired for more than 90 days but less than one year, the person may become registered by making application and paying to the board a renewal fee that is equal to two times the renewal fee for the registration as specified in § 297.4 of this title.

    (C) If a pharmacy technician registration has expired for more than one year, the pharmacy technician may not renew the registration and must complete the requirements for initial registration as specified in subsection (c) of this section.

(4) After review, the board may determine that paragraph (3)(C) of this subsection does not apply if the registrant is the subject of a pending investigation or disciplinary action.

(e) An individual may use the title "Registered Pharmacy Technician" or "Ph.T.R." if the individual is registered as a pharmacy technician in this state.

Source: The provisions of this § 297.3 adopted to be effective December 23, 2003, 28 TexReg 11264; amended to be effective September 11, 2003, 30 TexReg 5367; amended to be effective June 11, 2006, 31 TexReg 4640; amended to be effective December 3, 2006, 31 TexReg 9611; amended to be effective September 18, 2007, 32 TexReg 6375; amended to be effective December 14, 2008, 33 TexReg 10028; amended to be effective September 12, 2011, 36 TexReg 5848; amended to be effective June 11, 2015, 40 TexReg 3667; amended to be effective June 12, 2016, 41 TexReg 4258; amended to be effective March 19, 2017, 42 TexReg 1128; amended to be effective March 7, 2018, 43TexReg 1279

§297.4   Fees

(a) Pharmacy technician trainee. The fee for registration shall be $ 55 for a two-year registration.

(b) Pharmacy technician.

    (1) Biennial Registration. The board shall require biennial renewal of all pharmacy technician registrations provided under Chapter 568 of the Act.

    (2) Initial Registration Fee. The fee for initial registration shall be $ 83 for a two-year registration.

    (3) Renewal Fee. The fee for biennial renewal shall be $ 80 for a two-year registration.

Source: The provisions of this § 297.4 adopted to be effective December 23, 2003, 28 TexReg 11264; amended to be effective June 11, 2006, 31 TexReg 4640; amended to be effective November 1, 2006, 31 TexReg 6734; amended to be effective October 1, 2007, 32 TexReg 6375; amended to be effective October 1, 2009, 34 TexReg 6116; amended to be effective September 14, 2010, 35 TexReg 8365; amended to be effective December 1, 2011, 36 TexReg 5848; amended to be effective October 1, 2012, 37 TexReg 6939; amended to be effective January 1, 2014, 38 TexReg 8888; amended to be effective September 11, 2014, 39 TexReg 7138; amended to be effective January 4, 2018, 42 TexReg 7709; amended to be effective June 20, 2019, 44 TexReg 2956

§297.5   Pharmacy Technician Trainees

(a) A person designated as a pharmacy technician trainee shall be registered with the board prior to beginning training in a Texas licensed pharmacy.

(b) A person may be designated as a pharmacy technician trainee for no more than two years and the requirements for registration as a pharmacy technician must be completed within the two year period.

Source: The provisions of this §297.5 adopted to be effective December 23, 2003, 28 TexReg 11264; amended to be effective June 11, 2006, 31 TexReg 4640

§297.6   Pharmacy Technician and Pharmacy Technician Trainee Training

(a) Pharmacy technicians and pharmacy technician trainees shall complete initial training as outlined by the pharmacist-in-charge in a training manual. Such training:

    (1) shall meet the requirements of subsections (d) or (e) of this section; and

    (2) may not be transferred to another pharmacy unless:

        (A) the pharmacies are under common ownership and control and have a common training program; and

        (B) the pharmacist-in-charge of each pharmacy in which the pharmacy technician or pharmacy technician trainee works certifies that the pharmacy technician or pharmacy technician trainee is competent to perform the duties assigned in that pharmacy.

(b) The pharmacist-in-charge shall assure the continuing competency of pharmacy technicians and pharmacy technician trainees through in-service education and training to supplement initial training.

(c) The pharmacist-in-charge shall document the completion of the training program and certify the competency of pharmacy technicians and pharmacy technician trainees completing the training. A written record of initial and in-service training of pharmacy technicians and pharmacy technician trainees shall be maintained and contain the following information:

    (1) name of the person receiving the training;

    (2) date(s) of the training;

    (3) general description of the topics covered;

    (4) a statement that certifies that the pharmacy technician or pharmacy technician trainee is competent to perform the duties assigned;

    (5) name of the person supervising the training; and

    (6) signature of the pharmacy technician or pharmacy technician trainee and the pharmacist-in-charge or other pharmacist employed by the pharmacy and designated by the pharmacist-in-charge as responsible for training of pharmacy technicians and pharmacy technician trainees.

(d) A person who has previously completed the training program outlined in subsection (e) of this section, a licensed nurse, or physician assistant is not required to complete the entire training program outlined in subsection (e) of this section if the person is able to show competency through a documented assessment of competency. Such competency assessment may be conducted by personnel designated by the pharmacist-in-charge, but the final acceptance of competency must be approved by the pharmacist-in-charge.

(e) Pharmacy technician and pharmacy technician trainee training shall be outlined in a training manual. Such training manual shall, at a minimum, contain the following:

Phr. Rules

(1) written procedures and guidelines for the use and supervision of pharmacy technicians and pharmacy technician trainees. Such procedures and guidelines shall:

    (A) specify the manner in which the pharmacist responsible for the supervision of pharmacy technicians and pharmacy technician trainees will supervise such personnel and verify the accuracy and completeness of all acts, tasks, and functions performed by such personnel; and

    (B) specify duties which may and may not be performed by pharmacy technicians and pharmacy technician trainees; and

(2) instruction in the following areas and any additional areas appropriate to the duties of pharmacy technicians and pharmacy technician trainees in the pharmacy:

    (A) Orientation;

    (B) Job descriptions;

    (C) Communication techniques;

    (D) Laws and rules;

    (E) Security and safety;

    (F) Prescription drugs:

        (i) Basic pharmaceutical nomenclature;

        (ii) Dosage forms;

    (G) Drug orders:

        (i) Prescribers;

        (ii) Directions for use;

        (iii) Commonly-used abbreviations and symbols;

        (iv) Number of dosage units;

        (v) Strengths and systems of measurement;

        (vi) Routes of administration;

        (vii) Frequency of administration; and

        (viii) Interpreting directions for use;

    (H) Drug order preparation:

        (i) Creating or updating patient medication records;

        (ii) Entering drug order information into the computer or typing the label in a manual system;

        (iii) Selecting the correct stock bottle;

        (iv) Accurately counting or pouring the appropriate quantity of drug product;

        (v) Selecting the proper container;

        (vi) Affixing the prescription label;

        (vii) Affixing auxiliary labels, if indicated; and

        (viii) Preparing the finished product for inspection and final check by pharmacists;

    (I) Other functions;

    (J) Drug product prepackaging;

    (K) Written policy and guidelines for use of and supervision of pharmacy technicians and pharmacy technician trainees; and

    (L) Confidential patient medication records.

(f) Pharmacy technicians and pharmacy technician trainees compounding non-sterile pharmaceuticals shall meet the training and education requirements specified in the rules for the class of pharmacy in which the pharmacy technician or pharmacy technician trainee is working.

(g) Pharmacy technicians and pharmacy technician trainees compounding sterile pharmaceuticals shall meet the training and education requirements specified in the rules for class of pharmacy in which the pharmacy technician or pharmacy technician trainee is working.

Source: The provisions of this §297.6 adopted to be effective December 23, 2003, 28 TexReg 11264; amended to be effective June 11, 2006, 31 TexReg 4640; amended to be effective June 3, 2007, 32 TexReg 2862

§297.7 Exemption from Pharmacy Technician Certification Requirements

(a) Purpose. This section outlines procedures to petition the board for an exemption to the certification requirements established by § 568.002 of the Act (relating to Pharmacy Technician Registration Required). The board will consider petitions for exemption on a case by case basis.

(b) Long-term exempt pharmacy technicians. Long-term exempt pharmacy technicians are pharmacy technicians who, on September 1, 2001, had been continuously employed as a pharmacy technician in this state for at least 10 years and who received an exemption from the board.

(c) Rural county exempt pharmacy technicians. Rural county exempt pharmacy technicians are pharmacy technicians working in counties with a population of 50,000 or less and meet the following requirements.

    (1) Eligibility. An individual may petition the board for an exemption from the certification requirements established by § 568.002 of the Act (relating to Pharmacy Technician Registration Required) if the individual works in a county with a population of 50,000 or less.

    (2) Petition process.

        (A) An individual shall petition the board for the exemption. The petition shall contain the following:

            (i) name of the individual;

            (ii) name, address, and license number of the pharmacy where the individual is employed;

            (iii) name of the county in which the pharmacy is located and the most recent official population estimate for the county from the Texas State Data Center;

            (iv) a notarized statement signed by the individual stating:

                (I) the reason(s) the individual is asking for the exemption, including reason(s) the individual has not taken and passed a pharmacy technician certification examination approved by the board; and

Phr. Rules

(II) that the information provided in the petition is true and correct; and
   (v) a notarized statement signed by the pharmacist-in-charge of the pharmacy the individual is currently working, stating that the:
     (I) pharmacist-in-charge supports the individual's petition for exemption;
     (II) individual has completed the pharmacy technician training program at the pharmacy; and
     (III) pharmacist-in-charge has personally worked with and observed that the individual is competent to perform the duties of a pharmacy technician.
(B) Each petition shall be considered on an individual basis. In determining whether to grant the exemption, the board shall consider the information contained in the petition and additional information including the following:
   (i) the accuracy and completeness of the petition;
   (ii) reason(s) the individual is asking for the exemption;
   (iii) the population of the county;
   (iv) the number of pharmacies located in the county and adjacent counties and the number of pharmacy technicians working in these pharmacies;
   (v) unemployment rate in the county and adjacent counties; and
   (vi) the following information concerning the pharmacy where the individual is currently working:
     (I) the degree of compliance on previous compliance inspections; and
     (II) history of disciplinary action by the board or other regulatory agencies against the licenses held by the pharmacy or pharmacists working at the pharmacy.
(C) After review of the petition, the individual and the pharmacist-in-charge of the pharmacy where the individual is working shall be notified in writing of approval or denial of the petition.
(D) If the petition is approved, the individual shall register with the board as a pharmacy technician.
(3) Limitations.
(A) The exemption granted under this subsection may only be used at the pharmacy noted in the petition and may not be transferred to another pharmacy. If the pharmacy technician ceases employment at the pharmacy or changes employment, the exemption is canceled.
(B) If the population of the county exceeds 50,000, the board shall cancel the exemption. The pharmacy technician and the pharmacist-in-charge of the pharmacy shall be notified when an exemption is canceled.
(C) If the exemption granted under subparagraphs (A) or (B) of this paragraph is cancelled, the pharmacy technician's registration is void and the registration certificate must be surrendered to the Board.

Source: The provisions of this § 297.7 adopted to be effective December 23, 2003, 28 TexReg 11264; amended to be effective September 7, 2004, 29 TexReg 8525; amended to be effective June 11, 2006, 31 TexReg 4640; amended to be effective June 8, 2008, 33 TexReg 4310; amended to be effective January 4, 2018, 42 TexReg 7709

§297.8 Continuing Education Requirements

(a) Pharmacy Technician Trainees. Pharmacy technician trainees are not required to complete continuing education.
(b) Pharmacy Technicians.
(1) All pharmacy technicians shall be exempt from the continuing education requirements during their initial registration period.
(2) All pharmacy technicians must complete and report 20 contact hours of approved continuing education obtained during the previous renewal period in pharmacy related subjects in order to renew their registration as a pharmacy technician. No more than 5 of the 20 hours may be earned at the pharmacy technician's workplace through in-service education and training under the direct supervision of the pharmacist(s).
(3) A pharmacy technician may satisfy the continuing education requirements by:
(A) successfully completing the number of continuing education hours necessary to renew a registration as specified in paragraph (2) of this subsection;
(B) successfully completing during the preceding license period, one credit hour for each year of the renewal period, in pharmacy related college course(s); or
(C) taking and passing a pharmacy technician certification examination approved by the board during the preceding renewal period, which shall be equivalent to the number of continuing education hours necessary to renew a registration as specified in paragraph (2) of this subsection.
(4) To renew a registration, a pharmacy technician must report on the renewal application completion of at least twenty contact hours of continuing education. The following is applicable to the reporting of continuing education contact hours.
(A) At least one contact hour of the 20 contact hours specified in paragraph (2) of this subsection shall be related to Texas pharmacy laws or rules.
(B) Any continuing education requirements which are imposed upon a pharmacy technician as a part of a board order or agreed board order shall be in addition to the requirements of this section.
(5) Pharmacy technicians are required to maintain records of completion of continuing education for three years from the date of reporting the hours on a renewal application. The records must contain at least the following information:
(A) name of participant;
(B) title and date of program;
(C) program sponsor or provider (the organization);
(D) number of hours awarded; and
(E) dated signature of sponsor representative.
(6) The board shall audit the records of pharmacy technicians for verification of reported continuing education credit. The following is applicable for such audits.
(A) Upon written request, a pharmacy technician shall provide to the board copies of the record required to be maintained in paragraph (5) of this subsection or certificates of completion for all continuing education contact hours reported during

a specified registration period. Failure to provide all requested records by the specified deadline constitutes prima facie evidence of a violation of this rule.

 (B) Credit for continuing education contact hours shall only be allowed for programs for which the pharmacy technician submits copies of records reflecting that the hours were completed during the specified registration period(s). Any other reported hours shall be disallowed.

 (C) A pharmacy technician who submits false or fraudulent records to the board shall be subject to disciplinary action by the board.

(7) The following is applicable if a pharmacy technician fails to report completion of the required continuing education.

 (A) The registration of a pharmacy technician who fails to report completion of the required number of continuing education contact hours shall not be renewed and the pharmacy technician shall not be issued a renewal certificate for the license period until such time as the pharmacy technician successfully completes the required continuing education and reports the completion to the board.

 (B) A person shall not practice as a pharmacy technician without a current renewal certificate.

(8) A pharmacy technician who has had a physical disability, illness, or other extenuating circumstances which prohibits the pharmacy technician from obtaining continuing education credit during the preceding license period may be granted an extension of time to complete the continued education requirement. The following is applicable for this extension:

 (A) The pharmacy technician shall submit a petition to the board with his/her registration renewal application which contains:

  (i) the name, address, and registration number of the pharmacy technician;

  (ii) a statement of the reason for the request for extension;

  (iii) if the reason for the request for extension is health related, a statement from the attending physician(s) treating the pharmacy technician which includes the nature of the physical disability or illness and the dates the pharmacy technician was incapacitated; and

  (iv) if the reason for the request for the extension is for other extenuating circumstances, a detailed explanation of the extenuating circumstances and if because of military deployment, documentation of the dates of the deployment.

 (B) After review and approval of the petition, a pharmacy technician may be granted an extension of time to comply with the continuing education requirement which shall not exceed one license renewal period.

 (C) An extension of time to complete continuing education credit does not relieve a pharmacy technician from the continuing education requirement during the current license period.

 (D) If a petition for extension to the reporting period for continuing education is denied, the pharmacy technician shall:

  (i) have 60 days to complete and report completion of the required continuing education requirements; and

  (ii) be subject to the requirements of paragraph (6) of this subsection relating to failure to report completion of the required continuing education if the required continuing education is not completed and reported within the required 60-day time period.

(9) The following are considered approved programs for pharmacy technicians.

 (A) Any program presented by an Accreditation Council for Pharmacy Education (ACPE) approved provider subject to the following conditions.

  (i) Pharmacy technicians may receive credit for the completion of the same ACPE course only once during a renewal period.

  (ii) Pharmacy technicians who present approved ACPE continuing education programs may receive credit for the time expended during the actual presentation of the program. Pharmacy technicians may receive credit for the same presentation only once during a license period.

  (iii) Proof of completion of an ACPE course shall contain the following information:

   (I) name of the participant;

   (II) title and completion date of the program;

   (III) name of the approved provider sponsoring or cosponsoring the program;

   (IV) number of contact hours awarded;

   (V) the assigned ACPE universal program number and a "T" designation indicating that the CE is targeted to pharmacy technicians; and

   (VI) either:

    (-a-) a dated certifying signature of the approved provider and the official ACPE logo; or

    (-b-) the Continuing Pharmacy Education Monitor logo.

 (B) Pharmacy related college courses which are part of a pharmacy technician training program or part of a professional degree program offered by a college of pharmacy.

  (i) Pharmacy technicians may receive credit for the completion of the same course only once during a license period. A course is equivalent to one credit hour for each year of the renewal period. One credit hour is equal to 15 contact hours.

  (ii) Pharmacy technicians who teach these courses may receive credit towards their continuing education, but such credit may be received only once for teaching the same course during a license period.

 (C) Basic cardiopulmonary resuscitation (CPR) courses which lead to CPR certification by the American Red Cross or the American Heart Association or its equivalent shall be recognized as approved programs. Pharmacy technicians may receive credit for one contact hour towards their continuing education requirement for completion of a CPR course only once during a renewal period. Proof of completion of a CPR course shall be the certificate issued by the American Red Cross or the American Heart Association or its equivalent.

 (D) Advanced cardiovascular life support courses (ACLS) or pediatric advanced life support (PALS) courses which lead to initial ACLS or PALS certification by the American Heart Association or its equivalent shall be recognized as approved programs. Pharmacy technicians may receive credit for twelve contact hours towards their continuing education requirement for completion of an ACLS or PALS course only once during a renewal period. Proof of completion of an ACLS or PALS course shall be the certificate issued by the American Heart Association or its equivalent.

(E) Advanced cardiovascular life support courses (ACLS) or pediatric advanced life support (PALS) courses which lead to ACLS or PALS recertification by the American Heart Association or its equivalent shall be recognized as approved programs. Pharmacy may receive credit for four contact hours towards their continuing education requirement for completion of an ACLS or PALS recertification course only once during a renewal period. Proof of completion of an ACLS or PALS recertification course shall be the certificate issued by the American Heart Association or its equivalent.

(F) Attendance at Texas State Board of Pharmacy Board Meetings shall be recognized for continuing education credit as follows.
   (i) Pharmacy technicians shall receive credit for three contact hours towards their continuing education requirement for attending a full, public board business meeting in its entirety.
   (ii) A maximum of six contact hours are allowed for attendance at a board meeting during a renewal period.
   (iii) Proof of attendance for a complete board meeting shall be a certificate issued by the Texas State Board of Pharmacy.

(G) Participation in a Texas State Board of Pharmacy appointed Task Force shall be recognized for continuing education credit as follows.
   (i) Pharmacy technicians shall receive credit for three contact hours towards their continuing education requirement for participating in a Texas State Board of Pharmacy appointed Task Force.
   (ii) Proof of participation for a Task Force shall be a certificate issued by the Texas State Board of Pharmacy.

(H) Attendance at programs presented by the Texas State Board of Pharmacy or courses offered by the Texas State Board of Pharmacy as follows:
   (i) Pharmacy technicians shall receive credit for the number of hours for the program or course as stated by the Texas State Board of Pharmacy.
   (ii) Proof of attendance at a program presented by the Texas State Board of Pharmacy or completion of a course offered by the Texas State Board of Pharmacy shall be a certificate issued by the Texas State Board of Pharmacy.

(I) Pharmacy technicians shall receive credit toward their continuing education requirements for programs or courses approved by other state boards of pharmacy as follows:
   (i) Pharmacy technicians shall receive credit for the number of hours for the program or course as specified by the other state board of pharmacy.
   (ii) Proof of attendance at a program or course approved by another state board of pharmacy shall be a certificate or other documentation that indicates:
      (I) name of the participant;
      (II) title and completion date of the program;
      (III) name of the approved provider sponsoring or cosponsoring the program;
      (IV) number of contact hours awarded;
      (V) a dated certifying signature of the provider; and
      (VI) documentation that the program is approved by the other state board of pharmacy.

(J) Completion of an Institute for Safe Medication Practices' (ISMP) Medication Safety Self-Assessment for hospital pharmacies or for community/ambulatory pharmacies shall be recognized for continuing education credit as follows.
   (i) Pharmacy technicians shall receive credit for three contact hours towards their continuing education requirement for completion of an ISMP Medication Safety Self-Assessment.
   (ii) Proof of completion of an ISMP Medication Safety Self-Assessment shall be:
      (I) a continuing education certificate provided by an ACPE approved provider for completion of an assessment; or
      (II) a document from ISMP showing completion of an assessment.

(K) Programs approved by the American Medical Association (AMA) as Category 1 Continuing Medical Education (CME) and accredited by the Accreditation Council for Continuing Medical Education subject to the following conditions.
   (i) Pharmacy technicians may receive credit for the completion of the same CME course only once during a license period.
   (ii) Pharmacy technicians who present approved CME programs may receive credit for the time expended during the actual presentation of the program. Pharmacy technicians may receive credit for the same presentation only once during a license period.
   (iii) Proof of completion of a CME course shall contain the following information:
      (I) name of the participant;
      (II) title and completion date of the program;
      (III) name of the approved provider sponsoring or cosponsoring the program;
      (IV) number of contact hours awarded; and
      (V) a dated certifying signature of the approved provider.

(L) In-service education provided under the direct supervision of a pharmacist shall be recognized as continuing education as follows:
   (i) Pharmacy technicians shall receive credit for the number of hours provided by pharmacist(s) at the pharmacy technician's place of employment.
   (ii) Proof of completion of in-service education shall contain the following information:
      (I) name of the participant;
      (II) title or description of the program;
      (III) completion date of the program;
      (IV) name of the pharmacist supervising the in-service education;
      (V) number of hours; and
      (VI) a dated signature of the pharmacist providing the in-service education.

Source: The provisions of this § 297.8 adopted to be effective December 23, 2003, 28 TexReg 11264; amended to be effective June 11, 2006, 31 TexReg 4640; amended to be effective June 12, 2013, 38 TexReg 3603; amended to be effective September 14, 2015, 40 TexReg 6132; amended to be effective January 4, 2018, 42 TexReg 7709

Phr. Rules

§297.9 Notifications

(a) Change of Address and/or Name.

    (1) Change of address. A pharmacy technician or pharmacy technician trainee shall notify the board electronically or in writing within 10 days of a change of address, giving the old and new address and registration number.

    (2) Change of name.

        (A) A pharmacy technician or pharmacy technician trainee shall notify the board in writing within 10 days of a change of name by:

            (i) sending a copy of the official document reflecting the name change (e.g., marriage certificate, divorce decree, etc.); and

            (ii) paying a fee of $ 20.

        (B) An amended registration and/or certificate reflecting the new name of the pharmacy technician or pharmacy technician trainee will be issued by the board.

(b) Change of Employment. A pharmacy technician or pharmacy technician trainee shall report electronically or in writing to the board within 10 days of a change of employment giving the name and license number of the old and new pharmacy and registration number.

Source: The provisions of this § 297.9 adopted to be effective December 23, 2003, 28 TexReg 11264; amended to be effective June 11, 2006, 31 TexReg 4640; amended to be effective March 15, 2015, 40 TexReg 1090

§297.10 Registration for Military Service Members, Military Veterans, and Military Spouses

(a) Definitions. The following words and terms, when used in this section, shall have the following meanings, unless the context clearly indicates otherwise.

    (1) Active duty—Current full-time military service in the armed forces of the United States or active duty military service as a member of the Texas military forces, or similar military service of another state.

    (2) Armed forces of the United States—The army, navy, air force, coast guard, or marine corps of the United States or a reserve unit of one of those branches of the armed forces.

    (3) Military service member—A person who is on active duty.

    (4) Military spouse—A person who is married to a military service member.

    (5) Military veteran—A person who has served on active duty and who was discharged or released from active duty.

(b) Alternative registration procedure. For the purpose of § 55.004, Occupations Code, an applicant for a pharmacy technician registration who is a military service member, military veteran, or military spouse may complete the following alternative procedures for registering as a pharmacy technician.

    (1) An applicant who holds a current registration as a pharmacy technician issued by another state but does not have a current pharmacy technician certification certificate shall meet the requirements for registration as a pharmacy technician trainee as specified in § 297.3 of this chapter (relating to Registration Requirements).

    (2) An applicant who held a pharmacy technician registration in Texas that expired within the five years preceding the application date who meets the following requirements may be granted a pharmacy technician registration. The applicant:

        (A) shall complete the Texas application for registration that includes the following:

            (i) name;

            (ii) addresses, phone numbers, date of birth, and social security number; and

            (iii) any other information requested on the application;

        (B) shall provide documentation to include:

            (i) military identification indicating that the applicant is a military service member, military veteran, or military dependent, if a military spouse; and

            (ii) marriage certificate, if the applicant is a military spouse; applicant's spouse is on active duty status;

        (C) be exempt from the application fees paid to the board set forth in § 297.4(a) and (b)(2) of this chapter;

        (D) shall meet all necessary requirements in order for the board to access the criminal history records information, including submitting fingerprint information and such criminal history check does not reveal any charge or conviction for a crime that § 281.64 of this title (relating to Sanctions for Criminal Offenses) indicates a sanction of denial, revocation, or suspension; and

        (E) is not required to have a current pharmacy technician certification certificate.

(c) Expedited registration procedure. For the purpose of § 55.005, Occupations Code, an applicant for a pharmacy technician registration who is a military service member, military veteran or military spouse and who holds a current registration as a pharmacy technician issued by another state or who held a pharmacy technician registration in Texas that expired within the five years preceding the application date may complete the following expedited procedures for registering as a pharmacy technician.

    (1) The applicant shall:

        (A) have a high school or equivalent diploma (e.g., GED), or be working to achieve a high school or equivalent diploma. For the purpose of this clause, an applicant for registration may be working to achieve a high school or equivalent diploma for no more than two years; and

        (B) have taken and passed a pharmacy technician certification examination approved by the board and have a current certification certificate; and

        (C) complete the Texas application for registration that includes the following information:

            (i) name;

            (ii) addresses, phone numbers, date of birth, and social security number; and

            (iii) any other information requested on the application.

        (D) meet all requirements necessary in order for the Board to access the criminal history record information, including submitting fingerprint information and paying the required fees;

        (E) shall be exempt from the registration fee as specified in § 297.4(b)(2) of this chapter (relating to Fees).

Phr. Rules

    (2) Once an applicant has successfully completed all requirements of registration, and the board has determined there are no grounds to refuse registration, the applicant will be notified of registration as a registered pharmacy technician and of his or her pharmacy technician registration number.

    (3) All applicants for renewal of an expedited pharmacy technician registration issued to a military service member, military veteran, or military spouse shall comply with the renewal procedures as specified in § 297.3 of this chapter (relating to Registration Requirements).

(d) License renewal. As specified in § 55.003, Occupations Code, a military service member who holds a pharmacy technician registration is entitled to two years of additional time to complete any requirements related to the renewal of the military service member's registration as follows:

    (1) A military service member who fails to renew their pharmacy technician registration in a timely manner because the individual was serving as a military service member shall submit to the board:

        (A) name, address, and registration number of the pharmacy technician;

        (D) military identification indicating that the individual is a military service member; and

        (C) a statement requesting up to two years of additional time to complete the renewal.

    (2) A military service member specified in paragraph (1) of this subsection shall be exempt from fees specified in § 297.3(d)(4) of this chapter (relating to Registration Requirements).

    (3) A military service member specified in paragraph (1) of this subsection is entitled to two additional years of time to complete the continuing education requirements specified in § 297.8 of this title (relating to Continuing Education Requirements).

Source: The provisions of this § 297.10 adopted to be effective March 13, 2012, 37 TexReg 1706; amended to be effective January 7, 2014, 39 TexReg 78; amended to be effective December 6, 2015, 40 TexReg 8789; amended to be effective June 12, 2016, 41 TexReg 4258; amended to be effective January 4, 2018, 42 TexReg 7709

§297.11. Temporary Emergency Registration

(a) Definitions. The following words and terms, when used in this chapter, shall have the following meanings, unless the context clearly indicates otherwise.

    (1) Emergency situation—An emergency caused by a natural or manmade disaster or any other exceptional situation that causes an extraordinary demand for pharmacist services.

    (2) State—One of the 50 United States of America, the District of Columbia, and Puerto Rico.

(b) Emergency Temporary Pharmacy Technician Registration. In an emergency situation, the board may grant a pharmacy technician who holds a current registration in another state an emergency temporary pharmacy technician registration to practice in Texas. The following is applicable for the emergency temporary pharmacy technician registration.

    (1) An applicant for an emergency temporary pharmacy technician registration under this section must hold a current pharmacy technician registration in another state and that registration and other registrations held by the applicant in any other state may not be suspended, revoked, canceled, surrendered, or otherwise restricted for any reason.

    (2) To qualify for an emergency temporary pharmacy technician registration, the applicant must submit an application including the following information:

        (A) name, address, and phone number of the applicant; and

        (B) any other information the required by the board.

    (3) An emergency temporary pharmacy technician registration shall be valid for a period as determined by the board not to exceed six months. The executive director of the board, in his/her discretion, may renew the registration for an additional six months, if the emergency situation still exists.

(c) Exception. This section is not applicable to pharmacy technicians enrolled in a volunteer health registry maintained by the Texas Department of State Health Services.

Source: The provisions of this § 297.11 adopted to be effective June 11, 2015, 40 TexReg 3667

CHAPTER 303. DESTRUCTION OF DRUGS

§303.1 Destruction of Dispensed Drugs

(a) Drugs dispensed to patients in health care facilities or institutions.

    (1) Destruction by the consultant pharmacist. The consultant pharmacist, if in good standing with the Texas State Board of Pharmacy, is authorized to destroy dangerous drugs dispensed to patients in health care facilities or institutions. A consultant pharmacist may destroy controlled substances as allowed to do so by federal laws or rules of the Drug Enforcement Administration. Dangerous drugs may be destroyed provided the following conditions are met.

        (A) A written agreement exists between the facility and the consultant pharmacist.

        (B) The drugs are inventoried and such inventory is verified by the consultant pharmacist. The following information shall be included on this inventory:

            (i) name and address of the facility or institution;

            (ii) name and pharmacist license number of the consultant pharmacist;

            (iii) date of drug destruction;

            (iv) date the prescription was dispensed;

            (v) unique identification number assigned to the prescription by the pharmacy;

            (vi) name of dispensing pharmacy;

            (vii) name, strength, and quantity of drug;

            (viii) signature of consultant pharmacist destroying drugs;

            (ix) signature of the witness(es); and

            (x) method of destruction.

(C) The signature of the consultant pharmacist and witness(es) to the destruction and the method of destruction specified in subparagraph (B) of this paragraph may be on a cover sheet attached to the inventory and not on each individual inventory sheet, provided the cover sheet contains a statement indicating the number of inventory pages that are attached and each of the attached pages are initialed by the consultant pharmacist and witness(es).

(D) The drugs are destroyed in a manner to render the drugs unfit for human consumption and disposed of in compliance with all applicable state and federal requirements.

(E) The actual destruction of the drugs is witnessed by one of the following:

    (i) a commissioned peace officer;

    (ii) an agent of the Texas State Board of Pharmacy;

    (iii) an agent of the Texas Health and Human Services Commission, authorized by the Texas State Board of Pharmacy to destroy drugs;

    (iv) an agent of the Texas Department of State Health Services, authorized by the Texas State Board of Pharmacy to destroy drugs; or

    (v) any two individuals working in the following capacities at the facility:

        (I) facility administrator;

        (II) director of nursing;

        (III) acting director of nursing; or

        (IV) licensed nurse.

(F) If the actual destruction of the drugs is conducted at a location other than the facility or institution, the consultant pharmacist and witness(es) shall retrieve the drugs from the facility or institution, transport, and destroy the drugs at such other location.

(2) Destruction by a waste disposal service. A consultant pharmacist may utilize a waste disposal service to destroy dangerous drugs dispensed to patients in health care facilities or institutions. A consultant pharmacist may destroy controlled substances as allowed to do so by federal laws or rules of the Drug Enforcement Administration. Dangerous drugs may be transferred to a waste disposal service for destruction provided the following conditions are met.

(A) The waste disposal service is in compliance with applicable rules of the Texas Commission on Environmental Quality and United States Environmental Protection Agency relating to waste disposal.

(B) The drugs are inventoried and such inventory is verified by the consultant pharmacist prior to placing the drugs in an appropriate container, and sealing the container. The following information must be included on this inventory:

    (i) name and address of the facility or institution;

    (ii) name and pharmacist license number of the consultant pharmacist;

    (iii) date of packaging and sealing of the container;

    (iv) date the prescription was dispensed;

    (v) unique identification number assigned to the prescription by the pharmacy;

    (vi) name of dispensing pharmacy;

    (vii) name, strength, and quantity of drug;

    (viii) signature of consultant pharmacist packaging and sealing the container; and

    (ix) signature of the witness(es).

(C) The consultant pharmacist seals the container of drugs in the presence of the facility administrator and the director of nursing or one of the other witnesses listed in paragraph (1)(E) of this subsection as follows:

    (i) tamper resistant tape is placed on the container in such a manner that any attempt to reopen the container will result in the breaking of the tape; and

    (ii) the signature of the consultant pharmacist is placed over this tape seal.

(D) The sealed container is maintained in a secure area at the facility or institution until transferred to the waste disposal service by the consultant pharmacist, facility administrator, director of nursing, or acting director of nursing.

(E) A record of the transfer to the waste disposal service is maintained and attached to the inventory of drugs specified in subparagraph (B) of this paragraph. Such record shall contain the following information:

    (i) date of the transfer;

    (ii) signature of the person who transferred the drugs to the waste disposal service;

    (iii) name and address of the waste disposal service; and

    (iv) signature of the employee of the waste disposal service who receives the container.

(F) The waste disposal service shall provide the facility with proof of destruction of the sealed container. Such proof of destruction shall contain the date, location, and method of destruction of the container and shall be attached to the inventory of drugs specified in subparagraph (B) of this paragraph.

(3) Record retention. All records required in this subsection shall be maintained by the consultant pharmacist at the health care facility or institution for two years from the date of destruction.

(b) Drugs returned to a pharmacy. A pharmacist in a pharmacy may accept and destroy dangerous drugs that have been previously dispensed to a patient and returned to a pharmacy by the patient or an agent of the patient. A pharmacist may accept controlled substances that have been previously dispensed to a patient as allowed by federal laws of the Drug Enforcement Administration. The following procedures shall be followed in destroying dangerous drugs.

(1) The dangerous drugs shall be destroyed in a manner to render the drugs unfit for human consumption and disposed of in compliance with all applicable state and federal requirements.

(2) Documentation shall be maintained that includes the following information:

    (A) name and address of the dispensing pharmacy;

    (B) unique identification number assigned to the prescription, if available;

    (C) name and strength of the dangerous drug; and

    (D) signature of the pharmacist.

Source: The provisions of this §303.1 adopted to be effective September 20, 1977, 2 TexReg 3396; amended to be effective August 2, 1983, 8 TexReg 2698; amended to be effective August 30, 1984, 9 TexReg 4451; amended to be effective September 14, 1988, 13 TexReg 4326; amended to be effective June 11, 1991, 16 TexReg 2953; amended to be effective May

6, 1993, 18 TexReg 2625; amended to be effective September 30, 1993, 18 TexReg 6463; amended to be effective March 25, 1999, 24 TexReg 2024; amended to be effective March 12, 2003, 28 TexReg 2083; amended to be effective March 4, 2004, 29 TexReg 2013; amended to be effective September 13, 2009, 34 TexReg 6117; amended to be effective September 12, 2011, 36 TexReg 5850; amended to be effective March 15, 2015, 40 TexReg 1090

§303.2   Disposal of Stock Prescription Drugs

(a) Definition of stock. "Stock" as used in these sections means dangerous drugs or controlled substances which are packaged in the original manufacturer's container.

(b) Disposal of stock dangerous drugs. A pharmacist, licensed by the board, is authorized to destroy stock dangerous drugs owned by a licensed pharmacy if such dangerous drugs are destroyed in a manner to render the drugs unfit for human consumption and disposed of in compliance with all applicable state and federal requirements.

(c) Disposal of stock controlled substances. A pharmacist, licensed by the board, shall dispose of stock controlled substances owned by a licensed pharmacy in accordance with procedures authorized by the Federal and Texas Controlled Substances Acts and sections adopted pursuant to such Acts.

Source: The provisions of this § 303.2 adopted to be effective April 25, 1984, 9 TEXREG 2019; amended to be effective February 17, 1988, 13 TEXREG 614; amended to be effective September 30, 1993, 18 TexReg 6463; amended to be effective March 25, 1999, 24 TexReg 2024; amended to be effective March 12, 2003, 28 TexReg 2083; amended to be effective September 13, 2009, 34 TexReg 6117; amended to be effective March 15, 2015, 40 TexReg 1090

§303.3   Records

All inventory records and forms of disposed drugs shall be maintained for two years from the date of transfer, disposal, or destruction and be available for inspection by an agent of the board, Texas Department of Public Safety, Drug Enforcement Administration, or any other agent authorized to inspect such records.

Source: The provisions of this §303.3 adopted to be effective April 25, 1984, 9 TexReg 2019.

CHAPTER 305. EDUCATIONAL REQUIREMENTS

§305.1   Pharmacy Education Requirements

The minimum standards for the professional practice degree programs of a university, school, or college of pharmacy whose graduates shall be eligible for licensing in this state, shall be the minimum standards required by the Accreditation Council for Pharmacy Education. The universities, schools, and colleges of pharmacy whose professional practice degree programs have been approved by the board shall be published in the minutes of each annual meeting of the board.

Source: The provisions of this §305.1 adopted to be effective February 17, 1988, 13 TexReg 614; amended to be effective March 19, 1998, 23 TexReg 2819; amended to be effective June 11, 2006, 31 TexReg 4641

§305.2   Pharmacy Technician Training Programs

(a) Purpose. The purpose of this section is to set standards for Board approval of pharmacy technician training programs to ensure that graduates of the programs have the basic knowledge and experience in general pharmacy to practice in most pharmacy settings. Pharmacy technician training programs are not required to be approved by the Board. However, the Board maintains a list of Board-approved pharmacy technician training programs that meet the standards established in this section.

(b) Board-approved pharmacy technician training programs.

    (1) The approval by the Board of pharmacy technician training programs do not change any requirements for on-site training required of all pharmacy technicians as outlined in the rules for each class of pharmacy.

    (2) The standard for Board-approved pharmacy technician training programs shall be the American Society of Health-System Pharmacists' and Accreditation Council on Pharmacy Educations' (ASHP/ACPE) Accreditation Standards for Pharmacy Technician Education and Training Programs which are based on goals specified in ASHP's Model Curriculum for Pharmacy Technician Education and Training Programs.

    (3) The Board may approve pharmacy technician training programs which are currently ASHP/ACPE accredited, and maintain such accreditation.

    (4) The Board may approve pharmacy technician training programs not accredited by ASHP/ACPE provided:

    (A) the program meets ASHP/ACPE Accreditation Standards for Pharmacy Technician Education and Training Programs, modified as follows:

       (i) entities providing the pharmacy technician training programs are not required to be health care organizations or academic institutions;

       (ii) entities that offer or participate in offering pharmacy technician training programs are not required to be accredited by the Joint Commission on Accreditation of Healthcare Organizations, the American Osteopathic Association, or the National Committee on Quality Assurance; and

       (iii) students enrolled in pharmacy technician training programs must have a high school or equivalent diploma, e.g., GED, or they may be currently enrolled in a program which awards such a diploma;

    (B) the program:

       (i) makes an application to the Board;

       (ii) provides all information requested by the Board, necessary to confirm that the program meets the requirements outlined in subparagraph (A) of this paragraph;

       (iii) assists with any inspections requested by the Board of the facilities, records, and/or program guidelines necessary to confirm that the program meets the requirements outlined in subparagraph (A) of this paragraph; and

       (iv) pays an application processing fee to the Board of $ 100.00;

(C) the program director provides written status reports upon request of the Board and at least every three years to assist in evaluation of continued compliance with the requirements; and

(D) the program is subject to an on-site inspection at least every six years.

(5) The Board may require an outside entity to conduct any evaluations and/or inspections of a pharmacy technician training program as outlined in paragraph (4) of this subsection. This outside entity shall report to the Board whether a pharmacy technician training program meets the ASHP/ACPE Accreditation Standards for Pharmacy Technician Education and Training Programs as modified. Cost of these evaluations shall be the responsibility of the pharmacy technician training program.

(c) Students enrolled in Board-approved pharmacy technician training programs. A student enrolled in a Board-approved pharmacy technician training program must be registered as a pharmacy technician trainee or pharmacy technician prior to working in a pharmacy as part of the experiential component of the Board-approved pharmacy technician training program.

(d) Review of accreditation standards. The Board shall review the ASHP/ACPE Accreditation Standard for Pharmacy Technician Education and Training Programs periodically and whenever the Standard is revised.

(e) Listing of Board-approved Pharmacy Technician Training Programs. The Board shall maintain a list of the pharmacy technician training programs approved by the Board and periodically publish this list in the minutes of the Board. If the Board determines that a training program does not meet or no longer meets any of the requirements set forth in this section, the training program will not be listed as a Board-approved pharmacy technician training program.

Source: The provisions of this § 305.2 adopted to be effective March 7, 2001, 26 TexReg 1865; amended to be effective June 11, 2006, 31 TexReg 4641; amended to be effective September 7, 2008, 33 TexReg 7242; amended to be effective September 16, 2018, 43 TexReg 5805

CHAPTER 309. SUBSTITUTION OF DRUG PRODUCTS

§309.1 Objective

These sections govern the substitution of lower-priced generically equivalent drug products for certain brand name drug products and the substitution of interchangeable biological products for certain biological products.

Source: The provisions of this § 309.1 adopted to be effective June 1, 2002, 27 TexReg 1782; amended to be effective December 6, 2015, 40 TexReg 8790

§309.2 Definitions

The following words and terms, when used in this chapter, shall have the following meanings, unless the context clearly indicates otherwise. Any term not defined in this section shall have the definition set out in the Act, § 551.003 and Chapter 562.

(1) Act—The Texas Pharmacy Act, Occupations Code, Subtitle J, as amended.

(2) Biological product—A virus, therapeutic serum, toxin, antitoxin, vaccine, blood, blood component or derivative, allergenic product, protein (except any chemically synthesized polypeptide), or analogous product, or arsphenamine or derivative of arsphenamine (or any other trivalent organic arsenic compound), applicable to the prevention, treatment, or cure of a disease or condition of human beings.

(3) Biosimilar—A biological product that is highly similar to the reference product notwithstanding minor differences in clinically inactive components and there are no clinically meaningful differences between the biological product and the reference product in terms of the safety, purity, and potency of the product.

(4) Data communication device—An electronic device that receives electronic information from one source and transmits or routes it to another (e.g., bridge, router, switch, or gateway).

(5) Electronic prescription drug order—A prescription drug order which is transmitted by an electronic device to the receiver (pharmacy).

(6) Generically equivalent—A drug that is pharmaceutically equivalent and therapeutically equivalent to the drug prescribed.

(7) Interchangeable—Referencing a biological product that is:

(A) biosimilar to the reference product and can be expected to produce the same clinical result as the reference product in any given patient; and if the biological product is administered more than once to an individual, the risk in terms of safety or diminished efficacy of alternating or switching between use of the biological product and the reference product is not greater than the risk of using the reference product without such alternation or switch may be substituted for the reference product without the intervention of the health care provider who prescribed the reference product; or

(B) designated as therapeutically equivalent to another product by the United States Food and Drug Administration in the most recent edition or supplement of the United States Food and Drug Administration's references.

(8) Pharmaceutically equivalent—Drug products that have identical amounts of the same active chemical ingredients in the same dosage form and that meet the identical compendial or other applicable standards of strength, quality, and purity according to the United States Pharmacopoeia or another nationally recognized compendium.

(9) Reference product—A single biological product against which a biological product is evaluated and is found to be biosimilar.

(10) Therapeutically equivalent—Pharmaceutically equivalent drug products that, if administered in the same amounts, will provide the same therapeutic effect, identical in duration and intensity.

(11) Original prescription—The:

(A) original written prescription drug orders; or

(B) original verbal or electronic prescription drug orders reduced to writing either manually or electronically by the pharmacist.

(12) Practitioner—

(A) A person licensed or registered to prescribe, distribute, administer, or dispense a prescription drug or device in the course of professional practice in this state, including a physician, dentist, podiatrist, therapeutic optometrist, or veterinarian but excluding a person licensed under this subtitle;

(B) A person licensed by another state, Canada, or the United Mexican States in a health field in which, under the law of this state, a license holder in this state may legally prescribe a dangerous drug;

    (C) A person practicing in another state and licensed by another state as a physician, dentist, veterinarian, or podiatrist, who has a current federal Drug Enforcement Administration registration number and who may legally prescribe a Schedule II, III, IV, or V controlled substance, as specified under Chapter 481, Health and Safety Code, in that other state; or

    (D) An advanced practice registered nurse or physician assistant to whom a physician has delegated the authority to carry out or sign prescription drug orders under §§ 157.0511, 157.0512, or 157.054, Occupations Code.

Source: The provisions of this § 309.2 adopted to be effective June 1, 2002, 27 TexReg 1782; amended to be effective June 12, 2005, 30 TexReg 3210; amended to be effective December 6, 2015, 40 TexReg 8790

§309.3   Substitution Requirements

(a) General requirements. In accordance with Chapter 562 of the Act, a pharmacist may dispense a generically equivalent drug or interchangeable biological product if:

    (1) the generic drug or interchangeable biological product costs the patient less than the prescribed drug product;

    (2) the patient does not refuse the substitution; and

    (3) the practitioner does not certify on the prescription form that a specific prescribed brand is medically necessary as specified in a dispensing directive described in subsection (c) of this section.

(b) Prescription format for written prescription drug orders.

    (1) A written prescription drug order issued in Texas may:

        (A) be on a form containing a single signature line for the practitioner; and

        (B) contain the following reminder statement on the face of the prescription: "A generically equivalent drug product may be dispensed unless the practitioner hand writes the words 'Brand Necessary' or 'Brand Medically Necessary' on the face of the prescription."

    (2) A pharmacist may dispense a prescription that is not issued on the form specified in paragraph (1) of this subsection, however, the pharmacist may dispense a generically equivalent drug or interchangeable biological product unless the practitioner has prohibited substitution through a dispensing directive in compliance with subsection (c)(1) of this section.

    (3) The prescription format specified in paragraph (1) of this subsection does not apply to the following types of prescription drug orders:

        (A) prescription drug orders issued by a practitioner in a state other than Texas;

        (B) prescriptions for dangerous drugs issued by a practitioner in the United Mexican States or the Dominion of Canada; or

        (C) prescription drug orders issued by practitioners practicing in a federal facility provided they are acting in the scope of their employment.

    (4) In the event of multiple prescription orders appearing on one prescription form, the practitioner shall clearly identify to which prescription(s) the dispensing directive(s) apply. If the practitioner does not clearly indicate to which prescription(s) the dispensing directive(s) apply, the pharmacist may substitute on all prescriptions on the form.

(c) Dispensing directive.

    (1) General requirements. The following is applicable to the dispensing directive outlined in this subsection.

        (A) When a prescription is issued for a brand name product that has no generic equivalent product, the pharmacist must dispense the brand name product. If a generic equivalent or interchangeable biological product becomes available, a pharmacist may substitute the generically equivalent or interchangeable biological product unless the practitioner has specified on the initial prescription that the brand name product is medically necessary.

        (B) If the practitioner has prohibited substitution through a dispensing directive in compliance with this subsection, a pharmacist shall not substitute a generically equivalent drug or interchangeable biological product unless the pharmacist obtains verbal or written authorization from the practitioner, notes such authorization on the original prescription drug order, and notifies the patient in accordance with § 309.4 of this title (relating to Patient Notification).

    (2) Written prescriptions.

        (A) A practitioner may prohibit the substitution of a generically equivalent drug or interchangeable biological product for a brand name drug product by writing across the face of the written prescription, in the practitioner's own handwriting, the phrase "brand necessary" or "brand medically necessary."

        (B) The dispensing directive shall:

            (i) be in a format that protects confidentiality as required by the Health Insurance Portability and Accountability Act of 1996 (29 U.S.C. Section 1181 et seq.) and its subsequent amendments; and

           (ii) comply with federal and state law, including rules, with regard to formatting and security requirements.

        (C) The dispensing directive specified in this paragraph may not be preprinted, rubber stamped, or otherwise reproduced on the prescription form.

        (D) A practitioner may prohibit substitution on a written prescription only by following the dispensing directive specified in this paragraph. Two-line prescription forms, check boxes, or other notations on an original prescription drug order which indicate "substitution instructions" are not valid methods to prohibit substitution, and a pharmacist may substitute on these types of written prescriptions.

    (3) Verbal Prescriptions.

        (A) If a prescription drug order is transmitted to a pharmacist orally, the practitioner or practitioner's agent shall prohibit substitution by specifying "brand necessary" or "brand medically necessary." The pharmacist shall note any substitution instructions by the practitioner or practitioner's agent, on the file copy of the prescription drug order. Such file copy may follow the one-line format indicated in subsection (b)(1) of this section, or any other format that clearly indicates the substitution instructions.

        (B) If the practitioner's or practitioner's agent does not clearly indicate that the brand name is medically necessary, the pharmacist may substitute a generically equivalent drug or interchangeable biological product.

        (C) To prohibit substitution on a verbal prescription reimbursed through the medical assistance program specified in 42 C.F.R., § 447.331:

        (i)   the practitioner or the practitioner's agent shall verbally indicate that the brand is medically necessary; and

        (ii) the practitioner shall mail or fax a written prescription to the pharmacy which complies with the dispensing directive for written prescriptions specified in paragraph (1) of this subsection within 30 days.

  (4) Electronic prescription drug orders.

     (A) To prohibit substitution, the practitioner or practitioner's agent shall clearly indicate substitution instructions in the electronic prescription drug order.

     (B) If the practitioner or practitioner's agent does not indicate or does not clearly indicate in the electronic prescription drug order that the brand is necessary, the pharmacist may substitute a generically equivalent drug or interchangeable biological product.

     (C) To prohibit substitution on an electronic prescription drug order reimbursed through the medical assistance program specified in 42 C.F.R., § 447.331, the practitioner shall comply with state and federal laws.

  (5) Prescriptions issued by out-of-state, Mexican, Canadian, or federal facility practitioners.

     (A) The dispensing directive specified in this subsection does not apply to the following types of prescription drug orders:

        (i)   prescription drug orders issued by a practitioner in a state other than Texas;

        (ii) prescriptions for dangerous drugs issued by a practitioner in the United Mexican States or the Dominion of Canada; or

        (iii) prescription drug orders issued by practitioners practicing in a federal facility provided they are acting in the scope of their employment.

     (B) A pharmacist may not substitute on prescription drug orders identified in subparagraph (A) of this paragraph unless the practitioner has authorized substitution on the prescription drug order. If the practitioner has not authorized substitution on the written prescription drug order, a pharmacist shall not substitute a generically equivalent drug product unless:

        (i)   the pharmacist obtains verbal or written authorization from the practitioner (such authorization shall be noted on the original prescription drug order); or

        (ii) the pharmacist obtains written documentation regarding substitution requirements from the State Board of Pharmacy in the state, other than Texas, in which the prescription drug order was issued. The following is applicable concerning this documentation.

           (I)   The documentation shall state that a pharmacist may substitute on a prescription drug order issued in such other state unless the practitioner prohibits substitution on the original prescription drug order.

           (II) The pharmacist shall note on the original prescription drug order the fact that documentation from such other state board of pharmacy is on file.

           (III) Such documentation shall be updated yearly.

(d) Refills.

  (1) Original substitution instructions. All refills shall follow the original substitution instructions unless otherwise indicated by the practitioner or practitioner's agent.

  (2) Narrow therapeutic index drugs.

     (A) The board and the Texas Medical Board shall establish a joint committee to recommend to the board a list of narrow therapeutic index drugs and the rules, if any, by which this paragraph applies to those drugs. The committee must consist of an equal number of members from each board. The committee members shall select a member of the committee to serve as presiding officer for a one year term. The presiding officer may not represent the same board as the presiding officer's predecessor.

     (B) The board, on the recommendation of the joint committee, has determined that no drugs shall be included on a list of narrow therapeutic index drugs as defined in § 562.014, Occupations Code.

        (i)   The board has specified in § 309.7 of this title (relating to dispensing responsibilities) that for drugs listed in the publication, pharmacist shall use as a basis for determining generic equivalency, Approved Drug Products with Therapeutic Equivalence Evaluations and current supplements published by the Federal Food and Drug Administration, within the limitations stipulated in that publication. For drugs listed in the publications, pharmacists may only substitute products that are rated therapeutically equivalent in the Approved Drug Products with Therapeutic Equivalence Evaluations and current supplements.

        (ii) Practitioners may prohibit substitution through a dispensing directive in compliance with subsection (c) of this section.

     (C) The board shall reconsider the contents of the list if:

        (i)   the Federal Food and Drug Administration determines a new equivalence classification which indicates that certain drug products are equivalent but special notification to the patient and practitioner is required when substituting these products; or

        (ii) any interested person petitions the board to reconsider the list. If the board receives a petition to include a drug on the list, the joint committee specified in subparagraph (A) of this paragraph shall review the request and make a recommendation to the board.

Source: The provisions of this § 309.3 adopted to be effective June 1, 2002, 27 TexReg 1782; amended to be effective June 12, 2005, 30 TexReg 3210; amended to be effective June 8, 2008, 33 TexReg 4311; amended to be effective September 7, 2008, 33 TexReg 7243; amended to be effective December 7, 2010, 35 TexReg 10693; amended to be effective December 6, 2015, 40 TexReg 8790

§309.4 Patient Notification

(a) Substitution notification. Before delivery of a prescription for a generically equivalent drug or interchangeable biological product as authorized by Chapter 562, Subchapter A of the Act, a pharmacist must:

  (1) personally, or through his or her agent or employee inform the patient or the patient's agent that a less expensive generically equivalent drug or interchangeable biological product is available for the brand prescribed; and ask the patient or the patient's agent to choose between the generically equivalent drug or interchangeable biological product and the brand prescribed.

    (2) A pharmacist shall offer the patient or the patient's agent the option of paying for a prescription drug at a lower price instead of paying the amount of the copayment under the patient's prescription drug insurance plan if the price of the prescribed drug is lower than the amount of the patient's copayment.

(b) Exceptions. A pharmacy is not required to comply with the provisions of subsection (a) of this section:

    (1) in the case of the refill of a prescription for which the pharmacy previously complied with subsection (a) of this section with regard to the same patient or patient's agent; or

    (2) if the patient's physician or physician's agent advises the pharmacy that:

        (A) the physician has informed the patient or the patient's agent that a less expensive generically equivalent drug or interchangeable biological product is available for the brand prescribed; and

        (B) the patient or the patient's agent has chosen either the brand prescribed or the less expensive generically equivalent drug or interchangeable biological product.

(c) Notification by pharmacies delivering prescriptions by mail.

    (1) A pharmacy that supplies a prescription by mail is considered to have complied with the provision of subsection (a) of this section if the pharmacy includes on the prescription order form completed by the patient or the patient's agent language that clearly and conspicuously:

        (A) states that if a less expensive generically equivalent drug or interchangeable biological product is available for the brand prescribed, the patient or the patient's agent may choose between the generically equivalent drug or interchangeable biological product and the brand prescribed; and

        (B) allows the patient or the patient's agent to indicate the choice of the generically equivalent drug or interchangeable biological product or the brand prescribed.

    (2) If the patient or patient's agent fails to indicate otherwise to a pharmacy on the prescription order form under paragraph (1) of this subsection, the pharmacy may dispense a generically equivalent drug or interchangeable biological product.

(d) Inpatient notification exemption. Institutional pharmacies shall be exempt from the labeling provisions and patient notification requirements of § 562.006 and § 562.009 of the Act, as respects drugs distributed pursuant to medication orders.

Source: The provisions of this § 309.4 adopted to be effective June 1, 2002, 27 TexReg 1782; amended to be effective December 4, 2005, 30 TexReg 7875; amended to be effective December 7, 2010, 35 TexReg 10693; amended to be effective December 6, 2015, 40 TexReg 8790

§309.5   Communication with Prescriber

(a) Not later than the third business day after the date of dispensing a biological product, the dispensing pharmacist or the pharmacist's designee shall communicate to the prescribing practitioner the specific product provided to the patient, including the name of the product and the manufacturer or national drug code number.

(b) The communication must be conveyed by making an entry into an interoperable electronic medical records system or through electronic prescribing technology or a pharmacy benefit management system or a pharmacy record, which may include information submitted for the payment of claims, that a pharmacist reasonably concludes is electronically accessible by the prescribing practitioner. Otherwise, the pharmacist or the pharmacist's designee shall communicate the biological product dispensed to the prescribing practitioner, using facsimile, telephone, electronic transmission, or other prevailing means, provided that communication is not required if:

    (1) there is no interchangeable biological product approved by the United States Food and Drug Administration for the product prescribed; or

    (2) a refill prescription is not changed from the product dispensed on the prior filling of the prescription.

(c) This section expires September 1, 2019.

Source: The provisions of this § 309.5 adopted to be effective December 6, 2015, 40 TexReg 8790

§309.6   Records

(a) When the pharmacist dispenses a generically equivalent drug or interchangeable biological product pursuant to the Subchapter A, Chapter 562 of the Act, the following information shall be noted on the original prescription or in the pharmacy's data processing system:

    (1) any substitution instructions communicated orally to the pharmacist by the practitioner or practitioner's agent or a notation that no substitution instructions were given; and

    (2) the name and strength of the actual drug product dispensed shall be noted on the original or hard-copy prescription drug order. The name shall be either:

        (A) the brand name and strength; or

        (B) the generic name or the name of the interchangeable biological product, strength, and name of the manufacturer or distributor of such generic drug or interchangeable biological product. (The name of the manufacturer or distributor may be reduced to an abbreviation or initials, provided the abbreviation or initials are sufficient to identify the manufacturer or distributor. For combination drug products having no brand name, the principal active ingredients shall be indicated on the prescription.)

(b) If a pharmacist refills a prescription drug order with a generically equivalent product or interchangeable biological product from a different manufacturer or distributor than previously dispensed, the pharmacist shall record on the prescription drug order the information required in subsection (a) of this section for the product dispensed on the refill.

(c) If a pharmacy utilizes patient medication records for recording prescription information, the information required in subsections (a) and (b) of this section shall be recorded on the patient medication records.

(d) The National Drug Code (NDC) of a drug or any other code may be indicated on the prescription drug order at the discretion of the pharmacist, but such code shall not be used in place of the requirements of subsections (a) and (b) of this section.

Source: The provisions of this § 309.6 adopted to be effective June 1, 2002, 27 TexReg 1782; amended to be effective December 6, 2015, 40 TexReg 8790; amended to be effective January 4, 2018, 42 TexReg 7710

§309.7 Dispensing Responsibilities

(a) The determination of the drug product to be substituted as authorized by the Subchapter A, Chapter 562 of the Act, is the professional responsibility of the pharmacist, and the pharmacist may not dispense any product that does not meet the requirements of the Subchapter A, Chapter 562 of the Act.

(b) Pharmacists shall use as a basis for the determination of generic equivalency or interchangeability as defined in the Subchapter A, Chapter 562 of the Act, most recent edition or supplement of the United States Food and Drug Administration's references (e.g., the Orange Book or Purple Book).

(c) Pharmacists. For drugs not listed in the Orange Book, pharmacists shall use their professional judgment to determine generic equivalency.

(d) Pharmacists shall use Lists of Licensed Biological Products with Reference Product Exclusivity and Biosimilarity or Interchangeability Evaluations (Purple Book) and current supplements published by the Federal Food and Drug Administration, within the limitations stipulated in that publication, to determine biosimilarity to or interchangeability with a reference biological product.

Source: The provisions of this § 309.7 adopted to be effective June 1, 2002, 27 TexReg 1782; amended to be effective June 12, 2005, 30 TexReg 3210; amended to be effective December 6, 2015, 40 TexReg 8790

§309.8 Advertising of Generic Drugs by Pharmacies

Prescription drug advertising comparing generic drugs or biological products and brand name drugs or biological products is subject to the § 554.054 of the Act and in compliance with federal law.

Source: The provisions of this § 309.8 adopted to be effective June 1, 2002, 27 TexReg 1782; amended to be effective December 6, 2015, 40 TexReg 8790

CHAPTER 311. CODE OF CONDUCT

§311.1 Procedures

(a) Complaints alleging violations of the Board Code of Conduct by a board employee shall be submitted in writing to the executive director. If a board member is notified of a complaint against an employee, the board member shall direct the complainant to file a written complaint with the executive director. Complaints filed against a peace officer employee must comply with §614.023 of the Government Code (relating to Copy of Complaint to be Given to Officer or Employee).

(b) The executive director shall notify the employee's supervisor that a complaint has been filed against the employee. The supervisor shall provide the employee with written notice that a complaint has been filed, which contains the date the complaint was filed and a description of the complaint. An anonymous complaint or a complaint filed by e-mail will not be considered a valid complaint for the purposes of this section.

(c) In order for a complaint concerning violations of the Code of Conduct to be considered valid, such complaint shall contain the following information:
  (1) the date the complaint is filed;
  (2) the date the violation occurred;
  (3) the complainant's name, address, and telephone number;
  (4) the name of the board employee;
  (5) detailed description of the alleged violation;
  (6) any written documentation or name of witnesses to the alleged violation; and
  (7) the signature of the complainant.

(d) The executive director shall acknowledge receipt of the complaint in writing to the complainant. Such acknowledgment may include a request for additional information concerning the complaint or questions about the occurrence or statements.

(e) In reviewing the complaint, the executive director may contact the complainant if necessary and shall conduct a personal interview with the employee and give the employee ample opportunity to present evidence to support his or her explanation of the circumstances surrounding the complaint. The employee shall have the right to submit any relevant records, materials, comments, and documents to the executive director for review. Additionally, the employee has the right to review all documents and records involving the complaint. The employee may request the executive director to allow the board's legal counsel to advise the employee of his or her rights.

(f) Upon completing the review of the complaint and relevant statements or documents, the executive director shall render a decision concerning the complaint within 10 days and provide written notification of the decision to the employee, and his or her supervisor within five days of rendering the decision. The executive director shall notify the complainant of the disposition of the complaint. If the disposition of the complaint affects the employee's employment status, the employee has the right to exercise the board's grievance procedure.

(g) Complaints alleging violations of the Board Code of Conduct by the executive director shall be directed to the president of the board. The procedures set out in this section shall be followed in disposing of such complaints; provided, however, that for the purposes of this subsection, where the term "executive director" appears in the procedures set out in this section, the term "president of the board" shall be substituted therefor.

Source: The provisions of this §311.1 adopted to be effective April 23, 1982, 7 TexReg 1481; amended to be effective September 8, 2002, 27 TexReg 8243; amended to be effective December 3, 2006, 31 TexReg 9612; amended to be effective March 10, 2011, 36 TexReg 1559

§311.2 Procedures Regarding Complaints Filed against Board Members

(a) The following procedures are applicable with regard to complaints against a board member, if the complaint alleges violations of the laws and rules governing the practice of pharmacy.
  (1) The complaint shall be reviewed by the executive director, who may refer the complaint to the appropriate board staff for handling, or if deemed necessary, the executive director may refer the complaint to another agency.

(2) If the complaint is investigated and the investigation produces evidence of a violation of the laws or rules regarding the practice of pharmacy, the board staff shall determine if the complaint merits the institution of disciplinary action. This decision shall be made in consultation with one board member who shall be a pharmacist, but who shall not be the subject of the complaint; the board member shall be the president of the board, unless such person is unable to serve because he or she does not meet the criteria of this paragraph or for some other valid reason. If the president is unable to serve, the order of succession shall be vice-president, then treasurer. If none of the pharmacist officers are able to serve, then the board president or designee shall designate another pharmacist board member to serve.

(b) If after consultation with the board member described in subsection (a)(2) of this section, the determination is made that the complaint merits the institution of disciplinary action, the following is applicable.

   (1) The complaint shall be directed to the assistant attorney general assigned to the board. The Office of the Attorney General should then assign an assistant attorney general to prosecute the complaint in accordance with board rules.

   (2) The board's legal counsel shall act as a liaison between the board's staff and the attorney general's office. The board's legal counsel shall ensure that the board's staff provides any information or assistance requested by the attorney general's office.

   (3) The board member shall be sent a preliminary notice letter and offered the opportunity to attend an informal conference for the purpose of settling the matter through an informal conference.

(c) If the board member accepts the opportunity to attend an informal conference, the conference participants shall be as follows:

   (1) the assistant attorney general assigned to the case, who shall conduct the informal conference;

   (2) the board member who is the subject of the complaint and/or his or her legal counsel;

   (3) board staff, as necessary or required; and

   (4) one board member, who shall be the same person who was initially consulted about the complaint, as described in subsection (a)(2) of this section, provided, however, if that board member is unable to serve for some valid reason, the board member that shall attend the informal conference shall be a pharmacist, but who shall not be the subject of the complaint; the board member designated to attend the informal conference shall be the president of the board, unless such person is unable to serve because he or she does not meet the criteria of this paragraph or for some other valid reason. If the president is unable to serve, the order of succession shall be vice-president, then treasurer. If none of the pharmacist officers are able to serve, then the board president or designee shall designate another pharmacist board member to attend the informal conference.

(d) The case shall proceed to hearing, if the board member who is the subject of the complaint waives his or her right to attend an informal conference, or if after an informal conference is conducted, the case is not dismissed or the board member does not accept the recommendation for settlement.

(e) If the case proceeds to hearing, the following procedures are applicable:

   (1) the assistant attorney general assigned to the case shall prosecute the hearing with the hearings officer presiding;

   (2) the hearings officer shall then draft an officer's report which discusses the evidence and contains proposed findings of fact and conclusions of law. The hearings officer shall, as authorized by law, recommend a sanction if he or she determines one is necessary; and

   (3) at the next scheduled board meeting, after the hearing officer has issued a proposal and all parties have accepted and replied, the following is applicable.

      (A) The board, absent the board member who is the subject of the complaint, shall vote to:
         (i) accept or reject each proposed finding of fact and conclusion of law; and
         (ii) accept or reject the recommended sanction, if applicable.

      (B) If the board rejects the recommended sanction, the board shall then vote on the sanction they deem appropriate.

      (C) If the board determines that additional evidence is needed, they can vote to remand the case for further hearing, as provided by law.

(f) For the purposes of this section, a board member is defined as any individual who is serving on the board on the date of the receipt of the complaint, or any individual who has previously served on the board, if the complaint is filed within two years from the date the board member's official duties ended.

Source: The provisions of this §311.2 adopted to be effective October 21, 1992, 17 TexReg 6896.

CHAPTER 315. CONTROLLED SUBSTANCES

§315.1   Definitions – Effective September 1, 2016
The following terms in this section, when used in this chapter, have the following meanings, unless the context clearly indicates otherwise.

   (1) TCSA—The Texas Controlled Substances Act (Texas Health and Safety Code, Chapter 481).

   (2) Advanced practice registered nurse—A registered nurse licensed by the Texas Board of Nursing to practice as an advanced practice registered nurse on the basis of completion of an advanced educational program. The term includes a nurse practitioner, nurse midwife, nurse anesthetist, and clinical nurse specialist. The term is synonymous with "advanced nurse practitioner" and "advanced practice nurse."

   (3) Day—A calendar day unless the context clearly indicates a business day.

   (4) Drug Enforcement Administration (DEA)—The Federal Drug Enforcement Administration.

   (5) Electronic transmission—The transmission of information in electronic form such as computer to computer, electronic device to computer, e-mail, or the transmission of the exact visual image of a document by way of electronic media.

   (6) Emergency situation—A situation described in the Code of Federal Regulations, Title 21, § 1306.11(d).

(7) Individual practitioner—A physician, dentist, veterinarian, optometrist, podiatrist, or other individual licensed, registered, or otherwise permitted to dispense a controlled substance in the course of professional practice, but does not include a pharmacist, a pharmacy, or an institutional practitioner.

(8) Institutional practitioner—A hospital or other person (other than an individual practitioner) licensed, registered, or otherwise permitted to dispense a controlled substance in the course of professional practice, but does not include a pharmacy.

(9) Locum tenen—An individual practitioner who practices in a temporary position in this state and licensed by the appropriate Texas state licensing board.

(10) Long-term care facility (LTCF)—An establishment licensed as such by the Texas Department of Aging and Disability Services.

(11) NDC #—A National Drug Code number.

(12) Physician assistant—An individual licensed as such by the Texas Physician Assistant Board.

(13) Record—A notification, order form, statement, invoice, prescription, inventory information, or other document for the acquisition or disposal of a controlled substance, precursor, or apparatus in any manner by a registrant or permit holder under a record keeping or inventory requirement of federal law, the TCSA, or this chapter.

(14) Reportable prescription—A prescription for a controlled substance:
   (A) listed in Schedule II through V; and
   (B) not excluded from this chapter by a rule adopted under the TCSA, § 481.0761(b).

(15) Temporary controlled substances registration (TCSR)—A controlled substances registration issued to a locum tenen or a health practitioner for a period of time not to exceed 90 days.

Source: The provisions of this § 315.1 adopted to be effective March 10, 2016, 41 TexReg 1690

§315.2 Official Prescription Form

(a) A practitioner may order official prescription forms from the board only if the practitioner is registered by the DEA to prescribe a Schedule II controlled substance.

(b) The board is the sole source for the official prescription forms.

(c) This subsection applies only to an institutional practitioner who is employed by a hospital or other training institution. An institutional practitioner authorized by a hospital or institution to prescribe a Schedule II controlled substance under the DEA registration of the hospital or institution may order official prescription forms under this section if:
   (1) the practitioner prescribes a controlled substance in the usual course of the practitioner's training, teaching program, or employment at the hospital or institution;
   (2) the appropriate state health regulatory agency has assigned an institutional permit or similar number to the practitioner; and
   (3) the hospital or institution:
      (A) maintains a current list of each institutional practitioner and each assigned institutional permit number; and
      (B) makes the list available to another registrant or a member of a state health regulatory or law enforcement agency for the purpose of verifying the authority of the practitioner to prescribe the substance.

(d) An advanced practice registered nurse or physician assistant operating under a prescriptive authority agreement pursuant to Texas Occupations Code, Chapter 157 may order official prescription forms under this section if authority to prescribe has been delegated by a physician. Upon withdrawal of the delegating physician's authority such forms are void and must be returned to the board.

Source: The provisions of this § 315.2 adopted to be effective March 10, 2016, 41 TexReg 1690; amended to be effective June 20, 2019, 44 TexReg 2957

§315.3 Prescriptions – Effective September 1, 2016

(a) Schedule II Prescriptions.
   (1) Except as provided by subsection (e) of this section, a practitioner, as defined in the TCSA, § 481.002(39)(A), must issue a written prescription for a Schedule II controlled substance only on an official Texas prescription form or through an electronic prescription that meets all requirements of the TCSA. This subsection also applies to a prescription issued in an emergency situation.
   (2) A practitioner who issues a written prescription for any quantity of a Schedule II controlled substance must complete an official prescription form.
   (3) A practitioner may issue multiple written prescriptions authorizing a patient to receive up to a 90-day supply of a Schedule II controlled substance provided:
      (A) each prescription is issued for a legitimate medical purpose by a practitioner acting in the usual course of professional practice;
      (B) the practitioner provides written instructions on each prescription, other than the first prescription if the practitioner intends for that prescription to be filled immediately, indicating the earliest date on which a pharmacy may dispense each prescription; and
      (C) the practitioner concludes that providing the patient with multiple prescriptions in this manner does not create an undue risk of diversion or abuse.
   (4) A schedule II prescription must be dispensed no later than 21 days after the date of issuance or, if the prescription is part of a multiple set of prescriptions, issued on the same day, no later than 21 days after the earliest date on which a pharmacy may dispense the prescription as indicated on each prescription.

(b) Schedules III through V Prescriptions.
   (1) A practitioner, as defined in the TCSA, § 481.002(39)(A), (C), (D), may use prescription forms and order forms through individual sources. A practitioner may issue, or allow to be issued by a person under the practitioner's direction or supervision, a Schedule III through V controlled substance on a prescription form for a valid medical purpose and in the course of medical practice.

(2)   Schedule III through V prescriptions may be refilled up to five times within six months after date of issuance.
(c) Electronic prescription. A practitioner is permitted to issue and to dispense an electronic controlled substance prescription only in accordance with the requirements of the Code of Federal Regulations, Title 21, Part 1311.
(d) Controlled substance prescriptions may not be postdated.
(e) Advanced practice registered nurses or physician assistants may only use the official prescription forms issued with their name, address, phone number, and DEA numbers, and the delegating physician's name and DEA number.
Source: The provisions of this § 315.3 adopted to be effective March 10, 2016, 41 TexReg 1690; amended to be effective June 11, 2017, 42 TexReg 2931

§315.4   Exceptions to Use of Form – Effective September 1, 2016

(a) An official prescription form is not required for a medication order written for a patient who is admitted to a hospital at the time the medication order is written and dispensed.
  (1) A practitioner may dispense or cause to be dispensed a Schedule II controlled substance to a patient who:
      (A) is admitted to the hospital; and
      (B) will require an emergency quantity of a controlled substance upon release from the hospital.
  (2) Under paragraph (1) of this subsection, the controlled substance:
      (A) may only be dispensed in a properly labeled container; and
      (B) may not be more than a seven-day supply or the minimum amount needed for proper treatment of the patient until the patient can obtain access to a pharmacy, whichever is less.
(b) Subsection (a) of this section applies to a patient who is admitted to a hospital, including a patient:
  (1) admitted to:
      (A) a general hospital, special hospital, licensed ambulatory surgical center, surgical suite in a dental school, or veterinary medical school; or
      (B) a hospital clinic or emergency room, if the clinic or emergency room is under the control, direction, and administration as an integral part of a general or special hospital;
  (2) receiving treatment with a Schedule II controlled substance from a member of a Life Flight or similar medical team or an emergency medical ambulance crew or a paramedic-emergency medical technician operating as an extension of an emergency room of a general or special hospital; or
  (3) receiving treatment with a Schedule II controlled substance while the patient is an inmate incarcerated in a correctional facility operated by the Texas Department of Criminal Justice or a correctional facility operating in accordance with the Health Services Plan adopted by the Texas Commission on Jail Standards.
(c) Subsection (a) of this section applies to an animal admitted to an animal hospital, including an animal that is a permanent resident of a zoo, wildlife park, exotic game ranch, wildlife management program, or state or federal research facility.
(d) An official prescription form is not required in a long-term care facility (LTCF) if:
  (1) an individual administers the substance to an inpatient from the facility's medical emergency kit;
  (2) the individual administering the substance is an authorized practitioner or an agent acting under the practitioner's order; and
  (3) the facility maintains the proper records as required for an emergency medical kit in an LTCF.
(e) An official prescription form is not required when a therapeutic optometrist administers a topical ocular pharmaceutical agent in compliance with:
  (1) the Texas Optometry Act; and
  (2) a rule adopted by the Texas Optometry Board under the authority of the Texas Optometry Act.
Source: The provisions of this § 315.4 adopted to be effective March 10, 2016, 41 TexReg 1690

§315.5   Pharmacy Responsibility – Generally – Effective September 1, 2016

(a) Upon receipt of a properly completed prescription form, a dispensing pharmacist must:
  (1) if the prescription is for a Schedule II controlled substance, ensure the date the prescription is presented is not later than 21 days after the date of issuance;
  (2) if multiple prescriptions are issued by the prescribing practitioner allowing up to a 90-day supply of Schedule II controlled substances, ensure each prescription is neither dispensed prior to the earliest date intended by the practitioner nor dispensed beyond 21 days from the earliest date the prescription may be dispensed;
  (3) record the date dispensed and the pharmacy prescription number;
  (4) indicate whether the pharmacy dispensed to the patient a quantity less than the quantity prescribed; and
  (5) if issued on an official prescription form, record the following information, if different from the prescribing practitioner's information:
      (A) the brand name or, if none, the generic name of the controlled substance dispensed; or
      (B) the strength, quantity, and dosage form of the Schedule II controlled substance used to prepare the mixture or compound.
(b) The prescription presented for dispensing is void, and a new prescription is required, if:
  (1) the prescription is for a Schedule II controlled substance, 21 days after issuance, or 21 days after any earliest dispense date; or
  (2) the prescription is for a Schedule III, IV, or V controlled substance, more than six months after issuance or has been dispensed five times during the six months after issuance.
Source: The provisions of this § 315.5 adopted to be effective March 10, 2016, 41 TexReg 1690

§315.6   Pharmacy Responsibility – Electronic Reporting

(a) Not later than the next business day after the date a controlled substance prescription is dispensed, a pharmacy must electronically submit to the board the following data elements:

    (1) the prescribing practitioner's DEA registration number including the prescriber's identifying suffix of the authorizing hospital or other institution's DEA number when applicable;

    (2) the official prescription form control number if dispensed from a written official prescription form for a Schedule II controlled substance;

    (3) the board's designated placeholder entered into the control number field if the prescription is electronic and meets the requirements of Code of Federal Regulations, Title 21, Part 1311;

    (4) the patient's name, date of birth, and address including city, state, and zip code; or such information on the animal's owner if the prescription is for an animal;

    (5) the date the prescription was issued and dispensed;

    (6) the NDC # of the controlled substance dispensed;

    (7) the quantity of controlled substance dispensed;

    (8) the pharmacy's prescription number; and

    (9) the pharmacy's DEA registration number.

(b) A pharmacy must electronically correct dispensing data submitted to the board within seven business days of identifying an omission, error, or inaccuracy in previously submitted dispensing data.

Source: The provisions of this § 315.6 adopted to be effective March 10, 2016, 41 TexReg 1690; amended to be effective December 6, 2018, 43 TexReg 7787

§315.7   Pharmacy Responsibility – Oral, Telephonic, or Emergency Prescription – Effective September 1, 2016

(a) If a pharmacy dispenses a controlled substance pursuant to an orally or telephonically communicated prescription from a practitioner or the practitioner's designated agent, the prescription must be promptly reduced to writing, including the information required:

    (1) by law for a standard prescription; and

    (2) by law and this subchapter for an official prescription, if issued for a Schedule II controlled substance in an emergency situation.

(b) After dispensing a Schedule II controlled substance pursuant to an orally or telephonically communicated prescription, the dispensing pharmacy must:

    (1) maintain the written record created under subsection (a) of this section;

    (2) note the emergency nature of the prescription;

    (3) upon receipt from the practitioner, attach the original official prescription to the orally or telephonically communicated prescription; and

    (4) retain both documents in the pharmacy records.

(c) A pharmacy that dispenses Schedule III, IV, or V controlled substances pursuant to an orally or telephonically communicated prescription must inform the prescribing practitioner in the event of an emergency refill of the prescription.

(d) All records generated under this section must be maintained for two years from the date the substance was dispensed.

Source: The provisions of this § 315.7 adopted to be effective March 10, 2016, 41 TexReg 1690

§315.8   Pharmacy Responsibility – Modification of Prescription – Effective September 1, 2016

The pharmacy is responsible for documenting the following information regarding a modified prescription:

    (1) date the change or adding of information was authorized;

    (2) information that was authorized to be added or changed;

    (3) name of the prescribing practitioner granting the authorization; and

    (4) initials or identification code of the pharmacist.

Source: The provisions of this § 315.8 adopted to be effective March 10, 2016, 41 TexReg 1690

§315.9   Pharmacy Responsibility – Out-of-State Practitioner – Effective September 1, 2016

(a) A Schedule II controlled substance prescription issued by a practitioner in another state not on the board's official prescription form may be dispensed if:

    (1) the practitioner is authorized by the other state to prescribe the substance;

    (2) the pharmacy has a plan approved by and on file with the board allowing the activity; and

    (3) the pharmacy processes and submits the prescription according to the reporting requirements approved in the plan.

(b) The pharmacy may dispense a prescription for a Schedule III through V controlled substance issued by a practitioner in another state if the practitioner is authorized by the other state to prescribe the substance.

Source: The provisions of this § 315.9 adopted to be effective March 10, 2016, 41 TexReg 1690

§315.10 Return of Unused Official Prescription Form – Effective September 1, 2016

(a) An unused official prescription form is invalid and the practitioner or another person acting on behalf of the practitioner must return the unused form to the board with an appropriate explanation not later than the 30th day after the date:

    (1) the practitioner's license to practice, DEA number is canceled, revoked, suspended, denied, or surrendered or amended to exclude the handling of all Schedule II controlled substances; or

    (2) the practitioner is deceased.

(b) An individual who is an institutional practitioner must return an unused official prescription form to the administrator of the hospital or other training institution upon completion or termination of the individual's training at the hospital or institution. The administrator must return an unused official prescription form to the board not later than the 30th day after the date the individual completes or terminates all training programs.

(c)   No individual may continue to use an official prescription form issued under an institutional practitioner's DEA number or similar number after the individual has been properly and individually licensed as a practitioner by the appropriate state health regulatory agency.

Source: The provisions of this § 315.10 adopted to be effective March 10, 2016, 41 TexReg 1690

§315.11 Release of Prescription Data – Effective September 1, 2016

(a)   A person listed under § 481.076(a) of the TCSA must show proper need for the information when requesting the release of prescription data. The showing of proper need is ongoing.

(b)   A pharmacist may delegate access to prescription data to a pharmacy technician as defined by Texas Occupations Code, § 551.003, employed at the pharmacy and acting under the direction of the pharmacist.

(c)   A practitioner may delegate access to prescription data to an employee or other agent of the practitioner and acting at the direction of the practitioner.

Source: The provisions of this § 315.11 adopted to be effective March 10, 2016, 41 TexReg 1690

§315.12 Schedule III through V Prescription Forms

(a)   A practitioner, as defined in the TCSA, § 481.002(39)(A), (C), and (D), may use prescription forms ordered through individual sources or through an electronic prescription that includes the controlled substances registration number issued by the United States Drug Enforcement Administration and meets all requirements of the TCSA.

(b)   If a written prescription form is to be used to prescribe a controlled substance the dispensing practitioner must be registered with the DEA under both state and federal law to prescribe controlled substances.

Source: The provisions of this § 315.12 adopted to be effective March 10, 2016, 41 TexReg 1690; amended to be effective March 12, 2019, 44 TexReg 1345

§315.13 Official Prescription Form – Effective September 1, 2016

(a)   Accountability. A practitioner who obtains from the board an official prescription form is accountable for each numbered form.

(b)   Prohibited acts. A practitioner may not:
      (1)   allow another practitioner to use the individual practitioner's official prescription form;
      (2)   pre-sign an official prescription blank;
      (3)   post-date an official prescription; or
      (4)   leave an official prescription blank in a location where the practitioner should reasonably believe another could steal or misuse a prescription.

(c)   While not in use. While an official prescription blank is not in immediate use, a practitioner may not maintain or store the book at a location so the book is easily accessible for theft or other misuse.

(d)   Voided. A practitioner must account for each voided official prescription form by sending the voided form to the board.

(e)   Types of forms. Forms may be single or multiple copy forms as provided by the board.

(f)   Faxed forms. Faxed official prescription forms will be accounted for as in the TCSA, § 481.074(o).

Source: The provisions of this § 315.13 adopted to be effective March 10, 2016, 41 TexReg 1690

§315.14 Official Prescription – Effective September 1, 2016

(a)   Report lost forms. Not later than close of business on the day of discovery, a practitioner must report a lost or stolen official prescription form to:
      (1)   the local police department or sheriff's office in an effective manner; and
      (2)   the board.

(b)   Recovery report. Not later than close of business on the day of recovery of an official prescription form previously reported lost or stolen, a practitioner must, before using the recovered form, notify:
      (1)   the local law enforcement agency to which the matter was originally reported; and
      (2)   the board.

(c)   Replacement/lost form. Not later than the close of business on the day that an official prescription is replaced or reported lost, with or without a replacement, the prescribing practitioner, or designated agent, shall report to the board the following:
      (1)   patient name, address, date of birth or age;
      (2)   all drug information; and
      (3)   official prescription form control number.

Source: The provisions of this § 315.14 adopted to be effective March 10, 2016, 41 TexReg 1690

§315.15 Access Requirements

(a)   Effective September 1, 2019, a pharmacist before dispensing an opioid, benzodiazepine, barbiturate, or carisoprodol for a patient shall consult the Texas Prescription Monitoring Program (PMP) database to review the patient's controlled substance history. The dispensing pharmacist of a prescription shall be responsible for the review of the PMP database prior to dispensing the prescription, unless the pharmacy has designated another pharmacist whose identity has been recorded in the pharmacy's data processing system as responsible for PMP review.

(b)   The duty to consult the PMP database as described in subsection (a) of this section does not apply in the following circumstances:
      (1)   the prescribing individual practitioner is a veterinarian;

(2)   it is clearly noted in the prescription record that the patient has a diagnosis of cancer or is in hospice care; or

(3)   the pharmacist is unable to access the PMP after making and documenting a good faith effort to do so.

(c)   If a pharmacist uses pharmacy management systems that integrate data from the PMP, a review of the pharmacy management system with the integrated data shall be deemed compliant with the review of the PMP database as required under § 481.0764(a) of the Texas Health and Safety Code and in subsection (a) of this section.

(d)   Pharmacists and pharmacy technicians acting at the direction of a pharmacist may only access information contained in the PMP as authorized in § 481.076 of Texas Controlled Substances Act. A person who is authorized to access the PMP may only do so utilizing that person's assigned identifier (i.e., login and password) and may not use the assigned identifier of another person. Unauthorized access of PMP information is a violation of Texas Controlled Substances Act, the Texas Pharmacy Act, and board rules.

Source: The provisions of this § 315.15 adopted to be effective December 6, 2018, 43 TexReg 7788; amended to be effective June 20, 2019, 44 TexReg 2957

TEXAS CONTROLLED SUBSTANCES ACT AND RULES

Table of Contents
SCHEDULES OF CONTROLLED SUBSTANCES

Cont. Sub.

TEXAS CONTROLLED SUBSTANCES ACT

HEALTH AND SAFETY CODE, CHAPTER 481

SUBCHAPTER A. GENERAL PROVISIONS

SUBCHAPTER B. SCHEDULES

SUBCHAPTER C. REGULATION OF MANUFACTURE, DISTRIBUTION, AND DISPENSATION OF CONTROLLED SUBSTANCES, CHEMICAL PRECURSORS, AND CHEMICAL LABORATORY APPARATUS

Cont. Sub.

SUBCHAPTER D. OFFENSES AND PENALTIES

SUBCHAPTER E. FORFEITURE

SUBCHAPTER F. INSPECTIONS, EVIDENCE, AND MISCELLANEOUS LAW ENFORCEMENT PROVISIONS

SUBCHAPTER G. THERAPEUTIC RESEARCH PROGRAM

SUBCHAPTER H. ADMINISTRATIVE PENALTY

SUBCHAPTER I. INTERAGENCY PRESCRIPTION MONITORING WORK GROUP

SIMULATED CONTROLLED SUBSTANCES

HEALTH AND SAFETY CODE, CHAPTER 482

ABUSABLE SYNTHETIC SUBSTANCES

HEALTH AND SAFETY CODE, CHAPTER 484

ABUSABLE VOLATILE CHEMICALS

HEALTH AND SAFETY CODE, CHAPTER 485

SUBCHAPTER A GENERAL PROVISIONS

SUBCHAPTER B. SALES PERMITS AND SIGNS

SUBCHAPTER C. CRIMINAL PENALTIES

SUBCHAPTER D. ADMINISTRATIVE PENALTY

Cont. Sub.

CONTROLLED SUBSTANCES AND PRECURSOR / APPARATUS RULES

37 TAC PART 1, CHAPTER 13

SUBCHAPTER A. GENERAL PROVISIONS

SUBCHAPTER B. PRECURSOR CHEMICAL LABORATORY APPARATUS (PCLA)

SUBCHAPTER C. PEYOTE DISTRIBUTORS

SUBCHAPTER D. MISCELLANEOUS PROVISIONS

SUBCHAPTER G. FORFEITURE AND DESTRUCTION

Cont. Sub.

SCHEDULES OF CONTROLLED SUBSTANCES

PURSUANT TO THE TEXAS CONTROLLED SUBSTANCES ACT, HEALTH AND SAFETY CODE, CHAPTER 481, THESE SCHEDULES SUPERCEDE PREVIOUS SCHEDULES AND CONTAIN THE MOST CURRENT VERSION OF THE SCHEDULES OF ALL CONTROLLED SUBSTANCES FROM THE PREVIOUS SCHEDULES AND MODIFICATIONS.

This annual publication of the Texas Schedules of Controlled Substances was signed by John Hellerstedt, M.D., Commissioner of Health, and will take effect 21 days following publication of this notice in the *Texas Register*.

Changes to the schedules are designated by an asterisk (*). Additional information can be obtained by contacting the Department of State Health Services, Drugs and Medical Devices Unit, P.O. Box 149347, Austin, Texas 78714-9347. The telephone number is (512) 834-6755 and the website address is http://www.dshs.state.tx.us/dmd.

SCHEDULES

Nomenclature: Controlled substances listed in these schedules are included by whatever official, common, usual, chemical, or trade name they may be designated.

SCHEDULE I

Schedule I consists of:

- **Schedule I opiates**

  The following opiates, including their isomers, esters, ethers, salts, and salts of isomers, esters, and ethers, unless specifically excepted, if the existence of these isomers, esters, ethers, and salts is possible within the specific chemical designation:

  (1) Acetyl-alpha-methylfentanyl (N-[1-(1-methyl-2-phenethyl)- 4-piperidinyl]- Nphenylacetamide);
  (2) AH-7921 (3,4-dichloro-N-[(dimethylamino)cyclohexymethyl[benzamide));
  (3) Acetyl fentanyl (N-(l-phenethylpiperidin-4-yl)-N-phenylacetamide);
  (4) Acryl fentanyl [N-(1-phenethylpiperidin-4-yl)-N-phenylacrylamide) (Other names: acryloylfentanyl);
  (5) AH-7921 (3,4-dichrloro-N-[(dimethylamino)cyclohexymethyl]benzamide));
  (6) Allylprodine;
  (7) Alphacetylmethadol (except levo-alphacetylmethadol, also known as levo-alphaacetylmethadol, levomethadyl acetate, or LAAM);
  (8) Alpha-methylfentanyl or any other derivative of Fentanyl;
  (9) Alpha-methylthiofentanyl (N-[1-methyl-2-(2-thienyl) ethyl-4-piperidinyl]-Nphenyl-propanamide);
  (10) Benzethidine;
  (11) Beta-hydroxyfentanyl (N-[1-(2-hydroxy-2-phenethyl)-4-piperidinyl]-N-phenylpropanamide);
  (12) Beta-hydroxy-3-methylfentanyl (N-[1-(2-hydroxy-2-phenethyl)-3- methyl- 4-piperidinyl]-N- phenylpropanamide);
  *(13) beta-hydroxythiofentanyl (N-[1-[2-hydroxy-2-(thiophen-2-yl)ethyl]piperidin-4-yl]-N-phenylproprionamide, also known as N-[1-[2-hydroxy-2-(2-thienyl)ethyl]-4-piperidnyl]-n-phenyl-propanamide);
  (14) Betaprodine;
  (15) Butyryl fentanyl (N-(1-phenethylpiperidin-4-yl)-N-phenylbutanamide);
  (16) Clonitazene;
  (17) Diampromide;
  (18) Diethylthiambutene;
  (19) Difenoxin;
  (20) Dimenoxadol;
  (21) Dimethylthiambutene;
  (22) Dioxaphetyl butyrate;
  (23) Dipipanone;
  (24) Ethylmethylthiambutene;
  (25) Etonitazene;
  (26) Etoxeridine;
  (27) 4-Fluoroisobutyryl fentanyl [N-(4-fluorophenyl)-N-(1-phenethylpiperidin-4-yl)isobutyramide] (Other names: para-fluoroisobutyryl fentanyl);
  (28) Furanyl fentanyl [N-(1-phenethylpiperdin-4-yl)-N-phenylfuran-2-carboxamide];
  (29) Furethidine;
  (30) Hydroxypethidine;
  (31) Ketobemidone;
  (31) Levophenacylmorphan;
  (32) Meprodine;
  (33) Methadol;
  (34) 3-methylfentanyl (N-[3-methyl-1-(2-phenylethyl)-4-piperidyl]-Nphenylpropanamide), its optical and geometric isomers;
  (35) 3-methylthiofentanyl (N-[3-methyl-1-(2-thienyl)ethyl-4-piperidinyl]-Nphenylpropanamide);

(36) Moramide;
(37) Morpheridine;
(38) MPPP (1-methyl-4-phenyl-4-propionoxypiperidine);
(39) MT-45 (1-cyclohexyl-4-(1,2-diphenylethyl)piperazine);
(40) Noracymethadol;
(41) Norlevorphanol;
(42) Normethadone;
(43) Norpipanone;
(44) Ocfentanil [N-(2-fluorophenyl)-2-methoxy-N-(1-phenethylpiperidin-4-yl)acetamide];
(45) Para-fluorofentanyl (N-(4-fluorophenyl)-N-[1-(2-phenethyl)-4-piperidinyl]-propanamide);
(46) PEPAP (1-(2-phenethyl)-4-phenyl-4-acetoxypiperidine);
(47) Phenadoxone;
(48) Phenampromide;
(49) Phencyclidine;
(50) Phenomorphan;
(51) Phenoperidine;
(52) Piritramide;
(53) Proheptazine;
(54) Properidine;
(55) Propiram;
(56) Tetrahydrofuranyl fentanyl [N-(1-phenethylpiperidin-4-yl)-N-phenyltetrahydrofuran-2-carboxamide];
(57) Thiofentanyl (N-phenyl-N-[1-(2-thienyl)ethyl-4-piperidinyl]-propanamide);
(58) Tilidine;
(59) Trimeperidine; and,
(60) U-47700 (3,4-dichloro-N-[2-(dimethylamino)cyclohexyl]-N-methylbenzamide).

Schedule I opium derivatives

The following opium derivatives, their salts, isomers, and salts of isomers, unless specifically excepted, if the existence of these salts, isomers, and salts of isomers is possible within the specific chemical designation:
(1) Acetorphine;
(2) Acetyldihydrocodeine;
(3) Benzylmorphine;
(4) Codeine methylbromide;
(5) Codeine-N-Oxide;
(6) Cyprenorphine;
(7) Desomorphine;
(8) Dihydromorphine;
(9) Drotebanol;
(10) Etorphine (except hydrochloride salt);
(11) Heroin;
(12) Hydromorphinol;
(13) Methyldesorphine;
(14) Methyldihydromorphine;
(15) Monoacetylmorphine;
(16) Morphine methylbromide;
(17) Morphine methylsulfonate;
(18) Morphine-N-Oxide;
(19) Myrophine;
(20) Nicocodeine;
(21) Nicomorphine;
(22) Normorphine;
(23) Pholcodine; and
(24) Thebacon.

Schedule I hallucinogenic substances

Unless specifically excepted or unless listed in another schedule, a material, compound, mixture, or preparation that contains any quantity of the following hallucinogenic substances or that contains any of the substance's salts, isomers, and salts of isomers if the existence of the salts, isomers, and salts of isomers is possible within the specific chemical designation (for the purposes of this Schedule I hallucinogenic substances section only, the term "isomer" includes optical, position, and geometric isomers):
(1) Alpha-ethyltryptamine (some trade or other names: etryptamine; Monase; alpha ethyl-1H-indole-3-ethanamine; 3-(2-aminobutyl) indole; alpha-ET; AET);
(2) 4-bromo-2,5-dimethoxyamphetamine (some trade or other names: 4-bromo-2,5-dimethoxy-alpha-methylphenethylamine; 4-bromo-2,5-DMA);
(3) 4-bromo-2,5-dimethoxyphenethylamine (some trade or other names: Nexus; 2C-B;2-(4-bromo-2,5-dimethoxyphenyl)-1-aminoethane; alpha-desmethyl DOB);
(4) 2,5-dimethoxyamphetamine (some trade or other names: 2,5-dimethoxyalpha-methylphenethylamine; 2,5-DMA);
(5) 2,5-dimethoxy-4-ethylamphetamine (some trade or other names: DOET);

(6)   2,5-dimethoxy-4-(n)-propylthiophenethylamine, its optical isomers, salts and salts of isomers (Other names: 2C-T-7);

(7)   4-methoxyamphetamine (Other names: 4-methoxy-alpha-methylphenethylamine; paramethoxyamphetamine; PMA);

(8)   5-methoxy-3,4-methylenedioxy-amphetamine;

(9)   4-methl-2,5-dimethoxyamphetamine (Other names: 4-methyl-2,5-dimethoxy-alpha-methyl-phenethylamine; "DOM"; and "STP");;

(10) 3,4-methylenedioxy-amphetamine;

(11) 3,4-methylenedioxy-methamphetamine (MDMA, MDM);

(12) 3,4-methylenedioxy-N-ethylamphetamine (some trade or other names: N-ethylalpha-methyl-3,4(methylenedioxy)phenethylamine; N-ethyl MDA; MDE; MDEA);

(13) N hydroxy 3,4 methylenedioxyamphetamine (Other names: N hydroxy MDA);

(14) 3,4,5-trimethoxy amphetamine;

(15) 5-methoxy-N,N-dimethyltryptamine (Some trade or other names: 5-methoxy-3-[2-(dimethylamino)ethyl]indole; 5-MeO-DMT;

(16) alpha-methyltryptamine (AMT), its isomers, salts, and salts of isomers;

(17) Bufotenine (Other names: 3-(beta-Dimethylaminoethyl) 5 hydroxyindole; 3 (2 dimethylaminoethyl) 5 indolol; N,N dimethylserotonin; 5 hydroxy N,N dimethyltryptamine; mappine);

(18) Diethyltryptamine (Other names: N,N Diethyltryptamine; DET);

(19) Dimethyltryptamine (Other names: DMT)

(20) 5-methoxy-N,N-diisopropyltryptamine, its isomers, salts, and salts of isomers (Other names: 5-MeO-DIPT);

(21) Ibogaine (Other names: 7 Ethyl 6,6-beta,7,8,9,10,12,13 octhydro 2 methoxy 6,9 methano-5H-pyrido[1',2':1,2] azepino [5,4-b] indole; taber-nanthe iboga);

(22) Lysergic acid diethylamide;

*(23) Marihuana;
The term marihuana does not include hemp, as defined in section 297A of the Agricultural Marketing Act of 1946.

(24) Mescaline;

(25) Parahexyl (Other names: 3 Hexyl 1 hydroxy 7,8,9,10 tetrahydro 6,6,9 trimethyl 6H dibenzo [b,d] pyran; Synhexyl);

(26) Peyote, unless unharvested and growing in its natural state, meaning all parts of the plant classified botanically as Lophophora williamsii Lemaire, whether growing or not, the seeds of the plant, an extract from a part of the plant, and every compound, manufacture, salt, derivative, mixture, or preparation of the plant, its seeds, or extracts;

(27) N-ethyl-3-piperidyl benzilate;

(28) N-methyl-3-piperidyl benzilate;

(29) Psilocybin;

(30) Psilocin;

*(31) Tetrahydrocannabinols;
meaning tetrahydrocannabinols naturally contained in a plant of the genus Cannabis (cannabis plant), except for tetrahydrocannabinols in hemp (as defined under section 297A(1) of the Agricultural Marketing Act of 1946),as well as synthetic equivalents of the substances contained in the cannabis plant, or in the resinous extractives of such plant, and/or synthetic substances, derivatives, and their isomers with similar chemical structure and pharmacological activity to those substances contained in the plant, such as the following:
1 cis or trans tetrahydrocannabinol, and their optical isomers;
6 cis or trans tetrahydrocannabinol, and their optical isomers;
3,4 cis or trans tetrahydrocannabinol, and its optical isomers;
(Since nomenclature of these substances is not internationally standardized, compounds of these structures, regardless of numerical designation of atomic positions covered.);

(32) Ethylamine Analog of Phencyclidine (Other names: N-ethyl-l-phenylcyclohexylamine; (l-phenylcyclohexyl) ethylamine; N-(l-phenylcyclohexyl)-ethylamine; cyclohexamine; PCE);

(33) Pyrrolidine analog of phencyclidine (Other names: l-[l-(2-thienyl)-cyclohexyl]-piperidine; 2-thienyl analog of phencyclidine; TPCP; TCP);

(34) Thiophene analog of phencyclidine (Other names: 1-[1-(2-thienyl)-cyclohexyl] piperidine; 2-thienyl analog of phencyclidine; TPCP);

(35) 1 [1 (2 thienyl)cyclohexyl]pyrrolidine (Other names: TCPy);

(36) 4-methylmethcathinone (Other names: 4-methyl-N-methylcathinone; mephedrone);

(37) 3,4-methylenedioxypyrovalerone (MDPV);

(38) 2-(2,5-Dimethoxy-4-ethylphenyl)ethanamine (Other names: 2C-E);

(39) 2-(2,5-Dimethoxy-4-methylphenyl)ethanamine (Other names: 2C-D);

(40) 2-(4-Chloro-2,5-dimethoxyphenyl)ethanamine (Other names: 2C-C);

(41) 2-(4-Iodo-2,5-dimethoxyphenyl)ethanamine (Other names: 2C-I);

(42) 2-[4-(Ethylthio)-2,5-dimethoxyphenyl]ethanamine (Other names: 2C-T-2);

(43) 2-[4-(Isopropylthio)-2,5-dimethoxyphenyl]ethanamine (Other names: 2C-T-4);

(44) 2-(2,5-Dimethoxyphenyl)ethanamine (Other names:2C-H);

(45) 2-(2,5-Dimethoxy-4-nitro-phenyl)ethanamine (Other names: 2C-N);

(46) 2-(2,5-Dimethoxy-4-(n)-propylphenyl)ethanamine (Other names: 2C-P).

(47) 3,4-Methylenedioxy-N-methylcathinone (Other name: Methylone);

(48) (1-pentyl-1H-indol-3-yl)(2,2,3,3-tetramethylcyclopropyl)methanone (Other names: UR-144 and 1-pentyl-3-(2,2,3,3-tetramethlcyclopropoyl)indole);

(49) [1-(5-fluoro-pentyl)-1H-indol-3-yl](2,2,3,3-tetramethylcyclopropyl)methanone (Other names: 5-fluoro-UR-144 and 5-F-UR-144 and XLR11 and 1-5(5-flouro-pentyl)-3-(2,2,3,3-tetramethylcyclopropoyl)indole);

(50) N-(1-adamantyl)-1-pentyl-1H-indazole-3-carboxamide (Other names: APINACA, AKB48);

(51) Quinolin-8-yl 1-pentyl-1H-indole-3-carboxylate, its optical, positional, and geometric isomers, salts and salts of isomers (Other names: PB-22; QUPIC);

(52) Quinolin-8-yl 1-(5-fluoropentyl)-1H-indole-3-carboxylate, its optical, positional, and geometric isomers, salts and salts of isomers (Other names: 5-fluoro-PB-22; 5F-PB-22);

(53) N-(1-amino-3-methyl-1-oxobutan-2-yl)-1-(4-fluorbenzyl)-1H-indazole-3-carboxamide, its optical, positional, and geometric isomers, salts and salts of isomers (Other names: AB-FUBINACA);

(54) N-(1-amino-3,3-dimethyl-1-oxobutan-2-yl)-1-pentyl-1H-indazole-3-carboxamide (ADB-PINACA);

(55) 2-(4-iodo-2,5-dimethoxyphenyl)-N-(2-methoxybenzyl)ethanamine (25I-NBOMe; 2CI-NBOMe; 25I; Cimbi-5);

(56) 2-(4-chloro-2,5-dimethoxyphenyl)-N-(2-methoxybenzyl)ethanamine (25C-NBOMe; 2C-C-NBOMe; 25C; Cimbi-82);

(57) 2-(4-bromo-2,5-dimethoxyphenyl)-N-(2-methoxybenzyl)ethanamine (25B-NBOMe; 2C-B-NBOMe; 25B; Cimbi-36);

(58) Marihuana Extract

Meaning an extract containing one or more cannabinoids that has been derived from any plant of the genus Cannabis. other than the separated resin (whether crude or purified) obtained from the plant;

(59) 4-methyl-N-ethylcathinone (4-MEC);

(60) 4-methyl-alpha- pyrrolidinopropiophenone (4-MePPP);

(61) alpha-pyrrolidinopentiophenone ([alpha]-PVP);

(62) 1-(1,3-benzodioxol-5-yl)-2-(methylamino)butan-1-one (butylone, bk-MBDB);

(63) 2-(methy I amino)-1-phenylpentan-1-one (pentedrone);

(64) 1-(1,3-benzodioxol-5-yl)-2-(methylamino)pentan-1-one (pentylone, bk-MBDP);

(65) 4-fluoro-N-methylcathinone (4-FMC, flephedrone);

(66) 3-fluoro-N-methylcathinone (3-FMC);

(67) l-(naphthalen-2-yl)-2-(pyrrolidin-1-yl)pentan-l-one (naphyrone);

(68) alpha-pyrrolidinobutiophenone ([alpha]-PBP);

(69) N-(l-amino-3-methyl-l-oxobutan-2-yl)-l-(cyclohexy-methyl)-lH-indazole-3-carboxamide (Other names: AB-CHMINACA');

(70) N-(l-amino-3-methyl-l-oxobutan-2-yl)-l-pentyl-lH-indazole-3-carboxamide (Other names: AB-PINACA);

(71) [1-(5-fluoropentyl)-lH-indazol-3-yl](naphthalen-l-yl)methanone (Other names: THJ-220 I);

(72) 1-methyl-4-phenyl-1,2,5,6-tetrahydro-pyridine (MPTP); and,

(73) N-(l-amino03,3-dimethyl-l-oxobutan-2-yl)-l-(cyclohexyl-methyl)-1H-indazole-3-carboxamide (OTher names: MAB-CHMINACA and ABD-CHMINACA).

• Schedule I depressants

Unless specifically excepted or unless listed in another schedule, a material, compound, mixture, or preparation that contains any quantity of the following substances having a depressant effect on the central nervous system, including the substance's salts, isomers, and salts of isomers if the existence of the salts, isomers, and salts of isomers is possible within the specific chemical designation:

(1) Gamma-hydroxybutyric acid (other names: GHB; gamma-hydroxybutyrate; 4-hydroxybutyrate; 4-hydroxybutanoic acid; sodium oxybate; sodium oxybutyrate);

(2) Mecloqualone; and

(3) Methaqualone.

• Schedule I stimulants

Unless specifically excepted or unless listed in another schedule, a material, compound, mixture, or preparation that contains any quantity of the following substances having a stimulant effect on the central nervous system, including the substance's salts, isomers, and salts of isomers if the existence of the salts, isomers, and salts of isomers is possible within the specific chemical designation:

(1) Aminorex (some other names: aminoxaphen; 2-amino-5-phenyl-2-oxazoline; 4,5-dihydro- 5-phenyl-2-oxazolamine);

(2) N-benzylpiperazine (Other names: BZP; 1-benzylpiperazine), its optical isomers, salts and salts of isomers;

(3) Cathinone (Other names: 2-amino-1-phenyl-1-propanone; alphaaminopropiophenone; 2-aminopropiophenone and norephedrone);

(4) Fenethylline;

(5) Methcathinone (Other names: 2-(methylamino)-propiophenone; alpha-(methylamino) propiophenone; 2-(methylamino)-1-phenylpropan-1-one; alpha-N-methylaminopropiophenone; monomethylpropion; ephedrone; N-methylcathinone; methylcathinone; AL-464; AL-422; AL-463; and UR1432);

(6) 4-methylaminorex;

(7) N-ethylamphetamine; and

(8) N,N-dimethylamphetamine (Other names: N,N-alpha-trimethylbenzeneethaneamine; N,N-alpha-trimethylphenethylamine).

• Schedule I Cannabimimetic agents

Unless specifically exempted or unless listed in another schedule, any material, compound, mixture, or preparation which contains any quantity of cannabimimetic agents, or which contains their salts, isomers, and salts of isomers whenever the existence of such salts, isomers, and salts of isomers is possible within the specific chemical designation.

(1) The term 'cannabimimetic agents' means any substance that is a cannabinoid receptor type 1 (CB1 receptor) agonist as demonstrated by binding studies and functional assays within any of the following structural classes:

(1-1) 2-(3-hydroxycyclohexyl)phenol with substitution at the 5-position of the phenolic ring by alkyl or alkenyl, whether or not substituted on the cyclohexyl ring to any extent.

(1-2) 3-(1-naphthoyl)indole or 3-(1-naphthylmethane)indole by substitution at the nitrogen atom of the indole ring, whether or not further substituted on the indole ring to any extent, whether or not substituted on the naphthoyl or naphthyl ring to any extent.

(1-3) 3-(1-naphthoyl)pyrrole by substitution at the nitrogen atom of the pyrrole ring, whether or not further substituted in the pyrrole ring to any extent, whether or not substituted on the naphthoyl ring to any extent.

    (1-4) 1-(1-naphthylmethylene)indene by substitution of the 3-position of the indene ring, whether or not further substituted in the indene ring to any extent, whether or not substituted on the naphthyl ring to any extent.

    (1-5) 3-phenylacetylindole or 3-benzoylindole by substitution at the nitrogen atom of the indole ring, whether or not further substituted in the indole ring to any extent, whether or not substituted on the phenyl ring to any extent.

(2) 5-(1,1-dimethylheptyl)-2-[(1R,3S)-3-hydroxycyclohexyl]-phenol (Other names: CP-47,497);

(3) 5-(1,1-dimethyloctyl)-2-[(1R,3S)-3-hydroxycyclohexyl]-phenol (Other names: cannabicyclohexanol or CP-47,497 C8 homolog);

(4) 1-pentyl-3-(1-naphthoyl)indole (Other names:JWH-018 and AM678);

(5) 1-butyl-3-(1-naphthoyl)indole (Other names: JWH-073);

(6) 1-hexyl-3-(1-naphthoyl)indole (JWH-019);

(7) 1-[2-(4-Morpholinyl)ethyl]-3-(1-naphthoyl)indole (Other names: JWH-200);

(8) 1-pentyl-3-(2-methoxyphenylacetyl)indole (Other names: JWH-250);

(9) 1-pentyl-3-[1-(4-methoxynaphthoyl)]indole (Other names: JWH-081);

(10) 1-pentyl-3-(4-methyl-1-naphthoyl)indole (Other names: JWH-122);

(11) 1-pentyl-3-(4-chloro-1-naphthoyl)indole (Other names: JWH-398);

(12) 1-(5-fluoropentyl)-3-(1-naphthoyl)indole (Other names: AM2201);

(13) 1-(5-fluoropentyl)-3-(2-iodobenzoyl)indole (Other names: AM694);

(14) 1-pentyl-3-[(4-methoxy)-benzoyl]indole (Other names: SR-19 and RCS-4);

(15) 1-cyclohexylethyl-3-(2-methoxyphenylacetyl)indole (Other names: SR-18 and RCS-8); and

(16) 1-pentyl-3-(2-chlorophenylacetyl)indole (Other names: JWH- 203).

- **Schedule I temporarily listed substances subject to emergency scheduling by the United States Drug Enforcement Administration.**

    Unless specifically excepted or unless listed in another schedule, a material, compound, mixture, or preparation that contains any quantity of the following substances or that contains any of the substance's salts, isomers, and salts of isomers if the existence of the salts, isomers, and salts of isomers is possible within the specific chemical designation.

(1) N-[l-[2-hydroxy-2-(thiophen-2-yl)ethyl]piperidin-4-yl]-N-phenyl-proprionamide, also known as N-[1-[2-hydroxy-2-(2-thienyl) ethyl]-4-piperidnyl]-N-phenylpropanamide (Other name: beta-hydroxythiofentanyl);

(2) methyl 2-(l-(5-fluoropentyl)-lH-indazole-3-carboxamido)-3,3-dimethylbutanoate (Other names: 5F-ADB; 5F-MDMB-PINACA);

(3) methyl 2-(l-(5-fluoropentyl)-lH-indazole-3-caboxamido)-3-methylbutanoate (Other names: 5F-AMB);

(4) N-(adamantan-l-yl)-l-(5-fluoropentyl)-lH-indazole-3-carboxamide (Other names: 5F-APINACA, 5F-AKB48);

(5) N-(l-amino-3,3-dimethyl-l-oxobutan-2-yl)-l-(4-fluorobenzyl)-lH-indazole-3-carboxamide (Other names: ADB-FUBINACA);

(6) methyl 2-(l-(cyclohexylmethyl)-lH-indole-3-carboxamido)-3,3-dimethylbutanoate (Other names: MDMB-CHMICA, MMB-CHMINACA);

(7) methyl 2-(l-(4-fluorobenzyl)-lH-indazole-3-carboxamido)-3,3-dimethylbutanolate (Other names: MDMB-FUBINACA);

(8) methyl 2-(l-(4-fluorobenzyl)-1H-indazole-3-carboxamido)-3-methylbutanoate (Other names: FUB-AMB, MMB-FUBINACA, AMB-FUBINACA);

(9) N-(2-fluorophenyl)-N-(l-phenethylpiperidin-4-yl)propionamide (Other names: ortho-fluorofentanyl, 2-fluorofentanyl);

(10) 2-methoxy-N-(l-phenethylpiperidin-4-yl)-N-phenylacetamide, its isomers, esters, salts and salts of isomers, esters and ethers (Other names: methoxyacetyl fentanyl);

(11) N-(l-phenethylpiperidin-4-yl)-N-phenylcyclopropanecarboxamide (Other name: cyclopropyl fentanyl);

(12) N-(l-phenethylpiperidin-4-yl)-N-phenylpentanamide, its isomers, esters, ethers, salts and salts of isomers, esters and ethers (Other name: valeryl fentanyl);

(13) N-(4-fluorophenyl)-N-(l-phenethylpiperidin-4-yl)butyramide, its isomers, esters, ethers, salts and salts of isomers, esters and ethers (Other name: para-fluorobutyryl fentanyl);

(14) N-(4-methoxyphenyl)-N-(l-phenethylpiperidin-4-yl)butyramide, its isomers, esters, ethers, salts and salts of isomers, esters and ethers (Other name: para-methoxybutyryl fentanyl);

(15) N-(4-chlorophenyl)-N-(l-phenethylpiperidin-4-yl)isobutyramide, its isomers, esters, ethers salts and salts of isomers, esters and ethers (Other name: para-chloroisobutyryl fentanyl);

(16) N-(l-phenethylpiperidin-4-yl)-N-phenylisobutyramide, its isomers, esters, ethers salts and salts of isomers, esters and ethers (Other name: isobutyryl fentanyl);

(17) N-(1-phenethylpiperidin-4-yl)-N-phenylcyclopentanecarboxamide, its isomers, esters, ethers salts and salts of isomers, esters and ethers (Other name: cyclopentyl fentanyl);

(18) Fentanyl-related substances, their isomers, esters, ethers salts and salts of isomers, esters and ethers.

    (18-1) Fentanyl-related substance means any substance not otherwise listed under another Administration Controlled Substance Code Number, and for which no exemption or approval is in effect under section 505 of the Federal Food, Drug, and Cosmetic Act, that is structurally related to fentanyl by one or more of the following modifications:

        (18-1-1) Replacement of the phenyl portion of the phenethyl group by any monocycle, whether or not further substituted in or on the monocycle;

        (18-1-2) Substitution in or on the phenethyl group with alkyl, alkenyl, alkoxyl, hydroxyl, halo, haloalkyl, amino or nitro groups:

        (18-1-3) Substitution in or on the piperidine ring with alky, alkenyl, alkoxyl, ester, ether, hydroxyl, halo, haloalkyl, amino or nitro groups:

        (18-1-4) Replacement of the aniline right with any aromatic monocycle whether or not further substituted in or on the aromatic monocycle; and or

        (18-1-5) Replacement of the N-propionly group by another acyl group.

    (18-2) This defintion includes, but is not limited to, the following substances:

        (18-2-1) N-(1-2-fluorophenethyl)piperidin-4-yl)-N-(2-fluorophenyl)propionamide (2'fluoro ortho-fluorofentanyl);

        (18-2-2) N-(2-methylphenyl)-N-(1-phenethylpiperidin-4-yl)acetamide (ortho-methyl acetylfentanyl);

(18-2-3) N-(1-phenethylpiperidin-4-yl)-N,3-diphenylpropaniamide (beta'-phenyl fentanyl; hydrocinnamoyl fentanyl);

(18-2-4) N-(1-phenethylpiperidin-4-yl)-N-phenylthiophene-2-carboxamide (thiofuranyl fentanyl);

(18-2-5) (E)-N-(1-phenethylpiperidin-4-yl)-Nphenylbut-2-enamide (crotonyl fentanyl);

(19) Naphthalen-l-yl 1-(5-fluoropentyl)-1H-indole-3-carboxylate (other name: NM2201; CBL2201);

(20) N-(1-amino-3-methyl-l-oxobutan-2-yl)-1-(5-fluoropentyl)-1H-indazole-3-carboxamide (other name: 5F-AB-PINACA);

(21) 1-(4-cyanobutyl)-N-(2-phenylpropan-2-yl)-1H-indazole-3-carboxamide (other names: 4-CN-CUMYL-BUINACA; 4-cyano-CUMYL-BUTINACA; 4-CN-CUMYL BINANCA; CUMYL-4CN-BINACA; SGT-78);

(22) methyl 2-(1-(cyclohexylmethyl)-1H-indole-3-carboxamido)-3-methylbutanoate (other names: MMB-CHMICA, AMB-CHMICA);

(23) 1-(5-fluoropentyl)-N-(2-phenylpropan-2-yl)-1H-pyrrolo pyridine-3-carboxamide (other name: 5F-CUMYL-P7AICA); and,

(24) N-ethylpentylone (Other names: ephylone; 1-(1,3-benzodioxil-5-yl)-2-(ethylamino)-pentan-1-one);

(25) ethyl 2-(1-(5-fluoropentyl)-1H-indazole-3-carboxamido)-3,3-dimethylbutanoate and their optical, positional, and geometric isomers, salts, and salts of isomers (Other names: 5FEDMB-PINACA);

(26) methyl 2-(1-(5-fluoropentyl)-1H-indazole-3-carboxamido)-3,3-dimethylbutanoate and their optical, positional, and geometric isomers, salts, and salts of isomers (Other names: 5F-MDMB-PICA);

(27) N-(adamantan-l-yl)-1-(4-fluorobenzyl)-1Hindazole-3-carboxamide and their optical, positional, and geometric isomers, salts, and salts of isomers (Other names: FUB-AKB48; FUB-APINANCA); AKB48 N-(4-FLUOROBENZYL));

(28) 1-(5-fluoropentyl)-N-(2-phenylporpan-2-yl)-1H-indazole-3-carboxamode and their optical, positional, and geometric isomers, salts, and salts of isomers (Other names:5F-CUMYL-PINACA; SGT-25); and,

(29) (1-(4-fluorobenzyl)-1H-indol-3-yl)(2,2,3,3-tetramethylcyclopropyl)methanone their optical, positional, and geometric isomers, salts, and salts of isomers (Other name: FUB-144).

*(30) N-ethylhexedrone (Other name: 2-(ethylamino)-l-phenylhexan-l-one);

*(31) alpha-pyrrolidinohexanophenone (Other names: alpha-PHP, alpha-pyrrolidinohexiophenone, l-phenyl-2-(pyrrolidin-l-yl)hexan-l-one);

*(32) 4-Methyl-alpha-ethylaminopentiophenone (Other names: 4-MEAP, 2-(ethylamino)-l-(4-methylphenyl)pentan-l-one);

*(33) 4-Methyl-alpha-pyrrolidinohexiophenone (Other names: MPHP; 4'-methyl-alpha-pyrrolidinohexanophenone, l-(4-methylphenyl)-2-(pyrrolidin-l-yl)hexan-l-one;

*(34) alpha-Pyrrolidinoheptaphenone (Other names: PV8; l-phenyl-2-(pyrrolidin-l-yl)heptan-l-one); and

*(35) 4-Chloro-alpha-pyrrolidinovalerophenone (Other names: 4-chloro-alpha-PVP, 4-chloro-alpha-pyrrolidinopentiophenone, l-(4-chlorophenyl)-2-(pyrrolidin-l-yl)pentan-l-one).

SCHEDULE II

Schedule II consists of:

- ### Schedule II substances, vegetable origin or chemical synthesis
  The following substances, however produced, except those narcotic drugs listed in other schedules:
  (1) Opium and opiate, and a salt, compound, derivative, or preparation of opium or opiate, other than thebaine-derived butorphanol, *naldermidine, naloxone and its salts, naltrexone and its salts, and nalmefene and its salts, but including:
    - (1-1) Codeine;
    - (1-2) Dihydroetorphine;
    - (1-3) Ethylmorphine;
    - (1-4) Etorphine hydrochloride;
    - (1-5) Granulated opium;
    - (1-6) Hydrocodone;
    - (1-7) Hydromorphone;
    - (1-8) Metopon;
    - (1-9) Morphine;
    - *(1-10) Noroxymorphone;
    - (1-11) Opium extracts;
    - (1-12) Opium fluid extracts;
    - (1-13) Oripavine
    - (1-14) Oxycodone;
    - (1-15) Oxymorphone;
    - (1-16) Powdered opium;
    - (1-17) Raw opium;
    - (1-18) Thebaine; and
    - (1-19) Tincture of opium.
  (2) A salt, compound, isomer, derivative, or preparation of a substance that is chemically equivalent or identical to a substance described by Paragraph (1) of Schedule II substances, vegetable origin or chemical synthesis, other than the isoquinoline alkaloids of opium;
  (3) Opium poppy and poppy straw;
  (4) Cocaine, including:
    - (4-1) its salts, its optical, position, and geometric isomers, and the salts of those isomers;
    - (4-2) coca leaves and any salt, compound, derivative, or preparation of coca leaves and ecgonine and their salts, isomers, derivatives and salts of isomers and derivatives and any salt, compound derivative or preparation thereof which is chemically equivalent or identical to a substance described by this paragraph, except that the substances shall not include:
      - (4-2-1) decocainized coca leaves or extractions of coca leaves which extractions do not that do not contain cocaine or ecgonine; or
      - (4-2-2) ioflupane.
  (5) Concentrate of poppy straw, meaning the crude extract of poppy straw in liquid, solid, or powder form that contains the phenanthrene alkaloids of the opium poppy.

- ### Opiates
  The following opiates, including their isomers, esters, ethers, salts, and salts of isomers, if the existence of these isomers, esters, ethers, and salts is possible within the specific chemical designation:
  (1) Alfentanil;
  (2) Alphaprodine;
  (3) Anileridine;
  (4) Bezitramide;
  (5) Carfentanil;
  (6) Dextropropoxyphene, bulk (nondosage form);
  (7) Dihydrocodeine;
  (8) Diphenoxylate;
  (9) Fentanyl;
  (10) Isomethadone;
  (11) Levo-alphacetylmethadol (some trade or other names: levo-alpha-acetylmethadol, levomethadyl acetate, LAAM);
  (12) Levomethorphan;
  (13) Levorphanol;
  (14) Metazocine;
  (15) Methadone;
  (16) Methadone-Intermediate, 4-cyano-2-dimethylamino-4,4-diphenyl butane;
  (17) Moramide-Intermediate, 2-methyl-3-morpholino-1,1-diphenyl-propane-carboxylic acid;
  (18) Pethidine (meperidine);
  (19) Pethidine-Intermediate-A, 4-cyano-1-methyl-4-phenylpiperidine;
  (20) Pethidine-Intermediate-B, ethyl-4-phenylpiperidine-4-carboxylate;
  (21) Pethidine-Intermediate-C, 1-methyl-4-phenylpiperidine-4-carboxylic acid;

(22) Phenazocine;

(23) Piminodine;

(24) Racemethorphan;

(25) Racemorphan;

(26) Remifentanil

(27) Sufentanil;

(28) Tapentadol; and

*(29) Thiafentanil (methyl 4-(2-methoxy-N-phenylacetamido)-1-(2-(thiophen-2-yl)ethyl)piperidine-4-carboxylate).

- ## Schedule II stimulants

Unless listed in another schedule and except as provided by the Texas Controlled Substances Act, Health and Safety Code, Section 181.033, a material, compound, mixture, or preparation that contains any quantity of the following substances having a potential for abuse associated with a stimulant effect on the central nervous system:

(1)   Amphetamine, its salts, optical isomers, and salts of its optical isomers;

(2)   Methamphetamine, including its salts, optical isomers, and salts of optical isomers;

(3)   Methylphenidate and its salts;

(4)   Phenmetrazine and its salts; and,

(5)   Lisdexamfetamine, including its salts, isomers, and salts of its isomers.

- ## Schedule II depressants

Unless listed in another schedule, a material, compound, mixture or preparation that contains any quantity of the following substances having a depressant effect on the central nervous system, including the substance's salts, isomers, and salts of isomers if the existence of the salts, isomers, and salts of isomers is possible within the specific chemical designation:

(1)   Amobarbital;

(2)   Glutethimide;

(3)   Pentobarbital; and

(4)   Secobarbital.

- ## Schedule II hallucinogenic substances

(1)   Nabilone (Another name for nabilone: (±)-trans-3-(1,1-dimethylheptyl)-6,6a,7,8, 10,10a-hexahydro-1-hydroxy-6,6-dimethyl-9H-dibenzo[b,d]pyran-9-one); and,

*(2) Dronabinol in oral solution in drug products approved for marketing by the United States Food and Drug Administration.

- ## Schedule II precursors

Unless specifically excepted or listed in another schedule, a material, compound, mixture, or preparation that contains any quantity of the following substances:

(1)   Immediate precursor to methamphetamine:

(1-1)Phenylacetone and methylamine if possessed together with intent to manufacture methamphetamine;

(2)   Immediate precursor to amphetamine and methamphetamine:

(2-1)Phenylacetone (some trade or other names: phenyl-2-propanone; P2P; benzyl methyl ketone; methyl benzyl ketone); and,

(3)   Immediate precursors to phencyclidine (PCP):

(3-1)1-phenylcyclohexylamine;

(3-2)1-piperidinocyclohexanecarbonitrile (PCC); and,

(4)   Immediate precursor to fentanyl:

(4-1)4-anilino-N-phenethyl-4-piperidine (ANPP).

SCHEDULE III

Schedule III consists of:

- ### Schedule III depressants

  Unless listed in another schedule and except as provided by the Texas Controlled Substances Act, Health and Safety Code, Section 481.033, a material, compound, mixture, or preparation that contains any quantity of the following substances having a potential for abuse associated with a depressant effect on the central nervous system:

  (1) a compound, mixture, or preparation containing amobarbital, secobarbital, pentobarbital, or any of their salts and one or more active medicinal ingredients that are not listed in a schedule;

  (2) a suppository dosage form containing amobarbital, secobarbital, pentobarbital, or any of their salts and approved by the Food and Drug Administration for marketing only as a suppository;

  (3) a substance that contains any quantity of a derivative of barbituric acid, or any salt of a derivative of barbituric acid, except those substances that are specifically listed in other schedules;

  (4) Chlorhexadol;

  (5) Any drug product containing gamma hydroxybutyric acid, including its salts, isomers, and salts of isomers, for which an application is approved under section 505 of the Federal Food Drug and Cosmetic Act;

  (6) Ketamine, its salts, isomers, and salts of isomers. Some other names for ketamine: (±)-2-(2-chlorophenyl)-2-(methylamino)-cyclohexanone;

  (7) Lysergic acid;

  (8) Lysergic acid amide;

  (9) Methyprylon;

  (10) Perampanel, and its salts, isomers, and salts of isomers;

  (11) Sulfondiethylmethane;

  (12) Sulfonethylmethane;

  (13) Sulfonmethane; and,

  (14) Tiletamine and zolazepam or any salt thereof. Some trade or other names for a tiletamine-zolazepam combination product: Telazol. Some trade or other names for tiletamine: 2-(ethylamino)-2-(2-thienyl)-cyclohexanone. Some trade or other names for zolazepam: 4-(2-fluorophenyl)-6,8-dihydro-1,3,8-trimethyl-pyrazolo-[3,4-e][1,4]-diazepin-7(1H)-one, flupyrazapon.

- ### Nalorphine

- ### Schedule III narcotics

  Unless specifically excepted or unless listed in another schedule:

  (1) a material, compound, mixture, or preparation containing limited quantities of any of the following narcotic drugs, or any of their salts:

  (1-1) not more than 1.8 grams of codeine, or any of its salts, per 100 milliliters or not more than 90 milligrams per dosage unit, with an equal or greater quantity of an isoquinoline alkaloid of opium;

  (1-2) not more than 1.8 grams of codeine, or any of its salts, per 100 milliliters or not more than 90 milligrams per dosage unit, with one or more active, nonnarcotic ingredients in recognized therapeutic amounts;

  (1-3) not more than 1.8 grams of dihydrocodeine, or any of its salts, per 100 milliliters or not more than 90 milligrams per dosage unit, with one or more active, nonnarcotic ingredients in recognized therapeutic amounts;

  (1-4) not more than 300 milligrams of ethylmorphine, or any of its salts, per 100 milliliters or not more than 15 milligrams per dosage unit, with one or more active, nonnarcotic ingredients in recognized therapeutic amounts;

  (1-5) not more than 500 milligrams of opium per 100 milliliters or per 100 grams, or not more than 25 milligrams per dosage unit, with one or more active, nonnarcotic ingredients in recognized therapeutic amounts; and

  (1-6) not more than 50 milligrams of morphine, or any of its salts, per 100 milliliters or per 100 grams with one or more active, nonnarcotic ingredients in recognized therapeutic amounts.

  (2) any material, compound, mixture, or preparation containing any of the following narcotic drugs or their salts:

  (2-1) Buprenorphine.

- ### Schedule III stimulants

  Unless listed in another schedule, a material, compound, mixture or preparation that contains any quantity of the following substances having a stimulant effect on the central nervous system, including the substance's salts, optical, position, or geometric isomers, and salts of the substance's isomers, if the existence of the salts, isomers, and salts of isomers is possible within the specific chemical designation:

  (1) Benzphetamine;

  (2) Chlorphentermine;

  (3) Clortermine; and,

  (4) Phendimetrazine.

- ### Schedule III anabolic steroids and hormones

  Anabolic steroids, including any drug or hormonal substance, chemically and pharmacologically related to testosterone (other than estrogens, progestins, corticosteroids, and dehydroepiandrosterone), and include the following:

  (1) androstanediol

  (1-1) 3 beta,17 beta-dihydroxy-5 alpha-androstane;

(1-2)3 alpha,17 beta -dihydroxy-5 alpha-androstane;

(2) androstanedione (5 alpha-androstan-3,17-dione);

(3) androstenediol

    (3-1)1-androstenediol (3 beta,17 beta-dihydroxy-5 alpha-androst-1-ene);

    (3-2)1-androstenediol (3 alpha,17 beta-dihydroxy-5 alpha-androst-1-ene);

    (3-3)4-androstenediol (3 beta,17 beta-dihydroxy-androst-4-ene);

    (3-4)5-androstenediol (3 beta,17 beta-dihydroxy-androst-5-ene);

(4) androstenedione

    (4-1)1-androstenedione ([5 alpha]-androst-1-en-3,17-dione);

    (4-2)4-androstenedione (androst-4-en-3,17-dione);

    (4-3)5-androstenedione (androst-5-en-3,17-dione);

(5) bolasterone (7 alpha,17 alpha-dimethyl-17 beta-hydroxyandrost-4-en-3-one);

(6) boldenone (17 beta-hydroxyandrost-1,4,-diene-3-one);

(7) boldione (androsta-1,4-diene-3,17-dione)

(8) calusterone (7 beta,17 alpha-dimethyl-17 beta-hydroxyandrost-4-en-3-one);

(9) clostebol (4-chloro-17 beta-hydroxyandrost-4-en-3-one);

(10) dehydrochloromethyltestosterone (4-chloro-17 beta-hydroxy-17alpha-methyl-androst-1,4-dien-3-one);

(11) delta-1-dihydrotestosterone (a.k.a. '1-testosterone') (17 beta-hydroxy-5 alpha-androst-1-en-3-one);

(12) desoxymethyltestosterone (17[alpha]-methyl-5[alpha]-androst-2-en-17[beta]-ol; madol)

(13) 4-dihydrotestosterone (17 beta-hydroxy-androstan-3-one);

(14) drostanolone (17 beta-hydroxy-2 alpha-methyl-5 alpha-androstan-3-one);

(15) ethylestrenol (17 alpha-ethyl-17 beta-hydroxyestr-4-ene);

(16) fluoxymesterone (9-fluoro-17 alpha-methyl-11 beta,17 beta-dihydroxyandrost-4-en-3-one);

(17) formebolone (2-formyl-17 alpha-methyl-11 alpha,17 beta-dihydroxyandrost-1,4-dien-3-one);

(18) furazabol (17 alpha-methyl-17 beta-hydroxyandrostano[2,3-c]-furazan);

(19) 13 beta-ethyl-17 beta-hydroxygon-4-en-3-one;

(20) 4-hydroxytestosterone (4,17 beta-dihydroxy-androst-4-en-3-one);

(21) 4-hydroxy-19-nortestosterone (4,17 beta-dihydroxy-estr-4-en-3-one);

(22) mestanolone (17 alpha-methyl-17 beta-hydroxy-5 alpha-androstan-3-one);

(23) mesterolone (1 alpha-methyl-17 beta-hydroxy-[5 alpha]-androstan-3-one);

(24) methandienone (17 alpha-methyl-17 beta-hydroxyandrost-1,4-dien-3-one);

(25) methandriol (17 alpha-methyl-3 beta,17 beta-dihydroxyandrost-5-ene);

(26) methenolone (1-methyl-17 beta-hydroxy-5 alpha-androst-1-en-3-one);

(27) 17 alpha-methyl-3 beta, 17 beta-dihydroxy-5 alpha-androstane;

(28) methasterone (2 alpha, 17 alpha-dimethyl-5-alpha-androstan-17 beta-ol-3-one;

(29) 17alpha-methyl-3 alpha,17 beta-dihydroxy-5 alpha-androstane;

(30) 17 alpha-methyl-3 beta,17 beta-dihydroxyandrost-4-ene;

(31) 17 alpha-methyl-4-hydroxynandrolone (17 alpha-methyl-4-hydroxy-17 beta-hydroxyestr-4-en-3-one);

(32) methyldienolone (17 alpha-methyl-17 beta-hydroxyestra-4,9(10)-dien-3-one);

(33) methyltrienolone (17 alpha-methyl-17 beta-hydroxyestra-4,9-11-trien-3-one);

(34) methyltestosterone (17 alpha-methyl-17 beta-hydroxyandrost-4-en-3-one);

(35) mibolerone (7 alpha,17 alpha-dimethyl-17 beta-hydroxyestr-4-en-3-one);

(36) 17 alpha-methyl-delta-1-dihydrotestosterone (17 beta-hydroxy-17 alpha-methyl-5 alphaandrost-1-en-3-one) (a.k.a. '17-alpha-methyl-1-testosterone');

(37) nandrolone (17 beta-hydroxyestr-4-en-3-one);

(38) norandrostenediol—

    (38-1)   19-nor-4-androstenediol (3 beta, 17 beta-dihydroxyestr-4-ene);

    (38-2)   19-nor-4-androstenediol (3 alpha, 17 beta-dihydroxyestr-4-ene);

    (38-3)   19-nor-5-androstenediol (3 beta, 17 beta-dihydroxyestr-5-ene);

    (38-4)   19-nor-5-androstenediol (3 alpha, 17 beta-dihydroxyestr-5-ene);

(39) norandrostenedione—

    (39-1)   19-nor-4-androstenedione (estr-4-en-3,17-dione);

    (39-2)   19-nor-5-androstenedione (estr-5-en-3,17-dione;

(40) 19-nor-4,9(10)-androstadienedione (estra-4,9(10)-diene-3,17-dione)

(41) norbolethone (13 beta,17alpha-diethyl-17 beta-hydroxygon-4-en-3-one);

(42) norclostebol (4-chloro-17 beta-hydroxyestr-4-en-3-one);

(43) norethandrolone (17 alpha-ethyl-17 beta-hydroxyestr-4-en-3-one);

(44) normethandrolone (17 alpha-methyl-17 beta-hydroxyestr-4-en-3-one);

(45) oxandrolone (17 alpha-methyl-17 beta-hydroxy-2-oxa-[5 alpha]-androstan-3-one);

(46) oxymesterone (17 alpha-methyl-4,17 beta-dihydroxyandrost-4-en-3-one);

(47) oxymetholone (17 alpha-methyl-2-hydroxymethylene-17 beta-hydroxy-[5 alpha]-androstan-3-one);

(48) prostanozol (17 beta-hydroxy-5-alpha-androstano[3,2-c]pyrazole);

(49) stanozolol (17 alpha-methyl-17 beta-hydroxy-[5 alpha]-androst-2-eno[3,2-c]-pyrazole);

(50) stenbolone (17 beta-hydroxy-2-methyl-[5 alpha]-androst-1-en-3-one);

(51) testolactone (13-hydroxy-3-oxo-13,17-secoandrosta-1,4-dien-17-oic acid lactone);

(52) testosterone (17 beta-hydroxyandrost-4-en-3-one);

(53) tetrahydrogestrinone (13 beta,17 alpha-diethyl-17 beta-hydroxygon-4,9,11-trien-3-one);

(54) trenbolone (17 beta-hydroxyestr-4,9,11-trien-3-one); and

(55) any salt, ester, or ether of a drug or substance described in this paragraph.

- ## Schedule III hallucinogenic substances
  (1) Dronabinol (synthetic) in sesame oil and encapsulated in a soft gelatin capsule in U.S. Food and Drug Administration approved drug product. (Some other names for dronabinol:(6aR-trans)-6a,7,8,10a-tetrahydro-6,6,9-tri-methyl-3-pentyl-6Hdibenzo[b,d] pyran-1-ol, or (-)-delta-9-(trans)-tetrahydrocannabinol).

SCHEDULE IV

Schedule IV consists of:

- ### Schedule IV depressants

  Except as provided by the Texas Controlled Substances Act, Health and Safety Code, Section 481.033, a material, compound, mixture, or preparation that contains any quantity of the following substances having a potential for abuse associated with a depressant effect on the central nervous system, including the substance's salts, optical, positional, or geometric isomers, and salts of those isomers if the existence of the salts, isomers, and salts of isomers is possible within the specified chemical designation:

  (1) Alfaxalone (5[alpha]-pregnan-3[alpha]-ol-11,20-dione)
  (2) Alprazolam;
  (3) Barbital;
  *(4) Brexanolone (3[alpha]-hydroxy-5[alpha]-pregnan-20-one) (Other name: allopregnanolone);
  (5) Bromazepam;
  (6) Camazepam;
  (7) Chloral betaine;
  (8) Chloral hydrate;
  (9) Chlordiazepoxide;
  (10) Clobazam;
  (11) Clonazepam;
  (12) Clorazepate;
  (13) Clotiazepam;
  (14) Cloxazolam;
  (15) Delorazepam;
  (16) Diazepam;
  (17) Dichloralphenazone;
  (18) Estazolam;
  (19) Ethchlorvynol;
  (20) Ethinamate;
  (21) Ethyl loflazepate;
  (22) Fludiazepam;
  (23) Flunitrazepam;
  (24) Flurazepam;
  (25) Fospropofol;
  (26) Halazepam;
  (27) Haloxazolam;
  (28) Ketazolam;
  (29) Loprazolam;
  (30) Lorazepam;
  (31) Lormetazepam;
  (32) Mebutamate;
  (33) Medazepam;
  (34) Meprobamate;
  (35) Methohexital;
  (36) Methylphenobarbital (mephobarbital);
  (37) Midazolam;
  (38) Nimetazepam;
  (39) Nitrazepam;
  (40) Nordiazepam;
  (41) Oxazepam;
  (42) Oxazolam;
  (43) Paraldehyde;
  (44) Petrichloral;
  (45) Phenobarbital;
  (46) Pinazepam;
  (47) Prazepam;
  (48) Quazepam;
  (49) Suvorexant;
  (50) Temazepam;
  (51) Tetrazepam;
  (52) Triazolam;
  (53) Zaleplon;
  (54) Zolpidem; and,
  (55) Zopiclone, its salts, isomers, and salts of isomers.

- ## Schedule IV stimulants

Unless listed in another schedule, a material, compound, mixture, or preparation that contains any quantity of the following substances having a stimulant effect on the central nervous system, including the substance's salts, optical, positional, or geometric isomers, and salts of those isomers if the existence of the salts, isomers, and salts of isomers is possible within the specific chemical designation:

(1) Cathine [(+)-norpseudoephedrine];
(2) Diethylpropion;
(3) Fencamfamin;
(4) Fenfluramine;
(5) Fenproporex;
(6) Mazindol;
(7) Mefenorex;
(8) Modafinil;
(9) Pemoline (including organometallic complexes and their chelates);
(10) Phentermine;
(11) Pipradrol;
*(12) Solriamfetol ((R)-2-amino-3-phenylpropyl carbamate)) (Other names: benzenepropanol, beta-amino-carbamate (ester));
(13) Sibutramine; and
(14) SPA [(-)-1-dimethylamino-1,2-diphenylethane].

- ## Schedule IV narcotics

Unless specifically excepted or unless listed in another schedule, a material, compound, mixture, or preparation containing limited quantities of the following narcotic drugs or their salts:

(1) Not more than 1 milligram of difenoxin and not less than 25 micrograms of atropine sulfate per dosage unit; and
(2) Dextropropoxyphene (Alpha-(+)-4-dimethylamino-1,2-diphenyl-3-methyl-2-propionoxybutane); and,
(3) 2-[(dimethylamino)methyl]-1-(3-methoxyphenyl)cyclohexanol (other name: tramadol).

- ## Schedule IV other substances

Unless specifically excepted or unless listed in another schedule, a material, compound, substance's salts:

(1) Butorphanol, including its optical isomers;
(2) Carisoprodol
(3) Eluxadoline (other names: 5-[[[(2S-2-amino-3-[4-aminocarbonyl)-2,6-dimethylphenyl]-l-oxopropyl][(1S)-l-(4-phenyl-1H-imidazol-2-yl)ethyl]amino]methyl]-2-methoxybenzoic acid) including its salts, isomers, and salts of isomers;
(4) Lorcarserin including its salts, isomers and salts of isomers, whenever the existence of such salts, isomers, and salts of isomers is possible; and,
(5) Pentazocine, its salts, derivatives, compounds, or mixtures.

Cont. Sub.

SCHEDULE V

Schedule V consists of:

- **Schedule V narcotics containing non-narcotic active medicinal ingredients**

  A compound, mixture, or preparation containing limited quantities of any of the following narcotic drugs that also contain one or more nonnarcotic active medicinal ingredients in sufficient proportion to confer on the compound, mixture or preparation valuable medicinal qualities other than those possessed by the narcotic drug alone:
  (1) Not more than 200 milligrams of codeine, or any of its salts, per 100 milliliters or per 100grams;
  (2) Not more than 100 milligrams of dihydrocodeine, or any of its salts, per 100 milliliters or per 100 grams;
  (3) Not more than 100 milligrams of ethylmorphine, or any of its salts, per 100 milliliters or per 100 grams;
  (4) Not more than 2.5 milligrams of diphenoxylate and not less than 25 micrograms of atropine sulfate per dosage unit,
  (5) Not more than 15 milligrams of opium per 29.5729 milliliters or per 28.35 grams; and,
  (6) Not more than 0.5 milligram of difenoxin and not less than 25 micrograms of atropine sulfate per dosage unit.

- **Schedule V stimulants**

  Unless specifically exempted or excluded or unless listed in another schedule, a compound, mixture, or preparation which contains any quantity of the following substances having a stimulant effect on the central nervous system, including its salts, isomers and salts of isomers:
  (1) Pyrovalerone.

- **Schedule V depressants**

  Unless specifically exempted or excluded or unless listed in another schedule, any material, compound, mixture, or preparation, which contains any quantity of the following substances having a depressant effect on the central nervous system, including its salts:
  (1) Brivaracetam ((2S0-2-[4R0-2-oxo-4-propylpyrrolidin-1-yl]butanamide) (Other names: BRV, UCB-34714, and Briviact);
  (2) Ezogabine including its salts, isomers and salts of isomers, whenever the existence of such salts, isomers and salts of isomers is possible;
  (3) Lacosamide [(R)-2-acetoamido-N-benzyl-3-methoxy-propionamide];
  (4) Pregabalin [(S)-3-(aminomethyl)-5-methylhexanoic acid]; and
  *(5) Approved cannabidiol drugs.

  A drug product in finished dosage formulation that has been approved by the U.S. Food and Drug Administration that contains cannabidiol (2-[1R-3-methyl-6R-(1-methylethenyl)-2-cyclohexen-1-yl]-5-pentyl-1,3- benzenediol) derived from cannabis and no more than 0.1 percent (w/w) residual tetrahydrocannabinols

SUBCHAPTER A. GENERAL PROVISIONS

Sec. 481.001. Short Title.

This chapter may be cited as the Texas Controlled Substances Act.

Leg.H. Stats. 1989 71st Leg. Sess. Ch. 678, effective September 1, 1989.

Sec. 481.002. Definitions.

In this chapter:

(1) "Administer" means to directly apply a controlled substance by injection, inhalation, ingestion, or other means to the body of a patient or research subject by:
   (A) a practitioner or an agent of the practitioner in the presence of the practitioner; or
   (B) the patient or research subject at the direction and in the presence of a practitioner.

(2) "Agent" means an authorized person who acts on behalf of or at the direction of a manufacturer, distributor, or dispenser. The term does not include a common or contract carrier, public warehouseman, or employee of a carrier or warehouseman acting in the usual and lawful course of employment.

(3) "Commissioner" means the commissioner of public health or the commissioner's designee.

(4) "Controlled premises" means:
   (A) a place where original or other records or documents required under this chapter are kept or are required to be kept; or
   (B) a place, including a factory, warehouse, other establishment, or conveyance, where a person registered under this chapter may lawfully hold, manufacture, distribute, dispense, administer, possess, or otherwise dispose of a controlled substance or other item governed by the federal Controlled Substances Act (21 U.S.C. Section 801 et seq.) or this chapter, including a chemical precursor and a chemical laboratory apparatus.

(5) "Controlled substance" means a substance, including a drug, an adulterant, and a dilutant, listed in Schedules I through V or Penalty Group 1, 1-A, 2, 2-A, 3, or 4. The term includes the aggregate weight of any mixture, solution, or other substance containing a controlled substance. The term does not include hemp, as defined by Section 121.001, Agriculture Code, or the tetrahydrocannabinols in hemp.

(6) "Controlled substance analogue" means:
   (A) a substance with a chemical structure substantially similar to the chemical structure of a controlled substance in Schedule I or II or Penalty Group 1, 1-A, or 2; or
   (B) a substance specifically designed to produce an effect substantially similar to, or greater than, the effect of a controlled substance in Schedule I or II or Penalty Group 1, 1-A, or 2.

(7) "Counterfeit substance" means a controlled substance that, without authorization, bears or is in a container or has a label that bears an actual or simulated trademark, trade name, or other identifying mark, imprint, number, or device of a manufacturer, distributor, or dispenser other than the person who in fact manufactured, distributed, or dispensed the substance.

(8) "Deliver" means to transfer, actually or constructively, to another a controlled substance, counterfeit substance, or drug paraphernalia, regardless of whether there is an agency relationship. The term includes offering to sell a controlled substance, counterfeit substance, or drug paraphernalia.

(9) "Delivery" or "drug transaction" means the act of delivering.

(10) "Designated agent" means an individual designated under Section 481.074(b-2) to communicate a practitioner's instructions to a pharmacist in an emergency.

(11) "Director" means the director of the Department of Public Safety or an employee of the department designated by the director.

(12) "Dispense" means the delivery of a controlled substance in the course of professional practice or research, by a practitioner or person acting under the lawful order of a practitioner, to an ultimate user or research subject. The term includes the prescribing, administering, packaging, labeling, or compounding necessary to prepare the substance for delivery.

(13) "Dispenser" means a practitioner, institutional practitioner, pharmacist, or pharmacy that dispenses a controlled substance.

(14) "Distribute" means to deliver a controlled substance other than by administering or dispensing the substance.

(15) "Distributor" means a person who distributes.

(16) "Drug" means a substance, other than a device or a component, part, or accessory of a device, that is:
   (A) recognized as a drug in the official United States Pharmacopoeia, official Homeopathic Pharmacopoeia of the United States, official National Formulary, or a supplement to either pharmacopoeia or the formulary;
   (B) intended for use in the diagnosis, cure, mitigation, treatment, or prevention of disease in man or animals;
   (C) intended to affect the structure or function of the body of man or animals but is not food; or
   (D) intended for use as a component of a substance described by Paragraph (A), (B), or (C).

(17) "Drug paraphernalia" means equipment, a product, or material that is used or intended for use in planting, propagating, cultivating, growing, harvesting, manufacturing, compounding, converting, producing, processing, preparing, testing, analyzing, packaging, repackaging, storing, containing, or concealing a controlled substance in violation of this chapter or in injecting, ingesting, inhaling, or otherwise introducing into the human body a controlled substance in violation of this chapter. The term includes:
   (A) a kit used or intended for use in planting, propagating, cultivating, growing, or harvesting a species of plant that is a controlled substance or from which a controlled substance may be derived;

12/1/2019

(B)　a material, compound, mixture, preparation, or kit used or intended for use in manufacturing, compounding, converting, producing, processing, or preparing a controlled substance;

(C)　an isomerization device used or intended for use in increasing the potency of a species of plant that is a controlled substance;

(D)　testing equipment used or intended for use in identifying or in analyzing the strength, effectiveness, or purity of a controlled substance;

(E)　a scale or balance used or intended for use in weighing or measuring a controlled substance;

(F)　a dilutant or adulterant, such as quinine hydrochloride, mannitol, inositol, nicotinamide, dextrose, lactose, or absorbent, blotter-type material, that is used or intended to be used to increase the amount or weight of or to transfer a controlled substance regardless of whether the dilutant or adulterant diminishes the efficacy of the controlled substance;

(G)　a separation gin or sifter used or intended for use in removing twigs and seeds from or in otherwise cleaning or refining marihuana;

(H)　a blender, bowl, container, spoon, or mixing device used or intended for use in compounding a controlled substance;

(I)　a capsule, balloon, envelope, or other container used or intended for use in packaging small quantities of a controlled substance;

(J)　a container or other object used or intended for use in storing or concealing a controlled substance;

(K)　a hypodermic syringe, needle, or other object used or intended for use in parenterally injecting a controlled substance into the human body; and

(L)　an object used or intended for use in ingesting, inhaling, or otherwise introducing marihuana, cocaine, hashish, or hashish oil into the human body, including:

　(i)　a metal, wooden, acrylic, glass, stone, plastic, or ceramic pipe with or without a screen, permanent screen, hashish head, or punctured metal bowl;

　(ii)　a water pipe;

　(iii)　a carburetion tube or device;

　(iv)　a smoking or carburetion mask;

　(v)　a chamber pipe;

　(vi)　a carburetor pipe;

　(vii)　an electric pipe;

　(viii)　an air-driven pipe;

　(ix)　a chillum;

　(x)　a bong; or

　(xi)　an ice pipe or chiller.

(18)　"Federal Controlled Substances Act" means the Federal Comprehensive Drug Abuse Prevention and Control Act of 1970 (21 U.S.C. Section 801 et seq.) or its successor statute.

(19)　"Federal Drug Enforcement Administration" means the Drug Enforcement Administration of the United States Department of Justice or its successor agency.

(20)　"Hospital" means:

(A)　a general or special hospital as defined by Section 241.003;

(B)　an ambulatory surgical center licensed under Chapter 243 and approved by the federal government to perform surgery paid by Medicaid on patients admitted for a period of not more than 24 hours; or

(C)　a freestanding emergency medical care facility licensed under Chapter 254.

(21)　"Human consumption" means the injection, inhalation, ingestion, or application of a substance to or into a human body.

(22)　"Immediate precursor" means a substance the director finds to be and by rule designates as being:

(A)　a principal compound commonly used or produced primarily for use in the manufacture of a controlled substance;

(B)　a substance that is an immediate chemical intermediary used or likely to be used in the manufacture of a controlled substance; and

(C)　a substance the control of which is necessary to prevent, curtail, or limit the manufacture of a controlled substance.

(23)　"Institutional practitioner" means an intern, resident physician, fellow, or person in an equivalent professional position who:

(A)　is not licensed by the appropriate state professional licensing board;

(B)　is enrolled in a bona fide professional training program in a base hospital or institutional training facility registered by the Federal Drug Enforcement Administration; and

(C)　is authorized by the base hospital or institutional training facility to administer, dispense, or prescribe controlled substances.

(24)　"Lawful possession" means the possession of a controlled substance that has been obtained in accordance with state or federal law.

(25)　"Manufacture" means the production, preparation, propagation, compounding, conversion, or processing of a controlled substance other than marihuana, directly or indirectly by extraction from substances of natural origin, independently by means of chemical synthesis, or by a combination of extraction and chemical synthesis, and includes the packaging or repackaging of the substance or labeling or relabeling of its container. However, the term does not include the preparation, compounding, packaging, or labeling of a controlled substance:

(A)　by a practitioner as an incident to the practitioner's administering or dispensing a controlled substance in the course of professional practice; or

(B)　by a practitioner, or by an authorized agent under the supervision of the practitioner, for or as an incident to research, teaching, or chemical analysis and not for delivery.

(26)　"Marihuana" means the plant Cannabis sativa L., whether growing or not, the seeds of that plant, and every compound, manufacture, salt, derivative, mixture, or preparation of that plant or its seeds. The term does not include:

(A)　the resin extracted from a part of the plant or a compound, manufacture, salt, derivative, mixture, or preparation of the resin;

(B)　the mature stalks of the plant or fiber produced from the stalks;

(C)　oil or cake made from the seeds of the plant;

(D)　a compound, manufacture, salt, derivative, mixture, or preparation of the mature stalks, fiber, oil, or cake;

(E) the sterilized seeds of the plant that are incapable of beginning germination; or

(F) hemp, as that term is defined by Section 121.001, Agriculture Code.

(27) "Medical purpose" means the use of a controlled substance for relieving or curing a mental or physical disease or infirmity.

(28) "Medication order" means an order from a practitioner to dispense a drug to a patient in a hospital for immediate administration while the patient is in the hospital or for emergency use on the patient's release from the hospital.

(29) "Narcotic drug" means any of the following, produced directly or indirectly by extraction from substances of vegetable origin, independently by means of chemical synthesis, or by a combination of extraction and chemical synthesis:

(A) opium and opiates, and a salt, compound, derivative, or preparation of opium or opiates;

(B) a salt, compound, isomer, derivative, or preparation of a salt, compound, isomer, or derivative that is chemically equivalent or identical to a substance listed in Paragraph (A) other than the isoquinoline alkaloids of opium;

(C) opium poppy and poppy straw; or

(D) cocaine, including:

(i) its salts, its optical, position, or geometric isomers, and the salts of those isomers;

(ii) coca leaves and a salt, compound, derivative, or preparation of coca leaves; and

(iii) a salt, compound, derivative, or preparation of a salt, compound, or derivative that is chemically equivalent or identical to a substance described by Subparagraph (i) or (ii), other than decocainized coca leaves or extractions of coca leaves that do not contain cocaine or ecgonine.

(30) "Opiate" means a substance that has an addiction-forming or addiction-sustaining liability similar to morphine or is capable of conversion into a drug having addiction-forming or addiction-sustaining liability. The term includes its racemic and levorotatory forms. The term does not include, unless specifically designated as controlled under Subchapter B, the dextrorotatory isomer of 3-methoxy-n-methylmorphinan and its salts (dextromethorphan).

(31) "Opium poppy" means the plant of the species Papaver somniferum L., other than its seeds.

(32) "Patient" means a human for whom or an animal for which a drug:

(A) is administered, dispensed, delivered, or prescribed by a practitioner; or

(B) is intended to be administered, dispensed, delivered, or prescribed by a practitioner.

(33) "Person" means an individual, corporation, government, business trust, estate, trust, partnership, association, or any other legal entity.

(34) "Pharmacist" means a person licensed by the Texas State Board of Pharmacy to practice pharmacy and who acts as an agent for a pharmacy.

(35) "Pharmacist-in-charge" means the pharmacist designated on a pharmacy license as the pharmacist who has the authority or responsibility for the pharmacy's compliance with this chapter and other laws relating to pharmacy.

(36) "Pharmacy" means a facility licensed by the Texas State Board of Pharmacy where a prescription for a controlled substance is received or processed in accordance with state or federal law.

(37) "Poppy straw" means all parts, other than the seeds, of the opium poppy, after mowing.

(38) "Possession" means actual care, custody, control, or management.

(39) "Practitioner" means:

(A) a physician, dentist, veterinarian, podiatrist, scientific investigator, or other person licensed, registered, or otherwise permitted to distribute, dispense, analyze, conduct research with respect to, or administer a controlled substance in the course of professional practice or research in this state;

(B) a pharmacy, hospital, or other institution licensed, registered, or otherwise permitted to distribute, dispense, conduct research with respect to, or administer a controlled substance in the course of professional practice or research in this state;

(C) a person practicing in and licensed by another state as a physician, dentist, veterinarian, or podiatrist, having a current Federal Drug Enforcement Administration registration number, who may legally prescribe Schedule II, III, IV, or V controlled substances in that state; or

(D) an advanced practice registered nurse or physician assistant to whom a physician has delegated the authority to prescribe or order a drug or device under Section 157.0511, 157.0512, or 157.054, Occupations Code.

(40) "Prescribe" means the act of a practitioner to authorize a controlled substance to be dispensed to an ultimate user.

(41) "Prescription" means an order by a practitioner to a pharmacist for a controlled substance for a particular patient that specifies:

(A) the date of issue;

(B) the name and address of the patient or, if the controlled substance is prescribed for an animal, the species of the animal and the name and address of its owner;

(C) the name and quantity of the controlled substance prescribed with the quantity shown numerically followed by the number written as a word if the order is written or, if the order is communicated orally or telephonically, with the quantity given by the practitioner and transcribed by the pharmacist numerically;

(D) directions for the use of the drug;

(E) the intended use of the drug unless the practitioner determines the furnishing of this information is not in the best interest of the patient; and

(F) the legibly printed or stamped name, address, Federal Drug Enforcement Administration registration number, and telephone number of the practitioner at the practitioner's usual place of business.

(42) "Principal place of business" means a location where a person manufactures, distributes, dispenses, analyzes, or possesses a controlled substance. The term does not include a location where a practitioner dispenses a controlled substance on an outpatient basis unless the controlled substance is stored at that location.

(43) "Production" includes the manufacturing, planting, cultivating, growing, or harvesting of a controlled substance.

(44) "Raw material" means a compound, material, substance, or equipment used or intended for use, alone or in any combination, in manufacturing a controlled substance.

(45) "Registrant" means a person who has a current Federal Drug Enforcement Administration registration number.

(46) "Substitution" means the dispensing of a drug or a brand of drug other than that which is ordered or prescribed.

(47) "Official prescription form" means a prescription form that is used for a Schedule II controlled substance under Section 481.0755 and contains the prescription information required by Section 481.0755(e).

(48) "Ultimate user" means a person who has lawfully obtained and possesses a controlled substance for the person's own use, for the use of a member of the person's household, or for administering to an animal owned by the person or by a member of the person's household.

(49) "Adulterant or dilutant" means any material that increases the bulk or quantity of a controlled substance, regardless of its effect on the chemical activity of the controlled substance.

(50) "Abuse unit" means:
  (A) except as provided by Paragraph (B):
    (i) a single unit on or in any adulterant, dilutant, or similar carrier medium, including marked or perforated blotter paper, a tablet, gelatin wafer, sugar cube, or stamp, or other medium that contains any amount of a controlled substance listed in Penalty Group 1-A, if the unit is commonly used in abuse of that substance; or
    (ii) each quarter-inch square section of paper, if the adulterant, dilutant, or carrier medium is paper not marked or perforated into individual abuse units; or
  (B) if the controlled substance is in liquid form, 40 micrograms of the controlled substance including any adulterant or dilutant.

(51) "Chemical precursor" means:
  (A) Methylamine;
  (B) Ethylamine;
  (C) D-lysergic acid;
  (D) Ergotamine tartrate;
  (E) Diethyl malonate;
  (F) Malonic acid;
  (G) Ethyl malonate;
  (H) Barbituric acid;
  (I) Piperidine;
  (J) N-acetylanthranilic acid;
  (K) Pyrrolidine;
  (L) Phenylacetic acid;
  (M) Anthranilic acid;
  (N) Ephedrine;
  (O) Pseudoephedrine;
  (P) Norpseudoephedrine; or
  (Q) Phenylpropanolamine.

(52) "Department" means the Department of Public Safety.

(53) "Chemical laboratory apparatus" means any item of equipment designed, made, or adapted to manufacture a controlled substance or a controlled substance analogue, including:
  (A) a condenser;
  (B) a distilling apparatus;
  (C) a vacuum drier;
  (D) a three-neck or distilling flask;
  (E) a tableting machine;
  (F) an encapsulating machine;
  (G) a filter, Buchner, or separatory funnel;
  (H) an Erlenmeyer, two-neck, or single-neck flask;
  (I) a round-bottom, Florence, thermometer, or filtering flask;
  (J) a Soxhlet extractor;
  (K) a transformer;
  (L) a flask heater;
  (M) a heating mantel; or
  (N) an adaptor tube.

(54) "Health information exchange" means an organization that:
  (A) assists in the transmission or receipt of health-related information among organizations transmitting or receiving the information according to nationally recognized standards and under an express written agreement;
  (B) as a primary business function, compiles or organizes health-related information that is designed to be securely transmitted by the organization among physicians, health care providers, or entities within a region, state, community, or hospital system; or
  (C) assists in the transmission or receipt of electronic health-related information among physicians, health care providers, or entities within:
    (i) a hospital system;
    (ii) a physician organization;
    (iii) a health care collaborative, as defined by Section 848.001, Insurance Code;
    (iv) an accountable care organization participating in the Pioneer Model under the initiative by the Innovation Center of the Centers for Medicare and Medicaid Services; or
    (v) an accountable care organization participating in the Medicare shared savings program under 42 U.S.C. Section 1395jjj.

(55) [2 Versions: As added by Acts 2015, 84th Leg., ch. 1] "Executive commissioner" means the executive commissioner of the Health and Human Services Commission.

(55) [2 Versions: As added by Acts 2015, 84th Leg., ch. 1268; Effective September 1 2016] "Board" means the Texas State Board of Pharmacy.

Leg.H. Stats. 1989, 71st Leg., ch. 678 (H.B. 2136), § 1, effective September 1, 1989; am. Acts 1989, 71st Leg., ch. 1100 (S.B. 1046), § 5.02(b), effective September 1, 1989; am. Acts 1993, 73rd Leg., ch. 351 (S.B. 621), § 27, effective September 1, 1993; am. Acts 1993, 73rd Leg., ch. 789 (S.B. 472), § 15, effective September 1, 1993; am. Acts 1993, 73rd Leg., ch. 900 (S.B. 1067), § 2.01, effective September 1, 1994; am. Acts 1997, 75thLeg., ch. 745 (H.B. 1070), §§ 1, 2, effective January 1, 1998; am. Acts 1999, 76th Leg., ch. 145 (S.B. 254), §§ 1, 5(1), effective September 1, 1999; am. Acts 2001, 77th Leg., ch. 251 (S.B. 753), § 1, effective September 1, 2001; am. Acts 2001, 77th Leg., ch. 1188 (H.B. 3351), § 1, effective September 1, 2001; am. Acts 2003, 78th Leg., ch. 88 (H.B. 1095), § 9, effective May 20, 2003; am. Acts 2003, 78th Leg., ch. 1099 (H.B. 2192), § 4, effective September 1, 2003; am. Acts 2013, 83rd Leg., ch. 418 (S.B. 406), § 23, effective November 1, 2013; am. Acts 2013, 83rd Leg., ch. 1226 (S.B. 1643), § 1, effective September 1, 2013; am. Acts 2015, 84th Leg., ch. 1 (S.B. 219), § 3.1227, effective April 2, 2015; am. Acts 2015, 84th Leg., ch. 64 (S.B. 172), § 1, effective September 1, 2015; am. Acts 2015, 84th Leg., ch. 65 (S.B. 173), § 1, effective September 1, 2015; am. Acts 2015, 84th Leg., ch. 712 (H.B. 1212), § 3, effective September 1, 2015; am. Acts 2015, 84th Leg., ch. 1268 (S.B. 195), § 2, effective September 1, 2016; am. Acts 2019, 86th Leg., ch. 764 (H.B. 1325), § 8, effective June 10, 2019; am. Acts 2019, 86th Leg., ch. 1105 (H.B. 2174), § 2, effective September 1, 2019.

Sec. 481.003. Rules.

(a) [As amended by Acts 2019, 86th Leg., ch. 1105 (H.B. 2174)] The director may adopt rules to administer and enforce this chapter, other than Sections 481.074, 481.075, 481.0755, 481.0756, 481.076, 481.0761, 481.0762, 481.0763, 481.07635, 481.07636, 481.0764, 481.0765, and 481.0766. The board may adopt rules to administer Sections 481.074, 481.075, 481.0755, 481.0756, 481.076, 481.0761, 481.0762, 481.0763, 481.07635, 481.07636, 481.0764, 481.0765, and 481.0766.

(a) [As amended by Acts 2019, 86th Leg., ch. 1166 (H.B. 3284)] The director may adopt rules to administer and enforce this chapter, other than Sections 481.073, 481.074, 481.075, 481.076, 481.0761, 481.0762, 481.0763, 481.0764, 481.0765, 481.0766, 481.0767, 481.0768, and 481.0769. The board may adopt rules to administer Sections 481.073, 481.074, 481.075, 481.076, 481.0761, 481.0762, 481.0763, 481.0764, 481.0765, 481.0766, 481.0767, 481.0768, and 481.0769.

(b) The director by rule shall prohibit a person in this state, including a person regulated by the Texas Department of Insurance under the Insurance Code or the other insurance laws of this state, from using a practitioner's Federal Drug Enforcement Administration number for a purpose other than a purpose described by federal law or by this chapter. A person who violates a rule adopted under this subsection commits a Class C misdemeanor.

Leg.H. Stats. 1997, 75th Leg., ch. 745 (H.B. 1070), § 3, effective January 1, 1998; am. Acts 1999, 76th Leg., ch. 1266 (S.B. 1235), § 1, effective September 1, 1999; am. Acts 2015, 84th Leg., ch. 1268 (S.B. 195), § 3, effective June 20, 2015; am. Acts 2017, 85th Leg., ch. 485 (H.B. 2561), § 1, effective September 1, 2017; am. Acts 2019, 86th Leg., ch. 1105 (H.B. 2174), § 3, effective September 1, 2019; am. Acts 2019, 86th Leg., ch. 1166 (H.B. 3284), § 5, effective September 1, 2019.

SUBCHAPTER B. SCHEDULES

Sec. 481.031. Nomenclature.

Controlled substances listed in Schedules I through V and Penalty Groups 1 through 4 are included by whatever official, common, usual, chemical, or trade name they may be designated.

Leg.H. Stats. 1997 75th Leg. Sess. Ch. 745, effective January 1, 1998.

Sec. 481.032. Schedules.

(a) The commissioner shall establish and modify the following schedules of controlled substances under this subchapter: Schedule I, Schedule II, Schedule III, Schedule IV, and Schedule V.

(b) A reference to a schedule in this chapter means the most current version of the schedule established or altered by the commissioner under this subchapter and published in the Texas Register on or after January 1, 1998.

Leg.H. Stats. 1997 75th Leg. Sess. Ch. 745, effective September 1, 1997; Stats. 2001 77th Leg. Sess. Ch. 251, effective September 1, 2001.

Sec. 481.033. Exclusion from Schedules and Application of Act.

(a) A nonnarcotic substance is excluded from Schedules I through V if the substance may lawfully be sold over the counter without a prescription, under the Federal Food, Drug, and Cosmetic Act (21 U.S.C. Section 301 et seq.).

(b) The commissioner may not include in the schedules:
    (1) a substance described by Subsection (a); or
    (2) distilled spirits, wine, malt beverages, or tobacco.

(c) A compound, mixture, or preparation containing a stimulant substance listed in Schedule II and having a potential for abuse associated with a stimulant effect on the central nervous system is excepted from the application of this chapter if the compound, mixture, or preparation contains one or more active medicinal ingredients not having a stimulant effect on the central nervous system and if the admixtures are included in combinations, quantity, proportions, or concentrations that vitiate the potential for abuse of the substance having a stimulant effect on the central nervous system.

(d) A compound, mixture, or preparation containing a depressant substance listed in Schedule III or IV and having a potential for abuse associated with a depressant effect on the central nervous system is excepted from the application of this chapter if the compound, mixture, or preparation contains one or more active medicinal ingredients not having a depressant effect on the central nervous system and if the admixtures are included in combinations, quantity, proportions, or concentrations that vitiate the potential for abuse of the substance having a depressant effect on the central nervous system.

(e) A nonnarcotic prescription substance is exempted from Schedules I through V and the application of this chapter to the same extent that the substance has been exempted from the application of the Federal Controlled Substances Act, if the substance is listed as an exempt prescription product under 21 C.F.R. Section 1308.32 and its subsequent amendments.

(f)   A chemical substance that is intended for laboratory, industrial, educational, or special research purposes and not for general administration to a human being or other animal is exempted from Schedules I through V and the application of this chapter to the same extent that the substance has been exempted from the application of the Federal Controlled Substances Act, if the substance is listed as an exempt chemical preparation under 21 C.F.R. Section 1308.24 and its subsequent amendments.

(g)   An anabolic steroid product, which has no significant potential for abuse due to concentration, preparation, mixture, or delivery system, is exempted from Schedules I through V and the application of this chapter to the same extent that the substance has been exempted from the application of the Federal Controlled Substances Act, if the substance is listed as an exempt anabolic steroid product under 21 C.F.R. Section 1308.34 and its subsequent amendments.

Leg.H. Stats. 1997 75th Leg. Sess. Ch. 745, effective January 1, 1998 (renumbered from Sec. 481.037).

Sec. 481.034. Establishment and Modification of Schedules by Commissioner.

(a)   The commissioner shall annually establish the schedules of controlled substances. These annual schedules shall include the complete list of all controlled substances from the previous schedules and modifications in the federal schedules of controlled substances as required by Subsection (g). Any further additions to and deletions from these schedules, any rescheduling of substances and any other modifications made by the commissioner to these schedules of controlled substances shall be made:
  (1)   in accordance with Section 481.035;
  (2)   in a manner consistent with this subchapter; and
  (3)   with approval of the executive commissioner.

(b)   Except for alterations in schedules required by Subsection (g), the commissioner may not make an alteration in a schedule unless the commissioner holds a public hearing on the matter in Austin and obtains approval from the executive commissioner.

(c)   The commissioner may not:
  (1)   add a substance to the schedules if the substance has been deleted from the schedules by the legislature;
  (2)   delete a substance from the schedules if the substance has been added to the schedules by the legislature; or
  (3)   reschedule a substance if the substance has been placed in a schedule by the legislature.

(d)   In making a determination regarding a substance, the commissioner shall consider:
  (1)   the actual or relative potential for its abuse;
  (2)   the scientific evidence of its pharmacological effect, if known;
  (3)   the state of current scientific knowledge regarding the substance;
  (4)   the history and current pattern of its abuse;
  (5)   the scope, duration, and significance of its abuse;
  (6)   the risk to the public health;
  (7)   the potential of the substance to produce psychological or physiological dependence liability; and
  (8)   whether the substance is a controlled substance analogue, chemical precursor, or an immediate precursor of a substance controlled under this chapter.

(e)   After considering the factors listed in Subsection (d), the commissioner shall make findings with respect to those factors. If the commissioner finds the substance has a potential for abuse, the executive commissioner shall adopt a rule controlling the substance.

(f)   [Repealed by Acts 2003, 78th Leg., ch. 1099 (H.B. 2192), § 17, effective September 1, 2003.]

(g)   Except as otherwise provided by this subsection, if a substance is designated, rescheduled, or deleted as a controlled substance under federal law and notice of that fact is given to the commissioner, the commissioner similarly shall control the substance under this chapter. After the expiration of a 30-day period beginning on the day after the date of publication in the Federal Register of a final order designating a substance as a controlled substance or rescheduling or deleting a substance, the commissioner similarly shall designate, reschedule, or delete the substance, unless the commissioner objects during the period. If the commissioner objects, the commissioner shall publish the reasons for the objection and give all interested parties an opportunity to be heard. At the conclusion of the hearing, the commissioner shall publish a decision, which is final unless altered by statute. On publication of an objection by the commissioner, control as to that particular substance under this chapter is stayed until the commissioner publishes the commissioner's decision.

(h)   Not later than the 10th day after the date on which the commissioner designates, deletes, or reschedules a substance under Subsection (a), the commissioner shall give written notice of that action to the director and to each state licensing agency having jurisdiction over practitioners.

Leg.H. Stats. 1997 75th Leg. Sess. Ch. 745, effective January 1, 1998; Stats. 2003 78th Leg. Sess. Ch. 1099, effective September 1, 2003; am. Acts 2015, 84th Leg., ch. 1 (S.B. 219), § 3.1228, effective April 2, 2015.

Sec. 481.035. Findings.

(a)   The commissioner shall place a substance in Schedule I if the commissioner finds that the substance:
  (1)   has a high potential for abuse; and
  (2)   has no accepted medical use in treatment in the United States or lacks accepted safety for use in treatment under medical supervision.

(b)   The commissioner shall place a substance in Schedule II if the commissioner finds that:
  (1)   the substance has a high potential for abuse;
  (2)   the substance has currently accepted medical use in treatment in the United States; and
  (3)   abuse of the substance may lead to severe psychological or physical dependence.

(c)   The commissioner shall place a substance in Schedule III if the commissioner finds that:
  (1)   the substance has a potential for abuse less than that of the substances listed in Schedules I and II;
  (2)   the substance has currently accepted medical use in treatment in the United States; and

    (3) abuse of the substance may lead to moderate or low physical dependence or high psychological dependence.

(d) The commissioner shall place a substance in Schedule IV if the commissioner finds that:

    (1) the substance has a lower potential for abuse than that of the substances listed in Schedule III;

    (2) the substance has currently accepted medical use in treatment in the United States; and

    (3) abuse of the substance may lead to a more limited physical or psychological dependence than that of the substances listed in Schedule III.

(e) The commissioner shall place a substance in Schedule V if the commissioner finds that the substance:

    (1) has a lower potential for abuse than that of the substances listed in Schedule IV;

    (2) has currently accepted medical use in treatment in the United States; and

    (3) may lead to a more limited physical or psychological dependence liability than that of the substances listed in Schedule IV.

Leg.H. Stats. 1997 75th Leg. Sess. Ch. 745, effective January 1, 1998 (renumbered from Sec. 481.039).

Sec. 481.0355. Emergency Scheduling; Legislative Report.

(a) Except as otherwise provided by Subsection (b) and subject to Subsection (c), the commissioner may emergency schedule a substance as a controlled substance if the commissioner determines the action is necessary to avoid an imminent hazard to the public safety.

(b) The commissioner may not emergency schedule a substance as a controlled substance under this section if:

    (1) the substance is already scheduled;

    (2) an exemption or approval is in effect for the substance under Section 505, Federal Food, Drug, and Cosmetic Act (21 U.S.C. Section 355); or

    (3) the substance is an over-the-counter drug that qualifies for recognition as safe and effective under conditions established by federal regulations of the United States Food and Drug Administration governing over-the-counter drugs.

(c) Before emergency scheduling a substance as a controlled substance under this section, the commissioner shall consult with the Department of Public Safety and may emergency schedule the substance only in accordance with any recommendations provided by the department.

(d) In determining whether a substance poses an imminent hazard to the public safety, the commissioner shall consider:

    (1) the scope, duration, symptoms, or significance of abuse;

    (2) the degree of detriment that abuse of the substance may cause;

    (3) whether the substance has been temporarily scheduled under federal law; and

    (4) whether the substance has been temporarily or permanently scheduled under the law of another state.

(e) If the commissioner emergency schedules a substance as a controlled substance under this section, an emergency exists for purposes of Section 481.036(c) and the action takes effect on the date the schedule is published in the Texas Register.

(f) Except as otherwise provided by Subsection (f-1), an emergency scheduling under this section expires on September 1 of each odd-numbered year for any scheduling that occurs before January 1 of that year.

(f-1) The commissioner may extend the emergency scheduling of a substance under this section not more than once and for a period not to exceed one year by publishing the extension in the Texas Register. If the commissioner extends the emergency scheduling of a substance, an emergency exists for purposes of Section 481.036(c) and the action takes effect on the date the extension is published in the Texas Register.

(g) The commissioner shall post notice about each emergency scheduling of a substance or each extension of an emergency scheduling of a substance under this section on the Internet website of the Department of State Health Services.

(h) Not later than December 1 of each even-numbered year, the commissioner shall submit a report about each emergency scheduling action taken under this section during the preceding two-year period to the governor, the lieutenant governor, the speaker of the house of representatives, and each legislative standing committee with primary jurisdiction over the department and each legislative standing committee with primary jurisdiction over criminal justice matters.

Leg.H. Stats. 2015, 84th Leg., ch. 712 (H.B. 1212), § 4, effective September 1, 2015; am. Acts 2017, 85th Leg., ch. 499 (H.B. 2804), §§ 1, 2, effective September 1, 2017.

Sec. 481.036. Publication of Schedules.

(a) The commissioner shall publish the schedules by filing a certified copy of the schedules with the secretary of state for publication in the Texas Register not later than the fifth working day after the date the commissioner takes action under this subchapter.

(b) Each published schedule must show changes, if any, made in the schedule since its latest publication.

(c) An action by the commissioner that establishes or modifies a schedule under this subchapter may take effect not earlier than the 21st day after the date on which the schedule or modification is published in the Texas Register unless an emergency exists that necessitates earlier action to avoid an imminent hazard to the public safety.

Leg.H. Stats. 1997 75th Leg. Sess. Ch. 745, effective January 1, 1998 (renumbered from Sec. 481.040).

Sec. 481.037. Carisoprodol.

Schedule IV includes carisoprodol.

Leg.H. 2009 81st Leg. Sess. Ch. 774, effective June 19, 2009.

Cont. Sub.

SUBCHAPTER C. REGULATION OF MANUFACTURE, DISTRIBUTION, AND DISPENSATION OF CONTROLLED SUBSTANCES, CHEMICAL PRECURSORS, AND CHEMICAL LABORATORY APPARATUS

Sec. 481.061. Federal Registration Required.

(a) Except as otherwise provided by this chapter, a person who is not registered with or exempt from registration with the Federal Drug Enforcement Administration may not manufacture, distribute, prescribe, possess, analyze, or dispense a controlled substance in this state.

(b) A person who is registered with the Federal Drug Enforcement Administration to manufacture, distribute, analyze, dispense, or conduct research with a controlled substance may possess, manufacture, distribute, analyze, dispense, or conduct research with that substance to the extent authorized by the person's registration and in conformity with this chapter.

(c), (d) [Repealed by Acts 2015, 84th Leg., ch. 1268 (S.B. 195), § 25(1), effective September 1, 2016.]

Leg.H. Stats. 1997 75th Leg. Sess. Ch. 745, effective January 1, 1998; Stats. 2011 82nd Leg. Sess. Ch. 1342, effective September 1, 2011; Stats. 2013, 83rd Leg., ch. 956 (H.B. 1803), § 1, effective January 1, 2014; am. Acts 2015, 84th Leg., ch. 1268 (S.B. 195), § 4, 5, 25(1), effective September 1, 2016.

Sec. 481.062. Exemptions.

(a) The following persons may possess a controlled substance under this chapter without registering with the Federal Drug Enforcement Administration:

(1) an agent or employee of a manufacturer, distributor, analyzer, or dispenser of the controlled substance who is registered with the Federal Drug Enforcement Administration and acting in the usual course of business or employment;

(2) a common or contract carrier, a warehouseman, or an employee of a carrier or warehouseman whose possession of the controlled substance is in the usual course of business or employment;

(3) an ultimate user or a person in possession of the controlled substance under a lawful order of a practitioner or in lawful possession of the controlled substance if it is listed in Schedule V;

(4) an officer or employee of this state, another state, a political subdivision of this state or another state, or the United States who is lawfully engaged in the enforcement of a law relating to a controlled substance or drug or to a customs law and authorized to possess the controlled substance in the discharge of the person's official duties;

(5) if the substance is tetrahydrocannabinol or one of its derivatives:

(A) a Department of State Health Services official, a medical school researcher, or a research program participant possessing the substance as authorized under Subchapter G; or

(B) a practitioner or an ultimate user possessing the substance as a participant in a federally approved therapeutic research program that the commissioner has reviewed and found, in writing, to contain a medically responsible research protocol.

(6) a dispensing organization licensed under Chapter 487 that possesses low-THC cannabis.

(b) [Repealed by Acts 2015, 84th Leg., ch. 1268 (S.B. 195), § 25(1), effective September 1, 2016.]

Leg.H. Stats. 1997 75th Leg. Sess. Ch. 745, effective January 1, 1998; Stats. 2001 77th Leg. Sess. Ch. 251, effective September 1, 2001; am. Acts 2015, 84th Leg., ch. 1 (S.B. 219), § 3.1229, effective April 2, 2015; am. Acts 2015, 84th Leg., ch. 301 (S.B. 339), § 2, effective June 1, 2015; am. Acts 2015, 84th Leg., (S.B. 195), § 6, 25(1), effective September 1, 2016.

Sec. 481.0621. Exceptions.

(a) This subchapter does not apply to an educational or research program of a school district or a public or private institution of higher education. This subchapter does not apply to a manufacturer, wholesaler, retailer, or other person who sells, transfers, or furnishes materials covered by this subchapter to those educational or research programs.

(b) The department and the Texas Higher Education Coordinating Board shall adopt a memorandum of understanding that establishes the responsibilities of the board, the department, and the public or private institutions of higher education in implementing and maintaining a program for reporting information concerning controlled substances, controlled substance analogues, chemical precursors, and chemical laboratory apparatus used in educational or research activities of institutions of higher education.

(c) The department and the Texas Education Agency shall adopt a memorandum of understanding that establishes the responsibilities of the agency, the department, and school districts in implementing and maintaining a program for reporting information concerning controlled substances, controlled substance analogues, chemical precursors, and chemical laboratory apparatus used in educational or research activities of those schools and school districts.

Leg.H. Stats. 1997 75th Leg. Sess. Ch. 165, effective September 1, 1997, Ch. 745, effective January 1, 1998.

Sec. 481.063. Registration Application; Issuance or Denial. [Repealed]

Leg.H. Stats. 1995 74th Leg. Sess. Ch. 76, Stats. 1997 75th Leg. Sess. Ch. 745, effective January 1, 1998; Stats. 2001 77th Leg. Sess. Ch. 251, effective September 1, 2001; Stats. 2013, 83rd Leg., ch. 956 (H.B. 1803), § 2, effective January 1, 2014; Repealed by Acts 2015, 84th Leg., ch. 1268 (S.B. 195), § 25(1), effective September 1, 2016.

Sec. 481.064. Registration Fees. [Repealed]

Leg.H. Stats. 1997 75th Leg. Sess. Ch. 745, effective January 1, 1998; Stats. 2001 77th Leg. Sess. Ch. 251, effective September 1, 2001; Stats. 2007, 80th Leg. Sess. Ch. 1391, effective September 1, 2007; Stats. 2013, 83rd Leg., ch. 956 (H.B. 1803), § 3, effective January 1, 2014; Repealed by Acts 2015, 84th Leg., ch. 1268 (S.B. 195), § 25(1), effective September 1, 2016.

Sec. 481.0645. Registration, Renewal, and Fees for Physicians. [Repealed]

Leg.H. Stats. 2013, 83rd Leg., ch. 956 (H.B. 1803), § 4, effective January 1, 2014; Repealed by Acts 2015, 84th Leg., ch. 1268 (S.B. 195), § 25(1), effective September 1, 2016.

Sec. 481.065. Authorization for Certain Activities.

(a) The director may authorize the possession, distribution, planting, and cultivation of controlled substances by a person engaged in research, training animals to detect controlled substances, or designing or calibrating devices to detect controlled substances. A person who obtains an authorization under this subsection does not commit an offense involving the possession or distribution of controlled substances to the extent that the possession or distribution is authorized.

(b) A person may conduct research with or analyze substances listed in Schedule I in this state only if the person is a practitioner registered under federal law to conduct research with or analyze those substances and the person provides the director with evidence of federal registration.

Leg.H. Stats. 1989 71st Leg. Sess. Ch. 678, effective September 1, 1989.

Sec. 481.066. Voluntary Surrender, Cancellation, Suspension, Probation, or Revocation of Registration. [Repealed]

Leg.H. Stats. 1997 75th Leg. Sess. Ch. 745, effective January 1, 1998; Stats. 2001 77th Leg. Sess. Ch. 251, effective September 1, 2001; Repealed by Acts 2015, 84th Leg., ch. 1268 (S.B. 195), § 25(1), effective September 1, 2016.

Sec. 481.067. Records.

(a) A person who is registered with the Federal Drug Enforcement Administration to manufacture, distribute, analyze, or dispense a controlled substance shall keep records and maintain inventories in compliance with recordkeeping and inventory requirements of federal law and with additional rules the board or director adopts.

(b) The pharmacist-in-charge of a pharmacy shall maintain the records and inventories required by this section.

(c) A record required by this section must be made at the time of the transaction that is the basis of the record. A record or inventory required by this section must be kept or maintained for at least two years after the date the record or inventory is made.

Leg.H. Stats. 2001 77th Leg. Sess. Ch. 251, effective September 1, 2001; am. Acts 2015, 84th Leg., (S.B. 195), § 7, effective September 1, 2016.

Sec. 481.068. Confidentiality.

(a) The director may authorize a person engaged in research on the use and effects of a controlled substance to withhold the names and other identifying characteristics of individuals who are the subjects of the research. A person who obtains the authorization may not be compelled in a civil, criminal, administrative, legislative, or other proceeding to identify the individuals who are the subjects of the research for which the authorization is obtained.

(b) Except as provided by Sections 481.074 and 481.075, a practitioner engaged in authorized medical practice or research may not be required to furnish the name or identity of a patient or research subject to the department, the Department of State Health Services, or any other agency, public official, or law enforcement officer. A practitioner may not be compelled in a state or local civil, criminal, administrative, legislative, or other proceeding to furnish the name or identity of an individual that the practitioner is obligated to keep confidential.

(c) The director may not provide to a federal, state, or local law enforcement agency the name or identity of a patient or research subject whose identity could not be obtained under Subsection (b).

Leg.H. Stats. 2001 77th Leg. Sess. Ch. 251, effective September 1, 2001; am. Acts 2015, 84th Leg., ch. 1 (S.B. 219), § 3.1230, effective April 2, 2015.

Sec. 481.069. Order Forms. [Repealed]

Leg.H. Stats. 1989, 71st Leg. Sess. Chs. 678, 1100, effective September 1, 1989; Repealed by Acts 2015, 84th Leg., ch. 1268 (S.B. 195), § 25(1), effective September 1, 2016.

Sec. 481.070. Administering or Dispensing Schedule I Controlled Substance.

Except as permitted by this chapter, a person may not administer or dispense a controlled substance listed in Schedule I.

Leg.H. Stats. 1989, 71st Leg. Sess. Ch. 678, effective September 1, 1989.

Sec. 481.071. Medical Purpose Required before Prescribing, Dispensing, Delivering, or Administering Controlled Substance.

(a) A practitioner defined by Section 481.002(39)(A) may not prescribe, dispense, deliver, or administer a controlled substance or cause a controlled substance to be administered under the practitioner's direction and supervision except for a valid medical purpose and in the course of medical practice.

(b) An anabolic steroid or human growth hormone listed in Schedule III may only be:

(1) dispensed, prescribed, delivered, or administered by a practitioner, as defined by Section 481.002(39)(A), for a valid medical purpose and in the course of professional practice; or

(2) dispensed or delivered by a pharmacist according to a prescription issued by a practitioner, as defined by Section 481.002(39) (A) or (C), for a valid medical purpose and in the course of professional practice.

(c) For the purposes of Subsection (b), bodybuilding, muscle enhancement, or increasing muscle bulk or strength through the use of an anabolic steroid or human growth hormone listed in Schedule III by a person who is in good health is not a valid medical purpose.

Leg.H. Stats. 1989, 71st Leg. Sess. Chs. 678, 1100, effective September 1, 1989; Stats. 1997 75th Leg. Sess. Ch. 745, effective January 1, 1998.

Sec. 481.072. Medical Purpose Required before Distributing or Dispensing Schedule V Controlled Substance.

A person may not distribute or dispense a controlled substance listed in Schedule V except for a valid medical purpose.

Leg.H. Stats. 1989, 71st Leg. Sess. Ch. 678, effective September 1, 1989.

Sec. 481.073. Communication of Prescriptions by Agent. [Repealed]

Leg.H. Stats. 1989, 71st Leg., ch. 678 (H.B. 2136), § 1, effective September 1, 1989; am. Acts 2001, 77th Leg., ch. 251 (S.B. 753), § 9, effective September 1, 2001; am. Acts 2001, 77th Leg., ch. 1420 (H.B. 2812), § 14.794, effective September 1, 2001; am. Acts 2015, 84th Leg., ch. 1 (S.B. 219), § 3.1231, effective April 2, 2015; am. Acts 2015, 84th Leg., ch. 1268 (S.B. 195), § 8, effective September 1, 2016; Repealed by Acts 2019, 86th Leg., ch. 1105 (H.B. 2174), § 16, effective September 1, 2019.

Sec. 481.074. Prescriptions.

(a) A pharmacist may not:

(1) dispense or deliver a controlled substance or cause a controlled substance to be dispensed or delivered under the pharmacist's direction or supervision except under a valid prescription and in the course of professional practice;

(2) dispense a controlled substance if the pharmacist knows or should have known that the prescription was issued without a valid patient-practitioner relationship;

(3) fill a prescription that is not prepared or issued as prescribed by this chapter;

(4) permit or allow a person who is not a licensed pharmacist or pharmacist intern to dispense, distribute, or in any other manner deliver a controlled substance even if under the supervision of a pharmacist, except that after the pharmacist or pharmacist intern has fulfilled his professional and legal responsibilities, a nonpharmacist may complete the actual cash or credit transaction and delivery; or

(5) permit the delivery of a controlled substance to any person not known to the pharmacist, the pharmacist intern, or the person authorized by the pharmacist to deliver the controlled substance without first requiring identification of the person taking possession of the controlled substance, except as provided by Subsection (n).

(b) Except in an emergency as defined by board rule under Subsection (b-1) or as otherwise provided by Section 481.075(j) or (m) or 481.0755, a person may not dispense or administer a controlled substance without an electronic prescription that meets the requirements of and is completed by the practitioner in accordance with Section 481.075.

(b-1) In an emergency as defined by board rule, a person may dispense or administer a controlled substance on the oral or telephonically communicated prescription of a practitioner. The person who administers or dispenses the substance shall:

(1) if the person is a prescribing practitioner or a pharmacist, promptly comply with Subsection (c); or

(2) if the person is not a prescribing practitioner or a pharmacist, promptly write the oral or telephonically communicated prescription and include in the written record of the prescription the name, address, and Federal Drug Enforcement Administration number issued for prescribing a controlled substance in this state of the prescribing practitioner, all information required to be provided by a practitioner under Section 481.075(e)(1), and all information required to be provided by a dispensing pharmacist under Section 481.075(e)(2).

(b-2) In an emergency described by Subsection (b-1), an agent designated in writing by a practitioner defined by Section 481.002(39) (A) may communicate a prescription by telephone. A practitioner who designates a different agent shall designate that agent in writing and maintain the designation in the same manner in which the practitioner initially designated an agent under this subsection. On the request of a pharmacist, a practitioner shall furnish a copy of the written designation. This subsection does not relieve a practitioner or the practitioner's designated agent from the requirement of Subchapter A, Chapter 562, Occupations Code. A practitioner is personally responsible for the actions of the designated agent in communicating a prescription to a pharmacist.

(c) Not later than the seventh day after the date a prescribing practitioner authorizes an emergency oral or telephonically communicated prescription, the prescribing practitioner shall cause an electronic prescription, completed in the manner required by Section 481.075, to be delivered to the dispensing pharmacist at the pharmacy where the prescription was dispensed. On receipt of the electronic prescription, the pharmacist shall annotate the electronic prescription record with the original authorization and date of the emergency oral or telephonically communicated prescription.

(d) Except as specified in Subsections (e) and (f), the board, by rule and in consultation with the Texas Medical Board, shall establish the period after the date on which the prescription is issued that a person may fill a prescription for a controlled substance listed in Schedule II. A person may not refill a prescription for a substance listed in Schedule II.

(d-1) Notwithstanding Subsection (d), a prescribing practitioner may issue multiple prescriptions authorizing the patient to receive a total of up to a 90-day supply of a Schedule II controlled substance if:

    (1) each separate prescription is issued for a legitimate medical purpose by a prescribing practitioner acting in the usual course of professional practice;

    (2) the prescribing practitioner provides instructions on each prescription to be filled at a later date indicating the earliest date on which a pharmacy may fill each prescription;

    (3) the prescribing practitioner concludes that providing the patient with multiple prescriptions in this manner does not create an undue risk of diversion or abuse; and

    (4) the issuance of multiple prescriptions complies with other applicable state and federal laws.

(e) The partial filling of a prescription for a controlled substance listed in Schedule II is permissible in accordance with applicable federal law.

(f) A prescription for a Schedule II controlled substance for a patient in a long-term care facility (LTCF) or for a hospice patient with a medical diagnosis documenting a terminal illness may be filled in partial quantities to include individual dosage units. If there is any question about whether a hospice patient may be classified as having a terminal illness, the pharmacist must contact the practitioner before partially filling the prescription. Both the pharmacist and the practitioner have a corresponding responsibility to assure that the controlled substance is for a terminally ill hospice patient. The pharmacist must record the prescription in the electronic prescription record and must indicate in the electronic prescription record whether the patient is a "terminally ill hospice patient" or an "LTCF patient." A prescription that is partially filled and does not contain the notation "terminally ill hospice patient" or "LTCF patient" is considered to have been filled in violation of this chapter. For each partial filling, the dispensing pharmacist shall record in the electronic prescription record the date of the partial filling, the quantity dispensed, the remaining quantity authorized to be dispensed, and the identification of the dispensing pharmacist. Before any subsequent partial filling, the pharmacist must determine that the additional partial filling is necessary. The total quantity of Schedule II controlled substances dispensed in all partial fillings may not exceed the total quantity prescribed. Schedule II prescriptions for patients in a long-term care facility or hospice patients with a medical diagnosis documenting a terminal illness are valid for a period not to exceed 60 days following the issue date unless sooner terminated by discontinuance of the medication.

(g) A person may not dispense a controlled substance in Schedule III or IV that is a prescription drug under the Federal Food, Drug, and Cosmetic Act (21 U.S.C. Section 301 et seq.) without a prescription of a practitioner defined by Section 481.002(39)(A) or (D), except that the practitioner may dispense the substance directly to an ultimate user. A prescription for a controlled substance listed in Schedule III or IV may not be filled or refilled later than six months after the date on which the prescription is issued and may not be refilled more than five times, unless the prescription is renewed by the practitioner. A prescription under this subsection must comply with other applicable state and federal laws.

(h) A pharmacist may dispense a controlled substance listed in Schedule III, IV, or V under a prescription issued by a practitioner defined by Section 481.002(39)(C) only if the pharmacist determines that the prescription was issued for a valid medical purpose and in the course of professional practice. A prescription described by this subsection may not be filled or refilled later than six months after the date the prescription is issued and may not be refilled more than five times, unless the prescription is renewed by the practitioner.

(i) A person may not dispense a controlled substance listed in Schedule V and containing 200 milligrams or less of codeine, or any of its salts, per 100 milliliters or per 100 grams, or containing 100 milligrams or less of dihydrocodeine, or any of its salts, per 100 milliliters or per 100 grams, without the prescription of a practitioner defined by Section 481.002(39)(A), except that a practitioner may dispense the substance directly to an ultimate user. A prescription issued under this subsection may not be filled or refilled later than six months after the date the prescription is issued and may not be refilled more than five times, unless the prescription is renewed by the practitioner.

(j) A practitioner or institutional practitioner may not allow a patient, on the patient's release from the hospital, to possess a controlled substance prescribed by the practitioner unless:

    (1) the substance was dispensed under a medication order while the patient was admitted to the hospital;

    (2) the substance is in a properly labeled container; and

    (3) the patient possesses not more than a seven-day supply of the substance.

(k) A prescription for a controlled substance must show:

    (1) the quantity of the substance prescribed:

        (A) numerically, if the prescription is electronic; or

        (B) if the prescription is communicated orally or telephonically, as transcribed by the receiving pharmacist;

    (2) the date of issue;

    (2-a) if the prescription is issued for a Schedule II controlled substance to be filled at a later date under Subsection (d-1), the earliest date on which a pharmacy may fill the prescription;

    (3) the name, address, and date of birth or age of the patient or, if the controlled substance is prescribed for an animal, the species of the animal and the name and address of its owner;

    (4) the name and strength of the controlled substance prescribed;

    (5) the directions for use of the controlled substance;

    (6) the intended use of the substance prescribed unless the practitioner determines the furnishing of this information is not in the best interest of the patient; and

    (7) the name, address, Federal Drug Enforcement Administration number, and telephone number of the practitioner at the practitioner's usual place of business.

(l) A pharmacist may exercise his professional judgment in refilling a prescription for a controlled substance in Schedule III, IV, or V without the authorization of the prescribing practitioner provided:

    (1) failure to refill the prescription might result in an interruption of a therapeutic regimen or create patient suffering;

Cont. Sub.

(2)   either:
  (A)   a natural or manmade disaster has occurred which prohibits the pharmacist from being able to contact the practitioner; or
  (B)   the pharmacist is unable to contact the practitioner after reasonable effort;
(3)   the quantity of prescription drug dispensed does not exceed a 72-hour supply;
(4)   the pharmacist informs the patient or the patient's agent at the time of dispensing that the refill is being provided without such authorization and that authorization of the practitioner is required for future refills; and
(5)   the pharmacist informs the practitioner of the emergency refill at the earliest reasonable time.

(*l*-1) Notwithstanding Subsection (l), in the event of a natural or manmade disaster, a pharmacist may dispense not more than a 30-day supply of a prescription drug, other than a controlled substance listed in Schedule II, without the authorization of the prescribing practitioner if:
(1)   failure to refill the prescription might result in an interruption of a therapeutic regimen or create patient suffering;
(2)   the natural or manmade disaster prohibits the pharmacist from being able to contact the practitioner;
(3)   the governor has declared a state of disaster under Chapter 418, Government Code; and
(4)   the Texas State Board of Pharmacy, through its executive director, has notified pharmacies in this state that pharmacists may dispense up to a 30-day supply of a prescription drug.

(*l*-2) The prescribing practitioner is not liable for an act or omission by a pharmacist in dispensing a prescription drug under Subsection (l-1).

(m) A pharmacist may permit the delivery of a controlled substance by an authorized delivery person, by a person known to the pharmacist, a pharmacist intern, or the authorized delivery person, or by mail to the person or address of the person authorized by the prescription to receive the controlled substance. If a pharmacist permits delivery of a controlled substance under this subsection, the pharmacist shall retain in the records of the pharmacy for a period of not less than two years:
(1)   the name of the authorized delivery person, if delivery is made by that person;
(2)   the name of the person known to the pharmacist, a pharmacist intern, or the authorized delivery person if delivery is made by that person; or
(3)   the mailing address to which delivery is made, if delivery is made by mail.

(n) A pharmacist may permit the delivery of a controlled substance to a person not known to the pharmacist, a pharmacist intern, or the authorized delivery person without first requiring the identification of the person to whom the controlled substance is delivered if the pharmacist determines that an emergency exists and that the controlled substance is needed for the immediate well-being of the patient for whom the controlled substance is prescribed. If a pharmacist permits delivery of a controlled substance under this subsection, the pharmacist shall retain in the records of the pharmacy for a period of not less than two years all information relevant to the delivery known to the pharmacist, including the name, address, and date of birth or age of the person to whom the controlled substance is delivered.

(o) [Repealed.]
(p) [Repealed.]
(q) Each dispensing pharmacist shall send all required information to the board by electronic transfer or another form approved by the board not later than the next business day after the date the prescription is completely filled.

Leg.H. Stats. 1989, 71st Leg., ch. 678 (H.B. 2136), § 1, effective September 1, 1989; am. Acts 1989, 71st Leg., ch. 1100 (S.B. 1046), § 5.02, effective September 1, 1989; am. Acts 1991, 72nd, Leg., ch. 615 (S.B. 1497), § 10, effective September 1, 1991; am. Acts 1991, 72nd, Leg., ch. 761 (S.B. 314), § 6, effective September 1, 1991; am. Acts 1993, 73rd Leg., ch. 351 (S.B. 621), § 28, effective September 1, 1993; am. Acts 1993, 73rd Leg., ch. 789 (S.B. 472), § 16, effective September 1, 1993; am. Acts 1997, 75th Leg., ch. 745 (H.B. 1070), §§ 12, 13, effective January 1, 1998; am. Acts 1999, 76th Leg., ch. 145 (S.B. 254), § 2, effective September 1, 1999; am. Acts 2001, 77th Leg., ch. 251 (S.B. 753), § 10, effective September 1, 2001; am. Acts 2001, 77th Leg., ch. 1254 (S.B. 768), § 10, effective September 1, 2001; am. Acts 2005, 79th Leg., ch. 349 (S.B. 1188), § 21(a), effective September 1, 2005; am. Acts 2005, 79th Leg., ch. 1345 (S.B. 410), § 44(a), effective June 18, 2005; am. Acts 2007, 80th Leg., ch. 535 (S.B. 994), § 1, effective September 1, 2007; am. Acts 2007, 80th Leg., ch. 567 (S.B. 1658), § 2, effective September 1, 2007; am. Acts 2007, 80th Leg., ch. 1391 (S.B. 1879), § 2, effective September 1, 2007 (subsections (k) and (q) effective September 1, 2008); am. Acts 2009, 81st Leg., ch. 774 (S.B. 904), § 1, effective June 19, 2009; am. Acts 2011, 82nd Leg., ch. 91 (S.B. 1303), § 12.007, effective September 1, 2011; am. Acts 2011, 82nd Leg., ch. 1228 (S.B. 594), § 2, effective September 1, 2011; am. Acts 2011, 82nd Leg., ch. 1342 (S.B. 1273), § 2, effective September 1, 2011; am. Acts 2015, 84th Leg., ch. 1268 (S.B. 195), § 9, effective September 1, 2016; am. Acts 2017, 85th Leg., ch. 485 (H.B. 2561), § 2, effective September 1, 2017; am. Acts 2019, 86th Leg., ch. 1105 (H.B. 2174), §§ 4, 16, effective September 1, 2019.

Sec. 481.075. Schedule II Prescriptions.

(a) A practitioner who prescribes a controlled substance listed in Schedule II shall, except as provided by Section 481.074(b-1) or 481.0755 or a rule adopted under Section 481.0761, record the prescription in an electronic prescription that includes the information required by this section.
(b) [Repealed.]
(c) [Repealed.]
(d) [Repealed.]
(e) Each prescription used to prescribe a Schedule II controlled substance must contain:
(1)   information provided by the prescribing practitioner, including:
  (A)   the date the prescription is issued;
  (B)   the controlled substance prescribed;
  (C)   the quantity of controlled substance prescribed, shown numerically;
  (D)   the intended use of the controlled substance, or the diagnosis for which the controlled substance is prescribed, and the instructions for use of the substance;

(E)   the practitioner's name, address, and Federal Drug Enforcement Administration number issued for prescribing a controlled substance in this state;

(F)   the name, address, and date of birth or age of the person for whom the controlled substance is prescribed; and

(G)   if the prescription is issued to be filled at a later date under Section 481.074(d-1), the earliest date on which a pharmacy may fill the prescription;

   (2)   information provided by the dispensing pharmacist, including the date the prescription is filled; and

   (3)   the prescribing practitioner's electronic signature or other secure method of validation authorized by federal law.

(f)   [Repealed.]

(g)   Except for an emergency oral or telephonically communicated prescription described by Section 481.074(b-1), the prescribing practitioner shall:

   (1)   record or direct a designated agent to record in the electronic prescription each item of information required to be provided by the prescribing practitioner under Subsection (e)(1), unless the practitioner determines that:

(A)   under rule adopted by the board for this purpose, it is unnecessary for the practitioner or the practitioner's agent to provide the patient identification number; or

(B)   it is not in the best interest of the patient for the practitioner or practitioner's agent to provide information regarding the intended use of the controlled substance or the diagnosis for which it is prescribed; and

   (2)   electronically sign or validate the electronic prescription as authorized by federal law and transmit the prescription to the dispensing pharmacy.

(h)   In the case of an emergency oral or telephonically communicated prescription described by Section 481.074(b-1), the prescribing practitioner shall give the dispensing pharmacy the information needed to complete the electronic prescription record.

(i)   [As amended by Acts 2019, 86th Leg., chs. 1144 and 965 (H.B. 2847 and SB 683)] Each dispensing pharmacist shall:

   (1)   fill in on the official prescription form or note in the electronic prescription record each item of information given orally to the dispensing pharmacy under Subsection (h) and the date the prescription is filled, and:

(A)   for a written prescription, fill in the dispensing pharmacist's signature; or

(B)   for an electronic prescription, appropriately record the identity of the dispensing pharmacist in the electronic prescription record;

   (2)   retain with the records of the pharmacy for at least two years:

(A)   the official prescription form or the electronic prescription record, as applicable; and

(B)   the name or other patient identification required by Section 481.074(m) or (n);

   (3)   send all required information, including any information required to complete an official prescription form or electronic prescription record, to the board by electronic transfer or another form approved by the board not later than the next business day after the date the prescription is completely filled; and

   (4)   if the pharmacy does not dispense any controlled substance prescriptions during a period of seven consecutive days, send a report to the board indicating that the pharmacy did not dispense any controlled substance prescriptions during that period, unless the pharmacy has obtained a waiver or permission to delay reporting to the board.

(i)   [As amended by Acts 2019, 86th Leg., ch. 1105 (H.B. 2174)] Each dispensing pharmacist shall:

   (1)   note in the electronic prescription record each item of information given orally to the dispensing pharmacy under Subsection (h) and the date the prescription is filled and appropriately record the identity of the dispensing pharmacist in the electronic prescription record;

   (2)   retain with the records of the pharmacy for at least two years:

(A)   the electronic prescription record; and

(B)   the name or other patient identification required by Section 481.074(m) or (n); and

   (3)   send all required information, including any information required to complete an electronic prescription record, to the board by electronic transfer or another form approved by the board not later than the next business day after the date the prescription is completely filled

(j)   A medication order written for a patient who is admitted to a hospital at the time the medication order is written and filled is not required to be recorded in an electronic prescription record that meets the requirements of this section.

(k)   [Repealed.]

(l)   [Repealed.]

(m)   A pharmacy in this state may fill a prescription for a controlled substance listed in Schedule II issued by a practitioner in another state if:

   (1)   a share of the pharmacy's business involves the dispensing and delivery or mailing of controlled substances;

   (2)   the prescription is issued by a prescribing practitioner in the other state in the ordinary course of practice; and

   (3)   the prescription is filled in compliance with a written plan providing the manner in which the pharmacy may fill a Schedule II prescription issued by a practitioner in another state that:

(A)   is submitted by the pharmacy to the board; and

(B)   is approved by the board.

(n)   A person dispensing a Schedule II controlled substance under a prescription shall provide written notice, as defined by board rule adopted under Subsection (o), on the safe disposal of controlled substance prescription drugs, unless:

   (1)   the Schedule II controlled substance prescription drug is dispensed at a pharmacy or other location that:

(A)   is authorized to take back those drugs for safe disposal; and

(B)   regularly accepts those drugs for safe disposal; or

   (2)   the dispenser provides to the person to whom the Schedule II controlled substance prescription drug is dispensed, at the time of dispensation and at no cost to the person:

(A)   a mail-in pouch for surrendering unused controlled substance prescription drugs; or

(B)   chemicals to render any unused drugs unusable or non-retrievable.

(o)   The board shall adopt rules to prescribe the form of the written notice on the safe disposal of controlled substance prescription drugs required under Subsection (n). The notice must include information on locations at which Schedule II controlled substance prescription drugs are accepted for safe disposal. The notice, in lieu of listing those locations, may provide the address of an Internet website specified by the board that provides a searchable database of locations at which Schedule II controlled substance prescription drugs are accepted for safe disposal.

(p)   The board may take disciplinary action against a person who fails to comply with Subsection (n).

Leg.H. Stats. 1989, 71st Leg., ch. 678 (H.B. 2136), § 1, effective September 1, 1989; am. Acts 1989, 71st Leg., ch. 1100 (S.B. 1046), § 5.02(i), effective September 1, 1989; am. Acts 1993, 73rd Leg., ch. 789 (S.B. 472), § 17, effective September 1, 1993; am. Acts 1997, 75th Leg., ch. 745 (H.B. 1070), § 14, effective January 1, 1998; am. Acts 1999, 76th Leg., ch. 145 (S.B. 254), §§ 3, 5(2), effective September 1, 1999; am. Acts 2001, 77th Leg., ch. 251 (S.B. 753), § 11, effective September 1, 2001; am. Acts 2009, 81st Leg., ch. 774 (S.B. 904), § 2, effective June 19, 2009; am. Acts 2011, 82nd Leg., ch. 1228 (S.B. 594), § 3, effective September 1, 2011; am. Acts 2011, 82nd Leg., ch. 1342 (S.B. 1273), § 3, effective September 1, 2011; am. Acts 2015, 84th Leg., ch. 1268 (S.B. 195), § 10, effective September 1, 2016; am. Acts 2017, 85th Leg., ch. 485 (H.B. 2561), § 3, effective September 1, 2017; am. Acts 2019, 86th Leg., ch. 798 (H.B. 2088), § 1, effective September 1, 2019; am. Acts 2019, 86th Leg., ch. 965 (S.B. 683), § 1, effective September 1, 2019; am. Acts 2019, 86th Leg., ch. 1105 (H.B. 2174), §§ 5, 6, 16, effective September 1, 2019; am. Acts 2019, 86th Leg., ch. 1144 (H.B. 2847), § 4.001, effective September 1, 2019.

Sec. 481.0755. Written, Oral, and Telephonically Communicated Prescriptions.

(a)   Notwithstanding Sections 481.074 and 481.075, a prescription for a controlled substance is not required to be issued electronically and may be issued in writing if the prescription is issued:

(1)   by a veterinarian;

(2)   in circumstances in which electronic prescribing is not available due to temporary technological or electronic failure, as prescribed by board rule;

(3)   by a practitioner to be dispensed by a pharmacy located outside this state, as prescribed by board rule;

(4)   when the prescriber and dispenser are in the same location or under the same license;

(5)   in circumstances in which necessary elements are not supported by the most recently implemented national data standard that facilitates electronic prescribing;

(6)   for a drug for which the United States Food and Drug Administration requires additional information in the prescription that is not possible with electronic prescribing;

(7)   for a non-patient-specific prescription pursuant to a standing order, approved protocol for drug therapy, collaborative drug management, or comprehensive medication management, in response to a public health emergency or in other circumstances in which the practitioner may issue a non-patient-specific prescription;

(8)   for a drug under a research protocol;

(9)   by a practitioner who has received a waiver under Section 481.0756 from the requirement to use electronic prescribing;

(10)   under circumstances in which the practitioner has the present ability to submit an electronic prescription but reasonably determines that it would be impractical for the patient to obtain the drugs prescribed under the electronic prescription in a timely manner and that a delay would adversely impact the patient's medical condition; or

(11)   before January 1, 2021.

(b)   A dispensing pharmacist who receives a controlled substance prescription in a manner other than electronically is not required to verify that the prescription is exempt from the requirement that it be submitted electronically. The pharmacist may dispense a controlled substance pursuant to an otherwise valid written, oral, or telephonically communicated prescription consistent with the requirements of this subchapter.

(c)   Except in an emergency, a practitioner must use a written prescription to submit a prescription described by Subsection (a). In an emergency, the practitioner may submit an oral or telephonically communicated prescription as authorized under Section 481.074(b-1).

(d)   A written prescription for a controlled substance other than a Schedule II controlled substance must include the information required under Section 481.074(k) and the signature of the prescribing practitioner.

(e)   A written prescription for a Schedule II controlled substance must be on an official prescription form and include the information required for an electronic prescription under Section 481.075(e), the signature of the practitioner, and the signature of the dispensing pharmacist after the prescription is filled.

(f)   The board by rule shall authorize a practitioner to determine whether it is necessary to obtain a particular patient identification number and to provide that number on the official prescription form.

(g)   On request of a practitioner, the board shall issue official prescription forms to the practitioner for a fee covering the actual cost of printing, processing, and mailing the forms. Before mailing or otherwise delivering prescription forms to a practitioner, the board shall print on each form the number of the form and any other information the board determines is necessary.

(h)   Each official prescription form must be sequentially numbered.

(i)   A person may not obtain an official prescription form unless the person is a practitioner as defined by Section 481.002(39)(A) or an institutional practitioner.

(j)   Not more than one Schedule II prescription may be recorded on an official prescription form.

(k)   Not later than the 30th day after the date a practitioner's Federal Drug Enforcement Administration number or license to practice has been denied, suspended, canceled, surrendered, or revoked, the practitioner shall return to the board all official prescription forms in the practitioner's possession that have not been used for prescriptions.

(l)   Each prescribing practitioner:

(1)   may use an official prescription form only to submit a prescription described by Subsection (a);

(2)   shall date or sign an official prescription form only on the date the prescription is issued; and

(3)   shall take reasonable precautionary measures to ensure that an official prescription form issued to the practitioner is not used by another person to violate this subchapter or a rule adopted under this subchapter.

(m) In the case of an emergency oral or telephonically communicated prescription described by Section 481.074(b-1), the prescribing practitioner shall give the dispensing pharmacy the information needed to complete the official prescription form if the pharmacy is not required to use the electronic prescription record.

(n) Each dispensing pharmacist receiving an oral or telephonically communicated prescription under Subsection (m) shall:
  (1) fill in on the official prescription form each item of information given orally to the dispensing pharmacy under Subsection (m) and the date the prescription is filled and fill in the dispensing pharmacist's signature;
  (2) retain with the records of the pharmacy for at least two years:
    (A) the official prescription form; and
    (B) the name or other patient identification required by Section 481.074(m) or (n); and
  (3) send all required information, including any information required to complete an official prescription form, to the board by electronic transfer or another form approved by the board not later than the next business day after the date the prescription is completely filled.

Leg.II. Stats. 2019, 86th Leg., ch. 1105 (H.B. 2174), § 7, effective September 1, 2019.

Sec. 481.0756. Waivers From Electronic Prescribing.

(a) The appropriate regulatory agency that issued the license, certification, or registration to a prescriber is authorized to grant a prescriber a waiver from the electronic prescribing requirement under the provisions of this section.

(b) The board shall convene an interagency workgroup that includes representatives of each regulatory agency that issues a license, certification, or registration to a prescriber.

(c) The work group described by Subsection (b) shall establish recommendations and standards for circumstances in which a waiver from the electronic prescribing requirement is appropriate and a process under which a prescriber may request and receive a waiver.

(d) The board shall adopt rules establishing the eligibility for a waiver, including:
  (1) economic hardship;
  (2) technological limitations not reasonably within the control of the prescriber; or
  (3) other exceptional circumstances demonstrated by the prescriber.

(e) Each regulatory agency that issues a license, certification, or registration to a prescriber shall adopt rules for the granting of waivers consistent with the board rules adopted under Subsection (d).

(f) A waiver may be issued to a prescriber for a period of one year. A prescriber may reapply for a subsequent waiver not earlier than the 30th day before the date the waiver expires if the circumstances that necessitated the waiver continue.

Leg.H. Stats. 2019, 86th Leg., ch. 1105 (H.B. 2174), § 7, effective September 1, 2019.

Sec. 481.076. Official Prescription Information; Duties of Texas State Board of Pharmacy.

(a) The board may not permit any person to have access to information submitted to the board under Section 481.074(q) or 481.075 except:
  (1) the board, the Texas Medical Board, the Texas Department of Licensing and Regulation, with respect to the regulation of podiatrists, the State Board of Dental Examiners, the State Board of Veterinary Medical Examiners, the Texas Board of Nursing, or the Texas Optometry Board for the purpose of:
    (A) investigating a specific license holder; or
    (B) monitoring for potentially harmful prescribing or dispensing patterns or practices under Section 481.0762;
  (2) an authorized employee of the board engaged in the administration, investigation, or enforcement of this chapter or another law governing illicit drugs in this state or another state;
  (3) the department or other law enforcement or prosecutorial official engaged in the administration, investigation, or enforcement of this chapter or another law governing illicit drugs in this state or another state, if the board is provided a warrant, subpoena, or other court order compelling the disclosure;
  (4) a medical examiner conducting an investigation;
  (5) provided that accessing the information is authorized under the Health Insurance Portability and Accountability Act of 1996 (Pub. L. No. 104-191) and regulations adopted under that Act:
    (A) a pharmacist or a pharmacist-intern, pharmacy technician, or pharmacy technician trainee, as defined by Section 551.003, Occupations Code, acting at the direction of a pharmacist, who is inquiring about a recent Schedule II, III, IV, or V prescription history of a particular patient of the pharmacist; or
    (B) a practitioner who:
      (i) is a physician, dentist, veterinarian, podiatrist, optometrist, or advanced practice nurse or is a physician assistant described by Section 481.002(39)(D) or an employee or other agent of a practitioner acting at the direction of a practitioner; and
      (ii) is inquiring about a recent Schedule II, III, IV, or V prescription history of a particular patient of the practitioner;
  (6) a pharmacist or practitioner who is inquiring about the person's own dispensing or prescribing activity or a practitioner who is inquiring about the prescribing activity of an individual to whom the practitioner has delegated prescribing authority;
  (7) one or more states or an association of states with which the board has an interoperability agreement, as provided by Subsection (j);
  (8) a health care facility certified by the federal Centers for Medicare and Medicaid Services; or
  (9) the patient, the patient's parent or legal guardian, if the patient is a minor, or the patient's legal guardian, if the patient is an incapacitated person, as defined by Section 1002.017(2), Estates Code, inquiring about the patient's prescription record, including persons who have accessed that record.

(a-1) A person authorized to receive information under Subsection (a)(4), (5), or (6) may access that information through a health information exchange, subject to proper security measures to ensure against disclosure to unauthorized persons.

(a-2) A person authorized to receive information under Subsection (a)(5) may include that information in any form in the medical or pharmacy record of the patient who is the subject of the information. Any information included in a patient's medical or pharmacy record under this subsection is subject to any applicable state or federal confidentiality or privacy laws.

(a-3) [Repealed.]

(a-4) [Repealed.]

(a-5) [Repealed.]

(a-6) A patient, the patient's parent or legal guardian, if the patient is a minor, or the patient's legal guardian, if the patient is an incapacitated person, as defined by Section 1002.017(2), Estates Code, is entitled to a copy of the patient's prescription record as provided by Subsection (a)(9), including a list of persons who have accessed that record, if a completed patient data request form and any supporting documentation required by the board is submitted to the board. The board may charge a reasonable fee for providing the copy. The board shall adopt rules to implement this subsection, including rules prescribing the patient data request form, listing the documentation required for receiving a copy of the prescription record, and setting the fee.

(b) This section does not prohibit the board from creating, using, or disclosing statistical data about information submitted to the board under this section if the board removes any information reasonably likely to reveal the identity of each patient, practitioner, or other person who is a subject of the information.

(c) The board by rule shall design and implement a system for submission of information to the board by electronic or other means and for retrieval of information submitted to the board under this section and Sections 481.074 and 481.075. The board shall use automated information security techniques and devices to preclude improper access to the information. The board shall submit the system design to the director and the Texas Medical Board for review and comment a reasonable time before implementation of the system and shall comply with the comments of those agencies unless it is unreasonable to do so.

(d) Information submitted to the board under this section may be used only for:

    (1) the administration, investigation, or enforcement of this chapter or another law governing illicit drugs in this state or another state;

    (2) investigatory, evidentiary, or monitoring purposes in connection with the functions of an agency listed in Subsection (a)(1);

    (3) the prescribing and dispensing of controlled substances by a person listed in Subsection (a)(5); or

    (4) dissemination by the board to the public in the form of a statistical tabulation or report if all information reasonably likely to reveal the identity of each patient, practitioner, or other person who is a subject of the information has been removed.

(e) The board shall remove from the information retrieval system, destroy, and make irretrievable the record of the identity of a patient submitted under this section to the board not later than the end of the 36th calendar month after the month in which the identity is entered into the system. However, the board may retain a patient identity that is necessary for use in a specific ongoing investigation conducted in accordance with this section until the 30th day after the end of the month in which the necessity for retention of the identity ends.

(f) If the board accesses information under Subsection (a)(2) relating to a person licensed or regulated by an agency listed in Subsection (a)(1), the board shall notify and cooperate with that agency regarding the disposition of the matter before taking action against the person, unless the board determines that notification is reasonably likely to interfere with an administrative or criminal investigation or prosecution.

(g) If the board provides access to information under Subsection (a)(3) relating to a person licensed or regulated by an agency listed in Subsection (a)(1), the board shall notify that agency of the disclosure of the information not later than the 10th working day after the date the information is disclosed.

(h) If the board withholds notification to an agency under Subsection (f), the board shall notify the agency of the disclosure of the information and the reason for withholding notification when the board determines that notification is no longer likely to interfere with an administrative or criminal investigation or prosecution.

(i) Information submitted to the board under Section 481.074(q) or 481.075 is confidential and remains confidential regardless of whether the board permits access to the information under this section.

(j) The board may enter into an interoperability agreement with one or more states or an association of states authorizing the board to access prescription monitoring information maintained or collected by the other state or states or the association, including information maintained on a central database such as the National Association of Boards of Pharmacy Prescription Monitoring Program InterConnect. Pursuant to an interoperability agreement, the board may authorize the prescription monitoring program of one or more states or an association of states to access information submitted to the board under Sections 481.074(q) and 481.075, including by submitting or sharing information through a central database such as the National Association of Boards of Pharmacy Prescription Monitoring Program InterConnect.

(k) A person authorized to access information under Subsection (a)(4) or (5) who is registered with the board for electronic access to the information is entitled to directly access the information available from other states pursuant to an interoperability agreement described by Subsection (j).

Leg.H. Stats. 1989, 71st Leg., ch. 678 (H.B. 2136), § 1, effective September 1, 1989; am. Acts 1995, 74th Leg., ch. 965 (S.B. 673), § 81, effective June 16, 1995; am. Acts 1997, 75th Leg., ch. 745 (H.B. 1070), § 15, effective January 1, 1998; am. Acts 1999, 76th Leg., ch. 145 (S.B. 254), §§ 4, 5(3), effective September 1, 1999; am. Acts 2007, 80th Leg., ch. 1391 (S.B. 1879), § 3, effective September 1, 2008; am. Acts 2011, 82nd Leg., ch. 1228 (S.B. 594), § 4, effective September 1, 2011; am. Acts 2011, 82nd Leg., ch. 1342 (S.B. 1273), § 4, effective September 1, 2011; am. Acts 2013, 83rd Leg., ch. 1226 (S.B. 1643), § 2, effective September 1, 2013; am. Acts 2015, 84th Leg., ch. 1268 (S.B. 195), § 11, effective September 1, 2016; am. Acts 2015, 84th Leg., ch. 1268 (S.B. 195), § 12, effective June 20, 2015; am. Acts 2015, 84th Leg., ch. 1268 (S.B. 195), § 12, effective September 1, 2016; am. Acts 2017, 85th Leg., ch. 485 (H.B. 2561), § 4, effective September 1, 2017; am. Acts 2019, 86th Leg., ch. 467 (H.B. 4170), § 19.009, effective September 1, 2019; am. Acts 2019, 86th Leg., ch. 965 (S.B. 683), § 2, effective September 1, 2019; am. Acts 2019, 86th Leg., ch. 1144 (H.B. 2847), § 4.002, effective September 1, 2019; am. Acts 2019, 86th Leg., ch. 1166 (H.B. 3284), §§ 1, 10, effective September 1, 2019.

Sec. 481.0761. Rules; Authority to Contract.

(a) The board shall by rule establish and revise as necessary a standardized database format that may be used by a pharmacy to transmit the information required by Sections 481.074(q) and 481.075(i) to the board electronically or to deliver the information on storage media, including disks, tapes, and cassettes.

(b) The director shall consult with the Department of State Health Services, the Texas State Board of Pharmacy, and the Texas Medical Board and by rule may:

    (1) remove a controlled substance listed in Schedules II through V from the official prescription program, if the director determines that the burden imposed by the program substantially outweighs the risk of diversion of the particular controlled substance; or

    (2) return a substance previously removed from Schedules II through V to the official prescription program, if the director determines that the risk of diversion substantially outweighs the burden imposed by the program on the particular controlled substance.

(c) The board by rule may:

    (1) establish a procedure for the issuance of multiple prescriptions of a Schedule II controlled substance under Section 481.074(d-1);

    (2) remove from or return to the official prescription program any aspect of a practitioner's or pharmacist's hospital practice, including administering or dispensing;

    (3) waive or delay any requirement relating to the time or manner of reporting;

    (4) establish compatibility protocols for electronic data transfer hardware, software, or format, including any necessary modifications for participation in a database described by Section 481.076(j);

    (5) establish a procedure to control the release of information under Sections 481.074, 481.075, and 481.076; and

    (6) establish a minimum level of prescription activity below which a reporting activity may be modified or deleted.

(d) The board by rule shall authorize a practitioner to determine whether it is necessary to obtain a particular patient identification number and to provide that number in the electronic prescription record.

(e) In adopting a rule relating to the electronic transfer of information under this subchapter, the board shall consider the economic impact of the rule on practitioners and pharmacists and, to the extent permitted by law, act to minimize any negative economic impact, including the imposition of costs related to computer hardware or software or to the transfer of information.

(f) The board may authorize a contract between the board and another agency of this state or a private vendor as necessary to ensure the effective operation of the official prescription program.

(g) The board may adopt rules providing for a person authorized to access information under Section 481.076(a)(5) to be enrolled in electronic access to the information described by Section 481.076(a) at the time the person obtains or renews the person's applicable professional or occupational license or registration.

(h) The board, in consultation with the department and the regulatory agencies listed in Section 481.076(a)(1), shall identify prescribing practices that may be potentially harmful and patient prescription patterns that may suggest drug diversion or drug abuse. The board shall determine the conduct that constitutes a potentially harmful prescribing pattern or practice and develop indicators for levels of prescriber or patient activity that suggest a potentially harmful prescribing pattern or practice may be occurring or drug diversion or drug abuse may be occurring.

(i) The board, based on the indicators developed under Subsection (h), may send an electronic notification to a dispenser or prescriber if the information submitted under Section 481.074(q) or 481.075 indicates a potentially harmful prescribing pattern or practice may be occurring or drug diversion or drug abuse may be occurring.

(j) The board by rule may develop guidelines identifying behavior suggesting a patient is obtaining controlled substances that indicate drug diversion or drug abuse is occurring. A pharmacist who observes behavior described by this subsection by a person who is to receive a controlled substance shall access the information under Section 481.076(a)(5) regarding the patient for whom the substance is to be dispensed.

(k) The board by rule may develop guidelines identifying patterns that may indicate that a particular patient to whom a controlled substance is prescribed or dispensed is engaging in drug abuse or drug diversion. These guidelines may be based on the frequency of prescriptions issued to and filled by the patient, the types of controlled substances prescribed, and the number of prescribers who prescribe controlled substances to the patient. The board may, based on the guidelines developed under this subsection, send a prescriber or dispenser an electronic notification if there is reason to believe that a particular patient is engaging in drug abuse or drug diversion.

Leg.H. Stats. 1997, 75th Leg., ch. 745 (H.B. 1070), § 16, effective September 1, 1997; am. Acts 1999, 76th Leg., ch. 145 (S.B. 254), § 5(4), effective September 1, 1999; am. Acts 2007, 80th Leg., ch. 1391 (S.B. 1879), § 4, effective September 1, 2007; am. Acts 2009, 81st Leg., ch. 774 (S.B. 904), § 3, effective June 19, 2009; am. Acts 2011, 82nd Leg., ch. 1228 (S.B. 594), § 5, effective September 1, 2011; am. Acts 2015, 84th Leg., ch. 1268 (S.B. 195), § 13, effective June 20, 2015; am. Acts 2015, 84th Leg., ch. 1268 (S.B. 195), § 13, effective September 1, 2016; am. Acts 2017, 85th Leg., ch. 485 (H.B. 2561), § 5, effective September 1, 2017; am. Acts 2019, 86th Leg., ch. 1105 (H.B. 2174), § 8, effective September 1, 2019.

Sec. 481.0762. Monitoring by Regulatory Agency.

(a) Each regulatory agency that issues a license, certification, or registration to a prescriber shall promulgate specific guidelines for prescribers regulated by that agency for the responsible prescribing of opioids, benzodiazepines, barbiturates, or carisoprodol.

(b) A regulatory agency that issues a license, certification, or registration to a prescriber shall periodically access the information submitted to the board under Sections 481.074(q) and 481.075 to determine whether a prescriber is engaging in potentially harmful prescribing patterns or practices.

(c) If the board sends a prescriber an electronic notification authorized under Section 481.0761(i), the board shall immediately send an electronic notification to the appropriate regulatory agency.

(d) In determining whether a potentially harmful prescribing pattern or practice is occurring, the appropriate regulatory agency, at a minimum, shall consider:

(1)   the number of times a prescriber prescribes opioids, benzodiazepines, barbiturates, or carisoprodol; and

(2)   for prescriptions described by Subdivision (1), patterns of prescribing combinations of those drugs and other dangerous combinations of drugs identified by the board.

(e)   If, during a periodic check under this section, the regulatory agency finds evidence that a prescriber may be engaging in potentially harmful prescribing patterns or practices, the regulatory agency may notify that prescriber.

(f)   A regulatory agency may open a complaint against a prescriber if the agency finds evidence during a periodic check under this section that the prescriber is engaging in conduct that violates this subchapter or any other statute or rule.

Leg.H. Stats. 2017, 85th Leg., ch. 485 (H.B. 2561), § 6, effective September 1, 2017.

Sec. 481.0763. Registration by Regulatory Agency.

A regulatory agency that issues a license, certification, or registration to a prescriber or dispenser shall provide the board with any necessary information for each prescriber or dispenser, including contact information for the notifications described by Sections 481.0761(i) and (k), to register the prescriber or dispenser with the system by which the prescriber or dispenser receives information as authorized under Section 481.076(a)(5).

Leg.H. Stats. 2017, 85th Leg., ch. 485 (H.B. 2561), § 6, effective September 1, 2017.

Sec. 481.07635. Continuing Education.

(a)   A person authorized to receive information under Section 481.076(a)(5) shall, not later than the first anniversary after the person is issued a license, certification, or registration to prescribe or dispense controlled substances under this chapter, complete two hours of professional education related to approved procedures of prescribing and monitoring controlled substances.

(b)   A person authorized to receive information may annually take the professional education course under this section to fulfil hours toward the ethics education requirement of the person's license, certification, or registration.

(c)   The regulatory agency that issued the license, certification, or registration to a person authorized to receive information under Section 481.076(a)(5) shall approve professional education to satisfy the requirements of this section.

Leg.H. Stats. 2019, 86th Leg., ch. 1105 (H.B. 2174), § 9, effective September 1, 2019.

Sec. 481.07636. Opioid Prescription Limits.

(a)   In this section, "acute pain" means the normal, predicted, physiological response to a stimulus such as trauma, disease, and operative procedures. Acute pain is time limited. The term does not include:

(1)   chronic pain;

(2)   pain being treated as part of cancer care;

(3)   pain being treated as part of hospice or other end-of-life care; or

(4)   pain being treated as part of palliative care.

(b)   For the treatment of acute pain, a practitioner may not:

(1)   issue a prescription for an opioid in an amount that exceeds a 10-day supply; or

(2)   provide for a refill of an opioid.

(c)   Subsection (b) does not apply to a prescription for an opioid approved by the United States Food and Drug Administration for the treatment of substance addiction that is issued by a practitioner for the treatment of substance addiction.

(d)   A dispenser is not subject to criminal, civil, or administrative penalties for dispensing or refusing to dispense a controlled substance under a prescription that exceeds the limits provided by Subsection (b).

Leg.H. Stats. 2019, 86th Leg., ch. 1105 (H.B. 2174), § 9, effective September 1, 2019.

Sec. 481.0764. Duties of Prescribers, Pharmacists, and Related Health Care Practitioners.

(a)   A person authorized to receive information under Section 481.076(a)(5), other than a veterinarian, shall access that information with respect to the patient before prescribing or dispensing opioids, benzodiazepines, barbiturates, or carisoprodol.

(b)   A person authorized to receive information under Section 481.076(a)(5) may access that information with respect to the patient before prescribing or dispensing any controlled substance.

(c)   A veterinarian authorized to access information under Subsection (b) regarding a controlled substance may access the information for prescriptions dispensed only for the animals of an owner and may not consider the personal prescription history of the owner.

(d)   A violation of Subsection (a) is grounds for disciplinary action by the regulatory agency that issued a license, certification, or registration to the person who committed the violation.

(e)   This section does not grant a person the authority to issue prescriptions for or dispense controlled substances.

(f)   [Expires August 31, 2023] A prescriber or dispenser whose practice includes the prescription or dispensation of opioids shall annually attend at least one hour of continuing education covering best practices, alternative treatment options, and multi-modal approaches to pain management that may include physical therapy, psychotherapy, and other treatments. The board shall adopt rules to establish the content of continuing education described by this subsection. The board may collaborate with private and public institutions of higher education and hospitals in establishing the content of the continuing education. This subsection expires August 31, 2023.

Leg.H. Stats. 2017, 85th Leg., ch. 485 (H.B. 2561), § 6, effective September 1, 2017; am. Acts 2019, 86th Leg., ch. 1167 (H.B. 3285), § 7, effective September 1, 2019.

Sec. 481.0765. Exceptions.

(a) A prescriber is not subject to the requirements of Section 481.0764(a) if:
   (1) the patient has been diagnosed with cancer or sickle cell disease or the patient is receiving hospice care; and
   (2) the prescriber clearly notes in the prescription record that the patient was diagnosed with cancer or sickle cell disease or is receiving hospice care, as applicable.
(b) A dispenser is not subject to the requirements of Section 481.0764(a) if it is clearly noted in the prescription record that the patient has been diagnosed with cancer or sickle cell disease or is receiving hospice care.
(c) A prescriber or dispenser is not subject to the requirements of Section 481.0764(a) and a dispenser is not subject to a rule adopted under Section 481.0761(j) if the prescriber or dispenser makes a good faith attempt to comply but is unable to access the information under Section 481.076(a)(5) because of circumstances outside the control of the prescriber or dispenser.

Leg.H. Stats. 2017, 85th Leg., ch. 485 (H.B. 2561), § 6, effective September 1, 2017; am. Acts 2019, 86th Leg., ch. 640 (S.B. 1564), § 1, effective June 10, 2019.

Sec. 481.0766. Reports of Wholesale Distributors.

(a) A wholesale distributor shall report to the board the distribution of all Schedules II, III, IV, and V controlled substances by the distributor to a person in this state. The distributor shall report the information to the board in the same format and with the same frequency as the information is reported to the Federal Drug Enforcement Administration.
(b) Information reported to the board under Subsection (a) is confidential and not subject to disclosure under Chapter 552, Government Code.
(c) The board shall make the information reported under Subsection (a) available to the State Board of Veterinary Medical Examiners for the purpose of routine inspections and investigations.

Leg.H. Stats. 2017, 85th Leg., ch. 485 (H.B. 2561), § 6, effective September 1, 2017; am. Acts 2019, 86th Leg., ch. 449 (S.B. 1947), § 1, effective September 1, 2019; am. Acts 2019, 86th Leg., ch. 965 (S.B. 683), § 3, effective September 1, 2019; am. Acts 2019, 86th Leg., ch. 1144 (H.B. 2847), § 4.003, effective September 1, 2019; am. Acts 2019, 86th Leg., ch. 1166 (H.B. 3284), § 2, effective September 1, 2019.

Sec. 481.0767. Advisory Committee.

(a) The board shall establish an advisory committee to make recommendations regarding information submitted to the board and access to that information under Sections 481.074, 481.075, 481.076, and 481.0761, including recommendations for:
   (1) operational improvements to the electronic system that stores the information, including implementing best practices and improvements that address system weaknesses and workflow challenges;
   (2) resolutions to identified data concerns;
   (3) methods to improve data accuracy, integrity, and security and to reduce technical difficulties; and
   (4) the addition of any new data set or service to the information submitted to the board or the access to that information.
(b) The board shall appoint the following members to the advisory committee:
   (1) a physician licensed in this state who practices in pain management;
   (2) a physician licensed in this state who practices in family medicine;
   (3) a physician licensed in this state who performs surgery;
   (4) a physician licensed in this state who practices in emergency medicine at a hospital;
   (5) a physician licensed in this state who practices in psychiatry;
   (6) an oral and maxillofacial surgeon;
   (7) a physician assistant or advanced practice registered nurse to whom a physician has delegated the authority to prescribe or order a drug;
   (8) a pharmacist working at a chain pharmacy;
   (9) a pharmacist working at an independent pharmacy;
   (10) an academic pharmacist; and
   (11) two representatives of the health information technology industry, at least one of whom is a representative of a company whose primary line of business is electronic medical records.
(c) Members of the advisory committee serve three-year terms. Each member shall serve until the member's replacement has been appointed.
(d) The advisory committee shall annually elect a presiding officer from its members.
(e) The advisory committee shall meet at least two times a year and at the call of the presiding officer or the board.
(f) A member of the advisory committee serves without compensation but may be reimbursed by the board for actual expenses incurred in performing the duties of the advisory committee.

Leg.H. Stats. 2019, 86th Leg., ch. 1166 (H.B. 3284), § 3, effective September 1, 2019.

Sec. 481.0768. Administrative Penalty: Disclosure or Use of Information.

(a) A person authorized to receive information under Section 481.076(a) may not disclose or use the information in a manner not authorized by this subchapter or other law.
(b) A regulatory agency that issues a license, certification, or registration to a prescriber or dispenser shall periodically update the administrative penalties, or any applicable disciplinary guidelines concerning the penalties, assessed by that agency for conduct that violates Subsection (a).
(c) The agency shall set the penalties in an amount sufficient to deter the conduct.

Leg.H. Stats. 2019, 86th Leg., ch. 1166 (H.B. 3284), § 3, effective September 1, 2019.

Cont. Sub.

Sec. 481.0769. Criminal Offenses Related to Prescription Information.

(a) A person authorized to receive information under Section 481.076(a) commits an offense if the person discloses or uses the information in a manner not authorized by this subchapter or other law.

(b) A person requesting information under Section 481.076(a-6) commits an offense if the person makes a material misrepresentation or fails to disclose a material fact in the request for information under that subsection.

(c) An offense under Subsection (a) is a Class A misdemeanor.

(d) An offense under Subsection (b) is a Class C misdemeanor.

Leg.H. Stats. 2019, 86th Leg., ch. 1166 (H.B. 3284), § 3, effective September 1, 2019.

Sec. 481.077. Chemical Precursor Records and Reports.

(a) Except as provided by Subsection (l), a person who sells, transfers, or otherwise furnishes a chemical precursor to another person shall make an accurate and legible record of the transaction and maintain the record for at least two years after the date of the transaction.

(b) The director by rule may:

    (1) name an additional chemical substance as a chemical precursor for purposes of Subsection (a) if the director determines that public health and welfare are jeopardized by evidenced proliferation or use of the chemical substance in the illicit manufacture of a controlled substance or controlled substance analogue; or

    (2) exempt a chemical precursor from the requirements of Subsection (a) if the director determines that the chemical precursor does not jeopardize public health and welfare or is not used in the illicit manufacture of a controlled substance or a controlled substance analogue.

(b-1) If the director names a chemical substance as a chemical precursor for purposes of Subsection (a) or designates a substance as an immediate precursor, a substance that is a precursor of the chemical precursor or the immediate precursor is not subject to control solely because it is a precursor of the chemical precursor or the immediate precursor.

(c) This section does not apply to a person to whom a registration has been issued by the Federal Drug Enforcement Agency or who is exempt from such registration.

(d) Before selling, transferring, or otherwise furnishing to a person in this state a chemical precursor subject to Subsection (a), a manufacturer, wholesaler, retailer, or other person shall:

    (1) if the recipient does not represent a business, obtain from the recipient:

        (A) the recipient's driver's license number or other personal identification certificate number, date of birth, and residential or mailing address, other than a post office box number, from a driver's license or personal identification certificate issued by the department that contains a photograph of the recipient;

        (B) the year, state, and number of the motor vehicle license of the motor vehicle owned or operated by the recipient;

        (C) a complete description of how the chemical precursor is to be used; and

        (D) the recipient's signature; or

    (2) if the recipient represents a business, obtain from the recipient:

        (A) a letter of authorization from the business that includes the business license or comptroller tax identification number, address, area code, and telephone number and a complete description of how the chemical precursor is to be used; and

        (B) the recipient's signature; and

    (3) for any recipient, sign as a witness to the signature and identification of the recipient.

(e) [Repealed.]

(f) [Repealed.]

(g) [Repealed.]

(h) [Repealed.]

(i) A manufacturer, wholesaler, retailer, or other person who discovers a loss or theft of a chemical precursor subject to Subsection (a) shall:

    (1) submit a report of the transaction to the director in accordance with department rule; and

    (2) include in the report:

        (A) any difference between the amount of the chemical precursor actually received and the amount of the chemical precursor shipped according to the shipping statement or invoice; or

        (B) the amount of the loss or theft.

(j) A report under Subsection (i) must:

    (1) be made not later than the third day after the date that the manufacturer, wholesaler, retailer, or other person learns of the discrepancy, loss, or theft; and

    (2) if the discrepancy, loss, or theft occurred during a shipment of the chemical precursor, include the name of the common carrier or person who transported the chemical precursor and the date that the chemical precursor was shipped.

(k) A manufacturer, wholesaler, retailer, or other person who sells, transfers, or otherwise furnishes any chemical precursor subject to Subsection (a), or a commercial purchaser or other person who receives a chemical precursor subject to Subsection (a):

    (1) shall maintain records and inventories in accordance with rules established by the director;

    (2) shall allow a member of the department or a peace officer to conduct audits and inspect records of purchases and sales and all other records made in accordance with this section at any reasonable time; and

    (3) may not interfere with the audit or with the full and complete inspection or copying of those records.

(l) This section does not apply to the sale or transfer of any compound, mixture, or preparation containing ephedrine, pseudoephedrine, or norpseudoephedrine that is in liquid, liquid capsule, or liquid gel capsule form.

Leg.H. Stats. 1989, 71st Leg., ch. 678 (H.B. 2136), § 1, effective September 1, 1989; am. Acts 1989, 71st Leg., ch. 1100 (S.B. 1046), § 5.02(k), effective September 1, 1989; am. Acts 1997, 75th Leg., ch. 745 (H.B. 1070), § 17, effective January 1, 1998; am. Acts 2001, 77th Leg., ch. 251 (S.B. 753),

Cont. Sub.

§ 12, effective September 1, 2001; am. Acts 2003, 78th Leg., ch. 570 (H.B. 1629), § 1, effective September 1, 2003; am. Acts 2003, 78th Leg., ch. 1099 (H.B. 2192), § 6, effective September 1, 2003; am. Acts 2005, 79th Leg., ch. 282 (H.B. 164), § 4, effective August 1, 2005; am. Acts 2019, 86th Leg., ch. 595 (S.B. 616), §§ 4.001, 4.011(1), effective September 1, 2019.

Sec. 481.0771. Records and Reports on Pseudoephedrine.

(a) A wholesaler who sells, transfers, or otherwise furnishes a product containing ephedrine, pseudoephedrine, or norpseudoephedrine to a retailer shall:
  (1) before delivering the product, obtain from the retailer the retailer's address, area code, and telephone number; and
  (2) make an accurate and legible record of the transaction and maintain the record for at least two years after the date of the transaction.
(b) The wholesaler shall make all records available to the director in accordance with department rule, including:
  (1) the information required by Subsection (a) (1);
  (2) the amount of the product containing ephedrine, pseudoephedrine, or norpseudoephedrine delivered; and
  (3) any other information required by the director.
(c) Not later than 10 business days after receipt of an order for a product containing ephedrine, pseudoephedrine, or norpseudoephedrine that requests delivery of a suspicious quantity of the product as determined by department rule, a wholesaler shall submit to the director a report of the order in accordance with department rule.
(d) A wholesaler who, with reckless disregard for the duty to report, fails to report as required by Subsection (c) may be subject to disciplinary action in accordance with department rule.

Leg.H. Stats. 2005 79th Leg. Sess. Ch. 282, effective August 1, 2005.

Sec. 481.078. Chemical Precursor Transfer Permit. [Repealed]

Leg.H. Stats. 1989, 71st Leg., ch. 1100 (S.B. 1046), § 5.02(l), effective September 1, 1989; am. Acts 1997, 75th Leg., ch. 745 (H.B. 1070), § 18, effective January 1, 1998; am. Acts 2001, 77th Leg., ch. 251 (S.B. 753), § 13, effective September 1, 2001; Repealed by Acts 2019, 86th Leg., ch. 595 (S.B. 616), § 4.011(2), effective September 1, 2019.

Sec. 481.079. Repealed.

Repealed Stats. 1997 75th Leg. Sess. Ch. 745, repealed effective January 1, 1998.

Sec. 481.080. Chemical Laboratory Apparatus Record-Keeping Requirements.

(a) A manufacturer, wholesaler, retailer, or other person who sells, transfers, or otherwise furnishes a chemical laboratory apparatus shall make an accurate and legible record of the transaction and maintain the record for at least two years after the date of the transaction.
(b) The director may adopt rules to implement this section.
(c) The director by rule may:
  (1) name an additional item of equipment as a chemical laboratory apparatus for purposes of Subsection (a) if the director determines that public health and welfare are jeopardized by evidenced proliferation or use of the item of equipment in the illicit manufacture of a controlled substance or controlled substance analogue; or
  (2) exempt a chemical laboratory apparatus from the requirement of Subsection (a) if the director determines that the apparatus does not jeopardize public health and welfare or is not used in the illicit manufacture of a controlled substance or a controlled substance analogue.
(d) This section does not apply to a person to whom a registration has been issued by the Federal Drug Enforcement Agency or who is exempt from such registration.
(d-1) This section does not apply to a chemical manufacturer engaged in commercial research and development:
  (1) whose primary business is the manufacture, use, storage, or transportation of hazardous, combustible, or explosive materials;
  (2) that operates a secure, restricted location that contains a physical plant not open to the public, the ingress into which is constantly monitored by security personnel; and
  (3) that holds:
    (A) a Voluntary Protection Program Certification under Section (2)(b)(1), Occupational Safety and Health Act of 1970 (29 U.S.C. Section 651 et seq.); or
    (B) a Facility Operations Area authorization under the Texas Risk Reduction Program (30 T.A.C. Chapter 350).
(e) Before selling, transferring, or otherwise furnishing to a person in this state a chemical laboratory apparatus subject to Subsection (a), a manufacturer, wholesaler, retailer, or other person shall:
  (1) if the recipient does not represent a business, obtain from the recipient:
    (A) the recipient's driver's license number or other personal identification certificate number, date of birth, and residential or mailing address, other than a post office box number, from a driver's license or personal identification certificate issued by the department that contains a photograph of the recipient;
    (B) the year, state, and number of the motor vehicle license of the motor vehicle owned or operated by the recipient;
    (C) a complete description of how the apparatus is to be used; and
    (D) the recipient's signature; or
  (2) if the recipient represents a business, obtain from the recipient:
    (A) a letter of authorization from the business that includes the business license or comptroller tax identification number, address, area code, and telephone number and a complete description of how the apparatus is to be used; and

Cont. Sub.

      (B) the recipient's signature; and

  (3) for any recipient, sign as a witness to the signature and identification of the recipient.

(f) [Repealed.]

(g) [Repealed.]

(h) [Repealed.]

(i) [Repealed.]

(j) A manufacturer, wholesaler, retailer, or other person who discovers a loss or theft of such an apparatus shall:

  (1) submit a report of the transaction to the director in accordance with department rule; and

  (2) include in the report:

      (A) any difference between the number of the apparatus actually received and the number of the apparatus shipped according to the shipping statement or invoice; or

      (B) the number of the loss or theft.

(k) A report under Subsection (j) must:

  (1) be made not later than the third day after the date that the manufacturer, wholesaler, retailer, or other person learns of the discrepancy, loss, or theft; and

  (2) if the discrepancy, loss, or theft occurred during a shipment of the apparatus, include the name of the common carrier or person who transported the apparatus and the date that the apparatus was shipped.

(l) This subsection applies to a manufacturer, wholesaler, retailer, or other person who sells, transfers, or otherwise furnishes any chemical laboratory apparatus subject to Subsection (a) and to a commercial purchaser or other person who receives such an apparatus. A person covered by this subsection:

  (1) shall maintain records and inventories in accordance with rules established by the director;

  (2) shall allow a member of the department or a peace officer to conduct audits and inspect records of purchases and sales and all other records made in accordance with this section at any reasonable time; and

  (3) may not interfere with the audit or with the full and complete inspection or copying of those records.

Leg.H. Stats. 1989, 71st Leg., ch. 1100 (S.B. 1046), § 5.02(l), effective September 1, 1989; am. Acts 1997, 75th Leg., ch. 745 (H.B. 1070), § 19, effective January 1, 1998; am. Acts 2001, 77th Leg., ch. 251 (S.B. 753), § 14, effective September 1, 2001; am. Acts 2015, 84th Leg., ch. 83 (S.B. 1666), § 1, effective May 22, 2015; am. Acts 2015, 84th Leg., ch. 1268 (S.B. 195), § 15, effective September 1, 2016; am. Acts 2019, 86th Leg., ch. 595 (S.B. 616), §§ 4.002, 4.003, 4.011(3), effective September 1, 2019.

Sec. 481.081. Chemical Laboratory Apparatus Transfer Permit. [Repealed]

Leg.H. Stats. 1989, 71st Leg., ch. 1100 (S.B. 1046), § 5.02(l), effective September 1, 1989; am. Acts 1997, 75th Leg., ch. 745 (H.B. 1070), § 20, effective January 1, 1998; am. Acts 2001, 77th Leg., ch. 251 (S.B. 753), § 15, effective September 1, 2001; Repealed by Acts 2019, 86th Leg., ch. 595 (S.B. 616), § 4.011(4), effective September 1, 2019.

Sec. 481.082. Repealed.

Repealed Stats. 1997 75th Leg. Sess. Ch. 745, repealed effective January 1, 1998.

SUBCHAPTER D. OFFENSES AND PENALTIES

Sec. 481.101. Criminal Classification.

For the purpose of establishing criminal penalties for violations of this chapter, controlled substances, including a material, compound, mixture, or preparation containing the controlled substance, are divided into Penalty Groups 1 through 4.

Leg.H. Stats. 1989 71st Leg. Sess. Chs. 678, 1100, effective September 1, 1989.

Sec. 481.102. Penalty Group 1.

Penalty Group 1 consists of:

  (1) the following opiates, including their isomers, esters, ethers, salts, and salts of isomers, esters, and ethers, unless specifically excepted, if the existence of these isomers, esters, ethers, and salts is possible within the specific chemical designation:

      Alfentanil;

      Allylprodine;

      Alphacetylmethadol;

      Benzethidine;

      Betaprodine;

      Clonitazene;

      Diampromide;

      Diethylthiambutene;

      Difenoxin not listed in Penalty Group 3 or 4;

      Dimenoxadol;

      Dimethylthiambutene;

      Dioxaphetyl butyrate;

      Dipipanone;

      Ethylmethylthiambutene;

        Etonitazene;
        Etoxeridine;
        Furethidine;
        Hydroxypethidine;
        Ketobemidone;
        Levophenacylmorphan;
        Meprodine;
        Methadol;
        Moramide;
        Morpheridine;
        Noracymethadol;
        Norlevorphanol;
        Normethadone;
        Norpipanone;
        Phenadoxone;
        Phenampromide;
        Phenomorphan;
        Phenoperidine;
        Piritramide;
        Proheptazine;
        Properidine;
        Propiram;
        Sufentanil;
        Tilidine; and
        Trimeperidine;

(2) the following opium derivatives, their salts, isomers, and salts of isomers, unless specifically excepted, if the existence of these salts, isomers, and salts of isomers is possible within the specific chemical designation:
        Acetorphine;
        Acetyldihydrocodeine;
        Benzylmorphine;
        Codeine methylbromide;
        Codeine-N-Oxide;
        Cyprenorphine;
        Desomorphine;
        Dihydromorphine;
        Drotebanol;
        Etorphine, except hydrochloride salt;
        Heroin;
        Hydromorphinol;
        Methyldesorphine;
        Methyldihydromorphine;
        Monoacetylmorphine;
        Morphine methylbromide;
        Morphine methylsulfonate;
        Morphine-N-Oxide;
        Myrophine;
        Nicocodeine;
        Nicomorphine;
        Normorphine;
        Pholcodine; and
        Thebacon;

(3) the following substances, however produced, except those narcotic drugs listed in another group:
    (A) Opium and opiate not listed in Penalty Group 3 or 4, and a salt, compound, derivative, or preparation of opium or opiate, other than thebaine derived butorphanol, nalmefene and its salts, naloxone and its salts, and naltrexone and its salts, but including:
        Codeine not listed in Penalty Group 3 or 4;
        Dihydroetorphine;
        Ethylmorphine not listed in Penalty Group 3 or 4;
        Granulated opium;
        Hydrocodone not listed in Penalty Group 3;
        Hydromorphone;
        Metopon;
        Morphine not listed in Penalty Group 3;
        Opium extracts;
        Opium fluid extracts;
        Oripavine;
        Oxycodone;
        Oxymorphone;

Cont. Sub.

Powdered opium;

Raw opium;

Thebaine; and

Tincture of opium;

(B) a salt, compound, isomer, derivative, or preparation of a substance that is chemically equivalent or identical to a substance described by Paragraph (A), other than the isoquinoline alkaloids of opium;

(C) Opium poppy and poppy straw;

(D) Cocaine, including:

(i) its salts, its optical, position, and geometric isomers, and the salts of those isomers;

(ii) coca leaves and a salt, compound, derivative, or preparation of coca leaves; and

(iii) a salt, compound, derivative, or preparation of a salt, compound, or derivative that is chemically equivalent or identical to a substance described by Subparagraph (i) or (ii), other than decocainized coca leaves or extractions of coca leaves that do not contain cocaine or ecgonine; and

(E) concentrate of poppy straw, meaning the crude extract of poppy straw in liquid, solid, or powder form that contains the phenanthrine alkaloids of the opium poppy;

(4) the following opiates, including their isomers, esters, ethers, salts, and salts of isomers, if the existence of these isomers, esters, ethers, and salts is possible within the specific chemical designation:

Acetyl-alpha-methylfentanyl (N-[1-(1-methyl-2- phenethyl)-4-piperidinyl]-N-phenylacetamide);

Alpha-methylthiofentanyl (N-[1-methyl-2-(2- thienyl)ethyl-4-piperidinyl]-N-phenylpropanamide);

Alphaprodine;

Anileridine;

Beta-hydroxyfentanyl (N-[1-(2-hydroxy-2- phenethyl)-4-piperidinyl] -N-phenylpropanamide);

Beta-hydroxy-3-methylfentanyl;

Bezitramide;

Carfentanil;

Dihydrocodeine not listed in Penalty Group 3 or 4;

Diphenoxylate not listed in Penalty Group 3 or 4;

Fentanyl or alpha-methylfentanyl, or any other derivative of Fentanyl;

Isomethadone;

Levomethorphan;

Levorphanol;

Metazocine;

Methadone;

Methadone-Intermediate, 4-cyano-2-dimethylamino- 4, 4-diphenyl butane;

3-methylfentanyl(N-[3-methyl-1-(2-phenylethyl)- 4-piperidyl]-N-phenylpropanamide);

3-methylthiofentanyl(N-[3-methyl-1-(2-thienyl) ethyl-4-piperidinyl]-N-phenylpropanamide);

Moramide-Intermediate, 2-methyl-3-morpholino-1, 1-diphenyl-propane-carboxylic acid;

Para-fluorofentanyl(N-(4-fluorophenyl)-N-1-(2- phenylethyl)-4-piperidinylpropanamide);

PEPAP (1-(2-phenethyl)-4-phenyl-4- acetoxypiperidine);

Pethidine (Meperidine);

Pethidine-Intermediate-A, 4-cyano-1-methyl-4- phenylpiperidine;

Pethidine-Intermediate-B, ethyl-4- phenylpiperidine-4 carboxylate;

Pethidine-Intermediate-C, 1-methyl-4- phenylpiperidine-4-carboxylic acid;

Phenazocine;

Piminodine;

Racemethorphan;

Racemorphan;

Remifentanil; and

Thiofentanyl(N-phenyl-N-[1-(2-thienyl)ethyl-4-pi peridinyl]-propanamide);

(5) Flunitrazepam (trade or other name: Rohypnol);

(6) Methamphetamine, including its salts, optical isomers, and salts of optical isomers;

(7) Phenylacetone and methylamine, if possessed together with intent to manufacture methamphetamine;

(8) Phencyclidine, including its salts;

(9) Gamma hydroxybutyric acid (some trade or other names: gamma hydroxybutyrate, GHB), including its salts;

(10) Ketamine;

(11) Phenazepam;

(12) U-47700;

(13) AH-7921;

(14) ADB-FUBINACA;

(15) AMB-FUBINACA; and

(16) MDMB-CHMICA.

Leg.H. Stats. 1989, 71st Leg., ch. 678 (H.B. 2136), § 1, effective September 1, 1989; am. Acts 1989, 71st Leg., ch. 1100 (S.B. 1046), § 5.02(n), effective September 1, 1989; am. Acts 1991, 72nd Leg., ch. 761 (S.B. 314), § 1, effective September 1, 1991; am. Acts 1997, 75th Leg., ch. 745 (H.B. 1070), § 21, effective January 1, 1998; am. Acts 2001, 77th Leg., ch. 251 (S.B. 753), § 16, effective September 1, 2001; am. Acts 2001, 77th Leg., ch. 459 (H.B. 139), § 1, effective September 1, 2001; am. Acts 2003, 78th Leg., ch. 1099 (H.B. 2192), § 7, effective September 1, 2003; am. Acts 2009, 81st Leg., ch. 739 (S.B. 449), § 1, effective September 1, 2009; am. Acts 2017, 85th Leg., ch. 491 (H.B. 2671), § 1, effective September 1, 2017.

Sec. 481.1021. Penalty Group 1-A.

(a) Penalty Group 1-A consists of:

  (1) lysergic acid diethylamide (LSD), including its salts, isomers, and salts of isomers; and

  (2) compounds structurally derived from 2,5-dimethoxyphenethylamine by substitution at the 1-amino nitrogen atom with a benzyl substituent, including:

    (A) compounds further modified by:

      (i) substitution in the phenethylamine ring at the 4-position to any extent (including alkyl, alkoxy, alkylenedioxy, haloalkyl, or halide substituents); or

      (ii) substitution in the benzyl ring to any extent (including alkyl, alkoxy, alkylenedioxy, haloalkyl, or halide substituents); and

    (B) by example, compounds such as:

      4-Bromo-2,5-dimethoxy-N-(2-methoxybenzyl) phenethylamine (trade or other names: 25B-NBOMe, 2C-B-NBOMe);

      4-Chloro-2,5-dimethoxy-N-(2-methoxybenzyl) phenethylamine (trade or other names: 25C-NBOMe, 2C-C-NBOMe);

      2,5-Dimethoxy-4-methyl-N-(2-methoxybenzyl) phenethylamine (trade or other names: 25D-NBOMe, 2C-D-NBOMe);

      4-Ethyl-2,5-dimethoxy-N-(2-methoxybenzyl) phenethylamine (trade or other names: 25E-NBOMe, 2C-E-NBOMe);

      2,5-Dimethoxy-N-(2- methoxybenzyl)phenethylamine (some trade and other names: 25H-NBOMe, 2C-H-NBOMe);

      4-Iodo-2,5-dimethoxy-N-(2-methoxybenzyl) phenethylamine (some trade and other names: 25I-NBOMe, 2C-I-NBOMe);

      4-Iodo-2,5-dimethoxy-N- benzylphenethylamine (trade or other name: 25I-NB);

      4-Iodo-2,5-dimethoxy-N-(2,3- methylenedioxybenzyl)phenethylamine (trade or other name: 25I-NBMD);

      4-Iodo-2,5-dimethoxy-N-(2- fluorobenzyl)phenethylamine (trade or other name: 25I-NBF);

      4-Iodo-2,5-dimethoxy-N-(2-hydroxybenzyl) phenethylamine (trade or other name: 25I-NBOH);

      2,5-Dimethoxy-4-nitro-N-(2-methoxybenzyl) phenethylamine (trade or other names: 25N-NBOMe, 2C-N-NBOMe); and

      2,5-Dimethoxy-4-(n)-propyl-N-(2- methoxybenzyl)phenethylamine (some trade and other names: 25P-NBOMe, 2C-P-NBOMe).

(b) To the extent Subsection (a)(2) conflicts with another provision of this subtitle or another law, the other provision or the other law prevails.

Leg.H. Stats. 1997 75th Leg. Sess. Ch. 745, effective January 1, 1998; am. Acts 2015, 84th Leg., ch. 64 (S.B. 172), § 2, effective September 1, 2015.

Sec. 481.103. Penalty Group 2.

(a) Penalty Group 2 consists of:

  (1) any quantity of the following hallucinogenic substances, their salts, isomers, and salts of isomers, unless specifically excepted, if the existence of these salts, isomers, and salts of isomers is possible within the specific chemical designation:

    5-(2-aminopropyl)benzofuran (5-APB);

    6-(2-aminopropyl)benzofuran (6-APB);

    5-(2-aminopropyl)-2,3-dihydrobenzofuran (5-APDB);

    6-(2-aminopropyl)-2,3-dihydrobenzofuran (6-APDB);

    5-(2-aminopropyl)indole (5-IT,5-API);

    6-(2-aminopropyl)indole (6-IT,6-API);

    1-(benzofuran-5-yl)-N-methylpropan-2-amine (5-MAPB);

    1-(benzofuran-6-yl)-N-methylpropan-2-amine (6-MAPB);

    Benzothiophenylcyclohexylpiperidine (BTCP);

    8-bromo-alpha-methyl-benzo[1,2-b:4,5-b']difuran- 4-ethanamine (trade or other name: Bromo-DragonFLY);

    Desoxypipradrol (2-benzhydrylpiperidine);

    2, 5-dimethoxyamphetamine (some trade or other names: 2, 5-dimethoxy-alpha-methylphenethylamine; 2, 5-DMA);

    Diphenylprolinol (diphenyl(pyrrolidin-2-yl) methanol, D2PM);

    Dronabinol (synthetic) in sesame oil and encapsulated in a soft gelatin capsule in a U.S. Food and Drug Administration approved drug product (some trade or other names for Dronabinol: (a6aR-trans)-6a,7,8,10a-tetrahydro- 6,6, 9-trimethyl-3-pentyl-6H- dibenzo [b,d]pyran-1-ol or (-)-delta-9- (trans)- tetrahydrocannabinol);

    Ethylamine Analog of Phencyclidine (some trade or other names: N-ethyl-1-phenylcyclohexylamine, (1- phenylcyclohexyl) ethylamine, N-(1-phenylcyclohexyl) ethylamine, cyclohexamine, PCE);

    2-ethylamino-2-(3-methoxyphenyl)cyclohexanone (trade or other name: methoxetamine);

    Ibogaine (some trade or other names: 7-Ethyl-6, 6, beta 7, 8, 9, 10, 12, 13-octahydro-2-methoxy-6, 9-methano-5H- pyrido [1', 2':1, 2] azepino [5, 4-b] indole; tabernanthe iboga.);

    5-iodo-2-aminoindane (5-IAI);

    Mescaline;

    5-methoxy-3, 4-methylenedioxy amphetamine;

    4-methoxyamphetamine (some trade or other names: 4-methoxy-alpha-methylphenethylamine; paramethoxyamphetamine; PMA);

    4-methoxymethamphetamine (PMMA);

    2-(2-methoxyphenyl)-2-(methylamino)cyclohexanone (some trade and other names: 2-MeO-ketamine; methoxyketamine);

    1-methyl- 4-phenyl-4-propionoxypiperidine (MPPP, PPMP);

    4-methyl-2, 5-dimethoxyamphetamine (some trade and other names: 4-methyl-2, 5-dimethoxy-alpha- methylphenethylamine; "DOM"; "STP");

    3,4-methylenedioxy methamphetamine (MDMA, MDM);

3,4-methylenedioxy amphetamine;

3,4-methylenedioxy N-ethylamphetamine (Also known as N-ethyl MDA);

5,6-methylenedioxy-2-aminoindane (MDAI);

Nabilone (Another name for nabilone: (+)-trans- 3-(1,1-dimethylheptyl)- 6,6a, 7,8,10,10a-hexahydro-1-hydroxy- 6, 6-dimethyl-9H-dibenzo[b,d] pyran-9-one;

N-benzylpiperazine (some trade or other names: BZP; 1-benzylpiperazine);

N-ethyl-3-piperidyl benzilate;

N-hydroxy-3,4-methylenedioxyamphetamine (Also known as N-hydroxy MDA);

4-methylaminorex;

N-methyl-3-piperidyl benzilate;

Parahexyl (some trade or other names: 3-Hexyl-1- hydroxy-7, 8, 9, 10-tetrahydro-6, 6, 9-trimethyl-6H-dibenzo [b, d] pyran; Synhexyl);

1-Phenylcyclohexylamine;

1-Piperidinocyclohexanecarbonitrile (PCC);

Pyrrolidine Analog of Phencyclidine (some trade or other names: 1-(1-phenylcyclohexyl)-pyrrolidine, PCPy, PHP);

Tetrahydrocannabinols, other than marihuana, and synthetic equivalents of the substances contained in the plant, or in the resinous extractives of Cannabis, or synthetic substances, derivatives, and their isomers with similar chemical structure and pharmacological activity such as:

delta-1 cis or trans tetrahydrocannabinol, and their optical isomers;

delta-6 cis or trans tetrahydrocannabinol, and their optical isomers;

delta-3, 4 cis or trans tetrahydrocannabinol, and its optical isomers; or

compounds of these structures, regardless of numerical designation of atomic positions, since nomenclature of these substances is not internationally standardized;

Thiophene Analog of Phencyclidine (some trade or other names: 1-[1-(2-thienyl) cyclohexyl] piperidine; 2-Thienyl Analog of Phencyclidine; TPCP, TCP);

1-pyrrolidine (some trade or other name: TCPy);

1-(3-trifluoromethylphenyl)piperazine (trade or other name: TFMPP); and

3,4,5-trimethoxy amphetamine;

(2) Phenylacetone (some trade or other names: Phenyl-2-propanone; P2P, Benzymethyl ketone, methyl benzyl ketone);

(3) unless specifically excepted or unless listed in another Penalty Group, a material, compound, mixture, or preparation that contains any quantity of the following substances having a potential for abuse associated with a depressant or stimulant effect on the central nervous system:

Aminorex (some trade or other names: aminoxaphen; 2-amino-5-phenyl-2-oxazoline; 4,5-dihydro-5- phenyl-2-oxazolamine);

Amphetamine, its salts, optical isomers, and salts of optical isomers;

Cathinone (some trade or other names: 2-amino-1- phenyl-1-propanone, alpha-aminopropiophenone, 2-aminopropiophenone);

Etaqualone and its salts;

Etorphine Hydrochloride;

Fenethylline and its salts;

Lisdexamfetamine, including its salts, isomers, and salts of isomers;

Mecloqualone and its salts;

Methaqualone and its salts;

Methcathinone (some trade or other names: 2- methylamino-propiophenone; alpha-(methylamino)propriophenone; 2-(methylamino)-1-phenylpropan-1-one; alpha-N- methylaminopropriophenone; monomethylpropion; ephedrone, N-methylcathinone; methylcathinone; AL-464; AL-422; AL-463; and UR 1431);

N-Ethylamphetamine, its salts, optical isomers, and salts of optical isomers; and

N,N-dimethylamphetamine (some trade or other names: N,N,alpha-trimethylbenzeneethanamine; N,N,alpha-trimethylphenethylamine), its salts, optical isomers, and salts of optical isomers;

(4) any compound structurally derived from 2-aminopropanal by substitution at the 1-position with any monocyclic or fused-polycyclic ring system, including:

(A) compounds further modified by:

(i) substitution in the ring system to any extent (including alkyl, alkoxy, alkylenedioxy, haloalkyl, or halide substituents), whether or not further substituted in the ring system by other substituents;

(ii) substitution at the 3-position with an alkyl substituent; or

(iii) substitution at the 2-amino nitrogen atom with alkyl, benzyl, dialkyl, or methoxybenzyl groups, or inclusion of the 2-amino nitrogen atom in a cyclic structure; and

(B) by example, compounds such as:

4-Methylmethcathinone (Also known as Mephedrone);

3,4-Dimethylmethcathinone (Also known as 3,4-DMMC);

3-Fluoromethcathinone (Also known as 3-FMC);

4-Fluoromethcathinone (Also known as Flephedrone);

3,4-Methylenedioxy-N-methylcathinone (Also known as Methylone);

3,4-Methylenedioxypyrovalerone (Also known as MDPV);

alpha-Pyrrolidinopentiophenone (Also known as alpha-PVP);

Naphthylpyrovalerone (Also known as Naphyrone);

alpha-Methylamino-valerophenone (Also known as Pentedrone);

beta-Keto-N-methylbenzodioxolylpropylamine (Also known as Butylone);

beta-Keto-N-methylbenzodioxolylpentanamine (Also known as Pentylone);

beta-Keto-Ethylbenzodioxolylbutanamine (Also known as Eutylone); and

3,4-methylenedioxy-N-ethylcathinone (Also known as Ethylone);

    (5)   any compound structurally derived from tryptamine (3-(2-aminoethyl)indole) or a ring-hydroxy tryptamine:

        (A)   by modification in any of the following ways:

            (i)   by substitution at the amine nitrogen atom of the sidechain to any extent with alkyl or alkenyl groups or by inclusion of the amine nitrogen atom of the side chain (and no other atoms of the side chain) in a cyclic structure;

            (ii)   by substitution at the carbon atom adjacent to the nitrogen atom of the side chain (alpha-position) with an alkyl or alkenyl group;

            (iii)   by substitution in the 6-membered ring to any extent with alkyl, alkoxy, haloalkyl, thioaklyl, alkylenedioxy, or halide substituents; or

            (iv)   by substitution at the 2-position of the tryptamine ring system with an alkyl substituent; and

        (B)   including:

            (i)   ethers and esters of the controlled substances listed in this subdivision; and

            (ii)   by example, compounds such as:

alpha-ethyltryptamine;

alpha-methyltryptamine;

Bufotenine (some trade and other names: 3-(beta-Dimethylaminoethyl)-5-hydroxyindole; 3-(2-dimethylaminoethyl)- 5- indolol; N, N-dimethylserotonin; 5-hydroxy-N, N- dimethyltryptamine; mappine);

Diethyltryptamine (some trade and other names: N, N-Diethyltryptamine, DET);

Dimethyltryptamine (trade or other name: DMT);

5-methoxy-N, N-diisopropyltryptamine (5-MeO-DiPT);

O-Acetylpsilocin (Trade or other name: 4-Aco-DMT);

Psilocin; and

Psilocybin;

    (6)   2,5-Dimethoxyphenethylamine and any compound structurally derived from 2,5-Dimethoxyphenethylamine by substitution at the 4-position of the phenyl ring to any extent (including alkyl, alkoxy, alkylenedioxy, haloalkyl, or halide substituents), including, by example, compounds such as:

4-Bromo-2,5-dimethoxyphenethylamine (trade or other name: 2C-B);

4-Chloro-2,5-dimethoxyphenethylamine (trade or other name: 2C-C);

2,5-Dimethoxy-4-methylphenethylamine (trade or other name: 2C-D);

4-Ethyl-2,5-dimethoxyphenethylamine (trade or other name: 2C-E);

4-Iodo-2,5-dimethoxyphenethylamine (trade or other name: 2C-I);

2,5-Dimethoxy-4-nitrophenethylamine (trade or other name: 2C-N);

2,5-Dimethoxy-4-(n)-propylphenethylamine (trade or other name: 2C-P);

4-Ethylthio-2,5-dimethoxyphenethylamine (trade or other name: 2C-T-2);

4-Isopropylthio-2,5-dimethoxyphenethylamine (trade or other name: 2C-T-4); and

2,5-Dimethoxy-4-(n)-propylthiophenethylamine (trade or other name: 2C-T-7); and

    (7)   2,5-Dimethoxyamphetamine and any compound structurally derived from 2,5-Dimethoxyamphetamine by substitution at the 4-position of the phenyl ring to any extent (including alkyl, alkoxy, alkylenedioxy, haloalkyl, or halide substituents), including, by example, compounds such as:

4-Ethylthio-2,5-dimethoxyamphetamine (trade or other name: Aleph-2);

4-Isopropylthio-2,5-dimethoxyamphetamine (trade or other name: Aleph-4);

4-Bromo-2,5-dimethoxyamphetamine (trade or other name: DOB);

4-Chloro-2,5-dimethoxyamphetamine (trade or other name: DOC);

2,5-Dimethoxy-4-ethylamphetamine (trade or other name: DOET);

4-Iodo-2,5-dimethoxyamphetamine (trade or other name: DOI);

2,5-Dimethoxy-4-methylamphetamine (trade or other name: DOM);

2,5-Dimethoxy-4-nitroamphetamine (trade or other name: DON);

4-Isopropyl-2,5-dimethoxyamphetamine (trade or other name: DOIP); and

2,5-Dimethoxy-4-(n)-propylamphetamine (trade or other name: DOPR).

  (b)   For the purposes of Subsection (a)(1) only, the term "isomer" includes an optical, position, or geometric isomer.

  (c)   To the extent Subsection (a)(4), (5), (6), or (7) conflicts with another provision or this subtitle or another law, the other provision or the other law prevails. If a substance listed in this section is also listed in another penalty group, the listing in the other penalty group controls.

  (d)   [Repealed.]

Leg.H. Stats. 1989, 71st Leg., ch. 678 (H.B. 2136), § 1, effective September 1, 1989; am. Acts 1989, 71st Leg., ch. 1100 (S.B. 1046), § 5.02(n), effective September 1, 1989; am. Acts 1991, 72nd Leg., ch. 761 (S.B. 314), § 2, effective September 1, 1991; am. Acts 1997, 75th Leg., ch. 745 (H.B. 1070), § 23, effective January 1, 1998; am. Acts 2001, 77th Leg., ch. 251 (S.B. 753), § 17, effective September 1, 2001; am. Acts 2003, 78th Leg., ch. 1099 (H.B. 2192), § 8, effective September 1, 2003; am. Acts 2009, 81st Leg., ch. 739 (S.B. 449), § 2, effective September 1, 2009; am. Acts 2011, 82nd Leg., ch. 784 (H.B. 2118), § 1, effective September 1, 2011; am. Acts 2015, 84th Leg., ch. 64 (S.B. 172), § 3, effective September 1, 2015; am. Acts 2017, 85th Leg., ch. 384 (S.B. 227), § 1, effective September 1, 2017; am. Acts 2017, 85th Leg., ch. 491 (H.B. 2671), § 3, effective September 1, 2017.

Cont. Sub.

Sec. 481.1031. Penalty Group 2-A.

  (a) In this section:
- (1) "Core component" is one of the following: azaindole, benzimidazole, benzothiazole, carbazole, imidazole, indane, indazole, indene, indole, pyrazole, pyrazolopyridine, pyridine, or pyrrole.
- (2) "Group A component" is one of the following: adamantane, benzene, cycloalkylmethyl, isoquinoline, methylpiperazine, naphthalene, phenyl, quinoline, tetrahydronaphthalene, tetramethylcyclopropane, amino oxobutane, amino dimethyl oxobutane, amino phenyl oxopropane, methyl methoxy oxobutane, methoxy dimethyl oxobutane, methoxy phenyl oxopropane, or an amino acid.
- (3) "Link component" is one of the following functional groups: carboxamide, carboxylate, hydrazide, methanone (ketone), ethanone, methanediyl (methylene bridge), or methine.

  (b) Penalty Group 2-A consists of any material, compound, mixture, or preparation that contains any quantity of a natural or synthetic chemical substance, including its salts, isomers, and salts of isomers, listed by name in this subsection or contained within one of the structural classes defined in this subsection:
- (1) WIN-55,212-2;
- (2) Cyclohexylphenol: any compound structurally derived from 2-(3-hydroxycyclohexyl)phenol by substitution at the 5-position of the phenolic ring, (N-methylpiperidin-2-yl)alkyl, (4-tetrahydropyran)alkyl, or 2-(4-morpholinyl)alkyl, whether or not substituted in the cyclohexyl ring to any extent, including:
  JWH-337;
  JWH-344;
  CP-55,940;
  CP-47,497; and
  analogues of CP-47,497;
- (3) Cannabinol derivatives, except where contained in marihuana, including tetrahydro derivatives of cannabinol and 3-alkyl homologues of cannabinol or of its tetrahydro derivatives, such as:
  Nabilone;
  HU-210; and
  HU-211;
- (4) Tetramethylcyclopropyl thiazole: any compound structurally derived from 2,2,3,3-tetramethyl-N-(thiazol-2-ylidene) cyclopropanecarboxamide by substitution at the nitrogen atom of the thiazole ring, whether or not further substituted in the thiazole ring to any extent, whether or not substituted in the tetramethylcyclopropyl ring to any extent, including:
  A-836,339;
- (5) any compound containing a core component substituted at the 1-position to any extent, and substituted at the 3-position with a link component attached to a group A component, whether or not the core component or group A component are further substituted to any extent, including:
  Naphthoylindane;
  Naphthoylindazole (THJ-018);
  Naphthyl methyl indene (JWH-171);
  Naphthoylindole (JWH-018);
  Quinolinoyl pyrazole carboxylate (Quinolinyl fluoropentyl fluorophenyl pyrazole carboxylate);
  Naphthoyl pyrazolopyridine; and
  Naphthoylpyrrole (JWH-030);
- (6) any compound containing a core component substituted at the 1-position to any extent, and substituted at the 2-position with a link component attached to a group A component, whether or not the core component or group A component are further substituted to any extent, including:
  Naphthoylbenzimidazole (JWH-018 Benzimidazole); and
  Naphthoylimidazole;
- (7) any compound containing a core component substituted at the 3-position to any extent, and substituted at the 2-position with a link component attached to a group A component, whether or not the core component or group A component are further substituted to any extent, including:
  Naphthoyl benzothiazole; and
- (8) any compound containing a core component substituted at the 9-position to any extent, and substituted at the 3-position with a link component attached to a group A component, whether or not the core component or group A component are further substituted to any extent, including:
  Naphthoylcarbazole (EG-018).

Leg.H. Stats. 2011, 82nd Leg. Sess. Ch., ch. 170, effective September 1, 2011; am. Acts 2015, 84th Leg., ch. 65 (S.B. 173), § 2, effective September 1, 2015.

Sec. 481.104. Penalty Group 3.

  (a) Penalty Group 3 consists of:
- (1) a material, compound, mixture, or preparation that contains any quantity of the following substances having a potential for abuse associated with a stimulant effect on the central nervous system:
  Methylphenidate and its salts; and
  Phenmetrazine and its salts;
- (2) a material, compound, mixture, or preparation that contains any quantity of the following substances having a potential for abuse associated with a depressant effect on the central nervous system:

a substance that contains any quantity of a derivative of barbituric acid, or any salt of a derivative of barbituric acid not otherwise described by this subsection;

a compound, mixture, or preparation containing amobarbital, secobarbital, pentobarbital, or any salt of any of these, and one or more active medicinal ingredients that are not listed in any penalty group;

a suppository dosage form containing amobarbital, secobarbital, pentobarbital, or any salt of any of these drugs, and approved by the United States Food and Drug Administration for marketing only as a suppository;

Alprazolam;

Amobarbital;

Bromazepam;

Camazepam;

Carisoprodol;

Chlordiazepoxide;

Chlorhexadol;

Clobazam;

Clonazepam;

Clorazepate;

Clotiazepam;

Cloxazolam;

Delorazepam;

Diazepam;

Estazolam;

Ethyl loflazepate;

Etizolam;

Fludiazepam;

Flurazepam;

Glutethimide;

Halazepam;

Haloxzolam;

Ketazolam;

Loprazolam;

Lorazepam;

Lormetazepam;

Lysergic acid, including its salts, isomers, and salts of isomers;

Lysergic acid amide, including its salts, isomers, and salts of isomers;

Mebutamate;

Medazepam;

Methyprylon;

Midazolam;

Nimetazepam;

Nitrazepam;

Nordiazepam;

Oxazepam;

Oxazolam;

Pentazocine, its salts, derivatives, or compounds or mixtures thereof;

Pentobarbital;

Pinazepam;

Prazepam;

Quazepam;

Secobarbital;

Sulfondiethylmethane;

Sulfonethylmethane;

Sulfonmethane;

Temazepam;

Tetrazepam;

Tiletamine and zolazepam in combination, and its salts. (some trade or other names for a tiletamine-zolazepam combination product: Telazol, for tiletamine: 2-(ethylamino)- 2-(2-thienyl)-cyclohexanone, and for zolazepam: 4-(2- fluorophenyl)-6, 8-dihydro-1,3,8,-trimethylpyrazolo-[3,4- e](1,4)-d diazepin-7(1H)-one, flupyrazapon);

Tramadol;

Triazolam;

Zaleplon;

Zolpidem; and

Zopiclone;

(3) Nalorphine;

(4) a material, compound, mixture, or preparation containing limited quantities of the following narcotic drugs, or any of their salts:

not more than 1.8 grams of codeine, or any of its salts, per 100 milliliters or not more than 90 milligrams per dosage unit, with an equal or greater quantity of an isoquinoline alkaloid of opium;

not more than 1.8 grams of codeine, or any of its salts, per 100 milliliters or not more than 90 milligrams per dosage unit, with one or more active, nonnarcotic ingredients in recognized therapeutic amounts;

not more than 300 milligrams of dihydrocodeinone (hydrocodone), or any of its salts, per 100 milliliters or not more than 15 milligrams per dosage unit, with a fourfold or greater quantity of an isoquinoline alkaloid of opium;

not more than 300 milligrams of dihydrocodeinone (hydrocodone), or any of its salts, per 100 milliliters or not more than 15 milligrams per dosage unit, with one or more active, nonnarcotic ingredients in recognized therapeutic amounts;

not more than 1.8 grams of dihydrocodeine, or any of its salts, per 100 milliliters or not more than 90 milligrams per dosage unit, with one or more active, nonnarcotic ingredients in recognized therapeutic amounts;

not more than 300 milligrams of ethylmorphine, or any of its salts, per 100 milliliters or not more than 15 milligrams per dosage unit, with one or more active, nonnarcotic ingredients in recognized therapeutic amounts;

not more than 500 milligrams of opium per 100 milliliters or per 100 grams, or not more than 25 milligrams per dosage unit, with one or more active, nonnarcotic ingredients in recognized therapeutic amounts;

not more than 50 milligrams of morphine, or any of its salts, per 100 milliliters or per 100 grams with one or more active, nonnarcotic ingredients in recognized therapeutic amounts; and

not more than 1 milligram of difenoxin and not less than 25 micrograms of atropine sulfate per dosage unit;

(5)   a material, compound, mixture, or preparation that contains any quantity of the following substances:
Barbital;
Chloral betaine;
Chloral hydrate;
Ethchlorvynol;
Ethinamate;
Meprobamate;
Methohexital;
Methylphenobarbital (Mephobarbital);
Paraldehyde;
Petrichloral; and
Phenobarbital;

(6)   Peyote, unless unharvested and growing in its natural state, meaning all parts of the plant classified botanically as Lophophora, whether growing or not, the seeds of the plant, an extract from a part of the plant, and every compound, manufacture, salt, derivative, mixture, or preparation of the plant, its seeds, or extracts;

(7)   unless listed in another penalty group, a material, compound, mixture, or preparation that contains any quantity of the following substances having a stimulant effect on the central nervous system, including the substance's salts, optical, position, or geometric isomers, and salts of the substance's isomers, if the existence of the salts, isomers, and salts of isomers is possible within the specific chemical designation:
Benzphetamine;
Cathine [(+)-norpseudoephedrine];
Chlorphentermine;
Clortermine;
Diethylpropion;
Fencamfamin;
Fenfluramine;
Fenproporex;
Mazindol;
Mefenorex;
Modafinil;
Pemoline (including organometallic complexes and their chelates);
Phendimetrazine;
Phentermine;
Pipradrol;
Sibutramine; and
SPA [(-)-1-dimethylamino-1,2-diphenylethane];

(8)   unless specifically excepted or unless listed in another penalty group, a material, compound, mixture, or preparation that contains any quantity of the following substance, including its salts:
Dextropropoxyphene (Alpha-(+)-4-dimethylamino- 1,2-diphenyl-3-methyl-2-propionoxybutane);

(9)   an anabolic steroid, including any drug or hormonal substance, or any substance that is chemically or pharmacologically related to testosterone, other than an estrogen, progestin, dehydroepiandrosterone, or corticosteroid, and promotes muscle growth, including the following drugs and substances and any salt, ester, or ether of the following drugs and substances:
Androstanediol;
Androstanedione;
Androstenediol;
Androstenedione;
Bolasterone;
Boldenone;
Calusterone;
Clostebol;
Dehydrochlormethyltestosterone;
Delta-1-dihydrotestosterone;

Dihydrotestosterone (4-dihydrotestosterone);
Drostanolone;
Ethylestrenol;
Fluoxymesterone;
Formebulone;
Furazabol;
13beta-ethyl-17beta-hydroxygon-4-en-3-one;
4-hydroxytestosterone;
4-hydroxy-19-nortestosterone;
Mestanolone;
Mesterolone;
Methandienone;
Methandriol;
Methenolone;
17alpha-methyl-3beta, 17 beta-dihydroxy-5alpha- androstane;
17alpha-methyl-3alpha, 17 beta-dihydroxy-5alpha- androstane;
17alpha-methyl-3beta, 17beta-dihydroxyandrost-4- ene;
17alpha-methyl-4-hydroxynandrolone;
Methyldienolone;
Methyltestosterone;
Methyltrienolone;
17alpha-methyl-delta-1-dihydrotestosterone;
Mibolerone;
Nandrolone;
Norandrostenediol;
Norandrostenedione;
Norbolethone;
Norclostebol;
Norethandrolone;
Normethandrolone;
Oxandrolone;
Oxymesterone;
Oxymetholone;
Stanozolol;
Stenbolone;
Testolactone;
Testosterone;
Tetrahydrogestrinone; and
Trenbolone; and

(10) Salvia divinorum, unless unharvested and growing in its natural state, meaning all parts of that plant, whether growing or not, the seeds of that plant, an extract from a part of that plant, and every compound, manufacture, salt, derivative, mixture, or preparation of that plant, its seeds, or extracts, including Salvinorin A.

(b) Penalty Group 3 does not include a compound, mixture, or preparation containing a stimulant substance listed in Subsection (a)(1) if the compound, mixture, or preparation contains one or more active medicinal ingredients not having a stimulant effect on the central nervous system and if the admixtures are included in combinations, quantity, proportion, or concentration that vitiate the potential for abuse of the substances that have a stimulant effect on the central nervous system.

(c) Penalty Group 3 does not include a compound, mixture, or preparation containing a depressant substance listed in Subsection (a) (2) or (a)(5) if the compound, mixture, or preparation contains one or more active medicinal ingredients not having a depressant effect on the central nervous system and if the admixtures are included in combinations, quantity, proportion, or concentration that vitiate the potential for abuse of the substances that have a depressant effect on the central nervous system.

Leg.H. Stats. 1989, 71st Leg., ch. 678 (H.B. 2136), § 1, effective September 1, 1989; am. Acts 1989, 71st Leg., ch. 1100 (S.B. 1046), § 5.02(n), effective September 1, 1989; am. Acts 1991, 72nd Leg., ch. 761 (S.B. 314), § 3, effective September 1, 1991; am. Acts 1997, 75th Leg., ch. 745 (H.B. 1070), § 24, effective January 1, 1998; am. Acts 2001, 77th Leg., ch. 251 (S.B. 753), § 18, effective September 1, 2001; am. Acts 2009, 81st Leg., ch. 739 (S.B. 449), § 3, effective September 1, 2009; am. Acts 2013, 83rd Leg., ch. 1254 (H.B. 124), § 1, effective September 1, 2013; am. Acts 2017, 85th Leg., ch. 491 (H.B. 2671), § 2, effective September 1, 2017.

Sec. 481.105. Penalty Group 4.

Penalty Group 4 consists of:
(1) a compound, mixture, or preparation containing limited quantities of any of the following narcotic drugs that includes one or more nonnarcotic active medicinal ingredients in sufficient proportion to confer on the compound, mixture, or preparation valuable medicinal qualities other than those possessed by the narcotic drug alone:

not more than 200 milligrams of codeine per 100 milliliters or per 100 grams;
not more than 100 milligrams of dihydrocodeine per 100 milliliters or per 100 grams;
not more than 100 milligrams of ethylmorphine per 100 milliliters or per 100 grams;
not more than 2.5 milligrams of diphenoxylate and not less than 25 micrograms of atropine sulfate per dosage unit;
not more than 15 milligrams of opium per 29.5729 milliliters or per 28.35 grams; and

not more than 0.5 milligram of difenoxin and not less than 25 micrograms of atropine sulfate per dosage unit;

(2) unless specifically excepted or unless listed in another penalty group, a material, compound, mixture, or preparation containing any quantity of the narcotic drug Buprenorphine or Butorphanol or a salt of either; and

(3) unless specifically exempted or excluded or unless listed in another penalty group, any material, compound, mixture, or preparation that contains any quantity of pyrovalerone, a substance having a stimulant effect on the central nervous system, including its salts, isomers, and salts of isomers.

Leg.H. Stats. 1997 75th Leg. Sess. Ch. 745, effective January 1, 1998; Stats. 2001 77th Leg. Sess. Ch. 251, effective September 1, 2001.

Sec. 481.106. Classification of Controlled Substance Analogue.

For the purposes of the prosecution of an offense under this subchapter involving the manufacture, delivery, or possession of a controlled substance, Penalty Groups 1, 1-A, 2, and 2-A include a controlled substance analogue that:

(1) has a chemical structure substantially similar to the chemical structure of a controlled substance listed in the applicable penalty group; or

(2) is specifically designed to produce an effect substantially similar to, or greater than, a controlled substance listed in the applicable penalty group.

Leg.H. Stats. 2003 78th Leg. Sess. Ch. 1099, effective September 1, 2003; am. Acts 2015, 84th Leg. ch. 65 (SB 173), § 3, effective September 1, 2015; am. Acts 2015, 84th Leg., ch. 712 (H.B. 1212), § 5, effective September 1, 2015.

Sec. 481.108. Preparatory Offenses.

Title 4, Penal Code, applies to an offense under this chapter.

Leg.H. Stats. 1995 74th Leg. Sess. Ch. 318, effective September 1, 1995.

Sec. 481.111. Exemptions.

(a) The provisions of this chapter relating to the possession and distribution of peyote do not apply to the use of peyote by a member of the Native American Church in bona fide religious ceremonies of the church or to a person who supplies the substance to the church. An exemption granted to a member of the Native American Church under this section does not apply to a member with less than 25 percent Indian blood.

(b) The provisions of this chapter relating to the possession of denatured sodium pentobarbital do not apply to possession by personnel of a humane society or an animal control agency for the purpose of destroying injured, sick, homeless, or unwanted animals if the humane society or animal control agency is registered with the Federal Drug Enforcement Administration. The provisions of this chapter relating to the distribution of denatured sodium pentobarbital do not apply to a person registered as required by Subchapter C, who is distributing the substance for that purpose to a humane society or an animal control agency registered with the Federal Drug Enforcement Administration.

(c) A person does not violate Section 481.113, 481.116, 481.1161, 481.121, or 481.125 if the person possesses or delivers tetrahydrocannabinols or their derivatives, or drug paraphernalia to be used to introduce tetrahydrocannabinols or their derivatives into the human body, for use in a federally approved therapeutic research program.

(d) The provisions of this chapter relating to the possession and distribution of anabolic steroids do not apply to the use of anabolic steroids that are administered to livestock or poultry.

(e) Sections 481.120, 481.121, 481.122, and 481.125 do not apply to a person who engages in the acquisition, possession, production, cultivation, delivery, or disposal of a raw material used in or by-product created by the production or cultivation of low-THC cannabis if the person:

(1) for an offense involving possession only of marihuana or drug paraphernalia, is a patient for whom low-THC cannabis is prescribed under Chapter 169, Occupations Code, or the patient's legal guardian, and the person possesses low-THC cannabis obtained under a valid prescription from a dispensing organization; or

(2) is a director, manager, or employee of a dispensing organization and the person, solely in performing the person's regular duties at the organization, acquires, possesses, produces, cultivates, dispenses, or disposes of:

(A) in reasonable quantities, any low-THC cannabis or raw materials used in or by-products created by the production or cultivation of low-THC cannabis; or

(B) any drug paraphernalia used in the acquisition, possession, production, cultivation, delivery, or disposal of low-THC cannabis.

(f) For purposes of Subsection (e):

(1) "Dispensing organization" has the meaning assigned by Section 487.001.

(2) "Low-THC cannabis" has the meaning assigned by Section 169.001, Occupations Code.

Leg.H. Stats. 1989, 71st Leg., ch. 678 (H.B. 2136), § 1, effective September 1, 1989; am. Acts 1989, 71st Leg., ch. 1100 (S.B. 1046), § 5.03(d), effective September 1, 1989; am. Acts 2011, 82nd Leg., ch. 170 (S.B. 331), § 2, effective September 1, 2011; am. Acts 2019, 86th Leg., ch. 595 (S.B. 616), § 4.004, effective September 1, 2019.

Sec. 481.112. Offense: Manufacture or Delivery of Substance in Penalty Group 1.

(a) Except as authorized by this chapter, a person commits an offense if the person knowingly manufactures, delivers, or possesses with intent to deliver a controlled substance listed in Penalty Group 1.

(b) An offense under Subsection (a) is a state jail felony if the amount of the controlled substance to which the offense applies is, by aggregate weight, including adulterants or dilutants, less than one gram.

(c)   An offense under Subsection (a) is a felony of the second degree if the amount of the controlled substance to which the offense applies is, by aggregate weight, including adulterants or dilutants, one gram or more but less than four grams.

(d)   An offense under Subsection (a) is a felony of the first degree if the amount of the controlled substance to which the offense applies is, by aggregate weight, including adulterants or dilutants, four grams or more but less than 200 grams.

(e)   An offense under Subsection (a) is punishable by imprisonment in the Texas Department of Criminal Justice for life or for a term of not more than 99 years or less than 10 years, and a fine not to exceed $100,000, if the amount of the controlled substance to which the offense applies is, by aggregate weight, including adulterants or dilutants, 200 grams or more but less than 400 grams.

(f)   An offense under Subsection (a) is punishable by imprisonment in the Texas Department of Criminal Justice for life or for a term of not more than 99 years or less than 15 years, and a fine not to exceed $250,000, if the amount of the controlled substance to which the offense applies is, by aggregate weight, including adulterants or dilutants, 400 grams or more.

Leg.H. Stats. 1989 71st Leg. Sess. Ch. 678, effective September 1, 1989; Stats. 1993 73rd Leg. Sess. Ch. 900, effective September 1, 1994; Stats. 2001 77th Leg. Sess. Ch. 1188, effective September 1, 2001; Stats. 2009 81st Leg. Sess. Ch. 87, effective September 1, 2009.

Sec. 481.1121. Offense: Manufacture or Delivery of Substance in Penalty Group 1-A.

(a)   Except as provided by this chapter, a person commits an offense if the person knowingly manufactures, delivers, or possesses with intent to deliver a controlled substance listed in Penalty Group 1-A.

(b)   An offense under this section is:

    (1)   a state jail felony if the number of abuse units of the controlled substance is fewer than 20;

    (2)   a felony of the second degree if the number of abuse units of the controlled substance is 20 or more but fewer than 80;

    (3)   a felony of the first degree if the number of abuse units of the controlled substance is 80 or more but fewer than 4,000; and

    (4)   punishable by imprisonment in the Texas Department of Criminal Justice for life or for a term of not more than 99 years or less than 15 years and a fine not to exceed $250,000, if the number of abuse units of the controlled substance is 4,000 or more.

Leg.H. Stats. 1997 75th Leg. Sess. Ch. 745, effective January 1, 1998; Stats. 2001 77th Leg. Sess. Ch. 1188, effective September 1, 2001; Stats. 2009 81st Leg. Sess. Ch. 87, effective September 1, 2009.

Sec. 481.1122. Manufacture of Substance in Penalty Group 1: Presence of Child.

If it is shown at the punishment phase of a trial for the manufacture of a controlled substance listed in Penalty Group 1 that when the offense was committed a child younger than 18 years of age was present on the premises where the offense was committed:

    (1)   the punishments specified by Sections 481.112(b) and (c) are increased by one degree;

    (2)   the minimum term of imprisonment specified by Section 481.112(e) is increased to 15 years and the maximum fine specified by that section is increased to $150,000; and

    (3)   the minimum term of imprisonment specified by Section 481.112(f) is increased to 20 years and the maximum fine specified by that section is increased to $300,000.

Leg.H. Stats. 2007, 80th Leg. Sess. Ch. 840, effective September 1, 2007.

Sec. 481.113. Offense: Manufacture or Delivery of Substance in Penalty Group 2 or 2-A.

(a)   Except as authorized by this chapter, a person commits an offense if the person knowingly manufactures, delivers, or possesses with intent to deliver a controlled substance listed in Penalty Group 2 or 2-A.

(b)   An offense under Subsection (a) is a state jail felony if the amount of the controlled substance to which the offense applies is, by aggregate weight, including adulterants or dilutants, less than one gram.

(c)   An offense under Subsection (a) is a felony of the second degree if the amount of the controlled substance to which the offense applies is, by aggregate weight, including adulterants or dilutants, one gram or more but less than four grams.

(d)   An offense under Subsection (a) is a felony of the first degree if the amount of the controlled substance to which the offense applies is, by aggregate weight, including adulterants or dilutants, four grams or more but less than 400 grams.

(e)   An offense under Subsection (a) is punishable by imprisonment in the Texas Department of Criminal Justice for life or for a term of not more than 99 years or less than 10 years, and a fine not to exceed $100,000, if the amount of the controlled substance to which the offense applies is, by aggregate weight, including adulterants or dilutants, 400 grams or more.

Leg.H. Stats. 1989 71st Leg. Sess. Ch. 678, effective September 1, 1989; Stats. 1993 73rd Leg. Sess. Ch. 900, effective September 1, 1994; Stats. 2001 77th Leg. Sess. Ch. 1188, effective September 1, 2001; Stats. 2009 81st Leg. Sess. Ch. 87, effective September 1, 2009; Stats. 2011 82nd Leg. Sess. Ch. 170, effective September 1, 2011.

Sec. 481.1131. Cause of Action for Sale or Provision of Synthetic Cannabinoid.

(a)   In this section, "synthetic cannabinoid" means a substance included in Penalty Group 2-A under Section 481.1031.

(b)   This section does not affect the right of a person to bring a common law cause of action against an individual whose consumption or ingestion of a synthetic cannabinoid resulted in causing the person bringing the suit to suffer personal injury or property damage.

(c)   Providing, selling, or serving a synthetic cannabinoid may be made the basis of a statutory cause of action under this section on proof that the intoxication of the recipient of the synthetic cannabinoid was a proximate cause of the damages suffered.

(d)   The liability provided under this section for the actions of a retail establishment's employees, customers, members, or guests who are or become intoxicated by the consumption or ingestion of a synthetic cannabinoid is in lieu of common law or other statutory law warranties and duties of retail establishments.

(e)   This chapter does not impose obligations on a retail establishment other than those expressly stated in this section.

Leg.H. Stats. 2017, 85th Leg., ch. 539 (S.B. 341), § 3, effective September 1, 2017.

          12/1/2019

Cont. Sub.

Sec. 481.114. Offense: Manufacture or Delivery of Substance in Penalty Group 3 or 4.

(a) Except as authorized by this chapter, a person commits an offense if the person knowingly manufactures, delivers, or possesses with intent to deliver a controlled substance listed in Penalty Group 3 or 4.

(b) An offense under Subsection (a) is a state jail felony if the amount of the controlled substance to which the offense applies is, by aggregate weight, including adulterants or dilutants, less than 28 grams.

(c) An offense under Subsection (a) is a felony of the second degree if the amount of the controlled substance to which the offense applies is, by aggregate weight, including adulterants or dilutants, 28 grams or more but less than 200 grams.

(d) An offense under Subsection (a) is a felony of the first degree, if the amount of the controlled substance to which the offense applies is, by aggregate weight, including adulterants or dilutants, 200 grams or more but less than 400 grams.

(e) An offense under Subsection (a) is punishable by imprisonment in the Texas Department of Criminal Justice for life or for a term of not more than 99 years or less than 10 years, and a fine not to exceed $100,000, if the amount of the controlled substance to which the offense applies is, by aggregate weight, including any adulterants or dilutants, 400 grams or more.

Leg.H. Stats. 1989 71st Leg. Sess. Ch. 678, effective September 1, 1989; Stats. 1993 73rd Leg. Sess. Ch. 900, effective September 1, 1994; Stats. 2001 77th Leg. Sess. Ch. 1188, effective September 1, 2001; Stats. 2009 81st Leg. Sess. Ch. 87, effective September 1, 2009.

Sec. 481.115. Offense: Possession of Substance in Penalty Group 1.

(a) Except as authorized by this chapter, a person commits an offense if the person knowingly or intentionally possesses a controlled substance listed in Penalty Group 1, unless the person obtained the substance directly from or under a valid prescription or order of a practitioner acting in the course of professional practice.

(b) An offense under Subsection (a) is a state jail felony if the amount of the controlled substance possessed is, by aggregate weight, including adulterants or dilutants, less than one gram.

(c) An offense under Subsection (a) is a felony of the third degree if the amount of the controlled substance possessed is, by aggregate weight, including adulterants or dilutants, one gram or more but less than four grams.

(d) An offense under Subsection (a) is a felony of the second degree if the amount of the controlled substance possessed is, by aggregate weight, including adulterants or dilutants, four grams or more but less than 200 grams.

(e) An offense under Subsection (a) is a felony of the first degree if the amount of the controlled substance possessed is, by aggregate weight, including adulterants or dilutants, 200 grams or more but less than 400 grams.

(f) An offense under Subsection (a) is punishable by imprisonment in the Texas Department of Criminal Justice for life or for a term of not more than 99 years or less than 10 years, and a fine not to exceed $100,000, if the amount of the controlled substance possessed is, by aggregate weight, including adulterants or dilutants, 400 grams or more.

Leg.H. Stats. 1989 71st Leg. Sess. Ch. 678, effective September 1, 1989; Stats. 1993 73rd Leg. Sess. Ch. 900, effective September 1, 1994; Stats. 2009 81st Leg. Sess. Ch. 87, effective September 1, 2009.

Sec. 481.1151. Offense: Possession of Substance in Penalty Group 1-A.

(a) Except as provided by this chapter, a person commits an offense if the person knowingly possesses a controlled substance listed in Penalty Group 1-A.

(b) An offense under this section is:
    (1) a state jail felony if the number of abuse units of the controlled substance is fewer than 20;
    (2) a felony of the third degree if the number of abuse units of the controlled substance is 20 or more but fewer than 80;
    (3) a felony of the second degree if the number of abuse units of the controlled substance is 80 or more but fewer than 4,000;
    (4) a felony of the first degree if the number of abuse units of the controlled substance is 4,000 or more but fewer than 8,000; and
    (5) punishable by imprisonment in the Texas Department of Criminal Justice for life or for a term of not more than 99 years or less than 15 years and a fine not to exceed $250,000, if the number of abuse units of the controlled substance is 8,000 or more.

Leg.H. Stats. 1997 75th Leg. Sess. Ch. 745, effective January 1, 1998; Stats. 2009 81st Leg. Sess. Ch. 87, effective September 1, 2009.

Sec. 481.116. Offense: Possession of Substance in Penalty Group 2.

(a) Except as authorized by this chapter, a person commits an offense if the person knowingly or intentionally possesses a controlled substance listed in Penalty Group 2, unless the person obtained the substance directly from or under a valid prescription or order of a practitioner acting in the course of professional practice.

(b) An offense under Subsection (a) is a state jail felony if the amount of the controlled substance possessed is, by aggregate weight, including adulterants or dilutants, less than one gram.

(c) An offense under Subsection (a) is a felony of the third degree if the amount of the controlled substance possessed is, by aggregate weight, including adulterants or dilutants, one gram or more but less than four grams.

(d) An offense under Subsection (a) is a felony of the second degree if the amount of the controlled substance possessed is, by aggregate weight, including adulterants or dilutants, four grams or more but less than 400 grams.

(e) An offense under Subsection (a) is punishable by imprisonment in the Texas Department of Criminal Justice for life or for a term of not more than 99 years or less than five years, and a fine not to exceed $50,000, if the amount of the controlled substance possessed is, by aggregate weight, including adulterants or dilutants, 400 grams or more.

Leg.H. Stats. 1989 71st Leg. Sess. Ch. 678, effective September 1, 1989; Stats. 1993 73rd Leg. Sess. Ch. 900, effective September 1, 1994; Stats. 2009 81st Leg. Sess. Ch. 87, effective September 1, 2009.

Sec. 481.1161. Offense: Possession of Substance in Penalty Group 2-A.

(a) Except as authorized by this chapter, a person commits an offense if the person knowingly possesses a controlled substance listed in Penalty Group 2-A, unless the person obtained the substance directly from or under a valid prescription or order of a practitioner acting in the course of professional practice.

(b) An offense under this section is:

    (1) a Class B misdemeanor if the amount of the controlled substance possessed is, by aggregate weight, including adulterants or dilutants, two ounces or less;

    (2) a Class A misdemeanor if the amount of the controlled substance possessed is, by aggregate weight, including adulterants or dilutants, four ounces or less but more than two ounces;

    (3) a state jail felony if the amount of the controlled substance possessed is, by aggregate weight, including adulterants or dilutants, five pounds or less but more than four ounces;

    (4) a felony of the third degree if the amount of the controlled substance possessed is, by aggregate weight, including adulterants or dilutants, 50 pounds or less but more than 5 pounds;

    (5) a felony of the second degree if the amount of the controlled substance possessed is, by aggregate weight, including adulterants or dilutants, 2,000 pounds or less but more than 50 pounds; and

    (6) punishable by imprisonment in the Texas Department of Criminal Justice for life or for a term of not more than 99 years or less than 5 years, and a fine not to exceed $50,000, if the amount of the controlled substance possessed is, by aggregate weight, including adulterants or dilutants, more than 2,000 pounds.

Leg.H. Stats. 2011, 82nd Leg. Sess. Ch. 170, effective September 1, 2011.

Sec. 481.117. Offense: Possession of Substance in Penalty Group 3.

(a) Except as authorized by this chapter, a person commits an offense if the person knowingly or intentionally possesses a controlled substance listed in Penalty Group 3, unless the person obtains the substance directly from or under a valid prescription or order of a practitioner acting in the course of professional practice.

(b) An offense under Subsection (a) is a Class A misdemeanor if the amount of the controlled substance possessed is, by aggregate weight, including adulterants or dilutants, less than 28 grams.

(c) An offense under Subsection (a) is a felony of the third degree if the amount of the controlled substance possessed is, by aggregate weight, including adulterants or dilutants, 28 grams or more but less than 200 grams.

(d) An offense under Subsection (a) is a felony of the second degree, if the amount of the controlled substance possessed is, by aggregate weight, including adulterants or dilutants, 200 grams or more but less than 400 grams.

(e) An offense under Subsection (a) is punishable by imprisonment in the Texas Department of Criminal Justice for life or for a term of not more than 99 years or less than five years, and a fine not to exceed $50,000, if the amount of the controlled substance possessed is, by aggregate weight, including adulterants or dilutants, 400 grams or more.

Leg.H. Stats. 1989 71st Leg. Sess. Ch. 678, effective September 1, 1989; Stats. 1993 73rd Leg. Sess Ch. 900, effective September 1, 1994; Stats. 2009 81st Leg. Sess. Ch. 87, effective September 1, 2009.

Sec. 481.118. Offense: Possession of Substance in Penalty Group 4.

(a) Except as authorized by this chapter, a person commits an offense if the person knowingly or intentionally possesses a controlled substance listed in Penalty Group 4, unless the person obtained the substance directly from or under a valid prescription or order of a practitioner acting in the course of practice.

(b) An offense under Subsection (a) is a Class B misdemeanor if the amount of the controlled substance possessed is, by aggregate weight, including adulterants or dilutants, less than 28 grams.

(c) An offense under Subsection (a) is a felony of the third degree if the amount of the controlled substance possessed is, by aggregate weight, including adulterants or dilutants, 28 grams or more but less than 200 grams.

(d) An offense under Subsection (a) is a felony of the second degree, if the amount of the controlled substance possessed is, by aggregate weight, including adulterants or dilutants, 200 grams or more but less than 400 grams.

(e) An offense under Subsection (a) is punishable by imprisonment in the Texas Department of Criminal Justice for life or for a term of not more than 99 years or less than five years, and a fine not to exceed $50,000, if the amount of the controlled substance possessed is, by aggregate weight, including adulterants or dilutants, 400 grams or more.

Leg.H. Stats. 1989 71st Leg. Sess. Ch. 678, effective September 1, 1989; Stats. 1993 73rd Leg. Sess. Ch. 900, effective September 1, 1994; Stats. 2009 81st Leg. Sess. Ch. 87, effective September 1, 2009.

Sec. 481.119. Offense: Manufacture, Delivery, or Possession of Miscellaneous Substances.

(a) A person commits an offense if the person knowingly manufactures, delivers, or possesses with intent to deliver a controlled substance listed in a schedule by an action of the commissioner under this chapter but not listed in a penalty group. An offense under this subsection is a Class A misdemeanor, except that the offense is:

    (1) a state jail felony, if the person has been previously convicted of an offense under this subsection; or

    (2) a felony of the third degree, if the person has been previously convicted two or more times of an offense under this subsection.

(b) A person commits an offense if the person knowingly or intentionally possesses a controlled substance listed in a schedule by an action of the commissioner under this chapter but not listed in a penalty group. An offense under this subsection is a Class B misdemeanor.

Leg.H. Stats. 1989 71st Leg. Sess. Ch. 678, effective September 1, 1989; Stats. 2001 77th Leg. Sess. Ch. 1188, effective September 1, 2001; am. Acts 2015, 84th Leg., (H.B. 1424), § 1, effective September 1, 2015.

Sec. 481.1191. Civil Liability for Engaging in or Aiding in Production, Distribution, Sale, or Provision of Synthetic Substances.

(a) In this section:

  (1) "Minor" means a person younger than 18 years of age.

  (2) "Synthetic substance" means an artificial substance that produces and is intended by the manufacturer to produce when consumed or ingested an effect similar to or in excess of the effect produced by the consumption or ingestion of a controlled substance or controlled substance analogue, as those terms are defined by Section 481.002.

(b) A person is liable for damages proximately caused by the consumption or ingestion of a synthetic substance by another person if the actor:

  (1) produced, distributed, sold, or provided the synthetic substance to the other person; or

  (2) aided in the production, distribution, sale, or provision of the synthetic substance to the other person.

(c) A person is strictly liable for all damages caused by the consumption or ingestion of a synthetic substance by a minor if the actor:

  (1) produced, distributed, sold, or provided the synthetic substance to the minor; or

  (2) aided in the production, distribution, sale, or provision of the synthetic substance to the minor.

(d) A person who is found liable under this section or other law for any amount of damages arising from the consumption or ingestion by another of a synthetic substance is jointly and severally liable with any other person for the entire amount of damages awarded.

(e) Chapter 33, Civil Practice and Remedies Code, does not apply to an action brought under this section or an action brought under Section 17.50, Business & Commerce Code, based on conduct made actionable under Subsection (f) of this section.

(f) Conduct for which Subsection (b) or (c) creates liability is a false, misleading, or deceptive act or practice or an unconscionable action or course of action for purposes of Section 17.50, Business & Commerce Code, and that conduct is:

  (1) actionable under Subchapter E, Chapter 17, Business & Commerce Code; and

  (2) subject to any remedy prescribed by that subchapter.

(g) An action brought under this section may include a claim for exemplary damages, which may be awarded in accordance with Section 41.003, Civil Practice and Remedies Code.

(h) Section 41.008, Civil Practice and Remedies Code, does not apply to the award of exemplary damages in an action brought under this section.

(i) Section 41.005, Civil Practice and Remedies Code, does not apply to a claim for exemplary damages in an action brought under this section.

(j) It is an affirmative defense to liability under this section that the synthetic substance produced, distributed, sold, or provided was approved for use, sale, or distribution by the United States Food and Drug Administration or other state or federal regulatory agency with authority to approve a substance for use, sale, or distribution.

(k) It is not a defense to liability under this section that a synthetic substance was in packaging labeled with "Not for Human Consumption" or other wording indicating the substance is not intended to be ingested.

Leg.H. Stats. 2017, 85th Leg., ch. 861 (H.B. 2612), § 1, effective September 1, 2017.

Sec. 481.120. Offense: Delivery of Marihuana.

(a) Except as authorized by this chapter, a person commits an offense if the person knowingly or intentionally delivers marihuana.

(b) An offense under Subsection (a) is:

  (1) a Class B misdemeanor if the amount of marihuana delivered is one-fourth ounce or less and the person committing the offense does not receive remuneration for the marihuana;

  (2) a Class A misdemeanor if the amount of marihuana delivered is one-fourth ounce or less and the person committing the offense receives remuneration for the marihuana;

  (3) a state jail felony if the amount of marihuana delivered is five pounds or less but more than one-fourth ounce;

  (4) a felony of the second degree if the amount of marihuana delivered is 50 pounds or less but more than five pounds;

  (5) a felony of the first degree if the amount of marihuana delivered is 2,000 pounds or less but more than 50 pounds; and

  (6) punishable by imprisonment in the Texas Department of Criminal Justice for life or for a term of not more than 99 years or less than 10 years, and a fine not to exceed $100,000, if the amount of marihuana delivered is more than 2,000 pounds.

Leg.H. Stats. 1989 71st Leg. Sess. Ch. 678, effective September 1, 1989; Stats. 1993 73rd Leg. Sess. Ch. 900, effective September 1, 1994; Stats. 2009 81st Leg. Sess. Ch. 87, effective September 1, 2009.

Sec. 481.121. Offense: Possession of Marihuana.

(a) Except as authorized by this chapter, a person commits an offense if the person knowingly or intentionally possesses a usable quantity of marihuana.

(b) An offense under Subsection (a) is:

  (1) a Class B misdemeanor if the amount of marihuana possessed is two ounces or less;

  (2) a Class A misdemeanor if the amount of marihuana possessed is four ounces or less but more than two ounces;

  (3) a state jail felony if the amount of marihuana possessed is five pounds or less but more than four ounces;

  (4) a felony of the third degree if the amount of marihuana possessed is 50 pounds or less but more than 5 pounds;

  (5) a felony of the second degree if the amount of marihuana possessed is 2,000 pounds or less but more than 50 pounds; and

  (6) punishable by imprisonment in the Texas Department of Criminal Justice for life or for a term of not more than 99 years or less than 5 years, and a fine not to exceed $50,000, if the amount of marihuana possessed is more than 2,000 pounds.

Leg.H. Stats. 1989 71st Leg. Sess. Ch. 678, effective September 1, 1989; Stats. 1993 73rd Leg. Sess. Ch. 900, effective September 1, 1994; Stats. 2009 81st Leg. Sess. Ch. 87, effective September 1, 2009.

Sec. 481.122. Offense: Delivery of Controlled Substance or Marihuana to Child.

(a)   A person commits an offense if the person knowingly delivers a controlled substance listed in Penalty Group 1, 1-A, 2, or 3 or knowingly delivers marihuana and the person delivers the controlled substance or marihuana to a person:

(1)   who is a child;

(2)   who is enrolled in a public or private primary or secondary school; or

(3)   who the actor knows or believes intends to deliver the controlled substance or marihuana to a person described by Subdivision (1) or (2).

(b)   It is an affirmative defense to prosecution under this section that:

(1)   the actor was a child when the offense was committed; or

(2)   the actor:

(A)   was younger than 21 years of age when the offense was committed;

(B)   delivered only marihuana in an amount equal to or less than one-fourth ounce; and

(C)   did not receive remuneration for the delivery.

(c)   An offense under this section is a felony of the second degree.

(d)   In this section, "child" means a person younger than 18 years of age.

(e)   If conduct that is an offense under this section is also an offense under another section of this chapter, the actor may be prosecuted under either section or both.

Leg.H. Stats. 1989 71st Leg. Sess. Ch. 678, effective September 1, 1989; Stats. 1993 73rd Leg. Sess. Ch. 900, effective September 1, 1994; Stats. 1997 75th Leg. Sess. Ch. 745, effective January 1, 1998; Stats. 2001 77th Leg. Sess. Ch. 251, effective September 1, 2001.

Sec. 481.123. Defense to Prosecution for Offense Involving Controlled Substance Analogue.

(a)   It is an affirmative defense to the prosecution of an offense under this subchapter involving the manufacture, delivery, or possession of a controlled substance analogue that the analogue:

(1)   was a substance for which there is an approved new drug application under Section 505 of the Federal Food, Drug, and Cosmetic Act (21 U.S.C. Section 355); or

(2)   was a substance for which an exemption for investigational use has been granted under Section 505 of the Federal Food, Drug, and Cosmetic Act (21 U.S.C. Section 355), if the actor's conduct with respect to the substance is in accord with the exemption.

(b)   For the purposes of this section, Section 505 of the Federal Food, Drug, and Cosmetic Act (21 U.S.C. Section 355) applies to the introduction or delivery for introduction of any new drug into intrastate, interstate, or foreign commerce.

Leg.H. Stats. 1989 71st Leg. Sess. Ch. 678, effective September 1, 1989; Stats. 1997 75th Leg. Sess. Ch. 745, effective January 1, 1998; Stats. 2003 78th Leg. Sess. Ch. 1099, effective September 1, 2003; am. Acts 2015, 84th Leg., ch. 712 (H.B. 1212), § 6, effective September 1, 2015.

Sec. 481.124. Offense: Possession or Transport of Certain Chemicals with Intent to Manufacture Controlled Substance.

(a)   A person commits an offense if, with intent to unlawfully manufacture a controlled substance, the person possesses or transports:

(1)   anhydrous ammonia;

(2)   an immediate precursor; or

(3)   a chemical precursor or an additional chemical substance named as a precursor by the director under Section 481.077(b)(1).

(b)   For purposes of this section, an intent to unlawfully manufacture the controlled substance methamphetamine is presumed if the actor possesses or transports:

(1)   anhydrous ammonia in a container or receptacle that is not designed and manufactured to lawfully hold or transport anhydrous ammonia;

(2)   lithium metal removed from a battery and immersed in kerosene, mineral spirits, or similar liquid that prevents or retards hydration; or

(3)   in one container, vehicle, or building, phenylacetic acid, or more than nine grams, three containers packaged for retail sale, or 300 tablets or capsules of a product containing ephedrine or pseudoephedrine, and:

(A)   anhydrous ammonia;

(B)   at least three of the following categories of substances commonly used in the manufacture of methamphetamine:

(i)   lithium or sodium metal or red phosphorus, iodine, or iodine crystals;

(ii)   lye, sulfuric acid, hydrochloric acid, or muriatic acid;

(iii)   an organic solvent, including ethyl ether, alcohol, or acetone;

(iv)   a petroleum distillate, including naphtha, paint thinner, or charcoal lighter fluid; or

(v)   aquarium, rock, or table salt; or

(C)   at least three of the following items:

(i)   an item of equipment subject to regulation under Section 481.080, if the person is not a registrant; or

(ii)   glassware, a plastic or metal container, tubing, a hose, or other item specially designed, assembled, or adapted for use in the manufacture, processing, analyzing, storing, or concealing of methamphetamine.

(c)   For purposes of this section, a substance is presumed to be anhydrous ammonia if the substance is in a container or receptacle that is:

(1)   designed and manufactured to lawfully hold or transport anhydrous ammonia; or

(2) not designed and manufactured to lawfully hold or transport anhydrous ammonia, if:
  (A) a properly administered field test of the substance using a testing device or instrument designed and manufactured for that purpose produces a positive result for anhydrous ammonia; or
  (B) a laboratory test of a water solution of the substance produces a positive result for ammonia.
(d) An offense under this section is:
  (1) a felony of the second degree if the controlled substance is listed in Penalty Group 1 or 1-A;
  (2) a felony of the third degree if the controlled substance is listed in Penalty Group 2;
  (3) a state jail felony if the controlled substance is listed in Penalty Group 3 or 4; or
  (4) a Class A misdemeanor if the controlled substance is listed in a schedule by an action of the commissioner under this chapter but not listed in a penalty group.
(e) If conduct constituting an offense under this section also constitutes an offense under another section of this code, the actor may be prosecuted under either section or under both sections.
(f) This section does not apply to a chemical precursor exempted by the director under Section 481.077(b)(2) from the requirements of that section.

Leg.H. Stats. 2001 77th Leg. Sess. Ch. 1188, effective September 1, 2001; 2003 78th Leg. Sess. Ch. 570, effective June 20, 2003; Stats. 2005 79th Leg. Sess. Ch. 282, effective August 1, 2005; am. Acts 2015, 84th Leg., (S.B. 195), § 16, effective September 1, 2016.

Sec. 481.1245. Offense: Possession or Transport of Anhydrous Ammonia; Use of or Tampering with Equipment.

(a) A person commits an offense if the person:
  (1) possesses or transports anhydrous ammonia in a container or receptacle that is not designed or manufactured to hold or transport anhydrous ammonia;
  (2) uses, transfers, or sells a container or receptacle that is designed or manufactured to hold anhydrous ammonia without the express consent of the owner of the container or receptacle; or
  (3) tampers with equipment that is manufactured or used to hold, apply, or transport anhydrous ammonia without the express consent of the owner of the equipment.
(b) An offense under this section is a felony of the third degree.

Leg.H. Stats. 2005 79th Leg. Sess. Ch. 282, effective August 1, 2005.

Sec. 481.125. Offense: Possession or Delivery of Drug Paraphernalia.

(a) A person commits an offense if the person knowingly or intentionally uses or possesses with intent to use drug paraphernalia to plant, propagate, cultivate, grow, harvest, manufacture, compound, convert, produce, process, prepare, test, analyze, pack, repack, store, contain, or conceal a controlled substance in violation of this chapter or to inject, ingest, inhale, or otherwise introduce into the human body a controlled substance in violation of this chapter.
(b) A person commits an offense if the person knowingly or intentionally delivers, possesses with intent to deliver, or manufactures with intent to deliver drug paraphernalia knowing that the person who receives or who is intended to receive the drug paraphernalia intends that it be used to plant, propagate, cultivate, grow, harvest, manufacture, compound, convert, produce, process, prepare, test, analyze, pack, repack, store, contain, or conceal a controlled substance in violation of this chapter or to inject, ingest, inhale, or otherwise introduce into the human body a controlled substance in violation of this chapter.
(c) A person commits an offense if the person commits an offense under Subsection (b), is 18 years of age or older, and the person who receives or who is intended to receive the drug paraphernalia is younger than 18 years of age and at least three years younger than the actor.
(d) An offense under Subsection (a) is a Class C misdemeanor.
(e) An offense under Subsection (b) is a Class A misdemeanor, unless it is shown on the trial of a defendant that the defendant has previously been convicted under Subsection (b) or (c), in which event the offense is punishable by confinement in jail for a term of not more than one year or less than 90 days.
(f) An offense under Subsection (c) is a state jail felony.

Leg.H. Stats. 1989 71st Leg. Sess. Ch. 678, effective September 1, 1989; Stats. 1993 73rd Leg. Sess. Ch. 900, effective September 1, 1994.

Sec. 481.126. Offense: Illegal Barter, Expenditure, or Investment.

(a) A person commits an offense if the person:
  (1) barters property or expends funds the person knows are derived from the commission of an offense under this chapter punishable by imprisonment in the Texas Department of Criminal Justice for life;
  (2) barters property or expends funds the person knows are derived from the commission of an offense under Section 481.121(a) that is punishable under Section 481.121(b)(5);
  (3) barters property or finances or invests funds the person knows or believes are intended to further the commission of an offense for which the punishment is described by Subdivision (1); or
  (4) barters property or finances or invests funds the person knows or believes are intended to further the commission of an offense under Section 481.121(a) that is punishable under Section 481.121(b)(5).
(b) An offense under Subsection (a)(1) or (3) is a felony of the first degree. An offense under Subsection (a)(2) or (4) is a felony of the second degree.

Leg.H. Stats. 1989 71st Leg. Sess. Ch. 678, effective September 1, 1989; Stats. 1993 73rd Leg. Sess. Ch. 900, effective September 1, 1994; Stats. 1995 74th Leg. Sess. Ch. 318, effective September 1, 1995; Stats. 2001 77th Leg. Sess. Ch. 251, effective September 1, 2001; Stats. 2003 78th Leg. Sess. Ch. 712, effective September 1, 2003; Stats. 2009 81st Leg. Sess. Ch. 87, effective September 1, 2009.

Sec. 481.127. Offense: Unauthorized Disclosure of Information.

(a) A person commits an offense if the person knowingly gives, permits, or obtains unauthorized access to information submitted to the board under Section 481.074(q) or 481.075.

(b) An offense under this section is a state jail felony.

Leg.H. Stats. 1989 71st Leg. Sess. Ch. 678, effective September 1, 1989; Stats. 1993 73rd Leg. Sess. Ch. 900, effective September 1, 1994; Stats. 1997 75th Leg. Sess. Ch. 745, effective January 1, 1998; Stats. 2013, 83rd Leg., ch. 1226 (S.B. 1643), § 3, effective September 1, 2013; am. Acts 2015, 84th Leg., (S.B. 195), § 17, effective September 1, 2016.

Sec. 481.128. Offense and Civil Penalty: Commercial Matters.

(a) A registrant or dispenser commits an offense if the registrant or dispenser knowingly:

    (1) distributes, delivers, administers, or dispenses a controlled substance in violation of Subchapter C;

    (2) manufactures a controlled substance not authorized by the person's Federal Drug Enforcement Administration registration or distributes or dispenses a controlled substance not authorized by the person's registration to another registrant or other person;

    (3) refuses or fails to make, keep, or furnish a record, report, notification, order form, statement, invoice, or information required by this chapter;

    (4) prints, manufactures, possesses, or produces an official prescription form without the approval of the board;

    (5) delivers or possesses a counterfeit official prescription form;

    (6) refuses an entry into a premise for an inspection authorized by this chapter;

    (7) refuses or fails to return an official prescription form as required by Section 481.0755(k);

    (8) refuses or fails to make, keep, or furnish a record, report, notification, order form, statement, invoice, or information required by a rule adopted by the director or the board; or

    (9) refuses or fails to maintain security required by this chapter or a rule adopted under this chapter.

(b) If the registrant or dispenser knowingly refuses or fails to make, keep, or furnish a record, report, notification, order form, statement, invoice, or information or maintain security required by a rule adopted by the director or the board, the registrant or dispenser is liable to the state for a civil penalty of not more than $5,000 for each act.

(c) An offense under Subsection (a) is a state jail felony.

(d) If a person commits an act that would otherwise be an offense under Subsection (a) except that it was committed without the requisite culpable mental state, the person is liable to the state for a civil penalty of not more than $1,000 for each act.

(e) A district attorney of the county where the act occurred may file suit in district court in that county to collect a civil penalty under this section, or the district attorney of Travis County or the attorney general may file suit in district court in Travis County to collect the penalty.

Leg.H. Stats. 1993, 73rd Leg., ch. 900 (S.B. 1067), § 2.02, effective September 1, 1994; am. Acts 1997, 75th Leg., ch. 745 (H.B. 1070), § 30, effective January 1, 1998; am. Acts 2001, 77th Leg., ch. 251 (S.B. 753), § 22, effective September 1, 2001; am. Acts 2019, 86th Leg., ch. 1105 (H.B. 2174), § 10, effective September 1, 2019; am. Acts 2019, 86th Leg., ch. 1166 (H.B. 3284), § 6, effective September 1, 2019.

Sec. 481.1285. Offense: Diversion of Controlled Substance by Registrants, Dispensers, and Certain Other Persons.

(a) This section applies only to a registrant, a dispenser, or a person who, pursuant to Section 481.062(a)(1) or (2), is not required to register under this subchapter.

(b) A person commits an offense if the person knowingly:

    (1) converts to the person's own use or benefit a controlled substance to which the person has access by virtue of the person's profession or employment; or

    (2) diverts to the unlawful use or benefit of another person a controlled substance to which the person has access by virtue of the person's profession or employment.

(c) An offense under Subsection (b)(1) is a state jail felony. An offense under Subsection (b)(2) is a felony of the third degree.

(d) If conduct that constitutes an offense under this section also constitutes an offense under any other law, the actor may be prosecuted under this section, the other law, or both.

Leg.H. Stats. 2011, 82nd Leg. Sess. Ch. 1200, effective September 1, 2011.

Sec. 481.129. Offense: Fraud.

(a) A person commits an offense if the person knowingly:

    (1) distributes as a registrant or dispenser a controlled substance listed in Schedule I or II, unless the person distributes the controlled substance as authorized under the federal Controlled Substances Act (21 U.S.C. Section 801 et seq.);

    (2) uses in the course of manufacturing, prescribing, or distributing a controlled substance a Federal Drug Enforcement Administration registration number that is fictitious, revoked, suspended, or issued to another person;

    (3) issues a prescription bearing a forged or fictitious signature;

    (4) uses a prescription issued to another person to prescribe a Schedule II controlled substance;

    (5) possesses, obtains, or attempts to possess or obtain a controlled substance or an increased quantity of a controlled substance:

(A) by misrepresentation, fraud, forgery, deception, or subterfuge;

(B) through use of a fraudulent prescription form;

(C) through use of a fraudulent oral or telephonically communicated prescription; or

(D) through the use of a fraudulent electronic prescription; or

(6) furnishes false or fraudulent material information in or omits material information from an application, report, record, or other document required to be kept or filed under this chapter.

(a-1) A person commits an offense if the person, with intent to obtain a controlled substance or combination of controlled substances that is not medically necessary for the person or an amount of a controlled substance or substances that is not medically necessary for the person, obtains or attempts to obtain from a practitioner a controlled substance or a prescription for a controlled substance by misrepresentation, fraud, forgery, deception, subterfuge, or concealment of a material fact. For purposes of this subsection, a material fact includes whether the person has an existing prescription for a controlled substance issued for the same period of time by another practitioner.

(b) A person commits an offense if the person knowingly or intentionally:

(1) makes, distributes, or possesses a punch, die, plate, stone, or other thing designed to print, imprint, or reproduce an actual or simulated trademark, trade name, or other identifying mark, imprint, or device of another on a controlled substance or the container or label of a container for a controlled substance, so as to make the controlled substance a counterfeit substance; or

(2) manufactures, delivers, or possesses with intent to deliver a counterfeit substance.

(c) A person commits an offense if the person knowingly or intentionally:

(1) delivers a prescription or a prescription form for other than a valid medical purpose in the course of professional practice; or

(2) possesses a prescription for a controlled substance or a prescription form unless the prescription or prescription form is possessed:

(A) during the manufacturing or distribution process;

(B) by a practitioner, practitioner's agent, or an institutional practitioner for a valid medical purpose during the course of professional practice;

(C) by a pharmacist or agent of a pharmacy during the professional practice of pharmacy;

(D) under a practitioner's order made by the practitioner for a valid medical purpose in the course of professional practice; or

(E) by an officer or investigator authorized to enforce this chapter within the scope of the officer's or investigator's official duties.

(d) An offense under Subsection (a) is:

(1) a felony of the second degree if the controlled substance that is the subject of the offense is listed in Schedule I or II;

(2) a felony of the third degree if the controlled substance that is the subject of the offense is listed in Schedule III or IV; and

(3) a Class A misdemeanor if the controlled substance that is the subject of the offense is listed in Schedule V.

(d-1) An offense under Subsection (a-1) is:

(1) a felony of the second degree if any controlled substance that is the subject of the offense is listed in Schedule I or II;

(2) a felony of the third degree if any controlled substance that is the subject of the offense is listed in Schedule III or IV; and

(3) a Class A misdemeanor if any controlled substance that is the subject of the offense is listed in Schedule V.

(e) An offense under Subsection (b) is a Class A misdemeanor.

(f) An offense under Subsection (c)(1) is:

(1) a felony of the second degree if the defendant delivers:

(A) a prescription form; or

(B) a prescription for a controlled substance listed in Schedule II; and

(2) a felony of the third degree if the defendant delivers a prescription for a controlled substance listed in Schedule III, IV, or V.

(g) An offense under Subsection (c)(2) is:

(1) a state jail felony if the defendant possesses:

(A) a prescription form; or

(B) a prescription for a controlled substance listed in Schedule II or III; and

(2) a Class B misdemeanor if the defendant possesses a prescription for a controlled substance listed in Schedule IV or V.

Leg.H. Stats. 1989, 71st Leg., ch. 678 (H.B. 2136), § 1, effective September 1, 1989; am. Acts 1989, 71st Leg., ch. 1100 (S.B. 1046), § 5.02(p), effective September 1, 1989; am. Acts 1993, 73rd Leg., ch. 900 (S.B. 1067), § 2.02, effective September 1, 1994; am. Acts 1997, 75th Leg., ch. 745 (H.B. 1070), § 31, effective January 1, 1998; am. Acts 2001, 77th Leg., ch. 251 (S.B. 753), § 23, effective September 1, 2001; am. Acts 2011, 82nd Leg., ch. 1200 (S.B. 158), § 2, effective September 1, 2011; am. Acts 2019, 86th Leg., ch. 1105 (H.B. 2174), § 11, effective September 1, 2019; am. Acts 2019, 86th Leg., ch. 1166 (H.B. 3284), § 7, effective September 1, 2019.

Sec. 481.130. Penalties Under Other Law.

A penalty imposed for an offense under this chapter is in addition to any civil or administrative penalty or other sanction imposed by law.

Leg.H. Stats. 1989 71st Leg. Sess. Ch. 678, effective September 1, 1989.

Sec. 481.131. Offense: Diversion of Controlled Substance Property or Plant.

(a) A person commits an offense if the person intentionally or knowingly:

(1) converts to the person's own use or benefit a controlled substance property or plant seized under Section 481.152 or 481.153; or

(2) diverts to the unlawful use or benefit of another person a controlled substance property or plant seized under Section 481.152 or 481.153.

(b) An offense under this section is a state jail felony.

Leg.H. Stats. 1991 72nd Leg. Sess. Ch. 141, effective September 1, 1991; Stats. 1993 73rd Leg. Sess. Ch. 900, effective September 1, 1994.

Sec. 481.132. Multiple Prosecutions.

(a) In this section, "criminal episode" means the commission of two or more offenses under this chapter under the following circumstances:
  (1) the offenses are committed pursuant to the same transaction or pursuant to two or more transactions that are connected or constitute a common scheme, plan, or continuing course of conduct; or
  (2) the offenses are the repeated commission of the same or similar offenses.

(b) A defendant may be prosecuted in a single criminal action for all offenses arising out of the same criminal episode. If a single criminal action is based on more than one charging instrument within the jurisdiction of the trial court, not later than the 30th day before the date of the trial, the state shall file written notice of the action.

(c) If a judgment of guilt is reversed, set aside, or vacated and a new trial is ordered, the state may not prosecute in a single criminal action in the new trial any offense not joined in the former prosecution unless evidence to establish probable guilt for that offense was not known to the appropriate prosecution official at the time the first prosecution began.

(d) If the accused is found guilty of more than one offense arising out of the same criminal episode prosecuted in a single criminal action, sentence for each offense for which the accused has been found guilty shall be pronounced, and those sentences run concurrently.

(e) If it appears that a defendant or the state is prejudiced by a joinder of offenses, the court may order separate trials of the offenses or provide other relief as justice requires.

(f) This section provides the exclusive method for consolidation and joinder of prosecutions for offenses under this chapter. This section is not a limitation of Article 36.09 or 36.10, Code of Criminal Procedure.

Leg.H. Stats. 1991 72nd Leg. Sess. Ch. 193, effective September 1, 1991; Stats. 1991 72nd Leg. Sess. 1st C.S. Ch. 14, effective November 12, 1991 (renumbered from Sec. 481.131).

Sec. 481.133. Offense: Falsification of Drug Test Results.

(a) A person commits an offense if the person knowingly or intentionally uses or possesses with intent to use any substance or device designed to falsify drug test results.

(b) A person commits an offense if the person knowingly or intentionally delivers, possesses with intent to deliver, or manufactures with intent to deliver a substance or device designed to falsify drug test results.

(c) In this section, "drug test" means a lawfully administered test designed to detect the presence of a controlled substance or marihuana.

(d) An offense under Subsection (a) is a Class B misdemeanor.

(e) An offense under Subsection (b) is a Class A misdemeanor.

Leg.H. Stats. 1991 72nd Leg. Sess. Ch. 274, effective September 1, 1991; Stats. 1991 72nd Leg. Sess. 1st C.S. Ch. 14, effective November 12, 1991 (renumbered from Sec. 481.131).

Sec. 481.134. Drug-Free Zones.

(a) In this section:
  (1) "Minor" means a person who is younger than 18 years of age.
  (2) "Institution of higher education" means any public or private technical institute, junior college, senior college or university, medical or dental unit, or other agency of higher education as defined by Section 61.003, Education Code.
  (3) "Playground" means any outdoor facility that is not on the premises of a school and that:
    (A) is intended for recreation;
    (B) is open to the public; and
    (C) contains three or more play stations intended for the recreation of children, such as slides, swing sets, and teeterboards.
  (4) "Premises" means real property and all buildings and appurtenances pertaining to the real property.
  (5) "School" means a private or public elementary or secondary school or a day-care center, as defined by Section 42.002, Human Resources Code.
  (6) "Video arcade facility" means any facility that:
    (A) is open to the public, including persons who are 17 years of age or younger;
    (B) is intended primarily for the use of pinball or video machines; and
    (C) contains at least three pinball or video machines.
  (7) "Youth center" means any recreational facility or gymnasium that:
    (A) is intended primarily for use by persons who are 17 years of age or younger; and
    (B) regularly provides athletic, civic, or cultural activities.

(b) An offense otherwise punishable as a state jail felony under Section 481.112, 481.1121, 481.113, 481.114, or 481.120 is punishable as a felony of the third degree, and an offense otherwise punishable as a felony of the second degree under any of those sections is punishable as a felony of the first degree, if it is shown at the punishment phase of the trial of the offense that the offense was committed:
  (1) in, on, or within 1,000 feet of premises owned, rented, or leased by an institution of higher learning, the premises of a public or private youth center, or a playground; or
  (2) in, on, or within 300 feet of the premises of a public swimming pool or video arcade facility.

(c) The minimum term of confinement or imprisonment for an offense otherwise punishable under Section 481.112(c), (d), (e), or (f), 481.1121(b)(2), (3), or (4), 481.113(c), (d), or (e), 481.114(c), (d), or (e), 81.115(c)-(f), 481.1151(b)(2), (3), (4), or (5), 481.116(c), (d), or (e), 481.1161(b)(4), (5), or (6), 481.117(c), (d), or (e), 481.118(c), (d), or (e), 481.120(b)(4), (5), or (6), or 481.121(b)(4), (5), or (6) is increased by five years and the maximum fine for the offense is doubled if it is shown on the trial of the offense that the offense was committed:

(1) in, on, or within 1,000 feet of the premises of a school, the premises of a public or private youth center, or a playground; or

(2) on a school bus.

(d) An offense otherwise punishable under Section 481.112(b), 481.1121(b)(1), 481.113(b), 481.114(b), 481.115(b), 481.1151(b)(1), 481.116(b), 481.1161(b)(3), 481.120(b)(3), or 481.121(b)(3) is a felony of the third degree if it is shown on the trial of the offense that the offense was committed:

(1) in, on, or within 1,000 feet of any real property that is owned, rented, or leased to a school or school board, the premises of a public or private youth center, or a playground; or

(2) on a school bus.

(e) An offense otherwise punishable under Section 481.117(b), 481.119(a), 481.120(b)(2), or 481.121(b)(2) is a state jail felony if it is shown on the trial of the offense that the offense was committed:

(1) in, on, or within 1,000 feet of any real property that is owned, rented, or leased to a school or school board, the premises of a public or private youth center, or a playground; or

(2) on a school bus.

(f) An offense otherwise punishable under Section 481.118(b), 481.119(b), 481.120(b)(1), or 481.121(b)(1) is a Class A misdemeanor if it is shown on the trial of the offense that the offense was committed:

(1) in, on, or within 1,000 feet of any real property that is owned, rented, or leased to a school or school board, the premises of a public or private youth center, or a playground; or

(2) on a school bus.

(g) Subsection (f) does not apply to an offense if:

(1) the offense was committed inside a private residence; and

(2) no minor was present in the private residence at the time the offense was committed.

(h) Punishment that is increased for a conviction for an offense listed under this section may not run concurrently with punishment for a conviction under any other criminal statute.

Leg.H. Stats. 1993 73rd Leg. Sess. Ch. 888, effective September 1, 1993; Stats. 1995 74th Leg. Sess. Ch. 260, effective May 30, 1995; Stats. 1995 74th Leg. Sess. Chs. 260, 318, Stats. 1997 75th Leg. Sess. Ch. 1063, effective September 1, 1997; Stats. 2003 78th Leg. Sess. Ch. 570, effective June 20, 2003; Stats. 2009 81st Leg. Sess. Ch. 452, effective September 1, 2009; Stats. 2011 82nd Leg. Sess. Ch. 170, effective September 1, 2011; am. Acts 2015, 84th Leg., ch. 839 (S.B. 236), § 1, effective September 1, 2015.

Sec. 481.135. Maps as Evidence of Location or Area.

(a) In a prosecution under Section 481.134, a map produced or reproduced by a municipal or county engineer for the purpose of showing the location and boundaries of drug-free zones is admissible in evidence and is prima facie evidence of the location or boundaries of those areas if the governing body of the municipality or county adopts a resolution or ordinance approving the map as an official finding and record of the location or boundaries of those areas.

(b) A municipal or county engineer may, on request of the governing body of the municipality or county, revise a map that has been approved by the governing body of the municipality or county as provided by Subsection (a).

(c) A municipal or county engineer shall file the original or a copy of every approved or revised map approved as provided by Subsection (a) with the county clerk of each county in which the area is located.

(d) This section does not prevent the prosecution from:

(1) introducing or relying on any other evidence or testimony to establish any element of an offense for which punishment is increased under Section 481.134; or

(2) using or introducing any other map or diagram otherwise admissible under the Texas Rules of Evidence.

Leg.H. Stats. 1993 73rd Leg. Sess. Ch. 888, effective September 1, 1993; Stats. 2005 79th Leg. Sess. Ch. 728, effective Sept. 1, 2005.

Sec. 481.136. Offense: Unlawful Transfer or Receipt of Chemical Precursor.

(a) A person commits an offense if the person sells, transfers, furnishes, or receives a chemical precursor subject to Section 481.077(a) and the person:

(1) does not comply with Section 481.077 or 481.0771;

(2) knowingly makes a false statement in a report or record required by Section 481.077 or 481.0771; or

(3) knowingly violates a rule adopted under Section 481.077 or 481.0771.

(b) An offense under this section is a state jail felony, unless it is shown on the trial of the offense that the defendant has been previously convicted of an offense under this section or Section 481.137, in which event the offense is a felony of the third degree.

Leg.H. Stats. 1997, 75th Leg., ch. 745 (H.B. 1070), § 32, effective January 1, 1998; am. Acts 2001, 77th Leg., ch. 251 (S.B. 753), § 24, effective September 1, 2001; am. Acts 2005, 79th Leg., ch. 282 (H.B. 164), § 8, effective August 1, 2005; am. Acts 2019, 86th Leg., ch. 595 (S.B. 616), § 4.005, effective September 1, 2019.

Sec. 481.137. Offense: Transfer of Precursor Substance for Unlawful Manufacture.

(a) A person commits an offense if the person sells, transfers, or otherwise furnishes a chemical precursor subject to Section 481.077(a) with the knowledge or intent that the recipient will use the chemical precursor to unlawfully manufacture a controlled substance or controlled substance analogue.

(b) An offense under this section is a felony of the third degree.

Leg.H. Stats. 1997 75th Leg. Sess. Ch. 745, effective January 1, 1998; Stats. 2001 77th Leg. Sess. Ch. 251, effective September 1, 2001.

Sec. 481.138. Offense: Unlawful Transfer or Receipt of Chemical Laboratory Apparatus.

(a) A person commits an offense if the person sells, transfers, furnishes, or receives a chemical laboratory apparatus subject to Section 481.080(a) and the person:

    (1) does not comply with Section 481.080;

    (2) knowingly makes a false statement in a report or record required by Section 481.080; or

    (3) knowingly violates a rule adopted under Section 481.080.

(b) An offense under this section is a state jail felony, unless it is shown on the trial of the offense that the defendant has been previously convicted of an offense under this section, in which event the offense is a felony of the third degree.

Leg.H. Stats. 1997, 75th Leg., ch. 745 (H.B. 1070), § 32, effective January 1, 1998; am. Acts 2001, 77th Leg., ch. 251 (S.B. 753), § 26, effective September 1, 2001; am. Acts 2019, 86th Leg., ch. 595 (S.B. 616), § 4.006, effective September 1, 2019.

Sec. 481.139. Offense: Transfer of Chemical Laboratory Apparatus for Unlawful Manufacture.

(a) A person commits an offense if the person sells, transfers, or otherwise furnishes a chemical laboratory apparatus with the knowledge or intent that the recipient will use the apparatus to unlawfully manufacture a controlled substance or controlled substance analogue.

(b) An offense under Subsection (a) is a felony of the third degree.

Leg.H. Stats. 1997 75th Leg. Sess. Ch. 745, effective January 1, 1998; Stats. 2001 77th Leg. Sess. Ch. 251, effective September 1, 2001.

Sec. 481.140. Use of Child in Commission of Offense.

(a) If it is shown at the punishment phase of the trial of an offense otherwise punishable as a state jail felony, felony of the third degree, or felony of the second degree under Section 481.112, 481.1121, 481.113, 481.114, 481.120, or 481.122 that the defendant used or attempted to use a child younger than 18 years of age to commit or assist in the commission of the offense, the punishment is increased by one degree, unless the defendant used or threatened to use force against the child or another to gain the child's assistance, in which event the punishment for the offense is a felony of the first degree.

(b) Notwithstanding Article 42.08, Code of Criminal Procedure, if punishment for a defendant is increased under this section, the court may not order the sentence for the offense to run concurrently with any other sentence the court imposes on the defendant.

Leg.H. Stats. 2001 77th Leg. Sess. Ch. 786, effective June 14, 2001.

Sec. 481.141. Manufacture or Delivery of Controlled Substance Causing Death or Serious Bodily Injury.

(a) If at the guilt or innocence phase of the trial of an offense described by Subsection (b), the judge or jury, whichever is the trier of fact, determines beyond a reasonable doubt that a person died or suffered serious bodily injury as a result of injecting, ingesting, inhaling, or introducing into the person's body any amount of the controlled substance manufactured or delivered by the defendant, regardless of whether the controlled substance was used by itself or with another substance, including a drug, adulterant, or dilutant, the punishment for the offense is increased by one degree.

(b) This section applies to an offense otherwise punishable as a state jail felony, felony of the third degree, or felony of the second degree under Section 481.112, 481.1121, 481.113, 481.114, or 481.122.

(c) Notwithstanding Article 42.08, Code of Criminal Procedure, if punishment for a defendant is increased under this section, the court may not order the sentence for the offense to run concurrently with any other sentence the court imposes on the defendant.

Leg.H. Stats. 2003 78th Leg. Sess. Ch. 712, effective September 1, 2003.

SUBCHAPTER E. FORFEITURE

Sec. 481.151. Definitions.

In this subchapter:

    (1) "Controlled substance property" means a controlled substance, mixture containing a controlled substance, controlled substance analogue, counterfeit controlled substance, drug paraphernalia, chemical precursor, chemical laboratory apparatus, or raw material.

    (2) "Controlled substance plant" means a species of plant from which a controlled substance listed in Schedule I or II may be derived.

    (3) "Summary destruction" or "summarily destroy" means destruction without the necessity of any court action, a court order, or further proceedings.

    (4) "Summary forfeiture" or "summarily forfeit" means forfeiture without the necessity of any court action, a court order, or further proceedings.

Leg.H. Stats. 1991 72nd Leg. Sess. Ch. 141, effective September 1, 1991; Stats. 2001 77th Leg. Sess. Ch. 251, effective September 1, 2001; Stats. 2007, 80th Leg. Sess. Ch. 152, effective May 21, 2007.

Sec. 481.152. Seizure, Summary Forfeiture, and Summary Destruction of Controlled Substance Plants.

(a) Controlled substance plants are subject to seizure and summary forfeiture to the state if:

    (1) the plants have been planted, cultivated, or harvested in violation of this chapter;

    (2) the plants are wild growths; or

    (3) the owners or cultivators of the plants are unknown.

(b) Subsection (a) does not apply to unharvested peyote growing in its natural state.

(c)　If a person who occupies or controls land or premises on which the plants are growing fails on the demand of a peace officer to produce an appropriate registration or proof that the person is the holder of the registration, the officer may seize and summarily forfeit the plants.

(d)　If a controlled substance plant is seized and forfeited under this section, a court may order the disposition of the plant under Section 481.159, or the department or a peace officer may summarily destroy the property under the rules of the department.

Leg.H. Stats. 1989 71st Leg. Sess. Ch. 678, effective September 1, 1989; Stats. 1991 72nd Leg. Sess. Ch. 141, effective September 1, 1991; Stats. 2007, 80th Leg. Sess. Ch. 152, effective May 21, 2007.

Sec. 481.153. Seizure, Summary Forfeiture, and Summary Destruction of Controlled Substance Property.

(a)　Controlled substance property that is manufactured, delivered, or possessed in violation of this chapter is subject to seizure and summary forfeiture to the state.

(b)　If an item of controlled substance property is seized and forfeited under this section, a court may order the disposition of the property under Section 481.159, or the department or a peace officer may summarily destroy the property under the rules of the department.

Leg.H. Amended by Stats. 1991 72nd Leg. Sess. Ch. 141, effective September 1, 1991; Stats. 2007, 80th Leg. Sess. Ch. 152, effective May 21, 2007.

Sec. 481.154. Rules.

(a)　The director may adopt reasonable rules and procedures, not inconsistent with the provisions of this chapter, concerning:
　　(1)　summary forfeiture and summary destruction of controlled substance property or plants;
　　(2)　establishment and operation of a secure storage area;
　　(3)　delegation by a law enforcement agency head of the authority to access a secure storage area; and
　　(4)　minimum tolerance for and the circumstances of loss or destruction during an investigation.

(b)　The rules for the destruction of controlled substance property or plants must require:
　　(1)　more than one person to witness the destruction of the property or plants;
　　(2)　the preparation of an inventory of the property or plants
destroyed; and
　　(3)　the preparation of a statement that contains the names of the persons who witness the destruction and the details of the destruction.

(c)　A document prepared under a rule adopted under this section must be completed, retained, and made available for inspection by the director.

Leg.H. Amended by Stats. 1991 72nd Leg. Sess. Ch. 141, effective September 1, 1991; Stats. 2007, 80th Leg. Sess. Ch. 152, § 6, effective May 21, 2007.

Sec. 481.159. Disposition of Controlled Substance Property or Plant.

(a)　If a district court orders the forfeiture of a controlled substance property or plant under Chapter 59, Code of Criminal Procedure, or under this code, the court shall also order a law enforcement agency to:
　　(1)　retain the property or plant for its official purposes, including use in the investigation of offenses under this code;
　　(2)　deliver the property or plant to a government agency for official purposes;
　　(3)　deliver the property or plant to a person authorized by the court to receive it;
　　(4)　deliver the property or plant to a person authorized by the director to receive it; or
　　(5)　destroy the property or plant that is not otherwise disposed of in the manner prescribed by this subchapter.

(b)　The district court may not require the department to receive, analyze, or retain a controlled substance property or plant forfeited to a law enforcement agency other than the department.

(c)　In order to ensure that a controlled substance property or plant is not diluted, substituted, diverted, or tampered with while being used in the investigation of offenses under this code, law enforcement agencies using the property or plant for this purpose shall:
　　(1)　employ a qualified individual to conduct qualitative and quantitative analyses of the property or plant before and after their use in an investigation;
　　(2)　maintain the property or plant in a secure storage area accessible only to the law enforcement agency head and the individual responsible for analyzing, preserving, and maintaining security over the property or plant; and
　　(3)　maintain a log documenting:
　　　　(A)　the date of issue, date of return, type, amount, and concentration of property or plant used in an investigation; and
　　　　(B)　the signature and the printed or typed name of the peace officer to whom the property or plant was issued and the signature and the printed or typed name of the individual issuing the property or plant.

(d)　A law enforcement agency may contract with another law enforcement agency to provide security that complies with Subsection (c)　　for controlled substance property or plants.

(e)　A law enforcement agency may adopt a written policy with more stringent requirements than those required by Subsection (c). The director may enter and inspect, in accordance with Section 481.181, a location at which an agency maintains records or controlled substance property or plants as required by this section.

(f)　If a law enforcement agency uses a controlled substance property or plant in the investigation of an offense under this code and the property or plant has been transported across state lines before the forfeiture, the agency shall cooperate with a federal agency in the investigation if requested to do so by the federal agency.

(g)　Under the rules of the department, a law enforcement agency head may grant to another person access to a secure storage facility under Subsection (c)(2).

Cont. Sub.

(h) A county, justice, or municipal court may order forfeiture of a controlled substance property or plant, unless the lawful possession of and title to the property or plant can be ascertained. If the court determines that a person had lawful possession of and title to the controlled substance property or plant before it was seized, the court shall order the controlled substance property or plant returned to the person, if the person so desires. The court may only order the destruction of a controlled substance property or plant that is not otherwise disposed of in the manner prescribed by Section 481.160.

(i) If a controlled substance property or plant seized under this chapter was forfeited to an agency for the purpose of destruction or for any purpose other than investigation, the property or plant may not be used in an investigation unless a district court orders disposition under this section and permits the use of the property or plant in the investigation.

Leg.H. Stats. 1989 71st Leg. Sess. Ch. 678, effective September 1, 1989; Stats. 1989 71st Leg., 1st C.S., Ch. 12, effective October 18, 1989; Stats. 1991 72nd Leg. Sess. Ch 141, effective September 1, 1991; am. Acts 2015, 84th Leg., (S.B. 195), § 20, effective September 1, 2016.

Sec. 481.160. Destruction of Excess Quantities.

(a) If a controlled substance property or plant is forfeited under this code or under Chapter 59, Code of Criminal Procedure, the law enforcement agency that seized the property or plant or to which the property or plant is forfeited may summarily destroy the property or plant without a court order before the disposition of a case arising out of the forfeiture if the agency ensures that:

    (1) at least five random and representative samples are taken from the total amount of the property or plant and a sufficient quantity is preserved to provide for discovery by parties entitled to discovery;

    (2) photographs are taken that reasonably depict the total amount of the property or plant; and

    (3) the gross weight or liquid measure of the property or plant is determined, either by actually weighing or measuring the property or plant or by estimating its weight or measurement after making dimensional measurements of the total amount seized.

(b) If the property consists of a single container of liquid, taking and preserving one representative sample complies with Subsection (a)(1).

(c) A representative sample, photograph, or record made under this section is admissible in civil or criminal proceedings in the same manner and to the same extent as if the total quantity of the suspected controlled substance property or plant was offered in evidence, regardless of whether the remainder of the property or plant has been destroyed. An inference or presumption of spoliation does not apply to a property or plant destroyed under this section.

(d) If hazardous waste, residuals, contaminated glassware, associated equipment, or by-products from illicit chemical laboratories or similar operations that create a health or environmental hazard or are not capable of being safely stored are forfeited, those items may be disposed of under Subsection (a) or may be seized and summarily forfeited and destroyed by a law enforcement agency without a court order before the disposition of a case arising out of the forfeiture if current environmental protection standards are followed.

(e) A law enforcement agency seizing and destroying or disposing of materials described in Subsection (d) shall ensure that photographs are taken that reasonably depict the total amount of the materials seized and the manner in which the materials were physically arranged or positioned before seizure.

(f) [Repealed by Stats. 2005 79th Leg. Sess., Ch. 1224, effective September 1, 2005.]

Leg.H. Stats. 1989 71st Leg. Sess. Ch. 678, effective September 1, 1989; Stats. 1989 71st Leg. Sess. Ch. 1100, effective September 1, 1989; Stats. 1991 72nd Leg. Sess. Ch. 14, effective September 1, 1991; Stats. 1991 72nd Leg. Sess. Ch. 285, effective September 1, 1991; Stats. 1997 75th Leg. Sess. Ch. 745, effective January 1, 1998; Stats. 2001 77th Leg. Sess. Ch. 251, effective September 1, 2001; Stats. 2005 79th Leg. Sess., Ch. 1224, effective September 1, 2005.

SUBCHAPTER F. INSPECTIONS, EVIDENCE, AND MISCELLANEOUS LAW ENFORCEMENT PROVISIONS

Sec. 481.181. Inspections.

(a) The director may enter controlled premises at any reasonable time and inspect the premises and items described by Subsection (b) in order to inspect, copy, and verify the correctness of a record, report, or other document required to be made or kept under this chapter and to perform other functions under this chapter. For purposes of this subsection, "reasonable time" means any time during the normal business hours of the person or activity regulated under this chapter or any time an activity regulated under this chapter is occurring on the premises. The director shall:

    (1) state the purpose of the entry;

    (2) display to the owner, operator, or agent in charge of the premises appropriate credentials; and

    (3) deliver to the owner, operator, or agent in charge of the premises a written notice of inspection authority.

(b) The director may:

    (1) inspect and copy a record, report, or other document required to be made or kept under this chapter;

    (2) inspect, within reasonable limits and in a reasonable manner, the controlled premises and all pertinent equipment, finished and unfinished drugs, other substances, and materials, containers, labels, records, files, papers, processes, controls, and facilities as appropriate to verify a record, report, or document required to be kept under this chapter or to administer this chapter;

    (3) examine and inventory stock of a controlled substance and obtain samples of the controlled substance;

    (4) examine a hypodermic syringe, needle, pipe, or other instrument, device, contrivance, equipment, control, container, label, or facility relating to a possible violation of this chapter; and

    (5) examine a material used, intended to be used, or capable of being used to dilute or adulterate a controlled substance.

(c) Unless the owner, operator, or agent in charge of the controlled premises consents in writing, the director may not inspect:

    (1) financial data;

    (2) sales data other than shipment data; or

    (3) pricing data.

Leg.H. Stats. 1989 71st Leg. Sess. Ch. 678, effective September 1, 1989; Stats. 2003 78th Leg. Sess. Ch. 1099, effective September 1, 2003.

Sec. 481.182. Evidentiary Rules Relating to Offer of Delivery.

For the purpose of establishing a delivery under this chapter, proof of an offer to sell must be corroborated by:

    (1) a person other than the person to whom the offer is made; or

    (2) evidence other than a statement of the person to whom the offer is made.

Leg.H. Stats. 1989 71st Leg. Sess. Ch. 678, effective September 1, 1989; Stats. 2003 78th Leg. Sess. Ch. 1099, effective September 1, 2003.

Sec. 481.183. Evidentiary Rules Relating to Drug Paraphernalia.

(a) In considering whether an item is drug paraphernalia under this chapter, a court or other authority shall consider, in addition to all other logically relevant factors, and subject to rules of evidence:

    (1) statements by an owner or person in control of the object concerning its use;

    (2) the existence of any residue of a controlled substance on the object;

    (3) direct or circumstantial evidence of the intent of an owner or other person in control of the object to deliver it to a person whom the person knows or should reasonably know intends to use the object to facilitate a violation of this chapter;

    (4) oral or written instructions provided with the object concerning its use;

    (5) descriptive material accompanying the object that explains or depicts its use;

    (6) the manner in which the object is displayed for sale;

    (7) whether the owner or person in control of the object is a supplier of similar or related items to the community, such as a licensed distributor or dealer of tobacco products;

    (8) direct or circumstantial evidence of the ratio of sales of the object to the total sales of the business enterprise;

    (9) the existence and scope of uses for the object in the community;

    (10) the physical design characteristics of the item; and

    (11) expert testimony concerning the item's use.

(b) The innocence of an owner or other person in charge of an object as to a direct violation of this chapter does not prevent a finding that the object is intended or designed for use as drug paraphernalia.

Leg.H. Stats. 1989 71st Leg. Sess. Ch. 678, effective September 1, 1989; Stats. 2003 78th Leg. Sess. Ch. 1099, effective September 1, 2003.

Sec. 481.184. Burden of Proof; Liabilities.

(a) The state is not required to negate an exemption or exception provided by this chapter in a complaint, information, indictment, or other pleading or in any trial, hearing, or other proceeding under this chapter. A person claiming the benefit of an exemption or exception has the burden of going forward with the evidence with respect to the exemption or exception.

(b) In the absence of proof that a person is the duly authorized holder of an appropriate registration or order form issued under this chapter, the person is presumed not to be the holder of the registration or form. The presumption is subject to rebuttal by a person charged with an offense under this chapter.

(c) This chapter does not impose a liability on an authorized state, county, or municipal officer engaged in the lawful performance of official duties.

Leg.H. Stats. 1989 71st Leg. Sess. Ch. 678, effective September 1, 1989; Stats. 2003 78th Leg. Sess. Ch. 1099, effective September 1, 2003.

Sec. 481.185. Arrest Reports.

(a) Each law enforcement agency in this state shall file monthly with the director a report of all arrests made for drug offenses and quantities of controlled substances seized during the preceding month. The agency shall make the report on a form provided by the director and shall provide the information required by the form.

(b) The director shall publish an annual summary of all drug arrests and controlled substances seized in the state.

Leg.H. Stats. 1989 71st Leg. Sess. Ch. 678, effective September 1, 1989.

Sec. 481.186. Cooperative Arrangements.

(a) The director shall cooperate with federal and state agencies in discharging the director's responsibilities concerning traffic in controlled substances and in suppressing the abuse of controlled substances. The director may:

    (1) arrange for the exchange of information among government officials concerning the use and abuse of controlled substances;

    (2) cooperate in and coordinate training programs concerning controlled substances law enforcement at local and state levels;

    (3) cooperate with the Federal Drug Enforcement Administration and state agencies by establishing a centralized unit to accept, catalog, file, and collect statistics, including records on drug-dependent persons and other controlled substance law offenders in this state and, except as provided by Section 481.068, make the information available for federal, state, and local law enforcement purposes; and

    (4) conduct programs of eradication aimed at destroying wild or illegal growth of plant species from which controlled substances may be extracted.

(b) In the exercise of regulatory functions under this chapter, the director may rely on results, information, and evidence relating to the regulatory functions of this chapter received from the Federal Drug Enforcement Administration or a state agency.

Leg.H. Stats. 1989 71st Leg. Sess. Ch. 678, effective September 1, 1989; Stats. 2003 78th Leg. Sess. Ch. 1099, effective September 1, 2003.

SUBCHAPTER G. THERAPEUTIC RESEARCH PROGRAM

Sec. 481.201. Research Program; Review Board.

  (a) The executive commissioner may establish a controlled substance therapeutic research program for the supervised use of tetrahydrocannabinols for medical and research purposes to be conducted in accordance with this chapter.

  (b) If the executive commissioner establishes the program, the executive commissioner shall create a research program review board. The review board members are appointed by the executive commissioner and serve at the will of the executive commissioner.

  (c) The review board shall be composed of:

    (1) a licensed physician certified by the American Board of Ophthalmology;

    (2) a licensed physician certified by the American Board of Internal Medicine and certified in the subspecialty of medical oncology;

    (3) a licensed physician certified by the American Board of Psychiatry;

    (4) a licensed physician certified by the American Board of Surgery;

    (5) a licensed physician certified by the American Board of Radiology; and

    (6) a licensed attorney with experience in law pertaining to the practice of medicine.

  (d) Members serve without compensation but are entitled to reimbursement for actual and necessary expenses incurred in performing official duties.

Leg.H. Stats. 1989 71st Leg. Sess. Ch. 678, effective September 1, 1989; am. Acts 2015, 84th Leg., ch. 1 (S.B. 219), § 3.1232, effective April 2, 2015.

Sec. 481.202. Review Board Powers and Duties.

  (a) The review board shall review research proposals submitted and medical case histories of persons recommended for participation in a research program and determine which research programs and persons are most suitable for the therapy and research purposes of the program. The review board shall approve the research programs, certify program participants, and conduct periodic reviews of the research and participants.

  (b) The review board, after approval of the executive commissioner, may seek authorization to expand the research program to include diseases not covered by this subchapter.

  (c) The review board shall maintain a record of all persons in charge of approved research programs and of all persons who participate in the program as researchers or as patients.

  (d) The executive commissioner may terminate the distribution of tetrahydrocannabinols and their derivatives to a research program as the executive commissioner determines necessary.

Leg.H. Stats. 1989 71st Leg. Sess. Ch. 678, effective September 1, 1989; am. Acts 2015, 84th Leg., ch. 1 (S.B. 219), § 3.1233, effective April 2, 2015.

Sec. 481.203. Patient Participation.

  (a) A person may not be considered for participation as a recipient of tetrahydrocannabinols and their derivatives through a research program unless the person is recommended to a person in charge of an approved research program and the review board by a physician who is licensed by the Texas Medical Board and is attending the person.

  (b) A physician may not recommend a person for the research program unless the person:

    (1) has glaucoma or cancer;

    (2) is not responding to conventional treatment for glaucoma or cancer or is experiencing severe side effects from treatment; and

    (3) has symptoms or side effects from treatment that may be alleviated by medical use of tetrahydrocannabinols or their derivatives.

Leg.H. Stats. 1989 71st Leg. Sess. Ch. 678, effective September 1, 1989; am. Acts 2015, 84th Leg., ch. 1 (S.B. 219), § 3.1234, effective April 2, 2015.

Sec. 481.204. Acquisition and Distribution of Controlled Substances.

  (a) The executive commissioner shall acquire the tetrahydrocannabinols and their derivatives for use in the research program by contracting with the National Institute on Drug Abuse to receive tetrahydrocannabinols and their derivatives that are safe for human consumption according to the regulations adopted by the institute, the United States Food and Drug Administration, and the Federal Drug Enforcement Administration.

  (b) The executive commissioner shall supervise the distribution of the tetrahydrocannabinols and their derivatives to program participants. The tetrahydrocannabinols and derivatives of tetrahydrocannabinols may be distributed only by the person in charge of the research program to physicians caring for program participant patients, under rules adopted by the executive commissioner in such a manner as to prevent unauthorized diversion of the substances and in compliance with all requirements of the Federal Drug Enforcement Administration. The physician is responsible for dispensing the substances to patients.

Leg.H. Stats. 1989 71st Leg. Sess. Ch. 678, effective September 1, 1989; am. Acts 2015, 84th Leg., ch. 1 (S.B. 219), § 3.1235, effective April 2, 2015.

Sec. 481.205. Rules; Reports.

  (a) The executive commissioner shall adopt rules necessary for implementing the research program.

  (b) If the executive commissioner establishes a program under this subchapter, the commissioner shall publish a report not later than January 1 of each odd-numbered year on the medical effectiveness of the use of tetrahydrocannabinols and their derivatives and any other medical findings of the research program.

Leg.H. Stats. 1989 71st Leg. Sess. Ch. 678, effective September 1, 1989; am. Acts 2015, 84th Leg., ch. 1 (S.B. 219), § 3.1236, effective April 2, 2015.

SUBCHAPTER H. ADMINISTRATIVE PENALTY

Sec. 481.301. Imposition of Penalty.

The department may impose an administrative penalty on a person who violates Section 481.067, 481.077, 481.0771, or 481.080 or a rule or order adopted under any of those sections.

Leg.H. Acts 2007, 80th Leg., ch. 1391 (S.B. 1879), § 5, effective September 1, 2007; am. Acts 2019, 86th Leg., ch. 595 (S.B. 616), § 4.007, effective September 1, 2019.

Sec. 481.302. Amount of Penalty.

(a) The amount of the penalty may not exceed $1,000 for each violation, and each day a violation continues or occurs is a separate violation for purposes of imposing a penalty. The total amount of the penalty assessed for a violation continuing or occurring on separate days under this subsection may not exceed $20,000.

(b) The amount shall be based on:

(1) the seriousness of the violation, including the nature, circumstances, extent, and gravity of the violation;

(2) the threat to health or safety caused by the violation;

(3) the history of previous violations;

(4) the amount necessary to deter a future violation;

(5) whether the violator demonstrated good faith, including when applicable whether the violator made good faith efforts to correct the violation; and

(6) any other matter that justice may require.

Leg.H. Stats. 2007, 80th Leg. Sess. Ch. 1391, effective September 1, 2007.

Sec. 481.303. Report and Notice of Violation and Penalty.

(a) If the department initially determines that a violation occurred, the department shall give written notice of the report to the person by certified mail, registered mail, personal delivery, or another manner of delivery that records the person's receipt of the notice.

(b) The notice must:

(1) include a brief summary of the alleged violation;

(2) state the amount of the recommended penalty; and

(3) inform the person of the person's right to a hearing on the occurrence of the violation, the amount of the penalty, or both.

Leg.H. Stats. 2007, 80th Leg. Sess. Ch. 1391, effective September 1, 2007.

Sec. 481.304. Penalty to Be Paid or Informal Hearing Requested.

(a) Before the 21st day after the date the person receives notice under Section 481.303, the person in writing may:

(1) accept the determination and recommended penalty; or

(2) make a request for an informal hearing held by the department on the occurrence of the violation, the amount of the penalty, or both.

(b) At the conclusion of an informal hearing requested under Subsection (a), the department may modify the amount of the recommended penalty.

(c) If the person accepts the determination and recommended penalty, including any modification of the amount, or if the person fails to timely respond to the notice, the director by order shall approve the determination and impose the recommended penalty.

Leg.H. Stats. 2007, 80th Leg. Sess. Ch. 1391, effective September 1, 2007.

Sec. 481.305. Formal Hearing.

(a) The person may request a formal hearing only after participating in an informal hearing.

(b) The request must be submitted in writing and received by the department before the 21st day after the date the person is notified of the decision from the informal hearing.

(c) If a timely request for a formal hearing is not received, the director by order shall approve the determination from the informal hearing and impose the recommended penalty.

(d) If the person timely requests a formal hearing, the director shall refer the matter to the State Office of Administrative Hearings, which shall promptly set a hearing date and give written notice of the time and place of the hearing to the director and to the person. An administrative law judge of the State Office of Administrative Hearings shall conduct the hearing.

(e) The administrative law judge shall make findings of fact and conclusions of law and promptly issue to the director a proposal for a decision about the occurrence of the violation and the amount of any proposed penalty.

(f) If a penalty is proposed under Subsection (e), the administrative law judge shall include in the proposal for a decision a finding setting out costs, fees, expenses, and reasonable and necessary attorney's fees incurred by the state in bringing the proceeding. The director may adopt the finding and impose the costs, fees, and expenses on the person as part of the final order entered in the proceeding.

Leg.H. Stats. 2007, 80th Leg. Sess. Ch. 1391, effective September 1, 2007.

Sec. 481.306. Decision.

(a) Based on the findings of fact, conclusions of law, and proposal for a decision, the director by order may:
  (1) find that a violation occurred and impose a penalty; or
  (2) find that a violation did not occur.

(b) The notice of the director's order under Subsection (a) that is sent to the person in the manner provided by Chapter 2001, Government Code, must include a statement of the right of the person to judicial review of the order.

Leg.H. Stats. 2007, 80th Leg. Sess. Ch. 1391, effective September 1, 2007.

Sec. 481.307. Options Following Decision: Pay or Appeal.

Before the 31st day after the date the order under Section 481.306 that imposes an administrative penalty becomes final, the person shall:
  (1) pay the penalty; or
  (2) file a petition for judicial review of the order contesting the occurrence of the violation, the amount of the penalty, or both.

Leg.H. Stats. 2007, 80th Leg. Sess. Ch. 1391, effective September 1, 2007.

Sec. 481.308. Stay of Enforcement of Penalty.

(a) Within the period prescribed by Section 481.307, a person who files a petition for judicial review may:
  (1) stay enforcement of the penalty by:
    (A) paying the penalty to the court for placement in an escrow account; or
    (B) giving the court a supersedeas bond approved by the court that:
      (i) is for the amount of the penalty; and
      (ii) is effective until all judicial review of the order is final; or
  (2) request the court to stay enforcement of the penalty by:
    (A) filing with the court a sworn affidavit of the person stating that the person is financially unable to pay the penalty and is financially unable to give the supersedeas bond; and
    (B) sending a copy of the affidavit to the director by certified mail.

(b) Following receipt of a copy of an affidavit under Subsection (a)(2), the director may file with the court, before the sixth day after the date of receipt, a contest to the affidavit. The court shall hold a hearing on the facts alleged in the affidavit as soon as practicable and shall stay the enforcement of the penalty on finding that the alleged facts are true. The person who files an affidavit has the burden of proving that the person is financially unable to pay the penalty or to give a supersedeas bond.

Leg.H. Stats. 2007, 80th Leg. Sess. Ch. 1391, effective September 1, 2007.

Sec. 481.309. Collection of Penalty.

(a) If the person does not pay the penalty and the enforcement of the penalty is not stayed, the penalty may be collected.

(b) The attorney general may sue to collect the penalty.

Leg.H. Stats. 2007, 80th Leg. Sess. Ch. 1391, effective September 1, 2007.

Sec. 481.310. Decision by Court.

(a) If the court sustains the finding that a violation occurred, the court may uphold or reduce the amount of the penalty and order the person to pay the full or reduced amount of the penalty.

(b) If the court does not sustain the finding that a violation occurred, the court shall order that a penalty is not owed.

Leg.H. Stats. 2007, 80th Leg. Sess. Ch. 1391, effective September 1, 2007.

Sec. 481.311. Remittance of Penalty and Interest.

(a) If the person paid the penalty and if the amount of the penalty is reduced or the penalty is not upheld by the court, the court shall order, when the court's judgment becomes final, that the appropriate amount plus accrued interest be remitted to the person before the 31st day after the date that the judgment of the court becomes final.

(b) The interest accrues at the rate charged on loans to depository institutions by the New York Federal Reserve Bank.

(c) The interest shall be paid for the period beginning on the date the penalty is paid and ending on the date the penalty is remitted.

Leg.H. Stats. 2007, 80th Leg. Sess. Ch. 1391, effective September 1, 2007.

Sec. 481.312. Release of Bond.

(a) If the person gave a supersedeas bond and the penalty is not upheld by the court, the court shall order, when the court's judgment becomes final, the release of the bond.

(b) If the person gave a supersedeas bond and the amount of the penalty is reduced, the court shall order the release of the bond after the person pays the reduced amount.

Leg.H. Stats. 2007, 80th Leg. Sess. Ch. 1391, effective September 1, 2007.

Sec. 481.313. Administrative Procedure.

A proceeding to impose the penalty is considered to be a contested case under Chapter 2001, Government Code.

Leg.H. Stats. 2007, 80th Leg. Sess. Ch. 1391, effective September 1, 2007.

Sec. 481.314. Disposition of Penalty.

The department shall send any amount collected as a penalty under this subchapter to the comptroller for deposit to the credit of the general revenue fund.

Leg.H. Stats. 2007, 80th Leg. Sess. Ch. 1391, effective September 1, 2007.

SUBCHAPTER I. INTERAGENCY PRESCRIPTION MONITORING WORK GROUP

Sec. 481.351. Interagency Prescription Monitoring Work Group.

The interagency prescription monitoring work group is created to evaluate the effectiveness of prescription monitoring under this chapter and offer recommendations to improve the effectiveness and efficiency of recordkeeping and other functions related to the regulation of dispensing controlled substances by prescription.

Leg.H. Stats. 2013, 83rd Leg., ch. 1226 (S.B. 1643), § 4, effective September 1, 2013.

Sec. 481.352. Members.

The work group is composed of:
(1) the executive director of the board or the executive director's designee, who serves as chair of the work group;
(2) the commissioner of state health services or the commissioner's designee;
(3) the executive director of the Texas Medical Board or the executive director's designee;
(4) the executive director of the Texas Board of Nursing or the executive director's designee;
(5) the executive director of the Texas Physician Assistant Board or the executive director's designee;
(6) the executive director of the State Board of Dental Examiners or the executive director's designee;
(7) the executive director of the Texas Optometry Board or the executive director's designee;
(8) the executive director of the Texas Department of Licensing and Regulation or the executive director's designee;
(9) the executive director of the State Board of Veterinary Medical Examiners or the executive director's designee; and
(10) a medical examiner appointed by the board.

Leg.H. Stats. 2013, 83rd Leg., ch. 1226 (S.B. 1643), § 4, effective September 1, 2013; am. Acts 2015, 84th Leg., ch. 1268 (S.B. 195), § 22, effective June 20, 2015; am. Acts 2017, 85th Leg., ch. 282 (H.B. 3078), § 61, effective September 1, 2017.

Sec. 481.353. Meetings.

(a) The work group shall meet when necessary as determined by the board.
(b) The work group is subject to Chapter 551, Government Code.
(c) The work group shall proactively engage stakeholders and solicit and take into account input from the public.

Leg.H. Stats. 2013, 83rd Leg., ch. 1226 (S.B. 1643), § 4, effective September 1, 2013; am. Acts 2019, 86th Leg., ch. 965 (S.B. 683), § 4, effective September 1, 2019; am. Acts 2019, 86th Leg., ch. 1144 (H.B. 2847), § 4.004, effective September 1, 2019.

Sec. 481.354. Report.

Not later than December 1 of each even-numbered year, the work group shall submit to the legislature its recommendations relating to prescription monitoring.

Leg.H. Stats. 2013, 83rd Leg., ch. 1226 (S.B. 1643), § 4, effective September 1, 2013.

SIMULATED CONTROLLED SUBSTANCES
HEALTH AND SAFETY CODE, CHAPTER 482

Sec. 482.001. Definitions.

In this chapter:
  (1) "Controlled substance" has the meaning assigned by Section 481.002 (Texas Controlled Substances Act).
  (2) "Deliver" means to transfer, actually or constructively, from one person to another a simulated controlled substance, regardless of whether there is an agency relationship. The term includes offering to sell a simulated controlled substance.
  (3) "Manufacture" means to make a simulated controlled substance and includes the preparation of the substance in dosage form by mixing, compounding, encapsulating, tableting, or any other process.
  (4) "Simulated controlled substance" means a substance that is purported to be a controlled substance, but is chemically different from the controlled substance it is purported to be.

Leg.H. Stats. 1989 71st Leg. Sess. Ch. 678, effective September 1, 1989.

Sec. 482.002. Unlawful Delivery or Manufacture with Intent to Deliver; Criminal Penalty.

  (a) A person commits an offense if the person knowingly or intentionally manufactures with the intent to deliver or delivers a simulated controlled substance and the person:
   (1) expressly represents the substance to be a controlled substance;
   (2) represents the substance to be a controlled substance in a manner that would lead a reasonable person to believe that the substance is a controlled substance; or
   (3) states to the person receiving or intended to receive the simulated controlled substance that the person may successfully represent the substance to be a controlled substance to a third party.
  (b) It is a defense to prosecution under this section that the person manufacturing with the intent to deliver or delivering the simulated controlled substance was:
   (1) acting in the discharge of the person's official duties as a peace officer;
   (2) manufacturing the substance for or delivering the substance to a licensed medical practitioner for use as a placebo in the course of the practitioner's research or practice; or
   (3) a licensed medical practitioner, pharmacist, or other person authorized to dispense or administer a controlled substance, and the person was acting in the legitimate performance of the person's professional duties.
  (c) It is not a defense to prosecution under this section that the person manufacturing with the intent to deliver or delivering the simulated controlled substance believed the substance to be a controlled substance.
  (d) An offense under this section is a state jail felony.

Leg.H. Stats. 1989 71st Leg. Sess. Ch. 678, effective September 1, 1989; Stats. 1993 73rd Leg. Sess. Ch. 900, effective September 1, 1994.

Sec. 482.003. Evidentiary Rules.

  (a) In determining whether a person has represented a simulated controlled substance to be a controlled substance in a manner that would lead a reasonable person to believe the substance was a controlled substance, a court may consider, in addition to all other logically relevant factors, whether:
   (1) the simulated controlled substance was packaged in a manner normally used for the delivery of a controlled substance;
   (2) the delivery or intended delivery included an exchange of or demand for property as consideration for delivery of the substance and the amount of the consideration was substantially in excess of the reasonable value of the simulated controlled substance; and
   (3) the physical appearance of the finished product containing the substance was substantially identical to a controlled substance.
  (b) Proof of an offer to sell a simulated controlled substance must be corroborated by a person other than the offeree or by evidence other than a statement of the offeree.

Leg.H. Stats. 1989 71st Leg. Sess. Ch. 678, effective September 1, 1989.

Sec. 482.004. Summary Forfeiture.

A simulated controlled substance seized as a result of an offense under this chapter is subject to summary forfeiture and to destruction or disposition in the same manner as is a controlled substance property under Subchapter E, Chapter 481.

Leg.H. Stats. 1989 71st Leg. Sess. Ch. 678, effective September 1, 1989; Stats. 1991 72nd Leg. Sess. Ch. 141, effective September 1, 1991.

Sec. 482.005. Preparatory Offenses.

Title 4, Penal Code, applies to an offense under this chapter.

Leg.H. Stats. 1995 74th Leg. Sess. Ch. 318, effective September 1, 1995.

Cont. Sub.

ABUSABLE SYNTHETIC SUBSTANCES
HEALTH AND SAFETY CODE, CHAPTER 484

Sec. 484.001. Definitions.

In this chapter:
   (1) "Abusable synthetic substance" means a substance that:
       (A) is not otherwise regulated under this title or under federal law;
       (B) is intended to mimic a controlled substance or controlled substance analogue; and
       (C) when inhaled, ingested, or otherwise introduced into a person's body:
           (i)   produces an effect on the central nervous system similar to the effect produced by a controlled substance or controlled substance analogue;
           (ii) creates a condition of intoxication, hallucination, or elation similar to a condition produced by a controlled substance or controlled substance analogue; or
           (iii) changes, distorts, or disturbs the person's eyesight, thinking process, balance, or coordination in a manner similar to a controlled substance or controlled substance analogue.
   (2) "Business" includes trade and commerce and advertising, selling, and buying service or property.
   (3) "Mislabeled" means varying from the standard of truth or disclosure in labeling prescribed by law or set by established commercial usage.
   (4) "Sell" and "sale" include offer for sale, advertise for sale, expose for sale, keep for the purpose of sale, deliver for or after sale, solicit and offer to buy, and every disposition for value.

Leg.H. Stats 2015, 84th Leg., ch. 187 (S.B. 461), § 1, effective September 1, 2015.

Sec. 484.002. Prohibited Acts.

   (a) A person commits an offense if in the course of business the person knowingly produces, distributes, sells, or offers for sale a mislabeled abusable synthetic substance.
   (b) An offense under this section is a Class C misdemeanor, except that the offense is a Class A misdemeanor if it is shown on the trial of the offense that the actor has previously been convicted of an offense under this section or of an offense under Section 32.42(b)(4), Penal Code, and the adulterated or mislabeled commodity was an abusable synthetic substance.
   (c) If conduct constituting an offense under this section also constitutes an offense under another provision of law, the person may be prosecuted under either this section or the other provision.

Leg.H. Stats 2015, 84th Leg., ch. 187 (S.B. 461), § 1, effective September 1, 2015.

Sec. 484.003. Civil Penalty.

   (a) The attorney general or a district, county, or city attorney may institute an action in district court to collect a civil penalty from a person who in the course of business produces, distributes, sells, or offers for sale a mislabeled abusable synthetic substance.
   (b) The civil penalty may not exceed $25,000 a day for each offense. Each day an offense is committed constitutes a separate violation for purposes of the penalty assessment.
   (c) The court shall consider the following in determining the amount of the penalty:
       (1) the person's history of any previous offenses under Section 484.002 or under Section 32.42(b)(4), Penal Code, relating to the sale of a mislabeled abusable synthetic substance;
       (2) the seriousness of the offense;
       (3) any hazard posed to the public health and safety by the offense; and
       (4) demonstrations of good faith by the person charged.
   (d) Venue for a suit brought under this section is in the city or county in which the offense occurred or in Travis County.
   (e) A civil penalty recovered in a suit instituted by a local government under this section shall be paid to that local government.

Leg.H. Stats 2015, 84th Leg., ch. 187 (S.B. 461), § 1, effective September 1, 2015.

Sec. 484.004. Affirmative Defense.

It is an affirmative defense to prosecution or liability under this chapter that:
   (1) the abusable synthetic substance was approved for use, sale, or distribution by the United States Food and Drug Administration or other state or federal regulatory agency with authority to approve the substance's use, sale, or distribution; and
   (2) the abusable synthetic substance was lawfully produced, distributed, sold, or offered for sale by the person who is the subject of the criminal or civil action.

Leg.H. Stats 2015, 84th Leg., ch. 187 (S.B. 461), § 1, effective September 1, 2015.

Sec. 484.005. No Defense.

In a prosecution or civil action under this chapter, the fact that the abusable synthetic substance was in packaging labeled with "Not for Human Consumption," or other wording indicating the substance is not intended to be ingested, is not a defense.

Leg.H. Stats 2015, 84th Leg., ch. 187 (S.B. 461), § 1, effective September 1, 2015.

ABUSABLE VOLATILE CHEMICALS
HEALTH AND SAFETY CODE, CHAPTER 485

SUBCHAPTER A. GENERAL PROVISIONS

Sec. 485.001. Definitions.

In this chapter:
  (1) "Abusable volatile chemical" means:
      (A) a chemical, including aerosol paint, that:
          (i) is packaged in a container subject to the labeling requirements concerning precautions against inhalation established under the Federal Hazardous Substances Act (15 U.S.C. Section 1261 et seq.), as amended, and regulations adopted under that Act and is labeled with the statement of principal hazard on the principal display panel "VAPOR HARMFUL" or other labeling requirement subsequently established under that Act or those regulations;
          (ii) when inhaled, ingested, or otherwise introduced into a person's body, may:
              (a) affect the person's central nervous system;
              (b) create or induce in the person a condition of intoxication, hallucination, or elation; or
              (c) change, distort, or disturb the person's eyesight, thinking process, balance, or coordination; and
          (iii) is not:
              (a) a pesticide subject to Chapter 76, Agriculture Code, or to the Federal Environmental Pesticide Control Act of 1972 (7 U.S.C. Section 136 et seq.), as amended;
              (b) a food, drug, or cosmetic subject to Chapter 431 or to the Federal Food, Drug, and Cosmetic Act (21 U.S.C. Section 301 et seq.), as amended; or
              (c) a beverage subject to the Federal Alcohol Administration Act (27 U.S.C. Section 201 et seq.), as amended; or
      (B) nitrous oxide that is not:
          (i) a pesticide subject to Chapter 76, Agriculture Code, or to the Federal Environmental Pesticide Control Act of 1972 (7 U.S.C. Section 136 et seq.), as amended;
          (ii) a food, drug, or cosmetic subject to Chapter 431 or to the Federal Food, Drug, and Cosmetic Act (21 U.S.C. Section 301 et seq.), as amended; or
          (iii) a beverage subject to the Federal Alcohol Administration Act (27 U.S.C. Section 201 et seq.), as amended.
  (2) "Aerosol paint" means an aerosolized paint product, including a clear or pigmented lacquer or finish.
  (3) [Repealed by Acts 2015, 84th Leg., ch. 1 (S.B. 219), § 3.1639(94), effective April 2, 2015.]
  (4) "Commissioner" means the commissioner of state health services.
  (5) "Deliver" means to make the actual or constructive transfer from one person to another of an abusable volatile chemical, regardless of whether there is an agency relationship. The term includes an offer to sell an abusable volatile chemical.
  (6) "Delivery" means the act of delivering.
  (7) "Department" means the Department of State Health Services.
  (7-a) "Executive commissioner" means the executive commissioner of the Health and Human Services Commission.
  (8) "Inhalant paraphernalia" means equipment or materials of any kind that are intended for use in inhaling, ingesting, or otherwise introducing into the human body an abusable volatile chemical. The term includes a tube, balloon, bag, fabric, bottle, or other container used to concentrate or hold in suspension an abusable volatile chemical or vapors of the chemical.
  (9) "Sell" includes a conveyance, exchange, barter, or trade.

Leg.H. Stats. 1989 71st Leg. Sess. Ch. 678, effective September 1, 1989; Stats. 2001 77th Leg. Sess. Ch. 1463, effective September 1, 2001; am. Acts 2015, 84th Leg., ch. 1 (S.B. 219), § 3.1241, 3.1639(94), effective April 2, 2015.

Sec. 485.002. Rules.

The executive commissioner may adopt rules necessary to comply with any labeling requirements concerning precautions against inhalation of an abusable volatile chemical established under the Federal Hazardous Substances Act (15 U.S.C. Section 1261 et seq.), as amended, or under regulations adopted under that Act.

Leg.H. Stats. 1989, 71st Leg., ch. 678 (H.B. 2136), § 1, effective September 1, 1989; am. Acts 2001, 77th Leg., ch. 1463 (H.B. 2950), § 2, effective September 1, 2001; am. Acts 2015, 84th Leg., ch. 1 (S.B. 219), §§ 3.1241, 3.1639(94), effective April 2, 2015.

SUBCHAPTER B. SALES PERMITS AND SIGNS

Sec. 485.011. Permit Required.

A person may not sell an abusable volatile chemical at retail unless the person or the person's employer holds, at the time of the sale, a volatile chemical sales permit for the location of the sale.

Leg.H. Stats. 1989 71st Leg. Sess. Ch. 678, effective September 1, 1989; Stats. 2001 77th Leg. Sess. Ch. 1463, effective September 1, 2001 (renumbered from Sec. 485.012).

Cont. Sub.

Sec. 485.012. Issuance and Renewal of Permit.

(a) To be eligible for the issuance or renewal of a volatile chemical sales permit, a person must:

    (1) hold a sales tax permit that has been issued to the person;

    (2) complete and return to the department an application as required by the department; and

    (3) pay to the department the application fee established under Section 485.013 for each location at which an abusable volatile chemical may be sold by the person holding a volatile chemical sales permit.

(b) The executive commissioner shall adopt rules as necessary to administer this chapter, including application procedures and procedures by which the department shall give each permit holder reasonable notice of permit expiration and renewal requirements.

(c) The department shall issue or deny a permit and notify the applicant of the department's action not later than the 60th day after the date on which the department receives the complete application and appropriate fee. If the department denies an application, the department shall include in the notice the reasons for the denial.

(d) A permit issued or renewed under this chapter is valid for two years from the date of issuance or renewal.

(e) A permit is not valid if the permit holder has been convicted more than once in the preceding year of an offense committed:

    (1) at a location for which the permit is issued; and

    (2) under Section 485.031, 485.032, or 485.033.

(f) A permit issued by the department is the property of the department and must be surrendered on demand by the department.

(g) The department shall prepare an annual roster of permit holders.

(h) The department shall monitor and enforce compliance with this chapter.

Leg.H. Stats. 1989 71st Leg. Sess. Ch. 678, effective September 1, 1989; Stats. 2001 77th Leg. Sess. Ch. 1463, effective September 1, 2001 (renumbered from Sec. 485.013); am. Acts 2015, 84th Leg., ch. 1 (S.B. 219), § 3.1243, effective April 2, 2015.

Sec. 485.013. Fee.

The executive commissioner by rule may establish fees in amounts as prescribed by Section 12.0111.

Leg.H. Stats. 1989 71st Leg. Sess. Ch. 678, effective September 1, 1989; Stats. 1991 72nd Leg. Sess. Ch. 14, effective September 1, 1991; Stats. 2001 77th Leg. Sess. Ch. 1463, effective September 1, 2001; am. Acts 2015, 84th Leg., ch. 1 (S.B. 219), § 3.1244, effective April 2, 2015.

Sec. 485.014. Permit Available for Inspection.

A permit holder must have the volatile chemical sales permit or a copy of the permit available for inspection by the public at each location where the permit holder sells an abusable volatile chemical.

Leg.H. Stats. 1989 71st Leg. Sess. Ch. 678, effective September 1, 1989; Stats. 2001 77th Leg. Sess. Ch. 1463, effective September 1, 2001.

Sec. 485.015. Refusal to Issue or Renew Permit.

A proceeding for the failure to issue or renew a volatile chemical sales permit under Section 485.012 or for an appeal from that proceeding is governed by the contested case provisions of Chapter 2001, Government Code.

Leg.H. Stats. 1989 71st Leg. Sess. Ch. 678, effective September 1, 1989; Stats. 1995 74th Leg. Sess. Ch. 76; Stats. 2001 77th Leg. Sess. Ch. 1463, effective September 1, 2001.

Sec. 485.016. Disposition of Funds; Education and Prevention Programs.

(a) The department shall account for all amounts received under Section 485.013 and send those amounts to the comptroller.

(b) The comptroller shall deposit the amounts received under Subsection (a) in the state treasury to the credit of the general revenue fund to be used only by the department to:

    (1) administer, monitor, and enforce this chapter; and

    (2) finance statewide education projects concerning the hazards of abusable volatile chemicals and the prevention of inhalant abuse.

Leg.H. Stats. 1989 71st Leg. Sess. Ch. 678, effective September 1, 1989; Stats. 1991 72nd Leg. Sess. Ch. 14, effective September 1, 1991; Stats. 2001 77th Leg. Sess. Ch. 1463, effective September 1, 2001.

Sec. 485.017. Signs.

A business establishment that sells an abusable volatile chemical at retail shall display a conspicuous sign, in English and Spanish, that states the following:

It is unlawful for a person to sell or deliver an abusable volatile chemical to a person under 18 years of age. Except in limited situations, such an offense is a state jail felony.

It is also unlawful for a person to abuse a volatile chemical by inhaling, ingesting, applying, using, or possessing with intent to inhale, ingest, apply, or use a volatile chemical in a manner designed to affect the central nervous system. Such an offense is a Class B misdemeanor.

Leg.H. Stats. 1989 71st Leg. Sess. Ch. 678, effective September 1, 1989; Stats. 2001 77th Leg. Sess. Ch. 1463, effective September 1, 2001.

Sec. 485.018. Prohibited Ordinance and Rule.

(a) A political subdivision or an agency of this state may not enact an ordinance or rule that requires a business establishment to display an abusable volatile chemical, other than aerosol paint, in a manner that makes the chemical accessible to patrons of the business only with the assistance of personnel of the business.

(b) This section does not apply to an ordinance or rule that was enacted before September 1, 1989.

Leg.H. Stats. 1991 72nd Leg. Sess. Ch. 14, effective September 1, 1991; Stats. 2001 77th Leg. Sess. Ch. 1463, effective September 1, 2001; Stats. 2009 81st Leg. Sess. Ch. 1130, effective September 1, 2009.

Sec. 485.019. Restriction of Access to Aerosol Paint.

(a) A business establishment that holds a permit under Section 485.012 and that displays aerosol paint shall display the paint:

    (1) in a place that is in the line of sight of a cashier or in the line of sight from a workstation normally continuously occupied during business hours;

    (2) in a manner that makes the paint accessible to a patron of the business establishment only with the assistance of an employee of the establishment; or

    (3) in an area electronically protected, or viewed by surveillance equipment that is monitored, during business hours.

(b) This section does not apply to a business establishment that has in place a computerized checkout system at the point of sale for merchandise that alerts the cashier that a person purchasing aerosol paint must be over 18 years of age.

(c) A court may issue a warning to a business establishment or impose a civil penalty of $50 on the business establishment for a first violation of this section. After receiving a warning or penalty for the first violation, the business establishment is liable to the state for a civil penalty of $100 for each subsequent violation.

(d) For the third violation of this section in a calendar year, a court may issue an injunction prohibiting the business establishment from selling aerosol paint for a period of not more than two years. A business establishment that violates the injunction is liable to the state for a civil penalty of $100, in addition to any other penalty authorized by law, for each day the violation continues.

(e) If a business establishment fails to pay a civil penalty under this section, the court may issue an injunction prohibiting the establishment from selling aerosol paint until the establishment pays the penalty, attorney's fees, and court costs.

(f) The district or county attorney for the county in which a violation of this section is alleged to have occurred, or the attorney general, if requested by the district or county attorney for that county, may file suit for the issuance of a warning, the collection of a penalty, or the issuance of an injunction.

(g) A penalty collected under this section shall be sent to the comptroller for deposit in the state treasury to the credit of the general revenue fund.

(h) This section applies only to a business establishment that is located in a county with a population of 75,000 or more.

Leg.H. Stats. 1997 75th Leg. Sess. Ch. 593, effective September 1, 1997; Stats. 2001, 77th Leg. Sess. Ch. 1463, effective September 1, 2001.

SUBCHAPTER C. CRIMINAL PENALTIES

Sec. 485.031. Possession and Use.

(a) A person commits an offense if the person inhales, ingests, applies, uses, or possesses an abusable volatile chemical with intent to inhale, ingest, apply, or use the chemical in a manner:

    (1) contrary to directions for use, cautions, or warnings appearing on a label of a container of the chemical; and

    (2) designed to:

        (A) affect the person's central nervous system;

        (B) create or induce a condition of intoxication, hallucination, or elation; or

        (C) change, distort, or disturb the person's eyesight, thinking process, balance, or coordination.

(b) An offense under this section is a Class B misdemeanor.

Leg.H. Stats. 1989 71st Leg. Sess. Ch. 678, effective September 1, 1989; Stats. 2001 77th Leg. Sess. Ch. 1463, effective September 1, 2001.

Sec. 485.032. Delivery to a Minor.

(a) A person commits an offense if the person knowingly delivers an abusable volatile chemical to a person who is younger than 18 years of age.

(b) It is a defense to prosecution under this section that:

    (1) the abusable volatile chemical that was delivered contains additive material that effectively discourages intentional abuse by inhalation; or

    (2) the person making the delivery is not the manufacturer of the chemical and the manufacturer of the chemical failed to label the chemical with the statement of principal hazard on the principal display panel "VAPOR HARMFUL" or other labeling requirement subsequently established under the Federal Hazardous Substances Act (15 U.S.C. Section 1261 et seq.), as amended, or regulations subsequently adopted under that Act.

(c) It is an affirmative defense to prosecution under this section that:

    (1) the person making the delivery is an adult having supervisory responsibility over the person younger than 18 years of age and:

        (A) the adult permits the use of the abusable volatile chemical only under the adult's direct supervision and in the adult's presence and only for its intended purpose; and

        (B) the adult removes the chemical from the person younger than 18 years of age on completion of that use; or

(2) the person to whom the abusable volatile chemical was delivered presented to the defendant an apparently valid Texas driver's license or an identification certificate, issued by the Department of Public Safety of the State of Texas and containing a physical description consistent with the person's appearance, that purported to establish that the person was 18 years of age or older.

(d) Except as provided by Subsections (e) and (f), an offense under this section is a state jail felony.

(e) An offense under this section is a Class B misdemeanor if it is shown on the trial of the defendant that at the time of the delivery the defendant or the defendant's employer held a volatile chemical sales permit for the location of the sale.

(f) An offense under this section is a Class A misdemeanor if it is shown on the trial of the defendant that at the time of the delivery the defendant or the defendant's employer:

(1) did not hold a volatile chemical sales permit but did hold a sales tax permit for the location of the sale; and

(2) had not been convicted previously under this section for an offense committed after January 1, 1988.

Leg.H. Stats. 1989 71st Leg. Sess. Ch. 678, effective September 1, 1989; Stats. 2001 77th Leg. Sess. Ch. 1463, effective September 1, 2001 (renumbered from Sec. 485.033).

Sec. 485.033. Inhalant Paraphernalia.

(a) A person commits an offense if the person knowingly uses or possesses with intent to use inhalant paraphernalia to inhale, ingest, or otherwise introduce into the human body an abusable volatile chemical in violation of Section 485.031.

(b) A person commits an offense if the person:

(1) knowingly:

(A) delivers or sells inhalant paraphernalia;

(B) possesses, with intent to deliver or sell, inhalant paraphernalia; or

(C) manufactures, with intent to deliver or sell, inhalant paraphernalia; and

(2) at the time of the act described by Subdivision (1), knows that the person who receives or is intended to receive the paraphernalia intends that it be used to inhale, ingest, apply, use, or otherwise introduce into the human body a volatile chemical in violation of Section 485.031.

(c) An offense under Subsection (a) is a Class B misdemeanor, and an offense under Subsection (b) is a Class A misdemeanor.

Leg.H. Stats. 1989 71st Leg. Sess. Ch. 678, effective September 1, 1989; Stats. 1991, 72nd Leg. Sess. Ch. 14, effective September 1, 1991; Stats. 2001 77th Leg. Sess. Ch. 1463, effective September 1, 2001 (renumbered from Sec. 485.034).

Sec. 485.034. Failure to Post Sign.

(a) A person commits an offense if the person sells an abusable volatile chemical in a business establishment and the person does not display the sign required by Section 485.017.

(b) An offense under this section is a Class C misdemeanor.

Leg.H. Stats. 1989 71st Leg. Sess. Ch. 678, effective September 1, 1989; Stats. 2001 77th Leg. Sess. Ch. 1463, effective September 1, 2001 (renumbered from Sec. 485.035).

Sec. 485.035. Sale without Permit.

(a) A person commits an offense if the person sells an abusable volatile chemical in violation of Section 485.011 and the purchaser is 18 years of age or older.

(b) An offense under this section is a Class B misdemeanor.

Leg.H. Stats. 1989 71st Leg. Sess. Ch. 678, effective September 1, 1989; Stats. 2001 77th Leg. Sess. Ch. 1463, effective September 1, 2001 (renumbered from Sec. 485.036).

Sec. 485.036. Proof of Offer to Sell.

Proof of an offer to sell an abusable volatile chemical must be corroborated by a person other than the offeree or by evidence other than a statement of the offeree.

Leg.H. Stats. 1989 71st Leg. Sess. Ch. 678, effective September 1, 1989; Stats. 2001 77th Leg. Sess. Ch. 1463, effective September 1, 2001 (renumbered from Sec. 485.037).

Sec. 485.037. Summary Forfeiture.

An abusable volatile chemical or inhalant paraphernalia seized as a result of an offense under this chapter is subject to summary forfeiture and to destruction or disposition in the same manner as controlled substance property under Subchapter E, Chapter 481.

Leg.H. Stats. 1989 71st Leg. Sess. Ch. 678, effective September 1, 1989; Stats. 2001 77th Leg. Sess. Ch. 1463, effective September 1, 2001 (renumbered from Sec. 485.038).

Sec. 485.038. Preparatory Offenses.

Title 4, Penal Code, applies to an offense under this subchapter.

Leg.H. Stats. 1995 74th Leg. Sess. Ch. 318; Stats. 2001 77th Leg. Sess. Ch. 1463, effective September 1, 2001 (renumbered from Sec. 485.039).

SUBCHAPTER D. ADMINISTRATIVE PENALTY

Sec. 485.101. Imposition of Penalty.

(a) The department may impose an administrative penalty on a person who sells abusable glue or aerosol paint at retail who violates this chapter or a rule or order adopted under this chapter.

(b) A penalty collected under this subchapter shall be deposited in the state treasury in the general revenue fund.

Leg.H. Stats. 1999 76th Leg. Sess. Ch. 1411, effective September 1, 1999.

Sec. 485.102. Amount of Penalty.

(a) The amount of the penalty may not exceed $1,000 for each violation, and each day a violation continues or occurs is a separate violation for purposes of imposing a penalty. The total amount of the penalty assessed for a violation continuing or occurring on separate days under this subsection may not exceed $5,000.

(b) The amount shall be based on:

    (1) the seriousness of the violation, including the nature, circumstances, extent, and gravity of the violation;

    (2) the threat to health or safety caused by the violation;

    (3) the history of previous violations;

    (4) the amount necessary to deter a future violation;

    (5) whether the violator demonstrated good faith, including when applicable whether the violator made good faith efforts to correct the violation; and

    (6) any other matter that justice may require.

Leg.H. Stats. 1999 76th Leg. Sess. Ch. 1411, effective September 1, 1999.

Sec. 485.103. Report and Notice of Violation and Penalty.

(a) If the department initially determines that a violation occurred, the department shall give written notice of the report by certified mail to the person.

(b) The notice must:

    (1) include a brief summary of the alleged violation;

    (2) state the amount of the recommended penalty; and

    (3) inform the person of the person's right to a hearing on the occurrence of the violation, the amount of the penalty, or both.

Leg.H. Stats. 1999 76th Leg. Sess. Ch. 1411, effective September 1, 1999.

Sec. 485.104. Penalty to Be Paid or Hearing Requested.

(a) Within 20 days after the date the person receives the notice sent under Section 485.103, the person in writing may:

    (1) accept the determination and recommended penalty of the department; or

    (2) make a request for a hearing on the occurrence of the violation, the amount of the penalty, or both.

(b) If the person accepts the determination and recommended penalty or if the person fails to respond to the notice, the department by order shall impose the recommended penalty.

Leg.H. Stats. 1999 76th Leg. Sess. Ch. 1411, effective September 1, 1999; ; am. Acts 2015, 84th Leg., ch. 1 (S.B. 219), § 3.1245, effective April 2, 2015.

Sec. 485.105. Hearing.

(a) If the person requests a hearing, the department shall refer the matter to the State Office of Administrative Hearings, which shall promptly set a hearing date. The department shall give written notice of the time and place of the hearing to the person. An administrative law judge of the State Office of Administrative Hearings shall conduct the hearing.

(b) The administrative law judge shall make findings of fact and conclusions of law and promptly issue to the department a written proposal for a decision about the occurrence of the violation and the amount of a proposed penalty.

Leg.H. Stats. 1999 76th Leg. Sess. Ch. 1411, effective September 1, 1999; am. Acts 2015, 84th Leg., ch. 1 (S.B. 219), § 3.1246, effective April 2, 2015.

Sec. 485.106. Decision by Department.

(a) Based on the findings of fact, conclusions of law, and proposal for a decision, the department by order may:

    (1) find that a violation occurred and impose a penalty; or

    (2) find that a violation did not occur.

(b) The notice of the department's order under Subsection (a) that is sent to the person in accordance with Chapter 2001, Government Code, must include a statement of the right of the person to judicial review of the order.

Leg.H. Stats. 1999 76th Leg. Sess. Ch. 1411, effective September 1, 1999; am. Acts 2015, 84th Leg., ch. 1 (S.B. 219), § 3.1247, effective April 2, 2015.

Sec. 485.107. Options Following Decision: Pay or Appeal.

Within 30 days after the date the order of the department under Section 485.106 that imposes an administrative penalty becomes final, the person shall:

(1) pay the penalty; or

(2) file a petition for judicial review of the department's order contesting the occurrence of the violation, the amount of the penalty, or both.

Leg.H. Stats. 1999 76th Leg. Sess. Ch. 1411, effective September 1, 1999; am. Acts 2015, 84th Leg., ch. 1 (S.B. 219), § 3.1248, effective April 2, 2015.

Sec. 485.108. Stay of Enforcement of Penalty.

(a) Within the 30-day period prescribed by Section 485.107, a person who files a petition for judicial review may:

(1) stay enforcement of the penalty by:

(A) paying the penalty to the court for placement in an escrow account; or

(B) giving the court a supersedeas bond approved by the court that:

(i) is for the amount of the penalty; and

(ii) is effective until all judicial review of the department's order is final; or

(2) request the court to stay enforcement of the penalty by:

(A) filing with the court a sworn affidavit of the person stating that the person is financially unable to pay the penalty and is financially unable to give the supersedeas bond; and

(B) sending a copy of the affidavit to the department by certified mail.

(b) If the department receives a copy of an affidavit under Subsection (a)(2), the department may file with the court, within five days after the date the copy is received, a contest to the affidavit. The court shall hold a hearing on the facts alleged in the affidavit as soon as practicable and shall stay the enforcement of the penalty on finding that the alleged facts are true. The person who files an affidavit has the burden of proving that the person is financially unable to pay the penalty or to give a supersedeas bond.

Leg.H. Stats. 1999 76th Leg. Sess. Ch. 1411, effective September 1, 1999; am. Acts 2015, 84th Leg., ch. 1 (S.B. 219), § 3.1249, effective April 2, 2015.

Sec. 485.109. Collection of Penalty.

(a) If the person does not pay the penalty and the enforcement of the penalty is not stayed, the penalty may be collected.

(b) The attorney general may sue to collect the penalty.

Leg.H. Stats. 1999 76th Leg. Sess. Ch. 1411, effective September 1, 1999.

Sec. 485.110. Decision by Court.

(a) If the court sustains the finding that a violation occurred, the court may uphold or reduce the amount of the penalty and order the person to pay the full or reduced amount of the penalty.

(b) If the court does not sustain the finding that a violation occurred, the court shall order that a penalty is not owed.

Leg.H. Stats. 1999 76th Leg. Sess. Ch. 1411, effective September 1, 1999.

Sec. 485.111. Remittance of Penalty and Interest.

(a) If the person paid the penalty and if the amount of the penalty is reduced or the penalty is not upheld by the court, the court shall order, when the court's judgment becomes final, that the appropriate amount plus accrued interest be remitted to the person within 30 days after the date that the judgment of the court becomes final.

(b) The interest accrues at the rate charged on loans to depository institutions by the New York Federal Reserve Bank.

(c) The interest shall be paid for the period beginning on the date the penalty is paid and ending on the date the penalty is remitted.

Leg.H. Stats. 1999 76th Leg. Sess. Ch. 1411, effective September 1, 1999.

Sec. 485.112. Release of Bond.

(a) If the person gave a supersedeas bond and the penalty is not upheld by the court, the court shall order, when the court's judgment becomes final, the release of the bond.

(b) If the person gave a supersedeas bond and the amount of the penalty is reduced, the court shall order the release of the bond after the person pays the reduced amount.

Leg.H. Stats. 1999 76th Leg. Sess. Ch. 1411, effective September 1, 1999.

Sec. 485.113. Administrative Procedure.

A proceeding to impose the penalty is considered to be a contested case under Chapter 2001, Government Code.

Leg.H. Stats. 1999 76th Leg. Sess. Ch. 1411, effective September 1, 1999.

CONTROLLED SUBSTANCES RULES
37 TAC, PART 1, CHAPTER 13

SUBCHAPTER A. GENERAL PROVISIONS

§13.1 Definitions

(a) The terms in this section, when used in this chapter, have the following meanings, unless the context clearly indicates otherwise.

(1) Act—The Texas Controlled Substances Act (Texas Health and Safety Code, Chapter 481).

(2) Day—A calendar day unless otherwise indicated as a business day.

(3) Department (DPS) —The Texas Department of Public Safety.

(4) Drug Enforcement Administration (DEA) —The Federal Drug Enforcement Administration.

(5) Electronic transmission—The transmission of information in electronic form such as computer to computer, electronic device to computer, email, or the transmission of the exact visual image of a document by way of electronic media.

(6) Record—A notification, order form, statement, invoice, inventory information, or other document for the acquisition or disposal of a controlled substance, precursor, or apparatus created or maintained in any manner by a distributor or permit holder under a record keeping or inventory requirement of federal law, the Act, or this chapter.

(b) For purposes of this chapter, the terms "precursor chemical" and "chemical precursor" are interchangeable.

Source: The provisions of this § 13.1 adopted to be effective November 6, 2016, 41 TexReg 8619

SUBCHAPTER B. PRECURSOR CHEMICAL LABORATORY APPARATUS (PCLA)

§ 13.11. Application

(a) Applicants for a precursor chemical laboratory apparatus (PCLA) permit under this subchapter must apply in a manner prescribed by the department.

(b) An application for an annual PCLA permit is complete when it contains all information required by the department, including:

(1) Business name;

(2) Business owner/representative;

(3) Storage facility address;

(4) Multiple businesses owned by applicant of agent;

(5) Identification of the PCLA to be obtained;

(6) Description of how the PCLA will be used;

(7) Consent to inspect acknowledgement; and

(8) Any supporting documentation or other information requested by the department.

(c) An application for a one-time PCLA permit is complete when it contains all information required by the department, including:

(1) Applicant's name, address, telephone number, email address (if available), driver license number or Texas identification card number, and date of birth;

(2) Quantity of PCLA associated with the request;

(3) Description of how the PCLA will be used;

(4) Consent to inspect acknowledgement; and

(5) Any supporting documentation or other information requested by the department.

(d) The application form and any additional document or statement required by the department must be signed or electronically acknowledged by:

(1) The applicant, if the applicant is an individual;

(2) A general partner of the applicant, if the applicant is a partnership;

(3) An officer of the applicant, if the applicant is a corporation or other business association; or

(4) The administrator of the applicant, if the applicant is a hospital or teaching institution.

(e) If an incomplete application is received, notice of the deficiency will be sent to the applicant. The applicant will have 60 calendar days after receipt of notice to provide the required information and submit a complete application. If an applicant fails to furnish the documentation, the application will be considered withdrawn, and a new application will be required.

(f) By submitting the application, the applicant agrees to allow the department to conduct a criminal history background check as authorized by law.

(g) No fee is required for a permit under this subchapter.

Source: The provisions of this § 13.11 adopted to be effective November 6, 2016, 41 TexReg 8619

§ 13.12. Expiration and Renewal

(a) An annual permit expires one year from the end of the month of issuance.

(b) A permit may be renewed for up to 180 days after the expiration date. If the permit has been expired for more than 180 days, a new application must be submitted.

(c) An expired permit that has not been renewed within the 180 days cannot be used to receive or transfer chemical precursor or laboratory apparatus.

Source: The provisions of this § 13.12 adopted to be effective November 6, 2016, 41 TexReg 8619

§ 13.13. Reporting

(a)   The department issued precursor chemical laboratory apparatus (PCLA) transaction form or its electronic equivalent must be completed by a PCLA distributor to report the required transactional details, including information relating to the recipient of a precursor or apparatus. The distributor must complete all applicable sections of the form.

(b)   Except as provided by subsection (c) of this section, the report must be filed not later than the 7th day after the distributor completes the transaction and returned to the department.

(c)   A distributor may make the comprehensive monthly report by submitting a computer generated report. This form of reporting must be pre-approved by the department and must include the same information as the PCLA transaction form. The comprehensive monthly report is due by the 30th day following the end of the reported month.

(d)   All required reports must be submitted to the department in the form and manner required by the department.

Source: The provisions of this § 13.13 adopted to be effective November 6, 2016, 41 TexReg 8619

§ 13.14. Transactions

(a)   A prospective precursor chemical laboratory apparatus (PCLA) recipient must present to the distributor an original one-time permit or an original or electronic file copy of an annual permit.

(b)   The distributor must take reasonable steps to ensure proper identification of a potential recipient.

Source: The provisions of this § 13.14 adopted to be effective November 6, 2016, 41 TexReg 8619

§ 13.15. Notification of Changes

(a)   An applicant for or holder of an annual permit must notify the department before the seventh day following any modification or change in the individual's business name, address, telephone number or other information required on the application, registration, or permit.

(b)   The notification must be in writing and include the signature of the permit holder, applicant, or other individual who is authorized to sign an original application.

Source: The provisions of this § 13.13 adopted to be effective November 6, 2016, 41 TexReg 8619

§ 13.16. Security

(a)   A permit holder must establish and maintain effective controls and procedures to prevent unauthorized access, theft, or diversion of any precursor chemical laboratory apparatus (PCLA). The following constitute the minimum security requirements to protect these controlled items. The permit holder must:

   (1)   Establish and maintain a building, an enclosure within a building, or an enclosed yard that provides reasonably adequate security against the diversion of a controlled item;

   (2)   Limit access to each storage area to the minimum number of individuals or employees necessary for the permit holder's activities; and

   (3)   Designate an individual or a limited number of individuals with responsibility for each area in which a controlled item is stored, and authority to enter or control entry into the area.

(b)   In the absence of a physical barrier, such as a wall, partition, fence, or similar divider, the permit holder may comply with this section by another form of substantially increased security to limit physical access to the storage area under subsection (a)(2) of this section.

(c)   The permit holder will make the designation required by subsection (a)(3) of this section in writing and will make the designation available upon request in the same manner as a record kept under this chapter. The holder may update the designation record as necessary to reflect current practice.

(d)   When maintenance personnel or a business guest, visitor, or similar individual is present in or passes through an area addressed by this section, the permit holder must provide for reasonably adequate observation of the area by an employee specifically designated under subsection (a)(3) of this section.

(e)   If a permit holder has an alarm system that is in operation and being monitored, the permit holder must immediately report each unauthorized intrusion or other security breach to the department and to the permit holder's local law enforcement agency.

(f)   A permit holder is not required to make the alarm report required under subsection (e) of this section if there is a reasonable explanation for the security breach that does not involve potential diversion.

Source: The provisions of this § 13.16 adopted to be effective November 6, 2016, 41 TexReg 8619

§ 13.17. Record Keeping

(a)   A distributor or recipient of a precursor or apparatus must make an accurate and legible record of each distribution; and maintain the record for two years after the date of the transaction.

(b)   A distributor satisfies the record keeping requirement under this section by recording and maintaining the record of distribution as a readily retrievable record in an automated data processing system, if the system provides a comprehensive monthly report to the department.

Source: The provisions of this § 13.17 adopted to be effective November 6, 2016, 41 TexReg 8619

§ 13.18. Inventory

(a) Unless exempt under the Act, a distributor or recipient of a precursor or apparatus must establish and maintain an inventory under this section.

(b) A distributor or recipient must conduct an initial inventory to include each precursor chemical laboratory apparatus (PCLA) that is covered by this subchapter and in stock at the time of the inventory. The distributor or recipient must conduct the initial inventory not later than the 90th day after the date the department issues the initial permit under this chapter.

(c) After the initial inventory, a distributor or recipient must conduct another inventory not later than the 24th month following the month of the last inventory.

(d) The department may deem a distributor or recipient to be in compliance with the inventory requirements of this section if the distributor or recipient:

   (1) Is a business that routinely conducts an annual inventory of all items; and

   (2) Maintains a readily retrievable record of each precursor or apparatus located during the inventory.

Source: The provisions of this § 13.18 adopted to be effective November 6, 2016, 41 TexReg 8619

§ 13.19. Inspection

(a) Upon request of the department, a registrant or permit holder may be provided up to 24 hours, excluding weekends and holidays, to produce any or all records required to be maintained on site for inspection by the department.

(b) All registrants authorized to maintain an offsite central record keeping system shall, upon request, produce the requested records within two business days.

(c) If an individual maintains a record under this chapter using an automated data processing system and if the individual does not have a printer available on site, the individual must:

   (1) Make a useable copy available to the department at the close of business the day after the audit; and

   (2) Certify that the information contained within the copy is true and correct as of the date of audit and has not been altered, amended, or modified.

(d) No individual in charge of a premise, item, or record covered by the Act or this subchapter may refuse, or interfere with, an inspection. Refusal or interference by an applicant or permit holder may be a ground for the department to deny the application or suspend or revoke the permit.

Source: The provisions of this § 13.19 adopted to be effective November 6, 2016, 41 TexReg 8619

§ 13.20. Denial, Suspension, Revocation

(a) First time violations of this chapter may result in suspension or revocation for a period of up to three months. A second violation within two years may result in the suspension of the registration for a period of up to 6 months. Three or more violations within two years may result in the revocation of the registration, and the denial of any subsequent application for a period of two years.

(b) Denial, suspension, and revocation for violations of the Act and this chapter proceedings will be conducted under the procedures described in Subchapter H of the Act.

Source: The provisions of this § 13.20 adopted to be effective November 6, 2016, 41 TexReg 8619

§ 13.21. Administrative Violations and Penalties

The violations detailed in this section will be subject to an administrative fine of $ 500 per violation, subject to the factors provided in § 481.302 of the Act. These fines may be imposed in lieu of or in addition to suspension or revocation, under the procedures described in Subchapter H of the Act for violations of the Act and this chapter.

   (1) Failure to maintain records/inventories.

   (2) Failure to provide required reports.

   (3) Inaccurate or fraudulent reporting.

   (4) Failure to surrender required documents.

   (5) Failure to display required signage/license.

   (6) Failure to maintain adequate security.

   (7) Operating outside scope of license.

   (8) Failure to notify of license changes.

   (9) Refusing to allow or failure to cooperate with inspections.

   (10) Misrepresentation of information on application, record, or report.

   (11) Unlawful transfer or receipt of precursor chemical.

   (12) Transfer of precursor substance for unlawful manufacture.

   (13) Unlawful transfer or receipt of lab apparatus.

   (14) Transfer of lab apparatus for unlawful manufacture.

Source: The provisions of this § 13.21 adopted to be effective November 6, 2016, 41 TexReg 8619

§ 13.22. Disqualifying Criminal Offenses

(a)   Pursuant to Texas Occupations Code, § 53.021(a)(1) the department may revoke a precursor chemical laboratory apparatus (PCLA) permit or deny an application for a PCLA permit if the applicant or permit holder has been convicted of a felony or misdemeanor that directly relates to the duties and responsibilities of a PCLA permit holder.

(b)   The department has determined the criminal offenses within Texas Health and Safety Code, Chapters 481 - 486 directly relate to the duties and responsibilities of PCLA permit holder. A conviction for such an offense may result in the denial of an initial or renewal application for a PCLA permit or the revocation of a PCLA permit.

(c)   A felony conviction for an offense within Texas Health and Safety Code, Chapters 481 - 486, or a substantially similar offense, is disqualifying for 10 years from the date of the conviction unless a full pardon has been granted.

(d)   A Class A or B misdemeanor conviction for an offense within Texas Health and Safety Code, Chapters 481 - 486, or a substantially similar offense, is disqualifying for five years from the date of conviction unless a full pardon has been granted.

(e)   For the purposes of this chapter, all references to conviction are to those for which the judgment has become final.

(f)   The department may consider the factors specified in Texas Occupations Code, § 53.022 and § 53.023 in determining whether to grant, deny, or revoke any certificate of registration.

   Source: The provisions of this § 13.22 adopted to be effective November 6, 2016, 41 TexReg 8619

§ 13.23. Notice and Hearings

(a)   Hearings on administrative penalties, and denials, suspensions or revocations, are governed by Subchapter H of the Act (§ 481.301 et seq.).

(b)   The department may rely on the mailing and electronic mail address and facsimile number currently on file for all purposes relating to notification. The failure to maintain a current mailing and electronic mail address and facsimile number with the department is not a defense to any action based on the registrant's or applicant's failure to respond. Service upon the registrant or applicant of notice is complete and receipt is presumed upon the date the notice is sent, if sent before 5:00 p.m. by facsimile or electronic mail, and 3 days following the date sent if by regular United States mail.

(c)   Following adequate notice of a hearing on a contested case before the State Office of Administrative Hearings (SOAH), failure of the respondent to appear at the time of hearing shall entitle the department to request from the administrative law judge an order dismissing the case from the SOAH docket and to informally dispose of the case on a default basis.

(d)   In cases brought before SOAH, in the event that the respondent is adjudicated to be in violation of the Act or this chapter after a trial on the merits, the department has authority to assess, in addition to the penalty imposed, the actual costs of the administrative hearing. Such costs include, but are not limited to, investigative costs, witness fees, deposition expenses, travel expenses of witnesses, costs of adjudication before SOAH and any other costs that are necessary for the preparation of the department's case including the costs of any transcriptions of testimony.

(e)   The costs of transcribing the testimony and preparing the record for an appeal by judicial review shall be paid by the respondent.

   Source: The provisions of this § 13.23 adopted to be effective November 6, 2016, 41 TexReg 8619

§ 13.24. Additional or Exempted Chemical Precursor or Laboratory Apparatus

(a)   Under the authority of § 481.077(b) and § 481.080(c) of the Act, the department has determined that the items detailed in the section should be added to or exempted from the chemical precursor or laboratory apparatus lists.

(b)   Chemical precursor additions. The department hereby names the following chemical substances as chemical precursors subject to the Act, § 481.077(b):

    (1)   Red phosphorus; and

    (2)   Hypophosphorous acid.

(c)   Chemical precursor exemptions. The department has not exempted any substances from the list of chemical precursor subject to the Act, § 481.077(b).

(d)   Laboratory apparatus additions. The department has not added any items to the list of items of chemical laboratory apparatus subject to the Act, § 481.080(a).

(e)   Laboratory apparatus exemptions. The department has not exempted any items from those chemical laboratory apparatus subject to the Act, § 481.080(a).

   Source: The provisions of this § 13.24 adopted to be effective November 6, 2016, 41 TexReg 8619

§ 13.25. Immediate Chemical Precursor List

The substances detailed in this section are designated as being an immediate precursor as provided under the Act, § 481.002(22):

    (1)   Benzaldehyde;

    (2)   Gamma-butyrolactone (other names include: GBL; dihydro-2(3H)-furanone; 1,2-butanolide; 1,4-butanolide; 4-hydroxybutanoic acid lactone; gamma-hydroxybutyric acid lactone);

    (3)   Isosafrole;

    (4)   3,4-methylenedioxyphenyl-2-propanone;

    (5)   N-methylephedrine, its salts, optical isomers, and salts of optical isomers;

    (6)   N-methylpseudoephedrine, its salts, optical isomers, and salts of optical isomers;

    (7)   Piperonal;

(8) Safrole; and

(9) Lithium metal removed from a battery and immersed in kerosene, mineral spirits, or similar liquid that prevents or retards hydration.

Source: The provisions of this § 13.25 adopted to be effective November 6, 2016, 41 TexReg 8619

SUBCHAPTER C. PEYOTE DISTRIBUTORS

§ 13.31. Application for Peyote Distributor Registration

(a) An applicant for registration as a peyote distributor must:

(1) Register with the Federal Drug Enforcement Administration (DEA) in compliance with Title 21, USC 21 §§ 821 - 831;

(2) Submit a complete application to the department;

(3) Submit the names and addresses of all individuals who are to be employed by or under contract with the distributor to engage in any peyote transactions or otherwise come into contact with or possess peyote on behalf of the distributor; and

(4) Certify the individuals listed pursuant to subsection (a)(3) of this section have been instructed in proper peyote harvesting techniques, as provided in § 13.34 of this title, relating to Harvesting.

(b) No fee is required for a registration under this subchapter.

Source: The provisions of this § 13.31 adopted to be effective November 6, 2016, 41 TexReg 8620

§ 13.32. Expiration and Renewal

A peyote distributor registration expires one year from the anniversary of the date of issuance, and must be renewed prior to expiration. An expired registration provides no authority to engage in the business of a distributor.

Source: The provisions of this § 13.32 adopted to be effective November 6, 2016, 41 TexReg 8620

§ 13.33. Employee/Contractor Information

(a) The distributor must furnish to the department the name and identifying information of each employee or independent contractor who will possess peyote on behalf of the distributor, and certify the individual has been trained in proper harvesting techniques as provided in § 13.34 of this title, relating to Harvesting.

(b) The distributor is responsible for maintaining the accuracy of the information provided to the department, and must notify the department of any change to the information within seven days of the change.

Source: The provisions of this § 13.33 adopted to be effective November 6, 2016, 41 TexReg 8620

§ 13.34. Harvesting

(a) Distributors must ensure the peyote is harvested in compliance with proper harvesting techniques, whereby only the crown is harvested and the non-chlorophyllous stem and root are left intact. Any improperly harvested peyote, including any stems or roots, must be identified as such to prospective buyers, and may not be represented as properly harvested.

(b) Harvested peyote must be protected from insects, mold, and contaminants.

(c) When a distributor or the distributor's employee or contractor is hunting, harvesting, cutting, collecting, transporting, or otherwise in possession of peyote, the individual must carry:

(1) Proof of the distributor's current registration, and in the case of an employee or contractor, an employee identification card or other documentation establishing a current employment or contractual relationship with the registrant; and

(2) Documentation sufficient to show lawful access to the land where the peyote was harvested, including the name and location of the person granting the access.

(d) The documentation required by subsection (b) of this section must be presented upon demand of a representative of the department, a peace officer, a federal official, or the landowner or landowner's representative.

Source: The provisions of this § 13.34 adopted to be effective November 6, 2016, 41 TexReg 8620

§ 13.35. Sales

Distributors are only authorized to sell peyote to those authorized to possess peyote under Texas Health and Safety Code, § 481.111. Distributors are responsible for confirming the purchaser's identification and legal authority to possess peyote.

Source: The provisions of this § 13.35 adopted to be effective November 6, 2016, 41 TexReg 8620

§ 13.36. Transactional Records

(a) A distributor must maintain for two years records of all transactions involving peyote. The records must reflect:

(1) The date of the transaction;

(2) The quantity purchased or sold, expressed as both the number of buttons and the weight in pounds and ounces;

(3) The total purchase price;

(4) As applicable, signatures of the purchaser and seller, names, addresses, DPS and DEA registration numbers, tribal identification or government issued identification number, and church affiliation;

(5) If applicable, the name(s) of any employee(s) or contractors engaged in the transaction; and

(6) Any other records required under Title 21 CFR Part 1304.

(b) A distributor must:
    (1) Make the records available for inspection and copying by the department upon request, and submit the records to the department upon request;
    (2) Create the records contemporaneously with the event recorded; and
    (3) Ensure the records are current.

Source: The provisions of this § 13.36 adopted to be effective November 6, 2016, 41 TexReg 8620

§ 13.37. Security

(a) A distributor must establish and maintain effective controls and procedures in order to prevent unauthorized access, theft, or diversion of peyote.

(b) A distributor may not allow access to the peyote storage area to anyone other than an employee identified to the department in compliance with § 13.33 of this title, relating to Employee/Contractor Information, or who is otherwise authorized under Texas Health and Safety Code, § 481.111.

Source: The provisions of this § 13.37 adopted to be effective November 6, 2016, 41 TexReg 8620

§ 13.38. Inventory

A distributor must conduct a monthly inventory of all peyote in stock and maintain readily retrievable records of the inventory. The records must be made available for inspection and copying by the department upon request, and the records must be submitted to the department upon request.

Source: The provisions of this § 13.38 adopted to be effective November 6, 2016, 41 TexReg 8620

§ 13.39. Reporting of Loss or Theft

(a) A distributor must notify the department not later than the three days after the date the distributor learns of:
    (1) A discrepancy in the amount of peyote ordered from a source inside or outside this state and the amount received, if not back ordered;
    (2) A loss or theft during shipment from a source inside or outside this state; or
    (3) A loss or theft from current inventory.

(b) A distributor must notify the department of a loss of theft by submitting a report to the department in the manner required by the department.

(c) A report submitted under this section must contain:
    (1) The name, address, and telephone number of the business or other person submitting the report;
    (2) The printed or typed name of the person preparing the report; and
    (3) The date the person prepared the report.

(d) If the report under this section concerns a:
    (1) Discrepancy, the report must include:
        (A) The name of the item ordered;
        (B) The difference in the amount actually received; and
        (C) The amount shipped according to the shipping statement or invoice;
    (2) Loss or theft from current inventory, the report must include:
        (A) The name and amount of the item lost or stolen;
        (B) The physical location where the loss or theft occurred; and
        (C) The date of discovery of the loss or theft.
    (3) Discrepancy, loss, theft, or other potential diversion that occurred during shipment of the item, the report must include:
        (A) The name of the common carrier or person who transported the item; and
        (B) The date the item was shipped.

Source: The provisions of this § 13.39 adopted to be effective November 6, 2016, 41 TexReg 8620

§ 13.40. Denial, Suspension, Revocation

(a) First time violations of this chapter or Texas Health and Safety Code, § 481.111 may result in suspension or revocation for a period of up to three months. A second violation within two years may result in the suspension of the registration for a period of up to six months. Three or more violations within two years may result in the revocation of the registration, and the denial of any subsequent application for a period of two years.

(b) Denial, suspension, and revocation proceedings will be conducted under the procedures described in Subchapter H of the Texas Health and Safety Code, Chapter 481 (§ 481.301 et seq.) for violations of the Texas Health and Safety Code, § 481.111 and this chapter.

Source: The provisions of this § 13.40 adopted to be effective November 6, 2016, 41 TexReg 8620

§ 13.41. Administrative Penalties

The following reflect the department's guidelines for administrative penalties to be used in lieu of or in addition to suspension or revocation actions, under the procedures described in Subchapter H of Texas Health and Safety Code, Chapter 481 (§ 481.301 et seq.) for violations of Texas Health and Safety Code, § 481.111 and this chapter. The violations detailed in this section will be subject to a fine of $ 500 per violation, subject to the factors provided in § 481.302.

(1) Failure to maintain required records.

(2) Failure to provide reports upon request.

(3) Inaccurate or fraudulent reports.

(4) Failure to maintain adequate security.

(5) Operating outside scope of license.

(6) Failure to notify of changes to licensee's employees.

(7) Refusing to allow or failure to cooperate with inspections.

(8) Misrepresentation of information on application, record, or report.

(9) Unlawful transfer or receipt of peyote.

(10) Failure to validate authority of purchaser.

(11) Sale of contaminated peyote.

(12) Improper harvesting.

(13) Misrepresentation relating to sale, including misrepresenting the peyote as properly harvested or as crown material.

Source: The provisions of this § 13.41 adopted to be effective November 6, 2016, 41 TexReg 8620

§ 13.42. Notice and Hearings

(a) Hearings on administrative penalties and other disciplinary actions are governed by Subchapter H of Texas Health and Safety Code, Chapter 481 (§ 481.301 et seq.).

(b) The department may rely on the mailing and electronic mail address and facsimile number currently on file for all purposes relating to notification. The failure to maintain a current mailing and electronic mail address with the department is not a defense to any action based on the registrant's or applicant's failure to respond. Service upon the registrant or applicant of notice is complete and receipt is presumed upon the date the notice is sent, if sent before 5:00 p.m. by facsimile or electronic mail, and three days following the date sent if by regular United States mail.

(c) Following adequate notice of a hearing on a contested case before the State Office of Administrative Hearings (SOAH), failure of the respondent to appear at the time of hearing shall entitle the department to request from the administrative law judge an order dismissing the case from the SOAH docket and to informally dispose of the case on a default basis.

(d) In cases brought before SOAH, if the respondent is adjudicated to be in violation of Texas Health and Safety Code, § 481.111 or this chapter after a trial on the merits, the department has authority to assess, in addition to the penalty imposed, the actual costs of the administrative hearing. Such costs include, but are not limited to, investigative costs, witness fees, deposition expenses, travel expenses of witnesses, costs of adjudication before SOAH and any other costs that are necessary for the preparation of the department's case including the costs of any transcriptions of testimony.

(e) The costs of transcribing the testimony and preparing the record for an appeal by judicial review shall be paid by the respondent.

Source: The provisions of this § 13.42 adopted to be effective November 6, 2016, 41 TexReg 8620

§ 13.43. Exemption from Penalty for Failure to Renew in Timely Manner

An individual who holds a registration issued under Texas Health and Safety Code, § 481.111 is exempt from any increased fee or other penalty for failing to renew the license or registration in a timely manner if the individual establishes to the satisfaction of the department the individual failed to renew the license or registration in a timely manner because the individual was serving as a military service member, as defined in Texas Occupations Code, § 55.001.

Source: The provisions of this § 13.43 adopted to be effective November 6, 2016, 41 TexReg 8620

§ 13.44. Extension of License Renewal Deadlines for Military Members

A military service member, as defined in Texas Occupations Code, § 55.001, who holds a registration issued under Texas Health and Safety Code, § 481.111 is entitled to two years of additional time to complete any requirement related to the renewal of the license.

Source: The provisions of this § 13.44 adopted to be effective November 6, 2016, 41 TexReg 8620

SUBCHAPTER D. MISCELLANEOUS PROVISIONS

§ 13.51. Ephedrine, Pseudoephedrine, and Norpseudoephedrine

(a) A wholesale distributor who sells, transfers, or otherwise furnishes a product containing ephedrine, pseudoephedrine, or norpseudoephedrine to a retailer shall obtain before delivering the product:

(1) The retailer's business name, address, area code, and telephone number;

(2) The name of the person making the purchase;

(3) The amount of the product containing ephedrine, pseudoephedrine, or norpseudoephedrine ordered; and

(4) Any other information required by the department.

(b) A wholesale distributor shall make an accurate and legible record of the information in subsection (a) of this section and the amount of the product containing ephedrine, pseudoephedrine, or norpseudoephedrine actually delivered. A wholesale distributor shall retain the record for a period of at least two years after the date of the transaction. The record shall be made available to the department upon request.

(c)   Not later than ten business days after receipt of an order for a product containing ephedrine, pseudoephedrine, or norpseudoephedrine requesting delivery of a suspicious quantity of that product, the wholesale distributor shall report the suspicious order to the department on the form and in the manner approved by the department.

(d)   A wholesale distributor who distributes a product containing ephedrine, pseudoephedrine, or norpseudoephedrine to a retailer shall make available for immediate inspection to any member of the department during regular business hours upon presentation of proper credentials all files, papers, processes, controls, or facilities appropriate for verification of a required record or report. If the wholesaler is no longer in operation or closed, the records shall be made available within three business days.

(e)   A wholesale distributor who fails to comply with the requirements of this section may be subject to administrative penalties, pursuant to Subchapter H of the Act and notification of the proper administrative or law enforcement authorities.

Source: The provisions of this § 13.51 adopted to be effective November 6, 2016, 41 TexReg 8621

SUBCHAPTER G. FORFEITURE AND DESTRUCTION

§13.151 Subchapter Definitions

The following words and terms, when used in this subchapter, have the following meanings, unless the context clearly indicates otherwise.

(1)   Abusable volatile chemical—Has the meaning given that term by the Texas Health and Safety Code, Chapter 485. In addition, abusable volatile chemicals also include any derivative products, such as, glues, aerosol paint, aerosol adhesives, aerosol spray air, and cement adhesives or any other product containing an abusable volatile chemical.

(2)   Excess quantity—Unless otherwise modified under § 13.157(d) of this title (relating to SOP for Destruction By Laboratory or Agency—Security Control), more than:

   (A)   one kilogram of bulk dry evidence, such as powder;

   (B)   500 milliliters of bulk liquid evidence, such as a chemical precursor or liquid controlled substance;

   (C)   200 dosage or abuse units of an item, such as tablets, capsules, liquids, or other items so measured;

   (D)   250 grams of bulk packaged marihuana;

   (E)   five individual controlled substance plants, such as marihuana or peyote; or

   (F)   five miscellaneous items of drug or inhalant paraphernalia.

(3)   Hazardous material—An item that:

   (A)   creates a health or environmental hazard or prohibits safe storage because of its nature and quantity; or

   (B)   meets the hazardous waste criteria of the United States Environmental Protection Agency (EPA), because of its nature, including its corrosivity, ignitability, reactivity, toxicity, or other hazardous characteristic.

(4)   Item—Controlled substance property, controlled substance plant, simulated controlled substance, volatile chemical or related inhalant paraphernalia, or abusable glue, aerosol paint, or related inhalant paraphernalia, as those terms are used in the Texas Health and Safety Code, Chapters 481 - 485.

(5)   Laboratory—A crime laboratory located in this state that holds a registration number for the analysis of a controlled substance from the DEA.

(6)   Lawful possession—Includes the possession of an item obtained in accordance with state or federal law.

(7)   Simulated controlled substance—Has the meaning given that term by the Texas Health and Safety Code, Chapter 482.

(8)   SOP—A standard operation procedure established under this subchapter.

Source: The provisions of this § 13.151 adopted to be effective July 18, 2001, 26 TexReg 5266; amended to be effective March 30, 2017, 42 TexReg 1574

§13.152 Summary Forfeiture

(a)   Generally. An item may be forfeited to the state under this subchapter if:

   (1)   the lawful possession of the item cannot be readily ascertained; and

   (2)   the law enforcement agency or peace officer seizing the item makes every reasonable effort to investigate lawful possession.

(b)   Forfeiture requirements. Except as provided in subsection (c) of this section, an item is summarily forfeited to the state under this subchapter, if the item is of a type commonly abused and:

   (1)   an apparently legitimate possessor has voluntarily surrendered the item to a laboratory, law enforcement agency, or peace officer for the express purpose of destruction;

   (2)   no known lawful possessor can be determined; or

   (3)   no lawful possessor is reasonably likely to be located.

(c)   Pharmaceuticals. A legitimately manufactured pharmaceutical item is not subject to summary forfeiture to the state under subsection (b) of this section, unless it:

   (1)   has been voluntarily surrendered by an apparently legitimate possessor to a laboratory, law enforcement agency, or peace officer for the express purpose of destruction; or

   (2)   was illegally sold or possessed under the Texas Health and Safety Code, Chapters 481 - 485.

(d)   Doubtful case. If there is doubt about legitimacy or lawfulness, the laboratory, law enforcement agency, or peace officer contemplating destruction must seek a court order of destruction.

(e)   Not required to accept an item. This subchapter only applies to an item that has been accepted by a laboratory, law enforcement agency, or peace officer for summary forfeiture or destruction. It does not require a laboratory, agency, or officer to accept a particular item for summary forfeiture or destruction.

Source: The provisions of this §13.152 adopted to be effective July 18, 2001, 26 TexReg 5266

§13.153 Item Legally Worthless as Criminal Evidence

(a) Generally. This subchapter describes the documentation and security provisions to use once the decision to destroy has been made.

(b) Reasonable effort. Before a laboratory, law enforcement agency, or peace officer destroys an item under this subchapter, the director recommends but does not require a responsible party to make a reasonable effort to ensure the item:

    (1) has no continuing evidentiary value or significance to any pending or contemplated criminal case; or

    (2) is in excess quantity.

(c) If case filed. If a criminal case was filed involving an item, the person seeking destruction authorization or contemplating the giving of authorization to destroy must contact the office of the appropriate prosecutor or court before destruction to determine whether the item has any continuing evidentiary significance.

Source: The provisions of this §13.153 adopted to be effective July 18, 2001, 26 TexReg 5266

§13.154 Destruction Authority – Controlled Substance Property or Plant

(a) Generally. Destruction with or without court order. A laboratory, law enforcement agency, or peace officer may destroy controlled substance property or a controlled substance plant covered by this section:

    (1) with a court order under the authority of that order; or

    (2) without a court order under the authority of one of the summary destruction provisions of the Act, Subchapter E.

(b) Statutory sources. A laboratory, law enforcement agency, or peace officer may destroy without a court order:

    (1) a controlled substance plant under the authority of the Act, §481.152(d);

    (2) an item of controlled substance property under the authority of the Act, §481.153(b); or

    (3) an excess quantity of certain items under the authority of the Act, §481.160.

(c) Subchapter applies. The documentation and security provisions of this subchapter apply to destruction of an item of controlled substance property or plant under this section, except where provided otherwise in a court order of destruction.

Source: The provisions of this §13.154 adopted to be effective July 18, 2001, 26 TexReg 5266

§13.155 Destruction Authority – Other Item

(a) Destruction with or without court order. A laboratory, law enforcement agency, or peace officer may destroy certain miscellaneous items covered by this section:

    (1) with a court order under the authority of that order; or

    (2) without a court order under the authority of one of the summary destruction provisions of the Texas Health and Safety Code, Chapters 482 - 485.

(b) Statutory sources. A laboratory, law enforcement agency, or peace officer may destroy without a court order:

    (1) a simulated controlled substance under the authority of the Texas Health and Safety Code, §482.004; or

    (2) an abusable volatile chemical or inhalant paraphernalia under the authority of the Texas Health and Safety Code, §485.037.

(c) Dangerous drug. At the direction of the Texas State Board of Pharmacy, a law enforcement agency or peace officer may destroy without a court order a dangerous drug under the authority of the Texas Health and Safety Code, §483.074.

(d) Subchapter applies. The documentation and security provisions of this subchapter apply to destruction of a miscellaneous item under this section, except where provided otherwise in a court order of destruction.

Source: The provisions of this §13.155 adopted to be effective July 18, 2001, 26 TexReg 5266; amended to be effective October 28, 2007, 32 TexReg 7492

§13.156 Destruction Authority – Court Order

(a) Statutory authority. A court may issue an order of destruction for an item that:

    (1) is controlled substance property or plant under the authority of the Act, §481.159; or

    (2) was stolen or acquired in any other manner that made the acquisition a penal offense under the authority of the Texas Code of Criminal Procedure, Chapter 47.

(b) Security provisions required by the court. A laboratory, law enforcement agency, or peace officer carrying out a court order of destruction must comply with the documentation and security provisions of the order, if any.

(c) No security provisions required by the court. If the court order is silent about the manner of destruction, or if it does not specify or direct another manner of destruction inconsistent with this subchapter, the laboratory, law enforcement agency, or peace officer must comply with the documentation and security provisions of this subchapter.

Source: The provisions of this §13.156 adopted to be effective July 18, 2001, 26 TexReg 5266

§13.157 SOP for Destruction by Laboratory or Agency – Security Control

(a) SOP required. Before allowing anyone, whether peace officer or civilian, to destroy an item under this subchapter, a laboratory or law enforcement agency must adopt a written SOP for the destruction of the kind of item sought to be destroyed.

(b) Compliance required. A laboratory or law enforcement agency must require that each person engaged in destruction under this subchapter must strictly follow each SOP. A written SOP may exceed a minimum requirement contained within this subchapter.

(c) Generally. In order to minimize the likelihood of pilferage or other unlawful diversion, an SOP must include requirements that are reasonably likely to:

    (1) uncover the occurrence of a discrepancy, loss, theft, or other potential diversion; and

    (2) identify and destroy the excess quantity of an item, in order to reduce the size of an exhibit while preserving its evidentiary value.

(d) Modify definition of "excess quantity." With the express approval of each appropriate prosecuting authority, an SOP may increase or decrease the amount of an item necessary to meet the definition of an "excess quantity" under that SOP.

(e) Specifically. An SOP must include a requirement that:

   (1) a specific person or category of persons must seek destruction authorization for an item after it exceeds the maximum limits for item storage established by the SOP, including the duration and amount;

   (2) a specific person or category of persons must make an immediate report to a supervisor of an unusual or suspicious incident or probable breach of security reasonably related to potential discrepancy, loss, theft, or other diversion;

   (3) a supervisor must make a thorough investigation of the incident, including laboratory reanalysis if necessary; and

   (4) a specific person or category of persons must contact the submitting peace officer, the submitting law enforcement agency, or the office of the prosecutor responsible for the case to seek:

      (A) written authorization to destroy all or part of a particular exhibit; or

      (B) blanket written authorization to destroy all or part of each exhibit that meets certain criteria

Source: The provisions of this §13.157 adopted to be effective July 18, 2001, 26 TexReg 5266

§13.158 Manner of Destruction – Security Control

(a) Destruction by anyone. A person may accomplish routine destruction of an item under this subchapter by burning in a suitable incinerator or by another method as long as the person performs the destruction in:

   (1) a safe and responsible manner;

   (2) compliance with all relevant federal, state, and local laws; and

   (3) compliance with all requirements of the Texas Commission on Environmental Quality and the EPA.

(b) Private contract. If a laboratory, law enforcement agency, or peace officer contracts with a private entity to destroy the item, the private contractor must:

   (1) hold a controlled substances registration number from the director and DEA; and

   (2) obtain full permitting from the EPA as a hazardous waste transportation, storage, or disposal facility, as appropriate.

(c) Destruction by officer. The director recommends but does not require that an individual peace officer should §not destroy hazardous material, unless that officer possesses the special expertise required to handle the material safely and lawfully.

Source: The provisions of this §13.158 adopted to be effective July 18, 2001, 26 TexReg 5266; amended to be effective October 28, 2007, 32 TexReg 7492

§13.159 Two-Witness Rule – Security Control

(a) Destruction by anyone. A laboratory, law enforcement agency, or peace officer may not destroy an item under this subchapter without at least two individuals present to witness the actual destruction. One witness must be:

   (1) a supervisor; or

   (2) another individual expressly designated by a supervisor to witness that specific destruction incident.

(b) Destruction by laboratory. If a laboratory destroys the item, destruction must comply with:

   (1) the security provisions of this chapter for a controlled substances registrant; and

   (2) the documentation and security provisions of this subchapter that reference a laboratory.

(c) Destruction by agency or officer. If a law enforcement agency or peace officer destroys the item:

   (1) no two individuals may serve as the sole witnesses to consecutive destruction incidents; and

   (2) the director recommends but does not require both of the two witnesses should be peace officers from different law enforcement agencies.

Source: The provisions of this §13.159 adopted to be effective July 18, 2001, 26 TexReg 5266

§13.160 Destruction Inventory – Security Control

(a) After laboratory analysis. If destruction under this subchapter follows a laboratory analysis process that has resulted in adequate repackaging and sealing of an item, the director will deem a destruction inventory to be sufficient if it consists of an inspection, accomplished without breaking the seal, in order to:

   (1) verify the nature, kind, and quantity of the items sought to be destroyed as compared with the original laboratory submission; and

   (2) determine the status of the packaging and seal integrity.

(b) No laboratory analysis. If destruction does not follow a laboratory analysis process that has resulted in adequate repackaging and sealing of an item, a destruction inventory must include:

   (1) the relevant case or file number;

   (2) the name of the seizing law enforcement agency or peace officer;

   (3) a description of the packaging;

   (4) a description of the status of the packaging and seal integrity; and

   (5) the count and weight of the item, including the exact nature, kind, and quantity.

Source: The provisions of this §13.160 adopted to be effective July 18, 2001, 26 TexReg 5266

§13.161 Witness Responsibility – Security Control

(a) Generally. For purposes of accountability, at least two of the witnesses to a destruction under this subchapter must, during a process conducted immediately before the physical destruction of an item:

   (1) examine each item in a manner sufficient to complete the destruction inventory required by this subchapter;

(2)   compare that destruction inventory with each previous inventory of the item, including one that may have been made as part of an evidence submission form, a laboratory analysis, or as part of the destruction authorization;

(3)   examine each package for the integrity or breach of the package or seal;

(4)   refuse to destroy an item that reasonably appears to have been tampered with or to be at variance with its purported count or weight; and

(5)   ensure destruction of each item as soon as reasonably possible.

(b)   Suspicious incident. Each witness must:

(1)   investigate a suspicious incident or probable breach of security, including a discrepancy, loss, theft, or other potential diversion of an item to be destroyed; or

(2)   report the incident or breach to an appropriate law enforcement agency or peace officer for investigation.

(c)   Registrant security provisions may also apply. The registrant security provisions of this chapter apply if a witness to destruction under this subchapter is also registered individually as a controlled substances registrant or employed by a registrant. If so, the witness is responsible for making a written report to the director through the Narcotics Regulation Bureau of a probable breach of security under those provisions.

Source: The provisions of this §13.161 adopted to be effective July 18, 2001, 26 TexReg 5266; amended to be effective February 25, 2010, 35 TexReg 1476

§13.162 Laboratory Retesting for Possible Tampering – Security Control

(a)   Suspicious incident. Unless there is an obvious, reasonable explanation for the event in question, each witness to a destruction under this subchapter is responsible for returning an item to a laboratory for testing to detect a discrepancy, loss, theft, or other potential diversion if:

(1)   the count or weight of the item is substantially incorrect;

(2)   a package has been opened; or

(3)   there is another suspicious incident or probable breach of security.

(b)   Laboratory options. If an individual returns an item to a laboratory for testing under this section, the laboratory may conduct an analysis sufficient to detect discrepancy, loss, theft, or other potential diversion or to resolve the particular suspicion surrounding the incident.

Source: The provisions of this §13.162 adopted to be effective July 18, 2001, 26 TexReg 5266

§13.163 Destruction Documentation – Security Control

(a)   Contemporaneous written statement. At or immediately after the time of a destruction under this subchapter, one of the witnesses to destruction must complete a written statement containing a detailed description of the destruction of the item, including all the relevant information required by this subchapter.

(b)   Private contract. If a laboratory, law enforcement agency, or peace officer contracts with a private entity to destroy the item, the witnesses need not be present during the actual physical destruction of each item by the private contractor. A written statement under this subsection must document the status and handling of the item up to the point the laboratory, agency, or officer turned it over to the private contractor for destruction under the contract.

(c)   Contents of statement. A statement may incorporate other documents by reference and must contain:

(1)   relevant seizure information, including the seizing law enforcement agency or peace officer, the date and location of seizure, and the authority for seizure;

(2)   the destruction authority, including the name, position, and reason given by the individual authorizing destruction;

(3)   the manner of transportation to the destruction site, including the names of each individual transporting an item;

(4)   an inventory of the items destroyed, including the nature, kind, and quantity of the item;

(5)   the witnesses, including the name, title, agency, and signature of each witness;

(6)   the date and location of destruction;

(7)   manner of destruction; and

(8)   each unusual or suspicious event that occurred during the destruction incident.

Source: The provisions of this §13.163 adopted to be effective July 18, 2001, 26 TexReg 5266

§13.164 Document Maintenance, Inspection, and Transmittal – Security Control

(a)   Generally. The laboratory, law enforcement agency, or peace officer who destroys an item under this subchapter must maintain the original destruction documents in a readily retrievable form after the date of destruction.

(b)   Available to Director for inspection. The destroying laboratory, law enforcement agency, or peace officer must make the original destruction documents available for announced or unannounced inspection by the director.

(c)   Copy upon request. If the director requests a copy of the destruction documentation, a laboratory, law enforcement agency, or peace officer destroying an item subject to this subchapter must provide the copy to the director within seven days.

(d)   Destruction standard operating procedure (SOP). A laboratory or law enforcement agency adopting a written destruction SOP under this subchapter must:

(1)   maintain the original copy of the SOP;

(2)   make the original available for announced or unannounced inspection by the director or a member of the department; and

(3)   provide the copy to the director under this section in the same manner as another destruction document.

Source: The provisions of this §13.164 adopted to be effective July 18, 2001, 26 TexReg 5266

§13.165 Communication with Director (Crime Lab Service)

If a person is required or allowed by this subchapter to make a notification, report, or other written, telephonic, or personal communication to the director, the person must make the communication to the director through the Crime Laboratory Service at the address indicated in § 28.7 of this title (relating to Communications).

Source: The provisions of this § 13.165 adopted to be effective July 18, 2001, 26 TexReg 5266; amended to be effective August 18, 2015, 40 TexReg 5159

Cont. Sub.

DEA PHARMACIST'S MANUAL

An Informational Outline of the Controlled Substances Act

Revised 2010

Table of Contents

DEA Manual

DEA PHARMACIST'S MANUAL

An Information Outline of the Controlled Substances Act

Revised 2010

[Editor's Note: The Pharmacist's Manual is provided as of December 1, 2011, per the following website: www. DEAdiversion.usdoj.gov/pubs/manuals. Please reference that website for the latest information.]

AN INFORMATIONAL OUTLINE OF THE CONTROLLED SUBSTANCES ACT

Michele M. Leonhart
Administrator
Drug Enforcement Administration

Joseph T. Rannazzisi
Deputy Assistant Administrator/Deputy Chief of Operations
Office of Diversion Control

Mark W. Caverly
Chief, Liaison and Policy Section

This manual has been prepared by the Drug Enforcement Administration, Office of Diversion Control, as a guide to assist pharmacists in their understanding of the Federal Controlled Substances Act and its implementing regulations as they pertain to the pharmacy profession.

The 2010 edition replaces all previous editions of the Pharmacist's Manual issued by the Drug Enforcement Administration, both hard copy and electronic.

DEA Manual

SECTION I – INTRODUCTION

Disclaimer

This pharmacist's manual is intended to summarize and explain the basic requirements for prescribing, administering, and dispensing controlled substances under the Controlled Substances Act (CSA), Title 21 United States Code (21 U.S.C.) 801-971 and the DEA regulations, Title 21, Code of Federal Regulations (21 C.F.R.), Parts 1300 to 1316. Pertinent citations to the law and regulations are included in this manual.

Printed copies of the complete regulations implementing the CSA (21 C.F.R. Part 1300 to end) may be obtained from:

> Superintendent of Documents
> U.S. Government Printing Office
> Washington, D.C. 20402

Both the C.F.R. and the Federal Register (which includes proposed and final rules implementing the CSA) are available on the internet through the U.S. Government Printing Office website. This website, which provides information by section, citation, and keywords, can be accessed at:

> www.gpoaccess.gov

Unofficial copies of pertinent C.F.R. citations and this pharmacist's manual may be found on the internet at DEA's Diversion website (under "publications"):

> www.DEAdiversion.usdoj.gov

Should any pertinent provisions of the law or regulations be modified in the future, DEA will issue a revised electronic version of this document, which will be posted on the DEA Diversion website.

If you encounter errors in this document, please notify:

> Drug Enforcement Administration
> Attn: Liaison and Policy Section/ODL
> 8701 Morrissette Drive
> Springfield, Virginia 22152

Inquiries regarding topics within this document may be addressed to your local DEA Diversion Field Office (**Appendix K**) or the address above.

Authorization for Public Dissemination

All material in this publication is in the public domain and may be reproduced without the express permission of the Drug Enforcement Administration.

Message from the Administrator

The Drug Enforcement Administration is pleased to provide you with the 2010 edition of the Pharmacist's Manual to assist you in understanding the provisions of the Controlled Substances Act (CSA) and its implementing regulations. This manual will answer questions you may encounter in the practice of pharmacy and provide guidance in complying with the CSA regulations. This edition has been updated to include information on the provisions of the Combat Methamphetamine Epidemic Act of 2005, the Ryan Haight Online Pharmacy Consumer Protection Act of 2008, and the Interim Final Rule entitled Electronic Prescriptions for Controlled Substances.

Your role in the proper dispensing of controlled substances is critical to the health of patients and helps protect society against drug abuse and diversion. Your adherence to the CSA, together with its objectives and your compliance, is a powerful resource for protecting the public health, assuring patient safety, and preventing the diversion of controlled substances and drug products containing listed chemicals.

Sincerely,

Michele M. Leonhart
Administrator
Drug Enforcement Administration

DEA Manual

PREFACE

The Drug Enforcement Administration (DEA) was established in 1973 to serve as the primary agency responsible for the enforcement of federal drug laws. The Controlled Substances Act (CSA) and its implementing regulations establish federal requirements regarding both illicit and licit controlled substances. With respect to pharmaceutical controlled substances, DEA's responsibility is twofold: to prevent diversion and abuse of these substances while ensuring an adequate and uninterrupted supply is available to meet the country's legitimate medical, scientific, and research needs. In carrying out this mission, DEA works closely with state and local authorities and other federal agencies.

Under the framework of the CSA, all controlled substance transactions take place within a "closed system" of distribution established by Congress. Within this "closed system" all legitimate handlers of controlled substances – manufacturers, distributors, physicians, pharmacies, and others, must be registered with DEA (unless exempt) and maintain strict accounting for all controlled substance transactions.

To carry out this mission effectively, DEA seeks to educate its registrants regarding their legal obligations. It is DEA's goal to maintain a positive working relationship with all of its registrants, including pharmacies. DEA understands that it can best serve the public interest by working with the pharmacy community to prevent the diversion of pharmaceutical controlled substances and scheduled listed chemical products (SLCPs) into the illicit market.

Federal controlled substance laws are designed to function in tandem with state controlled substance laws. DEA works in cooperation with state professional licensing boards and state and local law enforcement officials to make certain that pharmaceutical controlled substances are prescribed, administered, and dispensed for a legitimate medical purpose in the usual course of professional practice. Within this framework, the majority of investigations into possible violations of controlled substance laws are carried out by state authorities. DEA focuses its investigations on cases involving violators of the highest level or most significant impact.

In the event a state board revokes the license of a pharmacy, DEA will request a voluntary surrender of the pharmacy's DEA registration. If the pharmacy refuses to surrender its registration, DEA will seek administrative action to revoke its DEA registration based on lack of state authorization. Additional administrative remedies that may be utilized to correct a lack of compliance include a letter of admonition or an administrative hearing. DEA may also pursue civil or criminal sanctions if there is sufficient evidence to justify a prosecution. All such actions are designed to protect the public health and safety.

In addition to the diversion of controlled substances, DEA is concerned with the diversion of certain chemicals used in the clandestine manufacture of controlled substances. Chemicals such as ephedrine and pseudoephedrine contained in over the counter and prescription substances are immediate precursors used in the illicit manufacture of methamphetamine and amphetamine. These products may be purchased or stolen from retail outlets, including pharmacies, for use in clandestine laboratories.

Pharmacies that sell over the counter products containing ephedrine and pseudoephedrine must be "self-certified" as required by the Combat Methamphetamine Epidemic Act of 2005 (CMEA). The CMEA created a new category of products designated as SLCPs. SLCPs are products containing ephedrine, pseudoephedrine, or phenylpropanolamine that may be marketed or distributed lawfully in the United States as a non-prescription drug under the Food, Drug, and Cosmetic Act. The retail provisions of the CMEA went into effect on September 30, 2006 and require, among other things, employee training, self certification, placement of SLCPs out of customer reach, required identification, sales logbooks, sales and purchase limits, and others.

DEA and the pharmacy profession have strong common interests in the appropriate use of controlled substances and SLCPs. An effective working relationship to ensure compliance with CSA requirements will continue to produce lasting benefits on a national scale.

SECTION II – SCHEDULES OF CONTROLLED SUBSTANCES

The drugs and other substances that are considered controlled substances under the CSA are divided into five schedules. A listing of the substances and their schedules is found in the DEA regulations, 21 C.F.R. Sections 1308.11 through 1308.15. A controlled substance is placed in its respective schedule based on whether it has a currently accepted medical use in treatment in the United States and its relative abuse potential and likelihood of causing dependence. Some examples of controlled substances in each schedule are outlined below.

NOTE: Drugs listed in schedule I have no currently accepted medical use in treatment in the United States and, therefore, may not be prescribed, administered, or dispensed for medical use. In contrast, drugs listed in schedules II-V have some accepted medical use and may be prescribed, administered, or dispensed for medical use.

Schedule I Controlled Substances

Substances in this schedule have a high potential for abuse, have no currently accepted medical use in treatment in the United States, and there is a lack of accepted safety for use of the drug or other substance under medical supervision.

Some examples of substances listed in schedule I are: heroin, lysergic acid diethylamide (LSD), marijuana (cannabis), peyote, methaqualone, and 3,4-methylenedioxymethamphetamine ("ecstasy").

Schedule II Controlled Substances

Substances in this schedule have a high potential for abuse which may lead to severe psychological or physical dependence.

Examples of single entity schedule II narcotics include morphine and opium. Other schedule II narcotic substances and their common name brand products include: hydromorphone (Dilaudid®), methadone (Dolophine®), meperidine (Demerol®), oxycodone (OxyContin®), and fentanyl (Sublimaze® or Duragesic®).

Examples of schedule II stimulants include: amphetamine (Dexedrine®, Adderall®), methamphetamine (Desoxyn®), and methylphenidate (Ritalin®). Other schedule II substances include: cocaine, amobarbital, glutethimide, and pentobarbital.

Schedule III Controlled Substances

Substances in this schedule have a potential for abuse less than substances in schedules I or II and abuse may lead to moderate or low physical dependence or high psychological dependence.

Examples of schedule III narcotics include combination products containing less than 15 milligrams of hydrocodone per dosage unit (Vicodin®) and products containing not more than 90 milligrams of codeine per dosage unit (Tylenol with codeine®). Also included are buprenorphine products (Suboxone® and Subutex®) used to treat opioid addiction.

Examples of schedule III non-narcotics include benzphetamine (Didrex®), phendimetrazine, ketamine, and anabolic steroids such as oxandrolone (Oxandrin®).

Schedule IV Controlled Substances

Substances in this schedule have a low potential for abuse relative to substances in schedule III.

An example of a schedule IV narcotic is propoxyphene (Darvon® and Darvocet-N 100®).

Other schedule IV substances include: alprazolam (Xanax®), clonazepam (Klonopin®), clorazepate (Tranxene®), diazepam (Valium®), lorazepam (Ativan®), midazolam (Versed®), temazepam (Restoril®), and triazolam (Halcion®).

Schedule V Controlled Substances

Substances in this schedule have a low potential for abuse relative to substances listed in schedule IV and consist primarily of preparations containing limited quantities of certain narcotics. These are generally used for antitussive, antidiarrheal, and analgesic purposes.

Examples include cough preparations containing not more than 200 milligrams of codeine per 100 milliliters or per 100 grams (Robitussin AC® and Phenergan with Codeine®).

Scheduled Listed Chemical Product (SLCP)

An SLCP is defined as a product that contains ephedrine, pseudoephedrine, or phenylpropanolamine and may be marketed or distributed lawfully in the United States under the Federal Food, Drug, and Cosmetic Act as a nonprescription drug.

SECTION III – REGISTRATION REQUIREMENTS

New Pharmacy Registration

Every pharmacy that dispenses a controlled substance must be registered with the DEA. First, a state license must be obtained.

To register as a new pharmacy, the DEA Form 224 must be completed. The cost of the application fee is indicated on the application form. The certificate of registration must be maintained at the registered location and kept available for official inspection. If a person owns and operates more than one pharmacy, each place of business must be registered.

The DEA Form 224 should be completed online (www.DEAdiversion.usdoj.gov).

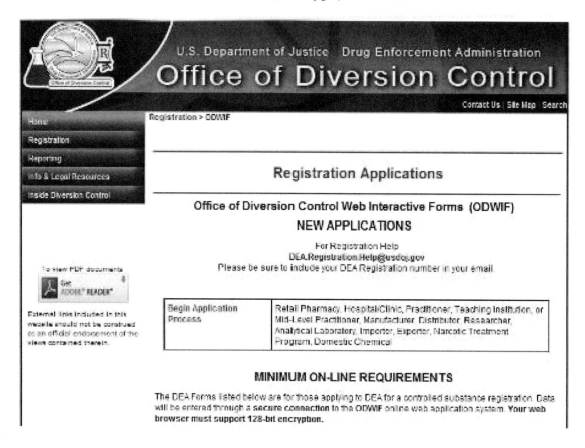

A paper version of the DEA Form 224 may be requested by writing to:

Drug Enforcement Administration
Attn: Registration Section/ODR
P.O. Box 2639
Springfield, Virginia 22152-2639

If a pharmacy needs a duplicate Certificate of Registration (DEA Form 223), a copy may be requested online via DEA's Diversion website, www.DEAdiversion.usdoj.gov, or contact DEA Headquarters at 1-800-882-9539 or via e-mail at DEA.Registration.Help@usdoj.gov.

Renewal of Pharmacy Registration

A pharmacy registration must be renewed every three years utilizing DEA Form 224a, Renewal Application for DEA Registration. The cost of the application fee is indicated on the application form.

To renew a registration, the most current information from the pharmacy's existing registration must be utilized. A registrant can renew online no more than 60 days prior to the current expiration date. The DEA Form 224a should be completed online and can be found at www. DEAdiversion.usdoj.gov.

If the registrant has not renewed online approximately 50 days before the registration expiration date, a renewal application is sent to the registrant at the mailing address listed on the current registration. If the renewal form is not received by the 30th day before the expiration date of the current registration, the pharmacy should contact the local DEA Registration Specialist (**Appendix J**) or DEA Headquarters at 1-800-882-9539 and request a renewal registration form.

NOTE: Once the expiration date has passed and no renewal has been received by DEA, the pharmacy has no authority to handle controlled substances.

Affidavit for Renewal of Retail Chain Pharmacy Registration

Corporations that own or operate a chain of pharmacies may submit a single DEA Form 224b, Retail Pharmacy Registration Affidavit for Chain Renewal. This affidavit, along with a list of the corporation's registrations, is provided in lieu of a separate registration application for each pharmacy registration. No registration may be issued unless the completed affidavit is received by DEA. The corporation should retain a copy of this affidavit with their readily retrievable records for the duration of the registrations covered by the affidavit. A responsible individual must answer the questions listed on the affidavit on behalf of the corporation as they pertain to each registrant.

The original affidavit along with the registration application fee and the list of registrations should be mailed to:

> Registration Chain Renewal
> Drug Enforcement Administration
> Attn: Registration Section/ODR
> P.O. Box 2639
> Springfield, Virginia 22152-2639

Change of Business Address

A pharmacy that moves to a new physical location must request a modification of registration. Modifications are handled in the same manner as applications and must be approved by DEA. A modification of registration can be requested online at www.DEAdiversion.usdoj.gov or in writing to the local DEA Registration Specialist (**Appendix J**) responsible for the area in which the pharmacy is located. If the change of address involves a change in state, the proper state issued license and, if applicable, controlled substances registration must be obtained prior to the approval of modification of the federal registration. If the modification is approved, DEA will issue a new certificate of registration and, if requested, new schedule II order forms (DEA Form 222). The registrant should maintain the new certificate with the old certificate until expiration. A Renewal Application for Registration (DEA Form 224a) will only be sent to the mailing address on file with DEA. It will not be forwarded.

Termination of Registration

A pharmacy that discontinues business activities either completely or only regarding controlled substances must return its DEA registration certificate and unused official order forms (DEA Form 222) to the local DEA Registration Specialist (**Appendix J**). In addition, DEA may ask for the location of where inventories, prescriptions, and other required controlled substance records will be stored during the requisite two-year retention period.

Unwanted controlled substances in the pharmacy's possession must be disposed of in accordance with DEA regulations (see **Section IV, Transfer or Disposal of Controlled Substances**).

Transfer of Business

A pharmacy registrant that transfers its business operations to another pharmacy registrant must submit in person or by registered or certified mail, return receipt requested, to the Special Agent in Charge in his/her area, at least 14 days in advance of the date of the proposed transfer (unless the Special Agent in Charge waives this time limitation in individual instances), the following information:

1. The name, address, registration number, and authorized business activity of the registrant discontinuing the business (registrant-transferor);

2. The name, address, registration number, and authorized business activity of the person acquiring the business (registrant-transferee);

3. Whether the business activities will be continued at the location registered by the person discontinuing business, or moved to another location (if the latter, the address of the new location should be listed); and

4. The date on which the transfer of controlled substances will occur.

On the day the controlled substances are transferred, a complete inventory must be taken and a copy of the inventory must be included in the records of both the person transferring the business and the person acquiring the business. This inventory will serve as the final inventory for the registrant going out of business and transferring the controlled substances. It will also serve as the initial inventory for the registrant acquiring the controlled substances. It is not necessary to send a copy of the inventory to the DEA unless requested by the Special Agent in Charge.

To transfer schedule II controlled substances, the receiving registrant must issue an official order form (DEA Form 222) or an electronic equivalent to the registrant transferring the drugs. The transfer of schedules III-V controlled substances must be documented in writing to show the drug name, dosage form, strength, quantity, and date transferred. The document must include the names, addresses, and DEA registration numbers of the parties involved in the transfer of the controlled substances.

All controlled substance records required to be kept by the registrant-transferor shall be transferred to the registrant-transferee. Responsibility for the accuracy of records prior to the date of transfer remains with the transferor, but responsibility for custody and maintenance shall be upon the transferee.

If the registrant acquiring the pharmacy owns at least one other pharmacy licensed in the same state as the pharmacy being transferred, the registrant may apply for a new DEA registration prior to the date of transfer. DEA will issue a registration which will authorize the registrant to obtain controlled substances at the time of transfer, but the registrant may not dispense controlled substances until the pharmacy has been issued a valid state pharmacy license.

A DEA registration application to transfer ownership of an existing pharmacy can be facilitated if the applicant includes an affidavit verifying that the pharmacy has been registered by the state licensing agency. The affidavit verifying the existence of the state license should be attached to the initial application for registration.

Denial, Suspension, or Revocation of Registration

Under the CSA (21 U.S.C. § 824 (a)), DEA has the authority to deny, suspend, or revoke a DEA registration upon a finding that the registrant:

1. Has materially falsified the application;

2. Has been convicted of a felony relating to a controlled substance or a List I chemical;

3. Had a State license or registration suspended, revoked, or denied by a competent State authority and is no longer authorized by State law to engage in the manufacturing, distribution, or dispensing of controlled substances or List I chemicals or has had the suspension, revocation, or denial of a registration recommended by competent State authority;

4. Has committed an act which would render the DEA registration inconsistent with the public interest; or

5. Has been excluded (or directed to be excluded) from participation in a program pursuant to Title 42 U.S.C. § 1320a-7(a), that is, a Medicaid or Medicare program.

Denial of Registration in the Public Interest

In determining the public interest, the CSA states the following factors are to be considered (21 U.S.C. § 823 (f)):

1. The recommendation of the appropriate State licensing board or professional disciplinary authority.

2. The applicant's experience in dispensing or conducting research with respect to controlled substances.

3. The applicant's conviction record under federal or state laws relating to the manufacture, distribution, or dispensing of controlled substances.

4. Compliance with applicable State, Federal, or local laws relating to controlled substances.

5. Such other conduct which may threaten the public health and safety.

Chemical Registration Requirements

Registration is not required for regulated sellers of SLCPs. However, a regulated seller must self-certify with DEA pursuant to federal law (see **Section XIV, Self-Certification**). A regulated seller is defined as a grocery store, general merchandise store, drug store, or other entity engaged in over-the-counter sales of ephedrine (both single-entity and combination products), pseudoephedrine, or phenylpropanolamine products, directly to walk-in customers or in face-to-face transactions by direct sales. A mobile retail vendor is defined as a person or entity that makes sales at retail from a stand that is intended to be temporary or is capable of being moved from one location to another.

Federal law requires any person who is engaged in the wholesale distribution of an SLCP to obtain a registration as a chemical distributor. A distributor who does not meet all the requirements for a regulated seller of SLCPs, or who does not meet the requirements for distributors required to submit "mail-order" reports, is a wholesale distributor.

Note: this would include those pharmacies that sell quantities of SLCPs to institutions, including long term care facilities, jails, and other institutional-type settings for non-patient specific use. Such pharmacies are often referred to as "closed door" pharmacies.

Retail pharmacies that are registered to handle controlled substances need not obtain a separate DEA chemical registration for retail distribution of SLCPs. If a pharmacy desires to engage in the wholesale distribution of bulk quantities of SLCPs, the pharmacy is required to register with DEA as a chemical distributor because these activities fall outside the definition of a regulated seller. Therefore, the pharmacy would be subject to the registration requirements that apply to wholesale distributors for those distribution activities, and subject to the pharmacy requirements for its pharmacy activities. To obtain a DEA chemical distributor registration, a pharmacy may complete the DEA Form 510 online at www.DEAdiversion.usdoj.gov. A paper version may be requested by writing to:

> Drug Enforcement Administration
> Attn: Registration Section/ODR
> P.O. Box 2639
> Springfield, Virginia 22152-2639

SECTION IV – TRANSFER OR DISPOSAL OF CONTROLLED SUBSTANCES

Transfer of Controlled Substances

A pharmacy may hire an outside firm to inventory, package, and arrange for the transfer of its controlled substances to another pharmacy, the original supplier, or the original manufacturer. The pharmacy is responsible for the actual transfer of the controlled substances and for the accuracy of the inventory and records. The records involving the transfer of controlled substances must be kept readily available by the pharmacy for two years for inspection by the DEA.

To transfer schedule II substances, the receiving registrant must issue an official order form (DEA Form 222) or an electronic equivalent to the registrant transferring the drugs. The transfer of schedules III-V controlled substances must be documented in writing to show the drug name, dosage form, strength, quantity, and date transferred. The document must include the names, addresses, and DEA registration numbers of the parties involved in the transfer of the controlled substances.

Transfer to a Pharmacy

If a pharmacy goes out of business or is acquired by a new pharmacy, it may transfer the controlled substances to another pharmacy. On the day the controlled substances are transferred, a complete inventory must be taken which documents the drug name, dosage form, strength, quantity, and date transferred. In addition, DEA Form 222 or the electronic equivalent must be prepared to document the transfer of schedule II controlled substances. This inventory will serve as the final inventory for the registrant going out of business and transferring the controlled substances. It will also serve as the initial inventory for the registrant acquiring the controlled substances. A copy of the inventory must be included in the records of each pharmacy. It is not necessary to send a copy of the inventory to the DEA. The pharmacy acquiring the controlled substances must maintain all records involved in the transfer of the controlled substances for two years.

Transfer to the Original Supplier or Original Manufacturer

Any pharmacy may transfer controlled substances to the original supplier or the original manufacturer that is appropriately registered with the DEA. The pharmacist must maintain a written record showing:

1. The date of the transaction.

2. The name, strength, dosage form, and quantity of the controlled substance.

3. The supplier or manufacturer's name, address, and registration number.

The DEA Form 222 or the electronic equivalent will be the official record for the transfer of schedule II controlled substances.

Disposal of Controlled Substances

A pharmacy may transfer controlled substances to a DEA registered reverse distributor who handles the disposal of controlled substances. The pharmacy should contact the local DEA Diversion Field Office (**Appendix K**) for an updated list of DEA registered reverse distributors. In no case should drugs be forwarded to the DEA unless the registrant has received prior approval from the DEA. The DEA procedures established for the disposal of controlled substances must not be construed as altering in any way the state laws or regulations for the disposal of controlled substances.

Reverse Distributors Authorized to Dispose Controlled Substances

A pharmacy may forward controlled substances to a DEA registered reverse distributor who handles the disposal of controlled substances. When a pharmacy transfers schedule II controlled substances to a reverse distributor for destruction, the reverse distributor must issue an official order form (DEA Form 222) or the electronic equivalent to the pharmacy. When schedules III-V controlled substances are transferred to a reverse distributor for destruction, the pharmacy must maintain a record of distribution that lists the drug name, dosage form, strength, quantity, and date transferred. The DEA registered reverse distributor who will destroy the controlled substances is responsible for submitting a DEA Form 41 (Registrants Inventory of Drugs Surrendered) to the DEA when the controlled substances have been destroyed. A DEA Form 41 should **not** be used to record the transfer of controlled substances between the pharmacy and the reverse distributor disposing of the drugs.

A paper version of the DEA Form 41 may be requested by writing to:

>Drug Enforcement Administration
>Attn: Registration Section/ODR
>P.O. Box 2639
>Springfield, Virginia 22152-2639

Disposal of Controlled Substances by Persons Not Registered with DEA

On January 21, 2009, DEA published in the Federal Register an Advance Notice of Proposed Rulemaking (ANPRM), *Disposal of Controlled Substances by Persons Not Registered with the Drug Enforcement Administration*. This ANPRM sought comments on how to address the issue of disposal of dispensed controlled substances held by DEA nonregistrants (i.e., ultimate users, long term care facilities). DEA was interested in the possible options that would enable nonregistrants to dispose of unwanted controlled substances, while also protecting public health and public safety, and minimizing the possibility of diversion. The public comment period for this ANPRM ended on March 23, 2009.

SECTION V – SECURITY REQUIREMENTS

Requests for Employment Waivers for Certain Pharmacy Employees

Under 21 C.F.R. § 1301.76(a), a registrant must not employ in a position which allows access to controlled substances any person who has been convicted of a felony relating to controlled substances, or who, at any time, has had an application for DEA registration denied, revoked, or surrendered for cause. "For cause" means surrendering a registration in lieu of, or as a consequence of, any federal or state administrative, civil, or criminal action resulting from an investigation of the individual's handling of controlled substances.

However, 21 C.F.R. § 1307.03 does permit registrants desiring to employ an individual who meets this definition to request an exception to this requirement. The employer must have a waiver approved before allowing such an employee or prospective employee to have access to controlled substances. A waiver request should be sent by the employer to the following address:

>Drug Enforcement Administration
>Attn: Regulatory Section/ODG
>8701 Morrissette Drive
>Springfield, Virginia 22152

A registrant that applies for such a waiver should understand that the following factors will be considered by the DEA in the approval process and should provide details relevant to each factor as part of the waiver request submitted, since a waiver will not be considered unless there are valid reasons to believe that diversion is unlikely to occur:

1. A detailed description of the nature and extent of the individual's past controlled substances violations, including all pertinent documentation;

2. Current status of the individual's state licensure;

3. Extent of individual's proposed access to controlled substances. "Access" is not limited to only physical access to controlled substances, but includes any influence over the handling of controlled substances;

4. Registrant's proposed physical and professional safeguards to prevent diversion by the individual;

5. Status of employing registrant regarding handling of controlled substances;

6. Other pertinent information uncovered by DEA in its investigation of the individual's or registrant's handling of controlled substances; and

7. All other relevant factors or materials.

Controlled Substance Theft or Significant Loss

Should a theft or significant loss of any controlled substance occur at a pharmacy, the following procedures must be implemented within one business day of the discovery of the theft or loss.

A. Notify DEA and Local Police

The theft of controlled substances from a registrant is a criminal act and a source of diversion that requires notification to DEA. A pharmacy must notify in writing the local DEA Diversion Field Office (**Appendix K**) within one business day of discovery of a theft or significant loss of a controlled substance. Although not specifically required by federal law or regulations, the registrant should also notify local law enforcement and state regulatory agencies. Prompt notification to enforcement agencies will allow them to investigate the incident and prosecute those responsible for the diversion. If there is a question as to whether a theft has occurred or a loss is significant, a registrant should err on the side of caution and report it to DEA and local law enforcement authorities.

DEA must be notified directly. This requirement is not satisfied by reporting the theft or significant loss in any other manner. For example, a corporation which owns or operates multiple registered sites and wishes to channel all notifications through corporate management or any other internal department responsible for security, must still provide notice directly to DEA in writing within one business day upon discovery and keep a copy of that notice for its records. The notice must be signed by an authorized individual of the registrant.

B. Complete DEA Form 106

A pharmacy must also complete a DEA Form 106 (*Report of Theft or Loss of Controlled Substances*) which can be found online at www.DEAdiversion.usdoj.gov under the *Quick Links* section. The DEA Form 106 is used to document the actual circumstances of the theft or significant loss and the quantities of controlled substances involved. A paper version of the form can be obtained by writing to:

Drug Enforcement Administration
Attn: Regulatory Section/ODG
8701 Morrissette Drive
Springfield, Virginia 22152

If completing the paper version, the pharmacy should send the original DEA Form 106 to the local DEA Diversion Field Office (**Appendix K**) and keep a copy for its records. Please see the **Guidelines for Completing the DEA Form 106 (Appendix I)** for additional guidance.

The DEA Form 106 must include the following information:

1. Name and address of the firm (pharmacy),
2. DEA registration number,
3. Date of theft or loss (or when discovered if not known),
4. Name and telephone number of local police department (if notified),
5. Type of theft (e.g., night break-in, armed robbery),
6. List of identifying marks, symbols, or price codes (if any) used by the pharmacy on the labels of the containers, and
7. A listing of controlled substances missing, including the strength, dosage form, and size of container (in milliliters if liquid form) or corresponding National Drug Code numbers.

C. If Investigation Finds No Theft or Loss

If, after the initial notification to DEA, the investigation of the theft or loss determines no such theft or loss of controlled substances occurred, a DEA Form 106 does not need to be filed. However, the registrant must notify DEA in writing of this fact in order to resolve the initial report and explain why no DEA Form 106 was filed regarding the incident.

D. Registrant's Responsibility for Identifying "Significant Loss"

Although the CSA regulations do not define the term "significant loss," it is the responsibility of the registrant to use his/her best judgment to take appropriate action. Whether a "significant loss" has occurred depends, in large part, on the business of the pharmacy and the likelihood of a rational explanation for a particular occurrence. What would constitute a significant loss for a pharmacy may be viewed as comparatively insignificant for a hospital or manufacturer.

Further, the loss of a small quantity of controlled substances, repeated over a period of time, may indicate a significant problem for a registrant, which must be reported. The burden of responsibility is on the registrant to identify what is a significant loss and make the required report to DEA.

When determining whether a loss is significant, a registrant should consider, among others, the following factors:

1. The actual quantity of controlled substances lost in relation to the type of business;
2. The specific controlled substances;
3. Whether the loss of the controlled substances can be associated with access to those controlled substances by specific individuals, or whether the loss can be attributed to unique activities that may take place involving the controlled substances;
4. A pattern of losses over a specific time period, whether the losses appear to be random, and the results of efforts taken to resolve the losses; and, if known
5. Whether the specific controlled substances are likely candidates for diversion; and

6.   Local trends and other indicators of the diversion potential of the missing controlled substances.

If it is determined that the loss is not significant, the registrant should place a record of the occurrence in a theft and loss file for future reference. Miscounts or adjustments to inventory involving clerical errors on the part of the pharmacy should not be reported on a DEA Form 106, but rather should be noted in a separate log at the pharmacy management's discretion.

In-Transit Loss

When all or part of an in-transit shipment of controlled substances fails to reach its intended destination, the supplier is responsible for reporting the in-transit loss of controlled substances to DEA. The purchaser is responsible for reporting any loss of controlled substances after he/she has signed for or taken custody of a shipment. If it is discovered after that point that an in-transit loss or theft has occurred; the purchaser must then submit a DEA Form 106. If the purchaser does not take custody of the shipment and instead returns it to the supplier, it is the supplier's responsibility for reporting any loss of controlled substances in the original shipment.

In-Transit Loss from Central Fill Pharmacy

Central fill pharmacies must comply with 21 C.F.R. § 1301.74(e) when selecting private, common or contract carriers to transport filled prescriptions to a retail pharmacy for delivery to an ultimate user. Pursuant to 21 C.F.R. § 1301.76(d), when a central fill pharmacy contracts with private, common or contract carriers to transport filled prescriptions to a retail pharmacy, the central fill pharmacy is responsible for reporting the in-transit loss upon discovery of such loss by use of a DEA Form 106. In addition, when a retail pharmacy contracts with private, common or contract carriers to retrieve filled prescriptions from a central fill pharmacy, the retail pharmacy is responsible for reporting in-transit losses upon discovery using a DEA Form 106.

Breakage and Spillage

The breakage or spillage of controlled substances does not constitute a "loss" of controlled substances. When there is breakage, damage, or spillage or some other form of destruction, any recoverable controlled substances must be disposed of according to DEA requirements. When this disposal occurs, it must be reported to DEA on a DEA Form 41 (*Registrants Inventory of Drugs Surrendered*). Damaged goods may also be disposed of through shipment to a reverse distributor or by a DEA approved process as defined in **Section IV, Transfer or Disposal of Controlled Substances**.

A paper version of the DEA Form 41 may be requested by writing to:

> Drug Enforcement Administration
> Attn: Regulatory Section/ODG
> 8701 Morrissette Drive
> Springfield, Virginia 22152

Robberies and Burglaries Involving Controlled Substances

The Controlled Substance Registrant Protection Act of 1984 (CSRPA) was enacted to protect DEA registrants against certain crimes (see Title 18 U.S.C. § 2118 for a complete text of CSRPA). The CSRPA provides for the federal investigation of controlled substances thefts and robberies if any of the following conditions are met:

1.   The replacement cost of the controlled substances taken is $500 or more.

2.   Interstate or foreign commerce was involved in the execution of the crime.

3.   A person was killed or suffered significant bodily injury as a result of the crime.

Penalties Upon Conviction – The perpetrator(s) convicted of violating CSRPA's provisions may be subject to the following penalties:

1.   Burglary or robbery – a maximum $25,000 fine and/or 20 years imprisonment.

2.   If a dangerous weapon was used to carry out the crime – a maximum $35,000 fine and/or 25 years imprisonment.

3.   If death resulted from the crime – a maximum $50,000 fine and/or life imprisonment.

SECTION VI – RECORDKEEPING REQUIREMENTS

Every pharmacy must maintain complete and accurate records on a current basis for each controlled substance purchased, received, stored, distributed, dispensed, or otherwise disposed of. These records are required to provide accountability of all controlled substances from the manufacturing process through the dispensing pharmacy and to the ultimate user. The closed system reduces the potential for diversion of controlled substances.

All required records concerning controlled substances must be maintained for at least two years for inspection and copying by duly authorized DEA officials. Records and inventories of schedule II controlled substances must be maintained separately from all other records of the registrant. All records and inventories of schedules III, IV, and V controlled substances must be maintained either separately from all other records or in such a form that the information required is readily retrievable from the ordinary business records. Recordkeeping requirements for prescriptions are detailed in **Section VI, Prescription Records**.

Readily retrievable is defined as:

1. Records kept by automatic data processing systems or other electronic or mechanized recordkeeping systems in such a manner that they can be separated out from all other records in a reasonable time, and/or

2. Records kept in such a manner that certain items are asterisked, redlined, or in some other manner visually identifiable apart from other items appearing on the records.

Required Records

The records which must be maintained by a pharmacy are:

1. Executed and unexecuted official order forms (DEA Form 222) or the electronic equivalent

2. Power of Attorney authorization to sign order forms

3. Receipts and/or invoices for schedules III, IV, and V controlled substances

4. All inventory records of controlled substances, including the initial and biennial inventories, dated as of beginning or close of business

5. Records of controlled substances distributed (i.e., sales to other registrants, returns to vendors, distributions to reverse distributors)

6. Records of controlled substances dispensed (i.e., prescriptions, schedule V logbook)

7. Reports of Theft or Significant Loss (DEA Form 106), if applicable

8. Inventory of Drugs Surrendered for Disposal (DEA Form 41), if applicable

9. Records of transfers of controlled substances between pharmacies

10. DEA registration certificate

11. Self-certification certificate and logbook (or electronic equivalent) as required under the Combat Methamphetamine Epidemic Act of 2005

Central Recordkeeping

A registrant desiring to maintain shipping and financial records (but not executed official order forms) at a central location rather than the registered location must submit written notification of his/her intention by registered or certified mail, return receipt requested, in triplicate, to the Special Agent in Charge of the local DEA Diversion Field Office in which the registrant is located (**Appendix K**). Unless the registrant is informed by the DEA that the permission to keep central records is denied, the registrant may begin maintaining central records 14 days after DEA receives this notification. Central recordkeeping requirements are described in 21 C.F.R. § 1304.04. Central recordkeeping permits are no longer issued by the DEA.

Prescription Records

Pharmacies have two options for filing prescription records under the C.F.R. If there is a conflict between federal and state requirements for filing prescriptions, DEA recognizes that the pharmacy must choose a filing system that would comply with both federal (21 U.S.C. § 903) and state law. All prescription records must be *readily retrievable* for DEA inspection. Controlled substance prescriptions must be filed in one of the following ways:

Paper Prescriptions Records Option 1 (Three separate files):

1. A file for schedule II controlled substances dispensed.

2. A file for schedules III, IV and V controlled substances dispensed.

3. A file for all noncontrolled drugs dispensed.

Paper Prescriptions Records Option 2 (Two separate files):

1. A file for all schedule II controlled substances dispensed.

2. A file for all other drugs dispensed (noncontrolled and those in schedules III, IV and V). If this method is used, a prescription for a schedule III, IV or V drug must be made readily retrievable by use of a red "C" stamp not less than one inch high. If a pharmacy has an electronic recordkeeping system for prescriptions which permits identification by prescription number and retrieval of original documents by prescriber's name, patient's name, drug dispensed, and date filled, the requirement to mark the hard copy with a red "C" is waived.

Electronic Prescription Records

1. If a prescription is created, signed, transmitted, and received electronically, all records related to that prescription must be retained electronically.

2. Electronic records must be maintained electronically for two years from the date of their creation or receipt. However, this record retention requirement shall not pre-empt any longer period of retention which may be required now or in the future, by any other Federal or State law or regulation, applicable to pharmacists or pharmacies.

3. Records regarding controlled substances must be readily retrievable from all other records. Electronic records must be easily readable or easily rendered into a format that a person can read.

Records of electronic prescriptions for controlled substances shall be maintained in an application that meets the requirements of 21 C.F.R. §1311. The computers on which the records are maintained may be located at another location, but the records must be readily retrievable at the registered location if requested by the DEA or other law enforcement agent. The electronic application must be capable of printing out or transferring the records in a format that is readily understandable to an Administration or other law enforcement agent at the registered location. Electronic copies of prescription records must be sortable by prescriber name, patient name, drug dispensed, and date filled.

SECTION VII – INVENTORY REQUIREMENTS

An "inventory" is a complete and accurate list of all stocks and forms of controlled substances in the possession of the registrant as determined by an actual physical count for schedule II controlled substances and an estimated count or measure of the contents of a schedule III, IV, or V controlled substance (unless the container holds more than 1,000 tablets or capsules in which case an exact count of the contents must be made). The CSA also requires that all inventory records be maintained at the registered location in a readily retrievable manner for at least two years for copying and inspection. In addition, the inventory records of schedule II controlled substances must be kept separate from all other controlled substances.

Initial Inventory

When issued a DEA registration, a registrant must take an initial inventory, which is an actual physical count of all controlled substances in their possession. If there are no stocks of controlled substances on hand, the registrant should make a record showing a zero inventory. There is no requirement to submit a copy of the inventory to the DEA. The C.F.R. requires that the inventory include:

1. The date of the inventory,

2. Whether the inventory was taken at the beginning or close of business,

3. The name of each controlled substance inventoried,

4. The finished form of each of the substances (e.g., 10 milligram tablet),

5. The number of dosage units of each finished form in the commercial container (e.g., 100 tablet bottle),

6. The number of commercial containers of each finished form (e.g., four 100 tablet bottles), and

7. A count of the substance – if the substance is listed in schedule II, an exact count or measure of the contents or if the substance is listed in schedules III, IV, or V, an estimated count or measure of the contents, unless the container holds more than 1,000 tablets or capsules in which case, an exact count of the contents is required.

DEA recommends, but does not require, an inventory record include the name, address, and DEA registration number of the registrant, and the signature of the person or persons responsible for taking the inventory.

Biennial Inventory

Following the initial inventory, the registrant is required to take a biennial inventory (every two years), which requires the same information as the initial inventory (see list above) of all controlled substances on hand. The biennial inventory may be taken on any date which is within two years of the previous inventory date. There is no requirement to submit a copy of the inventory to DEA.

Newly Scheduled Controlled Substance Inventory

When a drug not previously listed as a controlled substance is scheduled or a drug is rescheduled, the drug must be inventoried as of the effective date of scheduling or change in scheduling.

SECTION VIII – ORDERING CONTROLLED SUBSTANCES

Ordering Schedule II Controlled Substances

Only schedules I and II controlled substances are ordered with an official order form, DEA Form 222, or the electronic equivalent (see below, *Controlled Substance Ordering System (CSOS) – Electronic Order Forms*). A DEA Form 222 is required for each distribution, purchase, or transfer of a schedule II controlled substance.

When a controlled substance has been moved by DEA from schedule II to another schedule at the federal level, in many states it may remain a schedule II controlled substance pending any legislative or administrative action that may result from the federal action. Many states require transactions that involve substances they classify as schedule II be made via official order forms (DEA Form 222) or the electronic equivalent. When federal law or regulations differ from state law or regulations, a pharmacy is required to abide by the more stringent aspects of both the federal and state requirements. When the use of DEA Form 222 or the electronic equivalent for the transfer of a controlled substance is not required under federal law, its use as mandated by these states does not violate federal law and is therefore permitted.

Requesting Official Order Forms

The unexecuted DEA Form 222 can be requested initially by checking "block 3" on the application for a new registration (DEA Form 224). The DEA Form 224 can be found online at www.DEAdiversion.usdoj.gov.

Once a registrant has received a DEA registration number, additional DEA Forms 222 may be ordered online at www.DEAdiversion.usdoj. gov. When requesting additional DEA Forms 222 online, a valid DEA registration number, business name, and contact telephone number are required. The registrant may also request DEA Forms 222 by calling the DEA Headquarters Registration Section at 1-800-882-9539 or by contacting the local DEA Registration Specialist (**Appendix J**).

Each book of DEA Form 222 consists of seven sets of forms. Each pharmacy is provided a maximum of six books at one time unless its needs exceed this limit. In such a case, the pharmacy should contact the local DEA Registration Specialist (**Appendix J**) to request additional books.

Completing Official Order Forms

When ordering schedule II controlled substances, the purchaser is responsible for filling in the number of packages, the size of the package, and the name of the item. Each DEA Form 222 must be signed and dated by a person authorized to sign a registration application or a person granted power of attorney (see below, **Power of Attorney to Sign an Official Order Form**). When the items are received, the pharmacist must document on the purchaser's copy (copy three) the actual number of packages received and the date received.

The executed DEA Form 222 must be maintained separately from the pharmacy's other business records. However, this does not preclude a registrant from attaching a copy of the supplier's invoice to the related DEA Form 222.

Title 21 C.F.R. § 1305.15(a)(1) requires that, for orders using the DEA Form 222, an order must not be filled if the order is not complete, legible, or properly prepared, executed, or endorsed, or if the order shows any alteration, erasure, or change of any description. For a discussion of the circumstances in which an electronic order must not be filled see below, *Controlled Substance Ordering System (CSOS) – Electronic Order Forms*.

A supplier may refuse to accept an order for any reason as set forth under 21 C.F.R. § 1305.15(c). If a supplier refuses to accept an order, a statement that the order is not accepted is sufficient. If an order is refused, the supplier must return copies one and two of the DEA Form 222 to the purchaser with a statement explaining the reason the order was refused. For electronic orders, the supplier must notify the purchaser and provide a statement as to the reason (see below, *Controlled Substance Ordering System (CSOS) – Electronic Order Forms*).

DEA policy does not preclude the substitution of identical products differing in packaging size from those initially ordered, provided that the actual quantity received does not exceed the amount initially ordered and that the National Drug Code number reflected is that of the actual product shipped. For example, a distributor may substitute five bottles of 100, 2 milligram tablets for one bottle of 500, 2 milligram tablets or any variation thereof.

Cancellation and Voiding an Official Order Form

A purchaser may cancel an order (or partial order) on a DEA Form 222 by notifying the supplier in writing. The supplier must indicate the cancellation on Copies 1 and 2 of the DEA Form 222 by drawing a line through the cancelled item(s) and printing "cancelled" in the space provided for the number of items shipped.

A supplier may void part or all of an order on a DEA Form 222 by notifying the purchaser in writing. The supplier must indicate the voiding in Copies 1 and 2 of the DEA Form 222 by drawing a line through the cancelled item(s) and printing "void" in the space provided for the number of items shipped. For information regarding cancelled electronic orders, see below, *Controlled Substance Ordering System (CSOS) – Electronic Order Forms*.

Power of Attorney to Sign an Official Order Form

Any registrant (pharmacy) may authorize one or more individuals, whether or not they are located at the registered location, to obtain and execute DEA Forms 222 by granting a power of attorney to each such individual. The power of attorney must be signed by the same person who signed the most recent application for registration or renewal registration, as well as the individual being authorized to obtain and execute the DEA Forms 222.

The power of attorney may be revoked at any time by the person who granted and signed the power of attorney. Only if the renewal application is signed by a different person is it necessary to grant a new power of attorney when the pharmacy completes a renewal registration. The power of attorney should be filed with executed DEA Forms 222 as a readily retrievable record. The power of attorney is not submitted to DEA.

Suggested formats for granting and revoking a power of attorney follow:

Power of Attorney for DEA Forms 222 and Electronic Orders

_____(Name of registrant)
_____(Address of registrant)
_____(DEA registration number)

I, _____ (name of person granting power), the undersigned, who is authorized to sign the current application for registration of the above named registrant under the Controlled Substances Act or Controlled Substances Import and Export Act, have made, constituted, and appointed, and by these presents, do make, constitute, and appoint _____ _____ (name of attorney-in-fact), my true and lawful attorney for me in my name, place, and stead, to execute applications for books of official order forms and to sign such order forms in requisition for schedule I and II controlled substances, in accordance with Section 308 of the Controlled Substances Act (21 U.S.C. 828) and part 1305 of Title 21 of the Code of Federal Regulations. I hereby ratify and confirm all that said attorney shall lawfully do or cause to be done by virtue hereof.

_____

(Signature of person granting power)

I, _____(name of attorney-in-fact), hereby affirm that I am the person named herein as attorney-in-fact and that the signature affixed hereto is my signature.

_____

(Signature of attorney-in-fact)

Witnesses:

1. _____
2. _____

Signed and dated on the ___ day of _____ in the year ____ at _____.

Notice of Revocation

The foregoing power of attorney is hereby revoked by the undersigned, who is authorized to sign the current application for registration of the above-named registrant under the Controlled Substances Act. Written notice of this revocation has been given to the attorney-in-fact _____ this same day.

_____

(Signature of person revoking power)

Witnesses:

1. _____
2. _____

Signed and dated on the ___ day of _____ in the year ____ at _____.

Lost or Stolen Order Forms

When a pharmacist has not received an expected shipment of controlled substances, he/she should first contact the supplier to determine whether the original DEA Form 222 was received. If the original order form has been lost or stolen, the pharmacist must complete a second order form so the supplier can fill the original order. The pharmacist must also prepare a statement which includes the first order form's serial number and date, and verify that the drugs ordered were never received. The pharmacy must attach a copy of the statement to the second order form that is sent to the supplier. In addition, the pharmacist must keep a copy of the statement with copy three from the first and second order forms.

A pharmacy, upon discovery of the loss or theft of used or unused order forms, must immediately report the loss to the local DEA Diversion Field Office (**Appendix K**) and provide the serial numbers of each lost or stolen order form. If an entire book or multiple books of order forms are lost or stolen, and the serial numbers of the missing forms cannot be identified, the pharmacist must report the approximate date of issuance (in lieu of the serial numbers) to the DEA. If an unused order form reported stolen or lost is later recovered or found, the pharmacy must immediately notify the local DEA Diversion Field Office.

Controlled Substance Ordering System (CSOS) – Electronic Order Forms

Any registrant permitted to order schedule II controlled substances may do so electronically via the DEA Controlled Substance Ordering System (CSOS) and maintain the records of these orders electronically for two years. The use of electronic orders is optional; registrants may continue to issue orders on a paper DEA Form 222. CSOS allows for secure electronic transmission of controlled substance orders without the supporting paper DEA Form 222. The adoption of the CSOS standards is the only allowance for the electronic transmission of schedule II controlled substance orders between controlled substance manufacturers, distributors, pharmacies, and other DEA authorized entities. CSOS uses Public Key Infrastructure (PKI) technology, which requires CSOS users to obtain a CSOS digital certificate for electronic ordering. The electronic orders must be signed using a digital signature issued by a Certification Authority (CA) run by the DEA.

Digital certificates can be obtained only by registrants and individuals granted power of attorney by registrants to sign orders. A registrant must appoint a CSOS coordinator who will serve as that registrant's recognized agent regarding issues pertaining to issuance of, revocation of, and changes to, digital certificates issued under that registrant's DEA registration. A CSOS digital certificate will be valid until the DEA registration under which it is issued expires or until the CSOS CA is notified that the certificate should be revoked. Certificates will be revoked if the certificate holder is no longer authorized to sign schedule II orders for the registrant, if the information on which the certificate is based changes, or if the digital certificate used to sign electronic orders has been compromised, stolen, or lost.

A "Questions and Answers" page about the CSOS certificate is available on the DEA E-Commerce Program website at www.DEAecom. gov. Applicants can download the Diversion PKI CSOS Enrollment document and the CSOS Subscriber's Manual for assistance on the enrollment process. DEA maintains a support line to assist applicants and subscribers with issues pertaining to certificate enrollment, issuance, revocation, and renewal. Staff is available from 8:00 a.m. to 6:00 p.m. (Eastern Time), Monday through Friday at 1-877-332-3266 if further assistance is needed.

Unaccepted and Defective Electronic Orders

An electronic order for controlled substances may not be filled if any of the following occurs:

1. The required data fields have not been completed.

2. The order is not signed using a digital certificate issued by DEA.

3. The digital certificate used has expired or been revoked prior to signature.

4. The purchaser's public key will not validate the digital certificate.

5. The validation of the order shows that the order is invalid for any reason.

If an order cannot be filled, the supplier must notify the purchaser and provide a statement as to the reason (e.g., improperly prepared or altered). A supplier may, for any reason, refuse to accept any order. If a supplier refuses, a statement that the order is not accepted is sufficient.

When a purchaser receives an unaccepted electronic order from the supplier, the purchaser must electronically link the statement of nonacceptance to the original order. The original statement must be retained for two years. Neither a purchaser nor a supplier may correct a defective order. The purchaser must issue a new order for the order to be filled.

Cancellation and Voiding of Electronic Orders

A supplier may void all (or part) of an electronic order by notifying the purchaser of the voiding. If the entire order is voided, the supplier must make an electronic copy of the order and indicate "Void" on the copy and return it to the purchaser. The supplier is not required to retain a record of orders that are not filled. The purchaser must retain an electronic copy of the voided order. Should a supplier partially void an order, the supplier must indicate in the linked record that nothing was shipped for each item voided.

Lost Electronic Orders

If a purchaser determines that an unfilled electronic order has been lost before or after receipt, the purchaser must provide, to the supplier, a signed statement. This statement must include the unique tracking number and date of the lost order and state that the goods covered by the first order were not received through loss of that order. If the purchaser executes a new order to replace the lost order, the purchaser must electronically link an electronic record of the second order and a copy of the statement with the record of the first order and retain them both. If the supplier to whom the order was directed subsequently receives the first order, the supplier must indicate that it is "not accepted" and return it to the purchaser. The purchaser must link the returned order to the record of that order and the statement.

Ordering Schedules III-V Controlled Substances

The registrant must keep a receipt (invoice or packing slip) on which it records the date the drugs were received and confirm that the order is accurate. These receipts must also contain the name of each controlled substance, the finished form, the number of dosage units of finished form in each commercial container, and the number of commercial containers ordered and received. In addition, these receipts must be maintained in a readily retrievable manner for inspection by the DEA.

SECTION IX – VALID PRESCRIPTION REQUIREMENTS

To dispense controlled substances, a pharmacist must know the requirements for a valid prescription which are described in this section. A prescription is an order for medication which is dispensed to or for an ultimate user. A prescription is not an order for medication which is dispensed for immediate administration to the ultimate user (i.e., an order to dispense a drug to an inpatient for immediate administration in a hospital is not a prescription).

A prescription for a controlled substance must be dated and signed on the date when issued. The prescription must include the patient's full name and address, and the practitioner's full name, address, and DEA registration number.

The prescription must also include:

1. Drug name
2. Strength
3. Dosage form
4. Quantity prescribed
5. Directions for use
6. Number of refills authorized (if any)

A prescription must be written in ink or indelible pencil or typewritten and must be manually signed by the practitioner on the date when issued. An individual (i.e., secretary or nurse) may be designated by the practitioner to prepare prescriptions for the practitioner's signature. The practitioner is responsible for ensuring the prescription conforms to all requirements of the law and regulations, both federal and state.

Who May Issue

A prescription for a controlled substance may only be issued by a physician, dentist, podiatrist, veterinarian, mid-level practitioner, or other registered practitioner who is:

1. Authorized to prescribe controlled substances by the jurisdiction in which the practitioner is licensed to practice, and
2. Registered with DEA or exempted from registration (e.g., Public Health Service, Federal Bureau of Prisons, military practitioners), or
3. An agent or employee of a hospital or other institution acting in the normal course of business or employment under the registration of the hospital or other institution which is registered in lieu of the individual practitioner being registered, provided that additional requirements as set forth in the C.F.R. are met.

Purpose of Issue

To be valid, a prescription for a controlled substance must be issued for a legitimate medical purpose by a practitioner acting in the usual course of professional practice. The practitioner is responsible for the proper prescribing and dispensing of controlled substances.

A prescription may not be issued in order for an individual practitioner to obtain controlled substances for supplying the individual practitioner for the purpose of general dispensing to patients.

Corresponding Responsibility

A pharmacist also needs to know there is a corresponding responsibility for the pharmacist who fills the prescription. An order purporting to be a prescription issued not in the usual course of professional treatment or in legitimate and authorized research is an invalid prescription within the meaning and intent of the CSA (21 U.S.C. § 829). The person knowingly filling such a purported prescription, as well as the person issuing it, shall be subject to the penalties provided for violations of the provisions of law relating to controlled substances. A pharmacist is required to exercise sound professional judgment when making a determination about the legitimacy of a controlled substance prescription. Such a determination is made before the prescription is dispensed. The law does not require a pharmacist to dispense a prescription of doubtful, questionable, or suspicious origin. To the contrary, the pharmacist who deliberately ignores a questionable prescription when there is reason to believe it was not issued for a legitimate medical purpose may be prosecuted along with the issuing practitioner, for knowingly and intentionally distributing controlled substances. Such action is a felony offense, which may result in the loss of one's business or professional license (see *United States v. Kershman*, 555 F.2d 198 [United States Court Of Appeals, Eighth Circuit, 1977]).

Electronic Prescriptions

On March 31, 2010 the DEA published in the Federal Register an interim final rule *Electronic Prescriptions for Controlled Substances* which became effective June 1, 2010. The rule revises DEA regulations to provide practitioners with the option of writing prescriptions for controlled substances electronically. The regulations also permit pharmacies to receive, dispense, and archive these electronic prescriptions. These regulations are an addition to, not a replacement of, the existing rules.

Persons who wish to dispense controlled substances using electronic prescriptions must select software that meets the requirements of this rule. As of June 1, 2010, only those electronic pharmacy applications that comply with all of DEA's requirements as set forth in 21 C.F.R. §1311 may be used by DEA-registered pharmacies to electronically receive and archive controlled substances prescriptions and dispense controlled substances based on those prescriptions.

A registered pharmacy may process electronic prescriptions for controlled substances only if the following conditions are met:

1. The pharmacy uses a pharmacy application that meets all of the applicable requirements of 21 C.F.R. §1311, and

2. The prescription is otherwise in conformity with the requirements of the CSA and 21 C.F.R. §1311.

A pharmacy cannot process electronic prescriptions for controlled substances until its pharmacy application provider obtains a third party audit or certification review that determines that the application complies with DEA's requirements and the application provider provides the audit/certification report to the pharmacy. The audit report the pharmacy will receive from the pharmacy application provider will indicate if the application is capable of importing, displaying, and storing DEA-required prescription information accurately and consistently. If the third-party auditor or certification organization finds that a pharmacy application does not accurately and consistently import, store, and display the information related to the name, address, and registration number of the practitioner, patient name and address, and prescription information (drug name, strength, quantity, directions for use), the indication of signing, and the number of refills, the pharmacy must not accept electronic prescriptions for the controlled substance.

If the third-party auditor or certification organization finds that a pharmacy application does not accurately and consistently import, store, and display **other information** required for prescriptions, the pharmacy must not accept electronic prescriptions for controlled substances that are subject to the additional information requirements. For example, until the audit or certification report indicates that the pharmacy application can import, display, and store both a hospital DEA number and the individual practitioner's extension number, the pharmacy must not accept electronic prescriptions that include only a hospital DEA registration number. The pharmacy may, however, use the application to process other controlled substance prescriptions if the audit or certification report has found that the pharmacy application meets all other requirements.

The pharmacy must determine which employees are authorized to enter information regarding the dispensing of controlled substance prescriptions and annotate or alter records of these prescriptions (to the extent such alterations are permitted under DEA regulations). The pharmacy must ensure that logical access controls in the pharmacy application are set so that only such employees are granted access to perform these functions.

When a pharmacist fills a prescription in a manner that would require, under 21 C.F.R. §1306, the pharmacist to make notation on the prescription if the prescription were a paper prescription, the pharmacist must make the same notation electronically when filling an electronic prescription and retain the annotation electronically in the prescription record or linked files. ***When a prescription is received electronically, the prescription and all required annotations must be stored electronically.***

When a pharmacist receives a paper or oral prescription that indicates that it was originally transmitted electronically to the pharmacy, the pharmacist must check the pharmacy's records to ensure that the electronic version was not received and the prescription dispensed. If both prescriptions were received, the pharmacist must mark one as void.

When a pharmacist receives a paper or oral prescription that indicates that it was originally transmitted electronically to another pharmacy, the pharmacist must check with that pharmacy to determine whether the prescription was received and dispensed. If the pharmacy that received the original electronic prescription had not dispensed the prescription, that pharmacy must mark the electronic version as void or cancelled. If the pharmacy that received the original electronic prescription dispensed the prescription, the pharmacy with the paper version must not dispense the paper prescription and must mark the prescription as void.

Verification of Practitioner Registration

A pharmacist has a responsibility to ensure that a prescription has been issued by an appropriately registered or exempt practitioner (see above, **Who May Issue**). As such, it is helpful to be familiar with how a DEA registration number is constructed and to whom such registrations are issued.

Construction of Valid DEA Registration Number for Practitioners

Knowing how a DEA registration number is constructed can be a useful tool for recognizing a forged prescription (see **Appendix D, Pharmacist's Guide to Prescription Fraud**). Prior to October 1, 1985, DEA registration numbers for physicians, dentists, veterinarians, and other practitioners started with the letter A. New registration numbers issued to practitioners after that date begin with the letter B or F. Registration numbers issued to mid-level practitioners begin with the letter M. The first letter of the registration number is almost always followed by the first letter of the registrant's last name (e.g., J for Jones or S for Smith) and then a computer generated sequence of seven numbers (such as MJ3614511).

Practitioner's Use of a Hospital's DEA Registration Number

Practitioners (e.g., intern, resident, staff physician, mid-level practitioner) who are agents or employees of a hospital or other institution, may, when acting in the usual course of business or employment, administer, dispense, or prescribe controlled substances under the registration of the hospital or other institution in which he or she is employed, in lieu of individual registration, provided that:

1. The dispensing, administering, or prescribing is in the usual course of professional practice.

2. The practitioner is authorized to do so by the state in which they practice.

3. The hospital or institution has verified that the practitioner is permitted to administer, dispense, or prescribe controlled substances within the state.

4. The practitioner acts only within the scope of employment in the hospital or institution.

5. The hospital or institution authorizes the practitioner to administer, dispense, or prescribe under its registration and assigns a specific internal code number for each practitioner.

An example of a specific internal code number is depicted below:

A current list of internal codes and the corresponding individual practitioners is to be maintained by the hospital or other institution. This list is to be available at all times to other registrants and law enforcement agencies upon request for the purpose of verifying the authority of the prescribing individual practitioner. Pharmacists should contact the hospital or other institution for verification if they have any doubts in filling such a prescription.

Exemption of Federal Government Practitioners from Registration

The requirement of registration is waived for any official of the U.S. Army, Navy, Marine Corps, Air Force, Coast Guard, Public Health Service, or Bureau of Prisons, who is authorized to administer, dispense, or prescribe, but not to procure or purchase controlled substances in the course of his or her official duties. Such officials must follow procedures set forth in 21 C.F.R. part 1306 regarding prescriptions, but must also state the branch of service or agency (e.g., "U.S. Army" or "Public Health Service") and the service identification number of the issuing official in lieu of the registration number required on prescription forms. The service identification number for a Public Health Service employee is his or her Social Security identification number.

If federal government practitioners wish to maintain a DEA registration for a private practice, which would include prescribing for private patients, these practitioners must be fully licensed to handle controlled substances by the state in which they are located.

Registration Requirements for Mid-Level Practitioners

Mid-level practitioners (MLPs) are registered and authorized by the DEA and the state in *which* they practice to dispense, administer, and prescribe controlled substances in the course of professional practice (see **Appendix B, Definitions**). Examples of MLPs include, but are not limited to, nurse practitioners, nurse midwives, nurse anesthetists, clinical nurse specialists, physician assistants, optometrists, ambulance services, animal shelters, euthanasia technicians, nursing homes, and homeopathic physicians.

MLPs may apply for an individual DEA registration granting controlled substance privileges. However, such registration is contingent upon the authority granted by the state in which they are licensed. The DEA may register MLPs whose states clearly authorize them to prescribe, dispense, and administer controlled substances in one or more schedules.

It is incumbent upon the pharmacist who fills the prescription to ensure that the MLP is prescribing within the parameters established by the state in which he/she practices. MLP authority to prescribe controlled substances varies greatly by state. Pharmacists should check with the state licensing or controlled substances authority to determine which MLP disciplines are authorized to prescribe controlled substances in the state. Pharmacists may also visit the DEA Diversion website at www.DEAdiversion.usdoj.gov for a chart indicating the prescribing authority of MLPs by state (click on *Registration Support* and scroll down to *Mid-Level Practitioners Authorization by State*).

Schedule II Controlled Substances

Schedule II controlled substances require a written prescription which must be manually signed by the practitioner or an electronic prescription that meets all DEA requirements for electronic prescriptions for controlled substances. There is no federal time limit within which a schedule II prescription must be filled after being signed by the practitioner. However, the pharmacist must determine that the prescription is still needed by the patient. While some states and many insurance carriers limit the quantity of controlled substances dispensed to a 30-day supply, there are no express federal limits with respect to the quantities of drugs dispensed via a prescription. However, the amount dispensed must be consistent with the requirement that a prescription for a controlled substance be issued only for a legitimate medical purpose by a practitioner acting in the usual course of professional practice. For a schedule II controlled substance, an oral order is only permitted in an emergency situation (see **Section X, Emergency Dispensing**).

Refills

The refilling of a prescription for a controlled substance listed in schedule II is prohibited (21 U.S.C. § 829(a)).

Issuance of Multiple Prescriptions for Schedule II Controlled Substances

The DEA has revised its regulations regarding the issuance of multiple prescriptions for schedule II controlled substances. Under the new regulation, which became effective December 19, 2007, an individual practitioner may issue multiple prescriptions authorizing the patient to receive a total of up to a 90-day supply of a schedule II controlled substance provided the following conditions are met:

1. Each prescription must be issued on a separate prescription blank.

2. Each separate prescription must be issued for a legitimate medical purpose by an individual practitioner acting in the usual course of professional practice.

3. The individual practitioner must provide written instructions on each prescription (other than the first prescription, if the prescribing practitioner intends for that prescription to be filled immediately) indicating the earliest date on which a pharmacy may fill each prescription.

4. The individual practitioner concludes that providing the patient with multiple prescriptions in this manner does not create an undue risk of diversion or abuse.

5. The issuance of multiple prescriptions is permissible under applicable state laws.

6. The individual practitioner complies fully with all other applicable requirements under the CSA and C.F.R., as well as any additional requirements under state law.

It should be noted that the implementation of this change in the regulation should not be construed as encouraging individual practitioners to issue multiple prescriptions or to see their patients only once every 90 days when prescribing schedule II controlled substances. Rather, individual practitioners must determine on their own, based on sound medical judgment, and in accordance with established medical standards, whether it is appropriate to issue multiple prescriptions and how often to see their patients when doing so.

Facsimile Prescriptions for Schedule II Controlled Substances

In order to expedite the filling of a prescription, a prescriber may transmit a schedule II prescription to the pharmacy by facsimile. The original schedule II prescription must be presented to the pharmacist and verified against the facsimile at the time the controlled substance is actually dispensed. The pharmacist must make sure the original document is properly annotated and filed with the records that are required to be kept.

Exceptions for Schedule II Facsimile Prescriptions

DEA has granted three exceptions to the facsimile prescription requirements for schedule II controlled substances. The facsimile of a schedule II prescription may serve as the original prescription as follows:

1. A practitioner prescribing a schedule II narcotic controlled substance to be compounded for the direct administration to a patient by parenteral, intravenous, intramuscular, subcutaneous or intraspinal infusion may transmit the prescription by facsimile. The pharmacy will consider the facsimile prescription a "written prescription" and no further documentation is required. All normal requirements of a legal prescription must be followed.

2. Practitioners prescribing schedule II controlled substances for residents of Long Term Care Facilities may transmit a prescription by facsimile to the dispensing pharmacy. The facsimile prescription serves as the original written prescription for the pharmacy. No further documentation is required.

3. A practitioner prescribing a schedule II narcotic controlled substance for a patient enrolled in a hospice care program certified and/or paid for by Medicare under Title XVIII or a hospice program which is licensed by the state, may transmit a prescription to

the dispensing pharmacy by facsimile. The practitioner will note on the prescription that it is for a hospice patient. The facsimile serves as the original written prescription. No further documentation is required.

Schedules III-V Controlled Substances

A pharmacist may dispense directly a controlled substance listed in Schedule III, IV, or V only pursuant to either a paper prescription signed by a practitioner, a facsimile of a signed paper prescription transmitted by the practitioner or the practitioner's agent to the pharmacy, an electronic prescription that meets DEA's requirements for such prescriptions, or a call-in as indicated below (see **Telephone Authorization for Schedules III-V Controlled Substances**).

Refills

Schedules III and IV controlled substances may be refilled if authorized on the prescription. However, the prescription may only be refilled up to five times within six months after the date of issue. After five refills or after six months, whichever occurs first, a new prescription is required.

When a prescription for any controlled substance in schedules III or IV is refilled, the following information must be entered on the back of the prescription: the dispensing pharmacist's initials, the date the prescription was refilled, and the amount of drug dispensed on the refill. If the pharmacist only initials and dates the back of the prescription, the pharmacist will be deemed to have dispensed a refill for the full face amount of the prescription.

Electronic Recordkeeping of Schedules III-IV Prescription Information

A pharmacy is permitted to use an electronic recordkeeping system as an alternative to the manual method for the storage and retrieval of original paper prescription orders for schedules III and IV controlled substances.

The electronic system must provide online retrieval of original prescription information for those prescriptions which are currently authorized for refill. The information must include, but is not limited to: the original prescription number; date of issuance; full name and address of the patient; the prescriber's name, address, and DEA registration number; the name, strength, dosage form and quantity of the controlled substance prescribed (and quantity dispensed if different from the quantity prescribed); and the total number of refills authorized by the prescriber.

In addition, the electronic system must provide online retrieval of the current refill history for schedules III or IV controlled substance prescriptions. This information must include, but is not limited to: the name of the controlled substance, the date of refill, the quantity dispensed, the dispensing pharmacist's identification code or name/initials for each refill, and the total number of refills dispensed to date for that prescription.

The pharmacist must verify and document that the refill data entered into the system is correct. All computer generated prescription/refill documentation must be stored in a separate file at the pharmacy and must be maintained for a period of two years from the dispensing date. To meet the C.F.R. recordkeeping requirements, the pharmacy's electronic system must comply with the following guidelines:

1. If the system provides a hard copy printout of each day's controlled substance prescription refills, each pharmacist who refilled those prescriptions must verify his/her accuracy by signing and dating the printout as he/she would sign a check or legal document.

2. The printout must be provided to each pharmacy that uses the computer system within 72 hours of the date on which the refill was dispensed. The printout must be verified and signed by each pharmacist who dispensed the refills.

3. In lieu of such a printout, the pharmacy must maintain a bound logbook or a separate file in which each pharmacist involved in the day's dispensing signs a statement, verifying that the refill information entered into the computer that day has been reviewed by him/her and is correct as shown.

4. A pharmacy's electronic system must have the capability of printing out any refill data which the pharmacy must maintain under the CSA. For example, this would include a refill-by-refill audit trail for any specified strength and dosage form of any controlled substance, by either brand or generic name or both, dispensed by the pharmacy. Such a printout must include:

    •   Prescribing practitioner's name

    •   Patient's name and address

    •   Quantity and date dispensed on each refill

    •   Name or identification code of the dispensing pharmacist

    •   Original prescription number

    In any electronic system employed by a user pharmacy, the central recordkeeping location must be capable of providing a printout to a requesting pharmacy of the above information within 48 hours.

5. In case a pharmacy's electronic system experiences downtime, the pharmacy must have a back-up procedure to document in writing refills of schedules III or IV controlled substances. This procedure must ensure that refills are authorized by the original prescription, that the maximum number of refills has not been exceeded, and that all required data is retained for online entry as soon as possible.

A pharmacy may use only one of the two systems described (i.e., manual or electronic) for storage and retrieval of prescription order refill information of schedules III or IV controlled substances.

Facsimile Prescriptions for Schedules III-V Controlled Substances

Prescriptions for schedules III-V controlled substances may be transmitted by facsimile from the practitioner or the practitioner's agent to the dispensing pharmacy. The facsimile is considered to be equivalent to an original prescription as long as the practitioner has manually signed the prescription.

Telephone Authorization for Schedules III-V Prescriptions

A pharmacist may dispense a controlled substance listed in schedules III, IV, or V pursuant to an oral prescription made by an individual practitioner and promptly reduced to writing by the pharmacist containing all information required for a valid prescription except for the signature of the practitioner (see **Appendix D, Pharmacist's Guide to Prescription Fraud**).

Transfer of Schedules III-V Prescription Information

A DEA registered pharmacy may transfer original prescription information for schedules III, IV, and V controlled substances to another DEA registered pharmacy for the purpose of refill dispensing between pharmacies, on a one time basis only. However, pharmacies electronically sharing a real-time, on-line database may transfer up to the maximum refills permitted by law and the prescriber's authorization.

Transfers are subject to the following requirements:

The transfer must be communicated directly between two licensed pharmacists and the transferring pharmacist must record the following information:

1. Write the word "VOID" on the face of the invalidated prescription; for electronic prescriptions, information that the prescription has been transferred must be added to the prescription record.

2. Record on the reverse of the invalidated prescription the name, address, and DEA registration number of the pharmacy to which it was transferred and the name of the pharmacist receiving the prescription information; for electronic prescriptions, such information must be added to the prescription record.

3. Record the date of the transfer and the name of the pharmacist transferring the information.

For paper prescriptions and prescriptions received orally and reduced to writing by the pharmacist, the pharmacist receiving the transferred prescription information must write the word "transfer" on the face of the transferred prescription and reduce to writing all information required to be on a prescription and include:

1. Date of issuance of original prescription.

2. Original number of refills authorized on original prescription.

3. Date of original dispensing

4. Number of valid refills remaining and date(s) and locations of previous refill(s).

5. Pharmacy's name, address, DEA registration number, and prescription number from which the prescription information was transferred.

6. Name of pharmacist who transferred the prescription.

7. Pharmacy's name, address, DEA registration number, and prescription number from which the prescription was originally filled.

For electronic prescriptions being transferred electronically, the transferring pharmacist must provide the receiving pharmacist with the following information in addition to the original electronic prescription data:

1. The date of the original dispensing

2. The number of refills remaining and the date(s) and locations of previous refills

3. The transferring pharmacy's name, address, DEA registration number, and prescription number for each dispensing.

4. The name of the pharmacist transferring the prescription.

5. The name, address, DEA registration number, and prescription number from the pharmacy that originally filled the prescription, if different.

The pharmacist receiving a transferred electronic prescription must create an electronic record for the prescription that includes the receiving pharmacist's name and all of the information transferred with the prescription (listed above).

The original and transferred prescription(s) must be maintained for a period of two years from the date of last refill.

Pharmacies electronically accessing the same prescription record must satisfy all information requirements of a manual mode for prescription transferal.

The procedure allowing the transfer of prescription information for refill purposes is permissible only if allowable under existing State or other applicable law.

Prescription Monitoring Programs

A prescription monitoring program is a state-administered data collection system used to gather prescription information. This information may be made available to state and federal investigators on a need-to-know basis.

Many states have established an electronic prescription drug monitoring program because it has proven to be an effective tool for detecting pharmaceutical diversion and for developing pharmacist and physician medical education programs. These programs heighten awareness about diversion, prescription drug abuse, drug trends, and are useful for tracking prescription medication dispensed within a state. In some states, the data can be used by pharmacists to identify potential "doctor shoppers" and those who attempt to obtain controlled substances by fraud, forgery, or deceit.

In the states that have adopted these programs, a large part of their success has been attributed to the pharmacists' participation. The DEA strongly endorses prescription monitoring programs.

SECTION X – DISPENSING REQUIREMENTS

Required Information for Prescription Labels

The pharmacist dispensing a prescription for a controlled substance listed in schedules II, III, IV, or V must affix to the package a label showing date of filling, the pharmacy name and address, the serial (prescription) number, the name of the patient, the name of the prescribing practitioner, and directions for use and cautionary statements, if any, contained in such prescription or required by law. If a prescription is filled at a central fill pharmacy, the central fill pharmacy must affix to the package a label showing the retail pharmacy name and address and a unique identifier (i.e., the central fill pharmacy's DEA registration number) indicating that the prescription was filled at the central fill pharmacy.

Federal Food and Drug Administration regulations require that the label of any drug listed as a "controlled substance" in schedules II, III, or IV of the CSA must, when dispensed to or for a patient, contain the following warning: *CAUTION: Federal law prohibits the transfer of this drug to any person other than the patient for whom it was prescribed.* In addition, a pharmacist who receives a prescription for a controlled substance must dispense that prescription to the patient or a member of the patient's household. To provide the controlled substance to anyone other than the patient or a member of the patient's household is distribution, not dispensing.

Schedule II Controlled Substance Prescriptions

A pharmacist may dispense a schedule II controlled substance, which is a prescription drug as determined under the Federal Food, Drug, and Cosmetic Act, only pursuant to a written prescription signed by the practitioner, except in an emergency situation as described below.

Emergency Dispensing

An "emergency prescription" in this context, is defined to mean that the immediate administration of the drug is necessary for proper treatment of the intended ultimate user, that no alternative treatment is available (including a drug which is not a schedule II controlled substance), and it is not possible for the prescribing practitioner to provide a written prescription for the drug at that time. In a bona fide emergency, a practitioner may telephone a schedule II prescription to the pharmacist who may then dispense the prescription. The prescribing practitioner must provide a written and signed prescription to the pharmacy within seven days and meet the below requirements:

1. The drug prescribed and dispensed must be limited to the amount needed to treat the patient during the emergency period. Prescribing or dispensing beyond the emergency period must be pursuant to a written prescription order.

2. The prescription order must be immediately reduced to writing by the pharmacist and must contain all information, except for the prescribing practitioner's signature.

3. If the prescribing individual practitioner is not known to the pharmacist, he/she must make a reasonable effort to determine that the oral authorization came from a registered individual practitioner, which may include a call back to the prescribing individual

practitioner using his or her telephone number as listed in the telephone directory and/or other good faith efforts to insure his or her identity.

4. Within seven days after authorizing an emergency telephone prescription, the prescribing practitioner must furnish the pharmacist a written, signed prescription for the controlled substance prescribed. The prescription must have written on its face "Authorization for Emergency Dispensing" and the date of the oral order. The written prescription may be delivered to the pharmacist in person or by mail, but if delivered by mail, it must be postmarked within the seven day period. Upon receipt, the dispensing pharmacist must attach this written prescription to the oral emergency prescription which had earlier been reduced to writing by the pharmacist. By regulation, the pharmacist must notify the local DEA Diversion Field Office (**Appendix K**) if the prescriber fails to provide a written prescription within seven days. Failure of the pharmacist to do so will void the authority conferred on the pharmacy to dispense the controlled substance without a written prescription of a prescribing practitioner.

5. For electronic prescriptions, the pharmacist must annotate the record of the electronic prescription with the original authorization and date of the oral order.

Partial Dispensing

A prescription for a schedule II controlled substance may be partially dispensed if the pharmacist is unable to supply the full quantity of a written or emergency oral (telephone) prescription, provided the pharmacist notes the quantity supplied on the front of the written prescription, on a written record of the emergency oral prescription, or in the electronic prescription record. The remaining portion may be dispensed within 72 hours of the first partial dispensing. However, if the remaining portion is not or cannot be filled within the 72 hour period, the pharmacist must notify the prescribing practitioner. No further quantity may be supplied beyond 72 hours without a new prescription.

Partial Filling of Schedule II Prescriptions for Terminally Ill or Long Term Care Facility Patients

A prescription for a schedule II controlled substance written for a patient in a Long Term Care Facility (LTCF) or for a patient with a medical diagnosis documenting a terminal illness, may be filled in partial quantities to include individual dosage units. If there is any question whether a patient may be classified as having a terminal illness, the pharmacist must contact the practitioner prior to partially filling the prescription. Both the pharmacist and the prescribing practitioner have a corresponding responsibility to assure that the controlled substance is for a terminally ill patient.

The pharmacist must record on the prescription whether the patient is "terminally ill" or an "LTCF patient." A prescription that is partially filled and does not contain the notation "terminally ill" or "LTCF patient" must be deemed to have been filled in violation of the CSA. For each partial filling, the dispensing pharmacist must record on the back of the prescription (or on another appropriate record, uniformly maintained, and readily retrievable) the date of the partial filling, quantity dispensed, remaining quantity authorized to be dispensed, and the identification of the dispensing pharmacist. The total quantity of schedule II controlled substances dispensed in all partial fillings must not exceed the total quantity prescribed. Schedule II prescriptions for patients in an LTCF or terminally ill patients are valid for a period not to exceed 60 days from the issue date unless sooner terminated by the discontinuance of medication.

Schedules III-V Controlled Substance Prescriptions

A pharmacist may dispense a controlled substance in schedules III, IV, or V having received either a paper prescription signed by a practitioner, a facsimile of that prescription transmitted by the practitioner or their agent to the pharmacy, an electronic prescription that meets DEA's requirements for such prescriptions, or an oral prescription made by an individual practitioner. The pharmacist must promptly reduce the oral prescription to writing, including all required information except the signature of the prescribing practitioner.

Partial Dispensing

A pharmacist may partially dispense a prescription for schedules III-V controlled substances provided that each partial filling is recorded in the same manner as a refilling, the total quantity dispensed in all partial fillings does not exceed the total quantity prescribed, and no dispensing occurs beyond six months from the date on which the prescription was issued.

Dispensing Without a Prescription

Dispensing a controlled substance without a prescription is outlined in 21 C.F.R. § 1306.26. The regulation states that a controlled substance listed in schedules II, III, IV, or V which is not a prescription drug as determined under the Federal Food, Drug, and Cosmetic Act, may be dispensed by a pharmacist without a prescription to a purchaser at retail, provided that:

1. Such dispensing is made only by a pharmacist and not by a non-pharmacist employee even if under the supervision of a pharmacist (although after the pharmacist has fulfilled his or her professional and legal responsibilities, the actual cash, credit transaction, or delivery, may be completed by a non-pharmacist);

2. Not more than 240 cc. (8 ounces) of any such controlled substance containing opium, nor more than 120 cc. (4 ounces) of any other such controlled substance, nor more than 48 dosage units of any such controlled substance containing opium, nor more than 24 dosage units of any other such controlled substance, may be dispensed at retail to the same purchaser in any given 48-hour period;

3. The purchaser is at least 18 years of age and the pharmacist requires every purchaser of a controlled substance under this section not known to him or her to furnish suitable identification (including proof of age where appropriate);

4. A bound record book (which must be maintained in accordance with the recordkeeping requirement of 21 C.F.R. § 1304.04) for dispensing of controlled substances is maintained by the pharmacist, which contains the name and address of the purchaser, the name and quantity of the controlled substance purchased, the date of each purchase, and the name or initials of the pharmacist who dispensed the substance to the purchaser;

5. The prescription is not required for distribution or dispensing of the substance pursuant to any other Federal, State or local law; and

6. Central fill pharmacies may not dispense controlled substances at the retail level to a purchaser.

Delivery of a Controlled Substance to Persons in Other Countries

Controlled substances that are dispensed pursuant to a legitimate prescription may not be delivered or shipped to individuals in other countries without proper authorization. Any such delivery or shipment is an export under the CSA and cannot be conducted unless the person sending the controlled substances:

1. Has registered with DEA as an "exporter" (see 21 C.F.R. §§ 1301 and 1309).

2. Has obtained the necessary permit(s), or submitted the necessary declaration(s) for export (21 C.F.R. §§ 1312 or 1313).

SECTION XI – RYAN HAIGHT ONLINE PHARMACY CONSUMER PROTECTION ACT OF 2008

Summary of the Act's Major Provisions

On October 15, 2008, the President signed into law the *Ryan Haight Online Pharmacy Consumer Protection Act of 2008*, often referred to as the *Ryan Haight Act*. This law amends the CSA by adding a series of new regulatory requirements and criminal provisions designed to combat the proliferation of so-called "rogue Internet sites" that unlawfully dispense controlled substances by means of the Internet. The *Ryan Haight Act* applies to all controlled substances in all schedules.

This law became effective April 13, 2009. As of that date, it is illegal under federal law to deliver, distribute, or dispense a controlled substance by means of the Internet unless the online pharmacy holds a modification of DEA registration authorizing it to operate as an online pharmacy. Thus, any person who knowingly or intentionally dispenses a controlled substance by means of the Internet that does not have a modification of DEA registration allowing such activity is in violation of 21 U.S.C. § 841(h)(1) and subject to potential criminal prosecution and (in the case of DEA registrants) loss of DEA registration.

Note: The information contained in this section is meant to summarize the Ryan Haight Act but should not be relied upon as setting forth all the requirements. As is always the case, pharmacies are responsible for complying with the actual text of the CSA and DEA regulations.

Definition of an Online Pharmacy

An online pharmacy is a person, entity, or Internet site, whether in the United States or abroad, that knowingly or intentionally delivers, distributes, or dispenses, or offers or attempts to deliver, distribute, or dispense, a controlled substance by means of the Internet. Examples of an online pharmacy include (but are not limited to) the following:

- Any website that sells, or offers to sell, any controlled substance or a prescription therefor to a person in the United States.

- Any person who operates such a website.

- Any person who pays a practitioner to write prescriptions for controlled substances for customers of such a website.

- Any person who pays a pharmacy to fill prescriptions for controlled substances that were issued to customers of such a website.

- Any pharmacy that knowingly or intentionally fills prescriptions for controlled substances that were issued to customers of such a website.

- Any person who sends an e-mail that:

  (1) offers to sell a controlled substance or a prescription for a controlled substance in a manner not authorized by the Act;

  (2) directs buyers to a website operating in violation of the Act;

  (3) or otherwise causes or facilitates the delivery, distribution, or dispensing of a controlled substance in a manner not authorized by the Act.

Online Pharmacy Registration Exemptions

The following are exempt from the Ryan Haight Act's definition of an "online pharmacy" so long as their activities are limited solely to the exemptions provided:

- Manufacturers or distributors registered under 21 U.S.C. § 823(a), (b), (d), or (e) who do not dispense controlled substances to nonregistrants.

- Nonpharmacy practitioners who are registered under 21 U.S.C. § 823(f) and whose activities are authorized by that registration, provided that any website operated by such nonpharmacy practitioners complies with 21 C.F.R.§ 1304.50, which requires the website to post in a visible and clear manner on its homepage, or on a page directly linked thereto in which the hyperlink is also visible and clear on the homepage, a list of the DEA-registered nonpharmacy practitioners who are affiliated with the website.

- Any hospital or other medical facility registered under 21 U.S.C. § 823(f) that is operated by an agency of the United States (including the Armed Forces).

- A health care facility owned or operated by an Indian tribe or tribal organization carrying out a contract or compact under the Indian Self-Determination and Education Assistance Act.

- Any agent or employee of any hospital or facility that is operated by an agency of the United States, and any agent or employee of any hospital or facility owned or operated by an Indian tribe or tribal organization carrying out a contract or compact under the Indian Self-Determination and Education Assistance Act, provided such agent or employee is lawfully acting in the usual course of business or employment, and within the scope of the official duties of such agent or employee, with such hospital or facility, and, with respect to agents or employees of such health care facilities only to the extent such individuals are furnishing services pursuant to those contracts or compacts.

- Mere advertisements that do not attempt to facilitate an actual transaction involving a controlled substance.

- A person, entity, or Internet site that is not in the United States and does not facilitate the delivery, distribution, or dispensing of a controlled substance by means of the Internet to any person in the United States.

- A pharmacy registered under 21 U.S.C. § 823(f) whose dispensing of controlled substances via the Internet consists solely of "refilling prescriptions for controlled substances in schedule III, IV, or V," **as that term is defined in 21 C.F.R. § 1300.04(k).** (This definition is set forth at the end of this section.)

- A pharmacy registered under 21 U.S.C. § 823(f) whose dispensing of controlled substances via the Internet consists solely of "filling new prescriptions for controlled substances in schedule III, IV, or V," **as that term is defined in 21 C.F.R. § 1300.04(d).** (This definition is set forth at the end of this section.)

- Any registered pharmacy whose delivery, distribution, or dispensing of controlled substances by means of the Internet consists solely of filling prescriptions that were electronically prescribed in a manner authorized by the CSA.

- Any registered pharmacy whose delivery, distribution, or dispensing of controlled substances by means of the Internet consists solely of the transmission of prescription information between a pharmacy and an automated dispensing system located in a Long Term Care Facility when the registration of the automated dispensing system is held by that pharmacy as described in 21 C.F.R §§ 1301.17 and 1301.27 and the pharmacy is otherwise complying with the DEA regulations.

Notification Requirements

Thirty days prior to offering a controlled substance for sale, delivery, distribution, or dispensing by means of the Internet, the online pharmacy shall notify DEA and the State boards of pharmacy in any States in which the online pharmacy offers to sell, deliver, distribute, or dispense controlled substances. Completion of the *Application for Modification of Registration for Online Pharmacies* serves as the notification requirement to DEA.

The online pharmacy must make a separate thirty-day advance notice to the State boards of pharmacy in each State in which it intends to offer to sell, deliver, distribute, or dispense controlled substances. Online pharmacies that apply for the modification of registration are required to certify that the applicable State boards of pharmacy have been notified.

How to Register as an Online Pharmacy

To operate legally as an online pharmacy, the online pharmacy must first be registered with DEA as a pharmacy. Once registered with DEA as a pharmacy, the pharmacy may apply for a modification of registration to operate as an online pharmacy. To apply for a modification of registration, complete *the Application for Modification of Registration for Online Pharmacies* online at www.DEAdiversion.usdoj.gov. There is no fee to apply to modify a DEA registration to an online pharmacy.

If the modification of registration is approved, the pharmacy will be issued a modified DEA Certificate of Registration with the new business activity listed as online pharmacy. The registrant will keep the same DEA registration number. A pharmacy may perform the activities of a retail pharmacy and an online pharmacy at the same time.

State Licensure Requirements

An online pharmacy must comply with the requirements of all applicable State laws concerning the licensure of pharmacies in each State from which it, and in each State to which it, delivers, distributes, or dispenses, or offers to deliver, distribute, or dispense, controlled substances by means of the Internet. In addition, online pharmacies must certify they are in compliance with these requirements when completing the *Application for Modification of Registration for Online Pharmacies*.

The requirement that an online pharmacy list the States in which it is licensed to dispense controlled substances is designed to ensure that an online pharmacy only dispenses controlled substances to patients in States in which it is authorized to practice pharmacy. Dispensing beyond the scope of State licensure is one of the recurring transgressions of some rogue online pharmacies and generally violates State law. Under this Act, a State may bring civil action in federal court to enjoin any violation of the Ryan Haight Act – not merely those violations of State law – and to obtain other appropriate legal or equitable relief. 21 U.S.C. § 882(c).

Online Pharmacy Website Requirements

When a pharmacy applies for a modification of registration to become an online pharmacy, it must display on its homepage a declaration that it has done so. This declaration must state the following:

> *"In accordance with the Controlled Substances Act and the DEA regulations, this online pharmacy has made the notifications to the DEA Administrator required by 21 U.S.C. § 831 and 21 C.F.R. § 1304.40."*

Once approved to operate as an online pharmacy, the online pharmacy must display at all times on the homepage of its Internet site a declaration of compliance with the requirements of 21 U.S.C. § 831 with respect to the delivery or sale or offer for sale of controlled substances. This statement must include the name of the pharmacy as it appears on the DEA Certificate of Registration.

An online pharmacy is required to post Internet Pharmacy Site Disclosure Information on the homepage of each Internet site it operates. It must be posted in a visible and clear manner and contain the following information:

1. The name and address of the pharmacy as it appears on the pharmacy's DEA Certificate of Registration.

2. The pharmacy's telephone number and e-mail address.

3. Name of pharmacist-in-charge, professional degree, States of licensure, and telephone number.

4. List of State(s) in which the pharmacy is licensed to dispense controlled substances.

5. Certification that the pharmacy is registered to deliver, distribute, or dispense controlled substances by means of the Internet.

6. The name, address, telephone number, professional degree, and States of licensure of any practitioner who has a contractual relationship to provide medical evaluations or issue prescriptions for controlled substances, through referrals from the website or at the request of the owner or operator of the website, or any employee or agent thereof.

7. The following statement must be visible on the website:

> *"This online pharmacy is obligated to comply fully with the Controlled Substances Act and DEA regulations. As part of this obligation, this online pharmacy has obtained a modified DEA registration authorizing it to operate as an online pharmacy. In addition, this online pharmacy will only dispense a controlled substance to a person who has a valid prescription issued for a legitimate medical purpose based upon a medical relationship with a prescribing practitioner. This includes at least one prior in-person medical evaluation in accordance with section 309 of the Controlled Substances Act (21 U.S.C. § 829), or a medical evaluation via telemedicine in accordance with section 102(54) of the Controlled Substances Act (21 U.S.C. § 802(54))."*

If at any time an online pharmacy should change its Internet site web address, the online pharmacy must notify DEA at least thirty days in advance of this change.

Reporting Requirements

Each online pharmacy must submit a monthly report to DEA of the total quantity of each controlled substance that the online pharmacy has dispensed the previous calendar month. The report is required for every month in which the total amount of dispensing of controlled substances by the pharmacy is either (i) over 100 prescriptions filled or (ii) 5,000 or more dosage units dispensed of all controlled substances combined. Should an online pharmacy's total quantity of dispensed controlled substances fall below both of the thresholds listed above, a report is still required that indicates a negative response for that given month.

The report must include the total amount of such dispensing by any means including all controlled substances dispensed via Internet transactions, mail-order transactions, face-to-face transactions, or any other means. It is not required that the online pharmacy identify the means of the dispensing in its report. Reporting will be by National Drug Code (NDC) numbers. Report the total number of dosage units dispensed for each NDC number.

This report is due on or before the 15th day of the following month. For example, an online pharmacy would submit its report for the month of January no later than February 15th. Reports must be submitted electronically via online reporting, electronic upload, or other means as approved by DEA. All reports must be kept for at least two years and be readily retrievable for inspection.

Should an online pharmacy revert back to a retail pharmacy, the pharmacy is still required to report the monthly sales for the month in which it changes back to a retail pharmacy.

Prescription Requirements

In order for a prescription to be valid, it must be issued for a legitimate medical purpose in the usual course of professional practice by a practitioner who has conducted at least one in-person medical evaluation of the patient or by a covering practitioner. An in-person medical evaluation is a medical evaluation that is conducted with the patient in the physical presence of the practitioner, without regard to whether portions of the evaluation are conducted by other health professionals.

Definition of Prescription Terms

A pharmacy website is exempted from the Ryan Haight Act's definition of an "online pharmacy" if its Internet-facilitated activity relating to controlled substances is limited to filling new and/or refilling prescriptions for controlled substances in schedules III, IV, or V. If the pharmacy is so exempted from the definition of an "online pharmacy," it is not required under the Act to obtain a modification of its DEA registration authorizing it to operate as an online pharmacy. Thus, it is important to understand precisely the definitions of the following terms.

Filling New Prescriptions for Controlled Substances in Schedules III-V

As stated in 21 C.F.R. § 1300.04 (d), the term **"filling new prescriptions for controlled substances in schedule III, IV, or V"** means filling a prescription for an individual for a controlled substance in schedule III, IV, or V, if:

1. The pharmacy dispensing that prescription has previously dispensed to the patient a controlled substance other than by means of the Internet and pursuant to the valid prescription of a practitioner that meets the applicable requirements of [21 U.S.C. § 829(b) and (c)] and [21 C.F.R. §§ 1306.21 and 1306.22] (for purposes of this definition, such a prescription shall be referred to as the "original prescription");

2. The pharmacy contacts the practitioner who issued the original prescription at the request of that individual to determine whether the practitioner will authorize the issuance of a new prescription for that individual for the controlled substance described in [paragraph (1) of this definition] (i.e., the same controlled substance as described in [paragraph (1)]); and

3. The practitioner, acting in the usual course of professional practice, determines there is a legitimate medical purpose for the issuance of the new prescription.

Refilling Prescriptions for Controlled Substances in Schedules III-V

As stated in 21 C.F.R. § 1300.04(k), the term **"refilling prescriptions for controlled substances in schedule III, IV, or V"**:

1. Means the dispensing of a controlled substance in schedule III, IV, or V in accordance with refill instructions issued by a practitioner as part of a valid prescription that meets the requirements of [21 U.S.C. § 829(b) and (c)] and [21 C.F.R. §§ 1306.21 and 1306.22], as appropriate; and

2. Does not include the issuance of a new prescription to an individual for a controlled substance that individual was previously prescribed.

SECTION XII – OTHER PHARMACY OPERATIONS

Central Fill Pharmacy

A "central fill pharmacy" (see **Appendix B, Definitions**) fills prescriptions for controlled substances on behalf of retail pharmacies with which it has a contractual agreement to provide such services or with pharmacies who share a common owner. When one retail pharmacy receives a prescription and a second pharmacy prepares and subsequently delivers the controlled substance medication to the first retail pharmacy for dispensing to the patient, the second pharmacy is engaging in a "central fill" activity. Records must be maintained by both the central fill pharmacy and the retail pharmacy that completely reflect the disposition of all controlled substance prescriptions dispensed. Central fill pharmacies are required to comply with the same security requirements applicable to retail pharmacies including the general requirement to maintain effective controls and procedures to guard against theft and diversion of controlled substances. Retail pharmacies that also perform central fill activities are allowed to do so without a separate DEA registration, separate inventories, or separate records.

Central fill pharmacies are permitted to prepare both initial and refill prescriptions, subject to all applicable state and federal regulations. Only a licensed pharmacist may fill the prescription. Both the retail and central fill pharmacists have a corresponding responsibility to ensure that the prescription was issued for a legitimate medical purpose by an individual practitioner acting in the usual course of professional practice and otherwise in the manner specified by DEA regulations.

Prescription information may be provided to an authorized central fill pharmacy by a retail pharmacy for dispensing purposes. Prescriptions for controlled substances listed in schedules II, III, IV, or V may be transmitted electronically from a retail pharmacy to a central fill pharmacy including via facsimile. The retail pharmacy transmitting the prescription information must:

1. Write the word "CENTRAL FILL" on the face of the original prescription and record the name, address, and DEA registration number of the central fill pharmacy to which the prescription has been transmitted and the name of the retail pharmacy pharmacist transmitting the prescription, and the date of transmittal;

2. Ensure that all information required to be on a prescription is transmitted to the central fill pharmacy (either on the face of the prescription or in the electronic transmission of information);

3. Maintain the original prescription for a period of two years from the date the prescription was last refilled;

4. Keep a record of receipt of the filled prescription, including the date of receipt, the method of delivery (private, common, or contract carrier) and the name of the retail pharmacy employee accepting delivery;

5. For schedules III-V prescriptions, indicate in the information transmitted the number of refills already dispensed and the number of refills remaining (refills for schedule II prescriptions are not permitted).

The central fill pharmacy receiving the transmitted prescription must:

1. Keep a copy of the prescription (if sent via facsimile) or an electronic record of all the information transmitted by the retail pharmacy, including the name, address, and the DEA registration number of the retail pharmacy transmitting the prescription;

2. Keep a record of the date of receipt of the transmitted prescription, the name of the licensed pharmacist filling the prescription, and dates of filling or refilling of the prescription; and

3. Keep a record of the date the filled prescription was delivered to the retail pharmacy and the method of delivery (i.e. private, common, or contract carrier).

Central fill pharmacies must affix to the package a label showing the retail pharmacy name and address and a unique identifier (i.e. the central fill pharmacy's DEA registration number) indicating that the prescription was filled at the central fill pharmacy. Central fill pharmacies must comply with the provisions of the C.F.R. when selecting private, common, or contract carriers to transport filled prescriptions to a retail pharmacy (and likewise for retail pharmacies retrieving filled prescriptions from a central fill pharmacy) for delivery to the ultimate user.

For electronic prescriptions, the name, address, and DEA registration number of the central fill pharmacy to which the prescription has been transmitted, the name of the retail pharmacy pharmacist transmitting the prescription, and the date of transmittal must be added to the electronic prescription record.

Long Term Care Facilities

A Long Term Care Facility (LTCF) is defined in the C.F.R. as a nursing home, retirement care, mental care, or other facility or institution, which provides extended health care to resident patients. In most cases, these facilities are not registered with DEA, yet these health care facilities routinely maintain controlled substances issued via prescription to their residents. These controlled substances are already outside the CSA's closed drug distribution system since they have been dispensed to the ultimate user.

LTCFs frequently need to dispose of unused medications due to a change in the resident's medication or the resident's death. Accordingly, LTCFs should contact the local DEA Diversion Field Office (**Appendix K**) for drug disposal instructions. The DEA is aware of issues currently facing LTCFs concerning the dispensing and handling of controlled substances, which are affected by a variety of state laws and circumstances. Pharmacists should check with their state agency for guidelines concerning controlled substances at LTCFs.

Regulations concerning LTCFs can also be found under:

- Section IX, *Exceptions for Schedule II Facsimile Prescriptions*

- Section X, *Partial Filling of Schedule II Prescriptions for Terminally Ill or Long Term Care Facility Patients*

Use of Automated Dispensing Systems by Retail Pharmacies at Long Term Care Facilities

If state law or regulations permit, the DEA will allow a retail pharmacy to register at the site of the LTCF and store controlled substances in an Automated Dispensing System (ADS) as outlined in 21 C.F.R. § 1301.27. In an ADS, a pharmacy stores bulk drugs in the machine in separate bins or containers. The pharmacy programs and controls the ADS remotely. Only authorized LTCF staff are allowed access to its contents, which are dispensed on a single-dose basis at the time of administration pursuant to a valid prescription. The ADS electronically records each dispensing, thus maintaining dispensing records for the pharmacy. Because the drugs are not considered dispensed until the system provides them, drugs in the ADS are counted as pharmacy stock. A registered retail pharmacy that possesses additional registrations for ADS machines at LTCFs may keep all records required for those additional registered sites at the retail pharmacy or other approved central location.

DEA registered pharmacies wishing to operate an ADS at an LTCF must contact the DEA Office of Diversion Control, Registration Section, at 1-800-882-9539 for registration instructions. Additional requirements for maintaining an ADS can be found online at www. DEAdiversion.usdoj.gov.

Emergency Kits for Long Term Care Facilities

The DEA has issued a policy statement which provides individual state licensing and regulatory boards with general guidelines for establishing specific rules concerning controlled substances used in emergency kits at Long Term Care Facilities (see **Appendix H, Guidelines for Emergency Kits in Long Term Care Facilities**).

Opioid (Narcotic) Addiction Treatment Programs

The Narcotic Addiction Treatment Act of 1974 and the Drug Addiction Treatment Act (DATA) of 2000 amended the CSA with respect to the use of controlled substances in the medical treatment of opioid addiction. These laws established the procedures for approving and licensing practitioners involved in the treatment of opioid addiction as well as improving the quality and delivery of that treatment to the segment of society in need.

Practitioners wishing to prescribe and dispense FDA approved schedule II controlled substances (i.e., methadone) for maintenance and detoxification treatment must obtain a separate DEA registration as a Narcotic Treatment Program via a DEA Form 363 which may be completed online at www.DEAdiversion.usdoj.gov. In addition to obtaining this separate DEA registration, this type of activity also requires the approval and certification by the Center for Substance Abuse Treatment (CSAT) within the Substance Abuse and Mental Health Services Administration (SAMHSA) of the U.S. Department of Health and Human Services as well as the applicable state methadone authority.

If a practitioner wishes to prescribe or dispense schedules III, IV, or V controlled substances approved by the FDA for addiction treatment (i.e., Suboxone® or Subutex® drug products), the practitioner must request a waiver from CSAT which will then notify DEA of all waiver requests. These practitioners are referred to as DATA waived practitioners.

DATA waived practitioners may treat 30 or 100 patients at any one time, dependent on individual authorization from CSAT. Upon authorization by CSAT, DEA will issue a new DEA certificate of registration bearing (1) the DEA registration number, (2) a unique identification number, and (3) the corresponding business activity to identify whether the physician is authorized to treat 30 or 100 patients. Pursuant to 21 C.F.R. §1301.28(d), the practitioner is required to include the identification number on all records when dispensing and on all prescriptions when prescribing Schedules III, IV, or V narcotic controlled drugs for use in maintenance or detoxification treatment. The listing of the identification number on a prescription is in addition to all other information required on a valid prescription to include the practitioner's DEA registration number (see **Section IX, Valid Prescription Requirements**).

Dispensing Controlled Substances for the Treatment of Pain

On September 6, 2006, the DEA published in the Federal Register a Policy Statement, *Dispensing Controlled Substances for the Treatment of Pain*. The purpose of the Policy Statement was to make clear the longstanding requirement under the law that physicians may prescribe controlled substances only for a legitimate medical purpose in the usual course of professional practice. In no way should this interfere with the legitimate practice of medicine or cause any physician to be reluctant to provide legitimate pain treatment. The second purpose of the Policy Statement was for the DEA to dispel the mistaken notion among a small number of medical professionals that the agency has embarked on a campaign to "target" physicians who prescribe controlled substances for the treatment of pain or that physicians must curb their legitimate prescribing of pain medications to avoid legal liability.

To achieve these aims, the document summarized the relevant legal principles and provided an explanation of DEA's role with respect to the regulation of controlled substances. The document also addressed specific issues and questions that have been raised on a recurring basis by physicians who seek guidance on the subject of dispensing controlled substances for the treatment of pain.

To review the Policy Statement, it may be accessed at www.DEAdiversion.usdoj.gov. Click *on Info & Legal Resources*, then *Federal Register Notices*, then *Notices 2006*, then *Policy Statement: Dispensing Controlled Substances for the Treatment of Pain, September 6, 2006*. For additional guidance on the responsibilities of the pharmacist where it pertains to the treatment of pain, see **Section IX, Corresponding Responsibility**.

SECTION XIII – OTHER CONTROLLED SUBSTANCE REGULATIONS

Controlled Substance Distribution by a Pharmacy – "Five Percent Rule"

A pharmacy registered to dispense controlled substances may distribute such substances (without being registered as a distributor) to another pharmacy or to a registered practitioner for the purpose of general dispensing by the practitioner to patients, provided that the following conditions are met:

1. The pharmacy or practitioner that will receive the controlled substances is registered under the CSA to dispense controlled substances;

2. The distribution is recorded by the distributing practitioner in accordance with 21 C.F.R. § 1304.22(c) and the receipt is recorded by the receiving practitioner in accordance with 21 C.F.R. § 1304.22(c);

3. If the pharmacy distributes a schedule II controlled substance, it must document the transfer on an official order form (DEA Form 222) or the electronic equivalent. For instructions on completing this form, see Section VIII, *Ordering Controlled Substances.*

4. **"Five Percent Rule"** – total number of dosage units of all controlled substances distributed by a pharmacy may not exceed five percent of all controlled substances dispensed by the pharmacy during a calendar year. If at any time the controlled substances distributed exceed five percent, the pharmacy is required to register as a distributor.

United States Postal Service Mailing Requirements for Controlled Substances

United States Postal Services regulations permit the mailing of controlled substances by drug manufacturers or their agents, pharmacies, or other authorized handlers when distribution is lawful under DEA regulations and if the mailer or the addressee meets one of the following conditions:

1. The mailer or the addressee is registered with DEA.

2. The mailer or the addressee is exempt from DEA registration as permissible by law.

United States Postal Service regulations permit mailing of any controlled substance, provided it is not outwardly dangerous and will not cause injury to a person's life or health, and if the following preparation and packaging standards are met:

1. The inner container of any parcel containing controlled substances is marked and sealed as required by the provisions of the CSA and its implementing regulations, and is placed in a plain outer container or securely wrapped in plain paper.

2. If the controlled substance consists of prescription medicines, the inner container is also labeled to show the name and address of the pharmacy, practitioner, or other person dispensing the prescription.

3. The outside wrapper or container is free of markings that would indicate the nature of the contents.

SECTION XIV – COMBAT METHAMPHETAMINE EPIDEMIC ACT OF 2005

Summary of the Act's Major Provisions

In March 2006, the President signed the *Combat Methamphetamine Epidemic Act of 2005* (CMEA). As a result of the new law, the DEA issued an Interim Final Rule in the Federal Register on September 26, 2006, which outlined the retail provisions of the CMEA.

Under the CMEA, regulated sellers must follow new requirements for retail sales of over-the-counter products containing the List I chemicals ephedrine, pseudoephedrine, and phenylpropanolamine (PPA), which can be used to manufacture methamphetamine illegally. The CMEA defined *"regulated seller"* to mean a retail distributor (including a pharmacy and mobile retail vendors) and *"at retail"* to mean sale or purchase for personal use.

Scheduled Listed Chemical Products

The CMEA created a new category of products called *"scheduled listed chemical product* (SLCP)." It includes any product that may be marketed or distributed lawfully in the United States under the Federal Food, Drug, and Cosmetic Act as a nonprescription drug that contains ephedrine, pseudoephedrine, or PPA (includes salts, optical isomers, and salts of optical isomers) (21 U.S.C. § 802(45)). This applies to nonprescription drug products only, not prescription drug products. Retail sales of SLCPs are excluded from the definition of a "regulated transaction" and from the registration requirement under 21 U.S.C. § 823, but are subject to a separate system of retail sales controls under 21 U.S.C. § 830.

Other requirements of the law include:

* Requirement of regulated sellers to place the products behind the counter or in locked cabinets.

* Requirement of regulated sellers to check the identity of purchasers and maintain a log of each sale that includes the purchaser's name and address, signature of the purchaser, product sold, quantity sold, date, and time.

* Requirement of regulated sellers to maintain the logbook for at least two years.

* Requirement of regulated sellers to train employees in the requirements of the law and certify to DEA that the training has occurred.

* Places a quantity limit of each of the chemicals that may be sold to an individual in a day to 3.6 grams of the chemical (base) without regard to the number of transactions.

* For nonliquids, product packaging is limited to blister packs containing no more than 2 dosage units per blister. Where blister packs are not technically feasible, the product must be packaged in unit dose packets or pouches.

- For individuals, purchases in a 30-day period are limited to 9 grams, of which not more than 7.5 grams may be imported by means of a common or contract carrier or the U.S. Postal Service.

While many states have enacted their own legislation regarding the regulation of these products, the federal law also requires regulated sellers to complete a self-certification process with the DEA that includes training their employees on the new regulations and procedures. The self-certification process must be completed online at process must be completed online at process must be completed online at www. DEAdiversion.usdoj.gov. If state law differs from federal law regarding the regulation of these products, retail outlets are to adhere to the stricter provisions of both.

Copies of the Interim Final Rule are available at www.DEAdiversion.usdoj.gov (click on the *Combat Meth Act of 2005*, then *Interim Final Rule – Retail Sales of Scheduled Listed Chemical Products*). Details on specific provisions of the CMEA that may impact a pharmacy that engages in retail sales of SLCPs are outlined below.

Recordkeeping Requirements

Regulated sellers are required to maintain a written (bound logbook) or electronic list of sales that identifies the transactions with the following information:

1. The name of the purchaser
2. The address of the purchaser
3. The date and time of the sale
4. The amount of product sold

The logbook requirement does not apply to any purchase by an individual of a single sales package that contains not more than 60 milligrams of pseudoephedrine.

Concurrently, purchasers are required to:

1. Present a photo identification issued by a State or the Federal Government (see **Proof of Identity Requirements** below for a complete list of acceptable forms of identification).
2. Sign a logbook and enter his or her name, address, date, and time of sale.

Once identification of the purchaser is presented to the seller, the seller is required to:

1. Determine that the name in the logbook corresponds to the name on the identification and that the date and time are correct.
2. Enter into the logbook the name of the product and the quantity sold.

The logbook must include a notice to purchasers that entering false statements or misrepresentations in the logbook may subject purchasers to criminal penalties under 18 U.S.C. § 1001. Sellers must maintain each entry in the logbook for not fewer than two years after the date on which the entry is made.

Loss or Theft of Scheduled Listed Chemical Products

A report should be made orally to the local DEA Diversion Field Office (**Appendix K**) in the area where the pharmacy is located. Per 21 C.F.R. § 1314.15(c), a written report of losses must be filed within 15 days after the pharmacist becomes aware of the loss or theft. A written report should include the DEA registration number (if applicable), name, business address, date of loss, type of loss, and a description of the circumstances of the loss (e.g., in-transit, theft from premises).

Proof of Identity Requirements

The CMEA requires an individual to present an identification card that includes a photograph and is issued by a State or the Federal Government or a document considered acceptable under 8 C.F.R. § 274a.2(b)(1)(v)(A) and (B). Those documents currently include the following:

- United States passport;
- Alien Registration Receipt Card or Permanent Resident Card, Form I-551;
- An unexpired foreign passport that contains a temporary I-551 stamp, or temporary I–551 printed notation on a machine-readable immigrant visa;
- An Employment Authorization Document which contains a photograph (Form I–766);
- In the case of a nonimmigrant alien authorized to work for a specific employer incident to status, a foreign passport with form I-94 or Form I-94A bearing the same name as the passport and containing an endorsement of the alien's nonimmigrant status, as long as the period of endorsement has not yet expired and the proposed employment is not in conflict with any restrictions or limitations identified on the Form;

- A passport from the Federated States of Micronesia (FSM) or the Republic of the Marshall Islands (RMI) with Form I–94 or Form I–94A indicating nonimmigrant admission under the Compact of Free Association Between the United States and the FSM or RMI;

- In the case of an individual lawfully enlisted for military service in the Armed Forces under 10 U.S.C. § 504, a military identification card issued to such individual may be accepted only by the Armed Forces.

For individuals 16 years of age or older:

- A driver's license or identification card containing a photograph, issued by a state or an outlying possession of the United States. If the driver's license or identification card does not contain a photograph, identifying information shall be included such as: name, date of birth, sex, height, color of eyes, and address;

- School identification card with a photograph;

- Voter's registration card;

- U.S. military card or draft record;

- Identification card issued by federal, state, or local government agencies or entities. If the identification card does not contain a photograph, identifying information shall be included such as: name, date of birth, sex, height, color of eyes, and address;

- Military dependent's identification card;

- Native American tribal documents;

- United States Coast Guard Merchant Mariner Card;

- Driver's license issued by a Canadian government authority.

For individuals under age 18 who are unable to produce a document from the list above, the following documents are acceptable to establish identity only:

- School record or report card;

- Clinic doctor or hospital record;

- Daycare or nursery school record.

NOTE: *The list of acceptable forms of identification, as cited in the CMEA, may change ("in effect on or after the date of enactment"). The DEA has no discretion to alter the list.*

Product Placement

SLCPs must be stored behind the counter or, if in an area where the public has access, in a locked cabinet. Although DEA is not including cabinet specifications in the rule, a locked cabinet should be substantial enough that it cannot be easily picked up and removed. In a store setting, the cabinet should be similar to those used to store items, such as cigarettes, that can be accessed only by sales staff.

Self-Certification

As part of the requirements of CMEA, an annual self-certification is required for all regulated sellers of SLCPs. A regulated seller must not sell SLCPs unless it has self-certified with DEA. In self-certifying, the regulated seller is confirming:

- The employees who will be engaged in the sale of SLCPs have undergone training regarding provisions of CMEA.

- Records of the training are maintained.

- Sales to individuals do not exceed 3.6 grams of ephedrine, pseudoephedrine, or phenylpropanolamine per day.

- Nonliquid forms are packaged as required.

- SLCPs are stored behind the counter or in a locked cabinet.

- A written or electronic logbook containing the required information on sales of these products is properly maintained.

- The logbook information will be disclosed only to Federal, State, or local law enforcement and only to ensure compliance with Title 21 of the United States Code or to facilitate a product recall.

The only way to self-certify is through DEA's Diversion website at www.DEAdiversion.usdoj.gov. Self-certification can be accomplished on any computer (e.g., at the store, at home, at the library, or at any other location).

A certificate will be generated by DEA upon receipt of the self-certification application. The regulated seller may print this certificate, or if the regulated seller is unable to print it, DEA will print and mail the certificate to the regulated seller. Chain stores wishing to file self-certifications for more than 10 locations must print or copy the form electronically and submit the information to DEA by mail. DEA will

DEA Manual

work with these persons to facilitate this process. Persons interested in this self-certification option should contact DEA for assistance at 1-800-882-9539. For current DEA registrants, the system will pre-populate the form with basic information if the registrant enters his DEA registration number in the field provided.

The regulated seller must self-certify to DEA as described above on an **annual basis**. It is the responsibility of the regulated seller to ensure that all employees have been trained prior to self-certifying each time.

It is the regulated seller's responsibility to annually renew before the certificate expires if the regulated seller intends to continue selling SLCPs at retail. The certificate contains a self-certification number in the upper right corner. The expiration date of the certificate is listed under the self-certification number. Regulated sellers may verify the expiration date of their certificate at www.DEAdiversion.usdoj.gov.

The self-certification requirement is subject to the provisions of 18 U.S.C. § 1001. A regulated seller who knowingly or willfully certifies to facts that are not true is subject to fines and imprisonment.

Required Training

Training materials designed by DEA must be used, although a regulated seller may include information in addition to that provided by DEA. DEA training materials may be found at www.DEAdiversion.usdoj.gov.

Training Records

Each employee of a regulated seller who is responsible for delivering SLCPs to purchasers or who deals directly with purchasers by obtaining payment for the SLCPs must undergo training and must sign an acknowledgement of training received prior to selling SLCPs. This record must be kept in the employee's personnel file.

Self-Certification Fee

On December 29, 2008, the DEA published a Final Rule in the Federal Register entitled *Combat Methamphetamine Epidemic Act of 2005: Fee for Self-Certification for Regulated Sellers of Scheduled Listed Chemical Products*. The rule established a self-certification fee for regulated sellers of SLCPs that are not DEA pharmacy registrants.

APPENDICES

Appendix A

This summary is provided as a quick reference to the provisions of the Controlled Substances Act. It is not intended to replace any statutory or regulatory requirement thereof. For complete guidance as to the provisions of each area indicated below, please check the appropriate section of this manual.

Summary of Controlled Substances Act Requirements

	Schedule II	Schedules III & IV	Schedule V
Registration	Required	Required	Required
Receiving Records	DEA Form 222	Invoices, readily retrievable	Invoices, readily retrievable
Prescriptions	Written[1] prescriptions[2]	Written, oral, or fax	Written, oral, or fax
Refills	No	No more than 5 within 6 months	As authorized when prescription is issued or if renewed by a practitioner
Maintenance of Prescriptions	Separate file	Separate file or readily retrievable	Separate file or readily retrievable[3]
Distribution Between Registrants	DEA Form 222	Invoices	Invoices
Security	Locked cabinet or dispersed among non-controlled pharmaceuticals	Locked cabinet or dispersed among non-controlled pharmaceuticals	Locked cabinet or dispersed among non-controlled pharmaceuticals
Theft or Significant Loss	Report to DEA and complete DEA Form 106	Report to DEA and complete DEA Form 106	Report to DEA and complete DEA Form 106

Note: *All records* must be maintained for 2 years, unless state law requires a longer period.

---

[1] *Written prescriptions include paper prescriptions and electronic prescriptions that meet DEA's requirements for such prescriptions.*

[2] *Emergency prescriptions require a signed follow-up prescription within seven days.* **Exceptions:** *A facsimile prescription serves as the original prescription when issued to residents of Long Term Care Facilities, hospice patients, or patients with a diagnosed terminal illness, or for immediate administration (21 C.F.R. § 1306.11(e), (f) and (g)).*

[3] *The record of dispensing can also be a schedule V logbook, if state law allows.*

12/1/2019

Appendix B

Definitions Based on the Controlled Substances Act
and the Code of Federal Regulations

Administer

The direct application of a controlled substance to the body of a patient or research subject by 1) a practitioner or (in his/her presence) by his/her authorized agent, or 2) the patient or research subject at the direction and in the presence of the practitioner, whether such application is by injection, inhalation, ingestion, or any other means.

Central Fill Pharmacy

A pharmacy which is permitted by the state in which it is located to prepare controlled substance orders for dispensing pursuant to a valid prescription transmitted to it by a registered retail pharmacy and to return the labeled and filled prescriptions to the retail pharmacy for delivery to the ultimate user. Such central fill pharmacy shall be deemed "authorized" to fill prescriptions on behalf of a retail pharmacy only if the retail pharmacy and central fill pharmacy have a contractual relationship providing for such activities or share a common owner.

Chemicals

Please see the definitions for List I Chemical, Retail Distributor and Scheduled Listed Chemical Product.

Dispense

To deliver a controlled substance to an ultimate user or research subject by, or pursuant to the lawful order of, a practitioner, including the prescribing and administering of a controlled substance and the packaging, labeling, or compounding necessary to prepare the substance for such delivery.

Individual Practitioner

A physician, dentist, veterinarian, or other individual licensed, registered or otherwise permitted, by the United States or the jurisdiction in which they practice, to dispense a controlled substance in the course of professional practice, but does not include a pharmacist, a pharmacy, or an institutional practitioner.

Institutional Practitioner

A hospital or other person (other than an individual) licensed, registered or otherwise permitted, by the United States or the jurisdiction in which it practices, to dispense a controlled substance in the course of professional practice, but does not include a pharmacy.

Inventory

All factory and branch stocks in finished form of a basic class of controlled substance manufactured or otherwise acquired by a registrant, whether in bulk, commercial containers, or contained in pharmaceutical preparations in the possession of the registrant (including stocks held by the registrant under separate registration as a manufacturer, importer, exporter, or distributor).

List I Chemical

A chemical specifically designated by the [DEA] Administrator in 21 C.F.R. § 1310.02(a)… that, in addition to legitimate uses, is used in manufacturing a controlled substance in violation of the [Controlled Substances] Act and is important to the manufacture of a controlled substance.

Long Term Care Facility (LTCF)

A nursing home, retirement care, mental care, or other facility or institution that provides extended health care to resident patients.

Mid-level Practitioner (MLP)

An individual practitioner, other than a physician, dentist, veterinarian, or podiatrist, who is licensed, registered or otherwise permitted by the United States or the jurisdiction in which he/she practices, to dispense a controlled substance in the course of professional practice. Examples of MLPs include, but are not limited to, nurse practitioners, nurse midwives, nurse anesthetists, clinical nurse specialists, and physician assistants who are authorized to dispense controlled substances by the state in which they practice. Because this authority varies greatly by state, check with the state licensing authority to determine which MLP disciplines are authorized to dispense controlled substances in a particular state or visit, www.DEAdiversion.usdoj.gov (click on *Registration Support*, then *Resources*, then *Mid-level Practitioners Authorization by State*).

Online Pharmacy

An online pharmacy is a person, entity, or Internet site, whether in the United States or abroad, that knowingly or intentionally delivers, distributes, or dispenses, or offers or attempts to deliver, distribute, or dispense, a controlled substance by means of the Internet.

Pharmacist

Any pharmacist licensed by a state to dispense controlled substances, and shall include any other person (e.g., pharmacist intern) authorized by a state to dispense controlled substances under the supervision of a pharmacist licensed by such state.

Prescription

An order for medication which is dispensed to or for an ultimate user but does not include an order for medication which is dispensed for immediate administration to the ultimate user (e.g., an order to dispense a drug to a bed patient for immediate administration in a hospital is not a prescription).

Readily Retrievable

Certain records which are kept by automatic data processing systems or other electronic or mechanized recordkeeping systems in such a manner that they can be separated out from all other records in a reasonable time and/or records kept in such a manner that certain items are asterisked, redlined, or in some other manner visually identifiable apart from other items appearing on the records.

Regulated Seller

A retail distributor (including a pharmacy or a mobile retail vendor), except that the term does not include an employee or agent of the distributor.

Retail Distributor

A grocery store, general merchandise store, drug store, or other entity or person whose activities as a distributor relating to drug products containing ephedrine, pseudoephedrine or phenylpropanolamine are limited almost exclusively to sales for personal use, both in number of sales and volume of sales, either directly to walk-in customers or in face-to-face transactions by direct sales.

Scheduled Listed Chemical Product (SLCP)

A product that contains ephedrine, pseudoephedrine, or phenylpropanolamine which may be marketed or distributed lawfully in the United States under the Federal, Food, Drug, and Cosmetic Act as a nonprescription drug. Ephedrine, pseudoephedrine, and phenylpropanolamine include their salts, optical isomers, and salts of optical isomers.

Ultimate User

A person who has lawfully obtained, and who possesses, a controlled substance for his [her] own use or for the use of a member of his [her] household or for an animal owned by him [her] or by a member of his [her] household.

Appendix C

Definitions of Abbreviations

C.F.R. ....Code of Federal Regulations

CMEA ....Combat Methamphetamine Epidemic Act of 2005

CSA.......................Controlled Substances Act

CSAT......................Center for Substance Abuse Treatment

CSOS.....................Controlled Substance Ordering System

CSRPA ....Controlled Substance Registrant Protection Act of 1984

DEA.......................Drug Enforcement Administration

FDA.......................Food and Drug Administration

HHS.......................Department of Health and Human Services

SAMHSA ....Substance Abuse and Mental Health Services Administration

U.S.C.....................United States Code

Appendix D
Pharmacist's Guide to Prescription Fraud

The purpose of this guide is to ensure that controlled substances continue to be available for legitimate medical and scientific purposes while preventing diversion into the illicit market. It is not the intent of this publication to discourage or prohibit the use of controlled substances where medically indicated. However, nothing in this guide should be construed as authorizing or permitting any person to conduct any act that is not authorized or permitted under federal or state laws.

Pharmacist's Responsibilities

The abuse of prescription drugs—especially controlled substances—is a serious social and health problem in the United States today. As a healthcare professional, pharmacists share responsibility for preventing prescription drug abuse and diversion.

- Pharmacists have a personal responsibility to protect their practice from becoming an easy target for drug diversion. They need to know of the potential situations where drug diversion can occur, and establish safeguards to prevent drug diversion.

- The dispensing pharmacist must maintain a constant vigilance against forged or altered prescriptions. The CSA holds the pharmacist responsible for knowingly dispensing a prescription that was not issued in the usual course of professional treatment.

Types of Fraudulent Prescriptions

Pharmacists should be aware of the various kinds of forged prescriptions that may be presented for dispensing. Some patients, in an effort to obtain additional amounts of legitimately prescribed drugs, alter the practitioner's prescription. They may have prescription pads printed using a legitimate doctor's name, but with a different call back number that is answered by an accomplice to verify the prescription. Drug seeking individuals may also call in their own prescriptions and give their own telephone number as a call-back for confirmation. Drug abusers sometimes steal legitimate prescription pads from practitioner's offices and/or hospitals and prescriptions are written using fictitious patient names and addresses.

In addition, individuals may go to emergency rooms complaining of pain in the hopes of receiving a controlled substance prescription. The prescription can then be altered or copied to be used again. Computers are often used to create prescriptions for nonexistent doctors or to copy legitimate doctors' prescriptions. The quantity of drugs prescribed and frequency of prescriptions filled are not lone indications of fraud or improper prescribing, especially if a patient is being treated with opioids for pain management. Pharmacists should also recognize that drug tolerance and physical dependence may develop as a consequence of a patient's sustained use of opioid analgesics for the legitimate treatment of chronic pain.

The following criteria may indicate that a prescription was not issued for a legitimate medical purpose:

- The prescriber writes significantly more prescriptions (or in larger quantities) compared to other practitioners in the area.

- The patient appears to be returning too frequently. A prescription which should last for a month in legitimate use is being refilled on a biweekly, weekly or even a daily basis.

- The prescriber writes prescriptions for antagonistic drugs, such as depressants and stimulants, at the same time. Drug abusers often request prescriptions for "uppers and downers" at the same time.

- The patient presents prescriptions written in the names of other people.

- A number of people appear simultaneously, or within a short time, all bearing similar prescriptions from the same physician.

- People who are not regular patrons or residents of the community, show up with prescriptions from the same physician.

The following criteria may indicate a forged prescription:

- Prescription looks "too good". The prescriber's handwriting is too legible.

- Quantities, directions, or dosages differ from usual medical usage.

- Prescription does not comply with the acceptable standard abbreviations or appears to be textbook presentations.

- Prescription appears to be photocopied.

- Directions are written in full with no abbreviations.

- Prescription is written in different color inks or written in different handwriting.

Prevention Techniques

- Know the prescriber and his/her signature.

- Know the prescriber's DEA registration number.

- Know the patient.

- Check the date on the prescription order to determine if it has been presented in a reasonable length of time since being issued by the prescriber.

When there is a question about any aspect of the prescription order, the pharmacist should contact the prescriber for verification or clarification.

If at any time a pharmacist is in doubt, he /she should require proper identification. Although this procedure is not foolproof (identification papers can also be stolen/forged), it does increase the drug abuser's risk. If a pharmacist believes the prescription is forged or altered, he/she should not dispense it and call the local police. If a pharmacist believes he/she has discovered a pattern of prescription abuse, he/she should contact the state Board of Pharmacy or the local DEA Diversion Field Office (**Appendix K**). Both DEA and state authorities consider retail-level diversion a priority issue.

Proper Controls

Dispensing procedures without control and professional caution are an invitation to the drug abuser. Proper controls can be accomplished by following common sense, sound professional practice, and proper dispensing procedures. In addition, pharmacy staff should have knowledge of these safeguards, as it will help prevent and protect the pharmacy from becoming a source of diversion.

Most drug abusers seek out areas where communication and cooperation between health care professionals are minimal because it makes the drug abuser's work easier. Thus, a pharmacist should encourage other local pharmacists and physicians to develop a working relationship which will promote teamwork and camaraderie. In addition, the pharmacist should become familiar with those controlled substances that are popular for abuse and resale on the streets in the area and should discuss those findings with other pharmacists and practitioners in the community.

Appendix E

Affidavit for a New Pharmacy[1]

I, _____, the _____ (Title of officer, official, partner, or other position) of
_____ (Corporation, partnership, or sole proprietor), doing business as _____
(Store name) at _____ (Number and Street), _____ (City) _____ (State)
_____ (Zip Code), hereby certify that said store was issued a pharmacy permit No. _____ by the
_____ (Board of Pharmacy or Licensing Agency) of the State of _____ on
_____ (Date).

This statement is submitted in order to obtain a Drug Enforcement Administration registration number. I understand that if any information is false, the Administration may immediately suspend the registration for this store and commence proceedings to revoke under 21 U.S.C. § 824(a) because of the danger to public health and safety. I further understand that any false information contained in this affidavit may subject me personally and the above-named corporation/partnership/business to prosecution under 21 U.S.C. § 843, the penalties for conviction of which include imprisonment for up to 4 years, a fine of not more than $30,000.00 or both.

_____

Signature (Person who signs Application for Registration)

State of _____ County of _____ Subscribed to and sworn before me this _____ day of _____,
20_____.

_____

Notary Public

---

[1] *21 C.F.R. § 1301.17(a).*

Appendix F

Affidavit for Transfer of a Pharmacy[1]

I, _____, the _____ (Title of officer, official, partner, or other position) of _____ (Corporation, partnership, or sole proprietor), doing business as _____
___ (Store name) hereby certify:

(1) That said company was issued a pharmacy permit No. _____ by the _____ (Board of Pharmacy or Licensing Agency) of the State of _____ and a DEA Registration Number _____ for a pharmacy located at _____ (Number and Street), _____ (City) _____ (State) _____ (Zip Code); and

(2) That said company is acquiring the pharmacy business of _____ (Name of Seller) doing business as _____ with DEA Registration Number _____ on or about _____ (Date of Transfer) and that said company has applied (or will apply on _____ (Date)) for a pharmacy permit from the Board of Pharmacy (or Licensing Agency) of the State of _____ to do business as _____ _____ (Store name) at _____ (Number and Street) _____ (City) _____ (State) _____ (Zip Code).

This statement is submitted in order to obtain a Drug Enforcement Administration registration number.

I understand that if a DEA registration number is issued, the pharmacy may acquire controlled substances but may not dispense them until a pharmacy permit or license is issued by the State board of pharmacy or licensing agency.

I understand that if any information is false, the Administration may immediately suspend the registration for this store and commence proceedings to revoke under 21 U.S.C. § 824(a) because of the danger to public health and safety. I further understand that any false information contained in this affidavit may subject me personally and the above-named corporation/partnership/business to prosecution under 21 U.S.C. § 843, the penalties for conviction of which include imprisonment for up to 4 years, a fine of not more than $30,000.00 or both.

_____

Signature (Person who signs Application for Registration)

State of _____ County of _____ Subscribed to and sworn before me this _____ day of _____, 20_____.

_____

Notary Public

---

[1] 21 C.F.R. § 1301.17(b).

Appendix G
Equivalency Tables for Ephedrine, Pseudoephedrine, and Phenylpropanolamine
Under the Combat Methamphetamine Epidemic Act of 2005

RETAIL DAILY SALE LIMITS ARE NOT TO EXCEED THE FOLLOWING AMOUNTS PER PURCHASER	
Ingredient	Number of Tablets = 3.6 grams
25 mg Ephedrine HCl	175
25 mg Ephedrine Sulfate	186
30 mg Pseudoephedrine HCl	146
60 mg Pseudoephedrine HCl	73
120 mg Pseudoephedrine HCl	36
30 mg Pseudoephedrine Sulfate	155
60 mg Pseudoephedrine Sulfate	77
120 mg Pseudoephedrine Sulfate	38
Phenylpropanolamine (PPA)	The Food and Drug Administration issued a voluntary recall of this ingredient as being unsafe for human consumption. Veterinary use is by prescription only.

30-DAY SALE LIMITS ARE NOT TO EXCEED THE FOLLOWING AMOUNTS PER PURCHASER		
Ingredient	Number of tablets at retail = 9 grams	Number of tablets for mail orders = 7.5 grams
25 mg Ephedrine HCl	439	366
25 mg Ephedrine Sulfate	466	389
30 mg Pseudoephedrine HCl	366	305
60 mg Pseudoephedrine HCl	183	152
120 mg Pseudoephedrine HCl	91	76
30 mg Pseudoephedrine Sulfate	389	324
60 mg Pseudoephedrine Sulfate	194	162
120 mg Pseudoephedrine Sulfate	97	81
Phenylpropanolamine (PPA)	The Food and Drug Administration issued a voluntary recall of this ingredient as being unsafe for human consumption. Veterinary use is by prescription only.	

DEA Manual

Appendix H

Guidelines for Emergency Kits in Long Term Care Facilities

A pharmacy may place an emergency kit with controlled substances in a non-DEA registered Long Term Care Facility (LTCF), if the appropriate state agency or regulatory authority specifically approves the placement and promulgates procedures that delineate:

1. The source from which the LTCF may obtain controlled substances for emergency kits and that the source of supply is a DEA-registered hospital/clinic, pharmacy, or practitioner.

2. The security safeguards for each emergency kit stored at the LTCF, including who may have access to the emergency kit, and specific limitation of the type and quantity of controlled substances permitted in the kit.

3. The responsibility for proper control and accountability of the emergency kit within the LTCF, including the requirement that the LTCF and the supplying registrant maintain complete and accurate records of the controlled substances placed in the emergency kit, the disposition of the controlled substances, and the requirement to take and maintain periodic physical inventories.

4. The emergency medical conditions under which the controlled substances may be administered to LTCF patients, including the requirement that controlled substances be administered by authorized personnel only as expressly authorized by an individual practitioner and in compliance with the provisions of 21 C.F.R. §§ 1306.11 and 1306.21.

5. The prohibited activities that if violated could result in state revocation, denial, or suspension of the privilege to supply or possess emergency kits containing controlled substances.

The requirements for emergency kits in LTCFs were published in a *Federal Register* notice on April 9, 1980 (**45 FR 24128**). Pharmacies and LTCFs may wish to consult the notice to ensure compliance with the requirements.

Appendix I

Guidelines for Completing the DEA Form 106

Instructions for completing the DEA Form 106 are provided when filling out either the paper or electronic version of the form. Listed below are additional guidelines:

- Do not use a DEA Form 106 to report an accidental spillage. Save the broken bottles, salvage the product if possible, and contact the local DEA Diversion Field Office (**Appendix K**) for additional instructions. This type of a loss must be reported on a DEA Form 41, Registrants Inventory of Drugs Surrendered.

- If thefts have occurred due to employee pilferage over a period of time, document on the DEA Form 106 the date of discovery in block 4. Provide estimated beginning and ending dates of the thefts in box 17 with an explanation.

- If there are multiple thefts or losses on the same day (e.g. mail-order pharmacy), report each theft or loss on a separate DEA Form 106.

- Miscounts or adjustments to inventory involving clerical errors on the part of the pharmacy should not be reported on a DEA Form 106. A separate log documenting the discrepancies may be kept at the management's discretion.

- In block 9, enter the number of thefts or losses experienced in the last 24 months, but do not include the current theft or loss being reported. If the current theft or loss was the only theft or loss in the last 24 months, enter 0 (zero).

- In block 12, enter the amount the pharmacy paid for the controlled substances, not the retail value.

- In blocks 14 b & c, if the customer accepted the controlled substance before discovering a loss in transit, identify the supplier and its DEA registration number.

- In block 14f, when explaining how many losses occurred from the same carrier, do not include the current loss.

- The date next to the signature and title on page 2 should be the date the form was completed, signed, and sent to the local DEA Diversion Field Office (**Appendix K**).

- Document the National Drug Code (NDC) number of the controlled substance, and if the loss was a partial container, document the actual amount of theft or loss within the container.

- If the controlled substance contains hydrocodone, oxycodone or a similar controlled substance and contains acetaminophen, aspirin or ibuprofen, indicate the strength of the non-controlled substance as well as the strength of the controlled substance contained in the product.

- If amending a paper version of a prior DEA Form 106, print Amended in the upper front page margin, with the date of the theft.

DEA Manual

Appendix J

DEA Registration Specialists in Field Divisions

Registration assistants are available during normal business hours to provide information about new applications, renewals, order forms, or changes to a DEA registration. Addresses and telephone numbers are subject to change. Please refer to the DEA's Diversion website, www. DEAdiversion.usdoj.gov, for the most current listing.

Appendix K

Drug Enforcement Administration
Diversion Field Office Locations

Visit www.DEAdiversion.usdoj.gov for current addresses and telephone numbers.

DEA Manual

Appendix L

Internet Resources

DEA's Diversion Control Program Website

www.DEAdiversion.usdoj.gov

DEA Homepage

www.dea.gov

U.S. Government Printing Office

www.gpoaccess.gov/cfr/index.html

Provides access to the C.F.R., Parts 1300 to end, primary source for the Pharmacist's Manual, and the Federal Register which contains proposed and finalized amendments to the C.F.R.

Office of National Drug Control Policy (ONDCP)

www.whitehousedrugpolicy.gov

Food and Drug Administration

www.FDA.gov

HHS & SAMHSA's National Clearinghouse for Alcohol and Drug Information

www.health.org

SAMHSA/CSAT

www.csat.samhsa.gov

Federation of State Medical Boards

www.FSMB.org

National Association of Boards of Pharmacy

www.nabp.net

National Association of State Controlled Substances Authorities

www.nascsa.org

Appendix M

Small Business and Agriculture
Regulatory Enforcement Ombudsman

The Small Business and Agriculture Regulatory Enforcement Ombudsman and 10 Regional Fairness Boards were established to receive comments from small businesses about federal agency enforcement actions. The Ombudsman will annually evaluate the enforcement activities and rate each agency's responsiveness to small business. If you wish to comment on DEA enforcement actions, you may contact the Ombudsman at 1-888-REG-FAIR (1-888-734-3247).

DEA Manual

Appendix N

Additional Assistance

This publication is intended to provide guidance and information on the requirements of the CSA and its implementing regulations. If you require additional clarification or assistance, or wish to comment on any matter regarding the DEA's requirements or regulatory activities, please contact your local DEA Diversion Field Office (**Appendix K**). Every effort will be made to respond promptly to your inquiry.

Plain Language

The Drug Enforcement Administration has made every effort to write this manual in clear, plain language. If you have suggestions as to how to improve the clarity of this manual, please contact us at:

> Drug Enforcement Administration
> Attn: Liaison and Policy Section/ODL
> 8701 Morrissette Drive
> Springfield, Virginia 22152
> Telephone: 1-202-307-7297

TEXAS DANGEROUS DRUG ACT
HEALTH AND SAFETY CODE, CHAPTER 483

SUBCHAPTER A. GENERAL PROVISIONS

SUBCHAPTER B. DUTIES OF PHARMACISTS, PRACTITIONERS, AND OTHER PERSONS

SUBCHAPTER C. CRIMINAL PENALTIES

SUBCHAPTER D. CRIMINAL AND CIVIL PROCEDURE

SUBCHAPTER E. OPIOID ANTAGONISTS

Dang. Drugs

SUBCHAPTER A. GENERAL PROVISIONS

Sec. 483.0001. Short Title.

This Act may be cited as the Texas Dangerous Drug Act.

Leg.H. Stats. 1993 73rd Leg. Sess. Ch. 789, effective September 1, 1993.

Sec. 483.001. Definitions.

In this chapter:
(1) "Board" means the Texas State Board of Pharmacy.
(2) "Dangerous drug" means a device or a drug that is unsafe for self-medication and that is not included in Schedules I through V or Penalty Groups 1 through 4 of Chapter 481 (Texas Controlled Substances Act). The term includes a device or a drug that bears or is required to bear the legend:
   (A) "Caution: federal law prohibits dispensing without prescription" or "Rx only" or another legend that complies with federal law; or
   (B) "Caution: federal law restricts this drug to use by or on the order of a licensed veterinarian."
(3) "Deliver" means to sell, dispense, give away, or supply in any other manner.
(4) "Designated agent" means:
   (A) a licensed nurse, physician assistant, pharmacist, or other individual designated by a practitioner to communicate prescription drug orders to a pharmacist;
   (B) a licensed nurse, physician assistant, or pharmacist employed in a health care facility to whom the practitioner communicates a prescription drug order; or
   (C) a registered nurse or physician assistant authorized by a practitioner to carry out a prescription drug order for dangerous drugs under Subchapter B, Chapter 157, Occupations Code.
(5) "Dispense" means to prepare, package, compound, or label a dangerous drug in the course of professional practice for delivery under the lawful order of a practitioner to an ultimate user or the user's agent.
(6) "Manufacturer" means a person, other than a pharmacist, who manufactures dangerous drugs. The term includes a person who prepares dangerous drugs in dosage form by mixing, compounding, encapsulating, entableting, or any other process.
(7) "Patient" means:
   (A) an individual for whom a dangerous drug is prescribed or to whom a dangerous drug is administered; or
   (B) an owner or the agent of an owner of an animal for which a dangerous drug is prescribed or to which a dangerous drug is administered.
(8) "Person" includes an individual, corporation, partnership, and association.
(9) "Pharmacist" means a person licensed by the Texas State Board of Pharmacy to practice pharmacy.
(10) "Pharmacy" means a facility where prescription drug or medication orders are received, processed, dispensed, or distributed under this chapter, Chapter 481 of this code, and Subtitle J, Title 3, Occupations Code. The term does not include a narcotic drug treatment program that is regulated by Chapter 466, Health and Safety Code.
(11) "Practice of pharmacy" means:
   (A) provision of those acts or services necessary to provide pharmaceutical care;
   (B) interpretation and evaluation of prescription drug orders or medication orders;
   (C) participation in drug and device selection as authorized by law, drug administration, drug regimen review, or drug or drug-related research;
   (D) provision of patient counseling;
   (E) responsibility for:
      (i) dispensing of prescription drug orders or distribution of medication orders in the patient's best interest;
      (ii) compounding and labeling of drugs and devices, except labeling by a manufacturer, repackager, or distributor of nonprescription drugs and commercially packaged prescription drugs and devices;
      (iii) proper and safe storage of drugs and devices; or
      (iv) maintenance of proper records for drugs and devices. In this subdivision, "device" has the meaning assigned by Subtitle J, Title 3, Occupations Code; or
   (F) performance of a specific act of drug therapy management for a patient delegated to a pharmacist by a written protocol from a physician licensed by the state under Subtitle B, Title 3, Occupations Code.
(12) "Practitioner" means:
   (A) a person licensed by:
      (i) the Texas Medical Board, State Board of Dental Examiners, Texas Optometry Board, or State Board of Veterinary Medical Examiners to prescribe and administer dangerous drugs; or
      (ii) the Texas Department of Licensing and Regulation, with respect to podiatry, to prescribe and administer dangerous drugs;
   (B) a person licensed by another state in a health field in which, under the laws of this state, a licensee may legally prescribe dangerous drugs;

(C) a person licensed in Canada or Mexico in a health field in which, under the laws of this state, a licensee may legally prescribe dangerous drugs; or

(D) an advanced practice registered nurse or physician assistant to whom a physician has delegated the authority to prescribe or order a drug or device under Section 157.0511, 157.0512, or 157.054, Occupations Code.

(13) "Prescription" means an order from a practitioner, or an agent of the practitioner designated in writing as authorized to communicate prescriptions, or an order made in accordance with Subchapter B, Chapter 157, Occupations Code, or Section 203.353, Occupations Code, to a pharmacist for a dangerous drug to be dispensed that states:

(A) the date of the order's issue;

(B) the name and address of the patient;

(C) if the drug is prescribed for an animal, the species of the animal;

(D) the name and quantity of the drug prescribed;

(E) the directions for the use of the drug;

(F) the intended use of the drug unless the practitioner determines the furnishing of this information is not in the best interest of the patient;

(G) the name, address, and telephone number of the practitioner at the practitioner's usual place of business, legibly printed or stamped; and

(H) the name, address, and telephone number of the licensed midwife, registered nurse, or physician assistant, legibly printed or stamped, if signed by a licensed midwife, registered nurse, or physician assistant.

(14) "Warehouseman" means a person who stores dangerous drugs for others and who has no control over the disposition of the drugs except for the purpose of storage.

(15) "Wholesaler" means a person engaged in the business of distributing dangerous drugs to a person listed in Sections 483.041(c) (1)-(6).

Leg.H. Stats. 1989, 71st Leg., ch. 678 (H.B. 2136), § 1, effective September 1, 1989; am. Acts 1989, 71st Leg., ch. 1100 (S.B. 1046), §§ 5.03(h), 5.04(b), effective September 1, 1989; am. Acts 1991, 72nd Leg., ch. 14 (S.B. 404), § 200, effective September 1, 1991; am. Acts 1991, 72nd Leg., ch. 237 (H.B. 1495), § 10, effective September 1, 1991; am. Acts 1991, 72nd Leg., ch. 588 (S.B. 774), § 26, effective September 1, 1991; am. Acts 1993, 73rd Leg., ch. 351 (S.B. 621), § 29, effective September 1, 1993; am. Acts 1993, 73rd Leg., ch. 789 (S.B. 472), § 18, effective September 1, 1993; am. Acts 1995, 74th Leg., ch. 965 (S.B. 673), §§ 6, 82, effective June 16, 1995; am. Acts 1997, 75th Leg., ch. 1095 (H.B. 2088), § 18, effective September 1, 1997; am. Acts 1997, 75th Leg., ch. 1180 (S.B. 609), § 22, effective September 1, 1997; am. Acts 2001, 77th Leg., ch. 112 (S.B. 1166), § 6, effective May 11, 2001; am. Acts 2001, 77th Leg., ch. 1254 (S.B. 768), § 11, effective September 1, 2001; am. Acts 2001, 77th Leg., ch. 1420 (H.B. 2812), § 14.795, effective September 1, 2001; am. Acts 2003, 78th Leg., ch. 88 (H.B. 1095), § 10, effective May 20, 2003; am. Acts 2005, 79th Leg., ch. 1240 (H.B. 1535), § 54, effective September 1, 2005; am. Acts 2013, 83rd Leg., ch. 418 (S.B. 406), § 24, effective November 1, 2013; am. Acts 2019, 86th Leg., ch. 467 (H.B. 4170), § 19.010, effective September 1, 2019.

Sec. 483.002. Rules.

The board may adopt rules for the proper administration and enforcement of this chapter.

Leg.H. Stats. 1989 71st Leg. Sess. Ch. 678, effective September 1, 1989.

Sec. 483.003. Department of State Health Services Hearings Regarding Certain Dangerous Drugs.

(a) The Department of State Health Services may hold public hearings in accordance with Chapter 2001, Government Code, to determine whether there is compelling evidence that a dangerous drug has been abused, either by being prescribed for nontherapeutic purposes or by the ultimate user.

(b) On finding that a dangerous drug has been abused, the Department of State Health Services may limit the availability of the abused drug by permitting its dispensing only on the prescription of a practitioner described by Section 483.001(12)(A), (B), or (D).

Leg.H. Stats. 1989 71st Leg. Sess. Ch. 678, effective September 1, 1989; Stats. 1995 74th Leg. Sess. Ch. 76, Stats. 1997 75th Leg. Sess. Ch. 1180, effective September 1, 1997; Stats. 2001 77th Leg. Sess. Ch. 112, effective May 11, 2001; am. Acts 2015, 84th Leg., ch. 1 (S.B. 219), § 3.1237, effective April 2, 2015.

Sec. 483.004. Commissioner of State Health Services Emergency Authority Relating to Dangerous Drugs.

If the commissioner of state health services has compelling evidence that an immediate danger to the public health exists as a result of the prescription of a dangerous drug by practitioners described by Section 483.001(12)(C), the commissioner may use the commissioner's existing emergency authority to limit the availability of the drug by permitting its prescription only by practitioners described by Section 483.001(12)(A), (B), or (D).

Leg.H. Stats. 1989 71st Leg. Sess. Ch. 678, effective September 1, 1989; Stats. 2001 77th Leg. Sess. Ch. 112, effective May 11, 2001; am. Acts 2015, 84th Leg., ch. 1 (S.B. 219), § 3.1238, effective April 2, 2015.

SUBCHAPTER B. DUTIES OF PHARMACISTS, PRACTITIONERS, AND OTHER PERSONS

Sec. 483.021. Determination by Pharmacist on Request to Dispense Drug.

(a) A pharmacist who is requested to dispense a dangerous drug under a prescription issued by a practitioner shall determine, in the exercise of the pharmacist's professional judgment, that the prescription is a valid prescription. A pharmacist may not dispense a dangerous drug if the pharmacist knows or should have known that the prescription was issued without a valid patient-practitioner relationship.

(b) A pharmacist who is requested to dispense a dangerous drug under a prescription issued by a therapeutic optometrist shall determine, in the exercise of the pharmacist's professional judgment, whether the prescription is for a dangerous drug that a therapeutic optometrist is authorized to prescribe under Section 351.358, Occupations Code.

Leg.H. Stats. 1989 71st Leg. Sess. Ch. 678, effective September 1, 1989; Stats. 1991 72nd Leg. Sess. Ch. 588, effective September 1 1991; Stats. 2001 77th Leg. Sess. Chs. 1254, 1420, effective September 1, 2001.

Sec. 483.022. Practitioner's Designated Agent; Practitioner's Responsibilities.

(a) A practitioner shall provide in writing the name of each designated agent as defined by Section 483.001(4)(A) and (C), and the name of each healthcare facility which employs persons defined by Section 483.001(4)(B).

(b) The practitioner shall maintain at the practitioner's usual place of business a list of the designated agents or healthcare facilities as defined by Section 483.001(4).

(c) The practitioner shall provide a pharmacist with a copy of the practitioner's written authorization for a designated agent as defined by Section 483.001(4) on the pharmacist's request.

(d) This section does not relieve a practitioner or the practitioner's designated agent from the requirements of Subchapter A, Chapter 562, Occupations Code.

(e) A practitioner remains personally responsible for the actions of a designated agent who communicates a prescription to a pharmacist.

(f) A practitioner may designate a person who is a licensed vocational nurse or has an education equivalent to or greater than that required for a licensed vocational nurse to communicate prescriptions of an advanced practice nurse or physician assistant authorized by the practitioner to sign prescription drug orders under Subchapter B, Chapter 157, Occupations Code.

Leg.H. Stats. 1989 71st Leg. Sess. Ch. 678, effective September 1, 1989; Stats. 1991 72nd Leg. Sess. Ch. 14, effective September 1, 1991; Stats. 1991 72nd Leg. Sess. Ch. 237, effective September 1, 1991; Stats. 1993 73rd Leg. Sess. Ch. 789, effective September 1, 1993; Stats. 1999 76th Leg. Sess. Ch. 428, effective September 1, 1999; Stats. 2001 77th Leg. Sess. Ch. 1420, effective September 1, 2001.

Sec. 483.023. Retention of Prescriptions.

A pharmacy shall retain a prescription for a dangerous drug dispensed by the pharmacy for two years after the date of the initial dispensing or the last refilling of the prescription, whichever date is later.

Leg.H. Stats. 1989 71st Leg. Sess. Ch. 678, effective September 1, 1989.

Sec. 483.024. Records of Acquisition or Disposal.

The following persons shall maintain a record of each acquisition and each disposal of a dangerous drug for two years after the date of the acquisition or disposal:

(1) a pharmacy;

(2) a practitioner;

(3) a person who obtains a dangerous drug for lawful research, teaching, or testing purposes, but not for resale;

(4) a hospital that obtains a dangerous drug for lawful administration by a practitioner; and

(5) a manufacturer or wholesaler licensed by the Department of State Health Services under Chapter 431 (Texas Food, Drug, and Cosmetic Act).

Leg.H. Stats. 1989 71st Leg. Sess. Ch. 678, effective September 1, 1989; am. Acts 2015, 84th Leg., ch. 1 (S.B. 219), § 3.1239, effective April 2, 2015.

Sec. 483.025. Inspections; Inventories.

A person required to keep records relating to dangerous drugs shall:

(1) make the records available for inspection and copying at all reasonable hours by any public official or employee engaged in enforcing this chapter; and

(2) allow the official or employee to inventory all stocks of dangerous drugs on hand.

Leg.H. Stats. 1989 71st Leg. Sess. Ch. 678, effective September 1, 1989.

Dang. Drugs

SUBCHAPTER C. CRIMINAL PENALTIES

Sec. 483.041. Possession of Dangerous Drug.

(a) A person commits an offense if the person possesses a dangerous drug unless the person obtains the drug from a pharmacist acting in the manner described by Section 483.042(a)(1) or a practitioner acting in the manner described by Section 483.042(a)(2).

(b) Except as permitted by this chapter, a person commits an offense if the person possesses a dangerous drug for the purpose of selling the drug.

(c) Subsection (a) does not apply to the possession of a dangerous drug in the usual course of business or practice or in the performance of official duties by the following persons or an agent or employee of the person:

    (1) a pharmacy licensed by the board;

    (2) a practitioner;

    (3) a person who obtains a dangerous drug for lawful research, teaching, or testing, but not for resale;

    (4) a hospital that obtains a dangerous drug for lawful administration by a practitioner;

    (5) an officer or employee of the federal, state, or local government;

    (6) a manufacturer or wholesaler licensed by the Department of State Health Services under Chapter 431 (Texas Food, Drug, and Cosmetic Act);

    (7) a carrier or warehouseman;

    (8) a home and community support services agency licensed under and acting in accordance with Chapter 142;

    (9) a licensed midwife who obtains oxygen for administration to a mother or newborn or who obtains a dangerous drug for the administration of prophylaxis to a newborn for the prevention of ophthalmia neonatorum in accordance with Section 203.353, Occupations Code;

    (10) a salvage broker or salvage operator licensed under Chapter 432; or

    (11) a certified laser hair removal professional under Subchapter M, Chapter 401, who possesses and uses a laser or pulsed light device approved by and registered with the Department of State Health Services and in compliance with department rules for the sole purpose of cosmetic nonablative hair removal.

(d) An offense under this section is a Class A misdemeanor.

Leg.H. Stats. 1989 71st Leg. Sess. Chs. 678, 1100, effective September 1, 1989; Stats. 1993 73rd Leg. Sess. Ch. 16, effective April 2, 1993; Stats. 1993 73rd Leg. Sess. Ch. 789, effective September 1, 1993; Stats. 1995 74th Leg. Sess. Chs. 307, 318, Stats. 1997 75th Leg. Sess. Ch. 1095, effective September 1, 1997, Ch. 1129, effective September 1, 1997; Stats. 2001 77th Leg. Sess. Ch. 265, effective May 22, 2001; Stats. 2005 79th Leg. Sess. Ch. 1240, effective September 1, 2005; Stats. 2009 81st Leg. Sess. Ch. 303, effective September 1, 2010; am. Acts 2015, 84th Leg., ch. 1 (S.B. 219), § 3.1240, effective April 2, 2015.

Sec. 483.042. Delivery or Offer of Delivery of Dangerous Drug.

(a) A person commits an offense if the person delivers or offers to deliver a dangerous drug:

    (1) unless:

        (A) the dangerous drug is delivered or offered for delivery by a pharmacist under:

            (i) a prescription issued by a practitioner described by Section 483.001(12)(A) or (B);

            (ii) a prescription signed by a registered nurse or physician assistant in accordance with Subchapter B, Chapter 157, Occupations Code; or

            (iii) an original written prescription issued by a practitioner described by Section 483.001(12)(C); and

        (B) a label is attached to the immediate container in which the drug is delivered or offered to be delivered and the label contains the following information:

            (i) the name and address of the pharmacy from which the drug is delivered or offered for delivery;

            (ii) the date the prescription for the drug is dispensed;

            (iii) the number of the prescription as filed in the prescription files of the pharmacy from which the prescription is dispensed;

            (iv) the name of the practitioner who prescribed the drug and, if applicable, the name of the registered nurse or physician assistant who signed the prescription;

            (v) the name of the patient and, if the drug is prescribed for an animal, a statement of the species of the animal; and

            (vi) directions for the use of the drug as contained in the prescription; or

    (2) unless:

        (A) the dangerous drug is delivered or offered for delivery by:

            (i) a practitioner in the course of practice; or

             (ii) a registered nurse or physician assistant in the course of practice in accordance with Subchapter B, Chapter 157, Occupations Code; and

        (B) a label is attached to the immediate container in which the drug is delivered or offered to be delivered and the label contains the following information:

            (i) the name and address of the practitioner who prescribed the drug, and if applicable, the name and address of the registered nurse or physician assistant;

            (ii) the date the drug is delivered;

            (iii) the name of the patient and, if the drug is prescribed for an animal, a statement of the species of the animal; and

            (iv) the name of the drug, the strength of the drug, and directions for the use of the drug.

(b) Subsection (a) does not apply to the delivery or offer for delivery of a dangerous drug to a person listed in Section 483.041(c) for use in the usual course of business or practice or in the performance of official duties by the person.

(c) Proof of an offer to sell a dangerous drug must be corroborated by a person other than the offeree or by evidence other than a statement by the offeree.

(d) An offense under this section is a state jail felony.

(e) The labeling provisions of Subsection (a) do not apply to a dangerous drug prescribed or dispensed for administration to a patient who is institutionalized. The board shall adopt rules for the labeling of such a drug.

(f) Provided all federal requirements are met, the labeling provisions of Subsection (a) do not apply to a dangerous drug prescribed or dispensed for administration to food production animals in an agricultural operation under a written medical directive or treatment guideline from a veterinarian licensed under Chapter 801, Occupations Code.

Leg.H. Stats. 1989 71st Leg. Sess. Chs. 678, 1100, effective September 1, 1989; Stats. 1993 73rd Leg. Sess. Ch. 287, effective September 1, 1993; Stats. 1993 73rd Leg. Sess. Ch. 789, effective September 1, 1993; Stats. 1993 73rd Leg. Sess. Ch. 900, effective September 1, 1994; Stats. 1995 74th Leg. Sess. Ch. 965, Stats. 1997 75th Leg. Sess. Ch. 1180, effective September 1, 1997; Stats. 1999 76th Leg. Sess. Ch. 1404, effective September 1, 1999; Stats. 2001 77th Leg. Sess. Ch. 1420, effective September 1, 2001.

Sec. 483.043. Manufacture of Dangerous Drug.

(a) A person commits an offense if the person manufactures a dangerous drug and the person is not authorized by law to manufacture the drug.

(b) An offense under this section is a state jail felony.

Leg.H. Stats. 1989 71st Leg. Sess. Ch. 678, effective September 1, 1989; Stats. 1993 73rd Leg. Sess. Ch. 900, effective September 1, 1994.

Sec. 483.045. Forging or Altering Prescription.

(a) A person commits an offense if the person:
   (1) forges a prescription or increases the prescribed quantity of a dangerous drug in a prescription;
   (2) issues a prescription bearing a forged or fictitious signature;
   (3) obtains or attempts to obtain a dangerous drug by using a forged, fictitious, or altered prescription;
   (4) obtains or attempts to obtain a dangerous drug by means of a fictitious or fraudulent telephone call; or
   (5) possesses a dangerous drug obtained by a forged, fictitious, or altered prescription or by means of a fictitious or fraudulent telephone call.

(b) An offense under this section is a Class B misdemeanor unless it is shown on the trial of the defendant that the defendant has previously been convicted of an offense under this chapter, in which event the offense is a Class A misdemeanor.

Leg.H. Stats. 1989 71st Leg. Sess. Ch. 678, effective September 1, 1989.

Sec. 483.046. Failure to Retain Prescription.

(a) A pharmacist commits an offense if the pharmacist:
   (1) delivers a dangerous drug under a prescription; and
   (2) fails to retain the prescription as required by Section 483.023.

(b) An offense under this section is a Class B misdemeanor unless it is shown on the trial of the defendant that the defendant has previously been convicted of an offense under this chapter, in which event the offense is a Class A misdemeanor.

Leg.H. Stats. 1989 71st Leg. Sess. Ch. 678, effective September 1, 1989.

Sec. 483.047. Refilling Prescription Without Authorization.

(a) Except as authorized by Subsections (b) and (b-1), a pharmacist commits an offense if the pharmacist refills a prescription unless:
   (1) the prescription contains an authorization by the practitioner for the refilling of the prescription, and the pharmacist refills the prescription in the manner provided by the authorization; or
   (2) at the time of refilling the prescription, the pharmacist is authorized to do so by the practitioner who issued the prescription.

(b) A pharmacist may exercise his professional judgment in refilling a prescription for a dangerous drug without the authorization of the prescribing practitioner provided:
   (1) failure to refill the prescription might result in an interruption of a therapeutic regimen or create patient suffering;
   (2) either:
      (A) a natural or manmade disaster has occurred which prohibits the pharmacist from being able to contact the practitioner; or
      (B) the pharmacist is unable to contact the practitioner after reasonable effort;
   (3) the quantity of drug dispensed does not exceed a 72-hour supply;
   (4) the pharmacist informs the patient or the patient's agent at the time of dispensing that the refill is being provided without such authorization and that authorization of the practitioner is required for future refills; and
   (5) the pharmacist informs the practitioner of the emergency refill at the earliest reasonable time.

(b-1) Notwithstanding Subsection (b), in the event of a natural or manmade disaster, a pharmacist may dispense not more than a 30-day supply of a dangerous drug without the authorization of the prescribing practitioner if:
   (1) failure to refill the prescription might result in an interruption of a therapeutic regimen or create patient suffering;
   (2) the natural or manmade disaster prohibits the pharmacist from being able to contact the practitioner;
   (3) the governor has declared a state of disaster under Chapter 418, Government Code; and
   (4) the board, through the executive director, has notified pharmacies in this state that pharmacists may dispense up to a 30-day supply of a dangerous drug.

(b-2) The prescribing practitioner is not liable for an act or omission by a pharmacist in dispensing a dangerous drug under Subsection (b-1).

(c)   An offense under this section is a Class B misdemeanor unless it is shown on the trial of the defendant that the defendant has previously been convicted under this chapter, in which event the offense is a Class A misdemeanor.

Leg.H. Stats. 1989, 71st Leg., ch. 678 (H.B. 2136), § 1, effective September 1, 1989; am. Acts 1993, 73rd Leg., ch. 789 (S.B. 472), § 22, effective September 1, 1993; am. Acts 2015, 84th Leg., 599 (S.B. 460), § 1, effective September 1, 2015.

Sec. 483.048. Unauthorized Communication of Prescription.

(a)   An agent of a practitioner commits an offense if the agent communicates by telephone a prescription unless the agent is designated in writing under Section 483.022 as authorized by the practitioner to communicate prescriptions by telephone.

(b)   An offense under this section is a Class B misdemeanor unless it is shown on the trial of the defendant that the defendant has previously been convicted of an offense under this chapter, in which event the offense is a Class A misdemeanor.

Leg.H. Stats. 1989 71st Leg. Sess. Ch. 678, effective September 1, 1989.

Sec. 483.049. Failure to Maintain Records.

(a)   A person commits an offense if the person is required to maintain a record under Section 483.023 or 483.024 and the person fails to maintain the record in the manner required by those sections.

(b)   An offense under this section is a Class B misdemeanor unless it is shown on the trial of the defendant that the defendant has previously been convicted of an offense under this chapter, in which event the offense is a Class A misdemeanor.

Leg.H. Stats. 1989 71st Leg. Sess. Ch. 678, effective September 1, 1989.

Sec. 483.050. Refusal to Permit Inspection.

(a)   A person commits an offense if the person is required to permit an inspection authorized by Section 483.025 and fails to permit the inspection in the manner required by that section.

(b)   An offense under this section is a Class B misdemeanor unless it is shown on the trial of the defendant that the defendant has previously been convicted of an offense under this chapter, in which event the offense is a Class A misdemeanor.

Leg.H. Stats. 1989 71st Leg. Sess. Ch. 678, effective September 1, 1989.

Sec. 483.051. Using or Revealing Trade Secret.

(a)   A person commits an offense if the person uses for the person's advantage or reveals to another person, other than to an officer or employee of the board or to a court in a judicial proceeding relevant to this chapter, information relating to dangerous drugs required to be kept under this chapter, if that information concerns a method or process subject to protection as a trade secret.

(b)   An offense under this section is a Class B misdemeanor unless it is shown on the trial of the defendant that the defendant has previously been convicted of an offense under this chapter, in which event the offense is a Class A misdemeanor.

Leg.H. Stats. 1989 71st Leg. Sess. Ch. 678, effective September 1, 1989.

Sec. 483.052. Violation of Other Provision.

(a)   A person commits an offense if the person violates a provision of this chapter other than a provision for which a specific offense is otherwise described by this chapter.

(b)   An offense under this section is a Class B misdemeanor, unless it is shown on the trial of the defendant that the defendant has previously been convicted of an offense under this chapter, in which event the offense is a Class A misdemeanor.

Leg.H. Stats. 1989 71st Leg. Sess. Ch. 678, effective September 1, 1989.

Sec. 483.053. Preparatory Offenses.

Title 4, Penal Code, applies to an offense under this subchapter.

Leg.H. Stats. 1995 74th Leg. Sess. Ch. 318, effective September 1, 1995.

SUBCHAPTER D. CRIMINAL AND CIVIL PROCEDURE

Sec. 483.071. Exceptions; Burden of Proof.
(a) In a complaint, information, indictment, or other action or proceeding brought for the enforcement of this chapter, the state is not required to negate an exception, excuse, proviso, or exemption contained in this chapter.
(b) The defendant has the burden of proving the exception, excuse, proviso, or exemption.

Leg.H. Stats. 1989 71st Leg. Sess. Ch. 678, effective September 1, 1989.

Sec. 483.072. Uncorroborated Testimony.
A conviction under this chapter may be obtained on the uncorroborated testimony of a party to the offense.

Leg.H. Stats. 1989 71st Leg. Sess. Ch. 678, effective September 1, 1989.

Sec. 483.073. Search Warrant.
A peace officer may apply for a search warrant to search for dangerous drugs possessed in violation of this chapter. The peace officer must apply for and execute the search warrant in the manner prescribed by the Code of Criminal Procedure.

Leg.H. Stats. 1989 71st Leg. Sess. Ch. 678, effective September 1, 1989.

Sec. 483.074. Seizure and Destruction.
(a) A dangerous drug that is manufactured, sold, or possessed in violation of this chapter is contraband and may be seized by an employee of the board or by a peace officer authorized to enforce this chapter and charged with that duty.
(b) If a dangerous drug is seized under Subsection (a), the board may direct an employee of the board or an authorized peace officer to destroy the drug. The employee or authorized peace officer directed to destroy the drug must act in the presence of another employee of the board or authorized peace officer and shall destroy the drug in any manner designated as appropriate by the board.
(c) Before the dangerous drug is destroyed, an inventory of the drug must be prepared. The inventory must be accompanied by a statement that the dangerous drug is being destroyed at the direction of the board, by an employee of the board or an authorized peace officer, and in the presence of another employee of the board or authorized peace officer. The statement must also contain the names of the persons in attendance at the time of destruction, state the capacity in which each of those persons acts, be signed by those persons, and be sworn to by those persons that the statement is correct. The statement shall be filed with the board.

Leg.H. Stats. 1989 71st Leg. Sess. Ch. 678, effective September 1, 1989; Stats. 1991 72nd Leg. Sess. Ch. 237, effective September 1, 1991.

Sec. 483.075. Injunction.
The board may institute an action in its own name to enjoin a violation of this chapter.

Leg.H. Stats. 1989 71st Leg. Sess. Ch. 678, effective September 1, 1989.

Sec. 483.076. Legal Representation of Board.
(a) If the board institutes a legal proceeding under this chapter, the board may be represented only by a county attorney, a district attorney, or the attorney general.
(b) The board may not employ private counsel in any legal proceeding instituted by or against the board under this chapter.

Leg.H. Stats. 1989 71st Leg. Sess. Ch. 678, effective September 1, 1989.

SUBCHAPTER E. OPIOID ANTAGONISTS

Sec. 483.101. Definitions.

In this subchapter:

(1) "Emergency services personnel" includes firefighters, emergency medical services personnel as defined by Section 773.003, emergency room personnel, and other individuals who, in the course and scope of employment or as a volunteer, provide services for the benefit of the general public during emergency situations.

(2) "Opioid antagonist" means any drug that binds to opioid receptors and blocks or otherwise inhibits the effects of opioids acting on those receptors.

(3) "Opioid-related drug overdose" means a condition, evidenced by symptoms such as extreme physical illness, decreased level of consciousness, constriction of the pupils, respiratory depression, or coma, that a layperson would reasonably believe to be the result of the consumption or use of an opioid.

(4) "Prescriber" means a person authorized by law to prescribe an opioid antagonist.

Leg.H. Stats. 2015, 84th Leg., ch. 958 (S.B. 1462), § 1, effective September 1, 2015.

Sec. 483.102. Prescription of Opioid Antagonist; Standing Order.

(a) A prescriber may, directly or by standing order, prescribe an opioid antagonist to:

(1) a person at risk of experiencing an opioid-related drug overdose; or

(2) a family member, friend, or other person in a position to assist a person described by Subdivision (1).

(b) A prescription issued under this section is considered as issued for a legitimate medical purpose in the usual course of professional practice.

(c) A prescriber who, acting in good faith with reasonable care, prescribes or does not prescribe an opioid antagonist is not subject to any criminal or civil liability or any professional disciplinary action for:

(1) prescribing or failing to prescribe the opioid antagonist; or

(2) if the prescriber chooses to prescribe an opioid antagonist, any outcome resulting from the eventual administration of the opioid antagonist.

Leg.H. Stats. 2015, 84th Leg., ch. 958 (S.B. 1462), § 1, effective September 1, 2015.

Sec . 483.103. Dispensing of Opioid Antagonist.

(a) A pharmacist may dispense an opioid antagonist under a valid prescription to:

(1) a person at risk of experiencing an opioid-related drug overdose; or

(2) a family member, friend, or other person in a position to assist a person described by Subdivision (1).

(b) A prescription filled under this section is considered as filled for a legitimate medical purpose in the usual course of professional practice.

(c) A pharmacist who, acting in good faith and with reasonable care, dispenses or does not dispense an opioid antagonist under a valid prescription is not subject to any criminal or civil liability or any professional disciplinary action for:

(1) dispensing or failing to dispense the opioid antagonist; or

(2) if the pharmacist chooses to dispense an opioid antagonist, any outcome resulting from the eventual administration of the opioid antagonist.

Leg.H. Stats. 2015, 84th Leg., ch. 958 (S.B. 1462), § 1, effective September 1, 2015.

Sec. 483.104. Distribution of Opioid Antagonist; Standing Order.

A person or organization acting under a standing order issued by a prescriber may store an opioid antagonist and may distribute an opioid antagonist, provided the person or organization does not request or receive compensation for storage or distribution.

Leg.H. Stats. 2015, 84th Leg., ch. 958 (S.B. 1462), § 1, effective September 1, 2015.

Sec. 483.105. Possession of Opioid Antagonist.

Any person may possess an opioid antagonist, regardless of whether the person holds a prescription for the opioid antagonist.

Leg.H. Stats. 2015, 84th Leg., ch. 958 (S.B. 1462), § 1, effective September 1, 2015.

Sec. 483.106. Administration of Opioid Antagonist.

(a) A person who, acting in good faith and with reasonable care, administers or does not administer an opioid antagonist to another person whom the person believes is suffering an opioid-related drug overdose is not subject to criminal prosecution, sanction under any professional licensing statute, or civil liability, for an act or omission resulting from the administration of or failure to administer the opioid antagonist.

(b) Emergency services personnel are authorized to administer an opioid antagonist to a person who appears to be suffering an opioid-related drug overdose, as clinically indicated.

Leg.H. Stats. 2015, 84th Leg., ch. 958 (S.B. 1462), § 1, effective September 1, 2015.

Sec. 483.107. Conflict of Law.

To the extent of a conflict between this subchapter and another law, this subchapter controls.

Leg.H. Stats. 2015, 84th Leg., ch. 958 (S.B. 1462), § 1, effective September 1, 2015.

Dang. Drugs

Dang. Drugs

TEXAS FOOD, DRUG, AND COSMETIC ACT
HEALTH AND SAFETY CODE, CHAPTER 431

Table of Contents

Ts FD&C Act

Ts FD&C Act

SUBCHAPTER L. DEVICE DISTRIBUTORS AND MANUFACTURERS

SUBCHAPTER M. DRUG DONATION PROGRAM

SUBCHAPTER N. WHOLESALE DISTRIBUTORS OF PRESCRIPTION DRUGS

SUBCHAPTER O. PRESCRIPTION DRUG DONATION PILOT PROGRAM

Ts FD&C Act

SUBCHAPTER A. GENERAL PROVISIONS

Sec. 431.001. Short Title.

This chapter may be cited as the Texas Food, Drug, and Cosmetic Act.

Leg.H. Stats. 1989 71st Leg. Sess. Ch. 678, effective September 1, 1989.

Sec. 431.002. Definitions.

In this chapter:

(1) "Advertising" means all representations disseminated in any manner or by any means, other than by labeling, for the purpose of inducing, or that are likely to induce, directly or indirectly, the purchase of food, drugs, devices, or cosmetics.

(2) "Animal feed," as used in Subdivision (23), in Section 512 of the federal Act, and in provisions of this chapter referring to those paragraphs or sections, means an article intended for use as food for animals other than man as a substantial source of nutrients in the diet of the animals. The term is not limited to a mixture intended to be the sole ration of the animals.

(3), (4) [Repealed by Acts 2015, 84th Leg., ch. 1 (S.B. 219), § 3.1639(75), effective April 2, 2015.]

(5) "Butter" means the food product usually known as butter that is made exclusively from milk or cream, or both, with or without common salt or additional coloring matter, and containing not less than 80 percent by weight of milk fat, after allowing for all tolerances.

(6) (A) "Color additive" means a material that:

   (i) is a dye, pigment, or other substance made by a process of synthesis or similar artifice, or extracted, isolated, or otherwise derived, with or without intermediate or final change of identity from a vegetable, animal, mineral, or other source; and

   (ii) when added or applied to a food, drug, or cosmetic, or to the human body or any part of the human body, is capable, alone or through reaction with other substance, of imparting color. The term does not include any material exempted under the federal Act.

(B) "Color" includes black, white, and intermediate grays.

(C) Paragraph (A) does not apply to any pesticide chemical, soil or plant nutrient, or other agricultural chemical solely because of its effect in aiding, retarding, or otherwise affecting, directly or indirectly, the growth or other natural physiological processes of produce of the soil and thereby affecting its color, whether before or after harvest.

(7) [Repealed by Acts 2015, 84th Leg., ch. 1 (S.B. 219), § 3.1639(75), effective April 2, 2015.]

(8) "Consumer commodity," except as otherwise provided by this subdivision, means any food, drug, device, or cosmetic, as those terms are defined by this chapter or by the federal Act, and any other article, product, or commodity of any kind or class that is customarily produced or distributed for sale through retail sales agencies or instrumentalities for consumption by individuals, or for use by individuals for purposes of personal care or in the performance of services ordinarily rendered within the household, and that usually is consumed or expended in the course of the consumption or use. The term does not include:

(A) a meat or meat product, poultry or poultry product, or tobacco or tobacco product;

(B) a commodity subject to packaging or labeling requirements imposed under the Federal Insecticide, Fungicide, and Rodenticide Act (7 U.S.C. 136), or The Virus-Serum-Toxin Act (21 U.S.C. 151 et seq.);

(C) a drug subject to the provisions of Section 431.113(c)(1) or Section 503(b)(1) of the federal Act;

(D) a beverage subject to or complying with packaging or labeling requirements imposed under the Federal Alcohol Administration Act (27 U.S.C. 205(e)); or

(E) a commodity subject to the provisions of Chapter 61, Agriculture Code, relating to the inspection, labeling, and sale of agricultural and vegetable seed.

(9) "Contaminated with filth" applies to any food, drug, device, or cosmetic not securely protected from dust, dirt, and as far as may be necessary by all reasonable means, from all foreign or injurious contaminations.

(10) "Cosmetic" means articles intended to be rubbed, poured, sprinkled, or sprayed on, introduced into, or otherwise applied to the human body or any part of the human body for cleaning, beautifying, promoting attractiveness, or altering the appearance, and articles intended for use as a component of those articles. The term does not include soap.

(11) "Counterfeit drug" means a drug, or the container or labeling of a drug, that, without authorization, bears the trademark, trade name or other identifying mark, imprint, or device of a drug manufacturer, processor, packer, or distributor other than the person who in fact manufactured, processed, packed, or distributed the drug, and that falsely purports or is represented to be the product of, or to have been packed or distributed by, the other drug manufacturer, processor, packer, or distributor.

(12) [Repealed by Acts 2015, 84th Leg., ch. 1 (S.B. 219), § 3.1639(75), effective April 2, 2015.]

(13) "Device," except when used in Sections 431.003, 431.021(l), 431.082(g), 431.112(c) and 431.142(c), means an instrument, apparatus, implement, machine, contrivance, implant, in vitro reagent, or other similar or related article, including any component, part, or accessory, that is:

(A) recognized in the official United States Pharmacopoeia National Formulary or any supplement to it;

(B) intended for use in the diagnosis of disease or other conditions, or in the cure, mitigation, treatment, or prevention of disease in man or other animals; or

(C)   intended to affect the structure or any function of the body of man or other animals and that does not achieve any of its principal intended purposes through chemical action within or on the body of man or other animals and is not dependent on metabolization for the achievement of any of its principal intended purposes.

(14)   "Drug" means articles recognized in the official United States Pharmacopoeia National Formulary, or any supplement to it, articles designed or intended for use in the diagnosis, cure, mitigation, treatment, or prevention of disease in man or other animals, articles, other than food, intended to affect the structure or any function of the body of man or other animals, and articles intended for use as a component of any article specified in this subdivision. The term does not include devices or their components, parts, or accessories. A food for which a claim is made in accordance with Section 403(r) of the federal Act, and for which the claim is approved by the secretary, is not a drug solely because the label or labeling contains such a claim.

(15)   "Federal Act" means the Federal Food, Drug and Cosmetic Act (Title 21 U.S.C. 301 et seq.).

(16)   "Food" means:

    (A)   articles used for food or drink for man;

    (B)   chewing gum; and

    (C)   articles used for components of any such article.

(17)   "Food additive" means any substance the intended use of which results or may reasonably be expected to result, directly or indirectly, in its becoming a component or otherwise affecting the characteristics of any food (including any substance intended for use in producing, manufacturing, packing, processing, preparing, treating, packaging, transporting, or holding food; and including any source of radiation intended for any use), if such substance is not generally recognized, among experts qualified by scientific training and experience to evaluate its safety, as having been adequately shown through scientific procedures (or, in the case of a substance used in food prior to January 1, 1958, through either scientific procedures or experience based on common use in food) to be safe under the conditions of its intended use; except that such term does not include:

    (A)   a pesticide chemical in or on a raw agricultural commodity;

    (B)   a pesticide chemical to the extent that it is intended for use or is used in the production, storage, or transportation of any raw agricultural commodity;

    (C)   a color additive;

    (D)   any substance used in accordance with a sanction or approval granted prior to the enactment of the Food Additives Amendment of 1958, Pub. L. No. 85-929, 52 Stat. 1041 (codified as amended in various sections of 21 U.S.C.), pursuant to the federal Act, the Poultry Products Inspection Act (21 U.S.C. 451 et seq.) or the Meat Inspection Act of 1906 (21 U.S.C. 601 et seq.); or

    (E)   a new animal drug.

(18)   "Health authority" means a physician designated to administer state and local laws relating to public health.

(19)   "Immediate container" does not include package liners.

(20)   "Infant formula" means a food that is represented for special dietary use solely as a food for infants by reason of its simulation of human milk or its suitability as a complete or partial substitute for human milk.

(21)   "Label" means a display of written, printed, or graphic matter upon the immediate container of any article; and a requirement made by or under authority of this chapter that any word, statement, or other information that appears on the label shall not be considered to be complied with unless the word, statement, or other information also appears on the outside container or wrapper, if any, of the retail package of the article, or is easily legible through the outside container or wrapper.

(22)   "Labeling" means all labels and other written, printed, or graphic matter (1) upon any article or any of its containers or wrappers, or (2) accompanying such article.

(23)   "Manufacture" means:

    (A)   the process of combining or purifying food or packaging food for sale to a person at wholesale or retail, and includes repackaging, labeling, or relabeling of any food;

    (B)   the process of preparing, propagating, compounding, processing, packaging, repackaging, labeling, testing, or quality control of a drug or drug product, but does not include compounding that is done within the practice of pharmacy and pursuant to a prescription drug order or initiative from a practitioner for a patient or prepackaging that is done in accordance with Section 562.154, Occupations Code;

    (C)   the process of preparing, fabricating, assembling, processing, packing, repacking, labeling, or relabeling a device; or

    (D)   the making of any cosmetic product by chemical, physical, biological, or other procedures, including manipulation, sampling, testing, or control procedures applied to the product.

(24)   "New animal drug" means any drug intended for use for animals other than man, including any drug intended for use in animal feed:

    (A)   the composition of which is such that the drug is not generally recognized among experts qualified by scientific training and experience to evaluate the safety and effectiveness of animal drugs as safe and effective for use under the conditions prescribed, recommended, or suggested in the labeling of the drug (except that such an unrecognized drug is not deemed to be a "new animal drug" if at any time before June 25, 1938, it was subject to the Food and Drug Act of June 30, 1906, and if at that time its labeling contained the same representations concerning the conditions of its use);

    (B)   the composition of which is such that the drug, as a result of investigations to determine its safety and effectiveness for use under those conditions, has become recognized but that has not, otherwise than in the investigations, been used to a material extent or for a material time under those conditions; or

    (C)   is composed wholly or partly of penicillin, streptomycin, chloratetracycline, chloramphenicol, or bacitracin, or any derivative of those substances, unless:

        (i)   a published order of the secretary is in effect that declares the drug not to be a new animal drug on the grounds that the requirement of certification of batches of the drug, as provided by Section 512(n) of the federal Act, is not necessary to ensure that the objectives specified in Section 512(n)(3) of that Act are achieved; and

        (ii)   Paragraph (A) or (B) of this subdivision does not apply to the drug.

Ts FD&C Act

(25) "New drug" means:
   (A) any drug, except a new animal drug, the composition of which is such that such drug is not generally recognized among experts qualified by scientific training and experience to evaluate the safety and effectiveness of drugs, as safe and effective for use under the conditions prescribed, recommended, or suggested in the labeling thereof (except that such an unrecognized drug is not a "new drug" if at any time before May 26, 1985, it was subject to the Food and Drug Act of June 30, 1906, and if at that time its labeling contained the same representations concerning the conditions of its use); or
   (B) any drug, except a new animal drug, the composition of which is such that such drug, as a result of investigations to determine its safety and effectiveness for use under such conditions, has become so recognized, but which has not, otherwise than in such investigations, been used to a material extent or for a material time under such conditions.

(26) "Official compendium" means the official United States Pharmacopoeia National Formulary, or any supplement to it.

(27) "Package" means any container or wrapping in which a consumer commodity is enclosed for use in the delivery or display of that consumer commodity to retail purchasers. The term includes wrapped meats enclosed in papers or other materials as prepared by the manufacturers thereof for sale. The term does not include:
   (A) shipping containers or wrappings used solely for the transportation of a consumer commodity in bulk or in quantity to manufacturers, packers, or processors, or to wholesale or retail distributors;
   (B) shipping containers or outer wrappings used by retailers to ship or deliver a commodity to retail customers if the containers and wrappings do not bear printed matter relating to any particular commodity; or
   (C) containers subject to the provisions of the Standard Barrel Act (Apple Barrels) (15 U.S.C. 231, 21 U.S.C. 20) or the Standard Barrel Act (Fruits and Vegetables) (15 U.S.C. 234-236).

(28) "Person" includes individual, partnership, corporation, and association.

(29) "Pesticide chemical" means any substance which, alone, in chemical combination or in formulation with one or more other substances, is a "pesticide" within the meaning of the Federal Insecticide, Fungicide, and Rodenticide Act (7 U.S.C. 136(u)), as now in force or as amended, and that is used in the production, storage, or transportation of raw agricultural commodities.

(30) "Principal display panel" means that part of a label that is most likely to be displayed, presented, shown, or examined under normal and customary conditions of display for retail sale.

(31) "Raw agricultural commodity" means any food in its raw or natural state, including all fruits that are washed, colored, or otherwise treated in their unpeeled natural form prior to marketing.

(32) "Saccharin" includes calcium saccharin, sodium saccharin, and ammonium saccharin.

(33) "Safe" refers to the health of humans or animals.

(34) "Secretary" means the secretary of the United States Department of Health and Human Services.

Leg.H. Stats. 1989 71st Leg. Sess. Ch. 678, effective September 1, 1989; Stats. 1991 72nd Leg. Sess. Ch. 14, effective September 1, 1991; Stats. 1991 72nd Leg. Sess. Ch. 539, effective September 1, 1991; Stats. 1993 73rd Leg. Sess. Ch. 459, effective September 1, 1993; Stats. 1997 75th Leg. Sess. Ch. 629, effective September 1, 1997; Stats. 2003 78th Leg. Sess. Chs. 111, 383, 982, 1099, effective September 1, 2003; Stats. 2005 79th Leg. Sess., Ch. 28 (S.B. 492), §5, effective September 1, 2005; am. Acts 2015, 84th Leg., ch. 1 (S.B. 219), § 3.0941, 3.0942, 3.1639(75), effective April 2, 2015.

Sec. 431.003. Article Misbranded Because of Misleading Labeling or Advertising.

If an article is alleged to be misbranded because the labeling or advertising is misleading, then in determining whether the labeling or advertising is misleading, there shall be taken into account, among other things, not only representations made or suggested by statement, word, design, device, sound, or any combination of these, but also the extent to which the labeling or advertising fails to reveal facts material in the light of such representations or material with respect to consequences which may result from the use of the article to which the labeling or advertising relates under the conditions of use prescribed in the labeling or advertising thereof, or under such conditions of use as are customary or usual.

Leg.H. Stats. 1989 71st Leg. Sess. Ch. 678, effective September 1, 1989; Stats. 1991 72nd Leg. Sess. Ch. 14, effective September 1, 1991.

Sec. 431.004. Representation of Drug as Antiseptic.

The representation of a drug, in its labeling, as an antiseptic shall be considered to be a representation that the drug is a germicide, except in the case of a drug purporting to be, or represented as, an antiseptic for inhibitory use as a wet dressing, ointment, dusting powder, or such other use as involves prolonged contact with the body.

Leg.H. Stats. 1989 71st Leg. Sess. Ch. 678, effective September 1, 1989.

Sec. 431.005. Provisions Regarding Sale of Food, Drugs, Devices, or Cosmetics.

The provisions of this chapter regarding the selling of food, drugs, devices, or cosmetics, shall be considered to include the manufacture, production, processing, packaging, exposure, offer, possession, and holding of any such article for sale; and the sale, dispensing, and giving of any such article, and the supplying or applying of any such articles in the conduct of any food, drug, or cosmetic establishment.

Leg.H. Stats. 1989 71st Leg. Sess. Ch. 678, effective September 1, 1989.

Sec. 431.006. Certain Combination Products.

If the United States Food and Drug Administration determines, with respect to a product that is a combination of a drug and a device, that:
   (1) the primary mode of action of the product is as a drug, a person who engages in wholesale distribution of the product is subject to licensure under Subchapter I; and
   (2) the primary mode of action of the product is as a device, a distributor or manufacturer of the product is subject to licensure under Subchapter L.

Leg.H. Stats. 1999 76th Leg. Sess. Ch. 132, effective May 20, 1999.

Sec. 431.007. Compliance with Other Law; Molluscan Shellfish.

A person who is subject to this chapter and who handles molluscan shellfish, as that term is defined by Section 436.002, shall comply with Section 436.105.

Leg.H. Stats. 1999 76th Leg. Sess. Ch. 1298, effective June 18, 1999; Stats. 2001 77th Leg. Sess. Ch. 1420, effective September 1, 2001 (renumbered from Sec. 431.006).

Sec. 431.008. Applicability of Chapter to Distressed or Reconditioned Merchandise and Certain Licensed Entities.

    (a)   This chapter applies to a food, drug, device, or cosmetic that is distressed merchandise for purposes of Chapter 432 or that has been subject to reconditioning in accordance with Chapter 432.

    (b)   Except as provided by Subsection (c), this chapter applies to the conduct of a person licensed under Chapter 432.

    (c)   A person who holds a license under Chapter 432 and is engaging in conduct within the scope of that license is not required to hold a license as a wholesale drug distributor under Subchapter I, a food wholesaler under Subchapter J, or a device distributor under Subchapter L.

Leg.H. Stats. 2001 77th Leg. Sess. Ch. 265, effective May 22, 2001.

Sec. 431.009. Applicability of Chapter to Frozen Desserts.

    (a)   This chapter applies to a frozen dessert, an imitation frozen dessert, a product sold in semblance of a frozen dessert, or a mix for one of those products subject to Chapter 440. A frozen dessert, an imitation frozen dessert, a product sold in semblance of a frozen dessert, or a mix for one of those products is food for purposes of this chapter.

    (b)   Except as provided by Subsection (c), this chapter applies to the conduct of a person licensed under Chapter 440.

    (c)   A person who holds a license under Chapter 440 related to the manufacturing of a product regulated under that chapter and is engaging in conduct within the scope of that license is not required to hold a license as a food manufacturer or food wholesaler under Subchapter J.

Leg.H. Stats. 2003 78th Leg. Sess. Ch. 112, effective September 1, 2003.

Sec. 431.010. Applicability of Chapter to Milk and Milk Products.

    (a)   This chapter applies to milk or a milk product subject to Chapter 435. Milk or a milk product is a food for purposes of this chapter.

    (b)   Except as provided by Subsection (c), this chapter applies to the conduct of a person who holds a permit under Chapter 435.

    (c)   A person who holds a permit under Chapter 435 related to the processing, producing, bottling, receiving, transferring, or transporting of Grade A milk or milk products and who is engaging in conduct within the scope of that permit is not required to hold a license as a food manufacturer or food wholesaler under Subchapter J.

Leg.H. Stats. 2003 78th Leg. Sess. Ch. 757, effective September 1, 2003.

Sec. 431.011. Applicability of Chapter to Consumable Hemp Products and Manufacturers.

    (a)   This chapter applies to a consumable hemp product subject to Chapter 443. An article regulated under this chapter may not be deemed to be adulterated solely on the basis that the article is a consumable hemp product.

    (b)   Except as provided by Subsection (c), this chapter applies to the conduct of a person who holds a license under Chapter 443.

    (c)   A person who holds a license under Chapter 443 related to the processing of hemp or the manufacturing of a consumable hemp product regulated under that chapter and is engaging in conduct within the scope of that license is not required to hold a license as a food manufacturer or food wholesaler under Subchapter J.

Leg.H. Stats. 2019, 86th Leg., ch. 764 (H.B. 1325), § 4, effective June 10, 2019.

SUBCHAPTER B. PROHIBITED ACTS

Sec. 431.021. Prohibited Acts.

The following acts and the causing of the following acts within this state are unlawful and prohibited:

(a) the introduction or delivery for introduction into commerce of any food, drug, device, or cosmetic that is adulterated or misbranded;

(b) the adulteration or misbranding of any food, drug, device, or cosmetic in commerce;

(c) the receipt in commerce of any food, drug, device, or cosmetic that is adulterated or misbranded, and the delivery or proffered delivery thereof for pay or otherwise;

(d) the distribution in commerce of a consumer commodity, if such commodity is contained in a package, or if there is affixed to that commodity a label that does not conform to the provisions of this chapter and of rules adopted under the authority of this chapter; provided, however, that this prohibition shall not apply to persons engaged in business as wholesale or retail distributors of consumer commodities except to the extent that such persons:

(1) are engaged in the packaging or labeling of such commodities; or

(2) prescribe or specify by any means the manner in which such commodities are packaged or labeled;

(e) the introduction or delivery for introduction into commerce of any article in violation of Section 431.084, 431.114, or 431.115;

(f) the dissemination of any false advertisement;

(g) the refusal to permit entry or inspection, or to permit the taking of a sample or to permit access to or copying of any record as authorized by Sections 431.042-431.044; or the failure to establish or maintain any record or make any report required under Section 512(j), (l), or (m) of the federal Act, or the refusal to permit access to or verification or copying of any such required record;

(h) the manufacture within this state of any food, drug, device, or cosmetic that is adulterated or misbranded;

(i) the giving of a guaranty or undertaking referred to in Section 431.059, which guaranty or undertaking is false, except by a person who relied on a guaranty or undertaking to the same effect signed by, and containing the name and address of the person residing in this state from whom the person received in good faith the food, drug, device, or cosmetic; or the giving of a guaranty or undertaking referred to in Section 431.059, which guaranty or undertaking is false;

(j) the use, removal, or disposal of a detained or embargoed article in violation of Section 431.048;

(k) the alteration, mutilation, destruction, obliteration, or removal of the whole or any part of the labeling of, or the doing of any other act with respect to a food, drug, device, or cosmetic, if such act is done while such article is held for sale after shipment in commerce and results in such article being adulterated or misbranded;

(l) (1) forging, counterfeiting, simulating, or falsely representing, or without proper authority using any mark, stamp, tag, label, or other identification device authorized or required by rules adopted under this chapter or the regulations promulgated under the provisions of the federal Act;

(2) making, selling, disposing of, or keeping in possession, control, or custody, or concealing any punch, die, plate, stone, or other thing designed to print, imprint, or reproduce the trademark, trade name, or other identifying mark, imprint, or device of another or any likeness of any of the foregoing on any drug or container or labeling thereof so as to render such drug a counterfeit drug;

(3) the doing of any act that causes a drug to be a counterfeit drug, or the sale or dispensing, or the holding for sale or dispensing, of a counterfeit drug;

(m) the using by any person to the person's own advantage, or revealing, other than to the department, to a health authority, or to the courts when relevant in any judicial proceeding under this chapter, of any information acquired under the authority of this chapter concerning any method or process that as a trade secret is entitled to protection;

(n) the using, on the labeling of any drug or device or in any advertising relating to such drug or device, of any representation or suggestion that approval of an application with respect to such drug or device is in effect under Section 431.114 or Section 505, 515, or 520(g) of the federal Act, as the case may be, or that such drug or device complies with the provisions of such sections;

(o) the using, in labeling, advertising or other sales promotion of any reference to any report or analysis furnished in compliance with Sections 431.042-431.044 or Section 704 of the federal Act;

(p) in the case of a prescription drug distributed or offered for sale in this state, the failure of the manufacturer, packer, or distributor of the drug to maintain for transmittal, or to transmit, to any practitioner licensed by applicable law to administer such drug who makes written request for information as to such drug, true and correct copies of all printed matter that is required to be included in any package in which that drug is distributed or sold, or such other printed matter as is approved under the federal Act. Nothing in this subsection shall be construed to exempt any person from any labeling requirement imposed by or under other provisions of this chapter;

(q) (1) placing or causing to be placed on any drug or device or container of any drug or device, with intent to defraud, the trade name or other identifying mark, or imprint of another or any likeness of any of the foregoing;

(2) selling, dispensing, disposing of or causing to be sold, dispensed, or disposed of, or concealing or keeping in possession, control, or custody, with intent to sell, dispense, or dispose of, any drug, device, or any container of any drug or device, with knowledge that the trade name or other identifying mark or imprint of another or any likeness of any of the foregoing has been placed thereon in a manner prohibited by Subdivision (1); or

(3) making, selling, disposing of, causing to be made, sold, or disposed of, keeping in possession, control, or custody, or concealing with intent to defraud any punch, die, plate, stone, or other thing designed to print, imprint, or reproduce the trademark, trade name, or other identifying mark, imprint, or device of another or any likeness of any of the foregoing on any drug or container or labeling of any drug or container so as to render such drug a counterfeit drug;

(r) dispensing or causing to be dispensed a different drug in place of the drug ordered or prescribed without the express permission in each case of the person ordering or prescribing;

(s) the failure to register in accordance with Section 510 of the federal Act, the failure to provide any information required by Section 510(j) or (k) of the federal Act, or the failure to provide a notice required by Section 510(j)(2) of the federal Act;

(t) (1) the failure or refusal to:

    (A) comply with any requirement prescribed under Section 518 or 520(g) of the federal Act; or

    (B) furnish any notification or other material or information required by or under Section 519 or 520(g) of the federal Act;

    (2) with respect to any device, the submission of any report that is required by or under this chapter that is false or misleading in any material respect;

(u) the movement of a device in violation of an order under Section 304(g) of the federal Act or the removal or alteration of any mark or label required by the order to identify the device as detained;

(v) the failure to provide the notice required by Section 412(b) or 412(c), the failure to make the reports required by Section 412(d)(1) (B), or the failure to meet the requirements prescribed under Section 412(d)(2) of the federal Act;

(w) except as provided under Subchapter M of this chapter and Section 562.1085, Occupations Code, the acceptance by a person of an unused prescription or drug, in whole or in part, for the purpose of resale, after the prescription or drug has been originally dispensed, or sold;

(x) engaging in the wholesale distribution of drugs or operating as a distributor or manufacturer of devices in this state without obtaining a license issued by the department under Subchapter I, L, or N, as applicable;

(y) engaging in the manufacture of food in this state or operating as a warehouse operator in this state without having a license as required by Section 431.222 or operating as a food wholesaler in this state without having a license under Section 431.222 or being registered under Section 431.2211, as appropriate;

(z) unless approved by the United States Food and Drug Administration pursuant to the federal Act, the sale, delivery, holding, or offering for sale of a self-testing kit designed to indicate whether a person has a human immunodeficiency virus infection, acquired immune deficiency syndrome, or a related disorder or condition;

(aa) making a false statement or false representation in an application for a license or in a statement, report, or other instrument to be filed with or requested by the department under this chapter;

(bb) failing to comply with a requirement or request to provide information or failing to submit an application, statement, report, or other instrument required by the department;

(cc) performing, causing the performance of, or aiding and abetting the performance of an act described by Subsection (x);

(dd) purchasing or otherwise receiving a prescription drug from a pharmacy in violation of Section 431.411(a);

(ee) selling, distributing, or transferring a prescription drug to a person who is not authorized under state or federal law to receive the prescription drug in violation of Section 431.411(b);

(ff) failing to deliver prescription drugs to specified premises as required by Section 431.411(c);

(gg) failing to maintain or provide pedigrees as required by Section 431.412 or 431.413;

(hh) failing to obtain, pass, or authenticate a pedigree as required by Section 431.412 or 431.413;

(ii) the introduction or delivery for introduction into commerce of a drug or prescription device at a flea market;

(jj) the receipt of a prescription drug that is adulterated, misbranded, stolen, obtained by fraud or deceit, counterfeit, or suspected of being counterfeit, and the delivery or proffered delivery of such a drug for payment or otherwise; or

(kk) the alteration, mutilation, destruction, obliteration, or removal of all or any part of the labeling of a prescription drug or the commission of any other act with respect to a prescription drug that results in the prescription drug being misbranded.

Leg.H. Stats. 1991, 72nd Leg. Sess. Ch. 14, effective September 1, 1991; Stats 1991, 72nd Leg. Sess. Ch. 539, effective September 1, 1991; Stats 1993, 73rd Leg. Sess. Ch. 440, effective September 1, 1993; Stats 1995 74th Leg. Sess. Ch. 1047, effective September 1, 1995; Stats 1997 75th Leg. Sess. Ch. 282, effective September 1, 1997; Stats 2001 77th Leg. Sess. Ch. 262, effective September 1, 2001; Stats 2001, 77th Leg. Sess. Ch. 1138, effective January 1, 2002; Stats 2003, 78th Leg. Sess. Ch. 198, effective June 18, 2003; Stats 2003, 78th Leg. Sess. Ch. 321, effective June 18, 2003; Stats 2003, 78th Leg. Sess. Ch. 383, effective September 1, 2003; Stats 2003, 78th Leg. Sess. Ch. 982, effective September 1, 2003; Stats 2005 79th Leg. Sess. Ch. 282, effective March 1, 2006; Stats 2007, 80th Leg. Sess. Ch. 980, effective September 1, 2007; am. Acts 2015, 84th Leg., ch. 1 (S.B. 219), § 3.0943, effective April 2, 2015.

Sec. 431.0211. Exception.

Any provision of Section 431.021 that relates to a prescription drug does not apply to a prescription drug manufacturer, or an agent of a prescription drug manufacturer, who is obtaining or attempting to obtain a prescription drug for the sole purpose of testing the prescription drug for authenticity.

Leg.H. Stats. 2007, 80th Leg. Sess. Ch. 980, effective September 1, 2007.

Sec. 431.022. Offense: Transfer of Product Containing Ephedrine.

(a) A person commits an offense if the person knowingly sells, transfers, or otherwise furnishes a product containing ephedrine to a person 17 years of age or younger, unless:

    (1) the actor is:

        (A) a practitioner or other health care provider licensed by this state who has obtained, as required by law, consent to the treatment of the person to whom the product is furnished; or

        (B) the parent, guardian, or managing conservator of the person to whom the product is furnished;

    (2) the person to whom the product is furnished has had the disabilities of minority removed for general purposes under Chapter 31, Family Code; or

    (3) the product is a drug.

(b) An offense under this section is a Class C misdemeanor unless it is shown on the trial of the offense that the defendant has been previously convicted of an offense under this section, in which event the offense is a Class B misdemeanor.

(c) A product containing ephedrine that is not described in Subsection (a)(3) must be labeled in accordance with department rules to indicate that sale to persons 17 years of age or younger is prohibited.

Leg.H. Stats. 1999 76th Leg. Sess. Ch. 151, effective September 1, 1999; am. Acts 2015, 84th Leg., ch. 1 (S.B. 219), § 3.0944, effective April 2, 2015.

Sec. 431.023. Limited Exemption for Distressed Food, Drugs, Devices, or Cosmetics.

In relation to a food, drug, device, or cosmetic that is distressed merchandise for purposes of Chapter 432, Sections 431.021(a), (c), and (d) do not prohibit:

    (1) the introduction or delivery for introduction into commerce of the merchandise for the purpose of reconditioning in accordance with Chapter 432 and not for sale to the ultimate consumer;

    (2) the receipt in commerce of the merchandise for the purpose of reconditioning in accordance with Chapter 432 and not for sale to the ultimate consumer;

    (3) the holding of merchandise for the purpose of reconditioning in accordance with Chapter 432 and not for resale to the ultimate consumer; or

    (4) the reconditioning of the merchandise in accordance with Chapter 432.

Leg.H. Stats. 2001 77th Leg. Sess. Ch. 265, effective May 22, 2001.

Ts FD&C Act

SUBCHAPTER C. ENFORCEMENT

Sec. 431.041. Definition.

In this subchapter, "detained or embargoed article" means a food, drug, device, cosmetic, or consumer commodity that has been detained or embargoed under Section 431.048.

Leg.H. Stats. 1989 71st Leg. Sess. Ch. 678, effective September 1, 1989.

Sec. 431.042. Inspection.

(a) To enforce this chapter, the department or a health authority may, on presenting appropriate credentials to the owner, operator, or agent in charge:

    (1) enter at reasonable times an establishment, including a factory or warehouse, in which a food, drug, device, or cosmetic is manufactured, processed, packed, or held for introduction into commerce or held after the introduction;

    (2) enter a vehicle being used to transport or hold the food, drug, device, or cosmetic in commerce; or

    (3) inspect at reasonable times, within reasonable limits, and in a reasonable manner, the establishment or vehicle and all equipment, finished and unfinished materials, containers, and labeling of any item and obtain samples necessary for the enforcement of this chapter.

(b) The inspection of an establishment, including a factory, warehouse, or consulting laboratory, in which a prescription drug or restricted device is manufactured, processed, packed, or held for introduction into commerce extends to any place or thing, including a record, file, paper, process, control, or facility, in order to determine whether the drug or device:

    (1) is adulterated or misbranded;

    (2) may not be manufactured, introduced into commerce, sold, or offered for sale under this chapter; or

    (3) is otherwise in violation of this chapter.

(c) An inspection under Subsection (b) may not extend to:

    (1) financial data;

    (2) sales data other than shipment data;

    (3) pricing data;

    (4) personnel data other than data relating to the qualifications of technical and professional personnel performing functions under this chapter;

    (5) research data other than data:

        (A) relating to new drugs, antibiotic drugs, and devices; and

        (B) subject to reporting and inspection under regulations issued under Section 505(i) or (j), 519, or 520(g) of the federal Act; or

    (6) data relating to other drugs or devices that, in the case of a new drug, would be subject to reporting or inspection under regulations issued under Section 505(j) of the federal Act.

(d) An inspection under Subsection (b) shall be started and completed with reasonable promptness.

(e) This section does not apply to:

    (1) a pharmacy that:

        (A) complies with Subtitle J, Title 3, Occupations Code;

        (B) regularly engages in dispensing prescription drugs or devices on prescriptions of practitioners licensed to administer the drugs or devices to their patients in the course of their professional practice; and

        (C) does not, through a subsidiary or otherwise, manufacture, prepare, propagate, compound, or process a drug or device for sale other than in the regular course of its business of dispensing or selling drugs or devices at retail;

    (2) a practitioner licensed to prescribe or administer a drug who manufactures, prepares, propagates, compounds, or processes the drug solely for use in the course of the practitioner's professional practice;

    (3) a practitioner licensed to prescribe or use a device who manufactures or processes the device solely for use in the course of the practitioner's professional practice; or

    (4) a person who manufactures, prepares, propagates, compounds, or processes a drug or manufactures or processes a device solely for use in research, teaching, or chemical analysis and not for sale.

(f) The executive commissioner may exempt a class of persons from inspection under this section if the executive commissioner finds that inspection as applied to the class is not necessary for the protection of the public health.

(g) The department or a health authority who makes an inspection under this section to enforce the provisions of this chapter applicable to infant formula shall be permitted, at all reasonable times, to have access to and to copy and verify records:

    (1) in order to determine whether the infant formula manufactured or held in the inspected facility meets the requirements of this chapter; or

    (2) that are required by this chapter.

(h) If the department or a health authority while inspecting an establishment, including a factory or warehouse, obtains a sample, the department or health authority before leaving the establishment shall give to the owner, operator, or the owner's or operator's agent a receipt describing the sample.

Leg.H. Stats. 1989 71st Leg. Sess. Ch. 678, effective September 1, 1989; Stats. 2001 77th Leg. Sess. Ch. 1420, effective September 1, 2001; Stats. 2003 78th Leg. Sess. Ch. 111, effective September 1, 2003; am. Acts 2015, 84th Leg., ch. 1 (S.B. 219), § 3.0945, effective April 2, 2015.

Sec. 431.043. Access to Records.

A person who is required to maintain records under this chapter or Section 519 or 520(g) of the federal Act or a person who is in charge or custody of those records shall, at the request of the department or a health authority, permit the department or health authority at all reasonable times access to and to copy and verify the records, including records that verify that the hemp in a consumable hemp product was produced in accordance with Chapter 122, Agriculture Code, or 7 U.S.C. Chapter 38, Subchapter VII.

Leg.H. Stats. 1989, 71st Leg., ch. 678 (H.B. 2136), § 1, effective September 1, 1989; am. Acts 2015, 84th Leg., ch. 1 (S.B. 219), § 3.0946, effective April 2, 2015; am. Acts 2019, 86th Leg., ch. 764 (H.B. 1325), § 5, effective June 10, 2019.

Sec. 431.044. Access to Records Showing Movement in Commerce.

(a) To enforce this chapter, a carrier engaged in commerce or other person receiving a food, drug, device, or cosmetic in commerce or holding a food, drug, device, or cosmetic received in commerce shall, at the request of the department or a health authority, permit the department or health authority at all reasonable times to have access to and to copy all records showing:

    (1) the movement in commerce of the food, drug, device, or cosmetic;

    (2) the holding of the food, drug, device, or cosmetic after movement in commerce; and

    (3) the quantity, shipper, and consignee of the food, drug, device, or cosmetic.

(b) The carrier or other person may not refuse access to and copying of the requested record if the request is accompanied by a written statement that specifies the nature or kind of food, drug, device, or cosmetic to which the request relates.

(c) Evidence obtained under this section or evidence that is directly or indirectly derived from the evidence obtained under this section may not be used in a criminal prosecution of the person from whom the evidence is obtained.

(d) A carrier is not subject to other provisions of this chapter because of the carrier's receipt, carriage, holding, or delivery of a food, drug, device, or cosmetic in the usual course of business as a carrier.

Leg.H. Stats. 1989 71st Leg. Sess. Ch. 678, effective September 1, 1989; am. Acts 2015, 84th Leg., ch. 1 (S.B. 219), § 3.0947, effective April 2, 2015.

Sec. 431.045. Emergency Order.

(a) The commissioner or a person designated by the commissioner may issue an emergency order, either mandatory or prohibitory in nature, in relation to the manufacture or distribution of a food, drug, device, or cosmetic in the department's jurisdiction if the commissioner or the person designated by the commissioner determines that:

    (1) the manufacture or distribution of the food, drug, device, or cosmetic creates or poses an immediate and serious threat to human life or health; and

    (2) other procedures available to the department to remedy or prevent the occurrence of the situation will result in unreasonable delay.

(b) The commissioner or a person designated by the commissioner may issue the emergency order without notice and hearing if the commissioner or a person designated by the commissioner determines this is practicable under the circumstances.

(c) If an emergency order is issued without a hearing, the department shall propose a time and place for a hearing and refer the matter to the State Office of Administrative Hearings. An administrative law judge of that office shall set the time and place for the hearing at which the emergency order is affirmed, modified, or set aside. The hearing shall be held under the contested case provisions of Chapter 2001, Government Code, and the department's formal hearing rules.

(d) [Repealed by Acts 2015, 84th Leg., ch. 1 (S.B. 219), § 3.1639(75), effective April 2, 2015.]

Leg.H. Stats. 1989 71st Leg. Sess. Ch. 678, effective September 1, 1989; Stats. 1997 75th Leg. Sess. Ch. 629, effective September 1, 1997; Stats. 2001 77th Leg. Sess. Ch. 262, effective September 1, 2001; am. Acts 2015, 84th Leg., ch. 1 (S.B. 219), § 3.0948, 3.1639(75), effective April 2, 2015.

Sec. 431.046. Violation of Rules.

A violation of a rule adopted under this chapter is a violation of this chapter.

Leg.H. Stats. 1989 71st Leg. Sess. Ch. 678, effective September 1, 1989.

Sec. 431.047. Violation; Injunction.

(a) The department or a health authority may petition the district court for a temporary restraining order to restrain a continuing violation of Subchapter B or a threat of a continuing violation of Subchapter B if the department or health authority finds that:

    (1) a person has violated, is violating, or is threatening to violate Subchapter B; and

    (2) the violation or threatened violation creates an immediate threat to the health and safety of the public.

(b) A district court, on petition of the department or a health authority, and on a finding by the court that a person is violating or threatening to violate Subchapter B shall grant any injunctive relief warranted by the facts.

(c) Venue for a suit brought under this section is in the county in which the violation or threat of violation is alleged to have occurred or in Travis County.

(d) The department and the attorney general may each recover reasonable expenses incurred in obtaining injunctive relief under this section, including investigative costs, court costs, reasonable attorney fees, witness fees, and deposition expenses. The expenses recovered by the department may be used by the department for the administration and enforcement of this chapter. The expenses recovered by the attorney general may be used by the attorney general.

Leg.H. Stats. 1989 71st Leg. Sess. Ch. 678, effective September 1, 1989; Stats. 1991 72nd Leg. Sess. Ch. 539, effective September 1, 1991; am. Acts 2015, 84th Leg., ch. 1 (S.B. 219), § 3.0949, effective April 2, 2015.

Ts FD&C Act

12/1/2019

Sec. 431.048. Detained or Embargoed Article.

(a) The department shall affix to an article that is a food, drug, device, cosmetic, or consumer commodity a tag or other appropriate marking that gives notice that the article is, or is suspected of being, adulterated or misbranded and that the article has been detained or embargoed if the department finds or has probable cause to believe that the article:

    (1) is adulterated;

    (2) is misbranded so that the article is dangerous or fraudulent under this chapter; or

    (3) violates Section 431.084, 431.114, or 431.115.

(b) The tag or marking on a detained or embargoed article must warn all persons not to use the article, remove the article from the premises, or dispose of the article by sale or otherwise until permission for use, removal, or disposal is given by the department or a court.

(c) A person may not use a detained or embargoed article, remove a detained or embargoed article from the premises, or dispose of a detained or embargoed article by sale or otherwise without permission of the department or a court. The department may permit perishable goods to be moved to a place suitable for proper storage.

(d) The department shall remove the tag or other marking from an embargoed or detained article if the department finds that the article is not adulterated or misbranded.

(e) The department may not detain or embargo an article, including an article that is distressed merchandise, that is in the possession of a person licensed under Chapter 432 and that is being held for the purpose of reconditioning in accordance with Chapter 432, unless the department finds or has probable cause to believe that the article cannot be adequately reconditioned in accordance with that chapter and applicable rules.

Leg.H. Stats. 1989 71st Leg. Sess. Ch. 678, effective September 1, 1989; Stats. 1997 75th Leg. Sess. Ch. 282, effective September 1, 1997; Stats. 2001 77th Leg. Sess. Ch. 265, effective September 1, 2001; am. Acts 2015, 84th Leg., ch. 1 (S.B. 219), § 3.0950, effective April 2, 2015.

Sec. 431.049. Removal Order for Detained or Embargoed Article.

(a) If the claimant of the detained or embargoed articles or the claimant's agent fails or refuses to transfer the articles to a secure place after the tag or other appropriate marking has been affixed as provided by Section 431.048, the department may order the transfer of the articles to one or more secure storage areas to prevent their unauthorized use, removal, or disposal.

(b) The department may provide for the transfer of the article if the claimant of the article or the claimant's agent does not carry out the transfer order in a timely manner. The costs of the transfer shall be assessed against the claimant of the article or the claimant's agent.

(c) The claimant of the article or the claimant's agent shall pay the costs of the transfer.

(d) The department may request the attorney general to bring an action in the district court in Travis County to recover the costs of the transfer. In a judgment in favor of the state, the court may award costs, attorney fees, court costs, and interest from the time the expense was incurred through the date the department is reimbursed.

Leg.H. Stats. 1989 71st Leg. Sess. Ch. 678, effective September 1, 1989; Stats. 1991 72nd Leg. Sess. Ch. 14, effective September 1, 1991; Stats. 1997 75th Leg. Sess. Ch. 282, effective September 1, 1997; am. Acts 2015, 84th Leg., ch. 1 (S.B. 219), § 3.0951, effective April 2, 2015.

Sec. 431.0495. Recall Orders.

(a) In conjunction with the issuance of an emergency order under Section 431.045 or the detention or embargo of an article under Section 431.048, the commissioner may order a food, drug, device, cosmetic, or consumer commodity to be recalled from commerce.

(b) The commissioner's recall order may require the articles to be removed to one or more secure areas approved by the department.

(c) The recall order must be in writing and signed by the commissioner.

(d) The recall order may be issued before or in conjunction with the affixing of the tag or other appropriate marking as provided by Section 431.048(a) or in conjunction with the commissioner's issuance of an emergency order under Section 431.045.

(e) The recall order is effective until the order:

    (1) expires on its own terms;

    (2) is withdrawn by the commissioner;

    (3) is reversed by a court in an order denying condemnation under Section 431.050; or

    (4) is set aside at the hearing provided to affirm, modify, or set aside an emergency order under Section 431.045.

(f) The claimant of the articles or the claimant's agent shall pay the costs of the removal and storage of the articles removed.

(g) If the claimant or the claimant's agent fails or refuses to carry out the recall order in a timely manner, the commissioner may provide for the recall of the articles. The costs of the recall shall be assessed against the claimant of the articles or the claimant's agent.

(h) The commissioner may request the attorney general to bring an action in the district court of Travis County to recover the costs of the recall. In a judgment in favor of the state, the court may award costs, attorney fees, court costs, and interest from the time the expense was incurred through the date the department is reimbursed.

Leg.H. Stats. 2015, 84th Leg., ch. 1 (S.B. 219), § 3.0952, effective April 2, 2015.

Sec. 431.050. Condemnation.

An action for the condemnation of an article may be brought before a court in whose jurisdiction the article is located, detained, or embargoed if the article is adulterated, misbranded, or in violation of Section 431.084, 431.114, or 431.115.

Leg.H. Stats. 1989 71st Leg. Sess. Ch. 678, effective September 1, 1989.

Sec. 431.051. Destruction of Article.

(a) A court shall order the destruction of a sampled article or a detained or embargoed article if the court finds that the article is adulterated or misbranded.

(b) After entry of the court's order, an authorized agent shall supervise the destruction of the article.

(c) The claimant of the article shall pay the cost of the destruction of the article.

(d) The court shall tax against the claimant of the article or the claimant's agent all court costs and fees, and storage and other proper expenses.

Leg.H. Stats. 1989 71st Leg. Sess. Ch. 678, effective September 1, 1989.

Sec. 431.052. Correction by Proper Labeling or Processing.

(a) A court may order the delivery of a sampled article or a detained or embargoed article that is adulterated or misbranded to the claimant of the article for labeling or processing under the supervision of the department if:

    (1) the decree has been entered in the suit;

    (2) the costs, fees, and expenses of the suit have been paid;

    (3) the adulteration or misbranding can be corrected by proper labeling or processing; and

    (4) a good and sufficient bond, conditioned on the correction of the adulteration or misbranding by proper labeling or processing, has been executed.

(b) The claimant shall pay the costs of the supervision.

(c) The court shall order that the article be returned to the claimant and the bond discharged on the representation to the court by the department that the article no longer violates this chapter and that the expenses of the supervision are paid.

Leg.H. Stats. 1989 71st Leg. Sess. Ch. 678, effective September 1, 1989; am. Acts 2015, 84th Leg., ch. 1 (S.B. 219), § 3.0953, effective April 2, 2015.

Sec. 431.053. Condemnation of Perishable Articles.

(a) The department shall immediately condemn or render by any means unsalable as human food an article that is a nuisance under Subsection (b) and that the department finds in any room, building, or other structure or in a vehicle.

(b) Any meat, seafood, poultry, vegetable, fruit, or other perishable article is a nuisance if it:

    (1) is unsound;

    (2) contains a filthy, decomposed, or putrid substance; or

    (3) may be poisonous or deleterious to health or otherwise unsafe.

Leg.H. Stats. 1989 71st Leg. Sess. Ch. 678, effective September 1, 1989; am. Acts 2015, 84th Leg., ch. 1 (S.B. 219), § 3.0954, effective April 2, 2015.

Sec. 431.054. Administrative Penalty.

(a) The department may assess an administrative penalty against a person who violates Subchapter B or an order adopted or registration issued under this chapter.

(b) In determining the amount of the penalty, the department shall consider:

    (1) the person's previous violations;

    (2) the seriousness of the violation;

    (3) any hazard to the health and safety of the public;

    (4) the person's demonstrated good faith; and

    (5) such other matters as justice may require.

(c) The penalty may not exceed $25,000 a day for each violation.

(d) Each day a violation continues may be considered a separate violation.

Leg.H. Stats. 1989 71st Leg. Sess. Ch. 678, effective September 1, 1989; Stats. 1991 72nd Leg. Sess. Ch. 539, effective September 1, 1991; am. Acts 2015, 84th Leg., ch. 1 (S.B. 219), § 3.0955, effective April 2, 2015.

Sec. 431.055. Administrative Penalty Assessment Procedure.

(a) An administrative penalty may be assessed only after a person charged with a violation is given an opportunity for a hearing.

(b) If a hearing is held, an administrative law judge of the State Office of Administrative Hearings shall make findings of fact and shall issue to the department a written proposal for decision regarding the occurrence of the violation and the amount of the penalty that may be warranted.

(c) If the person charged with the violation does not request a hearing, the department may assess a penalty after determining that a violation has occurred and the amount of the penalty that may be warranted.

(d) After making a determination under this section that a penalty is to be assessed against a person, the department shall issue an order requiring that the person pay the penalty.

(e) [Repealed by Acts 2015, 84th Leg., ch. 1 (S.B. 219), § 3.1639(75), effective April 2, 2015.]

Leg.H. Stats. 1989 71st Leg. Sess. Ch. 678, effective September 1, 1989; am. Acts 2015, 84th Leg., ch. 1 (S.B. 219), § 3.0956, 3.1639(75), effective April 2, 2015.

Sec. 431.056. Payment of Administrative Penalty.

(a) Not later than the 30th day after the date an order finding that a violation has occurred is issued, the department shall inform the person against whom the order is issued of the amount of the penalty for the violation.

(b) Not later than the 30th day after the date on which a decision or order charging a person with a penalty is final, the person shall:
   (1) pay the penalty in full; or
   (2) file a petition for judicial review of the department's order contesting the amount of the penalty, the fact of the violation, or both.

(b-1) If the person seeks judicial review within the period prescribed by Subsection (b), the person may:
   (1) stay enforcement of the penalty by:
      (A) paying the amount of the penalty to the court for placement in an escrow account; or
      (B) posting with the court a supersedeas bond for the amount of the penalty; or
   (2) request that the department stay enforcement of the penalty by:
      (A) filing with the court a sworn affidavit of the person stating that the person is financially unable to pay the penalty and is financially unable to give the supersedeas bond; and
      (B) sending a copy of the affidavit to the department.

(b-2) If the department receives a copy of an affidavit under Subsection (b-1)(2), the department may file with the court, within five days after the date the copy is received, a contest to the affidavit. The court shall hold a hearing on the facts alleged in the affidavit as soon as practicable and shall stay the enforcement of the penalty on finding that the alleged facts are true. The person who files an affidavit has the burden of proving that the person is financially unable to pay the penalty or to give a supersedeas bond.

(c) A bond posted under this section must be in a form approved by the court and be effective until all judicial review of the order or decision is final.

(d) A person who does not send money to, post the bond with, or file the affidavit with the court within the period prescribed by Subsection (b) waives all rights to contest the violation or the amount of the penalty.

Leg.H. Stats. 1989 71st Leg. Sess. Ch. 678, effective September 1, 1989; am. Acts 2015, 84th Leg., ch. 1 (S.B. 219), § 3.0957, effective April 2, 2015.

Sec. 431.057. Refund of Administrative Penalty.

On the date the court's judgment that an administrative penalty against a person should be reduced or not assessed becomes final, the court shall order that:
   (1) the appropriate amount of any penalty payment plus accrued interest be remitted to the person not later than the 30th day after that date; or
   (2) the bond be released, if the person has posted a bond.

Leg.H. Stats. 1989 71st Leg. Sess. Ch. 678, effective September 1, 1989; am. Acts 2015, 84th Leg., ch. 1 (S.B. 219), § 3.0958, effective April 2, 2015.

Sec. 431.058. Recovery of Administrative Penalty by Attorney General.

The attorney general at the request of the department may bring a civil action to recover an administrative penalty under this subchapter.

Leg.H. Stats. 1989 71st Leg. Sess. Ch. 678, effective September 1, 1989; am. Acts 2015, 84th Leg., ch. 1 (S.B. 219), § 3.0959, effective April 2, 2015.

Sec. 431.0585. Civil Penalty.

(a) At the request of the department, the attorney general or a district, county, or city attorney shall institute an action in district court to collect a civil penalty from a person who has violated Section 431.021.

(b) The civil penalty may not exceed $25,000 a day for each violation. Each day of violation constitutes a separate violation for purposes of the penalty assessment.

(c) The court shall consider the following in determining the amount of the penalty:
   (1) the person's history of any previous violations of Section 431.021;
   (2) the seriousness of the violation;
   (3) any hazard posed to the public health and safety by the violation; and
   (4) demonstrations of good faith by the person charged.

(d) Venue for a suit brought under this section is in the city or county in which the violation occurred or in Travis County.

(e) A civil penalty recovered in a suit instituted by a local government under this section shall be paid to that local government.

Leg.H. Stats. 1991 72nd Leg. Sess. Ch. 14, effective September 1, 1991; am. Acts 2015, 84th Leg., ch. 1 (S.B. 219), § 3.0960, effective April 2, 2015.

Sec. 431.059. Criminal Penalty; Defenses.

(a) A person commits an offense if the person violates any of the provisions of Section 431.021 relating to unlawful or prohibited acts. A first offense under this subsection is a Class A misdemeanor unless it is shown on the trial of an offense under this subsection that the defendant was previously convicted of an offense under this subsection, in which event the offense is a state jail felony. In a criminal proceeding under this section, it is not necessary to prove intent, knowledge, recklessness, or criminal negligence of the defendant beyond the degree of culpability, if any, stated in Section 431.021 to establish criminal responsibility for the violation.

(a-1), (a-2) [Repealed by Acts 2007, 80th Leg., ch. 980 (S.B. 943), § 14, effective September 1, 2007.]

(b) A person is not subject to the penalties of Subsection (a):
   (1) for having received an article in commerce and having delivered or offered delivery of the article, if the delivery or offer was made in good faith, unless the person refuses to furnish, on request of the department or a health authority, the name and address of the person from whom the article was received and copies of any documents relating to the receipt of the article;

(2) for having violated Section 431.021(a) or (e) if the person establishes a guaranty or undertaking signed by, and containing the name and address of, the person residing in this state from whom the person received in good faith the article, to the effect that:

(A) in the case of an alleged violation of Section 431.021(a), the article is not adulterated or misbranded within the meaning of this chapter; and

(B) in the case of an alleged violation of Section 431.021(e), the article is not an article that may not, under the provisions of Section 404 or 405 of the federal Act or Section 431.084 or 431.114, be introduced into commerce;

(3) for having violated Section 431.021, if the violation exists because the article is adulterated by reason of containing a color additive not from a batch certified in accordance with regulations promulgated under the federal Act, if the person establishes a guaranty or undertaking signed by, and containing the name and address of, the manufacturer of the color additive, to the effect that the color additive was from a batch certified in accordance with the applicable regulations promulgated under the federal Act;

(4) for having violated Section 431.021(b), (c), or (k) by failure to comply with Section 431.112(i) with respect to an article received in commerce to which neither Section 503(a) nor Section 503(b)(1) of the federal Act applies if the delivery or offered delivery was made in good faith and the labeling at the time of the delivery or offer contained the same directions for use and warning statements as were contained in the labeling at the same time of the receipt of the article; or

(5) for having violated Section 431.021(l)(2) if the person acted in good faith and had no reason to believe that use of the punch, die, plate, stone, or other thing would result in a drug being a counterfeit drug, or for having violated Section 431.021(l)(3) if the person doing the act or causing it to be done acted in good faith and had no reason to believe that the drug was a counterfeit drug.

(c) A publisher, radio-broadcast licensee, or agency or medium for the dissemination of an advertisement, except the manufacturer, packer, distributor, or seller of the article to which a false advertisement relates, is not liable under this section for the dissemination of the false advertisement, unless the person has refused, on the request of the department, to furnish the department the name and post-office address of the manufacturer, packer, distributor, seller, or advertising agency, residing in this state who caused the person to disseminate the advertisement.

(d) A person is not subject to the penalties of Subsection (a) for a violation of Section 431.021 involving misbranded food if the violation exists solely because the food is misbranded under Section 431.082 because of its advertising, and a person is not subject to the penalties of Subsection (a) for such a violation unless the violation is committed with the intent to defraud or mislead.

(e) It is an affirmative defense to prosecution under Subsection (a) that the conduct charged is exempt, in accordance with Section 431.023, from the application of Section 431.021.

Leg.H. Stats. 1989 71st Leg. Sess. Ch. 678, effective September 1, 1989; Stats. 1991 72nd Leg. Sess. Ch. 14, effective September 1, 1991; Stats. 2001 77th Leg. Sess. Ch. 265, effective May 22, 2001; Stats. 2003 78th Leg. Sess. Chs. 111, 383, 392, effective September 1, 2003; Stats. 2005 79th Leg. Sess., Ch. 282 (H.B. 164), § 3(h), effective March 1, 2006; Stats 2007, 80th Leg. Sess. Ch. 980, effective September 1, 2007; am. Acts 2015, 84th Leg., ch. 1 (S.B. 219), § 3.0961, effective April 2, 2015.

Sec. 431.060. Initiation of Proceedings.

(a) The attorney general, or a district, county, or municipal attorney to whom the department or a health authority reports a violation of this chapter, shall initiate and prosecute appropriate proceedings without delay.

(b) The department or attorney general may, as authorized by Section 307 of the federal Act, bring in the name of this state a suit for civil penalties or to restrain a violation of Section 401 or Section 403(b) through (i), (k), (q), or (r) of the federal Act if the food that is the subject of the proceedings is located in this state.

(c) The department or attorney general may not bring a proceeding under Subsection (b):

(1) before the 31st day after the date on which the state has given notice to the secretary of its intent to bring a suit;

(2) before the 91st day after the date on which the state has given notice to the secretary of its intent to bring a suit if the secretary has, not later than the 30th day after receiving notice from the state, commenced an informal or formal enforcement action pertaining to the food that would be the subject of the suit brought by the state; or

(3) if the secretary is diligently prosecuting a suit in court pertaining to that food, has settled a suit pertaining to that food, or has settled the informal or formal enforcement action pertaining to that food.

Leg.H. Stats. 1989 71st Leg. Sess. Ch. 678, effective September 1, 1989; Stats. 1993 73rd Leg. Sess. Ch. 459, effective September 1, 1993; am. Acts 2015, 84th Leg., ch. 1 (S.B. 219), § 3.0962, effective April 2, 2015.

Sec. 431.061. Minor Violation.

This chapter does not require the department or a health authority to report for prosecution or the institution of proceedings under this chapter a minor violation of this chapter if the department or health authority believes that the public interest is adequately served by a suitable written notice or warning.

Leg.H. Stats. 1989 71st Leg. Sess. Ch. 678, effective September 1, 1989; am. Acts 2015, 84th Leg., ch. 1 (S.B. 219), § 3.0963, effective April 2, 2015.

SUBCHAPTER D.　FOOD

Sec. 431.081.　Adulterated Food.

A food shall be deemed to be adulterated:

(a)　if:

  (1)　it bears or contains any poisonous or deleterious substance which may render it injurious to health; but in case the substance is not an added substance the food shall not be considered adulterated under this subdivision if the quantity of the substance in the food does not ordinarily render it injurious to health;

  (2)　it:

    (A)　bears or contains any added poisonous or added deleterious substance, other than one that is a pesticide chemical in or on a raw agricultural commodity, a food additive, a color additive, or a new animal drug which is unsafe within the meaning of Section 431.161;

    (B)　is a raw agricultural commodity and it bears or contains a pesticide chemical which is unsafe within the meaning of Section 431.161(a);

    (C)　is, or it bears or contains, any food additive which is unsafe within the meaning of Section 431.161(a); provided, that where a pesticide chemical has been used in or on a raw agricultural commodity in conformity with an exemption granted or a tolerance prescribed under Section 431.161(a), and such raw agricultural commodity has been subjected to processing such as canning, cooking, freezing, dehydrating, or milling, the residue of such pesticide chemical remaining in or on such processed food shall, notwithstanding the provisions of Section 431.161 and Section 409 of the federal Act, not be deemed unsafe if such residue in or on the raw agricultural commodity has been removed to the extent possible in good manufacturing practice, and the concentration of such residue in the processed food, when ready to eat, is not greater than the tolerance prescribed for the raw agricultural commodity; or

    (D)　is, or it bears or contains, a new animal drug, or a conversion product of a new animal drug, that is unsafe under Section 512 of the federal Act;

  (3)　it consists in whole or in part of a diseased, contaminated, filthy, putrid, or decomposed substance, or if it is otherwise unfit for foods;

  (4)　it has been produced, prepared, packed or held under unsanitary conditions whereby it may have become contaminated with filth, or whereby it may have been rendered diseased, unwholesome, or injurious to health;

  (5)　it is, in whole or in part, the product of a diseased animal, an animal which has died otherwise than by slaughter, or an animal that has been fed upon the uncooked offal from a slaughterhouse;

  (6)　its container is composed, in whole or in part, of any poisonous or deleterious substance which may render the contents injurious to health; or

  (7)　it has been intentionally subjected to radiation, unless the use of the radiation was in conformity with a regulation or exemption in effect in accordance with Section 409 of the federal Act;

(b)　if:

  (1)　any valuable constituent has been in whole or in part omitted or abstracted therefrom;

  (2)　any substance has been substituted wholly or in part therefor;

  (3)　damage or inferiority has been concealed in any manner;

  (4)　any substance has been added thereto or mixed or packed therewith so as to increase its bulk or weight, or reduce its quality or strength or make it appear better or of greater value than it is;

  (5)　it contains saccharin, dulcin, glucin, or other sugar substitutes except in dietary foods, and when so used shall be declared; or

  (6)　it be fresh meat and it contains any chemical substance containing sulphites, sulphur dioxide, or any other chemical preservative which is not approved by the United States Department of Agriculture, the Animal and Plant Health Inspection Service (A.P.H.I.S.) or by department rules;

(c)　if it is, or it bears or contains, a color additive that is unsafe under Section 431.161(a); or

(d)　if it is confectionery and:

  (1)　has any nonnutritive object partially or completely imbedded in it; provided, that this subdivision does not apply if, in accordance with department rules, the object is of practical, functional value to the confectionery product and would not render the product injurious or hazardous to health;

  (2)　bears or contains any alcohol, other than alcohol not in excess of five percent by volume. Any confectionery that bears or contains any alcohol in excess of one-half of one percent by volume derived solely from the use of flavoring extracts and less than five percent by volume:

    (A)　may not be sold to persons under the legal age necessary to consume an alcoholic beverage in this state;

    (B)　must be labeled with a conspicuous, readily legible statement that reads, "Sale of this product to a person under the legal age necessary to consume an alcoholic beverage is prohibited ";

    (C)　may not be sold in a form containing liquid alcohol such that it is capable of use for beverage purposes as that term is used in the Alcoholic Beverage Code;

    (D)　may not be sold through a vending machine;

    (E)　must be labeled with a conspicuous, readily legible statement that the product contains not more than five percent alcohol by volume; and

    (F)　may not be sold in a business establishment which derives less than 50 percent of its gross sales from the sale of confectioneries; or

  (3)　bears or contains any nonnutritive substance; provided, that this subdivision does not apply to a nonnutritive substance that is in or on the confectionery by reason of its use for a practical, functional purpose in the manufacture, packaging, or storage of the confectionery if the use of the substance does not promote deception of the consumer or otherwise result in adulteration or misbranding in violation of this chapter; and provided further, that the executive commissioner may, for the purpose of avoiding or resolving uncertainty as to the application of this subdivision, adopt rules allowing or prohibiting the use of particular nonnutritive substances.

Leg.H. Stats. 1989 71st Leg. Sess. Ch. 678, effective September 1, 1989; Stats. 1993 73rd Leg. Sess. Ch. 439, effective September 1, 1993; am. Acts 2015, 84th Leg., ch. 1 (S.B. 219), § 3.0964, effective April 2, 2015.

Sec. 431.082. Misbranded Food.
A food shall be deemed to be misbranded:
- (a) if its labeling is false or misleading in any particular or fails to conform with the requirements of Section 431.181;
- (b) if, in the case of a food to which Section 411 of the federal Act applies, its advertising is false or misleading in a material respect or its labeling is in violation of Section 411(b)(2) of the federal Act;
- (c) if it is offered for sale under the name of another food;
- (d) if it is an imitation of another food, unless its label bears, in prominent type of uniform size, the word "imitation" and immediately thereafter the name of the food imitated;
- (e) if its container is so made, formed, or filled as to be misleading;
- (f) if in package form unless it bears a label containing:
  - (1) the name and place of business of the manufacturer, packer, or distributor; and
  - (2) an accurate statement, in a uniform location on the principal display panel of the label, of the quantity of the contents in terms of weight, measure, or numerical count; provided, that under this subsection reasonable variations shall be permitted, and exemptions as to small packages shall be established, by department rules;
- (g) if any word, statement, or other information required by or under the authority of this chapter to appear on the label or labeling is not prominently placed thereon with such conspicuousness (as compared with other words, statements, designs, or devices in the labeling) and in such terms as to render it likely to be read and understood by the ordinary individual under customary conditions of purchase and use;
- (h) if it purports to be or is represented as a food for which a definition and standard of identity has been prescribed by federal regulations or department rules as provided by Section 431.245, unless:
  - (1) it conforms to such definition and standard; and
  - (2) its label bears the name of the food specified in the definition and standard, and, in so far as may be required by those regulations or rules, the common names of ingredients, other than spices, flavoring, and coloring, present in such food;
- (i) if it purports to be or is represented as:
  - (1) a food for which a standard of quality has been prescribed by federal regulations or department rules as provided by Section 431.245, and its quality falls below such standard unless its label bears, in such manner and form as those regulations or rules specify, a statement that it falls below such standard; or
  - (2) a food for which a standard or standards of fill of container have been prescribed by federal regulations or department rules as provided by Section 431.245, and it falls below the standard of fill of container applicable thereto, unless its label bears, in such manner and form as those regulations or rules specify, a statement that it falls below such standard;
- (j) unless its label bears:
  - (1) the common or usual name of the food, if any; and
  - (2) in case it is fabricated from two or more ingredients, the common or usual name of each such ingredient, and if the food purports to be a beverage containing vegetable or fruit juice, a statement with appropriate prominence on the information panel of the total percentage of the fruit or vegetable juice contained in the food; except that spices, flavorings, and colors not required to be certified under Section 721(c) of the federal Act, other than those sold as such, may be designated as spices, flavorings, and colors, without naming each; provided that, to the extent that compliance with the requirements of this subdivision is impractical or results in deception or unfair competition, exemptions shall be established by department rules;
- (k) if it purports to be or is represented for special dietary uses, unless its label bears such information concerning its vitamin, mineral, and other dietary properties as the executive commissioner determines to be, and by rule prescribed, as necessary in order to fully inform purchasers as to its value for such uses;
- (l) if it bears or contains any artificial flavoring, artificial coloring, or chemical preservative, unless it bears labeling stating that fact; provided that, to the extent that compliance with the requirements of this subsection is impracticable, exemptions shall be established by department rules. The provisions of this subsection and Subsections (h) and (j) with respect to artificial coloring do not apply in the case of butter, cheese, and ice cream;
- (m) if it is a raw agricultural commodity that is the produce of the soil and bears or contains a pesticide chemical applied after harvest, unless the shipping container of the commodity bears labeling that declares the presence of the chemical in or on the commodity and the common or usual name and the function of the chemical, except that the declaration is not required while the commodity, after removal from the shipping container, is being held or displayed for sale at retail out of the container in accordance with the custom of the trade;
- (n) if it is a product intended as an ingredient of another food and if used according to the directions of the purveyor will result in the final food product being adulterated or misbranded;
- (o) if it is a color additive, unless its packaging and labeling are in conformity with the packaging and labeling requirements applicable to the color additive as may be contained in regulations issued under Section 721 of the federal Act;
- (p) if its packaging or labeling is in violation of an applicable regulation issued under Section 3 or 4 of the federal Poison Prevention Packaging Act of 1970 (15 U.S.C. 1472 or 1473);
- (q) (1) if it is a food intended for human consumption and is offered for sale, unless its label or labeling bears nutrition information that provides:
    - (A) (i) the serving size that is an amount customarily consumed and that is expressed in a common household measure that is appropriate to the food; or

        (ii) if the use of the food is not typically expressed in a serving size, the common household unit of measure that expresses the serving size of the food;

    (B) the number of servings or other units of measure per container;

    (C) the total number of calories in each serving size or other unit of measure that are:

        (i) derived from any source; and

        (ii) derived from fat;

    (D) the amount of total fat, saturated fat, cholesterol, sodium, total carbohydrates, complex carbohydrates, sugar, dietary fiber, and total protein contained in each serving size or other unit of measure; and

    (E) any vitamin, mineral, or other nutrient required to be placed on the label and labeling of food under the federal Act; or

  (2) (A) if it is a food distributed at retail in bulk display cases, or a food received in bulk containers, unless it has nutrition labeling prescribed by the secretary; and

    (B) if the secretary determines it is necessary, nutrition labeling will be mandatory for raw fruits, vegetables, and fish, including freshwater or marine finfish, crustaceans, mollusks including shellfish, amphibians, and other forms of aquatic animal life, except that:

  (3) (A) Subdivisions (1) and (2) do not apply to food:

        (i) that is served in restaurants or other establishments in which food is served for immediate human consumption or that is sold for sale or use in those establishments;

        (ii) that is processed and prepared primarily in a retail establishment, that is ready for human consumption, that is of the type described in Subparagraph (i), that is offered for sale to consumers but not for immediate human consumption in the establishment, and that is not offered for sale outside the establishment;

        (iii) that is an infant formula subject to Section 412 of the federal Act;

        (iv) that is a medical food as defined in Section 5(b) of the Orphan Drug Act (21 U.S.C. Section 360ee(b)); or

        (v) that is described in Section 405, clause (2), of the federal Act;

    (B) Subdivision (1) does not apply to the label of a food if the secretary determines by regulation that compliance with that subdivision is impracticable because the package of the food is too small to comply with the requirements of that subdivision and if the label of that food does not contain any nutrition information;

    (C) if the secretary determines that a food contains insignificant amounts of all the nutrients required by Subdivision (1) to be listed in the label or labeling of food, the requirements of Subdivision (1) do not apply to the food if the label, labeling, or advertising of the food does not make any claim with respect to the nutritional value of the food, provided that if the secretary determines that a food contains insignificant amounts of more than half the nutrients required by Subdivision (1) to be in the label or labeling of the food, the amounts of those nutrients shall be stated in a simplified form prescribed by the secretary;

    (D) if a person offers food for sale and has annual gross sales made or business done in sales to consumers that is not more than $500,000 or has annual gross sales made or business done in sales of food to consumers that is not more than $50,000, the requirements of this subsection do not apply to food sold by that person to consumers unless the label or labeling of food offered by that person provides nutrition information or makes a nutrition claim;

    (E) if foods are subject to Section 411 of the federal Act, the foods shall comply with Subdivisions (1) and (2) in a manner prescribed by the rules; and

    (F) if food is sold by a food distributor, Subdivisions (1) and (2) do not apply if the food distributor principally sells food to restaurants or other establishments in which food is served for immediate human consumption and the food distributor does not manufacture, process, or repackage the food it sells;

  (r) if it is a food intended for human consumption and is offered for sale, and a claim is made on the label, labeling, or retail display relating to the nutrient content or a nutritional quality of the food to a specific disease or condition of the human body, except as permitted by Section 403(r) of the federal Act; or

  (s) if it is a food intended for human consumption and its label, labeling, and retail display do not comply with the requirements of Section 403(r) of the federal Act pertaining to nutrient content and health claims.

Leg.H. Stats. 1989 71st Leg. Sess. Ch. 678, effective September 1, 1989; Stats. 1991 72nd Leg. Sess. Ch. 14, effective September 1, 1991; Stats. 1993 73rd Leg. Sess. Ch. 459, effective September 1, 1993; am. Acts 2015, 84th Leg., ch. 1 (S.B. 219), § 3.0965, effective April 2, 2015.

Sec. 431.083. Food Labeling Exemptions.

  (a) Except as provided by Subsection (c), the executive commissioner shall adopt rules exempting from any labeling requirement of this chapter:

    (1) small open containers of fresh fruits and fresh vegetables; and

    (2) food that is in accordance with the practice of the trade, to be processed, labeled, or repacked in substantial quantities at establishments other than those where originally processed or packed, on conditions that the food is not adulterated or misbranded under the provisions of this chapter when removed from the processing, labeling, or repacking establishment.

  (b) Food labeling exemptions adopted under the federal Act apply to food in this state except as modified or rejected by department rules.

  (c) The executive commissioner may not adopt rules under Subsection (a) to exempt foods from the labeling requirements of Sections 403(q) and (r) of the federal Act.

Leg.H. Stats. 1989 71st Leg. Sess. Ch. 678, effective September 1, 1989; Stats. 1993 73rd Leg. Sess. Ch. 459, effective September 1, 1993; am. Acts 2015, 84th Leg., ch. 1 (S.B. 219), § 3.0966, effective April 2, 2015.

Sec. 431.084. Emergency Permit for Foods Contaminated with Microorganisms.

(a) The department shall provide for the issuance of temporary permits to a manufacturer, processor, or packer of a class of food in any locality that provides conditions for the manufacture, processing, or packing for the class of food as necessary to protect the public health only if the department finds after investigation that:

   (1) the distribution in this state of a class of food may, because the food is contaminated with microorganisms during the manufacture, processing, or packing of the food in any locality, be injurious to health; and

   (2) the injurious nature of the food cannot be adequately determined after the food has entered commerce.

(b) The executive commissioner by rule shall establish standards and procedures for the enforcement of this section.

(c) During the period for which permits are issued for a class of food determined by the department to be injurious under Subsection (a), a person may not introduce or deliver for introduction into commerce the food unless the person is a manufacturer, processor, or packer who has a permit issued by the department as authorized by rules adopted under this section.

(d) The department may immediately suspend a permit issued under this section if a condition of the permit is violated. An immediate suspension is effective on notice to the permit holder.

(e) A holder of a permit that has been suspended may at any time apply for the reinstatement of the permit. Immediately after a hearing and an inspection of the permit holder's establishment, the department shall reinstate the permit if adequate measures have been taken to comply with and maintain the conditions of the permit as originally issued or as amended.

(f) A permit holder shall provide access to the permit holder's factory or establishment to the department to allow the department to determine whether the permit holder complies with the conditions of the permit. Denial of access is grounds for suspension of the permit until the permit holder freely provides the access.

Leg.H. Stats. 1989 71st Leg. Sess. Ch. 678, effective September 1, 1989; am. Acts 2015, 84th Leg., ch. 1 (S.B. 219), § 3.0967, effective April 2, 2015.

Ts FD&C Act

SUBCHAPTER E. DRUGS AND DEVICES

Sec. 431.111. Adulterated Drug or Device.

  (a) (1)   if it consists in whole or in part of any filthy, putrid, or decomposed substance; or

      (2) (A) if it has been prepared, packed, or held under insanitary conditions whereby it may have been contaminated with filth, or whereby it may have been rendered injurious to health; or

         (B) if it is a drug and the methods used in, or the facilities or controls used for, its manufacture, processing, packing, or holding do not conform to or are not operated or administered in conformity with current good manufacturing practice to assure that such drug meets the requirements of this chapter as to safety and has the identity and strength, and meets the quality and purity characteristics, which it purports or is represented to possess; or

      (3) if its container is composed, in whole or in part, of any poisonous or deleterious substance which may render the contents injurious to health; or

      (4) if it:

         (A) bears or contains, for purposes of coloring only, a color additive that is unsafe under Section 431.161(a); or

         (B) is a color additive, the intended use of which in or on drugs or devices is for purposes of coloring only, and is unsafe under Section 431.161(a); or

      (5) if it is a new animal drug that is unsafe under Section 512 of the federal Act;

  (b) if it purports to be or is represented as a drug, the name of which is recognized in an official compendium, and its strength differs from, or its quality or purity falls below, the standards set forth in such compendium. Such determination as to strength, quality or purity shall be made in accordance with the tests or methods of assay set forth in such compendium, or in the absence of or inadequacy of such tests or methods of assay, those prescribed under the authority of the federal Act. No drug defined in an official compendium shall be deemed to be adulterated under this subsection because it differs from the standards of strength, quality, or purity therefor set forth in such compendium, if its difference in strength, quality, or purity from such standards is plainly stated on its label. Whenever a drug is recognized in The United States Pharmacopeia and The National Formulary (USP-NF), it shall be subject to the requirements of the USP-NF;

  (c) if it is not subject to Subsection (b) and its strength differs from, or its purity or quality falls below, that which it purports or is represented to possess;

  (d) if it is a drug and any substance has been:

      (1) mixed or packed therewith so as to reduce its quality or strength; or

      (2) substituted wholly or in part therefor;

  (e) if it is, or purports to be or is represented as, a device that is subject to a performance standard established under Section 514 of the federal Act, unless the device is in all respects in conformity with the standard;

  (f) (1) if it is a class III device:

      (A) (i)   that is required by a regulation adopted under Section 515(b) of the federal Act to have an approval under that section of an application for premarket approval and that is not exempt from Section 515 as provided by Section 520(g) of the federal Act; and

         (ii) (I) for which an application for premarket approval or a notice of completion of a product development protocol was not filed with the United States Food and Drug Administration by the 90th day after the date of adoption of the regulation; or

            (II) for which that application was filed and approval was denied or withdrawn, for which that notice was filed and was declared incomplete, or for which approval of the device under the protocol was withdrawn;

         (B) that was classified under Section 513(f) of the federal Act into class III, which under Section 515(a) of the federal Act is required to have in effect an approved application for premarket approval, that is not exempt from Section 515 as provided by Section 520(g) of the federal Act, and that does not have the application in effect; or

         (C) that was classified under Section 520(l) of the federal Act into class III, which under that section is required to have in effect an approved application under Section 515 of the federal Act, and that does not have the application in effect, except that:

      (2) (A) in the case of a device classified under Section 513(f) of the federal Act into class III and intended solely for investigational use, Subdivision (1)(B) does not apply to the device during the period ending on the 90th day after the date of adoption of the regulations prescribing the procedures and conditions required by Section 520(g)(2) of the federal Act; and

         (B) in the case of a device subject to a regulation adopted under Section 515(b) of the federal Act, Subdivision (1) does not apply to the device during the period ending on whichever of the following dates occurs later:

           (i) the last day of the 30-day calendar month beginning after the month in which the classification of the device into class III became effective under Section 513 of the federal Act; or

           (ii) the 90th day after the date of adoption of the regulation;

  (g) if it is a banned device;

  (h) if it is a device and the methods used in, or the facilities or controls used for its manufacture, packing, storage, or installations are not in conformity with applicable requirements under Section 520(f)(1) of the federal Act or an applicable condition as prescribed by an order under Section 520(f)(2) of the federal Act; or

  (i) if it is a device for which an exemption has been granted under Section 520(g) of the federal Act for investigational use and the person who was granted the exemption or any investigator who uses the device under the exemption fails to comply with a requirement prescribed by or under that section.

    Leg.H. Stats. 1989 71st Leg. Sess. Ch. 678, effective September 1, 1989; Stats. 1993 73rd Leg. Sess. Ch. 440, effective September 1, 1993; am. Acts 2015, 84th Leg., ch. 1 (S.B. 219), § 3.0968, effective April 2, 2015.

Sec. 431.112. Misbranded Drug or Device.

A drug or device shall be deemed to be misbranded:

(a) (1) if its labeling is false or misleading in any particular; or

(2) if its labeling or packaging fails to conform with the requirements of Section 431.181.

(b) if in a package form unless it bears a label containing (1) the name and place of business of the manufacturer, packer, or distributor; and (2) an accurate statement of the quantity of the contents in terms of weight, measure, or numerical count; provided, that under Subdivision (2) reasonable variations shall be permitted, and exemptions as to small packages shall be allowed in accordance with regulations prescribed by the secretary under the federal Act;

(c) if any word, statement, or other information required by or under authority of this chapter to appear on the label or labeling is not prominently placed thereon with such conspicuousness (as compared with other words, statements, designs, or devices, in the labeling) and in such terms as to render it likely to be read and understood by the ordinary individual under customary conditions of purchase and use;

(d) (1) if it is a drug, unless:

(A) its label bears, to the exclusion of any other nonproprietary name (except the applicable systematic chemical name or the chemical formula):

(i) the established name (as defined in Subdivision (3)) of the drug, if any; and

(ii) in case it is fabricated from two or more ingredients, the established name and quantity of each active ingredient, including the quantity, kind, and proportion of any alcohol, and also including, whether active or not, the established name and quantity or proportion of any bromides, ether, chloroform, acetanilid, acetphenetidin, amidopyrine, antipyrine, atropine, hyoscine, hyoscyamine, arsenic, digitalis, digitalis glucosides, mercury, ouabain, strophanthin, strychnine, thyroid, or any derivative or preparation of any such substances, contained therein; provided, that the requirement for stating the quantity of the active ingredients, other than the quantity of those specifically named in this subparagraph shall apply only to prescription drugs; and

(B) for any prescription drug the established name of the drug or ingredient, as the case may be, on the label (and on any labeling on which a name for such drug or ingredient is used) is printed prominently and in type at least half as large as that used thereon for any proprietary name or designation for such drug or ingredient; and provided, that to the extent that compliance with the requirements of Paragraph (A)(ii) or this paragraph is impracticable, exemptions shall be allowed under regulations promulgated by the secretary under the federal Act;

(2) if it is a device and it has an established name, unless its label bears, to the exclusion of any other nonproprietary name, its established name (as defined in Subdivision (4)) prominently printed in type at least half as large as that used thereon for any proprietary name or designation for such device, except that to the extent compliance with this subdivision is impracticable, exemptions shall be allowed under regulations promulgated by the secretary under the federal Act;

(3) as used in Subdivision (1), the term "established name," with respect to a drug or ingredient thereof, means:

(A) the applicable official name designated pursuant to Section 508 of the federal Act; or

(B) if there is no such name and such drug, or such ingredient, is an article recognized in an official compendium, then the official title thereof in such compendium; or

(C) if neither Paragraph (A) nor Paragraph (B) applies, then the common or usual name, if any, of such drug or of such ingredient; provided further, that where Paragraph (B) applies to an article recognized in the United States Pharmacopoeia National Formulary, the official title used in the United States Pharmacopoeia National Formulary shall apply;

(4) as used in Subdivision (2), the term "established name" with respect to a device means:

(A) the applicable official name of the device designated pursuant to Section 508 of the federal Act;

(B) if there is no such name and such device is an article recognized in an official compendium, then the official title thereof in such compendium; or

(C) if neither Paragraph (A) nor Paragraph (B) applies, then any common or usual name of such device;

(e) unless its labeling bears:

(1) adequate directions for use; and

(2) such adequate warnings against use in those pathological conditions or by children where its use may be dangerous to health, or against unsafe dosage or methods or durations of administration or application, in such manner and form, as are necessary for the protection of users unless the drug or device has been exempted from those requirements by the regulations adopted by the secretary;

(f) if it purports to be a drug the name of which is recognized in an official compendium, unless it is packaged and labeled as prescribed therein unless the method of packing has been modified with the consent of the secretary. Whenever a drug is recognized in the United States Pharmacopoeia National Formulary, it shall be subject to the requirements of the United States Pharmacopoeia National Formulary with respect to packaging and labeling. If there is an inconsistency between the requirements of this subsection and those of Subsection (d) as to the name by which the drug or its ingredients shall be designated, the requirements of Subsection (d) prevail;

(g) if it has been found by the secretary to be a drug liable to deterioration, unless it is packaged in such form and manner, and its label bears a statement of such precautions, as the secretary shall by regulations require as necessary for the protection of public health;

(h) if:

(1) it is a drug and its container is so made, formed, or filled as to be misleading; or

(2) it is an imitation of another drug; or

(3) it is offered for sale under the name of another drug;

(i) if it is dangerous to health when used in the dosage, or manner or with the frequency or duration prescribed, recommended, or suggested in the labeling thereof;

(j) if it is a color additive, the intended use of which is for the purpose of coloring only, unless its packaging and labeling are in conformity with such packaging and labeling requirements applicable to such color additive, as may be contained in rules issued under Section 431.161(b);

(k) in the case of any prescription drug distributed or offered for sale in this state, unless the manufacturer, packer, or distributor thereof includes in all advertisements and other descriptive printed matter issued or caused to be issued by the manufacturer, packer, or distributor with respect to that drug a true statement of:

   (1) the established name as defined in Subsection (d), printed prominently and in type at least half as large as that used for any trade or brand name;

   (2) the formula showing quantitatively each ingredient of the drug to the extent required for labels under Subsection (d); and

   (3) other information in brief summary relating to side effects, contraindications, and effectiveness as required in regulations issued under Section 701(e) of the federal Act;

(l) if it was manufactured, prepared, propagated, compounded, or processed in an establishment in this state not registered under Section 510 of the federal Act, if it was not included in a list required by Section 510(j) of the federal Act, if a notice or other information respecting it was not provided as required by that section or Section 510(k) of the federal Act, or if it does not bear symbols from the uniform system for identification of devices prescribed under Section 510(e) of the federal Act as required by regulation;

(m) if it is a drug and its packaging or labeling is in violation of an applicable regulation issued under Section 3 or 4 of the federal Poison Prevention Packaging Act of 1970 (15 U.S.C. 1472 or 1473);

(n) if a trademark, trade name, or other identifying mark, imprint or device of another, or any likeness of the foregoing has been placed thereon or on its container with intent to defraud;

(o) in the case of any restricted device distributed or offered for sale in this state, if:

   (1) its advertising is false or misleading in any particular; or

   (2) it is sold, distributed, or used in violation of regulations prescribed under Section 520(e) of the federal Act;

(p) in the case of any restricted device distributed or offered for sale in this state, unless the manufacturer, packer, or distributor thereof includes in all advertisements and other descriptive printed matter issued by the manufacturer, packer, or distributor with respect to that device:

   (1) a true statement of the device's established name as defined in Section 502(e) of the federal Act, printed prominently and in type at least half as large as that used for any trade or brand name thereof; and

   (2) a brief statement of the intended uses of the device and relevant warnings, precautions, side effects, and contraindications and in the case of specific devices made subject to regulations issued under the federal Act, a full description of the components of such device or the formula showing quantitatively each ingredient of such device to the extent required in regulations under the federal Act;

(q) if it is a device subject to a performance standard established under Section 514 of the federal Act, unless it bears such labeling as may be prescribed in such performance standard; or

(r) if it is a device and there was a failure or refusal:

   (1) to comply with any requirement prescribed under Section 518 of the federal Act respecting the device; or

   (2) to furnish material required by or under Section 519 of the federal Act respecting the device.

Leg.H. Stats. 1989 71st Leg. Sess. Ch. 678, effective September 1, 1989; Stats. 1997 75th Leg. Sess. Ch. 282, effective September 1, 1997; Stats. 2003 78th Leg. Sess. Ch. 111, effective September 1, 2003; Stats. 2003 78 th Leg. Sess. Ch. 1099, effective September 1, 2003.

Sec. 431.113. Exemption for Certain Drugs and Devices.

(a) The executive commissioner shall adopt rules exempting from any labeling or packaging requirement of this chapter drugs and devices that are, in accordance with the practice of the trade, to be processed, labeled, or repacked in substantial quantities at establishments other than those where originally processed or packaged on condition that such drugs and devices are not adulterated or misbranded under the provisions of this chapter on removal from such processing, labeling, or repacking establishment.

(b) Drugs and device labeling or packaging exemptions adopted under the federal Act shall apply to drugs and devices in this state except insofar as modified or rejected by department rules.

(c) (1) A drug intended for use by man that:

   (A) because of its toxicity or other potentiality for harmful effect, or the method of its use, or the collateral measures necessary to its use, is not safe for use except under the supervision of a practitioner licensed by law to administer such drug; or

   (B) is limited by an approved application under Section 505 of the federal Act to use under the professional supervision of a practitioner licensed by law to administer such drug shall be dispensed only:

     (i) on a written prescription of a practitioner licensed by law to administer such drug; or

     (ii) on an oral prescription of such practitioner that is reduced promptly to writing and filed by the pharmacist; or

     (iii) by refilling any such written or oral prescription if such refilling is authorized by the prescriber either in the original prescription or by oral order that is reduced promptly to writing and filed by the pharmacist. The act of dispensing a drug contrary to the provisions of this paragraph shall be deemed to be an act that results in a drug being misbranded while held for sale.

(2) Any drug dispensed by filling or refilling a written or oral prescription of a practitioner licensed by law to administer such drug shall be exempt from the requirements of Section 431.112, except Sections 431.112(a)(1), (h)(2), and (h)(3), and the packaging requirements of Sections 431.112(f), (g), and (m), if the drug bears a label containing the name and address of the dispenser, the serial number and date of the prescription or of its filling, the name of the prescriber, and, if stated in the prescription, the name of the patient, and the directions for use and cautionary statements, if any, contained in such

prescription. This exemption shall not apply to any drugs dispensed in the course of the conduct of business of dispensing drugs pursuant to diagnosis by mail, or to a drug dispensed in violation of Subdivision (1).

(3) A drug that is subject to Subdivision (1) shall be deemed to be misbranded if at any time prior to dispensing its label fails to bear at a minimum, the symbol "RX Only." A drug to which Subdivision (1) does not apply shall be deemed to be misbranded if at any time prior to dispensing its label bears the caution statement quoted in the preceding sentence.

Leg.H. Stats. 1989 71st Leg. Sess. Ch. 678, effective September 1, 1989; 2003 78th Leg. Sess. Chs. 111, 1099, effective September 1, 2003; am. Acts 2015, 84th Leg., ch. 1 (S.B. 219), § 3.0969, effective April 2, 2015.

Sec. 431.114. New Drugs.

(a) A person shall not sell, deliver, offer for sale, hold for sale or give away any new drug unless:
(1) an application with respect thereto has been approved and the approval has not been withdrawn under Section 505 of the federal Act; and
(2) a copy of the letter of approval or approvability issued by the United States Food and Drug Administration is on file with the department if the product is manufactured in this state.
(b) A person shall not use in or on human beings or animals a new drug or new animal drug limited to investigational use unless the person has filed with the United States Food and Drug Administration a completed and signed investigational new drug (IND) application in accordance with 21 C.F.R. 312.20-312.38 and the exemption has not been terminated. The drug shall be plainly labeled in compliance with Section 505(i) of the federal Act.
(c) This section shall not apply:
(1) to any drug that is not a new drug as defined in the federal Act;
(2) to any drug that is licensed under the Public Health Service Act (42 U.S.C. 201 et seq.); or
(3) to any drug approved by the department by the authority of any prior law.

Leg.H. Stats. 1989 71st Leg. Sess. Ch. 678, effective September 1, 1989; Stats. 1991 72nd Leg. Sess. Ch. 14, effective September 1, 1991; 2003 78th Leg. Sess. Ch. 111, effective September 1, 2003; am. Acts 2015, 84th Leg., ch. 1 (S.B. 219), § 3.0970, effective April 2, 2015.

Sec. 431.115. New Animal Drugs.

(a) A new animal drug shall, with respect to any particular use or intended use of the drug, be deemed unsafe for the purposes of this chapter unless:
(1) there is in effect an approval of an application filed pursuant to Section 512(b) of the federal Act with respect to the use or intended use of the drug; and
(2) the drug, its labeling, and the use conforms to the approved application.
(b) A new animal drug shall not be deemed unsafe for the purposes of this chapter if the article is for investigational use and conforms to the terms of an exemption in effect with respect thereto under Section 512(j) of the federal Act.
(c) This section does not apply to any drug:
(1) licensed under the virus-serum-toxin law of March 4, 1913 (21 U.S.C. 151-159);
(2) approved by the United States Department of Agriculture; or
(3) approved by the department by the authority of any prior law.

Leg.H. Stats. 1989 71st Leg. Sess. Ch. 678, effective September 1, 1989; Stats. 1991 72nd Leg. Sess. Ch. 14, effective September 1, 1991; am. Acts 2015, 84th Leg., ch. 1 (S.B. 219), § 3.0971, effective April 2, 2015.

Sec. 431.116. Average Manufacturer Price.

(a) In this section, "average manufacturer price" has the meaning assigned by 42 U.S.C. Section 1396r-8(k), as amended.
(b) A person who manufactures a drug, including a person who manufactures a generic drug, that is sold in this state shall file with the department:
(1) the average manufacturer price for the drug; and
(2) the price that each wholesaler in this state pays the manufacturer to purchase the drug.
(c) The information required under Subsection (b) must be filed annually or more frequently as determined by the department.
(d) The department and the attorney general may investigate the manufacturer to determine the accuracy of the information provided under Subsection (b). The attorney general may take action to enforce this section.
(e) [Repealed by Acts 2005, 79th Leg., ch. 349 (S.B. 1188), § 29, effective September 1, 2007.]
(f) Notwithstanding any other state law, pricing information disclosed by manufacturers or labelers under this section may be provided by the department only to the Medicaid vendor drug program for its sole use. The Medicaid vendor drug program may use the information only as necessary to administer its drug programs, including Medicaid drug programs.
(g) Notwithstanding any other state law, pricing information disclosed by manufacturers or labelers under this section is confidential and, except as necessary to permit the attorney general to enforce state and federal laws, may not be disclosed by the Health and Human Services Commission or any other state agency in a form that discloses the identity of a specific manufacturer or labeler or the prices charged by a specific manufacturer or labeler for a specific drug.
(h) The attorney general shall treat information obtained under this section in the same manner as information obtained by the attorney general through a civil investigative demand under Section 36.054, Human Resources Code.
(i) Notwithstanding any other state law, the penalties for unauthorized disclosure of confidential information under Chapter 552, Government Code, apply to unauthorized disclosure of confidential information under this section.

Leg.H. Stats. 2001 77th Leg. Sess. Ch. 1003, effective September 1, 2001; Stats 2003 78th Leg. Sess. Ch. 198, effective September 1, 2003; Stats 2005 79th Leg. Sess. Ch. 349, effective September 1, 2007; am. Acts 2015, 84th Leg., ch. 1 (S.B. 219), § 3.0972, effective April 2, 2015.

Ts FD&C Act

Sec. 431.117. Priority for Health Care Providers in Distribution of Influenza Vaccine.

The executive commissioner shall study the wholesale distribution of influenza vaccine in this state to determine the feasibility of implementing a system that requires giving a priority in filling orders for influenza vaccine to physicians and other licensed health care providers authorized to administer influenza vaccine over retail establishments. The executive commissioner may implement such a system if it is determined to be feasible.

Leg.H. Stats. 2007, 80th Leg. Sess. Ch. 922, effective June 15, 2007; am. Acts 2015, 84th Leg., ch. 1 (S.B. 219), § 3.0973, effective April 2, 2015.

Ts FD&C Act

SUBCHAPTER F. COSMETICS

Sec. 431.141. Adulterated Cosmetic.

A cosmetic shall be deemed to be adulterated:

(a) if it bears or contains any poisonous or deleterious substance which may render it injurious to users under the conditions of use prescribed in the labeling thereof, or under such conditions of use as are customary or usual; provided, that this provision shall not apply to coal-tar hair dye, the label of which bears the following legend conspicuously displayed thereon; "Caution: This product contains ingredients which may cause skin irritation on certain individuals and a preliminary test according to accompanying directions should first be made. This product must not be used for dyeing the eyelashes or eyebrows; to do so may cause blindness"; and the labeling of which bears adequate directions for such preliminary testing. For the purposes of this subsection and Subsection (e) the term "hair dye" shall not include eyelash dyes or eyebrow dyes;

(b) if it consists in whole or in part of any filthy, putrid, or decomposed substance;

(c) if it has been produced, prepared, packed, or held under unsanitary conditions whereby it may have become contaminated with filth, or whereby it may have been rendered injurious to health;

(d) if its container is composed, in whole or in part, of any poisonous or deleterious substance which may render the contents injurious to health;

(e) if it is not a hair dye and it is, or it bears or contains, a color additive that is unsafe within the meaning of Section 431.161(a).

Leg.H. Stats. 1989 71st Leg. Sess. Ch. 678, effective September 1, 1989.

Sec. 431.142. Misbranded Cosmetic.

(1) A cosmetic shall be deemed to be misbranded:

  (a) if:

    (1) its labeling is false or misleading in any particular; and

    (2) its labeling or packaging fails to conform with the requirements of Section 431.181;

  (b) if in package form unless it bears a label containing (1) the name and place of business of the manufacturer, packer, or distributor; and (2) an accurate statement of the quantity of the contents in terms of weight, measure or numerical count, which statement shall be separately and accurately stated in a uniform location on the principal display panel of the label; provided, that under Subdivision (2) reasonable variations shall be permitted, and exemptions as to small packages shall be established by regulations prescribed by department rules;

  (c) if any word, statement, or other information required by or under authority of this chapter to appear on the label or labeling is not prominently placed thereon with such conspicuousness (as compared with other words, statements, designs, or devices, in the labeling) and in such terms as to render it likely to be read and understood by the ordinary individual under customary conditions of purchase and use;

  (d) if its container is so made, formed, or filled as to be misleading;

  (e) if it is a color additive, unless its packaging and labeling are in conformity with the packaging and labeling requirements, applicable to the color additive, prescribed under Section 721 of the federal Act. This subsection shall not apply to packages of color additives which, with respect to their use for cosmetics, are marketed and intended for use only in or on hair dyes, as defined by Section 431.141(a); or

  (f) if its packaging or labeling is in violation of an applicable regulation issued pursuant to Section 3 or 4 of the federal Poison Prevention Packaging Act of 1970 (15 U.S.C. 1472 or 1473).

(2) The executive commissioner shall adopt rules exempting from any labeling requirement of this chapter cosmetics that are in accordance with the practice of the trade, to be processed, labeled, or repacked in substantial quantities at an establishment other than the establishment where it was originally processed or packed, on condition that the cosmetics are not adulterated or misbranded under the provisions of this chapter on removal from the processing, labeling, or repacking establishment. Cosmetic labeling exemptions adopted under the federal Act shall apply to cosmetics in this state except insofar as modified or rejected by department rules.

Leg.H. Stats. 1989 71st Leg. Sess. Ch. 678, effective September 1, 1989; Stats. 1991 72nd Leg. Sess. Ch. 14, effective September 1, 1991; am. Acts 2015, 84th Leg., ch. 1 (S.B. 219), § 3.0974, effective April 2, 2015.

Ts FD&C Act

SUBCHAPTER G. POISONOUS OR DELETERIOUS SUBSTANCES

Sec. 431.161. Poisonous or Deleterious Substances.

(a) Any poisonous or deleterious substance, food additive, pesticide chemical in or on a raw agricultural commodity, or color additive shall, with respect to any particular use or intended use, be deemed unsafe for the purpose of Section 431.081(a)(2) with respect to any food, Section 431.111(a) with respect to any drug or device, or Section 431.141 with respect to any cosmetic. However, if a rule adopted under Section 431.181 or Subsection (b) is in effect that limits the quantity of that substance, and if the use or intended use of that substance conforms to the terms prescribed by the rule, a food, drug, or cosmetic shall not, by reason of bearing or containing that substance in accordance with the rules, be considered adulterated within the meaning of Section 431.081(a)(1), 431.111, or 431.141.

(b) The executive commissioner, whenever public health or other considerations in the state so require or on the petition of an interested party, may adopt rules prescribing tolerances for any added, poisonous, or deleterious substances, food additives, pesticide chemicals in or on raw agricultural commodities, or color additives, including zero tolerances and exemptions from tolerances in the case of pesticide chemicals in or on raw agricultural commodities. The rules may prescribe the conditions under which a food additive or a color additive may be safely used and may prescribe exemptions if the food additive or color additive is to be used solely for investigational or experimental purposes. Rules adopted under this section limiting the quantity of poisonous or deleterious substances in food must provide equal or stricter standards than those adopted by the federal Food and Drug Administration or its successor. A person petitioning for the adoption of a rule shall establish by data submitted to the executive commissioner that a necessity exists for the rule and that its effect will not be detrimental to the public health. If the data furnished by the petitioner are not sufficient to allow the executive commissioner to determine whether the rules should be adopted, the executive commissioner may require additional data to be submitted. The petitioner's failure to comply with the request is sufficient grounds to deny the request. In adopting rules relating to those substances, the executive commissioner shall consider, among other relevant factors, the following information furnished by the petitioner, if any:

   (1) the name and all pertinent information concerning the substance, including, if available, its chemical identity and composition, a statement of the conditions of the proposed use, directions, recommendations, and suggestions, specimens of proposed labeling, all relevant data bearing on the physical or other technical effect, and the quantity required to produce that effect;

   (2) the probable composition of any substance formed in or on a food, drug, or cosmetic resulting from the use of that substance;

   (3) the probable consumption of that substance in the diet of man and animals, taking into account any chemically or pharmacologically related substance in the diet;

   (4) safety factors that, in the opinion of experts qualified by scientific training and experience to evaluate the safety of those substances for the use or uses for which they are proposed to be used, are generally recognized as appropriate for the use of animal experimentation data;

   (5) the availability of any needed practicable methods of analysis for determining the identity and quantity of:

      (A) that substance in or on an article;

      (B) any substance formed in or on an article because of the use of that substance; and

      (C) the pure substance and all intermediates and impurities; and

   (6) facts supporting a contention that the proposed use of that substance will serve a useful purpose.

(c) The executive commissioner may adopt emergency rules under Chapter 2001, Government Code, to establish tolerance levels of poisonous or deleterious substances in food.

Leg.H. Stats. 1989 71st Leg. Sess. Ch. 678, effective September 1, 1989; Stats. 1995 74th Leg. Sess. Ch. 76, effective September 1, 1995; am. Acts 2015, 84th Leg., ch. 1 (S.B. 219), § 3.0975, effective April 2, 2015.

SUBCHAPTER G-1. ABUSABLE SYNTHETIC SUBSTANCES

Sec. 431.171. Designation of Consumer Commodity as Abusable Synthetic Substance.

(a)   The commissioner may designate a consumer commodity as an abusable synthetic substance if the commissioner determines that the consumer commodity is likely an abusable synthetic substance and the importation, manufacture, distribution, or retail sale of the commodity poses a threat to public health.

(b)   In determining whether a consumer commodity is an abusable synthetic substance, the commissioner may consider:

(1)   whether the commodity is sold at a price higher than similar commodities are ordinarily sold;

(2)   any evidence of clandestine importation, manufacture, distribution, or diversion from legitimate channels;

(3)   any evidence suggesting the product is intended for human consumption, regardless of any consumption prohibitions or warnings on the packaging of the commodity; or

(4)   whether any of the following factors suggest the commodity is an abusable synthetic substance intended for illicit drug use:

(A)   the appearance of the packaging of the commodity;

(B)   oral or written statements or representations of a person who sells, manufactures, distributes, or imports the commodity;

(C)   the methods by which the commodity is distributed; and

(D)   the manner in which the commodity is sold to the public.

Leg.H. Stats 2015, 84th Leg., ch. 712 (H.B. 1212), § 2, effective September 1, 2015.

Sec. 431.172. Applicability of Chapter to Abusable Synthetic Substance.

A commodity classified as an abusable synthetic substance by the commissioner under Section 431.171 is subject to:

(1)   the provisions of this chapter that apply to food and cosmetics, including provisions relating to adulteration, packaging, misbranding, and inspection; and

(2)   all enforcement actions under Subchapter C.

Leg.H. Stats 2015, 84th Leg., ch. 712 (H.B. 1212), § 2, effective September 1, 2015.

Ts FD&C Act

SUBCHAPTER H. FAIR PACKAGING AND LABELING; FALSE ADVERTISING

Sec. 431.181. Fair Packaging and Labeling.

(a) All labels of consumer commodities, as defined by this chapter, shall conform with the requirements for the declaration of net quantity of contents of Section 4 of the Fair Packaging and Labeling Act (15 U.S.C. 1451 et seq.) and the regulations promulgated pursuant thereto; provided, that consumer commodities exempted from the requirements of Section 4 of the Fair Packaging and Labeling Act shall also be exempt from this subsection.

(b) The label of any package of a consumer commodity that bears a representation as to the number of servings of the commodity contained in the package shall bear a statement of the net quantity (in terms of weight, measure, or numerical count) of each serving.

(c) No person shall distribute or cause to be distributed in commerce any packaged consumer commodity if any qualifying words or phrases appear in conjunction with the separate statement of the net quantity of contents required by Subsection (a), but nothing in this subsection shall prohibit supplemental statements at other places on the package describing in nondeceptive terms the net quantity of contents; provided, that the supplemental statements of net quantity of contents shall not include any term qualifying a unit of weight, measure, or count that tends to exaggerate the amount of the commodity contained in the package.

(d) Whenever the executive commissioner determines that rules containing prohibitions or requirements other than those prescribed by Subsection (a) are necessary to prevent the deception of consumers or to facilitate value comparisons as to any consumer commodity, the executive commissioner shall adopt with respect to that commodity rules effective to:

　(1) establish and define standards for the characterization of the size of a package enclosing any consumer commodity, which may be used to supplement the label statement of net quantity of contents of packages containing such commodity, but this subdivision shall not be construed as authorizing any limitation on the size, shape, weight, dimensions, or number of packages that may be used to enclose any commodity;

　(2) regulate the placement on any package containing any commodity, or on any label affixed to the commodity, of any printed matter stating or representing by implication that such commodity is offered for retail sale at a price lower than the ordinary and customary retail sale price or that a retail sale price advantage is accorded to purchasers thereof by reason of the size of that package or the quantity of its contents;

　(3) require that the label on each package of a consumer commodity (other than one which is a food within the meaning of Section 431.002) bear:

　　(A) the common or usual name of the consumer commodity, if any; and

　　(B) in case the consumer commodity consists of two or more ingredients, the common or usual name of each ingredient listed in order of decreasing predominance, but nothing in this paragraph shall be deemed to require that any trade secret be divulged; or

　(4) prevent the nonfunctional slack-fill of packages containing consumer commodities. For the purpose of this subdivision, a package shall be deemed to be nonfunctionally slack-filled if it is filled of substantially less than its capacity for reasons other than:

　　(A) protection of the contents of the package; or

　　(B) the requirements of the machine used for enclosing the contents in the package.

Leg.H. Stats. 1989 71st Leg. Sess. Ch. 678, effective September 1, 1989; am. Acts 2015, 84th Leg., ch. 1 (S.B. 219), § 3.0976, effective April 2, 2015.

Sec. 431.182. False Advertisement.

(a) An advertisement of a food, drug, device, or cosmetic shall be deemed to be false if it is false or misleading in any particular.

(b) The advertising of a food that incorporates a health claim not in conformance with or defined by Section 403(r) of the federal Act is deemed to be false or misleading for the purposes of this chapter.

Leg.H. Stats. 1989 71st Leg. Sess. Ch. 678, effective September 1, 1989; Stats. 1993 73rd Leg. Sess. Ch. 386, effective September 1, 1993.

Sec. 431.183. False Advertisement of Drug or Device.

(a) An advertisement of a drug or device is false if the advertisement represents that the drug or device affects:

　(1) infectious and parasitic diseases;

　(2) neoplasms;

　(3) endocrine, nutritional, and metabolic diseases and immunity disorders;

　(4) diseases of blood and blood-forming organs;

　(5) mental disorders;

　(6) diseases of the nervous system and sense organs;

　(7) diseases of the circulatory system;

　(8) diseases of the respiratory system;

　(9) diseases of the digestive system;

　(10) diseases of the genitourinary system;

　(11) complications of pregnancy, childbirth, and the puerperium;

　(12) diseases of the skin and subcutaneous tissue;

　(13) diseases of the musculoskeletal system and connective tissue;

　(14) congenital anomalies;

　(15) certain conditions originating in the perinatal period;

　(16) symptoms, signs, and ill-defined conditions; or

　(17) injury and poisoning.

(b) Subsection (a) does not apply to an advertisement of a drug or device if the advertisement does not violate Section 431.182 and is disseminated:
   (1) to the public for self-medication and is consistent with the labeling claims permitted by the federal Food and Drug Administration;
   (2) only to members of the medical, dental, and veterinary professions and appears only in the scientific periodicals of those professions; or
   (3) only for the purpose of public health education by a person not commercially interested, directly or indirectly, in the sale of the drug or device.
(c) The executive commissioner by rule shall authorize the advertisement of a drug having a curative or therapeutic effect for a disease listed under Subsection (a) if the executive commissioner determines that an advance in medical science has made any type of self-medication safe for the disease. The executive commissioner may impose conditions and restrictions on the advertisement of the drug necessary in the interest of public health.
(d) This section does not indicate that self-medication for a disease other than a disease listed under Subsection (a) is safe or effective.

Leg.H. Stats. 1989 71st Leg. Sess. Ch. 678, effective September 1, 1989; Stats. 1991 72nd Leg. Sess. Ch. 14, effective September 1, 1991; am. Acts 2015, 84th Leg., ch. 1 (S.B. 219), § 3.0977, effective April 2, 2015.

Ts FD&C Act

SUBCHAPTER I. WHOLESALE DISTRIBUTORS OF NONPRESCRIPTION DRUGS

Sec. 431.201. Definitions.

In this subchapter:
- (1) "Nonprescription drug" means any drug that is not a prescription drug as defined by Section 431.401.
- (2) "Place of business" means each location at which a drug for wholesale distribution is located.
- (3) "Wholesale distribution" means distribution to a person other than a consumer or patient, and includes distribution by a manufacturer, repackager, own label distributor, broker, jobber, warehouse, or wholesaler.

Leg.H. Stats. 1989 71st Leg. Sess., Ch. 678, { 1, effective September 1, 1989; Stats. 2005 79th Leg. Sess., Ch. 282 (H.B. 164), § 3(b), effective March 1, 2006.

Sec. 431.2011. Applicability of Subchapter.

This subchapter applies only to the wholesale distribution of nonprescription drugs.

Leg.H. Stats. 2005 79th Leg. Sess., Ch. 282 (H.B. 164), § 3(c), effective March 1, 2006.

Sec. 431.202. License Required.

- (a) A person may not engage in wholesale distribution of nonprescription drugs in this state unless the person holds a wholesale drug distribution license issued by the department under this subchapter or Subchapter N.
- (b) An applicant for a license under this subchapter must submit an application to the department on the form prescribed by the department or electronically on the state electronic Internet portal.
- (c) A license issued under this subchapter expires on the second anniversary of the date of issuance.

Leg.H. Stats. 1989 71st Leg. Sess. Ch. 678, effective September 1, 1989; Stats. 1991, 72nd Leg. Sess. Chs. 14, 539, effective September 1, 1991; Stats. 2005, Leg. Sess., Ch. 282 (H.B. 164), § 3(d), effective March 1, 2006; Stats. 2011 82nd Leg. Sess. Ch. 973, effective June 17, 2011.

Sec. 431.2021. Exemption from Licensing [Repealed].

Repealed by Acts 2015, 84th Leg., 1 (S.B. 219), § 3.1639(75), effective April 2, 2015.

Sec. 431.203. Contents of License Statement.

The license statement must contain:
- (1) the name under which the business is conducted;
- (2) the address of each place of business that is licensed;
- (3) the name and residence address of:
  - (A) the proprietor, if the business is a proprietorship;
  - (B) all partners, if the business is a partnership; or
  - (C) all principals, if the business is an association;
- (4) the date and place of incorporation, if the business is a corporation;
- (5) the names and residence addresses of the individuals in an administrative capacity showing:
  - (A) the managing proprietor, if the business is a proprietorship;
  - (B) the managing partner, if the business is a partnership;
  - (C) the officers and directors, if the business is a corporation; or
  - (D) the persons in a managerial capacity, if the business is an association; and
- (6) the residence address of an individual in charge of each place of business.

Leg.H. Stats. 1989 71st Leg. Sess. Ch. 678, effective September 1, 1989; Stats. 1991 72nd Leg. Sess. Ch. 539, effective September 1, 1991.

Sec. 431.2031. Effect of Operation in Other Jurisdictions; Reports.

- (a) A person who engages in the wholesale distribution of drugs outside this state may engage in the wholesale distribution of drugs in this state if the person holds a license issued by the department.
- (b) The department may accept reports from authorities in other jurisdictions to determine the extent of compliance with this chapter and the minimum standards adopted under this chapter.
- (c) The department may issue a license to a person who engages in the wholesale distribution of drugs outside this state to engage in the wholesale distribution of drugs in this state, if after an examination of the reports of the person's compliance history and current compliance record, the department determines that the person is in compliance with this subchapter and department rules.
- (d) The department shall consider each licensing statement filed by a person who wishes to engage in wholesale distribution of drugs in this state on an individual basis.

Leg.H. Stats. 1991 72nd Leg. Sess. Ch. 539, effective September 1, 1991; am. Acts 2015, 84th Leg., ch. 1 (S.B. 219), § 3.0978, effective April 2, 2015.

Sec. 431.204. Fees.

(a) The department shall collect fees for:
    (1) a license that is filed or renewed;
    (2) a license that is amended, including a notification of a change in the location of a licensed place of business required under Section 431.206; and
    (3) an inspection performed in enforcing this subchapter and rules adopted under this subchapter.

(b) The executive commissioner by rule shall set the fees in amounts that allow the department to recover the biennial expenditures of state funds by the department in:
    (1) reviewing and acting on a license;
    (2) amending and renewing a license;
    (3) inspecting a licensed facility; and
    (4) implementing and enforcing this subchapter, including a rule or order adopted or a license issued under this subchapter.

(c) Fees collected under this section shall be deposited to the credit of the food and drug registration fee account of the general revenue fund and appropriated to the department to carry out the administration and enforcement of this chapter.

Leg.H. Stats 1989 71st Leg. Sess. Ch. 678, effective September 1, 1989; Stats 1991 72nd Leg. Sess. Ch. 539, effective September 1, 1991; Stats. 2005, 79th Leg. Sess., Ch. 282 (H.B. 164), § 3 (e), effective March 1, 2006; am. Acts 2015, 84th Leg., ch. 1 (S.B. 219), § 3.0979, effective April 2, 2015.

Sec. 431.205. Expiration Date [Repealed].

Repealed by Stats. 2005 79th Leg. Sess., Ch. 282 (H.B. 164), § 3 (k), effective September 1, 2005.

Sec. 431.206. Change of Location of Place of Business.

(a) Not fewer than 30 days in advance of the change, the licensee shall notify the department in writing of the licensee's intent to change the location of a licensed place of business.

(b) The notice shall include the address of the new location, and the name and residence address of the individual in charge of the business at the new location.

(c) Not more than 10 days after the completion of the change of location, the licensee shall notify the department in writing to confirm the completion of the change of location and provide verification of the information previously provided or correct and confirm any information that has changed since providing the notice of intent.

(d) The notice and confirmation required by this section are deemed adequate if the licensee sends the notices by certified mail, return receipt requested, to the central office of the department or submits them electronically through the state electronic Internet portal.

Leg.H. Stats. 1989 71st Leg. Sess. Ch. 678, effective September 1, 1989; Stats. 1991 72nd Leg. Sess. Ch. 539, effective September 1, 1991; Stats. 2005 79th Leg. Sess., Ch. 282 (H.B. 164), § 3 (f), effective March 1, 2006; Stats. 2011 82nd Leg. Sess. Ch. 973, effective June 17, 2011.

Sec. 431.207. Refusal to License; Suspension or Revocation of License.

(a) The department may refuse an application for a license or may suspend or revoke a license if the applicant or licensee:
    (1) has been convicted of a felony or misdemeanor that involves moral turpitude;
    (2) is an association, partnership, or corporation and the managing officer has been convicted of a felony or misdemeanor that involves moral turpitude;
    (3) has been convicted in a state or federal court of the illegal use, sale, or transportation of intoxicating liquors, narcotic drugs, barbiturates, amphetamines, desoxyephedrine, their compounds or derivatives, or any other dangerous or habit-forming drugs;
    (4) is an association, partnership, or corporation and the managing officer has been convicted in a state or federal court of the illegal use, sale, or transportation of intoxicating liquors, narcotic drugs, barbiturates, amphetamines, desoxyephedrine, their compounds or derivatives, or any other dangerous or habit-forming drugs;
    (5) has not complied with this chapter or the rules implementing this chapter;
    (6) has violated Section 431.021(l)(3), relating to the counterfeiting of a drug or the sale or holding for sale of a counterfeit drug;
    (7) has violated Chapter 481 or 483;
    (8) has violated the rules of the public safety director of the Department of Public Safety, including being responsible for a significant discrepancy in the records that state law requires the applicant or licensee to maintain; or
    (9) fails to complete a license application or submits an application that contains false, misleading, or incorrect information or contains information that cannot be verified by the department.

(b) The executive commissioner by rule shall establish minimum standards required for the issuance or renewal of a license under this subchapter.

(c) The refusal to license an applicant or the suspension or revocation of a license by the department and the appeal from that action are governed by the procedures for a contested case hearing under Chapter 2001, Government Code.

Leg.H. Stats 1989 71st Leg. Sess. Ch. 678, effective September 1, 1989; Stats 1991 72nd Leg. Sess. Ch. 539, effective September 1, 1991; Stats. 1995 74th Leg. Sess. Ch. 76, effective September 1, 1995; Stats. 2005 79th Leg. Sess., Ch. 282 (H.B. 164), § 3 (f), effective March 1, 2006; am. Acts 2015, 84th Leg., ch. 1 (S.B. 219), § 3.0980, effective April 2, 2015.

Ts FD&C Act

Sec. 431.208. Reporting of Purchase Price.

(a) On the department's request, a person who engages in the wholesale distribution of drugs in this state shall file with the department information showing the actual price at which the wholesale distributor sells a particular drug to a retail pharmacy.

(b) The executive commissioner shall adopt rules to implement this section.

(c) The department and the attorney general may investigate the distributor to determine the accuracy of the information provided under Subsection (a). The attorney general may take action to enforce this section.

(d) [Repealed by Acts 2005, 79th Leg., ch. 349 (S.B. 1188), § 29, effective September 1, 2007.]

Leg.H. Stats. 2001 77th Leg. Sess. Ch. 1003, effective September 1, 2001; Stats 2005 79th Leg. Sess. Ch. 349, effective September 1, 2007; am. Acts 2015, 84th Leg., ch. 1 (S.B. 219), § 3.0981, effective April 2, 2015.

SUBCHAPTER J. FOOD MANUFACTURERS, FOOD WHOLESALERS, AND WAREHOUSE OPERATORS

Sec. 431.221. Definitions.

In this subchapter:

(1) "Place of business" means:

    (A) each location where:

        (i) a person manufactures food; or

        (ii) food for wholesale is distributed; or

    (B) a warehouse where food is stored.

(2) "Food manufacturer" means a person who combines, purifies, processes, or packages food for sale through a wholesale outlet. The term also includes a retail outlet that packages or labels food before sale and a person that represents itself as responsible for the purity and proper labeling of an article of food by labeling the food with the person's name and address. The term does not include a restaurant that provides food for immediate human consumption to a political subdivision or to a licensed nonprofit organization if the restaurant would not otherwise be considered a food manufacturer under this subdivision.

(3) "Food wholesaler" means a person who distributes food for resale, either through a retail outlet owned by that person or through sales to another person. The term "food wholesaler" shall not include:

    (A) a commissary which distributes food primarily intended for immediate consumption on the premises of a retail outlet under common ownership;

    (B) an establishment engaged solely in the distribution of nonalcoholic beverages in sealed containers; or

    (C) a restaurant that provides food for immediate human consumption to a political subdivision or to a licensed nonprofit organization if the restaurant would not otherwise be considered a food wholesaler under this subdivision.

(4) [Repealed September 1, 1997]

(5) "Direct seller" means an individual:

    (A) who is not affiliated with a permanent retail establishment and who engages in the business of:

        (i) in-person sales of prepackaged nonperishable foods, including dietary supplements, to a buyer on a buy-sell basis, a deposit-commission basis, or a similar basis for resale in a home; or

        (ii) sales of prepackaged nonperishable foods, including dietary supplements, in a home;

    (B) who receives substantially all remuneration for a service, whether in cash or other form of payment, which is directly related to sales or other output, including the performance of the service, and not to the number of hours worked; and

    (C) who performs services under a written contract between the individual and the person for whom the service is performed, and the contract provides that the individual is not treated as an employee with respect to federal tax purposes.

(6) "Licensed nonprofit organization" means an organization that is licensed under any statutory authority of the State of Texas and is exempt from federal income taxation under Section 501(a), Internal Revenue Code of 1986, and its subsequent amendments, as an organization described in Section 501(c)(3) of that code.

(7) "Warehouse operator" means a person that operates a warehouse where food is stored.

Leg.H. Stats. 1989 71st Leg. Sess. Ch. 678, effective September 1, 1989; Stats. 1993 73rd Leg. Sess. Ch. 713, effective September 1, 1993; Stats. 1995 74th Leg. Sess. Ch. 348, effective August 28, 1995; Stats. 1995 74th Leg. Sess. Ch. 1047, effective September 1, 1995; Stats. 1997 75th Leg. Sess. Ch. 629, effective September 1, 1997; Stats. 1997 75th Leg. Sess. Ch. 1378, effective September 1, 1997; Stats. 2003 78th Leg. Sess. Ch. 334, effective June 18, 2003, Ch. 383, effective September 1, 2003; Stats. 2005 79th Leg. Sess., Ch. 728 (H.B. 2018), § 23.001 (51), effective September 1, 2005.

Sec. 431.2211. Application of Subchapter.

(a) A person is not required to hold a license under this subchapter if the person is:

    (1) a person, firm, or corporation that only harvests, packages, or washes raw fruits or vegetables for shipment at the location of harvest;

    (2) an individual who only sells prepackaged nonperishable foods, including dietary supplements, from a private home as a direct seller;

    (3) a person who holds a license under Chapter 432 and who only engages in conduct within the scope of that license; or

    (4) a restaurant that provides food for immediate human consumption to a political subdivision or to a licensed nonprofit organization if the restaurant would not otherwise be required to hold a license under this subchapter.

(a-1) A person is not required to hold a license under this subchapter if the person holds a license under Chapter 440 and is engaging in conduct within the scope of that license.

(a-2) A person is not required to hold a license under this subchapter if the person holds a permit under Chapter 435 related to the processing, producing, bottling, receiving, transferring, or transporting of Grade A milk or milk products and is engaging in conduct within the scope of that permit.

(a-3) A person is not required to hold a license under this subchapter if the person holds a license under Chapter 443 and is engaging in conduct within the scope of that license.

(b) An exemption from the licensing requirements prescribed by this subchapter does not exempt the person from other provisions prescribed by this subchapter or from rules adopted by the executive commissioner to administer and enforce those provisions.

(c) This subchapter does not apply to the distribution of beverages in sealed containers by holders of licenses or permits issued under Chapter 19, 20, 23, or 64, Alcoholic Beverage Code. The provisions of the Alcoholic Beverage Code prevail to the extent of any conflict with this chapter.

(d) A food wholesaler is not required to obtain a license under this subchapter for a place of business if all of the food distributed from that place of business will be stored in a warehouse licensed under this subchapter.

(e) A food wholesaler that is not required to obtain a license for a place of business under Subsection (d) shall register that place of business with the department. The executive commissioner shall adopt rules for the registration of food wholesalers under this section.

Leg.H. Stats. 1993, 73rd Leg., ch. 713 (S.B. 565), § 1, effective September 1, 1993; am. Acts 1995, 74th Leg., ch. 348 (S.B. 955), § 2, effective August 28, 1995; am. Acts 1997, 75th Leg., ch. 629 (H.B. 492), § 3, effective September 1, 1997; am. Acts 1997, 75th Leg., ch. 1378 (H.B. 1362), § 2, effective September 1, 1997; am. Acts 2001, 77th Leg., ch. 262 (S.B. 1046), § 3, effective September 1, 2001; am. Acts 2003, 78th Leg., ch. 112 (S.B. 1454), § 2, effective September 1, 2003; am. Acts 2003, 78th Leg., ch. 334 (S.B. 381), § 2, effective June 18, 2003; am. Acts 2003, 78th Leg., ch. 383 (S.B. 1803), § 6, effective September 1, 2003; am. Acts 2003, 78th Leg., ch. 757 (H.B. 3542), § 2, effective September 1, 2003; am. Acts 2011, 82nd Leg., ch. 1317 (S.B. 81), § 1, effective September 1, 2012; am. Acts 2015, 84th Leg., ch. 1 (S.B. 219), § 3.0982, effective April 2, 2015; am. Acts 2019, 86th Leg., ch. 764 (H.B. 1325), § 6, effective June 10, 2019; am. Acts 2019, 86th Leg., ch. 1359 (H.B. 1545), § 392, effective September 1, 2019.

Sec. 431.222. License Required; Licensing Fees.

(a) Except as provided by Section 431.2211, a food manufacturer, food wholesaler, or warehouse operator in this state must apply for and obtain from the department every two years a license for each place of business that the food manufacturer, food wholesaler, or warehouse operator operates in this state. The food manufacturer, food wholesaler, or warehouse operator must pay a licensing fee for each establishment.

(b) The department shall require a food manufacturer that distributes only food manufactured by that firm to obtain only a license as a food manufacturer. A person that does not manufacture food and serves only as a food wholesaler must obtain only a food wholesaler's license. A person that distributes both its own manufactured food and food it does not manufacture must obtain only a food manufacturer's license. A warehouse operator who also distributes food is required to obtain only a warehouse operator license.

Leg.H. Stats. Stats. 1989 71st Leg. Sess. Ch. 678, effective September 1, 1989; Stats. 1991 72nd Leg. Sess. Ch. 14, effective September 1, 1991; Stats. 1993 73rd Leg. Sess. Ch. 713, effective September 1, 1993; 2003 78th Leg. Sess. Ch. 383, effective September 1, 2003; am. Acts 2015, 84th Leg., ch. 1 (S.B. 219), § 3.0983, effective April 2, 2015.

Sec. 431.223. Contents of License Application.

(a) The person applying for a license under this subchapter must provide, at a minimum, the following information in a license application:
  (1) the name under which the food manufacturer, wholesale distributor, or warehouse operator conducts business;
  (2) the address of each place of business in this state that is licensed;
  (3) if the food manufacturer, wholesale distributor, or warehouse operator is an individual, a partnership, or an association, the name or names of:
    (A) the proprietor, if the business is a sole proprietorship;
    (B) all partners, if the business is a partnership; or
    (C) all principals, if the business is an association;
  (4) if the food manufacturer, wholesale distributor, or wholesale operator is a corporation, the date and place of incorporation and the name and address of its registered agent in this state;
  (5) the names and residences of the individuals in an administrative capacity, showing:
    (A) the managing proprietor, if the business is a sole proprietorship;
    (B) the managing partner, if the business is a partnership;
    (C) the officers and directors, if the business is a corporation; or
    (D) the persons in a managerial capacity, if the business is an association; and
  (6) the residence address of a person in charge of each place of business.
(b) The license application must be signed, verified, and filed on a form furnished by the department according to department rules.

Leg.H. Stats. Stats. 1989 71st Leg. Sess. Ch. 678, effective September 1, 1989; Stats. 1993 73rd Leg. Sess. Ch. 713, effective September 1, 1993; 2003 78th Leg. Sess. Ch. 383, effective September 1, 2003; am. Acts 2015, 84th Leg., ch. 1 (S.B. 219), § 3.0984, effective April 2, 2015.

Sec. 431.224. Fees.

(a) The department shall collect fees for:
  (1) a license that is filed or renewed;
  (2) a license that is amended, including a notification of a change in the location of a licensed place of business required under Section 431.2251; and
  (3) an inspection performed to enforce this subchapter and rules adopted under this subchapter.
(b) The department may charge fees every two years.
(c) The executive commissioner by rule shall set the fees in amounts that allow the department to recover the biennial expenditures of state funds by the department in:
  (1) reviewing and acting on a license;
  (2) amending and renewing a license;
  (3) inspecting a licensed facility; and
  (4) implementing and enforcing this subchapter, including a rule or order adopted or a license issued under this subchapter.
(d) The department shall use not less than one-half of license fees collected for inspecting a licensed place of business or enforcing this subchapter, and the remainder for the administration of this subchapter.
(e) All license fees received by the department under this subchapter shall be deposited in the state treasury to the credit of the food and drug registration account.

Leg.H. Stats. 1989 71st Leg. Sess. Ch. 678, effective September 1, 1989; Stats. 1991 72nd Leg. Sess. Ch. 14, effective September 1, 1991; Stats. 1993 73rd Leg. Sess. Ch. 713, effective September 1, 1993; am. Acts 2015, 84th Leg., ch. 1 (S.B. 219), § 3.0985, effective April 2, 2015.

Sec. 431.2245. Processing of Licensing Fees.

(a)   The department shall establish a system for processing licensing fees under this chapter, including vended water facility licensing fees.

(b)   Under the fee processing system, the maximum time for processing a fee payment made by a negotiable instrument may not exceed 48 hours, beginning at the time that the negotiable instrument is first received by the department and ending at the time that the fee payment is submitted for deposit by the department to the treasury division of the office of the comptroller.

(c)   The comptroller shall cooperate with the department in developing the fee processing system.

Leg.H. Stats. 1999 76th Leg. Sess. Ch. 697, effective August 30, 1999; am. Acts 2015, 84th Leg., ch. 1 (S.B. 219), § 3.0986, effective April 2, 2015.

Sec. 431.225. Expiration Date.

(a)   The executive commissioner by rule may provide that licenses expire on different dates.

(b)   If the license expiration date is changed, license fees shall be prorated so that each license holder pays only that portion of the license fee allocable to the number of months during which the license is valid. On renewal of the license on the new expiration date, the total license renewal fee is payable.

Leg.H. Stats. 1989 71st Leg. Sess. Ch. 678, effective September 1, 1989; Stats. 1991 72nd Leg. Sess. Ch. 14, effective September 1, 1991; Stats. 1993 73rd Leg. Sess. Ch. 713, effective September 1, 1993; am. Acts 2015, 84th Leg., ch. 1 (S.B. 219), § 3.0987, effective April 2, 2015.

Sec. 431.2251. Change in Location of Place of Business.

Not later than the 31st day before the date of the change, the license holder shall notify in writing the department of the license holder's intent to change the location of a licensed place of business. The notice shall include the address of the new location and the name and residence address of the individual in charge of the place of business. Not later than the 10th day after the completion of the change of location, the license holder shall forward to the department the name and residence address of the individual in charge of the new place of business. Notice is considered adequate if the license holder provides the intent and verification notices to the department by certified mail, return receipt requested, mailed to the central office of the department.

Leg.H. Stats. 1993 73rd Leg. Sess. Ch. 713, effective September 1, 1993; am. Acts 2015, 84th Leg., ch. 1 (S.B. 219), § 3.0988, effective April 2, 2015.

Sec. 431.226. Refusal to Grant License; Suspension or Revocation of License.

(a)   The department may refuse an application for a license or may suspend or revoke a license.

(b)   The executive commissioner by rule shall establish minimum standards for granting and maintaining a license. In adopting rules under this section, the executive commissioner shall:

(1)   ensure that the minimum standards prioritize safe handling of fruits and vegetables based on known safety risks, including any history of outbreaks of food-borne communicable diseases; and

(2)   consider acceptable produce safety standards developed by a federal agency, state agency, or university.

(c)   The refusal or the suspension or revocation of a license by the department and the appeal from that action are governed by the procedures for a contested case hearing under Chapter 2001, Government Code.

Leg.H. Stats. 1989 71st Leg. Sess. Ch. 678, effective September 1, 1989; Stats. 1993 73rd Leg. Sess. Ch. 713, effective September 1, 1993; Stats. 1995 74th Leg. Sess. Ch. 76, effective September 1, 1995; Stats. 2011 82nd Leg. Sess. Ch. 1317, effective September 1, 2011; am. Acts 2015, 84th Leg., ch. 1 (S.B. 219), § 3.0989, effective April 2, 2015.

Sec. 431.227. Food Safety Best Practice Education Program.

(a)   The department shall approve food safety best practice education programs for places of business licensed under this chapter.

(b)   A place of business that completes a food safety best practice education program approved by the department shall receive a certificate valid for five years from the date of completion of the program.

(c)   When determining which places of business to inspect under Section 431.042, the appropriate inspecting authority shall consider whether the place of business holds a valid certificate from a food safety best practice education program under this section.

(d)   The executive commissioner shall adopt rules to implement this section.

Leg.H. Stats. 2011 82nd Leg. Sess. Ch. 1317, effective September 1, 2011; am. Acts 2015, 84th Leg., ch. 1 (S.B. 219), § 3.0990, effective April 2, 2015.

Ts FD&C Act

SUBCHAPTER K. GENERAL ADMINISTRATIVE PROVISIONS AND RULEMAKING AUTHORITY

Sec. 431.241. Rulemaking Authority.

(a) The executive commissioner may adopt rules for the efficient enforcement of this chapter.

(b) The executive commissioner may conform rules adopted under this chapter, if practicable, with regulations adopted under the federal Act.

(c) The enumeration of specific federal laws and regulations in Sections 431.244 and 431.245 does not limit the general authority granted to the executive commissioner in Subsection (b) to conform rules adopted under this chapter to those adopted under the federal Act.

(d) The executive commissioner may adopt the federal regulations issued by the secretary pursuant to the Prescription Drug Marketing Act of 1987 (21 U.S.C. Sections 331, 333, 353, and 381), as necessary or desirable so that the state wholesale drug distributor licensing program in Subchapter N may achieve compliance with that Act.

(e) The executive commissioner shall not establish a drug formulary that restricts by any prior or retroactive approval process a physician's ability to treat a patient with a prescription drug that has been approved and designated as safe and effective by the United States Food and Drug Administration, in compliance with federal law and subject to review by the executive commissioner.

(f) Nothing in this section shall effect a prior approval program in operation on the effective date of this section nor shall any portion of this chapter prohibit a prior approval process on any federally exempted products.

(g) The department may assess a fee for the issuance of a certificate of free sale and another certification issued under this chapter. The executive commissioner by rule shall set each fee in an amount sufficient to recover the cost to the department of issuing the particular certificate.

Leg.H. Stats. 1989 71st Leg. Sess. Ch. 678, effective September 1, 1989; Stats. 1991 72nd Leg. Sess. Ch. 539, effective September 1, 1991; Stats. 1993 73rd Leg. Sess. Ch. 675, effective September 1, 1993; am. Acts 2015, 84th Leg., ch. 1 (S.B. 219), § 3.0991, effective April 2, 2015.

Sec. 431.242. Contested Case Hearings and Appeals.

A hearing under this chapter or an appeal from a final administrative decision shall be conducted under Chapter 2001, Government Code.

Leg.H. Stats. 1989 71st Leg. Sess. Ch. 678, effective September 1, 1989; Stats. 1995 74th Leg. Sess. Ch. 76, effective September 1, 1995.

Sec. 431.243. Persons to Conduct Hearings [Repealed].

Repealed by Acts 2015, 84th Leg., ch. 1 (S.B. 219), § 3.1639(75), effective April 2, 2015.

Sec. 431.244. Federal Regulations Adopted as State Rules.

(a) A regulation adopted by the secretary under the federal Act concerning pesticide chemicals, food additives, color additives, special dietary use, processed low acid food, acidified food, infant formula, bottled water, or vended bottled water is a rule for the purposes of this chapter, unless the executive commissioner modifies or rejects the rule.

(b) A regulation adopted under the Fair Packaging and Labeling Act (15 U.S.C. 1451 et seq.) is a rule for the purposes of this chapter, unless the executive commissioner modifies or rejects the rule. The executive commissioner may not adopt a rule that conflicts with the labeling requirements for the net quantity of contents required under Section 4 of the Fair Packaging and Labeling Act (15 U.S.C. 1453) and the regulations adopted under that Act.

(c) A regulation adopted by the secretary under Sections 403(b) through (i) of the federal Act is a rule for the purposes of this chapter unless the executive commissioner modifies or rejects the rule. The executive commissioner may not adopt a rule that conflicts with the limitations provided by Sections 403(q) and (r) of the federal Act.

(d) A federal regulation that this section provides as a rule for the purposes of this chapter is effective:

　(1) on the date that the regulation becomes effective as a federal regulation; and

　(2) whether or not the executive commissioner or department has fulfilled the rulemaking provisions of Chapter 2001, Government Code.

(e) If the executive commissioner modifies or rejects a federal regulation, the executive commissioner shall comply with the rulemaking provisions of Chapter 2001, Government Code.

(f) For any federal regulation adopted as a state rule under this chapter, including a regulation considered to be a rule for purposes of this chapter under Subsection (a), (b), or (c), the department shall provide on its Internet website:

　(1) a link to the text of the federal regulation;

　(2) a clear explanation of the substance of and purpose for the regulation; and

　(3) information on providing comments in response to any proposed or pending federal regulation, including an address to which and the manner in which comments may be submitted.

Leg.H. Stats. 1989 71st Leg. Sess. Ch. 678, effective September 1, 1989; Stats. 1991 72nd Leg. Sess. Ch. 539, effective September 1, 1991; Stats. 1993 73rd Leg. Sess. Ch. 459, effective September 1, 1993; Stats. 1995 74th Leg. Sess. Ch. 76, effective September 1, 1995; Stats. 2011 82nd Leg. Sess. Ch. 1317, effective September 1, 2011; am. Acts 2015, 84th Leg., ch. 1 (S.B. 219), § 3.0992, effective April 2, 2015.

Sec. 431.245. Definition or Standard of Identity, Quality, or Fill of Container.

(a) A definition or standard of identity, quality, or fill of container of the federal Act is a definition or standard of identity, quality, or fill of container in this chapter, except as modified by department rules.

(b) The executive commissioner by rule may establish definitions and standards of identity, quality, and fill of container for a food if:
 (1) a federal regulation does not apply to the food; and
 (2) the executive commissioner determines that adopting the rules will promote honest and fair dealing in the interest of consumers.
(c) A temporary permit granted for interstate shipment of an experimental pack of food that varies from the requirements of federal definitions and standards of identity is automatically effective in this state under the conditions of the permit.
(d) The department may issue additional permits if the department determines that:
 (1) it is necessary for the completion of an otherwise adequate investigation; and
 (2) the interests of consumers are safeguarded.
(e) A permit issued under Subsection (d) is subject to the terms and conditions of department rules.

Leg.H. Stats. 1989 71st Leg. Sess. Ch. 678, effective September 1, 1989; am. Acts 2015, 84th Leg., ch. 1 (S.B. 219), § 3.0993, effective April 2, 2015.

Sec. 431.246. Removal of Adulterated Item from Stores.
The executive commissioner shall adopt rules that provide a system for removing adulterated items from the shelves of a grocery store or other retail establishment selling those items.

Leg.H. Stats. 1989 71st Leg. Sess. Ch. 678, effective September 1, 1989; am. Acts 2015, 84th Leg., ch. 1 (S.B. 219), § 3.0994, effective April 2, 2015.

Sec. 431.247. Delegation of Powers or Duties.
(a) [Repealed by Acts 2015, 84th Leg., ch. 1 (S.B. 219), § 3.1639(75), effective April 2, 2015.]
(b) A health authority may, unless otherwise restricted by law, delegate a power or duty imposed on the health authority by this chapter to an employee of the local health department, the local health unit, or the public health district in which the health authority serves.

Leg.H. Stats. 1989 71st Leg. Sess. Ch. 678, effective September 1, 1989; am. Acts 2015, 84th Leg., ch. 1 (S.B. 219), § 3.1639(75), effective April 2, 2015.

Sec. 431.2471. Texas Department of Health Peace Officers [Repealed].
Repealed by Acts 2015, 84th Leg., ch. 1 (S.B. 219), § 3.1639(75), effective April 2, 2015.

Sec. 431.248. Memorandum of Understanding with Department of Agriculture.
(a) The department and the Department of Agriculture shall execute a memorandum of understanding that:
 (1) requires each agency to disclose to the other agency any positive results of testing conducted by the agency for pesticides in food; and
 (2) specifies how each agency will assist the other in performing its duties regarding pesticides in food.
(b) The executive commissioner and the Department of Agriculture shall adopt the memorandum of understanding as a rule.
(c) The department and the Department of Agriculture shall request the federal Food and Drug Administration to join in execution of the memorandum of understanding.

Leg.H. Stats. 1989 71st Leg. Sess. Ch. 678, effective September 1, 1989; am. Acts 2015, 84th Leg., ch. 1 (S.B. 219), § 3.0995, effective April 2, 2015.

Sec. 431.249. Dissemination of Information.
(a) The department may publish reports summarizing the judgments, decrees, and court orders rendered under this chapter, including the nature and disposition of the charge.
(b) The department may disseminate information regarding a food, drug, device, or cosmetic in a situation that the department determines to involve imminent danger to health or gross deception of consumers.
(c) This section does not prohibit the department from collecting, reporting, and illustrating the results of an investigation by the department.

Leg.H. Stats. 1989 71st Leg. Sess. Ch. 678, effective September 1, 1989; am. Acts 2015, 84th Leg., ch. 1 (S.B. 219), § 3.0996, effective April 2, 2015.

Sec. 431.250. Public Comments for Federal Grants and Contracts.
(a) The department shall annually solicit comments from interested persons regarding the grants and contracts the department has requested from or entered into with the United States Food and Drug Administration for implementing the federal Act and its amendments, including the Food Safety Modernization Act (21 U.S.C. Section 2201 et seq.).
(b) The department shall solicit comments by posting on the department's Internet website a detailed description of and providing notice to interested persons of each grant and contract described by Subsection (a) requested or entered into during the previous year. The description and notice must include the benefits to this state, the department, the regulated community, and the public.
(c) The department shall respond to questions and comments about a grant or contract described by Subsection (a) to the best of the department's knowledge. If an interested person requests that the department decline to receive future federal funding from the grant or contract, the department shall consider the request and determine whether the benefits of the grant or contract outweigh the person's concerns.

Leg.H. Stats. 2015, 84th Leg., 749 (H.B. 1846), § 1, effective September 1, 2015.

SUBCHAPTER L. DEVICE DISTRIBUTORS AND MANUFACTURERS

Sec. 431.271. Definitions.

In this subchapter:

(1) "Distributor" means a person who furthers the marketing of a finished domestic or imported device from the original place of manufacture to the person who makes final delivery or sale to the ultimate consumer or user. The term includes an importer or an own-label distributor. The term does not include a person who repackages a finished device or who otherwise changes the container, wrapper, or labelling of the finished device or the finished device package.

(2) "Finished device" means a device, or any accessory to a device, that is suitable for use, without regard to whether it is packaged or labelled for commercial distribution.

(3) "Importer" means any person who initially distributes a device imported into the United States.

(4) "Manufacturer" means a person who manufactures, fabricates, assembles, or processes a finished device. The term includes a person who repackages or relabels a finished device. The term does not include a person who only distributes a finished device.

(5) "Place of business" means each location at which a finished device is manufactured or held for distribution.

Leg.H. Stats. 1993 73rd Leg. Sess. Ch. 440, effective September 1, 1993; Stats. 1995 74th Leg. Sess. Ch. 1047, effective September 1, 1995.

Sec. 431.272. License Required; Minimum Standards.

(a) Except as provided by Section 431.273, a person may not operate as a distributor or manufacturer of devices in this state unless the person has a license from the department for each place of business.

(b) A distributor or manufacturer of devices in this state must comply with the minimum requirements specified in the federal Act and in this chapter.

Leg.H. Stats. 1993, 73rd Leg., ch. 440 (S.B. 564), § 3, effective September 1, 1993; am. Acts 1995, 74th Leg., ch. 1047 (H.B. 2550), § 2, effective September 1, 1995; am. Acts 2015, 84th Leg., ch. SB219 (S.B. 219), § 3.0997, effective April 2, 2015.

Sec. 431.273. Exemption from Licensing.

(a) A person is exempt from licensing under this subchapter if the person engages only in the following types of device distribution:

(1) intracompany sales;

(2) distribution from a place of business located outside of this state; or

(3) the sale, purchase, or trade of a distressed or reconditioned device by a salvage broker or a salvage operator licensed under Chapter 432 (Texas Food, Drug, Device, and Cosmetic Salvage Act).

(a-1) A person is exempt from licensing under this subchapter if the person holds a registration certificate issued under Chapter 266, Occupations Code, and engages only in conduct within the scope of that registration.

(b) An exemption from the licensing requirements under this section does not constitute an exemption from the other provisions of this chapter or the rules adopted by the executive commissioner to administer and enforce this chapter.

Leg.H. Stats. 1993, 73rd Leg., ch. 440 (S.B. 564), § 3, effective September 1, 1993; am. Acts 1995, 74th Leg., ch. 1047 (H.B. 2550), § 3, effective September 1, 1995; am. Acts 2013, 83rd Leg., ch. 302 (H.B. 1395), § 1, effective September 1, 2013; am. Acts 2015, 84th Leg., ch. SB219 (S.B. 219), § 3.0998, effective April 2, 2015.

Sec. 431.274. License Application.

(a) A person applying for a license under this subchapter shall provide, at a minimum, the following information on a license application form furnished by the department:

(1) the name under which the business is conducted;

(2) the address of each place of business that is licensed;

(3) the name and residence address of:

(A) the proprietor, if the business is a proprietorship;

(B) all partners, if the business is a partnership; or

(C) all principals, if the business is an association;

(4) the date and place of incorporation if the business is a corporation;

(5) the names and residence addresses of the individuals in an administrative capacity showing:

(A) the managing proprietor, if the business is a proprietorship;

(B) the managing partner, if the business is a partnership;

(C) the officers and directors, if the business is a corporation; or

(D) the persons in a managerial capacity, if the business is an association; and

(6) the residence address of an individual in charge of each place of business.

(b) The license application must be signed, verified, and completed in a manner described in department rules.

(c) A person applying for a license under this subchapter must pay a licensing fee for each place of business.

Leg.H. Stats. 1993 73rd Leg. Sess. Ch. 440, effective September 1, 1993; am. Acts 2015, 84th Leg., ch. SB219 (S.B. 219), § 3.0999, effective April 2, 2015.

Sec. 431.275. Advisory Committee. [Repealed]

Repealed by Acts 2015, 84th Leg., ch. SB219 (S.B. 219), § 3.1639(75), effective April 2, 2015.

Sec. 431.276. Fees.

(a) The department shall collect fees for:
   (1) a license that is filed or renewed;
   (2) a license that is amended, including notification of a change of location of a licensed place of business required under Section 431.278, a change of the name of an association or corporation, or a change in the ownership of the licensee; and
   (3) an inspection performed to enforce this subchapter and rules adopted under this subchapter.
(b) The department may charge fees every two years.
(c) The executive commissioner by rule shall set the fees in amounts that allow the department to recover the biennial expenditures of state funds by the department in:
   (1) reviewing and acting on a license or renewal license;
   (2) amending a license;
   (3) inspecting a licensed facility; and
   (4) implementing and enforcing this subchapter, including a rule or order adopted or a license issued under this subchapter.
(d) At least half of the licensing fees collected shall be used to inspect an applicant or licensed place of business.
(e) Fees collected under this section shall be deposited to the credit of the food and drug registration fee account of the general revenue fund and may be appropriated to the department only to carry out this chapter.

Leg.H. Stats. 1993 73rd Leg. Sess. Ch. 440, effective September 1, 1993; am. Acts 2015, 84th Leg., ch. SB219 (S.B. 219), § 3.1000, effective April 2, 2015.

Sec. 431.277. License Expiration. [Repealed]

Repealed by Acts 2015, 84th Leg., ch. SB219 (S.B. 219), § 3.1639(75), effective April 2, 2015.

Sec. 431.278. Change of Location of Place of Business.

(a) Not fewer than 30 days in advance of the change, the licensee shall notify the department in writing of the licensee's intent to change the location of a licensed place of business. The notice shall include the address of the new location and the name and residence address of the individual in charge of the business at the new location.
(b) Not later than the 10th day after the date of completion of the change of location, the licensee shall notify the department in writing to verify the change of location, the address of the new location, and the name and residence address of the individual in charge of the business at the new address.
(c) Notice is adequate if the licensee provides the intent and verification notices to the department by certified mail, return receipt requested, mailed to the central office of the department.

Leg.H. Stats. 1993 73rd Leg. Sess. Ch. 440, effective September 1, 1993; am. Acts 2015, 84th Leg., ch. SB219 (S.B. 219), § 3.1001, effective April 2, 2015.

Sec. 431.279. Refusal to License; Suspension or Revocation of License.

(a) The department may refuse an application or may suspend or revoke a license if the applicant or licensee:
   (1) has been convicted of a felony or misdemeanor that involves moral turpitude;
   (2) is an association, partnership, or corporation and the managing officer has been convicted of a felony or misdemeanor that involves moral turpitude;
   (3) has been convicted in a state or federal court of the illegal use, sale, or transportation of intoxicating liquors, narcotic drugs, barbiturates, amphetamines, desoxyephedrine, their compounds or derivatives, or any other dangerous or habit-forming drugs;
   (4) is an association, partnership, or corporation and the managing officer has been convicted in a state or federal court of the illegal use, sale, or transportation of intoxicating liquors, narcotic drugs, barbiturates, amphetamines, desoxyephedrine, their compounds or derivatives, or any other dangerous or habit-forming drugs; or
   (5) has not complied with this chapter or the rules implementing this chapter.
(b) The department may refuse an application for a license or may suspend or revoke a license if the department determines from evidence presented during a hearing that the applicant or licensee:
   (1) has violated Section 431.021(l)(3), relating to the counterfeiting of a drug or the sale or holding for sale of a counterfeit drug;
   (2) has violated Chapter 481 (Texas Controlled Substances Act) or 483 (Dangerous Drugs); or
   (3) has violated the rules of the public safety director of the Department of Public Safety, including being responsible for a significant discrepancy in the records that state law requires the applicant or licensee to maintain.
(c) The refusal to license an applicant or the suspension or revocation of a license by the department and the appeal from that action are governed by the department's formal hearing procedures and the procedures for a contested case hearing under Chapter 2001, Government Code.

Leg.H. Stats. 1993 73rd Leg. Sess. Ch. 440, effective September 1, 1993; Acts 1995, 74th Leg., ch. 76 (S.B. 959), effective September 1, 1995; am. Acts 2015, 84th Leg., ch. SB219 (S.B. 219), § 3.1002, effective April 2, 2015.

Ts FD&C Act

SUBCHAPTER M. DRUG DONATION PROGRAM

Sec. 431.321. Definitions.

(a) "Charitable medical clinic" means a clinic, including a licensed pharmacy that is a community pharmaceutical access program provider, that provides medical care or drugs without charge or for a substantially reduced charge, complies with the insurance requirements of Chapter 84, Civil Practice and Remedies Code, and is exempt from federal income tax under Section 501(a) of the Internal Revenue Code of 1986 by being listed as an exempt organization in Section 501(c)(3) or 501(c)(4) of the code and is operated exclusively for the promotion of social welfare by being primarily engaged in promoting the common good and general welfare of the people in a community.

(b) "Seller" means a person, other than a charitable drug donor, as defined in Chapter 82, Civil Practice and Remedies Code.

(c) "Manufacturer" means a person, other than a charitable drug donor, as defined in Chapter 82, Civil Practice and Remedies Code.

(d) "Charitable drug donor" means a licensed convalescent or nursing home or related institution, licensed hospice, hospital, physician, pharmacy, or a pharmaceutical seller or manufacturer that donates drugs pursuant to a qualified patient assistance program, that donates drugs to a charitable medical clinic.

(d-1) In this subchapter, "community pharmaceutical access program" means a program offered by a licensed pharmacy under which the pharmacy assists financially disadvantaged persons to access prescription drugs at no charge or at a substantially reduced charge.

(e) In this subchapter, "patient assistance program" means a qualified program offered by a pharmaceutical manufacturer under which the manufacturer provides drugs to financially disadvantaged persons at no charge or at a substantially reduced cost. The term does not include the provision of a drug as part of a clinical trial.

Leg.H. Stats. 2001 77th Leg. Sess. Ch. 1138, effective January 1, 2001; Stats 2007, 80th Leg. Sess. Ch. 820, effective June 15, 2007.

Sec. 431.322. Donation of Unused Drugs to Charitable Medical Clinic.

(a) A charitable drug donor may donate certain unused prescription drugs to a charitable medical clinic, and a charitable clinic may accept, dispense, or administer the donated drugs in accordance with this subchapter.

(b) A seller or manufacturer of a drug may not donate drugs to a charitable medical clinic except pursuant to a qualified patient assistance program. A seller or manufacturer of a drug that donates drugs through a qualified patient assistance program shall be considered a charitable drug donor.

(c) The charitable drug donor shall use appropriate safeguards established by department rule to ensure that the drugs are not compromised or illegally diverted while being stored or transported to the charitable medical clinic.

(d) The charitable medical clinic may not accept the donated drugs unless:

(1) the charitable drug donor certifies that the drugs have been properly stored while in the possession of the donor or of the person for whom the drugs were originally dispensed;

(2) the charitable drug donor provides the clinic with a verifiable address and telephone number; and

(3) the person transferring possession of the drugs presents the charitable medical clinic with photographic identification.

Leg.H. Stats. Acts 2001, 77th Leg., ch. 1138 (H.B. 2729), § 1, effective January 1, 2002; am. Acts 2015, 84th Leg., ch. SB219 (S.B. 219), § 3.1003, effective April 2, 2015.

Sec. 431.323. Circumstances Under Which Donated Drugs May Be Accepted and Dispensed.

(a) A charitable medical clinic may accept and dispense or administer donated drugs only in accordance with this subchapter.

(b) The donated drugs must be drugs that require a prescription. A donated drug may not be a controlled substance under Chapter 481.

(c) The donated drugs must be approved by the federal Food and Drug Administration and:

(1) be sealed in the manufacturer's unopened original tamper-evident packaging and either:

(A) individually packaged; or

(B) packaged in unit-dose packaging;

(2) be oral or parenteral medication in sealed single-dose containers approved by the federal Food and Drug Administration;

(3) be topical or inhalant drugs in sealed units-of-use containers approved by the federal Food and Drug Administration; or

(4) be parenteral medication in sealed multiple-dose containers approved by the federal Food and Drug Administration from which no doses have been withdrawn; and

(5) must not be the subject of a mandatory recall by a state or federal agency or a voluntary recall by a drug seller or manufacturer.

(d) The charitable medical clinic may dispense or administer the donated drugs only:

(1) before the expiration date or within the recommended shelf life of the donated drugs, as applicable; and

(2) after a licensed pharmacist has determined that the drugs are of an acceptable integrity.

(e) The donated drugs may be accepted and dispensed or administered by the charitable medical clinic only in accordance with department rules.

Leg.H. Stats. 2001, 77th Leg., ch. 1138 (H.B. 2729), § 1, effective January 1, 2002; am. Acts 2015, 84th Leg., ch. SB219 (S.B. 219), § 3.1004, effective April 2, 2015.

Sec. 431.324. Rules.

The executive commissioner shall adopt rules to implement this subchapter that are designed to protect the public health and safety.

Leg.H. Stats. 2001 77th Leg. Sess. Ch. 1138, effective January 1, 2002 ; am. Acts 2015, 84th Leg., ch. SB219 (S.B. 219), § 3.1005, effective April 2, 2015.

Sec. 431.325. Limitation on Liability.

(a) Charitable drug donors, charitable medical clinics, and their employees are not liable for harm caused by the accepting, dispensing, or administering of drugs donated in strict compliance with this subchapter unless the harm is caused by:

   (i)   willful or wanton acts of negligence;

   (ii)   conscious indifference or reckless disregard for the safety of others; or

   (iii) intentional conduct.

(b) This section does not limit, or in any way affect or diminish, the liability of a drug seller or manufacturer pursuant to Chapter 82, Civil Practice and Remedies Code.

(c) This section shall not apply where harm results from the failure to fully and completely comply with the requirements of this subchapter.

(d) This section shall not apply to a charitable medical clinic that fails to comply with the insurance provisions of Chapter 84, Civil Practice and Remedies Code.

Leg.H. Stats. 2001 77th Leg. Sess. Ch. 1138, effective January 1, 2002.

Ts FD&C Act

SUBCHAPTER N. WHOLESALE DISTRIBUTORS OF PRESCRIPTION DRUGS

Sec. 431.401. Definitions.

In this subchapter:

(1) "Authentication" means to affirmatively verify before any wholesale distribution of a prescription drug occurs that each transaction listed on the pedigree for the drug has occurred.

(2) "Authorized distributor of record" means a distributor with whom a manufacturer has established an ongoing relationship to distribute the manufacturer's products in accordance with Section 431.4011.

(3) "Pharmacy warehouse" means a location for which a person holds a wholesale drug distribution license under this subchapter, that serves as a central warehouse for drugs or devices, and from which intracompany sales or transfers of drugs or devices are made to a group of pharmacies under common ownership and control.

(3-a) "Co-licensed product partner" means one of two or more parties that have the right to engage in the manufacturing or marketing of a prescription drug consistent with the United States Food and Drug Administration's regulations and guidances implementing the Prescription Drug Marketing Act of 1987 (Pub. L. No. 100-293).

(3-b) "Drop shipment" means the sale of a prescription drug to a wholesale distributor by the manufacturer of the prescription drug, or by the manufacturer's co-licensed product partner, third-party logistics provider, or exclusive distributor, in which:

    (A) the wholesale distributor takes title but not physical possession of the prescription drug;

    (B) the wholesale distributor invoices the pharmacy, pharmacy warehouse, or other person authorized by law to dispense or administer the drug to a patient; and

    (C) the pharmacy, pharmacy warehouse, or other authorized person receives delivery of the prescription drug directly from the manufacturer or the manufacturer's third-party logistics provider or exclusive distributor.

(4) "Logistics provider" means a person that receives prescription drugs only from the original manufacturer, delivers the prescription drugs at the direction of that manufacturer, and does not purchase, sell, trade, or take title to any prescription drug.

(4-a) "Manufacturer" means a person licensed or approved by the United States Food and Drug Administration to engage in the manufacture of drugs or devices, consistent with the federal agency's definition of "manufacturer" under the agency's regulations and guidances implementing the Prescription Drug Marketing Act of 1987 (Pub. L. No. 100-293). The term does not include a pharmacist engaged in compounding that is done within the practice of pharmacy and pursuant to a prescription drug order or initiative from a practitioner for a patient or prepackaging that is done in accordance with Section 562.154, Occupations Code.

(4-b) "Manufacturer's exclusive distributor" means a person who holds a wholesale distributor license under this subchapter, who contracts with a manufacturer to provide or coordinate warehousing, distribution, or other services on behalf of the manufacturer, and who takes title to, but does not have general responsibility to direct the sale or disposition of, the manufacturer's prescription drug. A manufacturer's exclusive distributor must be an authorized distributor of record to be considered part of the normal distribution channel.

(5) "Normal distribution channel" means a chain of custody for a prescription drug, either directly or by drop shipment, from the manufacturer of the prescription drug, the manufacturer to the manufacturer's co-licensed product partner, the manufacturer to the manufacturer's third-party logistics provider, or the manufacturer to the manufacturer's exclusive distributor, to:

    (A) a pharmacy to:

        (i) a patient; or

        (ii) another designated person authorized by law to dispense or administer the drug to a patient;

    (B) an authorized distributor of record to:

        (i) a pharmacy to a patient; or

        (ii) another designated person authorized by law to dispense or administer the drug to a patient;

    (C) an authorized distributor of record to an wholesale distributor licensed under this chapter to another designated person authorized by law to administer the drug to a patient;

    (D) an authorized distributor of record to a pharmacy warehouse to the pharmacy warehouse's intracompany pharmacy;

    (E) a pharmacy warehouse to the pharmacy warehouse's intracompany pharmacy or another designated person authorized by law to dispense or administer the drug to a patient;

    (F) a person authorized by law to prescribe a prescription drug that

    by law may be administered only under the supervision of the prescriber; or

    (G) an authorized distributor of record to one other authorized distributor of record to a licensed practitioner for office use.

(6) "Pedigree" means a document or electronic file containing information that records each wholesale distribution of a prescription drug, from sale by a manufacturer, through acquisition and sale by any wholesale distributor or repackager, until final sale to a pharmacy or other person dispensing or administering the prescription drug.

(7) "Place of business" means each location at which a drug for wholesale distribution is located.

(8) "Prescription drug" has the meaning assigned by 21 C.F.R. Section 203.3.

(9) "Repackage" means repackaging or otherwise changing the container, wrapper, or labeling of a drug to further the distribution of a prescription drug. The term does not include repackaging by a pharmacist to dispense a drug to a patient.

(10) "Repackager" means a person who engages in repackaging.

(10-a) "Third-party logistics provider" means a person who holds a wholesale distributor license under this subchapter, who contracts with a prescription drug manufacturer to provide or coordinate warehousing, distribution, or other services on behalf of the manufacturer, and who does not take title to the prescription drug or have general responsibility to direct the prescription drug's sale or disposition. A third-party logistics provider must be an authorized distributor of record to be considered part of the normal distribution channel.

(11) "Wholesale distribution" means distribution of prescription drugs to a person other than a consumer or patient. The term does not include:

(A) intracompany sales of prescription drugs, which means transactions or transfers of prescription drugs between a division, subsidiary, parent, or affiliated or related company that is under common ownership and control, or any transaction or transfer between co-license holders of a co-licensed product;

(B) the sale, purchase, distribution, trade, or transfer of prescription drugs or the offer to sell, purchase, distribute, trade, or transfer a prescription drug for emergency medical reasons;

(C) the distribution of prescription drug samples by a representative of a manufacturer;

(D) the return of drugs by a hospital, health care entity, or charitable institution in accordance with 21 C.F.R. Section 203.23;

(E) the sale of reasonable quantities by a retail pharmacy of a prescription drug to a licensed practitioner for office use;

(F) the sale, purchase, or trade of a drug, an offer to sell, purchase, or trade a drug, or the dispensing of a drug under a prescription;

(G) the sale, transfer, merger, or consolidation of all or part of the business of a pharmacy from or with another pharmacy, whether accomplished as a purchase and sale of stock or business assets;

(H) the sale, purchase, or trade of a drug, or the offer to sell, purchase, or trade a drug, for emergency medical reasons, including a transfer of a prescription drug by a retail pharmacy to another retail pharmacy to alleviate a temporary shortage;

(I) the delivery of, or offer to deliver, a prescription drug by a common carrier solely in the common carrier's usual course of business of transporting prescription drugs, if the common carrier does not store, warehouse, or take legal ownership of the prescription drug; or

(J) the sale or transfer from a retail pharmacy or pharmacy warehouse of expired, damaged, returned, or recalled prescription drugs to the original manufacturer or to a third-party returns processor.

(12) "Wholesale distributor" means a person engaged in the wholesale distribution of prescription drugs, including a manufacturer, repackager, own-label distributor, private-label distributor, jobber, broker, manufacturer warehouse, distributor warehouse, or other warehouse, manufacturer's exclusive distributor, authorized distributor of record, drug wholesaler or distributor, independent wholesale drug trader, specialty wholesale distributor, third-party logistics provider, retail pharmacy that conducts wholesale distribution, and pharmacy warehouse that conducts wholesale distribution.

Leg.H. Stats. 2005 79th Leg. Sess. Ch. 282, effective March 1, 2006; Stats 2007, 80th Leg. Sess. Ch. 980, effective September 1, 2007; Stats. 2009 81st Leg. Sess. Ch. 1384, effective June 19, 2009.

Sec. 431.4011. Ongoing Relationship.

In this subchapter, "ongoing relationship" means an association that exists when a manufacturer and distributor enter into a written agreement under which the distributor is authorized to distribute the manufacturer's products for a period of time or for a number of shipments. If the distributor is not authorized to distribute the manufacturer's entire product line, the agreement must identify the specific drug products that the distributor is authorized to distribute.

Leg.H. Stats. 2005 79th Leg. Sess., Ch. 282(H.B. 164), § 3(g), effective March 1, 2006.

Sec. 431.4012. Applicability of Subchapter.

This subchapter applies only to the wholesale distribution of prescription drugs.

Leg.H. Stats. 2005 79th Leg. Sess., Ch. 282 (H.B. 164), § 3 (g), effective March 1, 2006.

Sec. 431.402. License Required.

(a) A person may not engage in wholesale distribution of prescription drugs in this state unless the person holds a wholesale drug distribution license under this subchapter for each place of business.

(b) A license issued under this subchapter expires on the second anniversary of the date of issuance.

Leg.H. Stats. 2005 79th Leg. Sess., Ch. 282 (H.B. 164), § 3 (g), effective March 1, 2006.

Sec. 431.403. Exemption from Licensing.

(a) A person who engages in wholesale distribution of prescription drugs in this state for use in humans is exempt from this subchapter if the person is exempt under:

(1) the Prescription Drug Marketing Act of 1987(21 U.S.C. Section 353(c)(3)(B));

(2) the regulations adopted by the secretary to administer and enforce that Act; or

(3) the interpretations of that Act set out in the compliance policy manual of the United States Food and Drug Administration.

(b) An exemption from the licensing requirements under this section does not constitute an exemption from the other provisions of this chapter or the rules adopted under this chapter to administer and enforce the other provisions of this chapter.

Leg.H. Stats. 2005 79th Leg. Sess., Ch. 282 (H.B. 164), § 3 (g), effective March 1, 2006.

Sec. 431.4031. Exemption from Certain Provisions for Certain Wholesale Distributors.

(a) A wholesale distributor that distributes prescription drugs that are medical gases or a wholesale distributor that is a manufacturer or a third-party logistics provider on behalf of a manufacturer is exempt from Sections 431.404(a)(5) and (6), (b), and (c), 431.4045(2), 431.405, 431.407, and 431.408.

(b) A state agency or a political subdivision of this state that distributes prescription drugs using federal or state funding to nonprofit health care facilities or local mental health or mental retardation authorities for distribution to a pharmacy, practitioner, or patient is exempt from Sections 431.405(b), 431.407, 431.408, 431.412, and 431.413.

(c) The executive commissioner by rule may exempt specific purchases of prescription drugs by state agencies and political subdivisions of this state if the executive commissioner determines that the requirements of this subchapter would result in a substantial cost to the state or a political subdivision of the state.

Leg.H. Stats. 2005, 79th Leg., ch. 282 (H.B. 164), § 3(g), effective March 1, 2006; am. Acts 2007, 80th Leg., ch. 980 (S.B. 943), § 4, effective September 1, 2007; am. Acts 2009, 81st Leg., ch. 1384 (S.B. 1645), § 4, effective June 19, 2009; am. Acts 2015, 84th Leg., ch. SB219 (S.B. 219), § 3.1006, effective April 2, 2015.

Sec. 431.404. License Application.

(a) An applicant for a license under this subchapter must submit an application to the department on the form prescribed by the department. The application must contain:
  (1) the name, full business address, and telephone number of the applicant;
  (2) all trade or business names under which the business is conducted;
  (3) the address, telephone number, and name of a contact person for each of the applicant's places of business;
  (4) the type of business entity and:
    (A) if the business is a sole proprietorship, the name of the proprietor;
    (B) if the business is a partnership, the name of the partnership and each of the partners; or
    (C) if the business is a corporation, the name of the corporation, the place of incorporation, and the name and title of each corporate officer and director;
  (5) the name and telephone number of, and any information necessary to complete a criminal history record check on, a designated representative of each place of business; and
  (6) a list of all licenses and permits issued to the applicant by any other state under which the applicant is permitted to purchase or possess prescription drugs.
(b) Each person listed in Subsection (a)(5) shall provide the following to the department:
  (1) the person's places of residence for the past seven years;
  (2) the person's date and place of birth;
  (3) the person's occupations, positions of employment, and offices held during the past seven years;
  (4) the business name and address of any business, corporation, or other organization in which the person held an office under Subdivision (3) or in which the person conducted an occupation or held a position of employment;
  (5) a statement of whether during the preceding seven years the person was the subject of a proceeding to revoke a license or a criminal proceeding and the nature and disposition of the proceeding;
  (6) a statement of whether during the preceding seven years the person has been enjoined, either temporarily or permanently, by a court from violating any federal or state law regulating the possession, control, or distribution of prescription drugs, including the details concerning the event;
  (7) a written description of any involvement by the person as an officer or director with any business, including any investments, other than the ownership of stock in a publicly traded company or mutual fund during the past seven years, that manufactured, administered, prescribed, distributed, or stored pharmaceutical products and any lawsuits in which the businesses were named as a party;
  (8) a description of any misdemeanor or felony offense for which the person, as an adult, was found guilty, regardless of whether adjudication of guilt was withheld or whether the person pled guilty or nolo contendere;
  (9) a description of any criminal conviction of the person under appeal, a copy of the notice of appeal for that criminal offense, and a copy of the final written order of an appeal not later than the 15th day after the date of the appeal's disposition; and
  (10) a photograph of the person taken not earlier than 180 days before the date the application was submitted.
(c) The information submitted under Subsection (b) must be attested to under oath.
(d) An applicant or license holder shall submit to the department any change in or correction to the information required under this section in the form and manner prescribed by department rule.

Leg.H. Stats. 2005, 79th Leg., ch. 282 (H.B. 164), § 3(g), effective March 1, 2006; am. Acts 2007, 80th Leg., ch. 980 (S.B. 943), § 5, effective September 1, 2007; am. Acts 2015, 84th Leg., ch. SB219 (S.B. 219), § 3.1007, effective April 2, 2015.

Sec. 431.4045. Inspection Required.

The department may not issue a wholesale distributor license to an applicant under this subchapter unless the department:
  (1) conducts a physical inspection of the place of business at the address provided by the applicant under Section 431.404 or determines that an inspection is unnecessary after thoroughly evaluating the information in the application, the compliance history of the applicant and the applicant's principals, and the risk of counterfeiting in the applicant's product; and
  (2) determines that the designated representative of the place of business meets the qualifications required by Section 431.405.

Leg.H. Stats. 2007, 80th Leg. Sess. Ch. 980, effective September 1, 2007.

Sec. 431.405. Qualifications for License.

(a) The department may not issue a wholesale distributor license to an applicant without considering the minimum federal information and related qualification requirements published in federal regulations at 21 C.F.R. Part 205, including:
  (1) factors in reviewing the qualifications of persons who engage in wholesale distribution, 21 C.F.R. Section 205.6;
  (2) appropriate education and experience for personnel employed in wholesale distribution, 21 C.F.R. Section 205.7; and
  (3) the storage and handling of prescription drugs and the establishment and maintenance of prescription drug distribution records, 21 C.F.R. Section 205.50.

(b) In addition to meeting the minimum federal requirements as provided by Subsection (a), to qualify for the issuance or renewal of a wholesale distributor license under this subchapter, the designated representative of an applicant or license holder must:
  (1) be at least 21 years of age;
  (2) have been employed full-time for at least three years by a pharmacy or a wholesale distributor in a capacity related to the dispensing or distributing of prescription drugs, including recordkeeping for the dispensing or distributing of prescription drugs;
  (3) be employed by the applicant full-time in a managerial-level position;
  (4) be actively involved in and aware of the actual daily operation of the wholesale distributor;
  (5) be physically present at the applicant's place of business during regular business hours, except when the absence of the designated representative is authorized, including sick leave and vacation leave;
  (6) serve as a designated representative for only one applicant at any one time, except in a circumstance, as the department determines reasonable, in which more than one licensed wholesale distributor is colocated in the same place of business and the wholesale distributors are members of an affiliated group, as defined by Section 1504, Internal Revenue Code of 1986;
  (7) not have been convicted of a violation of any federal, state, or local laws relating to wholesale or retail prescription drug distribution or the distribution of controlled substances; and
  (8) not have been convicted of a felony under a federal, state, or local law.

Leg.H. Stats. 2005 79th Leg. Sess. Ch. 282, effective March 1, 2006; Stats 2007, 80th Leg. Sess. Ch. 980, effective September 1, 2007.

Sec. 431.406. Effect of Operation in Other Jurisdictions; Reports.

(a) A person who engages in the wholesale distribution of drugs outside this state may engage in the wholesale distribution of drugs in this state if the person holds a license issued by the department.
(b) The department may accept reports from authorities in other jurisdictions to determine the extent of compliance with this subchapter and the minimum standards adopted under this subchapter.
(c) The department may issue a license to a person who engages in the wholesale distribution of drugs outside this state to engage in the wholesale distribution of drugs in this state if, after an examination of the reports of the person's compliance history and current compliance record, the department determines that the person is in compliance with this subchapter and the rules adopted under this subchapter.
(d) The department shall consider each license application and any related documents or reports filed by or in connection with a person who wishes to engage in wholesale distribution of drugs in this state on an individual basis.

Leg.H. Stats. 2005 79th Leg. Sess., Ch. 282 (H.B. 164), § 3 (g), effective March 1, 2006.

Sec. 431.407. Criminal History Record Information.

The department shall submit to the Department of Public Safety the fingerprints provided by a person with an initial or a renewal license application to obtain the person's criminal history record information and may forward the fingerprints to the Federal Bureau of Investigation for a federal criminal history check.

Leg.H. Stats. 2005 79th Leg. Sess., Ch. 282 (H.B. 164), § 3 (g), effective March 1, 2006.

Sec. 431.408. Bond.

(a) A wholesale distributor applying for or renewing a license shall submit payable to this state a bond or other equivalent security acceptable to the department, including an irrevocable letter of credit or a deposit in a trust account or financial institution, in the amount of $100,000 payable to this state.
(a-1) A pharmacy warehouse that is not engaged in wholesale distribution is exempt from the bond requirement under Subsection (a).
(b) The bond or equivalent security submitted under Subsection (a) shall secure payment of any fines or penalties imposed by the department or imposed in connection with an enforcement action by the attorney general, any fees or other enforcement costs, including attorney's fees payable to the attorney general, and any other fees and costs incurred by this state related to that license holder, that are authorized under the laws of this state and that the license holder fails to pay before the 30th day after the date a fine, penalty, fee, or cost is assessed.
(c) The department or this state may make a claim against a bond or security submitted under Subsection (a) before the first anniversary of the date a license expires or is revoked under this subchapter.
(c-1) A single bond is sufficient to cover all places of business operated by a wholesale distributor in this state.
(d) The department shall deposit the bonds and equivalent securities received under this section in a separate account.

Leg.H. Stats. 2005 79th Leg. Sess. Ch. 282, effective March 1, 2006; Stats 2007, 80th Leg. Sess. Ch. 980, effective September 1, 2007.

Sec. 431.409. Fees.

(a) The department shall collect fees for:
  (1) a license that is filed or renewed;
  (2) a license that is amended, including a notification of a change in the location of a licensed place of business required under Section 431.410; and
  (3) an inspection performed in enforcing this subchapter and rules adopted under this subchapter.
(b) The executive commissioner by rule shall set the fees in amounts that are reasonable and necessary and allow the department to recover the biennial expenditures of state funds by the department in:

    (1)   reviewing and acting on a license;

    (2)   amending and renewing a license;

    (3)   inspecting a licensed facility; and

    (4)   implementing and enforcing this subchapter,

including a rule or order adopted or a license issued under this subchapter.

  (c)   Fees collected under this section shall be deposited to the credit of the food and drug registration fee account of the general revenue fund and appropriated to the department to carry out this chapter.

Leg.H. Stats. 2005, 79th Leg., ch. 282 (H.B. 164), § 3(g), effective March 1, 2006; am. Acts 2015, 84th Leg., ch. SB219 (S.B. 219), § 3.1008, effective April 2, 2015.

Sec. 431.4095. Renewal Notification; Change or Renewal.

  (a)   Before the expiration of a license issued under this subchapter, the department shall send to each licensed wholesale distributor a form containing a copy of the information the distributor provided to the department under Section 431.404.

  (b)   Not later than the 30th day after the date the wholesale distributor receives the form under Subsection (a), the wholesale distributor shall identify and state under oath to the department any change in or correction to the information.

Leg.H. Stats. 2007, 80th Leg. Sess. Ch. 980, effective September 1, 2007.

Sec. 431.410. Change of Location of Place of Business.

  (a)   Not fewer than 30 days in advance of the change, the license holder shall notify the department in writing of the license holder's intent to change the location of a licensed place of business.

  (b)   The notice shall include the address of the new location and the name and residence address of the individual in charge of the business at the new location.

  (c)   Not more than 10 days after the completion of the change of location, the license holder shall notify the department in writing to confirm the completion of the change of location and provide verification of the information previously provided or correct and confirm any information that has changed since providing the notice of intent.

  (d)   The notice and confirmation required by this section are considered adequate if the license holder sends the notices by certified mail, return receipt requested, to the central office of the department or submits the notices electronically through the state electronic Internet portal.

Leg.H. Stats. 2005 79th Leg. Sess., Ch. 282 (H.B. 164), § 3 (g), effective March 1, 2006; Stats. 2011 82nd Leg. Sess. Ch. 973, effective June 17, 2011.

Sec. 431.411. Minimum Restrictions on Transactions.

  (a)   A wholesale distributor shall receive prescription drug returns or exchanges from a pharmacy or pharmacy warehouse in accordance with the terms and conditions of the agreement between the wholesale distributor and the pharmacy or pharmacy warehouse. An expired, damaged, recalled, or otherwise nonsalable prescription drug that is returned to the wholesale distributor may be distributed by the wholesale distributor only to either the original manufacturer or a third-party returns processor. The returns or exchanges, salable or otherwise, received by the wholesale distributor as provided by this subsection, including any redistribution of returns or exchanges by the wholesale distributor, are not subject to the pedigree requirement under Section 431.412 if the returns or exchanges are exempt from pedigree under:

    (1)   Section 4 , Prescription Drug Marketing Act of 1987 (21 U.S.C. Section 353(c)(3)(B));

    (2)   the regulations adopted by the secretary to administer and enforce that Act; or

    (3)   the interpretations of that Act set out in the compliance policy guide of the United States Food and Drug Administration.

  (a-1)Each wholesale distributor and pharmacy shall administer the process of drug returns and exchanges to ensure that the process is secure and does not permit the entry of adulterated or counterfeit drugs into the distribution channel.

  (a-2)Notwithstanding any provision of state or federal law to the contrary, a person that has not otherwise been required to obtain a wholesale license under this subchapter and that is a pharmacy engaging in the sale or transfer of expired, damaged, returned, or recalled prescription drugs to the originating wholesale distributor or manufacturer and pursuant to federal statute, rules, and regulations, including the United States Food and Drug Administration's applicable guidances implementing the Prescription Drug Marketing Act of 1987 (Pub. L. No. 100-293), is exempt from wholesale licensure requirements under this subchapter.

  (b)   A manufacturer or wholesale distributor may distribute prescription drugs only to a person licensed by the appropriate state licensing authorities or authorized by federal law to receive the drug. Before furnishing prescription drugs to a person not known to the manufacturer or wholesale distributor, the manufacturer or wholesale distributor must verify that the person is legally authorized by the appropriate state licensing authority to receive the prescription drugs or authorized by federal law to receive the drugs.

  (c)   Except as otherwise provided by this subsection, prescription drugs distributed by a manufacturer or wholesale distributor may be delivered only to the premises listed on the license. A manufacturer or wholesale distributor may distribute prescription drugs to an authorized person or agent of that person at the premises of the manufacturer or wholesale distributor if:

    (1)   the identity and authorization of the recipient is properly established; and

    (2)   delivery is made only to meet the immediate needs of a particular patient of the authorized person.

  (d)   Prescription drugs may be distributed to a hospital pharmacy receiving area if a pharmacist or an authorized receiving person signs, at the time of delivery, a receipt showing the type and quantity of the prescription drug received. Any discrepancy between the receipt and the type and quantity of the prescription drug actually received shall be reported to the delivering manufacturer or wholesale distributor not later than the next business day after the date of delivery to the pharmacy receiving area.

Leg.H. Stats. 2005, 79th Leg., ch. 282 (H.B. 164), § 3(g), effective March 1, 2006; am. Acts 2007, 80th Leg., ch. 980 (S.B. 943), § 10, effective September 1, 2007; am. Acts 2015, 84th Leg., ch. SB219 (S.B. 219), § 3.1009, effective April 2, 2015.

Sec. 431.412. Pedigree Required.

(a) A person who is engaged in the wholesale distribution of a prescription drug, including a repackager but excluding the original manufacturer, shall provide a pedigree for each prescription drug for human consumption that leaves or at any time has left the normal distribution channel and is sold, traded, or transferred to any other person.

(b) [Repealed by Acts 2007, 80th Leg., ch. 980 (S.B. 943), § 14, effective September 1, 2007.]

(b-1)A retail pharmacy or pharmacy warehouse is required to comply with this section only if the pharmacy or warehouse engages in the wholesale distribution of a prescription drug.

(c) [Repealed by Acts 2007, 80th Leg., ch. 980 (S.B. 943), § 14, effective September 1, 2007.]

(d) A person who is engaged in the wholesale distribution of a prescription drug, including a repackager, but excluding the original manufacturer of the finished form of a prescription drug, and who is in possession of a pedigree for a prescription drug must verify before distributing the prescription drug that each transaction listed on the pedigree has occurred.

Leg.H. Stats. 2005 79th Leg. Sess. Ch. 282, effective March 1, 2006; Stats 2007, 80th Leg. Sess. Ch. 980, effective September 1, 2007.

Sec. 431.413. Pedigree Contents.

(a) A pedigree must include all necessary identifying information concerning each sale in the product's chain of distribution from the manufacturer, through acquisition and sale by a wholesale distributor or repackager, until final sale to a pharmacy or other person dispensing or administering the drug. At a minimum, the chain of distribution information must include:
   (1) the name, address, telephone number, and, if available, the e-mail address of each person who owns the prescription drug and each wholesale distributor of the prescription drug;
   (2) the name and address of each location from which the product was shipped, if different from the owner's name and address;
   (3) the transaction dates; and
   (4) certification that each recipient has authenticated the pedigree.

(b) The pedigree must include, at a minimum, the:
   (1) name of the prescription drug;
   (2) dosage form and strength of the prescription drug;
   (3) size of the container;
   (4) number of containers;
   (5) lot number of the prescription drug; and
   (6) name of the manufacturer of the finished dosage form.

(c) Each pedigree statement must be:
   (1) maintained by the purchaser and the wholesale distributor for at least three years; and
   (2) available for inspection and photocopying not later than the second business day after the date a request is submitted by the department or a peace officer in this state.

(d) The executive commissioner shall adopt rules to implement this section.

(e) [Expired pursuant to Acts 2005, 79th Leg., ch. 282 (H.B. 164), § 3(g), effective January 1, 2009.]

(e-1)If, after consulting with manufacturers, distributors, and pharmacies responsible for the sale and distribution of prescription drugs in this state, the department determines that electronic track and trace pedigree technology is universally available across the entire prescription pharmaceutical supply chain, the department shall establish a targeted implementation date for electronic track and trace pedigree technology. After the department has established a targeted implementation date, the department may revise the date. The targeted implementation date may not be earlier than July 1, 2010.

(f) [Expired pursuant to Acts 2005, 79th Leg., ch. 282 (H.B. 164), § 3(g), effective January 1, 2009.]

Leg.H. Stats. 2005, 79th Leg., ch. 282 (H.B. 164), § 3(g), effective March 1, 2006; am. Acts 2007, 80th Leg., ch. 980 (S.B. 943), §§ 11, 14, effective September 1, 2007; am. Acts 2015, 84th Leg., ch. SB219 (S.B. 219), § 3.1010, effective April 2, 2015.

Sec. 431.414. Refusal to License; Suspension or Revocation of License.

(a) The department may refuse an application for a license or may suspend or revoke a license if the applicant or license holder:
   (1) has been convicted of a felony or misdemeanor that involves moral turpitude;
   (2) is an association, partnership, or corporation and the managing officer has been convicted of a felony or misdemeanor that involves moral turpitude;
   (3) has been convicted in a state or federal court of the illegal use, sale, or transportation of intoxicating liquors, narcotic drugs, barbiturates, amphetamines, desoxyephedrine, their compounds or derivatives, or any other dangerous or habit-forming drugs;
   (4) is an association, partnership, or corporation and the managing officer has been convicted in a state or federal court of the illegal use, sale, or transportation of intoxicating liquors, narcotic drugs, barbiturates, amphetamines, desoxyephedrine, their compounds or derivatives, or any other dangerous or habit-forming drugs;
   (5) has not complied with this subchapter or the rules implementing this subchapter;
   (6) has violated Section 431.021(l)(3), relating to the counterfeiting of a drug or the sale or holding for sale of a counterfeit drug;
   (7) has violated Chapter 481 or 483; or
   (8) has violated the rules of the public safety director of the Department of Public Safety, including being responsible for a significant discrepancy in the records that state law requires the applicant or license holder to maintain.

(a-1)The department may suspend or revoke a license if the license holder no longer meets the qualifications for obtaining a license under Section 431.405.

(b) The executive commissioner by rule shall establish minimum standards required for the issuance or renewal of a license under this subchapter.

(c) The department shall deny a license application that is incomplete, contains false, misleading, or incorrect information, or contains information that cannot be verified by the department.

(d) The refusal to license an applicant or the suspension or revocation of a license by the department and the appeal from that action are governed by the procedures for a contested case hearing under Chapter 2001, Government Code.

Leg.H. Stats. 2005, 79th Leg., ch. 282 (H.B. 164), § 3(g), effective March 1, 2006; am. Acts 2007, 80th Leg., ch. 980 (S.B. 943), § 13, effective September 1, 2007; am. Acts 2015, 84th Leg., ch. SB219 (S.B. 219), § 3.1011, effective April 2, 2015.

Sec. 431.415. Order to Cease Distribution.

(a) The department shall issue an order requiring a person, including a manufacturer, distributor, or retailer of a prescription drug, to immediately cease distribution of the drug if the department determines there is a reasonable probability that:

  (1) a wholesale distributor has;

    (A) violated this subchapter;

    (B) falsified a pedigree; or

    (C) sold, distributed, transferred, manufactured, repackaged, handled, or held a counterfeit prescription drug intended for human use that could cause serious adverse health consequences or death; and

  (2) other procedures would result in unreasonable delay.

(b) An order under Subsection (a) must provide the person subject to the order with an opportunity for an informal hearing on the actions required by the order to be held not later than the 10th day after the date of issuance of the order.

(c) If, after providing an opportunity for a hearing, the department determines that inadequate grounds exist to support the actions required by the order, the commissioner shall vacate the order.

Leg.H. Stats. 2005, 79th Leg., ch. 282 (H.B. 164), § 3(g), effective March 1, 2006; am. Acts 2015, 84th Leg., ch. SB219 (S.B. 219), § 3.1012, effective April 2, 2015.

SUBCHAPTER O. PRESCRIPTION DRUG DONATION PILOT PROGRAM

Sec. 431.451. Definitions.

In this subchapter:
  (1) "Charitable drug donor" means:
    (A) a licensed convalescent or nursing facility or related institution, licensed hospice, hospital, physician, or pharmacy;
    (B) a pharmaceutical seller or manufacturer that donates drugs under a qualified patient assistance program; or
    (C) the licensed health care professional responsible for administration of drugs in a penal institution, as defined by Section 1.07, Penal Code, in this state.
  (2) "Charitable medical clinic" has the meaning assigned by Section 431.321.
  (3) "Manufacturer" means a person, other than a charitable drug donor, as defined in Chapter 82, Civil Practice and Remedies Code.
  (4) "Patient assistance program" means a qualified program offered by a pharmaceutical manufacturer under which the manufacturer provides drugs to financially disadvantaged persons at no charge or at a substantially reduced cost. The term does not include the provision of a drug as part of a clinical trial.
  (5) "Pilot program" means the prescription drug donation pilot program under this subchapter.
  (6) "Prescription drug" has the meaning assigned by Section 551.003, Occupations Code.
  (7) "Seller" means a person, other than a charitable drug donor, as defined in Chapter 82, Civil Practice and Remedies Code.

  Leg.H. Stats. 2015, 84th Leg., 1191 (S.B. 1243), § 1, effective September 1, 2015.

Sec. 431.452. Establishment of Pilot Program.

  (a) The department shall establish a pilot program for donation and redistribution of prescription drugs under this subchapter.
  (b) The department shall conduct the pilot program in one or more municipalities with a population of more than 500,000 but less than one million.

  Leg.H. Stats. 2015, 84th Leg., 1191 (S.B. 1243), § 1, effective September 1, 2015.

Sec. 431.453. Donation of Unused Drugs.

  (a) A charitable drug donor may donate certain unused prescription drugs to the department for the pilot program under this subchapter.
  (b) A seller or manufacturer of a drug that donates drugs through a qualified patient assistance program is considered a charitable drug donor.
  (c) A charitable drug donor shall use appropriate safeguards established by department rule to ensure that the drugs are not compromised or illegally diverted while being stored or transported.
  (d) The department may not accept the donated drugs unless:
    (1) the charitable drug donor certifies that the drugs have been properly stored while in the possession of the donor or of the person for whom the drugs were originally dispensed;
    (2) the charitable drug donor provides the department with a verifiable address and telephone number; and
    (3) the person transferring possession of the drugs presents photographic identification.

  Leg.H. Stats. 2015, 84th Leg., 1191 (S.B. 1243), § 1, effective September 1, 2015.

Sec. 431.454. Circumstances Under Which Donated Drugs May Be Accepted.

  (a) The department may accept donated drugs only in accordance with this subchapter.
  (b) The donated drugs must be:
    (1) prescription drugs; and
    (2) approved by the federal Food and Drug Administration and:
      (A) sealed in unopened tamper-evident unit dose packaging;
      (B) be oral medication in sealed single-dose containers approved by the federal Food and Drug Administration; or
      (C) be topical or inhalant drugs in sealed units-of-use containers approved by the federal Food and Drug Administration.
  (c) A drug packaged in single unit doses may be accepted and distributed if the outside packaging is opened but the single unit dose packaging is unopened.
  (d) Donated drugs may not:
    (1) be the subject of a mandatory recall by a state or federal agency or a voluntary recall by a drug seller or manufacturer;
    (2) be adulterated or misbranded;
    (3) be a controlled substance under Chapter 481;
    (4) be a parenteral or injectable medication;
    (5) require refrigeration;
    (6) expire less than 60 days after the date of the donation; or
    (7) be a drug that is prohibited from being dispensed to a patient other than a patient who is registered with the drug's manufacturer in accordance with federal Food and Drug Administration requirements.
  (e) The department may distribute the donated drugs only after a licensed pharmacist has determined that the drugs are of an acceptable integrity.
  (f) The department may not charge a fee for the drugs donated under the pilot program other than a nominal handling fee to defray the costs incurred in implementing the pilot program under this subchapter.
  (g) The department may not resell the drugs donated under the pilot program.

Leg.H. Stats. 2015, 84th Leg., 1191 (S.B. 1243), § 1, effective September 1, 2015.

Sec. 431.455. Prescription, Provision, and Administration of Donated Drugs.

(a) The donated drugs may be accepted and provided or administered to patients only by:

    (1) a charitable medical clinic;

    (2) a physician's office using the drugs for patients who receive assistance from the medical assistance program under Chapter 32, Human Resources Code, or for other indigent health care; or

    (3) a licensed health care professional responsible for administration of drugs in a penal institution, as defined by Section 1.07, Penal Code, in this state.

(b) A prescription drug provided or administered to a patient under the pilot program must be prescribed by a practitioner for use by that patient.

(c) The clinic or physician providing or administering the drug may charge a nominal handling fee in an amount prescribed by department rule.

(d) A clinic, physician, or other licensed health care professional receiving donated drugs may not resell the drugs.

Leg.H. Stats. 2015, 84th Leg., 1191 (S.B. 1243), § 1, effective September 1, 2015.

Sec. 431.456. Central Drug Repository.

The department shall establish a location to centrally store drugs donated under this subchapter for distribution to qualifying recipients.

Leg.H. Stats. 2015, 84th Leg., 1191 (S.B. 1243), § 1, effective September 1, 2015.

Sec. 431.457. Database of Donated Drugs.

The department shall establish and maintain an electronic database in which:

    (1) the department shall list the name and quantity of each drug donated to the department under the pilot program; and

    (2) a charitable medical clinic, physician, or other licensed health care professional may search for and request donated drugs.

Leg.H. Stats. 2015, 84th Leg., 1191 (S.B. 1243), § 1, effective September 1, 2015.

Sec. 431.458. Rules.

This subchapter shall be governed by department rules that are designed to protect the public health and safety, including:

    (1) the maximum handling fee that may be imposed by a clinic or physician providing or administering a donated drug to a patient;

    (2) provisions for maintenance of the database of donated drugs; and

    (3) any necessary forms for the administration of the pilot program.

Leg.H. Stats. 2015, 84th Leg., 1191 (S.B. 1243), § 1, effective September 1, 2015.

Sec. 431.459. Limitation on Civil and Criminal Liability.

(a) Charitable drug donors, manufacturers and sellers of donated drugs, charitable medical clinics, physicians, penal institutions, and their employees acting in good faith in providing or administering prescription drugs under the pilot program are not civilly or criminally liable or subject to professional disciplinary action for harm caused by providing or administering drugs donated under this subchapter unless the harm is caused by:

    (1) wilful or wanton acts of negligence;

    (2) conscious indifference or reckless disregard for the safety of others; or

    (3) intentional conduct.

(b) This section does not apply if the harm results from the failure to comply with the requirements of this subchapter.

(c) This section does not apply to a charitable medical clinic that fails to comply with the insurance provisions of Chapter 84, Civil Practice and Remedies Code.

Leg.H. Stats. 2015, 84th Leg., 1191 (S.B. 1243), § 1, effective September 1, 2015.

Sec. 431.460. Reports to Legislature.

Not later than January 1 of each odd-numbered year, the department shall report to the legislature on the results of the pilot program. The report must include:

    (1) the pilot program's efficacy in expanding access to prescription medications;

    (2) any cost savings to the state or local governments resulting from or projected to result from the pilot program;

    (3) an evaluation of the pilot program's database and system of distribution;

    (4) any health and safety issues posed by providing or administering donated drugs;

    (5) recommendations on improvements to the pilot program; and

    (6) an evaluation of potential expansion of the pilot program.

Leg.H. Stats. 2015, 84th Leg., 1191 (S.B. 1243), § 1, effective September 1, 2015.

Tx FD&C Act

OVER-THE-COUNTER SALES OF EPHEDRINE, PSEUDOEPHEDRINE, AND NORPSEUDOEPHEDRINE
HEALTH AND SAFETY CODE, CHAPTER 486

Table of Contents

SUBCHAPTER A. GENERAL PROVISIONS

SUBCHAPTER B. OVER-THE-COUNTER SALES

SUBCHAPTER C. ADMINISTRATIVE PENALTY

OVER-THE-COUNTER SALES OF EPHEDRINE, PSEUDOEPHEDRINE, AND NORPSEUDOEPHEDRINE
HEALTH AND SAFETY CODE, CHAPTER 486

SUBCHAPTER A. GENERAL PROVISIONS

Sec. 486.001. Definitions.
(a) In this chapter:
   (1) "Commissioner" means the commissioner of state health services.
   (2) [Repealed by Acts 2015, 84th Leg., ch. 1 (S.B. 219), § 3.1639(95), effective April 2, 2015.]
   (3) "Department" means the Department of State Health Services.
   (4) "Ephedrine," "pseudoephedrine," and "norpseudoephedrine" mean any compound, mixture, or preparation containing any detectable amount of that substance, including its salts, optical isomers, and salts of optical isomers. The term does not include any compound, mixture, or preparation that is in liquid, liquid capsule, or liquid gel capsule form.
   (4-a) "Executive commissioner" means the executive commissioner of the Health and Human Services Commission.
   (5) "Sale" includes a conveyance, exchange, barter, or trade.
   (6) "Real-time electronic logging system" means a system intended to be used by law enforcement agencies and pharmacies or other business establishments that:
      (A) is installed, operated, and maintained free of any one-time or recurring charge to the business establishment or to the state;
      (B) is able to communicate in real time with similar systems operated in other states and similar systems containing information submitted by more than one state;
      (C) complies with the security policy of the Criminal Justice Information Services division of the Federal Bureau of Investigation;
      (D) complies with information exchange standards adopted by the National Information Exchange Model;
      (E) uses a mechanism to prevent the completion of a sale of a product containing ephedrine, pseudoephedrine, or norpseudoephedrine that would violate state or federal law regarding the purchase of a product containing those substances; and
      (F) is equipped with an override of the mechanism described in Paragraph (E) that:
         (i) may be activated by an employee of a business establishment; and
         (ii) creates a record of each activation of the override.
(b) A term that is used in this chapter but is not defined by Subsection (a) has the meaning assigned by Section 481.002.

Leg.H. Stats. 2005 79th Leg. Sess., Ch. 282 (H.B. 164), § 9, effective August 1, 2005; Stats. 2011 82nd Leg. Sess. Ch. 742, effective September 1, 2011; am. Acts 2015, 84th Leg., ch. 1 (S.B. 219), § 3.1250, 3.1639(95), effective April 2, 2015.

Sec. 486.002. Applicability.
This chapter does not apply to the sale of any product dispensed or delivered by a pharmacist according to a prescription issued by a practitioner for a valid medical purpose and in the course of professional practice.

Leg.H. Stats. 2005 79th Leg. Sess., Ch. 282 (H.B. 164), § 9, effective August 1, 2005.

Sec. 486.003. Rules.
The executive commissioner shall adopt rules necessary to implement and enforce this chapter.

Leg.H. Stats. 2005 79th Leg. Sess., Ch. 282 (H.B. 164), § 9, effective August 1, 2005; am. Acts 2015, 84th Leg., ch. 1 (S.B. 219), § 3.1251, effective April 2, 2015.

Sec. 486.004. Fees.
(a) The department shall collect fees for an inspection performed in enforcing this chapter and rules adopted under this chapter.
(b) The executive commissioner by rule shall set the fees in amounts that allow the department to recover the biennial expenditures of state funds by the department in implementing and enforcing this chapter.
(c) Fees collected under this section shall be deposited to the credit of a special account in the general revenue fund and appropriated to the department to implement and enforce this chapter.

Leg.H. Stats. 2005, 79th Leg., ch. 282 (H.B. 164), § 9, effective August 1, 2005; am. Acts 2015, 84th Leg., ch. 1 (S.B. 219), § 3.1252, effective April 2, 2015; am. Acts 2017, 85th Leg., ch. 967 (S.B. 2065), § 4.001, effective September 1, 2017.

OTC Sales

12/1/2019

Sec. 486.005. Statewide Application and Uniformity.

(a) To ensure uniform and equitable implementation and enforcement throughout this state, this chapter constitutes the whole field of regulation regarding over-the-counter sales of products that contain ephedrine, pseudoephedrine, or norpseudoephedrine.

(b) This chapter preempts and supersedes a local ordinance, rule, or regulation adopted by a political subdivision of this state pertaining to over-the-counter sales of products that contain ephedrine, pseudoephedrine, or norpseudoephedrine.

(c) This section does not preclude a political subdivision from imposing administrative sanctions on the holder of a business or professional license or permit issued by the political subdivision who engages in conduct that violates this chapter.

Leg.H. Stats. 2005 79th Leg. Sess., Ch. 282 (H.B. 164), § 9, effective August 1, 2005.

SUBCHAPTER B. OVER-THE-COUNTER SALES

Sec. 486.011. Sales by Pharmacies.

A business establishment that operates a pharmacy licensed by the Texas State Board of Pharmacy may engage in over-the-counter sales of ephedrine, pseudoephedrine, and norpseudoephedrine.

Leg.H. Stats. 2005 79th Leg. Sess., Ch. 282 (H.B. 164), § 9, effective August 1, 2005.

Sec. 486.012. Sales by Establishments Other Than Pharmacies; Certificate of Authority [Repealed].

Repealed by Acts 2017, 85th Leg., ch. 967 (S.B. 2065), § 4.003, effective September 1, 2017.

Sec. 486.013. Restriction of Access to Ephedrine, Pseudoephedrine, and Norpseudoephedrine.

A business establishment that engages in over-the-counter sales of products containing ephedrine, pseudoephedrine, or norpseudoephedrine shall:

(1) if the establishment operates a pharmacy licensed by the Texas State Board of Pharmacy, maintain those products:
    (A) behind the pharmacy counter; or
    (B) in a locked case within 30 feet and in a direct line of sight from a pharmacy counter staffed by an employee of the establishment; or
(2) if the establishment does not operate a pharmacy licensed by the Texas State Board of Pharmacy, maintain those products:
    (A) behind a sales counter; or

(B) in a locked case within 30 feet and in a direct line of sight from a sales counter continuously staffed by an employee of the establishment.

Leg.H. Stats. 2005 79th Leg. Sess., Ch. 282 (H.B. 164), § 9, effective August 1, 2005.

Sec. 486.014. Prerequisites to and Restrictions on Sale.

(a) Before completing an over-the-counter sale of a product containing ephedrine, pseudoephedrine, or norpseudoephedrine, a business establishment that engages in those sales shall:
    (1) require the person making the purchase to:
        (A) display a driver's license or other form of government-issued identification containing the person's photograph and indicating that the person is 16 years of age or older; and
        (B) sign for the purchase;
    (2) make a record of the sale, including the name and date of birth of the person making the purchase, the address of the purchaser, the date and time of the purchase, the type of identification displayed by the person and the identification number, and the item and number of grams purchased; and
    (3) transmit the record of sale as required by Section 486.0141.
(b) A business establishment may not sell to a person who makes over-the-counter purchases of one or more products containing ephedrine, pseudoephedrine, or norpseudoephedrine:
    (1) within any calendar day, more than 3.6 grams of ephedrine, pseudoephedrine, norpseudoephedrine, or a combination of those substances; and
    (2) within any 30-day period, more than nine grams of ephedrine, pseudoephedrine, norpseudoephedrine, or a combination of those substances.

Leg.H. Stats. 2005 79th Leg. Sess., Ch. 282 (H.B. 164), § 9, effective August 1, 2005; Stats. 2011 82nd Leg. Sess. Ch. 742, effective September 1, 2011.

Sec. 486.0141. Transmission of Sales Information to Real-Time Electronic Logging System.

(a) Before completing an over-the-counter sale of a product containing ephedrine, pseudoephedrine, or norpseudoephedrine, a business establishment that engages in those sales shall transmit the information in the record made under Section 486.014(a)(2) to a real-time electronic logging system.
(b) Except as provided by Subsection (c), a business establishment may not complete an over-the-counter sale of a product containing ephedrine, pseudoephedrine, or norpseudoephedrine if the real-time electronic logging system returns a report that the completion of the sale would result in the person obtaining an amount of ephedrine, pseudoephedrine, norpseudoephedrine, or a combination of those substances greater than the amount described by Section 486.014(b), regardless of whether all or some of the products previously obtained by the buyer were sold at the establishment or another business establishment.
(c) An employee of a business establishment may complete a sale prohibited by Subsection (b) by using the override mechanism described by Section 486.001(a)(6)(F) only if the employee has a reasonable fear of imminent bodily injury or death from the person attempting to obtain ephedrine, pseudoephedrine, or norpseudoephedrine.
(d) On request of the Department of Public Safety, the administrators of a real-time electronic logging system shall make available to the department a copy of each record of an over-the-counter sale of a product containing ephedrine, pseudoephedrine, or norpseudoephedrine that is submitted by a business establishment located in this state.

Leg.H. Stats. 2011, 82nd Leg. Sess. Ch. 742, effective September 1, 2011.

OTC Sales

12/1/2019

Sec. 486.0142. Temporary Exemption.

(a) On application by a business establishment that operates a pharmacy and engages in over-the-counter sales of products containing ephedrine, pseudoephedrine, or norpseudoephedrine as authorized by Section 486.011, the Texas State Board of Pharmacy may grant that business establishment a temporary exemption, not to exceed 180 days, from the requirement of using a real-time electronic logging system under this chapter.

(b) On application by a business establishment that engages in over-the-counter sales of products containing ephedrine, pseudoephedrine, or norpseudoephedrine, the department may grant that business establishment a temporary exemption, not to exceed 180 days, from the requirement of using a real-time electronic logging system under this chapter

(c) A business establishment granted a temporary exemption under this section must keep records of sales in the same manner required under Section 486.0143 for a business establishment that experiences a mechanical or electronic failure of the real-time electronic logging system.

(d) An exemption granted under this section does not relieve a business establishment of any duty under this chapter other than the duty to use a real-time electronic logging system.

Leg.H. Stats. 2011, 82nd Leg., ch. 742 (H.B. 1137), § 3, effective September 1, 2011; am. Acts 2015, 84th Leg., ch. 1 (S.B. 219), § 3.1254, effective April 2, 2015; am. Acts 2017, 85th Leg., ch. 967 (S.B. 2065), § 4.002, effective September 1, 2017.

Sec. 486.0143. Written Log or Other Electronic Recordkeeping.

If a business establishment that engages in over-the-counter sales of a product containing ephedrine, pseudoephedrine, or norpseudoephedrine experiences a mechanical or electronic failure of the real-time electronic logging system, the business shall:

(1) maintain a written record or an electronic record made by any means that satisfies the requirements of Section 486.014(a)(2); and

(2) enter the information in the real-time electronic logging system as soon as practicable after the system becomes operational.

Leg.H. Stats. 2011, 82nd Leg. Sess. Ch. 742, effective September 1, 2011.

Sec. 486.0144. Online Portal.

The administrators of a real-time electronic logging system shall provide real-time access to the information in the system to the Department of Public Safety if the department executes a memorandum of understanding with the administrators.

Leg.H. Stats. 2011, 82nd Leg. Sess. Ch. 742, effective September 1, 2011.

Sec. 486.0145. Limitation on Civil Liability.

A person is not liable for an act done or omission made in compliance with the requirements of Section 486.014 or 486.0141.

Leg.H. Stats. 2011, 82nd Leg. Sess. Ch. 742, effective September 1, 2011.

Sec. 486.0146. Privacy Protections.

(a) The privacy protections provided an individual under 21 C.F.R. Section 1314.45 apply to information entered or stored in a real-time electronic logging system.

(b) A business establishment that engages in over-the-counter sales of a product containing ephedrine, pseudoephedrine, or norpseudoephedrine may disclose information entered or stored in a real-time electronic logging system only to the United States Drug Enforcement Administration and other federal, state, and local law enforcement agencies.

(c) A business establishment that engages in over-the-counter sales of a product containing ephedrine, pseudoephedrine, or norpseudoephedrine may not use information entered or stored in a real-time electronic logging system for any purpose other than for a disclosure authorized by Subsection (b) or to comply with the requirements of this chapter.

(d) Notwithstanding Subsection (c), a business establishment that engages in over-the-counter sales of a product containing ephedrine, pseudoephedrine, or norpseudoephedrine or an employee or agent of the business establishment is not civilly liable for the release of information entered or stored in a real-time electronic logging system unless the release constitutes negligence, recklessness, or wilful misconduct.

Leg.H. Stats. 2011, 82nd Leg. Sess. Ch. 742, effective September 1, 2011.

Sec. 486.015. Maintenance of Records.

(a) Except as provided by Subsection (b), a business establishment shall maintain each record made under Section 486.014(a)(2) until at least the second anniversary of the date the record is made and shall make each record available on request by the department or any local, state, or federal law enforcement agency, including the United States Drug Enforcement Administration.

(b) Subsection (a) does not apply to a business establishment that has used a real-time electronic logging system for longer than two years.

(c) A business establishment that has used a real-time electronic logging system for longer than two years shall destroy all paper records maintained under this section unless the destruction is otherwise prohibited by law.

Leg.H. Stats. 2005 79th Leg. Sess., Ch. 282 (H.B. 164), § 9, effective August 1, 2005; Stats. 2011 82nd Leg. Sess. Ch. 742, effective September 1, 2011.

SUBCHAPTER C. ADMINISTRATIVE PENALTY

Sec. 486.021. Imposition of Penalty.

The department may impose an administrative penalty on a person who violates this chapter.

Leg.H. Stats. 2005 79th Leg. Sess., Ch. 282 (H.B. 164), § 9, effective August 1, 2005.

Sec. 486.022. Amount of Penalty.

(a) The amount of the penalty may not exceed $1,000 for each violation, and each day a violation continues or occurs is a separate violation for purposes of imposing a penalty. The total amount of the penalty assessed for a violation continuing or occurring on separate days under this subsection may not exceed $20,000.

(b) The amount shall be based on:
   (1) the seriousness of the violation, including the nature, circumstances, extent, and gravity of the violation;
   (2) the threat to health or safety caused by the violation;
   (3) the history of previous violations;
   (4) the amount necessary to deter a future violation;
   (5) whether the violator demonstrated good faith, including when applicable whether the violator made good faith efforts to correct the violation; and
   (6) any other matter that justice may require.

Leg.H. Stats. 2005 79th Leg. Sess., Ch. 282 (H.B. 164), § 9, effective August 1, 2005.

Sec. 486.023. Report and Notice of Violation and Penalty.

(a) If the department initially determines that a violation occurred, the department shall give written notice of the report by certified mail to the person.

(b) The notice must:
   (1) include a brief summary of the alleged violation;
   (2) state the amount of the recommended penalty; and
   (3) inform the person of the person's right to a hearing on the occurrence of the violation, the amount of the penalty, or both.

Leg.H. Stats. 2005 79th Leg. Sess., Ch. 282 (H.B. 164), § 9, effective August 1, 2005.

Sec. 486.024. Penalty to be Paid or Hearing Requested.

(a) Before the 21st day after the date the person receives notice under Section 486.023, the person in writing may:
   (1) accept the determination and recommended penalty; or
   (2) make a request for a hearing on the occurrence of the violation, the amount of the penalty, or both.

(b) If the person accepts the determination and recommended penalty or if the person fails to respond to the notice, the department by order shall impose the penalty.

Leg.H. Stats. 2005 79th Leg. Sess., Ch. 282 (H.B. 164), § 9, effective August 1, 2005; am. Acts 2015, 84th Leg., ch. 1 (S.B. 219), § 3.1255, effective April 2, 2015.

Sec. 486.025. Hearing.

(a) If the person requests a hearing, the department shall refer the matter to the State Office of Administrative Hearings, which shall promptly set a hearing date, and the department shall give written notice of the time and place of the hearing to the person. An administrative law judge of the State Office of Administrative Hearings shall conduct the hearing.

(b) The administrative law judge shall make findings of fact and conclusions of law and promptly issue to the department a written proposal for a decision about the occurrence of the violation and the amount of a proposed penalty.

Leg.H. Stats. 2005 79th Leg. Sess., Ch. 282 (H.B. 164), § 9, effective August 1, 2005; am. Acts 2015, 84th Leg., ch. 1 (S.B. 219), § 3.1256, effective April 2, 2015.

Sec. 486.026. Decision.

(a) Based on the findings of fact, conclusions of law, and proposal for a decision, the department by order may:
   (1) find that a violation occurred and impose a penalty; or
   (2) find that a violation did not occur.

(b) The notice of the department's order under Subsection (a) that is sent to the person in the manner provided by Chapter 2001, Government Code, must include a statement of the right of the person to judicial review of the order.

Leg.H. Stats. 2005 79th Leg. Sess., Ch. 282 (H.B. 164), § 9, effective August 1, 2005; am. Acts 2015, 84th Leg., ch. 1 (S.B. 219), § 3.1257, effective April 2, 2015.

Sec. 486.027. Options Following Decision: Pay or Appeal.

Before the 31st day after the date the order under Section 486.026 that imposes an administrative penalty becomes final, the person shall:
   (1) pay the penalty; or

(2)   file a petition for judicial review of the order contesting the occurrence of the violation, the amount of the penalty, or both.

Leg.H. Stats. 2005 79th Leg. Sess., Ch. 282 (H.B. 164), § 9, effective August 1, 2005.

Sec. 486.028. Stay of Enforcement of Penalty.

(a)   Within the period prescribed by Section 486.027, a person who files a petition for judicial review may:
  (1)   stay enforcement of the penalty by:
    (A)   paying the amount of the penalty to the court for placement in an escrow account; or
    (B)   giving the court a supersedeas bond approved by the court that:
      (i)   is for the amount of the penalty; and
      (ii)   is effective until all judicial review of the order is final; or
  (2)   request the court to stay enforcement of the penalty by:
    (A)   filing with the court an affidavit of the person stating that the person is financially unable to pay the penalty and is financially unable to give the supersedeas bond; and
    (B)   sending a copy of the affidavit to the department by certified mail.

(b)   Following receipt of a copy of an affidavit under Subsection (a)(2), the department may file with the court, before the sixth day after the date of receipt, a contest to the affidavit. The court shall hold a hearing on the facts alleged in the affidavit as soon as practicable and shall stay the enforcement of the penalty on finding that the alleged facts are true. The person who files an affidavit has the burden of proving that the person is financially unable to pay the penalty or to give a supersedeas bond.

Leg.H. Stats. 2005 79th Leg. Sess., Ch. 282 (H.B. 164), § 9, effective August 1, 2005; am. Acts 2015, 84th Leg., ch. 1 (S.B. 219), § 3.1258, effective April 2, 2015.

Sec. 486.029. Collection of Penalty.

(a)   If the person does not pay the penalty and the enforcement of the penalty is not stayed, the penalty may be collected.
(b)   The attorney general may sue to collect the penalty.

Leg.H. Stats. 2005 79th Leg. Sess., Ch. 282 (H.B. 164), § 9, effective August 1, 2005.

Sec. 486.030. Decision by Court.

(a)   If the court sustains the finding that a violation occurred, the court may uphold or reduce the amount of the penalty and order the person to pay the full or reduced amount of the penalty.
(b)   If the court does not sustain the finding that a violation occurred, the court shall order that a penalty is not owed.

Leg.H. Stats. 2005 79th Leg. Sess., Ch. 282 (H.B. 164), § 9, effective August 1, 2005.

Sec. 486.031. Remittance of Penalty and Interest.

(a)   If the person paid the penalty and if the amount of the penalty is reduced or the penalty is not upheld by the court, the court shall order, when the court's judgment becomes final, that the appropriate amount plus accrued interest be remitted to the person before the 31st day after the date that the judgment of the court becomes final.
(b)   The interest accrues at the rate charged on loans to depository institutions by the New York Federal Reserve Bank.
(c)   The interest shall be paid for the period beginning on the date the penalty is paid and ending on the date the penalty is remitted.

Leg.H. Stats. 2005 79th Leg. Sess., Ch. 282 (H.B. 164), § 9, effective August 1, 2005.

Sec. 486.032. Release of Bond.

(a)   If the person gave a supersedeas bond and the penalty is not upheld by the court, the court shall order, when the court's judgment becomes final, the release of the bond.
(b)   If the person gave a supersedeas bond and the amount of the penalty is reduced, the court shall order the release of the bond after the person pays the reduced amount.

Leg.H. Stats. 2005 79th Leg. Sess., Ch. 282 (H.B. 164), § 9, effective August 1, 2005.

Sec. 486.033. Administrative Procedure.

A proceeding to impose the penalty under this subchapter is considered to be a contested case under Chapter 2001, Government Code.

Leg.H. Stats. 2005 79th Leg. Sess., Ch. 282 (H.B. 164), § 9, effective August 1, 2005.

OTC Sales

Table of Contents

PROCEDURES

ADDRESSES

WEB ADDRESSES

Proc./Forms

PROCEDURES

PHARMACISTS

Reporting a Theft or Significant Loss of Controlled Substances or Dangerous Drugs

A theft or loss of a significant amount of controlled substances and all dosage forms containing nalbuphine (*e.g.*, Nubain®) must be reported ***immediately upon discovery*** of the theft or loss. The following procedures should be followed.

Controlled Substances

(1)   Complete a DEA form 106 as directed and make four (4) copies.

(2)   Distribute the copies as follows:

Original and One (1) copy — mail to DEA Divisional Office

      Dallas Divisional Office *(For Texas zip codes other than Houston)*
          Drug Enforcement Administration
          10160 Technology Blvd., East
          Dallas, Texas 75220

      Houston Divisional Office *(For Texas zip codes other than Dallas)*
          Drug Enforcement Administration
          1433 West Loop South, Suite 600
          Houston, Texas 77027

      San Antonio District Office *(For central and western Texas)*
          Drug Enforcement Administration
          10127 Morocco, Suite 200
          San Antonio, Texas 78216

- One (1) copy — mail to TSBP at:
      Texas State Board of Pharmacy
      William P. Hobby Building, Suite 3-500
      333 Guadalupe Street
      Austin, Texas 78701

- One (1) copy — retain in the pharmacy's files for 2 years

*Note: Ambulatory surgical centers must also report any theft or loss of controlled substances to the Texas Department of State Health Services, Health Facility Licensing and Compliance Division, 1100 West 49th Street, Austin, Texas 78756.

Dangerous Drugs

(1)   Send a letter to the Board regarding the loss of dangerous drugs. Include in the letter the following information:

   (a)   name, address, and TSBP license number of the pharmacy;
   (b)   a list of the name(s) and quantities of dangerous drug(s) lost;
   (c)   a report of the circumstances of the loss; and
   (d)   date of the loss.

(2)   Distribute the copies as follows:

- Original copy — Mail to TSBP at:
      Texas State Board of Pharmacy
      William P. Hobby Building, Suite 3-500
      333 Guadalupe Street
      Austin, Texas 78701

- One (1) copy — retain in the pharmacy's files for 2 years

Proc./Forms

Reporting a Loss of Prescription Data from a Data Processing System

The pharmacist-in-charge of a Class A (Community) or Class C (Institutional) pharmacy that maintains prescription drug records in a data processing system shall report to the Board in writing any significant loss of information from the data processing system within 10 days of discovery of the loss.

   (1)   the notification should contain the following information:

      (a)   name, address, and TSBP license number of the pharmacy; and

      (b)   approximate number of records lost and/or dates covered by these records.

   (2)   Distribute the copies as follows:

- Original copy — Mail to TSBP at:

  Texas State Board of Pharmacy
  William P. Hobby Building, Suite 3-500
  333 Guadalupe Street
  Austin, Texas 78701

- One (1) copy — retain in the pharmacy's files for 2 years

Reporting Pharmacy Disasters, Accidents, and Emergencies

Any occurrence that may affect the strength, purity or labeling of drugs or devices must be ***immediately*** reported to the Board. This type of occurrence would include such disasters as fires, floods and hurricanes, which affect the pharmacy's drug stock. Specific requirements are contained in the Board Rule 291.3 titled *"Required Notifications."*

Distribution of Dangerous Drugs and Controlled Substances to Ambulances or EMS Units

A pharmacy may distribute dangerous drugs and if they have a valid (current) DPS and DEA registration, controlled substances to the following:

   (1)   hospitals;

   (2)   pharmacies;

   (3)   wholesalers, manufactures;

   (4)   practitioners (physicians, podiatrists, veterinaries, dentists, and therapeutic optometrists); and

   (5)   emergency medical service providers (EMSP).

Proc./Forms

Distribution of Controlled Substances and Dangerous Drugs to Registrants

Distributing Pharmacy

A pharmacy distributing controlled substances or dangerous drugs to another pharmacy (or doctor) must adhere to the following procedures.

Schedule II Controlled Substances

DEA Order Forms (DEA 222) must be used for distributing Schedule II controlled substances. The receiving registrant issues copy 1 (brown) and 2 (green) of the DEA order form to the distributing pharmacy. The distributing pharmacy must record the quantity of controlled substances distributed and the actual date of distribution on copy 1 (brown) and 2 (green). The distributing pharmacy must maintain copy 1 (brown) in their records and mail copy 2 (green) to the divisional office of the Drug Enforcement Administration by the end of the month during which the distribution occurred. For mailing addresses, see *State and Federal Agencies* in this section.

Schedule III-V Controlled Substances

Records for distribution must be maintained for Schedule III, IV or V controlled substances. These records (*e.g.*, invoices) must indicate the following information:*
(1) the actual date of distribution;
(2) name, strength, and quantity of the controlled substance distributed;
(3) name, address and DEA registration number of the distributing pharmacy; and
(4) name, address and DEA registration number of the pharmacy or practitioner to whom the controlled substances are distributed.
   Note: The distributing pharmacy must provide a copy of the record of distribution (invoice) to the receiving registrant.

Dangerous Drugs

Records of distribution must be maintained for dangerous drugs. These records (*e.g.*, invoices) must indicate the following information:*
(1) the actual date of distribution;
(2) name, strength, and quantity of the dangerous drug distributed;
(3) name and address of the distributing pharmacy; and
(4) name and address of the pharmacy or practitioner to whom the dangerous drugs are distributed.
   Note: The distributing pharmacy must provide a copy of the record of distribution (invoice) to the receiving pharmacy or doctor.

Maintenance of Records

All records must be maintained by the distributing pharmacy for a period of two years. Records of controlled substances listed in Schedule II must be maintained separately from all other records of the pharmacy. Records of controlled substances listed in Schedules III-V must be maintained separately from all other records of the pharmacy. If controlled substances, dangerous drugs, and/or non-prescription items are listed on the same record, the controlled substances must be asterisked, redlined, or in some other manner readily identifiable apart from all other items appearing on the record.

5% Rule — Controlled Substances

The total number of dosage units of controlled substances distributed by a pharmacy may not exceed 5% of all controlled substances distributed and dispensed by the pharmacy during each calendar year in which the pharmacy is registered. If at any time it does exceed 5%, the pharmacy is required to obtain an additional registration as a distributor. If at any time it does exceed 5%, the pharmacy is required to obtain an additional registration as a distributor from the DEA and Texas Department of State Health Services.

Proc./Forms

Excessive Purchases

When acting as a distributor (whether registered with DEA or not), the pharmacy must report any excessive purchases by a physician to the divisional office of the Drug Enforcement Administration.

Receiving Registrant

The registrant receiving the controlled substances must adhere to the following procedures.

Schedule II Controlled Substances

The receiving pharmacy must maintain copy 3 (blue) of all DEA order forms (DEA 222), including all copies of each unaccepted or defective order form and any attached statements or other documents. These forms must show the quantity of drugs received, the date the drug was received and the initials of the person responsible for the receipt of the Schedule II drugs.

Schedule III-V Controlled Substances

A copy of the distributing pharmacy's invoice for Schedule III, IV or V drugs must be maintained for two years. The receiving pharmacist, doctor, or other responsible individual must clearly initial and record the actual date of receipt of the drugs on the invoice.

Dangerous Drugs

A copy of the distributing pharmacy's invoice for dangerous drugs must be maintained for two years. The receiving pharmacist, doctor, or other responsible individual must clearly initial and record the actual date of receipt of the drugs on the invoice.

Maintenance of Records

All records must be maintained by the receiving pharmacy for a period of two years. Records of controlled substances listed in Schedule II must be maintained separately from all other records of the pharmacy. Records of controlled substances listed in Schedules III-V must be maintained separately from all other records of the pharmacy. If controlled substances, dangerous drugs, and/or nonprescription items are listed on the same record, the controlled substances must be asterisked, redlined, or in some other manner readily identifiable apart from all other items appearing on the record.

Although not required by law, the Board recommends that the distributing pharmacy have proof of delivery of controlled substances, *i.e.*, the signature of an authorized agent of the registrant receiving the controlled substances. If the pharmacy is distributing drugs to a doctor, the Board also recommends that the pharmacy have a signed order from the doctor, which indicates the doctor (not his/her agent) is requisitioning the controlled substances.

Since improperly documented distribution of controlled substances could indicate a source of diversion of the substances, the failure of a pharmacist to legally document the distribution of controlled substances may result in disciplinary action by the Board. In summary, the above procedures must be followed whenever a pharmacy distributes controlled substances to another registrant. A pharmacy cannot *loan* or *borrow* controlled substances.

How to Destroy Drugs

One of the most common questions received by the Board staff from pharmacists is *How do I destroy drugs?* The answer to this question may vary depending upon several factors: (1) whether the drugs are stock drugs in a pharmacy or drugs dispensed to a patient in a nursing home; (2) whether the stock drugs are dangerous drugs or controlled substances; and (3) whether the stock controlled drugs are in a Class A (Community) Pharmacy or a Class C (Institutional) Pharmacy.

The procedures for destroying drugs are described below. Please note that these procedures are divided into two main categories which relate to the type of drugs being destroyed: (1) dispensed drugs and (2) stock drugs.

Destruction of Dispensed Drugs

These procedures are set forth in Board Rule 303.1 and apply to drugs that have been: dispensed to patients in nursing homes and certain types of licensed health care facilities and institutions; and drugs previously dispensed to a patient and returned to the pharmacy by the patient or the patients agent. **A consultant pharmacist may not destroy controlled substances unless allowed to do so by federal laws or rules of the Drug Enforcement Administration.**

Destruction of dispensed drugs becomes necessary when drugs are discontinued, become outdated, or when nursing home patients are discharged from the nursing home or expire. These procedures do not apply to bulk or stock drugs belonging to a pharmacy or drugs that are supplied pursuant to a medication order to inpatients of a hospital by the hospitals pharmacy.

Drugs Dispensed to Patients in Healthcare Facilities or Institutions

(1) *Inventory of Drugs.* The drugs to be destroyed must be inventoried and such inventory verified by the consultant pharmacist. Controlled substances and dangerous drugs must be listed on separate forms. Each page of the inventory form must be consecutively numbered. The inventory must contain the following information:
- name and address of the facility or institution;
- name and pharmacist license number of the consultant pharmacist;
- date of destruction (if destroyed by the consultant pharmacist) or the date of packaging and sealing of the container (if destroyed by a waste disposal service);
- date the prescription was dispensed;
- unique identification number assigned to the prescription by the dispensing pharmacy;
- name of the dispensing pharmacy;
- name, strength, and quantity of the drug;
- signature of the consultant pharmacist who destroyed the drugs or who packaged and sealed the container for destruction by a waste disposal service;
- method of destruction; and
- signature of the witness(es).

(2) *Consultant Pharmacist.* A consultant pharmacist is defined as a pharmacist licensed in Texas in good standing with the Texas State Board of Pharmacy, who has a written agreement or contract with the nursing home (or other institution) specifying services, approximate time required and remuneration. A consultant pharmacist must have direct, immediate supervision of all pharmaceutical services within the nursing home or institution which concern the receiving and storing of drugs, and the destroying of dispensed drugs. A consultant pharmacist must maintain a permanent record of service and consultation at the nursing home or institution. Such record must be made available to any official witness who participates in the destruction of dangerous drugs or controlled substances in the nursing home or institution.

(3) *Authorized Witnesses.* The following persons may serve as official witnesses:
- a commissioned peace officer;
- an agent of the Texas State Board of Pharmacy;
- an authorized agent of the Texas Department of Human Services or Texas Department of State Health Services; or
- any two individuals working in the following capacities at the facility:
  - facility administrator;
  - director of nursing;
  - acting director of nursing; or
  - licensed nurse.

(4) *Drug Destruction.* The actual destruction of the dispensed drugs may be performed by the consultant pharmacist or by a waste disposal service.

Destruction by the Consultant Pharmacist.

(a) *Methods of Destruction.* In the presence of an authorized witness(es), drugs must be destroyed in a manner to render drugs unfit for human consumption and disposed of in compliance with all applicable state and federal requirements.

(b) *Destruction Site.* The drugs may be destroyed in the nursing home or off-site. If the actual destruction of the drugs is conducted at a location other than the nursing home or institution, the consultant pharmacist **AND** the authorized witness(es) must transport the drugs from the nursing home or institution to the alternative site.

Destruction by a Waste Disposal Service.

(a) *Waste Disposal Service.* The waste disposal service must be in compliance with applicable rules relating to waste disposal of the Texas Commission on Environmental Quality and United States Environmental Protection Agency (EPA).

(b) *Sealing Shipment Container.* In the presence of an authorized witness(es), the consultant pharmacist must seal the drugs container and place tamper resistant tape on the container so that any attempt to open the container will result in breaking of the tape. The consultant pharmacists signature must be placed over this tape seal.

Proc./Forms

    (c)   *Security of Shipment Container and Transfer to Waste Disposal Service.* The sealed container must be maintained in a secure area at the facility or institution until transferred to the waste disposal service by the consultant pharmacist, facility administrator, director of nursing, or acting director of nursing. A record of the transfer must be maintained which contains:

- date of the transfer;
- signature of the person who transferred the drugs to the waste disposal service;
- name and address of the waste disposal service; and
- signature of the employee of the waste disposal service who receives the container.

    (d)   *Proof of Destruction.* The waste disposal service must provide the facility with proof of destruction of the sealed container which contains the following information:

- date of destruction;
- location of the destruction; and
- method of destruction.

The proof of destruction from the waste disposal service must be attached to the inventory of drugs and maintained by the consultant pharmacist.

(5)   *Record Retention.* All required inventories and records must be maintained by the consultant pharmacist at the health care facility or institution for two (2) years from the date of destruction. Do NOT mail copies to the Texas State Board of Pharmacy or the Texas Department of State Health Services.

Previously Dispensed Drugs Returned to a Pharmacy

A pharmacist licensed by the Board is authorized to destroy dangerous drugs which have been previously dispensed to a patient and returned to the pharmacy. A pharmacist may not accept controlled substances that have been previously dispensed to a patient unless allowed by federal laws of the Drug Enforcement Administration. The following procedures should be followed when destroying drugs.

Dangerous Drugs other than Nalbuphine (e.g., Nubain)

(1)   *Record of Destruction.* A record of the drugs destroyed should be maintained by the pharmacy for two years. This record must contain the following information:

    (a)   name and address of the dispensing pharmacy;
    (b)   prescription number;
    (c)   name and strength of the drug;
    (d)   date of the destruction; and
    (e)   signature of the pharmacist destroying the drug.

(2)   *Methods of Destruction.* Drugs should be destroyed in a manner to render drugs unfit for human consumption and disposed of in compliance with all applicable state and federal requirements.

Destruction of Stock Prescription Drugs

These procedures apply to stock prescription drugs belonging to the pharmacy (drugs that are packaged in an original manufacturers container or have been prepackaged by the pharmacy for internal distribution).

Stock Dangerous Drugs

Dangerous drugs are prescription drugs which are not classified as controlled substances.

(1)   Pharmacists licensed by the Texas State Board of Pharmacy may destroy stock dangerous drugs if the drugs are destroyed in a manner to render the drugs unfit for human consumption (i.e., destroyed beyond reclamation) and disposed of in compliance with all applicable state and federal requirements. Records of destruction are not required except for Nalbuphine (e.g., Nubain).

(2)   Any brand of Nalbuphine (e.g., Nubain) must be inventoried prior to destruction and the destruction must be witnessed by another licensed pharmacist or commissioned peace officer. Records for destruction of these drugs must be maintained 2 years from the date of destruction.

Stock Controlled Substances

Class A and Class C Pharmacies

DEA will no longer accept outdated or unwanted controlled substances for destruction, except in unusual or extenuating circumstances. DEA offers the following alternatives for destroying controlled substances.

(1) Controlled substances may be personally delivered to an Environmental Protection Agency (EPA) approved incinerator. DEA must be notified 14 days in advance of the proposed destruction including the disposal site. Two responsible individuals from the pharmacy must accompany the controlled substances to the disposal site and actually witness their being rendered irretrievable. DEA Form 41 must be completed and forwarded to the attention of the appropriate DEA Divisional Office.

(2) Pharmacies may send (distribute) the unwanted controlled substances to a DEA registered disposal firm for destruction. Note that this constitutes a distribution by the pharmacy to another DEA registrant and must be documented through invoices and DEA Schedule II Order Forms (222). **Do not use** a DEA Form 41 to transfer possession of the controlled substances to the DEA registered disposal firm. Procedures for the distribution of controlled substances to another DEA registrant are outlined in this Section under the heading "*Distribution of Controlled Substances and Dangerous Drugs to Doctors or Pharmacies.*" Do not return controlled substances to a disposal firm unless they are DEA registered.

The following firms are registered by DEA for disposal of controlled substances at the time of publication of this reference. A current list of firms registered by DEA for disposal of controlled substances may be obtained by contacting one of the DEA Divisional Offices on the following pages.

If extenuating circumstances should arise concerning the destruction of unwanted or outdated controlled substances, contact a DEA Divisional Office for instructions. **DO NOT SEND THE CONTROLLED SUBSTANCES TO DEA.** Controlled substances received by the DEA Divisional Offices without DEA approval will not be accepted and will be returned to the sender. Regardless of the procedure followed, all federal, state, and local requirements for the handling of controlled substances and for waste disposal must be followed.

ARIZONA

Environmental Pharmaceuticals, LLC – (480) 659-9611
Covanta Environmental Pharmaceuticals, LLC DBA
Environmental Pharmaceuticals, LLC– 480-659-9611 ext. 203

CALIFORNIA

Far West Returns – (916) 524-6465
Outdate RX, LLC – (909) 335-7071

CONNECTICUT

Clean Harbors of Connecticut Inc. – (860) 583-3696

FLORIDA

Cavu Medical Products & Services LLC DBA Pharmatech Services – (813) 749-7113
Clean Harbors Florida LLC – (863) 519-6331 PharmaLink – (800) 257-3527
RX Return Services – (727) 754-7848
Rx Reverse Distributors Inc. – (772) 388-1212
Woodfield Distribution, LLC – (561) 998-3885

GEORGIA

Burke Horton, Inc. D/B/A The Rx Exchange – (678) 306-1866
Danox Environmental Services Inc. – (404) 671-9163
Maximum Rx Credit MRCI – (770) 985-2136
Return Logistics – (912) 748-5100
Zinvictus, Inc. – (770)-702-0446

ILLINOIS

Pharma Logistics – (847) 837-1224
Pharmaceutical Returns Services – (800) 215-5878 (Collector)
Qualanex, LLC – (800) 505-9291

INDIANA

Stericycle Inc. – (317) 860-1200 (Collector)

IOWA

National Pharmaceutical – (515) 252-7722

MICHIGAN

Drug & Laboratory Disposal Inc. – (269) 685-9824 (Collector)
Nortru LLC – (313) 824-5840
U S Industrial Technologies Inc. – (734) 462-4100

MINNESOTA

3M Drug Delivery Systems – (651) 733-2073
E Z Pharmacy Returns, LLC – (800) 440-0613

NEW JERSEY
  Advanced RX Returns D/B/A Omega 2000 RX Returns – (201) 222-3800

NEW YORK
  Ark Business Services Inc. Ark RX Returns Solutions – (347) 590-2779
  Devos Ltd. DBA Guaranteed Returns – (631) 689-0191
  Medwiz Solutions LLC, Returns Division – (845) 624-8080
  United RX Solutions, United Returns, Inc. – (844) 741-9718

NORTH CAROLINA
  ALMAC Clinical Services, Inc. ALMAC Clinical Services LLC – (919) 479-8850
  Assured Waste Solutions, LLC – (704) 865-7550
  Clean Harbors Reidsville LLC – (336) 342-6106
  Pharmaceutical Dimensions – (336) 664-5287

OHIO
  Achieva Group Returns, Inc. – (513) 474-9900
  Environmental Enterprises Inc. – (513) 541-1823 (Collector)
  Heritage Thermal Services Inc. – (330) 385-7336
  Stericycle Inc. – (317) 860-1175

OKLAHOMA
  Total Returns – (580) 276-3056

PENNSYLVANIA
  Chesapeake Waste Solutions – (717) 653-8882
  Complete RX Returns DBA CRX – (570) 706-9589
  HDS Returns LLC – (724) 856-7049
  Pharmareturns – (215) 653-7400 ext. 114
  Republic Environmental Systems (Pennsylvania), LLC - Stericycle Environmental Solutions – (215) 822-8995 ext. 111
  Specialty Disposal Services Inc. SDS – (973) 402-9246

TENNESSEE
  Clean Harbors Tennessee LLC – (615) 643-3177 ext. 3177
  Medsafe Waste LLC – (615) 431-2966 ext. 103
  Pharma-Mate Inc D/B/A Returnco – (706) 250-4831 (Collector) Reliable Pharmaceutical Returns,
  LLC – (615) 361-8856 (Collector) Return Solutions – (865) 675-1355 (Collector)

TEXAS
  Med-Turn, Inc. – (817) 868-5300 (Collector)
  Philip Reclamation Services-Stericycle Environmental Solutions, Inc. – (713) 679-2300
  Sharps Compliance, Inc. – (903) 693-2525 (Collector)
  Veolia ES Technical Solutions, L.L.C. – (409) 736-2821 (Collector)

UTAH
  Clean Harbors Aragonite – (435) 884-8100 (Collector)
  National Products Sales, Pharmaceutical Division – (801) 972-4132

WASHINGTON
  P.S. Industries Inc. – (206) 749-0739

WISCONSIN
  Capital Returns, Inc. DBA Genco Pharmaceutical Services – (414) 967-2800
  Veolia ES Technical Solutions, L.L.C. – (262) 255-6655

ADDRESSES

STATE AND FEDERAL AGENCIES

CHIROPRACTIC EXAMINERS, Texas State Board of

William P. Hobby Building
333 Guadalupe Street, Suite 3-825
Austin, Texas 78701-3942
Voice: (512) 305-6700
www.tbce.state.tx.us

DENTAL EXAMINERS, Texas State Board of

William P. Hobby Building
333 Guadalupe Street, Suite 3-800
Austin, Texas 78701-3942
Voice: (512) 463-6400
Complaints: (512) 821-3205
www.tsbde.texas.gov

DRUG ENFORCEMENT ADMINISTRATION (DEA)

HQ Registration Call Center (8:30 am-5:50 pm EST)
Phone: (800) 882-9539
HQ Mailing Address:
Drug Enforcement Administration
Attn: Registration Section/ODR
PO Box 2639
Springfield, VA 22152-2639
www.deadiversion.usdoj.gov

Dallas Divisional Office (For zip codes: 75000-75899*, 76000-76499, and 79000-79700)

Drug Enforcement Administration
10160 Technology Blvd., East
Dallas, Texas 75220
Voice: (214) 366-6900
Registration: (888) 366-4704

Houston Divisional Office (For zip codes: 75900-75999, 77000-78199, and 78900-78999)

Drug Enforcement Administration
1433 West Loop South, Suite 600
Houston, Texas 77027
Investigative Matters: (713) 693-3670
Fax 1: (713) 693-3661; Fax 2: (713) 693-3388
Registration: (800) 743-0595

San Antonio District Office (For zip codes: 75800-75899, 76500-76999, 7800-78299, 78600-78999, and 79700-79900)

Drug Enforcement Administration
10127 Morocco, Suite 200
San Antonio, Texas 78216
Investigative Matters: (210) 442-5678
Fax: (210) 442-5679
Registration: (800) 743-0595

*Note: Field office responsibility is assigned by county, therefore there may be some overlap in the zip codes listed above. If your zip code is listed for more than one of the field offices, contact any of the field offices and ask which office is responsible for your county.

Proc./Forms

12/1/2019

El Paso Divisional Office (For zip codes: 79900-79999)
660 Mesa Hills Drive
Suite 2000
El Paso, Texas 79912
Investigative Matters: (915) 231-4313
Fax 1: (915) 587 9502
Registration Assistance:
Phone 1: (915) 231 4310
Phone 2: (915) 892 9710
Fax 1: (915) 587 9504

FOOD AND DRUG ADMINISTRATION (FDA)
FDA U.S. Activities Branch
www.fda.gov

Dallas District
404 N. Central Expwy., Suite 300
Dallas, Texas 75204
Voice: (214) 253-5200

HEALTH AND HUMAN SERVICES
4900 N. Lamar, 4th Floor
Austin, Texas 78751
Voice: (512) 424-6500
hhs.texas.gov

Vendor Drug Program
4900 North Lamar Blvd.
Austin, TX 78751
1-800-435-4165 (HHS Pharmacy Benefits Access Help Desk)
Main: 512-730-7483
Pharmacy Benefits Access Help Desk: 512-491-1958
Formulary Management: 512-491-1961
Drug Utilization: 512-491-1962
www.txvendordrug.com

Pharmacy Prior Authorization
Phone: 1-877-PA-TEXAS (1-877-728-3927)
www.txvendordrug.com/formulary/prior-authorization

Licensing, Credentialing and Regulation
https://hhs.texas.gov/doing-business-hhs/licensing-credentialing-regulation

Long-Term Care – Regulatory
Voice: (512) 438-2625

INSURANCE, Texas Department of
William P. Hobby Building
333 Guadalupe Street, Suite
PO Box 149104
Austin, Texas 78701-3942
Voice: (800) 578-4677
Consumer Information: (800) 252-3439
www.tdi.texas.gov

LICENSING AND REGULATION, Texas Department of
920 Colorado Street
Austin, TX 78701
Voice: (512) 463-6599
www.tdlr.texas.gov

Proc./Forms

MEDICAL BOARD, Texas
William P. Hobby Building
333 Guadalupe Street, Suite 3-610
Austin, Texas 78701-3942
Voice: (512) 305-7010
Customer Service:
　　　(512) 305-7030 (outside Texas)
　　　(800) 248-4062 (Texas only)
www.tmb.state.tx.us

NURSING, Texas State Board of
William P. Hobby Building
333 Guadalupe Street, Suite 3-460
Austin, Texas 78701-3942
Voice: (512) 305-7400
Complaints: (800) 821-3205
www.bon.texas.gov

OPTOMETRY BOARD, Texas
William P. Hobby Building
333 Guadalupe Street, Suite 2-420
Austin, Texas 78701-3942
Voice: (512) 305-8500
Complaints: (800) 821-3205
www.tob.state.tx.us

PHARMACY, Texas State Board of
William P. Hobby Building
333 Guadalupe Street, Suite 3-500
Austin, Texas 78701-3942
www.pharmacy.texas.gov

STATE HEALTH SERVICES, Texas Department of
1100 West 49th Street
Austin, TX 78756
Voice: (512) 776-7111
Customer Service/Complaints: (512) 776-2150
www.dshs.texas.gov

Division for Regulatory Services, Drugs and Medical Devices Division
Voice: (512) 834-6770

Health Facility Licensing Division Hospital Licensing Program
Voice: (512) 834-6650

Long Term Care – Regulatory – see Health and Human Services Commission

Radiation Control, Bureau of
Rules and Regulations: (512) 834-6770, Ext. 2843
Enforcement: (512) 834-6665

VETERINARY MEDICAL EXAMINERS, Texas State Board of
William P. Hobby Building
333 Guadalupe Street, Suite 3-810
Austin, Texas 78701-3942
Voice: (512) 305-7555
Complaints: (800) 821-3205
www.veterinary.texas.gov

Proc./Forms

DRUG INFORMATION CENTERS

GALVESTON

Drug Information Center
University of Texas Medical Branch
Voice: (409) 772-2734

HOUSTON

Drug Information Center
M.D. Anderson Cancer Center
(accepts inquiries only from the University of Texas, M.D. Anderson Cancer Center staff, employees, and patients)
Voice: (713) 792-2858

Drug Information Center
Methodist Hospital
Voice: (713) 441-4190
Fax: (713) 441-0815
druginfo@tmh.tmc.edu

Drug Information Center
Texas Southern University College of Pharmacy and Health Sciences
Texas Medical Center
John P. McGovern Campus
2450 Holcombe Blvd, Houston, TX 77021
Voice: (713) 313-1242; (713) 313-1243
tsudic@tsu.edu

TEXAS POISON CENTER NETWORK

A statewide telecommunications network of poison centers has been implemented in Texas. A toll free telephone number will connect you to a poison center from anywhere in Texas. Poison centers have been opened in Amarillo, Dallas, El Paso, Galveston, San Antonio and Temple.

For poison information, dial the toll free number:

1-800-222-1222

In an emergency, dial 9-1-1

Public education materials such as brochures, phone stickers, and magnets are also available by dialing the 1-800 number above or at www.poisoncontrol.org.

Together, we can help reduce the incidences of poisonings in Texas!

Proc./Forms

Proc./Forms

FORMS – ONLINE

Forms are now fully accessible online. Web addresses for the items formerly included in this subsection are included below.

Complaint Process
https://www.pharmacy.texas.gov/consumer/complaint.asp

This page also contains the following information formerly included in this subsection:
- How Do I File a Complaint?
- How Are Complaints Resolved?
- What Happens If Disciplinary Action is Initiated?
- Will I Be Told of the Status and Resolution of My Complaint?

Complaint Report Form
https://www.pharmacy.texas.gov/consumer/complaintForm.asp

Professional Liability Claim Report Form
https://www.pharmacy.texas.gov/about/liabilityform.asp

MedWatch – The FDA Medical Products Reporting Program

Main program page
https://www.fda.gov/Safety/MedWatch/HowToReport/default.htm

Forms page
https://www.accessdata.fda.gov/scripts/medwatch/index.cfm?action=reporting.home

PROCEDURES AND POLICIES – ONLINE

Several procedures and policies previously published in the law book are also available online. Web addresses for these items are included below.

Drugs Which May Be Prescribed by Optometrists
https://www.pharmacy.texas.gov/files_pdf/Optometrists.pdf

Prescriptions Which May Be Dispensed in Texas
https://www.pharmacy.texas.gov/files_pdf/QUICK_REFERENCE_GUIDE.pdf

Guidelines for Establishing Pharmacist Peer Review Committees
https://www.pharmacy.texas.gov/files_pdf/PeerReview.PDF

Policy Statements and Guidelines
https://www.pharmacy.texas.gov/about/policyguidelines.asp

Each of the following statements formerly published in this subsection can also be found on the Policy Statements and Guidelines page, along with additional information.

Position Statement of the Treatment of Pain
https://www.pharmacy.texas.gov/files_pdf/Pain_Policy.PDF

Position Statement Regarding Working Conditions and Communication in Pharmacies
https://www.pharmacy.texas.gov/files_pdf/Working%20Conditions.pdf

Texas Board of Nurse Examiners/Board of Pharmacy Joint Position Statement on Medication Errors
https://www.pharmacy.texas.gov/about/medication_errors.asp

Proc./Forms

This index contains treatment of the laws compiled in the *Texas Pharmacy Laws and Regulations, 2020 Edition*. Statutory provisions from the Texas Annotated Statutes are referred to in the index by section number (*e.g.,* H-S §481.064).

A few basic rules for using this index are:

(1) *Consult the most pertinent subject.* For example, if you were looking in an evidence book for information about depositions, you would start with DEPOSITIONS rather than broader headings like EVIDENCE, TESTIMONY or WITNESSES. The broader headings may also exist, but to find the material more quickly, look for the specific subject first.

(2) *Cross references.* Pay close attention to and make full use of the index cross references. An index cross reference directs the index user to go to another part of the index to find treatment. This serves to keep indexes to a manageable size by reducing repetition of treatment under different headings.

(3) *Use definitions to aid in your search.* Starting a search under the DEFINED TERMS heading exposes the index user to a diverse sampling of statutory terminology which could suggest to the user other headings to consult.

The index benefits from customer suggestions. Especially helpful are popular names or legal terms specific to your area of practice. We are grateful for your assistance in the ongoing improvement of the index.

To contact the indexers, you may use any of the following methods:

- Contact the indexers via a toll-free number, 1-800-897-7922, for assistance in locating material within the index, or to make comments or suggestions.
- Contact the indexers by e-mail to lng-cho-indexing@lexisnexis.com.

For issues not directly related to the Index, such as missing pages, ordering or other customer service information, you may contact Customer Service via a toll-free number, 1-800-833-9844.

TABLE OF ABBREVIATIONS TO THE INDEX

INDEX

COMMUNITY PHARMACIES (CLASS A), 22 TAC 291.31 to 291.35

COMPOUNDING PHARMACIES.
Additional renewal requirements, Oc §561.0032.
Compounded and prepackaged drug products, Oc §562.151 to Oc §562.156.
Non-sterile preparations, 22 TAC 291.131.
Sterile preparations, 22 TAC 291.133.
Class E-S nonresident pharmacy compounding sterile preparations, 22 TAC 291.106.
Institutional pharmacies.
Pharmacies compounding sterile preparations (Class C-S), 22 TAC 291.77
Nonresident pharmacies.
Class E-S nonresident pharmacy compounding sterile preparations, 22 TAC 291.106

CONFLICT OF LAWS.
Texas pharmacy act, exclusive authority, Oc §551.006

CONSULTANT PHARMACIST
Freestanding emergency medical care centers (Class F), 22 TAC 291.151
Institutional pharmacies, 22 TAC 291.73

CONTINUING EDUCATION REQUIREMENTS
Official prescription program.
Controlled substances.
Continuing professional education requirements, H-S §481.07635
Pharmacists, Oc §559.051 to Oc §559.056
Certificate of completion, Oc §559.054
Demonstration of compliance, Oc §559.056
Method of obtaining, 22 TAC 295.8
Opioid drugs, education regarding, Oc §559.0525.
Program hours required, Oc §559.053
Recordkeeping requirements, 22 TAC 295.8; Oc §559.055
Reporting requirements, 22 TAC 295.8
Rulemaking authority, Oc §559.052
Satisfaction of requirements, Oc §559.051
Pharmacy technicians and trainees, 22 TAC 297.8; Oc §568.0045

CONTROLLED SUBSTANCES
Abusable synthetic substances, H-S §484.001 to 484.005
Additional assistance, DEA Manual, Appx. N
Administrative penalties and hearings.
Registration of pharmacy practitioners, H-S §481.301 to 481.314
Ambulances or EMS units.
Distribution of controlled substances, Bd. Pharm. P&A p. 500
Anhydrous ammonia.
Chemicals for manufacture of controlled substances, H-S §481.1245
Applicability to penal code, H-S §481.108, 482.005
Board of pharmacy.
Controlled substances prescription monitoring, 22 TAC 315.1 to 22 TAC 315.15. (*See* **PRESCRIPTIONS**)
Chemical laboratory apparatus.
Recordkeeping requirements, H-S §481.080
Transfer for unlawful manufacture, H-S §481.139
Unlawful transfer or receipt of, H-S §481.138

Chemicals for manufacture of controlled substances.
Anhydrous ammonia, H-S §481.1245
Possession or transfer of certain chemicals with intent to manufacture, H-S §481.124
Children and minors.
Child present on premises.
Manufacture of substance, H-S §481.1122
Delivery of controlled substance to child, H-S §481.122
Use of child in commission of offense, H-S §481.140
Commercial transactions, H-S §481.126 to 481.128
Controlled substance analogue.
Criminal classification, H-S §481.106
Deliver, manufacture or possession, H-S §481.123
Controlled substance property or plant.
Diversion of, H-S §481.131
Seizure. summary forfeiture, H-S §481.151 to 481.160
Criminal classification, H-S §481.101
Controlled substance analogue, H-S §481.106
Criminal law and procedure.
Burden of proof, H-S §481.184
Multiple prosecutions, H-S §481.132
Death or serious bodily injury.
Manufacture or delivery causing, H-S §481.141
Definitions, 37 TAC 13.1
CFR definitions, DEA Manual, Appx. B
Abbreviations, DEA Manual, Appx. C
Destruction of controlled substances, 22 TAC 303.1 to 22 TAC 303.3; DEA Manual p. 382; DEA Manual p. 383
Forfeiture. (*See* within this heading, "Forfeiture and destruction")
Registered DEA disposal facilities, Bd. Pharm. P&A p. 506
Disposal of controlled substances, DEA Manual p. 382
Distribution of controlled substances.
Ambulances or EMS units, Bd. Pharm. P&A p. 500
Doctors or pharmacies, Bd. Pharm. P&A p. 501; Bd. Pharm. P&A p. 502
Diversion of controlled substances.
Registrants, dispensers and certain persons not required to register, H-S §481.1285
Drug-free zones, H-S §481.134, 481.135
Drug paraphernalia.
Evidentiary rules relating to, H-S §481.183
Possession or delivery of, H-S §481.125
Drug test results.
Falsification of, H-S §481.133
Ephedrine, pseudoephedrine, norpseudoephedrine.
Wholesale distributors, duties, 37 TAC 13.51
Evidentiary rules relating to delivery, H-S §481.182
Exemption of certain substances, H-S §481.111
Five percent rule.
Pharmacy distribution of controlled substances, DEA Manual p. 404
Forfeiture and destruction.
Communication with director (crime lab service), 37 TAC 13.165
Definitions, 37 TAC 13.151
Destruction authority, 37 TAC 13.153 to 37 TAC 13.156
Security control, 37 TAC 13.157 to 37 TAC 13.164
Summary forfeiture.
Controlled substance property or plant, 37 TAC 13.152; H-S §481.151 to H-S §481.160
Fraud, H-S §481.129

Institutional pharmacies (Class C).
Freestanding ambulatory surgical center, pharmacies located in facility, 22 TAC 291.76
Limited prescription delivery pharmacy (Class H), 22 TAC 291.155
Ephedrine, over-the-counter sales, H-S §486.001 to 486.033
Equipment and supplies, 22 TAC 291.33
Clinic pharmacies (Class D), 22 TAC 291.93
Freestanding emergency medical care centers (Class F), 22 TAC 291.151
Institutional pharmacies, 22 TAC 291.74
Freestanding ambulatory surgical center, pharmacies located in facility, 22 TAC 291.76
Fire or other disaster, 22 TAC 291.3
Notification, Oc §562.106
Reporting requirements, Bd. Pharm. P&A p. 500
Floor stock.
Freestanding emergency medical care centers (Class F), 22 TAC 291.151
Institutional pharmacies, 22 TAC 291.74
Forged prescriptions, reporting of, 22 TAC 291.3
Formulary development, 22 TAC 291.74
Clinic pharmacies (Class D), 22 TAC 291.93
Fraud.
Pharmacist guide to prescription fraud, DEA Manual, Appx. D
Generic substitutions or interchangeable biological products.
Generally, 22 TAC 309.1 to 22 TAC 309.8. (See **GENERIC SUBSTITUTIONS OR INTERCHANGEABLE BIOLOGICAL PRODUCTS**)
Operational standards, 22 TAC 291.33; 22 TAC 291.104
Home.
Operating pharmacy in personal residence prohibited, 22 TAC 291.11
Identification of personnel, 22 TAC 291.32
Institutional pharmacies (Class C), 22 TAC 291.71 to 22 TAC 291.77
Rural hospitals, Oc §562.1011
Inventory requirements, 22 TAC 291.17
Labeling containers, 22 TAC 291.33
Clinic pharmacies (Class D), 22 TAC 291.93
Library.
Reference library, requirements, 22 TAC 291.33
Clinic pharmacies (Class D), 22 TAC 291.93
Freestanding emergency medical care centers (Class F), 22 TAC 291.151
Institutional pharmacies, 22 TAC 291.74
Freestanding ambulatory surgical center, pharmacies located in facility, 22 TAC 291.76
Limited prescription delivery pharmacy (Class H), 22 TAC 291.155
Nuclear pharmacies, 22 TAC 291.54
License to practice pharmacy.
General provisions, Oc §558.001 to 559.105. (See **PHARMACIST LICENSING**)
Licensing of pharmacies.
General provisions, Oc §560.001 to 561.005. (See **PHARMACY LICENSING**)
Linking internet sites, Oc §562.1045
Location and/or name, change of, 22 TAC 291.2
Written notification, Oc §562.106
Maintenance of records, Oc §562.105

Managing officer, change of.
Written notice requirements, 22 TAC 291.3
Medication orders.
Central prescription drug or medication order processing pharmacy (Class G), 22 TAC 291.153
Freestanding emergency medical care centers (Class F), 22 TAC 291.151
New pharmacy registration.
Controlled substances, DEA Manual p. 378
Affidavit for a new pharmacy, DEA Manual, Appx. E
Non-resident pharmacies (Class E), 22 TAC 291.101 to 22 TAC 291.106
Non-sterile preparations.
Pharmacies compounding, 22 TAC 291.131
Norpseudoephedrine, over-the-counter sales, H-S §486.001 to 486.033
Nuclear pharmacy (class B), 22 TAC 291.51 to 22 TAC 291.55
Off-site pharmacists, 22 TAC 291.33
Online pharmacy consumer protection.
Controlled substances, DEA Manual p. 399
Operational standards.
Central prescription drug or medication order processing pharmacy (Class G), 22 TAC 291.153
Clinic pharmacies (Class D), 22 TAC 291.93
Community pharmacies (Class A), 22 TAC 291.33
Freestanding emergency medical care centers (Class F), 22 TAC 291.151
Institutional pharmacies (Class C), 22 TAC 291.74
Freestanding ambulatory surgical center, pharmacies located in facility, 22 TAC 291.76
Limited prescription delivery pharmacy (Class H), 22 TAC 291.155
Non-resident pharmacies (Class E), 22 TAC 291.104
Nuclear pharmacy (class B), 22 TAC 291.54
Remote pharmacy services, 22 TAC 291.121
Out-of-date drugs or devices, 22 TAC 291.33
Over-the-counter sales of ephedrine products, H-S §486.001 to 486.033
Ownership, change of.
Written notification, 22 TAC 291.3; Oc §562.106
Owner's responsibilities, 22 TAC 291.32
Central prescription drug or medication order processing pharmacy (Class G), 22 TAC 291.153
Class C-institutional pharmacy.
Freestanding ambulatory surgical center, pharmacies located in facility, 22 TAC 291.76
Freestanding emergency medical care centers (Class F), 22 TAC 291.151
Nuclear pharmacy (Class B), 22 TAC 291.53
Personal residence.
Operating pharmacy in prohibited, 22 TAC 291.11
Personnel.
Clinic pharmacies (Class D), 22 TAC 291.92
Community pharmacies (Class A), 22 TAC 291.32
Institutional pharmacies (Class C), 22 TAC 291.73
Non-resident pharmacies (Class E), 22 TAC 291.103
Nuclear pharmacy (class B), 22 TAC 291.53
Petition to establish additional class of pharmacy, 22 TAC 291.22
Pharmaceutical care, 22 TAC 291.33; 22 TAC 291.54; 22 TAC 291.74
Pharmacist employment, change of, 22 TAC 291.3
Pharmacist-in-charge, 22 TAC 291.32